The Penguin India
REFERENCE YEARBOOK
2006

Compiled and Edited by
Derek O'Brien

PENGUIN BOOKS

PENGUIN BOOKS
Published by the Penguin Group
Penguin Books India Pvt Ltd, 11 Community Centre, Panchsheel Park, New Delhi 110 017, India
Penguin Group (USA) Inc., 375 Hudson Street, New York, NY 10014, USA
Penguin Group (Canada), 90 Eglinton Avenue East, Suite 700, Toronto, Ontario, M4P 2Y3, Canada (a division of Pearson Penguin Canada Inc.)
Penguin Books Ltd, 80 Strand, London WC2R 0RL, England
Penguin Ireland, 25 St Stephen's Green, Dublin 2, Ireland (a division of Penguin Books Ltd)
Penguin Group (Australia), 250 Camberwell Road, Camberwell, Victoria 3124, Australia (a division of Pearson Australia Group Pty Ltd)
Penguin Group (NZ), cnr Airborne and Rosedale Roads, Albany, Auckland 1310, New Zealand (a division of Pearson New Zealand Ltd)
Penguin Group (South Africa) (Pty) Ltd, 24 Sturdee Avenue, Rosebank, Johannesburg 2196, South Africa

Penguin Books Ltd, Registered Offices: 80 Strand, London WC2R 0RL, England

First published by Penguin Books India 2006
Copyright © Penguin Books India 2006
Colour maps copyright © Dorling Kindersley India 2006

All rights reserved

10 9 8 7 6 5 4 3 2 1

ISBN 10: 0144000644
ISBN 13: 9780144000647

Typeset in Humanst521 BT by InoSoft Systems, Noida
Printed at Brijbasi Art Press Ltd., Noida

Cover design by Hatch Design

Publisher's Note

After the phenomenal success of the inaugural edition of *The Penguin India Reference Yearbook* last year, we are proud to present the 2006 edition of the *Reference Yearbook*. The content of the book has been entirely revised, and every piece of information has been rechecked and updated for this year's edition. As a result, we are able to present to our readers the most up-to-date and comprehensive one-volume compendium of facts and figures on India and the world available today.

The cover story for the 2006 edition of *The Penguin India Reference Yearbook* is 'Building Confidence'. This section contains new and important essays by A.P.J. Abdul Kalam, Manmohan Singh, Amartya Sen, Bimal Jalan and Derek O'Brien. Other sections of the *Reference Yearbook* contain articles by Thomas L. Friedman, P.V. Narasimha Rao, Ashis Nandy, Vinay Lal and Satyajit Ray.

This year's *Reference Yearbook* features completely revised India and The World sections with a great deal of additional information on the states and union territories of India and the countries of the world. The sections on Politics, Economy, Science, Career, Sports, Arts and General Knowledge have been updated and revised too; these contain the latest news and updates from across the world and from India.

The Year in Review section contains a comprehensive day-by-day account of everything that has happened in India and the world over the last year, i.e. between 1 October 2004 and 30 September 2005. Separate listings highlight newsmakers of the year and obituaries. The Stop Press updates the account of important happenings right upto 1 November 2005.

Of course, *The Penguin India Reference Yearbook 2006* retains all the popular features of its first edition: historical timelines with detailed overviews of the last ten years; brief and informative who's whos; colour maps and flags of India and the world; 500 GK quiz questions on everything you need to know about what is happening in the world around you; and a detailed index.

Running to 976 pages, the *Reference Yearbook* packs in an incredible amount of data, and prides itself on the authenticity, currency and comprehensiveness of the information that it contains. Full of useful facts and statistics, it is presented in an easily accessible, reader-friendly format. For students, this is an ideal companion in their preparation for various competitive examinations. For the general reader, it is an immensely useful desk reference and ready-reckoner.

We are grateful for the very positive response we received from readers for the 2005 edition of the *Reference Yearbook*. Please do write to us with your thoughts and suggestions on the new edition. You can reach us at editorial@in.penguin group.com. For bulk purchases and institutional orders, please contact sales@in. penguingroup.com.

Content for *The Penguin India Reference Yearbook 2006* was provided by Suman Ray, Amit Ghosh, Nayan Chaudhury, Shalini Sinha, Sree Menon, Indrani Bhattacharjee and Debkumar Mitra at Derek O'Brien and Associates Pvt. Ltd. and supplemented by inputs from the editorial team at Penguin Books India.

Contents

STOP PRESS

Stop Press

Newsmakers and Happenings October 2005

Earthquake in Kashmir

A major earthquake measuring 7.6 on the Richter scale shook Kashmir on 8 October 2005 at 9.20 IST. Its epicentre was located in Pakistan-occupied Kashmir. The area around Muzaffarabad in PoK was completely devastated, while on the other side of the border, the town of Uri was badly hit. As of 21 October the Pakistan government's official death toll was 53,182, including more than 13,000 killed in the North West Frontier Province. The official death toll in Jammu and Kashmir was 1,360. However, some estimates say that the cumulative death toll could reach 100,000. Most of the affected areas are in mountainous regions and access is impeded by landslides that have blocked the roads. An estimated 3.3 million were left homeless in Pakistan, and many are at risk of dying from the spread of disease. It has been estimated that damages incurred are over $ 5 billion.

Here's a list of the world's major earthquakes in the last hundred years:

Date	Epicentre	Magnitude*	Number dead
1905	India	8.6	19,000
1908	Italy	7.2	100,000
1915	Italy	7.5	30,000
1920	China	7.8	200,000
1923	Japan	7.9	143,000
1927	China	7.9	200,000
1932	China	7.2	70,000
1934	India	8.1	11,000
1935	Pakistan (then India)	7.5	30,000
1939	Turkey	7.8	30,000
1939	Chile	8.3	28,000
1948	Turkmenistan	7.3	1,10,000
1970	Peru	7.9	66,000
1976	China	7.5	600,000
1988	Armenia	6.8	25,000
1993	India	6.2	10,000
1996	Chile	8.2	20,000
2001	India	7.7	13,000
2003	Iran	6.6	26,000
2004	Indonesia	9.0	283,000
2005	PoK	7.6	55,000+

* on Richter scale

Fernando Alonso

When the 2005 season concluded on 16 October, Formula 1 had a new world champion—Fernando Alonso of Spain. In fact it was on 25 September, with two races still to go, that Alonso became the youngest person to win the Formula One World Driver's Championship title, at the age of 24 years and 59 days. This broke the record earlier held by Emerson Fittipaldi. He is also the youngest driver in Formula 1 to start from the pole position on the grid (2002 Malaysian GP) and the youngest ever race winner (2002 Hungarian GP). The first Spanish Formula 1 champion, Alonso has been racing for the Renault team since 2002. The 2005 Formula 1 season also witnessed the debut of the first ever Indian driver to drive in the Formula 1 World Championship, Narain Karthikeyan.

Sania Mirza

In October 2005, the London-based *New Statesman* listed teenage tennis star Sania Mirza as one of the ten people capable of changing the world. 2005 was a remarkable year for Sania; in her first full-fledged season on the WTA tour, she saw her world ranking shoot up from no. 166 to no. 31. Sania registered her first win in a Grand Slam match in the first round of the 2005 Australian Open; later in the year she became the first Indian woman to win a WTA tour title when she won the Hyderabad Open. In August she became the first Indian woman to break into the top 50 list of tennis players worldwide. Her year-round performances made her feature on the cover of *Time* magazine, another first for an Indian sportsperson.

Man Booker Prize for John Banville

On 10 October, John Banville was named the winner of the 2005 Man Booker Prize for Fiction for *The Sea*. The internationally renowned literature award is worth L 50,000. The Irish-born John Banville was shortlisted for the Booker Prize in 1989 for his novel, *The Book of Evidence*, but lost out to Kazuo Ishiguro's *The Remains of the Day*. This year, however, the tables were turned with *The Sea* winning over Ishiguro's shortlisted *Never Let Me Go*. The other shortlisted novels were Julian Barnes's *Arthur and George*, Sebastian Barry's *A Long Long Way*, Ali Smith's *The Accidental* and Zadie Smith's *On Beauty*.

Harold Pinter wins Literature Nobel

English playwright Harold Pinter (b 1930) 'who in his plays uncovers the precipice under everyday prattle and forces entry into oppression's closed rooms' was awarded the Nobel Prize for Literature for 2005. Pinter is the author of such landmark plays as *The Birthday Party*, *The Dumb Waiter*, *The Caretaker* and *The Homecoming*.

Rain in South India

On 25 October, India's technology hub Bangalore became a flood zone after rains continued to lash the city, making it the wettest month in five decades. The city recorded 77.7 mm of rain on the 25th against an average rainfall of 180.44 mm in October. With total rainfall of 581.8 mm in October 2005, the previous record of 522.2 mm in October 1956 was broken. In neighbouring Tamil Nadu the Mettur dam was overflowing after nearly five decades. Chennai was also flooded subsequently. Life in the city came to a standstill and the army had to be called out.

Hurricane Wilma

It was the twelfth hurricane (sixth major) and the twenty-first named storm of the record-breaking 2005 Atlantic hurricane season. It was also the third

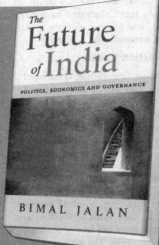

STOP PRESS

Category 5 hurricane of the season. At its peak, it was the most intense hurricane ever recorded in the Atlantic basin. Wilma made several landfalls, with the most destructive effects felt in the Yucatán Peninsula of Mexico (on 21 October), Cuba, and the US state of Florida. At least 33 deaths have been reported, and insured damage is estimated at between $8-12 billion.

Bihar Election Update

The Election Commission announced a four-phase re-election to the Bihar Assembly starting 18 October. The first phase on 18 October covers 61 constituencies, the second on 26 October 69 constituencies, the third on 13 November 72 constituencies and the fourth on 19 November 41 constituencies. Votes will be counted on 22 November and the results declared the same day. Bihar registered 43 per cent and 41 per cent votes in the first and second rounds of the four-phased elections respectively. The polling was by and large peaceful. People boycotted the polling process at quite a few booths. Deferred elections in seven constituencies were held on 29 October.

New Chief Justice of India

Supreme Court judge Yogesh Kumar Sabharwal has been appointed the new Chief Justice of India with effect from 1 November 2005. He replaces Chief Justice R.C. Lahoti.

Bomb blasts in Delhi

59 people were killed and more than 200 injured when three bomb blasts ripped through Sarojini Nagar, Paharganj and Govindpuri in Delhi on 29 October 2005. The markets were filled with shoppers in the last weekend before the Diwali and Eid celebrations and casualties were extensive. The terrorist group Lashkar-e-Toiba was suspected to be behind the serial blasts.

Obituaries

Chintamoni Kar

On 3 October sculptor Chintamoni Kar died in Kolkata at the age of 90. One of the most renowned sculptors of modern India, Kar was awarded the Padma Bhushan in 1972. In 2000, France's highest civilian honour was conferred on him.

Apollo Milton Obote

On 10 October Apollo Milton Obote died in Johannesburg at the age of 81. Prime Minister of Uganda from 1962 to 1966 and President of Uganda from 1966 to 1971 and from 1980 to 1985, he led Uganda to independence from the British colonial administration in 1962.

Rosa Parks

Rosa Parks, whose act of civil disobedience in 1955 inspired the modern civil rights movement, died on 24 October in Detroit, Michigan. She was 92.

José Simón Azcona del Hoyo

On 24 October the former President of Honduras (1986-90) died of a heart attack at the age of 78.

Nirmal Verma

On 25 October writer Nirmal Verma died at the age of 76. He together with Mohan Rakesh, Bhisham Sahni, Kamleshwar, Amarkant and others was the founder of the Nai Kahani (new short story) in Hindi literature. Some of his famous stories are 'Parinde', 'Andhere Mein', 'Dedh Inch Upar' and 'Kavve Aur Kala Pani'. He has also written some excellent novels like Lal Tin Ki Chhat and Antim Aranya. Nirmal Verma received the Jnanpith Award in 1999.

World Dateline October 2005

1: Dozens are killed in explosions at the Indonesian tourist destination of Bali. Gregory Olsen of USA is launched on board a Russian Soyuz spacecraft as the third fare-paying space tourist; he will travel to the International Space Station. The Ilamatepec volcano erupts in El Salvador.

3: Barry J. Marshall and Robin Warren are awarded the 2005 Nobel Prize in Physiology or Medicine.

4: Roy J. Glauber, John L. Hall and Theodor W. Hänsch are awarded the 2005 Nobel Prize in Physics.

5: Yves Chauvin, Robert H. Grubbs, and Richard R. Schrock are awarded the 2005 Nobel Prize in Chemistry. Hurricane Stan strikes Mexico and Central America.

8: An earthquake measuring 7.6 on the Richter scale strikes the Pakistan and India; the epicentre is in Pakistan occupied Kashmir, near Muzzafarabad.

10: In Germany, Christian Democrat leader Angela Merkel is named as the next Chancellor of Germany. Thomas Schelling and Robert Aumann are awarded the 2005 Nobel Prize for Economics.

13: British playwright Harold Pinter is named as the 2005 winner of the Nobel Prize for Literature.

15: Malawi President Bingu wa Mutharika declares a national disaster due to the worsening food shortages in the country. H5N1 avian influenza virus is confirmed in dead birds found in Turkey.

16: The re-entry module of the Chinese manned spacecraft Shenzhou 6 lands safely in Inner Mongolia, China.

17: Two are killed and nearly 90 injured in a collision between two ships in the Suez Canal. Jens Stoltenberg takes over as the Prime Minister of Norway. A new government is formed in New Zealand. Tropical Storm Wilma forms in the Atlantic, the 21st recorded storm in the season.

18: In UK, ex-chancellor Ken Clarke is eliminated from the leadership election of the Conservative Party. US authorities shut down a highway tunnel under the harbour of Baltimore, Maryland, following a threat to detonate explosive filled vehicles.

19: Hurricane Wilma intensifies into a Category 5 storm, the third in the Atlantic Hurricane season of 2005. Saddam Hussein goes on trial in Baghdad for crimes against humanity. China reports 2600 birds have died of the H5N1 virus near Hohhot, Inner Mongolia. Russia reports outbreaks of the virus in west Siberia and western Russia. An outbreak is also suspected in Macedonia, Europe.

21: A United Nations investigation concludes that high-ranking members of the Syrian and Lebanese governments were involved in the assassination of former Lebanese Prime Minister Rafik Hariri. An earthquake measuring 5.9 on the Richter scale hits the Turkish city of Ýzmir. Sadoun Nasouaf al-Janabi, a defence lawyer involved in the trial of former Iraqi President Saddam Hussein, is killed.

22: Tropical Storm Alpha forms in the Caribbean; it is the record-breaking 22nd named storm of the 2005 season. The first case of avian influenza (bird flu) is discovered in the United Kingdom from a South American parrot. Avian influenza is also detected in Croatia, in six swans found near Orahovica. The Australian Quarantine and Inspection Service discover antibodies of avian influenza in pigeons imported from Canada; Australia imposes a blanket ban on all live bird imports from Canada.

23: The Swedish National Veterinary Institute reports a dead duck discovered near Stockholm is infected with a strain of avian influenza. More than 100 are killed when Bellview Airlines Flight 210 crashes in Oyo State, Nigeria shortly after take-off from Lagos.

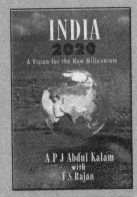

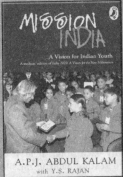

24: Lech Kaczyński wins the Polish presidential election.

25: Staff Sergeant George T. Alexander, Jr. becomes the 2,000th US military fatality in Iraq. Iraq's independent electoral commission announces that the country's draft constitution was approved in the vote held on 15 October.

26: What may be the first pyramid in Europe is discovered in Bosnia.

27: At least 20 Shia militia members and Iraqi police die following a Sunni Arab ambush in Nahrawan, southeast of Baghdad. Israeli Prime Minister Ariel Sharon calls for the expulsion of Iran from the United Nations after the Iranian President called for Israel to be 'wiped off the map'.

28: Sina-1, the first Iranian satellite built jointly with Russia is launched from Plesetsk Cosmodrome in Murmansk. Lewis 'Scooter' Libby, Chief of Staff to US Vice President Dick Cheney, accused of CIA leaks, resigns after being indicted for perjury and obstruction of justice by a grand jury.

India Dateline October 2005

1: Deepinder Singh Hooda, the 27-year-old son of Haryana CM Bhupinder Singh Hooda, wins the Lok Sabha by-election from Rohtak with a margin of 231,958 votes.

2: External Affairs Minister K. Natwar Singh travels to Pakistan leading a high-level official delegation to continue the India-Pakistan peace dialogue.

3: India and Pakistan sign an agreement to notify each other at least 72 hours before testing ballistic missiles within a 40-km radius of the International Boundary and the Line of Control (LoC). Bundelkhand Express derails and crashes into a signal cabin at Datia station, near Gwalior, killing 16. Brahmotsavam starts in Tirupati.

4: India and Pakistan issue a Joint Statement stating that the two countries will work towards a common understanding on demilitarization of the Siachen glacier before the next round of the composite dialogue in January. NCP leader Purno Sangma announces that he would resign as MP from Tura parliamentary constituency to protest against police brutalities on students in his constituency. The Allahabad High Court quashes the law that gives the Aligarh Muslim University its minority status; it also holds the reservation of seats for Muslims in its post-graduate medical courses as illegal.

5: Demostrations take place at Aligarh Muslim University following the quashing of its minority status. The Andhra Pradesh Legislative Assembly passes a Bill providing 5 per cent reservation for Muslims in educational institutions and government service. Jammu and Kashmir High Court Chief Justice Sachchidanand Jha is transferred to the Rajasthan High Court.

6: Former Union Minister and BJP MP, Ravi Shankar Prasad, is shot at and injured at an election meeting at Nokha in Rohtas district of Bihar. Chief Justice of the Madras High Court Markandeya Katju is re-assigned as Delhi High Court Chief Justice. The Supreme Court orders the transfer of the Chief Secretary of Uttar Pradesh, Neera Yadav, to some other post.

7: The Supreme Court declares the 23 May Presidential Proclamation dissolving the Bihar Assembly as unconstitutional but allows the present elections.

8: Kupwara, Baramulla and Poonch areas of Jammu and Kashmir are severely affected in an earthquake that originated near Muzzafarabad in Pakistan occupied Kasmir. Aftershocks are felt across north India, including Chandigarh and New Delhi.

9: Death toll in the previous day's earthquake reaches 588 in Jammu and Kashmir. An Air Sahara aircraft overshoots the runway while landing at Mumbai airport.

When ICT goes to the grassroots in Kerala ...

The world is watching, while the common man goes high-tech. In Kerala (India), e-learning, e-transaction, e-governance, information and communication are reaching out to the grass roots. Through the Akshaya Project which will soon make Kerala 100% computer literate state. A network of about 5000 Information and Communication Technology (ICT) centers called Akshaya e-kendras will ensure the power of networking and connectivity to the common man.

Mission Akshaya

- At least one computer literate person in every home.
- A network of about 5000 Akshaya e-kendras throughout the state.
- e-governance and public services through Akshaya e-centers
- Generation of locally relevant e-content.
- Massive employment opportunities.
- Economic communication through internet telephony, e-mail, chats etc.
- Increased PC penetration.
- Rural wireless Internet connectivity, net based transaction etc.

Akshaya addresses 3 major issues of ICT for development:
- Access • Skillset • Content

Kerala State Information Technology Mission
www.keralaitmission.org

AKSHAYA
www.akshaya.net

10: Earthquake death toll crosses 900 in Jammu and Kashmir. Purno Sangma resigns from the Lok Sabha.

13: Indian and Pakistani authorities deny that Indian troops crossed the Line of Control in the aftermath of the earthquake. The Petroleum and Natural Gas ministry announces India's bio-diesel policy; public sector oil marketing companies will buy bio-diesel from 1 January 2006 at Rs 25 a litre; this will be blended with diesel to the extent of 20 per cent in phases. The Public Investment Board approves the proposal of the Air-India board to buy 68 passenger aircraft from Boeing. Rahul Dravid is appointed the captain of the Indian cricket team for the forthcoming ODI series against Sri Lanka and South Africa. Union Agriculture Minister Sharad Pawar resigns from the marketing committee of the Board of Control for Cricket in India.

14: A curfew is imposed in the town of Mau in Uttar Pradesh following the outbreak of communal violence.

15: India announces that it is willing to allow Pakistani helicopters to fly in the no-fly zone along the Line of Control on a case-by-case basis. Communal violence continues in Mau.

16: Former PM H.D. Deve Gowda criticizes Infosys founder N. R Narayana Murthy on issues relating to the development of Bangalore and his role in the Bangalore International Airport. Communal clashes and subsequent police firing continue in Mau; the town remains under curfew.

17: Suspected militants kill 23 persons belonging to the Karbi tribe in central Assam's Karbi Anglong Hill district; they also burn down two buses in which the victims were travelling; suspected militants kill 10 more Karbis elsewhere in the state; authorities impose shoot-at-sight orders and an indefinite curfew in the affected areas of the district. The Bombay High Court sets aside the recent multi-crore sales of textile mill lands in Mumbai by the National Textile Corporation (NTC). Additional forces are deployed in Mau.

18: Jammu and Kashmir Minister of State for Education Ghulam Nabi Lone is shot dead; CPI (M) State secretary M.Y. Tarigami escapes unhurt in an attack. Supreme Court Justice Yogesh Kumar Sabharwal is appointed the new Chief Justice of India, with effect from 1 November. Police in Mau lodge FIRs against independent MLA Mukhtar Ansari and BJP Member of Legislative Council Ramji Singh for inciting communal riots. 43 per cent turnout in the first phase of Bihar Assembly polls

19: The first telephone calls from Jammu and Kashmir to Pakistan occupied Kashmir are made for the first time in 15 years. Curfew continues in Mau. The Supreme Court admits an appeal filed by the CBI challenging the Orissa High Court order modifying the death sentence awarded to Dara Singh in the Graham Staines murder case.

20: The Union Cabinet approves the limit of foreign direct investment (FDI) in telecom from 49 to 74 per cent. The Board of Control for Cricket in India (BCCI) awards the telecast rights of the two one-day series of 12 matches between India-Sri Lanka and India-South Africa to Prasar Bharati. Infosys founder N.R. Narayana Murthy resigns as Chairman of Bangalore International Airport Ltd. (BIAL) following remarks made by former PM H.D. Deve Gowda questioning his contribution to the project. Curfew relaxed in Mau.

21: Deferred election in the four Assembly constituencies of Gaya district in Bihar are held. In Andhra Pradesh, the Telangana Rashtra Samithi (TRS) party splits; its president and Union Labour Minister K. Chandrasekhar Rao and rebel MLA S. Santosh Reddy 'expel' each other. Onion prices shoot up across the country as heavy rains destroy crops in six major onion-producing states.

22: India proposes to open three relief and medical centres on Indian territory to help earthquake victims living across the Line of Control in Pakistan; they will be allowed to cross over across the LoC during daytime. Union government approves the import of onions to cope with the domestic shortage.

25: India defeats Sri Lanka by 152 runs in the first game of the seven-match Videocon Cup series in Nagpur; Sachin Tendulkar scores 93 in his comeback match. Heavy rain and flooding of riverbanks for the second day claim 11 lives in different parts of Tamil Nadu. The Reserve Bank of India raises the interest rate at which the central bank borrows from commercial banks (called the reverse repo rate) by one-fourth of one per cent (or 25 basis points), indicating a short-term rise in interest rates. The fragile infrastructure of Bangalore is exposed yet again under the fury of torrential rains that leaves nine people dead, several injured, vast expanses of low-lying residential areas and arterial roads marooned and many houses collapsed. With the consent of the contending parties, the Supreme Court appoints former Chief Election Commissioner T.S. Krishnamurthy as Observer for conducting the Board of Control for Cricket in India (BCCI) elections to be held in Kolkata before 30 November.

26: The second phase of the Bihar Assembly elections in 62 constituencies is by and large peaceful; about 41 per cent of the 1.3-crore voters exercise their franchise.

27: It is announced that Union Minister Ghulam Nabi Azad will be the new Chief Minister of Jammu and Kashmir. Rain cripples life in Chennai, 42 cm rain has fallen in 40 hours. India offers Rs 112.45 crore in assistance to Pakistan for relief and rehabilitation for the 8 October earthquake victims. The Union Cabinet decides to declare Sanskrit a classical language. So far, only Tamil enjoyed that status. The Sensex nosedives by 176 points.

28: K. Natwar Singh, India's External Affairs Minister, as well as the Congress Party are listed in the recently released report of the Volcker Committee as 'non-contractual beneficiaries' of Iraqi oil sales in 2001 under the United Nations oil-for-food programme. Storm batters coastal Andhra, Rayalaseema, at least 12 dead in three districts. India takes a 2-0 lead in the seven-match series for the Videocon Cup with a comprehensive eight-wicket win over Sri Lanka at Mohali. The BJP deals a severe blow to the Congress wresting the key Porbander Municipality. Vodafone picks up a 10 per cent share in Bharti Tele-Ventures. The Sensex plunges another 113 points.

29: Over 100 people are killed when seven bogies of the Repalle-Secunderabad passenger train derails in Andhra Pradesh after flash floods caused by the bursting of a reservoir near the tracks. 59 people are killed and over 200 injured in three bomb blasts at Sarojini Nagar, Paharganj and Govindpuri in Delhi; a terrorist hand is suspected behind the explosions. Senior Congress leader H.K.L. Bhagat passes away.

31: Ashfaq Arif, the prime accused in the 2000 Red Fort attack case, is sentenced to death by a Delhi court; two others are given life sentences. India announces it will open five points along the LoC on 7 November in order to help quake victims. The Sensex climbs by over 200 points. M.S. Dhoni slams an unbeaten 183, the highest score by a wicket-keeper in one-day cricket, as India beat Sri Lanka by 6 wickets in the third match of the Videocon Cup in Jaipur. Noted writer and Jnanpith winner Amrita Pritam passes away.

The Year in Review

Newsmakers and Happenings of the Year

London Bombings of 7 July 2005

The British capital city of London was struck by a series of four bomb attacks on Thursday 7 July 2005. The attacks targeted London's public transport system during the morning rush hour. At 8.50 a.m. (BST), three bombs exploded within 50 seconds of each other on three London Underground trains. Two of the bombs exploded on trains travelling to Liverpool Street and Edgware Road stations, while the third explosion took place on a train travelling between King's Cross and Russell Square stations. Around an hour later, a fourth bomb exploded on a bus. At 9.47 a.m. a blast took place in a number 30 double-decker bus at the junction of Tavistock Square and Upper Woburn Place. It was travelling from Marble Arch to Hackney. Ironically, the bus had been diverted from its normal route because of road closures in the wake of the tube bombings that had just taken place. The bomb was placed on a seat or the floor at the back of the upper deck. It killed 14 people including the bomber. The bombings led to a severe, day-long disruption of the city's transport and mobile telecommunications infrastructure. 56 people were killed in the attacks, including the four suspected bombers, with 700 injured. The incident was the deadliest single act of terrorism in the United Kingdom since the 1988 bombing of Pan Am Flight 103, and the worst bombing incident in London since the Second World War.

Four attempted bombings took place exactly two weeks after the deadly 7 July blasts, on 21 July. The police later recovered failed explosive devices on trains at Oval, Warren Street and Shepherd's Bush stations. A fourth device was found on a bus in Hackney. A fifth device was found in a rucksack abandoned in bushes at Little Wormwood Scrubs two days after the failed attacks. There were no fatalities in this incident.

Space Shuttle 'Return to Flight'

The US Space Shuttle returned to space flight when it was launched at 10.39 EDT, on 26 July 2005. This mission was denoted as STS-114, or the 'Return to Flight' Space Shuttle mission and was the first time the Shuttle was launched since the loss of Columbia in February 2003. The Shuttle was originally scheduled for launch on 13 July. However, problems with the fuel sensors led to the cancellation of this launch. The Shuttle was finally launched on 26 July, even though NASA scientists had failed to resolve the sensor problems. Video footage revealed that a small fragment of thermal tile had fallen off soon after launch. This prompted NASA to ground the entire Shuttle fleet.

The crew of STS-114 consisted of Eileen M. Collins (Commander), James M. Kelly, Soichi Noguchi, Stephen K.

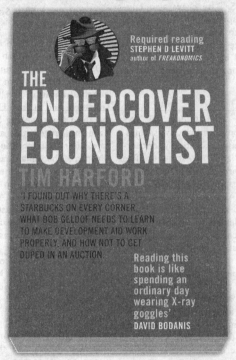

Robinson, Andrew Thomas, Wendy Lawrence and Charles Camarda. The STS-114 mission delivered supplies to the International Space Station (ISS), carried out tests on new Space Shuttle flight safety techniques and equipment and even replaced faulty equipment on the ISS. The mission was completed on 9 August 2005. The crew also conducted three spacewalks while at the station. Due to the poor weather at Kennedy Space Center, Florida, the shuttle landed at Edwards Air Force Base, California, an alternate landing site.

VAT

VAT stands for Value Added Tax. VAT is levied on consumption, not savings, and thus, at least theoretically, encourages savings and investment. The much-delayed arrival of VAT in India finally took place on 1 April 2005. Under the new VAT system, two rates of 4% and 12.5% are applied. The lower rate of 4% is levied on essential products like medicines and drugs, agricultural and industrial goods. The higher rate of 12.5% is applicable to the rest of the goods sold in India. Gold and silver ornaments are subject to a special VAT rate of 1%. Some products like petrol, diesel, aviation turbine fuel, liquor and lottery tickets are exempt from VAT. Under the VAT system, a dealer can take credit for the eligible input tax in a tax period as specified on the total purchases. The trader will charge VAT at the prescribed rate, in the same way as he used to charge sales tax. The VAT payable is compiled on a monthly basis. The dealer can adjust the input tax eligible on the entire purchase in the tax period against the output tax payable, irrespective of whether the entire goods purchased are sold or not.

One of the major advantages of VAT over sales tax is that VAT is non-cascading. The decision to introduce VAT was arrived at during the Conference of Chief Ministers of States/UTs held in 1999 and reiterated during the subsequent meetings held in June 2000 and July 2001.However, although it was earlier decided to implement VAT nationwide from 1 April 2003, this deadline was not met due to a lack of preparedness.

Spat between Shiv Sena and Narayan Rane

The Shiv Sena expelled its Maharashtra assembly leader Narayan Rane on 3 July 2005, a day after he announced his decision to resign from his post and launched an attack on Sena chief Bal Thackeray and his son Uddhav. Rane is the third front-ranking Sena leader to leave the party within a short span of time, after Chhagan Bhujbal and Sanjay Nirupam. The Sena headed towards a split as Rane claimed the support of 42 legislators. However, on 7 July, the Shiv Sena paraded 52 MLAs before the Speaker of the Maharashtra Assembly. On 23 July 2005, Narayan Rane resigned from the Maharashtra legislative assembly. On 30 July Rane formally joined the Congress party and was sworn in as a Cabinet Minister in the Vilasrao Deshmukh-led Democratic Front government.

Tsunami

A tsunami is a series of waves with a long wavelength and the period between crests of the wave can vary from a few minutes to over an hour. Tsunami is a Japanese word meaning 'harbour wave'. Tsunamis can occur at any time of day or night. At nearly 0800 local time on 26 December 2004, a titanic shift of tectonic plates triggered an immense magnitude 9.0 earthquake in the Indian Ocean, 250 kilometers from the west coast of Sumatra, Indonesia. The consequent tsunami devastated coastlines around the ocean and killed around 226,000 people, with millions left destitute. Thirty kilometres beneath the ocean

floor, a 1200-kilometre-stretch of the Indian plate slipped 20 metres beneath the Burma plate. This motion suddenly thrust the seafloor up by several metres, shaking the entire 5-kilometre-deep water column above the fault line. The colossal amount of energy released by the earthquake was roughly equivalent to 23,000 atomic bombs of the size that devastated Hiroshima. The tsunamis took between 15 minutes and 7 hours to reach the various coastlines affected. In India, it caused extensive damage in Andaman & Nicobar Islands, the states of Andhra Pradesh, Kerala and Tamil Nadu and Union Territory of Pondicherry. Aftershock activity, which continued for several days, reduced gradually and there was no aftershock of 6.0 and above magnitude on Richter scale after 9 January 2005. The death toll in India was close to 20,000. The total number of missing persons is at 5,640 of which 5,554 are from Andaman & Nicobar Islands, who are feared to be dead.

Gaza Pull-out

Gaza, a territory that covers about 200 sq km, lies on the Mediterranean coast, where Egypt and Israel meet. About 1.4 million Palestinians live in Gaza, of which 900,000 are refugees from conflicts with Israel. Gaza has been occupied by Israel since 1967. In 1988, The PLO declared an independent Palestinian state in the West Bank and Gaza and in 1993 Israel and the Palestine Liberation Organization (PLO) signed agreements that led to the withdrawal of Israeli troops from most of Gaza in 1994. In February 2005 the Israeli government voted to implement Prime Minister Ariel Sharon's plan for unilateral disengagement from the Gaza Strip beginning on 15 August 2005. The plan required the dismantling of all Israeli settlements there, and the removal of all Israeli settlers and military bases from the Strip, a process that was completed on 12 September 2005

as the Israeli cabinet formally declared an end to military rule in the Gaza Strip after 38 years of control. Approximately 8,000 settlers from Gaza, and the troops who protected them, left Gaza, though Israel will maintain control of Gaza's borders, coastline and airspace.

Maharashtra Floods

In late July many parts of Maharashtra including large areas of Mumbai were flooded. At least 1,000 people died as a result and many were left homeless. The floods occured a month after floods in Gujarat. The floods were caused by the eighth heaviest ever recorded 24-hour rainfall figure of 944 mm which lashed the metropolis on 26 July 2005 and continued on the 27th. Many middle class suburbs such as Andheri, Santa Cruz, Saki Naka, Sion and Goregaon—all thickly populated—came under 5 to 12 feet of water. The rains slackened between the 28th and 30th of July but picked up in intensity again on the 31st. The state government declared 27th and 28th as state holidays for the affected regions. The government also ordered all schools in the affected areas to close on 1 and 2 August. According to preliminary estimates the economic loss to Mumbai alone is close to Rs 450 crore and the figure is likely to go up.

Hurricane Katrina

With the second lowest pressure for an American hurricane in recorded history, Hurricane Katrina made landfall as a Category Four hurricane in Louisiana, USA on the morning of 29 August. The hurricane created massive storm surges and cut off highways connecting the city of New Orleans to mainland Louisiana. New Orleans, which is below sea-level, was completely flooded after levees failed. Many lost thier lives and hundreds of thousands of people were rendered homeless. The government of USA mounted a massive rescue opera-

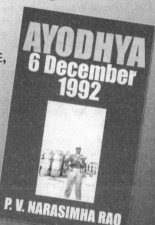

tion in collaboration with the American Red Cross for the victims of Hurricane Katrina. Oil prices soared as a result of the devastation.

Shane Warne

At the age of 36 he is still clearly at the peak of his powers with 40 wickets in the last Ashes series. On the same Old Trafford ground where he dismissed Mike Gatting with his 'ball of the century', Shane Warne became the first player to pass 600 Test wickets. He spearheaded six Ashes series wins for Australia and is one of five players named as Wisden's cricketers of the 20th century. He has also scored more runs than any other Test player without making a hundred.

Sourav Ganguly

Sourav Ganguly crossed the 10,000-run milestone in ODIs in the Indian Oil Cup versus Sri Lanka at Dambulla in 2005.He reached the mark with a single during an innings of 51, his 60th one-day half-century, and broke into what was a two-member club which includes Sachin Tendulkar and Inzaman-ul-Haq. Tendulkar took 259 innings and Inzamam 299 to reach the mark. Ganguly needed 262; he and Tendulkar formed the most productive opening partnership in the history of the game. He has been instrumental in several Indian victories, with 18 of his 22 centuries coming in games India won.

The Ashes

The Ashes is a biennial Test cricket contest played between England and Australia. Australia's first victory on English soil over England, on 29 August 1882, inspired a young London journalist, Reginald Shirley Brooks, to write a mock obituary which read 'In affectionate remembrance of English cricket which died at The Oval, 29th August, 1882. Deeply lamented by a large circle of sorrowing friends and acquaintances, RIP. NB The body will be cre-

mated and the Ashes taken to Australia.' It appeared in the *Sporting Times*. The series is named after this satirical obituary. In the Ashes till date 293 Test matches have been played, out of which Australia has won 117, lost 94 and drawn 82. The last time England had their hands on the tiny urn was in 1987. Since then, things were pretty quiet in England for the last 16 years. The longest journey of the English team came to an end when the 2005 Ashes series was played in England, and was won by England 2-1. The next Ashes series will be in Australia in 2006/2007.

Greg Chappell

Soon after John Wright ended his four-and-a-half year tenure, BCCI started discussions for the new coach of the Indian cricket team. The committee comprising Sunil Gavaskar, Ravi Shastri and Srinivas Venkata-raghavan interviewed four short-listed candidates— Mohinder Amarnath, Greg Chappell, Desmond Haynes and Tom Moody. Finally, former Australian captain Greg Chappell became India's new coach. It is second time lucky for Chappell, who was overlooked when New Zealander John Wright was given the job in 2000. It was a unanimous decision. His contract will be for two years until June 2007. The 56-year-old comes from a famous cricket family, with grandfather Victor Richardson and brothers Ian and Trevor also playing Test cricket for Australia. He led Australia in 48 of his 87 Tests, winning 21, although his spell in charge was interrupted by his involvement in Kerry Packer's World Series Cricket, which ran from 1977 to 1979. His feat of scoring centuries in each innings of his captaincy debut is unequalled.

Anil Kumble

When Anil Kumble trapped Mohammad Rafique of Bangladesh at Dhaka in 2004, he went past Kapil Dev to become India's leading wicket-

taker in Test cricket. Kumble's first 200 wickets took him 47 Tests, but since then he has been accumulating them at a much faster rate—236 more in just 44 games. The milestone came 14 years, four months and one day after he bowled his first ball in Tests—against England at Old Trafford in 1990.No bowler in India's history has won more Test matches than Anil Kumble. For most of his career Kumble struggled to make an impact outside India, but he turned that around magnificently in Australia in 2003-04, taking an incredible 24 wickets in three Test matches. Three months later, his 6 for 71 on a flat pitch at Multan helped India win a Test in Pakistan for the first time. His tally now stands at 461 wickets in 95 Test matches.

Harry Potter and the Half-Blood Prince

Set during Harry Potter's sixth year at Hogwarts, the sixth book in J.K. Rowling's phenomenally best-selling series prepares the reader for his last battles with Lord Voldemort. When it was released on 16 July 2005, it was the first book in the United Kingdom to have a simultaneous standard print, large print, and Braille edition release. In 24 hours, the book sold 6.9 million copies in the United States alone, roughly about 250,000 books per hour, making it the fastest selling book in history. It generated over $100 million in sales out of the gate, outpacing even the combined take of the top movies at the box office. Released simultaneously in India on 16 July, the book sold more than 100,000 copies in the first day alone. The Harry Potter series has sold more than 300 million copies worldwide so far.

Pope Benedict XVI

Pope Benedict XVI was elected on 19 April 2005, in a papal conclave over which he presided in his capacity as dean of the College of Cardinals. He was born on 16 April 1927 as Joseph Alois Ratzinger in Marktlam Inn, Bavaria, Germany.Presently, he is the 266th reigning pope, the head of the Roman Catholic Church and sovereign of Vatican City. He celebrated his Papal Inauguration Mass on 24 April 2005 and was enthroned in the Basilica of St. John Lateran (Basilica di San Giovanni in Laterano) on 7 May 2005.He served as professor at various German universities, Archbishop of Munich, Prefect of the Congregation for the Doctrine of the Faith and Dean of the College of Cardinals before becoming Pope.He is the oldest person to have been elected pope since Clement XII in 1730. He served longer as a cardinal before being elected pope than any pope since Benedict XIII (elected 1724). He is the 9th German pope, the last being the Dutch-German Adrian VI (1522–1523).

Condoleezza Rice

Condoleezza Rice, (born 14 November 1954), is the second United States Secretary of State in the administration of President George W. Bush. She replaced Colin Powell on 26 January 2005 to become the first African American woman, second African American (after Powell), and second woman (after Madeleine Albright) to serve in that post. She also was in government service from 1989 through March 1991, the period of German reunification and the final days of the Soviet Union, when she served in the Bush Administration as Director, and then Senior Director, of Soviet and East European Affairs in the National Security Council, and a Special Assistant to the President for National Security Affairs.She was a Professor of Political Science at Stanford University and served as Provost from 1993 to 1999.

Prakash Karat

The 56-year-old Prakash Karat was elected as the General Secretary of the Communist Party of India (Marxist) in

the 18th party congress on 11 April 2005. It elected a Central Committee with 85 members and 17-member Politburo.He takes over from Harkishen Singh Surjeet, who offered to step down from the post. His wife, Brinda, became the first woman entrant to the all-male politburo of the party. Prakash Karat was drawn into the Left movement in the 1960s, as a student in the Madras Christian College. He later went to the University of Edinburgh. He was elected to the party Central Committee in 1985 and the politburo in 1992.

British Elections and Tony Blair

The UK General Election was held on 5 May 2005 and was won by the Labour Party. Tony Blair, the leader of the Labour Party and Prime Minister, has won a historic third term in government for the Labour party. 645 parliamentary seats were contested at the general election with the winning party needing 324 seats to form the government.Tony Blair is the only Labour leader to have won three elections in a row but his margin of victory is less than half what it was in the Labour landslides of 1997 and 2001—and he has the lowest share of the vote for a ruling party in modern times. The Labour Party secured an overall majority of 66. Turnout figures showed that only about 61 percent of people eligible to vote went to the polls—a 2 per cent rise on the last general election.The major issues were 'War on terror', Aid and trade and Tax and spending.

Tenth Planet

Astronomers in the United States have announced the discovery of the '10th planet' to orbit our Sun. Designated 2003 UB313, it is about 3,000km across—a world of rock and ice and somewhat larger than Pluto. Scientists say it is three times as far away as Pluto, in an orbit at an angle to the or-

bits of the main planets. Its discoverers are Michael Brown of Caltech, Chad Trujillo of the Gemini Observatory in Hawaii, and David Rabinowitz of Yale University. It was picked up using the Samuel Oschin Telescope at Palomar Observatory and the 8m Gemini North telescope on Mauna Kea. The discoveries will once again ignite the debate about the qualifications of an object to be called a planet, an issue the International Astronomical Union is wrestling with as the official naming organization for this area of science.

G8 on Africa

Africa and Climate Change were the two main themes of the 2005 G8 Summit in Gleneagles.The international community set itself the eight UN Millennium Development Goals (MDGs) to achieve by 2015. These included targets on eradicating extreme poverty, combating HIV and AIDS and malaria, and ensuring that every child receives primary education. UK Prime Minister Tony Blair therefore made Africa a priority of the G8 Summit in Gleneagles. The comprehensive package agreed at Gleneagles were (a) A doubling of aid by 2010—an extra $50 billion worldwide and $25 billion for Africa, (b) Writing-off immediately the debts of 18 of the world's poorest countries, most of which are in Africa; this is worth $40 billion now, and as much as $55 billion as more countries qualify, (c) Writing off $17 billion of Nigeria's debt, in the biggest single debt deal ever, (d) As close to universal access to HIV/AIDS treatments as possible by 2010, (e) Up to an extra 25,000 trained peacekeeping troops, helping the Africa Union to better respond to security challenges like Darfur.

New Directive on Hijacking

Adopting tough measures to prevent hijacking, the Indian government has

decided to allow shooting down of a hijacked plane in case there is conclusive evidence that it is being used as a missile like the 9/11 terror attack. The anti-hijack policy, cleared by the Cabinet Committee on Security (CCS), rules out negotiations with hijackers on their demands and makes it clear that talks will only be aimed at preventing loss of life or ending the incident. The policy, which provides for death penalty to hijackers, also reduces bureaucratic hassles for getting permission for armed intervention due to shortage of reaction time. The Indian Air Force has been given the authority to take necessary steps for scrambling fighter jets to guard and guide the hijacked aircraft and force it to land on an Indian airport. However, a decision in this respect has to be taken by an official of the rank of Assistant Chief of Air Staff (Operations) or above. The policy says the decision to shoot down the hijacked aircraft should be taken after it is conclusively ascertained that the aircraft is being used as a missile.

World Year of Physics

The World Year of Physics (WYP 2005) is a worldwide celebration of physics and its importance in our everyday lives. Physics not only plays an important role in the development of science and technology but also has a tremendous impact on our society. The year 2005 marks the 100th anniversary of Albert Einstein's 'miraculous year' in which he published three important papers describing ideas that have since influenced all of modern physics. This year provides the opportunity to celebrate Einstein, his great ideas, and his influence on life in the 21st century. The International Union of Pure and Applied Physics declared the year 2005 as the World Year of Physics. The US physics community's efforts for 2005 are led by the American Physical Society, the American Association of Physics Teachers, and the American Institute of Physics, the premier organizations in the US for physicists, physics teachers, and physics societies.

Indian Idol

Indian Idol was one of the most popular prime-time shows on Indian television in 2005. The Sony Entertainment Television(India) program is co-produced with the makers of *American Idol*. The format is similar to *American Idol* and the British program *Pop Idol*. Approximately 120 finalists are chosen from auditions held throughout the country. The judges shortlist 30 performers on the basis of their performance on a given song. The TV audience votes by phone for 11 superfinalists. All but one contestant are eliminated each week by viewer votes. Abhijeet Sawant from Mumbai was crowned the Indian Idol beating out Amit Sana from Bhilai on 5 March 2005. The winner signed a contract worth Rs 1 crore with Sony Entertainment Television(India) along with a chance to record an album.

Kashmir Bus

India and Pakistan agreed to launch a landmark bus service across the ceasefire line dividing Kashmir on February 2005. The deal was announced after a meeting between the Indian and Pakistani foreign ministers in Islamabad. It gave millions of Kashmiris a chance to travel across the ceasefire line for the first time in more than 50 years. The two sides also agreed to use entry permits in place of passports once identities of the travellers are verified. India's Prime Minister Manmohan Singh flagged off the historic first bus to Muzaffarabad, capital of Pakistan administered Kashmir, in Srinagar on 7 April 2005.

Lakshmi Mittal

Lakshmi Mittal is a billionaire industrialist born in Sadulpur, Rajasthan, India, and currently residing in Kensington,

London, UK.He is chairman of the Mittal Steel Company NV, which is the world's largest producer of steel. He was the Fortune European Businessman of the Year for 2004. In March 2005, *Forbes* Magazine named him the 3rd richest man in the world (he was the 62nd richest in 2004) and the richest non-American, with an estimated wealth of US$25 billion. His residence in Kensington, bought in 2003 for £70 million ($128 million) from Formula One car racing boss Bernie Ecclestone, is the most expensive house ever purchased. He holds steel assets in Romania, Bosnia-Herzegovina, South Africa, Poland, Indonesia, Kazakhstan, the United States and other countries.

SENSEX 8500

The BSE Sensex or BSE Sensitive Index is a value-weighted index composed of 30 stocks with the base April 1979 = 100. It consists of the 30 largest and most actively traded stocks, representative of various sectors, on the Bombay Stock Exchange. The set of companies in the index is essentially fixed. The Sensex is generally regarded as the most popular and precise barometer of the Indian stock markets. The base value of the Sensex is 100 on 1 April 1979. At irregular intervals, the Bombay Stock Exchange (BSE) authorities review and modify its composition to make sure it reflects current market conditions. The stock market has grown by more than seven times from June 1990 to today. On 25 July 1990, the Sensex touched the magical four-digit figure for the first time and closed at 1,001 and on 8 October 1999, it crossed the 5,000-mark. The Sensex crossed the 8500 level on the Bombay Stock Exchange in September 2005 on brisk buying by funds in index-heavy shares of Reliance Industries, Infosys and some banking stocks. The Sensex jumped up from 8000 to 8500 in just eight trading sessions, the shortest ever period in the bourse's history. It appears that there is no stopping of the bull-run, which started in June 2003, unlike in the past when the bull-runs ended in disaster in 1992, 1995 and 2004. Foreign Institutional Investors continue to be in buoyant mood to increase their exposures in the Indian Stock Market. The trading volumes have also soared from Rs 37,801 crore to Rs 54,532 crore on Bombay Stock Exchange.

Amitabh Bachchan

Only five years ago, it looked like it was all over for the King of Bollywood. A succession of films flopped. Endorsements dried up. Even his company's 1996 production of the Miss World beauty pageant was plagued by protests from both Indian conservatives and feminists. By the turn of the millennium, Bachchan found himself $20 million in debt. Today the man known as the Big B is bigger than ever. The last two years have seen a string of box-office successes and a level of critical acclaim unprecedented in his 35-year career. Bachchan shot 11 films last year and has signed up for nine more this year, up from only four in 2002. He has endorsement contracts with a total of 17 brands, from Parker Pens to Pepsi. And in August, he returned to host a second series of the blockbuster television game show *Kaun Banega Crorepati*, the Indian version of *Who Wants to be a Millionaire?* At 62, he's still tall, dark and handsome.

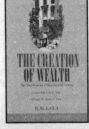

Obituaries

November 2004

Sheikh Zayed bin Sultan Al Nahayan: The ruler of Abu Dhabi and president of the United Arab Emirates passed away on 2 November. He became the Emir of Abu Dhabi in 1966. He played an instrumental role in the formation of the UAE and was its first president, first elected in 1971 and re-elected in 1976, 1981, 1986, and 1991.

Theo van Gogh: The Dutch film director, television producer, publicist and actor was murdered on 2 November. He was 47. He was the great-grandson of art dealer Theo van Gogh, brother of Vincent van Gogh. His notable films include *Blind Date* and *Submission*.

Iris Chang: The US-born historian and journalist passed away on 9 November 2004. She was 36. The daughter of Taiwanese immigrants, she was best known for her controversial account of the Nanjing Massacre, titled *The Rape of Nanking*.

Yasser Arafat: The Palestine leader, Chairman of the Palestine Liberation Organization and President of the Palestinian Authority passed away on 11 November 2004. He was 75. He was born Mohammed Abdel-Raouf Arafat As Qudwa al-Hussaeini. He was awarded the 1994 Nobel Peace Prize, along with Yitzhak Rabin and Shimon Peres. He also served as commander-in-chief of the Palestinian Revolutionary Forces and as the head of the PLO's political department. In 1989, he was elected as the future president of the proclaimed State of Palestine.

Arthur Hailey: The British-born best-selling novelist passed away on 24 November. He was 84. He was known for novels with different industrial or commercial backgrounds. His notable works include *Runway Zero-Eight*, *Hotel*, *Airport*, *Strong Medicine* and *The Evening News*.

John Drew Barrymore: The US actor passed away on 29 November 2004. He was 72. Born John Blythe Barrymore, Jr, he was a member of the Barrymore family, being the son of famous stage and screen actor John Barrymore. He was the father of current actor Drew Barrymore.

December 2004

Madurai Shanmukhavadivu (M.S.) Subbulakshmi: The Carnatic musician passed away on 11 December 2004. She was 88. Born Kunjamma in Madurai in 1916, she also acted in a few Tamil films. She received numerous awards, including the Ramon Magsaysay Award in 1974 and the Bharat Ratna in 1996.

Vijay Samuel Hazare: The former Indian cricket captain passed away on 18 December 2004. He was 89. A right-hand batsman and right-arm medium pace bowler, he made his Test debut against England at Lord's (June 1946). He was noted for his performance on India's first tour of Australia in 1947-48, when he scored a century in each innings of the Adelaide Test.

Pamulaparthi Venkata (P.V.) Narasimha Rao: The ninth Prime Minister of India (1991–1996) passed away on 23 December 2004. He was 83. He also served as Chief Minister of Andhra Pradesh and as Union Cabinet Minister (including home, defence and external affairs portfolios). He initiated free market reforms in the country. His tenure also witnessed the Babri Masjid crisis in 1992.

Nripendralal Chakraborty: The CPI (M) politician and former Tripura Chief Minister passed away on 25 December 2004. He was 99. A former member of the Politburo, he was elected to the Assembly for seven consecutive terms. He was the Chief Minister of Tripura from 1978 to 1988.

Artie Shaw: The American jazz musician, composer, bandleader, and writer, passed away on 30 December 2004. He was born Arthur Jacob Arshawsky. His notable hits include *Begin the Beguine*, *Lady Be Good*, and *Frenesi*.

January 2005

Jyotindra Nath Dixit: The Indian bureaucrat and incumbent National Security Adviser passed away on 3 January. He was 68. A former foreign secretary, he was also India's Alternate Permanent Representative and member of the Governing Bodies of the International Atomic Energy Agency.

Amrish Puri: The Indian actor passed away on 12 January. He was 72. He made his Bollywood debut in 1971 with *Reshma Aur Shera*. Notable Indian films include *Mr India*, *Shakti*, *Ghatak*. He also acted in Steven Spielberg's *Indiana Jones and the Temple of Doom*.

Zhao Ziyang: The People's Republic of China politician and former Premier passed away on 17 January. He was 85. He served as Premier of the People's Republic of China from 1980 to 1987, and General Secretary of the Communist Party of China from 1987 to 1989. A leading reformer, he was removed from power following his support of student demonstrators during the 1989 Tiananmen Square protests.

Parveen Babi: The actress passed away on 20 January. She was 49. Born as Parveen Wali Mohammad Khan Babi, she was the first Indian actress to be featured on *Time* magazine's cover. She made her debut in *Charitraheen*. Other notable films include *Namak Halaal* and *Kaalia*. She was a member of the royal family of Junagad.

February 2005

Maximillian Adolph Otto Siegfried 'Max' Schmeling: The former German world heavyweight boxing champion passed away on 2 February. He was 99. He won the world championship beating Jack Sharkey in 1930, thus becoming the first German heavyweight world champion. He lost his title to Sharkey in 1932 but came back to defeat the previously unbeaten Joe Louis in June, 1936.

Gnassingbe Eyadema: The president of Togo passed away on 5 February. He was 67. He became President on 14 April 1967 and stayed in power for the next 38 years.

Vinod Chandra Pande: The politician passed away on 7 February. A former governor of three states, he also served as a Cabinet Secretary.

Rafic Bahaa El Din Hariri: The Lebanese businessman, politician and former Prime Minister was assassinated on 14 February. He was 60. After making his fortune in businesses in Saudi Arabia, he played a key role in ending the civil war in Lebanon. In 1992, he returned to Lebanon and became the country's Prime Minister. He served in this role till 1998, and again from 2000 till his death. He also played a key role in the reconstruction of Lebanon following the end of the civil war.

Jef Raskin: The US human-computer interface expert passed away on 26 February. He was 61. He was best known for starting the Macintosh project for Apple Computer.

March 2005

Peter Zvi Malkin: The Israeli secret agent and member of the Israeli Mossad intelligence agency passed away on 1 March. He was 77. Born as Zvi Malchin, he rose to become the Chief of Operations in Mossad. He is best known for his role in the capture of senior Nazi official Adolf Eichmann in May 1960.

Gemini Ganesan: The actor passed away on 22 March. He was 85. Born as Ramaswamy Ganesan, he was known as *kadhal mannan* ('king of romance') of Tamil cinema; he was also a Lecturer at the Madras Christian College. He

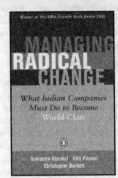

acted in more than 200 films, notable among which are *Avvai Shanmughi, Paava Mannipu, Kalyana Parisu and Hello Mr Zamindar.* He was awarded the Padma Shri in 1971.

April 2005

Pope John Paul II: The pope of the Catholic Church passed away on 2 April. He was 84. Born Karol Józef Wojtya in Poland, he became a bishop in 1958, the Archbishop of Krakow in 1963 and a cardinal in 1967. He was elected Pope in 1978, at the young age of 58. He survived an assassination attempt in the Vatican City in 1981.

Saul Bellow: The Canadian-born US author passed away on 5 April. He was 89. Born Solomon Bellows, he taught at a number of US universities. His first published novel was *Dangling Man,* published in 1944. His other notable works include *The Adventures of Augie March, Seize the Day, The Dean's December, Humboldt's Gift* and *Ravelstein.* He was awarded the Nobel Prize for Literature in 1976.

Rainier III, Louis-Henri-Maxence-Bertrand: The Sovereign Prince of Monaco passed away on 6 April. He was 81. He succeeded his grandfather, Prince Louis II on 9 May 1949. He is noted for revamping the economy of Monaco. He also promulgated a new constitution and renegotiated the relationship with France. He was once married to famous US actor, Grace Kelly. He was one of the longest serving monarchs at the time of his death.

Lucien Laurent: The French footballer passed away on 11 April. He was 97. He is famous for scoring the first ever World Cup goal.

Vishnu Kant Shastri: The Indian politician passed away on 17 April. He was 76. A member of Rajya Sabha, he was a former Governor of Himachal Pradesh and Uttar Pradesh and a President of Akhil Bhartiya Vidyarthi Parishad.

Ezer Weizman: The former Israeli president passed away on 24 April 2005. He was 80. He also served as a combat pilot in the British Royal Air Force and later in the Israeli Air Force. He later became the Chief of Operations on the General Staff of the Israeli Defence Forces.

May 2005

Robert Hunter: The Canadian environmentalist, journalist, author and politician passed away on 2 May. He was 63. He co-founded the international environmental organization, Greenpeace, in 1969.

Subodh Mukherjee: The Indian filmmaker passed away on 21 May. He was 84. He got his first break as a director in *Paying Guest.* The hits that he produced include *Junglee* and *Munimji.* He introduced Saira Banu in *Shagird* and Rakhee in *Sharmilee.*

Ismail Merchant: The Indian-born film producer passed away on 25 May. He was 68. He was born Ismail Noormohamed Abdul Rehman in Mumbai. His first film was *The Creation of Woman.* Other notable works include *The Householder, Shakespeare Wallah, In Custody* and *The Mystic Masseur.* In May 1961, he formed Merchant Ivory Productions along with James Ivory. He also wrote several books on cooking, such as *Ismail Merchant's Indian Cuisine, Ismail Merchant's Florence, Ismail Merchant's Passionate Meals* and *Ismail Merchant's Paris: Filming and Feasting in France.*

Sunil Dutt: The Bollywood actor and Union Minister passed away on 25 May. He was 75. Born as Balraj Dutt, he was noted for his role in *Mother India.* Other notable films are *Gumraah, Waqt* and *Humraaz.* He joined the Congress party in 1984 and was the serving Union Minister for Youth Affairs and Sports when he passed away.

June 2005

Anne Bancroft: The American actress passed away on 6 June. She was

73. She was born Anna Maria Louisa Italiano. She started off as a stage artist, and made her cinema debut in 1952 in *Don't Bother to Knock*. Her notable roles were in *The Miracle Worker*, *The Pumpkin Eater* and *7 Women*, but she is best remembered for her role of Mrs Robinson in *The Graduate*. She was also known for her numerous TV appearances.

Syed Mushtaq Ali: The Indian cricketer passed away on 18 June. He was 90. A Padma Shri recipient, he made his debut against England in Calcutta in 1933-34. He played 226 first-class matches, scoring more than 13000 runs and claiming 162 wickets.

Larry Collins: The US author passed away on 20 June. He was 75. He was born John Lawrence Collins Jr. and worked as a newspaper correspondent early in his career. He wrote a number of books along with French writer Dominique Lapierre. The most notable among these are *Is Paris Burning?*, *O Jerusalem!* and *Freedom at Midnight*.

Jack Kilby: The American engineer and inventor of the integrated circuit passed away on 20 June. He was 81. He was a co-recipient of the Nobel prize for Physics in 2000, as well as a large number of other awards and recognitions. He also taught Electrical Engineering at Texas A&M University in USA and held more than 60 patents. He is credited with co-inventing the hand-held calculator and the thermal printer used in portable data terminals.

Eknath Dhondu Solkar: The former Indian cricketer passed away on 26 June. He was 57. A left-hand batsman, he was also famous for his catching abilities. He made his Test debut against New Zealand at Hyderabad in October 1969. He took as many as 53 catches from 27 Tests, scored more than 1068 runs at an average of 25.42 and took 18 wickets.

July 2005

Luther Vandross: The US R&B singer passed away on 1 July. He was 54. Born as Luther Ronzoni Vandross Jr., his albums are estimated to have sold 25 million copies. He won eight Grammy awards including Best Male R&B Vocal Performance four times. He won four Grammy awards in 2004. His albums include *Never Too Much*, *Busy Body*, *The Night I Fell in Love*, and *Give Me the Reason*.

Balkrishna Pandharinath 'Baloo' Gupte: The former Indian Test cricketer passed away on 5 July. He was 70. He played three Tests for India between 1961 and 1965. He was also a leading wicket-taker in Ranji Trophy. His record of 9 for 55 for West Zone against South Zone in the 1962-63 Duleep Trophy final is still the best in the competition. He career figures stand at 417 wickets in 99 first-class games at an average of 24.88.

James Montgomery Doohan: The Canadian actor passed away on 20 July. He was 85. He was noted for his portrayal of Scotty on the original *Star Trek* television and film series.

John Garang de Mabior: The Sudanese Vice President and former leader of the rebel Sudan People's Liberation Army was killed in a helicopter crash on 30 July. He was 60.

Willem Frederik Duisenberg: The Dutch banker and politician and the first president of the European Central Bank (1998–2003), passed away on 31 July. He was 70. Commonly known as Wim Duisenberg, he played a key role in the introduction of the euro. Earlier in life, he worked at the International Monetary Fund and as an´ advisor to the director of the Nederlandsche Bank, the Dutch central bank. He also served as a professor at the University of Amsterdam. He was the Dutch Minister of Finance from 1973 to 1977, served as the vice president of the Dutch private bank, Rabobank and as the president of Nederlandsche Bank from 1982 to 1997.

August 2005

King Fahd bin Abdul Aziz al-Saud: The king and prime minister of Saudi Arabia and leader of the House of Saud passed away on 1 August. A son of the founder of the Saudi state, Ibn Saud, he had served as education minister, interior minister, and as deputy prime minister before becoming the crown prince in 1975. He ascended to the Saudi throne in 1982 following the death of King Khalid.

Robin Finlayson Cook: The Labour Party politician and former British Secretary of State for Foreign and Commonwealth Affairs (1997–2001) passed away on 6 August. He was 59. After the 2001 general elections, he was appointed the Leader of the House of Commons. He resigned from his post as Leader of the House of Commons and Lord President of the Council on 17 March 2003, in protest of the British government's decision to take part in military ation against Iraq. Earlier, he served as Shadow Social Services Secretary, Shadow Health Secretary, Shadow Trade Secretary and Shadow Foreign Secretary.

Lakshman Kadirgamar: The Sri Lankan politician and incumbent Foreign Minister was assassinated on 12 August. He was 73. He served as the foreign minister from 1994 to 2001 and again from April 2004 until his assassination. A trained lawyer, he was well known for his stance against negotiation with the Tamil rebels in Sri Lanka. In 2003, he was a candidate for the position of Secretary-General of the Commonwealth but lost to Don McKinnon of New Zealand.

Tonino Delli Colli: The Italian cinematographer passed away on 17 August. He was 81. He is noted for his work in films that include *The Good, the Bad and the Ugly*, *Once Upon a Time in the West*, *Once Upon a Time in America*, *Death and the Maiden*, *Bitter Moon*, *The Name of the Rose*, *The Decameron* and *The Canterbury Tales*. His last film was Roberto Benigni's 1997 film, *Life Is Beautiful*.

Marjorie 'Mo' Mowlam: The British Labour Party politician and former Secretary of State for Northern Ireland (1997–1999) passed away on 19 August. She was 55. She was the first woman to hold the post of Secretary of State for Northern Ireland. In 1999, she was appointed as Cabinet Office Minister. She also held the posts of Shadow Secretary of State for Northern Ireland and Shadow Secretary of State for National Heritage.

Robert Moog: The pioneer of electronic music, best known for his invention of the Moog synthesizer, passed away on 21 August. He was 71. He also received a Grammy Trustees Award for lifetime achievement in 1970.

Józef Rotblat: The Polish-born British physicist, anti-nuclear weapons campaigner and founder of Pugwash Conferences passed away on 31 August. He was 96. He was awarded the Nobel Peace Prize in 1995, along with the Pugwash Conferences on Science and World Affairs. He was also involved in the Manhattan Project, the US project to build atomic bombs during World War II, but later left it. He, along with famous philosopher and author Bertrand Russell, founded the Pugwash Conferences on Science and World Affairs in 1957.

September 2005

William Hubbs Rehnquist: The Chief Justice of the United States passed away on 3 September 2005. He was 80. He was an American attorney, jurist and political figure, who served as a United States Supreme Court justice from 1972 until 1986. He served as the Chief Justice from 1986 until his death in 2005.

Robert Wise: The US film producer and director passed away on 14 September. He was 91. He began his movie career as a sound and music editor and was nominated for the Academy Award for Film Editing for *Citizen Kane*. The first film that he directed was *The Curse of the Cat People*. His two most well known works are *West Side Story* and *The Sound of Music*. Other notable films are *The Day the Earth Stood Still* and *I Want to Live!* Nominated for the Oscars numerous times, he won for both Best Picture and Best Director for *West Side Story* and for *The Sound of Music*. He also won the Irving G. Thalberg Memorial Award in 1967.

Simon Wiesenthal: The Austrian architectural engineer, Holocaust survivor and Nazi hunter passed away on 20 September. He was 96. He was born Szymon Wiesenthal in what is now Ukraine. He is credited with the capture of more than a 1000 Nazi war criminals, including Adolf Eichmann, Karl Silberbauer, Franz Stangl and Hermine Braunsteiner-Ryan. He received a number of international awards and decorations, including the US Congressional Gold Medal and the French Legion of Honor.

World Dateline

October 2004

5: A fire breaks out on board the Canadian submarine, HMCS *Chicoutimi*. The submarine is subsequently stranded without power in the North Atlantic Ocean, off the north coast of Ireland. One crewmember is killed.

8: Kenneth Bigley, a British held hostage in Iraq is killed after a failed escape attempt. Philosopher Jacques Derrida, the founder of deconstruction, passes away.

9: Incumbent Australian PM, John Howard, leads the Liberal-National coalition to victory over the Labor Party in federal elections. Democratic elections are held in Afghanistan. However, the election is marred by widespread boycott by the presidential candidates and claims of irregularities. Even the counting of ballots is delayed but ultimately the UNICEF gives the go ahead after it decides that the irregularities would not affect the outcome. In UK, Queen Elizabeth II opens the new Scottish Parliament Building in a ceremony in Edinburgh.

10: Abdullahi Yusuf is chosen as the new president of Somalia. He was elected by a session of the transitional Parliament held in neighbouring Kenya on 10 October and sworn in on 14 October. American actor Christopher Reeve, who shot to fame after portraying Superman, passes away.

14: Prince Norodom Sihamoni is chosen as the new King of Cambodia. Previously Cambodia's ambassador to UNESCO, he is named the new ruler by a nine-member throne council.

20: Susilo Bambang Yudhoyono becomes President of Indonesia. He is a former military commander and served as a minister in the government of President Abdurrahman Wahid.

23: A powerful earthquake strikes Japan, north of Tokyo. The first quake measures 6.8 on the Richter Scale and is centred in Niigata state, 260km north of Tokyo. It kills over 15 people, injures nearly a 1000 more. It causes widespread damage to property and even derails a high-speed Bullet train.

24: Brazil successfully launches its first rocket into space. The VSV-30 vehicle is successfully launched from a launch centre at a place named Alcantara.

26: The Cassini probe passes within 1,200km of Titan. It sends back images of Saturn's moon Titan giving scientists the closest views yet of the satellite.

27: Details of the discovery of a new, recent, species of fossil hominid, *Homo floresiensis*, from the island of Flores, Indonesia are published. The one-metre-tall species has been dubbed 'the Hobbit' and is believed to have lived on Flores Island until at least 12,000 years ago. Australian archaeologists unearthed the bones while digging at a site named Liang Bua, a limestone cave on Flores.

29: A videotape of Osama bin Laden speaking is telecast on an Arabic television channel. He threatens more attacks on the USA.

November 2004

1: The deputy governor of Baghdad, Hatem Kamil, is assassinated.

2: Voting takes place in the US Presidential elections. NASA announces that it will resume its space shuttle program in May or early June, 2005. UAE president and founding father Sheikh Zayed passes away; Vice-President and Prime Minister Sheikh Maktoum becomes interim president. Controversial Dutch filmmaker Theo van Gogh is stabbed and shot dead in Amsterdam.

3: Khalifa bin Zayed Al Nahayan, the son of late UAE president Sheikh Zayed, is elected the new President of United Arab Emirates. President George W. Bush wins the popular vote in the US Presidential election. Senator John Kerry concedes defeat in the US presidential elections. US Democratic Senate Minority Leader Tom Daschle concedes defeat to Republican challenger John Thune, the first Senate leader in 52 years to lose a re-election bid. Hungary announces the withdrawal of its 300 troops in Iraq by the end of March 2005; Poland announces that it will scale back its 2,500 troops stationed in Iraq in 2005.

4: Russian President Vladimir Putin signs a bill approving the parliament's ratification of the Kyoto protocol.

6: Talks between Iran and three European Union members (France, Germany and the United Kingdom) on the Iranian nuclear program end without an agreement. Nine French peacekeepers and a US citizen are killed in the rebel-held town of Bouake in Côte d'Ivoire following a government air strike against insurgents. The French military retaliates by destroying two warplanes at Yamoussoukro airport.

7: Burt Rutan of Scaled Composites is officially awarded the Ansari X Prize for the first privately funded space flight.

8: US forces launch a major assault on the Iraqi town of Fallujah.

9: The Mozilla Foundation releases the first official version of its open source web browser, Firefox. Violence in Côte d'Ivoire results in 20 deaths and nearly 600 injuries; cocoa exports are halted. The Sudanese government and rebel leaders sign two accords over the Darfur conflict, including agreements on a no-fly zone over Darfur, the disarming of the Janjaweed militia and informing the location of forces to cease-fire monitors. United Nations officials arrive to investigate claims of genocide. United States Attorney General John Ashcroft and Secretary of Commerce Donald Evans resign. US forces reach the centre of Fallujah.

10: President George W. Bush announces White House Counsel Alberto R. Gonzales as his nominee for United States Attorney General. Three relatives of Iraqi Prime Minister Iyad Allawi are kidnapped. Kidnappers demand the lifting of the siege on Fallujah.

11: PLO leader Saeb Erakat announces that Palestinian Authority leader Yasser Arafat has died at the age of 75. Rawhi Fattouh becomes interim President of the Palestinian Authority. Lithuania becomes the first country to approve the new EU constitution.

12: Yasser Arafat's funeral procession is held in Cairo, Egypt. Later, he is 'temporarily' buried within his former headquarters in Ramallah in the West Bank.

13: Iran reaches an agreement with France, Germany and the UK to curb most of its uranium enrichment programme. 9 January 2005 is announced as the date for holding elections to choose the successor to Yasser Arafat.

15: The European Space Agency's ion propulsion spacecraft SMART-1 enters into lunar orbit. Bhutan announces a nation-wide ban on tobacco sales. US President George W. Bush accepts the resignation of Secretary of State Colin Powell.

16: US White House officials announce that Condoleezza Rice will be nominated to succeed Colin Powell as Secretary of State. NASA's hypersonic X-43 research aircraft reaches a speed of approximately Mach 10, breaking a record by reaching a velocity of about 7,000 mph in an unmanned experimental flight.

17: US retail giant Kmart purchases Sears in a deal worth $11.5 billion.

18: The US Department of Agriculture announces that a cow has tested positive for mad cow disease.

19: The government of Sudan and southern rebels sign an agreement at a special session of the United Nations Security Council in Nairobi, Kenya; both sides promise to commit themselves to ending the 21-year conflict by 31 December; the Council passes a resolution pledging substantial aid to the country after the war ceases.

20: NASA launches Swift, a satellite to investigate gamma ray bursts.

21: Hifikepunye Pohamba, of the ruling South-West Africa People's Organisation party, is declared the winner of the Namibian presidential election with 76% of the vote. The Electoral Commission of the Iraq interim government announces that par-liamentary elections will be held on 30 January 2005. In USA, the Grand Canyon is artificially flooded to bring natural sediment to the ecosystem.

22: Viktor Yanukovych is declared the official winner in the final round of the presidential election in Ukraine; opposition leader Viktor Yushchenko calls for supporters to protest what he calls 'the total falsification of the vote'; observers from the Organization for Security and Co-operation in Europe (OSCE) and senior US election observer, Senator Richard Lugar criticize the election. Iran declares that it will suspend its uranium enrichment programme, to meet a European Union-brokered deadline.

23: Ukrainian opposition leader Viktor Yushchenko declares himself winner in the Presidential election and takes a symbolic oath of office at a special parliament session; a 200,000 strong crowd surrounds the parliament building in Kiev.

24: The European Union rejects an Iranian request to continue using uranium enrichment centrifuges.

25: The Ukrainian Supreme Court disallows the publication of the presidential election results. Iran prevents the International Atomic Energy Agency (IAEA) from sealing centrifuges at the Natanz enrichment facility.

26: Several Ukrainian regions threaten to hold autonomy referendums; Yuschenko supporters blockade official buildings in Kiev; incumbent president Leonid Kuchma holds discussions with key European envoys; Yuschenko requests a new vote on 12 December. Palestinian organization Fatah officially picks former PM and PLO chairman Mahmoud Abbas as its candidate for January's presidential elections.

27: Ukraine's parliament votes for the annulment of the election results and asks President Leonid Kuchma to dissolve the country's Central Election Committee.

28: Swiss voters approve government proposals to permit research using stem cells of human embryos.

29: The People's Republic of China and Association of South East Asian Nations (ASEAN) sign a trade pact. The Ukrainian Supreme Court continues its public hearings of electoral fraud; outgoing President Leonid Kuchma asks for a new election. Chilean President Ricardo Lagos proposes special lifetime pensions for 28,000 survivors of the Pinochet regime's torture camps.

December 2004

1: Palestinian leader Marwan Barghouti joins the electoral race to succeed Yasser Arafat. The head of Brazil's AIDS programme says the government will violate patents on anti-AIDS drugs by copying them. Israeli Prime Minister Ariel Sharon sacks ministers from the secular Shinui party from his coalition government. Ukraine's parliament passes a vote of no confidence to dismiss Viktor Yanukovich as Prime Minister. The opposition led by Viktor Yushchenko agrees to continue negotiations and end the blockade of official buildings. A French appeals court reduces former Prime Minister Alain Juppé's disqualification from holding public office from ten years to one. UN personnel spot Rwandan troops in eastern Congo; Congolese officials say the troops are attacking and burning villages. Egypt and Israel hold talks in Jerusalem to discuss the planned Israeli withdrawal from the Gaza Strip.

2: The Swedish Supreme Court confirms the life sentence of Mijailo Mijailovic, killer of Swedish minister Anna Lindh. The European Union takes over from NATO in peacekeeping operations in Bosnia and Herzegovina.

3: Dragomir Milošević, the general who besieged Sarajevo for 3 years during the Bosnian Civil War, surrenders to the UN International Criminal Tribunal for the former Yugoslavia. 12,000 people died during the siege. A number of explosive devices explode in the Spanish capital Madrid following warnings by separatist group ETA. The Ukrainian Supreme Court rules that the 2004 second round presidential results are invalid and asks for a new vote to be completed within three weeks without determining whether the second round will be re-run or an entirely new election will be run. Rwanda denies sending any troops to Congo. Brazilian paleontologists of the University of Rio de Janeiro announce a find of a new dinosaur species, Unaysaurus tolentinoi. The find also shows links to Europe when both continents were part of Pangaea.

4: Peruvian-born María Julia Mantilla García is crowned Miss World.

5: Israel and Egypt carry out a prisoner exchange programme; Egypt releases an Israeli businessman held on charges of spying while Israel releases 6 Egyptian students who allegedly infiltrated Israel to kidnap soldiers.

6: Sinn Féin leader Gerry Adams recommends that Sinn Féin support a British-Irish power-sharing plan for Northern Ireland. Gunmen attack the US consular compound in Jeddah, Saudi Arabia; attackers kill nine Saudis in a four-hour battle but fail to enter the consulate building itself. The Basque separatist group ETA detonates seven bombs in public places across Spain.

7: Hamid Karzai is inaugurated as President of Afghanistan. New York State attorney general Eliot Spitzer announces his campaign for the Governor's office in 2006.

8: Delegates from 12 South American countries meeting in Cuzco, Peru, sign an agreement creating the South American Community of Nations, a group of nations along the lines of the European Union.

9: President George W. Bush nominates Jim Nicholson, US ambassador to the Vatican, as his nominee for Veterans Affairs Secretary replacing outgoing secretary Anthony Principi. Japan and Germany issue joint declarations that they want permanent seats on the UN Security Council with the veto power. The government of Lesotho announces plans to give women legal equality and property rights within a year.

10: Italian Prime Minister Silvio Berlusconi is acquitted of bribery. The 2004 Nobel Prizes are handed out at ceremonies in Oslo and Stockholm.

11: Doctors in Austria confirm that Ukrainian presidential candidate Viktor Yushchenko's illness was caused by dioxin poisoning. It is alleged that he first became ill after dining with the chairman of the Ukrainian Security Service in early September. Bernard Kerik withdraws his nomination for the post of Secretary of Homeland Security, in the wake of a scandal over the immigration status of a nanny in his employment.

12: The *Washington Post* alleges that the Bush administration used wire taps to intercept a number of phone conversations of Mohamed ElBaradei, Director General of the United Nations International Atomic Energy Agency. Palestinian leader Marwan Barghouti withdraws his nomination in the Palestinian presidential election just ten days after announcing his candidacy.

13: Chilean prosecutors charge former dictator Augusto Pinochet for alleged involvement in murder and 'disappearances' in Chile in the 1970s. Hundreds of protesters gather in Cairo outside Egypt's Supreme Judiciary buildings, calling for an end to Hosni Mubarak's 23-year presidency of Egypt. Romanian Prime Minister Adrian Nastase concedes defeat to opposition candidate Traian Basescu in the presidential election. Oracle Corporation announces a merger deal to acquire PeopleSoft for approximately US$10.3 billion.

14: French President Jacques Chirac inaugurates the world's highest road bridge in southern France, the Millau Viaduct over the River Tarn. A new species of monkey, the Arunachal Macaque, is discovered in India. It is the first new macaque discovered since 1903 and the first new primate in 49 years.

15: UK Home Secretary David Blunkett resigns from his post in the wake of numerous controversies; Charles Clarke, the Secretary of State for Education and Skills, is chosen as his successor. In USA, Sprint Corporation announces a US$35 billion deal to acquire Nextel Communications. The US authorities release evidence which shows that prisoners in Iraq were subject to electric shocks, mock executions and burns by US Marines.

16: Leaders of the European Union agree to invite Turkey to begin negotiations to join the EU from 3 October 2005. Former chess champion Bobby Fischer is offered residency in Iceland. Researchers at the University of Tübingen, Germany, report the discovery of a 30,000 to 37,000-year-old flute, believed to be the earliest musical instrument ever found.

17: US President George W. Bush signs the Intelligence Reform and Terrorism Prevention Act and creates the office of the Director of National Intelligence to oversee the country's fifteen spy agencies. The Israeli Labor party and Likud Party reach an agreement, forming a unity government in order to implement Israel's unilateral disengagement plan of 2004. The EU states that Turkey must recognize the ethnic-Greek government of EU member state Cyprus before it can begin negotiations for EU membership. In Bhutan, a nationwide ban on the sale of all tobacco products comes into effect.

18: The African Union issues to both sides involved in the Darfur conflict a deadline of 1700 GMT to halt the fighting in the region, failing which talks in Nigeria to find a solution to the conflict would end.

19: The Russian government auctions off the main production unit of oil giant YUKOS to the Baikalfinansgroup for 260.75bn roubles.

20: In Sudan, fighting fails to stop after a ceasefire between government troops and rebels.

21: UK Prime Minister Tony Blair makes a surprise visit to Baghdad. Author J.K. Rowling announces that the sixth book in her Harry Potter series, *Harry Potter and the Half-Blood Prince*, will be published on 16 July 2005. A court in Nigeria upholds the election of Nigerian president Olusegun Obasanjo, in the face of US, EU and Nigerian opposition criticism. Archaeologists in Abu Dhabi, United Arab Emirates, find the remains of a 7,500-year-old man on the island of Marawah.

22: The British charity organization Save the Children withdraws from Darfur after rebels kill its aid workers.

23: An earthquake of moment magnitude 8.1 occurs 305 miles north of Macquarie Island, in the Southern Ocean. A French UN worker in the Democratic Republic of the Congo is arrested for creating pornographic videos of young girls. UN troops from South Africa deploy in Democratic Republic of Congo to create a buffer zone between fighting factions.

25: The ESA's Huygens probe separates from NASA's *Cassini* spacecraft to travel to Saturn's moon Titan.

26: An earthquake of magnitude 9.0 strikes in the Indian Ocean off the western coast of Sumatra, triggering off a tsunami that kills hundreds of thousands of people in Thailand, Sri Lanka, the Maldives, India, Bangladesh, Burma, Indonesia and Malaysia. A re-run of the presidential runoff vote is held in Ukraine.

27: Fresh observations rule out the possibility that asteroid 2004 MN4 will hit Earth in 2029, as earlier predicted. Ukrainian Transport Minister Heorhiy Kyrpa, a staunch supporter of Viktor Yanukovych, is found dead from a gunshot. Israeli police arrest Palestinian presidential candidate Mustafa Barghouti. Ukrainian opposition presidential candidate Viktor Yushchenko claims victory. Iraq's main Sunni political movement, the Iraqi Islamic Party, withdraws from the upcoming general elections.

28: The Shiveluch volcano on Russia's Kamchatka Peninsula erupts, triggering an earthquake and a 6,500 foot plume of hot ash. Ukrainian presidential election: Prime Minister Viktor Yanukovych challenges the result of the re-run of the presidential election and threatens to take the issue to the Supreme Court.

29: The Popular Front for the Liberation of Palestine (PFLP) announces its support for Mustafa Al-Barghouti in the 2005 Palestinian presidential election. The Red Cross issues a statement saying that the number of dead in the Indian Ocean earthquake is likely to cross 100,000. The United States, Australia, Japan and India form an international coalition to lead aid efforts after the 2004 Indian Ocean earthquake. The Israeli parliament passes a law against terrorism and against support of terrorism. The Russian Aviation and Space Agency says that it will charge the US for transporting astronauts to the International Space Station from 2006.

30: Israel declares that Ariel Sharon and Shimon Peres have agreed on a deal to form a coalition government. In Sudan, the government and the rebel group SPLA have agreed to sign a ceasefire to end the civil war that began in 1983. The Ukrainian Central Election Commission rejects complaints of Prime Minister Viktor Yanukovych. In The Netherlands, a court imposes the country's first fines to spammers. In Senegal, President Abdoulaye Wade signs a peace deal with separatist rebels in the Casamance region, to end a 22-year conflict. The Canadian Food Inspection Agency reports a possible second case of mad cow disease.

31: Colombia extradites FARC leader Simón Trinidad to the USA to face conspiracy, kidnapping, and drug trafficking charges. Viktor Yanukovych resigns as Ukraine's Prime Minister. Taipei 101, the world's tallest skyscraper, is officially opened in Taipei, Taiwan. The Canadian government pledges to match dollar-for-dollar the donations of private Canadian citizens to the Indian Ocean Earthquake, besides the $40m in federal funds already committed; the government also announces plans to forgive the debt of the affected nations. The US government pledges $350m for relief; British charities raise £45m from public donations; the UK government increases its donation from £15m to £50m. Pakistani president Pervez Musharraf announces that he will retain his additional role as an army chief.

January 2005

1: The Turkish currency is revalued at a rate of 1,000,000 'old' lira for 1 New Turkish Lira. Luxembourg takes over the Presidency of the Council of the European Union.

2: The press report that the US government is preparing to keep suspected terrorists in detention without charge for life.

3: The United Nations accepts Singapore's offer to set up a UN Regional Coordination Centre to coordinate relief efforts to tsunami-affected areas. Three US Presidents—George W. Bush, Bill Clinton, and George H. W. Bush—make a joint appeal urging Americans to provide aid to the tsunami victims. In Croatia, incumbent President Stipe Mesic receives 49% of the vote in the presidential elections and goes into the second round.

4: Governor of Baghdad Ali al-Haidri is assassinated. Government forces and members of various armed groups begin to join to form a national army in Burundi.

6: Former South African President Nelson Mandela announces that AIDS caused the death of his sole surviving son, Makgatho Mandela. The US Department of Defense announces a new investigation into allegations of prisoner abuse at the Camp X-Ray detention center in Guantanamo Bay, Cuba. An Iraqi civilian testifies that US soldiers forced him and his cousin to jump into the Tigris River and caused his relative to be swept to death. World leaders gather in Jakarta, Indonesia, for an emergency summit with the United Nations.

7: Japan sends its largest military deployment since World War II to tsunami-hit countries. The Group of Seven Industrialized Nations (G7) agrees to a moratorium on the debt repayments of countries worst affected by the 26 December tsunami in Asia. Israeli police arrest Palestinian presidential candidate Mustafa Barghouti on the last day of the campaign as he tries to enter the Al-Aqsa mosque. The Ukrainian Supreme Court rejects Viktor Yanukovych's appeal against the electoral commission's decision confirming his loss in the presidential election. Chilean officials search the offices of former dictator Augusto Pinochet and investigate his US bank accounts.

8: US Navy nuclear submarine, USS *San Francisco*, runs aground south of the Pacific island of Guam. US Army sergeant Tracy Perkins is acquitted of manslaughter but found guilty of aggravated assault for forcing two Iraqi civilians to leap from a bridge into the River Tigris.

9: In Iraq, gunmen kill the deputy police chief of the city of Samarra, Major Muhammad Muzaffar. The US military frees about 230 prisoners it was holding at Abu Ghraib. A peace treaty is signed between warring factions in the Sudanese civil war, in Nairobi, Kenya.

10: Mahmoud Abbas is officially declared winner of the Palestinian presidential election, with 62.3% of the votes cast. A smoking ban comes into effect in Italy, prohibiting tobacco smoking in public places.

11: Severe flooding hits the Caribbean coasts of southern Central America.

12: British Airways flight 175 from London to New York is turned back by the US authorities, claiming that a suspected Moroccan terrorist is on board. US intelligence officials confirm that its search for weapons of mass destruction in Iraq ended in December 2004. In the USA, Lithuanian-born Vladas Zajanckauskas is charged with killing Jews in the Warsaw Ghetto during World War II. US space probe Deep Impact is successfully launched from Cape Canaveral.

13: The Paris Club, a group of financial officials from 19 of the world's richest countries, offers a debt freeze to nations affected by the 2004 Indian Ocean Earthquake. In Indonesia, rebels of the Free Aceh Movement call for ceasefire. Prince Harry of the United Kingdom apologizes for wearing a costume with a Nazi swastika at a party.

14: The Huygens probe successfully lands on Saturn's largest moon Titan. The World Health Organization reports that worldwide polio cases rose by more than one-third in 2004. Venezuela recalls its ambassador to Colombia over the dispute of the capture of FARC member Rodrigo Granda. Malaysia and Singapore agree to a truce on the disagreement over a land reclamation project in Johor Straits.

15: The first direct flights between mainland China and Taiwan since 1949 are announced to be carried out during the Chinese New Year holidays. Zhao Ziyang, former Premier of the People's Republic of China and General Secretary of the Communist Party of China, slips into a coma after multiple strokes. A British Museum report states that US-led forces in Iraq have destroyed and contaminated precious ancient Babylonian archaeological evidence and sites. Mahmoud Abbas is sworn in as president of the Palestinian Authority in a ceremony in the West Bank town of Ramallah.

16: Adriana Iliescu becomes the world's oldest woman to give birth, at age 66.

17: Zhao Ziyang, former Premier of the People's Republic of China and General Secretary of the Communist Party of China, dies at age 85. Croatian president Stipe Mesic is elected for a second term. Scandinavian prime ministers visit Thailand in the aftermath of the 2004 Indian Ocean Earthquake.

18: Syrian Catholic Archbishop of Mosul Basile Georges Casmoussa is kidnapped in Iraq. A UN World Conference on Disaster Reduction begins in Kobe, Japan. The Sudanese government signs a preliminary peace treaty with the National Democratic Alliance, an opposition umbrella group of rebels in the north and east of the country. The new largest passenger airliner in the world, the Airbus A380, is officially launched at a ceremony in the main French Airbus factory in Toulouse. The United Nations World Food Program appeals for aid to Mauritania, after drought and locust swarms destroy the harvest. Two former Bosnian Serb officers, Dragan Jokic and Vidoje Blagojevic, are convicted and imprisoned for their complicity in the Srebrenica massacre in 1995.

19: Israel lifts a ban on contacts with new Palestinian leader, Mahmoud Abbas. Japan Meteorological Agency issues tsunami warnings near the Izu island chain south of Tokyo after a strong undersea earthquake measuring 6.8 on the Richter scale. In Peru, Prime Minister Carlos Ferrero and Defence Minister Roberto Chiabra survive a censure motion in parliament.

20: US President George W. Bush is sworn in for his second term. Grenada switches recognition from the Republic of China (Taiwan) to the People's Republic of China, after a million dollar aid deal from the latter. In Belize, unrest over new taxes leads to burning down of the government offices and a union workers strike, shutting down ports and water supply. The Republic of Ireland, one of the last countries to use non-metric speed limits, officially changes over to the metric system. In Ukraine, the Supreme Court dismisses Prime Minister Viktor Yanukovych's appeal and confirms Viktor Yushchenko as the new president. Cuba announces a ban of smoking in public places, effective February 2005. The trial of Bernie Ebbers, former CEO of WorldCom, begins in New York. The Mars rover Opportunity uses its spectrometers to prove that Heat Shield Rock is a meteorite; it is the first such object to be found on another planet.

21: In France, teachers and civil servants join the strike in protest of job cuts in the public sector. The relatives of victims of the 2000 Kursk submarine disaster appeal to the European Court of Human Rights for an additional investigation into the accident.

22: The Tsunami relief concert is held at the Millennium Stadium, Cardiff, UK, in aid of the victims of the 2004 Indian Ocean earthquake. It raises over £1.25 million (•1.8 million or $2.4 million). The al-Aqsa Martyrs' Brigades agrees to a ceasefire on the condition that Israel fully stops its military operations inside the West Bank and Gaza Strip, including arrest raids and assassinations, and releases Palestinian

prisoners from its jails.

23: Viktor Yushchenko is invested as president of Ukraine at a ceremony in Kiev.

24: Yuliya Tymoshenko is appointed Prime Minister of Ukraine. The new 'Wall of Names' holocaust memorial is unveiled in Paris. JP Morgan Chase bank apologizes for its predecessors Canal Bank and Citizens' Bank which accepted slaves as collateral. A 6.2 Richter scale earthquake strikes in Palu, Central Sulawesi, Indonesia.

25: The nominees for the 77th Academy Awards are announced. Four British detainees at Camp X-Ray, Guantanamo Bay, Moazzam Begg, Feroz Abbasi, Martin Mubanga and Richard Belmar, are released and flown back to the UK, where the British police arrest them on arrival. Bill Gates donates $750 million through the Bill & Melinda Gates Foundation to the Global Alliance for Vaccines and Immunization, to provide vaccines to children in poor countries. The Bush administration requests an additional $80 billion from the US Congress for Iraq and Afghanistan. In Kenya, clashes take place between Kikuyu and Maasai tribes over water rights of the Ewaso Kedong River.

26: Condoleezza Rice is confirmed in the US Senate; she is the first African-American woman to serve as US Secretary of State. British authorities release Moazzam Begg, Feroz Abbasi, Martin Mubanga and Richard Belmar, without charge.

30: US soldiers are killed in a single day in Iraq when a helicopter crashes in western Iraq. It is the single worst loss of life for US forces since they invaded Iraq in March 2003. The World Economic Forum begins in Davos, Switzerland. The US Supreme Court rejects the appeal of Florida governor Jeb Bush to keep brain-damaged Terri Schiavo alive against the wishes of her husband. Her parents try to remove her husband as her guardian. In China, the death sentence of Tibetan lama Tenzin Delek Rinpoche is commuted to life imprisonment.

27: The African Union announces that around 100 people have been killed following an air raid into the Darfur region of Sudan. Holocaust survivors, leaders of more than 40 countries, former Soviet soldiers and other people gather in Oœwiêcim, Poland to mark the 60th anniversary of the liberation of the Auschwitz concentration camp. Israeli Prime Minister, Ariel Sharon, praises Palestinian President Mahmoud Abbas's efforts to restore calm, during a media interview. The fifth World Social Forum begins in Porto Alegre, Brazil.

28: In USA, the Riggs Bank agrees to pay a $16 million fine, after pleading guilty to violating the Bank Secrecy Act by hiding transfers of millions of dollars in accounts controlled by Chilean despot Augusto Pinochet and top officials of Equatorial Guinea. Nina Wang, considered to be Asia's richest woman, is formally charged with forgery of her kidnapped husband's will. Palestinian organization Hamas comes to power in local elections in Gaza. Latest investigation into the career of UK serial killer Dr Harold Shipman increases the count of his victims to 284. 70 Nobel Prize laureates release a statement supporting United Nations Secretary General Kofi Annan, as he faces a US Republican campaign calling for his resignation. In Bangladesh, former finance minister Shah AMS Kibria is killed in a grenade attack.

29: A series of moderate-intensity aftershocks strike the Andaman and Nicobar Islands and Sumatra in Indonesia.

30: Voting takes place in Iraq, marking the first multi-party election in 50 years.

31: US entertainer Michael Jackson pleads his innocence before his trial for alleged child molestation begins in California. The summit of the African Union begins in Nigeria. Sefer Halilovic, former head of the Bosnian army, goes on trial for killing Bosnian Croats during the Yugoslav wars.

February 2005

1: Pope John Paul II is taken to a hospital. King Gyanendra of Nepal sacks the government of Prime Minister Sher Bahadur Deuba and assumes direct power.

2: The German Federal Labour Agency reports that the German unemployment rate hit 12.1% in January; this is the highest rate in the country since the Great Depression and the Weimar Republic. *The Star Trek: Enterprise* television series is cancelled, marking the end of 18 consecutive years of *Star Trek* on television. King Gyanendra of Nepal forms a new cabinet and appoints himself as its head. Zimbabwean president Robert Mugabe announces that a general election will be held on 31 March. The Spanish parliament rejects an appeal from the Basque regional government for greater autonomy and a referendum for eventual independence. The parliament of Slovenia ratifies the European Union Constitution.

3: Zurab Zhvania, Prime Minister of Georgia, dies of gas poisoning. Greece hands over Dejan Milenkoviæ, the main suspect of the murder of Serbian Prime Minister Zoran Ðinðiæ, to Serbian authorities.

4: New observations confirm that asteroid 2004 MN4 (renamed as '99942 Apophis' in July 2005), previously considered to be an impact risk, will pass the Earth on 13 April 2029 at a distance of 36,350 km. In USA, Alberto Gonzales becomes the first Hispanic US Attorney General.

5: President Gnassingbé Eyadéma of Togo dies of a heart attack and is succeeded by his son Faure Gnassingbé. In

Afghanistan, NATO helicopters find the wreckage of a Kam Air Boeing 737 passenger aircraft in the mountains east of Kabul.

6: Thai Prime Minister Thaksin Shinawatra wins an unprecedented second term as prime minister. The Togolese parliament votes for a constitutional amendment, in an atteempt to legalize the accession to power of Faure Gnassingbé, son of Gnassingbé Eyadéma.

7: Englishwoman Ellen MacArthur sets a record for the quickest round-the-world solo sail when she completes the 27,354 mile journey in 71 days, 14 hours, 18 minutes and 33 seconds. Nigerian President Olusegun Obasanjo asks other African states not to recognize the installation of Faure Gnassingbé as Togolese president. Spanish police find a drifting boat containing 227 African migrants, off the Canary Islands. In Malawi, President Bingu wa Mutharika quits the governing party, the United Democratic Front, over criticism of his anti-corruption campaign.

8: Israel and the Palestinian Authority agree on a truce. Palestinian organization Hamas says it is not bound by the ceasefire. In Denmark, the centre-right coalition government of Prime Minister Anders Fogh Rasmussen retains power in the parliamentary election. In Nepal, phone lines and Internet connections are restored following their disconnection earlier in the month. A ban on tobacco smoking in public places becomes effective in Cuba. In China, the Ministry of Agriculture announces that it has developed a vaccine against bird flu spreading to humans. The Greek parliament elects Karolos Papoulias as the new president.

9: Carly Fiorina resigns her post as CEO of Hewlett-Packard. British survey ship HMS *Scott* produces the first sonar survey of the seabed site of the 2004 Indian Ocean earthquake. In Switzerland, the Federal Court rules that the money that former Nigerian dictator Sani Abacha took from Nigeria may be returned to the country.

10: A previously unreleased portion of the 9-11 Commission's report reveals that the US Federal Aviation Administration received 52 intelligence reports on potential terrorist attacks by al-Qaeda prior to 11 September 2001. The British Royal Family announces that Charles, Prince of Wales, will marry Camilla Parker Bowles on 8 April. North Korea announces that it has developed nuclear weapons for its self-defence; it suspends participation in multi-nation talks over its arms program. The first nationwide municipal elections take place in Saudi Arabia; however, only men in Riyadh are allowed to vote and only half of the municipal councils are open to voting; the monarchy will appoint the other half. In a meeting of the Economic Community of West African States (ECOWAS), West African leaders refuse to recognize Faure Gnassingbé as the new president of Togo and threaten to impose sanctions if the country does not hold presidential elections.

11: An estimated 2 million Iranians demonstrate against a possible US pre-emptive strike aimed at preventing Iran from deploying nuclear weapons. The 485-foot-long Shakidor Dam in Baluchistan, southwest Pakistan, bursts under the pressure of a week of heavy rainfall. Japan pledges over $21 million in support of a United Nations-backed independent tribunal of Khmer Rouge leaders in Cambodia.

12: Mass protests take place in the Togolese capital city, Lome, against President Faure Gnassingbé, leading to clashes between demonstrators and soldiers and police forces. A highly drug resistant strain of HIV is detected in a New York City individual.

13: Two strong aftershocks strike tsunami-hit Aceh province in Indonesia. Windsor Tower in central Madrid, Spain, one of the most prominent buildings in the city, is destroyed in a fire. Sister Lucia de Jesus dos Santos, the last survivor of three children to whom the Virgin Mary is said to have appeared at Fatima in central Portugal in 1917, passes away.

14: Researchers at the University of California, Los Angeles create a modified form of HIV which targets P-glycoproteins on cancer cells. Former Lebanese Prime Minister Rafik Hariri is killed along with others in a car bomb explosion in central Beirut.

15: USA recalls its ambassador to Syria, Margaret Scobey, in protest of alleged Syrian involvement in the assassination of former Lebanese Prime Minister Rafik Hariri. India, USA and European Union countries recall their ambassadors from Nepal in protest of the takeover by King Gyanendra.

16: The Kyoto Protocol on global warming comes into effect. Mohamed ElBaradei, head of the International Atomic Energy Agency (IAEA), states there is no evidence to suggest Iran is developing nuclear weapons. In USA, National Hockey League (NHL) Commissioner Gary Bettman announces the cancellation of the 2004-05 season because of the ongoing lockout; this is the first time that a North American professional sports league has cancelled an entire season due to a labour dispute. Iran and Syria announce the formation of a 'united front'.

17: US President George W. Bush names John Negroponte as his nominee to be the first United States Director of National Intelligence. The European Union introduces new laws that increase the rights of air passengers; they are now entitled to receive higher compensation for overbooking, delays and cancellation of flights. The government of Sudan rejects the United Nations' demand that the suspects of war crimes in Darfur region would be put before the International Criminal Court in The Hague.

18: The UK Food Standards Agency orders the withdrawal of over 350 food products from sale following the discovery of a possibly carcinogenic dye Sudan I in a batch of chilli powder used to make a batch of Worcestershire sauce. In the UK, the ban on hunting with dogs becomes effective. The American Civil Liberties Union releases documents obtained from the US Army alleging the destruction of evidence of abuse of prisoners in Afghanistan.

19: A massive demonstration in Rome asks for the release of an Italian journalist abducted in Iraq. Former US Presidents George Bush and Bill Clinton visit tsunami-affected areas of Thailand. An earthquake, measuring 6.9 on the Richter scale, strikes Southeast Sulawesi, Indonesia.

20: UN High Commissioner for Refugees Ruud Lubbers resigns over allegations of sexual harassment. The opposition Socialist party secures an absolute majority in the Portuguese parliament election. The disputed Turkish Republic of Northern Cyprus votes in its early general election. USA and EU join the protests against President Faure Gnassingbé of Togo. ECOWAS imposes sanctions and suspends Togo's membership; USA terminates all military assistance.

21: Israel releases 500 Palestinian prisoners, as a gesture of goodwill to the Palestinian Authority and to its chairman, Mahmoud Abbas. Former US Presidents Bill Clinton and George H. W. Bush visit tsunami-affected areas of Sri Lanka. Syrian President Bashar al-Assad appoints his brother-in-law Asef Shawkat as head of the country's military intelligence service. In UK, the Royal Navy announces that it will allow same-sex couples to live in family quarters if they are in registered partnership.

22: European Union countries renew sanctions against the government of

Robert Mugabe in Zimbabwe. Images from the European space probe, Mars Express, reveal the existence of a sea of ice close to the equator of Mars. An earthquake, measuring 6.4 on the Richter Scale, strikes the city of Zarand and a number of villages in Iran. Swiss medical company Novartis acquires US company Eon Labs and German Hexal AG. In Togo, the National Assembly reverses constitutional changes that allowed Faure Gnassingbé to become president. In Bolivia, former president Gonzalo Sánchez de Lozada and his cabinet are formally charged with genocide.

23: Three British soldiers are found guilty of abusing Iraqi prisoners. Rasim Deliæ, former commander of the Bosnian army in Bosnia during the Yugoslav Wars, announces he will surrender to the UN Tribunal to face charges of war crimes against ethnic Serbs.

24: In Somalia, Abdullahi Yusuf Ahmed and Mohammed Ali Ghedi, leaders of the exiled Somalian government, begin a tour of the country to evaluate the relocation of the government from Kenya to Somalia. A summit between US President George W. Bush and Russian President Vladimir Putin begins in the Slovak capital, Bratislava. In Colombia, the third anniversary of the capture of Ingrid Betancourt, former Colombian presidential candidate, by FARC rebels, is marked. An Italian court orders Argentine footballer Diego Maradona to pay 30 million euros of back taxes (almost US$ 40 million). New EU laws declare lottery scams illegal. The parliament of Turkey grants amnesty to 677,000 people who have been expelled from university in recent years. In Kyrgyzstan, mass protests in support of opposition politicians barred from elections take place.

25: Three British soldiers convicted earlier in the week of abusing Iraqi prisoners are dismissed from the army and jailed for periods ranging between five months and two years. King Gyanendra of Nepal requests foreign assistance against Maoist insurgents and states that the country will return to democracy in three years. In Switzerland, a court rules that Yeslam Binladin, a half-brother of Osama bin Laden, can market products using the 'Bin Ladin' brand name.

26: For the first time in his 26-year papacy, Pope John Paul II fails to bless the faithful at the weekly Angelus prayer service, instead following it from his hospital room. Egyptian President Hosni Mubarak suggests that the parliament amend the constitution to allow direct, secret elections for the next president. President Faure Gnassingbé of Togo announces that he will step down.

27: The World Health Organization's Framework Convention on Tobacco Control becomes legally binding upon ratifying nations. Russia agrees to sell nuclear reactor fuel to Iran, but with stringent measures to prevent diversion to a nuclear weapons programme.

28: In UK, Briton Saajid Badat pleads guilty to planning a suicide attack on a US bound aircraft. The entire Lebanese government resigns following public protests and a no confidence vote in the wake of Rafik Hariri's assassination. A vote on a new constitution takes place in Burundi. Ukraine reduces the retirement benefits of the ex-president Leonid Kuchma. Fresh clashes take place between rebels and government forces in Ivory Coast. Rebels subsequently declare the end of the peace effort. Bosnian Muslim general Rasim Delic surrenders to the International War Crimes Tribunal in The Hague, The Netherlands.

March 2005

1: In Afghanistan, president Hamid Karzai appoints Abdul Rashid Dostum as his chief-of-staff. President Saparmurat Niyazov of Turkmenistan orders the closure of all the hospitals in the country except those in the capital, as well as all rural libraries. In Burundi, a referendum approves the new constitution designed to end 12 years of civil war. In Uruguay, Dr Tabaré Vázquez becomes the country's first leftist president.

2: An earthquake measuring up to 7.5 on the Richter scale hits Darwin, Northern Territory in Australia. Microsoft founder Bill Gates conferred the title of Knight Commander of the British Empire. Demolition of Madrid's Windsor Tower, burnt down in a fire in February, starts.

3: In Pakistan, five men sentenced to death for the 2002 rape of Mukhtar Mai, are acquitted on appeal. In Indonesia, Muslim cleric Abu Bakar Bashir is found guilty of conspiracy for his involvement in the 2002 Bali bombing and is awarded a two and a half year jail sentence. However, he is found not guilty of all charges relating to the 2003 bombing of the Marriott hotel in Jakarta. Steve Fossett's GlobalFlyer touches down in Kansas, setting a new nonstop around-the-world flight record. US businesswoman Martha Stewart is released from prison after serving a five-month sentence. The World Trade Organisation upholds a ruling that orders USA to end subsidies to its cotton farmers. Scientists at Florida State University, USA, conclude that *Homo floresiensis* is a distinct species, separate from *Homo sapiens*.

4: Former interior minister of Ukraine, Yuri Kravchenko, is found dead in his country house.

5: Syrian President Bashar al-Assad announces that Syria will withdraw all of its troops in Lebanon.

6: Bolivian President Carlos Mesa announces his resignation.

7: Sony Corporation names its US operations chief, Howard Stringer, as its first-ever non-Japanese Chairman and Chief Executive Officer. In Moldova, the ruling Communist Party of the Republic of Moldova wins a narrow majority in parliamentary elections. In Norway, police recovers three paintings of Edvard Munch, one day after they were stolen.

8: In Lebanon, nearly 500,000 people take part in a pro-Syria rally. Significant quantities of ash and steam appear from the direction of active volcano Mount St. Helens in USA. Russian armed forces claim to have killed Chechen separatist leader Aslan Maskhadov. Kosovan Prime Minister Ramush Haradinaj resigns after the International Criminal Tribunal for the former Yugoslavia charges him with war crimes.

9: Bolivian President Carlos Mesa withdraws his resignation after the parliament declined to accept it. Syria announces that its troops will leave Lebanon before parliamentary elections are held in May 2005. In South Africa, the Hartebeestfontein gold mine south of Johannesburg collapses following an earthquake measuring 5.3 on the Richter scale.

10: USA withdraws from a part of the Vienna Convention that gave the International Criminal Court the right to intervene in cases of foreigners held in death rows in US jails. In Rwanda, traditional Gacaca community courts start to judge individuals accused of involvement in the 1994 Rwandan genocide. A US Judge dismisses a case brought by Vietnamese plaintiffs over the use of Agent Orange during the Vietnam War. Lebanese President, Emile Lahud, re-appoints Omar Karami as Prime Minister of Lebanon, within two weeks after his resignation. The Chief Executive of Hong Kong, Tung Chee Hwa, announces he will resign due to his poor health. The Islamic Commission of Spain issues a *fatwa* against al-Qaeda leader Osama bin Laden.

11: The first anniversary of the 11 March 2004 Madrid attacks is marked with a day of mourning. Released official documents confirm that US forces held young children at the Abu Ghraib prison in Iraq. Former Chess world champion Garry Kasparov announces he will retire from professional competitions.

12: The State Council of the People's Republic of China approves the resignation of Hong Kong's Chief Executive Tung Chee-Hwa; he assumes the post of vice-chairman of the Political Consultative Conference. Ukraine begins to withdraw its troops from Iraq.

13: Pope John Paul II leaves the Gemelli Polyclinic and returns to Vatican City. China begins conducting human trials of AIDS vaccine.

14: Massive protests take place in Beirut, Lebanon, against Syrian presence in the country. The Anti-Secession Law of the People's Republic of China, aimed at settling the issue of Taiwan, becomes effective. Bangladesh bans smoking in public places. In Italy, Alessandra Mussolini, granddaughter of Il Duce Benito Mussolini, is banned from regional elections for presenting fraudulent signatures. Former Macedonian interior minister, Ljube Boskowski, is indicted for war crimes.

15: OPEC announces that it is unable to control oil prices. The government of Italy announces that it will begin to withdraw its troops from Iraq within a few months. In Kosovo, an explosion hits the motorcade of President Ibrahim Rugova in the capital Pristina. The new Yad Vashem Holocaust museum is dedicated in Jerusalem. Japanese immigration officials declare that they will deport former chess player Bobby Fischer to USA, instead of allowing him to shift to Iceland. A

United Nations team investigating the murder of Rafik Hariri in Lebanon, completes its mission.

16: Israel formally hands Jericho to the Palestinian Authority control. Amnesty International declares that fair elections are impossible in Zimbabwe. The European Union postpones negotiations for Croatia's membership. The Zambian government files corruption charges against ex-president Frederick Chiluba in a British High Court; he is accused of defrauding the state of almost US$35 million. The United Nations withdraws its foreign personnel from the western parts of Darfur following threats from pro-government militias.

17: Physicist Horatiu Nastase claims to have achieved a black hole-like entity at the Relativistic Heavy Ion Collider particle accelerator in Upton, New York. In Zimbabwe, President Robert Mugabe states that the country is facing food shortages.

18: The Ukrainian government reveals that arms dealers have smuggled 18 nuclear-capable cruise missiles to Iran and China. In The Netherlands, businessman Frans van Anraat is put on trial for allegedly selling chemicals for making poison gas, to Saddam Hussein. The United Nations sacks one employee and suspends six others without pay over allegations of sexual abuse in the Democratic Republic of Congo. The Chinese government forces SMTH BBS, a popular newsgroup-like Bulletin Board System among Chinese university students, to shut down off-campus access. Private Johnson Beharry of the British Army receives the Victoria Cross, the highest bravery award in the British Commonwealth; he is the first person to receive the Victoria Cross since 1982 and the first living recipient since 1969.

19: The G20 group of the developing nations urges rich countries to end their farming subsidies in five years. A 7.0 magnitude earthquake strikes

Japan's Kyushu island; Japan's Meteorological Agency issues tsunami warnings. Pakistan successfully test-fires the Shaheen-II long-range nuclear-capable ballistic missile.

20: The Serbian government announces that Bosnian Serb general Vinko Pandureviæ will surrender to the war crimes tribunal at The Hague; he is facing charges related to genocide, connected to the 1995 Srebrenica massacre.

21: UN Secretary-General Kofi Annan proposes expansion of the Security Council from 15 members to 24 members. Opposition supporters take over the northern city of Osh and seize government buildings. In Namibia, Hifikepunye Pohamba succeeds President Sam Nujoma. In Estonia, Prime Minister Juhan Parts resigns following a vote of no confidence against justice minister Ken-Marti Vaher. Iceland's parliament grants citizenship to the US chess player Bobby Fischer. Israel announces plans to add 3,500 homes to a settlement in occupied territories near Jerusalem.

22: In Kyrgyzstan, President Askar Akayev's spokesman claims that opposition protests are a 'drug mafia' coup attempt. United Nations declares World Water Day, initiating a decade-long 'Water for Life' campaign for clean water. German airline Lufthansa announces its takeover of Swiss Airlines.

23: In Kyrgyzstan, police break up a demonstration in the capital Bishkek; President Askar Akayev sacks his interior minister and prosecutor general for failing to contain the protests.

24: In Kyrgyzstan, clashes take place between protesters and riot police in the capital, Bishkek; President Askar Akayev flees the country after his presidential palace is overrun. Paleontologists from North Carolina State University, USA, announce the discovery of structures resembling blood vessels and red blood cells inside a Tyrannosaurus rex fossil. Bobby Fischer leaves Japan for Iceland. The World Health Organization declares that tuberculosis cases in some African countries have tripled since 1990. France presents a draft resolution to vote at the United Nations, which would enable the International Criminal Court in The Hague to try war crime cases in the Darfur region of Sudan. The US Supreme Court refuses to hear an appeal filed by parents of Terri Schiavo to have her feeding tube reinserted.

25: Following the so-called Tulip Revolution in Kyrgyzstan, opposition leader Kurmanbek Bakiyev is named interim President of Kyrgyzstan; looting takes place in the capital city of Bishkek.

26: Hundreds of thousands of Taiwanese people hold a mass rally to protest against the People's Republic of China's anti-secession law, aimed at resolving the Taiwan-Mainland China dispute.

27: German Chancellor Gerhard Schröder comments in a German newspaper that German-based companies will stop outsourcing and invest in creating employment within Germany.

28: The first arrests are made for war crimes in Sudan's Darfur region as 15 officials are accused of rape, murder, and other crimes. A 34-member Taiwanese delegation travels to mainland China on a landmark official visit; this is the first such visit since the end of Chinese Civil War in 1949. An earthquake of magnitude 8.7 is reported off the west coast of North Sumatra. Lebanese officials announce that 2000 Syrian troops have left the country. In Zimbabwe, Archbishop Pius Ncube calls for a peaceful uprising against the government of Robert Mugabe. Russian state prosecutors start the sentencing of former oil tycoon Mikhail Khodorkovsky and his associate Platon Lebedev on charges of tax evasion and fraud.

29: Lord Paddy Ashdown, High Representative in Bosnia and Herzegovina, sacks Dragan Èoviæ, the Croat member of the Presidency of Bosnia and Herzegovina, on suspicion of financial corruption. In Kyrgyzstan, a new parliament appoints Kurmanbek Bakiyev as the official interim President; incumbent president, Aksar Akayev announces that he is ready to resign. An independent investigation clears the United Nations Secretary-General Kofi Annan of improper involvement in the Oil-for-Food Programme. Political activists in Mongolia demonstrate in capital city Ulan Bator for new elections. Kenya recalls 70 diplomats from overseas due to a cash shortage.

30: European nations pledge their support to UN secretary general Kofi Annan. In Egypt, thousands of demonstrators protest against the fifth term of president Hosni Mubarak.

31: The rebel Democratic Forces for the Liberation of Rwanda announces that it is ending its armed struggle. Pope John Paul II's condition deteriorates; he is believed to have been administered last rites. In USA, Terri Schiavo dies 13 days after her feeding tube was removed by court order. A UN report reveals that malnutrition rates in Iraqi children below the age of five have nearly doubled since the US-led invasion of Iraq. The UN-backed Millennium Ecosystem Assessment reveals an alarming rate of deterioration of the world's ecosystems. Elections are held in Zimbabwe.

April 2005

1: Hamas and Islamic Jihad declare their 'in principle' intention to join the Palestine Liberation Organisation. The Vatican announces that the Pope has suffered cardiovascular collapse and septic shock. The UN Security Council votes to refer Darfur war crimes suspects to the International Criminal Court. In Zimbabwe, the ruling Zanu-PF gains a two-thirds majority in the parliamentary election. The World Bank agrees to fund a controversial hydroelectric dam project in Laos.

2: Pope John Paul II passes away at the age of 84. In Nepal, former Prime Minister Girija Prasad Koirala is released from house arrest.

3: The body of Pope John Paul II is laid in state in the Vatican City. Deposed Kyrgysz president Askar Akayev agrees to tender an official resignation.

4: The USA awards its highest military award, the Medal of Honor, to Paul Ray Smith, killed in fighting at the Baghdad airport in 2003. The Vatican announces 8 April as the date for Pope John Paul II's funeral; he will be buried in the crypt of Saint Peter in the Vatican. The wedding of Prince Charles and Camilla Parker-Bowles, earlier scheduled for 8 April is postponed by one day to avoid clashing with the papal funeral and to allow Prince Charles to attend. Sudanese officials reject the UN resolution to use the International Criminal Court to prosecute people accused of Darfur atrocities. The Iraqi National Assembly elects Sunni Arab Hajim al-Hassani as its new speaker. Vandals deface the grave of slain Israeli Prime Minister Yitzhak Rabin and his wife Leah in the national cemetery in Jerusalem, Israel. The UN Security Council extends the mandate of UN and French peacekeepers in Côte d'Ivoire. The Moldovan parliament re-elects president Vladimir Voronin. Jörg Haider, the former leader of Freedom Party of Austria (FPÖ), leaves the party along with most of its parliamentary representatives, to set up a new party, the Alliance for Austria's Future.

5: British Prime Minister Tony Blair sets 5 May 2005 as the date for general elections in the United Kingdom.

6: Rival groups sign a peace treaty to end the civil war in Côte d'Ivoire. In Vatican City, the College of Cardinals sets 18 April as the date for a conclave for papal election to select a successor to Pope John Paul II. Kurdish leader, Jalal Talabani, is named as Iraq's new President. Monaco's ruler Prince Rainier III dies at age 81.

7: The Mexican Parliament votes to suspend the executive immunity of Mexico City Mayor Andrés Manuel López Obrador, effectively removing him from office to face criminal charges. Shia leader Ibrahim Jaafari is named as the new interim prime minister of Iraq. Sinn Féin leader Gerry Adams appeals to the IRA to stop violence. The Integrated Ocean Drilling Program (IODP) announces that it has drilled a hole to the lowest level of the Earth's crust.

8: The funeral of Pope John Paul II takes place. Presidential elections take place in Djibouti with incumbent president Ismail Omar Guelleh as the only candidate.

9: The South African New National Party, the successor to the National Party that ruled South Africa in the apartheid era, votes to dissolve itself. In UK, Prince Charles marries Camilla Parker Bowles. Tens of thousands of Iraqis stage an anti-American protest in Baghdad.

10: An earthquake of magnitude 6.7 strikes West Sumatra, Indonesia, while a second earthquake of magnitude 6.1 hits Tokyo. Former South African President F.W. de Klerk calls for the formation of a new political party, following the dissolution of the New National Party. Italian deputy Prime Minister Marco Follini calls for an early general election after the centre-right coalition of Prime Minister Silvio Berlusconi loses a regional vote.

11: The Parliament of Kyrgyzstan approves the resignation of deposed president Askar Akayev. The International Court of Justice at The Hague begins hearing a complaint by the

Democratic Republic of Congo that Uganda invaded its territory and committed human rights violations.

12: The Estonian Parliament confirms Andrus Ansip as the country's next prime minister.

13: Omar Karami resigns as the Prime Minister of Lebanon after he fails to form a government. The European Parliament votes to allow Bulgaria and Romania to join the European Union in 2007.

14: The Israeli soldier accused of shooting British cameraman James Miller is cleared by an Israeli Judge. The Czech coalition government agrees to form a new cabinet; the deal collapses later in the day.

15: NASA reports that the Gulf Stream ocean current is slowing down; the current stabilizes winter temperatures in North America and Europe. Amid growing political crisis and anti-government demonstrations, Ecuadorian President Lucio Gutiérrez declares a state of emergency in capital Quito and revokes the newly appointed Supreme Court of Justice. Prince Rainier III is buried in Monaco.

16: Najib Mikati becomes the new Prime Minister of Lebanon. State of Emergency is lifted in Quito, Ecuador.

17: In the Comoros Islands, the Mount Karthala volcano begins to erupt. Mehmet Ali Talat is elected as the new Turkish Cypriot president. In Austria, Jörg Haider launches his new party, Alliance for Austria's Future.

18: US Physicists at Brookhaven National Laboratory announce that they have created a newly discovered state of matter by smashing atoms in the Relativistic Heavy Ion Collider. The first ballot in the Papal conclave fails to elect a new pope. Adobe Systems buys Macromedia for $3.4 billion. The government of the Philippines begins talks with the rebel Moro Islamic Liberation Front. The Pakistani government releases 500 members of Pakistan People's Party it had earlier detained. The Rwandan Supreme Court hears appeals for Pasteur Bizimungu, the first president of Rwanda after the genocide.

19: German Cardinal Joseph Ratzinger is elected as the new Pope; he assumes the name of Pope Benedict XVI. The leading coalition in the new Government of Iraq, United Iraqi Alliance, demands the death penalty for Saddam Hussein. The tenth anniversary of the Oklahoma City bombing is commemorated. Peruvian authorities submit a $130 million plan to UNESCO to preserve the Inca site of Machu Picchu. Lebanese Prime Minister Najib Mikati forms a new government. The Kuwaiti parliament gives initial support to a law that would allow women to vote. The parliament of Greece ratifies the European Union Constitution. The first part of the Obelisk of Axum, a 1700-year-old artefact of the Axumite Kingdom taken to Rome by Benito Mussolini's troops in 1937, is returned to Ethiopia.

20: Italian Prime Minister Silvio Berlusconi resigns in order to form a new government. An earthquake measuring 5.8 on the Richter scale hits northern Kyushu, Japan. The Ecuadorian parliament removes President Lucio Gutiérrez from power; Vice President Alfredo Palacio is sworn in as new interim president. The United Nations Commission on Human Rights demands the restoration of civil liberties and democracy in Nepal.

21: The next launch of the Space Shuttle Discovery is postponed until at least 22 May. New Ecuadorian president Alfredo Palacio orders the arrest of former president Lucio Gutiérrez, who then takes refuge in the Brazilian embassy.

22: 9/11 suspect Zacarias Moussaoui pleads guilty to terror charges in US federal court. Saajid Badat, who had earlier pleaded guilty to involvement in Richard Reid's 'shoe-bombing' conspiracy, is sentenced to 13 years in jail in UK. Japanese Prime Minister Junichiro Koizumi publicly expresses 'deep remorse' for actions of Japanese troops in China during World War II. In the UK, the National Portrait Gallery reveals that the so-called 'Flower Portrait' of William Shakespeare is a forgery. A German court orders a retrial in the case of cannibal Armin Meiwes, who was earlier jailed in 2004 for eight years.

23: A rodent species from a new family of mammals, Laonastidae, is discovered in Laos; this is the first new family of mammals to be found since 1974.

24: Pope Benedict XVI is formally installed as Pope of the Catholic Church in an inaugural mass. About 1 million people march silently through Mexico City in support of the capital's mayor, Andrés Manuel López Obrador. The presidential election is held in Togo. The 90th anniversary of the mass killings of Armenians in the Ottoman Empire is commemorated. The 50th anniversary of the Bandung Conference is commemorated. Ousted Ecuadorian president, Lucio Gutiérrez, goes into exile in Brazil. Venezuelan president Hugo Chávez terminates military cooperation with USA. In Kuwait, around 7000 expatriate workers storm the embassy of Bangladesh in Kuwait City to protest against unpaid wages.

25: Bulgaria and Romania sign the accession treaty to the European Union. The 90th anniversary of the landing at Anzac Cove during World War I is marked at Anzac Cove, Gallipoli, Turkey. The third and final part of the Obelisk of Axum returns to Ethiopia. Czech Prime Minister Stanislav Gross resigns.

26: Members of the Taiwanese political party Kuomintang visit Mainland China; this is the first official visit by the highest leader of Kuomintang to Mainland China in 60 years. Faure Gnassingbé wins the Togolese presidential election; the announcement sparks off riots in capital city Lomé as the opposition denounces the result and alleges massive fraud. All Syrian troops leave Lebanon, fulfilling a UN Security Council Resolution.

27: The world's largest passenger aircraft, the Airbus A380, makes its maiden flight in Toulouse, France. Former Nepalese Prime Minister Sher Bahadur Deuba is arrested for alleged corruption. A Moscow court postpones the verdict on the case of Mikhail Khodorkovsky until 16 May.

29: May is set as the date of the next elections in Lebanon. In Togo, violence escalates as the opposition demonstrates against Faure Gnassingbé and opposition leader Bob Akitani declares himself president. In Zimbabwe, opposition party Movement for Democratic Change states that the country has run out of maize grain and asks President Mugabe to apply for foreign aid.

28: In Iraq, the National Assembly approves a Shi'a-led cabinet. The UN International Criminal Tribunal for Rwanda sentences former Hutu civic leader, Mika Muhimana, to life imprisonment for his role in the Rwandan genocide.

29: The next launch of the Space Shuttle Discovery is delayed until at least 13 July. Kuomintang Chairman Lien Chan meets with Communist Party of China Secretary-General Hu Jintao; this is the highest level contact between leaders of China and Taiwan since the meeting of Chiang Kai-shek and Mao Zedong in August 1945. An article in the state-owned *China Securities Journal* states that the country's policy of pegging the yuan to the US dollar can be altered. The currencies of Cyprus, Latvia, and Malta join the European Echange Rate Mechanism, one of the steps needed for a currency to join the Eurozone.

30: Terrorist attacks take place on tourists in Cairo, Egypt. King Gyanendra of Nepal lifts the state of emergency but continues press censorship and ban on political activities.

May 2005

1: In Nepal, 10,000 protesters march in Kathmandu against the policies of king Gyanendra and demand a return of democracy. Taiwanese president Chen Shui-bian requests a direct meeting with the Chinese government, following their meeting with opposition Kuomintang party leaders. Lenovo Group, the largest Chinese computer company, acquires the personal computer business of IBM for US$ 1.25 billion in cash.

2: In Togo, opposition party Union of Forces for Change refuses to join a new government. Foreign ministers meet in New York, USA, to review the Nuclear Non-Proliferation Treaty.

3: In Nepal, thousands of journalists march in protest to restore press freedoms on World Press Freedom Day. A Togolese constitutional court announces Faure Gnassingbé as a winner of presidential election; refugees continue to flee to neighboring countries. In Mogadishu, Somalia, an explosion kills 15 people when new prime minister Ali Mohammed Ghedi begins his speech in a football stadium; authorities later disclose that it was caused by an accidentally set off grenade.

4: Israel freezes the handover of West Bank Palestinian towns to the Palestinian Authority; Israel states it will resume handover after militant groups are disarmed. The Pakistani government announces that it has captured key Al-Qaeda suspect Abu Faraj al-Libbi. A Peruvian congressional committee accuses President Alejandro Toledo of electoral fraud.

5: The Orthodox Patriarch of Jerusalem Irineos is dismissed following a controversy over the leasing of church-owned lands. British general election takes place. An explosion occurs outside the United Kingdom consulate in New York City. There are no reported casualties. The Ugandan parliament votes to hold a referendum on returning to multi-party democracy.

6: Fatah wins 55 per cent of the seats in municipal elections held in 84 cities across the West Bank and Gaza; Hamas wins about one-third of the seats. In UK, the Labour Party wins a parliamentary majority but with a reduced margin; Tony Blair becomes the first Labour Prime Minister to lead his party to three election victories; Conservative Party leader Michael Howard announces that he will resign shortly.

7: Northern Ireland's Ulster Unionist Party leader and 1998 Nobel Peace Prize winner David Trimble resigns from the leadership after losing his seat in the British general election.

8: Worldwide celebrations are held to mark the 60th anniversary of V-E Day, the official end point of World War II in Europe. Abu Faraj al-Libbi, the al-Qaeda suspect captured in Pakistan on 2 May and thought to be the third-in-command in al-Qaeda, emerges to be a mid-level member in the organization. Seven Nepalese opposition parties join forces against King Gyanendra. In Belgium, two Rwandan men, Etienne Nzabonimana and Samuel Ndashyikirwa, are put on trial for involvement with the Rwandan genocide. Voting for the the second round of presidential election takes place in Central African Republic.

9: Iran admits to having converted 37 tons of raw uranium into gaseous form, a part of the uranium enrichment process. The crash site of the Mars Polar Lander, which failed in December 1999, is identified from images taken by the Mars Global Surveyor. Andrés Manuel López Obrador, mayor of Mexico City, announces that he will leave his post on 31 July to concentrate on his presidential election campaign.

10: G8 countries urge Ukraine to cover the Chernobyl nuclear plant. The Egyptian parliament approves a constitutional amendment allowing multiple candidates in presidential elections.

11: Riots over a *Newsweek* story about the desecration of the Quran lead to casualties in Jalalabad, Afghanistan. The White House and United States Capitol in Washington, DC are evacuated, in an incoming aircraft scare. The Austrian parliament ratifies the European Union constitution. The Bulgarian parliament ratifies the EU membership treaty.

14: Thousands of Uzbeks take over a high security jail in Andijan and set free thousands of prisoners in protest against the jail sentence of 23 businessmen who were accused of being Islamic extremists; violence breaks out in the city and in the Uzbek capital Tashkent; a political rally in Andijan demands the resignation of the government; at least 20 protesters are shot dead although some reports put the toll at around 500. A US Senate probe releases evidence showing two prominent British and French politicians received vouchers for millions of barrels of Iraqi oil in exchange for their support of Saddam Hussein's regime; those accused include prominent British politician George Galloway. South Korea announces it will restart bilateral talks with North Korea after a gap of one year. An earthquake measuring 6.9 on the Richter Scale strikes Sumatra in Indonesia. Thousands of protesters take to the streets of Andijan in Uzbekistan; Uzbek President Islam Karimov blames the violence on militants. In Taiwan, the Pan-Green Coalition wins the National Assembly election. In Sudan, 28 men are sentenced to 5–15 years in jail for a coup attempt. US Secretary of State

Condoleezza Rice promises action if investigations prove that US soldiers desecrated the Quran in Guantánamo Bay, Cuba; the Saudi Arabian government demands an investigation; seven people are killed during a protest in Afghanistan; protests also take place in Indonesia and Pakistan. The Vatican announces that the late Pope, John Paul II, will be beatified. A helicopter lands on top of the world's highest mountain, Mount Everest, for the first time. Malcolm Glazer gains control of British football team Manchester United after securing a 70% share. The European Court of Human Rights rules that Turkey's 1999 trial of Kurdish leader Abdullah Öcalan was not fair. Western countries pledge funds to Ukraine so that it can cover the Chernobyl nuclear reactor. La Cumbre volcano on Ferdinanda Island in the Galápagos Islands begins to erupt.

15: The Uzbek city of Andijan is sealed off. In Cote d'Ivoire, government and rebels agree to start disarmament and the formation of a unified army. Burundi president Domitien Ndayizeye and Agathon Rwasa, leader of the only existing rebel group, Hutu Forces of National Liberation, sign a peace deal in a meeting in Dar es Salaam, Tanzania.

16: The National Assembly of Kuwait votes 35-23 in favor of women's suffrage, effective for the 2007 parlimentary election. Ethiopian Prime Minister Meles Zenawi prohibits demonstrations in the capital Addis Ababa for one month following parliamentary elections; opposition parties accuse government of electoral fraud; Uzbek soldiers seal off the town of Korasuv after locals occupy government buildings; the government does not allow journalists or the Red Cross to enter the affected areas; telephone and Internet access is disconnected; some reports indicate 700 people dead; fighting continues in Andijan and other

towns; local leaders accuse the government troops of killing hundreds of civilliians and of carrying out mass arrests; opposition supporters and human rights campainers take out rallies in the capital Tashkent; hundreds of refugees have fled to Kyrgyzstan. Thousands take part in a rally in La Paz, Bolivia in support of higher taxes on foreign energy companies. The UN World Food Program declares that North Korea is in desperate need of food aid. Both Ethiopia's ruling party EPRDF and the opposition claim victories in the general election. Six African countries begin a two-day summit in Tripoli, Libya, to discuss the situation in Darfur, Sudan. The local rebel groups fail to send representatives.

17: British MP and anti-war campaigner, George Galloway, appears before the United States Senate to defend charges that he profited from Saddam Hussein's regime. In Russia, the trial of Nur-Pashi Kulayev, the only survivor of the attackers in the Beslan school hostage crisis, begins. The Uzbek government announces it will allow foreign diplomats to visit Andijan; survivors from Andijan who escaped to Kyrgyzstan reveal that government troops opened fire without warning; the opposition puts the number of dead at 745. Australian pop singer Kylie Minogue announces she has been diagnosed with the early stages of breast cancer. The Spanish parliament approves a plan to begin negotiations with the Basque ETA.

18: The Georgian Interior Ministry reveals that a hand grenade was found among spectators during a speech by US President George W. Bush earlier in the month in Tbilisi. Polish President Aleksander Kwaœniewski sets 25 September 2005 as the date for parliamentary elections and 9 October 2005 for presidential election. The World Health Organization announces an ebola outbreak in the Democratic Republic of Congo.

19: Scientific studies reveal that the 2004 Indian Ocean earthquake was the longest ever recorded (nearly 10 minutes), released the most energy(the equivalent of a 100 gigaton bomb), caused the longest fault rupture(800 miles) and had the longest duration of faulting. Uzbek President Islam Karimov rejects calls for international inquiry into unrest in the country. The UN Office for the Coordination of Humanitarian Affairs appeals for $16 million for food aid to Niger where drought and locust swarms destroyed the crop last year. Rwandan defence minister general Marcel Gatsinzi apologizes for being part of the Hutu government during the 1994 Rwandan genocide; this is the first instance of an apology from a government official. British scientists at Newcastle University announce that they have cloned human embryos for stem cells; a team of South Korean scientists at Seoul National University announce they have cloned the first embryonic cells customized to individual patients.

20: *Star Wars Episode III: Revenge of the Sith* is released in the United States; it sets a new record at the box office on the opening day with $50 million on 9,400 screens at 3,661 theaters worldwide. The last United Nations peacekeepers leave East Timor.

22: German Chancellor Gerhard Schröder announces that he will seek re-election in the next German federal election. Former Prime Minister of Mongolia Nambariin Enkhbayar wins the presidential election. In Nepal, thousands take part in an opposition demonstration against King Gyanendra and demand the restoration of parliament.

23: Supreme Leader of Iran, Ayatollah Ali Khamenei, urges the Council of Guardians to review applications of two reformist candidates, Mostafa Moin and Vice President Mohsen Mehralizadeh, after the council qualified only six candidates to the country's presidential election.

25: General elections take place in Suriname. The Baku-Tbilisi-Ceyhan pipeline, the longest oil pipeline in the world, begins operations.

26: The South African Geographical Names Council unanimously approves a recommendation to change the name of the country's executive capital, Pretoria, to Tshwane. US President George W. Bush promises the President of the Palestinian Authority, Abu Mazen, $50 million in aid. French authorities arrest a Chechen named Bislan Ismailov in connection to the murder of Theo van Gogh. In Egypt, a referendum is held for constitutional changes for presidential elections.

27: Protests take place in Egypt, Jordan, Lebanon, Malaysia Pakistan after the US military admits that its soldiers had 'mishandled' the Quran. The Germany parliament ratifies the Treaty establishing a Constitution for Europe. Former European Union Trade Commissioner, Pascal Lamy, becomes new Director-General of the World Trade Organization.

29: The French electorate rejects the Treaty establishing a Constitution for Europe.

30: Qatari Prince Hamid Bin Abdul Sani al-Thani is found guilty of sexually abusing girls younger than 15 in Prague, Czech Republic; he is sentenced to 30 months in prison. In Germany, the CDU/CSU opposition combine elects Angela Merkel as its candidate for Chancellor in the upcoming federal election. Amnesty International urges foreign governments to investigate human rights violations by senior US government officials in Afghanistan, Iraq, and Guantanamo Bay. The son of former Lebanese Prime Minister Rafiq Hariri, Saadettin Hariri, declares his victory in the first round of the general elections. Astronomers at the California Institute of Technology and Astronomical Observatory of Strasbourg state that the Andromeda galaxy is three times bigger than previously thought.

31: The police clashes with protesters demanding nationalization of the energy industry in the Bolivian capital La Paz. Serbia withdraws the arrest warrant for Mirjana Markovic, wife of Slobodan Milošević. United Nations Security Council votes to extend its peacekeeping mission in Haiti until 24 June. Russian billionaire and businessman Mikhail Khodorkovsky is sentenced to 9 years in prison in his tax evasion trial. In Bangkok, Canadian contestant Natalie Glebova is crowned Miss Universe 2005. *Vanity Fair* magazine reports that Ex-FBI official W. Mark Felt admitted he was the Watergate Scandal source known as 'Deep Throat'. In France, Prime Minister Jean-Pierre Raffarin resigns following the country's rejection of the Constitution for Europe; President Jacques Chirac appoints Interior Minister Dominique de Villepin as his successor. China opens the Three Gorges Dam to tourists. In Senegal, opposition leader Abdourahim Agne is charged with inciting rebellion after he asked for demonstrations against President Abdoulaye Wade. Bob Geldof announces plans for 'Live 8', a concert similar to the 1985 Live Aid charity concert, to coincide with the G8 Summit in Edinburgh; the concert is scheduled for July 2005 in London along with other concerts in Paris, Rome, Berlin and Philadelphia. The US Supreme Court overturns the conviction of defunct firm Arthur Andersen on charges relating to the Enron scandal; it states faulty jury instructions as the reason.

June 2005

2: In Lebanon, a bomb explosion kills journalist Samir Qasir, known for his criticism of Syria. The Latvian parliament ratifies the European Constitution.

3: In Bolivia, president Carlos Mesa calls for a referendum for regional autonomy on 16 October, in a bid to end opposition demonstrations. The commander of US forces at Guantánamo Bay, Cuba, reports five known incidents of mishandling of the Quran by guards.

4: Palestinian President Mahmoud Abbas postpones legislative elections originally scheduled for 17 July.

5: In Switzerland, voters decide to ratify the Schengen treaty, abolishing all its normal land border controls by 2007. In Kuwait, Sheikha Fatima al-Sabah and Fawziya al-Bahar become the first two women to be appointed to a municipal council.

6: Parliamentary elections are held in Ethiopia; the ruling EPRDF party claims victory. In Burundi, former rebel group Hutu Forces for the Defence of Democracy wins 75 out of 129 seats in municipal elections. Bolivian president Carlos Mesa offers his resignation. Apple Computer announces shift from IBM to Intel processors for their Macintosh computer range. The International Criminal Court announces an investigation into crimes against humanity in Darfur.

7: In Hungary, opposition candidate Laszlo Solyom wins the presidential election. Siemens announces the sale of its mobile phone business to the Taiwanese electronics company, BenQ.

8: Widespread demonstrations continue in Bolivia.

9: In Syria, the ruling Baath party votes to end the 40-year long state of emergency. In Bolivia, protesters take over seven oil fields managed by British Petroleum and Repsol.

10: Big explosions take place in the Colima volcano in Mexico. The Bolivian Congress accepts the resignation of President Carlos Mesa; Supreme Court justice Eduardo Rodríguez becomes the new interim president. In Australia, a government inquiry in the state of Queensland states that doctor Jayant Patel should be charged with murder, fraud, negligence and medical malpractice due to the death of 87 of his patients.

11: The G8 announces the cancellation of the multilateral debt of 18 of the poorest countries in the world.

12: Mike Tyson announces his retirement from boxing. Kuwait appoints Massuma al-Mubarak as the country's first female cabinet minister. The Kurdish parliament in Northern Iraq elects Masoud Barzani as the region's president.

13: An earthquake of magnitude 7.9 hits Chile. The last Australian peace-keeping troops leave East Timor. In USA, a California court clears Michael Jackson on all counts of child molestation and related charges. In Nigeria, president Olusegun Obasanjo orders the destruction of all illegal oil refineries in the Niger River delta. Swedish diplomat Jan Eliasson is unanimously elected President of the United Nations General Assembly.

14: A major earthquake strikes about 130 kilometres off the coast of northern California. Sudan rejects the UN's decision to use the International Criminal Court in relation to the Darfur conflict; it opens its own special court for this purpose. JP Morgan Chase & Co. announces a settlement of a lawsuit brought against it by Enron investors who claim that it helped the management of that company defraud them.

15: World leaders of the Group of 77 and China launch a two-day South Summit in Doha.

16: In Japan, former tycoon Yoshiaki Tsutsumi confesses to financial fraud and insider trading. Uzbekistan deports four members of human rights group International Helsinki Federation following their investigation in Andijan.

17: Presidential election begins in Iran. A United Nations investigation concludes that former Lebanese Prime Minister Rafik Hariri was killed in a truck bomb explosion. In Kyrgyzstan, protesters supporting presidential candidate Urmat Baryaktadasov seize a government building in the capital city, Bishkek; Baryaktadasov was denied registration on the grounds that he holds Kazakh citizenship. In the United Kingdom, the Ugandan-born bishop of Birmingham Rt. Rev. Dr John Sentamu is named the new Archbishop of York; he is the first ever black person to be appointed an Archbishop of the Church of England. In USA, Dennis Kozlowski, the former chief executive of Tyco International, and Mark Swartz, its erstwhile chief financial officer, are found guilty of grand larceny, conspiracy, falsifying business records and securities fraud.

20: The Anti-Syrian bloc led by Rafik Hariri's son, Saad al-Hariri, gains control of the Lebanese Legislature. An earthquake of magnitude 4.9 hits central Niigata prefecture in Japan. In UK, flash floods affect North Yorkshire villages and towns.

21: The Planetary Society launches the Cosmos 1 experimental solar sail spacecraft from a submarine submerged in the Barents Sea.

22: In Chad, a referendum votes to allow President Idriss Deby to stand elections for a third term in office. The Planetary Society announces that the Cosmos 1 experimental solar sail spacecraft has failed. An Italian military tribunal sentences 10 former Nazi officers in absentia to life imprisonment for their role in a World War II massacre of 560 civilians in the Tuscan village of Sant'Anna di Stazzema.

24: Second round of voting begins in presidential elections; Akbar Hashemi Rafsanjani and Mahmoud Ahmadinejad are the two remaining candidates. Sir Donald Tsang is sworn in as the second Chief Executive of Hong Kong. The Irish Republican Army issues an unreserved apology to the family of 14-year old Kathleen Feeney, whom it shot dead in November 1973.

25: In Iran, Mayor of Tehran, Mahmoud Ahmadinejad, wins the presidential election. General elections are held in Bulgaria.

27: The US Supreme Court releases a unanimous decision in MGM Studios, Inc. v. Grokster, Ltd., stating that peer-to-peer file sharing companies can be held liable for the copyright infringement of their users. Wal-Mart heir John T. Walton dies in a private aircraft crash. Kenya releases three men suspected of conspiracy to a suicide bombing in 2002 and links to al-Qaeda.

26: In Bulgaria, the Socialists win the most votes in the general elections, but fall short of the requirement to form a government on their own.

28: Chipmaker AMD files an antitrust lawsuit against rival Intel. Pakistan's Supreme Court suspends the acquittal of five men accused of raping Mukhtaran Bibi. Queen Elizabeth II conducts a fleet review of 167 naval, merchant and tall ships from UK and 35 other nations to commemorate the bicentenary of the Battle of Trafalgar. Guinea-Bissau's former president Kumba Yala declares his acceptance of the results of the presidential elections in the country. The Ugandan parliament votes to remove the law that restricts presidential tenure to two 5-year terms.

29: The United States Capitol building in Washington DC is briefly evacuated due to an aircraft that entered restricted airspace. New York City officials release the design for the centrepiece building of the proposed new World Trade Center; the name of the building is proposed to be 'The Freedom Tower'.

30: In Lebanon, former Minister of Finance Fouad Siniora is appointed the new prime minister. Survivors of the 1979 Iran hostage crisis claim that Iran's president-elect, Mahmoud Ahmadinejad, was involved in the hostage-taking crisis. International Criminal Court prosecutor Luis Moreno Ocampo states that there is credible evidence of crimes against humanity in Darfur. Somalian gunmen hijack a ship carrying United Nations food aid and demand $500,000 ransom for the crew.

July 2005

1: The UK assumes the rotating presidency of the European Union. Romania's legal tender, the leu, is re-valued; 10,000 old lei is now equivalent to 1 new leu; the ISO 4217 code is changed from ROL (Romanian leu) to RON (Romanian New leu).

2: The Live 8 concerts begin their tour in Tokyo.

3: Aviators Steve Fossett and Mark Rebholz re-enact the first non-stop transatlantic flight of Alcock and Brown in 1919, in a replica World War I Vickers Vimy bomber; they fly from Newfoundland, Canada to Ireland in about 18 hours. Parliamentary elections take place in Albania and Mauritius. In Japan, an underwater volcano causes a column of steam near the island of Iwo Jima.

4: Parliamentary elections start in Burundi. The impactor of NASA probe Deep Impact successfully hits comet Tempel 1. In the Philippines, president Gloria Arroyo announces that she would welcome impeachment proceedings as an opportunity to refute allegations about vote-rigging.

5: In Indonesia, an earthquake measuring 6.0-6.7 on the Richter scale hits Sumatra. In Germany, Sven Jaschan, suspected creator of the Sasser worm, goes on trial. In Germany, The unofficial Berlin Wall memorial in Berlin is dismantled.

6: New York Times reporter Judith Miller is jailed for refusing to divulge her source in an investigation into the leak of a CIA operative's name. The International Olympic Committee names London as the host of the 2012 Summer Olympics. The Bolivian parliament announces early elections and a referendum on regional autonomy. In Burundi, the former Hutu rebel group Forces for the Defence of Democracy wins 58% of the vote in parliamentary elections. Prince Albert II of Monaco admits publicly that he is a father of an illegitimate son by Nicole Coste, a flight attendant of Togolese origin. In Egypt, a court postpones the trial of presidential candidate Ayman Nour so that he can contest the election. In Chile, a court strips Augusto Pinochet of presidential immunity from prosecution in the investigation of disappearance of political opponents. In Myanmar, authorities release 249 dissidents from jail but continue to keep Aung San Suu Kyi under house arrest.

7: Explosions take place on the London Underground and bus system; the entire transport network is shut down. Malta ratifies the EU constitution unanimously. In the Philippines, president Gloria Arroyo asks all the members of her cabinet to resign. The United States raises the alert level from code yellow to code orange for mass transit systems, in response to the London bombings.

8: Hurricane Dennis, the first hurricane of the 2005 Atlantic hurricane season, approaches Cuba and appears to be heading towards the Gulf Coast of the United States. The first case of avian influenza in the Philippines is reported in the Bulacan province. Former Philippines ministers, other politicians and businessmen call upon president Gloria Arroyo to resign.

9: Authorities in the United Kingdom evacuate over 20,000 people from the centre of the city of Birmingham. World leaders at the G8 summit in Gleneagles, Scotland pledge 50 billion USD to fight poverty in Africa and US$3 billions to Palestinians for infrastructure development.

10: Italy announces that it will start its withdrawal of troops from Iraq in September, by pulling 300 of its 3,000 soldiers out of the country. Luxembourg approves the EU Constitution in a referendum. Former rebel leader John Garang is sworn in as vice president of Sudan. In Azerbaijan, thousands of opposition members stage demonstrations in the country's capital, demanding parliamentary elections.

11: The Indonesian government asks TV stations to close down between 1 am and 5 am daily for six months in order to conserve energy but broadcasts of live European football matches are exempt from the shutdown. In Kyrgyzstan, acting president Kurmanbek Bakiev wins the presidential elections.

12: London police identify four suspects in the 7 July 2005 London bombings. In Monaco, Prince Albert is inaugurated as the new ruling prince, in succession to his father Prince Rainier who died in April. In Singapore, President Sellapan Ramanathan announces that he will seek re-election. In Somalia, United Nations World Food Programme threatens to stop food shipments to the country for 10 years if its hijacked food ship and its crew are not released. The European Court of Justice fines France •20 million ($24 million) for violating European Union fishing quotas. In Fiji, head of the military, Frank Bainimarama threatens to declare martial law and topple the government if it grants amnesty to those involved with 2000 coup attempt.

13: US Supreme Court Chief Justice William Rehnquist is hospitalized with a fever. NASA's planned launch of Space Shuttle Discovery from Kennedy Space Center is delayed due to a problem with the fuel level sensors. In Indonesia, geologists raise the alert status of Mount Merapi volcano in Java that has been showing increased activity in the last one week. In the Philippines, thousands of protestors gather in Manila to demand the resignation of president Gloria Arroyo. In Pakistan, three express trains collide near Ghotki, killing over 100. In Chile, the Senate reforms the country's constitution, decreasing power of the military in the upper house and reducing the presidential term for four years.

14: US Supreme Court Chief Justice William Rehnquist announces he will not retire from the court as long as his health allows him to remain. Hurricane Emily causes flooding and mudslides in Grenada. Two minutes of silence is observed across Europe in memory of those who died in the 7 July 2005 London bombings. In Zimbabwe, a court sentences male athlete Samukeliso Sithole to 3.5 years in jail for masquerading as a female in women's sports.

15: The chemist Magdi al-Nashar, sought in relation to the 7 July London bombings, is arrested in Egypt. In the Philippines, opposition demonstrators demanding resignation of president Gloria Arroyo seize the building of the Department of Agriculture before dispersing. A 5.0 Richter scale earthquake hits central Philippines.

16: The English version of _Harry Potter and the Half-Blood Prince_ is released at midnight local time across the UK, Ireland and North America.

17: In Thailand, the authorities declare emergency in the three southern provinces of Narathiwat, Yala and Pattani due to increasing Muslim insurgency violence. In Yemen, president Ali Abdullah Saleh announces that he won't seek re-election next year. In Egypt, presidential aspirant and feminist Nawal el-Saadawi withdraws from the contest due to restrictive election regulations. In UK, the Sunni Council announces a _fatwa_ against suicide bombings. Representatives of the Indonesian government and the Free Aceh Movement reach a tentative peace deal in negotiations in Helsinki, Finland.

18: Hurricane Emily hits the Yucatán Peninsula in Mexico. Tens of thousands are evacuated. In Taiwan, authorities evacuate hundreds of people when Typhoon Haitang hits the country.

19: In the Philippines, President Gloria Arroyo announces that she will form a commission to investigate charges of poll fraud against her. In Lebanon, PM Fouad Siniora announces his new cabinet

20: In Pakistan, the police detain about 200 suspected Islamist extremists in a series of raids on religious properties. In China, authorities evacuate more than a million people from Fujian and Zhejiang provinces due to Typhoon Haitang.

21: German President Horst Köhler agrees to dissolve parliament and calls for early elections in mid-September 2005. Parts of the London Underground network are evacuated, following minor explosions in Shepherd's Bush, Warren Street and Oval stations. There are also reports of an incident on a bus in Hackney, East London. The People's Bank of China announces a 2 per cent revaluation of its currency, the Renminbi (yuan), and removes its peg to the US dollar. Indonesian president Susilo Bambang Yudhoyono orders the army to stop its offensive against separatist rebels in Aceh following a new peace deal. The Malaysian government removes the ringgit's peg to the US dollar.

22: In London, police chase and kill a South Asian-looking man, suspected of being an attempted suicide bomber, at the Stockwell tube station. The Pentagon confirms that 52 detainees of the Guantanamo camp have gone on hunger strike. Microsoft announces that the next version of its Windows operating system, codenamed 'Windows Longhorn' till now, will be officially known as 'Windows Vista'.

23: The strongest earthquake to hit Tokyo in more than a decade strikes eastern Japan. British police admit that the man killed the previous day in London, on suspicion of being a suicide bomber, had no connection with terrorists. The victim has been identified as Jean Charles de Menezes, a Brazilian. In Myanmar, former PM Khin Nyunt receives a suspended sentence of 44 years in prison for corruption.

24: A magnitude 7.2 earthquake occurs off the Nicobar Islands, close to the epicentre of the 26 December 2004 earthquake. American cyclist and cancer survivor Lance Armstrong wins his seventh consecutive Tour de France. Armstrong has announced that this will be his last tour and he will be retiring from the sport.

25: British PM Tony Blair apologizes for the accidental killing of Brazilian Jean Charles de Menezes, whom the police mistook for a suicide bomber. Bilateral negotiations resume between the US and North Korea. More arrests take place with connection to the recent London bombings. In the Philippines, the Opposition files impeachment complaint against president Gloria Arroyo for election fraud.

26: The Space Shuttle Discovery is successfully launched on mission STS-114, dubbed as 'Return to Flight'. Myanmar forgoes 2006 chairmanship of ASEAN. In The Netherlands, Mohammed Bouyeri is sentenced to life for the murder of filmmaker Theo van Gogh. In Mexico, a court rules that there is insufficient evidence to try former president Luis Echeverría for genocide for a student massacre in 1971. In Israel, Omri Sharon, MP and son of Ariel Sharon, is indicted for involvement in illegal campaign contributions, perjury and forgery. In Nepal, a court sentences former PM Sher Bahadur Deuba and three others to two years in jail on corruption charges.

27: The interim Prime Minister of Iraq, Ibrahim Jaafari, calls on US troops to leave Iraq. NASA cancels indefinitely future launches of the Space Shuttle after video footage reveals that a piece of insulation broke off the Space Shuttle external tank during the 26 July launch of the Discovery.

28: The Provisional IRA issues a statement formally asking its activists and members to end the armed campaign. The United States, India, China, Japan, South Korea and Australia form an alliance named the Asia Pacific Partnership on Clean Development and Climate, with the goal of reducing the emissions of gasses that lead to global warming. In the USA, some American-Muslim scholars announce a *fatwa* that condemns terrorism and religious extremism. In Bulgaria, the Bulgarian Socialist Party fails to form a government due to hung parliament; President Georgi Purvanov seeks the help of the National Movement of former king Simeon Saxe-Coburg-Gotha. In Guinea-Bissau, the electoral commission declares João Bernardo Vieira winner of the presidential election.

29: It is announced that astronomers have discovered a large new trans-Neptunian object, provisionally named 2003 UB_{313}, which is larger than Pluto. Three more London bombing suspects are arrested after raids in the UK and Italy. The President of Pakistan, Pervez Musharraf, announces that all foreign students have been asked to leave the nation's *madrassas* and return home.

30: Uzbekistan serves an ultimatum on the United States to move out of a base used for operations in Afghanistan within six months. Russia starts to withdraw its troops from the military bases in Georgia.

31: 7 more suspects are arrested in Brighton, UK, in connection with the 21 July 2005 London bombings. Wim Duisenberg, the first head of the European Central Bank, is found dead in his villa in the south of France. Chile's

Christian Democratic Party declares Michelle Bachelet as the presidential candidate of the ruling coalition. Russia's defence minister Sergei Ivanov prohibits the country's defense ministry from contacting ABC News after the channel broadcast an interview with Chechen rebel Shamil Basayev. In Iran, former president Akbar Hashemi Rafsanjani appeals for the release of an imprisoned dissident writer Akbar Ganji who has been on hunger strike for more than 50 days.

August 2005

1: Sudanese Vice-President and former rebel leader John Garang is killed in a helicopter crash; violence erupts in the capital city, Khartoum, when the news of his death breaks. New European Union directive banning tobacco advertising comes into effect. President Bush bypasses the Senate to end a five-month deadlock over the appointing of John Bolton as the US Ambassador to the UN. NASA announces that astronauts will carry out repairs on hull of the space shuttle Discovery to ensure its safety in re-entry.

2: Air France Flight 358 skids off the runway at Toronto's International Airport while landing during a lightning storm, and bursts into flames; all passengers and crew on board survive. In Zimbabwe, state prosecutors drop treason charges against opposition leader Morgan Tsvangirai. Malaysia, Indonesia and Singapore agree to conduct joint anti-piracy patrols in the Malacca Strait.

3: Mahmoud Ahmadinejad officially becomes the new president of Iran. In Saudi Arabia, Crown Prince Abdullah is invested as the new king. In Sudan, more than 800 people are wounded and 84 killed in violence following the death of ex-rebel and the country's vice-president, John Garang. Michaëlle Jean is chosen as the Governor General of Canada. In Malaysia, former deputy PM Anwar Ibrahim receives apology and compensation from former chief of police Rahim Noor, who beat him in September 1999 when he was arrested. Coup takes place in the African nation of Mauritania.

4: Al-Qaeda leader Ayman al-Zawahri issues a televised statement blaming Tony Blair and his government's foreign policy for the July 2005 London bombings. Coup leaders in Mauritania name Ely Ould Mohamed Vall, former national police chief, as the new president of the country. The African Union suspends Mauritania because of the recent coup. Scientists in Seoul National University, South Korea, announce they have cloned a dog, named Snuppy. Italian scientists discover cocaine residue in the Po River water. A Nepalese court rejects criminal Charles Sobhraj's appeal against his life sentence.

5: An earthquake hits Papua, Indonesia, measuring 6.0 on the Richter scale. Typhoon Matsa hits Taiwan. Russian Priz class mini-submarine AS-28 and its 7 crewmembers are trapped underwater off the Pacific coast of Russia.

6: A Tunisian ATR 72 passenger plane carrying 39 passengers and crew ditches in the sea off the coast of the Italian island of Sicily, killing 14.

7: Crewmembers trapped in the Russian mini-submarine AS-28 are rescued.

8: Iran resumes its nuclear programme at its uranium facility near the city of Isfahan. Bad weather prevents the Space Shuttle Discovery from landing at Kennedy Space Center. Japanese PM Junichiro Koizumi dissolves the Japanese House of Representatives and announces snap elections for 11 September.

9: Space Shuttle Discovery returns safely and lands at Edwards Air Force Base in California. Mahmoud Abbas, President of the Palestinian Authority, announces a Palestinian general election to be held in January 2006. Israeli authorities threaten Israeli settlers on the Gaza Strip with eviction if they do not leave their settlements voluntarily.

10: In Chile, Lucía Hiriart and Marco Antonio Pinochet, wife and youngest son of Augusto Pinochet, are indicted on charges of tax evasion. The United States and the African Union drop their demands that last week's coup in Mauritania be reversed.

11: Scientists at the German Primate Centre and the University of Göttingen, Germany announce the discovery of two new species of lemur, *Mirza zaza* and *Microcebus lehilahytsara*. Pakistan carries out a test launch of its first domestically designed cruise missile, the Babur missile. Salva Kiir is sworn in as the vice-president of Sudan, following the recent death of John Garang. The launch of the Mars Reconnaissance Orbiter is postponed due to technical problems. Malaysia announces a state of emergency in two towns after air pollution reaches dangerous levels.

12: A suspected Tamil Tigers sniper assassinates Sri Lankan Foreign Minister Lakshman Kadirgamar in Colombo. The Mars Reconnaissance Orbiter spacecraft is successfully launched from Cape Canaveral, Florida.

13: German Chancellor Gerhard Schröder warns the US not to initiate military action against Iran over its nuclear programme.

14: Kurmanbek Bakiyev is sworn in as Kyrgyzstan's new president. Helios Airways Flight 522 flying from Larnaca, Cyprus to Prague, Czech Republic crashes near Athens, Greece, with at least 121 on board.

15: The 60th anniversary of the Victory in the Pacific and the end of World War II is celebrated. The Parliament of Iraq grants an extension to leaders who are formulating the country's new Constitution.

16: Russian cosmonaut Sergei K. Krikalev sets a record for spending the most days in space (nearly 748 days over 20 years). A British news channel announces that it has uncovered classified documents that seem to show that Jean Charles de Menezes, the Brazilian man shot dead by British Police on 22 July 2005, was not wearing a heavy coat, nor did he jump the ticket barrier, was not given a warning, and did not attempt to evade the police. West Caribbean Airways Flight 708 flying from Colombia crashes in a remote region of Venezuela with 160 people on board. A magnitude 7.2 earthquake strikes the northeastern coast of Honshu, Japan.

17: Singapore president S.R. Nathan wins a second term in office.

18: Pope Benedict XVI makes his first foreign trip, to his homeland Germany.

19: Mounir El Motassadeq is re-convicted in Hamburg, Germany and sentenced to seven years in prison; he was the first person to be convicted for his role in the 9/11 attacks but had his conviction overturned in 2004. Pierre Nkurunziza, a former rebel leader of the Hutu majority in Burundi, is elected unopposed as the new president of Burundi; he is the first president to be chosen by a democratic process since the start of the civil war in 1993.

20: The original handwritten manuscript of a paper by Albert Einstein, entitled 'Quantum theory of the monatomic ideal gas' is found in the archives of Leiden University's Lorentz Institute for Theoretical Physics.

21: More than 800,000 people take part in the concluding Mass of World Youth Day 2005 in Cologne, Germany, along with Pope Benedict XVI.

22: Iraq's parliament receives a draft of that country's constitution, minutes before the revised deadline. In USA, Eric Rudolph is sentenced to three more life terms without possibility of parole for the

Centennial Olympic Park bombing of the 1996 Summer Olympics in Atlanta. Patriarch Theophilus III is unanimously elected 141st Orthodox Patriarch of Jerusalem by the Holy Synod of the Orthodox Church of Jerusalem. Israel PM Ariel Sharon announces that existing large West Bank Israeli settlements will be expanded.

23: More than 40 are killed when a Peruvian Boeing 737-200 aircraft crashes near Pucallpa, Peru, with 100 on board.

24: Heavy floods hit Austria, Germany and Switzerland, dislodging thousands of people from their homes. Chinese railroad workers in Tibet lay rail tracks on the Tanggula Mountain Pass in Tibet at 5,072 m (16,640 ft) above sea level, making it the highest railway in the world; this surpasses the previous record held by a Peruvian railway line at 255 m (837 ft).

25: French investigating magistrate Jean-Louis Bruguière warns that al-Qaeda is planning a terrorist attack in Asia and identifies Tokyo, Sydney and Singapore as potential targets.

26: 14 children and three adults are killed in a fire at a Paris building that housed African immigrants. Typhoon Mawar makes landfall at Chiba city, east of Tokyo.

27: Almost 1,000 detainees at the Abu Ghraib prison in Baghdad are released at the request of the Iraqi government.

28: Iraq's National Assembly signs the text of the proposed Iraqi constitution. Omri Sharon, son of the Israel PM, Ariel Sharon, is formally indicted on charges of corruption. Hurricane Katrina continues to strengthen and develops into a Category Five hurricane; it has the second lowest pressure for an American hurricane in recorded history (908 mb.); millions of people living in and around the below sea-level city in Louisiana, New Orleans, escape the city; the Mayor of New Orleans issues a mandatory evacuation order, as fears are raised that the levees protecting the city would not be able to withstand the hurricane's aftermath.

29: Hurricane Katrina makes landfall as a Category Four hurricane at 6.10 a.m. Central Daylight Time (CDT) and the eye passes just east of New Orleans, Louisiana; Venezuelan President Hugo Chávez offers to send food and fuel to the United States.

30: Hurricane Katrina creates storm surge higher than Hurricane Camille of 1969; US Highway 90 along Gulfport, Mississippi, and Interstate 10 causeway connecting the east side of New Orleans to mainland Louisiana are destroyed; New Orleans, Louisiana, is almost completely flooded after levees along Lake Pontchartrain fail; attempts to repair broken levees prove unsuccessful; fuel leaks pollute the floodwaters; the Louisiana Superdome is the primary evacuation site; Louisiana Governor Kathleen Blanco orders the evacuation of everyone remaining in New Orleans; the American Red Cross declares that the relief effort will be greater in scope than that following the 11 September 2001 attacks; Michael Brown, director of the United States Federal Emergency Management Agency, pledges full federal assistance. Oil prices reach US$70/bbl. Former Prime Minister of Israel, Binyamin Netanyahu, announces that he will challenge Ariel Sharon for leadership of the Likud party. In Paris, France, seven die and fourteen are injured in a fire in an apartment housing African immigrants. Indian PM Manmohan Singh announces that India will give US$50 million in additional aid for the reconstruction of Afghanistan.

31: In USA, the Federal government declares a public health emergency for the Gulf Coast of the United States and launches one of the largest search and rescue missions in history, in the wake of Hurricane Katrina. New Orleans mayor Ray Nagin states that thousands have possibly died in the city. At least 25,000 refugees from New Orleans will be moved to Houston, Texas. The government will release oil from its Strategic Petroleum Reserve to help refineries whose oil supplies have been affected by Hurricane Katrina. More than 900 people are killed in a stampede on the Al-Aaimmah bridge over the river Tigris in Baghdad during a Shia Muslim march to a shrine. All Palestinian Authority Assets held in the United States are frozen. A Philippine congressional committee stops all impeachment efforts against President Gloria Arroyo.

September 2005

1: Unidentified attackers open fire on a US military helicopter at New Orleans Superdome, while it was taking part in rescue operations; this incident halts the evacuations. Typhoon Talim passes over Taiwan. The first anniversary of the Beslan school tragedy is commemorated in Russia. The Common Chimpanzee genome sequence is released.

2: President Bush tours the area affected by Hurricane Katrina.

3: Qatar offers $100 million to the USA to help cope with Hurricane Katrina; Spain provides the United States with 70,000 barrels of oil a day during September; over 40,000 military personnel await deployment;these include active duty personnel and National Guard troops.

4: In USA, the Coast Guard asks people in the New Orleans area to hang brightly coloured or white objects to help them detect those who need help in the aftermath of Hurricane Katrina; Texas Governor Rick Perry orders emergency officials to begin preparations to airlift some of the 250,000 refugees already to other states that have offered to help; aerial photos of the affected areas are posted by the US National Oceanic and Atmospheric

Administration on the web; a number of nations and international organizations offer financial and humanitarian assistance. Typhoon Talim hits China's Anhui Province.

5: The National Elections Board of Ethiopia announces that the ruling EPRDF coalition has retained control of the government. Typhoon Nabi, classified as Category Three, reaches the Japanese coast. In USA, Senator and former First Lady Hillary Clinton calls for a '9/11 Style Inquiry' into the US federal government's response to Hurricane Katrina. US President George W. Bush nominates American jurist John G. Roberts, Jr. as the next Chief Justice of the United States. In Indonesia, Mandala Airlines Flight 091 crashes into a residential area of the Indonesian city of Medan, killing at least 100, including the governor and former governor of Sumatra Utara.

6: Typhoon Nabi hits Japan, forcing the evacuation of nearly 100,000 people. The plenary session of the House of Representatives of the Philippines drops the impeachment complaint filed against Philippine President Gloria Macapagal-Arroyo.

7: Michael Jackson announces that he will record and release a charity single dedicated to the victims of Hurricane Katrina with all proceeds going to the victims of Hurricane Katrina.

8: Hosni Mubarak wins the first multi-candidate presidential election in Egypt. Ayman Nour finishes second. Ukraine President Viktor Yushchenko removes PM Yulia Tymoshenko and most of the cabinet.

9: United States Department of Homeland Security Secretary Michael Chertoff appoints Vice Admiral Thad W. Allen, chief of staff of the United States Coast Guard, to direct Hurricane Katrina relief efforts in New Orleans, replacing Federal Emergency Management Agency director Michael D. Brown. An earthquake measuring 7.3 on the Richter scale is measured off the eastern coast of Papua New Guinea.

11: A videotape, purportedly from al-Qaeda, is delivered to American network ABC in Pakistan; it warns of future attacks on Los Angeles, California and Melbourne, Australia. Exit polls show that Japanese PM Junichiro Koizumi has won a landslide victory in the country's general election. Over 800,000 people are evacuated in the Zhejiang province of China after the province is hit by Typhoon Khanun.

12: In Norway, the Red-Green Coalition led by Jens Stoltenberg wins the 2005 legislature election. Michael D. Brown resigns as the head of the Federal Emergency Management Agency of the United States (FEMA) following criticism of his handling of the situation following Hurricane Katrina. Israel withdraws the last of its troops from the Gaza Strip.

13: The rebel National Liberation Front of Burundi breaks off peace negotiations with the new government of Pierre Nkurunziza.

14: For the first time ever, the President of Pakistan, Pervez Musharraf, shakes hands with the Israeli PM, Ariel Sharon, in public. UN High Commissioner for Refugees and World Food Programme appeal for more funds to provide food for two million refugees in Africa. Mandatory evacuation is ordered for parts of North Carolina, USA as Hurricane Ophelia approaches the state. Palestine organization Hamas blows a hole through the wall between Egypt and Gaza, allowing free passage for Palestinians to and from Egypt for the first time since 1967.

15: The Supreme court of Israel rejects the opinion of International Court of Justice for the removal of the Israeli West Bank barrier.

16: Hurricane Ophelia is downgraded to a tropical storm. The Bicentennial of the Battle of Trafalgar and the death of Admiral Lord Nelson is commemorated.

17: Iranian President Mahmoud Ahmadinejad rejects an offer from the European Union to halt its nuclear program while addressing the UN General Assembly.

18: Federal elections held in Germany produce a hung parliament.

19: North Korea agrees to abandon its nuclear weapons programmes and return to the Nuclear Non-Proliferation Treaty. Mayor Ray Nagin orders another evacuation of New Orleans as Hurricane Rita approaches.

20: North Korea announces that its offer to terminate its nuclear arms programme is subject to international approval to build a civilian nuclear reactor. German politician Joschka Fischer announces his retirement from the leadership of the Green party.

21: Hurricane Rita reaches Category 5 intensity.

22: Australia agrees to help Indonesia's fight against avian influenza by providing anti-viral drugs. The Parliament of Ukraine approves Yuriy Yekhanurov as the country's new PM.

23: In Germany, a proposed alliance between conservatives, liberals and greens is abandoned.

24: Hurricane Rita makes landfall as a Category 3 hurricane on the Texas-Louisiana border in USA.

25: An earthquake measuring 7.5 on the Richter Scale strikes northern Peru. Renault driver Fernando Alonso becomes the youngest ever Formula One champion. Swiss voters approve citizens from the 10 newest European Union member countries to travel and work in Switzerland.

26: Anti-Iraq War activist Cindy Sheehan is arrested while protesting outside the White House. In Spain, Imad Yarkas is convicted of conspiracy with al-Qaeda with connection to the 11 September 2001 attacks and sentenced to 27 years; Driss Chebli is convicted of collaborating with a terrorist group and sentenced to six years while Al Jazeera journalist Tayser Allouni is also convicted on the same charge and sentenced to seven years; Ghasoub al-Abrash Ghalyoun is acquitted on all counts.

27: Michaëlle Jean is sworn in as the 27th Governor General of Canada, replacing Adrienne Clarkson. Japanese scientists capture the first ever images of a living giant squid and recover one of its two longest tentacles. Israeli PM, Ariel Sharon, survives a major leadership challenge within the Likud Party.

28: US House Majority Leader Tom DeLay is indicted on one count of criminal conspiracy for allegedly funding Texas state elections secretly through the Republican national office.

29: *New York Times* reporter Judith Miller is released from jail after receiving a waiver from her news source, allowing her to testify in the investigation of the outing of CIA operative Valerie Plame. The US Senate confirms John G. Roberts, Jr. as Chief Justice of the US Supreme Court.

30: Judith Miller testifies before a federal grand jury and identifies Lewis Libby, Vice President Dick Cheney's chief of staff, as her confidential source for a non-published story about the revealing of a CIA agent.

India Dateline

October 2004

4: The Central government decides to wind up the Tehelka Commission headed by Justice S.N. Phukan and orders a probe by the Central Bureau of Investigation (CBI) into all allegations of corruption, including those against the former Defence Minister, George Fernandes, and others mentioned in the tapes by the Tehelka portal. Set up soon after tehelka.com's expose in March 2001, the National Democratic Alliance Government set up the Commission headed by Justice K. Venkataswami, who resigned in November 2002. Thereafter, Justice Phukan was appointed to continue the probe and the last extension given to the panel ended on 3 October 2004. The Board of Control for Cricket in India and Prasar Bharati sign an agreement giving the terrestrial and satellite rights for the telecast of all Test and one-day matches involving India, Australia, South Africa and Pakistan to Doordarshan. According to the agreement, Doordarshan will pay Rs 3 crore a day for the Test matches and Rs 7 crore for one-day matches. The overall agreement will be to the tune of Rs 100 crore.

10: Australia wins the first Test for the TVS Cup Border-Gavaskar Trophy at the Chinnaswamy Stadium by 217 runs to go up 1-0 in the four-match series. Michael Clarke, who scored a century on debut, was declared the man of the match and Virender Sehwag, who was charged with a level 2 breach of the ICC Code of Conduct, was imposed a penalty of 65 per cent of his match fee by match referee Ranjan Madugalle.

13: After failing to secure the resignation of the Chairman of the Central Board of Film Certification (CBFC), Anupam Kher, the Government appoints Sharmila Tagore as its Chairperson. She is appointed in an 'honorary capacity' for a period of three years from the day of taking charge.

15: Shane Warne breaks the world record for the most Test wickets as he overtakes Muttiah Muralitharan's tally of 532. Shane Warne created the record when he had Irfan Pathan caught at slip by Matthew Hayden.

16: The Congress-Nationalist Congress Party alliance in Mahararashtra

Assembly elections wins 141 seats in the 288-member Assembly — the Congress 69, the NCP 71 and the Republican Party of India (Athavale) one — four short of a simple majority. Their main opponents, the Shiv Sena-Bharatiya Janata Party alliance wins 117 seats, the Shiv Sena 62, the BJP 54 and the Swatantra Bharat Paksh one. Three parties that were allied to the Congress-NCP but decided to contest separately in the election won a small number of seats. Gegong Apang is sworn in as the 10th Chief Minister of Arunachal Pradesh for a record seventh time at a function at the Darbar Hall of the Raj Bhawan.

18: The elusive forest brigand Veerappan is shot dead by the Tamil Nadu Special Task Force (STF). At least four persons, including his close aide, Sethukuzhi Govindan, were killed in the exchange of fire in jungles in Dharmapuri district, which borders Karnataka. He was accused of more than 100 murders as well as kidnapping, smuggling and poaching and had been on the run for some 20 years and was involved in the kidnapping of former state minister of Karnataka, H. Nagappa, who was found dead after three months in captivity. He was also involved in the kidnapping of South Indian actor Rajkumar, who was released after 108 days in captivity. Since 1993, Veerappan had offered to surrender to the police on three occasions, always demanding that he be given a blanket amnesty. M. Venkaiah Naidu resigns as president of the Bharatiya Janata Party. The Leader of the Opposition, L.K. Advani, takes over as the new party chief. With his resignation, all party office-bearers lose their positions and the national executive council also stands dissolved. L. K. Advani will now be free to revamp the entire party structure.

25: Rajasthan Governor, Madan Lal Khurana, resigns from his post and declares his intention to take up issues af-fecting the people of Delhi, including the ongoing agitation against the closure of industries. He took charge as the Governor on 15 January 2004. A special court for CBI cases acquits Chandraswami in the St. Kitts forgery case. He was accused of conspiring to forge documents to frame Ajey Singh, son of the former Prime Minister, V.P. Singh. The other two accused in the case, the former Prime Minister, P.V. Narasimha Rao, and the former Union Minister, K.K. Tewari, were discharged in 1997 by the then Special Judge, Ajit Bharihoke, while the fourth accused, Kailash Nath Aggarwal alias Mamaji, died during the proceedings. Lakshmi N. Mittal's Ispat International announces the acquisition of LNM Holdings and a merger with the United States-based International Steel Group Inc. (ISG) in a deal worth $ 17.8 billion to form the world's largest steel firm, Mittal Steel Co.

27: Prithvi-III, a surface-to-surface missile, is successfully test-fired from the Interim-Test-Range at Chandipur, about 15 km from Balasore in Orissa. This is the first time that Prithvi-III is being launched. The Cabinet Committee on Economic Affairs (CCEA) approves the proposal for the creation of an Investment Commission after the Prime Minister, Manmohan Singh, decided that it would be located in the Finance Ministry and would enjoy operational autonomy and Government support. Originally proposed in the budget by the Finance Minister, P. Chidambaram, the Commission will comprise one chairperson, two members and three professional groups and will initially have a three-year term.

29: Congress approves Vilasrao Deshmukh's candidature as the new Chief Minister of Maharashtra. He became Chief Minister of the Democratic Front Government in 1999. He was asked to step down in January 2003 to make way for the Dalit face of the

Congress, Sushil Kumar Shinde. A protégé of the prominent Maratha politician, S. B. Chavan, he was the first Chief Minister from the backward Marathwada region. The Tamil Nadu Governor, P.S. Ramamohan Rao, resigns from the post. Andhra Pradesh Governor, Surjit Singh Barnala is most likely replacement for him. Australia captures its first Test series in India in 35 years with a resounding 342-run victory on the fourth day of the third Test match at the VCA Stadium, Nagpur.

30: The Andhra Pradesh Governor, Surjit Singh Barnala, is transferred and appointed as Governor of Tamil Nadu and former Maharashtra Chief Minister, Sushil Kumar Shinde, replaces him in the Raj Bhavan at Hyderabad. It is the second term in Chennai for Surjit Singh Barnala. His earlier term was during 1989-90. He was appointed Governor of Uttaranchal during the erstwhile National Democratic Alliance regime and was then shifted to Andhra Pradesh. The name of the former Madhya Pradesh Chief Minister, Uma Bharti, is not there in the list of office-bearers of the Bharatiya Janata Party. While five general secretaries, Pramod Mahajan, Arun Jaitley, Rajnath Singh, Shivraj Singh Chauhan and Sanjay Joshi, have been retained, the former Union Minister and Karnataka leader, Anantha Kumar, is the new general secretary in the list.

31: Shyam Benegal is honoured with the prestigious Indira Gandhi Award for National Integration. The award carries Rs 1.51 lakh in cash and a citation. The Air Officer Commanding-in-Chief of the Western Air Command, S. P. Tyagi, is named the next Chief of Air Staff (COAS) by the Government. Air Marshal Tyagi will take charge on 31 December when the present COAS, Air Chief Marshal S. Krishnaswami, retires. Kerala lifts the Santosh Trophy national footbal title with a 3-2 victory against Punjab.

November 2004

1: Vilasrao Deshmukh is sworn in as the new Chief Minister of Maharashtra and R.R. Patil becomes the Deputy Chief Minister. The Governor of Uttar Pradesh, T.V. Rajeshwar Rao, is sworn in as the acting Governor of Rajasthan and the Jharkhand Governor, Ved Prakash Marwah, as the acting Governor of Bihar.

2: Senior Congress leader Buta Singh is appointed Bihar Governor and Pratibha Patil Governor of Rajasthan. The Home Ministry sends an official invitation to the Hurriyat for talks. The Centre agrees on a three-tier system of compensation to states implementing the value-added tax from April next year. Raees Pathan, the second eyewitness who testified to the Best Bakery carnage, admits giving a false statement in court.

3: Zahira, the key eyewitness in the Best Bakery case, retracts her statements before a Mumbai court. The VSNL signs a Rs 500-crore-pact with Cisco Systems for deployment of India's largest broadband Metro Ethernet solution for Tata Indicom Broadband Services, in Mumbai. The naval version of Brahmos supersonic cruise missile is successfully test-fired off the Orissa coast. Surjit Singh Barnala is sworn in as Tamil Nadu Governor.

4: Sushil Kumar Shinde is sworn in Andhra Pradesh Governor. Uma Bharti is named BJP general secretary.

5: The Supreme Court declares that the Governor of a State can independently accord sanction for prosecution of a Minister in prevention of corruption cases without the 'aid and advice' of the Council of Ministers. The Supreme Court rules that computer software is liable to be taxed under the provisions of the Sales Tax Act. India wins the final Test in Mumbai but Australia clinches the Border-Gavaskar Trophy.

6: The NCP leader Babasaheb Kupekar is elected Maharashtra Assembly Speaker. The Congress president, Sonia Gandhi, announces Salman Khursheed as the president of the Uttar Pradesh unit.

7: India successfully test-fires the 350-km-range Dhanush missile from INS *Subhadra* along the east coast. Union Home Minister Shivraj Patil announces to install sensors along the International Border in Jammu and Kashmir to help in the surveillance and better monitoring of the belt.

8: The former Army Chief, Gen. S. F. Rodrigues is appointed Punjab Governor.

9: The Justice U. C. Bannerjee committee, appointed by the Railway Ministry to go into the technical, mechanical and other aspects of the Godhra train carnage, re-visits the site.

10: The BJP suspends the former MP Chief Minister Uma Bharti from the party's primary membership. The Public Investment Board (PIB) clears the Indian Airlines proposal to purchase 43 aircraft at a cost of Rs 9,475 crore and decides to recommend sovereign guarantee for the deal. East Bengal wins the Durand Cup in New Delhi.

11: Prime Minister Manmohan Singh announces to reduce troops in Jammu & Kashmir.

12: The Kanchi Sankaracharya Sri Jayendra Saraswathi is arrested in Mahbubnagar in Andhra Pradesh on charges of 'abetting the murder' of Sankararaman, manager of Varadarajaperumal temple in Kancheepuram on 3 September. Sensex hits 6000-mark.

13: Pakistan beats India in the one-off one-day International, played to commemorate the Platinum Jubilee of the Indian Board. Forex reserves cross $122 billion mark. Dronavalli Harika of India wins the world girls under-14 chess championship in Heraklion, Greece.

14: The Prime Minister Manmohan Singh launches the National Food-For-Work Programme (NFFWP) for 'generating employment to feed the poor,' covering 150 of the most backward districts in the country. Indian captain Sourav Ganguly is suspended for two Tests with immediate effect for breaching the ICC's Code of Conduct during the Board of Control for Cricket in India's Platinum Jubilee one-day International against Pakistan played at Eden Gardens.

15: The International Cricket Council (ICC) suspends its two-Test ban on Indian captain Sourav Ganguly.

16: The Prime Minister Manmohan Singh begins his first visit to Jammu and Kashmir for what is described as an attempt to touch the 'hearts and minds' of the people of the State. Zahira's sister-in-law Yasmin Sheikh, the fourth eyewitness in the Best Bakery case, identifies 11 accused.

17: The Prime Minister Manmohan Singh rejects the Pakistan President Pervez Musharraf's 'seven regions' proposal. The Chief Justice of the Madras High Court, B. Subhashan Reddy, is transferred and posted as Chief Justice of the Kerala High Court. Sensex touches nine-month high at 6016.

18: Salim Zarda, the Godhra carnage mastermind, is arrested on the outskirts of Godhra, Gujarat.

19: Thai Princess Maha Chakris wins the Rs 25-lakh Indira Gandhi Award for 2004 for peace, development and disarmament.

20: The Madras High Court dismisses the bail application of the Kanchi Sankaracharya, Sri Jayendra Saraswathi, in the case relating to the murder of Sankararaman, Manager of the Varadarajaperumal Temple, Kancheepuram, on 3 September.

21: The Common Admission Test (CAT) for the Indian Institute of Management and other management institutions for the next academic year ends peacefully. India wins the Kabaddi World Cup in Mumbai.

22: Onkar Kanwar is elected Federation of Indian Chambers of Commerce and Industry president. Plea for extension of police custody for Kanchi Acharya is rejected. Shilendra Kumar Singh is appointed Governor of Arunachal Pradesh. The term of office of the incumbent, Vinod Chandra Pande, has expired.

23: The Kanchi Sankaracharya Sri Jayendra Saraswathi is arrested. India and Pakistan agrees to press ahead with their composite dialogue. Justice Markandeya Katju, Judge of the Allahabad High Court, is appointed Chief Justice of the Madras High Court with effect from the date he assumes office.

24: The Union Cabinet decides to extend by three months the tenure of the high-level committee set up to inquire into the incident of fire on the Sabarmati Express at Godhra in February 2002 in which 58 persons died.

25: The Congress Jananayaga Peravai floated by the Finance Minister P. Chidambaram merges with the Congress. The Indian Railways announces its decision to increase freight rates for coal, iron ore and some other items to generate Rs 400 crore for the current year. Six out of 12 directors of Reliance Energy Limited resign from the Board of the company, which is headed by Anil Ambani.

26: The judicial custody for the Kanchi Acharya in the Sankararaman murder case is extended till 10 December. Akash, the indigenously developed surface-to-air missile, is test fired from the Integrated Test Range at Chandipur-on-Sea.

27: The Jharkhand Mukti Morcha leader Shibu Soren is reinducted into the Union Cabinet and gets back the Coal Ministry. S.M. Krishna, former Karnataka Chief Minister, is appointed Maharashtra Governor. Lt. Gen. Joginder Jaswant Singh is named the new Army Chief.

28: The first home-built Sukhoi-30 MKI multi-role fighter aircraft is handed over to the IAF. Justice Markandey Katju is sworn in Madras High Court Chief Justice. The 35th International Film Festival of India (IFFI) begins at Panaji.

29: India and Japan agrees to set up a multi-disciplinary group to enhance economic ties focussing on trade, investment and information technology.

30: The surface-to-air missile 'Akash' is test-fired with live warhead in Orissa. Wajahat Habibullah is named New Panchayati Raj Secretary. P. Harikrishna wins the world junior chess championship at Kochi.

December 2004

1: Indian cricketers sign contract for graded payment. The Union Law Minister H.R. Bhardwaj introduces in the Lok Sabha the Contempt of Courts (Amendment) Bill, 2004 providing for making truth a valid defence in the court of law.

2: The Government introduces in the Lok Sabha the Prevention of Terrorism (Repeal) Bill, 2004 seeking POTA repeal. The Department of Telecom (DoT) makes mobile service fully operational in Jammu and Kashmir and the Northeastern States. India defeats South Africa 1-0 in the two-Test series in India. Anil Kumble equals Kapil Dev's record of 434 Test victims.

3: India and Russia sign a joint declaration on bilateral ties, besides nine agreements, including one on Indian use of the Russian global satellite navigation system (Glonass). Gopalkrishna Gandhi is appointed West Bengal Governor. The Prime Minister Manmohan Singh sets up the Board for Reconstruction of Central Public Sector Enterprises.

4: Vladimir Putin declares that Russia will support India entering the UN

Security Council with veto power.

5: The Government names industrialist Ratan Tata to head the Investment Commission, with Deepak Parekh and Asoke Ganguly being the other two members. Christiano Junior of Dempo SC dies during the Federation Cup football tournament final against Mohun Bagan in Bangalore.

6: The Lok Sabha passes a bill repealing POTA. Somanahalli Mallaiah Krishna (72), former Karnataka Chief Minister, is sworn in Maharashtra Governor. The NDTV president Prannoy Roy is presented with the Award for Excellence in Journalism by the President A.P.J. Abdul Kalam for the channel's stories on the stamp paper scam.

7: Election Commission announces urban body elections in Jammu and Kashmir after two decades. The Central Bureau of Investigation (CBI) files an affidavit in the Supreme Court denying the allegation that the Rashtriya Janata Dal chief and Railway Minister, Lalu Prasad Yadav, and his wife and Bihar Chief Minister, Rabri Devi, were interfering in the Rs 900-crore fodder scam cases. The Government refers to the Standing Committee the Bill to repeal the Displaced Persons Claims Act, 1950 and certain other enactments.

8: Senior BJP leader and former MP Sunil Shastri quits party. Anil Ambani questions elder brother Mukesh's claims on Reliance ownership issue.

9: Parliament passes Prevention of Terrorism (Repeal) Bill and the Unlawful Activities (Prevention) Amendment Bill that replaces POTA. Iran's *Beautiful City* by Asghar Farhadi sweeps awards at the 35th edition of the IFFI in Panaji, Goa.

10: Kumble becomes the highest wicket-taker in Tests for India.

11: Legendary Carnatic musician, Madurai Shanmukhavadivu Subbulakshmi (88) dies. Sachin Tendulkar equals Sunil Gavaskar's record of 34 Test centuries in Dhaka.

12: Sachin Tendulkar equals Sunil Gavaskar's record for most double centuries by an Indian batsman.

13: The Nanavati-Shah judicial inquiry commission probing the Godhra train carnage and the communal riots that followed in Gujarat, visits Godhra. The Supreme Court issues notice to the Centre on a petition challenging the constitutional validity of Section 23 of the Hindu Succession Act, 1956 that provides for treating male and female heirs differently in the matter of inheritance.

14: The Kanchi Sankaracharya, Sri Jayendra Saraswathi, moves the Supreme Court seeking bail in the 'Sankararaman murder case'. India and Pakistan begin talks on nuclear confidence-building measures (CBMs) and exchange views on measures such as operationalization of a hotline between the Foreign Secretaries. India joins the select group of countries that telecast live proceedings in their legislatures, with the launch of two Doordarshan satellite channels dedicated exclusively to coverage of business in the Lok Sabha and the Rajya Sabha.

15: India and the US sign an agreement to prevent customs offences. The Union Cabinet approves the draft National Rural Employment Guarantee Bill, the draft Right to Information Bill, 2004. For the first time in the history of the BSE, the Sensex breaches the 6,400 mark.

16: The Prime Minister Manmohan Singh launches DD Direct Plus, the country's only free-to-air direct-to-home (DTH) service, with 33 television and 12 radio channels.

17: The Peruvian Film *Dias De Santiago* (Days of Santiago), directed by Josue Mendez wins the Golden Crow Pheasant Award for the best feature film at the Ninth International Film Festival of Kerala in

Thiruvananthapuram. The Supreme Court declines to grant interim bail to the Kanchi Sankaracharya arrested on 11 November in the 'Sankararaman murder case'.

18: The CEO of Baazee.com, Avnish Bajaj, is remanded to judicial custody in connection with the multi-media messaging scandal involving two school students in New Delhi. Former Indian cricket captain Vijay Hazare passes away in Vadodara.

19: Appu alias Krishnaswamy, prime accused in the Sankararaman murder case, is arrested at his farmhouse in Balakrishnapuram in Chittoor, Andhra Pradesh. M. Damodaran quits as Chairman and Managing Director of UTI Mutual Fund and administrator of UTI-I.

20: Election Commission lodges FIR against Lalu Prasad Yadav for distributing Rs 100 each to his partymen in Patna. India wins the Test series against Bangladesh. The Government introduces in the Rajya Sabha a Bill seeking to establish a Rail Land Development Authority to enable the Railways to use its land for commercial purposes for generating revenues by non-tariff measures. The Supreme Court declares that even in the case of an illegal second marriage, the wife is entitled to maintenance if the husband deserts her.

21: The Delhi High Court grants bail to Baazee.com CEO Avnish Bajaj.

22: The Union Cabinet clears a proposal of the Indian Space Research Organisation to launch a new high-power satellite with 24 C-band transponders—12 of them with India coverage and the remaining 12 with expanded coverage—in order to provide the much-needed back-up to the present C-band capacity in the country. A Constitution Bench of the Supreme Court declares that an acting Chief Justice of a High Court can discharge the functions of a Chief Justice. English author Upamanyu Chatterjee, Malayalam short story writer Paul Zachariah, Tamil and Hindi poets, Tamizhanban and Viren Dangwal, are declared among 22 winners of the Sahitya Akademi Awards for 2004.

23: The former Prime Minister, Pamulaparti Venkata Narasimha Rao (83), passes away. Mukesh Ambani gives up Rs 50-crore shares acquired as sweat equity from Reliance Infocomm (RIC). The Election Commission appoins six Special Observers for Bihar, Jharkhand and Haryana to supervise the Assembly elections scheduled to be held in these states in three phases in February 2005.

24: The former Madhya Pradesh Chief Minister Uma Bharti's suspension from the Bharatiya Janata Party is revoked by the party president, L.K. Advani.

25: Former Tripura Chief Minister, Nripen Chakraborty, passes away.

26: Over 15,000 people are killed, 10,000 in Andamans alone, and 7,397 in Tamil Nadu, as huge seismic waves (tsunami), triggered by a massive undersea earthquake off Sumatra in Indonesia, lash many coastal regions of India. The junior Sankaracharya of Kanchi Kamakoti Peetam, Sri Vijayendra Saraswathi, is questioned by the police in connection with the Sankararaman murder case. Ravi Subramanian, the prime accused in the Sankararaman murder case, is arrested in Guruvayur.

27: As the first step, the Union Cabinet allocates Rs 500 crores for the National Calamity Contingency Fund to meet the relief and rehabilitation requirements of the tsunami victims.

28: Onkar S. Kanwar, CMD, Apollo Tyres, takes over as the FICCI president.

29: The Government permits domestic private airlines to fly overseas except for the Gulf region. C. Rangarajan is appointed Chairman of the Economic Advisory Council to the Prime Minister with the Cabinet rank.

30: The Government promulgates an ordinance for setting up a Pension Fund Regulatory and Development Authority (PFRDA) on the lines of the Insurance Regulatory and Development Authority (IRDA).

31: S.P. Tyagi takes over as the Chief of Air Staff from S. Krishnaswamy.

January 2005

1: India, Pakistan exchange lists of nuclear installations. Madhya Pradesh government initiates disciplinary action against 540 doctors, mostly in rural areas, for unauthorized absence from duty for a long period. Assam Chief Minister, Tarun Gogoi, announces an insurance scheme for all bona fide residents of the state.

2: The Centre decides to send its team monitoring relief operations to the tsunami-affected states to speed up the rehabilitation process and further assess the assistance required for reconstruction. The Madhya Pradesh state government decides to wind up the loss-making Madhya Pradesh State Road Transport Corporation (MPSRTC).

3: Anil Ambani quits as IPCL Vice-Chairman. The National Security Adviser J.N. Dixit passes away.

4: Pravasi Bharatiya Samman Divas awards announced. Bharatiya Janata Party announces its first list of 39 candidates for the Haryana Assembly elections. Centre sets up new science advisory committee.

5: United Progressive Alliance forms a three-member group to suggest suitable follow-up action on the demand for carving out a separate Telangana state from Andhra Pradesh. The ocean research vessel, *Sagar Kanya*, sails on a two-month expedition to assess the impact of the tsunami in the Indian Ocean region, particularly around the Andaman and Nicobar Islands.

6: Union Communications Minister Dayanidhi Maran launches '.in' Internet domain for India.

7: Prime Minister Manmohan Singh announces dual citizenship to all those who migrated from the country after it became a Republic on 26 January 1950, provided their home countries allows them to do so.

8: Bharatiya Janata Party names all its candidates for the Jharkhand Assembly polls.

10: Supreme Court grants bail to the Kanchi Sankaracharya, Sri Jayendra Saraswathi, in the Sankararaman murder case. Mrinal Sen is chosen for the Dada Saheb Phalke Award for 2003 in recognition of his 'outstanding contribution' to Indian cinema.

11: The Government decides to offload a portion of its equity in Bharat Heavy Electricals Ltd. and Maruti Udyog in the market by the end of this fiscal.

12: Veteran film actor Amrish Puri passes away.

13: The Union Labour Ministry proposes to introduce a compensation to workers who lose employment due to the closure of industry or face retrenchment owing to the liberalization and privatization policy. The Telecom Regulatory Authority of India recommends one-time fee for all services.

14: Bharat Sanchar Nigam Limited (BSNL) launches its broadband service, DataOne.

16: India, US announce open skies aviation agreement. The Election Commission frames a new set of guidelines for mediapersons covering the elections, imposing a total ban on photography or videography inside polling stations.

17: Godhra fire accidental, says Justice U.C. Banerjee Committee.

18: The Finance Ministry revises all industry drawback rates factoring in the education cess. India, Singapore sign

MoU for army exercise.

19: The Union Cabinet approves Rs 2,731-crore relief and rehabilitation package for the victims of the tsunami in Tamil Nadu, Andhra Pradesh, Kerala and Pondicherry. 'Trishul' is successfully test-fired from the Integrated Test Range at Chandipur-on-Sea.

20: Supreme Court rules that states have no power to levy luxury tax on goods, including tobacco products such as cigarettes, gutkas and pan masalas.

22: Actress Parveen Babi passes away.

23: The Election Commission directs the Chief Electoral Officers of Haryana, Bihar and Jharkhand to videograph the proceedings inside polling stations without violating the secrecy of the vote.

25: Among others J.N. Dixit and R.K. Laxman awarded the Padma Vibhushan.

27: The Cabinet decides to set up a National Investment Fund—a corpus made of proceeds from disinvestment of PSUs. The Centre clears a Rs 60-crore proposal to help the Srinagar domestic airport go international.

28: The Cabinet Committee on Security (CCS) approves a Rs 742-crore scheme to strengthen maritime security by enhancing patrolling and surveillance in coastal areas.

29: Rajiv Gandhi Rehabilitation Package announced for tsunami-affected areas by granting loans and subsidies to fishermen for buying fishing vessels and nets.

30: The Group of Ministers (GoM) is formed to oversee the organization of the Commonwealth Games in India in 2010.

31: General Joginder Jaswant Singh becomes the first Sikh officer to take over as the Chief of Army Staff.

February 2005

1: Goa Governor S.C. Jamir asks the Chief Minister, Manohar Parrikar, to seek a vote of confidence in the State Assembly following the 32-month-old Bharatiya Janata Party-led coalition government losing the majority. Delhi government decides to ban students from using mobile phones in state-run schools.

2: Goa Governor S.C. Jamir dismisses the 32-month-old Manohar Parrikar-led Bharatiya Janata Party coalition government, even as the Government wins a vote of confidence. The senior Congressman, Pratap Singh Rane, is sworn in as the 16th Chief Minister of Goa. Foreign direct investment in telecom allowed up to 74 per cent. The Government decides to hike the interest rate on Employees Provident Fund to 9.5 per cent from the current 8.5 per cent with effect from 2002–03.

3: Indian driver Narain Karthikeyan and Tiago Monteiro of Portugal are named as Jordan's drivers for the 2005 season in Formula One.

4: The Government announces the fourth phase of National Highway Development Project that envisages broadening of 20,000-km of existing National Highways by the end of the 11th Five Year Plan period.

5: India's foreign exchange reserves grow by $291 million.

6: The Election Commission orders repolling in 660 polling stations in Bihar.

7: Goa Governor S.C. Jamir asks the Chief Minister, Pratapsinh Rane, to seek a vote of confidence on the floor of the Assembly on or before 4 March.

8: The Government reconstitutes the Central Board of Film Certification (CBFC), retaining three members in the newly-constituted 21-member set-up.

9: The Union Cabinet authorizes the Petroleum Ministry to hold negotiations with Pakistan, Bangladesh, Iran and Myanmar on the gas pipeline project. The Congress leader, Girija Vyas, is appointed chairperson of the National Commission for Women.

10: Madras High Court orders the release of the junior Sankaracharya of the Kanchi Mutt, Sri Vijayendra Saraswathi, on conditional bail in the Sankararaman murder case.

11: Supreme Court declares 112 private universities in Chhattisgarh illegal.

12: The Election Commission serves notice on the ruling RJD in Bihar on the screening of CDs allegedly containing footage of the post-Godhra riots in Gujarat.

14: Sania Mirza breaks into the top 100 of the world and is ranked No 99 with 371 points by the WTA Tour.

15: India and Italy sign a set of eight memorandums of understanding for cooperation in various areas of science and technology, including early warning of disasters and land-mapping for agriculture. The Centre extends the term of the National Commission on Enterprises in the Unorganized/Informal Sector to three years.

16: India and Pakistan agree to allow travel across the Line of Control (LoC) by bus between Srinagar and Muzaffarabad. Eminent Hindi writer Nirmal Verma and Malayalam novelist Kovilan are elected Fellows of the Sahitya Akademi.

17: The Congress-People Democratic Alliance gains a majority in the last phase of civic polls in Jammu and Kashmir. The Union Cabinet approves a Rs 821.88-crore relief and rehabilitation package for the tsunami-hit Andaman and Nicobar Islands. The Chairman and Managing Director of the Industrial Development Bank of India, M. Damodaran, is appointed Chairman of the Securities and Exchange Board of India.

18: India, UK sign pact on transfer of sentenced persons.

19: The Supreme Court holds that a member of the Scheduled Caste/Scheduled Tribe will not lose his status as SC/ST on migration to another state.

21: Akash, India's surface-to-air missile, is test-fired from a mobile launcher at the Integrated Test Range at Chandipur-on-sea, near Balasore, Orissa. The Supreme Court directs the Chief Secretaries of all the states and union territories to furnish details of the total post-graduate medical seats in government colleges and indicate 50 per cent seats to the Director-General of Health Services by 26 February for allocation to the all-India quota.

22: The Supreme Court directs the Election Commission to take up the counting of votes for the Assembly polls in Haryana on 27 February, as per its earlier notification, instead of on 23 February.

23: The prime witness in the Best Bakery case, Zahira Sheikh, fails to turn up before the G.T. Nanavati and K.G. Shah judicial inquiry commission.

24: The Government allows 100 per cent foreign direct investment in the construction industry through the automatic route.

25: The Election Commission orders repolling in 459 polling stations in Bihar.

26: New trains introduced and fares and freight spared in the Railway Budget. Shah Rukh Khan and Rani Mukherjee are adjudged best actors as the Yash Chopra-directed *Veer Zaara* bags the best film award at the 50th Filmfare awards.

27: Congress wins in Haryana with an absolute majority in the 90-member Assembly but Bihar deadlocked.

28: Bihar Chief Minister Rabri Devi quits. With an increased allocation from Rs 8,420 crore in the current year to Rs 10,280 crore, Finance Minister P. Chibambaram presents the budget. Finance Minister imposes a banking transaction tax of Rs 10 on cash withdrawals of over Rs 10,000 in a single day.

March 2005

1: The Bharatiya Janata Party-led National Democratic Alliance and the United Progressive Alliance stake claim to form the government in Jharkhand. TransWorld International (TWI) bags the production rights for the India-Pakistan cricket series even though the Board of Control for Cricket in India (BCCI) fails to take a decision on award of satellite overseas rights for the high profile series. The Pakistan President Pervez Musharraf orders the immediate release of 200 Indian civilian prisoners who have completed their term in Pakistan's jails. V.P. Shetty is appointed as Chairman of the Industrial Development Bank of India. The newly-elected Congress MLAs in Haryana unanimously authorize the AICC president, Sonia Gandhi, to select their leader.

2: Jharkhand Mukti Morcha (JMM) leader, Shibu Soren, is sworn in as the third Chief Minister of Jharkhand. Deputy Chief Minister, Filipe Neri Rodrigues, submits his resignation from the Council of Ministers.

4: Goa is brought under President's rule. Goa Chief Minister Pratapsinh Rane wins the vote of confidence in the Assembly with pro tem Speaker Francisco Sardinha casting his vote in favour of the Congress when there was a 16-16 tie. Bhupinder Singh Hooda, MP from Rohtak, is elected leader of the Haryana Congress Legislature Party.

5: Chief Minister of Bihar, Rabri Devi, stakes her claim to form a coalition government. The Board of Control for Cricket in India awards Sony Entertainment Television the satellite rights for the India-Pakistan cricket series. India wins the Davis Cup tie against China. Bhupinder Singh Hooda sworn in Haryana Chief Minister.

6: The Bihar Governor, Buta Singh, recommends President's rule in the State as no political party or a coalition of parties is in a position to form a stable government. Sania Mirza moves to an all-time career-high 77th spot in the latest WTA tour rankings.

7: President A.P.J. Abdul Kalam approves the Union Cabinet's decision recommending President's rule in Bihar following the stalemate in government formation. Jharkhand Mukti Morcha-led United Progressive Alliance government in Jharkhand appoints the Congress MLA, Pradeep Kumar Balmuchu, as pro tem Speaker in the Assembly.

9: The Sahara Group signs a three-year contract with the Indian women's cricket team. The Supreme Court directs the pro tem Speaker of the Jharkhand Legislative Assembly to conduct a composite floor test in the Assembly on 11 March. Sanjay Nirupam, two-time Shiv Sena Rajya Sabha MP, resigns from the party.

10: Central Zone clinches the Duleep Trophy.

11: Jharkhand Chief Minister, Shibu Soren, resigns. Calcutta High Court dismisses the caveatable interest of three Birla family members in the dispute over the property of the late M.P. Birla and his wife Priyamvada.

12: Arjun Munda sworn in Jharkhand Chief Minister. Exports touch $70 billion mark. Forex reserves up $1.9 billion. Navy places orders for BrahMos.

13: The World Bank agrees in principle to provide $500 million for India's National e-Governance Plan (NEGP) over the next four years.

14: Jet Airways becomes the first private airline to be listed at the National Stock Exchange. West Bengal Assembly passes a Bill incorporating a provision to appoint a caretaker for overseeing the functioning of the Darjeeling Gorkha Hill Council till elections are held to the Council following the expiry of its present term on 26 March. The Arjun Munda-led National Democratic Alliance Ministry demonstrates a majority in the Jharkhand Assembly.

15: The Union Government sets up a committee headed by Saumitra Chaudhuri, Member, Economic Advisory Council to the Prime Minister, to formulate the all-industry rates of duty drawback for the new fiscal.

16: The Jharkhand unit of the Nationalist Congress Party (NCP) merges with the ruling Bharatiya Janata Party. Sachin Tendulkar becomes only the fifth cricketer and the second from India to reach 10,000 Test runs.

17: Lok Sabha passes the vote on account for Rs 1,69,269 crore for defraying government expenditure for the first two months of 2005–06. India's Pankaj Advani makes a rare hat-trick of titles by becoming the 2005 IBSF point format World billiards champion.

18: The Patents (Amendment) Bill, 2005, is introduced in the Lok Sabha amid protests with a majority of members from across the political spectrum, including parties supporting the Government, objecting to the adoption of the ordinance route. The Gujarat Chief Minister, Narendra Modi, is denied a diplomatic visa to enter the United States and his business/tourist visa is cancelled by the US Embassy. India and China finalize a Memorandum of Understanding on the sharing of hydrological data about the Sutlej river during the flood season.

19: The Bharatiya Janata Party-ruled states decide not to implement the Value Added Tax from 1 April. Tamil writer D. Jayakanthan is conferred the Jnanpith Award for 2002. The Lok Sabha approves President's rule in Bihar. Forex reserves cross the $140 billion-mark. India defeats Pakistan to lead the three-Test series 1-0.

20: Finance Minister announces a deduction of Rs 1 lakh from taxable income for senior citizens.

21: Centre accepts all but two changes in Patents Bill. The Pension Fund Regulatory and Development Authority Bill 2005, is introduced in the Lok Sabha.

22: Lok Sabha passes the third Patents (Amendments) Bill 2005. Gemini Ganeshan, Tamil cinema's first acknowledged romantic hero, passes away. The Centre appoints the actor, Shabana Azmi, and the Congress leader, Syed Shahabuddin, members of the National Integration Council (NIC).

23: The Government refers the Pension Fund Regulatory and Development Authority (PFRDA) Bill, 2005, to the Parliamentary Standing Committee on Finance.

24: 21 states declare they will implement VAT from 1 April. The Union Cabinet decides to introduce the Bharat Stage-II grade diesel in all but seven states from 1 April. The Union Cabinet approves introduction of the Commission for the Protection of Child Rights Bill, 2005, in the current session of Parliament.

25: Buta Singh is sworn in as acting Governor of West Bengal.

26: Forex reserves cross $142 billion.

27: Amrita Thapar is crowned Pond's Femina Miss India-Universe.

28: The Supreme Court rules that the states are empowered to levy 'lifetime tax' in advance in lump sum at the time of registration of new motor vehicles based on their cost price. Pakistan wins the final Test against India in the TVS Cup series.

30: The Chattrapati Shivaji Terminus (formerly Victoria Terminus) in Mumbai finds a place in the World Heritage List. The Malayalam writer and political cartoonist, O.V. Vijayan, passes away.

31: The National Association of Software and Service Companies (Nasscom) announces the appointment of S. Ramadorai, CEO of Tata Consultancy Services, as its Chairman for 2005–06. India and Mauritius decide to pursue a Free Trade Agreement between the two countries.

April 2005

1: Twenty-one states shifts to the Value-Added Tax regime.

2: The External Affairs Minister, Natwar Singh, launches the India-European Union Parliamentary Forum.

3: Government reconstitutes the Board of Trade while Kumaramanglam Birla is named chairman of the 38-member board reconstituted with effect from 1 April.

4: The Prime Minister Manmohan Singh constitutes a task force to prepare a long-term plan for the social and economic development of Jammu and Kashmir.

5: Planning Commission endorses various sectoral 'corrective measures' contained in the Mid-Term Appraisal (MTA) of the Tenth Plan.

7: Srinagar-Muzaffarabad bus service flagged off.

8: The Government announces the setting up of an Inter-State Trade Council as part of measures to boost exports, especially in the key areas of agro-products, marine products and handlooms.

9: Forex reserves up $297 million. Home Minister Shivraj Patil decorates four officers and jawans of the Central Reserve Police Force with medals for their valiant role in the Gujarat Akshardham Temple terrorist attack of 2003.

10: Australia wins its fifth women's World Cup cricket title defeating India by 98 runs in the final.

11: China backs India's bid for UN Council seat. Prakash Karat elected CPI(M) general secretary. Second ISRO master control facility inaugurated in Bhopal.

12: Prime Minister Manmohan Singh launches National Rural Health Mission. The President, A.P.J. Abdul Kalam, presents the gallantry and distinguished service awards to 63 service personnel and civilians.

13: The Central Government files an additional affidavit in the Supreme Court stating that it decided to refer 23 more cases, including the Kargil coffin purchase deal, to the Central Bureau of Investigation for a fresh inquiry. Minister of Communications and Information Technology, Dayanidhi Maran, declares aim to accelerate connectivity by setting a target of 15 crore fresh connections in the next three years. India and China agree to an 11-point 'political parameters and guiding principles' to resolve their long-standing dispute.

14: India, US sign 'open skies' agreement.

15: BrahMos test-fired off west coast. Industrialist T.S. Santhanam passes away. The South Western Command of the Indian Army is established.

16: Forex reserves up $253 million.

17: Pakistan clinches one-day series against India. India and Pakistan decide to set up a Joint Business Council (JBC) of their apex industry associations. Pakistan President Pervez Musharraf visits India.

19: Vikram Seth is presented the Government of India's 'Pravasi Bharatiya Samman' 2005.

20: The Cabinet Committee on Economic Affairs (CCEA) decides to increase the minimum support price for paddy and other kharif crops for the 2005-06 season as recommended by the Commission on Agricultural Costs and Prices. The Union Cabinet decides to amend the Administrative Tribunals Act to provide for the abolition of the Central and State Administrative Tribunals in the wake of the Supreme Court's order, under which appeals against the tribunals' decision lay with the High Courts themselves instead of directly with the Supreme Court.

22: Indian Air Force opens talks with United States on joint production of F-16s and F-18s. FIFA, the world body governing football, forwards a donation of $1 million for reconstruction of sporting facilities in the country which were affected by the tsunami.

23: India decides to reverse its decision to suspend the supply of lethal weapons to the Royal Nepal Army. Forex reserves up $88 million.

25: A special court of the Central Bureau of Investigation frames charges against the Railway Minister and Rashtriya Janata Dal president, Lalu Prasad Yadav, in a case relating to the multi-crore fodder scam. Renowned scholar, philosopher and president of the Ramakrishna Mission, Swami Ranganathananda, passes away.

26: The indigenously-built short range surface-to-air missile 'Trishul' is successfully test-fired from the Integrated Test Range at Chandipur-on-sea. Twenty-one states, which have switched over to the Value-Added Tax, agrees to adopt uniform rates for industrial input, capital goods and essential commodities such as medicines, salt, bread and other items. Trinamool Congress splits. Aftab Ansari, six others convicted in the case of the terrorist attack on the American Centre.

27: A Special CBI Court sentences to death Aftab Ansari and six others for the attack on the American Centre three years ago.

28: Actress Nandita Das gets offer to be part of the jury at the 58th Cannes Film Festival in France.

29: The rocket launcher 'Pinaka' is test-fired at Chandipur-on-Sea.

30: India defeats Uzbekistan in the Davis Cup. Indians win eleven golds in the 17th Asian powerlifting championship.

May 2005

1: MP K. Karunakaran floats new party. All India Muslim Board adopts Nikahnama.

2: Finance Minister raises IT exemption limit for women, senior citizens and Savings accounts exempted from cash withdrawal tax; fringe benefit tax diluted to lessen burden. K. Karunakaran quits as Rajya Sabha member.

3: The Rajya Sabha passes the Coastal Aquaculture Authority Bill, 2004, for the regulation of all activities relating to coastal aquaculture. Prime Minister Manmohan Singh sets up a 'trade and economic relations committee', comprising senior ministers and officials, to take quick decisions on economic aspects of the country's foreign policy. The Union Finance Ministry sets up a committee to advise the Government on the extent of abatement for excise duty and service tax.

4: The Supreme Court reserves verdict in the four appeals—two by the Delhi Police and two by the accused—in the Parliament attack case challenging the verdict of the High Court acquitting two persons and upholding the death sentence for two others. India receives $ 465 million as IDA credit from the World Bank for reconstruction and recovery efforts in Tamil Nadu and Pondicherry.

5: India's Polar Satellite Launch Vehicle PSLV-C6 is launched from the spaceport at Sriharikota in Andhra Pradesh. The Supreme Court rules that erring companies are liable for criminal prosecution.

6: INS Himgiri, the second Indian-built multi-role warship, is decommissioned. The Supreme Court dismisses the petition seeking extension of the term of the Mukherjee Commission probing the disappearance of Netaji Subhash Chandra Bose in August 1945. Nobel Laureate Amartya Sen receives the Tagore Peace Award of the Asiatic Society for 2004 in recognition of his creative contribution to the development of human understanding towards global peace.

7: Two replicas of the stolen Nobel medallion of Rabindranath Tagore are handed over to the Visva-Bharati University by Sweden's Nobel Foundation.

8: The third major private airline Kingfisher's maiden flight takes off from Bangalore to Mumbai.

9: The Government clears the immediate dispatch of arms 'already in the pipeline' to Nepal. Parliament passes a bill to amend the Criminal Procedure Code providing relaxation in bail procedures and prohibiting the arrest of women between sunset and sunrise except in exceptional circumstances.

10: The Maharashtra Government decides to stop free supply of power to farmers from 1 June. The Lok Sabha passes the Special Economic Zone legislation by voice vote after incorporating the amendments suggested by the Left parties to ensure that states can take decisions on the extent of flexibility in labour laws. To regulate the functioning of private security agencies, the Government introduces legislation in the Rajya Sabha to make licences mandatory for operating such security agencies.

11: The Lok Sabha passes the Right to Information Bill, in keeping with a promise the United Progressive Alliance had made in its Common Minimum Programme. Union Finance Minister P. Chidambaram launches the system of online payment of excise duty and service tax through banks.

12: 'Prithvi' missile is test-fired from the Integrated Test Range (ITR) at Chandipur-on-sea. The Government decides to enact a law on disaster management to provide for requisite institutional mechanism for drawing up and monitoring the implementation of the National Disaster Management Plan. The Group of Ministers (GoM) on the print media clears a proposal to allow Foreign Institutional Investors (FIIs) to pick up stakes in print media companies provided it falls within the existing 26 per cent ceiling on foreign investment in such entities.

13: Parliament approves the Weapons of Mass Destruction and their De-livery System (Prohibition of Unlawful Activities) Bill, 2005. The Supreme Court gives a clean chit to the Board of Control for Cricket in India (BCCI) in cancelling the tender process for award of telecast rights for cricket matches till 2008.

14: Navin B. Chawla is appointed Election Commissioner to fill the vacancy in the Commission caused by the elevation of B.B. Tandon as Chief Election Commissioner.

16: The Government approves the new design of stamp papers of denominations varying from Re 1 to Rs 25,000 in its bid to counter the menace of fake stamps.

17: State-owned Bharat Sanchar Nigam Limited announces a 33 per cent reduction in tariffs for several countries, including the entire Gulf region, Africa and South Asian Association for Regional Cooperation (SAARC) nations. Committee on Rural Infrastructure approves a 'Bharat Nirman' proposal, entailing an investment of over Rs 1,74,000 crores in six critical areas over a four-year period (2005–09).

18: The Union Human Resource Development Ministry stops grants to 'Ekal Vidyalayas' (one-teacher schools) run by the Friends of Tribal Society (FTS) in tribal belts of the country in collaboration with the Vishwa Hindu Parishad.

19: The Union Cabinet approves the Planning Commission's mid-term appraisal (MTA) of the Tenth Plan for undertaking corrective action to put certain sectors of the economy back on track. Indian Government approves the implementation of the Sethusamudram Ship Channel Project off the Tamil Nadu coast at a cost of Rs 2,427.40 crores. Prime Minister Manmohan Singh reconstitutes the National Commission on Population (NPC). The Union Cabinet approves a new policy which provides for the release of two series of maps — defence and open. The Cabinet Committee on Economic Affairs (CCEA) approves the launch of the National Horticulture Mission under the Ministry of Agriculture with an outlay of Rs 2,300 crore for the remaining period of the Tenth Plan.

20: Greg Chappell appointed India coach. The Central POTA Review Committee sends its report to the Gujarat government in connection with the Godhra train carnage case.

21: Defence Minister Pranab Mukherjee inaugurates the first phase of Project Seabird, a futuristic, state-of-the-art operational naval base on the western seaboard at Karwar.

23: President Kalam signs Proclamation in Moscow to dissolve Bihar Assembly.

24: CPI (M) assures United Progressive Alliance of 'continuing cooperation'.

25: Union Cabinet Minister and actor Sunil Dutt passes away. Ruling Left Front wins 48 of the 79 civic bodies in West Bengal municipalities.

26: Government decides to divest 10 per cent equity in BHEL. Talks on Siachen demilitarization begin.

27: Multi-barrel rocket system 'Pinaka' undergoes a successful trial at Chandipur.

28: Sonia Gandhi is re-elected Congress chief. The Employees Provident Fund (EPF) Board recommends 9.5 per cent rate of interest on the EPF accumulations for its 40 million subscribers for the year 2004–05.

30: Prime Minister Manmohan Singh offers to work together with Pakistan President Pervez Musharraf to find a 'meaningful solution' to outstanding problems. The Vice-President, Bhairon Singh Shekhawat, inaugurates a special research project on 'post-Independence Indian Journalism' by advocating the cause of Hindi and asserting that methods should be explored to ensure that the 'rashtrabhasha (national language) becomes the rajbhasha (official language) of this country'.

31: The Election Commission rejects the demand for holding early Assembly elections in Bihar. From 1 August, smoking to be banned in movies, television serials. Amendments to the Tobacco Control Act notified.

June 2005

1: The Banking Cash Transaction Tax on cash withdrawals and receipts of term deposits in banks comes into effect. The Government decides to enhance the foreign investment cap under non-news category from 74 per cent to 100 per cent in Indian entities publishing scientific, technical and speciality magazines, periodicals and journals. The Indian Olympic Association (IOA) President, Suresh Kalmadi, is re-elected President of the Asian Athletics Association (AAA) for the second consecutive term (2005–09).

2: Hurriyat leaders visit Pakistan-occupied Kashmir (PoK) and Pakistan with a pledge to work as a bridge between India and Pakistan to resolve the long-standing Kashmir problem.

3: Board of Control for Cricket in India (BCCI) decides to bid for the 2011 World Cup. The Government reconstitutes the National Advisory Council (NAC), nominating two new members.

4: The Parliamentary Standing Committee on Law and Justice urges the Centre to change the names of the Madras, Calcutta and Bombay High Courts in line with the official names of these cities. $175 million rise in forex reserves.

6: Tamil Nadu Government abolishes the Common Entrance Test (CET) for admission to medical and engineering courses from this year. Veteran Congressman and six-time Chief Minister Pratapsinh Raoji Rane is sworn in as the Chief Minister of Goa.

7: Bharatiya Janata Party president L.K. Advani resigns from his party post, following the controversy over his description of Pakistan's founder Mohammad Ali Jinnah as 'secular' and his remark that the demolition of the Babri Masjid was the 'saddest day' of his life. Concerned by 'faculty shortage both in terms of quantity and quality' in many technical institutes across the country, the All-India Council for Technical Education (AICTE) stops 98 of the 3,849 institutions under it from admitting students for the coming academic year.

8: BJP rejects L.K. Advani's resignation.

9: The Government appoints eight judges to the Kerala, Gujarat and Rajasthan High Courts.

10: L.K. Advani withdraws his resignation. India, Sri Lanka sign agreements on developmental projects and education.

11: India becomes the first country to reprocess uranium-plutonium mixed carbide fuel.

12: Manmohan Singh becomes the first Prime Minister to visit Siachen. Sushma Chawla takes over as first woman Chairperson and Managing Director of Indian Airlines.

13: India signs $18-billion gas deal with Iran.

15: The Ministries of Health and Family Welfare and Information and Broadcasting (I&B) decide to delay the imposition of the ban on smoking scenes in television serials and movies by two months from 1 August to Gandhi Jayanti (2 October). Sensex crosses 6900 mark.

16: The Union Cabinet allows printing of facsimile editions of foreign newspapers and periodicals and increasing the syndication limits in Indian newspapers. The Union Cabinet approves amendments to the Citizenship Act, 1955, allowing all Persons of Indian Origin (PIOs) access to dual citizenship as long as their home countries permitted it in some form or the other.

17: The Maharashtra government sets up a committee to revive the controversial Dabhol Power Corporation (DPC) power plant.

18: Reliance announces family settlement. Former cricketer Syed Mushtaq Ali passes away.

20: Surface-to-air missile Akash is test-fired from the Integrated Test Range at Chandipur-on-sea. Sensex crosses 7000-mark.

21: Left Front wins 75 out of 141 seats in Kolkata civic elections.

22: Sensex crosses 7100-mark. The Home Ministry decides to set up a task force with the National AIDS Control Organisation (NACO) for dealing with HIV/AIDS among the paramilitary forces.

23: The Union Cabinet approves the introduction of a comprehensive Bill to protect women from domestic violence of any kind including dowry-related harassment.

25: Kerala bans camera cellphones in educational institutions. Forex reserves rise $1 billion.

26: Former cricketer Eknath Dhondu Solkar passes away. Anil D. Ambani is appointed Chairman of Reliance Infocomm Ltd. (RIC).

27: Sensex crosses 7200 mark.

28: Bharatiya Janata Party president L.K. Advani drops the former External Affairs Minister, Yashwant Sinha, from the list of party spokespersons.

29: Rajendra Singh Lodha is elected Chairman of the board of directors of Birla Corporation Ltd. (BCL), the flagship company of the M. P. Birla group.

30: The Cabinet decides to allow foreign radio stations to pick up stakes in private FM stations within the existing ceiling of 20 per cent of foreign capital but the ban on private stations to broadcast news continues. The former District Magistrate of Patna, Gautam Goswami, wanted in connection with the multi-crore flood relief scam, surrenders.

July 2005

1: Sensex crosses 7200 mark. Telecom Regulatory Authority of India (TRAI) asks phone companies to ensure that refunds are made within 60 days of surrender of the phone.

2: Sethusamudram project launched. Prasar Bharati evolves a new policy to promote sports by slashing charges for live telecast. Forex reserves drop $676 million.

3: Shiv Sena supremo Bal Thackeray expels Leader of the Opposition in the Maharashtra Assembly Narayan Rane from the party.

4: Mahesh Bhupathi and Mary Pierce win the 2005 Wimbledon mixed doubles title. The Supreme Court declines to stay the Madras High Court judgment quashing the Tamil Nadu Government order scrapping the Common Entrance Test (CET) for admissions to medicine, engineering and other professional courses for 2005–06.

5: Six heavily-armed terrorists make an attempt to storm the high-security makeshift Ram temple in Ayodhya and are killed by the security forces before they can strike at the shrine. The Union Cabinet withdraws the restriction on use of the national flag by the public as a portion of costumes.

6: Union Health and Family Welfare Minister A. Ramadoss announces the setting up of a task force to look into rural postings and continuing medical education.

7: All six Rajya Sabha candidates from West Bengal, including CPI (M) Polit Bureau members Sitaram Yechury and Brinda Karat, are declared elected unopposed. The Employees State Insurance Corporation (ESIC) decides to enhance the ceiling on reimbursement of medical care to state governments from Rs 750 to Rs 900 per insured person (IP) family unit per annum with effect from 1 May 2005.

9: The Central Advisory Board of Education (CABE) committee on regulatory mechanisms for textbooks and parallel textbooks taught in schools outside the government system recommends the setting up of a National Textbook Council to monitor material produced across the country. Centre agrees to pay a monthly 'ad hoc' compensation in case their revenue from the Value Added Tax (VAT) falls short of their projections on the basis of collections in earlier years through the erstwhile sales tax regime.

11: The Government announces liberal rules for granting student visas.

12: The Central Board of Secondary Education (CBSE) takes a series of measures from the next board examinations to make them 'stress-free'. These include giving extra time to the students to study the question paper.

13: The Empowered Committee of State Finance Ministers on Value Added Tax (VAT) decides that items which have at least 50 per cent industrial use will attract 4 per cent tax rate for that particular use.

14: The Panchayati Raj Ministry announces to spend over Rs 1,000 crore in the next two years towards installation of computers in 2.4 lakh panchayats, interlinking them with one another and also with a national panchayat portal. In a bid to check unfair practices by insurers and intermediaries to capture more business, the Insurance Regulatory and Development Authority (IRDA) tightens the norms for group insurance schemes and corporate agents.

15: The Nilgiri Mountain Railway (NMR) line between Udhagamandalam and Mettupalayam is granted World Heritage Site status by UNESCO.

18: The Supreme Court issues certain directions to control noise pollution caused by crackers, vehicles and loudspeakers, among other sources. The Postal Department proposes to start common service centres, whose functions will include issuing birth and death certificates.

19: India agrees 'reciprocally' to place its civilian nuclear facilities under International Atomic Energy Agency (IAEA) safeguards.

20: Sensex touches 7392. The Supreme Court approves the out-of-court settlement arrived at between the Maharashtra government and Dabhol Power Corporation.

21: The Maharashtra Legislative Assembly passes the controversial Bombay Police (Amendment) Bill prohibiting dance bars in the state.

22: Sensex crosses 7400-mark.

24: The 'Valley of Flowers,' part of the Nanda Devi National Park in the western Himalayas, is included on the world heritage list by the World Heritage Committee of UNESCO. Major quake rocks Nicobar Islands.

25: In a move towards giving more operational autonomy to public sector companies, the Government doubles their capacity to make investments without seeking clearances from administrative ministries. The Cabinet Committee on Economic Affairs (CCEA) approves the launch of a Plan scheme for financial support to 'public private partnerships' (PPPs) in projects for developing the country's infrastructure.

26: The Central Bureau of Investigation files a charge sheet in the Maharashtra Control of Organised Crime Act (MCOCA) Court in Pune against 67 persons, including Abdul Karim Ladsab Telgi. Trishul, India's most sophisticated short-range surface-to-air missile, is test-fired from the Integrated Test Range at Chandipur. The Standing Committee on Finance favours a foreign direct investment (FDI) to the extent of 26 per cent in the pension sector.

27: In one of the worst disasters in the history of India's petroleum industry, the offshore oil platform in the Bombay High area catches fire. Four persons are killed. All-time record rain in Mumbai; many Maharashtra villages marooned, death toll crosses 100;

thousands of Mumbai commuters stranded; Army, Navy called out. Sensex surpasses 7600-mark.

28: Prime Minister Manmohan Singh announces an immediate grant of Rs 500 crore to Maharashtra.

29: Maharashtra rain toll put at 749.

31: Pakistan bans import of films made in India.

August 2005

1: Dr V. Shanta, Chairperson of the Cancer Institute, Adyar, wins the Ramon Magsaysay Award for Public Service for 2005. Maharashtra receives heavy rain. In 24 hours the suburbs record 208.1 mm of rain and Mumbai 161 mm. Sania Mirza moves upto career-best ranking of 59 in the latest list released by the WTA.

2: Parliament approves the extension of President's rule in Bihar by another six months. Heavy rain continues in Maharashtra. 220 villages in Pune, 50 in Kolhapur,12 in Sangli cut off. Death toll in state goes up to 962. Cauvery tribunal gets one year extension. Pakistan lifts ban on sugar imports from India.

3: The Centre announces a second instalment of Rs 500 crore for flood relief in Mumbai and 18 districts of Maharashtra.

4: The flood situation in southern Maharashtra stabilizes as Karnataka releases 4.25 lakh cusecs of water from its Alamatti dam. Sensex moves upto 7797.

5: To prevent criminals from contesting the Bihar Assembly polls, the Election Commission decides to delete the names of all those persons against whom non-bailable warrants could not be executed for more than six months. The disinvestment of ten per cent equity stake in Bharat Heavy Electricals Limited (BHEL) is put on hold till the process of consultations is over. The Supreme Court holds that a doctor would be liable for criminal prosecution only for 'gross negligence' or if he did not possess the requisite skill.

6: India and Pakistan agree to notify each other of ballistic missile tests in a structured format and operationalize a hotline between the Foreign Secretaries to prevent 'misunderstandings.' Forex reserves cross $140 billion.

7: Three stupas, pottery and terracotta remains traced to the Asoka period are excavated in Jajpur district of Orissa.

8: Pollution Board approves using waste plastic to lay roads.

10: Jagdish Tytler submits resignation to Congress president Sonia Gandhi. He was named by the Nanavati Commission Report that went into the 1984 anti-Sikh riots.

11: The Union Cabinet clears the National Rural Employment Guarantee Bill that seeks to ensure 100 days of job guarantee to the unemployed youth of rural India.

12: The Supreme Court holds that admissions to unaided minority and non-minority professional educational institutions should be made only on the basis of a common entrance test. The Cabinet Committee on Economic Affairs approves revival of the 2185 MW Dabhol Power Project through Ratnagiri Gas and Power.

13: The Central Government constitutes two committees to implement a rehabilitation package, providing employment and compensation to families of the victims of the 1984 anti-Sikh riots.

14: The Government adopts an anti-hijack policy that empowers it to shoot down a hijacked commercial plane if it intrudes into sensitive areas. The Government announces an increase in the pension of freedom-fighters.

16: The Government calls off the strategic sale of shares in 13 public sector undertakings. Parliament approves the Citizenship (Amendment) Bill.

17: Parliament approves the Payment of Wages (Amendment) Bill, 2004. The Central Government exempts excise items such as cement and steel that are used in the construction of residential houses in tsunami-hit areas. Reliance files demerger scheme.

18: United Progressive Alliance Government moves the National Rural Employment Guarantee Bill in the Lok Sabha. It aims to provide 100 days of guaranteed wage employment to rural households in 200 districts. Sensex touches 7900-mark.

20: Bharatiya Janata Party president L.K. Advani orders the suspension of the former Rajasthan Governor, Madan Lal Khurana, from the party for 'gross indiscipline'. Forex reserves up $1.73 billion.

22: The Protection of Women from Domestic Violence Bill, 2005, seeking to provide effective protection to women from physical, sexual, verbal, emotional or economic violence at home, is introduced in the Lok Sabha.

23: The National Rural Employment Guarantee Bill, 2005, seeking to provide 100 days' assured employment every year to every rural household in 200 districts, is unanimously passed by the Lok Sabha with 52 amendments.

24: Maharashtra bans plastic bags. Rajyavardhan Singh Rathore gets the prestigious Rajiv Gandhi Khel Ratna Award for the year 2004.

25: P. Chidambaram unveils first-ever 'Outcome Budget'.

26: The Securities and Exchange Board of India decides to remove discretion in allotment of shares to qualified institutional buyers (QIBs) in public offerings and introduces a specific provision for allotment of shares to SEBI-registered mutual funds.

27: Forex reserves drop $1.1 billion.

28: India offers Afghanistan $50-million assistance for its reconstruction process.

29: The Central Board of Direct Taxes (CBDT) issues a circular explaining the provisions of the Fringe Benefit Tax (FBT) as introduced by the Finance Act, 2005.

31: The Drugs Controller of India approves the sale of 'Emergency Contraceptives' across the counter. These contraceptives were not available without a prescription until now.

September 2005

1: Sensex moves up to 7876. India and Pakistan agree to continue the composite dialogue and revive the 'Joint Commission' to be headed by the Foreign Ministers of the two countries.

2: The Government decides to divest 8 per cent shareholding in Maruti Udyog Limited (MUL). Sania Mirza reaches the third round of the US Open. India and Pakistan agree to start a truck service on the Srinagar-Muzaffarabad route as a first step towards promotion of trade across the Line of Control (LoC).

3: The Election Commission announces a four-phase polling schedule for the Bihar Assembly elections from 18 October to 19 November. India gives conditional support to nuclear energy programme of Iran.

4: No. 1 seed Maria Sharapova defeats Sania Mirza at the US Open.

5: Malayalam filmmaker Adoor Gopalakrishnan is selected for the Dada Saheb Phalke Award for 2004.

6: In a bid to resolve the crisis created by soaring world oil prices, the Government increases the prices of petrol and diesel. New Zealand defeats India by six wickets to win the Videocon tri-series at the Harare Sports Club.

7: Sensex touches 8,000.

8: Karnataka Administrative Tribunal (KAT) declares that HIV positive persons have a right to be considered for government service.

9: Hashim Abdul Halim is elected chairman of the Executive Committee of Commonwealth Parliamentary Association. Mahesh Bhupathi wins his seventh Grand Slam title with Daniela Hantuchova in the US Open.

10: Border Security Force (BSF) troops are withdrawn from Srinagar. Telangana Rashtra Samithi floats the Telangana Jagarana Sena.

11: Madan Lal Khurana gets expulsion order from BJP. India and Pakistan exchange nearly 500 civilian prisoners at the Wagah border.

12: The Bharatiya Janata Party revokes the expulsion order served on its Delhi leader, Madan Lal Khurana. Sensex crosses 8100-mark. Delhi government announces enhancement of the ex-gratia compensation to those injured in the 1984 riot violence to Rs 1.25 lakh each. The decision would benefit 2,996 people who had thus far received compensation of only up to Rs 2,000. Sania Mirza jumps to a career-best ranking of 34 in the list released by the WTA.

13: Nafisa Ali is nominated as chairperson of the Children's Film Society of India (CFSI).

14: The Asom Gana Parishad formally splits with the founder-president and former Chief Minister Prafulla Kumar Mahanta floating a new regional outfit. The resolution to form the Asom Gana Parishad (Progressive) is adopted at a political convention.

15: Sourav Ganguly confirms that he was asked to step down as captain of the Indian cricket team before the first Royal Stag Test match against Zimbabwe. In a bid to strengthen ties in the field of mining, India and China sign a memorandum of understanding for joint ventures in other countries and setting up a framework to promote cooperation in the field of metallic and non-metallic minerals research.

17: The Supreme Court declares that life imprisonment is not equivalent to imprisonment for 14 or 20 years. The Joint Admission Board (JAB) of the IITs announces the new format of the Joint Entrance Examination 2006, to be held on 9 April. The Centre issues an order to give effect to its decision to enhance the Swatantrata Sainik Samman Pension to freedom fighters and their eligible dependants.

19: The President gives assent to the National Rural Employment Guarantee Bill, 2005. The Bill provides for enhancement of livelihood security of rural households by providing at least 100 days of guaranteed wage employment in every financial year to every household, whose adult members volunteer to do unskilled manual work. This will be applicable to the whole of India, except Jammu and Kashmir. The Bombay Stock Exchange issues Dos and Don'ts for the benefit of investors as the Sensex touches an all time high of 8444.

20: The All-India Council for Technical Education (AICTE) approves an increase of 5,690 seats in 58 engineering colleges. Sensex moves up to 8500.

21: Central Board of Secondary Education (CBSE) officially announces the introduction of grading for Class X from 2008.

22: The Government decides to give a two-year term to certain senior public servants serving in the 'national security arena'. The Union Home Secretary, the Defence Secretary, the Director of the Intelligence Bureau (IB) and the chief of the external intelligence agency, Research and Analysis Wing (RAW), have been designated as those whose services could be available for a two-year period, even if it means an extension of service beyond the age of retirement. India wins its first overseas series victory in 19 years as Zimbabwe is defeated by 10 wickets in the second

Royal Stag Test at the Harare Sports Club. The Union Cabinet give its in-principle clearance of the sites for further expansion of the nuclear power stations in Koodankulam, Kakrapar and Rawatbhata and for setting up a new station at Jaitapur in Maharashtra.

23: Governor Buta Singh issues the notification for the Bihar assembly polls. The Union Ministry of Home Affairs sets up a high-level committee to draft a new Police Act that would take into account the ground realities of a modern nation. The leaking of Greg Chappell's confidential e-mail addressed to BCCI President triggers cricket controversy.

24: India votes against Iran nuclear issue at the International Atomic Energy Agency (IAEA).

25: The National Commission on Farmers calls for credit reforms in the farm sector to prevent farmers from committing suicide.

26: Amol Palekar's *Paheli* is chosen as India's official entry for the 2006 Academy Awards. The Supreme Court refuses to stay the implementation of the Rs 2,400-crore Sethusamudram Ship Channel Project (SSCP).

27: Indian captain Sourav Ganguly and coach Greg Chappell are asked by the Board of Control for Cricket in India (BCCI) to bury their differences.

28: Sensex crosses 8600 level.

30: The Supreme Court reiterates that lawyers have no right to go on strike or give a call for boycott or even a token strike to espouse their causes. Sachin Tendulkar informs the Board of Control for Cricket in India (BCCI) and the Chairman of selectors Kiran More about his availability for the Challenger Series.

Timeline of World History

Beginning of Time to 1994

4.4–4.3 million BC: Earliest known hominid fossils of *Ardipithecus ramidus* found in 1994 in Aramis, Ethiopia, by Tim White, Gen Suwa and Berhane Asfaw date back to this time.

4.2 million BC: First *Australopithecus anamensis* discovery in the Kanapoi region of East Lake Turkana, Kenya, in 1965 by a Harvard University expedition date back to this time.

Approximately 4 million BC: Discovery of tiny foot bones and tiny pelvic fossils indicates that the ancestors of humans walked upright by this time.

3.2 million BC: Appearance of *Australopithecus afarenis*. A near-complete female hominid skeleton nicknamed 'Lucy' was found in Ethiopia in 1974 by Donald Johanson and others.

2.5 million BC: Appearance of *Homo habilis*. This species had a larger brain than its ancestors and is widely believed to have used tools. Sileshi Semaw and Jack Harris published research on the tools in 1997.

1.8 million BC: Appearance of *Homo erectus*, who had a brain capacity of nearly 1,000ml.

1.7 million BC: *Homo erectus* leaves Africa. Researchers of ancient DNA, however, avidly debate this theory.

200,000 BC: In 1987, Rebecca Cann, Mark Stoneking and Allan Wilson report in the journal *Nature* that a common ancestor to all *Homo sapiens* was a woman who lived in Africa 200,000 years ago. They called her African 'Eve'.

100,000 BC: Appearance of *Homo sapiens* in South Africa. Many believe the 'human' migrations from Africa to Asia began during this period.

c.50,000 BC: *Homo sapiens* reaches Australia.

70,000 BC: Possible appearance of Neanderthal man. This species could make fire and use advanced tools.

35,000 BC: Neanderthal man replaced by later groups of *Homo sapiens* such as Cro-Magnons in Europe.

20,000 BC: The accepted date for Neanderthal extinction.

18,000 BC: Cro-Magnons replaced by later cultures.

15,000 BC: Possible human migrations across the Bering Strait into the Americas.

10,000 BC: Signs of semi-permanent agricultural settlements in Africa, Asia and Europe.

10,000–4,000 BC: Settlements turn into proto-cities and development of skills such as the wheel, pottery and improved methods of cultivation in Mesopotamia and elsewhere.

5500–3000 BC: Predynastic Egyptian cultures develop (5500–3100 BC). Agriculture in Egypt (c. 5000 BC). Earliest known civilization arises in Sumeria (4500–4000 BC). First phonetic writing appears (c. 3500 BC). Sumerians develop a city state civilization (c. 3000 BC). Egyptians and Sumerians start using copper. Neolithic age in Western Europe.

3000–2000 BC: Pharaonic rule begins in Egypt. King Khufu (Cheops),

4th dynasty (2700–2675 BC), completes construction of the Great Pyramid at Giza (c. 2680 BC). The Great Sphinx of Giza (c. 2540 BC) is built by King Khafre. The earliest Egyptian mummies. Invention of Papyrus. Phoenician settlements on the coast of what is now Syria and Lebanon. Semitic tribes settle in Assyria. Sargon, the first Akkadian king, builds the Mesopotamian empire. The Epic of Gilgamesh is composed (c. 3000 BC). Abraham leaves Ur (c. 2000 BC). Astronomical studies begin in Egypt, Babylon, India, China.

3000–1500 BC: Stonehenge erected in Britain. Its purpose, possibly astronomical, is still a matter of conjecture.

2000–1500 BC: Hyksos invaders drive Egyptians from Lower Egypt (17th century BC). Amosis I frees Egypt from Hyksos (c. 1600 BC). Assyrians rise to power—rise of the cities of Ashur and Nineveh. Twenty-four-character alphabet developed in Egypt. Israelites enslaved in Egypt. Cuneiform inscriptions used by Hittites. Peak of Minoan culture on the Isle of Crete and the appearance of the earliest form of written Greek. Hammurabi, the King of Babylon, develops oldest existing code of laws (18th century BC).

1500–1000 BC: Ikhnaton develops a monotheistic religion in Egypt (c. 1375 BC). His successor, Tutankhamen, returns to the earlier gods. Moses leads the Israelites out of Egypt into Canaan. The Ten Commandments. The Greeks destroy Troy (c. 1193 BC). End of Greek civilization in Mycenae with the invasion of the Dorians. Chinese civilization develops under the Shang Dynasty. The Olmec civilization exists in Mexico.

1000–900 BC: Solomon succeeds King David, builds Jerusalem temple. After Solomon's death, the kingdom is divided into Israel and Judah. Old Testament books of Bible begin to be written. Phoenicians colonize Spain with a settlement at Cadiz.

900–800 BC: Phoenicians establish Carthage (c. 810 BC). The *Iliad* and the *Odyssey* composed, perhaps by the Greek poet Homer.

800–700 BC: First recorded Olympic games (776 BC). The legendary founding of Rome by Romulus (753 BC). Assyrian King Sargon II conquers the Hittites, Chaldeans and Samaria (end of the Kingdom of Israel). Chariots introduced into Italy by Etruscans.

700–600 BC: End of Assyrian empire (616 BC)—Nineveh destroyed by Chaldeans (Neo-Babylonians) and Medes (612 BC). Founding of Byzantium by Greeks (c. 660 BC). Building of the Acropolis in Athens. Lifetime of Solon, the Greek lawmaker (640–560 BC). Time of Sappho of Lesbos, Greek poet (c. 610–580 BC). Times of Lao-tse, Chinese philosopher and founder of Taoism (born c. 604 BC).

600–500 BC: Babylonian King Nebuchadnezzar builds his empire and destroys Jerusalem (586 BC). Babylonian captivity of the Jews (starting 587 BC). Hanging Gardens of Babylon are designed. Cyrus the Great of Persia creates a great empire, conquers Babylon (539 BC) and frees the Jews. Athenian democracy develops. It is said Thales correctly predicted a solar eclipse (c.585 BC). Anaximander is said to have made the first map of the world in this time. Greeks discovered electric attraction produced by rubbing amber. Lifetime of Aeschylus, Greek dramatist (525–465 BC). Pythagoras, Greek philosopher and mathematician, probably lived between 582 and 507 BC. Confucius (551–479 BC) develops his ethical and social philosophy in China. The *Analects* or Lun-yü ('collected sayings') are compiled by the second generation of Confucian disciples.

500–400 BC: The Greeks defeat the Persians: battles of Marathon (490 BC), Thermopylae (480 BC), Salamis (480 BC). Peloponnesian Wars between Athens and Sparta (431–404 BC). Sparta emerges victorious. Pericles comes to power in Athens (462 BC). Flowering of Greek culture during the Age of Pericles (450–400 BC). The Parthenon is built in Athens as a temple of the goddess Athena (447–432 BC). Ictinus and Callicrates are the architects and Phidias is responsible for the sculpture. Sophocles, Greek dramatist lived between c.496 and 406 BC. Hippocrates the Greek 'Father of Medicine' born around 460 BC. Xerxes I, king of Persia, rules in the period between 485 and 465 BC.

400–300 BC: Pentateuch or the first five books of the Old Testament evolve in their final form. Philip of Macedon is assassinated after subduing the Greek city states (336 BC); his son Alexander the Great (356–323 BC) succeeds him. Alexander destroys Thebes (335 BC) and conquers Tyre and Jerusalem (332 BC). Alexander occupies Babylon (330 BC), invades India, and dies in Babylon. Alexander's empire is divided among his generals; General Seleucus I establishes his Middle East empire with capitals at Antioch (Syria) and Seleucia (in Iraq). The trial and execution of Greek philosopher Socrates (399 BC). Socrates's student Plato records the *Dialogues* (c. 427–348 BC). Euclid's work on geometry, *Elements of Geometry* is composed (323 BC). Aristotle, Greek philosopher, lived somewhere between 384 and 322 BC. Demosthenes, Greek orator, lived somewhere between 384 and 322 BC. Praxiteles, Greek sculptor, worked and lived in the time between 400 and 330 BC. Leucippus and Democritus proposed that matter is made of small, indestructible particles. They called these particles atoms.

300–251 BC: Aristarchus of Samos proposes that the earth revolves around the sun and calculates diameter of the earth. First Punic War (264–241 BC): Rome defeats the Carthaginians and begins its domination of the Medi-

terranean. Temple of the Sun at Teotihuacán, Mexico, is built (c. 300 BC). Invention of the Mayan calendar in Yucatán. First Roman gladiatorial games are played (264 BC). Archimedes, Greek mathematician, lived and worked between 287 and 212 BC.

250–201 BC: Second Punic War (219–201 BC): Hannibal, Carthaginian general, crosses the Alps (218 BC), reaches the gates of Rome (211 BC), retreats, and is defeated by Scipio Africanus at Zama (202 BC). Great Wall of China built (c. 215 BC).

200–151 BC: Romans defeat Seleucid King Antiochus III at Thermopylae (191 BC). The beginning of Roman world domination. Maccabean revolt against Seleucids (167 BC).

150–101 BC: Third Punic War (149–146 BC): Rome destroys Carthage, killing 450,000 and enslaving the remaining 50,000 inhabitants. Roman armies conquer Macedonia, Greece, Anatolia, Balearic Islands, and southern France. The Venus de Milo is sculpted (c. 140 BC). Cicero, Roman orator, lived between 106 and 43 BC.

100–51 BC: Julius Caesar (100–44 BC) invades Britain (55 BC) and conquers Gaul (France) (c. 50 BC). Spartacus leads a slave revolt against Rome (71 BC). Romans conquer the Seleucid empire. Roman General Pompey conquers Jerusalem (63 BC). Cleopatra sits on the Egyptian throne (51–31 BC). Chinese develop the use of paper (c. 100 BC). Virgil, Roman poet, lived between 70 and 19 BC. Lifetime of Horace, the Roman poet (65–8 BC).

50–1 BC: Caesar crosses Rubicon to fight Pompey (50 BC). Herod made Roman governor of Judea (37 BC). Caesar murdered (44 BC). Caesar's nephew, Octavian, defeats Mark Antony and Cleopatra at Battle of Actium (31 BC), and establishes Roman empire as Emperor Augustus; rules 27 BC–AD 14. Pantheon built for the first time under Agrippa, 27 BC. Lifetime of Ovid, Roman poet (43 BC–AD 18).

1–49 AD: Birth of Jesus Christ (variously given from 4 BC to AD 7). After Augustus, Tiberius becomes emperor (dies, AD 37), succeeded by Caligula (assassinated, AD 41), who is followed by Claudius. Crucifixion of Jesus (probably AD 30). Han dynasty in China founded by Emperor Kuang Wu Ti. Buddhism introduced into China.

50–99 AD: Claudius poisoned (AD 54), succeeded by Nero (who commits suicide in AD 68). Missionary journeys of Paul the Apostle (AD 34–60). Jews revolt against Rome; Jerusalem destroyed (AD 70). Roman persecutions of the Christians begin (AD 64). Colosseum built in Rome (AD 71–80). Trajan rules AD 98–116. Roman empire extends to Mesopotamia, Arabia, Balkans. First Gospels of St Mark, St John, St Matthew.

100–149 AD: Hadrian rules Rome (AD 117–38); codifies Roman law, rebuilds the Pantheon, establishes a postal system, as well as builds a wall between England and Scotland. Jews revolt under Bar Kokhba (AD 122–35); final Diaspora (dispersion) of Jews begins.

150–199 AD: Marcus Aurelius rules in Rome (AD 161–80). Oldest Mayan temples in Central America constructed at this time (c. AD 200). Ptolemy studies mathematics, science, geography; proposes that the earth is the centre of the solar system.

200–249 AD: Goths invade Asia Minor (c. AD 220). Roman persecutions of Christians increase. Persian (Sassanid) empire re-established. End of Chinese Han dynasty. Chinese mathematicians calculate the value of pi to five decimal places.

250–299 AD: Invasions of the Roman empire by Franks and Goths. Buddhism spreads in China. Chinese mathematicians invent the magnetic compass. Classic period of Mayan civilization (AD 250–900); development of

hieroglyphic writing, advances in art, architecture and science.

300–349 AD: Constantine the Great (rules AD 312–37) reunites eastern and western Roman empires, with a new capital (Constantinople) on the site of Byzantium (AD 330); issues Edict of Milan legalizing Christianity (AD 313) and becomes a Christian on his deathbed (AD 337). Council of Nicaea (AD 325) defines orthodox Christian doctrine.

350–399 AD: Huns invade Europe (c. AD 360). Theodosius the Great (rules AD 392–95) is the last emperor of a united Roman empire. Roman empire permanently divided in AD 395: western empire ruled from Rome; eastern empire ruled from Constantinople.

400–449 AD: Western Roman empire disintegrates under weak emperors. Alaric, king of the Visigoths, sacks Rome (AD 410). A mob of rioters burns down the Library of Alexandria, and much of the recorded knowledge of the western world is lost (415 AD). Attila the Hun attacks Roman provinces (AD 433). St Augustine's *City of God* is written (AD 411).

450–499 AD: Vandals destroy Rome (AD 455). Western Roman empire ends as Odoacer, German chieftain, overthrows the last Roman emperor, Romulus Augustulus, and becomes the king of Italy (AD 476). Ostrogothic kingdom of Italy established by Theodoric the Great (AD 493). Clovis, ruler of the Franks, is converted to Christianity (AD 496). First schism between western and eastern churches (AD 484). Beginning of the 'Dark Ages' in Europe.

500–549 AD: Eastern and western churches reconciled. Justinian I the Great (483–565), becomes Byzantine emperor (527), issues his first code of civil laws (529), conquers North Africa, Italy, and part of Spain. Plague in Europe. Arthur, legendary king of the Britons is killed (c. 537).

550–599: Beginnings of European silk industry after Justinian's missionaries smuggle silkworms out of China (553). The times of Prophet Muhammad, founder of Islam (570–632). Buddhism introduced in Japan (c. 560). St Augustine of Canterbury brings Christianity to Britain (597). After killing about half the population, plague in Europe subsides (594).

600–649: Prophet Mohammed flees from Mecca to Medina (the *Hejira*); first year of the Muslim calendar (622). Arabs conquer Jerusalem (637). Arabs conquer the Persians (641). Lifetime of Fatima, Prophet Mohammed's daughter (606–632).

650–699: Arabs attack North Africa (670) and destroy Carthage (697). Venerable Bede, an English monk, lived between 672 and 735.

700–749: Arab empire extends from Lisbon to China (by 716). Charles Martel, Frankish leader, defeats Arabs at Tours/Poitiers, halting the Arab advance in Europe (732). Charlemagne (742–814) is born. Introduction of pagodas in Japan from China.

750–799: Charlemagne becomes king of the Franks (771). Caliph Harun al-Rashid, immortalized in the Arabian Nights, rules the Arab empire from Baghdad (786–809): often noted as the 'golden age' of Arab culture. Vikings begin attacks on Britain (790) and land in Ireland (795). City of Machu Picchu flourishes in Peru.

800–849: Charlemagne crowned the first Holy Roman Emperor in Rome (800). Charlemagne dies (814), succeeded by his son, Louis the Pious, who divides France among his sons (817). The Arabs conquer Crete, Sicily, and Sardinia (826–827).

850–899: Norse attack as far south as the Mediterranean. However, they are repulsed (859). They discover Iceland (861). Alfred the Great is the king of Britain (871), defeats Danish invaders (878). Russian nation founded.

Prince Rurik establishes his capital at Novgorod (c. 862–879).

900–949: Beginning of Mayan post-classical period, which lasted till the Spanish conquest (900–1519). Vikings discover Greenland (c. 900). Arab Spain under Abd ar-Rahman III becomes a centre of learning (912–961). Otto I crowned in Aachen as king of Germany (936). West Saxon victory by the army of King Athelstan and his brother Edmund over the combined armies of Olaf III Guthfrithson, Viking king of Dublin and Constantine, and king of Scotland at the battle of Brunanburh(c. 936). Song dynasty (960–1126) reunifies China. Toltecs in Central America learn metal-smelting.

950–999: Mieszko I (c. 960–92), the first prince of the Piast dynasty, is the founder of the Polish state. Eric the Red, Viking explorer, sets up a colony in Greenland (c. 986). Reign of Hugh Capet, first Capetian king of France (987–96). Musical notation systematized by Guido D'Arezzo, a Benedictine prior of the Camaldolite monastery of Avellana around 990–1050. Vikings and Danes attack Britain repeatedly (988–99). Otto I crowned Holy Roman Emperor by Pope John XII (962).

c.1000–1300: Classic Pueblo period of Anasazi culture.

c. 1000: Viking explorer Leif Eriksson reaches North America. Hungary and Scandinavia convert to Christianity. The old English epic *Beowulf* is written.

c. 1008: Murasaki Shikibu writes one of the world's first novels *The Tale of Genji*.

1013: Danes take control of England.

1040: Macbeth murders Duncan, King of Scotland.

1053: Norman conquest of Italy. Norman invader Robert Guiscard establishes kingdom in Italy.

1054: Final separation between Eastern (Orthodox) and Western (Roman) churches.

1066: William of Normandy invades England, defeats last Saxon king, Harold II, at Battle of Hastings. He is later crowned William I of England, or William the Conqueror.

1068: Construction on the cathedral in Pisa, Italy, begins.

1095: At the Council of Clermont, Pope Urban II calls for a holy war to seize control of Jerusalem from the Muslims. This launches the First Crusade (1096).

1144: Second Crusade begins.

c. 1150: Angkor Wat is completed.

1150–67: The Universities of Paris and Oxford are established.

1162: Thomas á Becket becomes Archbishop of Canterbury.

1169: Ibn-Rushd begins translating the works of Aristotle.

1170: Followers of Henry II, King of England, assassinate Thomas á Becket.

1189: Richard I (Richard the Lionhearted) succeeds Henry II in England. Third Crusade.

1199: Richard the Lionhearted is killed in France. King John succeeds him to the English throne.

1312–37: In Africa, the Mali empire reaches its zenith under King Mansa Musa.

c. 1325: The beginning of the Renaissance in Italy. Development of *Noh* drama in Japan. Aztecs establish Tenochtitlán on the site of modern Mexico City. Peak of Muslim culture in Spain.

1337–1453: The Hundred Years War. English and French kings fight for control of France.

1347–51: Nearly 25 million people die in Europe's 'Black Death', a bubonic plague epidemic.

1368: Ming Dynasty begins in China.

1376–82: John Wycliffe, pre-Reformation religious reformer, and his followers translate the Latin Bible into English.

1378–1417: The Great Schism resulting in rival popes in Rome and Avignon, France, fighting for control of Roman Catholic Church.

c. 1387: Chaucer writes his *Canterbury Tales*.

1407: One of the world's first public banks, Casa di San Giorgio, is founded in Genoa.

1415: King of England Henry V defeats the French at Agincourt. Jan Hus, Bohemian preacher and follower of Wycliffe, burned at stake in Constance as heretic.

1418–60: Portugal's Prince Henry the Navigator sponsors exploration of Africa's coast.

1428: Joan of Arc leads the French against the English.

1430: The Burgundians capture Joan of Arc and turn her over to the English.

1431: Joan of Arc burned at the stake as a witch after an ecclesiastical trial.

1438: Rule of the Incas in Peru.

1450: Florence becomes centre of the Renaissance arts and learning under the Medicis.

1453: The Byzantine empire comes to an end when the Turks conquer Constantinople and found the Ottoman empire.

1455: The War of the Roses, a civil war between rival noble factions, start in England. It lasts till 1485. Johann Gutenberg invents the movable type at Mainz, Germany, and completes the first printed Bible.

1462: Ivan the Great begins his rule over Russia as its first czar. He rules till 1505.

1492: Troops of Queen Isabella I of Castile and King Ferdinand II of Aragon defeat the Moors. Christopher Columbus becomes the first European to visit the Caribbean Islands.

1493–96: Columbus's second voyage, to Dominica, Jamaica, Puerto Rico.

1498: Columbus's third voyage, to the Orinoco region.

1502–04: Columbus's fourth voyage, to Honduras and Panama.

1497–98: Portuguese explorer Vasco da Gama sails around the southern tip of Africa and discovers the sea route to India. John Cabot, Italian navigator and explorer in English employment, reaches and explores the Canadian coast. First black slaves in America are brought to the Spanish colony of Santo Domingo.

c. 1503: Leonardo da Vinci paints the *Mona Lisa*.

1504: Michelangelo sculpts his *David*.

1506: Construction of St Peter's Church begins in Rome. Artists and architects like Michelangelo, Leonardo da Vinci, Bramante, Raphael and Bernini are involved in its design and decoration.

1509: Henry VIII ascends the English throne. Michelangelo paints the ceiling of the Sistine Chapel.

1513: Vasco Nunez de Balboa becomes the first European to see the Pacific Ocean. Machiavelli writes *The Prince*.

1517: Turks gain control of Arabia and conquer Egypt. German theologian Martin Luther posts his 95 theses denouncing church abuses on a church door in Wittenberg. This starts the Reformation in Germany.

1519: Hernando Cortes conquers Mexico for Spain. Portuguese explorer Ferdinand Magellan sets out to circumnavigate the world. Charles I of Spain becomes Holy Roman Emperor Charles V. Ulrich Zwingli begins Reformation in Switzerland.

1520: Suleiman I ('the Magnificent') becomes Sultan of Turkey. He invades Hungary in 1521, Rhodes in 1522, attacks Austria in 1529, annexes Hungary in 1541, and Tripoli in 1551. He makes peace with Persia in 1553. In 1560, he destroys the Spanish fleet. He passes away in 1566. Pope Leo X excommunicates Martin Luther.

1521: Magellan reaches the Pacific but is killed in a skirmish with Philippine natives.

1522: One of Magellan's ships continues the circumnavigation under the leadership of Juan Sebastián del Cano and reaches Spain.

1524: Sailing under the French flag, Verrazano explores the coast of New England and New York Bay.

1527: Troops of the Holy Roman Empire attack Rome and imprison Pope Clement VII. This is regarded as the end of the Italian Renaissance. The Medici family is expelled from Florence.

1533: Spanish conquistador Francisco Pizarro marches to Peru and kills the last Inca ruler, Atahualpa.

1535: Reformation begins in England as Henry VIII makes himself head of the Church of England after a dispute with the Pope. Sir Thomas More, Lord Chancellor of England, executed as a traitor for his refusal to acknowledge the king's religious authority. Jacques Cartier sails up the St Lawrence River, which forms the basis of French claims to Canada.

1536: Henry VIII executes his second wife, Anne Boleyn. John Calvin establishes the Reformed and Presbyterian form of Protestantism in Switzerland, writes *Institutes of the Christian Religion*.

1541: John Knox leads Reformation in Scotland and establishes the Presbyterian Church there in 1560.

1543: Nicolaus Copernicus publishes *On the Revolution of Heavenly Bodies*. It details his heliocentric or Sun-centred theory of the solar system.

1547: Ivan IV ('the Terrible') crowned as czar of Russia.

1553: Queen Mary I restores Roman Catholicism in England.

1558: Queen Elizabeth I ascends the throne in England and rules till 1603. She restores Protestantism in England, establishes state Church of England, or Anglicanism.

1561: The Edict of Orleans stops the persecution of Huguenots, or members of the Protestant Reformed Church in France.

1572: French religious wars between Catholics and Protestants restart with St Bartholomew's Day Massacre, the killing of thousands of Huguenots at Vassy.

1570: Japan allows the visits of foreign ships. The Pope excommunicates Queen Elizabeth I. Turks attack Cyprus and declare war on Venice.

1571: Spanish and Italian fleets defeat the Turkish fleet at the Battle of Lepanto.

1572: Peace of Constantinople ends Turkish attacks on Europe.

1580: Francis Drake returns to England after circumnavigating the world.

1582: Pope Gregory XIII implements the Gregorian calendar.

1583: William of Orange rules the Netherlands.

1584: William of Orange assassinated on the orders of Philip II of Spain.

1587: Mary, Queen of Scots, executed for treason on the orders of Queen Elizabeth I.

1588: The English defeat the Spanish Armada and hence thwart a Spanish invasion of England. Henry, King of Navarre and Protestant leader, recognized as Henry IV, first Bourbon king of France.

1590: Henry IV assassinated. Edmund Spenser writes *The Faerie Queen*. Galileo conducts experiments with falling objects.

1592–1613: William Shakespeare's plays enacted in London.

1598: The Edict of Nantes grants religious freedom to the Huguenots.

1598: Tycho Brahe of Denmark describes his astronomical experiments.

1603: Elizabeth I passes away. James I of Scotland become King James I of England and Scotland. Japanese ruler shifts the capital to Edo (present-day Tokyo). Shakespeare writes *Hamlet*.

1605: Cervantes writes *Don Quixote de la Mancha*.

1607: Jamestown, Virginia, established as the first permanent English colony on American mainland.

1609: Samuel de Champlain establishes the French colony of Quebec.

1610: Galileo observes the moons of Jupiter through his telescope.

1611: Gustav II Adolph, or Gustavus Adolphus, elected King of Sweden. King James Version of the Bible is published in England. Rubens paints his *Descent from the Cross*.

1614: John Napier discovers logarithms.

1618–48: The Thirty Years War is fought in Europe as Protestants fight against Catholic oppression. The key players were Denmark, Sweden, Spain, Germany and France.

1618: Johannes Kepler postulates the last of three laws of planetary motion.

1619: A Dutch ship brings the first African slaves to British North America.

1620: The Pilgrim Fathers land in present-day USA after a three-month voyage in *Mayflower*. They had set sail from Plymouth, England.

1623: Dutch West India Company establishes New Netherland on the east coat of North America.

1626: Completion of St Peter's Church in Rome.

1632: Lord Baltimore founds Maryland.

1633: The Inquisition forces Galileo to recant his belief in Copernican theory of the solar system.

1642–46: Civil war breaks out in England between the supporters of Charles and the parliamentary forces, the New Model Army, also called Roundheads. Parliamentary leader Oliver Cromwell defeats the Royalists in 1646. The monarchy is overthrown.

1648: Charles I is put to trial. He is beheaded in 1649.

1653: Oliver Cromwell becomes Lord Protector of England, Scotland and Ireland.

1644: End of Ming Dynasty in China and the Manchus come to power.

Descartes writes *Principles of Philosophy*.

1658: Oliver Cromwell passes away and his son Richard takes over as Lord Protector.

1659: Richard Cromwell resigns and the Puritan government collapses.

1660: Restoration of monarchy in England under King Charles II.

1661: In France, Louis XIV begins personal rule as an absolute monarch and starts construction of his palace at Versailles.

1664: In North America, the British take New Amsterdam from the Dutch. New Amsterdam eventually grows into present-day New York City. Isaac Newton conducts experiments with gravity.

1665: The Great Plague kills 75,000 in London.

1666: Great Fire of London. Molière writes *Misanthrope*.

1667: Milton writes *Paradise Lost*.

1683–99: War of European powers against the Turks. Vienna survives a three-month Turkish siege.

1684: Gottfried Wilhelm Leibniz's calculus is published.

1685: James II succeeds Charles II in England.

1687: Newton's *Philosophiae Naturalis Principia Mathematica* (Mathematical Principles of Natural Philosophy), *Principia* or *Principia Mathematica* for short) is published, containing the statement of Newton's laws of motion and his law of universal gravitation.

1688: William of Orange invited to England amid apprehensions that James II will restore Catholicism. James II escapes to France. William III and his wife, Mary, are crowned rulers of England. In France, Louis XIV revokes the Edict of Nantes of 1598 leading to an exodus of thousands of Protestants.

1689: Peter the Great becomes czar of Russia and tries to westernize the country and develop Russia as a military power.

1690: William III of England defeats former King James II and Irish rebels at Battle of the Boyne in Ireland.

1701: War of Spanish Succession begins.

1707: United Kingdom of Great Britain formed as England, Wales, and Scotland are joined together by a parliamentary Act of Union.

1714: The Peace of Utrecht ends the War of Spanish Succession and marks the rise of the British empire as Britain gains Newfoundland, Hudson's Bay Territory, and Acadia from France, and Gibraltar and Minorca from Spain.

1729: Bach composes *St Matthew's Passion*. Isaac Newton's *Principia* translated from Latin into English.

1740: Capt. Vitus Bering, a Dane in Russian employment, discovers Alaska. Frederick II 'the Great' becomes king of Prussia.

1746: British defeat Scots under Stuart Pretender Prince Charles at Culloden Moor.

1755: Samuel Johnson's *Dictionary* is published for the first time. More than 60,000 die in an earthquake in Lisbon, Portugal.

1756–63: Seven Years War (called French and Indian Wars in America). Britain and Prussia defeat France, Spain, Austria, and Russia. It results in France losing its North American colonies, Spain handing over Florida to Britain in exchange for Cuba.

1759: British capture Quebec from the French. Voltaire writes *Candide*. Haydn composes *Symphony No. 1*.

1762: Catherine II 'the Great' becomes czarina of Russia. Jean Jacques Rousseau writes *Social Contract*. Mozart tours Europe as six-year-old prodigy.

1765: James Watt invents the steam engine. Britain imposes the Stamp Act on the American colonists.

1769: Sir William Arkwright patents a spinning machine. This is considered to be one of the first steps of the Industrial Revolution.

1770: The Boston Massacre, in which British troops open fire on an American mob. The event helped spark the American Revolution.

1772: Joseph Priestley and Daniel Rutherford independently discover nitrogen. Partition of Poland occurs. It takes place again in 1793 and in 1795. Austria, Prussia, and Russia divide the country and end its independence.

1773: The Boston Tea Party, in which a group of about 60 local Boston residents, named Sons of Liberty destroy the cargo of tea imported by the British authorities and throw it into the Boston Harbour. This event is considered as one of the starting points of the American Revolution.

1775: The American Revolution begins with battle of Lexington and Concord. Joseph Priestley discovers hydrochloric and sulphuric acids.

1776: US Declaration of Independence. Adam Smith writes *Wealth of Nations*. Edward Gibbon writes *Decline and Fall of the Roman Empire*.

1778: Capt. James Cook 'discovers' Hawaii.

1781: Immanuel Kant writes *Critique of Pure Reason*. German-born astronomer and musician William Herschel discovers Uranus, the seventh planet of the solar system.

1784: Russia annexes Crimea.

1787: Antoine Lavoisier conducts his work on chemical nomenclature. Mozart composes *Don Giovanni*.

1788: The French Parliament presents its grievances to King Louis XVI who agrees to hold the *Estates-General* in 1789 for the first time since 1613.

1789: French Revolution begins with the storming of the Bastille prison. George Washington is elected US President with all 69 votes of the electoral college; takes oath of office in New York City.

1790: Lavoisier formulates *Table of 31 chemical elements*.

1793: Louis XVI and Marie Antoinette are executed. The Reign of Terror begins in France. Eli Whitney invents the cotton gin resulting in the growth of the cotton industry.

1794: Reign of Terror ends in France with the execution of Maximilien Robespierre.

1796: French general Napoléon Bonaparte leads the French Army to victory against the Austrians. Edward Jenner introduces smallpox vaccine.

1798: Napoleon's fleet is defeated by the British at the Battle of the Nile, also known as the Battle of Aboukir Bay.

1799: Napoleon leads a coup that establishes himself as the effective ruler of France, as the First Consul.

1800: Napoleon conquers Italy. Strengthens his position as First Consul. In USA, the federal government moves to Washington DC. William Herschel discovers infrared radiation. Alessandro Volta develops the voltaic pile, a forerunner of the electric battery, which produces a steady electric current.

1801: United Kingdom of Great Britain and Ireland established with one monarch and one Parliament, but Catholics are excluded from voting.

1803: US negotiates the Louisiana Purchase from France. It pays $15 million to increase its territory by 827,000 sq. mi. (2,144,500 sq. km).

1804: Napoleon proclaims himself emperor of France and codifies French law under *Code Napoleon*.

1805: Lord Nelson defeats the combined French–Spanish fleets in the Battle of Trafalgar. Napoleon wins over Austrian and Russian forces at the Battle of Austerlitz.

1807: Robert Fulton carries out the first successful steamboat trip on *Clermont* between New York City and Albany.

1808: French armies occupy Rome and Spain. UK helps Spanish guerrillas against Napoleon in the Peninsular War. The US Congress bans the importation of slaves.

1812: Napoleon invades Russia in June but is forced to retreat in the severe winter. This results in the death of most of Napoleon's soldiers.

1814: The allied forces of Britain, Austria, Russia, Prussia, Sweden, and Portugal defeat the French. Napoleon is exiled to Elba, an island off the Italian coast. Bourbon King Louis XVIII takes over the French throne. George Stephenson builds the first practical steam locomotive.

1815: Napoleon returns to Paris on 20 March. Napoleon is defeated at the Battle of Waterloo, his last battle, on 18 June. King Louis XVIII is restored to the French throne on 28 June. Napoléon formally surrenders on board the British vessel HMS *Bellerophon* on 15 July. Napoléon is imprisoned and then exiled by the British to the island of Saint Helena from 15 October. Congress of Vienna is held. The political map of Europe is redrawn following the defeat of Napoleonic France.

1819: Simón Bolivar liberates New Granada (former Spanish colony in South America consisting of present-day Colombia, Venezuela, and Ecuador) from Spanish rule.

1821: Panama, Guatemala, and Santo Domingo proclaim independence from Spain.

1822: Greece proclaims independence from Turkey and becomes a republic. Turkey invades Greece. Brazil declares its independence from Portugal.

1825: Portugal recognizes Brazil as an independent nation.

1828: Russia declares war on Turkey. France and UK support Greece.

1829: War ends and Turkey recognizes Greek independence. Brazil becomes independent of Portugal.

1823: US Monroe Doctrine warns European nations not to interfere in the western hemisphere.

1824: Mexico becomes a republic. Simón Bolívar liberates Peru. Beethoven composes the *Ninth Symphony*.

c. 1826: Date of earliest known surviving photograph taken by Joseph-Nicéphore Niepce, considered to be the first successful permanent photograph.

1830: France invades Algeria. Louis Philippe becomes 'Citizen King' after a revolution forces Charles X to abdicate.

1831: Polish revolt against Russia fails. Belgium breaks away from the Netherlands.

1833: Slavery abolished in the British empire.

1834: Charles Babbage invents 'analytical engine', a precursor of the computer.

1836: Charles Dickens writes *Pickwick Papers*.

1837: Victoria becomes Queen of Great Britain.

1839–42: First Opium War between Britain and China.

1840: Lower and Upper Canada united.

1843: Wagner composes his opera *The Flying Dutchman*.

1844: Samuel F. B. Morse patents the telegraph.

1846: The eighth planet in the solar system, Neptune, is discovered. USA declares war on Mexico and annexes California and New Mexico. Elias Howe patents the sewing machine. Failure of potato crop causes famine in Ireland.

1848: Revolt in Paris leads to the abdication of Louis Philippe and election of Louis Napoleon as President of French Republic.

1848–49: Royalist troops suppress revolutions in Venice, Vienna, Berlin, Milan, Rome, and Warsaw. US–Mexico War ends with Mexico giving up claims to Texas, California, Arizona, New Mexico, Utah, and Nevada. Karl Marx and Friedrich Engels compile the *Communist Manifesto*.

1849: Gold rush begins in California.

1850: In USA, Henry Clay opens debate on slavery and warns the South against secession from the Union.

1851: Herman Melville writes *Moby-Dick*.

1852: South African Republic is established. Louis Napoleon proclaims himself Napoleon III. Harriet Beecher Stowe writes *Uncle Tom's Cabin*.

1853: Crimean War begins as Turkey declares war on Russia.

1854: UK and France join Turkey in war on Russia. Japanese allow American trade. Lord Alfred Tennyson writes *Charge of the Light Brigade*.

1855: Armed clashes between pro- and anti-slavery groups take place in Kansas, USA.

1856: Gustave Flaubert writes *Madame Bovary*.

1857: US Supreme Court rules that a slave is not a citizen.

1858: Pro-slavery Constitution rejected in Kansas. Republican politician Abraham Lincoln makes strong anti-slavery speech in Springfield, Illinois.

1859: The process of unification of Italy starts under the leadership of Sardinian premier Count Cavour. Construction of the Suez Canal starts. Jean-Joseph-Étienne Lenoir builds first practical internal-combustion engine. Edward Fitzgerald translates *The Rubaiyat of Omar Khayyam*. Charles Darwin writes *Origin of Species*.

1860: South Carolina breaks away from the Union.

1861: US Civil War begins. Alabama, Florida, Georgia, Louisiana, Mississippi and Texas break away from the Union and join with South Carolina to form the Confederate States of America, with Jefferson Davis as President. Arkansas, North Carolina, Tennessee and Virginia secede and join the Confederacy. First Battle of Bull Run (Manassas). Abraham Lincoln inaugurated as US President. Independent Kingdom of Italy proclaimed under Sardinian King Victor Emmanuel II. Serfs emancipated in Russia. Louis Pasteur postulates his theory of germs.

1862: US Civil War continues.

1863: Battle of Gettysburg.

1864: Gen. Sherman's Atlanta campaign.

1865: Confederate general Robert E. Lee surrenders to Union Army General Ulysses S. Grant at Appomattox to end the US Civil War. President Lincoln is assassinated. Joseph Lister begins antiseptic surgery. Gregor Mendel postulates *Law of Heredity*. Lewis Carroll writes *Alice's Adventures in Wonderland*.

1866: Alfred Nobel invents dynamite. Prussia and Italy defeat Austria in Seven Weeks War.

1867: Austria–Hungary Dual Monarchy established. Dominion of Canada is established. USA buys Alaska from Russia for $7,200,000. South African diamond field discovered. 675-year shogun rule comes to an end in Japan. Volume I of Marx's *Das Kapital* is published. Johann Strauss II composes *Blue Danube*.

1868: Revolution in Spain deposes Queen Isabella who then flees to France. In US, the Fourteenth Amendment giving civil rights to blacks is ratified.

1869: Suez Canal opens. German Lothar Meyer and Russian Dmitry Ivanovich Mendeleev almost simultaneously develop the first periodic table.

1870: Franco–Prussian War starts. Revolt in Paris. Third Republic is proclaimed in France.

1871: Franco-Prussian War ends. France surrenders Alsace-Lorraine to Germany. German empire proclaimed with Prussian king as Kaiser Wilhelm I. Henry Morton Stanley meets David Livingstone in Africa.

1872: Jules Verne writes *Around the World in 80 Days*.

1873: Economic crisis in Europe.

1875: The first performance of Georges Bizet's *Carmen*.

1876: Alexander Graham Bell patents the telephone.

1877: Russo-Turkish War starts. Thomas Alva Edison patents the phonograph. Pyotr Ilyich Tchaikovsky composes *Swan Lake*.

1878: Russo-Turkish War ends. Congress of Berlin revises Treaty of San Stefano that ended the Russo-Turkish War and redivides south-east Europe.

1879: UK and the Zulus fight the Anglo-Zulu War.

1880: Construction of the Panama Canal begins. US–China treaty allows USA to restrict immigration of Chinese labour.

1881: US President James Garfield assassinated.

1882: UK conquers Egypt. Germany, Austria, and Italy form Triple Alliance. In Berlin, Robert Koch announces the discovery of the tuberculosis germ.

1883: In Barcelona, Spain, architect Antoni Gaudi begins to build his masterpiece, the La Sagrada Familia cathedral.

1884–85: The Berlin West Africa Conference is held in Berlin at which major European nations discuss expansion in Africa.

1886: UK annexes Burma, now Myanmar. The Statue of Liberty is dedicated. Karl Benz patents his first successful petrol-driven automobile.

1887: Queen Victoria's Golden Jubilee. Sir Arthur Conan Doyle writes his first Sherlock Holmes story, *A Study in Scarlet*.

1888: John Boyd Dunlop develops commercially practical pneumatic tyres. 'Jack the Ripper' murders take place in London. The true identity of the murderer is yet to be ascertained.

1889: The Eiffel Tower is built for the Paris exposition.

1890: Elizabeth Jane Cochran, better known as Nellie Bly, pioneer of undercover journalism, travels round the world in '72 days, six hours, eleven minutes and fourteen seconds', mimicking Jules Verne's book *Around the World in Eighty Days*.

1892: Rudolf Diesel invents and patents the Diesel engine.

1893: New Zealand becomes first country in the world to grant women the right to vote.

1894: Sino-Japanese War begins. In France, Capt. Alfred Dreyfus convicted on false treason charge.

1895: Sino-Japanese War ends with China accepting defeat in the Treaty of Shimonoseki. German physicist Wilhelm Roentgen discovers X-rays Auguste and Louis Lumière show their first motion pictures in Paris.

1896: Alfred Nobel's will establishes the Nobel Prizes for peace, science, and literature. Guglielmo Marconi receives his first wireless patent in UK. First modern Olympic Games are held in Athens, Greece.

1897: Theodor Herzl launches the Zionist movement.

1898: Pierre and Marie Curie discover radium and polonium. US Battleship *Maine* is sunk in Havana Harbour. Spanish–American War begins and USA destroys a Spanish fleet near Santiago, Cuba.

1899: Boer War, or South African War, starts as a conflict between British and the Boers.

1900: Sigmund Freud writes *The Interpretation of Dreams*.

1901: The first Nobel Prizes are awarded. Queen Victoria passes away. Her son, Edward VII succeeds her to the British throne. US President William McKinley assassinated.

1902: Boer War ends in British victory.

1903: The Wright brothers, Orville and Wilbur, fly their first powered, controlled, heavier-than-air plane at Kitty Hawk.

1904: Russo-Japanese War begins. UK and France settle their differences by signing a series of agreements, the Entente Cordiale. Ernest Rutherford and Frederick Soddy postulate the General Theory of Radioactivity.

1905: Russo-Japanese War ends in defeat for Russia and Japan gains control of Korea but restores southern Manchuria to China. The Russian Revolution of 1905 begins when troops open fire on unarmed demonstrators in

St Petersburg. Strikes and riots follow and sailors on battleship *Potemkin* mutiny. In response, Czar Nicholas II announces reforms including first Duma or Parliament. Albert Einstein publishes Special Theory of Relativity and other significant theories in physics.

1906: San Francisco earthquake on the San Andreas Fault destroys much of San Francisco. Norwegian explorer Roald Amundsen fixes magnetic North Pole.

1907: Second Hague Peace Conference of 46 nations adopts 10 conventions on rules of war. Pablo Picasso's *Les Demoiselles d'Avignon* introduces cubism.

1908: Earthquake kills 150,000 in southern Italy and Sicily. Union of South Africa established as a confederation of colonies.

1909: American explorers Robert E. Peary and Matthew Henson are reported to have reached North Pole.

1910: South Africa becomes a British dominion.

1911: Ernest Rutherford discovers the structure of the atom. Roald Amundsen reaches South Pole. Italy defeats Turks in the Turkish-Italian War and annexes Tripoli and Libya. Chinese Republic is proclaimed after a revolution overthrows the Manchu dynasty. Sun Yat-sen is named President. A revolution in Mexico results in the replacement of President Porfirio Diaz with Francisco Madero.

1912–13: Balkan Wars take place. Turkey defeated by an alliance of Bulgaria, Greece, Montenegro, and Serbia. In the second war of 1913, Bulgaria is defeated after it attacks Serbia and Greece and Romania intervenes and Turks recapture Adrianople.

1912: The *Titanic* sinks on its maiden voyage.

1913: Greece annexes Crete. Francisco Madero, President of Mexico, assassinated. George I, king of Greece, assassinated.

1914: Austrian Archduke Francis Ferdinand and wife Sophie are assassinated in Sarajevo. Austria declares war on Serbia, Germany on Russia and France, and Britain on Germany. World War I begins. Panama Canal is officially opened.

1915: World War I continues. German submarine sinks British passenger liner and cargo ship *Lusitania*. This event plays a key role in the entry of the USA into World War I. Second Battle of Ypres takes place. Genocide of estimated 600,000 to one million Armenians by Turkish soldiers. Albert Einstein publishes *General Theory of Relativity*.

1916: World War I continues. Battle of Verdun and Battle of the Somme take place. USA buys the Virgin Islands from Denmark for $25 million. British troops suppress Easter Rebellion in Ireland.

1917: World War I continues. USA declares war on Germany. First US combat troops arrive in France. Third Battle of Ypres takes place. Russian Revolution of 1917 ends the rule of the Romanov family in Russia. February Revolution forces Czar Nicholas II to abdicate. A provisional government takes office in Russia with Alexander Fedorovich Kerensky as prime minister. Bolsheviks seize power in armed coup d'état led by Lenin and Trotsky in Russia. Kerensky flees the country. Balfour Declaration promises Jewish homeland in Palestine. US declares war on Austria and Hungary. Armistice signed between new Russian Bolshevik government and Germans. Sigmund Freud writes *Introduction to Psychoanalysis*.

1918: Bolsheviks execute Czar Nicholas II and his family. Russian Civil War breaks out between Reds (Bolsheviks) and Whites (anti-Bolsheviks). Second Battle of the Marne. German Kaiser abdicates. Hostilities cease on the Western Front. Worldwide influenza epidemic kills nearly 20 million.

1919: Third International (Comintern) establishes Soviet control over international communist movements. Allies and Germany sign Versailles Treaty incorporating Woodrow Wilson's draft Covenant of League of Nations. Aviators John Alcock and Arthur Brown make the first transatlantic non-stop flight.

1920: Bolsheviks emerge victorious in the Russian Civil War. League of Nations holds its first meeting at Geneva, Switzerland. Treaty of Sèvres dissolves the Ottoman empire.

1921: US Congress formally ends war. Reparations Commission fixes German liability for World War I at 132 billion gold marks. German inflation begins. Major treaties signed at Washington Disarmament Conference limit naval tonnage and pledge to respect territorial integrity of China.

1922: Benito Mussolini marches on Rome and forms a fascist government. Irish Free State, a self-governing dominion of British empire, is officially proclaimed. Kemal Atatürk, founder of modern Turkey, overthrows the country's last sultan. James Joyce writes *Ulysses*.

1923: Adolf Hitler's 'Beer Hall Putsch' coup attempt in Munich fails. French and Belgian troops occupy Ruhr region of Germany to enforce reparations payments. Earthquake destroys large parts of Tokyo.

1924: Death of Lenin. Stalin wins Russian power struggle and rules as Soviet dictator until death in 1953. Adolf Hitler is sentenced to five years in prison where he writes *Mein Kampf*, his autobiography.

1925: Locarno conferences seek to secure European peace through mutual guarantees. John Logie Baird, Scottish inventor, transmits human features by television.

1926: Gertrude Ederle of USA becomes the first woman to swim English Channel. Ernest Hemingway writes *The Sun Also Rises*.

1927: German economy collapses. Socialists riot in Vienna. General strike follows acquittal of Nazis for political murder. Leon Trotsky expelled from Russian Communist Party. Charles A. Lindbergh flies the first successful solo non-stop flight from New York to Paris. Philo T. Farnsworth demonstrates working television model. Georges Lemaître proposes Big Bang Theory. *The Jazz Singer*, with Al Jolson, is the first part-talking motion picture.

1928: 65 nations sign the Kellogg-Briand Pact, outlawing war. Alexander Fleming discovers penicillin. Richard E. Byrd starts expedition to the Antarctic. *Oxford English Dictionary* published after 44 years of research.

1929: Leon Trotsky expelled from USSR. Lateran Treaty establishes an independent Vatican City. In USA, stock market prices collapse resulting in the first phase of Depression and global economic crisis. Edwin Powell Hubble proposes theory of expanding universe. St Valentine's Day gangland massacre in Chicago.

1930: UK, USA, Japan, France, and Italy sign naval disarmament treaty. Nazis achieve gains in German elections. US physicist Ernest O. Lawrence develops the cyclotron. Clyde W. Tombaugh discovers Pluto, the ninth planet in the solar system.

1931: Spain becomes a republic with the ouster of King Alfonso XIII. In Germany, the Nazi Party gets the support of German industrialists. Mukden Incident, also called Manchurian Incident, in which the Japanese blow up a section of a Japanese railroad near Mukden (present-day Shenyang) in northern Manchuria, begins Japanese occupation of Manchuria. The *Star Spangled Banner* officially becomes US national anthem.

1932: Nazis lead in German elections with 230 Reichstag seats. Famine in USSR. Amelia Earhart becomes the first woman to fly solo across the Atlantic Ocean.

1933: Adolf Hitler is appointed German chancellor and assumes dictatorial powers. Germany and Japan withdraw from League of Nations. President Franklin D. Roosevelt launches New Deal to revive US economy. Prohibition repealed in USA. USA recognizes USSR.

1934: Nazis assassinate Chancellor Englebert Dollfuss of Austria. Hitler becomes Führer. USSR admitted to League of Nations. In China, Mao Zedong begins the Long March north with 100,000 soldiers.

1935: Saar becomes a part of Germany following a plebiscite. Nazis repudiate Versailles Treaty and introduce compulsory military service. Mussolini invades Ethiopia. President Roosevelt opens second phase of New Deal in USA.

1936: Germany occupies Rhineland. Italy annexes Ethiopia. Rome–Berlin Axis is proclaimed. Leon Trotsky is exiled to Mexico. King George V dies and is succeeded by his son, Edward VIII who abdicates the throne in the same year to marry an American-born divorcée. His brother, George VI succeeds him. Spanish civil war begins. War breaks out between China and Japan. Japan and Germany sign anti-Comintern pact.

1937: Hitler repudiates war guilt clause of Versailles Treaty. Italy withdraws from League of Nations. Japan invades China and conquers most of its coastal area. Amelia Earhart lost somewhere in the Pacific on her round-the-world flight. Picasso paints the *Guernica* mural.

1938: Hitler marches into Austria. Political and geographical union of Germany and Austria is proclaimed. The Munich Pact is signed whereby UK, France and Italy agree to allow Germany partition Czechoslovakia.

1939: Germany invades Poland, occupies Bohemia and Moravia. Germany renounces pact with England and concludes 10-year non-aggression pact with USSR. Russo-Finnish War begins. World War II begins. President Roosevelt proclaims US neutrality. Albert Einstein writes to President Roosevelt about the feasibility of an atomic bomb. *Gone with the Wind* premieres. General Franco's fascist forces defeat loyalist forces in the Spanish civil war.

1940: World War II continues. Japan joins the Axis powers. Hitler invades Norway, Denmark, the Netherlands, Belgium, Luxembourg and France. Winston Churchill becomes Britain's PM. Leon Trotsky is assassinated in Mexico. USSR annexes Estonia, Latvia and Lithuania. Russia and Finland sign a peace treaty whereby Finland loses one-tenth of its territory.

1941: World War II continues. Germany attacks the Balkans and Russia. Japanese surprise attack on US fleet at Pearl Harbour brings US into World War II. USA and UK declare war on Japan. Manhattan Project on atomic bomb research begins.

1942: World War II continues. Declaration of United Nations signed in Washington DC. Nazi leaders attend Wannsee Conference to discuss the 'final solution to the Jewish question', the systematic extermination of Jews now called the Holocaust. Enrico Fermi achieves nuclear chain reaction. More than 120,000 Japanese and persons of Japanese ancestry living in western US moved to 'relocation centres', some for the entire duration of the war.

1943: World War II continues. British PM Churchill and US President Roosevelt meet at the Casablanca Conference. Italian dictator Mussolini is deposed and killed.

1944: Allied forces invade Normandy on D-Day. Bretton Woods Conference creates International Monetary Fund and World Bank. USA, British Commonwealth and USSR propose establishment of United Nations at the Dumbarton Oaks Conference. Battle of the Bulge, or the Ardennes Offensive, the last major German offensive on the Western Front.

1945: Roosevelt, Churchill, Stalin meet at the Yalta Conference and plan the final defeat of Germany. President Roosevelt dies. Adolf Hitler is believed to have committed suicide. Germany surrenders. 8 May is declared V-E Day. Harry Truman, Churchill and Stalin meet at the Potsdam Conference to establish the basis of German reconstruction. US drops atomic bombs on the Japanese cities of Hiroshima and Nagasaki forcing Japan to surrender on V-J Day, 2 September. World War II ends. The United Nations is established. First electronic computer, ENIAC, is built.

1946: The First meeting of UN General Assembly opens in London. League of Nations is dissolved. Winston Churchill's 'Iron Curtain' speech warns of Soviet expansion. Italy abolishes monarchy. The verdict is passed in the Nuremberg war trial. 12 Nazi leaders (including one tried in absentia) are sentenced to death, seven are imprisoned, three are acquitted. Hermann Goering commits suicide a few hours before 10 other Nazi leaders are executed. Juan Perón becomes President of Argentina.

1947: Peace treaties for Bulgaria, Finland, Hungary, Italy, and Romania are signed in Paris. Soviet Union rejects US plan for UN atomic energy control. President Truman proposes Truman Doctrine to help Greece and Turkey in resisting communist expansion. Marshall Plan for European recovery is proposed. It envisages a coordinated programme to help European nations recover from the war. US Air Force pilot Chuck Yeager becomes the first person to break the sound barrier. Anne Frank's *The Diary of a Young Girl* is published.

1948: UK grants independence to Burma, now Myanmar and Ceylon, now Sri Lanka. Communists seize power in Czechoslovakia. Organization of American States (OAS) Charter is signed at Bogotá, Colombia. Nation of Israel proclaimed. Arab armies attack the newborn state the following day. The Berlin Blockade begins when the Soviet Union block Western rail and road access to Berlin from 24 June 1948–11 May 1949. This leads to an Allied airlift of essential supplies to the Western-held sectors of Berlin. Independent Republic of Korea is proclaimed. Verdict in Japanese war trial: 18 are imprisoned, Tôjô Hideki (Japanese PM and general during the war) and six others are hanged. United States of Indonesia is established. Alger Hiss, former US State Department official, indicted on perjury charges after denying passing secret documents to a communist spy ring and sentenced to five-year prison term. Alfred Kinsey publishes *Sexual Behavior in the American Male*. Tennessee Williams's *A Streetcar Named Desire* wins Pulitzer.

1949: Berlin Blockade ends ceasefire in Palestine. Truman proposes Point Four Program to help world's less developed areas. Israel signs armistice with Egypt. Start of North Atlantic Treaty Organization (NATO). Federal Republic of Germany (West Germany) is established. First successful Soviet atomic test. Chairman Mao Zedong formally proclaims Communist People's Republic of China. German Democratic Republic (East Germany) is established under Soviet rule. South Africa institutionalizes apartheid.

1950: Start of the Korean War following North Korean invasion of South Korea. Assassination attempt on President Truman by Puerto Rican nationalists. McCarthyism begins. Alger Hiss is convicted in second trial.

1951: 49 nations sign Japanese peace treaty in San Francisco. Libya becomes independent.

1952: British monarch George VI dies and his daughter becomes Queen Elizabeth II. Japan officially regains independence, marking the end of the period of Occupied Japan. Military coup in Egypt ousts King Farouk.

1953: Gen. Dwight D. Eisenhower becomes President of USA. Stalin dies. Dag Hammarskjöld becomes UN Secretary General. Edmund Hillary of New Zealand and Tenzing Norgay of Nepal become the first to reach the summit of Mt. Everest. Egypt becomes a republic. Korean armistice is signed. USSR explodes a hydrogen bomb. Tito becomes President of Yugoslavia. James Watson, Francis Crick, and Rosalind Franklin discover structure of DNA. Ernest Hemingway wins Pulitzer for *The Old Man and the Sea.*

1954: Soviet Union grants sovereignty to East Germany. Dien Bien Phu, French military outpost in Vietnam, falls to Vietminh army. Eight-nation Southeast Asia defence treaty (SEATO) is signed at Manila. Dr Jonas Salk starts inoculating children against polio. Algerian War of Independence against France begins.

1955: Churchill resigns as British PM and Anthony Eden succeeds him. West Germany becomes a sovereign state. Western European Union (WEU) comes into being. Warsaw Pact, East European mutual defence agreement, is signed. Juan Peron ousted in Argentina.

1956: First aerial Hydrogen bomb tested over Namu islet, Bikini Atoll. Egypt takes control of Suez Canal. Hungarian rebellion forces Soviet troops to withdraw from Budapest. Israel attacks Egypt's Sinai peninsula. Hungarian PM Imre Nagy announces Hungary's withdrawal from Warsaw Pact. Soviet troops occupy Budapest. British and French forces invade Port Said on the Suez Canal. Ceasefire forced by US pressure stops British, French and Israeli advance. Morocco gains independence.

1957: Eisenhower Doctrine calls for aid to mid-east countries which resist armed aggression from Communist-controlled nations. Russians launch *Sputnik I*, the first Earth-orbiting satellite.

1958: European Economic Community (Common Market) comes into effect. First US Earth satellite, *Explorer I*, is launched into orbit. Egypt and Syria merge to form United Arab Republic. US President Eisenhower orders US Marines into Lebanon at the request of President Chamoun. New French constitution adopted.

1959: Cuban President Batista resigns and flees the country as Fidel Castro takes over the country. The Dalai Lama escapes Tibet and arrives in India.

1960: American U-2 spy plane, piloted by Francis Gary Powers, is shot down over Russia. USSR sentences Gary Powers to 10 years in prison. Israelis capture Nazi leader Adolf Eichmann in Argentina. Senegal, Ghana, Nigeria, Madagascar, and Zaire (Belgian Congo) gain independence. Cuba starts to confiscate $770 million of US property. John F. Kennedy becomes US President.

1961: USA severs diplomatic relations with Cuba. Maj. Yuri A. Gagarin of USSR becomes the first man in orbit around Earth. An invasion by an estimated 1,200 anti-Castro exiles aided by USA is crushed. Alan B. Shepard Jr. is the first American in space. Berlin Wall is erected between East and West Berlin to stop East Germans from crossing over into West Germany. USSR tests 50-megaton hydrogen bomb.

1962: Nazi leader Adolf Eichmann is executed in Israel. Lt Col. John H. Glenn Jr. becomes the first American to orbit Earth. Algeria gains independence. Cuban missile crisis. Burundi, Jamaica, Western Samoa, Uganda, and Trinidad and Tobago become independent. Gary Powers is freed in exchange for Soviet spy.

1963: France and West Germany sign treaty of cooperation. Pope John XXIII dies and is succeeded by Cardinal Montini who becomes Pope Paul VI. Profumo scandal in UK. Martin Luther King Jr. delivers his 'I have a dream' speech at a civil rights rally attended by 200,000 people in Washington, DC. US President John F. Kennedy assassinated. Kenya becomes independent.

1964: Nelson Mandela is sentenced to life imprisonment in South Africa. President's Commission on the Assassination of President Kennedy issues Warren Report and concludes that Lee Harvey Oswald acted alone.

1965: Malcolm X, US black-nationalist leader, shot dead in New York City.

1966: The People's Republic of China explodes its first hydrogen bomb.

1967: Biafra secedes from Nigeria. Six Day war ends with Israel occupying Sinai peninsula, Golan Heights, Gaza Strip, and east bank of Suez Canal. Dr Christiaan N. Barnard and his team of South African surgeons perform the world's first successful human heart transplant but the patient dies 18 days later.

1968: Tet offensive and My Lai massacre take place in Vietnam War. Martin Luther King Jr., civil rights leader, is killed in Memphis. Sen. Robert F. Kennedy, younger brother of President John F. Kennedy is assassinated. Russian and Warsaw Pact forces invade Czechoslovakia to remove a liberal regime.

1969: Stonewall riot in New York City marks beginning of gay rights movement. *Apollo 11* astronauts—Neil A. Armstrong, Edwin E. Aldrin Jr. and Michael Collins are the first men to walk on Moon. Woodstock Festival ARPAnet, forerunner of Internet, goes online.

1970: Biafra surrenders after a 32-month fight for independence from Nigeria. Rhodesia declares itself a racially segregated republic. US troops invade Cambodia.

1971: UN gives its seat to Communist China and expels Nationalist China (Taiwan).

1972: UK takes over direct rule of Northern Ireland. In USA, police arrests five men who were trying to plant listening devices at the Democratic National Committee headquarters in Washington DC's Watergate complex. This starts the Watergate scandal. Eleven Israeli athletes are killed at the Munich Olympic Games after eight members of an Arab terrorist group invade the Olympic Village.

1973: Vietnam War ends with signing of peace pacts. In USA, President Nixon appears on national TV and accepts responsibility, but not blame, for the Watergate scandal. Greek military junta abolishes monarchy and proclaims a republic. Chile's Marxist President Salvadore Allende is ousted. Yom Kippur War is fought between Israel, Egypt and Syrian forces.

1974: In USA, the House Judiciary Committee adopts three articles of impeachment charging President Nixon with obstruction of justice, failure to uphold laws, and refusal to produce material subpoenaed by the committee. Richard M. Nixon announces he will resign the next day, the first US President to do so.

1975: Pol Pot and Khmer Rouge take over Cambodia. Two assassination attempts take place on US President Gerald Ford.

1976: Israeli airborne commandos attack Uganda's Entebbe Airport and free 103 hostages held by pro-Palestinian hijackers of Air France plane.

1977: Chinese leader Deng Xiaoping is restored to power as 'Gang of Four' is expelled from the Communist Party.

1978: Rhodesia's PM Ian Smith and black leaders agree on a transfer to black majority rule. Former Italian PM Aldo Moro kidnapped by Left wing terrorists and killed. Pope Paul VI dies and is succeeded by new Pope, John Paul I, who also dies after 34 days in office. He is succeeded by Karol Wojtyla of Poland as Pope John Paul II. Egypt's President Anwar Sadat and Israeli PM Menachem Begin sign a peace deal.

1979: Vietnam and Vietnam-backed Cambodian insurgents announce the fall of Phnom Penh, capital of Cambodia and the collapse of the Pol Pot regime. The Shah of Iran leaves the country and revolutionary forces under Muslim leader Ayatollah Ruhollah Khomeini take over the country. Margaret Thatcher becomes new British PM. Nicaraguan President Gen. Anastasio Somoza Debayle resigns and flees to Miami paving the way for Sandinistas to take over the country. Iranian militants seize US embassy in Teheran and take hostages. Soviet Union invades Afghanistan.

1980: Six US embassy aides escape from Iran. US breaks off diplomatic ties with Iran. Ousted Nicaragua ruler. Anastasio Somoza Debayle, assassinated in Asunción, capital of Paraguay. 8-year Iran–Iraq war begins. John Lennon of the Beatles is shot dead in New York City. Smallpox eradicated.

1981: US–Iran agreement frees 52 hostages held in Teheran since 1979. Assassination attempt on Pope John Paul II. AIDS is first identified.

1982: UK defeats Argentina in Falklands war. Israel invades Lebanon in attack on PLO. Princess Grace of Monaco dies of injuries in a car crash.

1983: Benigno S. Aquino Jr., political rival of Philippines President Marcos, is killed in Manila. A South Korean Boeing 747 jetliner bound for Seoul apparently flies into Soviet airspace by mistake and is shot down by a Soviet fighter aircraft, killing all 269 on board. More than 200 US marines are killed in an explosion in Beirut. US and its Caribbean allies invade Grenada.

1984: US and the Vatican exchange diplomats after 116 years. Italy and Vatican agree to end Roman Catholicism as state religion Soviet Union and its allies withdraw from the Summer Olympic Games in Los Angeles.

1985: Mikhail Gorbachev becomes Soviet leader. Two gunmen capture an American airliner with 133 on board,

104 of them Americans. Italian cruise ship *Achille Lauro* hijacked with 80 passengers and crew on board. Egyptian Boeing 737 airliner seized after take-off from Athens. 59 die after Egyptian forces storm the plane on Malta.

1986: Spain and Portugal join European Economic Community. USA freezes Libyan assets in the US. US Space shuttle *Challenger* explodes after launch at Cape Canaveral killing all seven on board. Haiti President Jean-Claude Duvalier flees to France. President Marcos flees the Philippines after ruling for 20 years and is succeeded by Corazon Aquino. Swedish PM Olof Palme is shot dead. Austrian President Kurt Waldheim's secret past as a Nazi army officer is revealed. US military aircraft attack Libyan targets. Desmond Tutu is elected archbishop in South Africa. Major nuclear accident at Soviet Union's Chernobyl power plant.

1987: Iraq apologizes after its missiles killed 37 in attack on US frigate *Stark* in the Persian Gulf. World War II Nazi leader Klaus Barbie sentenced to life imprisonment by French court for war crimes. In USA, Oliver North Jr. tells congressional inquiry that senior officials approved his secret Iran-Contra operations. Admiral John M. Poindexter, former national security adviser, testifies that he authorized use of Iran arms sale profits to aid Contras. Secretary of State George P. Shultz testifies he was deceived repeatedly on Iran-Contra affair. Defence Secretary Caspar W. Weinberger reveals official deception and intrigue. President Reagan accepts responsibility for Iran arms-Contra policy. Severe earthquake strikes Los Angeles.

1988: USA and Canada reach free trade agreement. Robert C. McFarlane, former national security adviser, pleads guilty in Iran-Contra case. US Navy ship shoots down Iranian airliner in Persian Gulf after mistaking it for a military aircraft, killing 290. Explosion on board his official aircraft kills Pakistani

President Mohammad Zia ul-Haq. Pan-Am 747 crashes in Lockerbie, Scotland, killing all 259 on board and 11 on ground.

1989: US planes shoot down two Libyan fighters over international waters in Mediterranean. Emperor Hirohito of Japan dies. Iran's Ayatollah Khomeini declares author Salman Rushdie's book *The Satanic Verses* offensive and issues a fatwa on him. Tanker *Exxon Valdez* discharges 11 million gallons of crude oil into Alaska's Prince William Sound. Tens of thousands of Chinese students take over Beijing's Tiananmen Square in a pro-democracy demonstration. Thousands are killed when the Chinese authorities decide to adopt a hard-line approach towards the demonstrators. US jury convicts Oliver North in Iran-Contra affair. Mikhail S. Gorbachev becomes Soviet President. P.W. Botha quits as South Africa's President. Deng Xiaoping resigns as China's leader. Berlin Wall comes down. Czech Parliament ends Communist domination in the country. Uprising in Romania ousts communist government. President Ceausescu and his wife are executed. US troops invade Panama to capture its leader Gen. Manuel Noriega on drug-related charges. The Dalai Lama wins the Nobel Peace Prize.

1990: Start of the World Wide Web and the Internet. Gen. Manuel Noriega surrenders in Panama. Yugoslav communists end 45-year grip on power. Communists give up power in USSR. South Africa frees Nelson Mandela after more than 27 years in prison. Hubble Space Telescope is launched. Iraqi troops invade Kuwait leading to Persian Gulf War. East and West Germany are reunited. Soviet President Gorbachev assumes emergency powers. Margaret Thatcher resigns as British PM after three terms in office; John Major is new PM. Solidarity Party leader Lech Walesa wins Poland's run-off presidential election. Haiti elects leftist priest Jean Bertrand Aristide as President in its first democratic election.

1991: US and Allies at war with Iraq. Warsaw Pact dissolves military alliance. Ceasefire ends Persian Gulf War. European countries end sanctions on South Africa. Communist government of Albania resigns. Jiang Qing, widow of Mao Zedong, commits suicide. South African Parliament repeals apartheid laws. Warsaw Pact is dissolved. Boris Yeltsin is inaugurated as the first freely elected President of Russian Republic. Lithuania, Estonia, and Latvia become independent. Haitian troops seize President Aristide in an uprising. USA suspends assistance to Haiti. Israel and Soviet Union resume relations after 24 years. USA indicts two Libyans in 1988 bombing of Pan Am Flight 103 over Lockerbie, Scotland. USSR breaks up after President Gorbachev resigns. Its constituent republics form Commonwealth of Independent States (CIS).

1992: Yugoslav Federation breaks up. President Bush of USA and President Yeltsin of Russia formally proclaim an end to 'Cold War'. US lifts trade sanctions against China. US recognizes three former Yugoslav republics. Former Panama leader Gen. Manuel Noriega is convicted in a US court and sentenced to 40 years imprisonment on drug charges. Caspar W. Weinberger indicted in Iran-Contra affair. Last Western hostages freed in Lebanon. UN expels Serbian-dominated Yugoslavia. US forces leave the Philippines after nearly a century of American military presence. Czechoslovak Parliament approves its separation into two nations. In UK, Prince Charles and Princess Diana agree to separate. President Bush pardons former Reagan administration officials involved in Iran-Contra affair.

1993: Czechoslovakia breaks up into Czech Republic and Slovakia. Vaclav Havel is elected Czech President. USA begins airlifting of supplies to besieged Bosnia towns. President of Sri Lanka, Ranasinghe Premadasa, is assassinated. Iraq accepts UN weapons monitoring. Israel and Palestinian authorities reach an accord. President Yeltsin's forces crush a revolt in the Russian Parliament. Europe's Maastricht Treaty takes effect, creating the European Union. South Africa adopts majority rule constitution.

1994: NAFTA comes into effect. Vance-Owen peace plan for Bosnia & Herzegovina is announced. Eugene Ionesco passes away. Tutsi massacre in Rwandan capital Kigali. Nelson Mandela becomes South Africa's first black president after its first fully multiracial elections. Richard Nixon passes away. The Channel Tunnel opens. Ayrton Senna is killed. Jacqueline Kennedy passes away. Erich Honecker passes away. Israel and the Vatican establish full diplomatic ties. Fragments of Comet Shoemaker Levy 9 hit Jupiter. North Yemen occupies South Yemen capital Aden. Israel and Jordan sign the Washington Declaration. Kim Il-Sung passes away. Ferry MS *Estonia* sinks in Baltic Sea. NASA loses Magellan probe over Venus. Burt Lancaster passes away. Angolan government and UNITA rebels sign the Lusaka Protocol in Zambia. Sweden voters accept and Norwegian voters reject EU membership. Red Hat Linux 1.0 is released. Russia sends troops into Chechnya.

Last Ten Years in Review

1995

January: Austria, Finland and Sweden enter the European Union. World Trade Organization is established to replace GATT. A chemical fire in an apartment complex in Manila, Philippines leads to the discovery of a bomb factory. This unravels the plans for al-Qaeda's Project Bojinka, a mass terrorist attack masterminded by Ramzi Yousef, who is arrested one month later. The plan aimed to destroy 11 passenger aircraft over the Pacific Ocean during 21–22 January. Russia comes close to launching a nuclear attack after a Norwegian missile launch for scientific research is detected and interpreted to be an attack on Russia. US President Bill Clinton authorizes a $20 billion loan to Mexico to stabilize its economy. Valeri Poliakov completes 366 days in space while aboard the Mir space station breaking a duration record. Malcolm X's daughter, Qubilah Shabazz, is arrested for conspiring to kill Louis Farrakhan. An earthquake of magnitude 7.2 on Richter scale strikes Japan near Kobe and causes great property damage, killing over 5,000. Gerald Durrell, naturalist, zookeeper, author and television presenter, passes away.

February: Steve Fossett becomes the first person to make a solo flight across the Pacific Ocean in a balloon. UK's oldest investment banking firm, Barings PLC, collapses after a securities broker, Nick Leeson, lost the bank $1.4 billion on unauthorized investments at the Tokyo Stock Exchange. Dr Bernard A. Harris Jr. becomes the first African American astronaut to walk in space.

March: Members of the Aum Supreme Truth cult release sarin gas in Tokyo on five separate subway trains killing 12 and injuring around 5,500. The United Nations peacekeeping mission in Somalia ends. Astronaut Norman Thagard becomes the first American to travel to space on board a Russian launch vehicle. The Schengen treaty comes into force.

April: A bomb attack on the Alfred P. Murrah Federal Building in Oklahoma City kills 168 people. Ginger Rogers, actress, dancer, passes away.

May: In New York City, more than 170 countries decide to extend the Nuclear Non-proliferation Treaty indefinitely and unconditionally. The Dalai Lama proclaims 6-year-old Gedhun Choekyi Nyima as the 11th reincarnation of the Panchen Lama. Jacques Chirac becomes the president of France. The Java programming language is launched to the public. In Russia, an earthquake of magnitude 7.6 on the Richter scale hits Neftegorsk, killing at least 2000.

June: A US Air Force F-16 aircraft is shot down over Bosnia while patrolling the NATO no-fly zone. Its pilot, Captain Scott O'Grady is later rescued. The Bose–Einstein condensate is created for the first time. French president Jacques Chirac announces the resumption of nuclear tests in French Polynesia.

July: Iraq threatens to end all cooperation with UNSCOM and IAEA, if sanctions against the country are not lifted by 31 August. However, later in the month, Iraq admits the existence of an offensive biological weapons programme for the first time, but denies weaponization. In New York City, the NASDAQ stock index closes above the 1,000 mark for the first time. The People's Liberation Army of China fires missiles into the waters north of Taiwan.

August: Iraqi ruler Saddam Hussein reveals new information about the Iraqi biological and nuclear weapons programmes. Iraq also withdraws its last UN declaration of prohibited biological weapons and hands over a large amount of new documents on its WMD programmes. Jerry Garcia, musician and lead guitarist of The Grateful Dead, passes away.

September: The Fourth World Conference on Women opens in Beijing with over 4,750 delegates from 181 countries in attendance.

October: Ten people are found guilty of bombing the World Trade Center in New York City in 1994. US football star O. J. Simpson is found not guilty of double murder for the deaths of former wife Nicole Brown Simpson and her friend Ronald Goldman. The Million Man March is held in Washington DC.

November: A right-wing Israeli gunman, Yigal Amir, assassinates Israeli PM Yitzhak Rabin in Tel Aviv. The Nigerian government executes playwright and environmental activist Ken Saro-Wiwa along with eight others from the Movement for the Survival of the Ogoni People. A budget stand-off between Democrats and Republicans in the United States Congress leads to a closure of national parks and museums while most government offices are run with skeleton staff. The Dow Jones Industrial Average closes above 5,000 (5,023.55) for the first time.

December: Scuba divers working under the direction of UNSCOM find over 200 prohibited Russian-made missile instruments and components in the Tigris river near Baghdad. The last new *Calvin and Hobbes* cartoon strip is published.

1996

January: Yasser Arafat is elected president of the Palestinian Authority. Andreas Papandreou, PM of Greece, resigns due to health problems and a new government is formed under Costas Simitis. Polish Premier Jozef Oleksy resigns amid charges he spied for Moscow. Jorge Sampaio is elected president of Portugal. US First Lady Hillary Rodham Clinton testifies before a grand jury in the Whitewater scandal. Colonel Ibrahim Bare Mainassara deposes the first democratically elected president of Niger, Mahamane Ousmane, in a military coup. President Jacques Chirac of France announces a 'definitive end' to French nuclear testing. An explosives-filled truck explodes at the Central Bank in Colombo, Sri Lanka, killing at least 86 and injuring 1,400. François Mitterrand, French politician and former President of France, passes away. Jerry Siegel, cartoonist and the creator of *Superman*, passes away.

February: Recently defected Iraqi weapons programme leader and Saddam Hussein's son-in-law, Hussein Kamel, is murdered on his return to Iraq.

March: Iraqi authorities cause a delay of 17 hours in providing UNSCOM inspection teams access to five sites designated for inspection. John Howard becomes PM of Australia. The Dunblane Massacre occurs at a primary school in the town of Dunblane, Scotland, UK, when Thomas Hamilton, a man in his forties, walks into the school and fires 105 rounds killing 16 children between 4–6 years of age and one adult teacher. US President Bill Clinton commits $100 million to an anti-terrorism agreement with Israel. The British government announces that bovine spongiform encephalopathy (BSE) or Mad Cow Disease is likely to have been transmitted to humans. The Republic of China (Taiwan) holds its first direct elections for president, electing Lee Teng-hui as president. The International Monetary Fund (IMF) approves a $10.2 billion loan to Russia for economic reform. Krzysztof Kieslowski, film director, passes away. George Burns, actor and singer, passes away.

April: In USA, suspected 'Unabomber' Theodore Kaczynski is arrested. Over 100 Lebanese civilians are killed after Israel shells the UN compound in Qana.

May: In USA, ValuJet's Douglas DC-9 Flight 592 on a Miami–Atlanta trip crashes in the Florida Everglades region killing all on board. Nearly 600 killed in severe thunderstorms and tornado in Bangladesh. Russian President Boris Yeltsin meets with Chechnya rebels for the first time and negotiates a ceasefire in the ongoing First Chechnya War.

June: UNSCOM supervises the destruction of Al-Hakam, Iraq's main biological warfare agents production facility. USA fails to build support for military action against Iraq in the UN Security Council even as Iraq continues to refuse access to a number of sites. A bomb explosion hits Manchester City Centre in UK. 19 US servicemen are killed in a bombing attack at Khobar Towers in Saudi Arabia. Ella Fitzgerald, jazz singer, passes away. Andreas Papandreou, Greek politician and former PM, passes away.

July: Dolly the sheep, the first mammal to be successfully cloned from an adult cell, is born. Iraqi officials block UN Inspector Ritter's attempt to conduct surprise inspections on the Republican Guard facility. Martina Hingis becomes the youngest person in history (age 15 years and 282 days) to win at Wimbledon when she takes the Ladies Doubles event. A Paris-bound Boeing 747 operating as TWA flight 800 explodes off the coast of Long Island killing all 230 on board. The 1996 Summer Olympics start in Atlanta, Georgia, USA.

August: NASA announces that the ALH 84001 meteorite, believed to have originated from Mars, contains evidence of primitive life forms. In UK, Prince Charles and Princess Diana are formally divorced at the High Court in London. Iraqi forces launch an offensive into the northern no-fly zone and capture Arbil.

September: Colombian Revolutionary Armed Forces (FARC) attack a military base in Guaviare, Colombia starting three weeks of guerrilla warfare that claims at least 130 lives. The Panhellenic Socialist Movement under the leadership of Costas Simitis wins the Greek legislative election. In Afghanistan, the Taliban capture capital city Kabul.

October: Opening statements in the O.J. Simpson trial begin in the USA.

November: Bill Clinton defeats Bob Dole in the US presidential election. UNSCOM inspectors discover buried prohibited missile parts. Iraq refuses to allow UNSCOM teams to remove remnants of missile engines for analysis outside of the country. NASA launches the Mars Global Surveyor. Mother Teresa gets honorary US citizenship.

December: In Afghanistan, Taliban forces retake the strategic Bagram air base. The Guatemalan government and leaders of Guatemalan National Revolutionary Union sign a peace accord that ends a 36-year civil war. Saddam Hussein's son Uday Hussein is seriously injured in an assassination attempt. Carl Sagan, US astronomer, passes away.

1997

January: Yasser Arafat returns to Hebron after more than 30 years and joins celebrations over the handover of the last Israeli-controlled West Bank city. Bill Clinton starts his second term as President of the United States. Newt Gingrich becomes the first leader of the United States House of Representatives to be internally disciplined for ethical misconduct. Madeleine Albright becomes the first female Secretary of State after confirmation by the US Senate. Clyde Tombaugh, astronomer and discoverer of Pluto, passes away.

February: O. J. Simpson is found to have civil liabilities for the deaths of Nicole Brown Simpson and Ron Goldman. The so-called 'Big Three' banks in Switzerland announce the creation of a $71 million fund to aid Holocaust survivors and their families. Morgan Stanley and Dean Witter investment banks announce a $10 billion merger. Astronauts from the space shuttle Discovery carry out repair work on the Hubble Space Telescope. The last of the People's Republic of China's major revolutionary leaders, Deng Xiaoping, passes away.

March: US President Bill Clinton bans federal funding for any research on human cloning. Picasso's work *Tete de Femme* is stolen from a London gallery but is recovered a week later. An explosion at a nuclear waste reprocessing plant in Japan exposes 35 workers to low-level radioactive contamination. It is one of the worst nuclear accidents in the country. A Russian An-24 charter plane flying to Turkey crashes after its tail section breaks off, killing all 50 on board. 14-year-and-10-month-old Tara Lipinski becomes the youngest champion of the women's world figure skating competition. 39 found dead in the Heaven's Gate cult suicide.

April: A 126-day hostage crisis at the residence of the Japanese ambassador in Lima, Peru, ends after government commandos storm and capture the building and rescue 71 hostages. Allen Ginsberg, US poet, passes away.

May: In UK, Labour Party victory in the general election ends 18 years of Conservative rule. Labour Party leader Tony Blair appointed PM of the United Kingdom. An earthquake near Ardekul in north-eastern Iran kills at least 2,400. IBM's chess computer Deep Blue defeats Garry Kasparov.

June: Timothy McVeigh is sentenced to death for his role in the 1995 terrorist bombing of the Alfred P. Murrah Federal Building in Oklahoma City, Oklahoma. In Cambodia, Khmer Rouge leader Pol Pot orders the killing of his defence chief Son Sen and 11 of Sen's family members.

July: UK hands over sovereignty of Hong Kong to the People's Republic of China. NASA's Pathfinder space probe lands on the surface of Mars. NATO invites the Czech Republic, Hungary and Poland to join the organization in 1999. In Miami, Florida, USA, serial killer Andrew Phillip Cunanan kills fashion designer Gianni Versace outside his home. The F.W. Woolworth Company closes after more than 100 years in business.

August: Aviation giants Boeing and McDonnell Douglas complete their merger. Microsoft buys a $150 million share of Apple Computer. The Independent International Commission on Decommissioning is set up in Northern Ireland, as part of the peace process. Diana, Princess of Wales, is severely injured in a car crash in Paris on 31 August and dies the next day.

September: Scotland votes to create its own Parliament after nearly 300 years of union with England. Agnes Gonxha Bojaxhiu, better known as Mother Teresa, passes away.

October: The Thrust SSC team from the United Kingdom sets the first supersonic land speed record. Iraq threatens to shoot down U-2 surveillance planes being used by UNSCOM inspectors.

November: Telecom giants WorldCom and MCI announce a US $37 billion merger to form MCI-WorldCom. Mary McAleese is elected President of Ireland. After nearly 18 years of imprisonment, the People's Republic of China releases pro-democracy dissident Wei Jingsheng for medical reasons. 62 people are killed in an attack outside the Temple of Hatshepsut in Luxor, Egypt.

December: Representatives from 121 countries sign a treaty prohibiting manufacture and deployment of anti-personnel landmines in Ottawa, Canada. Notable absentees are USA, People's Republic of China, and Russia. Hong Kong starts killing all the chickens within its territory to stop the spread of a potentially lethal influenza strain. 400 people are killed in four villages in an insurgency-related attack in Algeria.

1998

January: Russia begins to circulate a new Ruble to curb inflation and promote confidence. The Lunar Prospector spacecraft is launched into orbit around the Moon. It finds evidence of frozen water on the moon's surface. Ramzi Yousef is sentenced to life in prison for planning the World Trade Center bombing. European nations agree to forbid human cloning. Paula Jones accuses President Bill Clinton of sexual harassment. Bill Clinton denies, on American television, that he had 'sexual relations' with former White House intern Monica Lewinsky. US First Lady Hillary Rodham Clinton appears on television calling the attacks against her husband part of a right-wing conspiracy. In USA, suspected 'Unabomber' Theodore Kaczynski pleads guilty and accepts a sentence of life without the possibility of parole. Compaq buys Digital Equipment Corporation. Gunmen hold around 400 children and teachers hostage for several hours at an elementary school in Manila, Philippines. Helen Wills Moody, first women's champion at Wimbledon, passes away.

February: A US military pilot causes the death of 20 skiers in Italy riding on a lift suspended by a cable when his low-flying aircraft snaps the cable. An earthquake measuring 6.1 on the Richter scale hits north-east Afghanistan killing more than 5,000. Crown Prince Abdullah becomes the ruler of Jordan by decree of his father, King Hussein. Iraqi President Saddam Hussein negotiates a deal with UN Secretary General Kofi Annan, allowing the return of weapons inspectors to Baghdad and thus preventing US and British military action. Osama bin Laden publishes fatwa declaring jihad against all 'Jews and Crusaders'.

March: Data from the Galileo probe indicate that Jupiter's moon Europa has a liquid ocean under a thick crust of ice. PM Poul Nyrup Rasmussen returns to power following parliamentary elections in Denmark. An earthquake measuring 6.9 on the Richter scale hits south-eastern Iran. *Titanic* wins 11 Oscars at the Academy

Awards ceremony. Four students and one teacher are killed and 10 injured when two young boys aged 11 and 13 years fire upon students at Westside Middle School in Jonesboro, Arkansas. In USA, the government approves Viagra for use as a treatment for male impotence. Benjamin Spock, pediatrician, writer, Olympian, passes away.

April: UNSCOM reports to the UN Security Council that Iraq's declaration on its biological weapons program is incomplete and inadequate. On Good Friday, the Belfast Agreement is signed between the Irish and British governments and most Northern Ireland political parties. In Japan, the Akashi-Kaikyo Bridge linking Shikoku with Honshu opens to traffic, becoming the largest suspension bridge in the world. Citicorp and Travelers Group announce plans to merge creating the largest financial-services conglomerate in the world, Citigroup. The Cambodian dictator, Pol Pot, passes away.

May: Apple Computer unveils the iMac. Mercedes-Benz buys Chrysler for US $40 billion and forms DaimlerChrysler. The US Department of Justice and 20 US states file an antitrust case against Microsoft. Indonesian President Suharto resigns after 32 years as President and 7th consecutive re-elections. Vice-President B. J. Habibie becomes new President. An earthquake of magnitude 6.6 on the Richter scale hits northern Afghanistan killing up to 5,000. Frank Sinatra, singer, actor, passes away.

June: An ICE high-speed train derails at Eschede, Germany, causing 101 deaths.

July: In St Petersburg, Nicholas II of Russia and his family are buried in St Catherine Chapel, 80 years after being killed by the Bolsheviks. A tsunami triggered by an undersea earthquake destroys 10 villages in Papua New Guinea killing an estimated 1,500, leaving 2,000 more unaccounted for and thousands more homeless. Former White House intern, Monica Lewinsky, receives transactional immunity in exchange for her grand jury testimony concerning her relationship with US President Bill Clinton.

August: Iraq officially suspends all cooperation with UNSCOM teams. Bombing of the US embassies in Dar es Salaam, Tanzania, and Nairobi, Kenya, kills 224 people and injures over 4,500. In retaliation, the United States military launches cruise missile attacks against alleged al-Qaeda camps in Afghanistan and a suspected chemical plant in Sudan. US President Bill Clinton admits in taped testimony that he had an 'improper physical relationship' with White House intern Monica Lewinsky. On the same day he admits before the nation that he 'misled people' about his relationship.

September: A McDonnell Douglas MD-11 airliner operating as Swissair flight 111 crashes near Peggy's Cove, Nova Scotia, while flying from New York City to Geneva. All 229 people on board are killed. A UN court finds Jean-Paul Akayesu, a former mayor of a small Rwandan town, guilty of nine counts of genocide. The US Congress passes the 'Iraq Liberation Act' that states the US government's intention to remove Saddam Hussein from power in Iraq and replace the government with a democratic institution. Akira Kurosawa, Japanese film director, passes away. Florence 'Flo-Jo' Griffith-Joyner, track and field sprinter, passes away.

October: In South Africa, the Truth and Reconciliation Commission presents its report, condemning both sides for committing atrocities. 77-year old John Glenn, the first American to orbit Earth, becomes the oldest person to go into space when he is launched on board space shuttle Discovery.

November: The European Court of Human Rights is instituted. US President Clinton orders air strikes on Iraq but calls it off at the last minute when

Iraq promises unconditional support to UNSCOM. UNSCOM inspectors subsequently return to Iraq. The US House of Representatives' Judiciary Committee begins impeachment hearings against US President Bill Clinton. America Online (AOL) announces it will acquire Netscape Communications in a stock-for-stock transaction. Tony Blair becomes the first UK PM to address the Republic of Ireland's Parliament. Deutsche Bank announces a US $10 billion deal to buy Bankers Trust, thus creating one of the largest financial institutions in the world.

December: US President Clinton orders American and British air strikes on Iraq. UNSCOM withdraws all weapons inspectors from Iraq. Iraq announces its intention to fire upon US and British warplanes that patrol the northern and southern no-fly zones. Exxon announces a US $73.7 billion deal to buy Mobil, thus creating Exxon-Mobil. Venezuelan military leader and politician Hugo Chávez Frías is elected President of Venezuela. Khmer Rouge leaders apologize for the genocide in Cambodia that claimed over one million lives in the 1970s.

1999

January: The EU common currency, the Euro, is introduced. An earthquake measuring 6.0 on the Richter scale hits western Colombia killing at least 1,000.

February: The United States Senate acquits US President Bill Clinton in his impeachment trial. Assassination attempt against President Islam Karimov of Uzbekistan. Kurdish rebels take over embassies across Europe and hold hostages after Turkey arrests Kurdish leader Abdullah Ocalan. Colin Prescot and Andy Elson set a new endurance record after being in a hot air balloon for 233 hours and 55 minutes. Olusegun Obasanjo becomes Nigeria's first elected President since 1983. Former boxing champion Mike Tyson is

sentenced to one year in prison for an August 1998 assault on two people following a car accident. King Hussein of Jordan passes away.

March: In its first-ever attack on a sovereign country, NATO launches air strikes on Federal Republic of Yugoslavia. A fire in the Mont Blanc Tunnel in Europe kills 39 people and closes the tunnel for nearly three years. Hungary, Poland and the Czech Republic join NATO. Bertrand Piccard and Brian Jones become the first to circumnavigate the Earth in a hot air balloon. Paraguay's Vice President Luis Maria Argana assassinated. The Angolan embassy in Lusaka, Zambia, is destroyed in an explosion. Hutu rebels kill eight tourists in Uganda. The Convention on the Prohibition of Anti-Personnel Mines comes into force. A jury in Michigan, USA, finds Dr Jack Kevorkian guilty of second-degree murder for administering a lethal injection to a terminally ill man. In New York City, the Dow Jones Industrial Average closes above the 10,000 mark for the first time. Stanley Kubrick, American film director and writer, passes away. Joe DiMaggio, American baseball player, passes away. American violinist Yehudi Menuhin passes away,

April: Serbian forces close Kosovo's main border crossings to prevent ethnic Albanians from leaving. Columbine High School massacre takes place as two teenagers named Eric Harris and Dylan Klebold open fire on their teachers and fellow students in Littleton, Colorado, killing 12 students and one teacher, after which they take their own lives. Cambodia joins the Association of South-east Asian Nations (ASEAN) bringing the total members to 10. Nunavut, an Inuit homeland, part of the Northwest Territories becomes Canada's third territory. Two Libyans suspected of causing the crash of Pan Am flight 103 in 1988 are handed over for trial in the Netherlands. Lord

Killanin, former chairman of the IOC, passes away.

May: Elections are held in Scotland and Wales for the new Scottish Parliament and National Assembly for Wales. In the Federal Republic of Yugoslavia, three Chinese embassy workers are killed and 20 wounded when a NATO aircraft bombs the Chinese embassy in Belgrade in an apparent mistake. David Steel becomes the first presiding officer /Speaker of the modern Scottish Parliament. Carlo Azeglio Ciampi is elected President of Italy. Ehud Barak is elected PM of Israel. The International Criminal Tribunal for the Former Yugoslavia in The Hague, Netherlands, indicts Slobodan Milosevic and four others for war crimes and crimes against humanity committed in Kosovo. Leonardo da Vinci's masterpiece *The Last Supper* is put back on display in Milan, Italy, after 22 years of restoration work. English actor Dirk Bogarde passes away.

June: Federal Republic of Yugoslavia and NATO sign a peace treaty. The Kosovo War nears an end when NATO suspends its air strikes after Slobodan Milosevic agrees to withdraw Serbian forces from Kosovo. Operation Joint Guardian begins as NATO-led UN peacekeeping force KFor enter Kosovo. The government of Colombia announces it will include the estimated value of the country's illegal drug crops, over half a billion US dollars, in its GNP.

July: A plane piloted by John F. Kennedy Jr. crashes off the coast of Martha's Vineyard. His wife Carolyn Bessette Kennedy and her sister Lauren Bessette were on board and all three are killed. NASA intentionally crashes the Lunar Prospector spacecraft into the moon, thus ending its mission to detect frozen water on the moon's surface. King Hassan of Morocco passes away.

August: Russian President Boris Yeltsin removes his PM, Sergei Stepashin, and his entire cabinet. An earthquake of magnitude 7.4 on the Richter scale hits north-western Turkey, killing more than 17,000 and injuring 44,000. In Belgrade, tens of thousands of Serbians rally to demand the resignation of Yugoslav President Slobodan Milosevic.

September: Former US Senator John Danforth is appointed the head of an independent investigation of the 1993 fire at the Branch Davidian compound in Waco, Texas.

October: A military coup led by Pakistani Army Chief General Pervez Musharraf ousts the government of Prime Minister Nawaz Sharif and takes control of Pakistan. The US Senate rejects ratification of the Comprehensive Test Ban Treaty (CTBT). Gunmen open fire in the Armenian Parliament killing PM Vazgan Sarkisian, Parliament Chairman Karen Demirchian and six other members. EgyptAir Flight 990 on a New York City to Cairo flight crashes off the coast of Massachusetts, killing all 217 on board. The world human population crosses six billion. Tanzanian leader Julius Nyerere passes away.

November: Australians vote to keep the British Queen as their head of state. In Seattle, Washington, the first major demonstration of the anti-globalization movement forces the cancellation of opening ceremonies of a World Trade Organization meeting.

December: UK devolves political power in Northern Ireland to the Northern Ireland Executive. Tori Murden becomes the first woman to cross the Atlantic Ocean by rowboat alone when she reaches Guadeloupe from the Canary Islands. President Lt. General Omar Hasan Ahmad al-Bashir of Sudan dismisses the National Assembly during an internal power struggle between him and Speaker of the Parliament, Hasan al-Turabi. Algerian Ahmed Ressam is arrested while crossing the United States–Canada border when United States Customs finds explosives in the trunk of his vehicle. He is later convicted in a plot to bomb Los Angeles International Airport on New Year's Eve. The United Nations Monitoring, Verification and Inspection Commission (UNMOVIC) is created to replace UNSCOM. Boris Yeltsin resigns as President of Russia. Vladimir Putin succeeds him.

2000

January: America Online (AOL) announces an agreement to buy Time Warner for $162 billion making it the largest-ever corporate merger. A UN tribunal sentences five Bosnian Croats up to 25 years for the 1993 killing of over 100 Muslims in a Bosnian village.

February: French movie director Roger Vadim passes away. Charles M. Schulz, creator of the *Peanuts* comic strip, passes away.

March: The Constitution of Finland is rewritten. Hans Blix becomes executive chairman of UNMOVIC. Chen Shui-bian is elected President of the Republic of China (Taiwan). Presidential elections are held in Russia and Vladimir Putin is elected President.

April: Japanese PM Keizo Obuchi suffers a stroke and slips into a coma. Yoshiro Mori replaces Obuchi as PM of Japan. Microsoft is ruled to have violated US anti-trust laws.

May: The Tate Modern Art gallery opens in London. Portions of Lebanese land are liberated after 22 years of Israeli occupation. Barbara Cartland, romance novel author, passes away. British actor Sir John Gielgud passes away. Former Japanese PM Keizo Obuchi passes away.

June: Hafez al-Assad, President of Syria, passes away.

July: A Concorde supersonic passenger jet crashes soon after take-off from Paris killing all 109 aboard and five on the ground. Russian submarine Kursk sinks in the Barents Sea with the loss of all lives on board. US actor Walter Matthau passes away.

August: British actor Sir Alec Guinness passes away.

September: The 2000 Summer Olympics start in Sydney, Australia. The United Nations Millennium Summit begins in New York City. Swedish-owned arms manufacturer, Bofors, is sold to American arms manufacturer United Defense. Ariel Sharon leads several hundred armed Israelis in a visit to the Temple Mount, provoking Palestinian civil disorder that ultimately develops into the Al-Aqsa Intifada. Pierre Trudeau, former PM of Canada, passes away.

October: In Aden, Yemen, the US destroyer USS *Cole* is severely damaged in a suicide attack launched by a small boat laden with explosives. 250 million gallons of coal sludge spill in Martin County, Kentucky, USA.

November: Iraq rejects new UN Security Council weapons inspection proposals. Republican George W. Bush defeats Democrat Vice-President Al Gore in the US presidential election, but the final result is delayed for over a month because of disputed votes in Florida. Hillary Rodham Clinton is elected to the United States Senate. She is the first First Lady of the United States to win a public office. Alberto Fujimori is removed from office as President of Peru. Jean Chrétien is re-elected as the Canadian PM. Netscape Navigator version 6.0 is launched. Bill Clinton becomes the first serving US President to visit Vietnam.

December: A series of bombs explode in various places in Metro Manila, Philippines, within a span of a few hours, killing 22 and injuring nearly a hundred more. In Mexico, Vicente Fox becomes the new President.

2001

January: A major earthquake measuring 7.6 on the Richter scale hits El Salvador. George W. Bush succeeds Bill Clinton as President of the United States. Thousands of student protesters in Indonesia storm Parliament and demand that President Abdurrahman Wahid resign due to alleged involvement in corruption scandals. In the Netherlands, a Scottish court convicts a Libyan agent but acquits another for their part in the bombing of Pan Am Flight 103 that crashed at Lockerbie, Scotland, in 1988. William Hewlett, co-founder of Hewlett-Packard, passes away. Laurent-Desire Kabila, President of the Democratic Republic of the Congo is assassinated.

February: British and US forces carry out bombing raids attempting to disable Iraq's air defence network. Hollywood actors Tom Cruise and Nicole Kidman announce that they have separated. Likud Party leader Ariel Sharon wins election as prime minister of Israel. American submarine USS *Greeneville* accidentally strikes and sinks Japanese fishing vessel *Ehime-Maru*. NEAR Shoemaker spacecraft touches down on asteroid 433 Eros, becoming the first spacecraft to land on an asteroid. US and UK warplanes bomb Baghdad suburb. US motor racing driver Dale Earnhardt is killed in a crash during the Daytona 500 race. In USA, FBI agent Robert Hanssen is arrested and charged with spying for Russia for 15 years. Foot and mouth disease crisis begins in UK. Landmark Treaty of Nice signed. Cricket legend Sir Donald Bradman passes away.

March: Apple Computer's Mac OS X version 10.0 is released. Author Robert Ludlum passes away. William Hanna, co-founder (with Joseph Barbera) of famous Hanna-Barbera animation studio passes away.

April: An American EP-3E spy plane collides with a Chinese F-8 fighter jet and is forced to make an emergency landing in Hainan, China. Former President of the Federal Republic of Yugoslavia, Slobodan Milosevic, surrenders to police special forces. In the Netherlands, the Act on the Opening up of Marriage allowing same-sex couples to marry legally comes into effect for the first time in the world.

May: The Japanese cities of Urawa, Omiya and Yono merge to form the city of Saitama. Douglas Adams, author of *Hitchhiker's Guide to the Galaxy*, passes away. Government officials in the People's Republic of China put Zhonghua Sun to death because she refused to be sterilized, in violation of the country's one-child policy. Large trans-Neptunian object '28978 Ixion' found during the Deep Ecliptic Survey. 32-year old Erik Weihenmayer, from Boulder, Colorado, USA, becomes the first blind person to reach the summit of Mount Everest.

June: King Birendra, Queen Aishwarya and other members of the Nepalese royal family are killed when Crown Prince Dipendra goes on a drunken shooting spree. The prince then shoots himself. Although the wounded prince is proclaimed the new king, he succumbs to his injuries and King Birendra's brother, Prince Gyanendra, is crowned the new king. The cartoonist who was the creator of *Dennis the Menace*, Hank Ketcham, passes away. Control of the United States Senate switches from the Republican Party to the Democratic Party after Senator Jim Jeffords leaves the Republican Party. Tony Blair's Labour Party is elected for a second term in UK general election. In USA, Timothy McVeigh is executed for the 1995 Oklahoma City bombing. 23 people are killed and 11 more wounded when an American missile hits a soccer field in northern Iraq. General Pervez Musharraf takes over as President of Pakistan. Actor and film director Jack Lemmon passes away. Actor Anthony Quinn passes away.

July: The world's first self-contained artificial heart implanted in a patient, Robert Tools. British politician and novelist Jeffrey Archer is sentenced to four years in prison for perjury and perverting the course of justice.

August: US President George W. Bush announces his support for federal funding of limited research on embryonic stem cells. Astronomer Fred Hoyle passes away. Country musician Chet Atkins passes away.

September: Peru's Attorney General files homicide charges against ex-President Alberto Fujimori. The United States Justice Department announces that it is no longer seeking to break-up Microsoft and will instead seek a lesser anti-trust penalty. In Afghanistan, Ahmed Shah Massoud, leader of the Northern Alliance, is assassinated. Around 3,000 killed in the 11 September 2001(9/11) attack on the World Trade Center in New York City, The Pentagon in Arlington, Virginia, and rural Pennsylvania. Christiaan Barnard, South African heart surgeon who was the first to perform a human-to-human heart transplant, passes away.

October: First case of anthrax attack in the USA is reported. US attack on Afghanistan begins. US President George W. Bush presents a list of 22 most wanted terrorists. NASA's Galileo spacecraft passes within 112 miles of Jupiter's moon Io.

November: At the Doha Round of World Trade Organization conference, the Doha Declaration relaxes the international intellectual property laws. The Police Service of Northern Ireland is established. The supersonic commercial aircraft Concorde resumes flying after a 15-month break. Microsoft releases the X-Box console gaming system to the public. In New York City, an Airbus A300 carrying American Airlines Flight 587 crashes minutes after takeoff from John F. Kennedy International Airport, killing all 260 on board. Taliban forces abandon Kabul, the capital of Afghanistan, ahead of advancing Northern Alliance troops who then capture the city. In the first such instance since World War II, US President George W. Bush signs an executive order allowing military tribunals against any foreigners suspected of having connections to terrorist acts or planned acts on the United States. The first Harry Potter film, *Harry Potter and the Sorcerer's Stone*, is released. Nintendo releases the *Gamecube* console gaming system to the public. Former Beatle George Harrison passes away.

December: Enron files for Chapter 11 bankruptcy protection. Sultan of Selangor and 11th Yang di-Pertuan Agong of Malaysia passes away. The People's Republic of China gains permanent normal trade status with the United States.

2002

January: Euro banknotes and coins become legal tender in 12 member states of the European Union. Enron hearings begin. Kenneth Lay, CEO of the bankrupt Enron Corporation, resigns. Terrorist suspect John Walker Lindh's hearing begins.

February: Prince Willem-Alexander of the Netherlands, heir to the Dutch throne, marries Máxima Zorreguieta Cerruti in Amsterdam. Academy-Award-winning animator Chuck Jones dies.

March: Elizabeth Bowes-Lyon, the British Queen Mother, passes away. Film director Billy Wilder passes away. Actor Dudley Moore passes away. President Robert Mugabe wins the Zimbabwe elections with 54% of the vote to Morgan Tsvangirai's 40% on a turnout of 55.9%. Israeli ground troops invade the West Bank and Gaza Strip while dozens of tanks occupy Ramallah. In Rome, millions of trade union members protest against labour legislations filed by PM Silvio Berlusconi and against the assassination of Marco Biagi, an advisor to the labour minister.

April: Alexander Lebed, former Russian general who ran for the presidency against Boris Yeltsin, passes away. Ruth Handler, creator of the Barbie Doll, passes away. Ten nations deposit their ratifications for the International Criminal Court at a UN ceremony, bringing the total to 66. A minimum of 60 was needed to bring the statute into force. Coup d'etat takes place in Venezuela. President Hugo Chávez is taken to military barracks. Military announces a transitional government. Hugo Chávez returns to power in Venezuela barely days after the coup.

May: Jacques Chirac wins the French presidential elections with 82.21% of the vote to 17.79% for Jean-Marie Le Pen. Chirac appoints Jean-Pierre Raffarin as his new prime minister, replacing Lionel Jospin. In the Netherlands, controversial right-wing politician Pim Fortuyn is shot dead nine days before the general election for the Lower House of Parliament. The CDA (Christen Democratisch Appèl) led by Jan Peter Balkenende emerges as the single largest party in the elections with 43 seats. East Timor becomes an independent state. Stephen Jay Gould passes away. An article in a science journal reports that a new naturally occurring amino acid has been found in a certain type of archaic bacteria. Scientists are calling this new amino acid Pyrrolysine. The media reports that the NASA space probe Mars Odyssey has found signs of huge ice deposits on the planet Mars. A wordless ceremony takes place at the World Trade Center site to mark the end of the recovery effort. The European Union ratifies the Kyoto Protocol treaty. Japan states its intention to do so shortly.

June: Lennox Lewis knocks out Mike Tyson in an IBF and WBC championship boxing match in Memphis. Accountants Arthur Andersen convicted of obstructing justice by shredding documents related to the Enron inquiry. The World Health Organization declares Europe polio-free. A major earthquake hits Iran with its epicentre at Bou'in Zahra and having a magnitude of at least 6.0 on the Richter scale.

July: Organization of African Unity disbanded and African Union created. Assassination attempt on French President Jacques Chirac during Bastille Day celebrations. John Walker Lindh, the American who was found fighting for the Taliban in Afghanistan, pleads guilty to two charges. In the Netherlands, a new Cabinet is sworn in with Jan Peter Balkenende replacing Wim Kok as prime minister. An Israeli F-16 jet drops a bomb into a densely populated residential area of Gaza City killing 15 people including Salah Shehade, the leader of Hamas's military wing. The attack comes a few hours after the spiritual leader of Hamas, Ahmed Yassin, offered to stop all suicide attacks in exchange for full Israeli withdrawal from the West Bank and Gaza Strip. WorldCom files for bankruptcy protection. First near-earth object to be given a positive rating on the Palermo Technical Impact Hazard Scale for potential Earth collision is 2002 NT7 with a potential impact on 1 February 2019. Cyclist Lance Armstrong wins his fourth consecutive Tour de France. A series of bomb blasts occurs in the Christian districts of the city of Ambon in Indonesia. Nine American miners are rescued from a mine in Pennsylvania. The Homeland Security Bill is passed by the US House of Representatives. The Foreign Relations Committee of the United States Senate starts hearings on the proposed invasion of Iraq.

August: Explosions take place near the Parliament building in Bogota as Colombia's President Álvaro Uribe is being sworn in. At least 10 people are killed. WorldCom announces it has discovered $3.3 billion in false accounting in addition to the $3.8 billion found earlier. Colombian President Álvaro Uribe declares state of emergency. Massive floods occur on the Danube and other rivers in Europe. Germany, Russia, Austria and the Czech Republic are among the worst hit. The death toll crosses 100. The damage is estimated at billions of dollars. Russian President Vladimir Putin announces that Belarus will be fully integrated into Russia and each of Belarus's six provinces will become a separate republic within the Russian Federation. US Airways declares bankruptcy.

September: President Hamid Karzai of Afghanistan survives an assassination attempt in Kandahar. Ramzi Binalshibh, a key al-Qaeda member who is believed to have taken part in the planning of the 11 September 2001 attack is held in Pakistan. Switzerland becomes a full member of the UN. Hundreds of thousands join marches in London, UK and Rome, Italy to protest US plan to invade Iraq. Thousands of people march in Denver, Colorado to protest the US plan to invade Iraq. East Timor becomes the 191st member of the United Nations. Colin Powell meets with the UN Security Council for stronger resolutions against Iraq. Iraq tells the UN it will allow weapons inspectors immediately and unconditionally. 200 US marines enter Côte d'Ivoire to rescue foreigners in the country after rebel soldiers attempt to overthrow the government. Belgium becomes the second European country to legalize euthanasia. Nazi collaborator Maurice Papon is released from jail due to health reasons. The governor of the Philippine state of Palawan sends Philippine soldiers to take possession of the uninhabited oil-rich Spratly Islands. Parliamentary elections take place in Germany. Gerhard Schröder defeats Edmund Stoiber to remain the chancellor. Israel destroys buildings in Yasser Arafat's Ramallah headquarters after a suicide bomber killed five and wounded more than 60 on a Tel Aviv bus. The Bush administration pressures Congress to pass a resolution giving President Bush authority to use all means, including force, to remove Saddam Hussein and disarm Iraq. After three days of negotiations in Thailand, the Tamil Tigers agree to drop their demand for independence from Sri Lanka and accept autonomy in the north and northwest of the country. Archaeologists use a remote-controlled robot to access a sealed chamber within the Great Pyramid of Giza.

October: Suspected Chechen guerrillas take hundreds of hostages when they seize a theatre in Moscow. They demand the withdrawal of Russian troops from Chechnya. Later, special forces of the Russian army attack the Chechen separatists. 50 of the 53 separatists and over 100 of the 800 hostages are killed. A bomb explodes outside a nightclub on the Indonesian island of Bali killing around 200 people, most of them foreign holidaymakers. Around 200 more are injured. Hundreds of Israeli soldiers backed by tanks and other military vehicles take control of the Palestinian city of Jenin in response to a suicide bombing that killed 14 people. A French oil tanker, *Limburg*, explodes off the coast of Yemen. Pope John Paul II canonizes Josemaria Escriva, founder of Opus Dei. The discovery of a planetoid named Quaoar circling the Sun is announced. The European Commission of the European Union announces that 10 countries (Cyprus, the Czech Republic, Estonia, Hungary, Latvia, Lithuania, Malta, Poland, Slovakia, and Slovenia) have met its criteria for entry, paving the way for an expansion of the EU from 15 member states to 25. The International Court of Justice grants sovereignty over the Bakassi peninsula to Cameroon. The US Senate votes to give war powers to President George W. Bush. Former US President Jimmy Carter is awarded the Nobel Peace Prize. Leftist Luis Inacio 'Lula' da Silva wins Brazil's presidential election. A bomb explodes in suburban Manila, destroying a bus and killing at least three people, while 23 others are wounded. Irish actor Richard Harris passes away.

Kenyan President Daniel Arap Moi dissolves the country's Parliament to officially start the campaign for general elections and ending his tenure as one of Africa's longest-ruling leaders. Canadian author Yann Martel wins the Booker Prize for *Life of Pi*. The Irish referendum on the Treaty of Nice approves Ireland's acceptance of the treaty. Chess champion Vladimir Kramnik and the computer program Deep Fritz draw the Brains in Bahrain match, a series of eight games, with 4 points each. In the Netherlands, the new cabinet of PM Balkenende resigns because of constant internal fighting. UK takes back control of the local government in Northern Ireland.

November: An earthquake kills 29 in the town of San Giuliano di Puglia, in Campobasso, Molise, Italy. An earthquake of magnitude 7.9. strikes Denali fault in Denali National Park in Alaska. In Yemen an American missile destroys a car carrying what the United States claims were six al-Qaeda members, including the mastermind of the USS *Cole* attack, Qaed Salim Sinan al-Harethi. The Islamist Turkish Justice and Development Party (AKP) wins the Turkish general election. Israel's PM, Ariel Sharon, dissolves Parliament and calls for elections early next year. USA signs the International Treaty on Plant Genetic Resources for Food and Agriculture. An unofficial referendum in Gibraltar shows that 99% of voters want to retain the colony's governmental status quo and reject a UK proposal to grant Spain a share of sovereignty over the colony. Iran bans advertising of US products. PM of Ethiopia, Meles Zenawi, announces that the famine threatening his country could be worse than the 1984 famine. Democratic Party members of the United States House of Representatives choose California Representative Nancy Pelosi as their minority leader. She is the first woman to lead a major American party. Human clinical trials of a new HIV vaccine developed by researchers at the US National Institute of Allergy and Infectious Diseases start. The Communist Party of China names former Vice-President Hu Jintao as its general secretary. Three suicide bombers detonate themselves at a hotel in Mombasa, Kenya, killing a number of people including Israeli tourists. At the same time two anti-aircraft missiles miss a passenger aircraft taking off at Mombassa airport. Henry Kissinger is appointed chairman of the independent panel investigating the September 11 attacks on America. British intelligence agency MI5A uncovers a plot to release poison gas in the London underground railway network. Abdullah Gül becomes the new prime minister of Turkey. The first UN arms inspectors' team arrive in Iraq and prepare for inspections for evidence of the development or possession of weapons of mass destruction. An Italian court sentences former PM Giulio Andreotti to 24 years in prison for his involvement in the 1979 murder of journalist Mino Pecorelli. In the Netherlands, Volkert van der Graaf confesses to the murder of Dutch politician Pim Fortuyn. The Miss World contest is shifted to London following riots and killings in Nigeria. In Ecuador, former coup leader Lucio Gutiérrez wins 54.4% of the vote to win the presidential election. The tanker *Prestige* which has been leaking oil off the north-west coast of Spain for several days, splits into two. Despite efforts, the oil reaches the coast. The controversial physician Severino Antinori claims that a project to clone human beings has succeeded, with the first human clone due to be born in 2003. The Clonaid organization also announces that they have five clones waiting to be born, one of whom would be born in December 2002. US President George W. Bush signs into law the creation of a new Department of Homeland Security. The conservative Austrian People's Party led by Federal Chancellor

Wolfgang Schüssel wins as much as 42.27% of the vote in the Austrian general elections.

December: President Pierre Buyoya of Burundi and Pierre Nkurunziza, leader of the Hutu insurgents' Forces for the Defence of Democracy (FDD), sign a ceasefire accord at Arusha, Tanzania, in a bid to end the nine-year civil war. A strike is declared at the state-owned oil company in Venezuela to force President Hugo Chávez to call early elections. Opposition intensifies its attempt to remove President Hugo Chávez from power. Israeli troops, tanks and helicopter gunships move into the Bureij refugee camp in the Gaza Strip. Two paintings by Vincent van Gogh are stolen from the Van Gogh Museum in Amsterdam. The Opposition National Rainbow Coalition (NARC) wins a landslide victory over the ruling KANU party in the Kenyan general elections, ending 40 years of single party rule. North Korea expels UN weapons inspectors, and announces plans to reactivate a dormant nuclear fuel-processing laboratory. A US federal judge orders Microsoft to distribute Sun Microsystem's Java programming language in its Microsoft Windows operating system. Scientists at California-based VaxGen Inc. finishes the first human trial of an AIDS vaccine. Palestinian leader Yasser Arafat announces the cancellation of presidential and legislative elections scheduled for January 2003. US officials state that Iraq has failed to account for all its chemical and biological agents and that Iraq is in material breach of a United Nations Security Council resolution. Roh Moo-hyun wins South Korea's presidential election. In the Congo, government, rebels and Opposition parties sign a peace accord to end four years of civil war and set up a transitional government. Former Bosnian Serb President Biljana Plavsic pleads guilty to crimes against humanity at The Hague tribunal for her part in persecuting Bosnian Muslims and Croats during the 1992–95 conflict. Former US vice-president and 2000 presidential candidate Al Gore announces that he will not seek election to the Presidency in 2004. Henry Kissinger steps down as the chairman of a panel investigating the 11 September attacks citing conflict of interest with his clients. The European Union invites the Czech Republic, Cyprus, Estonia, Hungary, Latvia, Lithuania, Malta, Poland, Slovakia, and Slovenia to join when the EU is scheduled for its next expansion in May 2004. First flight of the ESC-A variant of the Ariane 5 ends in failure and the rocket and the two communications satellites it was carrying are destroyed a few minutes after lift-off from Kourou, French Guiana. The government of Indonesia and rebel leaders from the province of Aceh in north Sumatra sign a peace accord.

2003

January: Luíz Inácio Lula Da Silva becomes the President of Brazil. Pascal Couchepin becomes President of the Confederation in Switzerland. Facing worldwide criticism and against the wishes of the majorities of their own electorates, leaders of Britain, Spain, Italy, Portugal, Hungary, Poland, Denmark, and the Czech Republic release a statement, the letter of the eight, demonstrating support for the United States' plans for an invasion of Iraq. Leopoldo Galtieri, former Argentine dictator, passes away. Maurice Gibb, musician, passes away. Gianni Agnelli, president of Italian carmaker Fiat, passes away.

February: The Space Shuttle Columbia disintegrates over Texas upon re-entry, killing all seven astronauts on board. The dead astronauts include Indian-born Kalpana Chawla and the first Israeli to go to space, Ilan Ramon. US Secretary of State Colin Powell addresses the UN Security Council on Iraq. Global protests against war on

Iraq take place as more than six million people protest in over 600 cities worldwide. Dolly the sheep, the world's first cloned mammal, dies.

March: The United Arab Emirates, Bahrain and Kuwait urge Iraqi president Saddam Hussein to step down to avoid another war. Authorities in Pakistan capture Khalid Shaikh Mohammed, suspected mastermind of the 11 September 2001 attacks. Iraqi fighter aircraft threaten two US U-2 surveillance planes on missions for UN weapons inspectors forcing them to abort their mission and return to base. Arab media reports that Saddam Hussein has opened terrorist training camps in Iraq for Arab volunteers who are willing to carry out suicide bombings against US forces if a US-led attack takes place. Serbian PM Zoran Djindjic assassinated in Belgrade. WHO issues a global alert on SARS. Media reports claim that 350,000-year-old upright-walking human footprints have been found in Italy. Hu Jintao becomes President of the People's Republic of China, replacing Jiang Zemin. On 17 March US President George W. Bush gives an ultimatum: Iraqi leader Saddam Hussein and his sons must either leave Iraq within 48 hours or face military action at a time of the US's choosing. President Saddam Hussein and his sons do not comply with this ultimatum. On 19 March, the first American bombs are dropped on Baghdad. On 20 March, land troops from USA, UK, Australia and Poland invade Iraq. On 22 March, USA and UK begin their 'shock and awe' campaign with a massive air strike on military targets in Baghdad. Cricket World Cup in South Africa ends as Australia win over India. Boxer Roy Jones Jr. beats John Ruiz to become WBA champion. WHO doctor Carlo Urbani, who first identified SARS, dies of the disease.

April: US forces seize control of Baghdad. This event is considered to be the end point of the regime of Saddam Hussein. Retired US Army General Jay Garner becomes interim civil administrator of Iraq. Dr Robert Atkins, who developed the Atkins Nutritional Approach, passes away.

May: George W. Bush lands on the aircraft carrier USS *Abraham Lincoln* and gives a speech announcing the end of major combat in the Iraq War. Anti-apartheid activist Walter Sisulu passes away. A truck-bomb attack kills at least 60 at a government compound in northern Chechnya. A female homicide bomber blows up explosives strapped to her waist in a crowd of thousands of Muslim pilgrims, killing at least 18 people in Chechnya. The attack is seen as an attempt on the life of President Akhmad Kadyrov. A draft version of the proposed European Constitution is unveiled. Three hundredth anniversary celebration of Saint Petersburg, Russia, begins.

June: The People's Republic of China starts filling the reservoir behind the Three Gorges Dam, raising the water level near the dam to over 100 metres. A female bomber detonates a bomb near a bus carrying soldiers and civilians to a military airfield in Mozdok, a key staging point for Russian troops in Chechnya, killing at least 16 people. Actor Gregory Peck passes away. Actress Katharine Hepburn passes away.

July: WHO declares that SARS has been contained. Double bomb attack at a Moscow rock concert kills the female attackers and 15 other people. Newspaper columnist Robert Novak reveals the identity of a CIA agent, Valerie Plame. The Convention on the Future of Europe finishes and proposes the first European Constitution. British government scientist Dr David Kelly's body is found a few miles from his home in UK. The government announces an independent judicial inquiry into the events leading to the death. Actor and comedian Bob Hope passes away.

August: A bomber drives a truck filled with explosives into a military hospital near Chechnya, killing 50 people including Russian troops. The United Nations authorizes an international peacekeeping force for Liberia. Scientists announce that the ozone layer may be showing signs of recovery. NATO takes over command of the peacekeeping force in Afghanistan. This is its first major operation outside Europe. Jemaah Islamiah leader Riduan Isamuddin, better known as Hambali, is arrested in the Thai capital Bangkok. Widespread power outage hits northeast USA and Canada. Former Ugandan dictator Idi Amin passes away. Sérgio Vieira de Mello, Brazilian diplomat and statesman, is killed in an attack on the UN coumpund in Baghdad. Charles Bronson, actor, passes away.

September: Swedish Foreign Minister Anna Lindh is stabbed to death in a Stockholm department store. Sweden rejects adopting the Euro in a referendum. Estonia approves joining the EU in a referendum. American movie director Elia Kazan passes away.

October: Ahmed Qurei is new Palestine PM. China launches its first astronaut, Yang Liwei, into orbit. D.B.C. Pierre wins the Booker Prize. Carlos Mesa is the new president of Bolivia. Pope beatifies Mother Teresa. Final Concorde flight from New York to London takes place. Russian authorities arrest Mikhail Khodorkovsky and seize control of Yukos. Mahathir bin Mohamad retires, Badawi is the new PM of Malaysia.

November: President Kumaratunga suspends Sri Lankan parliament and deploys troops. UN votes in favour of a resolution to end sanctions against Cuba. Junichiro Koizumi wins the general elections in Japan. Arnold Schwarzenegger is sworn in as California governor. Bomb attacks take place on the headquarters of the HSBC Bank and the British consulate in the Turkish city of Istanbul. Michael Jackson surrenders to the police in USA. Georgian opposition supporters seize the Parliament building in the capital city Tbilisi. Georgian President Eduard Shevardnadze resigns.

December: Zimbabwe withdraws from the Commonwealth of Nations. US forces capture Saddam Hussein. Pervez Musharraf survives two assassination attempts. Linus Torvalds releases Linux kernel 2.6.0. Italian dairy giant Parmalat announces an estimated 3.96 billion euro gap in its accounts. British scientists fail to make contact with its Mars probe, Beagle 2. A powerful earthquake destroys 70% of the southern Iranian city of Bam, including the ancient Bam Citadel, the initial death toll is estimated at 40,000.

2004

January: The Republic of Ireland takes over the presidency of the European Union. The first of the NASA Mars Exploration Rovers, Spirit, successfully lands on the planet and starts transmitting signals. In Afghanistan, the Grand Council, the *Loya Jirga*, adopts a new Constitution of Afghanistan. Mikhail Saakashvili wins the Presidential elections of the Republic of Georgia. Jaap de Hoop Scheffer of The Netherlands became the new Secretary General of NATO, replacing Britain's Lord Robertson. The inquest into the death of Diana, Princess of Wales, and Dodi Al-Fayed is officially opened. US lifestyle guru Martha Stewart pleads not guilty to five criminal counts that include conspiracy, obstruction of justice and securities fraud arising from a 2001 stock sale. Indonesia announces that millions of birds have died from avian flu in the last few months. The People's Republic of China announces an outbreak of the H5N1 strain of avian influenza in its Guangxi autonomous region. Senator John Kerry wins the New Hampshire primary round of the 2004 US presidential election. In UK, the Hutton Inquiry report is released and absolves the British government and PM Tony Blair of any wrongdoing in David Kelly's death. The discovery of a new form of matter, Fermionic condensate, is announced.

February: A team of Russian scientists and another of US scientists report the discovery of two new chemical elements. These are elements 113, given the temporary name Ununtrium (Uut), and element 115, designated Ununpentium (Uup). Over 100 Iranian MP resign in protest at the Council of Guardians' disqualification of nearly 2000 candidates from the forthcoming general elections. Pakistan removes Abdul Qadeer Khan, the founder of Pakistan's nuclear weapons programme, as a special adviser to the prime minister. Abdul Qadeer Khan later confesses to smuggling nuclear hardware, sharing secret designs necessary to develop a nuclear weapon, and giving personal briefings to nuclear scientists from Libya, Iran, and North Korea. Astronomers detect the presence of oxygen and carbon in the atmosphere of an extra-solar planet, provisionally named Osiris. An explosion on board a Moscow subway train kills around 40 people and injures around 120. Sri Lankan President Chandrika Kumaratunga dissolves the parliament. Nearly 400 members of Yasser Arafat's Fatah faction of the PLO resign in protest over corruption and mismanagement. Senator John Kerry wins the caucuses in in the race for the Democratic presidential nomination. South Korean scientists announce what they claim to be the world's first successfully cloned human embryo. The former Chechen President Zelimkhan Yandarbiyev is killed in an explosion in the Qatari capital, Doha. Scientists at the California Institute of Technology announce the discovery of a galaxy that is the farthest known object in the universe. Iran offers to sell nuclear reactor

fuel on the international market under the supervision of the International Atomic Energy Agency. International Space Station crew Michael Foale and Alexandr Kaleri perform the first ever spacewalk involving the station's entire crew. Haitian Pres. Jean-Bertrand Aristide resigns as president of Haiti and escapes to Central African Republic.

March: Russian President Vladimir Putin names Mikhail Fradkov as his new prime minister. USA, France and Canada sends in hundreds of troops to Haiti. The Serbian parliament approves a new government headed by Vojislav Kostunica. Libya admits to having stockpiled 23 metric tons of mustard gas in its declaration to the Organisation for the Prohibition of Chemical Weapons in The Hague. New Democracy led by Costas Karamanlis defeats the Panhellenic Socialist Movement led by George Papandreou in the 2004 Greek legislative election. Iraq's governing council unanimously approves the country's new constitution. 10 bombs explode on Madrid commuter trains killing nearly 200 people and wounding around 1400 more. The South Korean Parliament votes to impeach President Roh Moo-hyun for his alleged breach of election rules. PM Goh Kun takes over the presidential functions. The opposition Spanish Socialist Workers' Party (PSOE) wins the Spanish Legislative elections. Newly elected Spanish PM José Luis Rodríguez Zapatero announces his government's opposition to the invasion and occupation of Iraq. Astronomers announce the discovery of Sedna, a Pluto-like planetoid. It is the most distant individual object known to orbit the Sun. Taiwanese President Chen Shui-bian and Vice-President Annette Lu are shot while campaigning in Tainan. Both survive with minor injuries. The secular ruling coalition Barisan Nasional wins a two-thirds majority in the Malaysian general election. Hamas selects Abdel Aziz al-

Rantissi as its leader in the Gaza Strip. Its exiled politburo chief Khaled Meshaal is chosen as the movement's overall leader. A bomb is discovered on the high speed TGV railway between Paris and Geneva near Troyes, France. NASA succeeds in its second attempt to fly the X-43A experimental aircraft from the Hyper-X project. It attains speeds above of Mach 7 making it the fastest ever hypersonic flight.

April: Four persons suspected of involvement in the 11 March 2004 Madrid bombings blow themselves up in an apartment building in Madrid when police raid the apartment. US administrator in Iraq, Paul Bremer, declares Moqtada al-Sadr as an outlaw. Canadian authorities order the slaughter of 19 million chickens in British Columbia due to bird flu fears. West Indies captain Brian Lara sets the highest score in Test cricket - 400 not out on the third day of the fourth Test against England in Antigua. The African National Congress (ANC) led by President Thabo Mbeki is re-elected with an increased majority in the 2004 South African legislative election. An Arabic channel broadcasts an audiotape, believed to be that of Osama bin Laden. The voice in the tape offers to halt terrorist operations in European countries that withdrew their troops from Muslim nations. Socialist Party leader José Luis Rodríguez Zapatero is sworn in as Spain's prime minister. Hamas leader Abdel Aziz al-Rantissi is killed in an Israeli missile attack. Hamas selects a new leader but keeps his identity secret to prevent an assassination. Mordechai Vanunu, who leaked Israeli nuclear-weapons secrets in 1986, is released from prison after 18 years. Reunification referendum held in Cyprus. 65% of Turkish Cypriot voters accept and 75% of Greek Cypriot voters reject the Annan Plan. Photographs showing US troops abusing and humiliating Iraqi prisoners at the Abu Ghraib prison outside Baghdad appear in the press. Six soldiers face court martial. Their commanding officer is suspended.

May: Cyprus, the Czech Republic, Estonia, Hungary, Latvia, Lithuania, Malta, Poland, Slovakia and Slovenia join the European Union. The separatist region of Ajaria attempts to sever its links from Georgia by blowing up the three bridges connecting it to the rest of the country. Georgian president Mikhail Saakashvili forces Aslan Abashidze, President of the breakaway republic of Ajaria, to resign. Over 50 former high-ranking United States diplomats address an open letter to George W. Bush complaining about the Bush administration's policy towards the Middle East. The United States Senate approves John Negroponte as the head of the new US embassy in Iraq. Hamas co-founder Mohammad Taha is released from an Israeli prison. Vladimir Putin is sworn in for his second four-year term as Russian president. US Defense Secretary Donald Rumsfeld testifies before the US Congress taking full responsibility and apologizing for the abuse of Iraqi detainees at the Abu Ghraib Prison. Chechen president Akhmad Kadyrov is killed in a landmine bomb blast during a parade in Grozny. British tabloid newspaper *The Daily Mirror* acknowledges its photos of alleged British Army abuse of Iraqi prisoners as a hoax, tenders an apology and sacks its editor, Piers Morgan. Chen Shui-bian is sworn in to a second term as President of the Republic of China in Taipei. Michael Moore's controversial film *Fahrenheit 9/11* wins the Palme d'Or at the Cannes Film Festival. Horst Köhler is elected President of Germany. The signing of a peace accord marks an end to the 21-year civil war in Sudan.

June: Ghazi Mashal Ajil al-Yawer is named president of Iraq's incoming government. Norway bans smoking in all bars and restaurants. In USA, Central Intelligence Agency (CIA) director George Tenet tenders his resignation.

George W. Bush presents the US Presidential Medal of Freedom to Pope John Paul II. North Korea bans its citizens from using mobile phones. Former US President Ronald Reagan passes away. The first transit of Venus since 1882 takes place. The ICC suspends the Zimbabwean cricket team from playing Test Matches till the end of 2004 due to their policy of racial bias in team selection. Ken Livingstone is reelected Mayor of London for a second four-year term. In Russia, the trial of oil tycoon Mikhail Khodorkovsky begins on charges of tax evasion and fraud. Software experts announce the development of a computer virus named 'Cabir' that is capable of infecting cellphones running on the Symbian OS with Bluetooth capabilities. The latest meeting of the European Council in Brussels ends in the agreement of a constitution for the European Union. The Philippine Congress announces the re-election of Gloria Arroyo to a second term as President of the Philippines in the 2004 general election. SpaceShipOne successfully achieves its maiden flight to the edge of outer space, thus becoming the first privately funded spacecraft to travel into space. US administrator in Iraq, Paul Bremer, hands over power in Iraq two days before the US-imposed deadline. The currencies of Estonia (the Kroon), Lithuania (the Litas), and Slovenia (the Tolar) enter ERM II, the European Union's Exchange Rate Mechanism.

July: The Iraqi Special Tribunal holds the first hearing in the trial of Saddam Hussein. The Cassini-Huygens unmanned probe becomes the first spacecraft to orbit Saturn. The International Ship and Port Facility Security Code comes into effect. Greece wins the Euro 2004 football tournament. The first direct presidential election is held in Indonesia. The Cambodian parliament votes to reappoint Hun Sen as PM. Former chess World Champion Bobby Fischer is detained in Japan. The PM of the Palestinian Authority, Ahmed Qurei, submits his resignation. Yasser Arafat refuses to accept the resignation and Qurei later withdraws his resignation. Israeli PM Ariel Sharon calls on French Jews to move to Israel following a dramatic rise in French anti-semitism. In USA, the 9/11 Commission releases its unanimous final report that harshly criticizes US intelligence agencies. US Senator John Kerry formally accepts the 2004 Democratic Presidential candidate nomination. The UN Security Council passes US-drafted resolution 1556 demanding the Sudanese government end atrocities in the Darfur conflict.

August: US authorities raise the security alert level for the World Bank and the International Monetary Fund (IMF) offices in Washington, DC, the New York Stock Exchange and companies in the New York City area after intelligence reports a possible al-Qaeda attack. The FBI warns that Mumbai, Delhi, or Bangalore could be the target of terrorist attacks. A non-radioactive steam leak at a Japanese nuclear power plant kills four and injures eight others. The South Korean government announces the shifting of the country's capital from Seoul to a new site at Gongju. Libya agrees to pay US $35 million to victims of a 1986 Berlin discotheque bombing. British scientists at University of Newcastle-upon-Tyne become the first in Europe to be granted permission to clone human embryos. Lee Hsien Loong is sworn in as the 3rd PM of Singapore. The 2004 Summer Olympics are held in Athens, Greece. Venezuelan President Hugo Chávez defeats a recall vote with 58% support. 1,300 Iraqi delegates begin a three-day conference in Baghdad to select an interim national assembly. The Cassini-Huygens spacecraft discovers two new natural satellites of Saturn. Germany apologizes for the genocide in Namibia on the 100th anniversary of the Herero uprising. *Nature* magazine reveals that five new satellites and a further candidate moon have been discovered orbiting Neptune. The Trans-Atlantic Exoplanet Survey (TrES) announces its first discovery of an extrasolar planet. The Roman Catholic Church returns a precious icon, the Virgin of Kazan, to the Kremlin's Cathedral of the Assumption as a goodwill gesture to the Russian Orthodox Church. China passes a law making it illegal to buy and sell blood, in a bid to tackle the HIV epidemic. Former Yugoslav President Slobodan Milosevic opens his defence at the trial that accuses him of genocide, crimes against humanity and war crimes.

September: Alu Alkhanov wins the presidential election in Chechnya. Iran informs the International Atomic Energy Agency that it plans to convert 37 tons of yellowcake uranium into a form that can be made into weapons. Armed men and women seize a school in Beslan, North Ossetia, Russia, and hold over 1,300 adults and children hostage. The standoff ends in tragedy; the official reports list 335 confirmed dead, including 156 children, and more than 700 wounded; 176 remain missing.

Chechen warlord Shamil Basayev claims responsibility. US President George W. Bush accepts the Republican nomination for a second term in office. The UN war crimes tribunal in The Hague declares former Yugoslav President Slobodan Miloševiæ unfit to represent himself in his trial, and appoints two lawyers to his defence. Lebanon amends its constitution to allow President Émile Lahoud to serve an additional term. The management of US film company Metro-Goldwyn-Mayer accepts a take-over offer from Sony in a deal worth just under US$3 billion. Afghan President Hamid Karzai survives an assassination attempt after a rocket is fired at his helicopter. The US Department of Homeland Security intercepts a United Airlines flight from London, so that Yusuf Islam, the musician formerly known as Cat Stevens, can be arrested and deported. Syria begins a 'phased redeployment' of its forces in Lebanon. USA formally lifts its general trade and aviation sanctions against Libya. The United States Senate confirms the nomination of Porter Goss as Director of the Central Intelligence Agency.

Timeline of Indian History

Beginning of Time to 1994

100,000–75,000 BC: Paleolithic period.

9000 to 4000 BC: Mesolithic period: Paintings on walls of the rock shelters of Bhimbetka in the foothills of the Vindhya mountains begin to appear.

6000 BC: Neolithic settlements in Baluchistan.

2800–2700 BC: Beginning of Indus Valley Civilization; Kot Dijian phase.

c.2700 BC: Approximate date of Indus Valley Seals found at Kish.

2650 BC: Mature Harappan phase begins.

2600–1700 BC: Civilization of the great cities in the Indus Valley (Mohenjodaro, Harappa), Punjab (Kalibangan) and Gujarat (Lothal).

2000–1600 BC: Aryans invade the Indus Valley region. Research in 1999 reported that gene patterns confirmed that Caucasoid invaders entered this region during this period.

c.1375 BC: Worship of Aryan deities in the land of the Mitanni, in the region from the Iranian mountains to the Mediterranean.

1400–900 BC: Early Vedic period (*Rig Veda*).

1000 BC: Iron in India.

900–500 BC: Later Vedic period (*Brahmanas*).

817 BC: Traditional date of the birth of Parsvanatha, the 23rd Tirthankara in Jain tradition.

c.800 BC: *Baudhayana Sulbasutra* is composed. *Sulbasutras* are appendices to the Vedas which give rules for con-structing altars. They contained a wealth of geometrical knowledge.

800–500 BC: The Upanishads are thought to have been composed around this time.

c.750 BC: *Manava Sulbasutra* is composed.

c.600 BC: *Apastamba Sulbasutra* is composed.

6th century BC onwards: Early urbanization in the eastern Gangetic valley.

6th century BC: The life and times of Mahavira, the founder of Jainism.

c.563 BC: Gautama Siddhartha Buddha, the founder of Buddhism, is born in what is today Nepal, possibly in Lumbini.

c.543–491 BC: Magadha under King Bimbisara.

537 BC: Cyrus the Persian campaigns west of the Indus.

517–509 BC: Darius the Persian conquers the Indus Valley region making the area a province of the Persian Empire.

c.500 BC: The *Ramayana* composed.

500–200 BC: The *Mahabharata* put into its final form.

c.491–459 BC: Ajatshatru's rule of Magadha. Ajatshatru is believed to have killed his father Bimbisara in c.491 BC.

Somewhere in the time between 520 BC and 400 BC, famous grammarian Panini, major work *Astadhyayi*, born in Shalatula (now Pakistan). Now he is considered by many as the forerunner of the modern formal language theory used to specify computer languages.

486 BC: Traditional date of Buddha's Nirvana. First Buddhist Council at Rajagriha, under the patronage of King Ajatshatru.

386 BC: Second Buddhist council at Vaishali.

364 BC: Nanda dynasty under Mahapadma.

327–326 BC: Invasion of India by Alexander.

325 BC: Alexander leaves India.

321 BC: Maurya Dynasty founded by Chandragupta (Maurya).

c.305 BC: Indian Expedition of Seleucus Nikator, a general of Alexander's army.

302 BC: Kautilya, minister to Chandragupta Maurya, writes *Arthasastra*, a compendium of laws, administrative procedures and political advice for running a kingdom.

c.273–232 BC: The reign of the Mauryan Emperor Asoka.

250 BC: Third Buddhist Council at Pataliputra.

c.206 BC: Indian expedition of Antiochos III, King of Syria.

c.200 BC: *Katyayana Sulbasutra* is composed.

185 BC: Pushyamitra kills the last Maurya and establishes the Sunga dynasty.

175 BC: Foundation of the Indo-Greek empire.

c.180 BC: *Varttikas*, or the supplementary rules to Panini's work written by Katyayana.

c.155 BC: Bactrian king Menander invades north-western India.

c.150 BC: *Mahabhashya* of Patanjali written.

c.145–101 BC: Rule of Elara Chola, a general and possibly a prince of Cholas who conquered Sri Lanka.

138–88 BC: Conflict of the kings of Parthia with Sakas in Eastern Iran.

c.100 BC: Gandhara school of sculpture flourishes; appearance of a Buddha image based on the Greek god Apollo.

c.100 BC: Deccan domination by the Andhras (also known as Satavahanas or Satakarni according to Prakrit inscriptions) begins.

58 BC: Epoch of the Krita-Malava-Vikrama Era.

57–38 BC: Squared letters appear on Parthian coins.

c.30 BC: End of Sunga–Kanva rule in eastern Malwa. Satavahana supremacy in the Deccan.

c.26–20 BC: Pandya ambassador in Roman Emperor Augustus's court.

AD 20–46: Gondopharnes, Indo-Parthian king in Taxila.

Early 1st century AD: Kujala Kadphises unites the Yue-chi tribes and establishes Kushana empire.

1st century AD: Intensive trade connections with the Roman empire.

c.AD 64: The Chinese Emperor Ming-ti sends for Buddhist texts.

c.AD 70: Saka satrap Bhumaka establishes Scythian power on the north-west coast of India.

AD 78: Saka era begins, generally associated with Kushan ruler Kanishka I. Decline of the Parthian rulers and consolidation of the Kushan power in the Indus valley.

c.AD 100: Kanishka convenes Fourth Buddhist Council at Jalandhar or in Kashmir.

AD 89–105: Kushan king repulsed by the Chinese General Pan Chao.

c.AD 120: A Western Satrap Dynasty (c.AD 120–c.AD 395) in Ujjain in Malwa founded by Bhumaka's son Chashtana.

AD 125 onwards: Resurgence of Satvahanas under Gautamiputra and Vasishtiputra.

c.AD 126: Saurashtra conquest of Gautamiputra Sri Satakarni.

AD 130–150: Accession of Saka ruler Rudradaman I, Chashtana's grandson.

AD 148–170: An-Shih-Kao translates a work by Kanishka's chaplain.

AD 1st or 2nd century: *Buddhacarita* ('Acts of the Buddha') written by poet Ashvaghosha.

1st to 4th century AD: Sangama literature compiled in Tamil Nadu.

AD 248: Epoch of the Traikutaka-Kalachuri Era.

AD 250: Disintegration of the Satvahana empire.

276–293: Sassanian conquest of parts of north-west India.

4th century AD: Development of Vajrayana Buddhism. Final form of *Bhagavad Gita*.

320–550: Gupta dynasty.

c.320–330: Rule of Chandragupta I from Pataliputra.

335–375: Samudragupta's reign, expansion of Gupta kingdom throughout north India and extending to South India.

c.360: Ceylonese embassy to Samudragupta.

c.379: Accession of Chandragupta II.

c.388–401: Chandragupta II Vikramaditya ends the satrapy of Ujjain by conquest of Malwa, Gujarat, and Saurashtra.

AD 3rd century: Pingala, author of *Chandasutra* explores the relationship between combinatorics and musical theory.

405–411: Travels of Fa-Hien in the Gupta empire.

c.410: Iron Pillar constructed in Delhi possibly by Chandragupta II Vikramaditya.

c.415–455: Accession and rule of Kumara Gupta I.

436: Simhavarman, the Pallava King of Kanchi, mentioned in the *Lokavibhaga*.

455: Accession of Skanda Gupta. Defeat of White Huns by Skanda Gupta.

c.458: Decimal number system first published in *Lokavibhaga*.

c.465: Harisena of the Vakataka Dynasty begins work at the Ajanta caves.

467: Latest known date of the rule of Skanda Gupta.

473: Accession of Kumara Gupta II.

476: Birth of the astronomer Aryabhata, author of *Âryabhatîya*.

c.477–495: Reign of Budhagupta.

500–527: Huns rule over north India; decline of the classical urban culture of the north.

c.505: Famous astronomer and mathematician Varahamihira, author of *Pancasiddhantika*, is born.

510: Huns led by Mihiragula conquer Punjab, Gujarat and Malwa from the Guptas.

533: Yashodarman, king of Malwa, organizes a national uprising against the Hun ruler Mihiragula.

543–544: Gupta rule continues in north Bengal. Rise of the Chalukyas of Vatapi.

566–567: Accession of the Chalukya ruler Kirtivarman I.

574: Rise of the Pallavas of Kanchipuram.

598: Famous mathematician Brahmagupta, author of *Brahmasphutasiddhanta* and *Khandakhadyaka*, is born. Sometime in the 7th century he calculated the earth's circumference to be 36,800 kms.

Late 4th–early 5th century: Kalidasa, Sanskrit poet and dramatist, who wrote *Abhijnanasakuntalam*, was possibly active during this period.

About 600: Famous mathematician Bhaskara I, the author of *Mahabhaskariya*, the *Laghubhaskariya* and the *Aryabhatiyabhasya*, is born.

606: Accession of Harsha.

609: Coronation of the Chalukya ruler Pulakesin II.

619–620: Supremacy of Sasanka of Gauda in eastern India.

630: Pulakesin II defeats Harsha; end of north India's hegemony.

630–643: Chinese traveler Hiuentsang in India.

634: Reference to the fame of Kalidasa and Bharavi in the Aihole inscription.

637: Arab raid against Thana.

639: Foundation of Lhasa by Srong-tsan-Gompo.

641: Harsha's embassy to China.

c.642: Death of Pulakesin II.

c.642–668: Rule of Narasimha-varman I, the Great Pallava. In AD 642 he defeated Pulakesin II and took over Badami (Vatapi).

643: Harsha's meeting with Hiuen-Tsang.

c.646–647: Death of Harsha.

650: The Pallavas, who ruled from their capital at Kanchipuram, are defeated by the Chalukyas.

670: The Pallavas build a new city at Mamallapuram.

675–685: Itsing, a Chinese traveler, stays at Nalanda.

c.700: Conversion of King Srimaravarman to Saivism by Tirujnana Sambandhar, the first of 63 *Nayanars* or Tamil saints.

711: Invasion of Sind by Muhammad bin Qasim.

712: Arab conquest of Nirun and Aror. Defeat and death of Dahir, the ruler of Sind.

713: Capture of Multan by the Arabs.

c.722: The defeat of Narasimhavarman II at the hands of the Chalukya King Vikramaditya II, which marked the downfall of the Pallava power.

730–756: Rule of Nagabhatta I of the Pratihara Dynasty. He ruled over Broach and Jodhpur, and extended his dominion till Gwalior; was also known for repulsing the invasion of the Mlecchas.

731: Yasovarman (c.730–c.740), king of Kanauj and an author who patronized the Prakrit poet Vakpatiraja and Sanskrit poet Bhavabhuti, sends an ambassador to China.

733: Lalitaditya Muktapida, ruler of Kashmir, receives investiture as king from the emperor of China.

c.733–46: Rule of the Chalukya king Vikramaditya II. He thrice took Kanchi.

His queen commissioned 'the best southern architect' to build the temple of Virupaksha.

c.753: Rise of the Rashtrakuta empire.

c.760: Pala rule begins in Bengal.

783: Vatsaraja establishes Gurjara-Pratihara dynasty of Rajasthan.

793–815: The rule of Govinda III, a Rashtrakuta king. He defeated the Pratihara King Nagabhatta II. Both the Palas and the ruler of Kanauj submitted to his protection.

c.836: Accession of Bhoja I, King of Kanauj.

c.846: Rise of Cholas and defeat of Pallavas.

855: Accession of Avantivarman of Kashmir.

c.870: Famous mathematician Sridhara, author of two mathematical treatises, *Trisatika* (sometimes called *Patiganitasara*) and *Patiganita*, is born.

c.871–907: The rule of Aditya I, a Chola king.

892: Coronation of Bhima I, an eastern Chalukya ruler.

893: Mahendrapàla I, a Pratihara king, consolidates the territories he inherited, besides adding to them parts of north Bengal, Magadha, and western Assam.

907: Accession of the Chola ruler Parantaka I.

914: Continuance of Pratihara rule in Saurashtra.

933: Devasena writes *Shravakachar*, considered the first Hindi book, in Apabhransha.

945: Coronation of Amma II (Vijayaditya VI), an eastern Chalukya ruler.

c.950–1003: Rule of Queen Didda of Kashmir.

c.954–1002: Chandella Dynasty builds numerous Vaishnava temples, notably at Khajuraho, under Yasovarman (c.930–54) and Dhanga (954–1002).

c.962: Alptigin, a Turkish warrior slave, seizes the Afghan fortress of

Ghazni and founds Ghaznavid Dynasty.

973: Foundation of the later Chalukya empire of Kalyana.

977: Accession of Sabuktigin, son of Alptigin, as the ruler of Ghazni.

985: Accession of the Chola King Rajaraja the Great.

986–987: First invasion of Sabuktigin in the provinces of Kabul and Punjab.

c.995: Accession of Sindhuraja Navasahasanka to the throne of the Paramaras in Malwa.

997: Death of Sabuktigin.

998: Accession of Sultan Mahmud in Ghazni.

c.1000: Mahmud of Ghazni leads an expedition to India. Lingaraja temple is built at Bhubaneswar. Saktivarman become the ruler of the eastern Chalukyas. Rajaraja I builds the Rajarajeswara temple at Tanjore. Immadi Narasimha Yadava Rayalu, a king who reigns at Narayanavanam in the Karvetnagar zamindari, builds the Chandragiri fort.

1001: Defeat of Jaipal, ruler of Punjab at the hands of Sultan Mahmud. Al Baruni comes to India with Mahmud of Ghazni.

1003: Regent queen of Kashmir, Queen Didda, passes away.

1004: Mahmud of Ghazni attacks Bhera.

1005: Mahmud of Ghazni entrusts his Indian holdings to Sukhpala. Mahmud captures Bhatinda.

1006: Mahmud of Ghazni captures Multan.

1008: Mahmud of Ghazni defeats Anandapala's troops in the Second Battle of Peshawar.

1012–1044: Rajendra Chola I rules the area now known as Tamil Nadu.

1013: Mahmud of Ghazni captures Nandana, in the vicinity of Multan.

1014: Rajaraja Chola dies.

1018: Kanauj seized by Mahmud of Ghazni. This marks the end of the Pratihara Dynasty.

c.1018–1055: Four-decade rule of Bhoja of Dhara in Malwa begins. He is known to have engraved *Kurmashataka*, a poetical work in Prakrita on stone slabs.

1025: Rajendra I of Chola sends a naval expedition against the maritime empire known as Sri Vijaya.

1026: Sarnath inscription of the time of Mahipala I of Bengal. Fall of Nidar Bhim of the Shahiya Dynasty. Sack of Somnath (during the reign of Bhimdeva I) by Mahmud of Ghazni.

1027: Bhimadeva I, the Chalukya king, builds the Sun Temple at Modhera (Gujarat).

1029: The Khajuraho temples are completed by the Chandelas.

1030: Death of Sultan Mahmud of Ghazni. Rajendra Chola erects the temple of Gangaikondacholapuram in the area now known as Tamil Nadu. Al Baruni writes *Tahqiq-i-Hind*.

1032: Vimala Shah, the minister of the Chalukya (Solanki) king of Gujarat, completes the first of the Dilwara Jain temples in Mount Abu.

1038: Nayapala succeeds to the throne of Bengal. Atisha Dipankara, a Buddhist scholar, visits Tibet.

1039: Death of Gangeyadeva Kalachuri in Tripura who introduced the seated Lakshmi coins.

c.1040: Coronation of Lakshmi-karna of the Kalachuri Dynasty. Famous mathematician Bhaskara II, author of *Lilavati* on arithmetic and geometry and *Bijaganita* is born.

1052: Tomar ruler Anangpal builds a Rajput citadel and town containing the Lal Kot (red fort) in the area now known as Delhi.

1070–1122: Somadeva Bhatta writes *Kathasaritasagara*. Rajendra Chola, Kulottunga I rules in the area now known as Tamil Nadu.

1076–1127: Rule of Vikramaditya VI of Kalyana, now Basava Kaluyana in Bidar district in Karanataka.

c.1076–1148: Anantavarman Choda Ganga's reign begins in Orissa.

1089–1101: Rule of Harsha, one of Kashmir's last Hindu kings.

1090: Rise of the Gahadavalas in Kanauj.

1095: The Sena family, who came from the south, takes control of power in Bengal with Vijayasena.

c.1098: Kirtivarman Chandella comes to power in Bundelkhand.

1100: Construction of the Jagannath temple at Puri begins by Anantavarman Choda Ganga.

1150: Sena dynasty begins.

1153–64: Rule of Vigraharaja IV in parts of Rajasthan near Ajmer.

1156: Rawal Jaisal founds Jaisalmer.

1175: Muhammad of Ghur invades India and captures Multan.

1178: Muhammad of Ghur defeated in Gujarat.

c.1185–1205: The rule of Lakshmana Sena of Bengal. Jayadeva writes *Gitagovinda*.

1191: First battle of Tarain between Rajputs under Prithviraj Chauhan and Muhammad of Ghur.

1192: Second battle of Tarain. Fall of Prithviraj Chauhan.

1192–93: Qutb-ud-din Aibak takes Delhi. Begins constructing the Qutb Minar.

1202: Turkish conquerors defeat Sena ruler and overrun Bengal.

1206: Death of Muhammad of Ghur and accession of Qutb-ud-din Aibak in India.

1210: Death of Qutb-ud-din Aibak. Accession of Aram Shah.

1210–11: Accession of Iltutmish.

1221: Invasion of the Mongols under Chengiz Khan.

c.1228: Ahom rule begins in Assam.

1231–32: Completion of the Qutb Minar under Iltutmish.

1236: Death of Iltutmish. Accession and deposition of Iltutmish's son Rukn-ud-din Firuz Shah. Accession of Iltutmish's daughter Raziyya.

1240: Deposition and murder of Raziyya. Accession of Mu'iz-ud-din Bahram.

1241: Capture of Lahore by the Mongols.

1246: Deposition and death of Ma'sud, Sultan of Delhi. Accession of Nasir-ud-din Mahmud to the throne of Delhi.

1266: Death of Nasir-ud-din Mahmud. Accession of Ghiyas-ud-din Balban, a slave of Iltutumish, who became a Chaglan, a group of 40 most influential people in Iltutmish's court.

1279: Latest known date of Rajendra IV Chola's rule in Tamil Nadu. Rebellion of Tughril in Bengal.

1286: Death of Ghiyas-ud-din Balban. Accession of Mu'iz-ud-din Kaiqubad, grandson of Balban, whom he succeeded in 1286 on the throne of Delhi in the absence of his father Nasiruddin Bughra Khan, who was then in Bengal.

1288: Marco Polo, the Venetian traveller, visits Kollam in Kerala.

1290: Death of Kaiqubad. Accession of Jalal-ud-din Firuz Khalji.

1292: Ala-ud-din Khalji captures Bhilsa. Mongol invasion somewhere between Delhi and the Khyber pass.

1294: Devagiri in the Deccan pillaged by Ala-ud-din Khalji.

1296: Accession of Ala-ud-din Khalji.

1297: Conquest of Gujarat (from Karnadeva II) by Ala-ud-din Khalji.

1297–1306: Delhi Sultanate repulses several attacks by the Mongols.

1301: Capture of Ranthambhor by Ala-ud-din Khalji.

1302–03: Capture of Chittor by Ala-ud-din Khalji. Mongol invasion under Targhi.

1305: Conquest of Malwa, Ujjain, Mandu, Dhar and Chanderi by the Khaljis.

1306–07: Malik Kafur's (a general of Ala-ud-din Khalji) expedition to Devagiri.

1308: Khalji expedition to Warangal.

1310: Malik Naib's (Malik Kafur) expedition into the south indian peninsula.

1316: Death of Ala-ud-din Khalji. Accession of Shihab-ud-din Umar. Death of Malik Naib.

1318: Assassination of Malik Kafur, deposition of Shahabuddin Umar, accession of Qutbuddin Mubarak.

1320: Assassination of Qutbuddin Mubarak, usurpation of power by Khusro Khan, a Hindu convert. Khusro Khan overthrown by Ghazi Malik (later known as Ghiyas-ud-din Tughluq). Foundation of Tughlaq Dynasty by Ghiyas-ud-din Tughluq.

1321: Expedition to Warangal under Muhammad Jauna, the son of Ghiyas-ud-din Tughluq. Rebellion of Muhammad Jauna.

1323: Second expedition to Warangal under Muhammad Jauna. Mongol invasion in northwest India.

1325: Accession of Muhammad bin Tughluq (Muhammad Jauna).

1327: Destruction of Kampili, in Vijayanagar, by Muhammad bin Tughluq. Transfer of the capital from Delhi to Daulatabad.

1328: The Mongols invade India but are repelled by Delhi sultanate.

1329: Qarachil expedition of Muhammad bin Tughluq to gain access to Tibet. Issue of brass and copper coins by Muhammad bin Tughluq.

1333–34: Arrival of Ibn Batuta in India.

1334: Sayyid Jalal al-Din Ahsan of Kaythal, who had been appointed governor of Ma'bar, leads a rebellion at Madura. Capture of Anegundi by Muhammad bin Tughluq.

1336: Traditional date of the foundation of Vijayanagar.

1338: Separate Sultanate of Bengal.

1342: Ibn Batuta leaves Delhi on his mission to China.

1345: Accession of Shams-ud-din Iliyas in Bengal.

1347: Ala-ud-din Bahman Shah proclaimed King of the Deccan.

1350: Famous mathematician Madhava of Sangamagramma is born.

1351: Death of Muhammad bin Tughluq. Accession of Firuz Tughluq.

1353: Firuz Tughluq's first expedition to Bengal.

1359: Firuz Tughluq's second expedition to Bengal.

1360: Firuz Tughluq's expedition to Orissa.

1361: Capture of Nagarkot or Kangra by Firuz Tughluq.

1363: Firuz Tughluq's first expedition to Sind.

1370: Vijayanagara conquers Sultanate of Madurai.

1374: Bukka, ruler of Vijayanagar, sends an embassy to the Emperor of China.

1377: Vijayanagar kingdom destroys Sultanate of Madura.

1382: Rebellion of Raja Ahmad or Malik Raja in Khandesh.

1388: Death of Firuz Tughluq. Accession of Ghiyas-ud-din Tughluq II.

1389: Death of Ghiyas-ud-din Tughluq II.

1398: Timur invades India. He sacks Delhi on 17 December.

1399: Timur leaves India.

1403: Separate Sultanate of Gujarat.

1414: Khizr Khan, governor of Multan appointed by Timur, takes possession of Delhi and founds the Sayyid Dynasty. Raja Ganesha, a Hindu landlord of Bhaturia and Dinajpur becomes the king of Bengal by usurping power from the weak Iliyas Shahi sultans.

1424: Capture of Warangal by Ahmad Shah Bahmani, a ruler of the Bahamani Dynasty.

1429: Transfer of the Bahmani capital from Gulbarga to Bidar.

c.1430–69: Rule of Rana Kumbha in Chittor.

1435–67: Kapilendra establishes Suryavamsha dynasty of Orissa.

c.1444: Famous astronomer Nilakantha Somayaji, author of *Tantrasamgraha*, is born.

1451: Bahlul Lodi ascends the throne of Delhi.

1459: Foundation of Jodhpur by Rao Jodha.

1469: Birth of Guru Nanak.

1486–1543: Life of Chaitanya, Bengali founder of popular Vaishnava sect.

1486–87: Fall of the Sangama Dynasty of Vijayanagar. Beginning of the rule of the Saluva Dynasty in Vijayanagar.

1489: Accession of Sikandar Lodi.

1489–90: Foundation of the Adil Shahi Dynasty of Bijapur.

1490: Establishment of the independent Nizam Shahi Dynasty of Ahmadnagar.

1493: Husain Shah elected King of Bengal.

1494: Accession of Babur in Farghana.

1497–98: First voyage of Vasco da Gama; he lands at Calicut.

1504: Babur occupies Kabul.

1505: Beginning of the rule of the Tuluva Dynasty in Vijayanagar.

1509: Accession of Krishnadeva Raya to the Vijayanagar throne.

c.1509–27: Rule of Rana Sanga in Mewar, Rajasthan.

1510: The Portugese capture Goa. Albuquerque is the governor.

1511: Babur captures Samarqand again.

1513: Death of Albuquerque.

1517: Death of Sikandar Lodi. Accession of Ibrahim Lodi.

1518: Quli Qutb Shah, a Turkish governor of the Bahmani kingdom, declares his independence and moves his capital to Golconda where he establishes Qutb Shahi Dynasty.

1526: First battle of Panipat between Babur and Ibrahim Lodi.

1527: Battle of Khanua between Babur and Rana Sanga.

1528: Babri Masjid built in Ayodhya by Mir Baqi, a nobleman from Babur's court.

1529: Battle of Gogra between Babur and the allied Afghans of Bengal and Bihar.

1529–30: Death of Krishnadeva Raya.

1530: Death of Babur and accession of Humayun.

1533: Bahadur Shah, ruler of Gujarat, captures Chittor.

1534: Humayun marches to Malwa.

1535: Defeat of Bahadur Shah of Gujarat and his flight to Mandu.

1537: Death of Bahadur Shah of Gujarat. Pope Paul II makes Goa an Episcopal See.

1538: Sher Khan, the regent of Jalal Khan Lohani, defeats Ghiyasuddin Mahmud Shah, last sultan of the Husain Shahi dynasty of Bengal. Humayun enters Gaur. Death of Guru Nanak.

1539: Sher Khan defeats Humayun at Chaunsa and assumes sovereignty.

1540: Humayun's defeat near Kanauj.

1542: Birth of Akbar. Sher Shah (formerly Sher Khan) builds a fort in Patna and makes it the capital of Bihar. Sher Shah first mints the rupee, a silver coin.

1544: Humayun arrives in Persia.

1545: Death of Sher Shah. Accession of Islam Shah, son of Sher Shah, to the throne of Delhi.

1552: Death of Guru Angad, the second Sikh Guru.

1554: Death of Islam Shah. Accession of Muhammad Adil Shah, son of Islam Shah, to the throne of Delhi.

1555: Humayun recovers the throne of Delhi. Tashi Namgyal ascends Ladakhi throne of 'Lion' and reunifies the kingdom.

1556: Death of Humayun and accession of Akbar. Second battle of Panipat between Akbar and Hemu; Akbar is the winner. Italian traveller and art collector Niccolao Manucci arrives in India.

1560: Fall of Bairam Khan.

1561: Mughul invasion of Malwa.

1562: Akbar marries a princess of Amber.

1564: Abolition of the Jizya. Death of Rani Durgavati and annexation of the Gond kingdom by the Mughals.

1565: Battle of Talikota; Vijayanagar is ransacked by sultans of the Deccan.

1568: Akbar's army captures the fort of Chittor.

1569: Akbar's army captures of Ranthambhor and Kalinjar. Birth of Salim, son of Akbar.

1571: Foundation of Fatepur Sikri by Akbar.

1572: Akbar annexes Gujarat.

1573: Surat surrenders to Akbar.

1574: Death of Guru Amardas, the third Sikh guru.

1575: Battle of Tukaroi between Daud Khan Karrani, ruler of Bengal, and Munim Khan, Akbar's army general; Karrani is defeated.

1576: Subjugation of Bengal. The battle of Gogunda or Haldighat; Rana Pratap defeated by Akbar.

1577: Akbar's troops invade Khandesh.

1580: Accession of Ibrahim Adil Shah II in Bijapur. First Jesuit mission at Agra. Rebellion in Bihar and Bengal by Daud Khan Karrani.

1581: Akbar's march against Mirza Muhammad Hakim in Kabul and reconciliation with him. Death of Guru Ramdas, fourth Sikh guru.

1582: Din-I-Ilahi or Divine Faith promulgated by Akbar.

1589: Death of Todar Mal, finance minister of Akbar, and Bhagwan Das, Todar Mal's colleague in charge of Lahore.

1591: Mughul conquest of Sind.

1592: Annexation of Orissa by Akbar.

1595: Siege of Ahmadnagar by Mughal army. Acquisition of Quandahar by Akbar. Annexation of Baluchistan by Akbar. Death of Faizi, a poet in the court of Akbar, in Lahore.

1597: Death of Rana Pratap of Mewar.

1600: Governor and Company of Merchants of London Trading into the East Indies or British East India Company formed by royal charter. Ahmadnagar stormed by Mughal army.

1601: Golden Temple at Amritsar is completed.

1602: Death of Abul Fazl. Formation of the United East India Company of the Netherlands.

1604: Adi Granth, the holy book of Sikhs, compiled.

1605: Death of Akbar and accession of Jahangir.

1606: Rebellion of Khusrau , son of Jehangir. Qandahar invaded by the Persians. Execution of the fifth Sikh guru, Arjan Dev, by Jahangir.

1607: Qandahar relieved by the Mughuls. Sher Afghan, first husband of Nur Jahan, killed. Second revolt of Khusrau. First trading post set up in Surat by Dutch East India Company.

1608: Malik Ambar, the prime minister of Murtaza Nizam Shah II, and the founder of the city of Aurangabad takes Ahmadnagar.

1609: Dutch factory at Pulicat.

1611: Jahangir marries Nur Jahan. The English establish a factory at Masulipatam.

1612: Prince Khurram marries Mumtaz Mahal. First English factory at Surat.

1613: Jahangir's firman to East India Company to eastablish a factory at Surat.

1615: Submission of Mewar to the Mughuls. Arrival of Sir Thomas Roe, an ambassador of King James I, in India.

1616: Sir Thomas Roe received by Jahangir. The Dutch establish a factory at Surat.

1617: Revolt in southern states of empire subdued by Prince Khurram, who receives title of Shah Jahan.

1618: Sir Thomas Roe, after obtaining firmans for English trade, leaves the Imperial Court.

1620: Jahangir captures Kangra Fort.

1625: Dutch Factory at Chinsura.

1626: Death of Malik Ambar. Rebellion of Mahabat Khan.

1627: Jahangir dies and Shah Jahan assumes the throne.

1628: Shah Jahan proclaimed Emperor.

1629: Rebellion of Khan Jahan Lodi, governor of Deccan.

1631: Death of Mumtaz Mahal. Shah Jahan commissions building of her tomb, the Taj Mahal.

1632: Mughul invasion of Bijapur. Grant of the 'Golden Firman' to the English Company by the sultan of Golconda. Construction of Taj Mahal begins at Agra.

1633: End of Ahmadnagar Dynasty.

1636: Shahji, father of Shivaji, enters the service of Bijapur. Aurangzeb appointed Subedar of the Deccan by Shah Jahan

1639: Foundation of Fort St George at Madras by the English. Shuja appointed Subedar of Bengal.

1645: Shah Jahan grants the English exemption from customs duty on trade as a reward for curing Princess Jahanara.

1646: Shivaji captures Torna.

1648: Taj Mahal completed.

1651: English factory started at Hugli. Firman granted to the English Company by Shuja to trade in Bengal.

1653: Aurangzeb reappointed viceroy of the Deccan. The Dutch start a factory at Chinsura.

1656: Death of Muhammad Adil Shah of Bijapur. Another firman granted to the English by Shuja. Job Charnock first comes to Bengal, serves for a while in Cossimbazar, is then sent to Patna. He later returns to Cossimbazar.

1657: Invasion of Bijapur by Aurangzeb. Aurangzeb captures Bidar and Kalyani. Illness of Shah Jahan. The war of succession between Aurangzeb and his brothers begins.

1658: Aurangzeb executes his brothers, imprisons his father and ascends throne.

1659: Murder of Afzal Khan, a general of Bijapur court, by Shivaji.

1659–66: Bernier at the court of Aurangzeb.

1660: Mir Jumla appointed governor of Bengal.

1661: Cession of Bombay to the English by the Portuguese. Execution of Murad. Mughul capture of Cooch Behar.

1663: Death of Mir Jumla. Shaista Khan appointed governor of Bengal by Aurangzeb.

1664: Shivaji sacks Surat. Colbert, the French minister, founds an India Company. Shivaji assumes royal title.

1666: Death of Shah Jahan. Capture of Chittagong by Bujurg Umid Khan, eldest son of Mughal Subahdar Shaista Khan. Shivaji's visit to Agra and escape. Birth of Sikh Guru Gobind Singh.

1668: First French factory started at Surat.

1670: Shivaji raids Surat.

1672: Satnami Sikh rebellion against Mughals. Shaista Khan's firman to the English Company.

1674: Francois Martin founds Pondicherry. Shivaji assumes the title of Chhatrapati.

1675: Execution of Teg Bahadur, guru of the Sikhs, by Aurangzeb.

1677: Shivaji's conquests in the Carnatic. East India Company's charter of 1677 allows them to mint money.

1678: Marwar occupied by the Mughals.

1679: Reimposition of the Jizya by Aurangzeb. Mughul attack on Marwar.

1680: Death of Shivaji. Aurangzeb's firman to the English Company.

1681: Aurangzeb goes to the Deccan. Establishes Aurangabad as new Mughal capital.

1687: Fall of Golconda.

1688: Madras gets a municipal corporation.

1689: Execution of Shambhaji, son of Shivaji. Rajaram, brother of

Shambhaji, succeeds but retires to Jinji.

1698: The English obtain zamindari of Sutanati, Calcutta and Govindapur from Sabarna Raychaudhuris of Bengal.

1699: First Maratha raid on Malwa. Guru Gobind Singh creates Khalsa.

1700: Death of Rajaram and regency of his widow Tara Bai. Aurangzeb appoints Murshid Quli Khan diwan of Bengal.

1701: French East India Company establishes post at Calicut.

1703: The Marathas enter Berar.

1706: The Marathas raid Gujarat and sack Baroda. Murshid Quli Khan shifts capital of Bengal from Dhaka to Murshidabad.

1707: Death of Aurangzeb. Battle of Jajau between sons of Aurangzeb. Accession of Shah Alam I as the Mughal emperor in Lahore.

1708: Shambhaji's son Shahu becomes the king of the Marathas. Death of Guru Gobind Singh.

1712: Death of Shah Alam I. Accession of Jahandar Shah, third son of Shah Alam I, as Mughal emperor.

1713: Jahandar Shah murdered. Farrukhsiyar becomes Mughal emperor.

1714: Shahu dies of smallpox and his minister or Peshwa, Balaji Vishwanath, takes over the Maratha throne.

1716: Execution of Banda, the Sikh leader.

1717: Farrukhsiyar's firman to the English Company.

1719: Farrukhsiyar put to death. Accession of Muhammad Shah, grandson of Shah Alam I, as Mughal emperor.

1720: Accession of Peshwa Baji Rao at Poona. Fall of the Sayyid brothers Rafi-Ud-Darajat and Rafi-ud-Dallah, kingmakers during the late Mughal period. They were killed by Muhammad Shah.

1720–40: Peshwa Baji Rao I extends Maratha rule to north India, raids Delhi.

1724: Saadat Khan appointed governor of Avadh by Mughal emperor Muhammad Shah. Hyderabad becomes essentially independent of Delhi under Governor Nizam-ul-Mulk. Qamar-ud-din becomes wazir of Mughal emperor Muhammad Shah.

1727: East India Company establishes first post office in Calcutta.

1727–39: Rule of Shujauddin Muhammad Khan as governor of Bengal after the death of his father-in-law Murshid Quli Khan.

1739: Nadir Shah sacks Delhi. Death of Shujauddin Muhammad Khan and accession of Sarfaraz in Bengal. The Marathas capture Salsette and Bassein, in what is now Mumbai, from the Portuguese.

1740: Alivardi Khan becomes governor of Bengal. Accession of Balaji Rao Peshwa in Poona.

1742: Maratha invasion of Bengal. Dupleix becomes governor of Pondicherry. Murder of Safdar Ali, Nawab of the Carnatic.

1744–48: War between English and the French in Europe. This led to the conflict between the two parties in the Carnatic resulting in the First Carnatic War.

1746: Labourdonnais, governor of Mauritius, reaches India and occupies Madras, in spite of the opposition of the British fleet; the French colours are displayed on Fort St George.

1747: Invasion of Ahmad Shah Abdali in Lahore.

1748: Death of Nizam-ul-Mulk. Death of Muhammad Shah of Delhi and accession of his son Ahmad Shah.

1749: Death of Shahu. Through the Treaty of Aix-la-Chapelle between the French and the British, Fort St. George is restored to the British.

1750: Defeat and death of Nasir Jung, ruler of Hyderabad.

1750–54: War of the Deccan and Carnatic succession between Chanda Sahib, supported by the French, and Anwar-ud-din, claimant to the throne of Carnatic.

1751: Treaty of Alivardi with the Marathas. Robert Clive captures Arcot.

1754: Recall of Dupleix. End of the Second Carnatic War (1750–54). Accession of Alamgir II as Mughal emperor.

1755: Delhi plundered by Afghan invader Ahmed Shah Durrani.

1756: Death of Alivardi Khan. Accession of Siraj-ud-daulah in Murshidabad.

1756–63: Seven Years War of Austrian succession in Europe and Third Carnatic War between the English and the French in India.

1757: Sack of Delhi and Mathura by Ahmad Shah Abdali. The English capture Chandernagore. Battle of Plassey between Siraj-ud-daulah and the British led by Robert Clive. Mir Jafar made Nawab of Bengal by the victorious British.

1758: Thomas-Arthur, Comte de Lally, French general, reaches India. The Marathas march beyond Punjab to reach Attock in Paktoonistan.

1759: Siege of Masulipatam; the town, garrisoned by the French under Marshal de Conflans, is attacked by an English force of 2500 men under the command of Colonel Forde. After a two-hour bombardment, the post capitulates after putting up a largely symbolic fight.

1760: Battle of Wandiwash; French lose control of the Deccan to the English. Lally defeated by General Sir Eyre Coote and forced to retire to Pondicherry, where he is besieged. Marathas led by Sadashiv Rao Bhau invade Udgir and defeat the Nizam forces by taking Burhanpur, Daulatabad, Ahmadnagar and Bijapur. Mir Qasim, Nawab of Bengal.

1761: Third battle of Panipat between Ahmad Shah Abdali and the Marathas. Fall of Pondicherry; with no hope of reinforcements from France, Lally capitulated to Clive's troops. Shah Alam II becomes Mughal emperor. Accession of Madhava Rao Peshwa in central Maharashtra. Rise of Hyder Ali in Mysore. Clive is ill and leaves for England.

1763: Treaty of Paris. Pondicherry returns to France, but its fortifications are razed and limits set on French military strength on the Coromandel coast; French stations in Bengal are to be strictly commercial.

1764: Battle of Buxar. The British defeat Mir Qasim.

1765: Robert Clive is the governor of Bengal. Death of Mir Jafar. Grant of the Diwani of Bengal, Bihar and Orissa to the British governor of Bengal, Robert Clive, by the Mughal Emperor Shah Alam II. Treaty of Allahabad between Robert Clive and the nawab of Avadh.

1766: Grant of the Northern Sarkars, a district between the mouth of the Krishna and Puri, in Orissa, to the English by the Nizam.

1767: Departure of Clive to London.

1767–69: The First Anglo-Mysore War. The British conclude a humiliating peace pact with Hyder Ali.

1769: The French East India Company is dissolved.

1770: The Great Bengal Famine.

1772: Warren Hastings appointed governor of Bengal. Death of Madhava Rao Peshwa.

1773: The Regulating Act passed by the British Parliament.

1774: The Rohilla War in Rohilkhand near Avadh. Warren Hastings becomes first Governor-General. Establishment of Supreme Court of Judicature in Calcutta by the British.

1775: Trial and execution of Nanda Kumar, a titled member of the Mughal aristocracy who became a naib immediately after the acquisition of the Diwani by the company, for forgery, allegedly at the instigation of Warren Hastings.

1775–82: The First Anglo-Maratha War.

1776: The Treaty of Purandhar, between the British and the Marathas.

1780–84: Second Anglo-Mysore War. The British defeat Hyder Ali. Birth of Ranjit Singh (1780) at Gujranwala.

1780: First Indian newspaper, an English weekly named *Bengali Gazette*, published from Calcutta.

1781: Deposition of Chait Singh, Raja of Benaras. Act passed to amend the Regulating Act.

1782: Affair of the Begams of Avaoh, where Hastings forced them to surrender the treasure they inherited. The treaty of Salbai, between the Marathas and the British. Death of Hyder Ali.

1783: Death of Sir Eyre Coote. Fox's India Bills, introduced in the House of Commons by Charles James Fox, one of which effectively puts the political government of India under the control of a commission appointed by Parliament. The other bill puts the management of the Company's commerce under another commission.

1784: Treaty of Mangalore between Tipu Sultan and the East India Company. Pitt's India Act; it divides the control of governance and trade, with clearly demarcated borders between the Crown and the Company. After this point, the Company function as a regularized subsidiary of the Crown, with greater answerability for its actions. Judge and linguist Sir William Jones founds Calcutta's Royal Asiatic Society.

1785: Resignation of Warren Hastings.

1786: Lord Cornwallis becomes Governor General.

1790–92: Third Mysore War between Tipu Sultan and the British-Maratha-Nizam combine.

1792: Treaty of Seringapatam; Tipu's sons taken as hostage, he suffers huge monetary and territory losses.

1792: Ranjit Singh succeds his father Mahan Singh as leader of Sukrchakhia Misl.

1793: Cornwallis administration concludes Permanent Settlement—a contract between the East India Company and the Bengal landholders allowing the latter to be admitted into the state system as the absolute owners of landed property. The landowners are endowed with the privilege of holding their proprietary right at a rate which is to continue unchanged for ever. Renewal of the Company's Charter.

1794: Death of Mahadji Scindia of Gwalior.

1795: Death of Ahalya Bai Holkar; she ruled from Indore.

1797: Zaman Shah, ruler of Kabul, attacks Lahore. Death of Asaf-ud-daulah, nawab of Avadh.

1798: Wazir Ali becomes the nawab of Avadh after the death of Asaf-ud-daulah. British Lord Mornington (Wellesley) becomes Governor General. Wellesley signs Subsidiary Alliance Treaty with the Nizam.

1799: Fourth Anglo-Mysore War. Death of Tipu. Partition of Mysore. Ranjit Singh's appointment to the governorship of Lahore. William Carey opens Baptist Mission at Serampore.

1800: Death of Nana Fadnavis, a minister of the Peshwa. Establishment of Fort William College by Wellesley. First multilingual press set up in Serampore.

1801: Annexation of the Carnatic by the British.

1802: Treaty of Bassein between Peshwa Baji Rao II and the East India Company.

1803–05: The Second Anglo-Maratha War: British defeat the Marathas at Assaye.

1805: British siege of Bharatpur fails. Recall of Wellesley.

1806: Vellore Mutiny: Revolt in Madras army over order to change headdress, instigated by Tipu's sons and retainers.

1808: Mission of Malcolm to Persia and of Elphinstone to Kabul.

1809: Treaty of Amritsar between the Sikhs and the British defines the River Sutlej as the boundary between the two.

1813: Renewal of the Company's Charter by the British government.

1814–16: The Anglo-Gurkha War.

1817–18: British campaign against the Pindaris, irregular armies of looters in central India; Pindari forces dispersed.

1817–19: The last Anglo-Maratha War between the British and the armies of Peshwa Baji Rao II, Bhonsles of Nagpur, Holkars of Indore. Baji Rao II defeated and sent to Kanpur as a prisoner.

1819: Monststuart Elphinstone appointed governor of Bombay.

1820: Thomas Munro appointed governor of Madras. Missionaries at Serampore bring out the first ever Bengali weekly *Samachar Darpan.*

1822: *Bombay Samachar*, a Gujarati daily, is published; it is the longest surviving daily in India.

1823: General Committee of Public Instruction formed in Calcutta. Sanskrit College founded in Calcutta.

1824: Sepoys at Barrackpore revolt citing small pay and religious reasons when asked to move to Arakan. Many of them hanged and some shot dead.

1824–26: The First Anglo-Burmese War.

1827: Death of Sir Thomas Munro, governor of Madras. Sir John Malcolm appointed governor of Bombay.

1828: Lord William Bentinck becomes Governor General. Bengali reformer Raja Ram Mohun Roy founds the Brahmo Samaj, initially known as the Brahmo Sabha, in Calcutta.

1829: Prohibition of Sati by Governor General William Bentinck.

1829–37: Suppression of Thuggees, gangs of roving criminals who looted and strangled their victims, primarily in Bengal, by British officer William Sleeman.

1831: Raja Ram Mohun Roy in England as the ambassador of the Mughal Emperor Akbar Shah II. Raja of Mysore deposed and its administration taken over by the East India Company. Meeting of Ranjit Singh and Governor General Bentinck at Rupar: Ranjit Singh agrees to let British traders use the Sutlej River.

1832: Annexation of Jaintia by the British.

1833: Renewal of the Company's charter by the British Parliament. The Charter Act of 1833 also requires the Company to divest itself of administering religious endowments. The English are now allowed to acquire land in India.

1834: Annexation of Coorg by the British. Law Commission appointed with Thomas B. Macaulay at its head. Formation of the Agra Province by the Charter Act of 1833; Metcalfe is the first governor.

1835: Bentinck announces that the British government should promote European literature and science by making English the language of higher education. Macaulay's *Minute on Education* argues that English should be taught instead of Sanskrit and Arabic. English is declared the official language of the East India Company's administration. Civil service jobs in India are opened to Indians. After Bentinck is removed Charles Metcalfe serves as acting Governor General for one year; he removes the existing restrictions on the press. First tea garden opened at Lakhimpur, Assam.

1838: British ask Ranjit Singh to help Shah Shuja regain his throne at Kabul. A tripartite treaty is signed in July 1838.

1839: Death of Ranjit Singh. India gets 21-mile-long telegraph line between Calcutta and Diamond Harbour.

1839–42: Persian army lays siege to Herat, leading to the First Anglo-Afghan War.

1843: Conquest of Sind. Gwalior War and adoption of the child-heir Jayavi Rao Scindia to the vacant throne. Panjim becomes capital of Goa.

1844: India's oldest teak plantation set up in Nilambur in Malabar.

1845: Commercial Bank of India founded.

1845–46: First Anglo-Sikh War.

1848: Lord Dalhousie becomes Governor General.

1848–49: Second Anglo-Sikh War results in the defeat of the Sikhs and annexation of Punjab.

1849: Opening of a Hindu girls' school in Calcutta by John Drinkwater Bethune.

1850: First English translation of *Rig Veda* by H.H. Wilson.

1851: British India Association formed. Madras Medical College established. Geological Survey of India established.

1852: Second Anglo-Burmese War. First Indian stamp, Scinde Dawk, issued at Karachi.

1853: Railway line opened from Bombay to Thane. Telegraph line from Calcutta to Agra. Annexation of Nagpur by Lord Dalhousie using the 'Doctrine of Lapse'. Cession of Berar to the British. Renewal of the Company's charter. Indian Civil Services examination introduced. Bengal Chamber of Commerce comes into being.

1854: Sir Charles Wood's Education Despatch, aimed at creating a properly articulated system of education, from the primary school to the university. India's first railway bridge built over Thane creek. First textile mill opened at Tardeo, Bombay.

1855: Santhal insurrection breaks out under the leadership of two brothers Sidhu and Kanhu in Chhotanagpur area. Revolt crushed by the British.

1856: Annexation of Avadh by Dalhousie; Wajid Ali Shah leaves for Calcutta. Remarriage of widows legalized.

1857: The revolt of 1857. Uprising of Indian sepoys at Barrackpore,

Meerut, Lucknow and Kanpur joined by Rani of Jhansi, Nana Saheb, Tantia Tope. Bahadur Shah Zafar declared emperor; revolt crushed and emperor exiled. The University Act passed by the Indian Legislative Council for the establishment of a university at Calcutta.

1858: The Government of India Act: British India placed under the direct government of the Crown. Queen Victoria's Proclamation. Port Blair becomes a penal settlement.

1859: Indigo Revolt: Violent movement all over Bengal against European indigo planters.

1861: The Indian Councils Act passed, enables participation of Indians in the Governor General's council. The Indian High Courts Act establishes high court of judicature. Introduction of a professional police organization under the Police Act of 1861. Paper Currency Act gives India a legal tender paper currency. Jhansi is ceded to the Scindias.

1862: Introduction of the Indian Penal Code (IPC) on 1 January 1862. Earl of Elgin is the new viceroy.

1863: Bombay-Burma Trading Corporation and National Bank of India established.

1865: The Orissa Famine. Opening of telegraphic communication between India and Europe.

1867: Debendranath Tagore buys a vast tract of land in Birbhum district of Bengal and sets up an ashram now famous as Santiniketan.

1868: The Punjab Tenancy Act. Railway line opened from Ambala to Delhi. Vernacular Press Act passed.

1869: Lord Mayo becomes viceroy.

1870: Lord Mayo's Provincial Settlement. First submarine telegraph cable laid from UK to Bombay.

1872: First census in colonial India. Lord Mayo assassinated. Bombay Municipal Corporation established.

1874: The Bihar famine.

1875: Gaikwad of Baroda's succession case: Sayaji Rao III becomes ruler. Prince of Wales visits India.

1876: British Parliament passes the Royal Titles Act creating Queen Victoria Empress of India. Lord Lytton is the new viceroy.

1877: Delhi Durbar: Queen of England is proclaimed the Empress of India.

1878: Outbreak of the Second Anglo-Afghan War. The Vernacular Press Act intended to muzzle the periodicals in Indian languages.

1881: The Factories Act passed; minimum age of workers raised. Mysore restored to Wadiyars by the British.

1882: The Hunter Commission, officially known as Indian Education Commission, is the first education commission in India. Telephone exchanges opened at Bombay, Calcutta and Madras.

1883: The Ilbert Bill bans the protected status of the whites and seeks equality of all subjects, native or otherwise, in the eye of law. India's first public theatre Star inaugurated in Calcutta.

1885: Foundation of Indian National Congress by Alan Octavian Hume. Bengal Tenancy Act. Bengal Local Self-Government Act. Third Anglo-Burmese War.

1888: Durand Cup, the world's third oldest football tournament, started in Shimla.

1889: Abdication of Maharaja Pratap Singh of Kashmir.

1891: The Factories Act is passed covering all factories employing more than 50 workers. The Age of Consent Act is passed.

1892: The Indian Councils Act is passed to regulate Indian administration.

1893: The Indian Football Association is established. Swami Vivekananda delivers his landmark speech at the Parliament of Religions in Chicago.

1894: Cornelia Sorabjee becomes the first Indian woman law graduate.

1896: Lumiere Brothers' Cinematographic shows a motion picture for the first time in India at Watson's Hotel, Bombay.

1896–97: Plague in Bombay. A great famine sweeps through India.

1899: Lord Curzon becomes the viceroy. Mahatma Gandhi organizes Indian Ambulance Corps for the British during the Boer War in South Africa. Sir M. Monier Williams's Sanskrit-English Dictionary published.

1901: North West Frontier Province is created by the British. The Imperial Cadet Corps is established. Indian Mines Act enacted. J. Watson Harod opens the first branch of the Gramaphone Company Limited in Calcutta. These are the first gramaphones in India. Rabindranath Tagore inaugurates the ashram school at Shantiniketan. Queen Victoria dies and a plan to built the Victorial Memorial is drawn up.

1902: The first wireless communication is established between Sagar Islands and the Sandheads in Diamond Harbour near Calcutta.

1903: India's first 5-star hotel, the Taj Mahal at Bombay, starts doing business.

1904: British Expedition to Tibet. Universities Act: Allowing the universities to be a centre of research and learning from merely a rewarding agency. Co-operative Societies Act passed. The British establish an Archaeological Department in India. Gandhi establishes the weekly journal, *Indian Opinion*. Organizes Phoenix Settlement near Durban.

1905: The First Partition of Bengal. Swadeshi campaign, boycott of British goods in protest. Lord Minto becomes Governor-General. Aga Khan III meets Minto in Simla and demands political rights to Muslims in India. Morley becomes Secretary of State for India. The first rifle factory is established at

Icchapore. Hafiz Abdul Majeed founds Hamdard. Prince of Wales (later George V) lays the foundation stone for the Prince of Wales Museum in Bombay.

1906: Foundation of the Muslim League by Aga Khan III in Dhaka. Congress declaration regarding Swaraj. First satyagraha campaign began with meeting in Johannesburg by Mahatma Gandhi in protest against proposed Asiatic ordinance directed against Indian immigrants in Transvaal.

1907: Madame Bhikaji Cama unfurls the flag of India at the Stuttgart Congress of the Second International in August. Spirit of the National Congress into Moderates and Extremists. Tata Iron and Steel Company (TISCO) is founded with Indian capital at Sakchi.

1908: Newspapers Incitement to Offences Act gives a magistrate the power to seize a newspaper if it published anything malicious. Khudiram Bose is sentenced to death for assassination attempt on Magistrate Kingsford which resulted in the killing of two British ladies. The Explosive Substances Act is enacted. The Calcutta Stock Exchange is inaugurated.

1909: The Morley-Minto Reforms: Officially known as India Act of 1909, it introduced separate electorate for the Muslims, inclusion of an Indian on the central and provincial councils and also on the council of the Secretary of State for India. The Indian Institute of Science in Bangalore is set up.

1910: Lord Crewe becomes the Secretary of State for India. Mahatma Gandhi establishes Tolstoy Farm near Johannesburg.

1911: The Delhi Durbar and announcement that Imperial capital moves to Delhi from Calcutta. Partition of Bengal modified. Mohun Bagan Club of Calcutta defeats East Yorkshire Regiment 2-1 in the IFA Shield final. Jinnah first introduces the Wakf Bill in the Imperial Legislative Council.

1912: Tata Iron and Steel Company begins production.

1913: Government of India Resolution on Educational Policy passed. The self-educated Indian genius Srinivasa Ramanujan sends a long list of brilliant theorems to British mathematician G.H. Hardy, and begins to come to the attention of academia. *Raja Harishchandra*, the first totally indigenous Indian feature film, is released. Rabindranath Tagore is awarded the Nobel Prize for Literature.

1914: Indian Science Congress holds its first session at Calcutta.

1915: Defence of India Act passed to deal with revolutionary and German-inspired threats. Gopal Krishna Gokhale, leader of the 1907 split in Congress and former member of Imperial Legislative Congress, dies. Mahatma Gandhi establishes Sabarmati ashram near Ahmedabad.

1916: The Lucknow Pact of the Indian National Congress and the All-India Muslim League to strengthen the demand for self-government. The Home Rule League founded by Lokmanya Bal Gangadhar Tilak in Poona. Annie Besant founds Home Rule League in Madras. Foundation of the Women's University at Poona.

1917–18: Indians made eligible for the King's Commission. Report of the Industrial Commission is submitted. The Champaran Satyagraha led by Gandhi begins in Bihar in support of indigo peasants. Anne Besant is the president of Congress. Montagu-Chelmsford Report appears in the summer of 1918, aiming at introducing partial responsible government in the provinces of British India. The Indian National Liberal Federation is set up by moderate members of Congress.

1919: The Jallianwala Bagh massacre happens on 13 April at Amritsar. Rowlatt Act is passed to give the Government of India summary powers to curb seditious activities. Rabindranath

Tagore renounces knighthood protesting against Jallianwala Bagh massacre. *Orphans of the Storm* is the first film to be certified by the Censor Board in India. Montagu-Chelmsford Reforms (implemented in 1921) provides step to self-government within empire with greater provincialization. Moplah Revolt on Malabar coast.

1920: The Khilafat Movement initiated by the Ali brothers, Muhammad Ali and Shawkat Ali. The Non-Co-operation Movement begins as a spin off of the Khilafat Movement. Gandhi elected president of All-India Home Rule League. Gandhi appeals for satyagraha resolution at the Congress session in Delhi. First Indian Khilafat delegation reaches London.

1921: The Moplahs rebellion starts on the Malabar coast. The Prince of Wales visits India. The Duke of Connaught lays foundation stone of All India War Memorial or India Gate. The discovery of the Indus Valley Civilization in Sind. Subramania Bharti, the Tamil poet, dies a tragic death.

1922: The Royal Military College opens in Dehra Dun. Delhi University is incorporated. Tagore's school at Shantiniketan becomes Vishva Bharati University. 38th Session of Indian National Congress at Gaya. India granted the right to be represented at the International Labour Organization. Civil Disobedience Movement launched, followed by violence at Chauri-Chaura which leads Gandhi to suspend the movement.

1923: Swarajists led by Motilal Nehru and C.R. Das decide to participate in Indian Council elections. Franchise for women in the United Provinces and Rajkot. First May Day celebrations in Madras. Radio clubs of Bombay and Calcutta broadcast their programmes.

1924: 40th Session of the Congress at Belgaum, Gandhi presides. First All-India Communist Conference in Kanpur.

The Gateway of India opened by Viceroy Earl of Reading. Subhas Chandra Bose is elected Mayor of Calcutta Corporation. Sir John Marshall discovers relics of Indus Valley Civilization.

1925: Vaikom satyagraha led by Kerala Provincial Congress Committee starts near Travancore to allow 'untouchables' to use roads round a temple. Elected legislative council at Cochin. RSS is founded at Nagpur by K.B. Hegdewar. Reforms Enquiry Committee Report. C.R. Das dies at Darjeeling. Franchise for women in Bengal. Electric Railway declared open in Bombay. Moderate Congress leader Surendranath Bannerjee dies at Barrackpore. Maharaja Hari Singh is the new ruler of Kashmir. Indian Hockey Federation is born. Lord Irwin succeeds Earl Reading as Viceroy and Governor General of India.

1926: Royal Indian Navy is created. Lord Reading's letter to the seventh Nizam asserting sovereignty of the British government is supreme everywhere in India. Royal Commission on Agriculture. Public Service Commission is constituted. Factories Act. Kakori Case: Ashfaqullah, Rajendra Lahiri and Ram Prasad Bismil are accused of conspiring to blow up the viceroy's train at Kakori. Shri Aurobindo Ashram is set up in Pondicherry.

1927: Indian Navy Act. British Parliament appoints Simon Commission to study the political reforms in India. Accused in the Kakori Conspiracy case Ashfaqullah, Rajendra Lahiri and Ram Prasad Bismil are hanged. FICCI is established by Purshottamdas Thakurdas, G.D. Birla and others. Jawaharlal Nehru succeeds in passing a resolution declaring complete independence as the goal of Congress at the Madras session.

1928: Simon Commission arrives in India; Congress boycotts the Commission; hartal observed in all major Indian cities. Lala Lajpat Rai dies after receiving blows during his protest against Simon Commission. No-tax satyagraha campaign is launched at Bardoli, led by Sadar Patel. Bhagat Singh, Ajoy Ghosh and Jatindranath Sanyal set up Hindustan Socialist Republican Army(HSRA). India wins hockey gold at Amsterdam Olympics. The Nehru Report: Motilal Nehru chairs an all party meeting and publishes a report defining Dominion Status as the form of government desired by India. Gandhi moves resolution at Congress session at Calcutta, calling for complete independence within one year, or else the beginning of another all-Indian satyagraha campaign.

1929: Lord Irwin promises Dominion status for India. Congress calls for full independence. All-India Trade Union Congress splits National Trade Union Federation is established; Jawaharlal Nehru and the Communists stay with AITUC; moderates leave. HSRA members try to kill Lord Irwin by blowing up his train. Bhagat Singh and Batukeswar Dutta arrested for throwing a bomb in the central legislative assembly in Delhi. Child Marriage Restraint Bill better known as Sarda Act passed raising the age for marriage from 15 to 18 for girls and from 18 to 21 for boys. Lahore session of the Congress; Jawaharlal Nehru hoists the National Flag at Lahore. Weekly air mail service between India and UK inaugurated. Appointment of the Royal Commission on Indian Labour. Viceroy House, now Rashtrapati Bhawan, has its first occupant Lord Irwin. Abdul Gaffar Khan, a Pakhtoon leader and aide of Gandhi, or Frontier Gandhi, organizes Khudai Khitmatgar. Teen Murti Bhawan is built to house the British Commander-in chief in India.

1930: Congress Working Committee meeting at Sabarmati Ashram asks Gandhi to launch Civil Disobedience Movement. Salt satyagraha, Gandhi's Dandi March. C. Rajagopalachari leads a salt march from Trichinopoly to Vedaranniyam. Jawaharlal Nehru is arrested; soon Gandhi's arrest is ordered. Gandhi's arrest leads to massive protests, especially Bombay and Calcutta. Simon Commission submits report, does not mention Dominion Status; British PM Ramsay McDonald 'rejects' the commission's findings. First Round Table Conference opens in London: Congress leaders are absent from the conference which is supposed to decide the future of India. Bhagat Singh, Rajguru and Sukdev are sentenced to death in the Lahore conspiracy case. Chittagong armoury raid led by Surya Sen. Child Marriage Act comes into effect. C.V. Raman wins the Nobel prize in physics. Great Depression (fall of agrarian prices) hits India.

1931: Gandhi-Irwin Pact signed, ends the civil disobedience movement. Gandhi sails from Bombay accompanied by Mahadev Desai, Naidu, Mirabehn, Pandit Madan Mohan Malavia etc. for the second Round Table Conference. The Indian Statistical Institute (ISI) founded by Professor P.C. Mahalanobis in Kolkata. Motilal Nehru dies in Lucknow. Mother Teresa takes her vows in Darjeeling. India's first talkie *Alam Ara* directed by Ardeshir M. Irani is released. Karachi session of Congress appoints Gandhi as its representative at the Round Table conference. Lord Willingdon is the new Viceroy of India.

1932: Gandhi arrested in Bombay with Sardar Patel and detained without trial at Yeravda prison. Madan Mohan Malviya arrested on the eve of Congress session in Delhi. Third Round Table Conference in London. The Communal Award creates separate electorates for 'depressed' classes; Gandhi protests and starts fast at Yeravada jail. The Poona Pact modifies the communal award. Sheikh Abdullah establishes All J&K Muslim

Conference. The Indian Military Academy set up in Dehra Dun. J.R.D. Tata pilots pioneering flight from Karachi to Bombay. India are the hockey champions at the Los Angeles Olympics. India plays its first Test Match in England; India lost the Test.

1933: Publication of the White Paper on various issues discussed at the Round Table Conference. Gandhi begins weekly publication of *Harijan* in place of *Young India*. Civil Disobedience Movement restarts. Indian National Airways launches daily air service between Calcutta and Dhaka. Gandhi on a ten-month tour of every province in India to help end untouchability. Kasturba Gandhi arrested and imprisoned for sixth time in two years. First Test match on Indian soil at Bombay, Lala Amarnath is the first Indian to score a century.

1934: Civil Disobedience Movement called off. Gandhi escapes attempt on life at Poona. The Indian Factories Act, 1934. The Bihar Earthquake. Joint Committee on Indian Constitutional Reform. Ranji Trophy is instituted.

1935: New Government of India Act passed. Golden Jubilee year of the Indian National Congress. Reserve Bank of India is formally inaugurated on I April. India's first national park, the Corbett National Park, is created in Uttar Pradesh. R.K. Narayan publishes his first novel *Swami and Friends*. Subrahmanyan Chandrasekhar calculates mass limit for stellar collapse of a white dwarf star.

1936: Death of King-Emperor George V. Accession and abdication of Edward VIII. Accession of George VI. Jawaharlal Nehru is the president at the 52nd session of Congress at Lucknow. All India Kisan Sabha is formed. Madame Cama who unfurled the first Indian flag at the International Socialist Congress in Stuttgart, dies. India wins hockey gold at Berlin Olympics. Author Munshi Premchand

dies. All India Radio inaugurated. Lord Linlithgow succeeds Lord Willingdon as Viceroy. First-ever elections in India.

1937: Inauguration of Provincial Autonomy. First elections held, won by Congress. Congress ministries in the majority of Provinces. C. Rajagopalachari forms a ministry in Madras. Hindu Women's Right to Property Act passed. Scientist J.C. Bose dies.

1938: Subhas Chandra Bose elected president of the Congress at Haripura session. Vinoba Bhabe establishes ashram at Poona. Bharatiya Vidya Bhavan founded in Bombay by K. M. Munshi.

1939: Second World War begins (3rd September). Resignation of Congress Ministries and the beginning of political deadlock in India. U.N. Brahmachari establishes India's first blood bank at Calcutta. Subhas Chandra Bose resigns from Congress, forms Forward Bloc.

1940: Lahore Resolution ('Pakistan Resolution') of the Muslim League, 'two nations' theory articulated by Jinnah. Udham Singh murders Michael O'Dwyer in London. Singh hanged at a later date. Wardha session of CWC approves Gandhi's proposal for individual civil-disobedience. Maulana Azad is Congress President.

1941: Subhash Chandra Bose reaches Germany. First shipbuilding yard is completed at Vishakhapatnam. Rabindranath Tagore dies.

1942: Fall of Singapore to Japan. Evacuation of Rangoon followed by influx of refugees into India. Gandhi meets Sir Stafford Cripps in New Delhi but calls his proposals a post-dated cheque; they are ultimately rejected by Congress. Congress adopts the Quit India resolution. August Revolution and arrest of Indian Leaders. Forward Bloc is banned; Subhas Chandra Bose meets Hitler in Berlin.

1943: Lord Wavell is the new Viceroy. Subhas Chandra Bose is in

Tokyo. Bose organizes the Indian National Army; creates the provincial government of free India in Singapore. Gandhi on a 21-day fast at Aga Khan Palace to end deadlock of negotiations between Viceroy and Indian leaders. Lord Mountbatten is Supreme Commander of South-East Asia. Hyderabad bans the Communist Party in the state. Howrah Bridge over river Hooghly in Bengal is completed. C.D. Deshmukh is the first Indian governor of the Reserve Bank of India. Bombay Talkies' *Kismet* begins its three year eight month record run at Calcutta. Famine in Bengal; many die.

1944: Kasturba Gandhi dies in detention at Aga Khan Palace. Gandhi freed from jail. Gandhi-Jinnah talks opened in Bombay on Rajagopalachari's proposals for solution of constitutional deadlock. Talks break down on Pakistan issue. Battle of Kohima between the Japanese and Allied forces. Justice Party adopts a resolution to form a separate Dravida Nadu.

1945: Lord Wavell's broadcast announcing British Government's determination to go ahead with the task of fitting India for self-government. Lord Wavell invites Congress and Muslim League to Shimla for talks; talks fail. Subhas Chandra Bose mysteriously disappears after an 'air-crash' over Formosa. Telco launched. First trial of Indian National Army men opened.

1946: Mutiny in Royal Indian Navy. Announcement of special mission of Cabinet Ministers to India. Cabinet Mission's plan announced. British Cabinet's plan for Interim Government announced. Muslim League decides to participate in the Interim Government; Congress announces acceptance of the long-term part of 16 May plan, but refuses invitation to participate in Interim Government. Muslim League withdraws its acceptance and decides on a policy of direct action. This leads to outbreak of mob violence in Calcutta and Noakhali. Gandhi on a four-month tour of 49 villages in East Bengal to quell communal rioting over Muslim representation in provisional government. Interim Government formed. Muslim League members sworn in. Constituent Assembly's first meeting. Dr Rajendra Prasad elected president of the Constituent Assembly. Madan Mohan Malviya dies. Sheikh Abdullah organizes the Quit Kashmir movement against Maharaja Hari Singh. Communist-led Telengana movement in Andhra. Indian Telephone Industries is established. Tata Airlines renamed Air India. Nehru publishes *The Discovery of India* from the Ahmadnagar fort prison.

1947: British PM Clement Attlee's historic announcement of transfer of power to 'responsible Indian hands' not later than June 1948. Lord Mountbatten's appointment as Viceroy of India in succession to Lord Wavell. Announcement of Lord Mountbatten's plan for Partition of India. Indian Independence Act is passed. Creation of dominions of India and Pakistan act passed by British Parliament. Sir Cyril Radcliffe's Boundary Commission set up to create the borders in Bengal and Punjab in June; Radcliffe awards are announced a month later. Jinnah insists on the creation of Pakistan; Muslim League begins 'Direct Action'. Pakistan is created by partitioning India on 14 August 1947. Patel's efforts to include princely states in the Indian Union begin. India wins freedom on 15 August; Jawaharlal Nehru is the country's first PM. Hundreds of thousands die in widespread communal violence after partition. India appeals to UN to intercede in the Kashmir dispute. Junagarh accedes to Pakistan. Kashmir becomes part of India. The accession, not recognized by Pakistan, leads to Indo-Pak conflict. C.N. Annadurai forms DMK. Sarojini Naidu is the Governor of UP. Vijaylakshmi Pandit is the ambassador to UN. Shanmukham Chetty presents independent India's first budget. Kundanlal Saigal dies in Jalandhar.

1948: Mahatma Gandhi killed by Nathuram Vinayak Godse on 30 January at Birla House in Delhi. Sri Chakravarti Rajagopalachari appointed Governor-General of India. Reserve Bank of India nationalized. Death of Qaid-i-Azam Mohammad Ali Jinnah. Troops of Government of India enter Hyderabad state. War with Pakistan over disputed territory of Kashmir. Integration of princely states into Indian Union. B.R. Ambedkar presents first Draft Constitution to Constituent Assembly.

1949: Ceasefire in Kashmir. India's ceasefire line with Pakistan demarcated. New Constitution of India adopted and signed.

1950: New Constitution comes into force on 26 January; India becomes a republic. Rajendra Prasad becomes the first President of Republic of India. Inauguration of the Supreme Court. India's first home minister Sardar Patel dies. Nehru-Liaqat Pact on minorities. Sri Aurobindo is dead.

1951: Inauguration of First Five-Year Plan. First census is carried out in independent India. Debate on Kashmir begins in UN security Council. Shyama Prasad Mookherjee establishes Bhartiya Jan Sangh.

1952: First General Election of independent India. Accession of Queen Elizabeth II. Chandernagore incorporated into India. Dr Rajendra Prasad is elected President of India. G.V. Mavalankar becomes the first Speaker of the Lok Sabha. First Five-Year Plan. Construction of Chandigarh begins. Sheikh Abdullah's ministry in Kashmir confirms accession to India. India launches its family planning programmes.

1953: New state of Andhra inaugurated. Chandigarh inaugurated as capital of Punjab. Mount Everest scaled by Edmund Hillary and Tenzing Norgay. PM of Kashmir Sheikh Abdullah imprisoned. PMs of India and Pakistan agree to appoint a plebiscite administrator for Kashmir. First backward classes commission headed by Kaka Kalelkar instituted.

1954: Pondicherry, Karaikal, Mahe, Yanon incorporated into India. The Filmfare Awards are instituted. China and India sign the Panchsheel agreement. Special Marriages Act introduces divorces by mutual consent.

1955: Hindu Marriage Act. Congress session at Avadi adopts resolution signalling a socialistic pattern of growth for the country. Satyajit Ray's first feature film *Pather Panchali* released. Kalelkar Commission report fails to recommend reservations for the backward classes.

1956: Nationalization of insurance companies. Pakistan proclaimed an Islamic republic. Hindu Succession Act. Reorganization of states along linguistic lines. India becomes the first Asian country to reach the semi-finals of the Olympic football tournament. Inauguration of Second Five-Year Plan. Chairman Drafting Committee of Indian Constitution B.R. Ambedkar dies.

1957: Second General Election held. Introduction of the decimal system of coinage. First Communist government in a state of India—EMS Namboodiripad becomes the CM of Kerala.

1958: Introduction of the metric system of weights. Union Finance Minister T.T. Krishnamachari resigns over share scandal. Maulana Abul Kalam Azad is dead.

1959: The Dalai Lama enters Indian territory for political asylum. Namboodiripad's Kerala government is dismissed; President's Rule is imposed. Sino-Indian border disputes. Swatantra Party formed by C. Rajagopalachari. Indo-Portuguese dispute. Arrival of Dwight D. Eisenhower, President of the USA, in New Delhi.

1960: Meeting of the Afro-Asian Conference at New Delhi. Indus Water Treaty with Pakistan. Nehru-Ayub Khan talks. Bifurcation of Bombay into Maharashtra and Gujarat states. Visits of President Voroshilov and Premier Khrushchev of the USSR and President Nasser of the UAR.

1961: Arrival of Queen Elizabeth and the Duke of Edinburgh at New Delhi. Nehru-Chow En Lai talks in Delhi. Operation Vijay and liberation of Goa, Daman and Diu from Portugal.

1962: Dr S. Radhakrishnan and Dr Zakir Hussain sworn in as President and Vice-President of India. Chinese invasion of India. Border war with China. Third General Election; Indian National Congress forms government, Nehru is PM again.

1963: Rajendra Prasad dies.

1964: Jawaharlal Nehru dies (24 May); Lal Bahadur Shastri becomes the new PM. CPI splits into CPI and CPI(M).

1965: Indo-Pak war in the Rann of Kutch. General Thimayya dies in Cyprus leading UN Peacekeepers. Hindi is declared the official language of the Union. DMK leads agitation in Madras. Durgapur Steel Plant becomes operational. First Indian expedition on Everest, led by Commander M.S. Kohli.

1966: Indo-Pak Tashkent accord. Death of Lal Bahadur Shastri at Tashkent. Indira Gandhi is the new PM. Bal Thackeray forms Shiv Sena. Mihir Sen swims across the English Channel. Artist and designer of the Bharat Ratna medallion Nandalal Bose dies. Reita Faria is crowned Miss World. Homi Bhabha, chairman Atomic Energy Commission, dies in an air-crash.

1967: Fourth General Election, Congress wins majority. Dr Zakir Hussain becomes President. First DMK ministry in Madras. Socialist leader Ram Manohar Lohia dies. Earthquake in Maharashtra, 100 dead. India's first cricket captain C.K. Nayudu is dead.

1968: Nobel in physiology and medicine for Hargobind Khurana. Green Revolution begins. Fourth Five-Year Plan postponed. Ustad Bade Ghulam Ali Khan passes away. India's first overseas Test series win, against New Zealand; Mansoor Ali Khan Pataudi is the captain.

1969: President Dr Zakir Hussain passes away. V.V. Giri elected President of India. Congress splits over V.V. Giri's election as President. Indira Gandhi at the helm of Congress. Morarji Desai resigns from cabinet. 14 banks nationalized. Death of C.N. Annadurai.

1970: Prime Minister Indira Gandhi inaugurates Meghalaya. A Bill for setting up of 'North-Eastern Council', to co-ordinate the development and security of Assam, Meghalaya, Manipur, and Tripura passed. Prime Minister Indira Gandhi addresses the Silver Jubilee Session of the United Nations. Supreme court holds nationalization of banks illegal. Privy Purses and special privileges of former Indian rulers abolished. Foundation of Auroville near Pondicherry.

1971: Fifth General Election, Indira Gandhi is re-elected PM. Indo-Soviet 20-year Treaty of Peace, Friendship and Co-operation. Pakistan declares war on India after gunning down of its aircraft near Calcutta. India Army in East Pakistan in support of Mukti Bahini fighting for independence. Pakistan surrenders; Bangladesh is born and recognized by India. India under Ajit Wadekar wins the first-ever Test series in England.

1972: Indira Gandhi and Zulfikar Ali Bhutto sign an Agreement at Simla committing both 'to abjure the use of force in resolving differences'. Mizoram inaugurated as a Union Territory. Arrival of Bangladesh leader Sheikh Mujibur Rehman in Calcutta, and his talks with Prime Minister Indira Gandhi. Indira Gandhi visits Dhaka and a joint statement is issued by India and Bangladesh; India and Bangladesh sign a 25 years' treaty of friendship, co-operation and peace.

1973: India's first Field Marshal is Sam Manekshaw. Coal mines nationalized. Foreign Exchange Regulation Act (FERA) passed.

1974: India carries out an underground nuclear experiment in Pokhran. Fakhruddin Ali Ahmad sworn in as the President of India. Joint Communique by India and Bangladesh; Indo-Pakistan Trade Agreement.

1975: Dr S. Radhakrishnan, former President of India, passes away in Madras. Railway Minister L.N. Mishra killed in a bomb blast at Samastipur railway station. Allahabad High Court upholds Raj Narain's petition against Indira Gandhi on electoral malpractices. National Emergency declared. Sikkim joins India. *Aryabhata*, the first Indian satellite, launched from the Soviet Union. An Ordinance amending the Maintenance of Internal Security Act issued. Announcement of a package of economic measures—the.20 Point Economic Programme.

1976: Parliament approves a Bill extending the life of the Lok Sabha up to 1978. Private Oil companies nationalized. Urban Land Ceiling Regulation Act passed. Doordarshan is separated from Akashvani. Singer Mukesh is dead.

1977: President Fakhruddin Ali Ahmed passes away in New Delhi. Vice-President B.D. Jatti sworn in as acting President. General Elections: Morarji Desai, Atal Bihari Vajpayee, Madhu Dandavate elected to the Lok Sabha; Indira Gandhi defeated in Rae Bareli. Indira Gandhi resigns as PM after triumph of the Janata Party and its allies in the sixth general elections. Morarji Desai elected leader of the Janata Party and sworn in as Prime Minister. Internal emergency promulgated on 25 June 1975 withdrawn. Press Censorship removed. Government revokes the external emergency promulgated on 3 December 1971. N. Sanjeeva Reddy elected unopposed as President of India. Indira Gandhi arrested in New Delhi by CBI on charges of corruption, released unconditionally. Government files petition in Delhi High Court challenging the release order of Indira Gandhi. Prime Minister Morarji Desai and the Soviet President Leonid Brezhnev sign a Joint Declaration in Moscow. India and Bangladesh sign Farakka agreement on water sharing in Dacca. The 44th Constitution Amendment Bill passed by the Lok Sabha.

1978: Congress splits; Indira Gandhi forms Congress(I); gets 'hand' as electoral symbol. Indian Coast Guard is set up. Famous kathak dancer Lachhu Maharaj passes away. The Lok Sabha expels Indira Gandhi from the house and sentences her to imprisonment; she is released a week later.

1979: Mother Teresa receives the Nobel Peace prize. Famous hockey player Dhyan Chand passes away. No-confidence motion against Morarji Desai; Desai resigns. Charan Singh sworn in as Prime Minister of India; resigns. Lok Sabha is dissolved, elections announced. Second backward classes commission constituted; B.P. Mandal is the chairman. Socialist leader Loknayak Jaiprakash Narayan is dead.

1980: Indira Gandhi storms back to power. Mother Teresa receives the Bharat Ratna award. Prakash Padukone wins the All England Badminton Championship. Famous singer Mohammed Rafi passes away. Noted sculptor and painter Ramkinkar Baij passes away. Congress leader Sanjay Gandhi dies in an aircrash. Mandal Commission report tabled. Atal Bihari Vajpayee and Lal Krishna Advani inaugurate Bharatiya Janata Party(BJP).

1981: Census begins all over the country. President's rule is imposed in Assam. Famous actor Nargis Dutt passes away. Salman Rushdie's *Midnight's Children* wins Booker Prize.

1982: Giani Zail Singh is elected President of India. Acharya Vinoba Bhabe dies. 'Palace on Wheels' begins its journey. India hosts the 9th Asian Games in New Delhi. Jammu & Kashmir CM Sheikh Abdullah is dead; Farooq Abdullah is the new CM.

1983: Non-Aligned summit begins in New Delhi. Industrialist G.D. Birla passes away. Bhanu Athaiya wins Oscar for costumes in *Gandhi*. Indian cricket team led by Kapil Dev lifts the Prudential World Cup. Sunil Gavaskar breaks Sir Don Bradman's record of maximum Test centuries. The Vishwa Hindu Parishad (VHP) launches a campaign to build a temple on the disputed site in Ayodhya.

1984: President's Rule imposed in Punjab. Operation Blue Star is launched, Jarnail Singh Bhindranwale and his supporters who were hiding in the holy Golden Temple are flushed out by army operation in which Bhindranwale is killed. Indira Gandhi is assassinated by two security guards. Outbreak of riots in Delhi; Sikhs are targeted. Bachendri Pal is the first Indian woman on top of Mt Everest. Lok Sabha elections held; Congress led by Rajiv Gandhi gets an overwhelming majority. Rajiv Gandhi is sworn in as the Prime Minister of India. Squadron Leader Rakesh Sharma become India's first cosmonaut. Bhopal gas tragedy kills 2500.

1985: Supreme Courts invokes Article 125 in the Shah Bano case. Rajiv Gandhi and Akali leader Harchand Singh Longowal sign Punjab agreement. PM announces Assam accord. M. Azharuddin become the first batsman in the world to hit three centuries in successive Tests on his debut. Indian cricket team wins the Benson and Hedges World Championship cricket tournament. Indira Gandhi National Open University is established. Narmada Bachao Andolan begins. The 52nd Amendment of Constitution; Anti-Defection bill.

1986: Parliament enacts the Muslim Women (Protection of Rights on Divorce) Act, 1986 that gives a Muslim woman the right to maintenance for the period of *iddat* after the divorce.

'First' Indian test tube baby born in Bombay. Noted actor Smita Patil passes away. General K.M. Cariappa is conferred the rank of Field Marshal. 4th Pay Commission submits its report. President's Rule imposed in J&K. Government signs Mizo Accord with Laldenga. Rukmini Devi Arundale, founder of Kalakshetra, passes away. Mikhail Gorbachev visits Delhi. SAARC summit in Bangalore.

1987: Goa becomes the 25th state of India. India deploys troops for peacekeeping operation in Sri Lanka. Noted ornithologist Salim Ali passes away. Sunil Gavaskar scores 10,000th Test run. R. Venkataraman is elected President of India. Playback singer Kishore Kumar passes away.

1988: Janata Dal is formed in Bangalore. Securities and Exchange Board of India (SEBI) comes into existence. Raj Kapoor passes away. Morarji Dasai is bestowed the title of Nishan-e-Pakistan.

1989: More than 70 MPs resign over the Bofor's gun deal issue. PM Rajiv Gandhi tenders his resignation. Lok Sabha elections announced; Congress is the largest party in the Parliament. Ram Janambhoomi foundation stone laid at Ayodhya. V.P. Singh of the newly formed Janata Dal is sworn in as the Prime Minister of India. The Constitution (61st Amendment) Act lowers the voting age from 21 to 18. Supreme Court orders Union Carbide Corporation to pay a compensation of $470 million for the Bhopal Gas tragedy. Mufti Mohammad Sayeed's daughter Rubaiyya Sayeed kidnapped in Kashmir; Rubaiyya released in exchange of 5 secessionists. Osho Rajneesh is dead.

1990: Bofors kickback case FIR registered. Mandal Commission Report on reservation implemented; violence erupts. PM V.P. Singh resigns after losing no-confidence motion in Parliament. Chandra Shekhar become Prime Minister of India. Film director V. Shantaram passes away. BJP President L.K. Advani begins his Rath Yatra to win support for building temple at Ayodhya. Indian troops withdrawn from Sri Lanka.

1991: Congress withdraws support from the Chandra Shekhar government. Lok Sabha elections announced. Rajiv Gandhi dies in a powerful bomb explosion in Sriperambudur during election campaign. Congress gets a majority in the Lok Sabha elections. P.V. Narasimha Rao is the new PM. Liberalization initiated by finance minister Dr Manmohan Singh. Satellite TV makes its debut in the wake of Gulf War. Census in India. Earthquake in Uttarkashi with many casualties.

1992: Satyajit Ray receives an Oscar for lifetime achievement. Prithvi missile launched. Shankar Dayal Sharma becomes President of India. Destruction of Babri Masjid on 6 December leads to communal violence all over the country. Famous vocalist Kumar Gandharva passes away. Satyajit Ray passes away.

1993: Riots in Mumbai. Rupee made convertible on trade account. More than 300 people killed in bomb blasts in Mumbai. Latur and Osmanabad earthquake kill thousands. J.R.D. Tata passes away. Women army officers are commissioned into non-combatant departments of the Indian Army.

1994: R.D. Burman passes away. ONGC becomes a public limited company. Chimanbhai Patel passes away. Manmohan Desai passes away. Devika Rani Roerich passes away. Lt. Gen. Satish Nambiar is new Army Chief. S. Bangarappa sets up Karnataka Congress Party. Wilfred D'Souza is new Goa CM. Sushmita Sen is crowned Miss Universe. Vaikom Mohd. Basheer passes away. Kiran Bedi wins Magsaysay Award. Rupee becomes fully convertible on current account. Cable Television Regulation Ordinance issued. The Gandhi Peace Prize is set up. Government notifies increase in the ceiling on election expenses on Lok Sabha and assembly polls. A.M. Ahmadi sworn in as Chief Justice. Aishwarya Rai is crowned Miss World. Shankar Roy Choudhury becomes new Chief of Army Staff. Giani Zail Singh passes away. H.D. Deve Gowda becomes Karnataka CM. NTR becomes Andhra Pradesh CM. P.K. Chamling becomes Sikkim CM.

Last Ten Years in Review

1995

January: India becomes a member of World Trade Organization (WTO). India and Sudan form a Joint Committee for Economic, Technical, Commercial, Information, Trade and Cultural Co-operation. South African President Nelson Mandela and PM Narasimha Rao sign an agreement on Intergovernmental Joint Commission for Political, Trade, Economic, Cultural, Scientific and Technical Co-operation.

February: AIR launches its FM service in Delhi.

March: Manohar Joshi is sworn in as CM of Maharashtra. Gegong Apang is sworn in as CM of Arunachal Pradesh. Kerala CM K. Karunakaran resigns. A.K. Anthony is sworn in as Kerala CM. President's rule is imposed in Bihar.

April: Former PM Morarji Desai passes away.

May: The Eighth SAARC summit is held in Delhi.

June: Mayawati becomes CM of Uttar Pradesh.

July: Supreme Court upholds the appointment of two Election Commissioners with powers equivalent to those of the Chief Election Commissioner. This clarifies the appointment of M.S. Gill and G.V.G. Krishnamurthy as Election Commissioners for a period of six years.

August: Punjab CM Beant Singh is assassinated. Andhra Pradesh CM N.T. Rama Rao resigns. N. Chandrababu Naidu is elected president of Telugu Desam Party. VSNL launches Internet Access Service.

September: Harcharan Singh Brar is sworn in as CM of Punjab. Music director, composer and lyricist Salil Chowdhury passes away.

October: President's rule is imposed in Uttar Pradesh. Industrialist Aditya Birla passes away.

November: Jaspal Rana wins gold in the individual event in the Commonwealth Shooting Championship.

December: Air Marshal S.K. Sareen takes over as Chief of Air Staff. The first exclusive Indian communication satellite, INSAT-2C, is launched on board Ariane Space rocket from Kourou, French Guyana. Indian remote sensing satellite, IRS-1C, is launched on board Ariane Space rocket from Kourou, French Guyana. India hosts the seventh SAF Games. Unidentified aircraft drops arms over Purulia district in West Bengal.

1996

January: Karnataka agrees to release 6 tmcft of Kavery water to Tamil Nadu. Maharashtra government clears Enron Dhabol Power project at a tariff of Rs 1.86 per unit. PM unveils India's state-of-the-art Main Battle Tank (MBT) 'Arjun'. Supreme Court orders Arunachal Pradesh to give protection to Chakma refugees. Supreme Court holds that horse racing is not gambling, but a game of skill. Victoria Terminus station, Mumbai, is renamed Chhatrapati Shivaji Railway Terminus. Forward trading is revived on BSE. N. T. Rama Rao passes away.

February: Gold price zooms to all-time record high of Rs 5600 per 10 grams. Wills World Cup Cricket is in-

augurated at Calcutta. Delhi CM Madanlal Khurana resigns. North-Eastern Development Finance Corporation is inaugurated. Sahib Singh Verma sworn in as Delhi's CM.

March: Chaudhary Randhir Singh is appointed governor of Sikkim. Former Union Minister Kalpanath Rai quits Congress. President and governors issue notifications for India's elections to elect the 11th Lok Sabha and six state assemblies.

April: Tamil Maanila Congress (Moopanar) party is registered and recognized. Union Ministers P. Chidambaram and M. Arunachalam resign. Supreme Court rules that political parties without audited accounts cannot take advantage of an election law that exempts tax expenditure on candidates. Assam CM Hiteshwar Saikia passes away. Dr Bhumindhar Barman becomes new CM of Assam.

May: Kerala Governor P. Shiv Shanker resigns. Controversial godman Chandraswami is arrested. Reliance Industries become India's first private sector company to post a total income of over Rs 8000 crore. Kerala CM A. K. Antony resigns. Tamil Nadu CM J. Jayalalithaa resigns. PM P. V. Narsimha Rao and his council of ministers resign. M. Karunanidhi (DMK) sworn in as Tamil Nadu CM. Lok Sabha election results are announced (534 out of 537), giving BJP (161) the position of the largest single party. President invites BJP leader A.B. Vajpayee to form government at the Centre. 11th Lok Sabha constituted. Joint Opposition candidate Purno A. Sangma (Cong. MP from Meghalaya) is elected Speaker of 11th Lok Sabha. PM A.B. Vajpayee seeks vote of confidence. 13-day-old BJP led minority coalition government headed by A.B.Vajpayee quits. Janata Dal leader H.D. Deve Gowda, 13-party United Front's consensus candidate for PM, presents to the President letters from 190 MPs pledging support to him.

June: Former President N.Sanjiva Reddy passes away. H. D. Deve Gowda's 21-member Central Cabinet is sworn in. India's third currency note press inaugurated in Mysore. Ram Vilas Paswan is appointed leader of the House in Lok Sabha and I. K. Gujral in Rajya Sabha. United Front government announces common minimum programme.

July: Janata Dal expels Maneka Gandhi from primary membership of the party. Chief Election Commissioner T. N. Seshan wins Magsaysay award. Veteran freedom fighter Aruna Asaf Ali pases away.

August: Leander Paes wins a bronze at Atlanta Olympics. Dr Raj Kumar conferred Dada Saheb Phalke award. Disinvestment Commission set up with G.V. Ramakrishna as chairman. Supreme Court asks Harshad Mehta to pay Rs 217 crore to income tax department.

September: Lok Pal Bill is introduced in Lok Sabha. Suresh Mehta ministry in Gujarat is dismissed, President's rule imposed. Arunachal Chief Minister Apang resigns and forms new party Arunachal Congress. Narasimha Rao resigns from Congress Party president's post.

October: Mother Teresa is made honorary US citizen. President's rule re-imposed in Uttar Pradesh.

November: Madhavrao Scindia rejoins Congress. Indian cricket team wins Titan Cup, beating S. Africa. 'Competition Post Card' is introduced.

December: M.S. Gill is appointed as the new Election Commissioner. Mahashweta Devi is selected for the Jnanpith Award.

1997

January: 30-year Ganga water sharing treaty between India and Bangladesh takes effect. Former Tamil Nadu CM Jayalalithaa released on bail after 27 days in prison. CBI charge-sheets former Haryana CM, Bhajan Lal, former Union ministers, Ajit Singh, Ram Lakhan Singh Yadav and five others in the Rs 3.5-crore Jharkhand Mukti Morcha MPs bribery case. Justice Meera Sahib Fathima Beevi and Justice Sukhdev Singh Kang are appointed governors of Tamil Nadu and Kerala respectively. Fifth Central Pay Commission submits its proposals.

February: Supreme Court declines to grant interim 'stay' in the matter of construction of Alamatti irrigation and power dam in Karnataka beyond 1,680 feet. Shiromani Akali Dal (Badal) president, Parkash Singh Badal, sworn in CM of Punjab for the third time. Ramakrishna Hegde forms the 'Lok Shakti' national political party. J. M. Lyngdoh is appointed Election Commissioner. Justice J. S. Verma is appointed Chief Justice of India. CBI arrests Chandraswami for alleged offences in violation of Foreign Contributions (Regulation) Act, 1976.

March: G. K. Moopanar unanimously elected the first president of the Tamil Maanila Congress. Lok Sabha passes Income Tax (Amendment) Bill, 1997. BJP and BSP agree to form coalition government in UP. Congress (I) withdraws support to 10-month old Deve Gowda government. The Bombay Stock Exchange crashes by 300 points.

April: The Deve Gowda government loses its vote of confidence. Interest rates on domestic term deposits brought down from 10% to 9% by the RBI. I.K. Gujral is chosen United Front leader in place of Deve Gowda. He is then sworn in as PM. I.K. Gujral wins vote of confidence in Parliament.

May: Sonia Gandhi enrols as a primary member of Congress(I). Special judge, V.B. Gupta, discharges Arjun Singh, N. D. Tiwari, Madhavrao Scindia and R. K. Dhawan, former Union ministers, in the Jain Hawala case. Theatre personality Shambhu Mitra passes away.

June: Insat-2D, fourth indigenous communications satellite, put into orbit by Ariane launch vehicle from Kourou in French Guyana. Election Commission fixes 14 July for the election of the 11th president of India. Sitaram Kesri elected president of the Congress(I). Vice-President K. R. Narayanan files nomination papers for presidential election. Film-maker Basu Bhattacharya passes away.

July: K. Raghunath succeeds Salman Haidar as foreign secretary. Tamil actor Sivaji Ganesan gets 1996 Dada Saheb Phalke award. Janata Dal splits. Laloo Prasad Yadav announces formation of Rashtriya Janata Dal. Sharad Yadav elected president of Janata Dal. Environmental activist Mahesh Chander Mehta wins Ramon Magsaysay Award. V.S. Rama Devi is appointed governor of Himachal Pradesh. Vice-President K.R. Narayanan wins presidential election by a record margin. The Union Cabinet decides to implement Fifth Pay Commission recommendations on pay scales and allowances for Central government employees. Laloo Prasad Yadav resigns as Bihar CM after CBI designated court issues an arrest warrant against him in the fodder scam case. Laloo Prasad Yadav's wife Rabri Devi is sworn in as the CM of Bihar. New Bihar CM Rabri Devi proves majority in assembly.

August: The governor of Andhra Pradesh, Krishan Kant, is elected India's new vice-president. The Jain Commission, which looked into the first part of its terms of reference dealing with the sequence of events that led to the assassination of Rajiv Gandhi, submits interim report to government. Lok Sabha holds its longest-ever sitting of about 22 hours for a special golden jubilee session debating issues of national importance.

September: Mother Teresa passes away. Prasar Bharati Act comes into force. Kalyan Singh sworn in as CM of Uttar Pradesh. Gen. V. P. Malik takes over from Gen. Shankar Roychowdhury as Chief of Army Staff. Pravin Thipsay becomes India's third chess grand master.

October: India's first woman police officer, Kiran Bedi, is awarded Joseph Beuys prize for her work in reforming the country's largest prison, Tihar Jail. Arundhati Roy wins the Booker Prize for her novel *The God of Small Things*. Dilip Parikh is sworn in as Gujarat CM. Veena maestro Dr V. Doreswamy Iyengar passes away.

November: Diana Hayden becomes Miss World. Former RBI Governor Dr C. Rangarajan sworn in as governor of Andhra Pradesh. Election Commission derecognizes Janata Party and Congress (Tiwari) as national parties. Dr A.P.J. Abdul Kalam, scientific advisor to defence minister, awarded the Bharat Ratna.

December: Orissa Janata Dal unit splits with 29 of 43 legislature party members forming 'Biju Janata Dal'. Congress leader in West Bengal, Mamata Banerjee, declares that she would seek recognition and separate symbol for her 'Trinamool Congress' and contest elections on her own. Gujarat Assembly is dissolved.

1998

January: Defence Research and Development Organisation (DRDO) and the Indian Air Force (IAF) jointly conduct stealth aircraft experiments resulting in the achievement of 94% radar invisibility.

February: Reserve Bank of India (RBI) allows exporters to receive interest-bearing advance payments not exceeding 100 basis points over Libor (London Inter-Bank Offered Rate) from their overseas buyers.

March: A three-judge bench of the Supreme Court dismisses the special leave petition of the CBI challenging the Delhi High Court verdict quashing the charges against L.K. Advani and V.C. Shukla in the Hawala case. BJP forms government in Gujarat. The final report of the Jain Commission on the conspiracy aspect of Rajiv Gandhi's assassination is submitted to the Union home ministry by the one-man panel. Atal Bihari Vajpayee is sworn in as prime minister along with a 42-member, two-tier ministry. Communist leader and Kerala's former CM, E.M.S. Namboodiripad, passes away.

April: Supreme Court rules that the services of a confirmed employee in both private and government sectors cannot be legally terminated by a simple notice. Kushabhau Thakre is the new BJP president.

May: In Assam, the government decides to make Dispur the permanent state capital. Apart from the creation of a special non-lapsable fund of around Rs1,500 crore each year, PM Atal Behari Vajpayee announces a series of other measures as part of his special north-east package. Short-range triple-role 'Trishul' missile successfully test-fired. The Union government decides to scrap the Urban Land Ceiling Act (ULCA) and raise the retirement age of Central government employees from 58 to 60. India conducts nuclear test at Pokhran.

June: India and Russia reach an agreement on the Russian sale of six 9K81 S-300V mobile air defence systems to India for deployment at front and army level.

July: Centre announces a Rs250 crore assistance to Jammu and Kashmir to help overcome the state's financial crisis and resolves to meet the state's expenditure to combat militancy. The Cabinet clears two bills for introduction in current session of Parliament: Prevention of Money Laundering Bill and Foreign Exchange Management (FEMA). Pratapsingh Rane government in Goa is dismissed and Wilfred De Souza sworn in as the new CM to head the new coalition that includes the BJP. Lok Sabha passes Prasar Bharati Bill by voice vote.

August: Reserve Bank of India lowers the refinance rate for export credit to 7% from 9%. Goa CM Dr Wilfred D'Souza and nine other legislators, who broke away from the Congress in July to form the Goa Rajiv Congress (GRC), are disqualified from the membership of the House. Government launches the 'Kar Vivadh Samadhan Scheme' for quick and voluntary settlement of over five lakh direct and indirect tax disputes amounting to arrears of Rs 52,000 crore.

September: The Bihar assembly rejects the Vananchal Bill.

October: Amartya Sen is awarded the 1998 Nobel Prize in Economics. In a bid to bring more investors to the dematerialized form of trading, the core group on depositories appointed by SEBI decides to make it mandatory for investors to deliver only demat shares if their net outstanding delivery position for a settlement is more than 5,000 shares.

November: The Union Cabinet clears the way for a bill to allow foreign insurance companies to take a 26% stake in new insurance ventures in India. It also allows FIIs to pick up an additional 14% in these organizations. Congress leader in Goa assembly, Luizinho Faleiro is sworn in as CM by Governor Lt. Gen. J. F. R. Jacob.

December: Women's Reservation Bill is introduced in the Lok Sabha. Lok Sabha passes a bill that provides capital punishment to those using special category explosives like RDX, PETN and HMX with an intent to endanger life or property. Union Cabinet okays automatic approval of foreign equity up to 100% for undertaking construction and maintenance of roads, highways, bridges, toll roads and vehicular tunnels as also ports and harbours. Socialist leader Jayaprakash Narayan is posthumously conferred the Bharat Ratna.

1999

January: The government reduces interest rates on small savings schemes, deposit schemes for retired government/PSU employees and relief bonds with immediate effect. The Central government decides to issue a series of ordinances including the Companies Amendment Ordinance and the Patents Amendment Ordinance. Government approves sale of part of its equity in six cash-rich public sector companies through buyback or cross-holding, to meet the disinvestment target of Rs 5000 crore during 1998–99. Arunachal Pradesh CM Gegong Apang resigns as a confidence vote moved by him in a special session of the state assembly is defeated by a margin of 0–36 votes.

February: Shiv Sena leader Narayan Rane is sworn in as the 15th CM of Maharashtra. Anil Kumble creates history by becoming only the second bowler in 123 years of Test cricket to take all 10 wickets in an innings. Supreme Court allows resumption of the construction of Narmada Dam after almost five years. Lok Sabha ratifies President's rule in Bihar.

March: The Patents (Amendment) Bill to allow exclusive marketing rights (EMRs) for foreign pharmaceuticals and agro-chemical firms is passed in the Lok Sabha with Congress support. In Bihar, Congress helps RJD leader Rabri Devi to win a vote of confidence.

April: The 12th Lok Sabha is dissolved.

May: President K.R. Narayanan dismisses Arunachal Pradesh Governor Mata Prasad for refusing to resign. He also accepts the resignation of West Bengal Governor A.R. Kidwai. SENSEX crosses the 4,000 mark. The BJP and its allies decides to name themselves the National Democratic Alliance (*Rashtriya Jantantrik Gathbandhan*). Congress expels rebel leaders Sharad Pawar, P. A. Sangma and Tariq Anwar for six years. Government hikes salaries of PSU employees. India launches air strikes in Kargil.

June: Union government imposes an indefinite ban on receiving signals of the Pakistan Television (PTV) in India. Leander Paes and Mahesh Bhupathi win French Open men's doubles at the Roland Garros. USA lifts sanctions against India.

July: Indian forces regain control of Tiger Hill after a prolonged fight. Leander Paes and Mahesh Bhupathi win the Wimbledon Men's doubles title. Election Commission announces that the general elections for the 13th Lok Sabha will be held in five phases starting from 4 September. On the advice of the Election Commission, the President of India issues a notification debarring Shiv Sena leader Bal Thackeray from contesting elections and disenfranchising him till 10 December 2001. Film actor Rajendra Kumar passes away.

August: Election Commission rejects the Sharad Pawar-led Nationalist Congress Party's plea for allotment of the 'charkha' symbol and orders its freezing. PM Atal Bihari Vajpayee accepts the resignation of Railway Minister Nitish Kumar. Former Union minister Kalpanath Rai passes away.

September: Kapil Dev replaces Anshuman Gaekwad as India coach.

October: President K. R. Narayanan formally invites Atal Bihari Vajpayee to be the next PM. India, UAE sign extradition treaty. Several hundred people are feared killed and over 15 million affected as a super cyclone, with a velocity of more than 260km per hour, hits 10 coastal districts of Orissa for more than eight hours. Najma Heptullah is elected president of the Inter-Parliamentary Council.

November: The Darjeeling Himalayan Railway is included on the UNESCO list of World Heritage sites.

December: Lok Sabha clears IRDA Bill. Yukta Mookhey becomes Miss

World. Indian Airlines flight IC-814 with 178 passengers and 11 crew aboard is hijacked.

2000

January: The special court for CBI cases allows the investigating agency to retain the final set of Swiss Bank documents relating to the Bofors pay-off case for conducting further investigation. SENSEX rises sharply by over 369 points to reach an all-time high of 5375. The Uttar Pradesh assembly passes the UP Regulation of Public Religious Buildings and Places Bill, 2000, to regulate the use and construction of public buildings and places for religious purposes. The government reconstitutes the Indira Gandhi National Centre for Arts (IGNCA) Trust while retaining Sonia Gandhi as a trustee along with P. V. Narasimha Rao, Prof Yashpal and Dr Abid Hussain. T.S. Krishnamurthy is the new Election Commissioner. The government announces an across-the-board 1% cut in the deposit rates on all small savings schemes like Public Provident Fund (PPF), National Savings Certificates, Kisan Vikas Patras, Post Office fixed deposit and Post Office recurring deposit schemes. PM Atal Bihari Vajpayee announces a Rs 10,271-crore 'Agenda for Economic Development' for the North-east and Sikkim. The government issues an ordinance for the reconstitution of the Telecom Regulatory Authority of India and creation of a telecom dispute settlement and appellate tribunal. The Indian team wins the Under-19 World Cup for cricket.

February: Dara Singh alias Ravinder Kumar Pal, wanted in 14 cases including the murder of the Australian missionary Graham Stuart Staines and his two sons, is arrested. The government announces the setting up of an 11-member Constitution Review Commission to be chaired by Justice M.N. Venkatachalaiah. The BJP's allies in the NDA win in Orissa and Haryana but BJP loses in Bihar. Railway Minister Mamata Banerjee presents her first Railway Budget. National cricket selectors appoint Sourav Ganguly as the captain. Biju Janatal Dal president, Naveen Patnaik, is unanimously elected leader of the BJD Legislature Party. Finance Minister Yashwant Sinha presents the Budget for 2000–01 in Parliament.

March: A 34-member United Front ministry headed by Wahengbam Nipamacha Singh is sworn in Manipur. Samata Party leader Nitish Kumar is sworn in as CM of Bihar by the governor, V.C. Pande. A 25-member BJD–BJP coalition ministry headed by the BJD president, Naveen Patnaik, is administered the oath of office by the Orissa governor, M.M. Rajendran. Meghalaya CM, B. B. Lyngdoh, resigns making way for the Speaker, E. K. Mawlong. Supreme Court rules that women employees of municipal corporations and municipal bodies who have been working on 'daily wages' are also entitled to the benefits under the Maternity Benefit Act, 1961. Bihar CM Nitish Kumar resigns. RJD's Rabri Devi is sworn in as the CM of Bihar and administered the oath of office. The Union Cabinet approves a proposal to carry out certain additions and amendments to the Central list of OBCs (Other Backward Classes) as recommended by the National Commission for Backward Classes. The youngest mayor in the country, Panchamarthi Anuradha of the Telugu Desam Party assumes office as mayor of Vijayawada Corporation. Government announces the creation of two special economic zones (SEZs) on the Chinese model in Gujarat and Tamil Nadu.

April: The Reserve Bank of India announces a cut in the bank rate from 8% to 7%. The CM of West Bengal, Jyoti Basu, commissions the Haldia Petrochem Project. The government approves 57 cases of foreign direct investment. Jhumpa Lahiri wins the Pulitzer Prize for fiction for her debut collection of short stories *Interpreter of Maladies*. The nearly three-year-old report of the Chandrachud Committee on match-fixing is placed in the Lok Sabha. 'Nishant', the indigenously built unmanned air vehicle (UAV), is test-flown from the interim test range.

May: Lara Dutta becomes Miss Universe 2000. Former Indian cricketer Manoj Prabhakar releases secret video that reveals the results of his 'undercover investigations' carried out with the help of 'tehelka.com'. VSNL announces a 50% cut in the Internet rates and free access at night as part of a special 'monsoon package'.

June: Senior Congress leader and former Union Minister Rajesh Pilot killed in a car accident. CBI issues summons to several cricketers, including Indian coach Kapil Dev, former skipper Mohammed Azharuddin, former manager Ajit Wadekar and commentators Ravi Shastri and Sunil Gavaskar in the match-fixing case. The government announces disinvestment of its equity in 33 state-owned companies, including privatization or outright sale of 26 public sector undertakings (PSUs), during the current financial year.

July: Report of the 11th Finance Commission is submitted to President K.R. Narayanan. The report will determine the sharing of resources between the Centre and the states for next five years. Union Cabinet gives the five lakh-strong non-executive workforce of public sector undertakings the option of choosing the periodicity of wage revision. Karnataka commits itself to releasing 6 tmct of water to Tamil Nadu within the next 30 days to make good the deficit in the inflow of water into the Mettur reservoir from 1 June. India's first missile-firing submarine, INS *Sindushastra*, is commissioned in St Petersburg, Russia. RBI launches a series of measures to halt the slide of the rupee against the US dollar. The government announces a reduction in the prices of rice and wheat sold under the Public Distribution System. Sandalwood smuggler Veerappan kidnaps famous actor Rajkumar along with three others.

August: Lt Gen. Sundararajan Padmanabhan is announced as the next Chief of the Army Staff replacing Gen. V.P. Malik. Uttaranchal Bill, Jharkhand Bill and Chhattisgarh Bill passed in the Lok Sabha. Famous cricketer Lala Amarnath passes away. Bangaru Laxman is declared elected unopposed as the new BJP president. The Union Power Minister P.R. Kumaramangalam passes away. PM Atal Bihari Vajpayee announces a package of measures to strengthen the small scale sector including raising the ceiling on loans from Rs 10 lakh to Rs 25 lakh and bringing service-oriented units into the ambit of the priority lending programme.

September: Weightlifter Karnam Malleswari wins a bronze at the Sydney Olympics. A special court convicts the former PM P. V. Narasimha Rao and Buta Singh in the 'Jharkhand Mukti Morcha case' on charges of bribing members of Parliament to buy votes to save the minority Congress government in the no confidence motion in 1993. Election Commission derecognizes CPI(M) as a national party but keeps alive its registration as a state party in Kerala, Tripura and West Bengal.

October: The All-India Congress Committee spokesman Ajit Jogi elected Chattisgarh Congress Legislature Party (CLP) leader unanimously. CBI alleges that Azharuddin had fixed matches while Ajay Jadeja and Nayan Mongia helped him.

November: The Union Cabinet allows the private sector to operate direct-to-home (DTH) television services that will enable subscribers to view over 100 channels through a small satellite dish and a TV set-top box containing a SIM card. The Board of

Control for Cricket in India suspends five cricketers: Mohammad Azharuddin, Ajay Jadeja, Nayan Mongia, Ajay Sharma and Manoj Prabhakar. Uttaranchal is born as the 27th state of the country. Jharkhand becomes the 28th state of the Indian Union. Veerappan releases Kannada actor Rajkumar and his relative Nagesh.

December: Priyanka Chopra become Miss World. Election Commission modifies the criteria to determine the status of a political party as 'National' or 'State' party. Azharuddin, Sharma banned for life by the Board of Control for Cricket in India. Government introduces a bill in the Lok Sabha that seeks to reduce its equity in nationalized banks from 51 to 33 % and empowers it to supersede the board of directors of public sector banks and constitute a financial restructuring authority. India and Russia sign their biggest yet defence deal for licensed production of the SU-30MKI fighter jets.

2001

January: India's indigenously built Light Combat Aircraft (LCA) Technology Demonstrator 1 (TD 1) undertakes its landmark first flight. Samata Party splits for the third time. The pilotless target aircraft 'Lakshya' is successfully inducted into the IAF. Senior Congress leader Jitendra Prasad passes away. India successfully carries out the second test of the Agni-II missile. Over two crore take a dip at Sangam in the Kumbh Mela. Union Cabinet permits the Enron Power Development Corporation to increase its stake in the Dabhol Power Project in Maharashtra since the other major partner, the Maharashtra State Electricity Board (MSEB), has expressed its inability to pick up equity in the second phase of the project. Senior BJP leader Vijayaraje Scindia passes away. India, Algeria sign partnership declaration, trade accord.

Major earthquake measuring 6.9 on the Richter scale strikes Gujarat. Prime Minister A.B. Vajpayee sanctions Rs 10 crore for immediate assistance. World Bank offers an immediate assistance of $300 million for emergency rehabilitation work in Gujarat.

February: In an effort to mop up funds for quake-hit Gujarat, the Union Cabinet decides to levy a 2% additional surcharge on income tax and corporate tax for the current financial year. Cabinet Committee on Disinvestment decides to reduce the government's share in Videsh Sanchar Nigam Limited (VSNL) to 26% from the present 52.97%. Former Indian skipper Pankaj Roy passes away. Two Union ministers, N.T. Shan-mugham and E. Ponnuswamy, both from Pattali Makkal Katchi (PMK), resign from the Vajpayee government. Former Information and Broadcasting Minister V. N. Gadgil passes away. Country's largest cigarette manufacturer ITC Limited announces its withdrawal from all sports sponsorship. World's biggest census begins in India. Sitar maestro Pandit Ravi Shankar is bestowed the award of honorary Knight Commander of the Order of the British Empire by the Queen in recognition of his service to music. India and Russia sign a historic accord on massive Indian investment in the Sakhalin oil and gas fields. Cabinet Committee on Disinvestment formally decides to dilute the government's equity holding in the Maruti Udyog Limited (MUL). Manipur Chief Minister Wahengbam Nipamacha Singh submits his resignation to Governor Ved Marwah. Samata Party leader Radhabinod Koijam is sworn in as the chief minister of Manipur. Reserve Bank of India cuts the bank rate and the credit reserve ratio (CRR) by 0.5%. Veteran CPI leader and longest serving parliamentarian Indrajit Gupta passes away. 2000–01 Economic Survey is presented to Parliament by Finance Minister Yashwant Sinha. Chhattisgarh Chief Minister Ajit Jogi wins the Marwahi assembly seat. West Bengal Chief Minister Jyoti Basu retires from electoral politics. Mamata Banerjee presents the 2001–02 Railway Budget. Finance Minister Yashwant Sinha presents the Annual Budget.

March: Bombay Stock Exchange president, Anand Rathi, resigns in the wake of allegations of his involvement in a bear cartel. P. Gopi Chand wins the All England badminton championship. Harbhajan Singh becomes the first Indian to claim a hat-trick in Test cricket, against Australia. Bombay Stock Exchange Sensex crashes by 114 points. Securities and Exchange Board of India (SEBI) restrains all broker member directors from acting as governing board members of the Bombay Stock Exchange (BSE) till further orders. Chokila Iyer assumes charge as India's first-ever woman foreign secretary, replacing Lalit Mansingh. V.V.S. Laxman becomes India's highest individual scorer (281) in a Test innings in the Kolkata Test against Australia. Defence Minister George Fernandes resigns from the Vajpayee government while the Railway Minister and Trinamool Congress chief Mamata Banerjee quits the ministry and withdraws her party's support to the National Democratic Alliance government. Indian cricket team ends Australia's winning streak in Tests by winning the Kolkata Test. Former South African President Nelson Mandela honoured with the Gandhi Peace Prize by President K.R. Narayanan. External Affairs Minister Jaswant Singh is appointed the country's new defence minister in place of George Fernandes. Agriculture Minister Nitish Kumar is given additional charge of railways. Lata Mangeshkar is given the Bharat Ratna award. Indian cricket team retains the Border–Gavaskar trophy winning the Chennai Test. Among others, Amitabh Bachchan is presented the Padma Bhushan award. India touches a popu-

lation of over 1.02 billion. Central Bureau of Investigation (CBI) arrests Ketan Parekh, leading stock broker, in connection with the Rs 130 crore pay-order scam.

April: Board of Control for Cricket in India (BCCI) receives a letter from the government asking it not to take part in any cricket tournament in non-regular venues such as Sharjah, Singapore and Toronto for three years. Congress and the Trinamool Congress announce the formalization of alliance for assembly election in West Bengal scheduled for 10 May. Government decides to give an additional 2% DA to the Central Government staff and 2% Dearness Relief to pensioners. Former Deputy Prime Minister Devi Lal passes away. Uttar Pradesh Chief Minister Rajnath Singh registers a convincing victory in the state assembly by-election from Hydergarh. NASSCOM president Dewang Mehta passes away. DMK leader and Union Commerce and Industry Minister Murasoli Maran announces his intention to 'keep away from active politics on health grounds.' Securities and Exchange Board of India permanently debars Harshad Mehta from dealing in securities and orders his prosecution in connection with the 1998 price manipulations in the scrips of BPL, Videocon and Sterlite. Lok Sabha passes the Railway Budget without any discussion.

May: Centre permits the Food Corporation of India (FCI) to offer for export 30 lakh tonnes of rice during the current financial year. Bismillah Khan receives the Bharat Ratna. About 13 crore voters in Tamil Nadu, West Bengal, Kerala, Assam, and the Union territory of Pondicherry cast their votes for the assembly polls. Former Maharashtra Chief Minister Sudhakarrao Naik passes away. AIADMK, headed by Jayalalitha, secures a landslide victory in the Tamil Nadu Assembly election with 196 of the 234 seats. Congress-led United Democratic Front wins the assembly elections in Kerala, securing a record two-thirds majority. Left Front wins again in the assembly elections of West Bengal. Congress–TMC combine emerges as the largest group in the Pondicherry Assembly elections, but falls short of an absolute majority. Renowned novelist R.K. Narayan passes away. Gold prices zoom to a 14-month high on the bullion market when standard gold touches Rs 4,600 per 10 grams on heavy stockist buying on expectations of a further rise in international prices. Nagendra Nath Jha is sworn in as the seventh Lt Governor of the Andaman and Nicobar Islands.

June: Government declares use of its emblem and name of a Central ministry by private websites as illegal. Air Marshal S. Krishnaswamy is appointed the new Vice Chief of Air Staff. Mahesh Bhupathi and Leander Paes win their second French Open men's doubles title. James Michael Lyngdoh takes over as the Chief Election Commissioner of India. Uma Bharati joins Bajrang Dal. India, Turkey sign extradition treaty.

July: Excise department slaps a Rs 200-crore duty evasion show-cause notice on the country's premier car maker, Maruti Udyog Limited. Centre slashes by about 30% the central issue price of wheat and rice sold to the 'above the poverty line' population (APL) through the public distribution system (PDS). Bangladesh passenger train, the first after 36 years, arrives at the Indian border. 50 lakh people affected in Orissa floods. Actor 'Sivaji' Ganesan passes away. R. Rajagopalan is appointed Director-General of the National Security Guards. Government reconstitutes the Disinvestment Commission, appointing R.H. Patil, chief of the Clearing Corporation of India (CCI), as the new chairman. Samajwadi Party member of Parliament, Phoolan Devi, is killed.

August: Official mascot of the inaugural Afro-Asian Games, Sheroo the lion, is unveiled by Prime Minister Atal Bihari Vajpayee. Milkha Singh refuses to accept the Arjuna Award for lifetime contribution. Supreme Court quashes the reservation for the graduates of All-India Institute of Medical Sciences (AIIMS) for postgraduate courses throwing open almost 100 seats for meritorious students from across the country. Central Bureau of Investigation (CBI) receives the translated version of documents from Sweden relating to the Bofors pay-off case. Tamil Maanila Congress president G.K. Moopanar, passes away.

September: The indigenous anti-tank guided missile, Nag, is successfully test-fired from the interim test range at Chandipur-on-sea. Special court sentences the stock broker, Hiten Dalal, and the former general manager of Canbank Mutual Fund (CBMF), B.R. Acharya, to three years' rigorous imprisonment for various offences including defrauding the CBMF of Rs 32.5 lakh during 1991–92. Mira Nair's *Monsoon Wedding* is awarded the Golden Lion for best picture at the Venice film festival. Seventh Manipur Legislative Assembly is dissolved. Government announces a 2% increase in the dearness allowance for serving Central government employees and a similar hike in the dearness relief for pensioners. India's indigenous ship-to-ship missile, Dhanush, successfully launched from a navy vessel at sea. Congress politician and former Andhra Pradesh CM Kotla Vijaya-bhaskar Reddy passes away.

October: Congress leader Madhavrao Scindia dies in an accident. Lt Gen. Pankaj Joshi takes over as the country's first Chief of Integrated Defence Staff (CIDS) and Lt. Gen. N.C. Vij as the new Vice-Chief of Army Staff. Gujarat Chief Minister Keshubhai Patel submits his resignation to the governor, paving the way for Narendra Modi to take over. George Fernandes returns to the Union government. Prime Minister Atal Bihari Vajpayee inducts the National Democratic Alliance convener into his Cabinet as minister of defence. Asha Bhosle receives the Dada Saheb Phalke Award. Reserve Bank of India (RBI) cuts the bank rate by 50 basis points to 6.5 %—the lowest ever since May 1973. The cricket board's internal inquiry into the match-fixing scandal exonerates Kapil Dev from any wrongdoing and closes all cases pending against him. Government decides to sell six hotels owned by the India Tourism Development Corporation (ITDC).

November: Supreme Court orders a ban on smoking in public places throughout the country with immediate effect. Central Bureau of Investigation (CBI) arrests Harshad Mehta and his two brothers—Ashwin and Sudhir—in connection with a case relating to alleged misappropriation of 27 lakh shares of 90 blue-chip companies. Dr A.P.J. Abdul Kalam steps down as the principal scientific adviser to the government after over four decades of distinguished service in different posts in the government. President K.R. Narayanan confers the prestigious Indira Gandhi Award for Peace, Disarmament and Development on Mary Robinson, United Nations High Commissioner for Human Rights.

December: Acting CBI director P.C. Sharma is appointed full-time chief of the organization. Supreme Court makes fastening of seat belts mandatory for front seat occupants in cars and directs the chief secretaries of the states and Union territories to implement the same. Dr Flinder Anderson Khonglam, leader of the People's Forum of Meghalaya, is formally invited by the acting governor, Arvind Dave, to form a new government. Ashok Kumar, who dominated the Hindi celluloid scene with his inimitable acting for over seven decades, passes away. 250-km

extended range version of the 'Prithvi' missile, developed for the Indian Air Force, is successfully test-fired from the interim test range at Chandipur-on-sea. Suicide squad storms Parliament; 5 militants killed; army deployed. Admiral Madhvendra Singh, India's western naval fleet commander during the 1999 Kargil conflict, takes over as the new naval chief succeeding Admiral Sushil Kumar.

2002

January: STD and ISD services are withdrawn from all private public call offices (PCOs) and cybercafes in the Kashmir valley following reports of misuse by militants. Pakistan government relaxes ban on Indian TV channels. Satish Dhawan, leader of the country's space programme and the longest serving director of the Indian Institute of Science, passes away. BJP leader Govind-acharya quits RSS. Pakistan President Pervez Musharraf bans the Lashkar-e-Taiba and Jaish-e-Mohammad along with three other sectarian and religious extremist outfits. Cabinet Committee on Disinvestment (CCD) decides to refer a fresh group of public sector units (PSUs) to the reconstituted list. The Indian Railways decides to ban smoking in trains, railway stations and all railway offices. In West Bengal, gunmen kill four policemen and critically wound 20 persons in front of the American Center in Kolkata. A third generation communication satellite, Insat-3C, is successfully launched into space on board the European launch vehicle, Ariane-4. The former Indian Air Force chief, Arjan Singh, becomes the first-ever Marshal of the Indian Air Force. Mark Mascarenhas, WorldTel chief and marketing agent of cricketer Sachin Tendulkar, passes away. Supreme Court directs all states to confiscate ultrasound machines used to determine the sex of the foetus in clinics running without a licence.

February: Centre announces stringent punishment and penalties for various types of cyber crimes. Cabinet Committee on Disinvestment (CCD) decides on selling 25% equity in the Videsh Sanchar Nigam Limited (VSNL) to Tata Group. Union Cabinet approves a voluntary retirement scheme for permanent government employees rendered surplus in keeping with the announcement made by Finance Minister Yashwant Sinha in his Budget speech last year. Government amends the provisions of the valuation of perquisites for certain categories of salaried assesses. United Arab Emirates deports Aftab Ansari alias Farhan Malik, prime suspect in the American Center attack in Kolkata. *Lagaan* is nominated in the category of the best non-English language film for the Oscars. Russian and Indian energy officials sign a $1.5 billion contract for the delivery of two Russian reactors for a new Indian nuclear power plant. Foreign exchange reserves cross $50 billion. Jyotiraditya Scindia wins from Guna in the Lok Sabha by-elections. Former PM and JD(S) president, H.D. Deve Gowda, wins from Kanakapura in the Lok Sabha by-elections. Gujarat CM, Narendra Modi, wins the by-election from Rajkot-II assembly constituency. Goa governor Mohamad Fazal dissolves the state assembly. Railway Minister Nitish Kumar presents the Railway Budget. Union Finance Minister, Yashwant Sinha presents the Annual Budget.

March: Veteran Congress leader, Narain Dutt Tiwari, is sworn in as the first elected CM of Uttaranchal. Lok Sabha Speaker G.M.C. Balayogi killed in a helicopter crash. The boards of the Reliance Industries Ltd and Reliance Petroleum Ltd unanimously approve the merger of RPL with RIL. Union Cabinet approves 100 % foreign direct investment (FDI) in films and advertising through the automatic approval route, but holds back a decision on permitting FDI in print media. India's medium range surface-to-air missile 'Akash' is successfully test-fired from the interim test range (ITR) in Orissa's Chandipur. BSP politician Mayawati resigns from Lok Sabha to focus on Uttar Pradesh. Congress leader Ibobi Singh is sworn in as the Manipur CM. Lok Sabha passes the Prevention of Terrorism Ordinance (POTO) bill. The Union Cabinet decides to grant 4 % additional dearness allowance to Central government employees and a similar increase in dearness relief for pensioners. Supreme Court directs the Centre and the University Grants Commission (UGC) to provide reservation in identified teaching posts for physically and visually disabled persons. The CBI books the first-ever case of email spamming from the country. The indigenous pilotless target aircraft (PTA) 'Lakshya' is successfully test-flown from the interim test range at Chandipur-on-sea. Government announces reduction in interest rates on Special Deposit Scheme, General Provident Fund and on other deposits from 9.5% to 9%.

April: BJP leader and former Union minister, Sikander Bakht, is appointed the governor of Kerala. Indian business tycoon, Manohar Rajaram Chhabria, passes away. President K.R. Narayanan approves the appointment of Justice B.N. Kirpal as the Chief Justice of India with effect from 6 May. The Supreme Court directs the Uttar Pradesh government to hand over the security of the Taj Mahal in Agra to the Central Industrial Security Force (CISF) from 1 May. Union Coal Minister Ram Vilas Paswan resigns from the Cabinet. Lok Sabha passes the Finance Bill.

May: Government appoints the former director general of Punjab police, K. P. S. Gill, as Narendra Modi's security adviser. Chairman of the Oberoi Group, M. S. Oberoi, passes away. Urdu poet and a recipient of the Sahitya Akademi Fellowship, Kaifi Azmi, passes away. Ketan Parekh and his cousin, Kartik Parekh, and Jatin Sarvaiya are arrested by the economic offences wing of the Mumbai police for cheating a Mauritius-based company. Mayawati wins trust vote in Uttar Pradesh. Government approves the sale of its 26% stake in Indian Petrochemicals Corporation (IPCL) to the Reliance Industries, for Rs 1,440 crore.

June: BJP legislature party leader, Manohar Parrikar, is sworn in as the new CM of a BJP-led coalition government in Goa. Light Combat Aircraft (LCA) Technology Demonstrator-II is successfully test-flown. Former vice-president and acting president, B.D. Jatti, passes away. Democratic Front government in Maharashtra, headed by Vilasrao Deshmukh, wins the vote of confidence in the Assembly. The anti-tank guided missile 'Nag' is successfully test-fired from the interim test range (ITR) at Chandipur-on-sea. Cabinet clears 26% foreign direct investment (FDI) in print media. Union Home Minister L. K. Advani becomes the deputy prime minister.

July: Yashwant Sinha becomes new foreign minister and Jaswant Singh becomes new finance minister. Chairman of Reliance Industries Ltd, Dhirubhai Ambani, passes away. Maharashtra Governor P.C. Alexander resigns. The Tamil Nadu police arrests the general secretary of the Marumalarchi Dravida Munnetra Kazhagam (MDMK), Vaiko, under POTA. The 71-year-old scientist, A.P.J. Abdul Kalam, becomes the new President of India. Gujarat Governor Sunder Singh Bhandari dissolves the state assembly and accepts the resignation of CM, Narendra Modi. VSNL cuts its international call rates by up to 40%. Vice-President Krishan Kant passes away. Mukesh Ambani becomes the new Reliance Industries Ltd chairman.

August: Former Union home secretary and former Comptroller and Audi-tor General, T.N.Chaturvedi, is appointed the new governor of Karnataka. Indian Railways starts the facility of booking train tickets through the Internet. NDA candidate, Bhairon Singh Shekhawat, is elected as the country's 12th vice-president. Vice-captain of the Indian women's cricket team visiting England, Mithali Raj, scores an unbeaten 210, the highest individual Test score.

September: Cinema and theatre director, actor and musician, B.V. Karanth, passes away. Supreme Court directs Karnataka to release 1.25 tmcft (thousand million cubic feet) of water everyday to Tamil Nadu from its four reservoirs. Planning Commission Secretary P. Shankar is sworn in as Central Vigilance Commissioner. Sachin Tendulkar becomes the youngest cricketer in the world to play 100 Test matches. India's Mahesh Bhupathi wins the US Open men's doubles title along with Max Mirnyi of Belarus. India's first exclusive meteorological satellite (METSAT) is launched using the Polar Satellite Launch Vehicle PSLV–C4, from Sriharikota. Jagmohan Dalmiya is unanimously re-elected BCCI president. Noted actress and social activist Priya Tendulkar passes away. Goa Governor Mohammad Fazal is transferred and appointed governor of Maharashtra for the rest of his term. Short range supersonic surface-to-air missile, Trishul, is successfully test-fired from the interim test range (ITR) at Chandipur-on-sea. Trials of the country's first-ever sea-to-surface missile, Dhanush, successfully completed. Noted industrialist and founder chairman of the Apollo Group, Raunaq Singh, passes away.

October: The Vatican approves of a miracle attributed to Mother Teresa, moving her one step closer to sainthood. The President appoints Justice Gopal Ballav Pattanaik as the new Chief Justice of India. Delhi Police chargesheet the suspended Haryana inspector-general of Police (Prisons), R.K.

Sharma, for conspiring to murder the *Indian Express* journalist, Shivani Bhatnagar. Reserve Bank of India cuts bank rate by 25 basic points from 6.50 per cent to 6.25 per cent Anti-conversion Bill passed in Tamil Nadu assembly.

November: Election Commission directs the Gujarat government to remove all hoardings and posters that are displayed in the state 'on communal lines'. People's Democratic Party (PDP) president, Mufti Mohammad Sayeed, is sworn in as the CM of Jammu and Kashmir. The Union Cabinet decides to start the process for corporatization of the Industrial Development Bank of India (IDBI) and for its conversion into a stand-alone bank.

December: Unit Trust of India (Transfer of Undertaking and Repeal) Bill, 2002, providing for the bifurcation of the UTI, receives parliamentary approval. The Union Cabinet decides to increase the fine for ticketless travel in trains fivefold—from Rs 50 to Rs 250. Divestment of HPCL and BPCL announced. Jurist, statesman and former ambassador to the US, Nani Ardeshir Palkhivala passes away. Yash Chopra is selected for the 2001 Dada Saheb Phalke Award. BJP wins the Gujarat assembly elections winning 126 seats in the 182-member House. The government appoints former Union minister, Suresh Prabhu, as the chairman of the Task Force on Interlinking of Rivers. Parliament approves the Freedom of Information Bill which envisages access to government information and files to every citizen in an effort to promote greater transparency, openness and accountability in administration. Justice Visheshwar Nath Khare is sworn in as the 33rd Chief Justice of India. Narendra Modi begin his second stint as the Gujarat chief minister. Metro Railway in Delhi starts operations. Ratan Tata gives up all his executive posts in the Tata group. He becomes the non-executive chairman.

Surjit Singh Barnala is the new governor of Andhra Pradesh.

2003

January: World athletics body absolves Sunita Rani, distance runner, of doping charges. Government appoints Justice S.N. Phukan as the new chief of the Tehelka enquiry commission. India successfully test-fires the 800-km-range Agni missile. Election Commission announces that assembly elections to the four States of Himachal Pradesh, Meghalaya, Nagaland and Tripura would be held on 26 February. IPS officer, Kiran Bedi, becomes the first woman and also the first Indian to be appointed as a United Nations civilian police adviser. Sushil Kumar Shinde sworn in as the Maharashtra chief minister. Medium-range surface-to-air missile 'Akash' is successfully test-fired from the interim test range (ITR) at Chandipur-on-sea. Poet Harivanshrai Bachchan passes away. Eminent economist and president of the International Economic Association, P.R. Brahmananda, passes away. National Security Guards (NSG) commando, Suresh Chand Yadav, who was killed in the operation to clear terrorists from the Akshardham temple in Gujarat, is awarded the Ashok Chakra. Government decides to carry out a strategic sale of the Hindustan Petroleum Corporation Limited. Bharatiya Vidya Bhavan receives the coveted Gandhi Peace Prize for 2002. A special court convicts stockbroker Hiten Dalal and three others, sentencing them to seven years' rigorous imprisonment for allegedly defrauding the Canbank Mutual Fund.

February: Reserve Bank of India announces that the non-banking finance companies (NBFCs) not having the minimum net-owned fund (NOF) of Rs 25 lakhs as on 9 January would not be allowed to continue with their business. To save the standing 'samba' crop, the

Supreme Court orders Karnataka to release 4,500 cusecs a day to Tamil Nadu. President A.P.J. Abdul Kalam launches the national social security number, initiated by the Employees Provident Fund Organization. Jaswant Singh presents the Annual Budget. Reserve Bank of India reduces interest rate on saving accounts offered by banks and repurchase rate for government securities by 0.5%.

March: India beats Pakistan in the World Cup and Sachin Tendulkar becomes the first player in one-day internationals to cross 12,000 runs. D.D. Lapang sworn in as the CM of Meghalaya. CPI(M) leader, Manik Sarkar, is sworn in as the CM of Tripura. India successfully launches an indigenously built torpedo. Union Finance Minister Jaswant Singh rolls back the increases in fertilizer prices he had announced in the Union Budget on 28 February. Indian cricket team enters World Cup final but Australia retains the World Cup with a 125-run win in the final. The Election Commission issues revised directions, making it mandatory for candidates to declare their educational background, assets and criminal antecedants.

April: India's first confirmed case of Severe Acute Respiratory Syndrome (SARS) found in Goa. Reserve Bank of India cuts bank rate by 25 basic points reducing it to 6%. Former BJP general secretary, K.N. Govindacharya, announces that he is quitting active politics. India's first stealth warship *Shivalik* is launched. Delhi High Court awards compensation of about Rs 18 crore to the families of the 59 dead and 103 injured in the Uphaar fire case of 13 June 1997.

May: Noted communist scholar and United Communist Party of India general secretary, Mohit Sen, passes away. Air-to-air missile Astra is test-fired. Shivshankar Menon is appointed India's high commissioner to Pakistan. The Finance and Investment Committee of the Employees Provident Fund Organization (EPFO) recommends the lowering of interest rates on provident fund contributions by at least 1%. Agriculture Minister Ajit Singh resigns from the Union government. Supreme Court declares that once an employer accepts the Voluntary Retirement Scheme (VRS) application of an employee, he or she cannot withdraw from the scheme. India announces the resumption of the suspended Delhi–Lahore bus service. Delhi High Court announces that former Indian cricketer Ajay Jadeja is free to play all matches in the country's domestic circuit, if selected. Duty on import of set-top boxes reduced.

June: Former judge, M. Rama Jois, sworn in as the 27th governor of Bihar, while Ved Prakash Marwah and Arvind Dave are sworn in governors of Jharkhand and Manipur respectively. Maruti Udyog Limited opens its maiden public issue of shares. Surface-to-air high-altitude interception missile 'Akash' test-fired from a mobile launcher. The Union Cabinet clears a proposal to include new castes and communities in the Central list of other backward classes in respect of Andhra Pradesh, Karnataka, Rajasthan, Delhi, Chandigarh, Haryana, Orissa and West Bengal. Nalin Surie is appointed India's new ambassador to China. The International Cricket Council (ICC) decides to withhold the $9 million due to India for playing in the World Cup after the players sign an amended sponsorship contract.

July: The Madhya Pradesh government issues a notification to increase the reservation for other backward classes (OBCs) to 27% in the state. Raghuram Rajan is named as the International Monetary Fund's new chief economist. Leander Paes and Martina Navratilova win the Wimbledon mixed doubles title. Sania Mirza becomes the first Indian woman to win a Grand Slam title. The Appointments Committee of the Union Cabinet approves the choice of Y. Venugopal Reddy for the next governor of the Reserve Bank of India. East Bengal becomes the first Indian club to win an international tournament on foreign soil when it beats BEC Tero Sasana of Thailand. Famous comedian Johnny Walker passes away. Chief Election Commissioner, J.M. Lyngdoh and social worker Shantha Sinha honoured with the Ramon Magsaysay Award. Mahant Ramchandradas Paramhans, president of the Ramjanmabhoomi Nyas, passes away.

August: A 37-member United Democratic Front ministry, headed by Gegong Apang, is sworn in by the Arunachal Pradesh Governor V.C. Pandey at Itanagar. The Supreme Court bans the collection of capitation fees by professional colleges. Parliament appoints a 15-member Joint Parliamentary Committee (JPC) with the Nationalist Congress Party leader, Sharad Pawar, as chairman, to suggest appropriate safety standards for soft drinks, fruit juices and other beverages. The Archaeological Survey of India submits its final report relating to Ayodhya excavations before the Allahabad High Court. Mulayam Singh Yadav is sworn in as the new CM of Uttar Pradesh.

September: Yaga Venugopal Reddy takes over as the 21st governor of the Reserve Bank of India. INSAT-3E, the communication satellite of the Indian Space Research Organization, is launched successfully from a spaceport in Kourou, French Guyana, by a European Ariane 5 launch vehicle. India wins the sixth Asia Cup hockey title for the first time. BSP splits after 37 rebels join Samajwadi Party. The Mulayam Singh Yadav government wins vote of confidence in the Uttar Pradesh Legislative Assembly. Former Indian cricketer G.S. Ramchand passes away. The special CBI court hearing the Babri Masjid demolition conspiracy case discharges Deputy PM L.K. Advani. The Human Resource Development Minister Murli

Manohar Joshi tenders his resignation.

October: UP CM, Mulayam Singh Yadav, inducts 91 new ministers into his Cabinet. World billiards champion Wilson Jones passes away. CBI files a charge sheet against the Chhattisgarh CM, Ajit Jogi, for using a forged note. Anjali Bhagwat wins the air rifle gold in the World Cup Finals. Government of India resumes cricketing and other sporting links with Pakistan. Election Commission decides not to recognize three new MP districts of Burhanpur, Anuppur and Ashoknagar. Pankaj Advani wins the World snooker title at the IBSF World Snooker Championship. The Election Commission makes it mandatory for candidates contesting the assembly polls in five states to show accounts of poll expenditure to the observers or returning officers.

November: Sushil Sharma held guilty in the 'Tandoor case' and is awarded the death sentence. SENSEX crosses the 5000 mark for the first time in 42 months. India win Asian Under-19 cricket trophy. Tamil Nadu government sacks 587 employees for going on strike. BCCI suspends Maharashtra cricketer Abhijit Kale on alleged bribery charges. Murasoli Maran passes away. IIM Common Aptitude Test (CAT) is cancelled following the leaking of question papers. CBI exonerates Indian Institute of Management faculty. Light Combat Aircraft (LCA) prototype makes its first flight at subsonic speed. Abu Salem and Monica Bedi are given jail sentences in Portugal. Assembly polls take place in Mizoram, Delhi, Rajasthan, Madhya Pradesh and Chhattisgarh.

December: Former Mumbai Police Commissioner R.S. Sharma is arrested in the fake stamp paper scam case. More castes are added to the Central 'Other Backward Classes' lists. Congress wins the Delhi assembly elections, BJP wins in Madhya Pradesh, Rajasthan and Chhattisgarh.

Vasundhara Raje becomes the first woman CM of Rajasthan. CBI registers a corruption case against the former Chhattisgarh CM, Ajit Jogi. Dev Anand selected for the Dada Saheb Phalke Award. MP Cabinet decides to ban cow slaughter. India wins the second Test against Australia, its first Test win in Australia after 22 years. POTA Amendment Bill passed in Lok Sabha. Chhattisgarh bans cow slaughter in the state. DMK withdraws its ministers from the Union Cabinet. Foreign exchange reserves cross $100 billion. Parliament passes Dual Citizenship Bill. MDMK pulls out of the NDA government.

2004

January: SAARC nations agree on free trade regime. SENSEX reaches all-time high of 6,026 points. Union Cabinet raises the FDI limit in oil refining to 100% while the cap for oil marketing companies is increased from 74% to 100%. Cabinet Committee on Security approves the Rs 2,800 crore deal for the Russian aircraft-carrier Admiral Gorshkov. DMK launches Democratic Progressive Alliance. Padma Shree awarded to Sourav Ganguly and Rahul Dravid. UGC makes green studies compulsory. Padma Vibhushan awarded to Amrita Pritam, M.N. Venkatachaliah and Jayant Vishnu Narlikar. Central Government bans import of domestic and wild birds. Restrictions on imports of gold and silver removed. India becomes the first developing country to import LNG.

February: HRD Ministry passes an order asking IIMs to reduce its fees to Rs 30,000. Rajiv Gandhi acquitted in Bofors case. 13th Lok Sabha dissolved. Vaiko released from prison. Retest of the CAT held successfully. Sania Mirza wins first WTA title, the Hyderabad Open. RBI hikes limit on gifts to Rs 5 lakh. Government decides to roll back CAS. Election Commission bans political advertisements in electronic media.

March: Confederation of Indian Industry (CII) and the Lahore Chamber of Commerce and Industry (LCCI) signs memorandum of understanding (MoU) to exchange information on all economic and commercial matters. Delhi High Court directs the Union Government to apprise it of the details of the money spent on the 'India Shining' advertisement campaign. Major Rajyavardhan Singh Rathore wins a gold medal at the Shooting World Cup in Sydney. Jammu and Kashmir Assembly unanimously passes a Bill that disqualifies women from being permanent residents of the state after marriage with non-permanent residents. India and Israel sign their biggest ever bilateral defence deal worth $1.1 billion. Election Commission orders the immediate removal of 'India Shining' and other state-sponsored advertisements. Prasar Bharati signs a Memorandum of Understanding (MoU) with the Indian Space Research Organisation (ISRO) for supply of Ku Band transponders for Doordarshan's Direct-to-Home (DTH) service. India registers its first-ever ODI series win in Pakistan. IIM-Kozhikode Chairman A.C. Muthiah announces a cut in the annual fees in line with the directives of the Ministry of Human Resource Development.

April: Supreme Court bans surrogate advertisements on electronic media. Sahara becomes the global sponsor for field hockey and signs a contract for a period of three years with the International Hockey Federation (FIH). Election Commission suggests ordinance to ban opinion polls. Election Commission asks the media organizations to furnish it with details of the revenue collected from each political party and candidate for their political advertisements so that it could be added to their election expenditure. IIM-Ahmedabad challenges fee cut. Infosys Technologies become India's first listed IT firm to have crossed $1 billion in turnover. India records its first-ever Test series win in Pakistan. Virender Sehwag scores 309 against Pakistan, the highest Test score by an Indian. First phase of polling held for140 Lok Sabha seats in which an estimated 50-55% of the 175 million voters exercise their votes. Reliance Industries become the first private sector Indian company to cross the one billion milestone in net profit.

May: S. Rajendra Babu is sworn in the 34th Chief Justice of India. Second and third phases of Lok Sabha elections held. Congress emerges as largest party; United Progressive Alliance gets majority. Congress comes back to power in the Andhra Pradesh Assembly. Left parties achieve their highest ever tally in the Lok Sabha. Congress ousted from power in Karnataka. Election Commission issues a notification constituting the 14th Lok Sabha. President appoints Manmohan Singh as the PM. The CPI(M) Politburo unanimously decides on Somnath Chatterjee for the post of Speaker of the 14th Lok Sabha. The first-ever coalition government in Karnataka takes office. Foreign exchange reserves touch $118.62 billion. India's first indigenously built civilian aircraft, 'Saras', achieves its maiden test flight. Union Human Resource Development Ministry asks the Indian Institutes of Management (IIMs) to evolve a uniform fee structure. Viswanathan Anand wins his third Chess Oscar.

June: L.K. Advani is unanimously elected leader of the BJP's parliamentary party. Union Finance Ministry appoints National Securities Depository Ltd. for providing Permanent Account Numbers (PAN) to new taxpayers in 139 cities. Tata Consultancy Services files IPO prospectus. The Board of Governors of the Indian Institute of Management Indore (IIM-I) decides to charge the same fee for the academic session 2004–05. TRAI directs all the cellular operators to inform their prepaid subscribers through SMS whenever they roam into another area and charge roaming fees.

July: PM announces assistance to each family in Andhra Pradesh whose breadwinner has committed suicide. Foreign exchange reserves cross $120 billion. 87 schoolchildren burnt to death and 23 seriously injured in a fire at a primary school in Kumbakonam town of Thanjavur district in Tamil Nadu.

August: The Supreme Court rules that a doctor cannot be held criminally liable if a patient dies due to an error of judgment or carelessness or for want of due caution although she/he can be liable to pay compensation. The Union Cabinet announces the repeal of the controversial Prevention of Terrorism Act (POTA) before it lapses on 23 October. PM Manmohan Singh starts a 'Janata Durbar' to know the problems of the people first-hand. Major Rajyavardhan Singh Rathore gets the silver medal for India in shooting (double trap category) at the Olympic Games. Babulal Gaur sworn in as new CM of Madhya Pradesh. Oommen Chandy becomes the new Kerala Chief Minister. The UPA Government releases its first-ever foreign trade policy

September: Supreme Court orders the Directorate-General of Health Services to complete counselling for the 161 seats fallen vacant under the 15 per cent all-India quota in Government medical and dental colleges. Puneeta Arora become the first woman in the three services to reach the second highest rank in the armed forces, the new Commandant of the Armed Forces Medical College. First ever Census data on religion is released. Government allows the removal of essential items such as butter, cheese, processed foods, aerated water and petrochemical products from the factory of production to warehouse, without the payment of excise duty. Rahul Dravid wins 'Player of the Year' and 'Test Player of the Year' award at the inaugural ICC Awards. Government permits duty-free imports of raw sugar for domestic consumption. Jagmohan Dalmiya is nominated the BCCI's Patron-in-Chief for three years after his term as the BCCI president ends on 30 September. Anju Bobby George is chosen for the Rajiv Gandhi Khel Ratna award for 2003. Union Cabinet decides to create a new category of languages as 'classical languages' and declare Tamil as the first language under the category. Union Home Minister Shivraj Patil orders an enquiry into the release of religion-based Census figures. EDUSAT, India's first exclusive satellite for educational services, placed in orbit. Bibi Jagir Kaur become the first woman to be elected for the second time as the president of the Shiromani Gurdwara Parbandhak Committee. Noted physicist and key leader of India's nuclear programme, Raja Ramanna, passes away. Musician Shobha Gurtu passes away. Tata Motors become the first company in the Indian engineering sector to list its securities on the New York Stock Exchange (NYSE). Author Mulk Raj Anand passes away. Ranbir Singh Mahendra of Haryana is elected president of the Board of Control for Cricket in India. International Olympic Committee imposes life bans on weightlifters Pratima Kumari and Sanamacha Chanu.

Afghanistan   Albania   Algeria   Andorra*

Angola   Antigua & Barbuda   Argentina   Armenia

Australia   Austria*   Azerbaijan   The Bahamas

Bahrain   Bangladesh   Barbados   Belarus

Belgium   Belize   Benin   Bhutan

Bolivia*   Bosnia & Herzegovina   Botswana   Brazil

Brunei   Bulgaria   Burkina Faso   Burundi

Cambodia   Cameroon   Canada   Cape Verde

Civil flags are shown except where marked thus (*); in these cases, government flags are shown in order to illustrate emblems. Both styles are official national flags.

Central African Republic

Chad

Chile

China

Colombia

Comoros

Democratic Republic of the Congo

Republic of the Congo

Costa Rica*

Côte d'Ivoire

Croatia

Cuba

Cyprus

Czech Republic

Denmark

Djibouti

Dominica

Dominican Republic*

East Timor

Ecuador*

Egypt

El Salvador

Equatorial Guinea

Eritrea

Estonia

Ethiopia

Fiji

Finland*

France

Gabon

The Gambia

Georgia

Civil flags are shown except where marked thus (*); in these cases, government flags are shown in order to illustrate emblems. Both styles are official national flags.

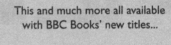

Germany   Ghana   Greece   Grenada

Guatemala*   Guinea   Guinea-Bissau   Guyana

Haiti*   Honduras   Hungary   Iceland

India   Indonesia   Iran   Iraq

Ireland   Israel   Italy   Jamaica

Japan   Jordan   Kazakhstan   Kenya

Kiribati   North Korea   South Korea   Kuwait

Kyrgyzstan   Laos   Latvia   Lebanon

Civil flags are shown except where marked thus (*); in these cases, government flags are shown in order to illustrate emblems. Both styles are official national flags.

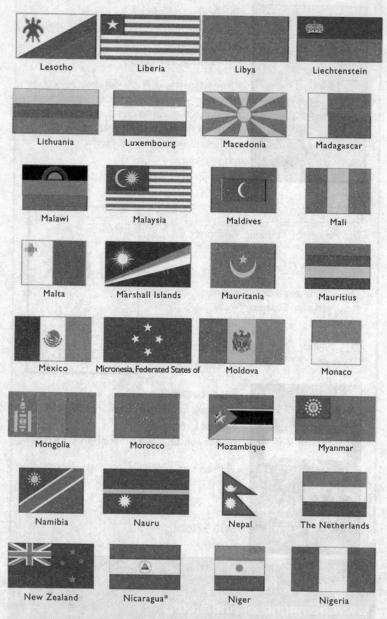

Lesotho

Liberia

Libya

Liechtenstein

Lithuania

Luxembourg

Macedonia

Madagascar

Malawi

Malaysia

Maldives

Mali

Malta

Marshall Islands

Mauritania

Mauritius

Mexico

Micronesia, Federated States of

Moldova

Monaco

Mongolia

Morocco

Mozambique

Myanmar

Namibia

Nauru

Nepal

The Netherlands

New Zealand

Nicaragua*

Niger

Nigeria

Civil flags are shown except where marked thus (*); in these cases, government flags are shown in order to illustrate emblems. Both styles are official national flags.

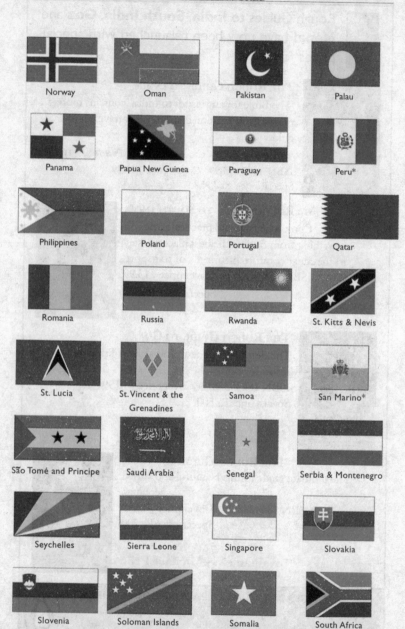

Norway

Oman

Pakistan

Palau

Panama

Papua New Guinea

Paraguay

Peru*

Philippines

Poland

Portugal

Qatar

Romania

Russia

Rwanda

St. Kitts & Nevis

St. Lucia

St. Vincent & the Grenadines

Samoa

San Marino*

São Tomé and Principe

Saudi Arabia

Senegal

Serbia & Montenegro

Seychelles

Sierra Leone

Singapore

Slovakia

Slovenia

Soloman Islands

Somalia

South Africa

Civil flags are shown except where marked thus (*); in these cases, government flags are shown in order to illustrate emblems. Both styles are official national flags.

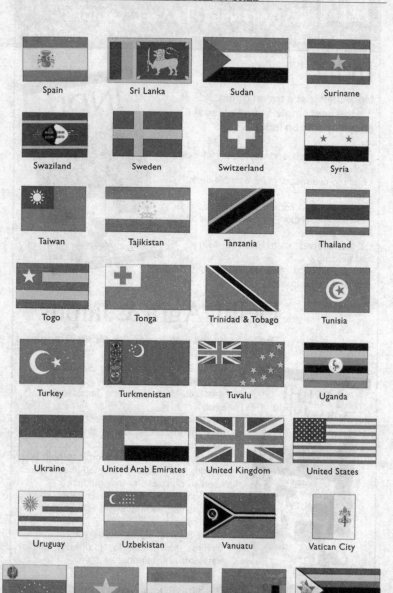

Spain   Sri Lanka   Sudan   Suriname

Swaziland   Sweden   Switzerland   Syria

Taiwan   Tajikistan   Tanzania   Thailand

Togo   Tonga   Trinidad & Tobago   Tunisia

Turkey   Turkmenistan   Tuvalu   Uganda

Ukraine   United Arab Emirates   United Kingdom   United States

Uruguay   Uzbekistan   Vanuatu   Vatican City

Venezuela*   Vietnam   Yemen   Zambia   Zimbabwe

Civil flags are shown except where marked thus (*); in these cases, government flags are shown in order to illustrate emblems. Both styles are official national flags.

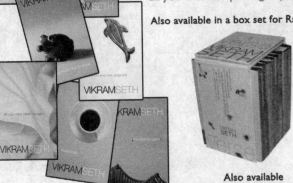

ARCTIC OCEAN
Chukchi Sea
Beaufort Sea
Brooks Range
Arctic Circle
Bering Strait
Aleutian Basin
Aleutian Islands
Aleutian Trench
Mt. McKinley 6194m
Gulf of Alaska
Victoria I.
Great Bear L.
Great Slave L.
Ellesmere I.
Baffin I.
Baffin Bay
Greenland
Denmark Strait
Iceland
Hudson Bay
Peninsule d'Ungava
Labrador Sea
Canadian Shield
Laurentian Highlands
L. Winnipeg
Great L.
St. Lawrence
Newfoundland
Grand Banks of Newfoundland
Vancouver I.
Coast Mts
Coast Ranges
Rocky Mountains
NORTH AMERICA
Great Plains
Appalachian Mts
Mississippi
Mendocino Fracture Zone
Murray Fracture Zone
Azores
Madeira
Canary Is.
Hawaiian Is.
Hawaii
Tropic of Cancer
Lower California
Sierra Madre
Gulf of Mexico
Yucatan Peninsula
West Indies
Caribbean Sea
Lesser Antilles
Cape Verde Is.
Orinoco
Angel Falls
Guiana Highlands
PACIFIC OCEAN
ATLANTIC OCEAN
Equator
Galapagos Is.
Amazon Basin
Amazon
SOUTH AMERICA
Purus
Phoenix Is.
Line Is.
Polynesia
Marquesas Is.
Cook Is.
Tonga
Andes
Planalto de Mato Grosso
Brazilian Highlands
Gran Chaco
Tropic of Capricorn
Pitcairn Is.
Easter I.
Kermadec Trench
Cerro Aconcagua 6959m
Juan Fernandez Is.
Pampas
Patagonia
Ascension
Tristan da Cunha
Falkland Is.
South Georgia
Tierra del Fuego
Cape Horn
Drake Passage
South Sandwich Is.
Antarctic Circle
SOUTHERN
ANTA

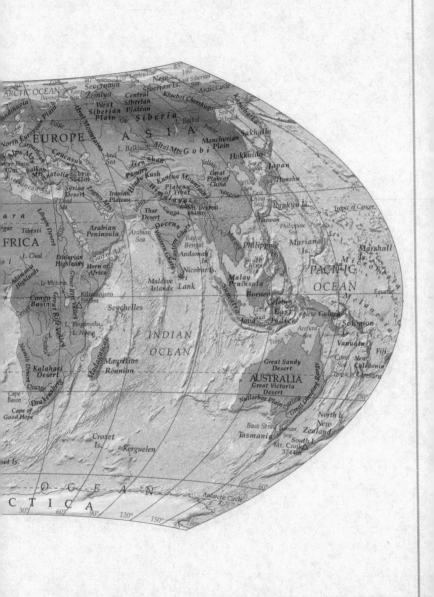

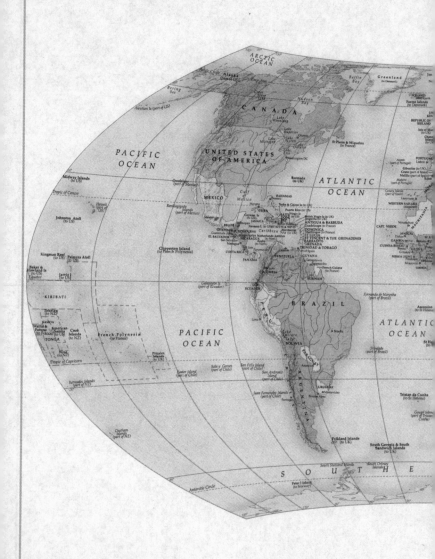

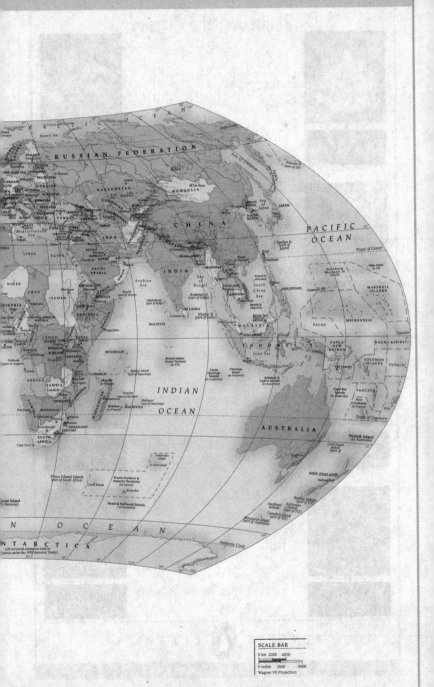

SCALE BAR

0 km 2000   4000

0 miles   2000   4000

Wagner VII Projection

The World

All the 192 countries that are members of the UN appear here in alphabetical order. There are detailed write-ups for the more significant countries, and all of India's neighbours, while the other nations appear in brief profiles. Historical, economic, political and demographic parameters of every country is part of this section. All dominions and dependencies appear under the respective countries.

Afghanistan

History

Alexander the Great used Afghanistan as the gateway to India in the 4th century BC. Islamic conquerors arrived in the 7th century AD, while Genghis Khan and Tamerlane reached in the 13th and 14th centuries.

Three Anglo-Afghan Wars were fought in the 19th and early 20th centuries. In 1893, UK denoted the Durand Line as the unofficial boundary between British India and Afghanistan.

In 1919, Afghanistan became independent. In 1926 Emir Amanullah established the Afghan monarchy and proclaimed himself king. He tried to introduce social reforms in the country but this led to opposition from conservative sections of the country. In 1929, Amanullah fled the country after civil unrest erupted over his reforms.

In 1953, General Mohammed Daud became the new prime minister. He contacted the Soviet Union for economic and military assistance and also introduced social reforms that included the abolition of purdah. But in 1963, Prime Minister Daud was forced to resign. In 1964, constitutional monarchy was established in the country.

In 1973, Mohammed Daud seized power in a coup and declared Afghanistan a republic. In 1978, the leftist People's Democratic Party ousted and killed him. However, the party's Khalq and Parcham factions began fighting amongst themselves. This led to a purge or exile of almost all the Parcham leaders. Meanwhile, conservative Islamic and ethnic leaders who had earlier objected to social changes began an armed revolt.

In 1979, a power struggle between leftist leaders Hafizullah Amin and Nur Mohammed Taraki in Kabul resulted in victory for Amin. However revolts in the countryside continued and the Afghan army faced collapse. In December 1979, the Soviet Union sent in its troops to remove Amin from power. Amin was deposed and executed. Babrak Karmal, leader of the party's Parcham faction, was installed as ruler, backed by Soviet troops.

Before long, the Soviet invasion reached a dead end as the local mujahideens put up a fierce resistance.

Although the invading force of about 100,000 Soviet troops controlled the cities, larger towns, and major garrisons, the mujahideens enjoyed relative freedom all over the countryside. Even the formidable Soviet war machine could not crush their uprising. Meanwhile, the USA provided money and sophisticated equipment to the Afghans and their allies in the region to fight the Soviets. But perhaps the greatest victims of the war were the millions of Afghans who were displaced in the war and became refugees in Pakistan and Iran. In 1988 USA, USSR, Pakistan, and Afghanistan signed an agreement that resulted in the complete withdrawal of Soviet troops in 1989.

In April 1992, Afghan rebel groups stormed Kabul and overthrew the communist president, Mohammad Najibullah. In 1993, the different mujahideen groups agreed on formation of a government with the ethnic Tajik, Burhanuddin Rabbani, proclaimed president. However, factional rivalry continued through 1994. It was around this point of time that Taliban, led by a former mujahideen commander named Mullah Mohammad Omar, emerged as a major challenge to the Rabbani government.

In 1996, the Taliban seized control of Kabul and introduced a strict puritan version of Islam. The new regime banned women from working outside their homes, introduced Islamic punishments that included stoning to death and amputations. Rabbani fled the capital to join the anti-Taliban Northern Alliance led by Ahmad Shah Masood. Soon, the Talibans extended their control over all parts of Afghanistan except for a small part that the Northern Alliance held. Soon after occupying Kabul, the Taliban dragged former President Najibullah and his brother from the UN compound and killed them.

In 1997, Pakistan and Saudi Arabia recognized Taliban as the legitimate rulers of Afghanistan even though most other countries continued to recognize Rabbani as the head of state. Meanwhile, the USA launched missile strikes at suspected bases of al-Qaeda leader Osama bin Laden, who was hiding in Afghanistan. In 1999, the UN imposed financial sanctions and an air embargo to force Afghanistan to hand over Osama bin Laden for trial. The sanctions were toughened in 2001. In March 2001, the Taliban destroyed giant Buddha statues in Bamiyan even as international organizations tried to save them. In May, the Taliban authorities ordered members of religious minorities to wear tags identifying themselves as non-Muslims. It also asked Hindu women to veil themselves. In September, Northern Alliance leader Ahmad Shah Masood was killed while giving a press briefing.

In October 2001, soon after the 9/11 attacks, USA and UK launched air strikes against Afghanistan when the Taliban refused to hand over Osama bin Laden. These air strikes were followed by ground attacks by US special operations forces allied with Northern Alliance fighters. These operations succeeded in driving the Taliban out of power by December. However, neither Mullah Mohammad Omar nor Osama bin Laden could be found.

On 5 December 2001, various Afghan groups meeting in the German city of Bonn agreed on an interim government pending general elections. On 22 December, Pashtun royalist Hamid Karzai was sworn in as head of a 30-member interim power-sharing government.

In January 2002, the first contingent of foreign peacekeepers arrived in the country. In April, former Afghan King Zahir Shah returned but assured the country that he would not stake claim to the throne. In September, President Karzai escaped an assassination attempt in his hometown Kandahar.

In June 2003, fresh clashes erupted between Taliban fighters and government forces in Kandahar province. In August 2003, NATO assumed its first-ever operational commitment outside Europe when it took control of security in Kabul. In January 2004, the Loya Jirga (grand council) adopted a new constitution that contained a strong emphasis on presidential power.

Geography

Location: Southern Asia, north and west of Pakistan, east of Iran.

Area: 647,500 sq. km.

Terrain: Mostly rugged mountains with plains in the north and south-west.

Natural resources: Natural gas, petroleum, coal, copper, chromite, talc, barites, sulphur, lead, zinc, iron ore, salt, precious and semiprecious stones.

Climate: The climate varies from arid to semi-arid. It has cold winters and hot summers.

People

Population: 29,928,987 (July 2005 est.).

Population growth rate: 4.77% (2005 est.).

Sex ratio: 1.06 male(s)/female (2003 est.).

Religions: Sunni Muslim 84%, Shi'a Muslim 15%, Others 1%.

Languages: Pashtu 35%, Afghan Persian (Dari) 50%, Turkic languages (primarily Uzbek and Turkmen) 11%, 30 minor languages (primarily Balochi and Pashai) 4%, much bilingualism.

Literacy rate: Total 36%, Male 51%, Female 21% (1999 est.).

Infant mortality rate: 163.07 deaths/1,000 live births (2005 est).

Life expectancy: Total 42.9 years, Male 42.71 years, Female 43.1 years (2005 est.).

Government

Capital: Kabul.

Government type: Transitional.

Independence: 19 August 1919 (from UK control over Afghan foreign affairs).

Legal system: According to the Bonn Agreement, a judicial commission will rebuild the country's justice system in accordance with Islamic principles, international standards, the rule of law, and Afghan legal traditions.

Executive branch:
Chief of state: President of the Transitional Islamic State of Afghanistan, Hamid Karzai (since 10 June 2002). The president is both chief of state and head of government.

Economy

Currency: Afghani.

Economy—overview:
The inflow of around $2 billion in international assistance has significantly improved Afghanistan's economic outlook. The agricultural sector is picking up after a four-year drought in most parts of the country. However, the problem of opium cultivation and manufacture of narcotics remains. As a matter of fact, by some estimates, it accounts for as much as one-third of the country's GDP. Tackling this problem will be difficult, mainly as it involves winning over the farmers to drop the profitable poppy cultivation and switch over to other crops. In March 2004, Afghanistan secured $8.2 billion in aid over the next three years. But as the situations stand now, Afghanistan is a very poor country that is heavily reliant on foreign aid and agriculture and trade with neighbouring countries. Most parts of the country suffer from lack of even basic infrastructure like housing, education, clean water, electricity, medical care, and jobs. The Afghan government and international donors face a daunting task of improving access to these basic necessities.

GDP: Purchasing power parity—$21.5 billion (2003 est.).

GDP—real growth rate: 7.5% (2004 est.).

GDP—per capita: Purchasing power parity—$800 (2003 est.).

Inflation rate: 5.2% (2003 est.).

Population below poverty line: 53% (2003).

Exports: $446 million (this figure does not include illicit exports) (2003 est.)—Fruits, nuts, carpets, wool, cotton, hides and pelts, precious and semi-precious gems.

Imports: $3.759 billion (2003 est.)—Capital goods, food, textiles, petroleum products.

External debt: $8 billion in bilateral debt plus $500 million in debt to multilateral development banks (2004).

Transport and Communications

Railways: 24.6 km.

Roads: 21,000 km.

Telephones: 33,100 (2002).

Mobile cellular: 12,000 (2002).

Internet users: 1,000 (2002).

Internet country code: .af

Albania

History

The Byzantine Empire ruled Albania from 535 to 1204. Thereafter, the Ottoman Turks ruled the country for about 400 years.

In 1912, Albania became independent from the Ottoman Empire. Italy invaded Albania just before World War II.

After World War II, Albanian Communist Party leader Enver Hoxha was installed as the country's leader. In 1948, the Soviet Union began supplying aid and assistance to Albania. In 1955, Albania was one of the founding members of the Warsaw Pact. However, in 1961, Soviet Union broke off diplomatic ties with Albania over an ideological difference and Albania allied itself with China.

In 1967, Albania declared itself the world's first atheist state. In 1968, Albania withdrew from the Warsaw Pact over the invasion of Czechoslovakia.

Following the collapse of communist regimes all over eastern Europe in 1990, thousands of Albanians attempted to flee through Western embassies. They seized ships at Albanian ports and sailed illegally to Italy.

Geography

Location: South-eastern Europe, bordering the Adriatic Sea and Ionian Sea, between Greece and Serbia and Montenegro.

Area: 28,748 sq. km.

Terrain: Mostly mountains and hills; small plains along coast.

Natural resources: Petroleum, natural gas, coal, bauxite, chromite, copper, iron ore, nickel, salt, timber, hydropower.

Climate: Albania has a mild temperate climate with cool, cloudy, wet winters and hot, clear, dry summers. The interior is cooler and wetter.

People

Population: 3,563,112 (July 2005 est.).

Population growth rate: 0.52% (2005 est.).

Sex ratio: 1.04 male(s)/female (2005 est.).

Religions: Muslim 70%, Albanian Orthodox 20%, Roman Catholic 10%.

Languages: Albanian (official—Tosk is the official dialect), Greek.

Literacy rate: Total 86.5%, Male 93.3%, Female 79.5% (2003 est.).

Infant mortality rate: 21.52 deaths/1,000 live births (2005 est.).

Life expectancy: Total 77.24 years, Male 74.6 years, Female 80.15 years (2005 est.).

Government

Capital: Tirana.

Government type: Democracy.

Independence: 28 November 1912 (from Ottoman Empire).

Legal system: Has a civil law system.

Executive branch:
Chief of state: President of the Republic Alfred Moisiu (since 24 July 2002).

Head of government: Prime Minister Fatos Nano (since 31 July 2002).

Economy

Currency: Lek.

GDP: Purchasing power parity—$17.46 billion (2004 est.).

GDP—real growth rate: 5.6% (2004 est.).

GDP—per capita: Purchasing power parity—$4,900 (2004 est.).

Inflation rate: 3.2% (2004).

Population below poverty line: 25% (2004 est.).

Unemployment rate: 15.8% officially; may be as high as 30% (2003 est.).

Exports: $552.4 million f.o.b. (2004 est.)—Textiles and footwear, asphalt, metals and metallic ores, crude oil, vegetables, fruits, tobacco.

Imports: $2.076 billion f.o.b. (2004 est.)—Machinery and equipment, foodstuff, textiles, chemicals.

External debt: $1.41 billion (2003).

Transport and Communications

Railways: 447 km.

Roads: 18,000 km.

Telephones: 255,000 (2003).

Mobile cellular: 1,100,000 (2003).

Internet users: 30,000 (2003).

Internet country code: .al

Algeria

History

Phoenicians settled in the coastal areas of Algeria in the first millennium BC. It later became a part of the Roman Empire and then, in the 16th century, became a part of the Ottoman Empire. In 1830, the French occupied Algeria and in 1848, it became a part of France. Around 250,000 people were killed in the Algerian War of Independence. Algeria gained independence in 1962.

The country witnessed serious rioting and demonstrations in the 1980s, due to the country's worsening economic condition. In 1991, the first ever parliamentary elections were held in Algeria and the fundamentalist Islamic party, the Front Islamique du Salut (FIS), emerged the largest party. The country's military leadership promptly called off the general elections and a five-member Higher State Council, with Mohamed Boudiaf as the head, took control of the country. This plunged the country into a violent civil war. It has been estimated that nearly 100,000 people have been killed in the conflict that has been noted for its brutality and violence.

Geography

Location: Northern Africa, bordering the Mediterranean Sea, between Morocco and Tunisia.

Area: 2,381,740 sq. km.

Terrain: Mostly high plateau and desert; some mountains; narrow, discontinuous coastal plain.

Natural resources: Petroleum, natural gas, iron ore, phosphates, uranium, lead, zinc.

Climate: The climate of Algeria varies from arid to semi-arid. During the summers, a hot dust/sand-laden wind named sirocco blows over the region.

People

Population: 32,531,853 (July 2005 est.).

Population growth rate: 1.22% (2005 est.).

Sex ratio: 1.02 male(s)/female (2005 est.).

Religions: Sunni Muslim (state religion) 99%, Christian and Jewish 1%.

Languages: Arabic (official), French, Berber dialects.

Literacy rate: Total 70%, Male 78.8%, Female 61% (2003 est.).

Infant mortality rate: 31 deaths/1,000 live births (2005 est.).

Life expectancy: Total 73 years, Male 71.45 years, Female 74.63 years (2005 est.).

Government

Capital: Algiers.

Government type: Republic.

Independence: 5 July 1962 (from France).

Legal system: Socialist, based on French and Islamic law.

Executive branch:
Chief of state: President Abdelaziz Bouteflika (since 28 April 1999).

Head of government: Prime Minister Ahmed Ouyahia (since 9 May 2003).

Economy

Currency: Algerian dinar.

GDP: Purchasing power parity—$212.3 billion (2004 est.).

GDP—real growth rate: 6.1% (2004 est.).

GDP—per capita: Purchasing power parity—$6,600 (2004 est.).

Inflation rate: 3.1% (2004 est.).

Population below poverty line: 23% (1999 est.).

Unemployment rate: 25.4% (2004 est.).

Exports: $32.16 billion f.o.b. (2004 est.)—Petroleum, natural gas, and petroleum products.

Imports: $15.25 billion f.o.b. (2004 est.)—Capital goods, foodstuff, consumer goods.

External debt: $21.9 billion (2004 est.).

Transport and Communications

Railways: 3,973 km.

Roads: 104,000 km.

Telephones: 2.2 million (2003).

Mobile cellular: 1,447,310 (2003).

Inernet users: 500,000 (2002).

Internet country code: .dz

Andorra

Geography

Location: South-western Europe, between France and Spain.

Area: 468 sq. km.

Natural resources: Hydropower, mineral water, timber, iron ore, lead.

Climate: Andorra has snowy, cold winters and warm, dry summers.

People

Population: 70,549 (July 2005 est.).

Population growth rate: 0.95% (2005 est.).

Sex ratio: 1.08 male(s)/female (2005 est.).

Religions: Roman Catholic (predominant).

Languages: Catalan (official), French, Castilian, Portuguese.

Literacy rate: 100%.

Infant mortality rate: 4.05 deaths/ 1,000 live births (2005 est.).

Life expectancy: Total 83.51 years, Male 80.56 years, Female 86.6 years (2005 est.).

Government

Capital: Andorra la Vella.

Government type: Parliamentary democracy (since March 1993) that retains as its chiefs of state a co-principality; the two princes are the President of France and the bishop of Seo de Urgel, Spain, who are represented locally by co-princes' representatives.

Independence: 1278 (was formed under the joint suzerainty of the French count of Foix and the Spanish bishop of Urgel).

Legal system: Based on French and Spanish civil codes.

Executive branch:
Chief of state: French co-prince Jacques Chirac (since 17 May 1995), represented by Philippe Massoni (since 26 July 2002); Spanish co-prince Bishop Joan Enric Vives i Sicilia (since 12 May 2003), represented by Nemesi Marques i Oste.

Head of government: Executive Council President Albert Pintat Santolania (since 27 May 2005).

Economy

Currency: Euro.

GDP: Purchasing power parity—$1.9 billion (2003 est.).

GDP—real growth rate: 2% (2003 est.).

GDP—per capita: Purchasing power parity—$26,800 (2003 est.).

Inflation rate: 4.3% (2000).

Exports: $58 million f.o.b. (1998)— Tobacco products, furniture.

Imports: $1.077 billion (1998)—Consumer goods, food, electricity.

Transport and Communications

Roads: 269 km.

Telephones: 35,000 (2001).

Mobile cellular: 23,500 (2001).

Internet users: 24,500 (2001).

Internet country code: .ad

Angola

History

People speaking the Khoisan language are believed to have been the original inhabitants of the area that is today Angola. Bantu-speaking people migrated to this region in large numbers after 1000 and emerged as the dominant group.

The Portuguese first arrived in the region in the 1480s and the present-day capital city of Luanda was founded in 1575. Soon, it emerged as an important point on the European trade route with India and South-east Asia. It also acted as a key source of slaves for the Portuguese colony of Brazil.

It was in the 1950s that the nationalist movement developed in Angola and the guerrilla war started. The socialist guerrilla independence movement, the Popular Liberation Movement of Angola (Movimento Popular de Libertacao de Angola, MPLA) originated in 1956 while the National Front for the Liberation of Angola (Frente Nacional de Libertacao de Angola, FNLA) was founded in 1957. Jonas Savimbi set up the National Union for the Total Independence of Angola (Uniao Nacional para a Independencia Total de Angola, UNITA) in 1966.

Angola gained independence in November 1975 when Portugal withdrew from the country without formally handing power to any one organization. A power struggle emerged between MPLA, backed by Cuba, and the FNLA–UNITA combine, backed by South Africa and the USA. The MPLA, which controlled Luanda, proclaimed itself as the government of independent Angola. On the other hand, UNITA and the FNLA set up a rival government in Huambo.

In 1994, the two warring factions signed a peace deal, the Lusaka Protocol peace accord. In 1996, Jose Eduardo dos Santos (MPLA) and Jonas Savimbi (UNITA) agreed to form a unified government; but the experiment did not work out.

In February 2002, Jonas Savimbi was killed by government troops. Following this, in April 2002, the Angolan Government and UNITA signed a ceasefire agreement.

Geography

Location: Southern Africa, bordering the South Atlantic Ocean, between Namibia and the Democratic Republic of the Congo.

Area: 1,246,700 sq. km.

Terrain: Narrow coastal plain; rises abruptly to vast interior plateau.

Natural resources: Petroleum, diamonds, iron ore, phosphates, copper, feldspar, gold, bauxite, uranium.

Climate: The climate of Angola is semi-arid in the south and along the coast. The northern part of the country has a cool, dry season from May to October and a hot, rainy season from November to April.

People

Population: 11,190,786 (July 2005 est.).

Population growth rate: 1.95% (2005 est.).

Sex ratio: 1.02 male(s)/female (2005 est.).

Religions: Indigenous beliefs 47%, Roman Catholic 38%, Protestant 15% (1998 est.).

Languages: Portuguese (official), Bantu and other African languages.

Literacy rate: Total 42%, Male 56%, Female 28% (1998 est.).

Infant mortality rate: 191.91 deaths/ 1,000 live births (2005 est.).

Life expectancy: Total 36.61 years, Male 36 years, Female 37.25 years (2005 est.).

Government

Capital: Luanda.

Government type: Republic, multi-party democracy with a strong presidential system.

Independence: 11 November 1975 (from Portugal).

Legal system: Based on Portuguese civil law system and customary law; modified to accommodate political pluralism and increased use of free markets.

Executive branch:
Chief of state: President Jose Eduardo Dos Santos (since 21 September 1979). The president is both the chief of state and head of government.

Economy

Currency: Kwanza.

GDP: Purchasing power parity—$23.17 billion (2004 est.).

GDP—real growth rate: 11.7% (2004 est.).

GDP—per capita: Purchasing power parity—$2,100 (2004 est.).

Inflation rate: 43.8% (2004 est.).

Population below poverty line: 70% (2003 est.).

Unemployment rate: Extensive unemployment and underemployment affecting more than half the population (2001 est.).

Exports: $12.76 billion f.o.b. (2004 est.)—Crude oil, diamonds, refined petroleum products, gas, coffee, sisal, fish and fish products, timber, cotton.

Imports: $4.896 billion f.o.b. (2004 est.)—Machinery and electrical equipment, vehicles and spare parts; medicines, food, textiles, military goods.

External debt: $9.2 billion (2003 est.).

Transport and Communications

Railways: 2,761 km.

Roads: 51,429 km.

Telephones: 96,300 (2003).

Mobile cellular: 130,000 (2002).

Internet users: 41,000 (2002).

Internet country code: .ao

Antigua and Barbuda

History

English settlers colonized Antigua in 1632. Barbuda was first colonized in 1678. In 1958, Antigua and Barbuda, then part of the Leeward Islands territory, joined the West Indies Federation. In November 1981, Antigua and Barbuda attained full independence.

Geography

Location: Caribbean, islands between the Caribbean Sea and the North Atlantic Ocean, east-south-east of Puerto Rico.

Area: 443 sq. km (Antigua 280 sq. km, Barbuda 161 sq. km).

Natural resources: Negligible.

Climate: Antigua and Barbuda has a pleasant tropical climate.

People

Population: 68,722 (July 2005 est.).

Population growth rate: 0.57% (2005 est.).

Sex ratio: 1 male(s)/female (2005 est.).

Religions: Christian (predominantly Anglican with other Protestant, and some Roman Catholic).

Languages: English (official), local dialects.

Literacy rate: Total 89%, Male 90%, Female 88% (1960 est.).

Infant mortality rate: 19.46 deaths/1,000 live births (2005 est.).

Life expectancy: Total 71.9 years, Male 69.53 years, Female 74.38 years (2005 est.).

Government

Capital: Saint John's.

Government type: Constitutional monarchy with UK-style parliament.

Independence: 1 November 1981 (from UK).

Legal system: Based on English common law.

Executive branch:
Chief of state: Queen Elizabeth II (since 6 February 1952), represented by Governor General James B. Carlisle (since 1993).

Head of government: Baldwin Spencer (since 2004).

Economy

Currency: East Caribbean dollar.

GDP: Purchasing power parity—$750 million (2002 est.).

GDP—real growth rate: 3% (2002 est.).

GDP—per capita: Purchasing power parity—$11,000 (2002 est.).

Inflation rate: 0.4% (2000 est.).

Exports: $689 million (2002)—Petroleum products, manufactured products, machinery and transport equipment, food and live animals.

Imports: $692 million (2002 est.)—Food and live animals, machinery and transport equipment, manufactures, chemicals, oil.

External debt: $231 million (1999).

Transport and Communications

Railways: 77 km.

Roads: 250 km (1999 est.).

Telephones: 38,000 (2002).

Mobile cellular: 38,200 (2002).

Internet users: 10,000 (2002).

Internet country code: .ag

Argentina

History

Prior to the arrival of the Europeans, indigenous people inhabited the area that is today Argentina. The north-western part of the country was a part of the Inca Empire.

In 1535, Spain sent an expedition led

by Pedro de Mendoza to settle Argentina. Although Mendoza met with initial success and even founded Santa María del Buen Aire, that later became Buenos Aires in 1536, lack of food doomed the expedition. In 1776, Spain created the viceroyalty of the Río de la Plata that consisted of modern-day Argentina, Uruguay, Paraguay, and southern Bolivia. Its capital was at Buenos Aires.

Between 1865 and 1870, Argentina, Brazil and Uruguay joined together to fight Latin America's bloodiest conflict, the War of the Triple Alliance, against Paraguay. It resulted in a humiliating defeat for Paraguay.

In 1881, Argentina and Chile agreed on their border along the Andes Mountains. Subsequently, Argentina gained exclusive rights to the Atlantic Ocean coast while Chile obtained the Pacific Ocean waters.

Argentina declared itself a neutral nation at the outbreak of World War II. However, in 1943, a military regime came to power. One of its key leaders was Colonel Juan Peron. Subsequently, in 1944, Argentina severed diplomatic relations with Japan and Germany and declared war on them in 1945. In 1946, Peron was elected the country's new President. His second wife, Eva Duarte de Peron (popularly called Evita), was put in unofficial charge of the department of social welfare. She was responsible for generous wage increases to the workers that helped her obtain considerable support for her husband. Juan Peron was overthrown in 1955, returned to power in 1973, but died the following year. His third wife and vice-president, Isabel, succeeded him as Argentina's next President.

In 1975, Argentina's inflation touched 300%. In 1976, a military junta led by General Jorge Videla seized power. The new regime dissolved the Parliament and initiated the so-called 'Dirty War' in which thousands of opponents of the regime disappeared.

In 1981, General Leopoldo Galtieri became the new head of the military regime. In April 1982, Argentine forces occupied the British territory of Falkland Islands that lay off its coast. This sparked off the Falklands Islands War and UK regained possession of the islands in June 1982. Defeat in the war cost Galtieri his job and General Reynaldo Bignone replaced him.

Civilian rule returned to Argentina in 1983 with Raul Alfonsin as President. Inflation levels touched 900%. In 1989, Carlos Menem was elected President. He introduced an economic austerity programme. However, this, along with the introduction of a new currency in 1992, could not prevent the economy from going into a recession in 1998. In November 2002, Argentina defaulted on an $800 million debt repayment to the World Bank, after it failed to re-secure IMF aid. In September 2003, Argentina and IMF reached an arrangement whereby Argentina would only pay interest on its loans.

Geography

Location: Southern South America, bordering the South Atlantic Ocean, between Chile and Uruguay.

Area: 2,766,890 sq. km.

Terrain: Argentina has the plains of the Pampas in the northern half, the plateau of Patagonia in the south and the Andes Mountains along the western border.

Natural resources: Lead, zinc, tin, copper, iron ore, manganese, petroleum, uranium, and the agricultural produce of the fertile plains of the Pampas.

Climate: The climate of Argentina is mostly temperate. However, the climate in the south-east is arid and in the south-west it is sub-antarctic.

People

Population: 39,537,943 (July 2005 est.).

Population growth rate: 0.98% (2005 est.).

Sex ratio: 0.97 male(s)/female (2005 est.).

Religions: Nominally Roman Catholic 92%, Protestant 2%, Jewish 2%, others 4%.

Languages: Spanish (official), English, Italian, German, French.

Literacy rate: Total 97.1%, Male 97.1%, Female 97.1% (2003 est.).

Infant mortality rate: 15.18 deaths/ 1,000 live births (2005 est.).

Life expectancy: Total 75.91 years, Male 72.17 years, Female 79.85 years (2005 est.).

Government

Capital: Buenos Aires.

Government type: Republic.

Independence: 9 July 1816 (from Spain).

Legal system: Mixture of US and west European legal systems.

Executive branch:
Chief of state: President Nestor Kirchner (since 25 May 2003). The president is both the chief of state and head of government.

Economy

Currency: Argentine peso.

Economy—overview:
Argentina is rich in natural resources, and has a diversified industrial base, a well-educated population and a well-developed export-oriented agricultural sector. In the last ten years, Argentina has suffered from chronic economic problems of high levels of external debt, runaway inflation, budget deficits and capital flight. The economic situation worsened in 2001 and government attempts at salvaging the economy proved inadequate. The peso's parity with the dollar was abandoned in January 2002, when the peso was devalued. The currency was subsequently floated in February that year. Soon after, the exchange rate plummeted and inflation rose sharply. The economy stabilized by mid-2002.

GDP: Purchasing power parity—$483.5 billion (2004 est.).

GDP—real growth rate: 8.3% (2004 est.).

GDP—per capita: Purchasing power parity—$12,400 (2004 est.).

Inflation rate: 6.1% (2004 est.).

Population below poverty line: 54.3% (June 2004).

Unemployment rate: 16.3% (September 2003).

Exports: $33.78 billion f.o.b. (2004 est.)—Edible oils, fuels and energy, cereals, food, motor vehicles.

Imports: $22.06 billion f.o.b. (2004 est.)—Machinery and equipment, motor vehicles, chemicals, metal manufactures, plastics.

External debt: $157.7 billion (2004 est.).

Transport and Communications

Railways: 34,091 km.

Roads: 215,471 km.

Telephones: 8,009,400 (2002).

Mobile cellular: 6,500,000 (2002).

Internet users: 4.1 million (2002).

Internet country code: .ar

Armenia

History

Armenia is one of the oldest civilizations in the world. It was the first country to officially adopt Christianity as its religion, around 300 AD.

The most notorious of the foreign powers to have ruled over Armenia were the Ottoman Turks. They massacred thousands of Armenians in 1894 and 1896 when they showed signs of growing nationalism. In 1915, in the middle of World War I, the Ottomans ordered the deportation of the Armenian population to the deserts of Middle East. It is estimated that between 600,000 and 1.5 million Armenians were either murdered or died of starvation.

Following Turkish defeat in World War I, Armenia declared its independence in May 1918. However, the Soviet Army annexed the nation in 1920. In 1936, Armenia became a Soviet republic. Armenia declared its independence from a collapsing Soviet Union in September 1991.

Geography

Location: South-western Asia, east of Turkey.

Area: 29,800 sq. km.

Terrain: The Armenian Highland region is mountainous. There is little forest-land but the rivers are fast-flowing.

Natural resources: Gold, copper, molybdenum, zinc, alumina.

Climate: Armenia has a highland climate with hot summers and cold winters.

People

Population: 2,982,904 (July 2005 est.).

Population growth rate: −0.25% (2005 est.).

Sex ratio: 0.9 male(s)/female (2005 est.).

Religions: Armenian Apostolic 94%, other Christian 4%, Yezidi (Zoroastrian/animist) 2%.

Languages: Armenian 96%, Russian 2%, others 2%.

Literacy rate: Total 98.6%, Male 99.4%, Female 98% (2003 est.).

Infant mortality rate: 23.28 deaths/1,000 live births (2005 est.).

Life expectancy: Total 71.55 years, Male 67.97 years, Female 75.75 years (2005 est.).

Government

Capital: Yerevan.

Government type: Republic.

Independence: 21 September 1991 (from the Soviet Union).

Legal system: Based on civil law system.

Executive branch:
Chief of state: President Robert Kocharian (since 30 March 1998).

Head of government: Prime Minister Andranik Markaryan (since 12 May 2000).

Economy

Economy—overview
Armenia had developed a modern industrial sector when it was a part of the Soviet Union. It used to exchange manufactured products and equipment for raw material. Since the collapse of the Soviet Union in 1991, Armenia has taken up small-scale agriculture, as against the large collective farms of the Soviet era. The process of privatization of industry has begun.

Currency: Dram.

GDP: Purchasing power parity—$13.65 billion (2004 est.).

GDP—real growth rate: 9% (2004 est.).

GDP—per capita: Purchasing power parity—$4,600 (2004 est.).

Inflation rate: 3.5% (2004 est.).

Population below poverty line: 50% (2002 est.).

Unemployment rate: 30% (2003 est.).

Exports: $850 million f.o.b. (2004 est.)—Diamonds, mineral products, foodstuff, energy.

Imports: $1.3 billion f.o.b. (2004 est.)—Natural gas, petroleum, tobacco products, foodstuff, diamonds.

External debt: $905 million (June 2001).

Transport and Communications

Railways: 852 km in common carrier service; does not include industrial lines.

Roads: 15,918 km.

Telephones: 562,600 (2003).

Mobile cellular: 114,400 (2003).

Internet users: 30,000 (2001).

Internet country code: .am

Australia

History

It is believed that the native aborigines arrived in Australia some 40,000–60,000 years ago. Europeans arrived on the scene in the 17th century. The first large-scale expedition was that of 1770 led by James Cook. The proliferation of Europeans in Australia had devastating effects on the local aborigine population.

The independence of the thirteen American colonies led the British to start colonizing Australia. In 1788, British Navy captain Arthur Phillip founded a penal settlement at Sydney when he arrived with a fleet of 11 vessels carrying nearly 800 convicts.

In 1901, the federation of Australia was achieved but the country remains under British sovereignty.

Geography

Location: Oceania, continent between the Indian Ocean and the South Pacific Ocean.

Area: 7,686,850 sq. km.

Terrain: The terrain of Australia consists mostly of low plateaus with deserts. There are fertile plains in the south-east of the country.

Natural resources: Bauxite, coal, iron ore, copper, tin, gold, silver, uranium, nickel, tungsten, mineral sands, lead, zinc, diamonds, natural gas, petroleum.

Climate: Australia features a wide range of climatic zones, from the tropical regions of the north to the arid expanses of the interior and the temperate regions of the south. Sometimes known as 'The Dry Continent', the land mass is relatively arid, with 80% of the country receiving a median rainfall of less than 600mm per year and 50% with less than 300mm. Summer starts in December, autumn in March, winter in June and spring in September. Seasonal fluctuations can be large, with temperatures ranging from above 50°C to well below zero. Although the climate is mostly of the continental type, the insular nature of the land mass results in modifications to the general continental pattern.

People

Population: 20,090,437 (July 2005 est.).

Population growth rate: 0.87% (2005 est.).

Sex ratio: 0.99 male(s)/female (2005 est.).

Ethnic groups: Caucasian 92%, Asian 7%, aboriginal and others 1%.

Religions: Anglican 26.1%, Roman Catholic 26%, other Christian 24.3%, non-Christian 11%, others 12.6%.

Languages: English, native languages.

Literacy rate: 100%.

Infant mortality rate: 4.69 deaths/ 1,000 live births (2005 est.).

Life expectancy: Total 80.39 years, Male 77.52 years, Female 83.4 years (2005 est.).

Government

Capital: Canberra.

Government type: Democratic, federal state system recognizing the British monarch as sovereign.

Independence: 1 January 1901 (federation of UK colonies).

Administrative divisions:

Six states and two territories*:

Australian Capital Territory*, New South Wales, Northern Territory*, Queensland, South Australia, Tasmania, Victoria, and Western Australia.

Legal system: Based on English common law.

Executive branch:

Chief of state: Queen of Australia Elizabeth II (since 6 February 1952), represented by Governor General Maj. Gen. (Ret.) Michael Jeffrey (since 11 August 2003).

Head of government: Prime Minister John Winston Howard (since 11 March 1996).

Elections and election results: Elections to the Senate were last held on 9 October 2004 and the next elections will be held by June 2008. Elections to the House of Representatives were last held on 9 October 2004 and will be next held by November 2007.

Economy

Currency: Australian dollar.

Economy—overview:
Australia has a Western-style capitalist economy and a per capita GDP on par with the top four West European economies. The country's rising output in the domestic economy has been a major factor in combating the global slump. Its emphasis on reforms is also a contributory reason behind the economy's strength.

GDP: Purchasing power parity—611.7 billion (2004 est.).

GDP—real growth rate: 3.5% (2004 est.).

GDP—per capita: Purchasing power parity—\$30,700 (2004 est.).

Inflation rate: 2.3% (2004 est.).

Unemployment rate: 5.1% (2004).

Exports: \$86.89 billion (2004 est.)— Coal, gold, meat, wool, alumina, iron ore, wheat, machinery and transport equipment.

Imports: \$98.1 billion (2004 est.)— Machinery and transport equipment, computers and office machines, telecommunication equipment and parts; crude oil and petroleum products.

External debt: $308.7 billion (2004 est.).

Transport and Communications

Railways: 43,802 km (5,290 km electrified).

Roads: 811,603 km.

Telephones: 10,815,000 (2003).

Mobile cellular: 14,347,000 (2003).

Internet users: 9,472,000 (2003).

Internet country code: .au

Austria

History

In the 5th century, sustained Hun and eastern German attacks destroyed the Roman provincial defence network on the Danube. Several Germanic tribes like the Goths, Rugii, Heruli and Langobardi settled in the Austrian lands. Charlemagne, who later became the Holy Roman Emperor, conquered the area in about 788. From the 13th century, the House of Hapsburg, also called the House of Austria, ruled over Austria till World War I.

The Congress of Vienna of 1814–15 that took place at the end of the Napoleonic Wars, reorganized Europe and changed the political landscape of the continent. Austria emerged as one of the major gainers. This helped turn the country into a dominant power in Europe. Between 1867 and 1918, the Hapsburg Empire that emerged from the constitutional compromise, or Ausgleich, of 1867 was known as Austria–Hungary, or the Austro-Hungarian empire.

The assassination of Archduke Francis Ferdinand of Austria in 1914 triggered off World War I. During the War, Austria fought alongside Germany, Bulgaria and the Ottoman Empire as one of the Central Powers. The war ended in ruin for Austria–Hungary and the empire collapsed.

In July 1934, the imprisonment of some Nazis led to an attempted Nazi coup and the assassination of Chancellor Dollfuss. In 1936, Austria acknowledged itself to be a 'German state'. In 1938 came the Anschluss, or the political union of Austria with Germany. This came about when Hitler annexed the country.

In 1945, Soviet troops liberated Vienna from German occupation and Austria came under occupation by British, French, Soviet and US forces. In 1955, Austria signed a treaty with France, UK, USA and USSR to establish an independent and 'permanently neutral' Austria. The country also joined the UN the same year.

In 1986, former UN Secretary General Kurt Waldheim was elected Austrian President. In 1995, Austria joined the European Union.

Geography

Location: Central Europe, north of Italy and Slovenia.

Area: 83,870 sq. km.

Terrain: The terrain of Austria is mostly mountainous in the west and south and mostly flat or gently sloping along the eastern and northern margins.

Natural resources: Oil, coal, lignite, timber, iron ore, copper, zinc, antimony, magnesite, tungsten, graphite, salt, hydropower.

Climate: Austria has a continental temperate climate. The winters are cold with frequent rain. There is some snowfall in the lowlands and in the mountains.

People

Population: 8,184,691 (July 2005 est.).

Population growth rate: 0.11% (2005 est.).

Sex ratio: 0.95 male(s)/female (2005 est.).

Religions: Roman Catholic 74%, Protestant 5%, Muslim 4%, others 17%.

Languages: German (official nationwide), Slovene (official in Carinthia), Croatian Hungarian (both official in Burgenland).

Literacy rate: 98% (2004 est.).

Infant mortality rate: 4.66 deaths/ 1,000 live births (2005 est.).

Life expectancy: Total 78.92 years, Male 76.03 years, Female 81.96 years (2005 est.).

Government

Capital: Vienna.

Government type: Federal republic.

Independence: 1156 (from Bavaria).

Legal system: Civil law system with Roman law origin; judicial review of legislative acts by the constitutional court; separate administrative and civil/penal supreme courts.

Executive branch:
Chief of state: President Heinz Fischer (since 8 July 2004).

Head of government: Chancellor Wolfgang Schuessel (since 4 February 2000).

Economy

Currency: Euro.

Economy—overview:
Austria has a prosperous well-developed market economy with high standard of living and has close relations with other EU economies, mainly Germany. There has been a strong inflow of foreign investors drawn by Austria's EU membership.

GDP: Purchasing power parity—$255.9 billion (2004 est.).

GDP—real growth rate: 1.9% (2004 est.).

GDP—per capita: Purchasing power parity—$31,300 (2004 est.).

Inflation rate: 1.8% (2004 est.).

Population below poverty line: 3.9% (1999).

Unemployment rate: 4.4% (2004 est.).

Exports: $102.7 billion f.o.b. (2004 est.)—Machinery and equipment, motor vehicles and parts, paper and paperboard, metal goods, chemicals, iron and steel; textiles, foodstuff.

Imports: $101.2 billion f.o.b. (2004 est.)—Machinery and equipment, motor vehicles, chemicals, metal goods, oil and oil products; foodstuff.

External debt: $15.5 billion (2003 est.).

Transport and Communications

Railways: 6,021 km (3,552 km electrified).

Roads: 200,000 km.

Telephones: 3,881,000 (2003).

Mobile cellular: 7,094,500 (2003).

Internet users: 3.73 million (2003).

Internet country code: .at

Azerbaijan

History

Nomadic Turkic tribes, Kurds, Iranian speakers and the Caucasian Albanians lived in Eastern Transcaucasia in ancient and medieval times. Following Arab incursions in the seventh century, local rulers called shahanshah set up an Islamic form of regime. In the early 16th century, Azerbaijan's Caucasian Muslims became Shiite Muslims.

In 1828, the Treaty of Turkmanchay between Russia and Persia divided Azerbaijan into a Soviet Azerbaijan (which is the present-day nation of Azerbaijan) and a southern region of Azerbaijan that is today a part of Iran. In 1918, following the Bolshevik Revolution in Russia, Azerbaijan declared its independence. However, in 1920, the Red Army invaded the country and declared it to be a Soviet Socialist Republic. In 1936, Azerbaijan became a full-fledged republic of the Soviet Union.

Since 1988, Azerbaijan has been involved in a territorial dispute with neighbouring Armenia over the enclave of Nagorno-Karabakh. The majority of the population of Nagorno-Karabakh is Armenian Christian by faith who want to become a part of Armenia or a separate independent nation. A ceasefire was reached in 1994, but the issue remains unresolved. In 2001, the Presidents of Armenia and Azerbaijan met peace negotiators from France, Russia and USA to work out a solution. In August 1991, Azerbaijan declared its independence from the disintegrating Soviet Union.

Geography

Location: South-western Asia, bordering the Caspian Sea, between Iran and Russia, with a small European portion north of the Caucasus range.

Area: 86,600 sq. km. This includes the area of exclave of Naxcivan Autonomous Republic and the Nagorno-Karabakh region.

Terrain: Azerbaijan consists of the large, flat Kur–Araz Ovaligi or Kura-Araks Lowland, much of which lies below sea level, the Great Caucasus Mountains in the north and Qarabag Yaylasi or Karabakh Upland in the west. Baku lies on Abseron Yasaqligi or Apsheron Peninsula that projects into Caspian Sea.

Natural resources: Petroleum, natural gas, iron ore, nonferrous metals, alumina.

Climate: The climate of Azerbaijan is of the dry semi-arid steppe type.

People

Population: 7,911,974 (July 2005 est.).

Population growth rate: 0.59% (2005 est.).

Sex ratio: 0.94 male(s)/female (2005 est.).

Religions: Muslim 93.4%, Russian Orthodox 2.5%, Armenian Orthodox 2.3%, others 1.8% (1995 est.).

Languages: Azerbaijani (Azeri) 89%, Russian 3%, Armenian 2%, others 6% (1995 est.).

Literacy rate: Total 97%, Male 99%, Female 96% (1989 est.).

Infant mortality rate: 81.74 deaths/1,000 live births (2005 est.).

Life expectancy: Total 63.35 years, Male 59.24 years, Female 67.66 years (2005 est.).

Government

Capital: Baku (Baki).

Government type: Republic.

Independence: 30 August 1991 (from the Soviet Union).

Legal system: Based on civil law system.

Executive branch:
Chief of state: President Ilham Aliyev (since 31 October 2003).

Head of government: Prime Minister Artur Rasizade (since 4 November 2003).

Economy

Currency: Azerbaijani manat.

Economy—overview:
Azerbaijan's biggest export is petroleum and the negotiation of production-sharing arrangements with foreign firms have so far resulted in the commitment of $60 billion to long-term development of oilfields. Azerbaijan suffers from problems that other former Soviet republics have faced in making the switch to a market economy. However, the country's sizable energy resources are a major help to its long-term prospects. Azerbaijan has also started on a process of economic reform.

GDP: Purchasing power parity—$30.01 billion (2004 est.).

GDP—real growth rate: 9.8% (2004 est.).

GDP—per capita: Purchasing power parity—$3,800 (2004 est.).

Inflation rate: 4.6% (2004 est.).

Population below poverty line: 49% (2002 est.).

Unemployment rate: 1.2% (2004 est.).

Exports: $3.168 billion f.o.b. (2004)—oil and gas 90%, machinery, cotton, foodstuff.

Imports: $3.622 billion f.o.b. (2004 est.)—Machinery and equipment, oil products, foodstuff, metals, chemicals.

External debt: $1.4 billion (2002).

Transport and Communications

Railways: 2,122 km.

Roads: 24,981 km.

Telephones: 923,800 (2002).

Mobile cellular: 870,000 (2002).

Internet users: 25,000 (2002).

Internet country code: .az

The Bahamas

History

The present-day Bahamian island of San Salvador was the first New World land that Christopher Columbus landed on in October 1492. British settlements on the islands first appeared in the 17th century.

Between 1717 and 1964, Bahamas remained a British crown colony. In 1964, it was granted self-government. In June 1973, it became an independent country.

Geography

Location: Caribbean chain of islands in the North Atlantic Ocean, south-east of the US state of Florida, north-east of Cuba.

Area: 13,940 sq. km.

Natural resources: Salt, aragonite, timber, arable land.

Climate: The Bahamas has a tropical marine climate that is moderated by the influence of the warm waters of the Gulf Stream.

People

Population: 301,790 (2005 est.).

Population growth rate: 0.67% (2005 est.).

Sex ratio: 0.96 male(s)/female (2005 est.).

Religions: Baptist 32%, Anglican 20%, Roman Catholic 19%, Methodist 6%, Church of God 6%, other Protestant 12%, none or unknown 3%, others 2%.

Languages: English (official), Creole (among Haitian immigrants).

Literacy rate: Total 95.6%, Male 94.7%, Female 96.5% (2003 est.).

Infant mortality rate: 25.21 deaths/1,000 live births (2005 est.).

Life expectancy: Total 65.54 years, Male 62.11 years, Female 69.04 years (2005 est.).

Government

Capital: Nassau.

Government type: Constitutional parliamentary democracy.

Independence: 10 July 1973 (from the UK).

Legal system: Based on English common law.

Executive branch:
Chief of state: Queen Elizabeth II (since 6 February 1952), represented by Governor General Ivy Dumont (since May 2002).

Head of government: Prime Minister Perry Christie (since 3 May 2002).

Economy

Currency: Bahamian dollar (BSD).

GDP: Purchasing power parity—$5.295 billion (2004 est.).

GDP—real growth rate: 3% (2004 est.).

GDP—per capita: Purchasing power parity—$17,700 (2004 est.).

Inflation rate: 1.2% (2004 est.).

Unemployment rate: 10.2% (2004 est.).

Exports: $636 million (2003 est.)—fish and crawfish; rum, salt, chemicals; fruits and vegetables.

Imports: $1.63 billion (2003 est.)—Machinery and transport equipment, manufactures, chemicals, mineral fuels; food and live animals.

External debt: $308.5 million (2002).

Transport and Communications

Railways: None.

Roads: 2,693 km.

Telephones: 131,700 (2003).

Mobile cellular: 121,800 (2002).

Internet users: 84,000 (2003).

Internet country code: .bs

Bahrain

History

Persians ruled the islands of Bahrain in the fourth century AD and then returned to claim Bahrain again in 1602 after Arab and Portuguese rule. Ahmad ibn al-Khalifah took over in 1783. The al-Khalifahs remain the ruling family in Bahrain.

In 1820, Bahrain became a British protectorate and became fully independent in 1971. In 1975, the Emir, Sheikh

Isa Bin-Salman Al Khalifah, dissolved the assembly and started ruling by decree.

Bahrain has been a key ally of the US, serving as a airbase during the Persian Gulf War in 1991. It is also the base of the US Navy's Fifth Fleet.

Geography

Location: Middle East, archipelago in the Persian Gulf, east of Saudi Arabia.

Area: 665 sq. km.

Terrain: Bahrain is mostly a low desert plain that rises gently to a low central escarpment.

Natural resources: Oil, natural gas, fish, pearls.

Climate: Bahrain has an arid climate with mild winters and hot, humid summers.

People

Population: 688,345. This includes 235,108 non-nationals (July 2005 est.).

Population growth rate: 1.51% (2005 est.).

Sex ratio: 1.27 male(s)/female (2005 est.).

Religions: Shi'a Muslim 70%, Sunni Muslim 30%.

Languages: Arabic, English, Farsi, Urdu.

Literacy rate: Total 89.1%, Male 91.9%, Female 85% (2003 est.).

Infant mortality rate: 17.27 deaths/1,000 live births (2005 est.).

Life expectancy: Total 74.23 years, Male 71.76 years, Female 76.78 years (2005 est.).

Government

Capital: Manama.

Government type: Constitutional hereditary monarchy.

Independence: 15 August 1971 (from the UK).

Legal system: Based on Islamic law and English common law.

Executive branch:
Chief of state: King Hamad bin Isa Al Khalifa (since 6 March 1999); heir apparent Crown Prince Salman bin Hamad (the monarch's son).

Head of government: Prime Minister Khalifa bin Salman Al Khalifa (since 1971).

Economy

Currency: Bahraini dinar.

Economy—overview:
60% of export receipts, 60% of government revenues and 30% of GDP of Bahrain come from petroleum production and refining. The country has well-developed communication and transport facilities, which has attracted many multinational firms with business interests in the Persian Gulf region.

GDP: Purchasing power parity—$13.01 billion (2004 est.).

GDP—real growth rate: 5.6% (2004 est.).

GDP—per capita: Purchasing power parity—$19,200 (2004 est.).

Inflation rate: 2.1% (2004 est.).

Unemployment rate: 15% (1998 est.).

Exports: $8.205 billion (2004 est.)—Petroleum and petroleum products, aluminum, textiles.

Imports: $5.87 billion (2004 est.)—Crude oil, machinery, chemicals.

External debt: $6.215 billion (2004 est.).

Transport and Communications

Railways: None.

Roads: 3,459 km.

Telephones: 185,800 (2003).

Mobile cellular: 443,100 (2003).

Internet users: 140,200 (2002).

Internet country code: .bh

Bangladesh

History

The earliest reference to the region that is today West Bengal and Bangladesh was to a kingdom called Vanga or Banga. In 1576 Bengal became a part of the Mughal Empire and majority of East Bengalis converted to Islam. With the decline and subsequent fall of the Mughals, the Suba, or Dominion, of Bengal became semi-independent. In 1608, the capital was moved from Rajmahal to Dhaka and in 1704 to Murshidabad. It was during this period that the English East India Company established its base at Calcutta.

At the time of partition in 1947, the two predominantly Islamic regions of the Indian subcontinent were made into one Islamic country—Pakistan. What is today Bangladesh was then known as East Pakistan. Inspite of sharing a common religion, all other characteristics of these two regions were vastly different.

Tension between East and West Pakistan developed because of their widespread disparities. Soon, in East Pakistan, the Awami League, a political party founded by Sheikh Mujibur Rahman, sought independence from West Pakistan. The Awami League swept the elections of December 1970, winning 167 of the 169 seats allotted to East Pakistan in the National Assembly (out of a total of 313 seats). This gave the League an overall majority. On the other hand, in West Pakistan, the Pakistan People's Party, led by Zulfikar Ali Bhutto, won 81 of 144 seats.

President Yahya Khan of Pakistan carried out negotiations in March 1971 even though military forces continued to reach East Pakistan in large numbers from West Pakistan. On 25 March, the army launched a massive attack in East Pakistan inflicting heavy casualties that included many students. Mujib himself was arrested and flown to West Pakistan. Most other leaders of the Awami League set up a government-in-exile in Calcutta and declared East Pakistan as an independent state named Bangladesh. In the vicious conflict that followed, around ten million people, mainly Hindus, fled to India. When the situation assumed alarming proportions, Indian military forces invaded the territory of East Pakistan on 3 December 1971. The Pakistani military surrendered on 16 December. Mujib was released from jail and returned to assume leadership of the newly born Bangladesh government in January 1972.

After independence, Bangladesh passed through successive phases of martial law, military coups and political assassinations. President Zia-ur-Rahman was assassinated in 1981 and Abdus Sattar assumed power. The following year, General Ershad seized power in a military coup. In 1990, General Ershad was ousted from power and lost the elections that followed in 1991. Democracy was re-established in the country and Begum Khaleda Zia, the widow of President Zia, became Prime Minister. Soon afterwards, General Ershad was imprisoned on charges of corruption and possession of illegal arms. The Constitution was altered, making the President a largely ceremonial designation and vesting primary executive power in the

Prime Minister's office. A general election was held in 1996, but a boycott by opposition parties reduced its credibility. The re-elected Khaleda Zia subsequently resigned and a caretaker government under Muhammad Habibur Rahman was appointed. A coalition government headed by Sheikh Hasina Wazed of the Awami League (Sheikh Mujib's daughter) was voted into power in a second set of elections held in the same year. In October 2001 the Bangladesh Nationalist Party won the parliamentary elections and Khaleda Zia returned to power.

Geography

Location: Southern Asia, bordering the Bay of Bengal, between Myanmar and India.

Area: 144,000 sq. km.

Terrain: Mostly flat alluvial plain; hilly in south-east.

Natural resources: Natural gas, arable land, timber, coal.

Climate: Bangladesh has a tropical climate with a mild winter from November to February and a hot, humid summer from March to June. The humid, warm rainy monsoon season is from June to October.

People

Population: 144,319,628 (July 2005 est.).

Population growth rate: 2.09% (2005 est.).

Sex ratio: 1.05 male(s)/female (2005 est.).

Religions: Muslim 83%, Hindu 16%, others 1% (1998).

Languages: Bangla (official, also known as Bengali), English.

Literacy rate: Total 43.1%, Male 53.9%, Female 31.8% (2003 est.).

Infant mortality rate: 62.6 deaths/ 1,000 live births (2005 est.).

Life expectancy: Total 62.08 years, Male 62.13 years, Female 62.02 years (2005 est.).

Government

Capital: Dhaka.

Government type: Parliamentary democracy.

Independence: 16 December 1971 (from Pakistan). 26 March 1971 is the date of independence from Pakistan while 16 December 1971 is known as Victory Day and commemorates the official creation of the state of Bangladesh.

Legal system: Based on English common law.

Executive branch:
Chief of state: President Tajuddin Ahmed (since 6 September 2002).

Head of government: Prime Minister Khaleda Zia of the Bangladesh Nationalist Party (since 10 October 2001).

Elections: The National Parliament elects the president for a five-year term. The election scheduled for 16 September 2002 was not held, as Tajuddin Ahmed was the only presidential candidate. He was sworn in on 6 September 2002 (the next election will be held by 2007). After the legislative elections, the leader of the party that wins the majority is usually appointed prime minister by the president.

Legislative branch:
There is a unicameral National Parliament or Jatiya Sangsad of 300 seats. Members are elected by popular vote from single territorial constituencies and they serve five-year terms.

Elections: Last held on 1 October 2001 (next elections are to be held before October 2006).
Note: the election of October 2001 brought a majority BNP government aligned with three other smaller parties—Jamaat-i-Islami, Islami Oikya Jote, and Jatiya Party (Naziur).

Economy

Currency: Taka (BDT).

Economy—overview:
Sustained domestic and international efforts to improve the economic situation of Bangladesh has succeeded little in delivering tangible improvements to this poor and densely populated nation. As much as half of the country's GDP is generated through the service sector. The agriculture sector accounts for the employment of nearly two-thirds of Bangladeshis. Rice is the single most important product. There are various major constraints to growth. These include frequent natural calamities such as cyclones and floods, inefficient public sector enterprises, underdeveloped ports, a rapidly growing labour force in excess of agricultural requirement. Other reasons include delays in exploiting energy resources such as natural gas, insufficient power supplies, and slow implementation of economic reforms.

GDP: Purchasing power parity—$275.7 billion (2004 est.).

GDP—real growth rate: 4.9% (2004 est.).

GDP—per capita: Purchasing power parity—$2,000 (2004 est.).

Inflation rate: 6% (2004 est.).

Population below poverty line: 45% (2004 est.).

Unemployment rate: 40% (includes underemployment) (2004 est.).

Exports: $7.478 billion (2004 est.).

Imports: $10.03 billion (2004 est.).

External debt: $19.97 billion (2004 est.).

Transport and Communications

Railways: 2,706 km.

Roads: 207,486 km.

Telephones: 740,000 (2003).

Mobile cellular: 1,365,000 (2003).

Internet users: 243,000 (2003).

Internet country code: .bd

Barbados

History

It s believed that Arawak Indians were the first inhabitants of the island of Barbados. The Portuguese were the first Europeans to visit the island but the British were the first to set up a colony there, in 1627. The initial cotton and tobacco plantations that were started on the island soon gave way to more profitable sugar plantations. African slaves were brought in to work on the plantations and soon they amounted for 90% of the population on the island. Later on, Barbados became the administrative headquarters of the Windward Islands but became a separate colony in 1885. UK granted it independence in 1966.

Geography

Location: Caribbean island in the North Atlantic Ocean, north-east of Venezuela.

Area: 431 sq. km.

Natural resources:
Petroleum, fish, natural gas.

Climate: Barbados has a tropical climate with a rainy season between June and October.

People

Population: 279,254 (July 2005 est.).

Population growth rate: 0.33% (2005 est.).

Sex ratio: 0.93 male(s)/female (2005 est.).

Religions: Protestant 67% (Anglican 40%, Pentecostal 8%, Methodist 7%, others 12%), Roman Catholic 4%, none 17%, others 12%.

Languages: English.

Literacy rate: Total 97.4%, Male 98%, Female 96.8% (1995 est.).

Infant mortality rate: 12.5 deaths/1,000 live births (2005 est.).

Life expectancy: Total 71.41 years, Male 69.46 years, Female 73.39 years (2005 est.).

Government

Capital: Bridgetown.

Government type: Parliamentary democracy; independent sovereign state within the Commonwealth.

Independence: 30 November 1966 (from the UK).

Legal system: English common law; no judicial review of legislative acts.

Executive branch:
Chief of state: Queen Elizabeth II (since 6 February 1952), represented by Governor General Sir Clifford Straughn Husbands (since 1 June 1996).

Head of government: Prime Minister Owen Seymour Arthur (since 6 September 1994).

Economy

Currency: Barbadian dollar.

GDP: Purchasing power parity—$4.569 billion (2004 est.).

GDP—real growth rate: 2.3% (2004 est.).

GDP—per capita: Purchasing power parity—$16,400 (2004 est.).

Inflation rate: –0.5% (2004 est.).

Unemployment rate: 10.7% (2003 est.).

Exports: $206 million (2004 est.)—Sugar and molasses, rum, other foods and beverages, chemicals, electrical components.

Imports: $1.039 billion (2004 est.)—Consumer goods, machinery, foodstuff, construction materials, chemicals, fuel, electrical components.

External debt: $692 million (2002).

Transport and Communications

Railways: None.

Roads: 1,600 km.

Telephones: 134,000 (2003).

Mobile cellular: 140,000 (2003).

Internet users: 100,000 (2003).

Internet country code: .bb

Belarus

History

In the fifth century AD, eastern Slavic tribes colonized Belarus, also known as Byelorussia or White Russia in historical times. The territory became a part of the Grand Duchy of Lithuania and later, in 1569, it was integrated with Poland. As a result of the repeated partitions of Poland, Belarus became a part of Russia.

In the aftermath of World War I, Belarus proclaimed its independence in 1918. But soon after, the Soviet Red Army invaded Belarus and in 1919, the

Belarusian Soviet Socialist Republic was proclaimed.

The 1930s saw the execution of hundreds of thousands in Belarus as a result of the Stalinist purges. More than a million people were killed during the German invasion of Belarus in 1941 and the capital city, Minsk, was severely damaged. The Soviet Army finally drove the Germans out in 1944.

In 1986, Belarus was heavily affected by the fallout of the nuclear explosion at Chernobyl in neighbouring Ukraine. In 1991, Belarus declared its independence from the collapsing Soviet Union.

Geography

Location: Eastern Europe, east of Poland.

Area: 207,600 sq. km.

Terrain: Generally flat terrain with extensive marshlands.

Natural resources: Forests, peat deposits, small quantities of oil and natural gas, granite, dolomitic limestone, marl, chalk, sand, gravel, clay.

Climate: Belarus has cold winters, cool and moist summers. Its climate is of a transitional type between continental and maritime climates.

People

Population: 10,300,483 (July 2005 est.).

Population growth rate: −0.09%. (2005 est.).

Sex ratio: 0.88 male(s)/female (2005 est.).

Religions: Eastern Orthodox 80%, others (including Roman Catholic, Protestant, Jewish, and Muslim) 20% (1997 est.).

Languages: Belarusian, Russian.

Literacy rate: Total 99.6%, Male 99.8%, Female 99.5% (2003 est.).

Infant mortality rate: 13.37 deaths/ 1,000 live births (2005 est.).

Life expectancy: Total 68.72 years, Male 63.03 years, Female 74.69 years (2005 est.).

Government

Capital: Minsk.

Government type: Republic.

Independence: 25 August 1991 (from the Soviet Union).

Legal system: Based on civil law system.

Executive branch:
Chief of state: President Aleksandr Lukashenko (since 20 July 1994).

Head of government: Prime Minister Sergei Sidorsky (since 19 December 2003).

Economy

Currency: Belarusian ruble.

GDP: Purchasing power parity—$70.5 billion (2004 est.)

GDP—real growth rate: 6.4% (2004 est.).

GDP—per capita: Purchasing power parity—$6,800 (2004 est.).

Inflation rate: 17.4% (2004 est.).

Population below poverty line: 27.1% (2003 est.).

Unemployment rate: 2% officially registered unemployed; large number of underemployed workers (2004).

Exports: $11.47 billion f.o.b. (2004 est.)—Machinery and equipment, mineral products, chemicals, metals; textiles, foodstuff.

Imports: $13.57 billion f.o.b. (2004 est.)—Mineral products, machinery and equipment, chemicals, foodstuff, metals.

External debt: $600 million (2004 est.).

Transport and Communications

Railways: 5,523 km.
Roads: 79,990 km.

Telephones: 3,071,300 (2003).
Mobile cellular: 1,118,000 (2003).
Internet users: 1,391,900 (2003).
Internet country code: .by

Belgium

History

Roman ruler Julius Caesar occupied the area that is today Belgium in the period between 57–50 BC. In the 16th century, it became a part of the Holy Roman Empire. In 1555, the Low Countries (a region consisting of modern-day the Netherlands, Belgium and Luxembourg) was united with Spain. The Treaty of Utrecht of 1713 gave the control of this region to Austria. Later on, France annexed the region. After the ouster of Napoleon, the Congress of Vienna (1814–15) gave Belgium to the Netherlands. But in 1830, Belgians rebelled against Dutch rule and declared their independence.

During World War II, Germany invaded Belgium and held the king, Leopold III, as prisoner. Allied forces liberated Belgium from German occupation in 1944. King Leopold III attempted to return to the throne in 1950 but social unrest forced him to abdicate in favour of his son, Baudouin. In the 1960s, Belgium granted independence to its African colonies.

The headquarters of both the European Union and North Atlantic Treaty Organization (NATO) are at the Belgian capital city, Brussels. It is also one of the homes of the European Parliament.

Geography

Location: Western Europe, bordering the North Sea, between France and the Netherlands.

Area: 30,528 sq. km.

Terrain: Belgium has flat coastal plains in the north-west, rolling hills in the central part of the country and mountains of the Ardennes Forest in the south-east.

Natural resources: Coal, natural gas, construction materials, silica sand, carbonates.

Climate: Belgium has a temperate climate with mild winters and cool summers.

People

Population: 10,364,388 (July 2005 est.).

Population growth rate: 0.15% (2005 est.).

Sex ratio: 0.96 male(s)/female (2005 est.).

Religions: Roman Catholic 75%, Protestant and others 25%.

Languages: Dutch (official) 60%, French (official) 40%, German (official) less than 1%, legally bilingual (Dutch and French).

Literacy rate: 98%.

Infant mortality rate: 4.68 deaths/1,000 live births (2005 est.).

Life expectancy: Total 78.62 years, Male 75.44 years, Female 81.94 years (2005 est.).

Government

Capital: Brussels.

Government type: Federal parliamentary democracy under a constitutional monarch.

Independence: 4 October 1830 (date on which a provisional government declared independence from the Netherlands).

Legal system: Civil law system influenced by English constitutional theory; judicial review of legislative acts.

Executive branch:
Chief of state: King Albert II (since 9 August 1993).

Head of government: Prime Minister Guy Verhofstadt (since 13 July 1999).

Economy

Currency: Euro.

Economy—overview:
Belgium has a modern private enterprise-based economy. The country enjoys a central geographic location, well-developed transport network and a diversified industrial and commercial base. However, a major drawback is the lack of natural resources. Almost three-quarters of Belgium's trade is with other EU countries. Public debt is about 100% of GDP.

GDP: Purchasing power parity—$316.2 billion (2004 est.).

GDP—real growth rate: 2.6% (2004 est.).

GDP—per capita: Purchasing power parity—$30,600 (2004 est.).

Inflation rate: 1.9% (2004 est.).

Population below poverty line: 4% (1989 est.).

Unemployment rate: 12% (2004 est.).

Exports: $255.7 billion f.o.b. (2003 est.)—Machinery and equipment, chemicals, diamonds, metals and metal products, foodstuff.

Imports: $235 billion f.o.b. (2003 est.)—Machinery and equipment, chemicals, diamonds, pharmaceuticals, foodstuff, transportation equipment, oil products.

External debt: $28.3 billion (1999 est.).

Transport and Communications

Railways: 3,518 km.

Roads: 148,216 km.

Telephones: 5,120,400 (2002).

Mobile cellular: 8,135,500 (2002).

Internet users: 3,400,000 (2002).

Internet country code: .be

Belize

History

The Mayan Civilization flourished in the area that is today Belize till about 1200. A few shipwrecked British sailors began the first recorded European settlement in 1638. In 1840, it officially became the Colony of British Honduras. In January 1964, it was granted full internal self-government. In 1981, the country was granted full independence.

However, Guatemala still lays claim to a substantial portion of land under Belize.

Geography

Location: Middle America, bordering the Caribbean Sea, between Guatemala and Mexico.

Area: 22,966 sq. km.

Natural resources: Arable land potential, timber, fish, hydropower.

Climate: Belize has a hot and humid tropical climate.

People

Population: 279,457 (July 2005 est.).

Population growth rate: 2.33% (2005 est.).

Sex ratio: 1.03 male(s)/female (2005 est.).

Religions: Roman Catholic 49.6%, Protestant 27%, none 9.4%, others 14%.

Languages: English (official), Spanish, Mayan, Garifuna (Carib), Creole.

Literacy rate: 94.1% (2003 est.).

Infant mortality rate: 25.69 deaths/1,000 live births (2005 est.).

Life expectancy: Total 67.49 years, Male 65.02 years, Female 70.08 years (2005 est.).

Government

Capital: Belmopan.

Government type: Parliamentary democracy.

Independence: 21 September 1981 (from the UK).

Legal system: English law.

Executive branch:
Chief of state: Queen Elizabeth II (since 6 February 1952), represented by Governor General Sir Colville Young Sr (since 17 November 1993).

Head of government: Prime Minister Said Wilbert Musa (since 28 August 1998).

Economy

Currency: Belizean dollar.

GDP: Purchasing power parity—$1.28 billion (2002 est.).

GDP—real growth rate: 3.7% (2002 est.).

GDP—per capita: Purchasing power parity—$4,900 (2002 est.).

Inflation rate: 2.9% (2004 est.).

Population below poverty line: 33% (1999 est.).

Unemployment rate: 12.9% (2003 est.).

Exports: $401.4 million f.o.b. (2004 est.)—Sugar, banana, citrus, clothing, fish products, molasses, wood.

Imports: $579.9 million c.i.f. (2004 est.)—Machinery and transport equipment, manufactured goods; fuels, chemicals, pharmaceuticals; food, beverages, tobacco.

External debt: $1.362 billion (2004 est.).

Transport and Communications

Railways: None.

Roads: 2,872 km.

Telephones: 33,300 (2003).

Mobile cellular: 60,400 (2003).

Internet users: 30,000 (2002).

Internet country code: .bz

Benin

History

The Abomey Kingdom of Dahomey was formed in 1625. France annexed Dahomey in 1893 and incorporated it into French West Africa in 1904. It attained independence in 1960 and Hubert Maga became the country's first President. In 1963 a coup led by the army's Chief of Staff, Colonel Christophe Soglo deposed President Maga.

In 1975, Dahomey was renamed as the People's Republic of Benin and the Parti de la Revolution Populaire du Benin (PRPB) was created as the country's only political party. In 1991, Nicephore Soglo defeated Kerekou in the first multi-candidate presidential elections. Kerekou returned to power in 1996 and was re-elected in 2001.

Geography

Location: Western Africa, bordering the Bight of Benin, between Nigeria and Togo.

Area: 112,620 sq. km.

Natural resources: Offshore oil deposits, limestone, marble, timber.

Climate: Benin has a tropical climate.

People

Population: 7,460,025 (July 2005 est.).

Population growth rate: 2.82% (2005 est.).

Sex ratio: 0.98 male(s)/female (2005 est.).

Religions: Indigenous beliefs 50%, Christian 30%, Muslim 20%.

Languages: French (official), Fon and Yoruba, tribal languages.

Literacy rate: Total 40.9%, Male 56.2%, Female 26.5% (2000).

Infant mortality rate: 85 deaths/ 1,000 live births (2005 est.).

Life expectancy: Total 50.51 years, Male 50.14 years, Female 50.89 years (2005 est.).

Government

Capital: Porto Novo (official capital). Cotonou (seat of government).

Government type: Republic under multiparty democratic rule.

Independence: 1 August 1960 (from France).

Legal system: Based on French civil law and customary law.

Executive branch:
Chief of state: President Mathieu Kerekou (since 4 April 1996). The president is both the chief of state and head of government.

Economy

Currency: Communaute Financiere Africaine franc (CFA Franc).

GDP: Purchasing power parity—$8.338 billion (2004 est.).

GDP—real growth rate: 5% (2004 est.).

GDP—per capita: Purchasing power parity—$1200 (2004 est.).

Inflation rate: 2.8% (2004 est.).

Population below poverty line: 33% (2001 est.).

Exports: $720.9 million f.o.b. (2004 est.)—Cotton, crude oil, palm products, cocoa.

Imports: $934.5 million f.o.b. (2004 est.)—Foodstuffs, capital goods, petroleum products.

External debt: $1.6 billion (2000).

Transport and Communications

Railways: 578 km.

Roads: 6,787 km.

Telephones: 66,500 (2003).

Mobile cellular: 236,200 (2003).

Internet users: 70,000 (2003).

Internet country code: .bj

Bhutan

History

The name Bhutan is believed to be derived from the Sanskrit 'Bhotant' which means 'the end of Tibet', or from 'Bhu-uttan', meaning 'high land'. Historically, the Bhutanese refer to their country as Druk Yul or the 'land of the thunder dragon'. A Tibetan lama named Shabdrung Ngawang Namgyal arrived in Bhutan in 1616. He is the one who introduced the present dual system of religious and secular government. He also created the system of Dzongs in Bhutan. He unified the country and established himself as the supreme leader with civil power vested in a high officer known as the Druk Desi. Religious affairs were charged to another leader, the Je Khenpo who is the Chief Abbot of Bhutan.

Civil wars plagued Bhutan in the two centuries following Shabdrung's death. This meant that the regional Penlops or governors gained more and more power. This ended with the election of the Penlop of Trongsa, Ugyen Wangchuck, as the first King of Bhutan in 1907.

In 1865, British troops invaded the area. In 1910, Bhutan allowed its foreign affairs to be taken care of by UK. In 1949, it entered into the Treaty of Friendship and Cooperation with India.

Geography

Location: Southern Asia, between China and India.

Area: 47,000 sq. km.

Terrain: Mostly mountainous with some fertile valleys and savanna.

Natural resources: Timber, hydropower, gypsum, dolomite, limestone, calcium carbide.

Climate: Bhutan's climate varies from tropical in the southern plains to cool winters and hot summers in the central valleys and severe winters and cool summers in the Himalayas.

People

Population: 2,232,291 (July 2005 est.).

Population growth rate: 2.11% (2005 est.).

Sex ratio: 1.07 male(s)/female (2005 est.).

Religions: Lamaistic Buddhist 75%, Indian- and Nepalese-influenced Hinduism 25%.

Languages: Dzongkha (official); Bhotes speak various Tibetan dialects; Nepalese speak various Nepalese dialects.

Literacy rate: Total 42.2%, Male 56.2%, Female 28.1% (1995 est.).

Infant mortality rate: 100.44 deaths/1,000 live births (2005 est.).

Life expectancy: Total 54.39 years, Male 54.65 years, Female 54.11 years (2005 est.).

Government

Capital: Thimphu.

Government type: Monarchy. There is a special treaty relationship with India.

Independence: 8 August 1949 (from the UK).

Legal system: Based on Indian law and English common law.

Executive branch:
Chief of state: King Jigme Singye Wangchuck (since 24 July 1972).

Head of government: Chairman of the council of ministers Lyonpo Jigme Y. Thinley (since 30 August 2003).

Legislative branch:
There is a unicameral National Assembly or Tshogdu with 150 seats of which 105 are elected from village constituencies, 10 represent religious bodies and 35 are designated by the monarch to represent government and other secular interests. The members serve three-year terms.

Economy

Currency: Ngultrum.

Economy—overview:
Bhutan has one of the world's smallest and least developed economies. Agriculture and forestry are the main sources of livelihood for more than 90% of the population. Agriculture consists largely of subsistence farming and animal husbandry. The mountainous terrain makes it tough to set up and develop roads and other forms of infrastructure. The country has close ties with India. There are strong trade (India is its single biggest source of imports and the biggest destination for its exports) and monetary links (the Ngultrum is treated at par with the Indian rupee and is also legal tender in Bhutan). It also depends heavily on India's financial assistance. Some of Bhutan's five-year plans have been financed by India. The industrial sector is technologically underdeveloped and most of the production is of the small sector cottage industry type. Bhutan's resources include its hydropower potential and its attraction as a tourism destination.

GDP: Purchasing power parity—$2.9 billion (2003 est.).

GDP—real growth rate: 5.3% (2003 est.).

GDP—per capita: Purchasing power parity—$1,400 (2003 est.).

Inflation rate: 3% (2002 est.).

Exports: $154 million f.o.b. (2000 est.).

Imports: $196 million c.i.f. (2000 est.).

External debt: $ 245 million (2000).

Transport and Communications

Railways: None.

Roads: 4,007 km.

Telephones: 25,200 (2003).

Mobile cellular: 22,000 (2005).

Internet users: 15,000 (2003).

Internet country code: .bt

Bolivia

History

The area that comprises modern-day Bolivia was once a part of the Inca Empire. In 1824, Venezuelan statesman Simon Bolivar, from whom Bolivia takes its name, liberated the country from

Spanish rule and in 1825, Bolivia gained its independence with Simon Bolivar as its President. In the later part of the 19th century, Bolivia lost great expanses of territory to its neighbouring countries.

Bolivia witnessed numerous coups and internal conflicts in the 1950s and 1960s. In 1967, USA helped the Bolivian government suppress a peasant uprising led by Ernesto 'Che' Guevara, who was killed after being betrayed by peasants. A string of military rulers followed till 1983, when the military junta handed over power to a civilian administration led by Siles Zuazo.

Geography

Location: Central South America, south-west of Brazil.

Area: 1,098,580 sq. km.

Terrain: The lofty Andes Mountains and a highland plateau (Altiplano), along with lower hills and the lowland plains of the Amazon Basin.

Natural resources: Tin, natural gas, petroleum, zinc, tungsten, antimony, silver, iron, lead, gold, timber, hydropower.

Climate: Bolivia's climate varies from humid and tropical to cold and semiarid.

People

Population: 8,857,870 (July 2005 est.).

Population growth rate: 1.49% (2005 est.).

Sex ratio: 0.98 male(s)/female (2005 est.).

Religions: Roman Catholic 95%, Protestant (Evangelical Methodist).

Languages: Spanish (official), Quechua (official), Aymara (official).

Literacy rate: Total 87.2%, Male 93.1%, Female 81.6% (2003 est.).

Infant mortality rate: 53.11 deaths/ 1,000 live births (2005 est.).

Life expectancy: Total 65.5 years, Male 62.89 years, Female 68.25 years (2005 est.).

Government

Capital: La Paz (seat of government). Sucre (legal capital and seat of judiciary).

Government type: Republic.

Independence: 6 August 1825 (from Spain).

Legal system: Based on Spanish law and Napoleonic code.

Executive branch:
Chief of state: Interim President Eduardo Rodrigrez Veltzé (since 10 June 2005). The president is both the chief of state and head of government.

Economy

Currency: Boliviano.

GDP: Purchasing power parity—$22.33 billion (2004 est.).

GDP—real growth rate: 3.7% (2004 est.).

GDP—per capita: Purchasing power parity—$2,600 (2004 est.).

Inflation rate: 2% (2001 est.).

Population below poverty line: 64% (2004 est.).

Unemployment rate: 9.2% in urban areas; there is widespread underemployment (2003 est.).

Exports: $1.986 billion f.o.b. (2004 est.)—Soybeans, natural gas, zinc, gold, wood (2000).

Imports: $1.595 billion f.o.b. (2004 est.)—Capital goods, raw materials and semi-manufactures, chemicals, petroleum, food.

External debt: $5.439 billion (2004 est.).

Transport and Communications

Railways: 3,519 km.

Roads: 60,282 km.

Telephones: 600,100 (2003).

Mobile cellular: 1,401,500 (2003).

Internet users: 270,000 (2002).

Internet country code: .bo

Bosnia and Herzegovina

History

The Romans annexed the area that is today Bosnia and Herzegovina in the second and first centuries BC. The Slavs started settling in the region in the seventh century. In 1463, the Ottoman Turks conquered Bosnia. The Congress of Berlin that followed the Russo-Turkish War of 1877–8 gave Austria–Hungary the mandate to govern Bosnia and Herzegovina.

On 28 June 1914, a Bosnian Serb student named Gavrilo Princip assassinated the Austrian Archduke Franz Ferdinand in Sarajevo. This triggered off World War I. By the time the War ended, the kingdom of Austria–Hungary had collapsed and Bosnia and Herzegovina became a part of the kingdom of Serbs, Croats and Slovenes in 1918. The country was renamed Yugoslavia in 1929.

Following the collapse of communism elsewhere in Europe in the 1990s, Bosnia and Herzegovina declared its independence from Yugoslavia in 1992. However, the state was beset by grave problems from the very start. While Muslim nationalists wanted a centralized independent state of Bosnia, the Croats wanted to join an independent Croatian state while Serb nationalists wanted to remain within the Belgrade-dominated remains of Yugoslavia. In the 1992 referendum on independence, Croat and Muslim nationalists formed a tactical alliance and outvoted Serbs, enraging the latter. A bloody civil war erupted and the Bosnian Serbs gained control over half of the country by August 1992.

In August and September 1995, NATO carried out air strikes against Serb positions. This enabled Muslims and Croats to retake substantial chunks of territory from the Serbs. Soon afterwards, the Dayton Peace Accord was signed. This led to the formation of two entities—one Muslim–Croat federation and a Serb entity (Republika Srpska) within the greater state of Bosnia and Herzegovina.

Geography

Location: South-eastern Europe, bordering the Adriatic Sea and Croatia.

Area: 51,129 sq. km.

Terrain: Mountains and valleys.

Natural resources: Coal, iron ore, bauxite, copper, lead, zinc, chromite, cobalt, manganese, nickel, clay, gypsum, salt, sand, forests, hydropower.

Climate: Bosnia and Herzegovina has hot summers and cold winters.

People

Population: 4,025,476 (July 2005 est.).

Population growth rate: 0.44% (2005 est.).

Sex ratio: 1.01 male(s)/female (2005 est.).

Religions: Muslim 40%, Orthodox 31%, Roman Catholic 15%, others 14%.

Languages: Bosnian, Croatian, Serbian.

Infant mortality rate: 21.05 deaths/ 1,000 live births (2005 est.).

Life expectancy: Total 72.85 years, Male 70.09 years, Female 75.8 years (2005 est.).

Government

Capital: Sarajevo.

Government type: Federal democratic republic.

Independence: 1 March 1992 (from Yugoslavia; date on which referendum for independence was completed); 3 March 1992 (date on which independence was declared).

Legal system: Based on civil law system.

Executive branch:
Chief of state: The presidency rotates between a Serb, a Bosnian Muslim and a Croat. Each member holds office for eight months. The current members are Borislav Paravac (Serb), Bulejman Tihic (Bosnian Muslim) and Ivo Miro Jovic (Croat).

Head of government: Prime Minister Adnan Terzic (since 20 December 2002).

Economy

Currency: Marka.

GDP: Purchasing power parity—$26.21 billion (2004 est.).

GDP—real growth rate: 5% (2004 est.).

GDP—per capita: Purchasing power parity—$6,500 (2004 est.).

Inflation rate: 1.1% (2004 est.).

Population below poverty line: 25% (2004 est.).

Unemployment rate: 44% (2004 est.).

Exports: $1.7 billion f.o.b. (2004 est.)—Metals, clothing, wood products.

Imports: $5.2 billion f.o.b. (2004 est.)—Machinery and equipment, chemicals, fuels, foodstuff.

External debt: $3 billion (2004 est.).

Transport and Communications

Railways: 1,021 km (795 km electrified).

Roads: 21,846 km.

Telephones: 938,000 (2003).

Mobile cellular: 1,050,000 (2003).

Internet users: 100,000 (2002).

Internet country code: .ba

Botswana

History

In 1885, UK established a protectorate named Bechuanaland, which they expanded in 1890. In 1966, UK granted it full independence. It became the Republic of Botswana with Seretse Khama as President.

In 2000, faced with one of the world's worst AIDS incidence rates, President Mogae announced that AIDS drugs would be made available for free from 2001.

Geography

Location: Southern Africa, north of South Africa.

Area: 600,370 sq. km.

Terrain: Predominantly flat to gently rolling tableland. The Kalahari Desert lies in the south-west.

Natural resources: Diamonds, copper, nickel, salt, soda ash, potash, coal, iron ore, silver.

Climate: Botswana has a semi-arid climate with warm winters and hot summers.

People

Population: 1,640,115 (July 2005 est.).

Population growth rate: 0% (2005 est.).

Sex ratio: 0.96 male(s)/female (2004 est.).

Religions: Indigenous beliefs 85%, Christian 15%.

Languages: English (official), Setswana.

Literacy rate: Total 79.8%, Male 76.9%, Female 82.4% (2003 est.).

Infant mortality rate: 54.58 deaths/1,000 live births (2005 est.).

Life expectancy: Total 33.87 years, Male 33.89 years, Female 33.84 years (2005 est.).

Government

Capital: Gaborone.

Government type: Parliamentary republic.

Independence: 30 September 1966 (from UK).

Legal system: Based on Roman–Dutch law and local customary law.

Executive branch:
Chief of state: President Festus Mogae (since 1 April 1998) and Vice-President Seretse Ian Khama (since 13 July 1998). The president is both the chief of state and head of government.

Economy

Currency: Pula.

GDP: Purchasing power parity—$15.05 billion (2004 est.).

GDP—real growth rate: 3.5% (2004 est.).

GDP—per capita: Purchasing power parity—$9,200 (2004 est.).

Inflation rate: 7% (2004 est.).

Population below poverty line: 47% (2002 est.).

Unemployment rate: 23.8% (2004 est.).

Exports: $2.94 billion f.o.b. (2004 est.)—Diamond, copper, nickel, soda ash, meat, textiles.

Imports: $2.255 billion f.o.b. (2004 est.)—Foodstuff, machinery, electrical goods, transport equipment, textiles, fuel and petroleum products, wood and paper products, metal and metal products.

External debt: $360 million (2002).

Transport and Communications

Railways: 888 km.

Roads: 10,217 km.

Telephones: 142,400 (2002).

Mobile cellular: 435,000 (2002).

Internet users: 60,000 (2002).

Internet country code: .bw

Brazil

History

Archaeological evidence shows that the region that is today called Brazil has been inhabited since at least 9000 BC. The indigenous 'Indians' who inhabited the coastal region at the time of first contact with Europeans is believed to have numbered between two million and six million.

In 1500, Portuguese explorer Pedro Alvares Cabral reached the area while on a voyage to India. Portugal initially called its new territory Vera Cruz, but later renamed it Brazil because of the large amounts of brazilwood, source of a valuable dye, that was found there. Before long, Brazil also became an important sugar-producing region for Portugal.

In 1789, Jose Joaquim da Silva Xavier, popularly known as Tiradentes, led the first rebellion against the Portuguese. The Portuguese authorities suppressed the rebellion and executed Tiradentes. In 1807, when Napoleon invaded Portugal, the Portuguese prince regent Dom Joao took refuge in Brazil. On 16 December 1815, he designated the Portuguese territories as the United Kingdom of Portugal, Brazil, and the Algarves. This had the effect of granting Brazil equality with Portugal. In 1822, Dom Joao's son, Dom Pedro, proclaimed the independence of Brazil. On 1 December, he was crowned Emperor of Brazil. In 1889, the monarchy was overthrown and a federal republic established in Brazil. Brazil had already begun to rise as a coffee-producing giant and by 1902, it was producing over 60% of the world's total coffee.

A revolt in 1930 saw Getulio Vargas taking charge as the head of a provisional revolutionary government. In 1937, Vargas led a coup and began ruling as a dictator. This was also the start of the welfare state in Brazil.

In 1960, the capital city was moved to Brasilia. From the 1980s, an economic crisis loomed over Brazil, and by 1991, inflation touched 1500%.

Geography

Location: Eastern South America, bordering the Atlantic Ocean.

Area: 8,511,965 sq. km.

Terrain: The terrain of Brazil is mostly flat with rolling lowlands in the north, a narrow coastal belt, some plains, hills, and mountains.

Natural resources: Bauxite, gold, iron ore, manganese, nickel, phosphates, platinum, tin, uranium, petroleum, hydropower, timber.

Climate: The climate of Brazil is mostly tropical but temperate in the south.

People

Population: 186,112,794 (July 2005 est.).

Population growth rate: 1.06% (2005 est.).

Sex ratio: 0.98 male(s)/female (2005 est.).

Religions: Roman Catholic (nominal) 80%.

Languages: Portuguese (official), Spanish, English, French.

Literacy rate: Total 86.4%, Male 86.1%, Female 86.6% (2003 est.).

Infant mortality rate: 29.61 deaths/ 1,000 live births (2005 est.).

Life expectancy: Total 71.69 years, Male 67.74 years, Female 75.85 years (2005 est.).

Government

Capital: Brasilia.

Government type: Federative republic.

Independence: 7 September 1822 (from Portugal).

Legal system: Based on Roman codes.

Executive branch:
Chief of state: President Luiz Inacio 'Lula' Da Silva (since 1 January 2003). Vice-President Jose Alencar (since 1 January 2003). The president is both the chief of state and head of government.

Economy

Currency: Real.

Economy—overview:
The Brazilian economy is the largest of all South American economies. It has large and well-developed agricultural, service, mining and manufacturing sectors. Between 2001 and 2003, the economy has successfully withstood a number of external and internal crises. Nevertheless, the economy is not without its fair share of problems, the most significant ones being debt related.

GDP: Purchasing power parity—$1.492 trillion (2004 est.).

GDP—real growth rate: 5.1% (2004 est.).

GDP—per capita: Purchasing power parity—$8,100 (2004 est.).

Inflation rate: 7.6% (2004 est.).

Population below poverty line: 22% (1998 est.).

Unemployment rate: 11.5% (2004 est.).

Exports: $95 billion f.o.b. (2004 est.)—Transport equipment, iron ore, soybeans, footwear, coffee, automobiles.

Imports: $61 billion f.o.b. (2004 est.)—Machinery, electrical and transport equipment, chemical products, oil.

External debt: $219.8 billion (2004).

Transport and Communications

Railways: 29,412 km.

Roads: 1,724,929 km.

Telephones: 38,810,000 (2002).

Mobile cellular: 46,373,300 (2003).

Internet users: 14,300,000 (2002).

Internet country code: .br

Brunei

History

In the sixth century AD, Brunei enjoyed trade relations with China. Later on, it came under Hindu influence by means of its connections with the Majapahit kingdom in Java. The power of Brunei started to decline towards the end of the 16th century when internal conflict affected the country. This decline continued through the 19th century. In 1841, Sarawak passed to the English. Later, it lost the island of Labuan in Brunei Bay and Sabah in present-day eastern East Malaysia. Petroleum was first produced in 1929.

In 1888, Brunei became a British protectorate. During World War II, the Japanese occupied Brunei between 1941–5. The British returned to power after the World War was over.

Geography

Location: South-eastern Asia, bordering the South China Sea and Malaysia.

Area: 5,770 sq. km.

Terrain: Brunei consists mostly of flat coastal plain that rises to mountains in the east.

Natural resources: Petroleum, natural gas, timber.

Climate: Brunei has a tropical hot, humid and rainy climate.

People

Population: 372,361 (July 2005 est.).

Population growth rate: 1.9% (2005 est.).

Sex ratio: 1.09 male(s)/female (2005 est.).

Religions: Muslim (official) 67%, Buddhist 13%, Christian 10%, indigenous beliefs and others 10%.

Languages: Malay (official), English, Chinese.

Literacy rate: Total 93.9%, Male 96.3%, Female 91.4% (2005 est.).

Infant mortality rate: 12.61 deaths/ 1,000 live births (2005 est.).

Life expectancy: Total 74.8 years, Male 72.36 years, Female 77.36 years (2005 est.).

Government

Capital: Bandar Seri Begawan.

Government type: Constitutional sultanate.

Independence: 1 January 1984 (from UK).

Legal system: Based on English common law; for Muslims, Islamic Shari'a law supersedes civil law in a number of areas.

Executive branch:
Chief of state: Sultan and Prime Minister Sir Hassanal Bolkiah (since 5 October 1967). The monarch is both the chief of state and head of government.

Economy

Currency: Bruneian dollar.

Economy—overview:
Brunei has a small and wealthy economy. Crude oil and natural gas production account for almost 50% of GDP. Per capita GDP is much higher than most other Third World countries and Brunei earns a lot of income from overseas investments. The government provides for all medical services and subsidizes rice and housing.

GDP: Purchasing power parity— $6.842 billion (2003 est.).

GDP—real growth rate: 3.2% (2003 est.).

GDP—per capita: Purchasing power parity—$23,600 (2003 est.).

Inflation rate: 0.3% (2003 est.).

Unemployment rate: 3.2% (2002 est.).

Exports: $7.7 billion f.o.b. (2003 est.)—Crude oil, natural gas, refined products.

Imports: $5.2 billion c.i.f. (2003 est.)—Machinery and transport equipment, manufactured goods, food, chemicals.

External debt: None.

Transport and Communications

Railways: 13 km (private line).

Roads: 2,525 km.

Telephones: 90,000 (2002).

Mobile cellular: 137,000 (2002).

Internet users: 35,000 (2002).

Internet country code: .bn

Bulgaria

History

Thracians lived in the country that is today Bulgaria from around 3500 BC. Thereafter, the Roman Empire annexed the lands and by about first century AD, it was a part of the Empire. After the fall of the Roman Empire, numerous tribes invaded that area, the most important of which were the Bulgars.

The Ottoman Turks conquered Bulgaria in 1836. The Russians forced Turkey to grant Bulgaria independence following the Russo-Turkish War of 1877–8.

Bulgaria fought numerous wars in the first half of the 20th century in the hope of gaining territory, mainly Macedonia, but most of these ended in failure. In 1944, the Soviet army invaded German-occupied Bulgaria. In 1946, a referendum abolished the monarchy and declared a republic. The Communist Party won the ensuing election and Georgi Dimitrov was elected prime minister.

Geography

Location: South-eastern Europe, bordering the Black Sea, between Romania and Turkey.

Area: 110,910 sq. km.

Terrain: Mostly mountains. There are lowlands in the north and the south-east.

Natural resources: Bauxite, copper, lead, zinc, coal, timber, arable land.

Climate: Bulgaria has a temperate climate with cold, damp winters and hot, dry summers.

People

Population: 7,450,349 (July 2005 est.).

Population growth rate: –0.89% (2005 est.).

Sex ratio: 0.93 male(s)/female (2005 est.).

Religions: Bulgarian Orthodox 82.6%, Muslim 12.2%, Roman Catholic 1.7%, Jewish 0.1%, Protestant, Gregorian–Armenian, and others 3.4% (1998).

Languages: Bulgarian, secondary languages closely correspond to ethnic breakdown.

Literacy rate: Total 98.6%, Male 99.1%, Female 98.2% (2003 est.).

Infant mortality rate: 20.55 deaths/1,000 live births (2005 est.).

Life expectancy: Total 72.03 years, Male 68.41 years, Female 75.87 years (2005 est.).

Government

Capital: Sofia.

Government type: Parliamentary democracy.

Independence: 3 March 1878 (from Ottoman Empire).

Legal system: Civil law and criminal law based on Roman law.

Executive branch:
Chief of state: President Georgi Parvanov (since 22 January 2002); Vice-President Angel Marin (since 22 January 2002).

Head of government: Chairman of the Council of Ministers (Prime Minister) Simeon Saxe-Coburg-Gotha (since 24 July 2001).

Economy

Currency: Lev.

GDP: Purchasing power parity—$61.63 billion (2004 est.).

GDP—real growth rate: 5.3% (2004 est.).

GDP—per capita: Purchasing power parity—$8,200 (2004 est.).

Inflation rate: 6.1% (2004 est.).

Population below poverty line: 13.4% (2002 est.).

Unemployment rate: 12.7% (2004 est.).

Exports: $7.337 billion f.o.b. (2003 est.)—Clothing, footwear, iron and steel, machinery and equipment, fuels.

Imports: $9.723 billion f.o.b. (2003 est.)—Fuels, minerals, and raw materials; machinery and equipment; metals and ores; chemicals and plastics; food, textiles.

External debt: $16.1 billion (2004 est.).

Transport and Communications

Railways: 4,294 km.

Roads: 37,077 km.

Telephones: 2,868,200 (2002).

Mobile cellular: 2,597,500 (2002).

Internet users: 630,000 (2002).

Internet country code: .bg

Burkina Faso

History

In 1947, Upper Volta was established as a separate territory within French West Africa. In 1960, it became independent.

In the first 30 years after independence, Upper Volta saw one coup after another. In 1984, the country was renamed as Burkina Faso. The country has one of the highest infection rates of HIV in the region.

Geography

Location: Western Africa, north of Ghana.

Area: 274,200 sq. km.

Natural resources: Manganese, limestone, marble; small deposits of gold, antimony, copper, nickel, bauxite, lead, phosphates, zinc, silver.

Climate: Burkina Faso has a tropical climate with warm, dry winters and hot, wet summers.

People

Population: 13,925,313 (July 2005 est.).

Population growth rate: 2.53% (2005 est.).

Sex ratio: 0.97 male(s)/female (2005 est.).

Religions: Indigenous beliefs 40%, Muslim 50%, Christian (mainly Roman Catholic) 10%.

Languages: French (official), native African languages belonging to Sudanic family.

Literacy rate: Total 26.6%, Male 36.9%, Female 16.6% (2003 est.).

Infant mortality rate: 97.57 deaths/1,000 live births (2005 est.).

Life expectancy: Total 43.92 years, Male 42.19 years, Female 45.7 years (2005 est.).

Government

Capital: Ouagadougou.

Government type: Parliamentary republic.

Independence: 5 August 1960 (from France).

Legal system: Based on French civil law system and customary law.

Executive branch:
Chief of state: President Blaise Compaore (since 15 October 1987).

Head of government: Prime Minister Ernest Paramanga Yonli (since 6 November 2000).

Economy

Currency: Communaute Financiere Africaine franc.

GDP: Purchasing power parity—$15.74 billion (2004 est.).

GDP—real growth rate: 4.8% (2004 est.).

GDP—per capita: Purchasing power parity—$1,200 (2004 est.).

Inflation rate: 2.4% (2004 est.).

Population below poverty line: 45% (2003 est.).

Exports: $418.6 million f.o.b. (2004 est.)—Cotton, livestock, gold.

Imports: $866.3 million f.o.b. (2004 est.)—Capital goods, foodstuff, petroleum.

External debt: $1.3 billion (2000).

Transport and Communications

Railways: 622 km.

Roads: 12,506 km.

Telephones: 65,400 (2003).

Mobile cellular: 227,000 (2003).

Internet users: 48,000 (2003).

Internet country code: .bf

Burundi

History

In 1890, the Tutsi kingdom of Urundi and neighbouring Ruanda (present-day Rwanda) was incorporated into German East Africa. In 1923, Belgium was granted League of Nations mandate to administer Ruanda–Urundi. In 1962, Urundi was separated from Ruanda–Urundi, and granted independence as Burundi, a monarchy under King Mwambutsa IV. The next four decades saw constant coups, massacres and assassinations, mostly along ethnic lines.

In October 2001, talks brokered by Nelson Mandela led to a transitional government in Burundi. Hutu and Tutsi leaders were meant to share power. However, the main Hutu rebel groups refused to sign ceasefire and fighting intensified. Fighting continued into 2004.

Geography

Location: Central Africa, east of the Democratic Republic of the Congo.

Area: 27,830 sq. km.

Natural resources: Nickel, uranium, rare earth oxides, peat, cobalt, copper, platinum (not yet exploited), vanadium, arable land, hydropower.

Climate: Burundi has an equatorial climate.

People

Population: 6,370,609 (July 2005 est.).

Population growth rate: 2.22% (2005 est.).

Sex ratio: 0.99 male(s)/female (2005 est.).

Religions: Christian 67% (Roman Catholic 62%, Protestant 5%), indigenous beliefs 23%, Muslim 10%.

Languages: Kirundi (official), French (official), Swahili (along Lake Tanganyika and in the Bujumbura area).

Literacy rate: Total 51.6%, Male 58.5%, Female 45.2% (2003 est.).

Infant mortality rate: 69.29 deaths/1,000 live births (2005 est.).

Life expectancy: Total 43.5 years, Male 42.91 years, Female 44.12 years (2005 est.).

Government

Capital: Bujumbura.

Government type: Republic.

Independence: 1 July 1962 (from UN trusteeship under Belgian administration).

Legal system: Based on German and Belgian civil codes and customary law.

Executive branch:
Chief of state: President Domitien Ndayizeye (since 30 April 2003).

Economy

Currency: Burundi franc.

GDP: Purchasing power parity—$4.001 billion (2004 est.).

GDP—real growth rate: 3% (2004 est.).

GDP—per capita: Purchasing power parity—$600 (2004 est.).

Inflation rate: 8.5% (2004 est.).

Population below poverty line: 68% (2002 est.).

Exports: $31.84 million f.o.b. (2004 est.)—Coffee, tea, sugar, cotton, hides.

Imports: $138.2 million f.o.b. (2004 est.).

External debt: $1,132.5 million (2002).

Transport and Communications

Railways: None.

Roads: 14,480 km.

Telephones: 23,900 (2003).

Mobile cellular: 64,000 (2003).

Internet users: 14,000 (2003).

Internet country code: .bi

Cambodia

History

In the first century AD, Chinese and Indian pilgrims and traders stopped on the coast of present-day Cambodia. A kingdom which Chinese writers called 'Funan' existed in southern Cambodia at this point of time.

The region that is today Cambodia came under the rule of the Hindu Khmers in around 600. It was during Khmer rule that the famous Angkor Wat and Angkor Thom temple complexes were constructed. The period of the Khmer rule from the ninth to the 15th century is considered as the Classical Era of Cambodian history.

France colonized the region in 1863 and joined together Cambodia, Laos and Vietnam into one protectorate called French Indochina. In 1941, Norodom Sihanouk came to power on the ceremonial throne of Cambodia. In 1953, France granted Cambodia independence. In 1955, Norodom Sihanouk abdicated the throne to his parents but remained as the head of government.

In March 1970, Gen. Lon Nol overthrew Sihanouk while he was away on foreign tours. In 1975, Lon Nol was himself overthrown by Pol Pot, leader of the Khmer Rouge forces. This was the starting point of one of the most gruesome periods of modern world history. Millions of Cambodians were killed by state sponsored terrorism or due to forced labour. The country was renamed Kampuchea.

In January 1979, Vietnamese forces removed Pol Pot from power. Pol Pot, along with tens of thousands of Khmer Rouge fighters, withdrew into the hills of western Cambodia. They joined forces with pro-Sihanouk forces to launch a guerilla movement aimed at overthrowing the pro-Vietnam government that had been installed in the country. In 1993, a deal was worked out whereby power would be shared by pro-Vietnamese leader Hun Sen and Sihanouk's son, Prince Ranariddh. The two of them would be co-prime ministers.

Geography

Location: South-eastern Asia, bordering the Gulf of Thailand, between Thailand, Vietnam, and Laos.

Area: 181,040 sq. km.

Terrain: The terrain of Cambodia is mostly made up of low, flat plains with mountains in the south-west and north.

Natural resources: Timber, gemstones, some iron ore, manganese, phosphates, hydropower potential.

Climate: Cambodia has a tropical climate. The monsoon season is from May to November while the dry season is from December to April.

People

Population: 13,607,069 (July 2005 est.).

Population growth rate: 1.81% (2005 est.).

Sex ratio: 0.94 male(s)/female (2005 est.).

Religions: Theravada Buddhist 95%, others 5%.

Languages: Khmer (official) 95%, French, English.

Literacy rate: Total 69.9%, Male 80.5%, Female 60.3% (2003 est.)

Infant mortality rate: 71.48 deaths/ 1,000 live births (2005 est.).

Life expectancy: Total 58.87 years, Male 55.92 years, Female 61.96 years (2005 est.).

Government

Capital: Phnom Penh.

Government type: Multiparty democracy under a constitutional monarchy.

Independence: 9 November 1953 (from France).

Legal system: Primarily a civil law mixture of French-influenced codes from the United Nations Transitional Authority in Cambodia (UNTAC) period, royal decrees, and acts of the legislature.

Executive branch:
Chief of state: King Norodom Sihamoni (since November 2004).

Head of government: Prime Minister Hun Sen (since 30 November 1998).

Economy

Currency: Riel.

Economy—overview:
The long-term development of the Cambodian economy after years of strife and conflict remains a formidable task. Its infrastructure is undeveloped, its population lacking in technical skills and higher education. Foreign investment and foreign aid suffer due to the lack of confidence in the country.

GDP: Purchasing power parity—$26.99 billion (2004 est.).

GDP—real growth rate: 5.4% (2004 est.).

GDP—per capita: Purchasing power parity—$2,000 (2004 est.).

Inflation rate: 3.1% (2004 est.).

Population below poverty line: 40% (2004 est.).

Unemployment rate: 2.5% (2000 est.).

Exports: $2.311 billion f.o.b. (2004 est.)—Timber, garments, rubber, rice, fish.

Imports: $3.129 billion f.o.b. (2004 est.)—Petroleum products, cigarettes, gold, construction materials, machinery, motor vehicles.

External debt: $2.4 billion (2002 est.).

Transport and Communications

Railways: 602 km.

Roads: 12,323 km.

Telephones: 35,400 (2002).

Mobile cellular: 380,000 (2002).

Internet users: 30,000 (2002).

Internet country code: .kh

Cameroon

History

The Portuguese and the Dutch were among the first European powers to colonize Cameroon. In 1919, the London Declaration divided Cameroon into a British administrative zone (20% of the land) and a French zone (80%). In 1922, the League of Nations granted a mandate to UK and France for their respective administrative zones.

In 1958, French Cameroon was granted self-government with Ahmadou Ahidjo as prime minister. Following a UN-sponsored referendum in 1961, one part of the British-administered Cameroon, Southern Cameroon, joined the Republic of Cameroon to become the Federal Republic of Cameroons. The other part, Northern Cameroon joined Nigeria. In 1972, a national referendum was held and subsequently Cameroon became a unitary state. It was renamed the United Republic of Cameroon.

Geography

Location: Western Africa, bordering the Bight of Biafra, between Equatorial Guinea and Nigeria.

Area: 475,440 sq. km.

Terrain: Diverse, with coastal plain in the south-west, dissected plateau in the centre, mountains in the west, and plains in the north.

Natural resources: Petroleum, bauxite, iron ore, timber, hydropower.

Climate: The climate of Cameroon is tropical along the coast but semi-arid and hot in the northern part of the country.

People

Population: 16,063,678 (July 2005 est.).

Population growth rate: 1.93% (2005 est.).

Sex ratio: 1.01 male(s)/female (2005 est.).

Religions: Indigenous beliefs 40%, Christian 40%, Muslim 20%.

Languages: English (official), French (official), 24 major African language groups.

Literacy rate: Total 79%, Male 84.7%, Female 73.4% (2003 est.).

Infant mortality rate: 68.26 deaths/1,000 live births (2005 est.).

Life expectancy: Total 47.84 years, Male 47.04 years, Female 48.67 years (2005 est.).

Government

Capital: Yaounde.

Government type: Unitary republic; multiparty presidential regime.

Independence: 1 January 1960 (from French-administered UN trusteeship).

Legal system: Based on French civil law system, with common law influence.

Executive branch:
Chief of state: President Paul Biya (since 6 November 1982).

Head of government: Prime Minister Ephraim Inoni (since 8 December 2004).

Economy

Currency: Communaute Financiere Africaine franc.

GDP: Purchasing power parity—$30.17 billion (2004 est.).

GDP—real growth rate: 4.9% (2004 est.).

GDP—per capita: Purchasing power parity—$1,900 (2004 est.).

Inflation rate: 1% (2004 est.).

Population below poverty line: 48% (2000 est.).

Unemployment rate: 30% (2001 est.).

Exports: $2.445 billion f.o.b. (2004 est.)—Crude oil and petroleum products, lumber, cocoa beans, aluminium, coffee, cotton.

Imports: $1.979 billion f.o.b. (2004 est.)—Machinery, electrical equipment, transport equipment, fuel, food.

External debt: $8.46 billion (2004 est.).

Transport and Communications

Railways: 1,008 km.

Roads: 34,300 km.

Telephones: 110,900 (2002).

Mobile cellular: 1,077,000 (2003).

Internet users: 60,000 (2002).

Internet country code: .cm

Canada

History

The first inhabitants of what is today Canada were people like the Inuits (Eskimos). It is thought that the Norse explorer Leif Eriksson reached either Labrador or Nova Scotia in 1000. In 1534, Jacques Cartier took and claimed Canada for France. It soon came to be called New France. The British responded to the French inroads into Canada by setting up the British Hudson's Bay Company in 1670. The main reasons behind French and British interest in Canada were the prospects in fisheries and the fur trade.

Soon the rivalries took a serious course and in 1713, the French lost Hudson Bay, Nova Scotia and Newfoundland. The British added to their conquests during the Seven Years War (1756–63). Ultimately, the French took leave of the North American mainland.

In 1849, the UK recognized Canada's right to self-government. The British North American Act of 1867 created the dominion of Canada by confederating Upper and Lower Canada, New Brunswick and Nova Scotia. In 1869, Canada purchased the vast lands in the Middle West. This led to the formation of the states of Manitoba (in 1870), Alberta and Saskatchewan (both in 1905).

The Statute of Westminister of 1931 recognized the equal status of UK and its dominions including Canada. Hence, Canada was recognized as a partner nation of UK, which was not subordinate in any form to UK and only associated to the common crown.

Geography

Location: Northern North America, bordering the North Atlantic Ocean on the east, North Pacific Ocean on the west, and the Arctic Ocean on the north, north of the USA.

Area: 9,984,670 sq. km.

Terrain: Canada consists mostly of plains with mountains in the west and lowlands in the south-east.

Natural resources: Iron ore, nickel, zinc, copper, gold, lead, molybdenum, potash, diamonds, silver, fish, timber, wildlife, coal, petroleum, natural gas, hydropower.

Climate: The climate of Canada varies from temperate in the south to subarctic and arctic in the north.

People

Population: 32,805,041 (July 2005 est.).

Population growth rate: 0.9% (2005 est.).

Sex ratio: 0.98 male(s)/female (2005 est.).

Religions: Roman Catholic 46%, Protestant 36%, others 18% (1991).

Languages: English 59.3% (official), French 23.2% (official), others 17.5%.

Literacy rate: 97% (1986 est.).

Infant mortality rate: 4.75 deaths/1,000 live births (2005 est.).

Life expectancy: Total 80.1 years, Male 76.73 years, Female 83.63 years (2005 est.).

Government

Capital: Ottawa.

Government type: Confederation with parliamentary democracy.

Independence: 1 July 1867 (from UK).

Legal system: Based on English common law, except in Quebec, where civil law system based on French law prevails.

Executive branch:
Chief of state: Queen Elizabeth II (since 6 February 1952), represented by Governor General Adrienne Clarkson (since 7 October 1999).

Head of government: Prime Minister Paul Martin (since 12 December 2003); Deputy Prime Minister Anne Mclellan (since 12 December 2003).

Elections and election results: Elections to the House of Commons were last held on 27 November 2000 and the next elections are scheduled for 2005.

Legislative branch:
Canada has a bicameral parliament or parlement that consists of the Senate or Senat (the Governor General appoints the members with the advice of the prime minister and they serve until reaching 75 years of age; the normal limit is 105 senators) and the House of Commons or Chambre des Communes (301 seats; members elected by direct, popular vote to serve for up to five-year terms).

Elections and election results: Elections to the House of Commons were last held on 27 November 2000 and the next elections are scheduled for 2005.

Economy

Currency: Canadian dollar.

Economy—overview:

Canada has an affluent, high-tech industrial society, with a market-oriented economic system, pattern of production, and high living standards. Since World War II, the high growth of its manufacturing, mining, and service sectors has transformed Canada from a largely rural economy into a primarily industrial and urban one. The 1989 US-Canada Free Trade Agreement (FTA) and the 1994 North American Free Trade Agreement (NAFTA) (which includes Mexico) resulted in substantial increase in trade and economic relations with the US. A key feature of the economy is the substantial trade surplus.

GDP: Purchasing power parity—$1.023 trillion (2004 est.).

GDP—real growth rate: 2.4% (2004 est.)

GDP—per capita: Purchasing power parity—$31,500 (2004 est.).

Inflation rate: 1.9% (2004 est.).

Unemployment rate: 7% (2004 est.).

Exports: $315.6 billion f.ob. (2004 est.)—Motor vehicles and parts, industrial machinery, aircraft, telecommunications equipment; chemicals, plastics, fertilizers; wood pulp, timber, crude petroleum, natural gas, electricity, aluminium.

Imports: $256.1 billion f.o.b. (2004 est.)—Machinery and equipment, motor vehicles and parts, crude oil, chemicals, electricity, durable consumer goods.

External debt: $570 billion (2004).

Transport and Communications

Railways: 48,909 km.

Roads: 1,408,000 km.

Telephones: 19,950,900 (2003).

Mobile cellular: 13,221,800 (2003).

Internet users: 16,840,000 (2002).

Internet country code: .ca

Cape Verde

History

In 1495, the islands of Cape Verde became a part of the Portuguese Empire. In 1975, Cape Verde achieved independence.

Geography

Location: Western Africa, group of islands in the North Atlantic Ocean, west of Senegal.

Area: 4,033 sq. km.

Natural resources: Salt, basalt rock, limestone, kaolin, fish.

Climate: Cape Verde has a temperate climate with warm dry summers.

People

Population: 418,224 (July 2005 est.).

Population growth rate: 0.67% (2005 est.).

Sex ratio: 0.94 male(s)/female (2005 est.).

Religions: Roman Catholic (infused with indigenous beliefs); Protestant (mostly Church of the Nazarene).

Languages: Portuguese, Crioulo (a mixture of Portuguese and West African words).

Literacy rate: Total 76.6%, Male 85.8%, Female 69.2% (2003 est.).

Infant mortality rate: 47.77 deaths/1,000 live births (2005 est.).

Life expectancy: Total 70.45 years, Male 67.13 years, Female 73.86 years (2005 est.).

Government

Capital: Praia.

Government type: Republic.

Independence: 5 July 1975 (from Portugal).

Legal system: Derived from the legal system of Portugal.

Executive branch:
Chief of state: President Pedro de Verona Rodrigues Pires (since 22 March 2001).

Head of government: Prime Minister Jose Maria Pereira Neves (since 1 February 2001).

Economy

Currency: Cape Verdean escudo.

GDP: Purchasing power parity—$600 million (2002 est.).

GDP—real growth rate: 5% (2004 est.).

GDP—per capita: Purchasing power parity—$1,400 (2002 est.).

Inflation rate: 1.5% (2004 est.).

Population below poverty line: 3% (2002).

Unemployment rate: 21% (2000 est.).

Exports: $61.11 million f.o.b. (2004 est.)—Fuel, shoes, garments, fish, hides.

Imports: $387.3 million f.o.b. (2004 est.)—Foodstuff, industrial products, transport equipment, fuels.

External debt: $325 million (2002).

Transport and Communications

Railways: None.

Roads: 1,350 km.

Telephones: 71,700 (2003).

Mobile cellular: 53,300 (2003).

Internet users: 20,400 (2003).

Internet country code: .cv

Central African Republic

History

France occupied the region that is today Central African Republic in the 1880s and in 1894 it set up the colony of Ubanghi Shari. In 1960, The Central African Republic became independent.

Geography

Location: Central Africa, north of the Democratic Republic of the Congo.

Area: 622,984 sq. km.

Terrain: Flat to rolling plateau; scattered hills in the north-east and south-west.

Natural resources: Diamond, uranium, timber, gold, oil, hydropower.

Climate: Central African Republic has a tropical climate with hot, dry winters and mild to hot, wet summers.

People

Population: 3,799,897 (July 2005 est.).

Population growth rate: 1.49% (2005 est.).

Sex ratio: 0.98 male(s)/female (2005 est.).

Religions: Indigenous beliefs 35%, Protestant 25%, Roman Catholic 25% (animistic beliefs and practices strongly influence the Christians), Muslim 15%.

Languages: French (official), Sangho (lingua franca and national language), tribal languages.

Literacy rate: Total 51%, Male 63.3%, Female 39.9% (2003 est.).

Infant mortality rate: 91 deaths/ 1,000 live births (2005 est.).

Life expectancy: Total 41.01 years, Male 39.21 years, Female 42.86 years (2005 est.).

Government

Capital: Bangui.

Government type: Republic.

Independence: 13 August 1960 (from France).

Legal system: Based on French law.

Executive branch:
Chief of state: President Francois Bozize (since 15 March 2003).

Head of government: Prime Minister Celestin Gaombalet (since 12 December 2003).

Economy

Currency: Communaute Financiere Africaine franc.

GDP: Purchasing power parity—$4.248 billion (2004 est.).

GDP—real growth rate: 0.5% (2004 est.).

GDP—per capita: Purchasing power parity—$1,100 (2004 est.).

Inflation rate: 3.6% (2001 est.).

Unemployment rate: 8% (2001 est.).

Exports: $172 million f.o.b. (2002 est.)—Diamond, timber, cotton, coffee, tobacco.

Imports: $136 million f.o.b. (2002 est.)—Food, textiles, petroleum products, machinery, electrical equipment, motor vehicles, chemicals, pharmaceuticals.

External debt: $881.4 million (2000 est.).

Transport and Communications

Railways: None.

Roads: 23,810 km.

Telephones: 9,000 (2002).

Mobile cellular: 13,000 (2003).

Internet users: 5,000 (2002).

Internet country code: .cf

Chad

History

Berbers began arriving in the area around Lake Chad in the eighth century AD. The onset of Islam happened around 1085. By 1913, France completed its conquest of Chad. In 1960, Chad became independent with Francois Ngarta Tombalbaye as President.

Geography

Location: Central Africa, south of Libya.

Area: 1.284 million sq. km.

Terrain: Broad, arid plains in the centre, desert in the north, mountains in the north-west, lowlands in the south.

Natural resources: Petroleum, uranium, natron, kaolin, fish.

Climate: The climate of Chad is tropical in the south and arid in the north.

People

Population: 9,826,419 (July 2005 est.).

Population growth rate: 2.95% (2005 est.).

Sex ratio: 0.95 male(s)/female (2005 est.).

Religions: Muslim 51%, Christian 35%, animist 7%, others 7%.

Languages: French (official), Arabic (official), Sara (in south), more than 120 different languages and dialects.

Literacy rate: Total 47.5%, Male 56%, Female 39.3% (2003 est.).

Infant mortality rate: 93.82 deaths/ 1,000 live births (2005 est.).

Life expectancy: Total 47.94 years, Male 46.84 years, Female 49.09 years (2005 est.).

Government

Capital: N'Djamena.

Government type: Republic.

Independence: 11 August 1960 (from France).

Legal system: Based on French civil law system and Chadian customary law.

Executive branch:
Chief of state: President Lt Gen. Idriss Deby (since 4 December 1990).

Head of government: Prime Minister Pascal Yoadimmadji (since 3 February 2005).

Economy

Currency: Communaute Financiere Africaine franc.

GDP: Purchasing power parity—$15.66 billion (2004 est.).

GDP—real growth rate: 38% (2004 est.).

GDP—per capita: Purchasing power parity—$1,600 (2004 est.).

Inflation rate: 8% (2004 est.).

Population below poverty line: 80% (2001 est.).

Exports: $365 million f.o.b. (2003 est.)—Cotton, cattle, gum Arabic, petroleum.

Imports: $500.7 million f.o.b. (2004 est.)—Machinery and transportation equipment, industrial goods, petroleum products, foodstuff, textiles.

External debt: $1.1 billion (2000 est.).

Transport and Communications

Railways: None.

Roads: 33,400 km.

Telephones: 11,800 (2002).

Mobile cellular: 65,000 (2003).

Internet users: 15,000 (2002).

Internet country code: .td

Chile

History

There were at least 500,000 natives living in the region that is today Chile when Spanish conquest of the area began in the middle of the 16th century. The most significant of these were the Araucanian Indian group. They put up a strong resistance to the Spanish right up to the 1880s.

In the 16th century, numerous English and Dutch pirates and adventurers raided the Chilean coast in search of easy wealth. In 1810, a junta of locally elected leaders in Santiago proclaimed autonomy for Chile. In 1818, Chile became independent with Bernardo O' Higgins as the supreme director.

In 1970, Salvador Allende became the world's first democratically elected Marxist President and initiated an extensive programme of nationalization and social reform. However, a US-sponsored coup toppled Allende in 1973 and installed General Augusto Pinochet as the country's new dictator. After Pinochet lost a referendum on whether he should remain in power in 1988, Patricio Aylwin was elected Chile's new President in 1989–90. Although Pinochet stepped down as head of state in 1990, he remained commander-in-chief of the army.

Geography

Location: Southern South America, bordering the South Pacific Ocean, Argentina, Bolivia and Peru.

Area: 756,950 sq. km. This includes Easter Island (Isla de Pascua) and Isla Sala y Gomez.

Terrain: The terrain of Chile consists of low coastal mountains, a fertile central valley and the Andes Mountains in the east.

Natural resources: Copper, timber, iron ore, nitrates, precious metals, molybdenum, hydropower.

Climate: Chile is mostly temperate.

People

Population: 15,980,912 (July 2005 est.).

Population growth rate: 0.97% (2005 est.).

Sex ratio: 0.98 male(s)/female (2005 est.).

Religions: Roman Catholic 89%, Protestant 11%, Jewish.

Languages: Spanish.

Literacy rate: Total 96.2%, Male 96.4%, Female 96.1% (2003 est.).

Infant mortality rate: 8.8 deaths/1,000 live births (2005 est.).

Life expectancy: Total 76.58 years, Male 73.3 years, Female 80.03 years (2005 est.).

Government

Capital: Santiago.

Government type: Republic.

Independence: 18 September 1810 (from Spain).

Legal system: Based on Code of 1857 derived from Spanish law and subsequent codes influenced by French and Austrian law.

Executive branch:
Chief of state: President Ricardo Lagos Escobar (since 11 March 2000). The president is both the chief of state and head of government.

Economy

Currency: Chilean peso.

Economy—overview:
Chile has a strong market-oriented

economy, one of the most robust ones in South America. It enjoys a reputation for strong financial institutions and good policy. Nevertheless, Chile experienced a recession in 1999, partly due to severe drought. Chile also suffers from chronic unemployment. Chile has also signed a free trade agreement with USA that became effective on 1 January 2004.

GDP: Purchasing power parity—$169.1 billion (2004 est.).

GDP—real growth rate: 5.8% (2004 est.).

GDP—per capita: Purchasing power parity—$10,700 (2004 est.).

Inflation rate: 2.4% (2004 est.).

Population below poverty line: 20.6% (2000 est.).

Unemployment rate: 8.5% (2004 est.).

Exports: $29.2 billion f.o.b. (2004 est.)—Copper, fish, fruits, paper and pulp, chemicals, wine.

Imports: $22.53 billion f.o.b. (2004 est.)—Consumer goods, chemicals, motor vehicles, fuels, electrical machinery, heavy industrial machinery, food.

External debt: $44.6 billion (2004 est.).

Transport and Communications

Railways: 6,585 km.

Roads: 79,605 km.

Telephone: 3,467,000 (2002).

Mobile cellular: 6,445,700 (2002).

Internet users: 3,575,000 (2002).

Internet country code: .cl

China

History

The recorded history of China goes back in time for nearly 4,000 years, although archeologists have traced the beginnings of human civilization in China to an even earlier time.

According to Chinese tradition, the Xia Dynasty (2070–1600 BC) was the first Chinese dynasty to rule a state. The Shang Dynasty (1600–1046 BC) overthrew the Xia Dynasty. The Western Zhou Dynasty (1046–771 BC) succeeded the Shang Dynasty. The Western Zhou Dynasty was followed by the Eastern Zhou Dynasty which itself is divided into two eras. The first of these two eras was the Spring and Autumn Era that lasted between 770 and 476 BC while the Warring States Era lasted between 475 and 221 BC.

Next came the Qin Dynasty (221–207 BC) The first emperor of the Qin Dynasty, Qin Shi Huang (259–210 BC) founded the first centralized, unified, multi-ethnic feudal state in Chinese history. He is also credited with the construction of the Great Wall of China, which stretches for 5,000 km in northern China.

A peasant uprising overthrew the Qin Dynasty and led to the founding of the Han Dynasty in 206 BC. After the Han Dynasty came the Three Kingdoms Period (AD 220–65), the Jin Dynasty (265–420), the Southern and Northern Dynasties (420–589), and the Sui Dynasty (581–618).

The Tang Dynasty followed the Sui Dynasty. During the Tang Dynasty, a successful government and administration system based on the Sui model was developed. Besides, it was a period of great cultural and artistic activity in the country. It is widely regarded as a golden period of Chinese history.

A period of almost continual warfare followed the demise of the Tang Dynasty. This was the period of Five Dynasties and Ten States. The Song Dynasty ruled over China between 960–1279.

In 1206, the famous Genghis Khan established the Mongolian Khanate. In 1271, his grandson, Kublai Khan, founded the Yuan Dynasty (1271–1368) after conquering the Central Plains. He founded a united country that also included Xinjiang, Tibet and Yunnan. It was during the Song-Yuan period, that the Chinese developed on their inventions—paper, printing, the compass and gunpowder and introduced them to the rest of the world.

Next came the Ming Dynasty (1368–1644) and the last Chinese royal dynasty, the Qing Dynasty (1644–1911). The rapid decline of the Qing Dynasty in the 19th century encouraged British nationals to import large quantities of opium into China. The Qing government's imposition of a ban on opium trafficking in China led to the Opium War with UK in 1840. It culminated in the signing of the Treaty of Nanking, which in many ways was an act of capitulation by the Chinese government to foreign forces on its own soil.

The Revolution of 1911 led by Dr Sun Yat-sen overthrew the 200-odd-year-old Qing Dynasty. It ended more than 2,000 years of feudal monarchy and established the Republic of China (1912–49).

The unequal terms and conditions imposed on China following World War I precipitated the 4th May Movement of 1919. In 1921, 12 communist delegates representing different parts of the Chinese nation, including Mao Zedong, held the First National Congress in Shanghai to found the Communist Party of China.

The years to follow witnessed the Chinese people led by the Communist Party of China fight the Northern Expeditionary War (1924–7), The War of Agrarian Revolution (1927–37), The War of Resistance against Japan (1937–45) and The War of Liberation (1945–9). Although the Communist Party succeeded in defeating the Kuomintang and the Japanese, another civil war erupted soon after the anti-Japanese war. The three-year war finally overthrew the Kuomintang government in 1949. On 1 October 1949, the People's Republic of China (PRC) was officially founded.

In October 1950 Chinese forces invaded eastern Tibet. In 1951 Tibet and China signed a treaty that guaranteed Tibetan autonomy and religion but also allowed the setting up of Chinese civil and military offices at Lhasa, the Tibetan capital. When a popular rebellion erupted at Lhasa in March 1959, the Dalai Lama escaped to India along with many of his aides. In 1962, China and India were involved in a brief border war. In 1979, China instituted a policy of 'reform and opening to the outside world', which aimed to modernize both the political and economic machinery of China. During 3–4 June 1989, the Chinese government used military forces including tanks and armed soldiers to suppress a dramatic series of pro-democracy student demonstrations resulting in the loss of hundreds of lives. In 1997, UK handed its colony of Hong Kong back to China. The Portuguese handover of Macao followed in 1999.

Geography

Location: Eastern Asia, bordering the East China Sea, Korea Bay, Yellow Sea, and South China Sea, between North Korea and Vietnam.

Area: Total: 9,596,960 sq. km.

Terrain: The terrain of China consists mostly of mountains and high plateaus. There are deserts in the west, and plains, deltas and hills in the east.

Natural resources: Coal, iron ore, petroleum, natural gas, mercury, tin, tungsten, antimony, manganese, molybdenum, vanadium, magnetite, aluminum, lead, zinc, uranium, hydropower potential.

Climate: The vast expanse of China means that the country's climate is extremely diverse. China has a tropical climate in the south but is subarctic in the north.

People

Population: 1,306,313,812 (July 2005 est.).

Population growth rate: 0.58% (2005 est.).

Sex ratio: 1.06 male(s)/female (2005 est.).

Religions: Officially atheist; unofficially: Daoist (Taoist), Buddhist, Muslim, Christian (2002 est.).

Languages: Standard Chinese or Mandarin (Putonghua, based on the Beijing dialect), Yue (Cantonese), Wu (Shanghaiese), Minbei (Fuzhou), Minnan (Hokkien-Taiwanese), Xiang, Gan, Hakka dialects, minority languages.

Literacy rate: Total 86%, Male 92.9%, Female 78.8% (2003 est.).

Infant mortality rate: 24.18 deaths/1,000 live births (2005 est.).

Life expectancy: Total 72.27 years, Male 70.65 years, Female 74.09 years (2005 est.).

Government

Capital: Beijing.

Government type: Communist state.

Independence: 221 BC (unification under the Qin or Ch'in Dynasty 221 BC; Qing or Ch'ing Dynasty replaced by the Republic on 12 February 1912; People's Republic established 1 October 1949).

Administrative divisions: 23 provinces (sheng), five autonomous regions* (zizhiqu), four municipalities** (shi), two Special Administrative Regions (SARs)***. 1. Anhui 2. Beijing** 3. Chongqing** 4. Fujian 5. Gansu 6. Guangdong 7. Guangxi* 8. Guizhou 9. Hainan 10. Hebei 11. Heilongjiang 12. Henan 13. Hong Kong*** 14. Hubei 15. Hunan 16. Jiangsu 17. Jiangxi 18. Jilin 19. Liaoning 20. Macao*** 21. Nei Mongol* 22. Ningxia* 23. Qinghai 24. Shaanxi 25. Shandong 26. Shanghai** 27. Shanxi 28. Sichuan 29. Tianjin** 30. Xinjiang* 31. Xizang* (Tibet) 32. Yunnan 33. Zhejiang. China considers Taiwan as its 23rd province.

Legal system: China's legal system is a complex combination of custom and statute, largely criminal law; rudimentary civil code in effect since 1 January 1987; new legal codes in effect since 1 January 1980.

Executive branch:
Chief of state: President Hu Jintao (since 15 March 2003) and Vice-President Zeng Qinghong (since 15 March 2003).

Head of government: Premier Wen Jiabao (since 16 March 2003).

Elections and election results: The National People's Congress elects the president and the vice-president for five-year terms. The last elections were held during 15–17 March 2003 and the next are scheduled for mid-March 2008. The president nominates the premier, and then it is to be confirmed by the National People's Congress.

Legislative branch:
China has a unicameral National People's Congress or Quanguo Renmin Daibiao Dahui (2,985 seats; members elected by municipal, regional, and provincial people's congresses to serve five-year terms).

Elections and election results: Last elections were held in December

2002– February 2003 and the next are scheduled for 2007–8.

Economy

Currency: Yuan, also referred to as the Renminbi.

Economy—overview:
China is one of the world's biggest economies with one of the highest growth rates. In 2003, China stood as the second-largest economy in the world after USA, measured on a purchasing power parity basis. Reform measures introduced since 1978 has quadrupled the GDP. China is one of those few economies, which can truly affect the global economy.

GDP: Purchasing power parity—$7.262 trillion (2004 est.).

GDP—real growth rate: 9.1% (official data) (2004 est.).

GDP—per capita: Purchasing power parity—$5,600 (2004 est.).

Inflation rate: 4.1% (2004 est.).

Population below poverty line: 10% (2001 est.).

Unemployment rate: Urban unemployment roughly 9.8%; substantial unemployment and underemployment in rural areas (2004 est.).

Exports: $583.1 billion f.o.b. (2004 est.)—Machinery and equipment; textiles and clothing, footwear, toys and sporting goods; mineral fuels.

Imports: $552.4 billion f.o.b. (2004 est.)—Machinery and equipment, mineral fuels, plastics, iron and steel, chemicals.

External debt: $233.3 billion (2004 est.).

Transport and Communications

Railways: 70,058 km.

Roads: 1,765,222 km.

Telephones: 263,000,000 (2003).

Mobile celluler: 269,000,000 (2003).

Internet users: 45,800,000 (2002).

Internet country code: .cn

Colombia

History

At the time of the Spanish conquest in the 16th century, native people speaking the Chibcha language were the most important of the local inhabitants of the area that is today Colombia.

In 1819, the South American liberator and statesman Simon Bolivar defeated the Spanish and formed the Republic of Gran Colombia, consisting of Colombia, Ecuador, Panama and Venezuela. However, Gran Colombia disintegrated in 1829–30 when Venezuela and Ecuador left. This led to the formation of the state of Nueva

Granada consisting of present-day Colombia and Panama. But even Nueva Granada collapsed with the War of the Thousand Days of 1899–1903 in which some 120,000 people perished. Colombia was rocked by a civil war again in 1948–57 when an estimated 250,000–300,000 were killed.

In 1978, the government started its campaign against the Colombian drug traffickers. Colombia's role as a key supplier in the international drug market gained significance following the major crackdown launched in Mexico in 1975. Before long, Colombia had become the source of almost 70% of the marijuana being imported into USA. As the volume of trafficking grew, it also gave rise to two major Mafia-like organizations. These were the so-called 'drug cartels'—the Medellin cartel led by Pablo Escobar and the Cali cartel. In July 2000 President Andres Pastrana launched 'Plan Colombia'. It succeeded in obtaining nearly US$1 billion in the form of military aid from USA, in order to fight drug trafficking and rebels who protected the traffickers.

Geography

Location: Northern South America, bordering the Caribbean Sea, between Panama and Venezuela, and bordering the North Pacific Ocean, between Ecuador and Panama.

Area: 1,138,910 sq. km. This includes Isla de Malpelo, Roncador Cay, Serrana Bank, and Serranilla Bank.

Terrain: Flat coastal lowlands, central highlands, high Andes Mountains, eastern lowland plains.

Natural resources: Petroleum, natural gas, coal, iron ore, nickel, gold, copper, emeralds, hydropower.

Climate: The climate of Colombia is tropical along coast and the eastern plains but cooler in the highlands.

People

Population: 42,954,279 (July 2005 est.).

Population growth rate: 1.49% (2005 est.).

Sex ratio: 0.96 male(s)/female (2005 est.).

Religions: Roman Catholic 90%.

Languages: Spanish.

Literacy rate: Total 92.5%, Male 92.4%, Female 92.6% (2003 est.).

Infant mortality rate: 20.97 deaths/ 1,000 live births (2005 est.).

Life expectancy: Total 71.72 years, Male 67.88 years, Female 75.7 years (2005 est.).

Government

Capital: Bogota.

Government type: Republic; executive branch dominates government structure.

Independence: 20 July 1810 (from Spain).

Legal system: Based on Spanish law; a new criminal code modelled after US procedures was enacted in 1992–3; judicial review of executive and legislative acts.

Executive branch:
Chief of state: President Alvaro Uribe Velez (since 7 August 2002). Vice-President Francisco Santos (since 7 August 2002). The President is both the chief of state and head of government.

Economy

Currency: Colombian peso.

Economy—overview:
Serious internal conflict is one of the main factors that hamper the Colombian economy. Other significant factors affecting the economy are austerity measures, weak domestic and foreign demand, high unemployment and an uncertain future for two of Colombia's leading exports—oil and coffee. The Colombian government's reform measures, economic policy and democratic security strategy have inspired confidence in the economy.

GDP: Purchasing power parity—$281.1 billion (2004 est.).

GDP—real growth rate: 3.6% (2004 est.).

GDP—per capita: Purchasing power parity—$6,600 (2004 est.).

Inflation rate: 5.9% (2004 est.).

Population below poverty line: 55% (2001).

Unemployment rate: 13.6% (2004 est.).

Exports: $15.5 billion f.o.b. (2004 est.)—Petroleum, coffee, coal, apparel, banana, cut flowers.

Imports: $15.34 billion f.o.b. (2004 est.)—Industrial equipment, transportation equipment, consumer goods, chemicals, paper products, fuels, electricity.

External debt: $38.7 billion (2004 est.).

Transport and Communications

Railways: 3,304 km.

Roads: 112,998 km.

Telephones: 8,768,100 (2003).

Mobile cellular: 6,186,200 (2003).

Internet users: 2,000,000 (2002).

Internet country code: .co

Comoros

History

In 1886, Comoros became a French protectorate. In 1961, it gained autonomy. In 1974, three of the islands forming the colony of Comoros voted for independence in a referendum.

Geography

Location: Southern Africa, group of islands at the northern mouth of the Mozambique Channel.

Area: 2,170 sq. km.

Natural resources: Negligible.

Climate: Tropical marine climate.

People

Population: 671,247 (July 2005 est.).

Population growth rate: 2.91% (2005 est.).

Sex ratio: 0.99 male(s)/female (2004 est.).

Religions: Sunni Muslim 98%, Roman Catholic 2%.

Languages: Arabic (official), French (official), Shikomoro (a blend of Swahili and Arabic).

Literacy rate: Total 56.5%, Male 63.6%, Female 49.3% (2003 est.).

Infant mortality rate: 74.93 deaths/ 1,000 live births (2005 est.).

Life expectancy: Total 61.96 years, Male 59.65 years, Female 64.33 years (2005 est.).

Government

Capital: Moroni.

Government type: Independent republic.

Independence: 6 July 1975 (from France).

Legal system: French and Sharia (Islamic) law in a new consolidated code.

Executive branch:
Chief of state: President Azali Assoumani (since 26 May 2002). The president is both the chief of state and the head of government.

Economy

Currency: Comoran franc.

GDP: Purchasing power parity—$441 million (2002 est.).

GDP—real growth rate: 2% (2002 est.).

GDP—per capita: Purchasing power parity—$700 (2002 est.).

Inflation rate: 3.5% (2001 est.).

Population below poverty line: 60% (2002 est.).

Unemployment rate: 20% (1996 est.).

Exports: $28 million f.o.b. (2002 est.)—Vanilla, ylang-ylang, cloves, perfume oil, copra.

Imports: $88 million f.o.b. (2002 est.)—Rice and other foodstuff, consumer goods; petroleum products, ce-ment, transport equipment.

External debt: $232 million (2000 est.).

Transport and Communications

Railways: None.

Roads: 880 km.

Telephones: 13,200 (2003).

Mobile cellular: 2,000 (2003).

Internet users: 5,000 (2003).

Internet country code: .km

Democratic Republic of the Congo

History

In the 1200s, the Kongo Empire included parts of modern-day Democratic Republic of the Congo. The first Europeans arrived in the 15th century. In the 16th–17th centuries, British, French, Dutch and Portuguese merchants carried out slave trade in the region.

Under the commission of the Belgian King Leopold II, British–American explorer Henry Morton Stanley sailed along the Congo River in 1877 and facilitated further exploration of the hinterlands. He also concluded treaties with local chiefs that later enabled Leopold II to obtain personal rights to the lands. In 1885, the Belgian king announced the creation of the Congo Free State with himself as the sovereign.

Congo Free State proved to be one of the most brutal colonial regimes ever. As Leopold attempted to derive the maximum possible benefit out of its people and resources, millions of natives perished in starvation, forced labour, torture and outright killings.

In June 1960, Belgian Congo became independent with Joseph Kasavubu as President and Patrice Lumumba as prime minister. Lumumba was murdered in January 1961. In 1965, commander-in-chief of the armed forces, Joseph Mobutu seized power in a coup.

In 1971, Joseph Mobutu embarked on a campaign of renaming. He renamed the country 'Zaire', Katanga province 'Shaba' and the river Congo 'River Zaire'. In 1973–4, he nationalized the foreign-owned firms in the country and drove out European investors. While the country's economic condition declined, Mobutu is believed to have amassed a huge personal fortune. In 1990–1, he finally ended his dictatorial rule and agreed to a multi-party system. Mobutu was finally ousted from power in May 1997 when the rebels (with Rwandan help) captured the capital, Kinshasa.

In January 2001, President Laurent Kabila was shot dead by a bodyguard. His son, Joseph Kabila became the new President.

Geography

Location: Central Africa, north-east of Angola.

Area: 2,345,410 sq. km.

Terrain: A vast central basin that is actually a low-lying plateau. There are mountains in the east.

Natural resources: Cobalt, copper, cadmium, petroleum, industrial and gem diamonds, gold, silver, zinc, manganese, tin, germanium, uranium, radium, bauxite, iron ore, coal, hydropower, timber.

Climate: Generally tropical climate. It is hot and humid in the equatorial river basin, cooler and wetter in the eastern highlands, cooler and drier in the southern highlands.

People

Population: 60,085,804 (2005 est.).

Population growth rate: 2.98% (2005 est.).

Sex ratio: 0.98 male(s)/female (2005 est.).

Religions: Roman Catholic 50%, Protestant 20%, Kimbanguist 10%, Muslim 10%, other syncretic sects and indigenous beliefs 10%.

Languages: French (official), Lingala (a lingua franca trade language), Kingwana (a dialect of Kiswahili or Swahili), Kikongo, Tshiluba.

Literacy rate: Total 65.5%, Male 76.2%, Female 55.1% (2003 est.).

Infant mortality rate: 92.87 deaths/1,000 live births (2005 est.).

Life expectancy: Total 49.35 years, Male 47.29 years, Female 51.47 years (2005 est.).

Government

Capital: Kinshasa.

Government type: Dictatorship.

Independence: 30 June 1960 (from Belgium).

Legal system: Based on Belgian civil law system and tribal law.

Executive branch:
Chief of state: President Joseph Kabila (since 26 January 2001). The president is both the chief of state and head of government.

Economy

Currency: Congolese franc.

GDP: Purchasing power parity—$42.74 billion (2004 est.).

GDP—real growth rate: 7.5% (2004 est.).

GDP—per capita: Purchasing power parity—$700 (2004 est.).

Inflation rate: 14% (2003 est.).

Exports: $1.417 billion f.o.b. (2002 est.)—Diamond, copper, crude oil, coffee, cobalt.

Imports: $933 million f.o.b. (2002 est.)—Foodstuff, mining and other machinery, transport equipment, fuels.

External debt: $11.6 billion (2000 est.).

Transport and Communications

Railways: 5,138 km.

Roads: 157,000 km (including 30 km of expressways) (1999 est.).

Telephones: 10,000 (2002).

Mobile cellular: 1,000,000 (2003).

Internet users: 50,000 (2002).

Internet country code: .cd

Republic of the Congo

History

In 1880, French explorer Pierre Savorgnan de Brazza negotiated an agreement with the Bateke ethnic group that led to the setting up of a French protectorate over the north bank of the Congo River. This new entity was initially called French Congo and later Middle Congo. In 1958, Congo gained autonomy and in 1960 it became independent with Fulbert Youlou as President.

Geography

Location: Western Africa, bordering the South Atlantic Ocean, between Angola and Gabon.

Area: 342,000 sq. km.

Terrain: A central plateau, coastal plain, southern basin, and northern basin.

Natural resources: Petroleum, timber, potash, lead, zinc, uranium, copper, phosphates, natural gas, hydropower.

Climate: Tropical climate with a rainy season between March and June and a dry season from June to October.

People

Population: 3,039,126 (July 2005 est.).

Population growth rate: 1.31% (2005 est.).

Sex ratio: 0.98 male(s)/female (2005 est.).

Religions: Christian 50%, animist 48%, Muslim 2%.

Languages: French (official), Lingala and Monokutuba (lingua franca trade languages), many local languages and dialects (of which Kikongo is the most widespread).

Literacy rate: Total 83.8%, Male 89.6%, Female 78.4% (2003 est.).

Infant mortality rate: 92.41 deaths/ 1,000 live births (2005 est.).

Life expectancy: Total 48.97 years, Male 47.94 years, Female 50.04 years (2005 est.).

Government

Capital: Brazzaville.

Government type: Republic.

Independence: 15 August 1960 (from France).

Legal system: Based on French civil law system and customary law.

Executive branch:
Chief of state: President Denis Sassou-Nguesso (since 25 October 1997). The president is both the chief of state and head of government.

Economy

Currency: Communaute Financiere Africaine franc.

GDP: Purchasing power parity—$2.324 billion (2004 est.).

GDP—real growth rate: 3.7% (2004 est.).

GDP—per capita: Purchasing power parity—$800 (2004 est.).

Inflation rate: 1.8% (2004 est.).

Exports: $2.224 billion f.o.b. (2004 est.)—Petroleum, lumber, plywood, sugar, cocoa, coffee, diamond.

Imports: $749.3 million f.o.b. (2004 est.)—Capital equipment, construction materials, foodstuff.

External debt: $5 billion (2000 est.).

Transport and Communications

Railways: 894 km.

Roads: 12,800 km.

Telephones: 7,000 (2003).

Mobile cellular: 330,000 (2003).

Internet users: 15,000 (2003).

Internet country code: .cg

Costa Rica

History

When Christopher Columbus visited the lands in 1502, native Indian tribes inhabited the area. The Spanish conquest began in 1563. In 1821, Costa Rica attained independence, but for two years it formed a part of the short-lived Mexican Empire. In 1848, Costa Rica became a republic.

Geography

Location: Middle America, bordering both the Caribbean Sea and the North Pacific Ocean, between Nicaragua and Panama.

Area: 51,100 sq. km (this includes Isla del Coco).

Natural resources: Hydropower.

Climate: Tropical; cooler in the highlands.

People

Population: 4,016,173 (July 2005 est.).

Population growth rate: 1.48% (2005 est.).

Sex ratio: 1.02 male(s)/female (2005 est.).

Religions: Roman Catholic 76.3%, Evangelical 13.7%, Jehovah's Witnesses 1.3%, other Protestant 0.7%, others 4.8%, none 3.2%.

Languages: Spanish (official), English.

Literacy rate: Total 96%, Male 95.9%, Female 96.1% (2003 est.).

Infant mortality rate: 9.95 deaths/1,000 live births (2005 est.).

Life expectancy: Total 76.84 years, Male 74.26 years, Female 79.55 years (2005 est.).

Government

Capital: San Jose.

Government type: Democratic republic.

Independence: 15 September 1821 (from Spain).

Legal system: Based on Spanish civil law system.

Executive branch:
Chief of state: President Abel Pacheco (since 8 May 2002). The president is both the chief of state and head of government.

Economy

Currency: Costa Rican colon.

GDP: Purchasing power parity—$37.97 billion (2004 est.).

GDP—real growth rate: 3.9% (2004 est.).

GDP—per capita: Purchasing power parity—$9,600 (2004 est.).

Inflation rate: 11.5% (2004 est.).

Population below poverty line: 18% (2004 est.).

Unemployment rate: 6.6% (2004 est.).

Exports: $6.184 billion (2004 est.)— Coffee, banana, sugar, pineapple, textiles, electronic components, medical equipment.

Imports: $7.842 billion (2004 est.)— Raw materials, consumer goods, capital equipment, petroleum.

External debt: $5.962 billion (2004 est.).

Transport and Communications

Railways: 950 km.

Roads: 35,303 km.

Telephones: 1,132,000 (2002).

Mobile cellular: 528,047 (2002).

Internet users: 800,000 (2002).

Internet country code: .cr

Cote d'Ivoire

History

In 1842, France established a protectorate over Ivory Coast and in 1893, made it a colony. In 1960, Cote d'Ivoire became independent under President Felix Houphouet-Boigny.

Geography

Location: Western Africa, bordering the North Atlantic Ocean, between Ghana and Liberia.

Area: 322,460 sq. km.

Terrain: Consists mostly of flat to undulating plains. There are mountains in the north-west.

Natural resources: Petroleum, natural gas, diamonds, manganese, iron ore, cobalt, bauxite, copper, hydropower.

Climate: Tropical along the coast and semiarid in the far north.

People

Population: 17,298,040 (July 2005 est.).

Population growth rate: 2.06% (2005 est.).

Sex ratio: 1 male(s)/female (2005 est.).

Religions: Christian 20–30%, Muslim 35–40%, indigenous 25–40% (2001).

The majority of foreigners (migratory workers) are Muslim (70%) and Christian (20%).

Languages: French (official), 60 native dialects with Dioula the most widely spoken.

Literacy rate: Total 50.9%, Male 57.9%, Female 43.6% (2003 est.).

Infant mortality rate: 90.83 deaths/1,000 live births (2005 est.).

Life expectancy: Total 48.62 years, Male 46.05 years, Female 51.27 years (2005 est.).

Government

Capital: Yamoussoukro. (Even though Yamoussoukro has been the official capital since 1983, Abidjan still remains the commercial and administrative centre.)

Government type: Republic.

Independence: 7 August 1960 (from France).

Legal system: Based on French civil law system and customary law.

Executive branch:
Chief of state: President Laurent Gbagbo (since 26 October 2000).

Head of government: Prime Minister Seydou Diarra (since 25 January 2003).

Economy

Currency: Communaute Financiere Africaine franc.

GDP: Purchasing power parity—$24.78 billion (2004 est.).

GDP—real growth rate: –1% (2004 est.).

GDP—per capita: Purchasing power parity—$1,500 (2004 est.).

Inflation rate: 1.4% (2004 est.).

Population below poverty line: 37% (1995).

Unemployment rate: 13% in urban areas (1998).

Exports: $5.124 billion f.o.b. (2004 est.)—Cocoa, coffee, timber, petroleum, cotton, banana, pineapple, palm oil, fish.

Imports: $3.36 billion f.o.b. (2004 est.)—Fuel, capital equipment, foodstuffs.

External debt: $11.81 billion (2004 est.).

Transport and Communications

Railways: 660 km.

Roads: 50,400 km.

Telephones: 328,000 (2002).

Mobile cellular: 1,236,000 (2003).

Internet users: 90,000 (2002).

Internet country code: .ci

Croatia

History

Croats settled the area that is today Croatia in the seventh century. In 925, Croats defeated the Byzantine and Frank invaders and set up their own independent kingdom. Civil war erupted in 1089 and led to the Hungarian conquest in 1091. In 1102, Croat tribal chiefs and Hungary signed a pact that caused the political union of Croatia with Hungary under the Hungarian monarch.

During World War II, Germany occupied Yugoslavia and installed a puppet regime in Croatia. The fascist puppet government under Ante Pavelic sought to create a Catholic, all-Croat republic and killed hundreds of thousands of Serbs and Jews.

The death of Yugoslav leader Josip Broz Tito in 1980 began the process of disintegration of the Yugoslav federation. The collapse of communism in the 1990s accelerated the process. In 1990, the first free elections in Croatia for more than 50 years were held.

In 1991, Croatia declared its independence from Yugoslavia. This led the Croatian Serbs in the eastern part of the country to expel Croats with the help of the Yugoslav army. A three-month-long Serbian siege of the eastern Croatian town of Vukovar resulted in a near-complete destruction of the city. When Serb forces captured the city in November 1991, they unleashed brutality on its inhabitants.

In 1992, Franjo Tudjman was elected Croatian President. The UN negotiated a ceasefire and set up four protected areas in Croatia, with 14,000 UN troops separating the Croats and Serbs to prevent hostilities.

Geography

Location: South-eastern Europe, bordering the Adriatic Sea, between Bosnia–Herzegovina and Slovenia.

Area: 56,542 sq. km.

Terrain: Geographically diverse terrain

with flat plains along the border with Hungary, low mountains and highlands near the Adriatic coastline and some islands.

Natural resources: Oil, some coal, bauxite, iron ore, calcium, gypsum, natural asphalt, silica, mica, clays, salt, hydropower.

Climate: Mediterranean and continental climate.

People

Population: 4,495,904 (July 2005 est.).

Population growth rate: −0.02% (2005 est.).

Sex ratio: 0.92 male(s)/female (2005 est.).

Religions: Roman Catholic 87.8%, Orthodox 4.4%, Muslim 1.3%, Protestant 0.3%, others and unknown 6.2% (2001).

Languages: Croatian 96%, others 4% (including Italian, Hungarian, Czech, Slovak, and German).

Literacy rate: Total 98.5%, Male 99.4%, Female 97.8% (2003 est.).

Infant mortality rate: 6.84 deaths/1,000 live births (2005 est.).

Life expectancy: Total 74.45 years, Male 70.79 years, Female 78.31 years (2005 est.).

Government

Capital: Zagreb.

Government type: Presidential/parliamentary democracy.

Independence: 25 June 1991 (from Yugoslavia).

Legal system: Based on civil law system.

Executive branch:

Chief of state: President Stjepan (Stipe) Mesic (since 18 February 2000).

Head of government: Prime Minister Ivo Sanader (since 9 December 2003).

Economy

Currency: Kuna.

GDP: Purchasing power parity—$50.33 billion (2004 est.).

GDP—real growth rate: 3.7% (2004 est.).

GDP—per capita: Purchasing power parity—$11,200 (2004 est.).

Inflation rate: 2.5% (2004 est.).

Population below poverty line: 11% (2003).

Unemployment rate: 13.8% (2004 est.).

Exports: $7.845 billion f.o.b. (2004 est.)—Transport equipment, textiles, chemicals, foodstuff, fuels.

Imports: $16.7 billion f.o.b. (2004 est.)—Machinery, transport and electrical equipment, chemicals, fuels and lubricants, foodstuff.

External debt: $26.4 billion (2004 est.).

Transport and Communications

Railways: 2,726 km (2003).

Roads: 28,344 km (2002).

Telephones: 1,825,000 (2002).

Mobile cellular: 2,553,000 (2003).

Internet users: 1,014,000 (2003).

Internet country code: .hr

Cuba

History

Arawak Indians inhabited Cuba when Christopher Columbus arrived in 1492. The first Spanish settlements came up in 1511, under the leadership of Diego de Velazquez. Between 1763 and 1860, Cuba's population increased from less than 150,000 to more than 1.3 million with slaves making up the biggest share of the increase. In the 19th century, the Cuban sugar industry underwent rapid expansion and at one point Cuba produced nearly one-third of the world's sugar.

The first war of independence raged between 1868 and 1878. As the economic and political situation in the colony worsened, the second War of Independence, led by the poet, Jose Marti, broke out in 1895. In 1898, an explosion took place on board the US battleship *Maine* in Havana harbour. The United States declared war on Spain in April 1898. In August, Spain signed a peace treaty ending all hostilities with USA and ceding Cuba.

Cuba became independent in 1902 with Tomas Estrada Palma as its President. However, under the Platt Amendment of 1901, USA had the right to oversee Cuba's international commitments, economy, and internal affairs. It also allowed the USA to establish a naval station at Guantánamo Bay.

In 1940, after a succession of puppet rulers, Fulgencio Batista became the President. In 1953, Fidel Castro launched an unsuccessful attempt to dethrone the Batista regime. He returned in 1956 and launched a guerilla campaign, aided by Ernesto 'Che' Guevara. Batista fled the country on New Year's Day 1959.

In 1960, the Cuban government nationalized all US businesses in Cuba, leading USA to break off diplomatic ties with Havana. In April 1961, USA sponsored an unsuccessful invasion attempt by Cuban exiles at the Bay of Pigs in south central Cuba. This, along with a US trade embargo and numerous US attempts to exterminate Fidel Castro prompted Cuba to drift towards the Soviet Union. Ultimately, Castro proclaimed Cuba a communist state.

In October 1962, a major confrontation brought the United States and the Soviet Union to the brink of nuclear war. The issue was the presence of Soviet nuclear-armed missiles in Cuba.

Geography

Location: Caribbean island between the Caribbean Sea and the North Atlantic Ocean.

Area: 110,860 sq. km.

Terrain: Mostly flat to rolling plains, with rugged hills and mountains in the south-east.

Natural resources: Cobalt, nickel, iron ore, copper, manganese, salt, timber, silica, petroleum, arable land.

Climate: Tropical climate moderated by trade winds.

People

Population: 11,346,670 (July 2005 est.).

Population growth rate: 0.33% (2005 est.).

Sex ratio: 0.99 male(s)/female (2005 est.).

Religions: Nominally 85% Roman Catholic before Castro assumed power; Protestants, Jehovah's Witnesses, Jews, and Santeria are also represented.

Languages: Spanish.

Literacy rate: Total 97%, Male 97.2%, Female 96.9% (2003 est.).

Infant mortality rate: 6.33 deaths/ 1,000 live births (2005 est.).

Life expectancy: Total 77.23 years, Male 74.94 years, Female 79.65 years (2005 est.).

Government

Capital: Havana.

Government type: Communist state.

Independence: 20 May 1902 (from Spain 10 December 1898; administered by the US from 1898 to 1902).

Legal system: Based on Spanish and American law, with large elements of communist legal theory.

Executive branch:
Chief of state: President of the Council of State and President of the Council of Ministers Fidel Castro Ruz (he served as prime minister from February 1959 to 24 February 1976 when the office was abolished; he has been president since 2 December 1976). The president is both the chief of state and head of government.

Economy

Currency: Cuban peso.

Economy—overview:
In general, the standard of living of the average Cuban is at a lower level than it was before the economic depression of the early 1990s. This was caused largely by the loss of Soviet aid following the collapse of the Soviet Union. The Cuban government has undertaken limited reforms in recent years to improve efficiency and solve numerous problems such as shortages of food, consumer goods and services. One unique feature of the economy is the contrast between efficient export zones and the inefficient domestic sector.

GDP: Purchasing power parity—$33.92 billion (2004 est.).

GDP—real growth rate: 3% (2004 est.).

GDP—per capita: Purchasing power parity—$3,000 (2004 est.).

Inflation rate: 3.1% (2004 est.).

Unemployment rate: 2.5% (2004 est.).

Exports: $2.014 billion f.o.b. (2004 est.)—Sugar, nickel, tobacco, fish, medical products, citrus, coffee.

Imports: $5.296 billion f.o.b. (2004 est.)—Petroleum, food, machinery and equipment, chemicals.

External debt: $12.09 billion (in convertible currency); another $15 billion–$20 billion owed to Russia (2004 est.).

Transport and Communications

Railways: 4,226 km.

Roads: 60,858 km.

Telephones: 574,400 (2002).

Mobile cellular: 17,900 (2002).

Internet users: 120,000 (2002).

Internet country code: .cu

Cyprus

History

Cyprus was the centre of Phoenician and Greek colonies in ancient times. In 1571, the island passed into Turkish hands and subsequently, a large Turkish colony was built on the island. UK annexed the island during World War I and in 1925, declared it to be a Crown colony. In August 1960, the island became an independent nation.

In 1974, a Greece-sponsored coup toppled Cypriot President Archbishop Makarios. Five days later, Turkey sent in troops with the objective of protecting the Turkish Cypriot community in the country. This invasion had the effect of partitioning the island into a Turkish Cypriot northern part and a Greek Cypriot part in the south. Meanwhile, the coup failed and the Greek military junta that had propped it up also collapsed. Archbishop Makarios returned to take up the presidency in December 1974. He offered self-government to the Turkish Cypriots but refused to transfer populations or partition the country.

In view of the impending Cypriot entry into European Union, twin referendums were held in the Greek and Turkish Cypriot areas on 24 April 2004. This was a last-minute attempt to achieve united EU entry. However, while the Greek part of the island endorsed the plan, Turkish Cypriots rejected it overwhelmingly. On 1 May 2004, Cyprus, but only the Greek part of it, joined the EU.

Geography

Location: Middle East, island in the Mediterranean Sea, south of Turkey.

Area: 9,250 sq. km (of which 3,355 sq. km is in the Turkish Cypriot area).

Natural resources: Copper, pyrites, asbestos, gypsum, timber, salt, marble, clay earth pigment.

Climate: Temperate Mediterranean climate with hot, dry summers and cool winters.

People

Population: 780,133 (July 2005 est.).

Population growth rate: 0.54% (2005 est.).

Sex ratio: 1 male(s)/female (2005 est.).

Religions: Greek Orthodox 78%, Muslim 18%, Maronite, Armenian Apostolic, and others 4%.

Languages: Greek, Turkish, English.

Literacy rate: Total 97.6%, Male 98.9%, Female 96.3% (2003 est.).

Infant mortality rate: 7.18 deaths/1,000 live births (2005 est.).

Life expectancy: Total 77.65 years, Male 75.29 years, Female 80.13 years (2005 est.).

Government

Capital: Nicosia.

Government type: Republic.

Independence: 16 August 1960 (from UK). The Turkish Cypriot area proclaimed self-rule on 13 February 1975.

Legal system: Based on common law, with civil law modifications.

Executive branch:
Chief of state: President Tassos Papadopoulos (since 1 March 2003). The president is both the chief of state and head of government.

Economy

Currency: Cypriot pound.

GDP: Republic of Cyprus: Purchasing power parity—$15.71 billion—(2004 est.); North Cyprus: Purchasing power parity—$4.54 billion (2004 est.).

GDP—real growth rate: Republic of Cyprus: 3.2% (2004 est.); North Cyprus: 2.6% (2004 est.).

GDP—per capita: Republic of Cyprus: Purchasing power parity— $20,300 (2004 est.); North Cyprus: Purchasing power parity—$7.135 (2004 est.).

Inflation rate: Republic of Cyprus: 2.4% (2003 est.); North Cyprus: 12.6% (2003 est.).

Exports: Republic of Cyprus: $1.094 billion f.o.b.; North Cyprus: $49.3 million f.o.b. (2004 est.)—Citrus, potatoe, pharmaceuticals, cement, clothing and cigarettes.

Imports: Republic of Cyprus: $7.327 billion; North Cyprus: NA (2004 est.).—Consumer goods, petroleum and lubricants, intermediate goods, machinery, transport equipment.

External debt: Republic of Cyprus: $5.258 billion f.o.b.; North Cyprus: $415.2 million f.o.b. (2004 est.)

Transport and Communications

Railways: None.

Roads: 13,943 km.

Telephones: Republic of Cyprus: 427,400 (2002).

Mobile cellular: Republic of Cyprus: 417,900 (2002).

Internet users: 210,000 (2002).

Internet country code: .cy

Czech Republic

History

Celtic, then Germanic and finally Slavic tribes settled in the lands that is today the Czech Republic. The Czechs founded the kingdom of Bohemia and the Premyslide dynasty that ruled Bohemia and Moravia from the 10th to the 16th century. After spending years under German domination, the Hussite Movement founded by reformer Jan Hus rekindled Czech nationalism in the 15th and 16th centuries. A Czech rebellion in 1618 led to the Thirty Years War (1618–48). As a result of defeat in the War, the Czechs had to submit to Austrian domination for the next 300 years. It was only after the collapse of the Austro-Hungarian Empire at the end of World War I that the Czechs gained freedom again.

The union of the Czech territories with Slovakia was announced in Prague in November 1918, leading to the creation of the Republic of Czechoslovakia with Thomas Masaryk as President. In March 1939, Germany occupied Czechoslovakia and made it a German protectorate. The country was freed from German occupation in 1945.

In 1960, Czechoslovakia became the Czechoslovak Socialist Republic under a new Constitution. In January 1968, the new Communist Party leader Alexander Dubcek launched a programme of liberalizing reforms known as 'Prague Spring'. In August 1968, Soviet-led Warsaw Pact troops invaded Czechoslovakia. The troops took Dubcek to Moscow and forced him to terminate the reforms he had initiated. In April 1969, Gustav Husak replaced Dubcek as the new Communist Party leader. In 1975, he took over as the new President. In 1977, a group of dissidents that included playwright Vaclav Havel published 'Charter 77'. It called for the restoration of civil and political rights in the country.

The country was rocked by mass demonstrations and protests in 1988 that continued into 1989. In November 1989, the leadership of the Communist Party resigned. In December, a new government took power. Vaclav Havel became the new President, Marian Calfa the new prime minister. Alexander Dubcek was elected chairman of Federal Assembly.

On 1 January 1993, Czechoslovakia split into two independent countries, the Czech Republic and Slovakia. Vaclav Havel was elected President of the new country while Vaclav Klaus became the prime minister.

Geography

Location: Central Europe, south-east of Germany.

Area: 78,866 sq. km.

Terrain: Bohemia in the western part of the country consists of rolling plains, hills, and plateaus surrounded by low mountains. In the eastern part of the country, Moravia consists of very hilly terrain.

Natural resources: Hard coal, soft coal, kaolin, clay, graphite, timber.

Climate: Temperate climate with cool summers and cold, cloudy and humid winters.

People

Population: 10,241,138 (July 2005 est.).

Population growth rate: −0.05% (2005 est.).

Sex ratio: 0.95 male(s)/female (2005 est.).

Religions: Roman Catholic 39.2%, Protestant 4.6%, Orthodox 3%, others 13.4%, atheist 39.8%.

Languages: Czech.

Literacy rate: 99.9% (1999 est.).

Infant mortality rate: 3.93 deaths/ 1,000 live births (2005 est.).

Life expectancy: Total 76.02 years, Male 72.74 years, Female 79.49 years (2005 est.).

Government

Capital: Prague.

Government type: Parliamentary democracy.

Independence: 1 January 1993 (date on which Czechoslovakia split into the Czech Republic and Slovakia).

Legal system: Civil law system based on Austro-Hungarian codes.

Executive branch:
Chief of state: President Vaclav Klaus (since 7 March 2003).

Head of government: Prime Minister Vladimir Spidla (since 12 July 2002).

Economy

Currency: Czech koruna.

GDP: Purchasing power parity—$172.2 billion (2004 est.).

GDP—real growth rate: 3.7% (2004 est.).

GDP—per capita: Purchasing power parity—$16,800 (2004 est.).

Inflation rate: 3.2% (2004 est.).

Unemployment rate: 10.6% (2004 est.).

Exports: $66.51 billion f.o.b. (2004 est.)—Machinery and transport equipment, intermediate manufactures, chemicals, raw materials and fuel (2000).

Imports: $68.19 billion f.o.b. (2004 est.)—Machinery and transport equipment, intermediate manufactures, raw materials and fuels, chemicals (2000).

External debt: $36.28 billion (2004 est.).

Transport and Communications

Railways: 9,520 km.

Roads: 127,204 km.

Telephones: 3,626,000 (2003).

Mobile cellular: 9,708,700 (2003).

Internet users: 2.7 million (2003).

Internet country code: .cz

Denmark

History

The initial settlers of the country were nomadic hunters and fishermen who developed into an agrarian community. Towards the end of the eighth century, the Danish were among the Vikings who raided the British Isles and other parts of western Europe. A unified Kingdom of Denmark first came about in the 10th century. This was also the time when Christianity was introduced to the country.

In 1849, Denmark became a constitutional monarchy with a bicameral Parliament. In 1944, the Danish territory of Iceland declared its independence from Denmark. In 1953, a significant change was made to the constitution. Subsequently, the Parliament was turned into a unicameral one. Also in 1953, Greenland became an integral part of Denmark.

Geography

Location: Northern Europe, bordering the Baltic Sea and the North Sea, on a peninsula north of Germany (Jutland); Denmark also includes two major islands—Sjaelland and Fyn.

Area: 43,094 sq. km.

Terrain: Low and flat to gently rolling plains.

Natural resources: Petroleum, natural gas, fish, salt, limestone, chalk, stone, gravel and sand.

Climate: Humid and overcast temperate climate. The country experiences mild and windy winter and cool summer.

People

Population: 5,432,335 (July 2005 est.).

Population growth rate: 0.34% (2005 est.).

Sex ratio: 0.98 male(s)/female (2005 est.).

Religions: Evangelical Lutheran 95%, other Protestant and Roman Catholic 3%, Muslim 2%.

Languages: Danish, Faroese, Greenlandic (an Inuit dialect), German; English is the predominant second language.

Literacy rate: 100%.

Infant mortality rate: 4.56 deaths/1,000 live births (2005 est.).

Life expectancy: Total 77.62 years, Male 75.34 years, Female 80.03 years (2005 est.).

Government

Capital: Copenhagen.

Government type: Constitutional monarchy.

Independence: Denmark was first organized as a unified state in the 10th century. In 1849, Denmark became a constitutional monarchy.

Legal system: Civil law system; judicial review of legislative acts.

Executive branch:
Chief of state: Queen Margrethe II (since 14 January 1972); Heir Apparent Crown Prince Frederik.

Head of government: Prime Minister Anders Fogh Rasmussen (since 27 November 2001).

Economy

Currency: Danish Krone.

Economy—overview:
Denmark has a modern market economy with well-developed and technologically advanced agricultural and industrial sectors. Notable features

of the Danish economy include high living standards, a stable currency, high level of dependence on foreign trade and government welfare measures. The country is also a net exporter of food and energy and also has a balance of payments surplus. Denmark has decided not to join 12 other EU members in the euro. The Danish Krone is pegged to the euro.

GDP: Purchasing power parity—$174.4 billion (2004 est.).

GDP—real growth rate: 2.1% (2004 est.).

GDP—per capita: Purchasing power parity—$32,200 (2004 est.).

Inflation rate: 1.4% (2004 est.).

Unemployment rate: 6.2% (2004).

Exports: $73.06 billion f.o.b. (2004 est.)—Machinery and instruments, meat and meat products, dairy products, fish, chemicals, furniture, ships, windmills.

Imports: $63.45 billion f.o.b. (2004 est.)—Machinery and equipment, raw materials and semi-manufactures for industry, chemicals, grain and foodstuff, consumer goods.

External debt: $21.7 billion (2000).

Transport and Communications

Railways: 3,002 km.

Roads: 71,591 km.

Telephones: 3,610,100 (2003).

Mobile cellular: 4,785,300 (2003).

Internet users: 2,756,000 (2002).

Internet country code: .dk

Djibouti

History

Immigrants from Arabia arrived in the region in the third century BC. The present-day Afars, one of the two most important ethnic groups of Djibouti, are the descendants of these immigrants. The Somali Issas, the other most important ethnic group, came later on. Islam was introduced to the region in 825 AD.

France came to control Djibouti in the 19th century by means of treaties with the local rulers. In 1888, France established the colony of Somaliland in the region and in 1892 Djibouti became the capital of this colony. In 1977, the French Territory of the Afars and the Issas became independent as Djibouti.

Geography

Location: Eastern Africa, bordering the Gulf of Aden and the Red Sea, between Eritrea and Somalia.

Area: 23,000 sq. km.

Natural resources: Geothermal areas.

Climate: Dry and torrid desert climate.

People

Population: 476,703 (July 2005 est.).

Population growth rate: 2.06% (2005 est.).

Sex ratio: 1.05 male(s)/female (2005 est.).

Religions: Muslim 94%, Christian 6%.

Languages: French (official), Arabic (official), Somali, Afar.

Literacy rate: Total 67.9%, Male 78%, Female 58.4% (2003 est.).

Infant mortality rate: 104.13 deaths/1,000 live births (2005 est.).

Life expectancy: Total 43.1 years, Male 41.84 years, Female 44.39 years (2005 est.).

Government

Capital: Djibouti.

Government type: Republic.

Independence: 27 June 1977 (from France).

Legal system: Based on French civil law system, traditional practices, and Islamic law.

Executive branch:
Chief of state: President Ismail Omar Guelleh (since 8 May 1999).

Head of government: Prime Minister Dileita Mohamed Dileita (since 4 March 2001).

Economy

Currency: Djiboutian franc.

GDP: Purchasing power parity—$619 million (2002 est.).

GDP—real growth rate: 3.5% (2002 est.).

GDP—per capita: Purchasing power parity—$1,300 (2002 est.).

Inflation rate: 2% (2002 est.).

Population below poverty line: 50% (2001 est.).

Unemployment rate: 50% (2004 est.).

Exports: $155 million f.o.b. (2002 est.)—Re-exports, hides and skins, coffee.

Imports: $665 million f.o.b. (2002 est.)—Foods, beverages, transport equipment, chemicals, petroleum products.

External debt: $366 million (2002 est.).

Transport and Communications

Railways: 100 km.

Roads: 2,890 km.

Telephones: 9,500 (2003).

Mobile cellular: 23,000 (2003).

Internet users: 6,500 (2003).

Internet country code: .dj

Dominica

History

Christopher Columbus gave the island its present name. The French were the first to colonize the island in 1632. Between 1748 and 1805, the control of Dominica shifted repeatedly between France and UK. Initially administered as part of the Leeward Islands, Dominica became a separate colony in 1771. The 1967 Constitution granted the island full self-governance in internal affairs.

Geography

Location: Caribbean island between the Caribbean Sea and the North Atlantic Ocean.

Area: 754 sq. km.

Natural resources: Timber, hydropower, arable land.

Climate: Tropical, moderated by north-east trade winds; heavy rainfall.

People

Population: 69,029 (July 2005 est.).

Population growth rate: −0.27% (2005 est.).

Sex ratio: 1.01 male(s)/female (2005 est.).

Religions: Roman Catholic 77%, Protestant 15%, none 2%, others 6%.

Languages: English (official), French patois.

Literacy rate: Total 94% (2003 est.).

Infant mortality rate: 14.15 deaths/1,000 live births (2005 est.).

Life expectancy: Total 74.65 years, Male 71.73 years, Female 77.71 years (2005 est.).

Government

Capital: Roseau.

Government type: Parliamentary democracy; republic within the Commonwealth.

Independence: 3 November 1978 (from UK).

Legal system: Based on English common law.

Executive branch:
Chief of state: President Nicholas Liverpool (since 10 November 2003).

Head of government: Prime Minister Roosevelt Skerrit (since 8 January 2004).

Economy

Currency: East Caribbean dollar.

GDP: Purchasing power parity—$384 million (2003 est.).

GDP—real growth rate: –1% (2003 est.).

GDP—per capita: Purchasing power parity—$5,500 (2003 est.).

Inflation rate: 1% (2001 est.).

Population below poverty line: 30% (2002 est.).

Unemployment rate: 23% (2000 est.).

Exports: $39 million f.o.b. (2003 est.)—Banana, soap, bay oil, vegetables, grapefruit, orange.

Imports: $98.2 million f.o.b. (2003 est.)—Manufactured goods, machinery and equipment, food, chemicals.

External debt: $161.5 million (2001).

Transport and Communications

Railways: None.

Roads: 780 km.

Telephones: 23,700 (2002).

Mobile cellular: 9,400 (2002).

Internet users: 12,500 (2002).

Internet country code: .dm

Dominican Republic

History

Christopher Columbus explored the island on which Dominican Republic is situated in 1492. He named the island 'La Espanola' and his son Diego was its first viceroy. In 1697, the eastern part of the island that later became the country of Haiti was given away to France. In 1809, the eastern two-thirds of the island was given back to Spain. In 1821, this part declared its independence. Haitian troops invaded it within weeks of independence and occupied it till 1844. In 1916, chaos and disorder in the island nation prompted the US to send in troops who remained on the island till 1934.

Geography

Location: Caribbean, eastern two-thirds of the island of Hispaniola, between the Caribbean Sea and the North Atlantic Ocean, east of Haiti.

Area: 48,730 sq. km.

Natural resources: Nickel, bauxite, gold, silver.

Climate: Tropical maritime climate with little seasonal temperature variation.

People

Population: 8,950,034 (July 2005 est.).

Population growth rate: 1.29% (2005 est.).

Sex ratio: 1.03 male(s)/female (2005 est.).

Religions: Roman Catholic 95%.

Languages: Spanish.

Literacy rate: Total 84.7%, Male 84.6%, Female 84.8% (2003 est.).

Infant mortality rate: 32.38 deaths/ 1,000 live births (2005 est.).

Life expectancy: Total 67.26 years (2005 est.).

Government

Capital: Santo Domingo.

Government type: Representative democracy.

Independence: 27 February 1844 (from Haiti).

Legal system: Based on French civil codes.

Executive branch:
Chief of state: President Leonel Fernandez Reyna (since 16 August 2004). Vice-President Rafael Albuquer-

que de Castro (since 16 August 2004). The president is both the chief of state and head of government.

Economy

Currency: Dominican peso.

GDP: Purchasing power parity—$55.68 billion (2004 est.).

GDP—real growth rate: 1.7% (2004 est.).

GDP—per capita: Purchasing power parity—$6,300 (2004 est.).

Inflation rate: 5.5% (2004 est.).

Population below poverty line: 25%.

Unemployment rate: 17% (2004 est.).

Exports: $5.446 billion f.o.b. (2004 est.)—Ferro-nickel, sugar, gold, silver, coffee, cocoa, tobacco, meats, consumer goods.

Imports: $8.093 billion f.o.b. (2004 est.)—Foodstuff, petroleum, cotton and fabrics, chemicals and pharmaceuticals.

External debt: $7.745 billion (2004 est.).

Transport and Communications

Railways: 1,743 km.

Roads: 12,600 km.

Telephones: 901,800 (2003).

Mobile cellular: 2,120,400 (2003).

Internet users: 500,000 (2003).

Internet country code: .do

East Timor

History

The Portuguese settled on Timor in 1520, while the Spanish reached in 1522. The Portuguese remained in control of the East Timor province until 1975. 1975 saw the formation of Democratic Republic of East Timor. However, independence proved to be shortlived. Indonesian forces invaded and occupied the territory and declared it to be an integral part of Indonesia. In 1999, Indonesia bowed to mounting international pressure and allowed a referendum to ascertain the future of East Timor. The majority vote in favour of independence led to East Timor finally gaining independence in 2002.

Geography

Location: South-eastern Asia, north-west of Australia in the Lesser Sunda Islands at the eastern end of the Indonesian archipelago.

Area: 15,007 sq. km.

Natural resources: Gold, petroleum, natural gas, manganese, marble.

Terrain: Mountainous terrain.

Climate: Hot and humid tropical climte with distinct rainy and dry seasons.

People

Population: 1,040,880 (July 2005 est.).

Poplation growth rate: 2.09% (2005 est.).

Sex ratio: 1.04 male(s)/female (2005 est.).

Religions: Roman Catholic 90%, Musim 4%, Protestant 3%, Hindu 0.5%, Buddhist, Animist.

Languages: Tetum (official), Portuguese (official), Indonesian, English.

Literacy rate: 58.6% (2002).

Infant mortality rate: 47.41 deaths/1,000 live births (2005 est.).

Life expectancy: Total 65.9 years, Male 63.63 years, Female 68.29 years (2005 est.).

Government

Capital: Dili.

Government type: Republic.

Independence: 20 May 2002 (official date of international recognition of East Timor's independence from Indonesia).

Legal system: UN-drafted legal system based on Indonesian law.

Executive branch:
Chief of state: President Jose Alexander Gusmao, also referred to as Xanana Gusmao (since 20 May 2002). The president plays a largely symbolic role but has the power to veto legislation.

Head of government: Prime Minister Mari Bin Amude Alkatiri (since 20 May 2002).

Economy

Currency: US dollar.

Economy—overview:
In 1999, almost 70% of East Timor's economic infrastructure was destroyed as a result of the freedom struggle. Since then, however, the country has been the site of a huge international reconstruction programme. Nevertheless, East Timor still faces a substantial task of reconstruction, administration and further development, such as that of the petroleum resources that are believed to lie in its waters.

GDP: Purchasing power parity—$370 million (2004 est.).

GDP—real growth rate: 1% (2004 est.).

GDP—per capita: Purchasing power parity—$400 (2004 est.).

Population below poverty line: 42% (2003 est.).

Unemployment rate: 50% (including underemployment) (1992 est.).

Exports: $8 million (2004 est.)—Coffee, sandalwood, marble.

Imports: $167 million (2004 est.)—Food.

Transport and Communications

Railways: None.

Roads: 3,800 km.

Internet country code .tp

Ecuador

History

Indigenous tribes ruled the area that is now Ecuador till the Incas conquered the lands in the 15th century. In the 16th century, the Spanish conquistadors vanquished the Incas and added it to the viceroyalty of Peru. In 1822, Ecuador established its independence from Spain and became a part of independent Gran Colombia, which also included modern-day Colombia, Panama and Venezuela. In 1830, Ecuador seceded from Gran Colombia. In 1942, Ecuador handed over around 200,000 square kilometres of disputed territory to Peru.

Geography

Location: Western South America, bordering the Pacific Ocean at the Equator, between Colombia and Peru.

Area: 283,560 sq. km. This includes Galapagos Islands.

Terrain: Central plain, inter-Andean central highlands, and flat and rolling eastern jungle.

Natural resources: Petroleum, fish, timber, hydropower.

Climate: Tropical climate along the coast and in the Amazonian jungle lowlands, but becomes cooler inland at higher altitudes.

People

Population: 13,363,593 (July 2005 est.).

Population growth rate: 1.24% (2005 est.).

Sex ratio: 1 male(s)/female (2005 est.).

Religions: Roman Catholic 95%.

Languages: Spanish (official), Amerindian languages (especially Quechua).

Literacy rate: Total 92.5%, Male 94%, Female 91% (2003 est.).

Infant mortality rate: 23.66 deaths/1,000 live births (2005 est.).

Life expectancy: Total 76.21 years, Male 73.35 years, Female 79.22 years (2005 est.).

Government

Capital: Quito.

Government type: Republic.

Independence: 24 May 1822 (from Spain).

Legal system: Based on civil law system.

Executive branch:
Chief of state: President Alfredo Palacio (since 20 April 2005); Vice-President Nicanor Alejandro (since 5

May 2005). The president is both the chief of state and head of government.

Economy

Currency: US dollar.

GDP: Purchasing power parity—$49.51 billion (2004 est.).

GDP—real growth rate: 5.8% (2004 est.).

GDP—per capita: Purchasing power parity—$3,700 (2004 est.).

Inflation rate: 2% (2004 est.).

Population below poverty line: 70% (2001 est.).

Unemployment rate: 11.1% (2004 est.).

Exports: $7.56 billion (2004 est.)—Petroleum, banana, shrimp, coffee, cocoa, cut flower, fish.

Imports: $7.65 billion (2004 est.)—Machinery and equipment, chemicals, raw materials, fuels; consumer goods.

External debt: $16.81 billion (2004 est.).

Transport and Communications

Railways: 966 km.

Roads: 43,197 km.

Telephones: 1,549,000 (2003).

Mobile cellular: 2,394,400 (2003).

Internet users: 569,700 (2003).

Internet country code: .ec

Egypt

History

Egypt is a cradle of human civilization. Settlement in the Nile Valley began around 7000 BC. Successive dynasties in Egypt ruled over a country that boasted of flourishing trade, prosperity and the unprecedented development of culture and traditions. Egypt's golden age coincided with the 18th and 19th dynasties, between the 16th to 13th centuries BC. This was the age of the pharaohs, of hieroglyphics, and the pyramids. Their construction in around 2500 BC remains one of the greatest engineering achievements of all times.

In 669 BC, Assyrians from Mesopotamia conquered Egypt and established their rule over the country. In 525 BC came the Persian conquest. In 332 BC, Alexander the Great of Macedonia conquered Egypt and founded the city of Alexandria. In 31 BC, the Roman Empire claimed Egypt following the death of Queen Cleopatra and Roman leader Octavian's defeat of her forces.

In AD 642, Arabs conquered Egypt. Between 1250 and 1517, the Mamluks/Mamelukes, or the slave soldiers, ruled the country.

In 1517, Egypt was absorbed into the Turkish Ottoman Empire. Between 1798 and 1801, Napoleon's forces occupied the country. However, in 1801, the British and the Turks drove the French out of Egypt and the country was restored to the Ottoman Empire.

The construction of the Suez Canal between 1859–69 was another turning point in the history of Egypt. In 1882, British troops seized control of Egypt and in 1914 it became a British protectorate. In 1922, Egypt gained independence and Fu'ad I became the King of Egypt.

On 14 May 1948, the proclamation of the State of Israel was made in Tel Aviv. The following day, armies from five Arab nations including Egypt invaded Israel but were beaten back. The subsequent armistices defined Israel's territorial limits. However, Egypt retained the Gaza Strip.

In 1952, Gamal Abdel Nasser led the Free Officers' Movement in a coup. This resulted in the installation of Muhammad Naguib as President and prime minister of Egypt. In June 1953, Naguib declared Egypt a republic and abolished the monarchy. In 1954, Gamal Abdel Nasser became the prime minister. In 1956, he became the new President.

On 26 July 1956, an international crisis erupted when President Nasser nationalized the Suez Canal to finance Egypt's construction of the Aswan High Dam. UK and France feared closure of the canal and the halting of petroleum shipments from the Persian Gulf region. In October, UK, France and Israel invaded Egypt. On 22 December, the UN evacuated British and French troops. This incident, now referred to as the Suez Crisis, proved to be a victory for Egypt and President Nasser.

President Nasser passed away in September 1970 and was succeeded by his Vice-President Anwar al-Sadat. In 1971, Egypt signed a Treaty of Friendship with the Soviet Union. The same year, the Aswan High Dam was completed, ushering in a new era for Egyptian irrigation, agriculture and industry.

On 6 October 1973, the Jewish holy day of Yom Kippur, Egypt and Syria attacked Israel, starting what is now called the Yom Kippur War. Israel and Egypt signed a ceasefire agreement in November and peace agreements on 18 January 1974.

In June 1975, the Suez Canal was reopened for the first time since the 1967 war. In 1977, Egypt became the first Arab country to recognize Israel when its president, Anwar Sadat, flew to Israel and even addressed its Parliament. In September 1978, Egypt and Israel signed the Camp David accords. On 6 October 1981, opponents of the peace dialogue with Israel assassinated Anwar Sadat. A national referendum approved Hosni Mubarak as the new President of Egypt.

Geography

Location: Northern Africa, bordering the Mediterranean Sea, between Libya and the Gaza Strip, and the Red Sea north of Sudan, and includes the Asian Sinai Peninsula.

Area: 1,001,450 sq. km.

Terrain: Mostly a vast desert plateau that is interrupted by the Nile Valley and Delta.

Natural resources: Petroleum, natural gas, iron ore, phosphates, manganese, limestone, gypsum, talc, asbestos, lead, zinc.

Climate: Desert climate with hot, dry summers and moderate winters.

People

Population: 77,505,756 (July 2005 est.).

Population growth rate: 1.78% (2005 est.).

Sex ratio: 1.02 male(s)/female (2005 est.).

Religions: Muslim (mostly Sunni) 94%, Coptic Christian and others 6%.

Languages: Arabic (official), English and French widely understood by educated classes.

Literacy rate: Total 57.7%, Male 68.3%, Female 46.9% (2003 est.)

Infant mortality rate: 32.59 deaths/1,000 live births (2005 est.).

Life expectancy: Total 71 years, Male 68.5 years, Female 73.62 years (2005 est.).

Government

Capital: Cairo.

Government type: Republic.

Independence: 28 February 1922 (from UK).

Legal system: Based on English common law, Islamic law, and Napoleonic codes.

Executive branch:
Chief of state: President Mohammed Hosni Mubarak (since 14 October 1981).

Head of government: Prime Minister Ahmed Nazif (since July 2004).

Economy

Currency: Egyptian pound.

Economy—overview:

Although the government proposed new privatization and reform measures in late 2003 and early 2004, there has been a lack of any substantial economic reform since the mid 1990s. This is reflected in the limited foreign direct investment in Egypt and low annual GDP growth. The government is apprehensive of possible negative public reaction to reforms.

GDP: Purchasing power parity—$316.3 billion (2004 est.).

GDP—real growth rate: 4.5% (2004 est.).

GDP—per capita: Purchasing power parity—$4,200 (2004 est.).

Inflation rate: 9.5% (2004 est.).

Population below poverty line: 16.7% (2000 est.).

Unemployment rate: 10.9% (2004 est.).

Exports: $11 billion f.o.b. (2004 est.) — Crude oil and petroleum products, cotton, textiles, metal products, chemicals.

Imports: $19.21 billion f.o.b. (2004 est.)—Machinery and equipment, foodstuff, chemicals, wood products, fuels.

External debt: $33.75 billion (2004 est.).

Transport and Communications

Railways: 5,063 km.

Roads: 64,000 km.

Telephones: 9,600,000 (2005).

Mobile cellular: 8,583,940 (2005).

Internet users: 1,900,000 (2002).

Internet country code: .eg

El Salvador

History

It is believed that the Pipil Indians who were descendants of the Aztecs migrated to the area in the 11th century. The Spanish arrived in the 1520s. In 1821, El Salvador declared its independence from Spain. Between 1931 and 1979, a succession of military dictators ruled El Salvador.

Geography

Location: Middle America, bordering the North Pacific Ocean, between Guatemala and Honduras.

Area: 21,040 sq. km.

Natural resources: Hydropower, geothermal power, petroleum, arable land.

Climate: Coastal El Salvador has a tropical climate while the uplands have a temperate climate.

People

Population: 6,704,932 (July 2005 est.).

Population growth rate: 1.75% (2005 est.).

Sex ratio: 0.95 male(s)/female (2005 est.).

Religions: Roman Catholic 83%.

Languages: Spanish, Nahua (among some Amerindians).

Literacy rate: Total 80.2%, Male 82.8%, Female 77.7% (2003 est.).

Infant mortality rate: 25.1 deaths/ 1,000 live births (2005 est.).

Life expectancy: Total 71.22 years, Male 67.61 years, Female 75.01 years (2005 est.).

Government

Capital: San Salvador.

Government type: Republic.

Independence: 15 September 1821 (from Spain).

Legal system: Based on civil and Roman law, with traces of common law.

Executive branch:
Chief of state: President Elias Antonio Saca Gonzalez (since 1 June 2004); Vice-President Ana Vilma De Escobar (since 1 June 2004). The president is both the chief of state and head of government.

Economy

Currency: US dollar.

GDP: Purchasing power parity—$32.35 billion (2004 est.).

GDP—real growth rate: 1.8% (2004 est.).

GDP—per capita: Purchasing power parity—$4,900 (2004 est.).

Inflation rate: 5.4% (2004 est.).

Population below poverty line: 36.1% (2003 est.).

Unemployment rate: 6.3% (2004 est.).

Exports: $3.249 billion (2004 est.)— Offshore assembly exports, coffee, sugar, shrimp, textiles, chemicals, electricity.

Imports: $5.968 billion (2004 est.)— Raw materials, consumer goods, capital goods, fuels, foodstuff, petroleum, electricity.

External debt: $4.792 billion (2004 est.).

Transport and Communications

Railways: 283 km.

Roads: 10,029 km.

Telephones: 752,600 (2003).

Mobile cellular: 1,149,800 (2003).

Internet users: 550,000 (2003).

Internet country code: .sv

Equatorial Guinea

History

Pygmies were the original inhabitants of the mainland part of the country. Fang and Bubi people, the two most important ethnic groups today, migrated to the region in the 17th century. The Portuguese arrived in the 15th century. In 1477, Portugal ceded the island of Fernando Po (present-day Bioko) to Spain.

In 1968, Spanish Guinea became independent as the Republic of Equatorial Guinea. In 1996, oil and natural gas was struck in Equatorial Guinea. Today, the country is a key producer of petroleum in Africa.

Geography

Location: Western Africa, bordering the Bight of Biafra, between Cameroon and Gabon.

Area: 28,051 sq. km.

Natural resources: Oil, petroleum, timber, small unexploited deposits of gold, manganese, uranium, titanium, iron ore.

Climate: Hot and humid tropical climate.

People

Population: 535,881 (July 2005 est.).

Population growth rate: 2.42% (2005 est.).

Sex ratio: 0.96 male(s)/female (2005 est.).

Religions: Nominally Christian and predominantly Roman Catholic, pagan practices.

Languages: Spanish (official), French (official), pidgin English, Fang, Bubi, Ibo.

Literacy rate: Total 85.7%, Male 93.3%, Female 78.4% (2003 est.).

Infant mortality rate: 85.13 deaths/1,000 live births (2005 est.).

Life expectancy: Total 55.56 years, Male 53.38 years, Female 57.8 years (2005 est.).

Government

Capital: Malabo.

Government type: Republic.

Independence: 12 October 1968 (from Spain).

Legal system: Based on Spanish civil law and tribal custom.

Executive branch:
Chief of state: President Brig. Gen. (Ret.) Teodoro Obiang Nguema Mbasogo

(since 3 August 1979).

Head of government: Miguel Abia Biteo Boriko (from June 2004).

Economy

Currency: Communaute Financiere Africaine franc.

GDP: Purchasing power parity—$1.27 billion (2002 est.).

GDP—real growth rate: 20% (2002 est.).

GDP—per capita: Purchasing power parity—$2,700 (2002 est.).

Inflation rate: 8.5% (2004 est.).

Unemployment rate: 30% (1998 est.).

Exports: $2.771 billion f.o.b. (2004 est.)—Petroleum, methanol, timber, cocoa.

Imports: $1.167 billion f.o.b. (2004 est.)—Petroleum sector equipment, other equipment.

External debt: $248 million (2000 est.).

Transport and Communications

Railways: None.

Roads: 2,880 km (1999 est.).

Telephones: 9,600 (2003).

Mobile cellular: 41,500 (2003).

Internet users: 1,800 (2002).

Internet country code: .gq

Eritrea

History

Between AD 300–600, Eritrea was a part of the Ethiopian kingdom of Aksum. In the 1500s the Ottoman Empire annexed Eritrea. In 1941, the UK occupied Eritrea and in 1949, it began administering Eritrea as a United Nations Trust Territory. In 1962 Ethiopia annexed Eritrea. In 1993, Eritreans voted almost unanimously for independence in a referendum. Eritrea became independent in June 1993. In 1999, border skirmishes with Ethiopia developed into a full-fledged war. In June 2000, the two countries signed a ceasefire agreement and later in December, a peace agreement.

Geography

Location: Eastern Africa, bordering the Red Sea, between Djibouti and Sudan.

Area: 121,320 sq. km.

Natural resources: Gold, potash, zinc, copper, salt, possibly oil and natural gas, fish.

Climate: Hot climate in the dry desert strip along the Red Sea coast. The central highlands are cooler and wetter.

People

Population: 4,561,599 (July 2005 est.).

Population growth rate: 2.51% (2005 est.).

Sex ratio: 0.99 male(s)/female (2005 est.).

Religions: Muslim, Coptic Christian, Roman Catholic, Protestant.

Languages: Afar, Arabic, Tigre and Kunama, Tigrinya, other Cushitic languages.

Literacy rate: Total 58.6%, Male 69.9%, Female 47.6% (2003 est.).

Infant mortality rate: 74.87 deaths/ 1,000 live births (2005 est.).

Life expectancy: Total 52.16 years, Male 51.14 years, Female 53.22 years (2005 est.).

Government

Capital: Asmara (formerly Asmera).

Government type: Transitional government.

Independence: 24 May 1993 (from Ethiopia).

Legal system: Primarily based on the Ethiopian legal code of 1957, with revisions.

Executive branch:
Chief of state: President Isaias Asewerki (since 8 June 1993). The president is the chief of state, head of government and the head of the State Council and National Assembly.

Economy

Currency: Nakfa.

GDP: Purchasing power parity— $4.154 billion (2004 est.).

GDP—real growth rate: 2.5% (2004 est.).

GDP—per capita: Purchasing power parity—$900 (2004 est.).

Inflation rate: 10% (2004 est.).

Population below poverty line: 50% (2004 est.).

Exports: $64.44 million f.o.b. (2004 est.)—Livestock, sorghum, textiles, food, small manufactures.

Imports: $622 million f.o.b. (2004 est.)—Machinery, petroleum products, food, manufactured goods.

External debt: $311 million (2000 est.).

Transport and Communications

Railways: 306 km.

Roads: 4,010 km.

Telephones: 38,100 (2003).

Internet users: 9,500 (2003).

Internet country code: .er

Estonia

History

In the 14th century, the Danes controlled the northern part of Estonia while the Teutonic Knights of Germany possessed the southern part of the country. In 1346, the Danes sold the part of Estonia in their control to the Teutonic Knights. The Teutonics now came to control all of Estonia, which they transformed into serfdom. In 1526, the Swedes came to control Estonia. In 1721, the Russians gained control of Estonia from Sweden. In 1918, Estonia proclaimed its independence. But in 1940, it was back under Soviet rule. Finally, in August 1991, Estonia gained independence.

Geography

Location: Eastern Europe, bordering the Baltic Sea and Gulf of Finland, between Latvia and Russia.

Area: 45,226 sq. km. This includes the area of 1,520 islands in the Baltic Sea.

Natural resources: Oil shale, peat, phosphorite, clay, limestone, sand, dolomite, arable land, sea mud.

Climate: Maritime climate with wet and moderate winters and cool summers.

People

Population: 1,332,893 (July 2005 est.).

Population growth rate: −0.65% (2005 est.)

Sex ratio: 0.84 male(s)/female (2005 est.).

Religions: Evangelical Lutheran, Russian Orthodox, Estonian Orthodox, Baptist, Methodist, Seventh-Day Adventist, Roman Catholic, Pentecostal, Word of Life, Jewish.

Languages: Estonian (official), Russian, Ukrainian, Finnish, others.

Literacy rate: Total 99.8%, Male 99.8%, Female 99.8% (2003 est.).

Infant mortality rate: 7.87 deaths/ 1,000 live births (2005 est.).

Life expectancy: Total 71.77 years, Male 66.28 years, Female 77.6 years (2005 est.).

Government

Capital: Tallinn.

Government type: Parliamentary republic.

Independence: 20 August 1991 (from Soviet Union).

Legal system: Based on civil law system.

Executive branch:
Chief of state: President Arnold Ruutel (since 8 October 2001).

Head of government: Prime Minister Andrus Ansip (since 12 April 2005).

Economy

Currency: Estonian kroon.

GDP: Purchasing power parity—$19.23 billion (2004 est.).

GDP—real growth rate: 6% (2004 est.).

GDP—per capita: Purchasing power parity—$14,300 (2004 est.).

Inflation rate: 3% (2004 est.).

Unemployment rate: 9.6% (2004 est.).

Exports: $5.701 billion f.o.b. (2004 est.)—Machinery and equipment 33%, wood and paper 15%, textiles 14%, food products 8%, furniture 7%, metals, chemical products.

Imports: $7.318 billion f.o.b. (2004 est.)—Machinery and equipment 33.5%, chemical products 11.6%, textiles 10.3%, foodstuff 9.4%, transportation equipment 8.9%.

External debt: $8.373 billion (2004 est.).

Transport and Communications

Railways: 958 km (2003).

Roads: 55,944 km (2003).

Telephones: 475,000 (2002).

Mobile cellular: 881,000 (2002).

Internet users: 444,000 (2002).

Internet country code: .ee

Ethiopia

History

Some of the oldest human remains found on Earth have been discovered in Ethiopia. Ethiopia was originally called Abyssinia. The Solomonic dynasty that once ruled the country claims its descent from the son of King Solomon and Queen Sheba.

In the seventh century BC, Ge'ez-speaking people established the kingdom of Da'amat in the northern parts of the country. Then in the second century AD, Semitic people originating from the Arabian Peninsula established the kingdom of Axum (Aksum).

In 1530-1, Muslim leader Ahmad Gran conquered most of Ethiopia. In 1868, a British expeditionary force defeated Emperor Tewodros II and he committed suicide to avoid capture. In 1889, the king of Shoa became Emperor Menelik II. He signed a bilateral friendship treaty at Wuchale with Italy.

In 1895, Italy invaded Ethiopia. But in 1896, the Ethiopians defeated the Italian forces in a battle fought at Adwa. The Ethiopians subsequently annulled the treaty of Wuchale.

In 1936, Italians invaded Ethiopia once again. They captured Addis Ababa, causing Haile Selassie to flee the country. The King of Italy was crowned Emperor of Ethiopia. Italy combined Ethiopia with Eritrea and Italian Somaliland to form Italian East Africa. In 1941, British and Commonwealth troops in association with the Ethiopian resistance, the Arbegnoch, defeated the Italians and restored Haile Selassie to his throne.

In 1952, United Nations federated Eritrea with Ethiopia and in 1962 Haile Selassie annexed Eritrea and turned it into an Ethiopian province. In 1973-4 an estimated 200,000 people died in Wallo province as a result of famine. In September 1974, Haile Selassie was deposed in a military coup and General Teferi Benti became the head of state. The Constitution was dissolved and Ethiopia was declared a socialist state under the rule of a Provisional Military Administrative Council, also known as the Derg. In 1975, Haile Selassie passed away under mysterious circumstances while in custody. Benti himself was killed in 1977.

In the late 1990s, border clashes between Ethiopia and Eritrea developed into full-scale warfare. In June 2000, the two countries signed a ceasefire agreement and later in December, a peace agreement.

Geography

Location: Eastern Africa, west of Somalia.

Area: 1,127,127 sq. km.

Terrain: High flat plateau with a central mountain range.

Natural resources: Gold, platinum, copper, potash, natural gas, hydropower.

Climate: Tropical monsoon climate with wide variation caused by topograpy.

People

Population: 73,058,286 (2005 est.).

Population growth rate: 2.36% (2005 est.).

Sex ratio: 1 male(s)/female (2004 est.).

Religions: Muslim 45%–50%, Ethiopian Orthodox 35%–40%, animist 12%, others 3%–8%.

Languages: Amharic, Tigrinya, Oromigna, Guaragigna, Somali, Arabic, other local languages, English.

Literacy rate: Total 42.7%, Male 50.3%, Female 35.1% (2003 est.).

Infant mortality rate: 95.32 deaths/1,000 live births (2005 est.).

Life expectancy: Total 48.83 years, Male 47.67 years, Female 50.03 years (2005 est.).

Government

Capital: Addis Ababa.

Government type: Federal republic.

Legal system: In a state of transition; mix of national and regional courts.

Executive branch:
Chief of state: President Girma Woldegiorgis (since 8 October 2001).

Head of government: Prime Minister Meles Zenawi (since August 1995).

Economy

Currency: Birr.

GDP: Purchasing power parity—$54.89 billion (2004 est.).

GDP—real growth rate: 11.6% (2004 est.).

GDP—per capita: Purchasing power parity—$800 (2004 est.).

Inflation rate: 2.4% (2004 est.).

Population below poverty line: 50% (2004 est.).

Exports: $562.8 million f.o.b. (2004 est.)—Coffee, gold, leather products, live animals, oilseeds.

Imports: $2.104 billion f.o.b. (2004 est.)—Food and live animals, petroleum and petroleum products, chemicals, machinery, motor vehicles, cereals, textiles.

External debt: $2.9 billion (2001 est.).

Transport and Communications

Railways: 681 km.

Roads: 33,297 km.

Telephones: 435,000 (2003).

Mobile cellular: 97,800 (2003).

Internet users: 75,000 (2003).

Internet country code: .et

Fiji

History

The first Europeans to see the islands were the Dutch Abel Janzsoon Tasman (in 1643) and the British Captain James Cook (in 1774). Foreign interest in the islands grew due to the availability of sandalwood and sea cucumber. Fiji became a British Crown colony on 10 October 1874. In order to promote its own policies and to foster the economic development of the colony, the government encouraged Indian migrants to take up permanent residency on the islands. Fiji achieved independence on 10 October 1970.

Geography

Location: Oceania, island group in the South Pacific Ocean, about two-thirds of the way from Hawaii to New Zealand.

Area: 18,270 sq. km.

Terrain: Mostly mountainous terrain. The mountains are of volcanic origin.

Natural resources: Timber, fish, gold, copper, hydropower.

Climate: Tropical marine climate with slight seasonal temperature variation.

People

Population 893,354 (July 2005 est.).

Population growth rate: 1.4% (2005 est.).

Sex ratio: 1.01 male(s)/female (2005 est.).

Religions: Christian 52% (Methodist 37%, Roman Catholic 9%), Hindu 38%, Muslim 8%, others 2%.

Languages: English (official), Fijian, Hindustani.

Literacy rate: Total 93.7%, Male 95.5%, Female 91.9% (2003 est.).

Infant mortality rate: 12.62 deaths/ 1,000 live births (2005 est.).

Life expectancy: Total 69.53 years, Male 67.05 years, Female 72.14 years (2005 est.).

Government

Capital: Suva.

Government type: Republic.

Independence: 10 October 1970 (from UK).

Legal system: Based on the British system.

Executive branch:
Chief of state: President Ratu Josefa Iloilovatu Uluivuda (since 2000); Vice-President Jope Seniloli (since 2000).

Head of government: Prime Minister Laisenia Qarase (since 10 September 2000).

Economy

Currency: Fijian dollar.

Economy—overview:
Fiji has forest, mineral and fish resources and is one of the most developed of the Pacific island economies. However, there is a large subsistence sector. Sugar exports and tourism industry are the major sources of foreign exchange. Sugar processing constitutes one-third of country's industrial activity.

GDP: Purchasing power parity— $5.173 billion (2004 est.).

GDP—real growth rate: 3.6% (2004 est.).

GDP—per capita: Purchasing power parity—$5,900 (2004 est.).

Inflation rate: 1.6% (2004 est.).

Population below poverty line: 25.5% (1990–1).

Unemployment rate: 7.6% (1999).

Exports: $609 million f.o.b. (2002)— Sugar, garments, gold, timber, fish, molasses, coconut oil.

Imports: $835 million c.i.f. (2002)— Manufactured goods, machinery and transport equipment, petroleum products, food, chemicals.

External debt: $188.1 million (2001).

Transport and Communications

Railways: 597 km.

Roads: 3,440 km.

Telephones: 102,000 (2003).

Mobile cellular: 109,900 (2003).

Internet users: 15,000 (2002).

Internet country code: .fj

Finland

History

The first inhabitants of the area that is today Finland were the Sami people, also called Lapp. Later on, Finnish-speaking people arrived in the region in the first millennium BC and drove the Samis northwards to the Arctic regions. In the eleventh century, repeated Finnish attacks on Swedish lands led to the Swedish conquest of Finland. In 1808, Russia invaded Sweden and the following year, Sweden handed over Finland to the Russians.

Finland declared its independence from Russia following the 1917 Revolution. In 1919, Finland became a republic.

During World War II, by the terms of the Treaty of Moscow of 1940, Finland surrendered a large part of south-eastern Finland to the Soviet Union. In 1944, the Soviet Red Army invaded the country. Finland had to hand over even more land to the Soviet Union and also had to pay hundreds of millions of dollars in war reparations. In 1995, Finland became a member state of the European Union.

Geography

Location: Northern Europe, bordering the Baltic Sea, Gulf of Bothnia, and Gulf of Finland, between Sweden and Russia.

Area: 337,030 sq. km.

Terrain: Mostly low, flat to rolling plains interspersed with lakes and low hills.

Natural resources: Timber, iron ore, copper, lead, zinc, chromite, nickel, gold, silver, limestone.

Climate: Cold temperate climate.

People

Population: 5,223,442 (July 2005 est.).

Population growth rate: 0.16% (2005 est.).

Sex ratio: 0.96 male(s)/female (2005 est.).

Religions: Evangelical Lutheran 89%, Russian Orthodox 1%, none 9%, others 1%.

Languages: Finnish 93.4% (official), Swedish 5.9% (official), small Sami- and Russian-speaking minorities.

Literacy rate: 100% (1980 est.).

Infant mortality rate: 3.57 deaths/1,000 live births (2005 est.).

Life expectancy: Total 78.35 years, Male 74.82 years, Female 82.02 years (2005 est.).

Government

Capital: Helsinki.

Government type: Republic.

Independence: 6 December 1917 (from Russia).

Legal system: Civil law system based on Swedish law.

Executive branch:
Chief of state: President Tarja Halonen (since 1 March 2000).

Head of government: Prime Minister Matti Vanhanen (since 24 June 2003) and Deputy Prime Minister Antti Kalliomaki (since 17 April 2003).

Economy

Currency: Euro.

Economy—overview:
Finland has a highly industrialized, largely free-market economy. The key economic sectors are manufacturing (such as telecommunications, electronics, wood, metals and engineering). One major success story in the manufacturing sector is that of Nokia. In 2000, Nokia accounted for 4% of Finland's GDP, nearly 30% of exports and 1% of jobs. Exports account for one-third of Finland's GDP. Other than timber and some minerals, Finland has to depend on imported raw materials, energy and components for producing manufactured products. Finland was one of the 12 countries joining the European Economic and Monetary Union (EMU).

GDP: Purchasing power parity—$151.2 billion (2004 est.).

GDP—real growth rate: 3% (2004 est.).

GDP—per capita: Purchasing power parity—$29,000 (2004 est.).

Inflation rate: 0.7% (2004 est.).

Unemployment rate: 8.9% (2004 est.).

Exports: $54.28 billion f.o.b. (2003 est.)—Machinery and equipment, chemicals, metals, timber, paper, pulp.

Imports: $37.35 billion f.o.b. (2003 est.)—Foodstuff, petroleum and petroleum products, chemicals, transport equipment, iron and steel, machinery, textile yarn and fabrics, grains.

External debt: $30 billion (December 1993).

Transport and Communications

Railways: 5,850 km.

Road: 78,197 km.

Telephones: 2,548,000 (2003).

Mobile cellular: 4,700,000 (2003).

Internet users: 2.65 million (2002).

Internet country code: .fi

France

History

Archaeological evidence shows that the area that is today France has been inhabited almost continuously since Paleolithic times. Around 1200 BC, the Celts (later called Gauls) migrated into the area. The Romans referred to the area as Transalpine Gaul. Roman emperor Augustus divided the country into four administrative provinces.

Between 751 and 987, the Carolingian dynasty ruled the territory. The greatest Carolingian ruler was Charlemagne, who later became the Holy Roman Emperor. In 843, the Treaty of Verdun divided the territories roughly corresponding with France, Germany and Italy among the three grandsons of Charlemagne. Consequently, Charles the Bald received what was then called Francia Occidentalis. France subsequently passed under the rule of the Capetian dynasty.

The House of Valois ruled France from 1328 to 1589. Between 1337 and 1453, France and England fought each other in the Hundred Years War that resulted in the return of British-held land to France. The House of Bourbon followed the Valois dynasty. The Bourbons ruled France from 1589 to the 1790s and from 1814 to 1830. The Bourbon–Orleans dynasty ruled for 18 years from 1830 to 1848.

Louis XIV, also called The Sun King, ruled from 1643 to 1715. His reign is widely regarded as a brilliant period of French history. Louis XIV extended France's eastern borders by defeating the Hapsburgs. He also fought the War of the Spanish Succession (1701–14) in which he took on a formidable European coalition but succeeded in securing the Spanish throne for his grandson.

In 1789, the French Revolution, also called the Revolution of 1789, swept the country and plunged it into a period of uncertainty and violence. On 14 July 1789, a mob of Parisians seized the Bastille prison, regarded as a symbol of royal tyranny and despotism. On 4 August 1789, the National Constituent Assembly decreed the abolition of the feudal regime. On 26 August, it introduced the Declaration of the Rights of Man and of the Citizen. On 20 September 1792, the National Convention was set up. It proclaimed the abolition of the monarchy and the establishment of the republic. On 19 January 1793, Louis XVI was condemned to death by 380 votes against 310. He was guillotined in Paris on 21 January 1793. Marie-Antoinette, his queen consort, was executed in October that year.

The period of the French Revolution from 5 September 1793, to 27 July 1794 is referred to as the 'Reign of Terror'. Faced with the dual problem of foreign war (with Austria) and civil war, the Revolutionary government decreed terror as the law of the day. It decided to take harsh measures against those suspected of being enemies of the Revolution. A wave of executions swept through Paris. The Committee of Public Safety, of which Maximilien Robespierre was the most prominent member, held virtual dictatorial control over the French government. It is now estimated that at least 300,000 suspects were arrested during the Reign of Terror, of which 17,000 were officially executed. Many died in prison, often without a trial.

Soon after the fall of Robespierre, and a crucial victory over Austria in the ongoing war, the government terminated its strict economic and social laws, even abandoning the aim of economic equality. The reactions that followed these moves ultimately led a young French general to defeat the Royalists and seize power in Paris. His name was Napoleon Bonaparte.

From 1799 to 1804, Napoleon served as the First Consul. Then, in 1804 he crowned himself Emperor of France in the presence of the Pope. Napoleon is widely regarded as one of the most influential personalities of Western history. Considered to be a brilliant military strategist, he also brought about the Napoleonic Code, which not only became the civil law of France but was also used as the starting point of civil-law codes in countries around the world.

Under Napolean's leadership, France was elevated to a position of dominance in Europe; its only major rival for European domination was the UK. Napoleon's ambitions of invading UK were dealt a deathblow on 21 October 1805 when a fleet of 33 ships under Admiral Pierre de Villeneuve was defeated by a British fleet of 27 ships under Admiral Horatio Nelson west of Cape Trafalgar, Spain. Napoleon's invasion of Russia in 1812 also ended in disaster. The warfare, shortage of supplies and the fierce cold of the Russian winter claimed 500,000 men. It also cost Napoleon his confidence and crucially, his allies.

A new coalition was formed in 1813 and the invasion of France was under way early in 1814. On 6 April, Napoleon abdicated. He was exiled to the island of Elba. In March 1815, he returned to France and formed a new army. However, the comeback proved to be shortlived and Napoleon suffered his final defeat at Waterloo in June 1815. Napoleon abdicated for the second time, on 22 June. The Bourbon monarchy was restored with Louis XVIII. Napoleon was imprisoned and exiled to the island of Saint Helena from October 1815. He passed away there, on 5 May 1821.

In 1848, the Second Republic was established with a nephew of Napoleon, Louis Napoleon, at its head. In 1852, he declared the Second Empire and took to the throne as Napoleon III. His abdication following defeat in the Franco-Prussian War (1870–1) led to the formation of the Third Republic.

World War I saw massive casualties in the trench warfare that took place in the northern parts of France. By the end of the war, nearly 1.3 million Frenchmen had been killed and more than twice that number wounded or crippled. The landmark peace document, the Treaty of Versailles, was signed at the end of the War.

Germany occupied France during World War II. General Charles de Gaulle, undersecretary of war, established a government-in-exile (Free French) in London and later in Algiers, Algeria. A sustained French Resistance campaign and the setting up of a subservient Vichy regime that owed allegiance to Nazi Germany characterized German occupation of France. The Allied invasion of western Europe began on 6 June 1944 from Normandy in northern France. This was the famous D-Day of World War II and led to the liberation of France. Charles de Gaulle returned to set up a provisional government.

The provisional government lasted till 1947, when the Fourth Republic was established. In the Fifth Republic, Charles de Gaulle returned as President and served till 1969.

The First Indochina War ended in French defeat in Vietnam in 1954. This led to French evacuation from the country. Algeria gained independence from France in 1962. Meanwhile, in 1956, French colonial rule came to an end in Morocco and Tunisia.

Geography

Location: Western Europe, bordering the Mediterranean Sea, between Italy and Spain; bordering the Bay of Biscay and English Channel, between Belgium and Spain, south-east of the UK.

Area: 547,030 sq. km (Includes only metropolitan France; excludes the overseas administrative divisions).

Terrain: Mostly flat plains or gently rolling hills in the north and west. Rest of the country is mountainous, with the Pyrenees in the south and the Alps in the east.

Natural resources: Coal, iron ore, bauxite, zinc, uranium, antimony, arsenic, potash, feldspar, fluorspar, gypsum, timber, fish.

Climate: Generally cool winters and mild summers. The Mediterranean areas have mild winters and hot summers.

People

Population: 60,656,178 (July 2005 est.).

Population growth rate: 0.37% (2005 est.).

Sex ratio: 0.95 male(s)/female (2005 est.).

Religions: Roman Catholic 83–88%, Protestant 2%, Jewish 1%, Muslim 5–10%, unaffiliated 4%.

Languages: French 100%, Provencal, Breton, Alsatian, Corsican, Catalan, Basque, Flemish.

Literacy rate: Total 99%, Male 99%, Female 99% (1980 est.).

Infant mortality rate: 4.26 deaths/1,000 live births (2005 est.).

Life expectancy: Total 79.6 years, Male 75.96 years, Female 83.42 years (2005 est.).

Government

Capital: Paris.

Government type: Republic.

Independence: AD 486 (unification under Clovis).

Legal system: Civil law system with indigenous concepts; review of administrative but not legislative acts.

Executive branch:

Chief of state: President Jacques Chirac (since 17 May 1995).

Head of government: Prime Minister Dominique Villepin (since 31 May 2005).

Elections and election results: The president is elected by popular vote for a five-year term. The election was last held on 21 April and 5 May 2002 and the next election is scheduled for April 2007 (first round) and May 2007 (second round). A majority of the National Assembly nominates the prime minister.

Legislative branch:

France has a bicameral parliament or Parlement that consists of the Senate or Senat and the National Assembly or Assemblee Nationale. The Senate has 331 seats. An electoral college indirectly elects members to serve nine-year terms by thirds every three years. In the period leading up to 2010, 25 new seats will be added to the Senate to make a total of 346 seats—326 for metropolitan France and overseas departments, two for New Caledonia, two for Mayotte, one for Saint-Pierre and Miquelon, three for overseas territories, and 12 for French nationals abroad. An electoral college will indirectly elect members to serve six-year terms, with one half of the seats being renewed every three years. The National Assembly has 577 seats. Members are elected by popular vote under a single-member majoritarian system to serve five-year terms.

Elections and election results: Senate elections were last held on 26 September 2004.

National Assembly elections were last held during 8–16 June 2002 and the next elections are scheduled for not later than June 2007.

Economy

Currency: Euro.

Economy—overview:

France has a prosperous modern economy undergoing transition from one that included widespread government ownership and control to a market-driven one. The list of large organizations that have been partially or fully privatized in recent times include Air France, Renault, and France Telecom. Income taxes have been lowered and measures introduced to boost employment. The country suffers from the problems of high cost of labour and the problems posed by the 35-hour workweek and restrictions on retrenchments. Efforts have also been initiated for pension reforms.

GDP: Purchasing power parity—$1.737 trillion (2004 est.).

GDP—real growth rate: 2.1% (2004 est.).

GDP—per capita: Purchasing power parity—$28,700 (2004 est.).

Inflation rate: 2.3% (2004 est.).

Population below poverty line: 6.5% (2000).

Unemployment rate: 10.1% (2004 est.).

Exports: $419 billion f.o.b. (2004 est.)—machinery and transportation equipment, aircraft, plastics, chemicals, pharmaceutical products, iron and steel, beverages.

Imports: $419.7 billion f.o.b. (2004 est.)—machinery and equipment, vehicles, crude oil, aircraft, plastics, chemicals.

External debt: 1,907,156 million Euros (2004 est.).

Transport and Communications

Railways: 32,175 km.

Roads: 893,100 km.

Telephones: 33,905,400 (2003).

Mobile cellular: 41,683,100 (2003).

Internet users: 18,716,000 (2002).

Internet country code: .fr

Gabon

History

The Portuguese were the first Europeans to arrive in the area in 1470. The Dutch arrived in 1593 and the French in 1630. In 1839, a local Mpongwe ruler signed away the sovereignty of the land to the French. In 1910, Gabon became a part of French Equatorial Africa. It gained independence in 1960.

Geography

Location: Western Africa, bordering the Atlantic Ocean at the Equator, between the Republic of the Congo and Equatorial Guinea.

Area: 267,667 sq. km.

Terrain: Narrow coastal plain with a hilly interior and savanna in the east and the north.

Natural resources: Petroleum, manganese, uranium, gold, timber, iron ore, hydropower.

Climate: Hot and humid tropical climate.

People

Population: 1,389,202 (July 2005 est.).

Population growth rate: 2.45% (2005 est.).

Sex ratio: 0.99 male(s)/female (2005 est.).

Religions: Christian 55%–75%, animist, Muslim less than 1%.

Languages: French (official), Fang, Myene, Nzebi, Bapounou/Eschira, Bandjabi.

Literacy rate: Total 63.2%, Male 73.7%, Female 53.3% (1995 est.).

Infant mortality rate: 53.64 deaths/1,000 live births (2005 est.).

Life expectancy: Total 55.75 years, Male 54.21 years, Female 57.34 years (2005 est.).

Government

Capital: Libreville.

Government type: Republic.

Independence: 17 August 1960 (from France).

Legal system: Based on French civil law system and customary law.

Executive branch:
Chief of state: President El Hadj Omar Bongo (since 2 December 1967).

Head of government: Prime Minister Jean-Francois Ntoutoume-Emane (since 23 January 1999).

Economy

Currency: Communaute Financiere Africaine franc.

GDP: Purchasing power parity—$7.966 billion (2004 est.).

GDP—real growth rate: 1.9% (2004 est.).

GDP—per capita: Purchasing power parity—$5,900 (2004 est.).

Inflation rate: 1.5% (2004 est.).

Unemployment rate: 21% (1997 est.).

Exports: $3.71 billion f.o.b. (2004 est.)—crude oil 77%, timber, manganese, uranium (2001).

Imports: $1.225 billion f.o.b. (2004 est.)—machinery and equipment, foodstuff, chemicals, construction materials.

External debt: $3.804 billion (2004 est.).

Transport and Communications

Railways: 814 km.

Roads: 8,464 km.

Telephones: 38,400 (2003).

Mobile cellular: 300,000 (2003).

Internet users: 35,000 (2003).

Internet country code: .ga

The Gambia

History

The present-day boundaries of the Gambia were demarcated by an agreement between Britain and France in 1889. In 1894, the Gambia became a British protectorate. In 1965, the Gambia became an independent country within the Commonwealth. In 1970, the Gambia became a republic.

Geography

Location: Western Africa, bordering the North Atlantic Ocean and Senegal.

Area: 11,300 sq. km.

Natural resources: Fish.

Climate: Tropical climate with a hot, rainy season from June to November and a cooler, dry season from November to May.

People

Population: 1,593,256 (July 2005 est.).

Population growth rate: 2.93% (2005 est.).

Sex ratio: 1 male(s)/female (2005 est.).

Religions: Muslim 90%, Christian 9%, indigenous beliefs 1%.

Languages: English (official), Mandinka, Wolof, Fula, other indigenous vernaculars.

Literacy rate: Total 40.1%, Male 47.8%, Female 32.8% (2003 est.).

Infant mortality rate: 72.02 deaths/1,000 live births (2005 est.).

Life expectancy: Total 55.2 years, Male 53.14 years, Female 57.31 years (2005 est.).

Government

Capital: Banjul.

Government type: Republic under multiparty democratic rule.

Independence: 18 February 1965 (from UK).

Legal system: Based on a composite of English common law, Koranic law, and customary law.

Executive branch:
Chief of state: President Yahya A.J.J. Jammeh (since 18 October 1996). The president is both the chief of state and head of government.

Economy

Currency: Dalasi.

GDP: Purchasing power parity—$2.799 billion (2004 est.).

GDP—real growth rate: 6% (2004 est.).

GDP—per capita: Purchasing power parity—$1,800 (2004 est.).

Inflation rate: 7% (2004 est.).

Exports: $114.4 million f.o.b. (2004 est.)—peanut products, fish, cotton lint, palm kernels, re-exports.

Imports: $180.9 million f.o.b. (2004 est.)—foodstuff, manufactures, fuel, machinery and transport equipment.

External debt: $476 million (2001 est.).

Transport and Communications

Railways: None.

Roads: 2,700 km.

Telephones: 38,400 (2002).

Mobile cellular: 100,000 (2002).

Internet users: 25,000 (2002).

Internet country code: .gm

Georgia

History

In around 4 BC, Georgia became a kingdom. In the later part of the 12th century, the kingdom enlarged to include the whole of Transcaucasia. In the 13th century, Mongols swept across the country and annihilated much of its population. In the 18th century, Georgia came under Russian control. Georgia declared its independence in 1918. In 1936, it became a separate Soviet republic. In 1991, Georgia announced its secession.

Geography

Location: South-western Asia, bordering the Black Sea, between Turkey and Russia.

Area: 69,700 sq. km.

Terrain: Mostly mountainous.

Natural resources: Forests, hydropower, manganese deposits, iron ore, copper, coal and oil deposits, coastal climate and soils.

Climate: Georgia has a warm and pleasant climate. The climate on the Black Sea coast resembles that of the Mediterranean region of Europe.

People

Population: 4,677,401 (July 2005 est.).

Population growth rate: −0.35% (2005 est.).

Sex ratio: 0.91 male(s)/female (2005 est.).

Religions: Georgian Orthodox 65%, Muslim 11%, Russian Orthodox 10%, Armenian Apostolic 8%, unknown 6%.

Languages: Georgian 71% (official), Russian 9%, Armenian 7%, Azeri 6%, others 7%.

Literacy rate: Total 99%, Male 100%, Female 98% (1999 est.).

Infant mortality rate: 18.59 deaths/ 1,000 live births (2005 est.).

Life expectancy: Total 75.88 years, Male 72.59 years, Female 79.67 years (2005 est.).

Government

Capital: T'bilisi.

Government type: Republic.

Independence: 9 April 1991 (from Soviet Union).

Legal system: Based on civil law system.

Executive branch:

Chief of state: President Mikhail Saakashvili (since 25 January 2004); the president is both the chief of state and head of government.

Economy

Currency: Lari.

Economy—overview:
The bulk of Georgia's economic activities are in the form of agricultural production, mining of manganese and copper are and the output of a small industrial sector. Georgia possesses substantial hydropower resources but has to import most of its energy, such as oil products and natural gas. The economy has suffered severe damage due to prolonged local conflict but Georgia has made good economic gains since 1995. This has been largely possible due to the help of the IMF and World Bank.

GDP: Purchasing power parity—$14.45 billion (2004 est.).

GDP—real growth rate: 4% (2004 est.).

GDP—per capita: Purchasing power parity—$3,100 (2004 est.).

Inflation rate: 5.5% (2004 est.).

Population below poverty line: 54% (2001 est.).

Unemployment rate: 17% (2001 est.).

Exports: $909.4 million (2004 est.)—scrap metal, machinery, chemicals, fuel re-exports, citrus fruits, tea, wine.

Imports: $1.806 billion (2004 est.)—fuels, machinery and parts, transport equipment, grain and other foods, pharmaceuticals.

External debt: $1.8 billion (2002).

Transport and Communications

Railways: 1,612 km.

Roads: 20,362 km.

Telephones: 650,500 (2003).

Mobile cellular: 522,300 (2003).

Internet users: 25,000 (2002).

Internet country code: .ge

Germany

History

It is believed that the Celts were the first inhabitants of the area that is to-day Germany. German tribes arrived in the area later. At the Battle of Teutoburg Forest in AD 9 German forces under Arminius defeated the Romans and wiped out three Roman legions. By the fourth century two powerful Germanic confederations had developed. These were the Alemanni on the Rhine and the Goths on the Danube. The arrival of nomadic non-German horsemen from the east pushed Germanic people into the Roman Empire. Meanwhile, the westward movement of the Huns put the frontiers of the Roman Empire under increasing pressure. The death of Hun leader, Attila, in 453, followed by the final demise of the remains of the Roman Empire put Germany in a position of dominance in Europe. Gradually, a number of German states arose all over the continent.

However, the states lacked political unity although some of them shared languages, customs and traditions. Before long, the Franks and the Ostrogoths clashed as both of them sought to expand their domination over Europe. Over time, the Franks emerged dominant.

Between 476 and 750, the Merovingians were the dominant Frankish dynasty. The Carolingian dynasty succeeded the Merovingians. The most famous Carolingian ruler was Charlemagne. At one point of time, he united in one single state almost all the Christian territories of western Europe. In 800, Pope Leo crowned him emperor of western Europe. Frankish and German kings ruled the empire for ten centuries, right upto 1806.

In the mid-19th century, Prussia became a formidable force under Fredrick the Great. In 1867, the German states north of the Main River joined together in a union named North German Confederation. The Prussians were the dominant force in the Confederation. The 1860s also saw the rise of Otto von Bismarck. He became the prime minister of Prussia in 1862. He also led Prussia to successive victories in wars against Austria, Denmark and France. These wars had the effect of creating a united Germany. The German Empire was founded on 18 January 1871, the date on which King Wilhelm I of Prussia was proclaimed Emperor of Germany at Versailles. Bismarck became the chancellor. In 1890, the new emperor, Wilhelm II, sought and obtained Bismarck's resignation as chancellor. Wilhelm II steered Germany on the 'New Course' policy. The foreign policy that he adopted led to the isolation of Germany in the global theatre.

On 28 June 1914, a Bosnian Serb named Gavrilo Princip assassinated Archduke Francis Ferdinand, heir presumptive to the Austrian throne, and his wife Sophie in Sarajevo. Austria–Hungary declared war on Serbia on 28 July. Russia responded by ordering a mobilization of its forces. On 1 August, Germany declared war against Russia and subsequently on France and Belgium. This brought a new country into the war, as the UK was committed to defend Belgium. It declared war against Germany on 4 August.

World War I ended in 1918 with the defeat of the Central Powers including the German Empire. The armistice that Germany had to sign as a result of the defeat meant the loss of its colonies to other European powers, surrender of land to its neighbours and the payment of substantial war reparations to the victors.

Soon after the end of the war, the Empire collapsed. A moderate state called the Weimar Republic was formed. The 1920s proved to be a dark period in German history. The economy was in a state of ruin, crippled by the war, a currency crisis, and the enormous burden of war reparations.

In 1920–1, Adolf Hitler became the leader of the National Socialist (Nazi) Party. On 30 January 1933, he became the chancellor. Following the death of President Paul von Hindenburg in 1934, he assumed the twin titles of Führer and chancellor. This also gave him the supreme command of the armed forces. Once at the helm of affairs in Germany, Hitler set up a strict totalitarian state. He fanned the population's suppressed pride in their fatherland by announcing his intentions of abrogating the Treaty of Versailles, territorial expansion of the country, reconstruction of the Reich's armed forces and restoration of the nation's wounded pride. On 30 June 1934, Hitler and his trusted SS forces carried out a bloody elimination of political rivals within the Nazi party itself. This is now known as the Night of the Long Knives.

Hitler then set about implementing his grandiose plans. He withdrew Germany from the League of Nations in October 1933. In January 1934, he signed a non-aggression treaty with Poland. In June 1935, he negotiated a naval treaty with UK that recognized Germany's right to a powerful navy once again. In March 1936, he used the excuse of a treaty between France and the Soviet Union to move into Rhineland. By 1937, Germany had linked up with Italy and Japan. The Third Reich had restored Germany to European dominance.

In 1936, Austria acknowledged itself to be a 'German state'. In 1938 came the Anschluss, or the political union of Austria with Germany. Hitler's next territorial demand was Czechoslovakia, which he took in 1939. He then forced Lithuania to give up some of its territories on the border with Prussia. On 1 September 1939, Germany invaded Poland. Two days later, UK and France declared war on Germany. World War II had started.

During the War, the Nazi government and its Axis collaborators carried out a systematic state-sponsored killing of six million Jewish people. The Germans called this 'the final solution to the Jewish question'. This is now referred to as the Holocaust. The Nazis set up 'ghettoes' of Jewish populations all across its new territorial acquisitions in Europe. Disease, hunger and malnutrition raged through the ghettoes and helped the Nazis eliminate the Jews without firing a single shot. When German forces moved into Russian territories, the Nazis set up special mobile killing units to murder Jews, Soviet commissars, and gypsies.

The War ended with German defeat and the division of the country into distinct occupation zones. In 1949, Germany was divided into West Germany and East Germany. The western zone that USA, France, and UK controlled became Federal Republic of Germany (West Germany). The Soviet zone became East Germany, or the communist German Democratic Republic. Konrad Adenauer became West Germany's first chancellor while Walter Ulbricht led East Germany. The city of Berlin became a divided city. In 1955, West Germany joined NATO while East Germany joined the Soviet Union-led Warsaw Pact.

On the evening of 9 November 1989, the communist authorities of East Germany announced new travel regulations. The government planned to issue official permissions for direct travel to the West. However, the general population misunderstood the announcement as a decision to open the Berlin Wall. Within hours, huge crowds had built up at the checkpoints, demanding to be allowed into West Berlin. The confused and uninformed border guards allowed them through. A night of euphoria and revelry followed as tens of thousands of East Germans swarmed into the free West and celebrated their new-found freedom with the West Berliners.

The opening of the Berlin wall proved to be the beginning of the end for East Germany and its communist regime. As the demonstrations grew in intensity, the Communist Party appointed a new reform-minded leader who promised free, multiparty elections. The communists suffered a crushing defeat in the March 1990 elections. In July, a monetary union of the two Germanys was achieved under the West German currency.

In July 1990, West German Chancellor Helmut Kohl struck a deal with Soviet leader Mikhail Gorbachev whereby Gorbachev dropped his objections to a unified Germany within NATO in return for a big West German financial aid to the Soviet Union. In 1991, Berlin was named as the capital of the united country.

Geography

Location: Central Europe, bordering the Baltic Sea and the North Sea, between the Netherlands and Poland, south of Denmark.

Area: 357,021 sq. km.

Terrain: The Bavarian Alps in the south, lowlands in the north, and uplands in the central part.

Natural resources: Coal, lignite, natural gas, iron ore, copper, nickel, uranium, potash, salt, construction materials, timber, arable land.

People

Population: 82,431,390 (July 2005 est.).

Population growth rate: 0.02% (2005 est.).

Sex ratio: 0.96 male(s)/female (2005 est.).

Religions: Protestant 34%, Roman Catholic 34%, Muslim 3.7%, unaffiliated or others 28.3%.

Languages: German.

Literacy rate: 99% (1977 est.).

Infant mortality rate: 4.16 deaths/1,000 live births (2005 est.).

Life expectancy: Total 78.65 years, Male 75.66 years, Female 81.81 years (2005 est.).

Government

Capital: Berlin.

Government type: Federal republic.

Independence: 3 October 1990 (date of unification of West Germany and East Germany).

Executive branch:
Chief of state: Horst Koehler (elected in May 2004; sworn in in July 2004).

Head of government: Chancellor Gerhard Schroeder (since 27 October 1998).

Elections and election results: A Federal Convention that includes all members of the Federal Assembly and an equal number of delegates elected by the state parliaments elect the president for a five-year term. The election was last held on 23 May 2004. The chancellor is elected by an absolute majority of the Federal Assembly for a four-year term. The election was last held on 22 September 2002 and the next election is scheduled for September 2006.

Legislative branch:
Germany has a bicameral parliament or Parlament that consists of the Federal Assembly or Bundestag and the Federal Council or Bundesrat. The Federal Assembly has 603 seats. Members are elected by popular vote under a system combining direct and proportional representation. A party must win 5% of the national vote or three direct mandates to gain representation. Members serve four-year terms. The Federal Council or Bundesrat has 69 votes. State governments are directly represented by votes and each state has three to six votes depending on population and is required to vote as a block.

Elections and election results:
There are no elections to the Federal Council. Federal Assembly elections were last held on 22 September 2002 and will be next held in September 2006.

Economy

Currency: Euro.

Economy—overview:
The prosperous and technologically advanced German economy is among the five largest economies of the world, no mean feat considering the situation of the country at the end of World War II and almost half a century of fractured existence as two separate countries.

However, Germany today is one of the slowest growing economies in the entire euro zone with slim chances of a rapid turnaround. One of the major challenges facing the country today is the ongoing process of integration and modernization of the erstwhile East German economy. Other constraints include the country's ageing population, high unemployment levels, and social security expenditure in excess of contributions from the working population. Germany's labour market suffers from structural rigidities, such as strict regulations on retrenchment and the determination of wages on a national basis. However, Germany has initiated corporate restructuring and structural reforms.

GDP: Purchasing power parity—$2.362 trillion (2004 est.).

GDP—real growth rate: 1.7% (2004 est.).

GDP—per capita: Purchasing power parity—$28,700 (2004 est.).

Inflation rate: 1.6% (2004 est.).

Unemployment rate: 10.6% (2004 est.).

Exports: $893.3 billion f.o.b. (2004 est.)—machinery, vehicles, chemicals, metals and manufactures, foodstuff, textiles.

Imports: $716.7 billion f.o.b. (2004 est.)—machinery, vehicles, chemicals, foodstuffs, textiles, metals.

External debt: 2,622,639 million Euros (2004 est.).

Transport and Communications

Railways: 46,039 km (21,000 km electrified).

Roads: 230,735 km (including 11,515 km of expressway).

Telephones: 54,350,000 (2003).

Mobile celluler: 64,800,000 (2003).

Internet users: 34 million (2002).

Internet country code: .de

Ghana

History

The Portuguese arrived in the Gold Coast area of Ghana in the 15th century. Later came the English, the Dutch and the Swedes. In 1874, UK proclaimed the coastal area of Ghana as a Crown colony. In March 1957, Ghana became the first among the African colonies to gain independence. In 1960, it became a republic.

Geography

Location: Western Africa, bordering the Gulf of Guinea, between Cote d'Ivoire and Togo.

Area: 239,460 sq. km.

Terrain: Mostly low plains with a dissected plateau in the south central area.

Natural resources: Gold, timber, industrial diamonds, bauxite, manganese, fish, rubber, hydropower.

Climate: Tropical climate.

People

Population: 21,029,853 (July 2005 est.).

Population growth rate: 1.25% (2004 est.).

Sex ratio: 1 male(s)/female (2005 est.).

Religions: Christian 63%, Muslim 16%, indigenous beliefs 21%.

Languages: English (official), African languages (including Akan, Moshi-Dagomba, Ewe, and Ga).

Literacy rate: Total 74.8%, Male 82.7%, Female 67.1% (2003 est.).

Infant mortality rate: 51.43 deaths/ 1,000 live births (2005 est.).

Life expectancy: Total 56 years, Male 55.04 years, Female 56.99 years (2005 est.).

Government

Capital: Accra.

Government type: Constitutional democracy.

Independence: 6 March 1957 (from UK).

Legal system: Based on English common law and customary law.

Executive branch:
Chief of state: President John Agyekum Kufuor (since 7 January 2001); Vice-President Alhaji Aliu Mahama (since 7 January 2001). The president is both the chief of state and head of government.

Economy

Currency: Cedi.

GDP: Purchasing power parity—$48.27 billion (2004 est.).

GDP—real growth rate: 5.4% (2004 est.).

GDP—per capita: Purchasing power parity—$2,300 (2004 est.).

Inflation rate: 13% (2004 est.).

Population below poverty line: 31.4% (1992 est.).

Unemployment rate: 20% (1997 est.).

Exports: $3.01 billion f.o.b. (2004 est.)—gold, cocoa, timber, tuna, bauxite, aluminum, manganese ore, diamond.

Imports: $3.699 billion f.o.b. (2004 est.)—capital equipment, petroleum, foodstuff.

External debt: $7.396 billion (2004 est.).

Transport and Communications

Railways: 953 km.

Roads: 46,176 km.

Telephones: 302,300 (2003).

Mobile cellular: 799,900 (2003).

Internet users: 170,000 (2002).

Internet country code: .gh

Greece

History

Advanced and prosperous civilizations flourished in the area of the Aegean Sea between 7000–3000 BC (Stone Age) and about 3000–1000 BC (Bronze Age). These were among the earliest advanced civilizations in Europe.

The period startig from around 1200 BC and upto the death of Alexander the Great (in 323 BC) is the period of the ancient Greek civilization. This was a period of great political, scientific, philosophical and artistic achievements and left a significant mark on Western civilization. Between 431and 404 BC, the two leading city states in ancient Greece, Athens and Sparta, fought each other in what is now called the Peloponnesian War. The consequent weakening of the nation resulted in its conquest by Phillip II of Macedon. His son was the famous Alexander the Great, widely regarded as one of the greatest conquerors of all times.

Thereafter, Greece became a province of the Roman Empire and remained so till the fall of Constantinople to the Crusaders in 1204. In 1453, Constantinople fell to the Turks and Greece became a Turkish province. An uprising erupted in 1821 and Greece gained independence in 1827, with France, Russia and UK guaranteeing sovereignty to the new state. Prince Otto of Bavaria was chosen as the first king of modern Greece.

In 1973, Greece was declared a republic and the monarchy was abolished. In 1974, a Greece-backed coup against President Makarios of Cyprus led to the Turkish invasion and occupation of the northern part of the island. In 1975, a new Constitution declared Greece to be a parliamentary republic with the President holding some executive powers.

Geography

Location: Southern Europe, bordering the Aegean Sea, Ionian Sea, and the Mediterranean Sea, between Albania and Turkey.

Area: 131,940 sq. km.

Terrain: Mostly mountanious with ranges extending into the sea as peninsulas or chain of islands.

Natural resources: Lignite, petroleum, iron ore, bauxite, lead, zinc, nickel, magnesite, marble, salt, hydropower potential.

Climate: Greece has a temperate climate with mild, wet winters and hot, dry summers.

People

Population: 10,668,354 (July 2005 est.).

Population growth rate: 0.19% (2005 est.).

Sex ratio: 0.97 male(s)/female (2004 est.).

Religions: Greek Orthodox (Christian) 98%, Muslim 1.3%, others 0.7%.

Languages: Greek 99% (official), English, French.

Literacy rate: Total 97.5%, Male 98.6%, Female 96.5% (2003 est.).

Infant mortality rate: 5.53 deaths/1,000 live births (2005 est.).

Life expectancy: Total 79.09 years, Male 76.59 years, Female 81.79 years (2005 est.).

Government

Capital: Athens.

Government type: Parliamentary republic.

Independence: 1829 (from the Ottoman Empire).

Legal system: Based on codified Roman law with a judiciary divided into civil, criminal, and administrative courts.

Executive branch:
Chief of state: President Konstandinos (Kostis) Stephanopoulos (since 10 March 1995).

Head of government: Prime Minister Konstandinos Karamanlis (since March 2004).

Economy

Currency: Euro.

GDP: Purchasing power parity—$226.4 billion (2004 est.).

GDP—real growth rate: 3.7% (2004 est.).

GDP—per capita: Purchasing power parity—$21,300 (2004 est.).

Inflation rate: 2.9% (2004 est.).

Unemployment rate: 10% (2004 est.).

Exports: $15.5 billion f.o.b. (2004 est.)—food and beverages, manufactured goods, petroleum products, chemicals, textiles.

Imports: $54.28 billion f.o.b. (2004 est.)—machinery, transport equipment, fuels, chemicals.

External debt: $67.23 billion (2004 est.).

Transport and Communications

Railways: 2,571 km (764 km electrified).

Roads: 117,000 km.

Telephones: 5,205,100 (2003).

Mobile cellular: 8,936,200 (2003).

Internet users: 1,718,400 (2003).

Internet country code: .gr

Grenada

History

The first inhabitants of Grenada were Arawak Indians who were later succeeded by Carib Indians. Although Christopher Columbus arrived in 1498, the Caribs continued to dominate the area for another 150 years. The French seized control in 1672 and held on to power till 1762 when the British arrived on the scene and invaded the territory. In 1833, the black slaves of the country were freed. Between 1885 and 1958, Grenada was the headquarters of the British Windward Islands territory. In 1967, it became a self-governing state in association with UK and finally gained independence in 1974.

Geography

Location: Caribbean, island between the Caribbean Sea and Atlantic Ocean, north of Trinidad and Tobago.

Area: 344 sq. km.

Natural resources: Timber, tropical fruit, deepwater harbours.

Climate: Tropical climate tempered by the north-east trade winds.

People

Population: 89,502 (July 2005 est.).

Population growth rate: 0.19% (2005 est.).

Sex ratio: 1.08 male(s)/female (2004 est.).

Religions: Roman Catholic 53%, Anglican 13.8%, Protestant 33.2%.

Languages: English (official), French patois.

Literacy rate: Total 98%, Male 98%, Female 98% (1970 est.).

Infant mortality rate: 14.62 deaths/1,000 live births (2005 est.).

Life expectancy: Total 64.53 years, Male 62.74 years, Female 66.31 years (2005 est.).

Government

Capital: Saint George's.

Independence: 7 February 1974 (from UK).

Legal system: Based on English common law.

Executive branch:

Chief of state: Queen Elizabeth II (since 6 February 1952), represented by Governor General Daniel Williams (since 9 August 1996).

Head of government: Prime Minister Keith Mitchell (since 22 June 1995).

Economy

Currency: East Caribbean dollar.

GDP: Purchasing power parity—$440 million (2002 est.).

GDP—real growth rate: 2.5% (2002 est.).

GDP—per capita: Purchasing power parity—$5,000 (2002 est.).

Inflation rate: 2.8% (2001 est.).

Population below poverty line: 32% (2000).

Unemployment rate: 12.5% (2000 est.).

Exports: $46 million (2002 est.)—bananas, cocoa, nutmeg, fruit and vegetables, clothing, mace.

Imports: $208 million (2002 est.)—food, manufactures, machinery, chemicals, fuel.

External debt: $196 million (2000).

Transport and Communications

Railways: None.

Roads: 1,040 km.

Telephones: 33,500 (2002).

Mobile cellular: 7,600 (2002).

Internet users: 15,000 (2002).

Internet country code: .gd

Guatemala

History

In ancient times, Guatemala was part of the Mayan civilization. The Spanish conquered the territories in the 1520s. Along with other Central American colonies, Guatemala declared independence from Spain in 1821 and became a part of the Mexican Empire that lasted till 1823. Thereafter, Guatemala became the political centre of the United Provinces of Central America. After the collapse of this union, Guatemala became an independent republic led by successive dictators. In 1960, the country lapsed into a 36-year civil war between the government and leftist forces which resulted in the loss of hundreds of thousands of lives. A peace agreement was finally signed in 1996.

Geography

Location: Middle America, bordering the North Pacific Ocean, between El Salvador and Mexico, and bordering the Gulf of Honduras (Caribbean Sea) between Honduras and Belize.

Area: 108,890 sq. km.

Terrain: Mostly mountainous with a narrow coastal plain and a rolling limestone plateau.

Natural resources: Petroleum, nickel, rare woods, fish, chicle, hydropower.

Climate: Tropical climate. The lowlands are hot and humid while the highlands are cooler.

People

Population: 14,655,189 (July 2005 est.).

Population growth rate: 2.57% (2005 est.).

Sex ratio: 1.03 male(s)/female (2005 est.).

Religions: Roman Catholic, Protestant, indigenous Mayan beliefs.

Languages: Spanish 60%, Amerindian languages 40% (23 officially recognized Amerindian languages, including Quiche, Cakchiquel, Kekchi, Mam, Garifuna and Xinca).

Literacy rate: Total 70.6%, Male 78%, Female 63.3% (2003 est.).

Infant mortality rate: 35.93 deaths/1,000 live births (2005 est.).

Life expectancy: Total 65.14 years, Male 64.27 years, Female 66.04 years (2005 est.).

Government

Capital: Guatemala City.

Government type: Constitutional democratic republic.

Independence: 15 September 1821 (from Spain).

Legal system: Civil law system; judicial review of legislative acts.

Executive branch:
Chief of state: President Oscar Berger (since 2004). The president is both the chief of state and head of government.

Economy

Currency: Quetzal, US dollar, others allowed.

GDP: Purchasing power parity—$59.47 billion (2004 est.).

GDP—real growth rate: 2.6% (2004 est.).

GDP—per capita: Purchasing power parity—$4,200 (2004 est.).

Inflation rate: 7.2% (2004 est.).

Population below poverty line: 75% (2004 est.).

Unemployment rate: 7.5% (2003 est.).

Exports: $2.911 billion f.o.b. (2004 est.)—coffee, sugar, banana, fruits and vegetables, cardamom, meat, apparel, petroleum, electricity.

Imports: $7.77 billion f.o.b. (2004 est.)—fuels, machinery and transport equipment, construction materials, grain, fertilizers, electricity.

External debt: $5.969 billion (2004 est.).

Transport and Communications

Railways: 886 km.

Roads: 14,118 km.

Telephones: 846,000 (2002).

Mobile cellular: 1,577,100 (2002).

Internet users: 400,000 (2002).

Internet country code: .gt

Guinea

History

In the 19th century, France made Guinea a protectorate and then a colony. In October 1958, Guinea became independent.

Geography

Location: Western Africa, bordering the North Atlantic Ocean, between Guinea-Bissau and Sierra Leone.

Area: 245,857 sq. km.

Terrain: Generally flat coastal plain with a hilly interior.

Natural resources: Bauxite, iron ore, diamonds, gold, uranium, hydropower, fish.

Climate: Generally hot and humid climate.

People

Population: 9,246,462 (July 2005 est.).

Population growth rate: 2.37% (2005 est.).

Sex ratio: 1 male(s)/female (2005 est.).

Religions: Muslim 85%, Christian 8%, indigenous beliefs 7%.

Languages: French (official), each ethnic group has its own language.

Literacy rate: Total 35.9%, Male 49.9%, Female 21.9% (1995 est.).

Infant mortality rate: 90.37 deaths/1,000 live births (2005 est.).

Life expectancy: Total 49.86 years, Male 48.61 years, Female 51.15 years (2005 est.).

Government

Capital: Conakry.

Government type: Republic.

Independence: 2 October 1958 (from France).

Legal system: Guinea's legal codes are currently undergoing revision. They are based on French civil law system, customary law, and decree.

Executive branch:
Chief of state: President Lansana Conte (head of military government since 5 April 1984, president since 19 December 1993).

Head of government: Prime Minister Cellou Dalein Diallo (since 4 December 2004).

Economy

Currency: Guinean franc.

GDP: Purchasing power parity—$19.5 billion (2004 est.).

GDP—real growth rate: 1% (2004 est.).

GDP—per capita: Purchasing power parity—$2,100 (2004 est.).

Inflation rate: 18% (2004 est.).

Population below poverty line: 40% (2003 est.).

Exports: $709.2 million f.o.b. (2004 est.)—bauxite, alumina, gold, diamond, coffee, fish, agricultural products.

Imports: $641.5 million f.o.b. (2004 est.)—petroleum products, metals, machinery, transport equipment, textiles, grain and other foodstuff.

External debt: $3.25 billion (2001 est.).

Transport and Communications

Railways: 837 km.

Roads: 30,500 km.

Telephones: 26,200 (2003).

Mobile cellular: 111,500 (2003).

Internet users: 40,000 (2003).

Internet country code: .gn

Guinea-Bissau

History

The area that is today Guinea-Bissau was once the Gabu kingdom, part of a greater Mali Empire. The Portuguese were the first Europeans to arrive, in the 15th century. In 1974, Portugal granted Guinea-Bissau independence with Amilcar Cabral's brother Luis Cabral as President.

Geography

Location: Western Africa, bordering the North Atlantic Ocean, between Guinea and Senegal.

Area: 36,120 sq. km.

Natural resources: Fish, timber, phosphates, bauxite, deposits of petroleum (unexploited).

Climate: Generally hot and humid tropical climate.

People

Population: 1,416,027 (July 2005 est.).

Population growth rate: 1.96% (2005 est.).

Sex ratio: 0.94 male(s)/female (2005 est.).

Religions: Indigenous beliefs 50%, Muslim 45%, Christian 5%.

Languages: Portuguese (official), Crioulo, African languages.

Literacy rate: Total 42.4%, Male 58.1%, Female 27.4% (2003 est.).

Infant mortality rate: 107.17 deaths/1,000 live births (2005 est.).

Life expectancy: Total 46.97 years, Male 45.09 years, Female 48.92 years (2005 est.).

Government

Capital: Bissau.

Government type: Republic.

Independence: 24 September 1973—date of unilateral declaration of independence by Guinea-Bissau.

Executive branch:
Chief of state: Interim President Henrique Rosa (since 28 September 2003).

Head of government: Prime Minister Carlos Gomes Jr (since 2004).

Economy

Currency: Communaute Financiere Africaine franc.

GDP: Purchasing power parity—$1.008 billion (2004 est.).

GDP—real growth rate: 2.6% (2004 est.).

GDP—per capita: Purchasing power parity—$700 (2004 est.).

Inflation rate: 4% (2002 est.).

Exports: $54 million f.o.b. (2002 est.)—cashew nuts, shrimp, peanuts, palm kernels, sawn lumber.

Imports: $104 million f.o.b. (2002 est.)—foodstuff, machinery and transport equipment, petroleum products.

External debt: $941.5 million (2000 est.).

Transport and Communications

Railways: None.

Roads: 4,400 km

Telephones: 10,600 (2003).

Mobile cellular: 1,300 (2003).

Internet users: 19,000 (2003).

Internet country code: .gw

Guyana

History

Christopher Columbus sighted Guyana during one of his voyages in 1498. In the 16th and 17th centuries, the English, the French and the Dutch had all established colonies. In 1831, it was formed into the colony of British Guiana. When slavery was abolished in 1834, a large number of indentured labourers from East Indies were imported to meet the labour shortage. In 1961, UK granted the colony full autonomy. Guyana attained independence in 1966.

Geography

Location: Northern South America, bordering the North Atlantic Ocean, between Surinam and Venezuela.

Area: 214,970 sq. km.

Terrain: Mostly rolling highlands. There is also a low coastal plain and a savanna in the south.

Natural resources: Bauxite, gold, diamonds, hardwood timber, shrimp, fish.

Climate: Hot and humid tropical climate moderated by north-east trade winds.

People

Population: 765,283 (July 2005 est.).

Population growth rate: 0.26% (2005 est.).

Sex ratio: 1.01 male(s)/female (2005 est.).

Religions: Christian 50%, Hindu 35%, Muslim 10%, others 5%.

Languages: English, Amerindian dialects, Creole, Hindi, Urdu.

Literacy rate: Total 98.8%, Male 99.1%, Female 98.5% (2003 est.).

Infant mortality rate: 33.26 deaths/ 1,000 live births (2005 est.).

Life expectancy: Total 65.5 years, Male 62.86 years, Female 68.28 years (2005 est.).

Government

Capital: Georgetown.

Government type: Republic within the Commonwealth.

Independence: 26 May 1966 (from UK).

Legal system: Based on English common law with certain admixtures of Roman–Dutch law.

Executive branch:
Chief of state: President Bharrat Jagdeo (since 11 August 1999).

Head of government: Prime Minister Samuel Hinds (since December 1997).

Economy

Currency: Guyanese dollar.

GDP: Purchasing power parity—$2.899 billion (2004 est.).

GDP—real growth rate: 1.9% (2004 est.).

GDP—per capita: Purchasing power parity—$3,800 (2004 est.).

Inflation rate: 4.5% (2004 est.).

Unemployment rate: 9.1% (2000).

Exports: $570.2 million f.o.b. (2004 est.)—sugar, gold, bauxite, rice, shrimp, molasses, rum, timber.

Imports: $650.1 million c.i.f. (2004 est.)—manufactures, machinery, petroleum, food.

External debt: $1.2 billion (2004 est.).

Transport and Communications

Railways: 187 km (entirely dedicated to ore transport).

Roads: 7,970 km.

Telephones: 80,400 (2002).

Mobile cellular: 87,300 (2002).

Internet users: 125,000 (2002).

Internet country code: .gy

Haiti

History

Arawak Indians were the original inhabitants of the island on which Haiti lies.

In 1492, Christopher Columbus landed on the island and named it Hispaniola, or Little Spain. In 1697, Spain ceded the western part of Hispaniola to

France, and this became the colony of Saint-Dominique. In 1791, the 480,000-strong slave population of the colony rose in rebellion against the colonial rulers. This resulted in the declaration of independence by Pierre-Dominique Toussant l'Ouverture, the leader of the slave uprising. Ultimately in 1804, the colony gained independence as Haiti, under its new leader, Jean-Jacques Dessalines.

After a succession of regimes and rulers, a physician named François Duvalier (or 'Papa Doc' Duvalier) became the President in September 1957. He promised political and economic power to the black masses. Violence, a shrinking economy, international isolation, vanishing US aid and continuing tension with Dominican Republic marked his regime. In July 1958, there was an unsuccessful attempt to overthrow Duvalier. This prompted him to set up a paramilitary group. This was the infamous Tontons Macoutes that terrorized the Haitian population during Duvalier's regime and effectively turned the country into a police state. In 1964 Duvalier engineered his election as 'President for life'.

In 1971, Duvalier passed away and was succeeded by his 19-year-old son, Jean-Claude Duvalier, or 'Baby Doc' who also declared himself President-for-life. His reign lasted till 1986 when he fled the country under mounting discontent.

In 1990, the former priest Jean-Bertrand Aristide was elected the President of Haiti. In 1991, a coup led by Brigadier-General Raoul Cedras ousted Aristide and led to sanctions by the US. In 1995, Aristide supporters won parliamentary elections and Rene Preval was installed as the new President of Haiti. Aristide returned as the President of Haiti in 2000. In 2004, Arisitide went into exile after an uprising against his regime intensified and rebel forces took one town after another and even reached the capital, Port-au-Prince.

Boniface Alexandre, the Supreme Court chief justice became the interim President.

Geography

Location: Caribbean, western one-third of the island of Hispaniola, between the Caribbean Sea and the North Atlantic Ocean, west of the Dominican Republic.

Area: 27,750 sq. km.

Natural resources: Bauxite, copper, calcium carbonate, gold, marble, hydropower.

Climate: Haiti has a tropical climate but is semi-arid in the part where mountains in the east cut off trade winds.

People

Population: 8,121,622 (July 2005 est.).

Population growth rate: 2.26% (2005 est.).

Sex ratio: 0.97 male(s)/female (2005 est.).

Religions: Roman Catholic 80%, Protestant 16% (Baptist 10%, Pentecostal 4%, Adventist 1%, others 1%), none 1%, others 3% (1982). Roughly half of the population also practises Voodoo.

Languages: French (official), Creole (official).

Literacy rate: Total 52.9%, Male 54.8%, Female 51.2% (2003 est.).

Infant mortality rate: 73.45 deaths/1,000 live births (2005 est.).

Life expectancy: Total 52.92 years, Male 54.8 years, Female 51.2 years (2005 est.).

Government

Capital: Port-au-Prince.

Government type: Elected government.

Independence: 1 January 1804 (from France).

Legal system: Based on Roman civil law system.

Executive branch:
Chief of state: Interim President Boniface Alexandre (since February 2004).

Head of government: Interim Prime Minister Gerard Latortue (since March 2004).

Economy

Currency: Gourde.

GDP: Purchasing power parity—$12.05 billion (2004 est.).

GDP—real growth rate: –3.5% (2004 est.).

GDP—per capita: Purchasing power parity—$1,500 (2004 est.).

Inflation rate: 22% (2004 est.).

Population below poverty line: 80% (2002 est.).

Unemployment rate: Widespread unemployment and underemployment.

Exports: $338.1 million f.o.b. (2004 est.)—manufactures, coffee, oils, cocoa.

Imports: $1.085 billion c.i.f. (2004 est.)—food, manufactured goods, machinery and transport equipment, fuels, raw materials.

External debt: $1.2 billion (2004 est.).

Transport and Communications

Railways: 40 km.

Roads: 4,160 km.

Telephones: 130,000 (2002).

Mobile cellular: 180,000 (2003).

Internet users: 80,000 (2002).

Internet country code: .ht

Honduras

History

In 1502, Christopher Columbus explored Honduras. It became a Spanish colony, although British elements briefly controlled the Mosquito Coast region. Honduras declared its independence from Spain in 1821.

Geography

Location: Middle America, bordering the Caribbean Sea, between Guatemala and Nicaragua.

Area: 112,090 sq. km.

Terrain: Mostly mountainous in the interior with narrow coastal plains.

Natural resources: Timber, gold, silver, copper, lead, zinc, iron ore, antimony, coal, fish, hydropower.

Climate: Subtropical in lowlands but temperate in the mountainous region.

People

Population: 6,975,204 (July 2005 est.).

Population growth rate: 2.16% (2005 est.).

Sex ratio: 1.01 male(s)/female (2005 est.).

Religions: Roman Catholic 97%, Protestant minority.

Languages: Spanish, Amerindian dialects.

Literacy rate: Total 76.2%, Male 76.1%, Female 76.3% (2003 est.).

Infant mortality rate: 29.32 deaths/1,000 live births (2005 est.).

Life expectancy: Total 65.6 years, Male 64.66 years, Female 66.59 years (2005 est.).

Government

Capital: Tegucigalpa.

Government type: Democratic constitutional republic.

Independence: 15 September 1821 (from Spain).

Legal system: Has its origins in Roman and Spanish civil law with increasing influence of English common law; recent judicial reforms have included the replacement of Napoleonic legal codes with the oral adversarial system.

Executive branch:
Chief of state: President Ricardo (Joest) Maduro (since 27 January 2002); First Vice-President Vicente Williams Agasse (since 27 January 2002). The president is both the chief of state and head of government.

Economy

Currency: Lempira.

GDP: Purchasing power parity—$18.79 billion (2004 est.).

GDP—real growth rate: 4.2% (2004 est.).

GDP—per capita: Purchasing power parity—$2,800 (2004 est.).

Inflation rate: 7.7% (2002 est.).

Population below poverty line: 53% (1993 est.).

Unemplyment rate: 28.5% (2004 est.).

Exports: $1.457 billion f.o.b. (2004 est.)—coffee, banana, shrimp, lobster, meat, zinc, lumber (2000).

Imports: $3.332 billion f.o.b. (2004 est.)—machinery and transport equipment, industrial raw materials, chemical products, fuels, foodstuff (2000).

External debt: $5.365 billion (2004 est.).

Transport and Communications

Railways: 699 km.

Roads: 13,603 km.

Telephones: 322,500 (2002).

Mobile cellular: 326,500 (2002).

Internet users: 168,600 (2002).

Internet country code: .hn

Hungary

History

The area that is today Hungary was once a part of the Roman Empire. The Magyars conquered all of Hungary in 896 and set up a kingdom. In 1241, a Mongol invasion wiped out almost half of the country's population. During the rule of Louis I the Great (1342–82), the Hungarian Empire reached the Baltic, the Black and the Mediterranean Seas. In 1389, war broke out between Hungary and the Turks. In the 16th century, Hungary accepted Hapsburg rule to avoid Turk subjugation. The dual monarchy of Austria–Hungary was formed in 1867.

During World War II, Hungary allied with Germany and took part in the 1941 German invasion of Russia. In 1945, Soviet forces drove the Germans out of Hungary. In 1946, the Parliament abolished the monarchy and set up a republic. The communists seized control in 1948. The country was turned into a one-party state, modelled on the Soviet Union.

In 1989, Hungarian communists in power voluntarily dismantled the one-party state and turned the country into a multiparty state. In 1999, Hungary joined NATO and in 2004, it became a member state of the EU.

Geography

Location: Central Europe, north-west of Romania.

Area: 93,030 sq. km.

Terrain: Mostly flat to rolling plains. There are hills and low mountains on the border with Slovakia.

Natural resources: Bauxite, coal, natural gas, fertile soils, arable land.

Climate: Temperate climate with cold, cloudy and humid winters and warm summers.

People

Population: 10,006,835 (July 2005 est.).

Population growth rate: −0.26% (2005 est.).

Sex ratio: 0.91 male(s)/female (2005 est.).

Religions: Roman Catholic 67.5%, Calvinist 20%, Lutheran 5%, atheist and others 7.5%.

Languages: Hungarian 98.2%, others 1.8%.

Literacy rate: Total 99.4%, Male 99.5%, Female 99.3% (2003 est.).

Infant mortality rate: 8.57 deaths/1,000 live births (2005 est.).

Life expectancy: Total 72.4 years, Male 68.18 years, Female 76.89 years (2005 est.).

Government

Capital: Budapest.

Government type: Parliamentary democracy.

Independence: 1001 (date of unification by King Stephen I).

Legal system: Rule of law based on Western model.

Executive branch:
Chief of state: President Ferenc Madl (since 4 August 2000).

Head of government: Prime Minister Fernec Gyurcsany (since 29 September 2004).

Economy

Currency: Forint.

Economy—overview:
Since the fall of communism, the Hungarian economy has been transformed from a centrally planned to a market economy. The country has recorded strong economic growth in recent years with the private sector accounting for more than 80% of GDP. In 2000, Hungarian sovereign debt was upgraded to the second-highest rating among all the central European economies making the transition to market economies.

GDP: Purchasing power parity—$149.3 billion (2004 est.).

GDP—real growth rate: 3.9% (2004 est.).

GDP—per capita: Purchasing power parity—$14,900 (2004 est.).

Inflation rate: 7% (2004 est.).

Population below poverty line: 8.6% (1993 est.).

Unemployment rate: 5.9% (2004 est.).

Exports: $54.62 billion f.o.b. (2004 est.)—machinery and equipment, other manufactures, food products, raw materials, fuels and electricity (2001).

Imports: $58.68 billion f.o.b. (2004 est.)—machinery and equipment 51.6%, other manufactures 35.3%, fuels and electricity 8.2%, food products 2.9%, raw materials 2.0% (2001).

External debt: $57 billion (2004 est.).

Transport and Communications

Railways: 7,937 km.

Roads: 159,568 km.

Telephones: 3,666,400 (2002).

Mobile cellular: 6,862,800 (2002).

Internet users: 1.6 million (2002).

Internet country code: .hu

Iceland

History

The first human settlers of the island of Iceland were Irish monks who left when the first Norse people arrived in the ninth century. In 930, a constitution was drawn up and a form of democratic system was initiated. Iceland was the world's oldest democracy and had the world's oldest functioning legislative assembly, the Althing, set up in 930. In 1000, Iceland adopted Christianity. During 1262–4, Iceland came under Norwegian rule and recognized the King of Norway as their monarch. Later on, it came under Danish control through the Kalmar union of 1397 that brought the kingdoms of Norway, Sweden, and Denmark together under a single monarch. This union lasted until 1523.

During 1402–4 and again between 1494–5, Iceland was hit by plague epidemics that wiped out half the population each time. In 1602, Denmark assumed a monopoly on all Icelandic trade. This monopoly remained in force for the next 200 years.

In 1904, Iceland attained home rule. In 1918, Iceland achieved full self-government under the Danish crown, with Denmark retaining control only over foreign affairs. In 1944, following a referendum, the Republic of Iceland was proclaimed on 17 June.

Geography

Location: Northern Europe, island between the Greenland Sea and the North Atlantic Ocean, north-west of the British Isles.

Area: 103,000 sq. km.

Terrain: Consists mostly of a plateau along with scattered mountain peaks and ice hills. The coast is deeply broken by bays and fjords.

Natural resources: Fish, hydropower, geothermal power, diatomite .

Climate: Temperate climate that is moderated by the North Atlantic Current. The country has mild, windy winters and damp, cool summers.

People

Population: 296,737 (July 2005 est.).

Population growth rate: 0.91% (2005 est.).

Sex ratio: 1 male(s)/female (2005 est.).

Religions: Evangelical Lutheran 87.1%, other Protestant 4.1%, Roman Catholic 1.7%, others 7.1% (2002).

Languages: Icelandic, English, Nordic languages, German is widely spoken.

Literacy rate: 99.9% (1997 est.).

Infant mortality rate: 3.31 deaths/1,000 live births (2005 est.).

Life expectancy: Total 80.19 years, Male 78.13 years, Female 82.34 years (2005 est.).

Government

Capital: Reykjavik.

Government type: Constitutional republic.

Independence: 17 June 1944 (from Denmark).

Legal system: Civil law system based on Danish law.

Executive branch:
Chief of state: President Olafur Ragnar Grimsson (since 1 August 1996).

Head of government: Prime Minister Halldor Asgrimsson (since 15 September 2004).

Economy

Currency: Icelandic krona.

GDP: Purchasing power parity—$9.373 billion (2004 est.).

GDP—real growth rate: 1.8% (2004 est.).

GDP—per capita: Purchasing power parity—$31,900 (2004 est.).

Inflation rate: 4% (2004 est.).

Unemployment rate: 3.1% (2004 est.).

Exports: $2.902 billion f.o.b. (2004 est.)—fish and fish products 70%, animal products, aluminum, diatomite, ferrosilicon.

Imports: $3.307 billion (2004 est.)—machinery and equipment, petroleum products; foodstuff, textiles.

External debt: $3.073 billion (2002).

Transport and Communications

Railways: None.

Roads: 13,004 km.

Telephones: 190,700 (2003).

Mobile cellular: 279,100 (2003).

Internet users: 195,000 (2003).

Internet country code: .is

India

History

The history of India is the story of a civilization that despite much internal strife and frequent invasions has retained its identity for five thousand years. The first known permanent settlements appeared 9,000 years ago and developed into the Indus Valley Civilization, which peaked between 2600 BC and 1900 BC.

After the gradual decline of the Indus Valley Civilization, the Vedic Civilization followed. The earliest literary source that sheds light on India's past is the Rig Veda, composed between 1,500 BC and 1,000 BC. Though warriors and conquerors, the Aryans lived alongside Indus, introducing them to the caste system and establishing the basis of the Indian religions. The Aryans inhabited the northern regions for about 700 years, and then moved further south and east when they developed iron tools and weapons. They eventually settled in the Ganges valley and built large kingdoms throughout much of northern India.

In the 6th Century BC the kingdom of Magadha—one of the 16 Mahajanapadas—had established paramountcy over other kingdoms of the Ganges valley. This was the time when Buddhism and Jainism emerged as popular movements to pose a serious challenge to Brahmanic orthodoxy.

Alexander the Great's invasion took place between 327 BC and 325 BC. Soon after Alexander's invasion, Chandragupta founded the Maurya Empire. Under the Mauryan king Asoka, this empire extended all over India except the extreme south. Asoka contributed greatly to India's cultural landscape. The empire began to disintegrate under weak successors. Pushyamitra Shunga, a Brahmin general usurped the throne after slaying the last Maurya king and presided over a loosely federal polity.

From 180 BC, a series of invasions from Central Asia followed, with the successive establishment in the northern Indian subcontinent of the Indo-Greek, Indo-Scythian and Indo-Parthian kingdoms, and finally the Kushan Empire. From the 3rd century onwards the Gupta dynasty oversaw the period referred to as India's 'Golden Age'. The rule of Harshavardhana from 606 to 647 AD was the only consolidated rule in India after the Guptas in the first millennium AD. The dominions of Harsha disintegrated into a multiplicity of warring petty states and principalities following his death. This anarchic state of affairs prevailed throughout India until the beginning of the 11th century.

In the south, several dynasties including the Chalukyas, Cheras, Cholas, Pallavas, and Pandyas prevailed during different periods. Science, art, literature, mathematics, astronomy, engineering, religion and philosophy flourished under the patronage of these kings.

The first Muslim victories in Indian territory had taken place in the 7th century, but it was not until the 11th century that the full-scale Islamic invasion began, headed by Mahmud of Ghazni. The Mongol invasion of Genghis Khan followed in 1219 and in 1397 Timur Lang's hordes poured in.

The Slave dynasty served as the first Sultans of Delhi in India from 1206 to 1290. From 1290 to 1526 the rule of the Khalji, Tughlaq, Sayyid and Lodi dynasties of the Delhi Sultanate followed. In 1526 the Mughal Empire was established by Babur, under which India once again achieved a large measure of political unity. Akbar was the greatest sovereign of the Mughal Empire. The Mughal Empire attained its peak of cultural splendour under the rule of Shah Jahan. His reign (1628–58) coincided with the golden age of Indian Saracenic architecture, best exemplified by the Taj Mahal. Shah Jahan was driven from the throne in 1658 by his son Aurangzeb. In the half century following the death of Aurangzeb, the Mughal Empire ceased to exist as an effective state. From the 11th to the 15th centuries, southern India was dominated by Hindu Chola and Vijayanagar dynasties.

Meanwhile from the 15th century onwards the struggle between European powers for dominance in Indian affairs had begun. With Vasco da Gama's discovery of the ocean route around Cape of Good Hope, Portugal, Holland and France began a race for the rich Indian and Spice Islands trade. England, France, the Netherlands and Denmark floated East India Companies. During the late 16th and 17th centuries, these companies competed with each other fiercely.

By the last quarter of the 18th century the English had vanquished all others and established themselves as the dominant power in India. The military campaigns of Robert Clive and the administrative enterprise of Warren Hastings (1772–1785) contributed significantly to this achievement. Once the British had consolidated their power through annexation of territories, commercial exploitation of the natural resources and native labour became ruthless. Bitterness at the annexations and confiscations, together with religious and racial hatred and resentment at the rapid westernizing policies of the white rulers, caused discontent and riots. Having crushed the rebellion of 1857 popularly known as the Sepoy Mutiny, the East India Company finally ceded its control over India to the British Crown in 1858.

By the end of the 19th century the first nationalist aspirations of India had begun to be revealed, expressing themselves in riots and rebellions fermented by the Congress party, which was founded in 1885. In the late 19th century the first steps were taken towards self-government in British India with the appointment of Indian councilors to advise the British viceroy and the establishment of provincial councils with Indian members.

Discontent with British rule became intense during the early 20th century. The British instituted a programme of power sharing, but Congress leaders like Motilal Nehru and Sarojini Naidu in the 1920s and Subhash Chandra Bose, Vallabhbhai Patel and Jawaharlal Nehru in the 1930s saw these reforms as instruments for continuing British control indefinitely. They organized movements of non-co-operation and civil disobedience from 1920 onwards. The government tried to suppress these mass movements brutally. A violent example was the Jallianwallah Bagh massacre of 1919.

A prolonged struggle for independence, the Indian independence movement, followed, led by Mahatma Gandhi, regarded officially as the father of modern India. The culmination of this path-breaking struggle was reached on 15 August1947 when India gained full independence from British rule, later becoming a republic on 26 January 1950. British India was divided into two independent nations; India with Nehru as prime minister and Pakistan with Muhammad Ali Jinnah as governor-general.

Nehru governed India until his death in 1964. Indira Gandhi was the prime minister from 1966 to 1977 and again from1980 to 1984. In 1975, beset with deepening political and economic problems, Mrs Gandhi declared a state of emergency and suspended many civil liberties. On 31 October 1984, Mrs Gandhi was assassinated and her son Rajiv Gandhi was chosen by the Congress (I) to take her place.

India's unresolved border disputes escalated into a brief war with China in 1962, and with Pakistan in 1947, 1965, and 1971, and a border altercation in the state of Kashmir (the Kargil conflict) in 1999. In 1998, India became one of the handful of countries in the world to attain full nuclear capability.

Significant economic reforms beginning in 1991 initiated by the present prime minister Dr Manmohan Singh, have transformed India into one of the fastest growing economies in the world.

Geography

Location: Southern Asia, bordering the Arabian Sea and the Bay of Bengal, between Myanmar and Pakistan.

Area: 3,300,000 sq. km.

Terrain: The terrain of India consists of the Himalayas in the north, the Deccan Plateau in the central and southern parts, the Gangetic plains, the coastal plains along the east and west coast, the mountains of the Eastern and Western Ghats, and the Thar desert in the west.

Natural resources: Coal, iron ore, manganese, mica, bauxite, titanium ore, chromite, natural gas, diamonds, petroleum, limestone, arable land.

Climate: India has a tropical climate with relatively high temperatures and dry winters. The Himalayas function as a meteorological barrier for the country. The monsoons play a very important role in the Indian climate.

People

Population: Total: 1,028,610,328 (2001 census); Scheduled Caste: 166,635,700; Scheduled Tribe: 84,326,240.

Population growth rate: 21.34% (decadal growth rate 1991–2001); 1.93% (average annual exponential growth rate).

Population density: 324 persons per sq km (2001 census).

Sex ratio: 1.07 male(s)/female (2001 census).

Ethnic groups: Indo-Aryan, Dravidian, Mongoloid, others.

Religions: Hindu, Muslim, Christian, Sikh, Buddhist, Jain, Parsi.

Languages: 18 languages recognized by the Indian Constitution. These are: Assamese, Bengali, Gujarati, Hindi, Kannada, Kashmiri, Konkani, Malayalam, Manipuri, Marathi, Nepali, Oriya, Punjabi, Sanskrit, Sindhi, Tamil, Telugu, Urdu. Hindi is the official language and the main link language.

Literacy rate: Total: 64.8%, Male: 75.3%, Female: 53.7% (2000 est.).

Infant mortality rate: 68 deaths/1000 live births (2000 est.).

Life expectancy: Total: 62.5 years, Male: 62.36 years, Female: 63.39 years (2000 est.).

Government

Capital: New Delhi.

Government type: Federal republic.

Independence: 15 August 1947 (from UK).

Administrative divisions: 28 states, 6 union territories* and 1 National Capital Territory (NCT) **.

1. Andaman and Nicobar Islands*
2. Andhra Pradesh
3. Arunachal Pradesh
4. Assam
5. Bihar
6. Chandigarh*
7. Chhattisgarh
8. Dadra and Nagar Haveli*
9. Daman and Diu*
10. Delhi**
11. Goa
12. Gujarat
13. Haryana
14. Himachal Pradesh
15. Jammu and Kashmir
16. Jharkhand
17. Karnataka
18. Kerala
19. Lakshadweep*
20. Madhya Pradesh
21. Maharashtra
22. Manipur
23. Meghalaya
24. Mizoram
25. Nagaland
26. Orissa
27. Pondicherry*
28. Punjab
29. Rajasthan
30. Sikkim
31. Tamil Nadu
32. Tripura
33. Uttaranchal
34. Uttar Pradesh
35. West Bengal

Constitution: 26 January 1950.

Legal system: Based on English common law with limited judicial review of legislative acts.

Executive branch:
Chief of state: President Dr Avul Pakir Jainulabdeen Abdul Kalam (since 25 July 2002). Vice President Bhairon Singh Sekhawat (since 16 August 2002).

Head of government: Prime Minister Dr Manmohan Singh (since 22 May 2004).

Legislative branch: India has a bicameral Parliament or Sansad that consists of the Council of States or Rajya Sabha and the People's Assembly or Lok Sabha. The Rajya Sabha consists of not more than 250 members. The number of members elected by each state is roughly in proportion to their population. At present, there are 233 members of the Rajya Sabha who have been elected by the Vidhan Sabhas. Besides these, there are 12 members nominated by the President as representatives of literature, science, art and social services. Rajya Sabha members serve for six years. The elections are held in a staggered manner with one third of the assembly being elected every 2 years. The Lok Sabha has 545 seats of which 543 are elected by popular vote and 2 appointed by the President. All members serve five-year terms.

Election and election results: Elections to the Lok Sabha were last held in May 2004. A United Progressive Alliance (UPA) government, headed by the Congress and including left parties, came to power, winning 278 seats.

Judicial branch: Supreme Court (the President appoints the judges and they remain in office until they reach the age of 65).

Economy

Currency: Rupee.

GDP—purchasing power parity: $3.022 trillion (2003 est.).

GDP—real growth rate: 7.6% (2003 est.).

GDP—per capita purchasing power parity: $2,900 (2003 est.).

Inflation rate (consumer prices): 4.6% (2003 est.).

Population below poverty line: 25% (2002 est.).

Unemployment rate: 9.1% (2003).

Exports: $57.24 billion f.o.b. (2003 est.)—Textile goods, gems and jewelry, engineering goods, chemicals, leather manufactures.

Imports: $74.15 billion f.o.b. (2003 est.)—Crude oil, machinery, gems, fertilizer, chemicals.

External debt: $95.3 billion (2003 est.).

Transportation and Communication

Railways: 108,706 km.

Roads: 3,300,000 km. (National Highways: 52,010 km.)

Telephones: 34,732,000 (2001 est.).

Mobile cellular: 5,725,000 (2001 est.).

Internet users: 7,000,000 (2001 est.).

Internet country code: in

Indonesia

History

In the first and second centuries AD, the islands of Indonesia came under Hindu influence. Muslims arrived in the 13th century. The Portuguese reached the islands in the 16th century but the Dutch drove them out by 1595. The latter established ports in Java with the objective of controlling the region's spice trade. The British took possession of the islands following Dutch defeat at the hands of the French in 1811 but returned them to the Dutch in 1816.

In 1922, Indonesia became an integral part of the Netherlands, as Dutch East Indies.

During World War II, Japan occupied Indonesia with the aim of gaining control over its petroleum resources. When the war ended, Indonesia declared its independence under nationalist leaders like Sukarno and Mohammed Hatta.

In September 1965, Sukarno was implicated in a coup in which six top Army generals were abducted, tortured and killed. On 11 March 1966, Sukarno handed over emergency powers to

General Suharto. He later became President of Indonesia.

In 1997, Indonesia was one of the worst hit in the Asian Economic Crisis. The economic downturn soon turned into a political crisis when anti-government protests and riots flared up across Indonesia. It ultimately forced Suharto to step down and hand over power to his vice-president Bacharuddin Jusuf Habibie.

In 1999, the first ever free parliamentary elections were held in Indonesia. Abdurrahman Wahid, also called Gus Dur, became the new Indonesian President, in a stunning upset, defeating the popular Megawati Sukarnoputri, daughter of Sukarno. In the same year ethnic violence broke out in Maluku and other parts of Indonesia, while the province of East Timor voted for independence in a UN-sponsored referendum. This resulted in brutal violence unleashed by pro-Indonesian militia. In July 2001, the Indonesian Parliament removed Wahid and appointed Megawati Sukarnoputri as the new President. In October 2004, Susilo B. Yudhoyouo became the new President after elections.

Geography

Location: South-eastern Asia, archipelago between the Indian Ocean and the Pacific Ocean.

Area: 1,919,440 sq. km.

Terrain: The islands of Indonesia consists mostly of coastal lowlands but the larger islands have mountains in the interiors.

Natural resources: Petroleum, tin, natural gas, nickel, timber, bauxite, copper, fertile soils, coal, gold, silver.

Climate: Hot and humid tropical climate which is more moderate in the highlands.

People

Population: 241,973,879 (July 2005 est.).

Population growth rate: 1.45% (2005 est.).

Sex ratio: 1 male(s)/female (2005 est.).

Religions: Muslim 88%, Protestant 5%, Roman Catholic 3%, Hindu 2%, Buddhist 1%, others 1% (1998).

Languages: Bahasa Indonesia (official), English, Dutch, local dialects (most widely spoken is Javanese).

Literacy rate: Total 88.5%, Male 92.9%, Female 84.1% (2003 est.).

Infant mortality rate: 35.06 deaths/ 1,000 live births (2005 est.).

Life expectancy: Total 69.57 years, Male 67.13 years, Female 72.13 years (2005 est.).

Government

Capital: Jakarta.

Government type: Republic.

Independence: 17 August 1945 (date of proclamation of independence); 27 December 1949 (date on which Indonesia became legally independent from the Netherlands).

Legal system: Based on Roman–Dutch law, modified by indigenous concepts and by new criminal procedure codes.

Executive branch:
Chief of state: President Susilo B. Yudhoyono (since 20 October 2004). The president is both the chief of state and head of government.

Economy

Currency: Indonesian rupiah.

Economy—overview:
Indonesia suffers from a multitude of internal problems that pose serious hurdles to economic development in the country. Internal reform and adoption of measures to boost investor confidence are two of the measures that would be beneficial to the economy.

GDP: Purchasing power parity—$827.4 billion (2004 est.).

GDP—real growth rate: 4.9% (2004 est.).

GDP—per capita: Purchasing power parity—$3,500 (2004 est.).

Inflation rate: 6.1% (2004 est.).

Population below poverty line: 27% (1999).

Unemployment rate: 9.2% (2004 est.).

Exports: $69.86 billion f.o.b. (2004 est.)—oil and gas, electrical appliances, plywood, textiles, rubber.

Imports: $45.07 billion f.o.b. (2004 est.)—machinery and equipment; chemicals, fuels, foodstuff.

External debt: $141.5 billion (2004 est.).

Transport and Communications

Railways: 6,458 km.

Roads: 342,700 km.

Telephones: 7,750,000 (2002).

Mobile cellular: 11,700,000 (2002).

Internet users: 4.4 million (2002).

Internet country code: .id

Iran

History

The Medes and Persians held sway over the region that we today call Iran till about 500 BC. The Persian ruler Cyrus the Great overthrew the Medes and began ruling as the head of the Persian or Achaemenid Empire. In around 331 BC, Alexander the Great took Persia. Thereafter, a succession of powers controlled Persia at different points of time. The Mongols invaded the area in the 12th century and the Safavid dynasty ruled from the 16th to the 18th century. It was during the reign of the Safavids that Shiite Islam became the dominant religion. After the Safavids came the Qajar dynasty. They ruled from 1794 to 1925.

In late February 1921, the military commander Reza Khan seized power. In 1925 the Iranian Parliament deposed the monarch, who was away undergoing prolonged treatment in Europe. The Parliament elected Reza Khan as the Shah of Persia. He founded the Pahlavi dynasty and assumed the name of Reza Shah Pahlavi. In 1935, Persia changed its name to Iran.

In 1941 the Soviet Union and Great Britain occupied Iran, apprehensive of the pro-German tendencies of the Shah. Mohammad Reza Shah Pahlavi replaced his father as the Shah of Iran on 16 September 1941. In the 1960s, the Shah initiated a campaign of modernization and westernization of Iran and launched the 'White Revolution'. However, his authoritarian rule sparked off widespread civil unrest in the late 1970s. In January 1979, the Shah, along with his family, were exiled out of Iran. In February that year, the Islamic fundamentalist leader, Ayatollah Ruhollah Khomeini, returned to Iran at the end of 14 years of exile. On 1 April 1979, the Islamic Republic of Iran was proclaimed following a referendum.

On 4 November 1979, revolutionaries forced their way into the US embassy in Tehran and took 52 Americans as hostage. USA retaliated by imposing an economic boycott, severing diplomatic relations and ordering the deportation of Iranian students studying in USA.

On 22 September 1980, Iraq invaded Iran in a culmination of a dispute over

Iranian oilfields. This was the start of the Iran–Iraq War. In August 1988 Iran accepted a UN-mediated ceasefire that it had previously rejected.

In May 1997, reformist politician Mohammad Khatami won the presidential election by a landslide, beating the dominant conservatives. In July 1999, pro-democracy students at Tehran University held a mass demonstration. Conservatives and hardliners regained control of the Iranian Parliament in legislative elections held in February and May 2004.

Geography

Location: Middle East, bordering the Gulf of Oman, the Persian Gulf, and the Caspian Sea, between Iraq and Pakistan.

Area: 1.648 million sq. km.

Terrain: Rugged terrain with a mountainous rim, high central basin with deserts and mountains. The coasts have small, discontinuous plains.

Natural resources: Petroleum, natural gas, coal, chromium, copper, iron ore, lead, manganese, zinc, sulphur.

Climate: Mostly arid or semi-arid but the Caspian coast has subtropical climate.

People

Population: 68,017,860 (July 2005 est.).

Population growth rate: 0.86% (2005 est.).

Sex ratio: 1.04 male(s)/female (2005 est.).

Religions: Shi'a Muslim 89%, Sunni Muslim 10%, Zoroastrian, Jewish, Christian, and Baha'i 1%.

Languages: Persian and Persian dialects 58%, Turkic and Turkic dialects 26%, Kurdish 9%, Luri 2%, Balochi 1%, Arabic 1%, Turkish 1%, others 2%.

Literacy rate: Total 79.4%, Male 85.6%, Female 73% (2003 est.).

Infant mortality rate: 41.58 deaths/1,000 live births (2005 est.).

Life expectancy: Total 69.96 years, Male 68.58 years, Female 71.4 years (2005 est.).

Government

Capital: Tehran.

Government type: Theocratic republic.

Independence: 1 April 1979 (proclamation of Islamic Republic of Iran).

Legal system: The constitution codifies Islamic principles of government.

Executive branch:
Chief of state: Supreme Leader Ayatollah Ali Hoseini-Khamenei (since 4 June 1989).

Head of government: President (Ali) Mohammad Khatami-Ardakani (since 3 August 1997); First Vice-President Dr Mohammad Reza Aref-Yazdi (since 26 August 2001).

Economy

Currency: Iranian rial.

Economy—overview:
Iran has a centrally planned economy with the state owning oil and other large enterprises. Although President Khatami has continued with the market reform measures started by his predecessor, Akbar Hashemi Rafsanjani, and also announced plans to diversify Iran's oil-reliant economy, his own political future is in serious doubt following the heavy defeat suffered by the reformist alliance at the 2004 parliamentary elections.

GDP: Purchasing power parity—$516.7 billion (2004 est.).

GDP—real growth rate: 6.3% (2004 est.).

GDP—per capita: Purchasing power parity—$7,700 (2004 est.).

Inflation rate: 15.5% (2004 est.).

Population below poverty line: 40% (2002 est.).

Unemployment rate: 11.2% (2004 est.).

Exports: $38.79 billion f.o.b. (2004 est.)—petroleum 85%, carpets, fruits and nuts, iron and steel, chemicals.

Imports: $31.3 billion f.o.b. (2004 est.)—industrial raw materials and intermediate goods, capital goods, foodstuff and other consumer goods, technical services, military supplies.

External debt: $13.4 billion (2004 est.).

Transport and Communications

Railways: 7,203 km.

Roads: 167,157 km.

Telephones: 14,571,100 (2003).

Mobile cellular: 3,376,500 (2003).

Internet users: 1.326 million (2002 est.).

Internet country code: .ir

Iraq

History

In ancient times, the area that is today Iraq was called Mesopotamia, the 'land between the rivers'. This was due to its location between the Tigris and the Euphrates rivers. Mesopotamia was home to one of the first advanced civilizations on the face of the Earth. After 2000 BC, the area became the home of the Babylonian and Assyrian Empires. Cyrus the Great of Persia conquered Mesopotamia in 538 BC while Alexander the Great claimed Mesopotamia in 331 BC. The Arabs conquered the country between AD 637–40 and set up the capital of the caliphate in Baghdad. Mongols plundered the country with much brutality in 1258. In the 16th, 17th and 18th centuries, the country became the subject of Turkish–Persian rivalry. Turkish suzerainty imposed in 1638 gave way to direct Turkish rule in 1831.

The UK occupied most parts of Mesopotamia during World War I and received a mandate for the country in 1920. The UK renamed the country Mesopotamia and in 1922 recognized a kingdom that was formed under Faysal, son of the Sharif of Mecca, who was crowned Iraq's first king in August 1921.

In October 1932, Iraq gained independence. However, the UK occupied the country once again during World War II. On 14 July 1958, a military coup deposed the monarchy and declared a republic with Abd-al-Karim Qasim as the prime minister.

In 1972, Iraq and the Soviet Union signed a 15-year Treaty of Friendship and Cooperation. The same year, the Iraqi government nationalized the Iraq Petroleum Company. In 1979, Saddam Hussein took over as the new President.

The Iran–Iraq war started on 4 September 1980 when Iran started shelling Iraqi border towns. On 22 September 1980, Iraq invaded Iran in a dispute over possessing the Iranian oilfields. In August 1988 Iran accepted a UN-mediated ceasefire that it had previously rejected.

On 2 August 1990, Iraq invaded Kuwait. This attracted UN condemnation. The United Nations Security Council (UNSC) Resolution 660 called for a full withdrawal of Iraqi forces from Kuwait. On 6 August, UNSC imposed economic sanctions on Iraq. On 8 August, Iraq announced the merger of Iraq and Kuwait. On 29 November, UNSC authorized the states cooperating with Kuwait to use all necessary means to uphold UNSC Resolution 660. The Gulf War started on 16–17 January 1991, when coalition forces began Operation Desert Storm with air attacks on Iraq. The ground operations started on 24 February 1991 and culminated in the liberation of Kuwait on 27 February. On 3 March, Iraq accepted the terms of a ceasefire.

On 15 October 1995 Saddam Hussein won a referendum that allowed him to remain President for another seven years. On 31 August 1996 Iraqi forces launched an offensive into the northern no-fly zone and captured the Kurdish city of Irbil.

In December 1998, USA and UK launched 'Operation Desert Fox', a bombing campaign to destroy Iraq's nuclear, chemical and biological weapons. In February 2001, USA and UK carried out bombing raids to eliminate Iraq's air defence network even though there was little international support in favour of such an attack.

In September 2002, US President George W. Bush called upon world leaders at a UN General Assembly session to deal with what he called 'grave and gathering danger' posed by Iraq. The same month, British Prime Minister Tony Blair released a dossier on the weapons capabilities of Iraq. On 17 March 2003, UK's ambassador to the UN declared that the diplomatic process on Iraq was over. Soon afterwards, arms inspectors left the country and President George W. Bush gave Saddam Hussein and his sons an ultimatum to leave the country within 48 hours or face war. On the expiry of the ultimatum, on 20 March, American missiles bombarded targets in Baghdad. US and British ground troops entered Iraq from the south in the following days. On 9 April, US forces advanced into central Baghdad. In the following days Kurdish fighters and US forces gained control of the northern cities of Kirkuk and Mosul.

In October 2003, the UN Security Council approved an amended US resolution on Iraq that bestowed legitimacy on the US-led administration in Iraq. The big break that the coalition forces were looking for in Iraq finally came on 14 December 2003, when Saddam Hussein was captured in Tikrit. On 1 July 2004, Saddam Hussein appeared in an Iraqi court for the first time. He was brought to the court in handcuffs and chains to stand trial on charges of war crimes and genocide. He remained defiant, describing President Bush as the 'real criminal', defending Iraq's 1990 invasion of Kuwait. He said he was still the Iraqi President and rejected the court's jurisdiction.

Geography

Location: Middle East, bordering the Persian Gulf, between Iran and Kuwait.

Area: 437,072 sq. km.

Terrain: Broad plains with marshlands along the Iranian border in the south.

Natural resources: Petroleum, natural gas, phosphates, sulphur.

Climate: Desert climate with winters that range from mild to cool. The summers are dry, hot, and cloudless.

People

Population: 26,074,906 (July 2005 est.).

Population growth rate: 2.7% (2005 est.).

Sex ratio: 1.02 male(s)/female (2005 est.).

Religions: Muslim 97% (Shi'a 60%–65%, Sunni 32%–37%), Christian and others 3%.

Languages: Arabic, Kurdish, Assyrian, Armenian.

Literacy rate: Total 40.4%, Male 55.9%, Female 24.4% (2003 est.).

Infant mortality rate: 50.25 deaths/ 1,000 live births (2005 est.).

Life expectancy: Total 68.7 years, Male 67.49 years, Female 69.97 years (2005 est.).

Government

Capital: Baghdad.

Government type: None. The Iraqi interim government was appointed on 1 June 2004.

Independence: 3 October 1932 (from League of Nations mandate under British administration).

Legal system: Based on civil and Islamic law under the Iraqi interim government and Transitional Administrative Law.

Executive branch:

Chief of state: Iraqi transitional government President Jalal Tolabani (since 6 April 2005); Deputy Presidents Abil Abd al-Mahdi and Ghazi al-Ujayal al-Yown (since 6 April 2005). The president and deputy presidents comprise the Presidency Council.

Head of government: Iraqi transitional government Prime Minister Ibrahim al-Jafari (since April 2005); Deputy Prime Ministers Rowsach Shaways, Ahmad Chaelabi and Abid al-Mutlaq al-jabbvm (since May 2005).

Economy

Currency: New Iraqi dinar.

Economy—overview:
The oil sector dominates Iraq's economy and has traditionally contributed about 95% of the country's foreign exchange earnings. Iraq faced severe financial problems in the 1980s due to heavy cost of waging war on Iran and the damage caused to the oil export facilities by the ongoing war. This forced the government to impose austerity measures. The government had to borrow heavily and reschedule foreign debt payments. The economic losses because of the war are estimated at around $100 billion. The end of the war in 1988 was followed by a gradual restoration of the infrastructure and the resumption of oil exports. But before the country could recover from this war fully, Iraq occupied Kuwait in August 1990. The consequent international economic sanctions and international military action severely affected the Iraqi economy. Legitimate oil exports ground to a halt following the imposition of a trade embargo on Iraq. Meanwhile the government pursued a policy of utilizing resources to support the military, security forces and important supporters of the regime. This had an adverse effect on the economy. The start of the UN's oil-for-food programme in December 1996 helped improve the situation. Under this program-me, Iraq was allowed to export limited amounts of oil in exchange for essential commodities like food and medicine, and some supplies to rebuild the country's infrastructure. In December 1999, the UN Security Council authorized Iraq to export as much oil as it was necessary in order to meet humanitarian needs. The military actions of 2003 have caused the shutdown of much of the central economic administrative system. The country's infrastructure is undergoing extensive rebuilding and production is creeping back towards pre-war levels. A joint UN and World Bank study released in 2003 put Iraq's key reconstruction needs through 2007 at $55 billion. In October 2003, international donors pledged assistance worth more than $33 billion.

GDP: Purchasing power parity—$89.8 billion (2004 est.).

GDP—real growth rate: 52.3% (2004 est.).

GDP—per capita: Purchasing power parity—$3,500 (2004 est.).

Inflation rate: 27.5% (2003 est.).

Exports: $10.1 billion f.o.b. (2004 est.)—crude oil.

Imports: $9.9 billion f.o.b. (2004 est.)—food, medicine, manufactures.

External debt: $125 billion (2004 est.).

Transport and Communications

Railways: 1,963 km.

Roads: 45,550 km.

Telephones: 675,000 (2003).

Mobile cellular: 20,000 (2002).

Internet users: 25,000 (2002).

Internet country code: .iq

Ireland

History

In the 12th century, the Vatican handed all of Ireland as a papal fief to the English Crown. However, it was only in the 17th century that the British achieved total control over the Irish.

The Act of Union of 1801 made Great Britain and Ireland into the 'United Kingdom of Great Britain and Ireland'. The Irish economy declined steadily in the following decades. The Irish Potato Famine, also called the Great Irish Famine, struck the nation in the 1840s when the potato crop failed for successive years. Nearly two million people migrated to North America.

In 1916, Irish Nationalists launched a rebellion against British rule. It is referred to as the Easter Rising or the Easter Rebellion and began on Easter Monday, 24 April 1916, in Dublin. The British crushed the rebellion and executed its leaders. However, the Easter Rising proved to be the beginning of the end of British rule over Ireland.

In 1919, the Sinn Fein (meaning 'Ourselves Alone') nationalist movement set up an assembly in Dublin. This proclaimed Irish independence. At the same time, the Irish Republican Army (IRA) launched a guerrilla campaign against British forces.

On Easter Monday 1949, the anniversary of the 1916 uprising, Eire became the Republic of Ireland (Ireland excluding Northern Ireland). Northern Ireland remains part of UK even today. Soon afterwards, Ireland withdrew from the British Commonwealth.

Geography

Location: Western Europe, occupying five-sixths of the island of Ireland in the North Atlantic Ocean, west of Great Britain.

Area: 70,280 sq. km.

Terrain: Mostly level to rolling interior plain surrounded by rugged hills and low mountains. There are sea cliffs on the west coast.

Natural resources: Natural gas, peat, copper, lead, zinc, silver, barite, gypsum, limestone, dolomite.

Climate: Temperate maritime climate that is modified by the North Atlantic Current. The country has mild winters and cool summers.

People

Population: 4,015,676 (July 2005 est.).

Population growth rate: 1.16% (2005 est.).

Sex ratio: 0.99 male(s)/female (2005 est.).

Religions: Roman Catholic 91.6%, Church of Ireland 2.5%, others 5.9% (1998).

Languages: English is the language generally used while Irish (Gaelic) is spoken in areas located along the western coast.

Literacy rate: 98% (1981 est.).

Infant mortality rate: 4.84 deaths/1,000 live births (2005 est.).

Life expectancy: Total 77.56 years, Male 74.95 years, Female 80.34 years (2005 est.).

Government

Capital: Dublin.

Government type: Republic.

Independence: 6 December 1921 (from UK).

Legal system: Based on English common law, substantially modified by indigenous concepts.

Executive branch:
Chief of state: President Mary McAleese (since 11 November 1997).

Head of government: Prime Minister Bertie Ahern (since 26 June 1997).

Economy

Currency: Euro.

Economy—overview:
The Irish economy is a small, modern economy with a high degree of reliance on trade. Industry accounts for over 40% of GDP, about 80% of exports and almost 30% of employment. Exports are a key driver for Ireland's growth. Increased levels of construction activity, consumer spending and business investment have also boosted the economy in recent times. Ireland was one of the 11 countries that launched the euro currency system in January 1999.

GDP: Purchasing power parity—$126.4 billion (2004 est.).

GDP—real growth rate: 5.1% (2004 est.).

GDP—per capita: Purchasing power parity—$31,900 (2004 est.).

Inflation rate: 2.2% (2004 est.).

Population below poverty line: 10% (1997 est.).

Unemployment rate: 4.3% (2004 est.).

Exports: $103.8 billion f.o.b. (2004 est.)—machinery and equipment, computers, chemicals, pharmaceuticals; live animals, animal products (1999).

Imports: $60.65 billion f.o.b. (2004 est.)—data-processing equipment, other machinery and equipment, chemicals, petroleum and petroleum products, textiles, clothing.

External debt: $11 billion (1998).

Transport and Communications

Railways: 3,312 km.

Roads: 95,736 km.

Telephones: 1,955,000 (2003).

Mobile cellular: 3,400,000 (2003).

Internet users: 1.26 million (2003).

Internet country code: .ie

Israel

History

In 1896, Austrian journalist Theodor Herzl proposed in his pamphlet 'Der Judenstaat' or 'The Jewish State' that a world council of nations should settle the Jewish question. By 1903, around 25,000 Zionist immigrants arrived in the area that is today Israel. Another 40,000 immigrants arrived in the period between 1904 and 1914. About half a million Arab residents already lived in the area that was then a part of the Turkish Ottoman Empire. In 1917, the British Foreign Secretary Arthur Balfour promised 'the establishment in Palestine of a national home for the Jewish people', in a letter to Baron Rothschild, a leading Zionist. However, in May 1939, the British government changed its policy and recommended a limit of 75,000 further immigrants and suggested a stop to immigration by 1944. Needless to say, Zionists condemned this new policy. Meanwhile, hundreds of thousands of Jews immigrated to British Mandate Palestine.

On 14 May 1948, the proclamation of the State of Israel was made in Tel Aviv. The following day, armies from five Arab nations, Egypt, Jordan, Iraq, Lebanon and Syria invaded Israel only to be beaten back. The armistices that followed helped define Israel's territorial limits mostly along the frontier of the earlier British Mandate Palestine. However, Egypt retained the Gaza Strip while Jordan kept the area around East Jerusalem and the territory now known as the West Bank.

In October 1956, Israel invaded the Sinai Peninsula. In five days the Israeli army captured Gaza, Rafah and Al-'Arish. The Israeli forces took thousands of prisoners and occupied most of the peninsula east of the Suez Canal.

In January 1964, Arab governments voted to create a body called the Palestine Liberation Organization (PLO). Its military force, the Palestine Liberation Army, was formed in 1968.

In 1967, rising tensions between Israel and its Arab neighbours boiled over and resulted in six days of warfare, starting on 5 June 1967 and ending on 11 June. This was the Six Day War. Israel seized Gaza and the Sinai from Egypt, the Golan Heights from Syria, and evicted Jordanian forces from the West Bank and East Jerusalem. In a stunning move, Israel eliminated Egypt's powerful air force on the first day of fighting by destroying its aircraft while they were still on the ground.

On 6 October 1973, which was the Jewish holy day of Yom Kippur, Egypt and Syria attacked Israel. This was the Yom Kippur War. Israel and Egypt signed a ceasefire agreement in November and peace agreements on 18 January 1974.

In the 1970s, Palestinians targeted Israelis all across the world. One of the most high-profile attacks was at the Munich Olympic Games in 1972 when Palestine attackers killed 11 Israeli athletes. In 1974, PLO Chairman Yasser Arafat made a dramatic first appearance at the United Nations.

In 1977, Egypt became the first Arab country to recognize Israel when its President Anwar Sadat flew to Israel and even addressed its Parliament. In September 1978, Egypt and Israel signed the Camp David accords. The Egyptian move attracted widespread criticism from other Arab countries. In 1981, opponents of the peace dialogue with Israel assassinated Anwar Sadat.

The peace process received a boost with the election of the left-wing Labour government in June 1992 with Yitzhak Rabin as prime minister. It culminated with the 'Declaration of Principles' and a historic handshake between Rabin and Yasser Arafat on the lawns of the White House in Washington DC. The 1994 Nobel Prize for Peace was jointly awarded to Yasser Arafat, Yitzhak Rabin and Shimon Peres. On 24 September 1995, the so-called Oslo II agreement was signed in Egypt. The agreement divided the West Bank into three zones, one zone under full Palestinian control, one under joint Israeli–Palestinian control and the third under Israeli control. On 4 November, a Jewish religious extremist, assassinated Israeli Prime Minister Yitzhak Rabin at a peace rally. Shimon Peres succeeded him as the Israeli prime minister. In May 1996, he lost the elections. In his place came Binyamin Netanyahu, a vocal critic of the peace process. In May 1999, Netanyahu lost the elections. The new Prime Minister Ehud Barak vowed to solve the conflict within one year. His tenure saw rising violence and a faltering peace process and ended with his resignation in 2001. The electorate swept Ariel Sharon into power, with an eye on a tougher approach to the Palestinian problem.

Geography

Location: Middle East, bordering the Mediterranean Sea, between Egypt and Lebanon.

Area: 20,770 sq. km.

Terrain: The Negev Desert in the south, a low coastal plain and central mountains.

Natural resources: Timber, potash, copper ore, natural gas, phosphate rock, magnesium bromide, clays, sand.

Climate: Temperate climate but hot and dry in the southern and eastern desert areas.

People

Population: 6,276,883 (July 2005 est.). This includes about 20,000 Israeli settlers in the Israeli-occupied Golan Heights, about 187,000 in the West Bank, more than 5,000 in the Gaza Strip, and fewer than 177,000 in East Jerusalem.

Population growth rate: 1.2% (2005 est.).

Sex ratio: 0.99 male(s)/female (2005 est.).

Religions: Jewish 80.1%, Muslim 14.6% (mostly Sunni Muslim), Christian 2.1%, others 3.2% (1996 est.).

Languages: Hebrew (official), Arabic is used officially for the Arab minority, English is the most commonly used foreign language.

Literacy rate: Total 95.4%, Male 97.3%, Female 93.6% (2003 est.).

Infant mortality rate: 7.03 deaths/ 1,000 live births (2005 est.).

Life expectancy: Total 79.32 years, Male 77.21 years, Female 81.55 years (2005 est.).

Government

Capital: Jerusalem.

Government type: Parliamentary democracy.

Independence: 14 May 1948 (from League of Nations mandate under British administration).

Legal system: Mixture of English common law, British mandate regulations, and, in personal matters, Jewish, Christian, and Muslim legal systems.

Executive branch:
Chief of state: President Moshe Katsav (since 31 July 2000).

Head of government: Prime Minister Ariel Sharon (since 7 March 2001).

Economy

Currency: New Israeli shekel.

Economy—overview:
Israel has a technologically advanced market economy. The country suffers

from limited natural resources. Yet it has developed its agricultural and industrial sectors over the last two decades. USA is the creditor of almost half of the government's external debt. It is also the major source of economic and military aid. Israel's economy grew at a fast pace in the early 1990s, thanks partly to the emigration of Jewish immigrants from the former Soviet Union during 1989–99 and the opening of new markets at the end of the Cold War. However, the violent Israeli–Palestinian conflict is a major drawback for the growth and development of the Israeli economy.

GDP: Purchasing power parity—$129 billion (2004 est.).

GDP—real growth rate: 3.9% (2004 est.).

GDP—per capita: Purchasing power parity—$20,800 (2004 est.).

Inflation rate: 0% (2004 est.).

Population below poverty line: 18% (2001 est.).

Unemployment rate: 10.7% (2004 est.).

Exports: $34.41 billion f.o.b. (2004 est.)—machinery and equipment, software, cut diamonds, agricultural products, chemicals, textiles and apparel.

Imports: $36.84 billion f.o.b. (2004 est.)—raw materials, military equipment, investment goods, rough diamonds, fuels, grain, consumer goods.

External debt: $74.46 billion (2004 est.).

Transport and Communications

Railways: 640 km.

Roads: 16,903 km.

Telephones: 3,006,000 (2002).

Mobile cellular: 6,334,000 (2002).

Internet users: 2 million (2002).

Internet country code: .il

Italy

History

Between the ninth and 3rd–4th centuries BC, the Etruscan civilization dominated the area that is modern-day Italy. The Romans followed the Etruscans and were in turn driven out by the Barbarian invasions of the fourth and fifth centuries AD.

Between the 15th and 18th centuries, France, the Holy Roman Empire, Spain and even Austria ruled the region. However, this could not stop Italy from becoming the nerve centre of European culture, mainly during the Renaissance period.

When Napoleonic rule came to an end in 1815, Italy was in the form of a collection of smaller independent states. The process of unification of peninsular Italy was completed by 1870 when Papal Rome was added to the kingdom. Italy was finally one nation under a constitutional monarchy.

In October 1922, the fascist leader Benito Amilcare Andrea Mussolini, or Il Duce (which means 'The Leader' in Italian) became the youngest prime minister of Italy. During World War II, Italy joined forces with Germany to form the Axis powers. It proved to be the undoing of both nations. By the time World War II ended, both dictators lay dead, their countries in ruins. In 1946, Italy declared itself a republic.

Geography

Location: Italy lies in southern Europe. It is a peninsula that extends into the central Mediterranean Sea, northeast of Tunisia.

Area: 301,230 sq. km (including Sardinia and Sicily).

Terrain: Mostly rugged and mountainous with some plains and coastal lowlands.

Natural resources: Mercury, potash, marble, sulphur, natural gas and crude oil reserves, fish, coal, and arable land.

Climate: Predominantly Mediterranean climate. However, the climate is of the Alpine type in the far north and hot and dry in the south.

People

Population: 58,103,033 (July 2005 est.).

Population growth rate: 0.07% (2005 est.).

Sex ratio: 0.96 male(s)/female (2005 est.).

Religions: Predominately Roman Catholic with mature Protestant and Jewish communities and a growing Muslim immigrant community.

Languages: Italian (official), German, French, Slovene.

Literacy rate: Total 98.6%, Male 99%, Female 98.3% (2003 est.).

Infant mortality rate: 5.94 deaths/1,000 live births (2005 est.).

Life expectancy: Total 79.68 years, Male 76.75 years, Female 82.81 years (2005 est.).

Government

Capital: Rome.

Government type: Republic.

Independence: 17 March 1861 (Kingdom of Italy proclaimed; Italy was not finally unified until 1870).

Legal system: Based on civil law system.

Executive branch:
Chief of state: President Carlo Azeglio Ciampi (since 13 May 1999).

Head of government: Prime Minister Silvio Berlusconi (since 10 June 2001).

Economy

Currency: Euro.

Economy—overview:
Italy has a diversified industrial economy and its per capita output is roughly the same as France and the UK. A striking feature of Italy's capitalistic economy is that it is divided into a developed industrial north and a less developed, welfare-dependent agriculture-dependent south with 20% unemployment. Italy imports most of the raw materials and 75% of the energy needed by its industries. Recently, Italy has pursued a tight fiscal policy in order to meet the requirements of the Economic and Monetary Unions. It has also benefited from lower interest and inflation rates. However, Italy has been sluggish on implementing much-needed structural reforms. These would have included reducing the high tax burden and overhauling of the rigid labour market and over-generous pension system.

GDP: Purchasing power parity—$1.609 trillion (2004 est.).

GDP—real growth rate: 1.3% (2004 est.).

GDP—per capita: Purchasing power parity—$27,700 (2004 est.).

Inflation rate: 2.3% (2004 est.).

Unemployment rate: 8.6% (2004 est.).

Exports: $336.4 billion f.o.b. (2004 est.).

Imports: $329.3 billion f.o.b. (2004 est.).

External debt: $913.9 billion (2004 est.).

Transport and Communications

Railways: 19,507 km.

Roads: 479,688 km.

Telephones: 26,596,000 (2003).

Mobile cellular: 55,918,000 (2003).

Internet users: 18.5 million (2003).

Internet country code: .it

Jamaica

History

At the time of arrival of Christopher Columbus in 1494, Arawak Indians inhabited the island of Jamaica. It remained a Spanish possession till 1655 when the British gained control. Black slaves were imported to work in the sugar plantations. The abolition of the slave trade in 1807, coupled with the global slump in sugar prices caused a depression in Jamaica that eventually led to an uprising in the island in 1865. In 1866, Jamaica became a Crown colony. In 1958, Jamaica played a leading role in the formation of the West Indian Federation. In 1962, Jamaica declared independence following a referendum.

Geography

Location: Caribbean, island in the Caribbean Sea, south of Cuba.

Area: 10,991 sq. km.

Natural resources: Bauxite, gypsum, limestone.

Climate: Hot and humid tropical climate. The interiors have temperate climate.

People

Population: 2,731,832 (July 2005 est.).

Population growth rate: 0.71% (2005 est.).

Sex ratio: 1 male(s)/female (2005 est.).

Religions: Protestant 61.3%, Roman Catholic 4%, others including some spiritual cults 34.7%.

Languages: English, patois English.

Literacy rate: Total 87.9%, Male 84.1%, Female 91.6% (2003 est.).

Infant mortality rate: 12.36 deaths/1,000 live births (2005 est.).

Life expectancy: Total 76.29 years, Male 74.23 years, Female 78.45 years (2005 est.).

Government

Capital: Kingston.

Government type: Constitutional parliamentary democracy.

Independence: 6 August 1962 (from UK).

Legal system: Based on English common law.

Executive branch:
Chief of state: Queen Elizabeth II (since 6 February 1952), represented by Governor General Sir Howard Felix Cooke (since 1 August 1991).

Head of government: Prime Minister Percival James Patterson (since 30 March 1992).

Economy

Currency: Jamaican dollar.

GDP: Purchasing power parity—$11.13 billion (2004 est.).

GDP—real growth rate: 1.9% (2004 est.).

GDP—per capita: Purchasing power parity—$4,100 (2004 est.).

Inflation rate: 12.4% (2004 est.).

Population below poverty line: 19.7% (2002 est.).

Unemployment rate: 15% (2004 est.).

Exports: $1.679 billion f.o.b. (2004 est.)—alumina, bauxite, sugar, banana, rum.

Imports: $3.624 billion f.o.b. (2004 est.)—machinery and transport equipment, construction materials, fuel, food, chemicals, fertilizers.

External debt: $5.964 billion (2004 est.).

Transport and Communications

Railways: 272 km.

Roads: 18,700 km.

Telephones: 444,400 (2002).

Mobile cellular: 1,400,000 (2002).

Internet users: 600,000 (2002).

Internet country code: .jm

Japan

History

The first unified Japanese state came about under the Yamato clan in 4th–5th century AD, which is also the time when Buddhism reached Japan via Korea. In 1192, Minamoto Yoritomo established the first shogunate in Japan. The first contact with Europe occurred in 1542 when an off-course Portuguese ship arrived in Japan. This was followed by traders from Portugal and other European countries. The Tokugawa shogunate (1603–1867) imposed a policy of isolation that prohibited all trade ties with the West, except one Dutch trading post. The shogun system was abolished when Emperor Meiji came to the throne in 1868. Under Emperor Meiji, Japan initiated a process of rapid modernization and westernisation. A Constitution was adopted, a parliamentary form of government took office and an imperial army was raised through conscription. Before long, Japan sought to expand its boundaries. This led to wars, first with China (1894–5) and then with Russia (1904–5). It annexed Korea in 1910 and Manchuria (now part of China) in 1931.

During World War II, Japan hastened the entry of USA into the war when it attacked its naval base at Pearl Harbour (7 December 1941). The War ended with the surrender of Japan, following the nuclear attacks on Hiroshima and Nagasaki in August 1945.

In 1947, Japan adopted a new Constitution. It embarked on a process of rebuilding of the nation from the ravages of the War that had left it in ruins. The decades to follow witnessed unprecedented growth that soon propelled Japan to become the world's second largest economy.

Geography

Location: Eastern Asia, island chain between the North Pacific Ocean and the Sea of Japan, east of the Korean Peninsula.

Area: 377,835 sq. km.

Terrain: Mostly rugged and mountainous. Consequently, the plains and valleys are densely populated.

Natural resources: Japan has negligible mineral resources but high in fish resources.

Climate: Varies from tropical in the south to cool temperate in the north.

People

Population: 127,417,244 (July 2005 est.).

Population growth rate: 0.05% (2005 est.).

Sex ratio: 0.96 male(s)/female (2005 est.).

Religions: Percentage of population observing both Shinto and Buddhism—84%, others 16% (including Christian 0.7%).

Languages: Japanese.

Literacy rate: 99% (2002 est.).

Infant mortality rate: 3.26 deaths/1,000 live births (2005 est.).

Life expectancy: Total 81.15 years, Male 77.86 years, Female 84.61 years (2005 est.).

Government

Capital: Tokyo.

Government type: Constitutional monarchy with a parliamentary government.

Independence: 660 BC, which is the traditional date of founding by Emperor Jimmu.

Legal system: Modelled after European civil law system with English–American influence.

Executive branch:
Chief of state: Emperor Akihito (since 7 January 1989).

Head of government: Prime Minister Junichiro Koizumi (since 26 April 2001).

Legislative branch:
Japan has a bicameral parliament. The Diet or the Kokkai consists of the House of Councillors or Sangi-in and the House of Representatives or Shugi-in. The House of Councillors has 247 seats. Members are elected for six-year terms, a half being elected every three years. One hundred forty-nine member are elected from members of multi-seat constituencies and 98 are elected by proportional representation.

The House of Representatives has 480 seats. Members are elected for four-year terms—300 from single-seat constituencies and 180 by proportional representation in 11 regional blocs.

Elections to the House of Councillors were last held on 29 July 2001. Elections to the House of Representatives were last held on 9 November 2003.

House of Councillors

LDP	115
DPJ	82
Komeito	24
JCP	9
SDP	5
Others	7

Distribution of seats as of October 2004 was:

LDP	114
DPJ	84
Komeito	24
JCP	9
SDP	5
Others	6

House of Representatives

Distribution of seats as of 13 November 2003 was:

LDP	244
DPJ	177
Komeito	34
JCP	9
SDP	6
Others	10

Economy

Currency: Yen.

Economy—overview:

In the years following the Second World War Japan rapidly achieved economic prosperity and became one of the world's largest economies. This was largely due to strong cooperation between the government and the industry, development of high technology, a strong work ethic and a comparatively low defence allocation (around 1% of GDP). For three decades, the country enjoyed high overall real economic growth. It averaged 10% in the 1960s, 5% in the 1970s and 4% in the 1980s. Things states deteriorating in the 1990s, mainly after the recession of 1997, with growth averaging just 1.7%.

One of the notable features of the Japanese economy is the interaction between manufacturers, suppliers, and distributors in closely-knit groups called keiretsu. Another significant feature has been the guarantee of lifetime employment for much of the urban labour force. Even today, a large part of the work force remain with the same employer all their working life. The recession in the mid-1990s has however contributed to the gradual erosion of both features in the Japanese society.

Japan has very little of its own natural resources and the country's industry is heavily dependent on imported raw materials and fuels. The much smaller agricultural sector is highly subsidised and protected and crop yields are among the highest in the world. Although the country is self-sufficient in rice, Japan needs to import about 50% of its requirements of other grain and fodder crops. Japan has one of the world's largest fishing fleets and accounts for nearly 15% of the global catch.

The slump of the 1990s was largely due to the over-investment in the late 1980s and policies that intended to extract speculative excesses from the stock and real estate markets. Government efforts to rejuvenate the economy have met with little success. The slowing down of the US, European, and Asian economies during 2000–03 further hampered recovery.

Two major long-term problems facing the economy are Japan's gigantic government debt (approaching 150% of GDP) and the ageing of the population. One remarkable feature is the country's robotic workforce. Japan has 410,000 of the world's 720,000 working robots population.

GDP: Purchasing power parity—$3.745 trillion (2004 est.).

GDP—real growth rate: 2.9% (2004 est.).

GDP—per capita: Purchasing power parity—$29,400 (2004 est.).

Inflation rate: –0.1% (2004 est.).

Unemployment rate: 4.7% (2004).

Exports: $538.8 billion f.o.b. (2004 est.).

Imports: $401.8 billion f.o.b. (2004 est.).

Transport and Communications

Railways: 23,705 km (15,995 km electrified).

Roads: 1,171,647 km.

Telephones: 71,149,000 (2002).

Mobile cellular: 86,658,600 (2002).

Internet users: 57,200,000 (2002).

Internet country code: .jp

Jordan

History

David and later Solomon incorporated parts of present-day Jordan into their kingdoms. Later, the Seleucids and the Arabs held sway. In the 16th century, Jordan became a part of the Turkish Ottoman Empire.

In 1920, the area comprising Transjordan, as it was then called, became a part of the British mandate of Palestine. In 1927, Transjordan became an independent state under British mandate. In 1949, Jordan annexed the West Bank territory. However, Israel snatched it back during the Six Day War of 1967. In 1994, Jordan signed a full peace agreement with Israel.

Geography

Location: Middle East, north-west of Saudi Arabia.

Area: 92,300 sq. km.

Terrain: Desert plateau in the east and highland area in the west. A great rift valley separates the east and west banks of the Jordan River.

Natural resources: Phosphates, potash, shale oil.

Climate: Mostly arid desert type.

People

Population: 5,759,732 (July 2005 est.).

Population growth rate: 2.56% (2005 est.).

Sex ratio: 1.1 male(s)/female (2005 est.).

Religions: Sunni Muslim 92%, Christian 6%, others 2% (2001 est.).

Languages: Arabic (official), English widely understood.

Literacy rate: Total 91.3%, Male 95.9%, Female 86.3% (2003 est.).

Infant mortality rate: 17.35 deaths/ 1,000 live births (2005 est.).

Life expectancy: Total 78.24 years, Male 75.75 years, Female 80.88 years (2005 est.).

Government

Capital: Amman.

Government type: Constitutional monarchy.

Independence: 25 May 1946 (from League of Nations mandate under British administration).

Legal system: Based on Islamic law and French codes.

Executive branch:

Chief of state: King Abdallah II (since 7 February 1999); Crown Prince Hamzah (half-brother of the monarch, born 29 March 1980).

Head of government: Prime Minister Adnan Badran (since 7 April 2005).

Economy

Currency: Jordanian dinar.

Economy—overview:
Jordan suffers from inadequate supplies of water and other natural resources like oil. The war in Iraq in 2003 hurt the Jordanian economy, as it was dependent on Iraq for discounted oil. Key among the problems that the Jordanian economy faces are poverty, debt and unemployment. The ascent of King Abdallah to the throne has also seen the institution of some amount of economic reforms.

GDP: Purchasing power parity—$25.5 billion (2004 est.).

GDP—real growth rate: 5.1% (2004 est.).

GDP—per capita: Purchasing power parity—$4,500 (2004 est.).

Inflation rate: 3.2% (2004 est.).

Population below poverty line: 30% (2001 est.).

Unemployment rate: 15% official rate (2004 est.).

Exports: $3.2 billion f.o.b. (2004 est.)—phosphates, fertilizers, potash, agricultural products, manufactures, pharmaceuticals.

Imports: $7.6 billion f.o.b. (2004 est.)—crude oil, machinery, transport equipment, food, live animals, manufactures.

External debt: $7.32 billion (2004 est.).

Transport and Communications

Railways: 505 km.

Roads: 7,301 km.

Telephones: 622,600 (2003).

Mobile cellular: 1,325,300 (2003).

Internet users: 212,000 (2002).

Internet country code: .jo

Kazakhstan

History

Turkic-speaking tribes and Mongols invaded and settled in what is now Kazakhstan between the first and eighth centuries AD. Arab invaders introduced Islam in the eighth century. It was in the late 15th century that the Kazakhs emerged as a distinct ethnic group with the formation of the Kazakh khanate.

In the 18th century, the Kazakhs formally joined Russia in order to gain protection from the invading Mongols. In 1920, Kazakhstan became an autonomous republic of the USSR. In 1936, Kazakhstan became a full-fledged union republic of the USSR. In December 1991, Kazakhstan declared its independence from the collapsing Soviet Union.

Geography

Location: Central Asia, north-west of China; a small portion west of the Ural River in easternmost Europe.

Area: 2,717,300 sq. km.

Terrain: Kazakhstan extends from the Volga to the Altai Mountains and from the plains in western Siberia to oases and desert in Central Asia.

Natural resources: Petroleum, natural gas, coal, iron ore, manganese, chrome ore, nickel, cobalt, copper, molybdenum, lead, zinc, bauxite, gold, uranium.

Climate: Continental climate with cold winters and hot summers.

People

Population: 15,185,844 (July 2005 est.).

Population growth rate: 0.03% (2005 est.).

Sex ratio: 0.93 male(s)/female (2005 est.).

Religions: Muslim 47%, Russian Orthodox 44%, Protestant 2%, others 7%.

Languages: Kazakh (Qazaq, state language) 64.4%, Russian 95% (2001 est.).

Literacy rate: Total 98.4%, Male 99.1%, Female 97.7% (1999 est.).

Infant mortality rate: 29.21 deaths/1,000 live births (2005 est.).

Life expectancy: Total 66.55 years, Male 61.21 years, Female 72.2 years (2005 est.).

Government

Capital: Astana.

Government type: Republic.

Independence: 16 December 1991 (from the Soviet Union).

Legal system: Based on civil law system.

Executive branch:
Chief of state: President Nursultan A. Nazarbayev (chairman of the Supreme Soviet from 22 February 1990, elected president 1 December 1991).

Head of government: Prime Minister Daniyal Akhmetov (since 13 June 2003).

Economy

Currency: Tenge.

Economy—overview:
Kazakhstan has large reserves of fossil fuel as well as other minerals and metals, a large livestock population and it is a globally significant producer of grain. Kazakhstan's industrial sector rests on the extraction and processing of these natural resources and also on a growing machine-building sector specializing in construction equipment, tractors, agricultural machinery, and some defence items. A short-term contraction of the economy followed immediately after the collapse of the Soviet Union in December 1991. The Caspian Consortium pipeline started in 2001, from western Kazakhstan's Tengiz oilfield to the Black Sea. Kazakhstan's new industrial policy aims to diversify the economy by removing the over-reliance on the oil sector.

GDP: Purchasing power parity— $118.4 billion (2004 est.).

GDP—real growth rate: 9.1% (2004 est.).

GDP—per capita: Purchasing power parity—$7,800 (2004 est.).

Inflation rate: 6.9% (2004 est.).

Population below poverty line: 19% (2004 est.).

Unemployment rate: 8% (2004 est.).

Exports: $18.47 billion f.o.b. (2004 est.)—oil and oil products, ferrous metals, chemicals, machinery, grain, wool, meat, coal.

Imports: $13.07 billion f.o.b. (2004 est.)—machinery and equipment 41%, metal products 28%, foodstuff 8%.

External debt: $26.03 billion (2004 est.).

Transport and Communications

Railways: 13,601 km.

Roads: 82,980 km.

Telephones: 2,081,900 (2002).

Mobile cellular: 1,027,000 (2002).

Internet users: 250,000 (2002).

Internet country code: .kz

Kenya

History

Evidence shows that Kenya was home to some of the earliest human settlements in the world. In the 1890s, Kenya became a part of the British East African Protectorate and in 1920 it became a British Crown colony. In 1944, the Kenyan African Union (KAU) was formed to campaign for African independence. In 1947, Jomo Kenyatta became a KAU leader. In 1952, a secret Kikuyu guerrilla group named Mau Mau began a violent campaign against white settlers. The following year, Kenyatta was charged with management of Mau Mau and jailed. The KAU was banned. In 1956, the government put down the Mau Mau rebellion but only after thousands were killed. In 1960, the Kenya African National Union (KANU) was formed. In 1961, Kenyatta took over the leadership of KANU. In 1963, Kenya became independent with Kenyatta as the prime minister. In 1964, Kenya became a republic with Kenyatta as the President.

Geography

Location: Eastern Africa, bordering the Indian Ocean, between Somalia and Tanzania.

Area: 582,650 sq. km.

Terrain: Low plains that rise to the central highlands bisected by the Great Rift Valley. There is a fertile plateau in the west.

Natural resources: Gold, limestone, soda ash, salt, rubies, fluorspar, garnets, wildlife, hydropower.

Climate: Varies from tropical along the coastal region to arid in the interiors.

People

Population: 33,829,590 (July 2005 est.).

Population growth rate: 2.56% (2005 est.).

Sex ratio: 1.01 male(s)/female (2005 est.).

Religions: Protestant 45%, Roman Catholic 33%, indigenous beliefs 10%, Muslim 10%, others 2%.

Languages: English (official), Kiswahili (official), several indigenous languages.

Literacy rate: Total 85.1%, Male 90.6%, Female 79.7% (2003 est.).

Infant mortality rate: 61.47 deaths/1,000 live births (2005 est.).

Life expectancy: Total 47.99 years, Male 48.87 years, Female 47.09 years (2005 est.).

Government

Capital: Nairobi.

Government type: Republic.

Independence: 12 December 1963 (from UK).

Legal system: Based on Kenyan statutory law, Kenyan and English common law, tribal law, and Islamic law.

Executive branch:
Chief of state: President Mwai Kibaki (since 30 December 2002) and Vice-President Moody Awori (since 25 September 2003). The president is both the chief of state and head of government.

Economy

Currency: Kenyan shilling.

Economy—overview:
Kenya is a regional centre for trade and finance in East Africa. Its economy has been hurt in recent times due to its reliance upon certain primary goods whose prices have remained low. In 1997, the IMF suspended Kenya's Enhanced Structural Adjustment Programme after the government failed to maintain reforms and curb corruption. A severe drought hit the country from 1999 to 2000, resulting in water and energy rationing and reduced agricultural output. The IMF resumed loans in 2000 to help Kenya through the drought period but stopped payments again in 2001 after the government failed to introduce suggested anti-corruption measures.

GDP: Purchasing power parity—$34.68 billion (2004 est.).

GDP—real growth rate: 2.2% (2004 est.).

GDP—per capita: Purchasing power parity—$1,100 (2004 est.).

Inflation rate: 9% (2004 est.).

Population below poverty line: 50% (2004 est.).

Unemployment rate: 40% (2001 est.).

Exports: $2.589 billion f.o.b. (2004 est.)—tea, horticultural products, coffee, petroleum products, fish, cement.

Imports: $4.19 billion f.o.b. (2004 est.)—machinery and transportation equipment, petroleum products, motor vehicles, iron and steel, resins and plastics.

External debt: $6.792 billion (2004 est.).

Transport and Communications

Railways: 2,778 km.

Roads: 63,942 km.

Telephones: 328,400 (2003).

Mobile cellular: 1,590,800 (2003).

Internet users: 400,000 (2002).

Internet country code: .ke

Kiribati

History

The islands comprising modern-day Kiribati were first settled in the first century AD. In 1892, the Gilbert Islands became a British protectorate while Banaba was annexed in 1900. These two were then joined with the Ellice Islands as the Gilbert and Ellice Islands Colony from 1916. The Gilbert Islands became independent as Kiribati in 1979.

Geography

Location: Oceania, group of 33 coral atolls in the Pacific Ocean, around the equator.

Area: 811 sq. km (this includes three island groups—Gilbert Islands, Line Islands, Phoenix Islands).

Natural resources: Phosphate (production discontinued in 1979).

Climate: Hot and humid tropical marine type of climate.

People

Population: 103,092 (July 2005 est.).

Population growth rate: 2.25% (2005 est.).

Sex ratio: 0.99 male(s)/female (2005 est.).

Religions: Roman Catholic 52%, Protestant (Congregational) 40%, some Seventh-day Adventist, Muslim, Baha'i, Latter-day Saints, and Church of God (1999).

Languages: I-Kiribati, English (official).

Infant mortality rate: 48.52 deaths/1,000 live births (2005 est.).

Life expectancy: Total 61.71 years, Male 58.71 years, Female 64.86 years (2005 est.).

Government

Capital: Tarawa.

Government type: Republic.

Independence: 12 July 1979 (from UK).

Executive branch:
Chief of state: President Anote Tong (since 10 July 2003). The president is both the chief of state and head of government.

Economy

Currency: Australian dollar.

GDP: Purchasing power parity—$79 million—supplemented by a nearly equal amount from external sources (2001 est.).

GDP—real growth rate: 1.5% (2001 est.).

GDP—per capita: Purchasing power parity—$800 (2001 est.).

Inflation rate: 2.5% (2001 est.).

Exports: $35 million f.o.b. (2002)—copra 62%, coconuts, seaweed, fish.

Imports: $83 million c.i.f. (2002)—foodstuff, machinery and equipment, miscellaneous manufactured goods, fuel.

External debt: $10 million (1999 est.).

Transport and Communications

Railways: None.

Roads: 670 km (1999 est.).

Telephones: 4,500 (2002).

Mobile cellular: 500 (2002).

Internet users: 2000 (2002).

Internet country code: .ki

Kuwait

History

It is believed that an ancient civilization dating back to the third millennium BC flourished in Kuwait. The modern history of Kuwait starts in the 18th century, when a group of Arabs migrated to the area that is today Kuwait. They set up an oligarchic principality of merchants engaged in fishing, pearling and trade. In course of time, Al Sabah emerged as the dominant clan and, in 1756, they were formally established as rulers.

In 1899, Kuwait became a British protectorate. In 1937, oil reserves were discovered in Kuwait. After the end of World War II, the country transformed itself, based on its petroleum riches.

In June 1961, Kuwait attained independence. During the Iran–Iraq war of the 1980s, Kuwait lent its support to Iraq. In July 1990, Iraq lodged a complaint with OPEC, accusing Kuwait of stealing oil from an Iraqi field near the border and threatened to use military force. In August 1990, more than 100,000 Iraqi troops invaded and annexed Kuwait. A US-led and UN-backed military campaign

was launched and by late February 1991, allied forces had reached Kuwait City. Retreating Iraqi forces carried out widespread looting, set fire to 742 of the country's 1,080 oil wells and allowed crude oil to flow into the desert and the sea. In 1993, the UN demarcated a new Kuwait–Iraq border.

Geography

Location: Middle East, bordering the Persian Gulf, between Iraq and Saudi Arabia.

Area: 17,820 sq. km.

Terrain: Flat to slightly undulating desert plain.

Natural resources: Petroleum, fish, shrimp, natural gas.

Climate: Dry desert type of climate with intensely hot summers and short, cool winters.

People

Population: 2,335,648. This includes 1,291,354 non-nationals (July 2003 est.).

Population growth rate: 3.44%. This rate reflects a return to pre-Gulf crisis immigration of expatriates (2005 est.).

Sex ratio: 1.52 male(s)/female (2005 est.).

Religions: Muslim 85% (Sunni 70%, Shi'a 30%), Christian, Hindu, Parsi, and others 15%.

Languages: Arabic (official), English widely spoken.

Literacy rate: Total 83.5%, Male 85.1%, Female 81.7% (2003 est.).

Infant mortality rate: 9.95 deaths/1,000 live births (2005 est.).

Life expectancy: Total 77.03 years, Male 76.01 years, Female 78.1 years (2005 est.).

Government

Capital: Kuwait City.

Government type: Nominal constitutional monarchy.

Independence: 19 June 1961 (from UK).

Legal system: Civil law system with Islamic law significant in personal matters.

Executive branch:
Chief of state: Amir Jabir al-Ahmad al-Jabir Al Sabah (since 31 December 1977).

Head of government: Prime Minister Sabah al-Ahmad al-Jabir Al Sabah (since 13 July 2003).

Economy

Currency: Kuwaiti dinar.

Economy—overview:
Kuwait is a small prosperous country with a relatively open economy and proven crude oil reserves of about 98 billion barrels. This is around 10% of total world reserves. Nearly half of Kuwait's GDP, 95% of export revenues and 80% of government income comes from petroleum. It depends almost wholly on food imports, except for fish. About 75% of drinking water is distilled from seawater or imported.

GDP: Purchasing power parity—$48 billion (2004 est.).

GDP—real growth rate: 6.8% (2004 est.).

GDP—per capita: Purchasing power parity—$21,300 (2004 est.).

Inflation rate: 2.3% (2004 est.).

Unemployment rate: 2.2% (2004 est.).

Exports: $27.42 billion f.o.b. (2004 est.)—oil and refined products, fertilizers.

Imports: $11.12 billion f.o.b. (2004 est.)—food, construction materials, vehicles and parts, clothing.

External debt: $15.02 billion (2004 est.).

Transport and Communications

Railways: None.

Roads: 4,450 km.

Telephones: 486,900 (2003).

Mobile cellular: 1,420,000 (2003).

Internet users: 567,000 (2003).

Internet country code: .kw

Kyrgyzstan

History

In the eighth century, Arab invaders conquered large parts of Central Asia, including what is today Kyrgyzstan, and introduced Islam. By 1685, Kyrgyz people settled in the area that is now Kyrgyzstan. In 1758, Chinese Manchus defeated the Oirat Mongols and the Kyrgyz people became nominal subjects of the Chinese empire. Early in the 19th century, the land passed into the jurisdiction of the Uzbek khanate of Kokand. In 1876, Russia conquered the khanate of Kokand and incorporated what is now Kyrgyzstan into the Russian empire. In 1926, the Kyrgyz Autonomous Region was upgraded to an Autonomous Soviet Socialist Republic. In 1991, Kirgizia was renamed Kyrgyzstan and declared its independence from the crumbling Soviet Union.

Geography

Location: Central Asia, west of China.

Area: 198,500 sq. km.

Terrain: Consists of the peaks of Tien Shan and its associated valleys and basins.

Natural resources: Hydropower, gold, rare earth metals, coal, oil, natural gas, nepheline, mercury, zinc, bismuth, lead.

Climate: Varies from dry continental to arctic in the Tien Shan areas. Ferghana Valley in the south-west has a subtropical climate while the northern foothill zone has a temperate climate.

People

Population: 5,146,281 (July 2005 est.).

Population growth rate: 1.29% (2005 est.).

Sex ratio: 0.96 male(s)/female (2004 est.).

Religions: Muslim 75%, Russian Orthodox 20%, others 5%.

Languages: Kyrgyz (official), Russian (official).

Literacy rate: Total 97%, Male 99%, Female 96% (1989 est.).

Infant mortality rate: 35.64 deaths/1,000 live births (2005 est.).

Life expectancy: Total 68.16 years, Male 64.16 years, Female 72.38 years (2005 est.).

Government

Capital: Bishkek.

Government type: Republic.

Independence: 31 August 1991 (from the Soviet Union).

Legal system: Based on civil law system.

Executive branch:
Chief of state: Acting President Kurwanbek Bakiyev (since 24 March 2005).

Head of government: Prime Minister Kurwanbek Bakiyev (since 24 March 2005).

Economy

Currency: Kyrgyzstani som.

Economy—overview:
Kyrgyzstan was the first CIS country to be accepted into the World Trade Organization. Kyrgyzstan has a poor, largely agricultural economy—cotton, tobacco, wool, and meat being the chief agricultural products. However, tobacco and cotton are significant export items. The country also exports gold, uranium, mercury, electricity, and natural gas. In recent times, Kyrgyzstan has implemented market reforms and land reform and the state has sold most of its stock in enterprises. The drastic reduction in production immediately after the break-up of the Soviet Union in December 1991 was recovered by mid-1995 and was accompanied by an increase in exports. In partnership with international financial institutions, the government has undertaken a comprehensive medium-term poverty reduction and economic growth strategy.

GDP: Purchasing power parity—$8.495 billion (2004 est.).

GDP—real growth rate: 6% (2004 est.).

GDP—per capita: Purchasing power parity—$1,700 (2004 est.).

Inflation rate: 3.2% (2004 est.).

Population below poverty line: 40% (2004 est.).

Unemployment rate: 18% (2004 est.).

Exports: $646.7 million f.o.b. (2004 est.)—cotton, wool, meat, tobacco, hydropower, natural gas, gold, mercury, uranium, machinery, shoes.

Imports: $775.1 million f.o.b. (2004 est.)—oil and gas, foodstuff, machinery and equipment, chemicals.

External debt: $1.97 billion (2004 est.).

Transport and Communications

Railways: 470 km.

Roads: 18,500 km.

Telephones: 394,800 (2002).

Mobile cellular: 53,100 (2002).

Internet users: 152,000 (2002).

Internet country code: .kg

Laos

History

It was in the eighth century that the Lao people started migrating into the area that is today Laos from southern China. The first Laotian state, the Lan Xang kingdom, was founded in the 14th century. In 1893, Laos became a French protectorate. It was subsequently integrated into Indochina. In March 1945 the Japanese took administrative control of Indochina. In April 1945, the independence of Laos was proclaimed.

In the 1960s, USA carried out large-scale aerial bombardment of Laos in an attempt to destroy North Vietnamese safe havens and to eliminate the supply lines. It has been estimated that more bombs were dropped on Laos than were used in the entire World War II. In 1973, a ceasefire agreement divided Laos between the communists and the royalists. In 1975, the Pathet Lao, renamed the Lao People's Front, seized power.

Geography

Location: South-eastern Asia, north-east of Thailand, west of Vietnam.

Area: 236,800 sq. km.

Terrain: Consists mostly of rugged mountains with some plains and plateaus.

Natural resources: Timber, hydropower, gypsum, tin, gold, gemstones.

Climate: Tropical monsoon type of climate with a rainy season from May to November and a dry season from December to April.

People

Population: 6,217,141 (July 2005 est.).

Population growth rate: 2.42% (2005 est.).

Sex ratio: 0.98 male(s)/female (2005 est.).

Religions: Buddhist 60%, animist and others 40%.

Languages: Lao (official), French, English, and various ethnic languages.

Literacy rate: Total 52.8%, Male 67.5%, Female 38.1% (2003 est.).

Infant mortality rate: 85.22 deaths/1,000 live births (2005 est.).

Life expectancy: Total 55.08 years, Male 53.07 years, Female 57.17 years (2005 est.).

Government

Capital: Vientiane.

Government type: Communist state.

Independence: 19 July 1949 (from France).

Legal system: The Laotian legal system is based on traditional customs, French legal norms and procedures, and socialist practice.

Executive branch:
Chief of state: President Gen. Khamtai Siphandon (since 26 February 1998).

Head of government: Prime Minister Boungnang Volachit (since 27 March 2001).

Economy

Currency: Kip.

Economy—overview:
Laos is one of the few remaining official Communist states. In 1986, it began decentralizing control over industries and encouraging private enterprise. The country has achieved a high growth rate ever since. The country suffers from inadequate infrastructure with no railways, limited availability of electricity, only a basic road network, and limited telecommunication networks. Subsistence agriculture accounts for nearly half of the country's GDP and 80% of total employment.

GDP: Purchasing power parity—$11.28 billion (2004 est.).

GDP—real growth rate: 6% (2004 est.).

GDP—per capita: Purchasing power parity—$1,900 (2004 est.).

Inflation rate: 12.3% (2004 est.).

Population below poverty line: 40% (2002 est.).

Unemployment rate: 5.7% (1997 est.).

Exports: $365.5 million f.o.b. (2004 est.)—garments, wood products, coffee, electricity, tin.

Imports: $579.5 million f.o.b. (2004 est.)—machinery and equipment, vehicles, fuel, consumer goods.

External debt: $2.49 billion (2001).

Transport and Communications

Railways: None.

Roads: 21,716 km.

Telephones: 61,900 (2002).

Mobile cellular: 55,200 (2002).

Internet users: 15,000 (2002).

Internet country code: .la

Latvia

History

Baltic tribes originally inhabited the region that is today Latvia. Then the region came under the influence of German knights. The Russians controlled the affairs of Latvia for 200 years till 1918. In 1918, Latvia declared its independence. But civil war ensued and ended in a peace treaty signed with the Soviet Union. In 1941, Germany invaded Latvia. In August 1991, Latvia declared full independence.

Geography

Location: Eastern Europe, bordering the Baltic Sea, between Estonia and Lithuania.

Area: 64,589 sq. km.

Terrain: A low plain.

Natural resources: Peat, limestone, dolomite, amber, hydropower, wood, arable land.

Climate: Maritime climate with wet, moderate winters.

People

Population: 2,290,237 (July 2005 est.).

Population growth rate: −0.69% (2005 est.).

Sex ratio: 0.86 male(s)/female (2005 est.).

Religions: Lutheran, Roman Catholic, Russian Orthodox.

Languages: Latvian (official), Lithuanian, Russian.

Literacy rate: 99.8% (2003 est.).

Infant mortality rate: 9.55 deaths/1,000 live births (2005 est.).

Life expectancy: Total 71.05 years, Male 65.78 years, Female 76.6 years (2005 est.).

Government

Capital: Riga.

Government type: Parliamentary democracy.

Independence: 21 August 1991 (from the Soviet Union).

Legal system: Based on civil law system.

Executive branch:
Chief of state: President Vaira Vike-Freiberga (since 8 July 1999).

Head of government: Prime Minister Aigars Kalvitis (since 2 December 2004).

Economy

Currency: Latvian lat.

GDP: Purchasing power parity—$26.53 billion (2004 est.).

GDP—real growth rate: 7.6% (2004 est.).

GDP—per capita: Purchasing power parity—$11,500 (2004 est.).

Inflation rate: 6% (2004 est.).

Unemployment rate: 8.8% (2004 est.).

Exports: $3.569 billion f.o.b. (2004 est.)—wood and wood products, machinery and equipment, metals, textiles, foodstuff.

Imports: $5.97 billion f.o.b. (2004 est.)—machinery and equipment, chemicals, fuels, vehicles.

External debt: $7.368 billion (2004 est.).

Transport and Communications

Railways: 2,303 km.

Roads: 60,472 km.

Telephones: 653,900 (2003).

Mobile cellular: 1,219,600 (2003).

Internet users: 936,000 (2003).

Internet country code: .lv

Lebanon

History

In about 3000 BC the Phoenicians are believed to have arrived in the coastal areas of Lebanon. This area came to be called Phoenicia. Byblos is regarded as the first urban settlement in the area and has been dated to around 3050–2850 BC. A period of close contact with Egypt followed under the

Amorites. However, Egypt lost its control over the area by the 14th century BC. This led to the emergence of a number of city states all over Phoenicia.

By the second millennium BC the Phoenicians had begun extending their influence along the eastern shores of the Mediterranean Sea by establishing a series of settlements. In the ninth century BC Assyrians threatened the independence of Phoenicia. In 868 BC, Ashurnasirpal II reached the Mediterranean and forced the Phoenician cities to pay tribute. When the Babylonian King Nebuchadnezzar II marched against Phoenicia and besieged Tyre, the city resisted successfully for 13 years but was finally taken.

In 538 BC, the control of Phoenicia passed from the Babylonians to their conquerors, the Persians. In 332 BC Tyre resisted a siege launched by Alexander the Great for eight months before Alexander finally captured the city. Most of the citizens were sold into slavery and Tyre lost its position as the dominant city of the region to Alexandria. Phoenicia was eventually incorporated into the Roman province of Syria.

By the end of the 11th century, Lebanon became a part of the crusaders' states. The northern part of the country became a part of Tripolis while the southern part of the country became a part of the kingdom of Jerusalem. Lebanon came under increasing French influence. At the end of World War I, Allied forces occupied Lebanon and placed it under a French military administration. In 1923, the League of Nations formally gave the mandate for Lebanon and Syria to France. In December 1943, France agreed to transfer power to the Lebanese government with effect from 1 January 1944.

In the 1960s, Palestine began using Lebanon as the base for their anti-Israeli activities. Civil war rocked Lebanon between 1975 and 1991. In June 1982, Israel launched a full-scale invasion of Lebanon, codenamed 'Operation Peace for Galilee'. In July 1986, Syrian observers were stationed in Beirut to monitor a peace agreement. In 1991, the Syrian-backed Lebanese government started retaking territory from the militia in southern Lebanon. This signalled the beginning of the end of the civil war in Lebanon.

Geography

Location: Middle East, between Israel and Syria, bordering the Mediterranean Sea.

Area: 10,400 sq. km.

Terrain: Consists mostly of a narrow coastal plain. The El Beqaa or Bekaa Valley separates Lebanon and the Anti-Lebanon Mountains.

Natural resources: Limestone, iron ore, salt, water, arable land.

Climate: Mediterranean climate with mild to cool wet winters and hot, dry summers.

People

Population: 3,826,218 (July 2005 est.).

Population growth rate: 1.26% (2005 est.).

Sex ratio: 0.94 male(s)/female (2005 est.).

Religions: Muslim 70% (including Shi'a, Sunni, Druze, Isma'ilite, Alawite or Nusayri), Christian 30% (including Orthodox Christian, Catholic, Protestant), Jewish.

Languages: Arabic (official), French, English, Armenian.

Literacy rate: Total 87.4%, Male 93.1%, Female 82.2% (2003 est.).

Infant mortality rate: 24.52 deaths/1,000 live births (2005 est.).

Life expectancy: Total 72.63 years, Male 70.17 years, Female 75.21 years (2005 est.).

Government

Capital: Beirut.

Government type: Republic.

Independence: 22 November 1943 (from League of Nations mandate under French administration).

Legal system: Combination of Ottoman law, Napoleonic code, canon law and civil law.

Executive branch:

Chief of state: President Emile Lahud (since 24 November 1998).

Head of government: Prime Minister Najib Mikati (since 19 April 2005).

Economy

Currency: Lebanese pound.

Economy—overview:
Lebanon's economic infrastructure suffered much damage in the 1975–91 civil war that also reduced national output by half. The prevailing atmosphere of peace since then has enabled the Central government to resume tax collections and regain access to ports and government facilities. A financially sound banking system and a resilient manufacturing sector have helped economic recovery in recent years. In 1993, the government launched 'Horizon 2000', a $20-billion reconstruction programme. In the 1990s, annual inflation has dropped to almost nil from over 100% at one point of time. Much of Lebanon's war-damaged infrastructure has been rebuilt. However, the economic battle is far from over. Most of the reconstruction was funded through heavy borrowing mostly from domestic banks. The government has initiated an economic austerity programme to cut down on government spending, increase revenue collection, and privatize state-held enterprises in a bid to reduce the mounting national debt. In November 2002, the government met with international donors at the Paris II Conference to seek bilateral assistance in restructuring its domestic debt at lower rates of interest.

GDP: Purchasing power parity—$18.83 billion (2004 est.).

GDP—real growth rate: 4% (2004 est.).

GDP—per capita: Purchasing power parity—$5,000 (2004 est.).

Inflation rate: 2% (2004 est.).

Population below poverty line: 28% (1999 est.).

Unemployment rate: 18% (1997 est.).

Exports: $1.783 billion f.o.b. (2004 est.)—jewellery, consumer goods, inorganic chemicals, fruit, tobacco, construction materials, paper, electric power machinery and switchgear, textile fibres.

Imports: $8.162 billion f.o.b. (2004 est.)—petroleum products, cars, medicinal products, clothing, tobacco, meat and live animals, consumer goods, textile fabrics.

External debt: $15.84 billion (2004 est.).

Transport and Communications

Railways: 401 km.

Roads: 7,300 km.

Telephones: 678,800 (2002).

Mobile cellular: 775,100 (2002).

Internet users: 400,000 (2002).

Internet country code: .lb

Lesotho

History

Native chief Moshoeshoe founded Basutoland, the forerunner of Lesotho, in the 1820s. In the 1860s, it became a British protectorate. Basutoland finally gained independence in 1966 as the Kingdom of Lesotho, with Moshoeshoe II as king and Chief Leabua Jonathan as prime minister.

Geography

Location: Southern Africa, an enclave of South Africa.

Area: 30,355 sq. km.

Natural resources: Water, agricultural and grazing land, diamond and other minerals.

Climate: Temperate; cool to cold, dry winters; hot, wet summers.

People

Population: 1,867,035 (2005 est.).

Population growth rate: 0.08% (2005 est.).

Sex ratio: 0.96 male(s)/female (2005 est.).

Religions: Christian 80%, indigenous beliefs 20%.

Languages: Sesotho (South Sotho), English (official), Zulu, Xhosa.

Literacy rate: Total 84.8%, Male 74.5%, Female 94.5% (2003 est.).

Infant mortality rate: 84.23 deaths/1,000 live births (2005 est.).

Life expectancy: Total 36.68 years, Male 36.86 years, Female 36.49 years (2005 est.).

Government

Capital: Maseru.

Government type: Parliamentary constitutional monarchy.

Independence: 4 October 1966 (from UK).

Legal system: Based on English common law and Roman–Dutch law.

Executive branch:
Chief of state: King Letsie III (since 7 February 1996).

Head of government: Prime Minister Pakalitha Mosisili (since 23 May 1998).

Economy

Currency: Loti, South African rand.

GDP: Purchasing power parity—$5.892 billion (2004 est.).

GDP—real growth rate: 3.3% (2004 est.).

GDP—per capita: Purchasing power parity—$3,200 (2004 est.).

Inflation rate: 5.3% (2004 est.).

Population below poverty line: 49% (1999).

Unemployment rate: 45% (2002 est.).

Exports: $484.5 million f.o.b. (2004 est.)—manufactures 75% (clothing, footwear, road vehicles), wool and mohair, food and live animals (2000).

Imports: $730.9 million f.o.b. (2004 est.)—food, building materials, vehicles, machinery, medicines, petroleum products (2000).

External debt: $735 million (2002).

Transport and Communications

Railways: 2.6 km.

Roads: 5,940 km.

Telephones: 28,600 (2002).

Mobile cellular: 92,000 (2002).

Internet users: 21,000 (2002).

Internet country code: .ls

Liberia

History

It was the American Colonization Society's efforts of settling slaves freed in USA that led to the creation of Liberia in 1822. The Society decided that the resettling of freed slaves in West Africa would be a viable solution to slavery. Some 12,000 slaves were subsequently taken to Liberia, initially called Monrovia.

In 1847, Monrovia became independent as the Free and Independent Republic of Liberia, Africa's oldest republic.

Geography

Location: Western Africa, bordering the North Atlantic Ocean, between Cote d'Ivoire and Sierra Leone.

Area: 111,370 sq. km.

Terrain: Mostly flat rolling coastal plain that rises in a rolling plateau and low mountains in the north-east.

Natural resources: Iron ore, timber, diamond, gold, hydropower.

Climate: Hot and humid tropical climate.

People

Population: 3,482,211 (July 2005 est.).

Population growth rate: 2.64% (2005 est.).

Sex ratio: 0.98 male(s)/female (2005 est.).

Religions: Indigenous beliefs 40%, Christian 40%, Muslim 20%.

Languages: English 20% (official), around 20 ethnic group languages.

Literacy rate: Total 57.5%, Male 73.3%, Female 41.6% (2003 est.).

Infant mortality rate: 128.87 deaths/ 1,000 live births (2005 est.).

Life expectancy: Total 47.69 years, Male 46.75 years, Female 48.65 years (2005 est.).

Government

Capital: Monrovia.

Government type: Republic.

Independence: 26 July 1847.

Legal system: Dual system of statutory law based on Anglo-American common law for the modern sector and customary law based on unwritten tribal practices for indigenous sector.

Executive branch:
Chief of state: Chairman Gyude Bryant (since 14 October 2003); this is an interim position, effective till presidential elections are held in 2005. The chairman is both the chief of state and head of government.

Economy

Currency: Liberian dollar.

GDP: Purchasing power parity—$2.903 billion (2004 est.).

GDP—real growth rate: 21.8% (2004 est.).

GDP—per capita: Purchasing power parity—$900 (2004 est.).

Inflation rate: 15% (2003 est.).

Population below poverty line: 80%.

Unemployment rate: 85% (2003 est.).

Exports: $1.079 billion f.o.b. (2002 est.)—rubber, timber, iron, diamond, cocoa, coffee.

Imports: $5.051 billion f.o.b. (2002 est.)—fuels, chemicals, machinery, transportation equipment, manufactures, foodstuff.

External debt: $2.1 billion (2000 est.).

Transport and Communications

Railways: 490 km.

Roads: 10,600 km.

Telephones: 7,000 (2001).

Mobile cellular: 2,000 (2001).

Internet users: 1,000 (2002).

Internet country code: .lr

Libya

History

In the seventh century BC, Phoenicians settled in Tripolitania in western Libya. In the fourth century BC, Greeks colonized Cyrenaica in the eastern part of the country. They gave it the name, Libya. In the sixth century AD, Libya became a part of the Byzantine Empire. But in 643, Arabs under Amr Ibn al-As conquered Libya and spread Islam. In the 16th century, Libya became a part of the Ottoman Empire. It joined together the three provinces of Tripolitania, Cyrenaica and Fezzan into a single regency in Tripoli. In 1911–12, Italy conquered Libya. In 1942, the Allied forces evicted Italians from Libya. They then divided the country amongst the French (who controlled Fezzan) and the British (who administered Cyrenaica and Tripolitania). In 1951, Libya became independent under King Idris al-Sanusi.

In 1969, Col. Muammar Abu Minyar al-Qadhafi deposed King Idris in a military coup. He subsequently pursued a pan-Arab agenda and tried to form mergers with several Arab countries. He also introduced state socialism and nationalized most of the country's economic activity, including the oil industry. In 1970, Libya ordered the closure of British and American airbases in the country.

In 1986, USA carried out air strikes against Libyan military facilities and residential areas in Tripoli and Benghazi, killing 101 people. Qadhafi's house was also attacked. USA justified the attacks by holding Libya responsible for the bombing of a Berlin discotheque that US military personnel frequented.

In 1992, UN imposed sanctions on Libya. This was in an attempt to force it to hand over two of its citizens suspected of involvement in the blowing up of a Pan Am airliner over the Scottish town of Lockerbie in December 1988. In August 2003, Libya signed a compensation deal worth $2.7 billion with lawyers representing families of Lockerbie bombing victims. Libya also formally took responsibility for the bombing in a letter to the UN Security Council. This led to the lifting of UN sanctions on Libya in September.

Geography

Location: Northern Africa, bordering the Mediterranean Sea, between Egypt and Tunisia.

Area: 1,759,540 sq. km.

Terrain: Mostly barren with flat to undulating plains, plateaus and depressions.

Natural resources: Petroleum, natural gas, gypsum.

Climate: Mediterranean type of climate along the coast and a dry extreme desert type of climate in the interiors.

People

Population: 5,765,563 including 166,510 non-nationals (July 2005 est.).

Population growth rate: 2.37% (2004 est.).

Sex ratio: 1.05 male(s)/female (2005 est.).

Religions: Sunni Muslim 97%.

Languages: Arabic, Italian, English.

Literacy rate: Total 82.6%, Male 92.4%, Female 72% (2003 est.).

Infant mortality rate: 24.6 deaths/ 1,000 live births (2005 est.).

Life expectancy: Total 76.5 years, Male 74.29 years, Female 78.82 years (2005 est.).

Government

Capital: Tripoli.

Government type: Military dictatorship.

Independence: 24 December 1951.

Legal system: Based on Italian civil law system and Islamic law.

Executive branch:
Chief of state: Revolutionary Leader Col. Muammar Abu Minyar al-Qadhafi (since 1 September 1969).

Head of government: Secretary of the General People's Committee (Prime Minister) Shukri Muhammad Ghanim (since 14 June 2003).

Economy

Currency: Libyan dinar.

Economy—overview:
The Libyan economy is primarily dependent upon revenues from the oil sector. Almost all of Libya's export earnings and about one-quarter of GDP comes from the petroleum industry. Libya enjoys one of the highest per capita GDPs in Africa, thanks to its oil revenues and small population. However, very little of this income trickles down to the lower orders of society. The process of economic reforms gathered momentum after UN sanctions were lifted in September 2003.

GDP: Purchasing power parity— $37.48 billion (2004 est.).

GDP—real growth rate: 4.9% (2004 est.).

GDP—per capita: Purchasing power parity—$6,700 (2004 est.).

Inflation rate: 2.9% (2004 est.).

Unemployment rate: 30% (2004).

Exports: $18.65 billion f.o.b. (2004 est.) —crude oil, refined petroleum products.

Imports: $7.224 billion f.o.b. (2004 est.)—machinery, transport equipment, food, manufactured goods (1999).

External debt: $4.069 billion (2004 est.).

Transport and Communications

Railways: None.

Roads: 83,200 km.

Telephones: 750,000 (2003).

Mobile cellular: 100,000 (2003).

Internet users: 160,000 (2003).

Internet country code: .ly

Liechtenstein

History

The present-day principality of Liechtenstein was founded in 1719 by combining the two Holy Roman Empire lordships of Vaduz and Schellenburg. Between 1815 and 1866, Liechtenstein was a part of the German Confederation. Liechtenstein became fully independent in 1866.

Geography

Location: Central Europe, between Austria and Switzerland.

Area: 160 sq. km.

Natural resources: Hydroelectric potential, arable land.

Climate: Continental climate with cold, cloudy winters with frequent snow or rain and cool to moderately warm summers.

People

Population: 33,717 (July 2005 est.).

Population growth rate: 0.82% (2005 est.).

Sex ratio: 0.95 male(s)/female (2005 est.).

Religions: Roman Catholic 76.2%, Protestant 7%, unknown 10.6%, others 6.2% (June 2002).

Languages: German (official), Alemannic dialect.

Literacy rate: 100%.

Infant mortality rate: 4.7 deaths/1,000 live births (2005 est.).

Life expectancy: Total 79.55 years, Male 75.96 years, Female 83.16 years (2005 est.).

Government

Capital: Vaduz.

Government type: Hereditary constitutional monarchy on a democratic and parliamentary basis.

Independence: 23 January 1719 (Imperial Principality of Liechtenstein established).

Legal system: Local civil and penal codes.

Executive branch:
Chief of state: Prince Hans Adam II (since 13 November 1989, assumed executive powers 26 August 1984); Heir Apparent Prince Alois, son of the monarch (born 11 June 1968).

Head of government: Head of Government Otmar Hasler (since 5 April 2001) and Deputy Head of Government Rita Kieber-Beck (since 5 April 2001).

Economy

Currency: Swiss franc.

GDP: Purchasing power parity—$825 million (1999 est.).

GDP—real growth rate: 11% (1999 est.).

GDP—per capita: Purchasing power parity—$25,000 (1999 est.).

Inflation rate: 1% (2001).

Unemployment rate: 1.3% (2002 est.).

Exports: $2.47 billion (1996)—small speciality machinery, connectors for audio and video, parts for motor vehicles, dental products, hardware, prepared foodstuff, electronic equipment, optical products.

Imports: $917.3 million (1996)—agricultural products, raw materials, machinery, metal goods, textiles, foodstuff, motor vehicles.

External debt: None.

Transport and Communications

Railways: 18.5 km.

Roads: 250 km.

Telephones: 19,900 (2002).

Mobile cellular: 11,400 (2002).

Internet users: 20,000 (2002).

Internet country code: .li

Lithuania

History

From the 14th to the 16th centuries, Lithuania and Poland was one of the strongest empires in the world and formed a confederation for about 200 years. Russians claimed Lithuania after the division of Poland in 1795. At the end of World War I, Lithuania took advantage of a weak Russia to declare its independence in 1918.

Geography

Location: Eastern Europe, bordering the Baltic Sea, between Latvia and Russia.

Area: 65,200 sq. km.

Terrain: Lowland with scattered small lakes.

Natural resources: Peat, arable land.

Climate: Transitional type of climate that lies between maritime and continental wet.

People

Population: 3,596,617 (July 2005 est.).

Population growth rate: −0.3% (2005 est.).

Sex ratio: 0.85 male(s)/female (2005 est.).

Religions: Roman Catholic (primarily), Lutheran, Russian Orthodox, Protestant, Evangelical Christian Baptist, Muslim, Jewish.

Languages: Lithuanian (official), Polish, Russian.

Literacy rate: 99.6% (2003 est.).

Infant mortality rate: 6.89 deaths/1,000 live births (2005 est.).

Life expectancy: Total 73.97 years, Male 68.94 years, Female 79.28 years (2005 est.).

Government

Capital: Vilnius.

Government type: Parliamentary democracy.

Independence: 11 March 1990—date of declaration of independence from Soviet Union.

Legal system: Based on civil law system; legislative acts can be appealed to the constitutional court.

Executive branch:
Chief of state: President Valdas Adamkus (since 12 July 2004).

Head of government: Premier Algirdas Mykolas Brazauskas (since 3 July 2001).

Economy

Currency: Litas.

GDP: Purchasing power parity—$45.23 billion (2004 est.).

GDP—real growth rate: 6.6% (2004 est.).

GDP—per capita: Purchasing power parity—$12,500 (2004 est.).

Inflation rate: 1.1% (2004 est.).

Unemployment rate: 8% (2004 est.).

Exports: $8.88 billion f.o.b. (2004 est.)—mineral products, textiles and clothing, machinery and equipment, chemicals, wood and wood products, foodstuff (2001).

Imports: $11.02 billion f.o.b. (2004 est.)—mineral products, machinery and equipment, transport equipment, chemicals, textiles and clothing, metals (2001).

External debt: $10.01 billion (2004 est.).

Transport and Communications

Railways: 1,998 km.

Roads: 77,148 km.

Telephones: 824,200 (2003).

Mobile cellular: 2,169,900 (2003).

Internet users: 695,700 (2003).

Internet country code: .lt

Luxembourg

History

Luxembourg became independent in 963, when Siegfried, Count de Ardennes, exchanged his lands for the Roman castle named Lucilinburhuc. This castle proved to be the birthplace of Luxembourg.

Geography

Location: Western Europe, between France and Germany.

Area: 2,586 sq. km.

Natural resources: Arable land.

Climate: Modified continental climate with mild winters and cool summers.

People

Population: 468,571 (July 2005 est.).

Population growth rate: 1.25% (2005 est.).

Sex ratio: 0.97 male(s)/female (2005 est.).

Religions: 87% Roman Catholic, 13% Protestants, Jews, and Muslims (2000).

Languages: Luxembourgish (national language), German (administrative language), French (administrative language).

Literacy rate: 100% (2000 est.).

Infant mortality rate: 4.81 deaths/ 1,000 live births (2005 est.).

Life expectancy: Total 78.74 years, Male 75.45 years, Female 82.24 years (2005 est.).

Government

Capital: Luxembourg.

Government type: Constitutional monarchy.

Independence: 1839 (from the Netherlands).

Legal system: Based on civil law system.

Executive branch:
Chief of state: Grand Duke Henri (since 7 October 2000); Heir Apparent Prince Guillaume (son of the monarch, born 11 November 1981).

Head of government: Prime Minister Jean-Claude Juncker (since 1 January 1995) and Vice Prime Minister Lydie Polfer (since 7 August 1999).

Economy

Currency: Euro.

GDP: Purchasing power parity—$27.27 billion (2004 est.).

GDP—real growth rate: 2.3% (2004 est.).

GDP—per capita: Purchasing power parity—$58,900 (2004 est.).

Inflation rate: 2.4% (2004 est.).

Unemployment rate: 4.5% (2004 est.).

Exports: $13.4 billion f.o.b. (2004)— machinery and equipment, steel products, chemicals, rubber products, glass.

Imports: $16.3 billion c.i.f. (2004)— minerals, metals, foodstuff, quality consumer goods.

Transport and Communications

Railways: 274 km.

Roads: 5,210 km.

Telephones: 355,400 (2002).

Mobile cellular: 473,000 (2002).

Internet users: 165,000 (2002).

Internet country code: .lu

Macedonia

History

Macedon gained prominence in the fourth century BC due to the conquests of Alexander the Great. Later on, Macedonia became a part of the Roman Empire, the Byzantine Empire and the Ottoman Empire. The 19th century saw constant rivalry for the possession of Macedonia, for its economic wealth and strategic location.

In 1991, the country declared its independence even as ethnic Albanians within Macedonia demanded their own territory while Greece objected to the use of the name Macedonia, as one of its provinces had the same name.

Geography

Location: South-eastern Europe, north of Greece.

Area: 25,333 sq. km.

Terrain: Mountanious with deep basins and valleys.

Natural resources: Low-grade iron ore, copper, lead, zinc, chromite, manganese, nickel, tungsten, gold, silver, asbestos, gypsum, timber, arable land.

Climate: Warm, dry summers and autumns and relatively cold winters with heavy snowfall.

People

Population: 2,045,262 (July 2005 est.).

Population growth rate: 0.26% (2005 est.).

Sex ratio: 1 male(s)/female (2005 est.).

Religions: Macedonian Orthodox 70%, Muslim 29%, others 1%.

Languages: Macedonian 68%, Albanian 25%, Turkish 3%, Serbo-Croatian 2%, others 2%.

Infant mortality rate: 10.09 deaths/1,000 live births (2005 est.).

Life expectancy: Total 73.73 years, Male 71.28 years, Female 76.37 years (2005 est.).

Government

Capital: Skopje.

Government type: Parliamentary democracy.

Independence: 8 September 1991—date of signing of referendum by registered voters endorsing independence (from Yugoslavia).

Legal system: Based on civil law system.

Executive branch:
Chief of state: President Branko Crvenkovski (sworn in on 12 May 2004).

Head of government: Prime Minister Vlado Buckovski (since 17 December 2004).

Economy

Currency: Macedonian denar.

GDP. Purchasing power parity—$14.4 billion (2004 est.).

GDP—real growth rate: 1.3% (2004 est.).

GDP—per capita: Purchasing power parity—$7,100 (2004 est.).

Inflation rate: 0.4% (2004 est.).

Population below poverty line: 30.2% (2004 est.).

Unemployment rate: 37.7% (2004 est.).

Exports: $1.629 billion f.o.b. (2004 est.)—food, beverages, tobacco, iron and steel.

Imports: $2.677 billion f.o.b. (2004 est.)—machinery and equipment, chemicals, fuels, food products.

External debt: $1.863 billion (2004 est.).

Transport and Communications

Railways: 699 km.

Roads: 8,684 km.

Telephones: 560,000 (2002).

Mobile cellular: 365,300 (2002).

Internet users: 100,000 (2002).

Internet country code: .mk

Madagascar

History

The first European known to have reach Madagascar was a Portuguese navigator named Diogo Dias, in 1500. The French soon followed.

In the early 19th century, a kingdom under Radama I took shape, uniting most of the island. The British allied with Radama I, giving him the title, King of Madagascar, and helped him against the French. In late 19th century, France succeeded in establishing a protectorate on the island. Madagascar gained independence in 1960 with Philibert Tsiranana as President.

Geography

Location: Southern Africa, island in the Indian Ocean, east of Mozambique.

Area: 587,040 sq. km.

Terrain: Narrow costal plain with a high plateau and mountains in the centre.

Natural resources: Graphite, chromite, coal, bauxite, salt, quartz, tar sands, semiprecious stones, mica, fish, hydropower.

Climate: Tropical along the coast, temperate further inland and arid in the south.

People

Population: 18,040,340 (July 2005 est.).

Population growth rate: 3.03% (2005 est.).

Sex ratio: 0.99 male(s)/female (2005 est.).

Religions: Indigenous beliefs 52%, Christian 41%, Muslim 7%.

Languages: French (official), Malagasy (official).

Literacy rate: Total 68.9%, Male 75.5%, Female 62.5% (2003 est.).

Infant mortality rate: 76.83 deaths/ live births (2005 est.).

Life expectancy: Total 56.95 years, Male 54.57 years, Female 59.4 years (2005 est.).

Government

Capital: Antananarivo.

Government type: Republic.

Independence: 26 June 1960 (from France).

Legal system: Based on French civil law system and traditional Malagasy law.

Executive branch:
Chief of state: President Marc Ravalomanana (since 6 May 2002).

Head of government: Prime Minister Jacques Sylla (since 27 May 2002).

Economy

Currency: Malagasy franc.

GDP: Purchasing power parity—$14.56 billion (2004 est.).

GDP—real growth rate: 5.5% (2004 est.).

GDP—per capita: Purchasing power parity—$800 (2004 est.).

Inflation rate: 7.5% (2004 est.).

Population below poverty line: 50% (2004 est.).

Exports: $868.2 million f.o.b. (2004 est.)—coffee, vanilla, shellfish, sugar, cotton cloth, chromite, petroleum products.

Imports: $1.147 billion f.o.b. (2004 est.)—capital goods, petroleum, consumer goods, food.

External debt: $4.6 billion (2002).

Transport and Communications

Railways: 732 km.

Roads: 49,827 km.

Ports and harbours: Antsiranana, Antsohimbondrona, Mahajanga, Toamasina, Toliara.

Airports: 116 (2003 est.).

Telephones: 59,600 (2003).

Mobile cellular: 279,500 (2003).

Internet users: 70,500 (2003).

Internet country code: .mg

Malawi

History

David Livingstone was the first European to carry out in-depth exploration of the area in the 19th century. In 1884, Cecil Rhodes' British South African Company received a charter to develop the region. This brought the company into conflict with the Arab slave traders in the 1880s. In 1891 UK annexed the territory and established the Nyasaland Districts Protectorate. It was called the British Central Africa Protectorate from 1893 and Nyasaland from 1907. In 1964, Nyasaland gained independence as Malawi.

Geography

Location: Southern Africa, east of Zambia.

Area: 118,480 sq. km.

Terrain: Narrow elongated plateau with rolling plains, hills and some mountains.

Natural resources: Limestone, arable land, hydropower, uranium (unexploited), coal, and bauxite.

Climate: Subtropical climate with a rainy season from November to May and dry season from May to November.

People

Population: 12,158,924 (2005 est.).

Population growth rate: 2.06% (2005 est.).

Sex ratio: 0.99 male(s)/female (2005 est.).

Religions: Protestant 55%, Roman Catholic 20%, Muslim 20%, indigenous beliefs 3%, others 2%.

Languages: English (official), Chichewa (official), regional languages.

Literacy rate: Total 62.7%, Male 76.1%, Female 49.8% (2003 est.).

Infant mortality rate: 103.32 deaths/ 1,000 live births (2005 est.).

Life expectancy: Total 36.97 years, Male 36.59 years, Female 37.36 years (2005 est.).

Government

Capital: Lilongwe.

Government type: Multiparty democracy.

Independence: 6 July 1964 (from UK).

Legal system: Based on English common law and customary law.

Executive branch:
Chief of state: President Bingu wa Mutharica (since 24 May 2004). The president is both the chief of state and head of government.

Economy

Currency: Malawian kwacha.

GDP: Purchasing power parity—$7.41 billion (2004 est.).

GDP—real growth rate: 4% (2004 est.).

GDP—per capita: Purchasing Power Parity—$600 (2004 est.).

Inflation rate: 12% (2004 est.).

Population below poverty line: 55% (2004 est.).

Exports: $503.4 million f.o.b. (2004 est.)—tobacco, tea, sugar, cotton, coffee, peanuts, wood products, apparel.

Imports: $521.1 million f.o.b. (2004 est.)—food, petroleum products, semi-manufactures, consumer goods, transportation equipment.

External debt: $3.129 billion (2004).

Transport and Communications

Railways: 797 km.

Roads: 28,400 km.

Telephones: 85,000 (2003).

Mobile cellular: 135,100 (2003).

Internet users: 36,000 (2003).

Internet country code: .mw

Malaysia

History

Malaya is believed to have been inhabited for about 6000–8000 years. It is thought that there were small kingdoms in the region in the second and third centuries AD. It was at this point of time that Indian explorers first arrived in the area. Malacca, which was founded by Sumatran exiles around 1400, was taken by the Portuguese in 1511 and the Dutch in 1641.

The area subsequently came under British influence by 1867, when they founded the Straits Settlements, which included Singapore, Malaya and Penang. In the 19th century, the Chinese began coming into this region. In 1941, the region was invaded by Japan.

In 1948, the British gave in to rising nationalism to form the semi-autonomous Federation of Malay. In 1957, Malay gained independence.

Geography

Location: South-eastern Asia, peninsula and northern one-third of the island of Borneo, bordering Indonesia and the South China Sea, south of Vietnam.

Area: 329,750 sq. km.

Terrain: Coastal plains that rise to hills and mountains.

Natural resources: Tin, timber, copper, iron ore, petroleum, natural gas, bauxite.

Climate: Tropical; annual south-west (April to October) and north-east (October to February) monsoons.

People

Population: 23,953,136 (July 2005 est.).

Population growth rate: 1.86% (2005 est.).

Sex ratio: 1.01 male(s)/female (2005 est.).

Religions: Muslim, Buddhist, Daoist, Hindu, Christian, Sikh. (In addition, Shamanism is practised in east Malaysia.)

Languages: Bahasa Melayu (official), English, Chinese dialects, Tamil, Telugu, Malayalam, Panjabi, Thai.

Literacy rate: Total 88.9%, Male 92.4%, Female 85.4% (2003 est.).

Infant mortality rate: 17 deaths/ 1,000 live births (2005 est.).

Life expectancy: Total 72.24 years, Male 69.56 years, Female 75.11 years (2005 est.).

Government

Capital: Kuala Lumpur.

Government type: Constitutional monarchy.

Independence: 31 August 1957 (from UK).

Legal system: Based on English common law.

Executive branch:
Chief of state: Paramount Ruler Tuanku Syed Sirajuddin ibni Almarhum Tuanku Syed Putra Jamalullail, the Raja of Perlis (since 12 December 2001).

Head of government: Prime Minister Abdullah bin Ahmad Badawi (since 31 October 2003).

Economy

Currency: Ringgit.

Economy—overview:
Malaysia is a middle-income country that transformed itself in the period between 1971 and the late 1990s from a producer of raw materials into an emerging multi-sector economy. In this period, growth was almost exclusively driven by exports, mainly of electronics. Consequently, the country was hard hit by the global economic downturn and the slump in the Information Technology (IT) sector in 2001. In 2001, GDP grew only by 0.5% mainly due to an estimated 11% fall in exports. However, a substantial fiscal stimulus package lessened the impact of the worst of the recession. The economy rebounded in 2002. It is unlikely that the country will experience a crisis similar to the one in 1997, thanks to its foreign exchange reserves and relatively small external debt. Nevertheless, the economy remains vulnerable to a prolonged slowdown in Japan and the US, which remain the top export destinations and key sources of foreign investment.

GDP: Purchasing power parity—$229.3 billion (2004 est.).

GDP—real growth rate: 7.1% (2004 est.).

GDP—per capita: Purchasing power parity—$9,700 (2004 est.).

Inflation rate: 1.3% (2004 est.).

Population below poverty line: 8% (1998 est.).

Unemployment rate: 3% (2004 est.).

Exports: $123.5 billion f.o.b. (2004 est.).

Imports: $99.3 billion f.o.b. (2004 est.).

External debt: $53.36 billion (2004 est.).

Transport and Communications

Railways: 2,418 km.

Roads: 65,877 km.

Telephones: 4,571,600(2003).

Mobile cellular: 11,124,100(2003).

Internet users: 8,692,000 (2003).

Internet country code: .my

Maldives

History

In ancient times, Maldives was known as the source of cowrie shells that acted as a currency in parts of India, South Asia and Middle East. Cowrie shells from Maldives have been found even at the centres of the Indus Valley Civilization.

The first people likely to have settled down in the Maldives were members of south-west Indian fishing communities. Mentions of what is today Maldives can be found in some of the ancient chronicles of south India.

On 16 December 1887, the ruling monarch, Sultan Muinuddheen II, signed an agreement with the British governor of Ceylon (now Sri Lanka). Under the terms of this agreement, Maldives became a British protectorate. On 26 July 1965, Maldives gained independence. On 11 November 1968, the sultanate was abolished and a republic was established.

Geography

Location: Southern Asia, group of atolls in the Indian Ocean, south-south-west of India.

Area: 300 sq. km.

Terrain: Flat, with white sandy beaches.

Natural resources: Fish.

Climate: Hot and humid tropical climate.

People

Population: 349,106 (July 2005 est.).

Population growth rate: 2.82% (2005 est.).

Sex ratio: 1.05 male(s)/female (2005 est.).

Religions: Sunni Muslim.

Languages: Maldivian Dhivehi (a dialect of Sinhala while the script is derived from Arabic), English spoken by most government officials.

Literacy rate: Total 97.2%, Male 97.1%, Female 97.3% (2003 est.).

Infant mortality rate: 56.52 deaths/1,000 live births (2005 est.).

Life expectancy: Total 64.04 years, Male 62.76 years, Female 65.42 years (2005 est.).

Government

Capital: Male.

Government type: Republic.

Independence: 26 July 1965 (from UK).

Legal system: Based on Islamic law with admixtures of English common law.

Executive branch:

Chief of state: President Maumoon Abdul Gayoom (since 11 November 1978). (The President is both the chief of state and head of government).

Economy

Currency: Rufiyaa.

Economy—overview:
Tourism is the largest industry of the country and accounts for 20% of GDP and more than 60% of its foreign exchange receipts. Import duties and tourism-related taxes contribute to over 90% of the government's tax revenue.

Fishing is another key sector of the Maldivian economy. In 1989, the Maldivian government initiated an economic reform process. It lifted import quotas and allowed the private sector to export its products. It has allowed greater foreign investment. The country suffers from a shortage of cultivable land and domestic labour, which in turn imposes constraints on agriculture and manufacturing. Even basic commodities like food has to be imported. Industry consists mainly of boat building, garment production and handicrafts and

accounts for about 18% of GDP. One major future source of concern for the Maldivian authorities is the global warming and subsequent rise in sea levels. Maldives is a low-lying country with 80% of the area lying at a height of one metre or less above sea level.

GDP: Purchasing power parity—$1.25 billion (2002 est.).

GDP—real growth rate: 2.3% (2002 est.).

GDP—per capita: Purchasing power parity—$3,900 (2002 est.).

Inflation rate: 1% (2002 est.).

Exports: $90 million f.o.b. (2002 est.).

Imports: $392 million f.o.b. (2002 est.).

External debt: $281 million (2003 est.).

Transport and Communications

Railways: None.

Roads: Not available.

Telephones: 28,700 (2002).

Mobile cellular: 41,900 (2002).

Internet users: 6,000 (2001).

Internet country code: .mv

Mali

History

Human remains dating back to 5000 BC have been found in Mali. The region's gold deposits and trade in a variety of commodities resulted in the developing of trading centres like Timbuktu and Djenne-Jeno. It has also been on the trans-Saharan caravan routes from the first century AD.

Towards the end of the 19th century, the area came under French domina-

tion. In 1904, it became a French colony. In 1920, it was renamed French Sudan. In November 1958, the territory became an autonomous state within the French Community, with the name Sudanese Republic. In September 1960, the Republic of Mali was proclaimed.

Geography

Location: Western Africa, bordering Algeria and Niger.

Area: 1,240,000 sq. km.

Terrain: Mostly flat or rolling northern plains covered by sand; savanna in the south and rugged hills in the north-east.

Natural resources: Gold, phosphates, kaolin, salt, limestone, uranium, hydropower; the country also has unexploited deposits of bauxite, iron ore, manganese, tin, and copper.

Climate: Subtropical to arid.

People

Population: 12,291,529 (July 2005 est.).

Population growth rate: 2.74% (2005 est.).

Sex ratio: 0.96 male(s)/female (2005 est.).

Religions: Muslim 90%, indigenous beliefs 9%, Christian 1%.

Languages: French (official), Bambara 80%, numerous African languages.

Literacy rate: Total 46.4%, Male 53.5%, Female 39.6% (2003 est.).

Infant mortality rate: 116.79 deaths/1,000 live births (2005 est.).

Life expectancy: Total 45.09 years, Male 44.69 years, Female 45.51 years (2005 est.).

Government

Capital: Bamako.

Government type: Republic.

Independence: 22 September 1960 (from France).

Legal system: Based on French civil law system and customary law.

Executive branch:
Chief of state: President Amadou Toumani Toure (since 8 June 2002).

Head of government: Prime Minister Ousmane Issoufi Maiga (since 30 April 2004).

Economy

Currency: Communaute Financiere Africaine franc.

GDP: Purchasing power parity—$11 billion (2004 est.).

GDP—real growth rate: 4% (2004 est.).

GDP—per capita: Purchasing power parity—$900 (2004 est.).

Inflation rate: 4.5% (2002 est.).

Population below poverty line: 64% (2001 est.).

Unemployment rate: 14.6% (2001 est.).

Exports: $915 million f.o.b. (2002 est.)—cotton, gold, livestock.

Imports: $927 million f.o.b. (2002 est.)—petroleum, machinery and equipment, construction materials, foodstuff, textiles.

External debt: $3.3 billion (2000).

Transport and Communications

Railways: 729 km.

Roads: 15,100 km.

Telephones: 56,600 (2002).

Mobile cellular: 250,000 (2003).

Internet users: 25,000 (2002).

Internet country code: .ml

Malta

History

Malta passed through to the Arabs, Normans and a series of feudal rulers. In 1530, the Order of the Hospital of St John of Jerusalem (the Knights Hospitalers), a religious and military order of the Roman Catholic Church, obtained control of the islands.

In the early 19th century, the Maltese people acknowledged British sovereignty. During World War II, the islands frustrated Axis invasion attempts and became one of the most heavily bombed targets during the War. UK rewarded the entire island with George Cross, its highest civilian decoration. Even today, the flag of Malta bears a representation of the medal of the George Cross.

Malta became an independent country within the Commonwealth on 21 September 1964 and a republic on 13 December 1974.

Geography

Location: Southern Europe, islands in the Mediterranean Sea, south of Sicily (Italy).

Area: 316 sq. km.

Natural resources: Limestone, salt, arable land.

Climate: Mediterranean climate with mild, rainy winters and hot, dry summers.

People

Population: 398,534 (July 2005 est.).

Population growth rate: 0.42% (2005 est.).

Sex ratio: 0.99 male(s)/female (2005 est.).

Religions: Roman Catholic 98%.

Languages: Maltese (official), English (official).

Literacy rate: Total 92.8%, Male 92%, Female 93.6% (2003 est.).

Infant mortality rate: 3.89 deaths/1,000 live births (2005 est.).

Life expectancy: Total 78.86 years, Male 76.7 years, Female 81.15 years (2005 est).

Government

Capital: Valletta.

Government type: Republic.

Independence: 21 September 1964 (from UK).

Legal system: Based on English common law and Roman civil law.

Executive branch:
Chief of state: President Eddie Fenech Adami (since 4 April 2004).

Head of government: Prime Minister Lawrence Gonzi (since 23 March 2004).

Economy

Currency: Maltese lira.

GDP: Purchasing power parity—$7.223 billion (2004 est.).

GDP—real growth rate: 1% (2004 est.).

GDP—per capita: Purchasing power parity—$18,200 (2004 est.).

Inflation rate: 2.9% (2004 est.).

Unemployment rate: 7% (2003 est.).

Exports: $2.625 billion f.o.b. (2004 est.)—machinery and transport equipment, manufactures.

Imports: $3.407 billion f.o.b. (2004 est.)—machinery and transport equipment, manufactured and semi-manufactured goods, food, drink, and tobacco.

External debt: $130 million (1997).

Transport and Communications

Railways: None.

Roads: 2,222 km.

Telephones: 208,300 (2003).

Mobile cellular: 290,000 (2003).

Internet users: 120,000 (2002).

Internet country code: .mt

Marshall Islands

History

The Spanish explored the islands in the 16th century. In 1788, they were named after a British captain. In 1947, the United Nations placed the Marshall Islands, along with the Mariana and Caroline Islands, under a US Trust Territory. Between 1946 and 1958, the US carried out nuclear tests on the Bikini and Enewetak islands. In 1983, the US paid $183.7 million as damages for contamination of the islands due to nuclear testing. Another $3.8 million was paid later to the displaced islanders of Bikini. In 1986, Marshall Islands attained self-government after entering into a Compact of Free Association.

Geography

Location: Oceania, group of atolls and reefs in the North Pacific Ocean.

Area: 181.3 sq. km (This includes the atolls of Bikini, Enewetak, Kwajalein, Majuro, Rongelap, and Utirik).

Natural resources: Coconut products, marine products, deep seabed minerals.

Climate: Hot and humid climate.

People

Population: 59,071 (July 2005 est.).

Population growth rate: 2.27% (2005 est.).

Sex ratio: 1.04 male(s)/female (2005 est.).

Religions: Christian (mostly Protestant).

Languages: English (widely spoken as a second language, both English and Marshallese are official languages), two major Marshallese dialects from the Malayo-Polynesian family, Japanese.

Literacy rate: Total 93.7%, Male 93.6%, Female 93.7% (1999).

Infant mortality rate: 29.45% (2005 est.).

Life expectancy: Total 70.01 years, Male 68.05 years, Female 72.06 years (2005 est.).

Government

Capital: Majuro.

Government type: Constitutional government in free association with the US.

Independence: 21 October 1986 (from the US-administered UN trusteeship).

Legal system: Based on adapted Trust Territory laws, acts of the legislature, municipal, common, and customary laws.

Executive branch:
Chief of state: President Kessai Hesa Note (since 5 January 2004). The president is both the chief of state and head of government.

Economy

Currency: US Dollar.

GDP: Purchasing power parity—$115 million (2001 est.).

GDP—real growth rate: 1% (2001 est.).

GDP—per capita: Purchasing power parity—$1,600 (2001 est.).

Inflation rate: 2% (2001 est.).

Exports: $9 million f.o.b. (2000)—copra cake, coconut oil, handicrafts, fish.

Imports: $54 million f.o.b. (2000)—foodstuff, machinery and equipment, fuels, beverages and tobacco.

External debt: $86.5 million (2000 est.).

Transport and Communications

Railways: None.

Roads: 64.5 km.

Telephones: 4,500 (2003).

Mobile cellular: 600 (2002).

Internet users: 1,400 (2003).

Internet country code: .mh

Mauritania

History

The earliest settlers of Mauritania were the sub-Saharan peoples and the Berbers. In the 15th century, Arab tribes reached Mauritania via a caravan route that linked the region with Morocco. This gave rise to a mixed Arab-Berber culture.

In 1904, Mauritania became a French colony. In 1920, it became a part of French West Africa and was administered from Senegal. Mauritania gained independence in November 1960.

Geography

Location: Northern Africa, bordering the North Atlantic Ocean, between Senegal and Western Sahara.

Area: 1,030,700 sq. km.

Terrain: Barren flat plains with some hills in the central part of the country.

Natural resources: Iron ore, gypsum, copper, phosphate, diamonds, gold, oil, fish.

Climate: Hot, dry, dusty desert climate.

People

Population: 3,086,859 (July 2005 est.).

Population growth rate: 2.9% (2005 est.).

Sex ratio: 0.98 male(s)/female (2005 est.).

Religions: Muslim 100%.

Languages: Hassaniya Arabic (official), Pulaar, Soninke, Wolof (official), French.

Literacy rate: Total 41.7%, Male 51.8%, Female 31.9% (2003 est.).

Infant mortality rate: 70.89 deaths/1,000 live births (2005 est.).

Life expectancy: Total 52.73 years, Male 50.52 years, Female 55 years (2005 est.).

Government

Capital: Nouakchott.

Government type: Republic.

Independence: 28 November 1960 (from France).

Legal system: A combination of Shari'a (Islamic law) and French civil law.

Executive branch:
Chief of state: President Maaouya Ould Sid Ahmed Taya (since 12 December 1984).

Head of government: Prime Minister Sghair Ould M'Bareck (since 6 July 2003).

Economy

Currency: Ouguiya.

GDP: Purchasing power parity—$5.534 billion (2004 est.).

GDP—real growth rate: 3% (2004 est.).

GDP—per capita: Purchasing power parity—$1,800 (2004 est.).

Inflation rate: 7% (2003 est.).

Population below poverty line: 40% (2004 est.).

Unemployment rate: 20% (2004 est.).

Exports: $541 million f.o.b. (2002)—iron ore, fish and fish products, gold.

Imports: $860 million f.o.b. (2002)—machinery and equipment, petroleum products, capital goods, foodstuff, consumer goods.

External debt: $2.5 billion (2000).

Transport and Communications

Railways: 717 km.

Roads: 7,660 km.

Telephones: 31,500 (2002).

Mobile cellular: 300,200 (2003).

Internet users: 10,000 (2002).

Internet country code: .mr

Mauritius

History

In 1498, Portuguese explorers chanced upon the island in the aftermath of Vasco da Gama's voyage around the Cape of Good Hope. In 1598, the Dutch laid claim to the still uninhabited island and renamed it after their head of state, Maurice, Prince of Orange.

In 1715, the French East India Company laid claim to Mauritius. They started settling the island from the 1720s and founded Port Louis as a staging ground for attacking the British in India. In 1834, the British abolished slavery. As a replacement for slavery, the British introduced the system of indentured labour. This led to the arrival of hundreds of thousands of workers from India.

In 1926, the first Indo-Mauritians were elected to government council. Internal self-government was introduced in 1957. Mauritius finally gained independence in March 1968.

Geography

Location: Southern Africa, island in the Indian Ocean, east of Madagascar.

Area: 2,040 sq. km (this includes Agalega Islands, Cargados Carajos Shoals [Saint Brandon], and Rodrigues).

Natural resources: Arable land, fish.

Climate: Tropical climate.

People

Population: 1,230,602 (July 2005 est.).

Population growth rate: 0.84% (2005 est.).

Sex ratio: 0.97 male(s)/female (2005 est.).

Religions: Hindu 52%, Christian 28.3% (Roman Catholic 26%, Protestant 2.3%), Muslim 16.6%, others 3.1%.

Languages: English (official), Creole, French (official), Hindi, Urdu, Hakka, Bhojpuri.

Literacy rate: Total 85.6%, Male 88.6%, Female 82.7% (2003 est.).

Infant mortality rate: 15.03 deaths/1,000 live births (2005 est.).

Life expectancy: Total 72.38 years, Male 68.4 years, Female 76.41 years (2005 est.).

Government

Capital: Port Louis.

Government type: Parliamentary democracy.

Independence: 12 March 1968 (from UK).

Legal system: Based on French civil law system with aspects of English common law in some areas.

Executive branch:
Chief of state: President Sir Anerood Jugnauth (since 7 October 2003).

Head of government: Prime Minister Paul Berenger (since 30 September 2003).

Economy

Currency: Mauritian rupee.

GDP: Purchasing power parity—$15.68 billion (2004 est.).

GDP—real growth rate: 4.7% (2004 est.).

GDP—per capita: Purchasing power parity—$12,800 (2004 est.).

Inflation rate: 6.4% (2002 est.).

Population below poverty line: 10% (2001 est.).

Unemployment rate: 10.8% (2004 est).

Exports: $2.012 billion f.o.b. (2004 est.)—clothing and textiles, sugar, cut flowers, molasses.

Imports: $2.245 billion f.o.b. (2004 est.)—manufactured goods, capital equipment, foodstuff, petroleum products, chemicals.

External debt: $1.78 billion (2004 est.).

Transport and Communications

Railways: None.

Roads: 2,000 km.

Telephones: 348,200 (2003).

Mobile cellular: 462,400 (2003).

Internet users: 150,000 (2003).

Internet country code: .mu

Mexico

History

The region that comprises present-day Mexico has been the home of ancient civilizations such as the Olmec, Toltec, Mayan and Aztec. The Aztec empire was still expanding when the Spanish appeared on the scene in 1519. The empire finally came to an end with the conquest of the Aztec capital, Tenochtitlan, in 1521 by forces led by the Spanish explorer, Hernan Cortes. The Spanish conquered the remains of the Mayan civilization in the mid-16th century and by 1681, Mexico had become a part of the viceroyalty of New Spain.

The first major revolt against the Spanish came in 1810 and independence was finally negotiated in 1821. In 1823, Mexico became a republic.

In 1845, Mexico lost Texas to the USA and following defeat in the Mexican War (1846-8) and the subsequent signing of the Treaty of Guadelupe Hidalgo, it had to give up vast stretches that today constitute western and south-western USA.

Geography

Location: Middle America, bordered with the Caribbean Sea and the Gulf of Mexico between Belize and the USA.

Area: 1,972,550 sq. km.

Terrain: High, rugged mountains, low coastal plains, high plateaus and even desert areas.

Natural resources: Mexico has deposits of petroleum, silver, copper, gold, lead, zinc, natural gas, timber.

Climate: Varies from tropical to desert.

People

Population: 106,202,903 (July 2005 est.).

Population growth rate: 1.17% (2005 est.).

Sex ratio: 0.96 male(s)/female (2005 est.).

Religions: Nominally Roman Catholic 89%, Protestant 6%, others 5%.

Languages: Spanish, various Mayan, Nahuatl, and other regional indigenous languages.

Literacy rate: 92.2% (2003 est.).

Infant mortality rate: 20.91 deaths/ 1,000 live births (2005 est.).

Life expectancy: Total 75.19 years, Male 72.42 years, Female 78.1 years (2005 est.).

Government

Capital: Mexico City.

Government type: Federal republic.

Independence: 24 September 1821, from Spain.

Legal system: Mixture of US constitutional theory and civil law system.

Executive branch:
Chief of state: President Vicente Fox Quesada (since 1 December 2000). The president is both the chief of state and head of government.

Economy

Currency: Mexican peso.

Economy—overview:
Mexico has a free market economy with a mixture of modern and obsolete industry and agriculture. There is an increasing level of domination of the private sector. Recent years have seen increased competition in key infrastructures like telecommunications, electricity, airports, seaports, railroads and natural gas distribution.

The economy is marked by a chronic unequal distribution of income. Ever since NAFTA was implemented in 1994, trade with the US and Canada has tripled. The economy registered a growth of 6.9% in 2000, but real GDP decreased by 0.3% in 2001. In 2002, there was only a nominal rise of 1%. The main cause behind this downturn was the slowdown in the USA.

Mexico has implemented free trade agreements with Guatemala, Honduras, El Salvador, and the European Free Trade Area. This means that more than 90% of the country's trade is now under free trade agreements. In 2001, foreign direct investment touched $25 billion although half of this came from one single case— Citigroup's acquisition of Mexico's second-largest bank, Banamex.

GDP: Purchasing power parity—$1.006 trillion (2004 est.).

GDP—real growth rate: 4.1% (2004 est.).

GDP—per capita: Purchasing power parity—$9,600 (2004 est.).

Inflation rate: 5.4% (2004 est.).

Population below poverty line: 40% (2003 est.).

Unemployment rate: 3.2% plus considerable underemployment (2004 est.).

Exports: $182.4 billion f.o.b. (2004 est.).

Imports: $190.8 billion f.o.b. (2004 est.).

External debt: $149.9 billion (2004 est.).

Transport and Communications

Railways: 19,510 km.

Roads: 329,532 km.

Telephones: 15,958,700 (2003).

Mobile cellular: 28,125,000 (2003).

Internet users: 10,033,000 (2003).

Internet country code: .mx

Federated States of Micronesia

History

In the 17th century, Spain colonized the islands of present-day Micronesia that were originally inhabited by Polynesians and Micronesians. In April 1947, the United Nations created the Trust Territory of the Pacific Islands that placed the Caroline, Northern Mariana and Marshall Islands under US administration. In 1979, the Micronesian Federation attained self-governance and in 1983, the islands accepted the Compact of Free Association with the USA. It became independent in 1986 when the US government declared the Trust Territory agreements no longer effective. In 1991, the Micronesian Federation became a member of the United Nations.

Geography

Location: Island group in the North Pacific Ocean.

Area: 702 sq. km. This includes Pohnpei (Ponape), Chuuk (Truk) Islands, Yap Islands, and Kosrae (Kosaie).

Natural resources: Forests, marine products, deep-seabed minerals.

Climate: Tropical climate with heavy rainfall round the year mainly in the eastern islands.

People

Population: 108,105 (July 2005 est.).

Population growth rate: −0.08% (2005 est.).

Sex ratio: 1.05 male(s)/female (2005 est.).

Religions: Roman Catholic 50%, Protestant 47%.

Languages: English (official and common language), Kapingamarangi, Kosrean, Nukuoro, Pohnpeian, Trukese, Ulithian, Woleaian, Yapese.

Literacy rate: Total 89%, Male 91%, Female 88% (1980 est.).

Infant mortality rate: 30.21 deaths/ 1,000 live births (2005 est.).

Life expectancy: Total 69.75 years, Male 67.96 years, Female 71.62 years (2005 est.).

Government

Capital: Palikir.

Government type: Constitutional government in free association with the US.

Independence: 3 November 1986 (from the US-administered UN Trusteeship).

Legal system: Based on adapted Trust Territory laws, acts of the legislature, municipal, common, and customary laws.

Executive branch:
Chief of state: President Joseph J. Urusemal (since 11 May 2003); Vice-President Redley Killion. The president is both the chief of state and head of government.

Economy

Currency: US Dollar.

GDP: Purchasing power parity—$277 million.

GDP—real growth rate: 1% (2002 est.).

GDP—per capita: Purchasing power parity—$2,000 (2002 est.).

Inflation rate: 1% (2002 est.).

Population below poverty line: 26.7% (1999 est.).

Unemployment rate: 16% (1999 est.).

Exports: $22 million f.o.b. (2000 est.)—fish, garments, banana, black pepper.

Imports: $149 million f.o.b. (2000 est.)—food, manufactured goods, machinery and equipment, beverages.

External debt: $53.1 million (2003 est.).

Transport and Communications

Railways: None.

Roads: 240 km.

Telephones: 10,100 (2001).

Internet users: 1,800 (2002).

Internet country code: .fm

Moldova

History

The Principality of Moldavia came under Ottoman Turk rule in the 16th century. Russia acquired Moldavian territory in 1791 and again in 1812. In 1918, Romania acquired the rest of the Moldavian territory that had remained with Turkey. In 1924, the Autonomous Soviet Socialist Republic of Moldavia was formed. In 1991, Moldavian Soviet Socialist Republic proclaimed its independence and changed its name to the Romanian spelling, Moldova.

Geography

Location: Eastern Europe, north-east of Romania.

Area: 33,843 sq. km.

Natural resources: Lignite, phosphorites, gypsum, arable land, limestone.

Climate: Moderate winters and warm summers.

People

Population: 4,455,421 (July 2005 est.).

Population growth rate: 0.22% (2005 est.).

Sex ratio: 0.91 male(s)/female (2005 est.).

Religions: Eastern Orthodox 98%, Jewish 1.5%, Baptist and others 0.5% (2000).

Languages: Moldovan (official), Russian, Gagauz (a Turkish dialect).

Literacy rate: Total 99.1%, Male 99.6%, Female 98.7% (2003 est.).

Infant mortality rate: 40.42 deaths/1,000 live births (2005 est.).

Life expectancy: Total 65.18 years, Male 61.12 years, Female 69.43 years (2005 est.).

Government

Capital: Chisinau.

Government type: Republic.

Independence: 27 August 1991 (from Soviet Union).

Legal system: Based on civil law system.

Executive branch:
Chief of state: President Vladimir Voronin (since 4 April 2001).

Head of government: Prime Minister Vasile Tarlev (since 15 April 2001).

Economy

Currency: Moldovan leu.

GDP: Purchasing power parity—$8.581 billion (2004 est.).

GDP—real growth rate: 6.8% (2004 est.).

GDP—per capita: Purchasing power parity—$1,900 (2004 est.).

Inflation rate: 11.5% (2004 est.).

Population below poverty line: 80% (2001 est.).

Unemployment rate: 8% (2002 est.).

Exports: $1.03 billion f.o.b. (2004 est.)—foodstuff, textiles, machinery.

Imports: $1.83 billion f.o.b. (2004 est.)—mineral products and fuel, machinery and equipment, chemicals, textiles (2000).

External debt: $1.4 billion (2004 est.).

Transport and Communications

Railways: 1,138 km.

Roads: 12,179 km.

Telephones: 706,900 (2002).

Mobile cellular: 338,200 (2002).

Internet users: 150,000 (2002).

Internet country code: .md

Monaco

History

In 1297 a member the Grimaldi family from the Italian city of Genoa, Francois Grimaldi, seized power in Monaco. Between 1524–1641, the Grimaldi family allied itself with Spain, and Monaco came under Spanish protection. In 1949, Prince Rainier III succeeded to the throne after the death of his grandfather, Louis II. In 1956, Prince Rainier married Hollywood actress Grace Kelly.

Geography

Location: Western Europe, bordering the Mediterranean Sea on the southern coast of France, near the border with Italy.

Area: 1.95 sq. km.

Terrain: Hilly, rugged and rocky terrain.

Natural resources: None.

Climate: Mediterranean climate.

People

Population: 32,409 (July 2005 est.).

Population growth rate: 0.43% (2005 est.).

Sex ratio: 0.91 male(s)/female (2005 est.).

Religions: Roman Catholic 90%.

Languages: French (official), English, Italian, Monegasque.

Literacy rate: 99%.

Infant mortality rate: 5.43 deaths/1,000 live births (2005 est.).

Life expectancy: Total 79.57 years, Male 75.53 years, Female 83.5 years (2005 est.).

Government

Capital: Monaco.

Government type: Constitutional monarchy.

Independence: 1419 (date on which the rule of the House of Grimaldi began in earnest).

Legal system: Based on French law.

Executive branch:
Chief of state: Prince Albert II (since 6 April 2005).

Head of government: Minister of State Jean-Paul Proust (since 1 June 2005).

Economy

Currency: Euro.

Economy—overview:
Monaco is a small prosperous nation famous for its high living standards, tourism industry and gambling. It is also a frequent destination for cruise ships, and a major construction project in 2001 installed a floating jetty to extend the pier used by cruise ships in the main harbour. In recent years, however, the country has initiated a process of diversification into services and small non-polluting industries. The state levies no income tax on residents of the principality and business taxes are low.

These two factors have established Monaco as a tax haven not only for wealthy individuals but also for foreign companies. Although the banking system in Monaco is run by the French banking commission, the principality has strict laws that restrict the revealing of information to outsiders. This has led to accusations of money laundering in the country. A number of industrial sectors are state-owned monopolies. However, Monaco does not publish national income figures. This makes it difficult to generate economic data for the country.

GDP: Purchasing power parity—$870 million (2000 est.).

GDP—real growth rate: 0.9% (2000 est.).

GDP—per capita: Purchasing power parity—$27,000 (2000 est.).

Inflation rate: 1.9% (2000).

Unemployment rate: 22% (1999).

External debt: $18 billion (2000 est.).

Transport and Communications

Railways: 1.7 km.

Roads: 50 km.

Telephones: 33,700 (2002).

Mobile cellular: 19,300 (2002).

Internet users: 16,000 (2002).

Internet country code: .mc

Mongolia

History

Between the fourth and 10th centuries, Turkic-speaking people dominated the region. The famous Genghis Khan united the Mongols under one umbrella and also conquered large swathes of Central Asia.

Inner Mongolia became a part of China in 1644. With the fall of the Ch'ing dynasty, Mongols declared independence from China in 1911 and finally drove away the Chinese with Russian assistance in 1921.

Geography

Location: Northern Asia, between China and Russia.

Area: 1,565,000 sq. km.

Terrain: Vast semi-desert and desert plains, grassy steppes, mountains in the west and south-west; Gobi Desert in south-central.

Natural resources: Oil, coal, copper, molybdenum, tungsten, phosphates, tin, nickel, zinc, wolfram, fluorspar, gold, silver, iron, phosphate.

Climate: Desert.

People

Population: 2,791,272 (July 2005 est.).

Population growth rate: 1.45% (2005 est.).

Sex ratio: 1 male(s)/female (2005 est.).

Religions: Tibetan Buddhist Lamaism 96%, Muslim (primarily in the south-west), Shamanism, and Christian 4%.

Languages: Khalkha Mongol 90%, Turkic, Russian.

Literacy rate: Total 99.1%, Male 99.2%, Female 99% (2003 est.).

Infant mortality rate: 53.79 deaths/1,000 live births (2005 est.).

Life expectancy: Total 64.52 years, Male 62.3 years, Female 66.86 years (2005 est.).

Government

Capital: Ulaanbaatar.

Government type: Parliamentary.

Independence: 11 July 1921 (from China).

Legal system: Mixture of Soviet, German, and US systems of law that combines aspects of a parliamentary system with some aspects of a presidential system.

Executive branch:
Chief of state: President Natsagiyn Bagabandi (since 20 June 1997).

Head of government: Prime Minister Tsakhiagiyn Elbegdorj (since 20 August 2004).

Economy

Currency: Togrog/Tugrik.

Economy—overview:
Traditionally, economic activity in Mongolia has been based on agriculture and breeding of livestock. But the country also possesses large deposits of metals like copper, coal, molybdenum, tin, tungsten, and gold that account for a substantial portion of industrial production. At one point of time, Soviet Russian assistance accounted for as much as one-third of GDP. But this vanished almost overnight at the time of the disintegration of the USSR in 1990–1. The deep recession that Mongolia experienced as a result was compounded by the ruling party's reluctance to launch any major and meaningful economic reform. The later Democratic Coalition (DC) government initiated widespread liberalization and the opening up of the country's economy across various sectors. Economic growth hit a roadblock in 1996 due to a number of natural disasters and falling prices of copper and cashmere, but picked up during 1997–99. Mongolia was hit by a temporary Russian ban on exports of oil and oil products in August and September 1999. Mongolia joined the World Trade Organization (WTO) in 1997 and the international donor community pledged over $300 million per year at the Consultative Group Meeting held in Ulaanbaatar in June 1999. The country also suffers from a heavy burden of external debt. Real GDP growth in 2000–1 was held down by a number of factors, namely

falling prices for Mongolia's primary sector exports, internal opposition to privatization, and adverse effects of weather on agriculture in early 2000 and 2001. In 2002, however, even though the country was hit by a drought, GDP rose by 4%. This was followed by a 5% rise in 2003. Russia claims Mongolia owes it $11 billion from the old Soviet period.

GDP: Purchasing power parity—$5.332 billion (2004 est.).

GDP—real growth rate: 10.6% official estimate (2004).

GDP—per capita: Purchasing power parity—$1,900 (2004 est.).

Inflation rate: 11% (2004 est.).

Population below poverty line: 36.1% (2004 est.).

Unemployment rate: 6.7% (2003).

Exports: $853 million f.o.b. (2004 est.).

Imports: $1 billion c.i.f. (2004 est.).

External debt: $1.191 billion (2004 est.).

Transport and Communications

Railways: 1,815 km.

Roads: 49,250 km.

Telephones: 142,300 (2004).

Mobile cellular: 404,400 (2004).

Internet users: 220,000 (2004).

Internet country code: .mn

Morocco

History

Since the second millennium BC, Morocco has been the home of the Berber people. The Arab invasion came around 685. In 1660, the Alawite dynasty came to power. This dynasty rules Morocco to this day. The European powers became interested in establishing colonies in Morocco in the 19th century. In 1904, France and Spain arrived at an agreement that divided Morocco into zones of French and Spanish control. In 1912, Morocco became a French protectorate under the Treaty of Fez. The French protectorate ended in 1956 after much unrest and nationalist activities.

Geography

Location: Northern Africa, bordering the North Atlantic Ocean and the Mediterranean Sea, between Algeria and Western Sahara.

Area: 446,550 sq. km.

Terrain: The northern coast and the interior are mountanious. There are extensive inter-montane valleys and bordering plateaus. There are also rich coastal plains.

Natural resources: Phosphates, iron ore, manganese, lead, zinc, fish, salt.

Climate: Mediterranean climate; more extreme in the interiors.

People

Population: 32,725,847 (July 2005 est.).

Population growth rate: 1.57% (2005 est.).

Sex ratio: 1 male(s)/female (2005 est.).

Religions: Muslim 98.7%, Christian 1.1%, Jewish 0.2%.

Languages: Arabic (official), Berber dialects, French.

Literacy rate: Total 51.7%, Male 64.1%, Female 39.4% (2003 est.).

Infant mortality rate: 41.62 deaths/1,000 live births (2005 est.).

Life expectancy: Total 70.66 years, Male 68.35 years, Female 73.07 years (2005 est.).

Government

Capital: Rabat.

Government type: Constitutional monarchy.

Independence: 2 March 1956 (from France).

Legal system: Based on Islamic law and French and Spanish civil law system.

Executive branch:
Chief of state: King Mohamed VI (since 30 July 1999).

Head of government: Prime Minister Driss Jettou (since 9 October 2002).

Economy

Currency: Moroccan dirham.

GDP: Purchasing power parity—$134.6 billion (2004 est.).

GDP—real growth rate: 4.4% (2004 est.).

GDP—per capita: Purchasing power parity—$4,200 (2004 est.).

Inflation rate: 2.1% (2004 est.).

Population below poverty line: 3.6% (2002 est.).

Unemployment rate: 12.1% (2004 est.).

Exports: $9.754 billion f.o.b. (2004 est.)—clothing, fish, inorganic chemicals, transistors, crude minerals, fertilizers, petroleum products, fruits, vegetables.

Imports: $15.63 billion f.o.b. (2004 est.)—crude petroleum, textile fabric, telecommunications equipment, wheat, gas and electricity, transistors, plastics.

External debt: $17.01 billion (2004 est.).

Transport and Communications

Railways: 1,907 km.

Roads: 57,694 km.

Telephones: 1,127,400 (2002).

Mobile cellular: 7,332,800 (2003).

Internet users: 800,000 (2003).

Internet country code: .ma

Mozambique

History

Bantu-speaking tribes moved into the region that is today Mozambique in the third century AD. Arabs and Swahili people came later. Vasco da Gama explored the area in 1498 and the Portuguese colonized it in 1505. Till 1752, Mozambique was administered as part of the Portuguese territory of Goa.

In the 18th and 19th centuries, Mozambique became an important slave-trading centre. In 1878, Portugal leased large areas of the colony to private organizations for commercial activity. In 1975, Mozambique became independent as a single-party state.

Geography

Location: South-eastern Africa, bordering the Mozambique Channel, between South Africa and Tanzania.

Area: 801,590 sq. km.

Terrain: Central lowlands with upland in the centre, high plateaus in the north-west, and mountains in the west.

Natural resources: Coal, titanium, natural gas, hydropower, tantalum, graphite.

Climate: Varies from tropical to subtropical.

People

Population: 19,406,703 (July 2005 est.).

Population growth rate: 1.48% (2005 est.).

Sex ratio: 0.96 male(s)/female (2005 est.).

Religions: Indigenous beliefs 50%, Christian 30%, Muslim 20%.

Languages: Portuguese (official), indigenous dialects.

Literacy rate: Total 47.8%, Male 63.5%, Female 32.7% (2003 est.).

Infant mortality rate: 130.79 deaths/ 1,000 live births (2005 est.).

Life expectancy: Total 40.32 years, Male 39.9 years, Female 40.75 years (2005 est.).

Government

Capital: Maputo.

Government type: Republic.

Independence: 25 June 1975 (from Portugal).

Legal system: Based on Portuguese civil law system and customary law.

Executive branch:
Chief of state: President Arwando Guebuza (since 2 February 2005).

Head of government: Prime Minister Luisa Diogo (since 17 February 2004).

Economy

Currency: Metical.

GDP: Purchasing power parity—$23.38 billion (2004 est.).

GDP—real growth rate: 8.2% (2004 est.).

GDP—per capita: Purchasing power parity—$1,200 (2004 est.).

Inflation rate: 12.8% (2004 est.).

Population below poverty line: 70% (2001 est.).

Unemployment rate: 21% (1997 est.).

Exports: $689.4 million f.o.b. (2004 est.)—aluminum, prawns, cashews, cotton, sugar, citrus, timber, bulk electricity.

Imports: $972.9 million f.o.b. (2004 est.)—machinery and equipment, vehicles, fuel, chemicals, metal products, foodstuff, textiles.

External debt: $966 million (2002 est.).

Transport and Communications

Railways: 3,123 km.

Roads: 30,400 km.

Telephones: 83,700 (2002).

Mobile cellular: 428,900 (2003).

Internet users: 50,000 (2002).

Internet country code: .mz

Myanmar

History

In the 16th–17th centuries, the British, Portuguese and the Dutch carried out trade activities in the area. The modern-day state of Myanmar (then Burma) was founded in the 18th century but was annexed by the British in 1885. Thereafter it became a province of India. The Government of India Act of 1935 separated Burma from India. During World War II, Japan occupied the country.

Geography

Location: South-eastern Asia, bordering the Andaman Sea and the Bay of Bengal, between Bangladesh and Thailand.

Area: 678,500 sq. km.

Terrain: Central lowlands ringed by steep, rugged highlands.

Natural resources: Petroleum, timber, tin, antimony, zinc, copper, tungsten, lead, coal, some marble, limestone, precious stones, natural gas, hydropower.

Climate: Tropical monsoon type of climate.

People

Population: 42,510,537 (July 2005 est.).

Population growth rate: 0.52% (2005 est.).

Sex ratio: 0.99 male(s)/female (2005 est.).

Religions: Buddhist 89%, Christian 4% (Baptist 3%, Roman Catholic 1%), Muslim 4%, animist 1%, others 2%.

Languages: Burmese, minority ethnic groups have their own languages.

Literacy rate: Total 83.1%, Male 88.7%, Female 77.7% (1995 est.).

Infant mortality rate: 70.35 deaths/1,000 live births (2005 est.).

Life expectancy: Total 55.79 years, Male 54.12 years, Female 57.56 years (2005 est.).

Government

Capital: Yangon.

Government type: Military regime.

Independence: 4 January 1948 (from UK).

Legal system: The country has not accepted compulsory ICJ jurisdiction.

Executive branch:

Chief of state: Chairman of the State Peace and Development Council Sr Gen. Than Shwe (since 23 April 1992). The chief of state is also the head of government.

Head of government: Chairman of the State Peace and Development Council Sr Gen. Than Shwe (since 23 April 1992). The appointed prime minister, Gen. Knin Nyunt (since 23 August 2003), is not the head of government.

Economy

Currency: Kyat.

Economy—overview:
Although Myanmar is rich in natural resources, it remains one of the poorest countries in the world with widespread poverty. In the early 1990s, the military regime took steps to liberalize the economy. But those efforts have met with little success and were consequently stalled. The country has not been able to achieve monetary or fiscal stability. Its economy suffers from serious imbalances. There is a steep inflation rate and the official exchange rate overvalues the Burmese currency, the kyat, by more than 100 times the market rate. Most overseas development assistance stopped after the military regime suppressed the democracy movement in 1988 and ignored the results of the 1990 election.

GDP: Purchasing power parity—$73.69 billion (2002 est.).

GDP—real growth rate: 5.3% (2002 est.).

GDP—per capita: Purchasing power parity—$1,700 (2002 est.).

Inflation rate: 49.7% (2003 est.).

Population below poverty line: 25% (2000 est.).

Unemployment rate: 5.1% (2001 est.).

Exports: $2.7 billion f.o.b. (2002).

Imports: $2.5 billion f.o.b. (2002).

External debt: $6.1 billion (2002 est.).

Transport and Communications

Railways: 3,955 km.

Roads: 28,200 km.

Telephones: Myanmar has an adequate telephone network that meets requirements for local and intercity as well as international service.

Internet users: 10,000 (2002).

Internet country code: .mm

Namibia

History

The Portuguese were the first Europeans to reach the area, in the late 15th century. In the late 19th century, the present international borders of Namibia were demarcated through German treaties with UK and Portugal. Subsequently, Germany annexed the territory as South West Africa. The Germans responded to uprisings by native populations by using brutal and overwhelming force that decimated as much as 90% of the Herero and Nama populations.

During World War I, South Africa invaded and captured South West Africa in 1914–15. In 1920, the League of Nations granted South Africa the mandate to govern South West Africa. In 1961, the UN General Assembly demanded the termination of South Africa's mandate over South West Africa and set its independence as an objective. In 1968, the UN General Assembly officially renamed South West Africa as Namibia. In March 1990, Namibia became independent.

Geography

Location: Southern Africa, bordering the South Atlantic Ocean, between Angola and South Africa.

Area: 825,418 sq. km.

Terrain: Deserts along the coast and in the east, the rest of the country is mostly a high plateau.

Natural resources: Diamonds, copper, uranium, gold, lead, tin, lithium, cadmium, zinc, salt, vanadium, natural gas, hydropower, fish.

Climate: Hot and dry desert climate.

People

Population: 2,030,692 (July 2005 est.).

Population growth rate: 0.73% (2005 est.).

Sex ratio: 1 male(s)/female (2005 est.).

Religions: Christian 80% to 90% (at least Lutheran), indigenous beliefs 10% to 20%.

Languages: English 7% (official), Afrikaans (it is the common language of most of the population including about 60% of the white population), German 32%, indigenous languages (Oshivambo, Herero, Nama).

Literacy rate: Total 84%, Male 84.4%, Female 83.7% (2003 est.).

Infant mortality rate: 48.98 deaths/1,000 live births (2005 est.).

Life expectancy: Total 43.93 years, Male 44.71 years, Female 43.13 years (2005 est.).

Government

Capital: Windhoek.

Government type: Republic.

Independence: 21 March 1990 (from South African mandate).

Legal system: Based on Roman–Dutch law and 1990 Constitution.

Executive branch:
Chief of state: President Hifikepunye Pohamba (since 15 November 2004).

Head of government: Prime Minister Nahas Angula (since 21 March 2005).

Economy

Currency: Namibian dollar.

GDP: Purchasing power parity—$14.76 billion (2004 est.).

GDP—real growth rate: 4.8% (2004 est.).

GDP—per capita: Purchasing power parity—$7,300 (2004 est.).

Inflation rate: 4.2% (2004 est.).

Population below poverty line: 50% (2002 est.).

Unemployment rate: 35% (1998 est.).

Exports: $1.356 billion f.o.b. (2004 est.)—diamond, copper, gold, zinc, lead, uranium; cattle, processed fish, karakul skins.

Imports: $1.473 billion f.o.b. (2004 est.)—foodstuff, petroleum products and fuel, machinery and equipment, chemicals.

External debt: $1.136 billion (2004 est.).

Transport and Communications

Railways: 2,382 km.

Roads: 66,467 km.

Telephones: 127,400 (2003).

Mobile cellular: 223,700 (2003).

Internet users: 65,000 (2003).

Internet country code: .na

Nauru

History

Germany incorporated Nauru into its Marshall Islands protectorate in late 1888. During World War I, Australian forces occupied Nauru and evicted German nationals. In 1920, Nauru became a mandated territory within the League of Nations, with Australia, UK and New Zealand as the responsible authorities. On 31 January 1968, Nauru became independent.

Geography

Location: Island in the South Pacific Ocean, south of the Marshall Islands.

Area: 21 sq. km.

Natural resources: Phosphates, fish.

Climate: Tropical monsoonal type of climate.

People

Population: 13,048 (July 2005 est.).

Population growth rate: 1.83% (2005 est.).

Sex ratio: 1 male(s)/female (2005 est.).

Religions: Christian (two-thirds Protestant, one-third Roman Catholic).

Languages: Nauruan (official, a distinct Pacific Island language), English widely understood, spoken, and used for most government and commercial purposes.

Infant mortality rate: 9.95 deaths/1,000 live births (2005 est.).

Life expectancy: Total 62.73 years, Male 59.16 years, Female 66.48 years (2005 est.).

Government

Capital: Nauru has no official capital; the government offices are in Yaren district.

Government type: Republic.

Independence: 31 January 1968 (from the UN trusteeship administered by Australia, NZ, and UK).

Legal system: Acts of the Nauru Parliament and British common law.

Executive branch:
Chief of state: President Ludwig Scotty (since 26 October 2004). The president is both the chief of state and head of government.

Economy

Currency: Australian dollar.

GDP: Purchasing power parity—$60 million (2001 est.).

GDP—per capita: Purchasing power parity—$5,000 (2001 est.).

Inflation rate: –3.6% (1993).

Exports: $640,000 f.o.b. (2004 est.)—phosphates.

Imports: $19.8 million c.i.f. (2004 est.)—food, fuel, manufactures, building materials, machinery.

External debt: $33.3 million (2003).

Transport and Communications

Railways: 5 km.

Roads: 30 km.

Telephones: 1,900 (2002).

Mobile cellular: 1,500 (2002).

Internet users: 300 (2002).

Internet country code: .nr

Nepal

History

The first civilizations of Nepal were largely confined to the Kathmandu Valley, due to its fertility. Nepal was also the birthplace of Gautama Buddha, founder of Buddhism.

The country assumed its current limits during the rule of the Malla kings (1200–1769). It was King Prithvi Narayan Shah who unified the region into one country in 1768. The UK recognized the independence of the country in 1923. Between 1846 and 1951, the Rana family ruled over Nepal as prime ministers. In 1951, however, the king assumed all powers and established a constitutional monarchy.

Geography

Location: Southern Asia, between China and India.

Area: 140,800 sq. km.

Terrain: Terai or flat river plain of the Ganga in south, central hill region, rugged Himalayas in north.

Natural resources: Quartz, scenic beauty, timber, hydropower, small deposits of lignite, copper, cobalt, iron ore.

Climate: Varies from cool summers and severe winters in the north to subtropical summers and mild winters in the south.

People

Population: 27,676,547 (July 2005 est.).

Population growth rate: 2.2% (2005 est.).

Sex ratio: 1.06 male(s)/female (2005 est.).

Religions: Hindu 86.2%, Buddhist 7.8%, Muslim 3.8%, others 2.2%. Nepal is the only official Hindu state in the world.

Languages: Nepali (official; spoken by 90% of the population), about a dozen other languages and about 30 major dialects. Many in the government and in the world of business also speak English.

Literacy rate: Total 45.2%, Male 62.7%, Female 27.6% (2003 est.).

Infant mortality rate: 66.98 deaths/ 1,000 live births (2005 est.).

Life expectancy: Total 59.8 years, Male 60.09 years, Female 59.5 years (2005 est.).

Government

Capital: Kathmandu.

Government type: Parliamentary democracy and constitutional monarchy.

Independence/date of formation: 1768 (when it was unified by Prithvi Narayan Shah).

Legal system: Based on Hindu legal concepts and English common law.

Executive branch:
Chief of state: King Gyanendra Bir Bikram Shah (succeeded the throne on 4 June 2001 following the death of his nephew, King Dipendra Bir Bikram Shah).

Head of government: The king dissolved the government and assumed power in February 2005.

Election results: None. The monarch is hereditary; following legislative elections, the leader of the majority party or leader of a majority coalition is usually appointed prime minister by the monarch. (King Birendra Bir Bikram Shah Dev died in a shooting at the royal palace on 1 June 2001 that also claimed the lives of most of the royal family. King Birendra's son, Crown Prince Dipendra, is believed to have been responsible for the shootings. He also shot himself. Dipendra was crowned king immediately after the shootings. He died three days later and was succeeded by his uncle, the present king.)

Legislative branch:
Nepal has a bicameral parliament consisting of the National Council (60 seats of which the House of Representatives appoints 35, the king appoints 10, and an electoral college elects 15. One-third of the members are elected every two years to serve six-year terms) and the House of Representatives (205 seats. Members are elected by popular vote to serve five-year terms.)

Economy

Currency: Nepalese rupee.

Economy—overview:
Nepal is one of the poorest and least developed countries in the world. As much as 42% of its population lives below the poverty line. Agriculture is the most important component of the economy. It provides livelihood for more than 80% of the population and accounts for 40% of GDP. The most important forms of industrial activity include the processing of agricultural produce including jute, tobacco, sugar cane and grain. As much as 80% of foreign exchange earnings in recent years have come from textile and carpet production. But this too has fallen in 2001–2 due to the overall slowdown in the world economy and attacks by Maoist insurgents on factory owners and workers. Tourism is another key source of foreign exchange. But this too suffered in the aftermath of 9/11 and the internal strife in Nepal on account of Maoist guerillas. Since 1991, the government has implemented economic reforms. These have taken the shape of reduction of business licences and registration requirements that aim to simplify investment in the country, reduction of subsidies, privatization of state industries, and trimming of the bureaucracy. Nepal has substantial potential in hydropower and tourism. Consequently, these areas have seen recent foreign investment interest. The small size of the economy, its remote landlocked

geographic location, and its susceptibility to natural calamities hampers foreign trade and investment in other sectors.

GDP: Purchasing power parity—$39.53 billion (2004 est.).

GDP—real growth rate: 3% (2004 est.).

GDP—per capita: Purchasing power parity—$1,500 (2004 est.).

Inflation rate: 2.9% (2002 est.).

Population below poverty line: 42% (1995–6).

Unemployment rate: 47% (2001 est.).

Exports: $568 million f.o.b., but does not include unrecorded border trade with India (2002 est.).

Imports: $1.419 billion f.o.b. (2002 est.).

External debt: $2.7 billion (2001 est.).

Transport and Communications

Railways: 59 km.

Roads: 13,223 km.

Telephones: 371,800 (2003).

Mobile cellular: 50,400 (2003).

Internet users: 80,000 (2002).

Internet country code: .np

The Netherlands

History

The Netherlands was a part of Charlemagne's empire in the eighth and ninth centuries. After passing through the control of Burgundy and the Hapsburgs, it came under Spanish rule in the 16th century. A revolt led by William of Orange broke out in 1568. The 1579 Union of Utrecht agreement led to the unification of the northern provinces into the United Provinces of the Netherlands. Spain finally recognized Dutch independence in the 17th century.

In 1602, the Dutch East India Company was set up. By the 17th century, the Netherlands emerged as one of the key European colonial powers. The Thirty Years War reaffirmed the Netherlands as an independent nation. In 1688, the British Parliament invited William of Orange and his wife, Mary Stuart, to take up the English throne as William III and Mary II.

When World War II broke out in 1939, the Netherlands declared itself to be neutral. In spite of this, Nazi Germany invaded the country in 1940 while in Asia, Japan occupied Dutch East Indies. Following the invasion, the Dutch royal family fled to England. The Germans were driven out in 1945. In 1949, Dutch East Indies was granted independence and it became the Republic of Indonesia. In 1963, the Netherlands handed over its remaining Asian territory, New Guinea, to Indonesia.

Geography

Location: Western Europe, bordering the North Sea, between Belgium and Germany.

Area: 41,526 sq. km.

Terrain: Mostly coastal lowlands and reclaimed land below sea level called polders. There are some hills in the south-eastern part of the country.

Natural resources: Natural gas, petroleum, peat, limestone, salt, sand and gravel, arable land.

Climate: Temperate marine type of climate with cool summers and mild winters.

People

Population: 16,407,491 (July 2005 est.).

Population growth rate: 0.53% (2005 est.).

Sex ratio: 0.98 male(s)/female (2005 est.).

Religions: Roman Catholic 31%, Protestant 21%, Muslim 4.4%, others 3.6%, unaffiliated 40%.

Languages: Dutch (official language), Frisian (official language).

Literacy rate: 99% (2000 est.).

Infant mortality: 5.04 deaths/1,000 live births (2005 est.).

Life expectancy: Total 78.81 years, Male 76.25 years, Female 81.51 years (2005 est.).

Government

Capital: Amsterdam; The Hague is the seat of government.

Government type: Constitutional monarchy.

Independence: 1579 (from Spain), (the year in which the Union of Utrecht was concluded, leading to the formation of the Netherlands.

Legal system: Civil law system incorporating French penal theory.

Executive branch:
Chief of state: Queen Beatrix (since 30 April 1980); Heir Apparent Willem-Alexander (born 27 April 1967), son of the monarch.

Head of government: Prime Minister Jan Peter Balkenende (since 22 July 2002).

Economy

Currency: Euro.

Economy—overview:
The prosperous open economy of The Netherlands is heavily reliant on foreign trade. Key features of the economy are moderate inflation and unemployment, a substantial current account surplus and stable industrial relations. It is also an important European transportation hub. Rotterdam is one of the world's busiest ports while Amsterdam's Schiphol Airport is among the busiest in the world. Besides a well-developed industrial sector, the country also has a highly mechanized agricultural sector that is a very important source of exports. The Netherlands was one of the 11 EU countries that launched the euro currency on 1 January 2002.

GDP: Purchasing power parity—$481.1 billion (2004 est.).

GDP—real growth rate: 1.2% (2004 est.).

GDP—per capita: Purchasing power parity—$29,500 (2004 est.).

Inflation rate: 1.4% (2004 est.).

Unemployment rate: 6% (2004 est.).

Exports: $293.1 billion f.o.b. (2004 est.)—machinery and equipment, chemicals, fuels; foodstuff.

Imports: $252.7 billion f.o.b. (2004 est.)—machinery and transport equipment, chemicals, fuels; foodstuff, clothing.

Transport and Communications

Railways: 2,808 km.

Roads: 116,500 km.

Telephones: 10,004,000 (2002).

Mobile cellular: 12,500,000 (2003).

Internet users: 8.5 million (2003).

Internet country code: .nl

New Zealand

History

British explorer James Cook charted the main islands in 1769. In 1840, New Zealand became a British Crown Colony. The landmark Treaty of Waitangi was signed in 1840 between the Maori tribes and the British. It provided for the recognition of Maori rights to territory in return for their acceptance of British rule. In 1893, New Zealand became the first country to give women the right to vote. In 1907, the Dominion of New Zealand was established.

Geography

Location: Oceania, islands in the South Pacific Ocean, southeast of Australia.

Area: 268,680 sq. km. (This includes Antipodes Islands, Auckland Islands, Bounty Islands, Campbell Island, Chatham Islands, and Kermadec Islands.)

Terrain: Predominantly mountainous with some large coastal plains.

Natural resources: Natural gas, iron ore, sand, coal, timber, hydropower, gold, limestone.

Climate: Temperate climate with sharp regional contrasts.

People

Population: 4,035,461 (July 2005 est.).

Population growth rate: 1.02% (2005 est.).

Sex ratio: 0.99 male(s)/female (2005 est.).

Religions: Anglican 24%, Presbyterian 18%, Roman Catholic 15%, Methodist 5%, Baptist 2%, other Protestant 3%, unspecified or none 33%.

Languages: English (official), Maori (official).

Literacy rate: 99% (1980 est.).

Infant mortality rate: 5.85 deaths/1,000 live births (2005 est.).

Life expectancy: Total 78.66 years, Male 75.67 years, Female 81.78 years (2005 est.).

Government

Capital: Wellington.

Government type: Parliamentary democracy.

Independence: 26 September 1907 (from UK).

Legal system: Based on English law, with special land legislation and land courts for the Maori.

Executive branch:
Chief of state: Queen Elizabeth II (since 6 February 1952), represented by Governor General Dame Silvia Cartwright (since 4 April 2001).

Head of government: Prime Minister Helen Clark (since 10 December 1999) and Deputy Prime Minister Michael Cullen (since July 2002).

Economy

Currency: New Zealand dollar.

Economy—overview:
Major economic restructuring since 1984 has transformed New Zealand from an agrarian economy that was dependent on access to the British market to a more industrialized, globally competitive free market economy. Per capita incomes, although rising, have remained below the level of the four largest EU economies. The growth rate of the economy is heavily dependent on trade and the global economic slowdown and the slump in commodity prices have affected it.

GDP: Purchasing power parity—$92.51 billion (2004 est.).

GDP—real growth rate: 4.8% (2004 est.).

GDP—per capita: Purchasing power parity—$23,200 (2004 est.).

Inflation rate: 2.4% (2004 est.).

Unemployment rate: 4.2% (2004 est.).

Exports: $19.85 billion (2004 est.)—dairy products, meat, wood and wood products, fish, machinery.

Imports: $19.77 billion (2004 est.)—machinery and equipment, vehicles and aircraft, petroleum, electronics, textiles, plastics.

External debt: $47.34 billion (2004 est.).

Transport and Communications

Railways: 3,898 km.

Roads: 92,382 km.

Telephones: 1,765,000 (2003).

Mobile cellular: 2,599,000 (2003).

Internet users: 2.11 million (2003).

Internet country code: .nz

Nicaragua

History

The Spanish governed Nicaragua till its independence in 1821. The dictatorial Somoza dynasty ruled Nicaragua during 1936–79. Thereafter, the Sandinistas came to power. The US-backed Contra rebels opposed their regime in the 1980s.

Geography

Location: Middle America, bordering both the Caribbean Sea and the North Pacific Ocean, between Costa Rica and Honduras.

Area: 129,494 sq. km.

Terrain: Extensive plains along the Atlantic coast which rise to central interior mountains. The Pacific coastal plain is narrow and interruted by volcanoes.

Natural resources: Gold, silver, copper, tungsten, lead, zinc, timber, fish.

Climate: Tropical in the lowlands but cooler in the highlands.

People

Population: 5,465,100 (July 2005 est.).

Population growth rate: 1.92% (2005 est.).

Sex ratio: 1 male(s)/female (2005 est.).

Religions: Roman Catholic 85%, Protestant.

Languages: Spanish (official), English and indigenous languages on the Caribbean coast.

Literacy rate: Total 67.5%, Male 67.2%, Female 67.8% (2003 est.).

Infant mortality rate: 29.11 deaths/1,000 live births (2005 est.).

Life expectancy: Total 70.33 years, Male 68.27 years, Female 72.49 years (2005 est.).

Government

Capital: Managua.

Government type: Republic.

Independence: 15 September 1821 (from Spain).

Legal system: Civil law system; Supreme court may review administrative acts.

Executive branch:
Chief of state: President Enrique Bolanos Geyer (since 10 January 2002);

Vice-President Jose Rizo Castellon (since 10 January 2002). The president is both chief of state and head of government

Economy

Currency: Gold Cordoba.

GDP: Purchasing power parity—$12.34 billion (2004 est.).

GDP—real growth rate: 4% (2004 est.).

GDP—per capita: Purchasing power parity—$2,300 (2004 est.).

Inflation rate: 9.3% (2004 est.).

Population below poverty line: 50% (2001 est.).

Unemployment rate: 7.8% (plus 46.5% underemployment) (2003 est.).

Exports: $750 million f.o.b. (2004 est.)—coffee, shrimp and lobster, cotton, tobacco, bananas, beef, sugar, gold.

Imports: $2.02 billion f.o.b. (2004 est.)—machinery and equipment, raw materials, petroleum products, consumer goods.

External debt: $4.573 billion (2004 est.).

Transport and Communications

Railways: 6 km.

Roads: 18,712 km.

Telephones: 171,600 (2002).

Mobile cellular: 202,800 (2002).

Internet users: 90,000 (2002).

Internet country code: .ni

Niger

History

In the 1890s, Niger became a part of French West Africa. In 1958, Niger became an autonomous republic of the French Community. In 1960, Niger became independent with Diori Haman as President.

Geography

Location: Western Africa, south-east of Algeria.

Area: 1,267,000 sq. km.

Terrain: Predominantly desert plains and sand dunes. There are plains in the south and hills in the north.

Natural resources: Uranium, coal, iron ore, tin, phosphates, gold, petroleum.

Climate: Hot, dry and dusty desert climate.

People

Population: 11,665,937 (July 2005 est.).

Population growth rate: 2.63% (2005 est.).

Sex ratio: 1 male(s)/female (2005 est.).

Religions: Muslim 80%, indigenous beliefs and Christian.

Languages: French (official), Hausa, Djerma.

Literacy rate: Total 17.6%, Male 25.8%, Female 9.7% (2003 est.).

Infant mortality rate: 121.69 deaths/1,000 live births (2005 est.).

Life expectancy: Total 42.13 years, Male 42.46 years, Female 41.8 years (2005 est.).

Government

Capital: Niamey.

Government type: Republic.

Independence: 3 August 1960 (from France).

Legal system: Based on French civil law system and customary law.

Executive branch:
Chief of state: President Tandja Mamadou (since 22 December 1999). The president is both chief of state and head of government.

Economy

Currency: Communaute Financiere Africaine franc.

GDP: Purchasing power parity—$9.716 billion (2004 est.).

GDP—real growth rate: 3.4% (2004 est.).

GDP—per capita: Purchasing power parity—$900 (2004 est.).

Inflation rate: 3% (2002 est.).

Population below poverty line: 63% (1993 est.).

Exports: $280 million f.o.b. (2002 est.)—uranium ore, livestock, cowpeas, onions.

Imports: $400 million f.o.b. (2002 est.)—foodstuff, machinery, vehicles and parts, petroleum, cereals.

External debt: $1.6 billion (1999 est.).

Transport and Communications

Railways: None.

Roads: 10,100 km.

Telephones: 22,400 (2002).

Mobile cellular: 24,000 (2003).

Internet users: 15,000 (2002).

Internet country code: .ne

Nigeria

History

Between the 11th and the 14th centuries, the Kanem Empire controlled the area. Islam was introduced in the 13th century. From the beginning of the 19th century and till 1851, the Fulani Empire controlled the region. In 1851, UK took Lagos and by 1886, it expanded its authority over all of the territory, which it called the 'Colony and Protectorate of Nigeria'. It governed the territory by 'indirect rule' through local leaders. Nigeria gained independence in 1960.

Geography

Location: Western Africa, bordering the Gulf of Guinea, between Benin and Cameroon.

Area: 923,768 sq. km.

Terrain: Southern lowlands that merge into central hills and plateaus. There are mountains in the south-east, and plains in the north.

Natural resources: Natural gas, petroleum, tin, columbite, iron ore, coal, limestone, lead, zinc, arable land.

Climate: Equatorial climate in the southern part of the country, tropical climate in the central part and arid climate in the northern part.

People

Population: 128,771,988 (July 2005 est.).

Population growth rate: 2.37% (2005 est.).

Sex ratio: 1.02 male(s)/female (2005 est.).

Religions: Muslim 50%, Christian 40%, indigenous beliefs 10%.

Languages: English (official), Hausa, Yoruba, Igbo (Ibo), Fulani.

Literacy rate: Total 68%, Male 75.7%, Female 60.6% (2003 est.).

Infant mortality rate: 98.8 deaths/ 1,000 live births (2005 est.).

Life expectancy: Total 46.74 years, Male 46.21 years, Female 47.29 years (2004 est.).

Government

Capital: Abuja.

Government type: Republic (in a state of transition from military to civilian rule).

Independence: 1 October 1960 (from UK).

Legal system: Based on English common law, Islamic Sharia law (only in some northern states), and traditional law.

Executive branch:
Chief of state: President Olusegun Obasanjo (since 29 May 1999). The president is both the chief of state and head of government.

Economy

Currency: Naira.

Economy—overview:
Nigeria possesses substantial petroleum resources. But years of political instability, poor macroeconomic management, corruption, and lack of infrastructure has negated the benefits of its mineral wealth. Nevertheless, the present civilian administration has initiated some reforms. Over the years, Nigeria has failed to diversify the economy away from its high degree of reliance on the oil sector that accounts for over 90% of foreign exchange earnings, around 20% of GDP, and over 60% of budgetary revenues. The mostly subsistence agricultural sector has also failed to keep pace with Nigeria's rapid population growth. Consequently, the country that was once a net exporter of food is now forced to import food. In August 2000, Nigeria entered into an IMF stand-by agreement by which the country received a debt-restructuring deal from the Paris Club and a $1 billion credit from the IMF. However, both of these were subject to economic reforms. However, Nigeria pulled out of its IMF programme in April 2002, when it failed to meet both spending and exchange rate targets, thus making it ineligible for further debt waivers from the Paris Club.

GDP: Purchasing power parity—$125.7 billion (2004 est.).

GDP—real growth rate: 6.2% (2004 est.).

GDP—per capita: Purchasing power parity—$1,000 (2004 est.).

Inflation rate: 11.7% (2002 est.).

Population below poverty line: 60% (2000 est.).

Unemployment rate: 28% (1992 est.).

Exports: $33.99 billion f.o.b. (2004 est.)—petroleum and petroleum products 95%, cocoa, rubber.

Imports: $17.14 billion f.o.b. (2004 est.)—machinery, chemicals, transport equipment, manufactured goods, food and live animals.

External debt: $30.55 billion (2004 est.).

Transport and Communications

Railways: 3,557 km.

Roads: 194,394 km.

Telephones: 853,100 (2003).

Mobile cellular: 3,149,500 (2003).

Internet users: 420,000 (2002).

Internet country code: .ng

North Korea

History

It is believed that the ancient kingdom of Choson was founded in the third millennium BC. China annexed it in 108 BC. The Yi Dynasty ruled it from 1392 to 1910 when Japan conquered all of Korea. Allied forces freed Korea from the Japanese in 1945. The part of the Korean peninsula north of the 38th parallel was occupied by the Soviet Union while USA occupied the region to the south of this line of latitude. In 1946, North Korea's Communist Party, the Korean Workers' Party, was inaugurated along with a Soviet-backed leadership that included Kim Il-sung, the future leader of the country. Independence came in 1948 with the withdrawal of Soviet troops and the proclamation of Democratic People's Republic of Korea. Kim Il-sung introduced the personal philosophy of Juche, or self-reliance, which became a guiding principle for North Korea's development. He served as premier from 1948 to 1972 and President and head of state from 1972 till his demise in 1994.

When South Korea declared its independence in 1950, North Korea launched an invasion attempt that soon developed into the Korean War. It ended inconclusively with the signing of the Armistice in 1953. It is believed to have resulted in an estimated 4,000,000 casualties, including civilians.

Geography

Location: Eastern Asia, northern half of the Korean Peninsula bordering the Korea Bay and the Sea of Japan, between China and South Korea.

Area: 120,540 sq. km.

Terrain: Mostly hilly and mountainous with deep and narrow valleys. There are wide coastal plains in the west and broken ones in the east.

Natural resources: Coal, lead, tungsten, zinc, graphite, magnesite, iron ore, copper, gold, pyrites, salt, fluorspar, hydropower.

Climate: Temperate climate with rainfall concentrated in the summer.

People

Population: 22,912,177 (July 2005 est.).

Population growth rate: 0.9% (2005 est.).

Sex ratio: 0.94 male(s)/female (2005 est.).

Religions: Traditionally Buddhist and Confucianist, some Christian and syncretic Chondogyo (Religion of the Heavenly Way).

Languages: Korean.

Literacy rate: 99%.

Infant mortality rate: 24.04 deaths/ 1,000 live births (2005 est.).

Life expectancy: Total 71.37 years, Male 68.65 years, Female 74.22 years (2005 est.).

Government

Capital: Pyongyang.

Government type: Authoritarian socialist; one-man dictatorship.

Independence: 15 August 1945 (from Japan).

Legal system: Based on German civil law system with Japanese influences and communist legal theory.

Executive branch:
Chief of state: Kim Jong-il (since July 1994). The late leader Kim Il-sung is now referred to as the 'Eternal President' of the country.

Head of government: Premier Pak Pong-ju (since 3 September 2003).

Economy

Currency: Won.

Economy—overview:
North Korea has a strict centrally planned economy. Its industry suffers from under-investment and shortages that have resulted in decline in industrial output and power generation. North Korea has suffered from successive years of food shortages created by severe droughts, chronic shortages of inputs, inefficient collective farming and lack of cultivable land. The country managed to prevent mass starvation in recent years due to huge international food aid deliveries. By some estimates, North Korea spends almost a third of its GDP on its armed forces. This eats up funds and resources that could otherwise have been used to develop other sectors. In recent times, the government has initiated some rationalization measures at earning hard currency, developing information technology industry and attracting foreign investments. However, it is still a far way off from full-fledged market reforms.

GDP: Purchasing power parity—$30.88 billion (2004 est.).

GDP—real growth rate: 1% (2004 est.).

GDP—per capita: Purchasing power parity—$1,400 (2004 est.).

Exports: $1.2 billion f.o.b. (2003 est.)—minerals, metallurgical products, manufactures (including armaments), textiles and fishery products.

Imports: $2.1 billion c.i.f. (2003 est.)—petroleum, coking coal, machinery and equipment, textiles, grain.

External debt: $12 billion (1996 est.).

Transport and Communications

Railways: 5,214 km.

Roads: 31,200 km.

Telephones: 1,100,000 (1997).

Internet country code: .kp

Norway

History

The oldest relics of human habitation in Norway date back to 9500 to 6000 BC. Between 3000 and 2500 BC new immigrants arrived in the eastern part of the country. These new settlers were predominantly farmers and herdsmen and they gradually replaced the original population of hunters and fishermen of the west coast.

Among the Norwegians were the Vikings or Norsemen, the group of seafaring warriors who raided and colonized large areas of Europe from the ninth to the 11th century. In 1015, Olaf II Haraldsson became the first effective ruler of all of Norway and initiated the conversion of Norwegians to Christianity. Between 1442 and 1814, Danish kings ruled over Norway. In 1814, Sweden gained control of the country but granted a lot of autonomy to the Norwegians. In 1905, Norway arranged an amicable separation with Sweden and invited a Danish prince to take up the Norwegian throne.

Geography

Location: Northern Europe, bordering the North Sea and the North Atlantic Ocean, west of Sweden.

Area: 324,220 sq. km.

Terrain: Glaciated terrain consisting mostly of high plateaus and mountains broken by valleys. The coastline is deeply indented by fjords. The northern part of the country is arctic tundra.

Natural resources: Petroleum, natural gas, iron ore, copper, lead, zinc, titanium, pyrites, nickel, fish, timber, hydropower.

Climate: Temperate along the coastal areas but modified by the effect of the North Atlantic Current. The interiors are colder with increased precipitation.

People

Population: 4,593,041 (July 2005 est.).

Population growth rate: 0.41% (2005 est.).

Sex ratio: 0.98 male(s)/female (2005 est.).

Religions: Evangelical Lutheran (state church), other Protestant and Roman Catholic.

Languages: Bokmal Norwegian (official), Nynorsk Norwegian (official), Sami, Finnish.

Literacy rate: 100%.

Infant mortality rate: 3.7 deaths/1,000 live births (2005 est.).

Life expectancy: Total 79.4 years, Male 76.78 years, Female 82.17 years (2005 est.).

Government

Capital: Oslo.

Government type: Constitutional monarchy.

Independence: 7 June 1905 (date on which Norway declared the dissolution of its union with Sweden).

Legal system: Mixture of customary law, civil law system, and common law traditions.

Executive branch:
Chief of state: King Harald V (since 17 January 1991); Heir Apparent Crown Prince Haakon Magnus, son of the monarch (born 20 July 1973).

Head of government: Prime Minister Kjell Magne Bondevik (since 19 October 2001).

Economy

Currency: Norwegian krone.

Economy—overview:
Norway is a prosperous welfare state with a mixture of free market and government control over key sectors like petroleum. Norway boasts a rich collection of natural resources like petroleum, minerals, hydropower, forests and fish. Oil and gas makes up one-third of exports. In fact, Norway is among the top oil exporters. Norway has remained outside the EU. Norway has realized its heavy reliance on petroleum exports. Therefore, with an eye on the future when petroleum will possibly run out, Norway has been saving its current budget surpluses in a Government Petroleum Fund. This fund is invested abroad and is valued at more than $40 billion.

GDP: Purchasing power parity—$183 billion (2004 est.).

GDP—real growth rate: 3.3% (2004 est.).

GDP—per capita: Purchasing power parity—$40,000 (2004 est.).

Inflation rate: 1% (2004 est.).

Unemployment rate: 4.3% (2004 est.).

Exports: $76.64 billion f.o.b. (2004 est.)—petroleum and petroleum products, machinery and equipment, metals, chemicals, ships, fish.

Imports: $45.96 billion f.o.b. (2004 est.)—machinery and equipment, chemicals, metals, foodstuff.

External debt: None.

Transport and Communications

Railways: 4,077 km.

Roads: 91,852 km.

Telephones: 3,343,000 (2002).

Mobile cellular: 4,163,400 (2003).

Internet users: 2.288 million (2002).

Internet country code: .no

Oman

History

The Arab migrations into what is today Oman began in the ninth century BC. Conversion into Islam took place in the seventh century AD. The Ibadi Imams ruled the country till 1154, when a royal dynasty was set up. The Portuguese held sway over the coastal areas between 1507 and 1650. In 1650, they were expelled from the country. The Al Bu Said dynasty was founded in the mid-18th century and still rules Oman. Oil was struck in 1964.

Geography

Location: Middle East, bordering the Arabian Sea, Gulf of Oman, and Persian Gulf, between Yemen and UAE.

Area: 212,460 sq. km.

Terrain: The central region is a desert plain while the north and south has rugged mountains.

Natural resources: Petroleum, natural gas, marble, limestone, copper, asbestos, chromium, gypsum.

Climate: Dry desert type of climate.

People

Population: 3,001,583 including 577,293 non-nationals (July 2005 est.).

Population growth rate: 3.38% (2005 est.).

Sex ratio: 1.26 male(s)/female (2005 est.).

Religions: Ibadhi Muslim 75%, Sunni Muslim, Shi'a Muslim, Hindu.

Languages: Arabic (official), English, Baluchi, Urdu, Indian dialects.

Literacy rate: Total 75.8%, Male 83.1%, Female 67.2% (2005 est.).

Infant mortality rate: 19.51 deaths/1,000 live births (2005 est.).

Life expectancy: Total 73.13 years, Male 70.92 years, Female 75.46 years (2005 est.).

Government

Capital: Muscat.

Government type: Monarchy.

Independence: 1650 (expulsion of the Portuguese).

Legal system: Based on English common law and Islamic law; ultimate appeal to the monarch.

Executive branch:
Chief of state: Sultan and Prime Minister Qaboos bin Said Al Said (since 23 July 1970); the monarch is both the chief of state and head of government.

Economy

Currency: Omani rial.

Economy—overview:
The recover of oil prices improved Oman's economic performance in 2000. The country has embarked on various reform measures that have taken the shape of privatization of utilities, the development of a body of commercial law to facilitate foreign investment, and increased budgetary outlays. Oman joined the World Trade Organization (WTO) in November 2000. In 2001, GDP growth improved in spite of a global slowdown. But in 2002, it slumped back to 2.2%. The government has been trying to replace expatriate workers with local workers in a bid to reduce unemployment. The government is also trying to develop Oman's gas resources.

GDP: Purchasing power parity—$38.09 billion (2004 est.).

GDP—real growth rate: 1.2% (2004 est.).

GDP—per capita: Purchasing power parity—$13,100 (2004 est.).

Inflation rate: –0.2% (2004 est.).

Unemployment rate: 15% (2004 est.).

Exports: $13.14 billion f.o.b. (2004 est.).

Imports: $6.373 billion f.o.b. (2004 est.).

External debt: $4.814 billion (2004 est.).

Transport and Communications

Railways: None.

Roads: 34,965 km.

Telephones: 233,900 (2002).

Mobile cellular: 464,900 (2002).

Internet users: 180,000 (2003).

Internet country code: .om

Pakistan

History

Pakistan was home to the settlements of the Indus Valley Civilization. Later on the area was controlled by a succession of invading forces such as the Aryans, the Persians, the Greeks, the Turks and the Arabs.

Islam was introduced in 711 and by 1526, it had become a part of the Mughal Empire. By 1857, the British had gained control of the region. At the time of India's independence in 1947, the region, along with what is today Bangladesh, was separated from India to form Pakistan, as a dominion within the Commonwealth in August 1947. Mohammed Ali Jinnah became the governor general and Liaquat Ali Khan the prime minister. The western part, what is today Pakistan, was then called West Pakistan. What is today Bangladesh formed the eastern part of the nascent nation and was then called East Pakistan. West Pakistan consisted of Sind, Baluchistan, North-west Frontier Province, along with a truncated part of Punjab. East Pakistan was formed by dividing Bengal. Full-fledged warfare between India and Pakistan followed in 1965 and 1971. The latter resulted in the formation of Bangladesh. Fighting over Kashmir broke out in May 1999 once again, in what is known as the Kargil War.

Geography

Location: Pakistan lies in Southern Asia, bordering the Arabian Sea, between India on the east, Iran and Afghanistan on the west.

Area: 803,940 sq. km.

Terrain: The flat Indus plain lies in the east. There are mountains in the north and north-west while the Baluchistan plateau lies in the west.

Natural resources: Land, extensive natural gas reserves, limited petroleum, poor quality coal, iron ore, copper, salt, limestone.

Climate: Hot, dry desert type of climate in most parts of the country. The climate is of the temperate type in the north-west.

People

Population: 162,419,946 (July 2005 est.).

Population growth rate: 2.03% (2005 est.).

Sex ratio: 1.05 male(s)/female (2005 est.).

Religions: Muslim 97% (Sunni 77%, Shi'a 20%), Christian, Hindu, and others 3%.

Languages: Punjabi 48%, Sindhi 12%, Siraiki (a Punjabi variant) 10%, Pashto 8%, Urdu (official) 8%, Baluchi 3%, Hindko 2%, Brahui 1%, English (official and lingua franca of Pakistani elite and most government ministries), Burushaski, and others 8%.

Literacy rate: Total 45.7%, Male 59.8%, Female 30.6% (2003 est.).

Infant mortality rate: 72.44 deaths/ 1,000 live births (2005 est.).

Life expectancy: Total 63 years, Male 62.04 years, Female 64.01 years (2005 est.).

Government

Capital: Islamabad.

Government type: Federal republic.

Independence: 14 August 1947 (from UK).

Administrative divisions:
Four provinces, one territory*, and one capital territory**
1. Baluchistan 2. Federally Administered Tribal Areas* 3. Islamabad Capital Territory** 4. North-West Frontier Province 5. Punjab 6. Sindh.

Legal system: Based on English common law with provisions to accommodate Pakistan's status as an Islamic state.

Executive branch:
Chief of state: President Pervez Musharraf (since 20 June 2001).

Head of government: Prime Minister Shaukat Aziz (since 28 August 2004).

Elections and election results: The parliament elects the President for a five-year term. In a referendum held on 30 April 2002, Musharraf's presidency was extended by five more years (the next referendum is scheduled to be held in 2007).

The 10 October 2002 elections resulted in the election of Prime Minister Mir Zafarullah Khan Jamali. Shaukat Aziz replaced Jamali as prime minister in 2004.

Legislative branch:
Pakistan has a bicameral parliament or Majlis-E-Shoora. It consist of the Senate (it has 100 seats; members indirectly elected by provincial assemblies to serve four-year terms, and the National Assembly (it has 342 seats of which 60 seats represent women, 10 seats represent minorities, members elected by popular vote to serve four-year terms).

Elections and election results: Senate last elections held 24 and 27 February 2003 (next to be held by February 2007); National Assembly—last elections held 10 October 2002 (next to be held by October 2006).

Economy

Currency: Pakistani Rupee.

Economy—overview:
Pakistan is an underdeveloped country that suffers from low levels of foreign investment. The country's economic prospects continued to improve in 2002 thanks to substantial inflows of foreign assistance beginning in 2001. Foreign exchange reserves have grown to record levels. This is largely due to fast growth in worker remittances. Since 2000, the country has witnessed some economic reform.

GDP: Purchasing power parity—$347.3 billion (2004 est.).

GDP—real growth rate: 6.1% (2004 est.).

GDP—per capita: Purchasing power parity—$2,200 (2004 est.).

Inflation rate: 4.8% (2004 est.).

Population below poverty line: 32% (2001 est.).

Unemployment rate: 8.3% plus substantial underemployment (2004 est.).

Exports: $15.07 billion f.o.b. (2004 est.).

Imports: $14.01 billion f.o.b. (2004 est.).

External debt: $33.97 billion (2004 est.).

Transport and Communications

Railways: 8,163 km.

Roads: 257,683 km.

Telephones: 3,982,800 (2003).

Mobile cellular: 2,624,800 (2003).

Internet users: 1.5 million (2002).

Internet country code: .pk

Palau

History

It is believed that the original settlers of Palau came from modern-day Indonesia in around 2500 BC. In 1543, the Spanish explorer Ruy Lopez de Villalobos visited the islands. For 300 years till 1899, the islands remained in Spanish possession. During World War I, Japan occupied the islands. During World War II, the islands served as a key base for the Japanese but were later taken by the US. In 1992, Palau signed a Compact of Free Association that meant that the USA would provide economic assistance to the islands in return for the right to build military installations. In 1994, Palau became a sovereign nation.

Geography

Location: Oceania, group of islands in the North Pacific Ocean, southeast of the Philippines.

Area: 458 sq. km.

Natural resources: Forests, gold, marine products, deep-seabed minerals.

Climate: Hot and humid climate.

People

Population: 20,303 (July 2005 est.).

Population growth rate: 1.39% (2005 est.).

Sex ratio: 1.13 male(s)/female (2005 est.).

Religions: Christian, Modekngei religion (one-third of the population observes this religion, which is indigenous to Palau).

Languages: English and Palauan (official).

Literacy rate: Total 92%, Male 93%, Female 90% (1980 est.).

Infant mortality rate: 14.84 deaths/ 1,000 live births (2005 est.).

Life expectancy: Total 70.14 years, Male 66.98 years, Female 73.48 years (2005 est.).

Government

Capital: Koror. A new capital is being built about 20 km north-east of Koror.

Government type: Constitutional government in free association with the US.

Independence: 1 October 1994 (from the US-administered UN Trusteeship).

Legal system: Based on Trust Territory laws, acts of the legislature, municipal, common, and customary laws.

Executive branch:
Chief of state: President Tommy

Esang Remengesau Jr (since 19 January 2001) and Vice-President Camsek Chin (since 1 January 2005). The president is both the chief of state and head of government.

Economy

Currency: US Dollar.

GDP: Purchasing power parity—$174 million.

GDP—real growth rate: 1% (2001 est.).

GDP—per capita: Purchasing power parity—$9,000 (2001 est.).

Inflation rate: 3.4% (2000 est.).

Exports: $18 million f.o.b. (2001 est.)—Shellfish, tuna, copra, garments.

Imports: $99 million f.o.b. (2001 est.).

External debt: None.

Transport and Communications

Railways: None.

Roads: 61 km.

Telephones: 6,700 (2002).

Mobile cellular: 1,000 (2002).

Internet country code: .pw

Panama

History

Panama was home to indigenous people when Spanish exploration started in the early 1500s. It declared its independence from Spain in 1821 but joined the confederacy of Gran Colombia. In 1903, it seceded from Colombia with US backing. The ceding of the Panama Canal Zone to USA followed soon after.

In 1988, US courts indicted Panamanian strongman General Manuel Noriega on drug charges. In 1989, the Panamanian Parliament named Noriega as the 'maximum leader'. He promptly announced a state of war between USA and Panama. In December that year, US forces seized the capital. Noriega surrendered in January 1990.

Geography

Location: Middle America, bordering both the Caribbean Sea and the North Pacific Ocean, between Colombia and Costa Rica.

Area: 78,200 sq. km.

Natural resources: Copper, mahogany forests, shrimp, hydropower.

Climate: Hot, humid, cloudy tropical maritime climate with a prolonged rainy season.

People

Population: 3,039,150 (July 2005 est.).

Population growth rate: 1.26% (2005 est.).

Sex ratio: 1.02 male(s)/female (2005 est.).

Religions: Roman Catholic 85%, Protestant 15%.

Languages: Spanish (official), English 14%.

Literacy rate: Total 92.6%, Male 93.2%, Female 91.9% (2003 est.).

Infant mortality rate: 20.47 deaths/1,000 live births (2005 est.)

Life expectancy: Total 71.94 years, Male 69.67 years, Female 74.31 years (2005 est.).

Government

Capital: Panama City.

Government type: Constitutional democracy.

Independence: 28 November 1821 (from Spain); 3 November 1903 (from Colombia).

Legal system: Based on civil law system.

Executive branch:

Chief of state: President Martin Torrijos Espino (since 1 September 2004). The president is both the chief of state and head of government.

Economy

Currency: Balboa, US dollar.

GDP: Purchasing power parity—$20.57 billion (2004 est.).

GDP—real growth rate: 0.6% (2004 est.).

GDP—per capita: Purchasing power parity—$6,900 (2004 est.).

Inflation rate: 2% (2004 est.).

Population below poverty line: 37% (1999 est.).

Unemployment rate: 12.6% (2004 est.).

Exports: $5.699 billion f.o.b. (2004 est.)—Banana, shrimp, sugar, coffee, clothing.

Imports: $7.164 billion f.o.b. (2004 est.)—Capital goods, crude oil, foodstuff, consumer goods, chemicals.

External debt: $8.78 billion (2004 est.).

Transport and Communications

Railways: 355 km.

Roads: 11,643 km.

Telephones: 386,900 (2002).

Mobile cellular: 834,000 (2003).

Internet users: 120,000 (2002).

Internet country code: .pa

Papua New Guinea

History

In 1906, the control of the British New Guinea territory was shifted to Australia. The name was changed to 'Territory of Papua'. In 1945, it became a United Nations trusteeship under Australian administration. The territories were combined under a new name, the Territory of Papua and New Guinea.

In 1951, partial home rule was granted while autonomy in internal affairs was granted nine years later. Full independence came in 1975.

Geography

Location: Oceania, group of islands including the eastern half of the island of New Guinea between the Coral Sea and the South Pacific Ocean, east of Indonesia.

Area: 462,840 sq. km.

Terrain: Mostly mountainous terrain with coastal lowlands and rolling foothills.

Natural resources: Gold, copper, silver, natural gas, timber, oil, fisheries.

Climate: Tropical climate.

People

Population: 5,545,268 (July 2005 est.).

Population growth rate: 2.26% (2005 est.).

Sex ratio: 1.05 male(s)/female (2005 est.).

Religions: Roman Catholic 22%, Lutheran 16%, Presbyterian/Methodist/London Missionary Society 8%, Anglican 5%, Evangelical Alliance 4%, Seventh-Day Adventist 1%, other Protestant 10%, indigenous beliefs 34%.

Languages: English spoken by 1–2%, pidgin English widespread, Motu spoken in Papua region. There are over 700 indigenous languages.

Literacy rate: Total 66%, Male 72.3%, Female 59.3% (2003 est.).

Infant mortality rate: 51.45 deaths/1,000 live births (2005 est.).

Life expectancy: Total 64.93 years, Male 62.76 years, Female 67.21 years (2005 est.).

Government

Capital: Port Moresby.

Government type: Constitutional monarchy with parliamentary democracy.

Independence: 16 September 1975 (from the Australian-administered UN trusteeship).

Legal system: Based on English common law.

Executive branch:
Chief of state: Queen Elizabeth II (since 6 February 1952), represented by Governor General Sir Paulius Matane (since 29 June 2004).

Head of government: Prime Minister Sir Michael Somare (since 2 August 2002); Deputy Prime Minister Andrew Baing (since 15 November 2003).

Economy

Currency: Kina.

Economy—overview:
Papua New Guinea is rich in natural resources, but exploitation is impeded by rugged terrain and the high cost of developing infrastructure. Eighty-five percent of the population depends on subsistence agriculture for livelihood. Mineral deposits such as oil, copper and gold, constitute 72% of export earnings.

GDP: Purchasing power parity—$11.99 billion (2004 est.).

GDP—real growth rate: –0.9% (2004 est.).

GDP—per capita: Purchasing power parity—$2,200 (2004 est.).

Inflation rate: 4.2% (2004 est.).

Population below poverty line: 37% (2002 est.).

Exports: $2.437 billion f.o.b. (2004 est.)—oil, gold, copper ore, logs, palm oil, coffee, cocoa, crayfish, prawns.

Imports: $1.353 billion f.o.b. (2004 est.)—machinery and transport equipment, manufactured goods, food, fuels, chemicals.

External debt: $2.463 billion (2004 est.).

Transport and Communications

Railways: None.

Roads: 19,600 km.

Telephones: 62,000 (2002).

Mobile cellular: 15,000 (2002).

Internet users: 135,000 (2001).

Internet country code: .pg

Paraguay

History

In 1776, Spain transferred Paraguay from the viceroyalty of Peru to the viceroyalty of La Plata with its capital at Buenos Aires in Argentina. In 1811, Paraguay became independent. Three dictators ruled the newborn nation over the next half-century. The third of them, Francisco Solano López, led

Paraguay to the bloodiest conflict in Latin American history. This was the War of the Triple Alliance, also called the Paraguayan War, in which Paraguay took on the allied forces of Argentina, Brazil, and Uruguay. The war not only resulted in a loss of territory but also a great loss of human life. Paraguay went back to war during 1932–5. This was the Chaco War and this time Paraguay won commercially important territory from Bolivia.

Geography

Location: Central South America, north-east of Argentina.

Area: 406,750 sq. km.

Terrain: Grassy plains and wooded hills east of Rio Paraguay; Gran Chaco region west of Rio Paraguay mostly low, marshy plain near the river; and dry forest and thorny scrub elsewhere.

Natural resources: Hydropower, timber, iron ore, manganese, limestone.

Climate: Varies from subtropical to temperate with substantial rainfall in the eastern parts but semi-arid in the far west.

People

Population: 6,347,884 (July 2005 est.).

Population growth rate: 2.48% (2005 est.).

Sex ratio: 1.01 male(s)/female (2005 est.).

Religions: Roman Catholic 90%, Mennonite, and other Protestant.

Languages: Spanish (official), Guarani (official).

Literacy rate: Total 94%, Male 94.9%, Female 93% (2003 est.).

Infant mortality rate: 25.63 deaths/ 1,000 live births (2005 est.).

Life expectancy: Total 74.89 years, Male 72.35 years, Female 77.55 years (2005 est.).

Government

Capital: Asuncion.

Government type: Constitutional republic.

Independence: 14 May 1811 (from Spain).

Legal system: Based on Argentine codes, Roman law, and French codes.

Executive branch:
Chief of state: President Nicanor Duarte Frutos (since 15 August 2003). Vice-President Luis Castiglioni (since 15 August 2003). The president is both the chief of state and head of government.

Economy

Currency: Guarani.

GDP: Purchasing power parity—$29.93 billion (2004 est.).

GDP—real growth rate: –2.8% (2004 est.).

GDP—per capita: Purchasing power parity—$4,800 (2004 est.).

Inflation rate: 5.1% (2004 est.).

Population below poverty line: 36% (2001 est.).

Unemployment rate: 15.1% (2004 est.).

Exports: $2.936 billion f.o.b. (2004 est.)—soybeans, animal feed, cotton, meat, edible oils, electricity.

Imports: $3.33 billion f.o.b. (2004 est.)—automobiles, consumer goods, tobacco, petroleum products, electrical machinery.

External debt: $3.239 billion (2004 est.).

Transport and Communications

Railways: 441 km.

Roads: 29,500 km.

Telephones: 273,200 (2002).

Mobile cellular: 1,770,300 (2003).

Internet users: 120,000 (2003).

Internet country code: .py

Peru

History

Cuzco in present-day Peru became the capital city of the Inca Empire in the 12th century. At the time of the Spanish conquest in the 1530s, the well-developed and prosperous Inca Empire was in the midst of a civil war. After the fall of the Inca empire, its territories became a part of the viceroyalty of Peru with its capital in Lima. In 1780, the Spanish suppressed a rebellion led by Tupac Amaru, who claimed descent from the Inca rulers. In 1821, Peru gained independence from Spain.

Between 1945 and 1980, the Shining Path, or Sendero Luminoso, guerrillas began their armed rebellion against the Peruvian government. Their violent movement intensified through the 1980s. It is estimated that the Shining Path's activities killed around 30,000 people and greatly harmed the Peruvian economy in the last 20 years of the 20th century.

Geography

Location: Western South America, bordering the South Pacific Ocean, between Chile and Ecuador.

Area: 1,285,220 sq. km.

Terrain: The Andes Mountains in the centre (the sierra), a coastal plain in the west (the costa) and the lowland jungle of Amazon basin in the east (selva).

Natural resources: Copper, silver, gold, petroleum, timber, fish, iron ore, coal, phosphate, potash, hydropower, natural gas.

Climate: Ranges from tropical in the east to dry desert in the west. The climate of the Andes region varies between temperate to frigid.

People

Population: 27,925,628 (July 2005 est.).

Population growth rate: 1.36% (2005 est.).

Sex ratio: 1.01 male(s)/female (2005 est.).

Religions: Roman Catholic 90%.

Languages: Spanish (official), Quechua (official), Aymara, numerous minor Amazonian languages.

Literacy rate: Total 90.9%, Male 95.2%, Female 86.8% (2003 est.).

Infant mortality rate: 31.94 deaths/ 1,000 live births (2004 est.).

Life expectancy: Total 69.53 years, Male 67.77 years, Female 71.37 years (2005 est.).

Government

Capital: Lima.

Government type: Constitutional republic.

Independence: 28 July 1821 (from Spain).

Legal system: Based on civil law system.

Executive branch:

Chief of state: President Alejandro Toledo Manrique (since 28 July 2001). The president is both the chief of state and head of government.

Economy

Currency: Nuevo Sol (PEN).

Economy—overview:
Peru has abundant mineral resources and rich fishing grounds. At the same time, lack of infrastructure hampers trade and investment while over-reliance on minerals exposes the economy to the dangers of fluctuations in global prices. The economy was one of the fastest growing in Latin America in 2002 and 2003. The Camisea natural gas pipeline project is scheduled to begin operations in 2004.

GDP: Purchasing power parity—$155.3 billion (2004 est.).

GDP—real growth rate: 4.5% (2004 est.).

GDP—per capita: Purchasing power parity—$5,600 (2004 est.).

Inflation rate: 3.8% (2004 est.).

Population below poverty line: 54% (2004 est.).

Unemployment rate: 13.4%; widespread underemployment (2003 est.).

Exports: $8.954 billion f.o.b. (2003 est.)—fish and fish products, gold, copper, zinc, crude petroleum and by-products, lead, coffee, sugar, cotton.

Imports: $9.6 billion f.o.b. (2004 est.)—machinery, transport equipment, foodstuff, petroleum, iron and steel, chemicals, pharmaceuticals.

External debt: $29.79 billion (2004 est.).

Transport and Communications

Railways: 3,462 km.

Roads: 78,230 km.

Telephones: 1,839,200 (2003).

Mobile cellular: 2,908,800 (2003).

Internet users: 2.85 million (2003).

Internet country code: .pe

The Philippines

History

The Spanish colonization of the Philippines began with the arrival of Ferdinand Magellan in 1521. In 1898, the Philippines became a colony of the United States after the Spanish-American War. The United States brought widespread education to the islands. The Philippines achieved independence in 1946. Ferdinand Marcos, who became the President in 1965, declared martial law in 1972. This spell of martial law in the country lasted till 1981 and Marcos was ousted in 1986.

Geography

Location: South-eastern Asia, archipelago between the Philippine Sea and the South China Sea, east of Vietnam.

Area: 300,000 sq. km.

Terrain: Mostly mountainous with coastal lowlands.

Natural resources: Timber, nickel, cobalt, petroleum, silver, gold, salt, copper.

Climate: Hot and dry between March to May, rainy from June to October, and cold from November to February.

People

Population: 87,857,473 (July 2005 est.).

Population growth rate: 1.84% (2005 est.).

Sex ratio: 1 male(s)/female (2005 est.).

Religions: Roman Catholic 83%, Protestant 9%, Muslim 5%, Buddhist and others 3%.

Languages: Filipino (based on Tagalog) and English.

Literacy rate: Total 95.9%, Male 96%, Female 95.8% (2003 est.).

Infant mortality rate: 23.51 deaths/1,000 live births (2005 est.).

Life expectancy: Total 69.91 years, Male 67.03 years, Female 72.92 years (2005 est.).

Government

Capital: Manila.

Government type: Republic.

Independence: 12 June 1898 (from Spain); 4 July 1946 (from USA).

Legal system: Based on Spanish and Anglo-American law.

Executive branch:
Chief of state: President Gloria Macapagal-Arroyo (since 20 January 2001). The president is both the chief of state and head of government.

Economy

Currency: Philippine peso.

Economy—overview:
The Philippine economy is a combination of agriculture, light industry, and supporting services. In 1998, the economy faltered due largely to the Asian financial crisis and adverse weather conditions. Growth plummeted to 0.6% in 1998 from 5% in 1997. There was some recovery in the following years (about 3.3% in 1999, 4.5% in 2000, and 4.5% in 2001). A growth of 4.4% in 2002 was marred by a record budget deficit. The Philippines has a public sector debt of more than 100% of GDP.

GDP: Purchasing power parity—$430.6 billion (2004 est.).

GDP—real growth rate: 5.9% (2004 est.).

GDP—per capita: Purchasing power parity—$5,000 (2004 est.).

Inflation rate: 5.5% (2004 est.).

Population below poverty line: 40% (2001 est.).

Unemployment rate: 11.7% (2004 est.).

Exports: $38.63 billion f.o.b. (2004 est.).

Imports: $37.5 billion f.o.b. (2004 est.).

External debt: $55.6 billion (2004 est.).

Transport and Communications

Railways: 897 km.

Roads: 202,124 km.

Telephones: 3,310,900 (2002).

Mobile cellular: 15,201,000 (2002).

Internet users: 3.5 million (2002).

Internet country code: .ph

Poland

History

In 966, Mieszko I of the Piast dynasty founded an entity known as Great Poland in the northern part of the present-day country. The tribes of southern Poland united to form Little Poland.The two entities joined together in 1047 under the reign of Casimir I the Restorer. In 1386, Poland united with Lithuania by virtue of a royal marriage. This united state emerged to be a formidable force in Europe, mainly between the 14th and 16th centuries when it defeated the Russians, the Ottoman Turks and the Knights of the Teutonic Order.

However, the monarchy declined in the 18th century with disastrous consequences. The Russians, the Austrians and the Prussians divided the country thrice. Consequently, the state of Poland ceased to exist. However, the Poles continued their efforts to regain a national identity through the 19th century. Their efforts bore fruit in 1918 when the independent Polish state was created after the end of World War I.

In 1939, Germany invaded Poland. This was the starting point of World War II as UK declared war on Germany in reaction to the invasion, while the Soviet Union invaded the country from the east. During the War, Poland was the scene of some of the worst atrocities ever. Germans built concentration camps in Poland that included Auschwitz, Treblinka and Majdanek. Millions of Jews from all over Europe were rounded up at these camps and exterminated.

The Soviet Army finally took Warsaw in January 1945. The Germans were driven out of the country by March 1945. The post-war Potsdam Conference demarcated the borders of the country. In 1947, Poland became a Communist People's Republic.

In the 1980s, Lech Walesa emerged as the leader of the first independent labour union in a Soviet bloc country. In 1990, Walesa was elected President of Poland. He introduced various worker reforms and steered the country away from communism.

Geography

Location: Central Europe, east of Germany.

Area: 312,685 sq. km.

Terrain: Mostly flat plain; mountains along the southern border.

Natural resources: Coal, sulphur, copper, natural gas, silver, lead, salt, amber, arable land.

Climate: Temperate climate. The winters are cold, cloudy and moderately severe with frequent precipitation. The summers are mild with frequent showers and thundershowers.

People

Population: 38,635,144 (July 2005 est.).

Population growth rate: 0.03% (2005 est.).

Sex ratio: 0.94 male(s)/female (2005 est.).

Religions: Roman Catholic 95%, Eastern Orthodox, Protestant, and others 5%.

Languages: Polish.

Literacy rate: 99.8% (2003 est.).

Infant mortality rate: 8.51 deaths/1,000 live births (2005 est.).

Life expectancy: Total 74.41 years, Male 70.3 years, Female 78.76 years (2005 est.).

Government

Capital: Warsaw.

Government type: Republic.

Independence: 11 November 1918 (date on which an independent republic was proclaimed).

Legal system: Mixture of Continental (Napoleonic) civil law and holdover communist legal theory.

Executive branch:
Chief of state: President Aleksander Kwasniewski (since 23 December 1995).

Head of government: Prime Minister Marek Belka (since 24 June 2004).

Economy

Currency: Zloty.

GDP: Purchasing power parity—$463.7 billion (2004 est.).

GDP—real growth rate: 5.6% (2004 est.).

GDP—per capita: Purchasing power parity—$12,000 (2004 est.).

Inflation rate: 3.4% (2004 est.).

Population below poverty line: 18.4% (2000 est.).

Unemployment rate: 17.5% (2004 est.).

Exports: $75.98 billion f.o.b. (2004 est.)—machinery and transport equipment, intermediate manufactured goods, miscellaneous manufactured goods, food and live animals.

Imports: $81.61 billion f.o.b. (2004 est.)—machinery and transport equipment, intermediate manufactured goods, chemicals, miscellaneous manufactured goods.

External debt: $99.15 billion (2004 est.).

Transport and Communications

Railways: 23,852 km.

Roads: 364,697 km.

Telephones: 12,300,000 (2003).

Mobile cellular: 17,401,000 (2003).

Internet users: 8,970,000 (2003).

Internet country code: .pl

Portugal

History

Portugal gained independence from Spain in 1143. The following centuries saw the rapid expansion of Portuguese rule all over the world. In 1488, Bartolomeu Dias reached Cape of Good Hope, the southernmost tip of the African mainland. In 1498, Vasco da Gama reached India. By the middle of the 16th century, the Portuguese Empire included Brazil, Indochina, East and West Africa and Malaya.

Spain invaded Portugal in 1581 and held it for the next 60 years, triggering a marked decline in Portuguese trade and commerce. The Portuguese hold over its far-flung colonies also suffered. Its European rivals wasted no time in snatching one territory after another from Portuguese rule. By the time the Spanish occupation was over, the only significant overseas possessions left for Portugal was Brazil, Angola and Mozambique.

In 1908, King Carlos and his heir were both assassinated in Lisbon. His second, Manuel, took to the throne. But he was ousted in a revolution. A republic was proclaimed in 1910. In 1911, a new Constitution separated the church from the state.

Geography

Location: South-western Europe, bordering the North Atlantic Ocean, west of Spain.

Area: 92,391 sq. km (this includes Azores and Madeira Islands).

Terrain: Rolling plains in the south and a mountainous area north of the Tagus River.

Natural resources: Fish, forests (cork), iron ore, copper, zinc, tin, tungsten, silver, gold, uranium, marble, clay, gypsum, salt, arable land, hydropower.

Climate: Maritime temperate climate.

People

Population: 10,566,212 (July 2005 est.).

Population growth rate: 0.39% (2005 est.).

Sex ratio: 0.94 male(s)/female (2005 est.).

Religions: Roman Catholic 94%, Protestant.

Languages: Portuguese (official), Mirandese (official).

Literacy rate: Total 93.3%, Male 95.5%, Female 91.3% (2003 est.).

Infant mortality rate: 5.05 deaths/1,000 live births (2005 est.).

Life expectancy: Total 77.53 years, Male 74.25 years, Female 81.03 years (2005 est.).

Government

Capital: Lisbon.

Government type: Parliamentary democracy.

Independence: 1143 (independent republic proclaimed on 5 October 1910).

Legal system: Civil law system.

Executive branch:
Chief of state: President Jorge Fernando Branco de Sampaio (since 9 March 1996).

Head of government: Prime Minister Jose Socrates (since 12 March 2005).

Economy

Currency: Euro.

Economy—overview:
Portugal has a well diversified service-based economy. It was one of the countries that started circulating the euro common currency on 1 January 2002. One of the major obstacles facing the country is its educational system.

GDP: Purchasing power parity—$188.7 billion (2004 est.).

GDP—real growth rate: –1.1% (2004 est.).

GDP—per capita: Purchasing power parity—$17,900 (2004 est.).

Inflation rate: 2.1% (2004 est.).

Unemployment rate: 6.5% (2004 est.).

Exports: $37.68 billion f.o.b. (2004 est.)—clothing and footwear, machinery, chemicals, cork and paper products, hides.

Imports: $52.1 billion f.o.b. (2004 est.)—machinery and transport equipment, chemicals, petroleum, textiles, agricultural products.

External debt: $274.7 billion (2004 est.).

Transport and Communications

Railways: 2,850 km.

Roads: 17,135 km.

Telephones: 4,278,800 (2003).

Mobile cellular: 9,341,400 (2003).

Internet users: 3,600,000 (2002).

Internet country code: .pt

Qatar

History

In 1783 the Âl Khalîfah family of Kuwait led the conquest of Bahrain, and installed themselves as the ruling family. They remained so in the 20th century. In 1867 a dispute arose between the Âl Khalîfahs of Bahrain and Qatar over the town of Az-Zubârah which escalated into a major confrontation. It was at this point of time that UK signed a separate treaty with Qatar, whom it had viewed as a Bahraini dependency till then. Between 1916 and 1971, Qatar was a British protectorate. In 1971, it declared independence.

Geography

Location: Middle East, peninsula bordering the Persian Gulf and Saudi Arabia.

Area: 11,437 sq. km.

Terrain: Flat and barren desert covered with loose sand and gravel.

Natural resources: Petroleum, natural gas, fish.

Climate: Summer lasts from May to September when temperatures and humidity are both very high. The winter months are from December to February. These are milder with pleasant and cool evenings.

People

Population: 863,051 (July 2005 est.).

Population growth rate: 2.61% (2005 est.).

Sex ratio: 1.88 male(s)/female (2005 est.).

Religions: Muslim 95%.

Languages: Arabic (official), English commonly used as a second language.

Literacy rate: Total 82.5%, Male 81.4%, Female 85% (2003 est.).

Infant mortality rate: 18.61 deaths/1,000 live births (2005 est.).

Life expectancy: Total 73.67 years, Male 71.15 years, Female 76.32 years (2005 est.).

Government

Capital: Doha.

Government type: Traditional monarchy.

Independence: 3 September 1971 (from UK).

Legal system: There is a discretionary system of law controlled by the amir. Civil codes are being implemented. Islamic law dominates family and personal matters.

Executive branch:
Chief of state: Amir Hamad bin Khalifa Al Thani (since 27 June 1995).

Head of government: Prime Minister Abdallah bin Khalifa Al Thani, brother of the monarch (since 30 October 1996); Deputy Prime Minister Muhammad bin Khalifa Al Thani (since 20 January 1998).

Economy

Currency: Qatari rial.

Economy—overview:
Oil and gas account for more than 55% of GDP, around 85% of export earnings and 70% of government revenues. Thanks to petroleum, Qatar has a per capita GDP that can be compared to that of the leading West European industrial countries. Qatar has proven oil reserves of 14.5 billion barrels. Qatar's proven reserves of natural gas exceed 17.9 trillion cubic metres, third largest in the world and about 5% of the world total. Since 2000, Qatar has posted trade surpluses,

mostly due to high oil prices and rising natural gas exports.

GDP: Purchasing power parity—$19.49 billion (2004 est.).

GDP—real growth rate: 8.7% (2004 est.).

GDP—per capita: Purchasing power parity—$23,200 (2004 est.).

Inflation rate: 3% (2004).

Unemployment rate: 2.7% (2001).

Exports: $15 billion f.o.b. (2004 est.).

Imports: $6.15 billion f.o.b. (2004 est.).

External debt: $18.82 billion (2004 est.).

Transport and Communications

Railways: None.

Roads: 1,230 km.

Telephones: 184,500 (2003).

Mobile cellular: 376,500 (2003).

Internet users: 126,000 (2003).

Internet country code: .qa

Romania

History

In May 1877, Romania proclaimed its independence from Turkey and in March 1881, the kingdom of Romania was proclaimed. The 1930s saw the rise of a fascist 'Iron Guard' movement in Romania. In 1938, King Carol II established a royal dictatorship in the country. During World War II, Romania joined the Axis powers and was part of the 1940 attack on Soviet Union. In August 1944, the Soviet Red Army invaded Romania. In 1945, a Soviet-backed government was installed in Romania. The Romanian People's Republic was proclaimed in December 1947.

In 1965, Nicolae Ceausescu became the new leader of the Communist Party. He not only promulgated a foreign policy independent from that of the Soviet Union but also denounced the Soviet invasion of Czechoslovakia in 1968. In 1975, USA granted Romania 'most favoured nation' status. However, Ceausescu's regime soon turned Romania into a police state.

Ceausescu and his wife were apprehended, given a trial and executed on Christmas Day, 1989. The opponents of communism set up the National Salvation Front to lead the country through this crucial phase. Ion Iliescu was chosen as the leader.

Geography

Location: South-eastern Europe, bordering the Black Sea, between Bulgaria and Ukraine.

Area: 237,500 sq. km.

Terrain: The country has the central Transylvanian Basin that is separated from the plains of Moldova on the east by the Caspainian Mountains and from the Walachian Plain on the south by the Transylvanian Alps.

Natural resources: Petroleum (reserves declining), timber, natural gas, coal, iron ore, salt, arable land, hydropower.

Climate: Temperate climate. The winters are cold and cloudy with frequent snow and fog.

People

Population: 22,329,977 (July 2005 est.).

Population growth rate: −0.12% (2005 est.).

Sex ratio: 0.95 male(s)/female (2005 est.).

Religions: Eastern Orthodox (including all sub-denominations) 87%, Protestant 6.8%, Catholic 5.6%, others (mostly Muslim) 0.4%, unaffiliated 0.2% (2002).

Languages: Romanian (official), Hungarian, German.

Literacy rate: Total 98.4%, Male 99.1%, Female 97.7% (2003 est.).

Infant mortality rate: 26.43 deaths/1,000 live births (2005 est.).

Life expectancy: Total 71.35 years, Male 67.86 years, Female 75.06 years (2004 est.).

Government

Capital: Bucharest.

Government type: Republic.

Independence: 9 May 1877 (date of proclamation of independence from Turkey); 30 December 1947 (date on which republic was proclaimed).

Legal system: Based on the constitution of France's Fifth Republic.

Executive branch:
Chief of state: President Traian Basescu (since 20 December 2004).

Head of government: Prime Minister Calin Popescu Tariceanu (since 29 December 2004).

Economy

Currency: Leu.

GDP: Purchasing power parity—$171.5 billion (2004 est.).

GDP—real growth rate: 8.1% (2004 est.).

GDP—per capita: Purchasing power parity—$7,700 (2004 est.).

Inflation rate: 14.3% (2003).

Population below poverty line: 44.5% (2000).

Unemployment rate: 6.3% (2004).

Exports: $23.54 billion f.o.b. (2004 est.)—textiles and footwear, metals and metal products, machinery and equipment, minerals and fuels, chemicals, agricultural products.

Imports: $28.43 billion f.o.b. (2004 est.)—machinery and equipment, fuels and minerals, chemicals, textile and products, basic metals, agricultural products.

External debt: $24.59 billion (2004 est.).

Transport and Communications

Railways: 11,385 km (3,888 km electrified).

Roads: 198,755 km.

Telephones: 4,300,000 (2003).

Mobile cellular: 6,900,000 (2003).

Internet users: 4,000,000 (2003).

Internet country code: .ro

Russia

History

According to tradition, the Viking Rurik reached Russia in 862 and established the first Russian dynasty. The various factions were united in the 10th and 11th centuries.

Between 1552 and 1556, Ivan IV 'the Terrible' conquered the Tartar khanates of Kazan and Astrakhan and established Russian rule over the lower and middle Volga region. He was the first person to be proclaimed tsar of Russia (in 1547). His reign saw the completion of the establishment of a centrally administered Russian state and the creation of an empire that also included non-Slav states. He gained notoriety for his reign of terror against the hereditary nobility.

In the 1580s, the Cossacks began invading Siberia. In 1613, the National Council elected Michael Romanov as tsar. This started the Romanov dynasty that ruled Russia until the 1917 revolution. His grandson. Peter the Great introduced far-reaching structural reforms in the government, creating a regular conscript army and navy, and subordinating the church to the crown.

From 1798–1814, Russia intervened in the Napoleonic wars in France. Napoleon's defeat in the 1812 invasion of Russia hastened his downfall. The Crimean War was fought between the Russians and the British, French, and Ottoman Turkish from 1853 to 1856. The 1856–64 Caucasian War completed the Russian annexation of the North Caucasus. The area of the present-day Central Asian republics was annexed between 1864–5.

In 1897, the Social Democratic Party was founded in Russia. In 1903, the party split into two factions—the Bolsheviks and the Mensheviks. In 1904–5, Russian expansion in Manchuria precipitated a war with Japan. Defeat in this war sparked the 1905 revolution that forced Tsar Nicholas II to grant a Constitution and establish a popularly elected constitutional body, the Duma.

The 1917 revolution had its roots in the riots that broke out in the city of Petrograd (now St Petersburg) over food scarcity. Tsar Nicholas II was forced to abdicate bringing more than 300 years of Romanov rule to an end. The Bolsheviks were installed in power. The first head of government was the founder of the Bolshevik Russian Communist Party, Vladimir Ilich Ulyanov, better known as Lenin. Lenin served till his death in 1924. The death of Lenin in 1924 resulted in a power struggle within the Communist Party, between Joseph Stalin and Leon Trotsky. After being dismissed from the office of Commissar of War, Trotsky was exiled in 1929. In 1940, he was murdered in Mexico City.

Stalin consolidated his stranglehold on power through a series of purges that eliminated his rivals and dissenters. He finally assumed premiership in 1941. Stalin successfully led USSR in World War II, in which he linked up with the Allied forces alongside UK and USA.

The Union of Soviet Socialist Republics, USSR, was formed as a federation on 30 December 1922. At its height, USSR, or Soviet Union, was the world's largest country. It was one of the only two global superpowers. The country covered around 22,400,000 square kilometres, seven times the area of India and more than twice the size of the United States. The country occupied nearly one-sixth of the Earth's land surface, covering 11 of the world's 24 time zones. It had the longest coastline and the longest frontiers of any country in the world.

Under the leadership of the Communist Party of the Soviet Union, USSR had an authoritarian and highly centralized political and economic system. The economic foundation of the USSR was described as 'Socialist ownership of the means of production, distribution, and exchange'. A series of five-year plans that set targets for all forms of production controlled the economy of the entire country.

In 1949, Soviet Union exploded its first atomic device. It followed this up with its first hydrogen bomb, exploded in 1953. In 1957, USSR launched the first-ever artificial earth satellite, Sputnik, to orbit the earth. In 1961, Soviet cosmonaut Yuri Gagarin accomplished the first manned orbital flight.

The emergence of two global giants, USSR and USA soon led to the development of a bipolar power structure in the world and heralded the Cold War. The Soviet cause was propagated through the installation of communist regimes in Eastern Europe, the formation of the Warsaw Pact, and the establishment of communist regimes in China, Cuba and North Korea. The Cold War reached a peak between 1948 and 1953. The death of Stalin in 1953 somewhat lulled the low-intensity conflict. But the tension resumed in the late 1950s and the early 1960s.

In October 1962, a major confrontation brought the United States and the Soviet Union to the brink of nuclear war. The issue was the presence of Soviet nuclear-armed missiles in Cuba. In May 1960, Soviet Premier Nikita Khrushchev pledged to defend Cuba with Soviet weapons. In July 1962, USA realized that the Soviet Union had begun missile shipments to Cuba. In retaliation, USA placed Cuba under a naval blockade. Finally, on 28 October, the Soviet Union informed USA it was stopping work on its missile sites in Cuba and taking back its missiles from the island. In return, the United States pledged never to invade Cuba and also secretly promised to withdraw US nuclear missiles stationed in Turkey.

The prevailing atmosphere of peace between USSR and USA came to an end when Soviet troops invaded Afghanistan in December 1979. The Soviet aim was to protect the regime of pro-Soviet leader Babrak Karmal.

The USA provided money and sophisticated equipment to the Afghans and their allies in the region to fight the Soviets. In 1988 USA, USSR, Pakistan, and Afghanistan signed an agreement that resulted in the complete withdrawal of Soviet troops in 1989.

In 1985, Mikhail Gorbachev became the new general secretary of the Communist Party while Andrey Gromyko became the new President. Gorbachev promulgated the policies of openness (glasnost) and restructuring (perestroika). In 1988, Gorbachev took over as the new President.

In 1989, Soviet troops suppressed a nationalist riot in the republic of Georgia. The same year, the Lithuanian Communist Party declared its independence from the Soviet communist Party. In 1990, Soviet troops were sent to Azerbaijan following inter-ethnic killings. Gorbachev opposed the independence of the Baltic states and imposed sanctions on Lithuania. Meanwhile, communist leader Boris Yeltsin was elected the President of the Russian Soviet Federative Socialist Republic. He left the Soviet Communist Party soon afterwards.

In August 1991, senior communist party officials detained Gorbachev at his holiday villa in Crimea. The coup however came to an end within days when the coup leaders themselves were arrested. This set off a chain of events leading to the ultimate collapse of the USSR.

Boris Yeltsin banned the Soviet Communist Party in Russia and seized its assets. He also recognized the independence of the Baltic republics. When the republic of Ukraine declared its independence from the Union, other republics followed suit and announced their breaking away. In September 1991, the Congress of People's Deputies voted for the dissolution of the Soviet Union. On Christmas Day 1991, Mikhail Gorbachev resigned as the Soviet President. On 31 December 1999, President Boris Yeltsin unexpectedly announced his resignation and named Prime Minister Putin as the acting President.

Geography

Location: Northern Asia and northern Europe, bordering the Arctic Ocean, North Pacific Ocean and the Black Sea.

Area: 17,075,200 sq. km.

Terrain: Broad plains and low hills west of the Urals. Siberia has vast stretches of coniferous forest and tundra. There are uplands and mountains along the southern border regions.

Natural resources: Russia is one of the world's largest oil and natural gas producers. Other natural resources present in the country include coal, various minerals and timber.

Climate: The vast expanse of Russia means that climate varies from one part of the country to another. The country has a humid continental type of climate in most parts of European Russia. The climate of Siberia is of the sub-arctic type although the polar north has tundra climate. The winters vary from cool along the Black Sea coast to frigid in Siberia while summers vary from warm in the steppes to cool along Arctic coast.

People

Population: 143,420,309 (July 2005 est.).

Population growth rate: −0.37% (2005 est.).

Sex ratio: 0.86 male(s)/female (2005 est.).

Religions: Russian Orthodox, Muslim, others.

Languages: Russian, local languages.

Literacy rate: 99.6% (2003 est.).

Infant mortality rate: 15.39 deaths/1,000 live births (2005 est.).

Life expectancy: Total 67.1 years, Male 60.55 years, Female 74.04 years (2005 est.).

Government

Capital: Moscow.

Government type: Federation.

Independence: 24 August 1991 (from Soviet Union).

Legal system: Based on civil law system; judicial review of legislative acts.

Executive branch:
Chief of state: President Vladimir Vladimirovich Putin (acting president since 31 December 1999, president since 7 May 2000).

Head of government: Premier Mikhail Yefimovich Fradkov (since 5 March 2004).

Elections and election results: The president is elected by popular vote for a four-year term. The election was last held on 14 March 2004 and will be held next in March 2008. The president appoints the premier with the approval of the Duma.

Legislative branch:
Russia has a bicameral Federal Assembly or Federalnoye Sobraniye that consists of the Federation Council or Sovet Federatsii and the State Duma or Gosudarstvennaya Duma. The Federation Council has 178 seats. Members serve four-year terms. The State Duma has 450 seats 225 seats are elected by proportional representation from party lists winning at least 5% of the vote. The remaining 225 seats are elected from single-member constituencies. Members are elected by direct, popular vote to serve four-year terms.

Elections and election results: State Duma elections were last held on 7 December 2003 and will be next held in December 2007.

Economy

Currency: Rouble.

Economy—overview:
The Russian economy has staged a recovery since the financial crisis of 1998. The year 2003 was its fifth straight year of growth and the country's average annual growth has been around 6.5%. The main drivers of this growth were high oil prices and a relatively cheap ruble. Besides, the economy has also seen significant investment and consumer-driven demand since 2000. Russia's international financial position has also improved since the 1998 financial crisis. One noteworthy feature has been that its foreign debt has dropped from around 90% of GDP to around 28%. Its foreign reserves have grown from only $12 billion a few years back to around $80 billion, largely due to oil export earnings. All these factors, along with the government effort to carry out structural reforms have raised business and investor confidence in the country. However, the economy is not without flaws. Petroleum, metals, and timber make up more than 80% of exports. This exposes the country to the potential dangers associated with world price swings. Another major problem facing the country is its outdated manufacturing sector, corruption, problematic banking system, and government intervention in the legal system. The recent controversy surrounding the arrest and trial of the head of one of Russia's largest oil companies has shaken foreign perception of the country.

GDP: Purchasing power parity—$1.408 trillion (2004 est.).

GDP—real growth rate: 6.7% (2004 est.).

GDP—per capita: Purchasing power parity—$9,800 (2004 est.).

Inflation rate: 11.5% (2004 est.).

Population below poverty line: 25% (January 2003 est.).

Unemployment rate: 8.3% (2004 est.).

Exports: $162.5 billion (2004 est.)—petroleum and petroleum products, natural gas, metals, chemicals, military products, wood and wood products.

Imports: $92.91 billion (2004 est.)—machinery and equipment, consumer goods, medicines, meat, sugar, semi-finished metal products.

External debt: $169.6 billion (2004 est.).

Transport and Communications

Railways: 87,157 km.

Roads: 537,289 km.

Telephones: 35,500,000 (2002).

Mobile cellular: 17,608,800 (2002).

Internet users: 6,000,000 (2002).

Internet country code: .ru

Rwanda

History

In 1890, Rwanda became a part of German East Africa. In 1916, Belgium occupied the territory. Subsequently, Belgium ruled the territory indirectly through Tutsi kings. In 1962, Rwanda became independent.

In 1988, around 50,000 Hutu refugees from Burundi escaped to Rwanda following ethnic violence there. In April 1994, the Rwandan and Burundian Presidents were both killed when their plane was shot down. This was followed by the systematic massacre of Tutsis by Hutu militia. Around 800,000 Tutsis and moderate Hutus were killed in 100 days.

In December 2001, Rwanda adopted a new flag and national anthem. In June 2002, the International Court of Justice in The Hague began to consider a suit filed by Democratic Republic of the Congo against Rwanda and its allies for human rights abuse, genocide and armed aggression. Paul Kagame won landslide victories in presidential and parliamentary elections held in 2003. In 2004, a French report concluded that it was Paul Kagame who ordered the 1994 shooting down of the aircraft carrying the Rwandan and Burundian Presidents.

Geography

Location: Central Africa, east of Democratic Republic of the Congo.

Area: 26,338 sq. km.

Natural resources: Gold, cassiterite (tin ore), wolframite (tungsten ore), methane, hydropower, arable land.

Climate: Temperate climate. There are two rainy seasons, one from February to April and the other from November to January.

People

Population: 8,440,820 (July 2005 est.).

Population growth rate: 2.43% (2005 est.).

Sex ratio: 0.99 male(s)/female (2005 est.).

Religions: Roman Catholic 56.5%, Protestant 26%, Adventist 11.1%, Muslim 4.6%, indigenous beliefs 0.1%, none 1.7%.

Languages: Kinyarwanda (official), French (official), English (official), Kiswahili (Swahili) used for commercial purpose.

Literacy rate: Total 70.4%, Male 76.3%, Female 64.7% (2003 est.).

Infant mortality rate: 91.23 deaths/1,000 live births (2005 est.).

Life expectancy: Total 46.96 years, Male 45.92 years, Female 48.03 years (2005 est.).

Government

Capital: Kigali.

Government type: Republic; presidential, multiparty system.

Independence: 1 July 1962 (from Belgium-administered UN trusteeship).

Legal system: Based on German and Belgian civil law systems and customary law.

Executive branch:
Chief of state: President Paul Kagame (since 22 April 2000).

Head of government: Prime Minister Bernard Makuza (since 8 March 2000).

Economy

Currency: Rwandan franc.

GDP: Purchasing power parity—$10.43 billion (2004 est.).

GDP—real growth rate: 0.9% (2004 est.).

GDP—per capita: Purchasing power parity—$1,300 (2004 est.).

Inflation rate: 7% (2004 est.).

Population below poverty line: 60% (2001 est.).

Exports: $69.78 million f.o.b. (2004 est.)—coffee, tea, hides, tin ore.

Imports: $260.8 million f.o.b. (2004 est.)—foodstuff, machinery and equipment, steel, petroleum products, cement and construction material.

External debt: $1.3 billion (2000 est.).

Transport and Communications

Railways: None.

Roads: 12,000 km.

Telephones: 23,200 (2002).

Mobile cellular: 134,000 (2003).

Internet users: 25,000 (2002).

Internet country code: .rw

Saint Kitts and Nevis

History

The British settled in St Kitts (formerly St Christopher) in 1623 and Nevis in 1628. The French arrived at St Kitts in 1627 and this sparked off a conflict between the two European powers that ended with a decisive French defeat in 1782. In 1958, the islands became a part of the West Indian federation and remained so till its dissolution in 1962. St Kitts and Nevis became independent in 1983.

Geography

Location: Caribbean islands in the Caribbean Sea, about one-third of the way from Puerto Rico to Trinidad and Tobago.

Area: 261 sq. km (Saint Kitts 168 sq. km; Nevis 93 sq. km).

Natural resources: Arable land.

Climate: Tropical climate with constant sea breezes. There is little seasonal temperature variation.

People

Population: 38,958 (July 2005 est.).

Population growth rate: 0.38% (2005 est.).

Sex ratio: 0.99 male(s)/female (2005 est.).

Religions: Anglican, other Protestant, Roman Catholic.

Languages: English.

Literacy rate: Total 97%, Male 97%, Female 98% (1980 est.).

Infant mortality rate: 14.49 deaths/1,000 live births (2005 est.).

Life expectancy: Total 72.15 years, Male 69.31 years, Female 75.16 years (2005 est.).

Government

Capital: Basseterre.

Government type: Constitutional monarchy with Westminster-style parliament.

Independence: 19 September 1983 (from UK).

Legal system: Based on English common law.

Executive branch:
Chief of state: Queen Elizabeth II (since 6 February 1952), represented by Governor General Cuthbert Montraville Sebastian (since 1 January 1996).

Head of government: Prime Minister Dr Denzil Douglas (since 6 July 1995) and Deputy Prime Minister Sam Condor (since 6 July 1995).

Economy

Currency: East Caribbean dollar.

GDP: Purchasing power parity—$339 million (2002 est.).

GDP—real growth rate: −1.9% (2002 est.).

GDP—per capita: Purchasing power parity—$8,800 (2002 est.).

Inflation rate: 1.7% (2001 est.).

Unemployment rate: 4.5% (1997).

Exports: $70 million (2002 est.)—machinery, food, electronics, beverages, tobacco.

Imports: $195 million (2002 est.)—machinery, manufactures, food, fuels.

External debt: $171 million (2001).

Transport and Communications

Railways: 50 km.

Roads: 320 km.

Telephones: 23,500 (2002).

Mobile cellular: 5,000 (2002).

Internet users: 10,000 (2002).

Internet country code: .kn

Saint Lucia

History

Saint Lucia became a British possession. In 1871, it became a part of the British territory of Windward Islands. In 1979, St Lucia achieved independence.

Geography

Location: Caribbean, island between the Caribbean Sea and North Atlantic Ocean, north of Trinidad and Tobago.

Area: 616 sq. km.

Natural resources: Forests, sandy beaches, minerals (pumice), mineral springs, geothermal potential.

Climate: Tropical climate with a moderating influence of the north-east trade winds.

People

Population: 166,312 (July 2005 est.).

Population growth rate: 1.28% (2005 est.).

Sex ratio: 0.97 male(s)/female (2005 est.).

Religions: Roman Catholic 90%, Anglican 3%, other Protestant 7%.

Languages: English (official), French patois.

Literacy rate: Total 67%, Male 65%, Female 69% (1980 est.).

Infant mortality rate: 13.53 deaths/1,000 live births (2005 est).

Life expectancy: Total 73.61 years, Male 70.05 years, Female 77.42 years (2005 est.).

Government

Capital: Castries.

Government type: Westminster-style parliamentary democracy.

Independence: 22 February 1979 (from UK).

Legal system: Based on English common law.

Executive branch:
Chief of state: Queen Elizabeth II (since 6 February 1952), represented by Governor General Dr Perlette Louisy (since September 1997).

Head of government: Prime Minister Kenneth Davis Anthony (since 24 May 1997) and Deputy Prime Minister Mario Michel (since 24 May 1997).

Economy

Currency: East Caribbean dollar.

GDP: Purchasing power parity—$866 million (2002 est.).

GDP—real growth rate: 3.3% (2002 est.).

GDP—per capita: Purchasing power parity—$5,400 (2002 est.).

Inflation rate: 3% (2001 est.).

Unemployment rate: 20% (2003 est.).

Exports: $66 million (2002 est.)—banana, clothing, cocoa, vegetables, fruits, coconut oil.

Imports: $267 million (2002 est.)—food 23%, manufactured goods 21%, machinery and transportation equipment 19%, chemicals, fuels.

External debt: $214 million (2000).

Transport and Communications

Railways: None.

Roads: 1,210 km.

Telephones: 51,100 (2002).

Mobile cellular: 14,300 (2002).

Internet users: 13,000 (2002).

Internet country code: .lc

Saint Vincent and the Grenadines

History

In 1763, the islands became a British colony. Between 1958 and 1962, the islands were part of the West Indies Federation. They finally gained independence in 1979.

Geography

Location: Caribbean, islands between the Caribbean Sea and North Atlantic Ocean, north of Trinidad and Tobago.

Area: 389 sq. km (Saint Vincent 344 sq. km).

Natural resources: Hydropower, cropland.

Climate: Tropical climate with little seasonal temperature variation.

People

Population: 117,534 (July 2005 est.).

Population growth rate: 0.27% (2005 est.).

Sex ratio: 1.03 male(s)/female (2005 est.).

Religions: Anglican 47%, Methodist 28%, Roman Catholic 13%, Hindu, Seventh-Day Adventist, other Protestant.

Languages: English, French patois.

Literacy rate: Total 96%, Male 96%, Female 96% (1970 est.).

Infant mortality rate: 15.24 deaths/1,000 live births (2004 est.).

Life expectancy: Total 73.35 years, Male 71.54 years, Female 75.21 years (2004 est.).

Government

Capital: Kingstown.

Government type: Parliamentary democracy; independent sovereign state within the Commonwealth.

Independence: 27 October 1979 (from UK).

Legal system: Based on English common law.

Executive branch:
Chief of state: Queen Elizabeth II (since 6 February 1952), represented by Governor General Sir Fredrick Nathaniel Ballantyne (since 2 September 2002).

Head of government: Prime Minister Ralph E. Gonsalves (since 29 March 2001).

Economy

Currency: East Caribbean dollar.

GDP: Purchasing power parity—$339 million (2002 est.).

GDP—real growth rate: –0.5% (2002 est.).

GDP—per capita: Purchasing power parity—$2,900 (2002 est.).

Inflation rate: –0.4% (2001 est.).

Unemployment rate: 15% (2001 est.).

Exports: $38 million (2002 est.).

Imports: $174 million (2002 est.).

External debt: $167.2 million (2000).

Transport and Communications

Railways: None.

Roads: 1,829 km.

Telephones: 27,300 (2002).

Mobile cellular: 10,000 (2002).

Internet users: 7,000 (2002).

Internet country code: .vc

Samoa

History

USA, UK and Germany all contested for the islands till they were divided between USA and Germany in 1899. In 1914, New Zealand occupied Western Samoa. In 1962, it became independent and in 1997 the word 'Western' was dropped from the name.

Geography

Location: Oceania, group of islands in the South Pacific Ocean, north-east of Australia.

Area: 2,944 sq. km.

Natural resources: Hardwood forests, fish, hydropower.

Climate: Tropical climate with a rainy season between October to March and a dry season from May to October.

People

Population: 177,287 (July 2005 est.).

Population growth rate: –0.23% (2005 est.).

Sex ratio: 1.39 male(s)/female (2005 est.).

Religions: Christian 99.7%.

Languages: Samoan (Polynesian), English.

Literacy rate: 99.7% (2003 est.).

Infant mortality rate: 27.71 deaths/1,000 live births (2005 est.).

Life expectancy: Total 70.72 years, Male 67.93 years, Female 73.65 years (2005 est.).

Government

Capital: Apia.

Government type: Constitutional monarchy under native chief.

Independence: 1 January 1962 (from New Zealand-administered UN trusteeship).

Legal system: Based on English common law and local customs.

Executive branch:
Chief of state: Chief Tanumafili II Malietoa. (He was the co-chief of state from 1 January 1962 and became the sole chief of state from 5 April 1963.)

Head of government: Prime Minister Sailele Malielegaoi Tuila'epa (since 1996).

Economy

Currency: Tala.

GDP: Purchasing power parity—$1 billion (2002 est.).

GDP—real growth rate: 5% (2002 est.).

GDP—per capita: Purchasing power parity—$5,600 (2002 est.).

Inflation rate: 4% (2001 est.).

Exports: $14 million f.o.b. (2002)—fish, coconut oil and cream, copra, taro, automotive parts, garments, beer.

Imports: $113 million f.o.b. (2002)—machinery and equipment, industrial supplies, foodstuffs.

External debt: $197 million (2000).

Transport and Communications

Railways: None.

Roads: 790 km.

Telephones: 11,800 (2002).

Mobile cellular: 2,700 (2002).

Internet users: 4,000 (2002).

Internet country code: .ws

San Marino

History

According to tradition, a Christian stonemason named Marinus founded San Marino in AD 301. In 1463, the Pope awarded the towns of Fiorentino, Montegiardino and Serravalle to San Marino. The town of Faetano joined the republic in 1464. In 1631, the papacy recognized San Marino's independence. In 1862, San Marino signed a customs union and treaty of friendship and cooperation with Italy.

Geography

Location: Southern Europe, an enclave in central Italy.

Area: 61.2 sq. km.

Natural resources: Building stone.

Climate: Mediterranean climate with mild to cool winters and warm, sunny summers.

People

Population: 28,880 (July 2005 est.).

Population growth rate: 1.3% (2005 est.).

Sex ratio: 0.92 male(s)/female (2005 est.).

Religions: Roman Catholic.

Languages: Italian.

Literacy rate: Total 96%, Male 97%, Female 95% (1976 est.).

Infant mortality rate: 5.73 deaths/1,000 live births (2005 est.).

Life expectancy: Total 81.62 years, Male 78.13 years, Female 85.43 years (2005 est.).

Government

Capital: San Marino.

Government type: Republic.

Independence: 3 September 301 (date of foundation of the republic).

Legal system: Based on civil law system with Italian law influences.

Executive branch:
Chief of state: Co-chiefs of state Captain Regent Cesare Gasperoni and Captain Regent Fausfa Morganti (for the period 1 April–30 September 2005).

Head of government: Secretary of State for Foreign and Political Affairs Fabio Berardi (since 15 December 2003).

Economy

Currency: Euro.

GDP: Purchasing power parity—$940 million (2001 est.).

GDP—real growth rate: 7.5% (2001 est.).

GDP—per capita: Purchasing power parity—$34,600 (2001 est.).

Inflation rate: 3.3% (2001).

Unemployment rate: 2.6% (2001).

Transport and Communications

Railways: None.

Roads: 220 km.

Telephones: 20,600 (2002).

Mobile cellular: 16,800 (2002).

Internet users: 14,300 (2002).

Internet country code: .sm

Sao Tome and Principe

History

The Portuguese explored the uninhabited islands in the 15th century and colonized them in the 16th century. In the 17th century, Sao Tome and Principe emerged as one of the world's leading sugar producers. Later on, coffee and cocoa cultivation was started. In 1908, Sao Tome and Principe was the world's largest producer of cocoa.

In 1951, Sao Tome and Principe became an overseas province of Portugal. In July 1975, Sao Tome and Principe became independent.

Geography

Location: Western Africa, islands in the Gulf of Guinea, straddling the equator, west of Gabon.

Area: 1,001 sq. km.

Natural resources: Fish, hydropower.

Climate: Hot and humid tropical climate.

People

Population: 187,410 (July 2005 est.).

Population growth rate: 3.16% (2005 est.).

Sex ratio: 0.97 male/female (2005 est.).

Religions: Christian 80% (Roman Catholic, Evangelical Protestant, Seventh-Day Adventist).

Languages: Portuguese (official).

Literacy rate: Total 79.3%, Male 85%, Female 62% (1991 est.).

Infant mortality rate: 43.11 deaths/1,000 live births (2005 est.).

Life expectancy: Total 66.99 years, Male 65.43 years, Female 68.59 years (2005 est.).

Government

Capital: Sao Tome.

Government type: Republic.

Independence: 12 July 1975 (from Portugal).

Legal system: Based on Portuguese legal system and customary law.

Executive branch:
Chief of state: President Fradique de Men zes (since 3 September 2001).

Head of government: Prime Minister Damiao Vaz d'Almeida (since 17 September 2004).

Economy

Currency: Dobra.

GDP: Purchasing power parity—$214 million (2003 est.).

GDP—real growth rate: 6% (2004 est.).

GDP—per capita: Purchasing power parity—$1,200 (2003 est.).

Inflation rate: 14% (2004 est.).

Exports: $6.7 million f.o.b. (2004 est.)—cocoa, copra, coffee, palm oil.

Imports: $41 million f.o.b. (2004 est.)—machinery and electrical equipment, food products, petroleum products.

External debt: $318 million (2002).

Transport and Communications

Railways: None.

Roads: 320 km.

Telephones: 7,000 (2003).

Mobile cellular: 4,800 (2003).

Internet users: 15,000 (2003).

Internet country code: .st

Saudi Arabia

History

In 622, Prophet Mohammed founded Islam in Medina. In medieval times, there were numerous conflicts between various rulers for the control of the Arabian Peninsula. The Ottomans gained control in 1517. Between 1915 and 1927, the British held the lands of what is today Saudi Arabia. In 1927, they recognized the sovereignty of the Kingdoms of Hejaz and Najd. These two kingdoms were united to form the Kingdom of Saudi Arabia in 1932.

Geography

Location: Middle East, bordering the Persian Gulf and the Red Sea, north of Yemen.

Area: 1,960,582 sq. km.

Terrain: Sandy desert with vast uninhabited stretches.

Natural resources: Petroleum, natural gas, iron ore, gold, copper.

Climate: Harsh, dry desert climate with great temperature extremes.

People

Population: 26,417,599. This includes 5,576,076 non-nationals (July 2005 est.).

Population growth rate: 2.31% (2005 est.).

Sex ratio: 1.21 male(s)/female (2005 est.).

Religions: Muslim 100%.

Languages: Arabic.

Literacy rate: Total 78.8%, Male 84.7%, Female 70.8% (2003 est.).

Infant mortality rate: 13.24 deaths/1,000 live births (2005 est.).

Life expectancy: Total 75.46 years, Male 73.46 years, Female 77.55 years (2005 est.).

Government

Capital: Riyadh.

Government type: Monarchy.

Independence: 23 September 1932 (unification of the kingdom).

Legal system: Based on Islamic law.

Executive branch:

Chief of state: King and Prime Minister Fahd bin Abd al-Aziz Al Saud (since 13 June 1982). Crown Prince and First Deputy Prime Minister Abdallah bin Abd al-Aziz Al Saud (half-brother to the monarch, heir to the throne since 13 June 1982). The monarch is both the chief of state and head of government.

Economy

Currency: Saudi riyal.

Economy—overview:
Saudi Arabia has an oil-based economy with strong governmental controls over major economic activities. Saudi Arabia has the largest reserves of petroleum in the world (26% of the proved reserves), ranks as the largest exporter of petroleum, and plays a leading role in OPEC. The petroleum sector accounts for roughly 75% of budget revenues, 45% of GDP, and 90% of export earnings. About 25% of GDP comes from the private sector. Roughly four million foreign workers play an important role in the Saudi economy, for example, in the oil and service sectors. The government in 1999 announced plans to begin privatizing the electricity companies, which follows the ongoing privatization of the telecommunications company. The government is supporting private sector growth to lessen the kingdom's dependence on oil and increase employment opportunities for the swelling Saudi population. Priorities for government spending in the short term include additional funds for the water and sewage systems and for education. Water shortages and rapid population growth constrain the government's efforts to increase self-sufficiency in agricultural products.

GDP: Purchasing power parity—$310.2 billion (2004 est.).

GDP—real growth rate: 5% (2004 est.).

GDP—per capita: Purchasing power parity—$12,000 (2004 est.).

Inflation rate: 0.8% (2004 est.).

Unemployment rate: 25% (2004 est.).

Exports: $113 billion f.o.b. (2004 est.); 90% of this is in the form of petroleum and petroleum products.

Imports: $36.21 billion f.o.b. (2004 est.).

External debt: $34.35 billion (2004 est.).

Transport and Communications

Railways: 1,392 km.

Roads: 152,044 km.

Telephones: 3,502,600 (2003).

Mobile cellular: 7,238,200 (2003).

Internet users: 1.5 million (2003).

Internet country code: .sa

Senegal

History

In the 1440s, Portuguese traders reached the estuary of the Senegal River. The Dutch set up a slave-trading centre on the island of Goree in the 16th century. The French set up their first settlement in the 17th century. During the Seven Years War of 1756–63, UK took over French settlements in Senegal and formed the colony of Senegambia. France regained its territories during American Revolutionary War of 1775–83.

In 1895, Senegal became a part of French West Africa. In June 1960, Senegal became independent as part of Mali Federation. In August 1960, Senegal withdrew from the Mali Federation and became a separate republic with Leopold Senghor as President. In 1982, Senegal and The Gambia formed a confederation named Senegambia. The confederation was dissolved in 1989.

Geography

Location: Western Africa, bordering the North Atlantic Ocean, between Guinea-Bissau and Mauritania.

Area: 196,190 sq. km.

Terrain: Low rolling plains rising to foothills in the south-west.

Natural resources: Fish, phosphates, iron ore.

Climate: Hot and humid tropical climate.

People

Population: 11,126,832 (July 2005 est.).

Population growth rate: 2.48% (2005 est.).

Sex ratio: 0.97 male(s)/female (2005 est.).

Religions: Muslim 94%, indigenous beliefs 1%, Christian 5% (mostly Roman Catholic).

Languages: French (official), Wolof, Pulaar, Jola, Mandinka.

Literacy rate: Total 40.2%, Male 50%, Female 30.7% (2003 est.).

Infant mortality rate: 55.51 deaths/1,000 live births (2005 est.).

Life expectancy: Total 56.75 years, Male 55.04 years, Female 58.52 years (2005 est.).

Government

Capital: Dakar.

Government type: Republic under multiparty democratic rule.

Independence: 4 April 1960 (from France).

Legal system: Based on French civil law system.

Executive branch:
Chief of state: President Abdoulaye Wade (since 1 April 2000).

Head of government: Prime Minister Macky Sall (since 21 April 2004).

Economy

Currency: Communaute Financiere Africaine franc.

GDP: Purchasing power parity—$18.36 billion (2004 est.).

GDP—real growth rate: 3.2% (2004 est.).

GDP—per capita: Purchasing power parity—$1,700 (2004 est.).

Inflation rate: 0.8% (2004 est.).

Population below poverty line: 54% (2001 est.).

Unemployment rate: 48% (2001 est.).

Exports: $1.374 billion f.o.b. (2004 est.)—fish, groundnut (peanut), petroleum products, phosphates, cotton.

Imports: $2.128 billion f.o.b. (2004 est.)—foods and beverages, capital goods, fuels.

External debt: $3.476 billion (2004 est.).

Transport and Communications

Railways: 906 km.

Roads: 14,576 km.

Telephones: 228,800 (2003).

Mobile cellular: 575,900 (2003).

Internet users: 225,000 (2003).

Internet country code: .sn

Serbia and Montenegro

History

The Kingdom of Serbs, Croats and Slovenes was formed in 1918. In 1929, the country was renamed Yugoslavia. When the Nazi German forces occupied the country, the partisans led by Josip Broz Tito and the Chetniks led by Draza Mihajlovic fought the Nazis till the end of the War in 1945.

Tito won the 1945 elections when the monarchists boycotted the vote. The new Parliament abolished the monarchy and proclaimed the Federal People's Republic of Yugoslavia with Tito as prime minister. In 1948, Tito led Yugoslavia away from the Soviet bloc. In 1953, Tito became the country's President and in 1963, he became President for life.

The death of Tito in 1980 was the beginning of the end of the federation. A system of rotating presidency designed to prevent internal strife between the constituent states— Serbia, Bosnia and Herzegovina, Croatia, Slovenia and Montenegro—was established.

In 1989, Slobodan Milosevic was elected President of Serbia. When barred by the Constitution from a third term as Serbian President, he took over as the President of the Federal Republic of Yugoslavia, now Serbia and Montenegro, in July 1997.

In 1991, Macedonia, Slovenia and Croatia proclaimed independence. By December 1991, the Yugoslav People's Army and Serbian separatists occupied nearly a third of Croatia's territory. Bosnia and Herzegovina declared its independence in 1992. A bloody civil war erupted and the Bosnian Serbs gained control over half of the country by August 1992. In August and September 1995, NATO carried out air strikes against Serb positions that enabled Muslims and Croats to retake substan-

tial chunks of territory from the Serbs. Soon afterwards, the Dayton Peace Accord was signed. This led to the formation of two entities: one Muslim-Croat federation and a Serb entity (Republika Srpska) within the greater state of Bosnia and Herzegovina.

Meanwhile, the situation in Montenegro and Kosovo grew tense. In May 1998, Milo Djukanovic was elected as the President of Montenegro. He openly proclaimed his intentions of severing ties with Serbia. On the other hand, the Yugoslav army and Serbian police started fighting against the Kosovo Liberation Army. The fact that Kosovo was legally an integral part of Serbia and Montenegro prevented NATO from intervening. Nevertheless, evidence of atrocities and massacres led to the first ever NATO intervention in the affairs of a sovereign nation regarding its own citizens. When negotiations in early 1999 failed to reach any conclusion, NATO initiated air strikes in March 1999.

Early in 2001, former President Milosevic was placed under 24-hour police surveillance in Belgrade. In February 2002, the trial of Slobodan Milosevic on charges of genocide and war crimes began in the Dutch capital, The Hague.

In February 2003, the Yugoslav Parliament signed Yugoslavia away into history when it approved a constitutional charter for the new Union of Serbia and Montenegro.

Geography

Location: South-eastern Europe, bordering the Adriatic Sea, between Albania and Bosnia and Herzegovina.

Area: 102,350 sq. km.

Terrain: Serbia and Montenegro has a widely varied terrain. There are fertile plains to the north, limestone ranges and basins to the east, mountains and hills to the south-east and a high shoreline to the south-west.

Natural resources: Oil, gas, coal, iron ore, bauxite, copper, lead, zinc, antimony, chromite, nickel, gold, silver, magnesium, pyrite, limestone, marble, salt, hydropower, arable land.

Climate: The northern part of the country has a continental climate with cold winters, hot, humid summers and well-distributed rainfall. The central portion of the country has a continental and Mediterranean climate while the southern part has Adriatic climate along the coast with hot, dry summers and autumns and relatively cold winters with heavy snowfall in the inland areas.

People

Population: 10,829,175 (July 2005 est.).

Population growth rate: 0.03% (2005 est.).

Sex ratio: 0.97 male(s)/female (2005 est.).

Religions: Orthodox 65%, Muslim 19%, Roman Catholic 4%, Protestant 1%, others 11%.

Languages: Serbian 95%, Albanian 5%.

Literacy rate: Total 93%, Male 97.2%, Female 88.9% (1991).

Infant mortality rate: 12.89 deaths/ 1,000 live births (2005 est.).

Life expectancy: Total 74.73 years, Male 72.15 years, Female 77.51 years (2005 est.).

Government

Capital: Belgrade.

Government type: Republic.

Independence: 27 April 1992 (date of formation of Federal Republic of Yugoslavia, now Serbia and Montenegro).

Legal system: Based on civil law system.

Executive branch:
Chief of state: President Svetozar Marovic (since 7 March 2003). The president is both the chief of state and head of government.

Economy

Currency: New Yugoslav dinar.

Economy—overview:
The country's economy has shrunk drastically over the last 14 years due to economic mismanagement in the Milosevic era, prolonged period under economic sanctions, and the damage inflicted to the country's infrastructure and industry in the 1999 NATO air strikes. Following the removal of President Slobodan Milosevic in October 2000, the new coalition government implemented measures to stabilize the economy and also started on an aggressive market reform programme. In December 2000, it renewed its IMF membership and then rejoined the World Bank (IBRD) and the European Bank for Reconstruction and Development (EBRD). The republic of Montenegro separated its economy from federal control and from Serbia during the Milosevic era. Even today, Montenegro has its own central bank. While Serbia uses the Yugoslav dinar as official currency, Montenegro uses the euro. It also makes its own budget and collects its own customs tariffs. Similarly, Kosovo enjoys a great degree of economic autonomy. Although it is technically still in Serbia and Montenegro, it is largely autonomous and is currently under United Nations Interim Administration Mission in Kosovo (UNMIK). It largely depends on the international community and Kosovars abroad for financial and technical assistance. Both the euro and the Yugoslav dinar are official currencies and the UNMIK manages the budget and collects taxes.

GDP: Purchasing power parity—$26.27 billion (2004 est.).

GDP—real growth rate: 6.5% (2004 est.).

GDP—per capita: Purchasing power parity—$2,400 (2004 est.).

Inflation rate: 11.6% (2003 est.).

Population below poverty line: 30% (1999 est.).

Unemployment rate: 30% (2004 est.).

Exports: $3.245 billion f.o.b. (2004 est.)—manufactured goods, food and live animals, raw materials.

Imports: $9.538 billion f.o.b. (2004 est.)—machinery and transport equipment, fuels and lubricants, manufactured goods, chemicals, food and live animals, raw materials.

External debt: $12.97 billion (2004 est.).

Transport and Communications

Railways: 4,380 km.

Roads: 45,290 km.

Telephones: 2,611,700 (2003).

Mobile cellular: 3,634,600 (2003).

Internet users: 847,000 (2003).

Internet country code: .yu

Seychelles

History

In 1903 the Seychelles became a British Crown Colony. Self-government was granted in 1975. Seychelles finally gained independence in 1976.

Geography

Location: Eastern Africa, group of islands in the Indian Ocean, north-east of Madagascar.

Area: 455 sq. km.

Terrain: The Mahe group is granitic, with a narrow coastal strip. Others are coral, flat, elevated reefs.

Natural resources: Fish, copra, cinnamon trees.

Climate: Humid tropical marine climate.

People

Population: 81,188 (July 2005 est.).

Population growth rate: 0.43% (2005 est.).

Sex ratio: 0.93 male(s)/female (2005 est.).

Religions: Roman Catholic 86.6%, Anglican 6.8%, other Christian 2.5%, others 4.1%.

Languages: English (official), French (official), Creole.

Literacy rate: Total 58%, Male 56%, Female 60% (1971 est.).

Infant mortality rate: 15.53 deaths/1,000 live births (2005 est.).

Life expectancy: Total 71.82 years, Male 66.41 years, Female 77.4 years (2005 est.).

Government

Capital: Victoria.

Government type: Republic.

Independence: 29 June 1976 (from UK).

Legal system: Based on English common law, French civil law, and customary law.

Executive branch:

Chief of state: President James Michel (since 14 April 2004). The president is both the chief of state and head of government.

Economy

Currency: Seychelles rupee.

GDP: Purchasing power parity—$626 million (2002 est.).

GDP—real growth rate: 1.5% (2002 est.).

GDP—per capita: Purchasing power parity—$7,800 (2002 est.).

Inflation rate: 5% (2004 est.).

Exports: $256.2 million f.o.b. (2004 est.)—canned tuna, frozen fish, cinnamon bark, copra, petroleum products (re-exports).

Imports: $393.4 million f.o.b. (2004 est.)—machinery and equipment, foodstuff, petroleum products, chemicals.

External debt: $218.1 million (2004 est.).

Transport and Communications

Railways: None.

Roads: 373 km.

Telephones: 21,700 (2002).

Mobile cellular: 54,500 (2003).

Internet users: 11,700 (2002).

Internet country code: .sc

Sierra Leone

History

The first Europeans to reach the region were the Portuguese, who gave it the name Sierra Leone. In 1787, British abolitionists and philanthropists established a settlement in Freetown for former slaves. In 1808, this settlement at Freetown became a British colony. In 1896, UK set up a protectorate over the hinterland of Freetown. In 1961, Sierra Leone became independent and in 1971, it became a republic. In 1978, a new constitution made Sierra Leone a one-party state with the All People's Congress as the only legal party.

Geography

Location: Western Africa, bordering the North Atlantic Ocean, between Guinea and Liberia.

Area: 71,740 sq. km.

Natural resources: Diamonds, titanium ore, bauxite, iron ore, gold, chromite.

Climate: Hot and humid tropical.

People

Population: 6,017,643 (July 2005 est.).

Population growth rate: 2.22% (2005 est.).

Sex ratio: 0.93 male(s)/female (2005 est.).

Religions: Muslim 60%, indigenous beliefs 30%, Christian 10%.

Languages: English (official), Mende, Temne, Krio.

Literacy rate: Total 31.4%, Male 45.4%, Female 18.2% (1995 est.).

Infant mortality rate: 143.64 deaths/1,000 live births (2005 est.).

Life expectancy: Total 42.52 years, Male 40.13 years, Female 44.98 years (2005 est.).

Government

Capital: Freetown.

Government type: Constitutional democracy.

Independence: 27 April 1961 (from UK).

Legal system: Based on English law and customary laws indigenous to local tribes.

Executive branch:
Chief of state: President Ahmad Tejan Kabbah (since 29 March 1996, reinstated 10 March 1998). The president is both the chief of state and head of government.

Economy

Currency: Leone.

GDP: Purchasing power parity—$3.335 billion (2004 est.).

GDP—real growth rate: 6% (2004 est.).

GDP—per capita: Purchasing power parity—$600 (2004 est.).

Inflation rate: 1% (2002 est.).

Population below poverty line: 68% (1989 est.).

Exports: $49 million f.o.b. (2002 est.)—diamond, rutile, cocoa, coffee, fish (1999).

Imports: $264 million f.o.b. (2002 est.)—foodstuff, machinery and equipment, fuels and lubricants, chemicals (1995).

External debt: $1.5 billion (2002 est.).

Transport and Communications

Railways: 84 km.

Roads: 11,330 km.

Telephones: 24,000 (2002).

Mobile cellular: 67,000 (2002).

Internet users: 8,000 (2002).

Internet country code: .sl

Singapore

History

The earliest known mention of Singapore is in a third century Chinese account that described Singapore as 'Pu-luo-chung' ('island at the end of a peninsula'). Fishermen and pirates originally inhabited Singapore and till the 14th century, it served as an outpost of the Sumatran empire of Shrivijaya. In the 14th century, it passed to Java and Siam and in the 15th century it became a part of the Malacca empire. The Portuguese in the 16th and the Dutch in the 17th century controlled the area. Then in 1819, the area was passed on to the British East India Company. It became a part of the Straits Settlements and the hub of British colonial activity in the region.

During World War II, during 1942–5, the Japanese occupied the islands. It became a British Crown Colony once again in 1946 but achieved full internal self-governance in 1959. In 1963, Singapore became a part of the Federation of Malaysia along with Malaya, Sabah and Sarawak. In 1965, Singapore withdrew from the federation to become an independent state.

Geography

Location: South-eastern Asia, islands between Malaysia and Indonesia.

Area: 692.7 sq. km.

Terrain: Lowland with a gently undulating central plateau that contains a water catchment area and a nature preserve.

Natural resources: Fish, deepwater ports.

Climate: Warm and humid climate.

People

Population: 4,425,720 (July 2005 est.).

Population growth rate: 1.56% (2005 est.).

Sex ratio: 0.96 male(s)/female (2005 est.).

Religions: Buddhist (Chinese), Muslim (Malays), Christian, Hindu, Sikh, Taoist, Confucianist.

Languages: Chinese (official), Malay (official and national), Tamil (official), English (official).

Literacy rate: Total 93.2%, Male 96.7%, Female 89.7% (2003 est.).

Infant mortality rate: 2.29 deaths/ 1,000 live births (2005 est.).

Life expectancy: Total 81.62 years, Male 79.05 years, Female 84.39 years (2005 est.).

Government

Capital: Singapore.

Government type: Parliamentary republic.

Independence: 9 August 1965 (from Malaysian Federation).

Legal system: Based on English common law.

Executive branch:
Chief of state: President Sellapan Rama Nathan (since 1 September 1999).

Head of government: Prime Minister Lee Hsien Loong (since 2004).

Economy

Currency: Singapore dollar.

Economy—overview:
Singapore is a highly developed free market economy marked by an open and corruption-free environment and stable prices. It also has one of the highest per capita GDPs in the world. The economy relies heavily on exports, mainly in the sphere of electronics and manufacturing. In 2001–2, the global recession and the slump in the technology sector hit Singapore's economy hard.

GDP: Purchasing power parity—$120.9 billion (2004 est.).

GDP—real growth rate: 8.1% (2004 est.).

GDP—per capita: Purchasing power parity—$27,800 (2004 est.).

Inflation rate: −1.7% (2004 est.).

Unemployment rate: 3.4% (2004 est.).

Exports: $127 billion f.o.b. (2002 est.).

Imports: $113 billion (2002 est.).

External debt: $19.4 billion (2004 est.).

Transport and Communications

Railways: 38.6 km.

Roads: 3,130 km.

Telephones: 1,896,100 (2004).

Mobile cellular: 3,521,800 (2004).

Internet users: 2,310,000 (2002).

Internet country code: .sg

Slovakia

History

Slavic Slovaks settled in the region that is present-day Slovakia in the sixth century. The Moravian Empire united the Slovaks in the ninth century. Germans and Magyars conquered Moravia in 907 and the Slovaks went under Hungarian rule that lasted till the collapse of the Hapsburg Empire in 1918. The Slovaks then joined Bohemia, Moravia and a part of Silesia to form the new country of Czechoslovakia.

Political reforms in Czechoslovakia began with the fall of communism in the 1990s and the election of Vaclav Havel as President of Czechoslovakia in 1989. Talks on the future of Czechoslovakia began in 1991. Finally, it was decided the two republics should separate and become two fully independent nations. The Republic of Slovakia came into existence on 1 January 1993.

Geography

Location: Central Europe, south of Poland.

Area: 48,845 sq. km.

Terrain: Rugged mountains in the central and northern parts and lowlands in the south.

Natural resources: Brown coal and lignite, iron ore, copper and manganese ore, salt, arable land.

Climate: Temperate climate with cool summers and cold, cloudy, and humid winters.

People

Population: 5,431,363 (July 2005 est.).

Population growth rate: 0.15% (2005 est.).

Sex ratio: 0.94 male(s)/female (2005 est.).

Religions: Roman Catholic 60.3%, atheist 9.7%, Protestant 8.4%, Orthodox 4.1%, others 17.5%.

Languages: Slovak (official), Hungarian.

Infant mortality rate: 7.41 deaths/ 1,000 live births (2005 est.).

Life expectancy: Total 74.5 years, Male 70.52 years, Female 78.68 years (2005 est.).

Government

Capital: Bratislava.

Government type: Parliamentary democracy.

Independence: 1 January 1993 (date on which Czechoslovakia split into the Czech Republic and Slovakia).

Legal system: Civil law system based on Austro-Hungarian codes.

Executive branch:
Chief of state: President Ivan Gasparovic (since 15 June 2004).

Head of government: Prime Minister Mikulas Dzurinda (since 30 October 1998).

Economy

Currency: Slovak koruna.

GDP: Purchasing power parity—$78.89 billion (2004 est.).

GDP—real growth rate: 5.3% (2004 est.).

GDP—per capita: Purchasing power parity—$14,500 (2004 est.).

Inflation rate: 7.5% (2004 est.).

Unemployment rate: 13.1% (2004 est.).

Exports: $29.24 billion f.o.b. (2004 est.)—machinery and transport equipment, intermediate manufactured goods, miscellaneous manufactured goods, chemicals (1999).

Imports: $29.67 billion f.o.b. (2004 est.)—machinery and transport equipment, intermediate manufactured goods, fuels, chemicals, miscellaneous manufactured goods (1999).

External debt: $19.54 billion (2004 est.).

Transport and Communications

Railways: 3,661 km.

Roads: 42,970 km.

Telephones: 1,294,700 (2003).

Mobile cellular: 3,678,800 (2003).

Internet users: 1,375,800 (2003).

Internet country code: .sk

Slovenia

History

The Slovene group of Slavic people settled in the area in the sixth century AD. In the seventh century, they set up the Slavic state of Samu. This state was allied with the Avars who dominated the Hungarian plains till Charlemagne defeated them in the late eighth century. In 1867, Slovenia became a part of the Austro-Hungarian Kingdom. Following the defeat of the Austro-Hungarian Kingdom in World War I, Slovenia declared its independence. In 1918, it joined Serbia, Montenegro and Croatia to form a new nation, later renamed Yugoslavia.

In the 1991, the Slovenia declared its independence.

Geography

Location: Central Europe, eastern Alps bordering the Adriatic Sea, between Austria and Croatia.

Area: 20,273 sq. km.

Terrain: A short coastal strip on the Adriatic, an alpine region adjacent to Italy and Austria, and valleys with numerous rivers to the east.

Natural resources: Lignite, coal, lead, zinc, mercury, uranium, silver, hydropower, forests.

Climate: Mediterranean climate in the coastal area. The plateaus and eastern valleys have continental climate with mild to hot summers and cold winters.

People

Population: 2,011,070 (July 2005 est.).

Population growth rate: −0.03% (2005 est.).

Sex ratio: 0.95 male(s)/female (2005 est.).

Religions: Roman Catholic (Uniate 2%) 70.8%, Lutheran 1%, Muslim 1%, atheist 4.3%, others 22.9%.

Languages: Slovenian 92%, Serbo-Croatian 6.2%, other 1.8%.

Literacy rate: 99.7% (2003 est.).

Infant mortality rate: 4.45 deaths/1,000 live births (2005 est.).

Life expectancy: Total 76.14 years, Male 72.42 years, Female 80.1 years (2005 est.).

Government

Capital: Ljubljana.

Government type: Parliamentary democratic republic.

Independence: 25 June 1991 (from Yugoslavia).

Legal system: Based on civil law system.

Executive branch:
Chief of state: President Janez Drnovsek (since 22 December 2002).

Head of government: Prime Minister Janez Jansa (since 9 November 2004).

Economy

Currency: Tolar.

GDP: Purchasing power parity—$39.41 billion (2004 est.).

GDP—real growth rate: 3.9% (2004 est.).

GDP—per capita: Purchasing power parity—$19,600 (2004 est.).

Inflation rate: 3.3% (2004 est.).

Unemployment rate: 6.4% (2004 est.).

Exports: $14.97 billion f.o.b. (2004 est.)—manufactured goods, machinery and transport equipment, chemicals, food.

Imports: $16.07 billion f.o.b. (2004 est.)—machinery and transport equipment, manufactured goods, chemicals, fuels and lubricants, food.

External debt: $14.65 billion (2004 est.).

Transport and Communications

Railways: 1,201 km.

Roads: 20,250 km.

Telephones: 812,300 (2003).

Mobile cellular: 1,739,100 (2003).

Internet users: 750,000 (2002).

Internet country code: .si

Solomon Islands

History

In 1893, the islands became a British protectorate. Japanese occupation of the islands during World War II sparked off bitter fighting with the Allies. In 1975, the islands attained self-governance. In 1978 Solomon Islands became independent.

Geography

Location: Oceania, group of islands in the South Pacific Ocean, east of Papua New Guinea.

Area: 28,450 sq. km.

Natural resources: Fish, forests, gold, bauxite, phosphates, lead, zinc, nickel.

Climate: Tropical monsoon type of weather with few extremes of temperature.

People

Population: 538,032 (July 2005 est.).

Population growth rate: 2.68% (2005 est.).

Sex ratio: 1.03 male(s)/female (2005 est.).

Religions: Anglican 45%, Roman Catholic 18%, United (Methodist/Presbyterian) 12%, Baptist 9%, Seventh-Day Adventist 7%, other Protestant 5%, indigenous beliefs 4%.

Languages: Melanesian pidgin is lingua franca in much of the country; English is official but spoken by only 1–2% of the population. There are 120 indigenous languages.

Infant mortality rate: 21.29 deaths/1,000 live births (2005 est.).

Life expectancy: Total 72.66 years, Male 70.16 years, Female 75.28 years (2005 est.).

Government

Capital: Honiara.

Government type: Parliamentary democracy.

Independence: 7 July 1978 (from UK).

Legal system: English common law.

Executive branch:
Chief of state: Queen Elizabeth II (since 6 February 1952), represented by Governor General Naihaniel Waena (since 7 July 2004).

Head of government: Prime Minister Sir Allan Kemakeza (since 17 December 2001); Deputy Prime Minister Snyder Rini (since 17 December 2001).

Economy

Currency: Solomon Islands dollar.

GDP: Purchasing power parity—$800 million (2002 est.).

GDP—real growth rate: −5.8% (2003 est.).

GDP—per capita: Purchasing power parity—$1,700 (2002 est.).

Inflation rate: 10% (2003 est.).

Exports: $74 million f.o.b. (2003 est.)—timber, fish, copra, palm oil, cocoa.

Imports: $67 million f.o.b. (2003 est.)—food, plant and equipment, manufactured goods, fuels, chemicals.

External debt: $180.4 million (2002 est.).

Transport and Communications

Railways: None.

Roads: 1,360 km.

Telephones: 6,600 (2002).

Mobile cellular: 1,000 (2002).

Internet users: 2,200 (2002).

Internet country code: .sb

Somalia

History

When UK occupied Aden (in present day Yemen) in 1839, Somalia became its source of foodstuffs. By the 1920s, the area that is today Somalia was under the control of two protectorates, one British and one Italian. UK gained control over the entire territory after 1941. In 1950, Italy returned as the UN-appointed trustee of its former territory. In 1960, UK and Italy granted independence to its Somali territories, British Somaliland and Italian Somaliland, thus enabling the creation of the United Republic of Somalia in July 1960.

In 1991, numerous clans that had grown up all across the country and had some access to weapons set up their own domains. The most significant among these domains was Somaliland. The Somali National Movement (SNM) secured control of the former British Somaliland region in the northern part of the country and declared an independent 'Somaliland Republic'. Even today, Somaliland has its own capital (Hargeisa), a working political system with its own President (Dahir Riyale Kahin), its government institutions, a security set-up and its own currency (Somaliland shilling). What it does not have, however, is the crucial international recognition of being a sovereign state separate from Somalia.

In December 1992, USA led a multinational force of more than 35,000 troops to Somalia. However, the international troops faced strong resistance. Fighting ravaged the food-growing regions, cutting off food supplies for the country's population. Mogadishu itself was devastated. This led to US withdrawal from the country. In 1995, even the UN retreated, having failed to restore peace and order.

In April 2002, warlords in the southwestern part of the country unilaterally declared autonomy for six districts and formed the 'South-western Regional Government'. In October 2002, the transitional government signed a ceasefire with 21 warring factions in order to stop hostilities for the duration of the peace talks.

Geography

Location: Eastern Africa, bordering the Gulf of Aden and the Indian Ocean, east of Ethiopia.

Area: 637,657 sq. km.

Terrain: Mostly flat to undulationg plateau rising to hills in the north.

Natural resources: Uranium, iron ore, tin, gypsum, bauxite, copper, salt, natural gas, likely oil reserves. (Besides uranium, the reserves of the other minerals are largely unexploited.)

Climate: Desert type of climate.

People

Population: 8,591,629 (July 2005 est.).

Population growth rate: 3.38% (2005 est.).

Sex ratio: 1 male(s)/female (2005 est.).

Religions: Sunni Muslim.

Languages: Somali (official), Arabic, Italian, English.

Literacy rate: Total 37.8%, Male 49.7%, Female 25.8% (2001 est.).

Infant mortality rate: 116.7 deaths/ 1,000 live births (2005 est.).

Life expectancy: Total 48.09 years, Male 46.36 years, Female 49.87 years (2005 est.).

Government

Capital: Mogadishu.

Government type: No permanent national government; transitional, parliamentary national government. A new transitioned faceted government concessions of a 275–member parliament was established or October 2004. However, it is based in Kendra and has not established effective governance inside Somalia.

Independence: 1 July 1960 (from a merger of British Somaliland.

Legal system: No national system; Shari'a and secular courts exist in some parts of the country.

Executive branch:
Chief of state: Abdullahi Yusuf Ahmed (since 14 October 2004).

Head of government: Prime Minister Ali Mohammed Ghedi (since 24 December 2004).

Economy

Currency: Somali shilling.

GDP: Purchasing power parity—$4.597 billion (2004 est.).

GDP—real growth rate: 2.8% (2004 est.).

GDP—per capita: Purchasing power parity—$600 (2004 est.).

Exports: $79 million f.o.b. (2002 est.)—livestock, banana, hides, fish, charcoal, scrap metal.

Imports: $344 million f.o.b. (2002 est.)—manufactured products, petroleum products, foodstuff, construction materials, qat.

External debt: $3 billion (2001 est.).

Transport and Communications

Railways: None.

Roads: 22,100 km.

Telephones: 100,000 (2002 est.).

Mobile cellular: 35,000 (2002).

Internet users: 89,000 (2002).

Internet country code: .so

South Africa

History

In the 1480s, Portuguese navigator Bartholomeu Dias became the first European to travel round the southern tip of Africa. In 1497, Portuguese explorer Vasco da Gama landed on the Natal coast. In 1652, Jan van Riebeeck, who represented the Dutch East India Company, established the Cape Colony at Table Bay. However, in 1795, British forces seized Cape Colony from the Dutch. A powerful Zulu Empire grew up in the region between 1816 and 1826. Between 1835 and 1840, the Boers (Africans of Dutch origin) founded Orange Free State and Transvaal.

In 1867, diamonds were discovered at Kimberley. Soon afterwards, UK annexed Transvaal. In 1879, the British defeated the Zulus in Natal. In 1880–1, the Boers rebelled against the British, resulting in the first Anglo-Boer War. In mid 1880s, gold was discovered in Transvaal and led to a gold rush. The second Anglo-Boer War began in 1899 when British troops gathered on the Transvaal border ignoring an ultimatum. Consequently, Transvaal and Orange Free State were made self-governing colonies of the British Empire.

In 1910, the Union of South Africa was formed out of the former British colonies of the Cape and Natal, and the Boer republics of Transvaal, and Orange Free State. In 1912, the Native National Congress, later renamed the African National Congress (ANC), was founded. In 1948, the National Party came to power and implemented a policy of apartheid. This was a policy of segregation and political and economic discrimination against non-European groups living in the country.

The ANC responded to this move by launching its campaign of civil disobedience under the leadership of Nelson Mandela. In 1956, Mandela was charged with high treason, along with 155 other activists. The government banned ANC. In 1961, South Africa was proclaimed a republic and left the Commonwealth. Mounting international pressure against the South African government led to the exclusion of South Africa from the Olympic Games. Meanwhile, ANC launched its military wing with Mandela as its head and embarked on a sabotage campaign.

In 1964, Nelson Mandela was arrested and charged with sabotage and attempt to overthrow the government. He was sentenced to life imprisonment.

In 1989, F.W. de Klerk replaced P.W. Botha as President. Soon afterwards, public facilities were desegregated and many ANC activists were freed from prison. In 1990, the ban on ANC was removed. Nelson Mandela was released after 27 years in prison. In 1991, talks began between the ANC and the National Party on the formation of a new multiracial democracy for South Africa. Remaining apartheid laws were repealed, leading to the lifting of international sanctions. The 1993 Nobel Peace prize was awarded to Nelson Mandela and F.W. de Klerk.

In April 1994, ANC won the country's first ever non-racial elections. Nelson Mandela became President. South Africa's Commonwealth membership was restored and the remaining international sanctions were lifted. In 1996, the Truth and Reconciliation Commission with Archbishop Desmond Tutu as its head began hearings on human rights violations committed by former government and liberation movements during the apartheid era. In 1998, the Truth and Reconciliation Commission released its report. It declared apartheid as a crime against humanity. The report also held the ANC accountable for human rights abuses. The ANC won the 1999 general elections. Nelson Mandela stepped down from power and handed the presidency to his vice-president, Thabo Mbeki.

Geography

Location: Southern Africa, at the southern tip of the continent of Africa.

Area: 1,219,912 sq. km.

Terrain: Vast interior plateau rimmed by rugged hills and a narrow coastal plain.

Natural resources: Gold, chromium, antimony, coal, iron ore, manganese, nickel, phosphates, tin, uranium, gemstones, diamond, platinum, copper, vanadium, salt, natural gas.

Climate: Mostly semi-arid but subtropical along the east coast.

People

Population: 44,344,136 (July 2005 est.).

Population growth rate: –0.31% (2005 est.).

Sex ratio: 0.94 male(s)/female (2005 est.).

Religions: Christian 68% (includes most whites and coloureds, about 60% of blacks and about 40% of Indians), Muslim 2%, Hindu 1.5% (60% of Indians), indigenous beliefs and animist 28.5%.

Languages: 11 official languages, including Afrikaans, English, Ndebele, Pedi, Sotho, Swazi, Tsonga, Tswana, Venda, Xhosa, Zulu.

Literacy rate: Total 86.4%, Male 87%, Female 85.7% (2003 est.).

Infant mortality rate: 61.81 deaths/ 1,000 live births (2005 est.).

Life expectancy: Total 43.27 years, Male 43.47 years, Female 43.06 years (2005 est.).

Government

Capital: Pretoria (Cape Town is the legislative centre and Bloemfontein the judicial centre).

Government type: Republic.

Independence: 31 May 1910 (from UK).

Legal system: Based on Roman–Dutch law and English common law.

Executive branch:
Chief of state: President Thabo Mbeki (since 16 June 1999). The president is both the chief of state and head of government.

Economy

Currency: Rand.

Economy—overview:
South Africa is an emerging market that enjoys numerous benefits. These include plenty of natural resources, well-developed service sectors, one of the largest stock exchanges in the world and a modern infrastructure. Nevertheless, it has been difficult to sustain a rate of growth high enough to make substantial dents in the country's unemployment problem. Besides, the country still suffers from the economic problems that continue from the apartheid era such as poverty and lack of economic empowerment among the backward sections. The country also suffers from high HIV/AIDS infection rates and crime rates, two significant detractors to foreign investment.

GDP: Purchasing power parity—$491.4 billion (2004 est.).

GDP—real growth rate: 3.5% (2004 est.).

GDP—per capita: Purchasing power parity—$11,100 (2004 est.).

Inflation rate: 4.5% (2004 est.).

Population below poverty line: 50% (2000 est.).

Unemployment rate: 26.2% (includes workers not looking for employment any longer) (2004 est.).

Exports: $41.97 billion f.o.b. (2004 est.)—gold, diamond, platinum, other metals and minerals, machinery and equipment (1998 est.).

Imports: $39.42 billion f.o.b. (2004 est.)—machinery and equipment, chemicals, petroleum products, scientific instruments, foodstuff (2000 est.).

External debt: $27.01 billion (2004 est.).

Transport and Communications

Railways: 22,298 km (includes a 2,228 km commuter rail system).

Roads: 275,971 km.

Telephones: 4,844,000 (2002).

Mobile cellular: 16,860,000 (2003).

Internet users: 3,100,000 (2002).

Internet country code: .za

South Korea

History

It is believed that the ancient kingdom of Choson was founded in the third millennium BC. In 108 BC, China annexed the region. The Yi Dynasty ruled it from 1392 to 1910. Japan conquered all of Korea in 1910. In 1945, Allied forces evicted the Japanese from Korea. The part of the Korean peninsula north of the 38th parallel was occupied by Soviet Union while USA occupied the region to the south of this line of latitude, present-day South Korea.

The Republic of Korea was proclaimed in 1948. South Korea declared its independence in 1950, prompting North Korea to launch an invasion attempt that soon developed into the Korean War. It ended with the signing of armistice in 1953. The war is believed to have claimed 4,000,000 casualties, including civilians.

A military coup took place in 1961, following which General Park Chung-

hee took power. Martial law was imposed in 1972 and General Park increased his powers by changing the Constitution. In 1979 General Park was assassinated. General Chun Doo-hwan replaced him as the nation's leader. Martial law was declared again in 1980. In 1987, President Chun was removed from office by student unrest and mounting international pressure.

In 2000, a historic summit took place in the North Korean capital city, Pyongyang, between President Kim Dae-jung and the North Korean leader, Kim Jong-il. The summit resulted in North Korea stopping propaganda broadcasts against the South. It also saw the re-opening of border liaison offices at the heavily fortified borders of the two countries. The same year, Kim Dae-jung was awarded the Nobel Peace Prize.

Geography

Location: Eastern Asia, southern half of the Korean Peninsula bordering the

Sea of Japan and the Yellow Sea.

Area: 98,480 sq. km.

Terrain: Mostly hills and mountains. There are wide coastal plains in the west and south.

Natural resources: Coal, tungsten, graphite, molybdenum, lead, hydropower potential.

Climate: Temperate climate.

People

Population: 48,422,644 (July 2005 est.).

Population growth rate: 0.38% (2005 est.).

Sex ratio: 1.01 male(s)/female (2005 est.).

Religions: Christian 49%, Buddhist 47%, Confucianist 3%, others 1%.

Languages: Korean, English.

Literacy rate: Total 98.1%, Male 99.3%, Female 97% (2003 est.).

Infant mortality rate: 7.05 deaths/ 1,000 live births (2005 est.).

Life expectancy: Total 75.82 years, Male 72.19 years, Female 79.76 years (2005 est.).

Government

Capital: Seoul.

Government type: Republic.

Independence: 15 August 1945 (from Japan).

Legal system: Combination of the elements of continental European civil law systems, Anglo-American law, and Chinese classical thought.

Executive branch:
Chief of state: President No Mu-hyun (Roh Moo-hyun) (since 25 February 2003). In March 2004, President Roh Moo-hyun was suspended after the parliament voted to impeach him over breach of election rules and for incom-

petence. However, in May 2004, a constitutional court overturned this parliamentary vote to impeach President Roh Moo-hyun. He was immediately reinstated.

Head of government: Prime Minister Lee Hae-chan (since 25 May 2004).

Economy

Currency: Won.

Economy—overview:
South Korea is one of the Four Tigers of East Asia that has achieved a high growth and has successfully emerged as a high-tech modern world economy. Thirty years ago, South Korea's GDP per capita was similar to those in the poorer African and Asian countries. The country achieved this success through the 1980s by means of close ties between government and the business enterprises and focused policy implementation. However, the Asian financial crisis of 1997–9 revealed the weaknesses in South Korea's economy such as its massive foreign borrowing and its flawed financial sector. In 2003 the six-day working week was shortened to five days.

GDP: Purchasing power parity—$925.1 billion (2004 est.).

GDP—real growth rate: 4.6% (2004 est.).

GDP—per capita: Purchasing power parity—$19,200 (2004 est.).

Inflation rate: 3.6% (2004 est.).

Population below poverty line: 4% (2001 est.).

Unemployment rate: 3.6% (2004 est.).

Exports: $250.6 billion f.o.b. (2004 est.)—electronic products, machinery and equipment, motor vehicles, steel, ships, textiles, clothing, footwear, fish.

Imports: $214.2 billion f.o.b. (2004 est.)—machinery, electronics and electronic equipment, oil, steel, transport equipment, textiles, organic chemicals, grains.

External debt: $160 billion (2004 est.).

Transport and Communications

Railways: 3,125 km.

Roads: 86,990 km.

Telephones: 22,877,000 (2003).

Mobile callular: 33,591,800 (2003).

Internet users: 29,220,000 (2003).

Internet country code: .kr

Spain

History

Celts, Basques and Iberians were the original inhabitants of Spain. In 711, the Muslims under Tariq ibn Ziyad arrived from Africa and in a few years time, gained control of most of the Iberian Peninsula. However, the reign of the Almohads saw the Christians regaining control of the Iberian Peninsula.

The accession of Ferdinand II to the throne of Aragon in 1479 resulted in the union of Aragon (eastern Spain) and Castile (western Spain). Consequently, Spain emerged as one of the most powerful monarchies in Europe. The completion of the Reconquest was followed by the establishment of Roman Catholicism as the state religion and the expulsion of Jews and Muslims, as a result of the Spanish Inquisition.

The 16th century was a period of Spanish exploration, conquest and colonization all over the world. In South America, the conquistadors wiped out the local Aztec, Inca and Mayan civilizations. Hernan Cortes led an expedition against Aztec Mexico and conquered the Aztec capital, Tenochtitlan, in 1521. The Pacific coastal regions were conquered between 1522 and 1524. In 1535, Spain established the viceroyalty of New Spain. It was charged with the governance of Spain's newly acquired territories in the New World.

In 1588, King Philip II of Spain sent a huge fleet of about 130 ships, around 8,000 sailors and an estimated 19,000 soldiers to invade England. This fleet is now referred to as the Spanish Armada. He planned to send in the Spanish army from present-day Belgium to coincide with the Armada's arrival on English shores. The consequent English defeat of the Armada not only saved England from Spanish invasion but also marked the simultaneous ascent of England and the decline of Spain as maritime powers.

On 1 October 1936, the Nationalist leader, General Franco, was named head of state and he set up a government in Burgos. Soon, foreign powers got embroiled in the Republican–Nationalist conflict. The Soviets directed Spanish communists to support the Republicans. The Mexican government also contributed to the Republican cause. Germany and Italy sent troops and vehicles to help the Nationalists. In August 1936, France, UK, the Soviet Union, Germany, and Italy signed a non-intervention agreement. General Francisco Franco served as the head of the government of Spain until 1973 and head of state until his death in 1975.

In 1959, an organization named Euzkadi Ta Askatasuna, meaning Basque Fatherland and Freedom, commonly referred to by its abbreviated form, ETA, was founded. The creation of an independent homeland in Spain's Basque region was declared to be its goal. In December 1973, Basque nationalists assassinated Prime Minister Admiral Luis Carrero Blanco in Madrid. Spain made the switch from dictatorship to monarchy in 1975 after General Franco passed away on 20 November. King Juan Carlos succeeded him as the head of state.

Geography

Location: South-western Europe, bordering the Bay of Biscay, Mediterranean Sea, North Atlantic Ocean, and Pyrenees Mountains, south-west of France.

Area: 504,782 sq. km.

Terrain: Large, flat to dissected plateau surrounded by rugged hills. The Pyrenees Mountains lie in the north of the country.

Natural resources: Coal, lignite, iron ore, copper, lead, zinc, uranium, tungsten, mercury, pyrite, magnesite, fluorspar, gypsum, sepiolite, kaolin, potash, hydropower, arable land.

Climate: Temperate climate with clear, hot summers in the interiors but more moderate and cloudy in the coastal parts.

People

Population: 40,341,462 (July 2005 est.).

Population growth rate: 0.15% (2005 est.).

Sex ratio: 0.96 male(s)/female (2005 est.).

Religions: Roman Catholic 94%, others 6%.

Languages: Castilian Spanish 74%, Catalan 17%, Galician 7%, Basque 2%.

Literacy rate: Total 97.9%, Male 98.7%, Female 97.2% (2003 est.).

Infant mortality rate: 4.42 deaths/1,000 live births (2005 est.).

Life expectancy: Total 79.52 years, Male 76.18 years, Female 83.08 years (2005 est.).

Government

Capital: Madrid.

Government type: Parliamentary monarchy.

Independence: 1492 (Date of seizure of Granada leading to the unification of several kingdoms. This is traditionally considered to be the creation of present-day Spain).

Legal system: Civil law system, with regional applications.

Executive branch:
Chief of state: King Juan Carlos I (since 22 November 1975). Heir Apparent Prince Felipe, son of the monarch, born 30 January 1968.

Head of government: President Jose Luis Rodriguez Zapatero (since 17 April 2004).

Economy

Currency: Euro.

Economy—overview:
Spain has a mixed capitalist economy. Spain was one of the countries that launched the European single currency (the euro) on 1 January 1999. The previous administration led by Jose Maria Aznar promoted a policy of economic deregulation, liberalization, and privatization, besides introducing tax reforms. One of the major problems facing the country is unemployment. Although unemployment levels fell steadily under the Aznar administration, it still remained high. The Spanish economy will also face challenges posed by its necessary adjustments required for integration to the monetary and economic policies of a united Europe.

GDP: Purchasing power parity—$937.6 billion (2004 est.).

GDP—real growth rate: 2.6% (2004 est.).

GDP—per capita: Purchasing power parity—$23,300 (2004 est.).

Inflation rate: 3.2% (2004 est.).

Unemployment rate: 10.4% (2004 est.).

Exports: $172.5 billion f.o.b. (2004 est.) —machinery, motor vehicles, foodstuffs.

Imports: $222 billion f.o.b. (2004 est.)—machinery and equipment, fuels, chemicals, semi-finished goods; foodstuff, consumer goods.

External debt: $771.1 billion (2004 est.).

Transport and Communications

Railways: 14,268 km.

Roads: 664,852 km.

Telephones: 17,567,500 (2003).

Mobile cellular: 37,506,700 (2003).

Internet users: 9,789,000 (2003).

Internet country code: .es

Sri Lanka

History

The first human settlers of Sri Lanka are thought to be tribes of the proto-Australoid ethnic group similar to the pre-Dravidian hill tribes of southern India. The Indo-Aryans immigrated from India in about the fifth century BC and combined with the early settlers to develop into the Sinhalese. The Tamils are believed to be later immigrants from Dravidian India. The time period of their movement into Sri Lanka is believed to have spread out from the third century BC to about AD 1200. The Tamil component of the island's population increased when south Indians were brought to work in the plantations in the 19th century.

The period between the 13th and 15th centuries saw foreign invasions from India, Malaya and China. The country was then called Ceylon. The Portuguese arrived in 1505 and by 1619, they controlled most of the island. The Sinhalese acquired the help of the Dutch to help throw out the Portuguese from the island. In 1796, the Dutch East India Company handed over power to the British. In 1808, Ceylon became a Crown Colony.

In 1948, Ceylon became an independent country. It changed its name to Sri Lanka in 1972.

Geography

Location: Southern Asia, island in the Indian Ocean, south of India.

Area: 65,610 sq. km.

Terrain: Flat to rolling plains .with mountains in the south-central interior region.

Natural resources: Limestone, graphite, mineral sands, gems, phosphates, clay, hydropower.

Climate: Tropical monsoon climate.

People

Population: 20,064,776 (July 2005 est.).

Population growth rate: 0.79% (2005 est.).

Sex ratio: 0.96 male(s)/female (2005 est.).

Religions: Buddhist 70%, Hindu 15%, Christian 8%, Muslim 7% (1999).

Languages: Sinhala (official and national language) 74%, Tamil (national language) 18%, others 8%.

Literacy rate: Total 92.3%, Male 94.8%, Female 90% (2003 est.).

Infant mortality rate: 14.35 deaths/ 1,000 live births (2005 est.).

Life expectancy: Total 73.17 years, Male 70.06 years, Female 75.86 years (2005 est.).

Government

Capital: Colombo. Sri Jayewardenepura Kotte is the legislative capital.

Government type: Republic.

Independence: 4 February 1948 (from UK).

Legal system: A mixture of English common law, Roman–Dutch, Muslim, Sinhalese and customary law.

Executive branch:
Chief of state: President Chandrika Bandaranaike Kumaratunga (since 12 November 1994). Mahinda Rajapakse (since April 2004) is the prime minister. The president is considered both the chief of state and head of government.

Election and election results: The president is elected by popular vote for a six-year term. The last elections were held on 21 December 1999 and the next elections are scheduled for December 2005. Chandrika Bandaranaike Kumaratunga was re-elected president.

Legislative branch:
Sri Lanka has a unicameral parliament of 225 seats and its members are elected by popular vote on the basis of a modified proportional representation system to serve six-year terms.

Election and election results:
The last election were held on 2 April 2004 and the next are due in 2010.

Economy

Currency: Sri Lankan rupee.

Economy—overview:
In 1977, Colombo gave up its import substitution trade policy for market-oriented policies and export-oriented trade. The key sectors now are food processing, textiles and apparel, food and beverages, telecommunications, and insurance and banking. GDP grew at an average annual rate of 5.5% in the early 1990s but a drought and a worsening security situation caused growth to slump to 3.8% in 1996. In the period 1997–2000, the economy rejuvenated with an average growth of 5.3%. In 2001, however, the first contraction in the country's history took place (–1.4%), due to a myriad of problems like the global slowdown, power shortages and budgetary problems. The prolonged civil conflict that has plagued the country for many years was also a contributory reason. In 2002, however, growth rebounded to 3.2%.

GDP: Purchasing power parity— $80.58 billion (2004 est.).

GDP—real growth rate: 5.2% (2004 est.).

GDP—per capita: Purchasing power parity—$41,000 (2005 est.).

Inflation rate: 5.8% (2004 est.).

Population below poverty line: 22% (1997 est.).

Unemployment rate: 7.8% (2004 est.).

Exports: $5.306 billion f.o.b. (2004 est.)—textiles and apparel, tea, diamond, coconut products, petroleum products.

Imports: $7.265 billion f.o.b. (2004 est.)—textiles, mineral products, petroleum, foodstuff, machinery and equipment.

External debt: $10.85 billion (2004 est.).

Transport and Communications

Railways: 1,449 km.

Roads: 11,650 km.

Telephones: 881,400 (2002).

Mobile cellular: 931,600 (2002).

Internet users: 200,000 (2002).

Internet country code: .lk

Sudan

History

An Egyptian and Nubian civilization named Kush grew up and flourished in the region till AD 350. The arrival of Arabs and their subsequent domination over the region resulted in a conversion to Islam. Between 1898 and 1955, the country was called Anglo-Egyptian Sudan. In 1953, UK and Egypt granted self-governance and in 1956, Sudan became independent. A succession of short-lived regimes ruled Sudan ever since it gained independence.

Geography

Location: Northern Africa, bordering the Red Sea, between Egypt and Eritrea.

Area: 2,505,810 sq. km.

Terrain: Generally flat, featureless plain; mountains in the far south, north-east and west; a desert dominates the south.

Natural resources: Petroleum, iron ore, copper, chromium ore, zinc, tungsten, mica, silver, gold, hydropower.

Climate: Tropical in the south, arid desert in the north.

People

Population: 40,187,486 (July 2005 est.).

Population growth rate: 2.6% (2005 est.).

Sex ratio: 1.02 male(s)/female (2005 est.).

Religions: Sunni Muslim 70% (in the north), indigenous beliefs 25%, Christian 5% (mostly in the south and in Khartoum).

Languages: Arabic (official), Nubian, Ta Bedawie, diverse dialects of Nilotic, Nilo-Hamitic, Sudanic languages, English.

Literacy rate: Total 61.1%, Male 71.8%, Female 50.5% (2003 est.).

Infant mortality rate: 62.5 deaths/ 1,000 live births (2005 est.).

Life expectancy: Total 58.54 years, Male 57.33 years, Female 59.8 years (2005 est.).

Government

Capital: Khartoum.

Government type: Authoritarian regime. An alliance of the military and the National Congress Party (NCP) runs the government.

Independence: 1 January 1956 (from Egypt and UK).

Legal system: Based on English common law and Islamic law.

Executive branch:
Chief of state: President Lt Gen. Umar Hassan Ahmad al-Bashir (since 16 October 1993). The President is both the chief of state and head of government. Gen. al-Bashir assumed supreme executive power in 1989. He subsequently retained power through many transitional governments in the early and mid-1990s. He was popularly elected for the first time in March 1996.

Economy

Currency: Sudanese dinar.

GDP: Purchasing power parity—$76.19 billion (2004 est.).

GDP—real growth rate: 6.4% (2004 est.).

GDP—per capita: Purchasing power parity—$1,900 (2004 est.).

Inflation rate: 9% (2004 est.).

Unemployment rate: 18.7% (2002 est.)

Exports: $3.395 billion f.o.b. (2004 est.)—oil and petroleum products; cotton, sesame, livestock, groundnuts, gum arabic, sugar.

Imports: $3.496 billion f.o.b. (2004 est.)—foodstuff, manufactured goods, refinery and transport equipment, medicines and chemicals, textiles, wheat.

External debt: $21 billion (2004 est.).

Transport and Communications

Railways: 5,978 km.

Roads: 11,900 km.

Telephones: 900,000 (2003).

Mobile cellular: 650,000 (2003).

Internet users: 300,000 (2003).

Internet country code: .sd

Suriname

History

A group of British planters set up the first permanent settlement of Europeans in Suriname in 1651. A Dutch fleet seized Suriname in 1667. The Netherlands held Suriname till its independence in 1975.

Geography

Location: Northern South America, bordering the North Atlantic Ocean, between French Guiana and Guyana.

Area: 163,270 sq. km.

Terrain: Mostly rolling hills; narrow coastal plain with swamps.

Natural resources: Timber, hydropower, fish, kaolin, shrimp, bauxite, gold, and small amounts of nickel, copper, platinum, iron ore.

Climate: Tropical climate.

People

Population: 438,144 (July 2005 est.).

Population growth rate: 0.25% (2005 est.).

Sex ratio: 1.04 male(s)/female (2005 est.).

Religions: Hindu 27.4%, Muslim 19.6%, Roman Catholic 22.8%, Protestant 25.2% (predominantly Moravian), indigenous beliefs 5%.

Languages: Dutch, English.

Literacy rate: Total 93%, Male 95%, Female 91% (1995 est.).

Infant mortality rate: 23.57 deaths/1,000 live births (2005 est.).

Life expectancy: Total 68.96 years, Male 66.75 years, Female 71.27 year (2005 est.).

Government

Capital: Paramaribo.

Government type: Constitutional democracy.

Independence: 25 November 1975 (from the Netherlands).

Legal system: Based on Dutch legal system incorporating French penal theory.

Executive branch:
Chief of state: President Runaldo Ronald Venetiaan (since 12 August 2000); Vice-President Jules Rattankoemar

Ajodhia (since 12 August 2000). The president is both the chief of state and head of government.

Economy

Currency: Surinamese guilder.

GDP: Purchasing power parity—$1.885 billion (2004 est.).

GDP—real growth rate: 4.2% (2004 est.).

GDP—per capita: Purchasing power parity—$4,300 (2004 est.).

Inflation rate: 23% (2003 est.).

Population below poverty line: 70% (2002 est.).

Unemployment rate: 17% (2000).

Exports: $495 million f.o.b. (2002)—alumina, crude oil, lumber, shrimp and fish, rice, banana.

Imports: $604 million f.o.b. (2002)—capital equipment, petroleum, foodstuff, cotton, consumer goods.

External debt: $321 million (2002 est.).

Transport and Communications

Railways: 166 km (single-track).

Roads: 4,492 km.

Telephones: 79,800 (2003).

Mobile cellular: 168,100 (2003).

Internet users: 20,000 (2002).

Internet country code: .sr

Swaziland

History

In the 18th century, a number of Bantu clans broke away from a bigger group in modern-day Mozambique and settled in the area that is today Swaziland. Prevailing tensions with the Zulu led their King Mswazi to appeal to the British for help in the 1840s. In 1881, the governments of UK and Transvaal assured the Swazi state of their independence. Between 1894 and 1899, Swaziland was a South African protectorate. In 1902, the control of the state was transferred to UK. Swaziland gained independence in 1968.

Geography

Location: Southern Africa, between Mozambique and South Africa.

Area: 17,363 sq. km.

Terrain: Mostly mountains and hills, with some moderately sloping plains.

Natural resources: Asbestos, coal, clay, cassiterite, hydropower, forests, small gold and diamond deposits, quarry stone, and talc.

Climate: Tropical.

People

Population: 1,173,900 (July 2005 est.).

Population growth rate: 0.25% (2005 est.).

Sex ratio: 1 male(s)/female (2005 est.).

Religions: Zionist (a combination of Christianity and indigenous ancestral worship) 40%, Roman Catholic 20%, Muslim 10%.

Languages: English (official, government business conducted in English), Siswati (official).

Literacy rate: Total 81.6%, Male 82.6%, Female 80.8% (2003 est.).

Infant mortality rate: 69.27 deaths/1,000 live births (2005 est.).

Life expectancy: Total 35.65 years, Male 37.18 years, Female 34.07 years (2005 est.).

Government

Capital: Mbabane; Lobamba is the royal and legislative capital.

Government type: Monarchy.

Independence: 6 September 1968 (from UK).

Legal system: Based on South African Roman–Dutch law in statutory courts and Swazi traditional law and custom in traditional courts.

Executive branch:
Chief of state: King Mswati III (since 25 April 1986).

Head of government: Prime Minister Absolom Themba Dlamini (since 14 November 2003).

Economy

Currency: Lilangeni.

GDP: Purchasing power parity—$6.018 billion (2004 est.).

GDP—real growth rate: 2.5% (2004 est.).

GDP—per capita: Purchasing power parity—$5,100 (2004 est.).

Inflation rate: 5.4% (2004 est.).

Population below poverty line: 40% (1995).

Unemployment rate: 34% (2000 est.).

Exports: $900.1 million f.o.b. (2004 est.)—soft drink concentrates, sugar, wood pulp, cotton yarn, refrigerators, citrus and canned fruit.

Imports: $1.14 billion f.o.b. (2004 est.)—motor vehicles, machinery, transport equipment, foodstuff, petroleum products, chemicals.

External debt: $320 million (2002 est.).

Transport and Communications

Railways: 301 km.

Roads: 3,247 km.

Telephones: 46,200 (2003).

Mobile cellular: 88,000 (2003).

Internet users: 27,000 (2003).

Internet country code: .sz

Sweden

History

The Kalmar Union of 1397 united Sweden with Norway and Denmark, with Denmark as the dominant state. However, this union failed and led to bitter conflict between the Swedes and the Danes. In 1520, the Danish king Christian II conquered Sweden and subsequently ordered the mass execution of Swedish nobles. This massacre is referred to as the Stockholm Bloodbath.

In June 1523 Gustav Vasa was elected king. Under his leadership, Sweden broke away from Danish domination. Sweden played a key role in the Thirty Years War (1618–48) and the 1648 Treaty of Westphalia gave Sweden substantial territories.

Geography

Location: Northern Europe, bordering the Baltic Sea, Gulf of Bothnia, Kattegat, and Skagerrak, between Finland and Norway.

Area: 449,964 sq. km.

Terrain: Mostly flat or in the form of gently rolling lowlands. There are mountains in the western part of the country.

Natural resources: Iron ore, copper, lead, zinc, gold, silver, tungsten, uranium, arsenic, feldspar, timber, hydropower.

Climate: Temperate in the south and subarctic in the north.

People

Population: 9,001,774 (July 2005 est.).

Population growth rate: 0.17% (2005 est.).

Sex ratio: 0.98 male(s)/female (2005 est.).

Religions: Lutheran 87%, Roman Catholic, Orthodox, Baptist, Muslim, Jewish, Buddhist.

Languages: Swedish, Sami, Finnish.

Literacy rate: 99% (1979 est.).

Infant mortality rate: 2.77 deaths/1,000 live births (2005 est.).

Life expectancy: Total 80.4 years, Male 78.19 years, Female 82.74 years (2005 est.).

Government

Capital: Stockholm.

Government type: Constitutional monarchy.

Independence: 6 June 1523 (date on which Gustav Vasa was elected king).

Legal system: Civil law system influenced by customary law.

Executive branch:

Chief of state: King Carl XVI Gustaf (since 19 September 1973); Heir Apparent Princess Victoria Ingrid Alice Desiree, daughter of the monarch (born 14 July 1977).

Head of government: Prime Minister Goran Persson (since 21 March 1996).

Economy

Currency: Swedish krona.

Economy—overview:
The Swedish economy is a combination of high-tech capitalism and an extensive welfare system that has led to a high standard of living. Sweden enjoys very good infrastructure, a skilled labour force, resources like hydropower, iron ore and timber. However, the Swedish economy is heavily reliant on foreign trade. On 14 September 2003, Swedish voters voted against an entry into the euro system.

GDP: Purchasing power parity—$255.4 billion (2004 est.).

GDP—real growth rate: 3.6% (2004 est.).

GDP—per capita: Purchasing power parity—$28,400 (2004 est.).

Inflation rate: 0.7% (2004 est.).

Unemployment rate: 5.6% (2004 est.).

Exports: $12.17 billion f.o.b. (2004 est.)—machinery, motor vehicles, paper products, pulp and wood, iron and steel products, chemicals.

Imports: $97.97 billion f.o.b. (2004 est.)—machinery, petroleum and petroleum products, chemicals, motor vehicles, iron and steel; foodstuff, clothing.

External debt: $66.5 billion (1994).

Transport and Communications

Railways: 11,481 km.

Roads: 212,402 km.

Telephones: 6,579,200 (2002).

Mobile cellular: 7,949,000 (2002).

Internet users: 5,125,000 (2002).

Internet country code: .se

Switzerland

History

Switzerland was known as Helvetia in ancient times. It later became a league of cantons in the Holy Roman Empire. The 1648 Treaty of Westphalia gave the country independence from the Holy Roman Empire. In 1798, French revolutionary troops occupied the country and proclaimed the Helvetic Republic. However, in 1803, Napoleon restored the old federal government. In the 19th century, the French-speaking and Italian-speaking citizens of Switzerland gained political equality.

In 1920, Switzerland joined the League of Nations and subsequently Geneva became the League's headquarters. Even today, the European headquarters of the United Nations are in Geneva. In both World Wars, Switzerland remained neutral.

Geography

Location: Central Europe, east of France, north of Italy.

Area: 41,290 sq. km.

Terrain: Mostly mountainous with the Alps in the south and the Jura in the north-west. There is a central plateau of rolling hills, plains, and large lakes.

Natural resources: Hydropower potential, timber, salt.

Climate: Temperate climate that varies with altitude.

People

Population: 7,489,370 (July 2005 est.).

Population growth rate: 0.49% (2005 est.).

Sex ratio: 0.97 male(s)/female (2005 est.).

Religions: Roman Catholic 46.1%, Protestant 40%, others 5%, none 8.9%.

Languages: German (official) 63.7%, French (official) 19.2%, Italian (official) 7.6%, Romansch (official) 0.6%, others 8.9%.

Literacy rate: 99% (1980 est.).

Infant mortality rate: 4.39 deaths/1,000 live births (2005 est.).

Life expectancy: Total 80.39 years, Male 77.58 years, Female 83.36 years (2005 est.).

Government

Capital: Berne.

Government type: Federal republic.

Independence: 1 August 1291 (Founding of the Swiss Confederation).

Legal system: Civil law system influenced by customary law.

Executive branch:
Chief of state: President Samuel Schmid (since 1 January 2005); Vice-President Moritz Leuenbuger (since 1 January 2005). The president is both the chief of state and head of government.

Economy

Currency: Swiss franc.

Economy—overview:
The Swiss economy is a prosperous and stable market economy. The characteristics of the economy are a highly skilled labour force, low unemployment and a high per capita GDP. Switzerland is the chosen destination for investors seeking a safe haven due to its secretive banking services.

GDP: Purchasing power parity—$251.9 billion (2004 est.).

GDP—real growth rate: −1.8% (2004 est.).

GDP—per capita: Purchasing power parity—$33,800 (2004 est.).

Inflation rate: 0.9% (2004 est.).

Exports: $130.7 billion f.o.b. (2004 est.)—machinery, chemicals, metals, watches, agricultural products.

Imports: $121.1 billion f.o.b. (2004 est.)—machinery, chemicals, vehicles, metals, agricultural products, textiles.

Transport and Communications

Railways: 4,511 km.

Roads: 71,011 km.

Telephones: 5,419,000 (2002).

Mobile cellular: 6,172,000 (2003).

Internet users: 2,556,000 (2002).

Internet country code: .ch

Syria

History

From the third century BC onwards, the area that is today Syria has been under control of the Sumerians, Assyrians, Babylonians, Egyptians, Hittites, Akkadians and Amorites. In the sixth century BC, it became a part of the Persian Achaemenian dynasty that in turn passed to Alexander the Great in 330 BC. It later formed parts of the Roman Empire, Byzantine Empire and the Ottoman Empire. UK invaded Syria during World War I and it became a French mandate after the War. Syria achieved independence in 1946. Between 1958 and 1961, it united with Egypt to form the United Arab Republic.

Geography

Location: Middle East, bordering the Mediterranean Sea, between Lebanon and Turkey.

Area: 185,180 sq. km (This includes 1,295 sq. km of Israeli-occupied territory).

Terrain: Primarily semi-arid and desert plateau; narrow coastal plain; mountains in the west.

Natural resources: Petroleum, phos-phates, chrome and manganese ores, asphalt, iron ore, rock salt, marble, gypsum, hydropower.

Climate: Mostly desert with hot, dry, sunny summers from June to August and mild, rainy winters from December to February along the coast.

People

Population: 18,448,752 (July 2005 est.) Besides this, about 40,000 people live in the Israeli-occupied Golan Heights, including above 20,000 Arab and above 20,000 Israeli letters.

Population growth rate: 2.34% (2005 est.).

Sex ratio: 1.05 male(s)/female (2005 est.).

Religions: Sunni Muslim 74%, Alawite, Druze, and other Muslim sects 16%, Christian (various sects) 10%, Jewish.

Languages: Arabic (official); Kurdish, Armenian, Aramaic, Circassian widely understood; French, English also understood.

Literacy rate: Total 76.9%, Male 89.7%, Female 64% (2003 est.).

Infant mortality rate: 29.53 deaths/ 1,000 live births (2005 est.).

Life expectancy: Total 70.03 years, Male 68.75 years, Female 71.38 years (2005 est.).

Government

Capital: Damascus.

Government type: Republic under military regime since March 1963.

Independence: 17 April 1946 (from League of Nations mandate under French administration).

Legal system: Based on Islamic law and civil law system; special religious courts.

Executive branch:
Chief of state: President Bashar al-Aasad (since 17 July 2000).

Head of government: Prime Minister Muhammad Naji al-Utri (since 10 September 2003).

Economy

Currency: Syrian pound.

Economy—overview:
Syria's slow economic growth rate, slower than its average annual population growth rate, has caused a persistent decline in its per capita GDP. External factors like the Israeli–Palestinian conflict, international war on terrorism, and the war between the US-led coalition and Iraq is likely to drive real annual GDP growth to healthier levels.

GDP: Purchasing power parity—$60.44 billion (2004 est.).

GDP—real growth rate: 2.3% (2004 est.).

GDP—per capita: Purchasing power parity—$3,400 (2004 est.).

Inflation rate: 2.1% (2004 est.).

Population below poverty line: 15%–25% (2002 est.).

Unemployment rate: 20% (2002 est.).

Exports: $6.086 billion f.o.b. (2004 est.)—crude oil , petroleum products, fruits and vegetables, cotton fibre, clothing, meat and live animals.

Imports: $5.042 billion f.o.b. (2004 est.)—machinery and transport equipment, food and livestock, metal and metal products, chemicals and chemical products.

External debt: $4 billion (2004 est.)—excchioes military dept and dobt to Russia.

Transport and Communications

Railways: 2,711 km.

Roads: 45,697 km.

Telephones: 2,099,300 (2002).

Mobile cellular: 400,000 (2002).

Internet users: 60,000 (2002).

Internet country code: .sy

Tajikistan

History

The Persians settled in the area in the sixth century BC. The region later formed parts of the empires of Persians and Alexander the Great. Uzbeks controlled the area in the 15th–19th centuries AD. The Russians annexed much of the region in the 1860s and in 1924 it became an autonomous republic administered by the Uzbek Republic. Tajikistan gained the status of a republic in 1929. In 1991, it gained independence after the disintegration of the Soviet Union.

Geography

Location: Central Asia, west of China.

Area: 143,100 sq. km.

Terrain: The Pamir and Alay Mountains dominate the landscape. The Western Fergana Valley lies to the north, while the Kofarnihon and Vakhsh Valleys feature in the south-west.

Natural resources: Hydropower, some petroleum, uranium, mercury, brown coal, lead, zinc, antimony, tungsten, silver, gold.

Climate: Mid-latitude continental with hot summers and mild winters; semi-arid to arctic in the Pamir Mountains.

People

Population: 7,163,506 (July 2005 est.).

Population growth rate: 2.15% (2005 est.).

Sex ratio: 0.99 male(s)/female (2005 est.).

Religions: Sunni Muslim 85%, Shi'a Muslim 5%.

Languages: Tajik (official), Russian widely used in government and business.

Literacy rate: 99.4% (2003 est.).

Infant mortality rate: 110.76 deaths/1,000 live births (2005 est.).

Life expectancy: Total 64.56 years, Male 61.39 years, Female 67.5 years (2005 est.).

Government

Capital: Dushanbe.

Government type: Republic.

Independence: 9 September 1991 (from Soviet Union).

Legal system: Based on civil law system. There is no judicial review of legislative acts.

Executive branch:
Chief of state: President Emomali Rahmonov (since 6 November 1994).

Head of government: Prime Minister Oqil Oqilov (since 20 January 1999).

Economy

Currency: Somoni.

Economy—overview:
As little as 8% to 10% of the land area is arable and cotton is the most important crop. There is a small amount of a variety of mineral resources in Tajikistan. These include silver, gold, uranium, and tungsten. Industrial activity is meagre. Tajikistan has the lowest per capita GDP among the 15 former Soviet republics. The civil war that raged in the country during 1992–7 caused further damage to the already weak infrastructure and caused industrial and agricultural production to plummet.

GDP: Purchasing power parity—$7.95 billion (2004 est.).

GDP—real growth rate: 10.5% (2004 est.).

GDP—per capita: Purchasing power parity—$1,100 (2004 est.).

Inflation rate: 8% (2004 est.).

Population below poverty line: 60% (2004 est.).

Unemployment rate: 40% (2002 est.).

Exports: $1.13 billion f.o.b. (2004 est.)—aluminum, electricity, cotton, fruits, vegetable oil, textiles.

Imports: $1.3 billion f.o.b. (2004 est.)—electricity, petroleum products, aluminum oxide, machinery and equipment, foodstuff.

External debt: $888 million (2004 est.).

Transport and Communications

Railways: 482 km.

Roads: 27,767 km (2000).

Telephones: 242,100 (2003).

Mobile cellular: 47,600 (2003).

Internet users: 4,100 (2003).

Internet country code: .tj

Tanzania

History

Portuguese explorers reached the coastal regions of Tanzania in 1500 and held some influence till the 17th century when the Sultan of Oman took over. In 1885, Tanganyika, along with what are today Rwanda and Burundi, was formed into the colony of German East Africa. After World War I, UK administered the territory, first under a League of Nations mandate and then as a UN trust territory.

In 1961, Tanganyika became independent with Julius Nyerere as prime minister. The following year, it became a republic. In 1964, the Afro-Shirazi Party ousted the Sultanate of Zanzibar in a left-wing revolution. Tanganyika and Zanzibar then merged together to form United Republic of Tanganyika and Zanzibar. In October 1964, it was renamed as United Republic of Tanzania.

Geography

Location: Eastern Africa, bordering the Indian Ocean, between Kenya and Mozambique.

Area: 945,087 sq. km. (This includes the islands of Mafia, Pemba, and Zanzibar.)

Terrain: Plains along the coast, a central plateau and highlands in the north and in the south.

Natural resources: Hydropower, tin, phosphates, iron ore, coal, diamond, gemstones, gold, natural gas, nickel.

Climate: Tropical climate along the coast and temperate climate in the highlands.

People

Population: 36,766,356 (July 2005 est.).

Population growth rate: 1.83% (2005 est.).

Sex ratio: 0.98 male(s)/female (2005 est.).

Religions: Mainland—Christian 30%, Muslim 35%, indigenous beliefs 35%. Zanzibar—99% Muslim.

Languages: Kiswahili or Swahili (official), Kiunguju (name for Swahili in Zanzibar), English, Arabic, many local languages.

Literacy rate: Total 78.2%, Male 85.9%, Female 70.7% (2003 est.).

Infant mortality rate: 98.54 deaths/1,000 live births (2005 est.).

Life expectancy: Total 45.24 years, Male 44.56 years, Female 45.94 years (2005 est.).

Government

Capital: Dar es Salaam; legislative offices have been transferred to Dodoma, the planned new national capital.

Government type: Republic.

Independence: 26 April 1964 (date on which Tanganyika united with Zanzibar to form the United Republic of Tanganyika and Zanzibar, renamed United Republic of Tanzania on 29 October 1964).

Legal system: Based on English common law.

Executive branch:

Chief of state: President Benjamin William Mkapa (since 23 November 1995). The president is both chief of state and head of government.

Economy

Currency: Tanzanian shilling.

GDP: Purchasing power parity—$23.71 billion (2004 est.).

GDP—real growth rate: 5.8% (2004 est.).

GDP—per capita: Purchasing power parity—$700 (2004 est.).

Inflation rate: 5.4% (2004 est.).

Population below poverty line: 36% (2002 est.).

Exports: $1.248 billion f.o.b. (2004 est.)—gold, coffee, cashew nuts, manufactures, cotton.

Imports: $1.972 billion f.o.b. (2004 est.)—consumer goods, machinery and transportation equipment, industrial raw materials, crude oil.

External debt: $7.321 billion (2004 est.).

Transport and Communications

Railways: 3,690 km.

Roads: 88,200 km

Ports and harbours: Bukoba, Dar es Salaam, Kigoma, Kilwa Masoko, Lindi, Mtwara, Mwanza, Pangani, Tanga, Wete, Zanzibar.

Airports: 123 (2003 est.).

Telephones: 149,100 (2003).

Mobile cellular: 891,200 (2003).

Internet users: 250,000 (2003).

Internet country code: .tz

Thailand

History

What is today Thailand was part of the Mon and Khmer kingdoms from the ninth century AD. Around the 10th century AD, Thai-speaking people migrated into the region from China. Later on, in the 13th century, two distinct kingdoms emerged in the region. The Sukhothai kingdom emerged around 1220 AD, while the Chiang Mai was founded in 1296. In 1350, the kingdom of Ayutthaya replaced the Sukhothai kingdom. In 1767, the Burmese destroyed the kingdom of Ayutthaya. In 1782, the Chakri dynasty came to power. The dynasty shifted the capital to Bangkok and expanded the kingdom into the Malay Peninsula and Laos and Cambodia. In 1856, the name Siam was adopted.

When Western powers extended their influence in the South-east Asian region in the 19th century, Siam was the only kingdom that avoided colonization. In 1932, the country became a constitutional monarchy subsequent to a military coup. In 1939, the present name of Thailand was adopted.

Geography

Location: South-eastern Asia, bordering the Andaman Sea and the Gulf of Thailand, south-east of Myanmar.

Area: 514,000 sq. km.

Terrain: The central area is a plain, the Khorat Plateau lies in the east and there are mountains in the other regions.

Natural resources: Tin, natural gas, tungsten, tantalum, timber, rubber, lead, fish, gypsum, lignite, fluorite, arable land.

Climate: Tropical climate. The rainy, warm, cloudy south-west monsoon season is from mid-May to September while the dry, cool north-east monsoon season is from November to mid-March.

People

Population: 65,444,371 (July 2005 est.).

Population growth rate: 0.87% (2005 est.).

Sex ratio: 0.98 male(s)/female (2005 est.).

Religions: Buddhist 95%, Muslim 3.8%, Christian 0.5%, Hindu 0.1%, others 0.6%.

Languages: Thai, English (secondary language of the elite), ethnic and regional dialects.

Literacy rate: Total 96%, Male 97.5%, Female 94.6% (2003 est.).

Infant mortality rate: 20.48 deaths/1,000 live births (2005 est.).

Life expectancy: Total 71.57 years, Male 69.39 years, Female 73.88 years (2005 est.).

Government

Capital: Bangkok.

Government type: Constitutional monarchy.

Independence: 1238 (traditional founding date).

Legal system: Based on civil law system, with influences of common law.

Executive branch:
Chief of state: King Bhumibol Adulyadej (since 9 June 1946).

Head of government: Prime Minister Thaksin Shinawatra (since 9 February 2001).

Economy

Currency: Baht.

Economy—overview:
Thailand has a free enterprise economy that is open to foreign investment. Between 1985 and 1995, Thailand enjoyed a very high growth rate averaging almost 9% annually. But this also increased speculative pressure on Thailand's currency, the baht. All this precipitated the 1997 crisis that revealed financial sector weaknesses and led the government to float the baht. Strong exports helped Thailand stage a recovery. The economy grew by 4.2% in 1999 and 4.4% in 2000 but growth slumped to 1.4% in 2001. GDP grew by 5.2% in 2002.

GDP: Purchasing power parity—$524.8 billion (2004 est.).

GDP—real growth rate: 6.1% (2004 est.).

GDP—per capita: Purchasing power parity—$8,100 (2004 est.).

Inflation rate: 2.8% (2004 est.).

Population below poverty line: 10% (2004 est.).

Unemployment rate: 1.5% (2004 est.).

Exports: $87.91 billion f.o.b. (2004 est.)—computers, seafood, clothing, transistors, rice (2000).

Imports: $80.84 billion f.o.b. (2004 est.)—fuels, capital goods, intermediate goods and raw materials, consumer goods.

External debt: $50.59 billion (2004 est.).

Transport and Communications

Railways: 4,071 km.

Roads: 57,403 km.

Telephones: 6,617,400 (2003).

Mobile cellular: 26,500,000 (2005).

Internet users: 6,971,500 (2003).

Internet country code: .th

Togo

History

In 1884, Germany set up the protectorate of Togoland. In 1914, British and French forces seized Togoland. In 1922, the League of Nations granted mandates to UK to administer the western part of Togoland and to France to rule the eastern part. In 1956, the British-held part of Togoland was included into Gold Coast that later became Ghana. In 1960, the French-administered part of Togoland became independent as Togo.

Geography

Location: Western Africa, bordering the Bight of Benin, between Benin and Ghana.

Area: 56,785 sq. km.

Terrain: Gently rolling savanna in the north, central hills, a southern plateau and a low coastal plain with extensive lagoons and marshes.

Natural resources: Phosphates, limestone, marble, arable land.

Climate: Tropical climate. Hot and humid in the south and semi-arid in the north.

People

Population: 5,681,519 (July 2005 est.).

Population growth rate: 2.17% (2005 est.).

Sex ratio: 0.97 male(s)/female (2004 est.).

Religions: Indigenous beliefs 51%, Christian 29%, Muslim 20%.

Languages: French (official and the language of commerce), Ewe and Mina (the two major African languages in the south), Kabye/Kabiye, Dagomba (the two major African languages in the north).

Literacy rate: Total 60.9%, Male 75.4%, Female 46.9% (2003 est.).

Infant mortality rate: 66.61 deaths/1,000 live births (2005 est.).

Life expectancy: Total 52.64 years, Male 50.64 years, Female 54.7 years (2005 est.).

Government

Capital: Lome.

Government type: Republic under transition to multiparty democratic rule.

Independence: 27 April 1960 (from French-administered UN trusteeship).

Legal system: French-based court system.

Executive branch:
Chief of state: President Faure Gnassingbe (since 6 Feburary 2005).

Head of government: Prime Minister Koffi Sama (since 29 June 2002).

Economy

Currency: Communaute Financiere Africaine franc.

GDP: Purchasing power parity—$8.684 billion (2004 est.).

GDP—real growth rate: 3% (2004 est.).

GDP—per capita: Purchasing power parity—$1,600 (2004 est.).

Inflation rate: 1% (2004 est.).

Population below poverty line: 32% (1989 est.).

Exports: $663.1 million f.o.b. (2004 est.)—re-exports, cotton, phosphates, coffee, cocoa.

Imports: $501.3 million f.o.b. (2003 est.)—machinery and equipment, foodstuff, petroleum products.

External debt: $1.4 billion (2000).

Transport and Communications

Railways: 568 km.

Roads: 7,520 km.

Telephones: 60,600 (2003).

Mobile cellular: 220,000 (2003).

Internet users: 210,000 (2003).

Internet country code: .tg

Tonga

History

Polynesians were the original settlers of Tonga. The Dutch arrived in 1616 while the British explorer James Cook came here in 1773 and 1777. Taufa'ahau Tupou founded the present ruling dynasty in 1831 and took the name George I. In 1900, his grandson George II signed a treaty of friendship with UK following which the kingdom became a British protectorate. In 1959, the treaty was revised but in 1970, Tonga became independent.

Geography

Location: Oceania, archipelago in the South Pacific Ocean.

Area: 748 sq. km.

Natural resources: Fish, fertile soil.

Climate: Tropical climate modified by trade winds.

People

Population: 112,422 (July 2005 est.).

Population growth rate: 1.9% (2005 est.).

Sex ratio: 0.99 male(s)/female (2005 est.).

Religions: Christian.

Languages: Tongan, English.

Literacy rate: Total 98.5%, Male 98.4%, Female 98.7% (1996 est.).

Infant mortality rate: 12.62 deaths/ 1,000 live births (2005 est.).

Life expectancy: Total 69.53 years, Male 67.05 years, Female 72.14 years (2005 est.).

Government

Capital: Nuku'alofa.

Government type: Hereditary constitutional monarchy.

Independence: 4 June 1970 (from UK protectorate).

Legal system: Based on English law.

Executive branch:
Chief of state: King Taufa'ahau Tupou IV (since 16 December 1965).

Head of government: Prime Minister Prince Lavaka ata Ulukalala (since February 2000) and Deputy Prime Minister Tevita Topou (since January 2001).

Economy

Currency: Pa'anga.

GDP: Purchasing power parity—$244 million (2004 est.).

GDP—real growth rate: 1.5% (2002 est.).

GDP—per capita: Purchasing power parity—$2,300 (2002 est.).

Inflation rate: 10.3% (2002 est.).

Unemployment rate: 13.3% (1996 est.).

Exports: $27 million f.o.b. (2002 est.)—squash, fish, vanilla beans, root crops.

Imports: $86 million f.o.b. (2002 est.)—foodstuff, machinery and transport equipment, fuels, chemicals.

External debt: $63.4 million (2001).

Transport and Communications

Railways: None.

Roads: 680 km.

Telephones: 11,200 (2002).

Mobile cellular: 9,000 (2004).

Internet users: 2,900 (2002).

Internet country code: .to

Trinidad and Tobago

History

When Christopher Columbus explored the two islands in 1498, Arawak Indians lived on Trinidad while Carib Indians lived on Tobago. The islands remained a Spanish possession till 1802 when they went into British possession. Thousands of indentured labourers were imported from India between 1845 and 1917. In 1889, the islands were united as one colony.

Limited self-government was granted in 1925. Between 1958 and 1962, the islands were a part of the West Indies Federation. In 1962, Trinidad and Tobago became independent. In 1976, the country became a republic.

Geography

Location: Caribbean islands between the Caribbean Sea and the North Atlantic Ocean, north-east of Venezuela.

Area: 5,128 sq. km.

Natural resources: Petroleum, natural gas, asphalt.

Climate: Tropical climate with a rainy season from June to December.

People

Population: 1,088,644 (July 2005 est.).

Population growth rate: −0.74% (2005 est.).

Sex ratio: 1.06 male(s)/female (2005 est.).

Religions: Roman Catholic 29.4%, Hindu 23.8%, Anglican 10.9%, Muslim 5.8%, Presbyterian 3.4%, others 26.7%.

Languages: English (official), Hindi, French, Spanish, Chinese.

Literacy rate: Total 98.6%, Male 99.1%, Female 98% (2003 est.).

Infant mortality rate: 24.31 deaths/ 1,000 live births (2005 est.).

Life expectancy: Total 68.91 years, Male 66.62 years, Female 71.3 years (2005 est.).

Government

Capital: Port-of-Spain.

Government type: Parliamentary democracy.

Independence: 31 August 1962 (from UK).

Legal system: Based on English common law.

Executive branch:
Chief of state: President George Maxwell Richards (since 17 March 2003).

Head of government: Prime Minister Patrick Manning (since 24 December 2001).

Economy

Currency: Trinidad and Tobago dollar.

GDP: Purchasing power parity—$11.48 billion (2004 est.).

GDP—real growth rate: 5.7% (2004 est.).

GDP—per capita: Purchasing power parity—$10,500 (2004 est.).

Inflation rate: 3.3% (2004 est.).

Population below poverty line: 21% (1992 est.).

Unemployment rate: 10.4% (2004 est.).

Exports: $6.671 billion f.o.b. (2004 est.)—petroleum and petroleum products, chemicals, steel products, fertilizer, sugar, cocoa, coffee, citrus, flowers.

Imports: $4.65 billion f.o.b. (2004 est.)—machinery, transportation equipment, manufactured goods, food, live animals.

External debt: $2.94 billion (2004 est.).

Transport and Communications

Railways: None.

Roads: 8,320 km.

Telephones: 325,100 (2002).

Mobile cellular: 361,900 (2002).

Internet users: 138,000 (2002).

Internet country code: .tt

Tunisia

History

In the 12th century BC, Phoenicians established settlements along the North African coast in the area that is today Tunisia. These included the city of Carthage, near present-day Tunis. However, the three Punic Wars between Carthage and Rome led to the destruction of Carthage. In the 1600s, Tunisia became a part of the Turkish Ottoman Empire. In 1881, French troops occupied the capital city, Tunis.

Thereafter, France took control of Tunisia's economic and foreign affairs. Tunisia formally became a French protectorate in 1883. In 1956, Tunisia became independent. In 1957, the monarchy was abolished and Tunisia became a republic.

Geography

Location: Northern Africa, bordering the Mediterranean Sea, between Algeria and Libya.

Area: 163,610 sq. km.

Terrain: Mountains in the north and a hot, dry central plain; the semi-arid region in the south merges into the Sahara.

Natural resources: Petroleum, phosphates, iron ore, lead, zinc, salt.

Climate: Temperate climate in the north and desert climate in the south.

People

Population: 10,074,951 (July 2005 est.).

Population growth rate: 1.99% (2005 est.).

Sex ratio: 1.02 male(s)/female (2005 est.).

Religions: Muslim 98%, Christian 1%, Jewish and others 1%.

Languages: Arabic (official and one of the languages of commerce), French (commerce).

Literacy rate: Total 74.2%, Male 84%, Female 64.4% (2003 est.).

Infant mortality rate: 24.77 deaths/1,000 live births (2005 est.).

Life expectancy: Total 74.89 years, Male 73.2 years, Female 76.71 years (2005 est.).

Government

Capital: Tunis.

Government type: Republic.

Independence: 20 March 1956 (from France).

Legal system: Based on French civil law system and Islamic law.

Executive branch:
Chief of state: President Zine El Abidine Ben Ali (since 7 November 1987).

Head of government: Prime Minister Mohamed Ghannouchi (since 17 November 1999).

Economy

Currency: Tunisian dinar.

GDP: Purchasing power parity—$70.88 billion (2004 est.).

GDP—real growth rate: 5.1% (2004 est.).

GDP—per capita: Purchasing power parity—$7,100 (2004 est.).

Inflation rate: 4.1% (2004 est.).

Population below poverty line: 7.6% (2001 est.).

Unemployment rate: 13.8% (2004 est.).

Exports: $9.926 billion f.o.b. (2004 est.)—textiles, mechanical goods, phosphates and chemicals, agricultural products, hydrocarbons.

Imports: $11.52 billion f.o.b. (2004 est.)—textiles, machinery and equipment, hydrocarbons, chemicals, food.

External debt: $14.71 billion (2004 est.).

Transport and Communications

Railways: 2,152 km.

Roads: 18,997 km.

Telephones: 1,163,800 (2003).

Mobile cellular: 1,899,900 (2003).

Internet users: 630,000 (2003 est.).

Internet country code: .tn

Turkey

History

In 1900 BC and thereafter, the Hittite Empire occupied the Asian part of the area that is today known as Turkey. In the sixth century BC, the Persian Empire annexed the area. The Roman Empire followed. Emperor Constantine declared Constantinople, now Istanbul, the capital of the Eastern Roman Empire. After the Romans came the Byzantine Empire, and in the 13th century AD came the Ottoman Empire. The Ottomans stamped their supremacy over the area for 600 years thereafter. At its height, the Ottoman Empire included large parts of south-eastern Europe, Syria, Israel, Iraq and most of the Arabian Peninsula in Asia and Egypt and North Africa till Algeria in the west. The Empire came to an end in 1922, succeeded by the Turkish Republic and a host of smaller states in south-eastern Europe and the Middle East.

The revolt of the Young Turks took place in 1909. Following this, the Sultan allowed for a Constitution and a liberal government. Furthermore, the country lost territory in the aftermath of World War I, consequent to its alliance with Germany.

The Republic of Turkey was declared in 1923 under the leadership of Kemal Ataturk and in 1924 the caliphate was abolished.

Geography

Location: Turkey straddles south-eastern Europe and south-western Asia. The portion of Turkey that lies west of the Bosporus is geographically a part of Europe. The country borders the Black Sea between Bulgaria and Georgia and the Aegean Sea and the Mediterranean Sea, between Greece and Syria.

Area: 780,580 sq. km.

Terrain: Turkey has a high central plateau (Anatolia), a narrow coastal plain and a number of mountain ranges.

Natural resources: Antimony, copper, borate, coal, chromium, mercury, sulphur, iron ore, arable land, hydropower.

Climate: Temperate climate with hot, dry summers and mild, wet winters.

People

Population: 69,660,559 (July 2005 est.).

Population growth rate: 1.09% (2005 est.).

Sex ratio: 1.02 male(s)/female (2005 est.).

Religions: Muslim 99.8% (mostly Sunni), other 0.2% (mostly Christians and Jews).

Languages: Turkish (official), Kurdish, Arabic, Armenian, Greek.

Literacy rate: Total 86.5%, Male 94.3%, Female 78.7% (2003 est.).

Infant mortality rate: 41.04 deaths/1,000 live births (2005 est.).

Life expectancy: Total 72.36 years, Male 69.94 years, Female 74.91 years (2005 est.).

Government

Capital: Ankara.

Government type: Republican parliamentary democracy.

Independence: 29 October 1923 (successor state to the Ottoman Empire).

Legal system: Derived from various European continental legal systems.

Executive branch:
Chief of state: President Ahmet Necdet Sezer (since 16 May 2000).

Head of government: Prime Minister Recep Tayyip Erdogan (14 March 2003).

Economy

Currency: Turkish lira.

Economy—overview:
Turkey's economy is a combination of modern industry and commerce and a traditional agriculture sector. While the country has a dynamic private sector, the state continues to play a major role in industry, transport, banking and communication. The dominated by the private sector textiles and clothing industry is not only the country's largest industry but also the single largest source of exports. Lately, the Turkish economy has suffered erratic growth and imbalances. Turkey has recorded real GNP growth in excess of 6% in many years but this has been offset by sharp declines in output in 1994, 1999 and 2001. The public sector fiscal deficit has consistently exceeded 10% of GDP, thanks to interest payments. This has exceeded 50% of central government spending. In 2003, the country recorded an inflation rate of 26%, a low figure in recent times. The bleak scenario because of these factors means that foreign investment the country has been low. In 2000–1, the Turkish economy faced a crisis created by a growing trade deficit and weak-nesses in the banking sector. This led to the floating of the lira, worsening recession.

GDP: Purchasing power parity—$508.7 billion (2004 est.).

GDP—real growth rate: 8.2% (2004 est.).

GDP—per capita: Purchasing power parity—$7,400 (2004 est.).

Inflation rate: 9.3% (2004 est.).

Unemployment rate: 9.3% (2004 est.).

Exports: $69.46 billion f.o.b. (2004 est.)—finished textiles, foodstuff, textiles, metal manufactures, transport equipment.

Imports: $94.5 billion c.i.f. (2004 est.).

External debt: $16.9 billion (2004 est.).

Transport and Communications

Railways: 8,671 km.

Roads: 354,421 km.

Telephones: 18,916,700 (2003).

Mobile cellular: 27,887,500 (2003).

Internet users: 5.5 million (2003).

Internet country code: .tr

Turkmenistan

History

The area that is today Turkmenistan was a part of the Parthian empire between the mid-third century BC and fourth century AD. Turkmens are believed to have arrived in the region in the 11th century. The Russian advance into Turkmenistan came in the 1860s and the 1870s. Turkmenistan was later carved out of Turkistan Autonomous Soviet Socialist Republic. In 1925, it became an independent Soviet Socialist Republic. In 1991, Turkmenistan proclaimed its independence from the Union of Soviet Socialist Republic (USSR).

Geography

Location: Central Asia, bordering

the Caspian Sea, between Iran and Kazakhstan.

Area: 488,100 sq. km.

Terrain: Largely flat, partly rolling, sandy desert with dunes that rise to form mountains in the south. There are low mountains along the border with Iran. The Caspian Sea lies to the west.

Natural resources: Petroleum, natural gas, coal, sulphur, salt.

Climate: Subtropical desert.

People

Population: 4,952,081 (July 2005 est.).

Population growth rate: 1.81% (2005 est.).

Sex ratio: 0.98 male(s)/female (2005 est.).

Ethnic groups: Turkmen 77%, Uzbek 9.2%, Russian 6.7%, Kazakh 2%, others 5.1%.

Religions: Muslim 89%, Eastern Orthodox 9%, unknown 2%.

Languages: Turkmen 72%, Russian 12%, Uzbek 9%, others 7%.

Literacy rate: Total 98%, Male 99%, Female 97% (1989 est.).

Infant mortality rate: 73.08 deaths/1,000 live births (2005 est.).

Life expectancy: Total 61.39 years, Male 58.02 years, Female 64.93 years (2005 est.).

Government

Capital: Ashgabat.

Government type: Republic.

Independence: 27 October 1991 (from the Soviet Union).

Legal system: Based on civil law system.

Executive branch:
Chief of state: President and Chairman of the Cabinet of Ministers Saparmurat Niyazov (since 27 October 1990). The president is both the chief of state and head of government.

Economy

Currency: Turkmen manat.

Economy—overview:
Turkmenistan's economic statistics are veiled in much secrecy and subject to error margins. Turkmenistan is mostly a desert. The country also has large gas and oil resources. Intensive agriculture is carried out in irrigated oases. Cotton occupies almost half of its irrigated land. Payment obligations arising out of short-term debts and distribution constraints faced by its petroleum and natural gas resources hurt the Turkmen economy. Nevertheless, there was a sizable rise in exports in 2003 along with an increase in GDP. This was mainly due to a smart recovery staged by the agriculture sector, industrial growth and rising international prices for petroleum and natural gas.

GDP: Purchasing power parity—$27.6 billion (2004 est.).

GDP—real growth rate: 7.5% (2004 est.).

GDP—per capita: Purchasing power parity—$5,700 (2004 est.).

Inflation rate: 9% (2005 est.).

Unemployment rate: 60% (2004 est.).

Population below poverty line: 58% (2003 est.).

Exports: $4 billion f.o.b. (2004 est.)—gas, oil, cotton fibre, textiles.

Imports: $2.85 billion f.o.b. (2004 est.)—machinery and equipment, foodstuff.

External debt: $2.4 billion to $5 billion (2001 est.).

Transport and Communications

Railways: 2,440 km.

Roads: 24,000 km.

Telephones: 374,000 (2002).

Mobile cellular: 52,000 (2004).

Internet users: 8,000 (2002).

Internet country code: .tm

Tuvalu

History

Tuvalu was formerly known as Ellice Islands. In 1892, the islands became a British protectorate and in 1915–16 the UK annexed them as part of the colony of the Gilbert and Ellice Islands. In 1975, the Ellice Islands were separated from the Gilbert Islands, renamed as Tuvalu and given home rule. Full independence was granted in 1978.

Geography

Location: Oceania, island group consisting of nine coral atolls in the South Pacific Ocean.

Area: 26 sq. km.

Natural resources: Fish.

Climate: Tropical climate.

People

Population: 11,636 (July 2005 est.).

Population growth rate: 1.47% (2005 est.).

Sex ratio: 0.95 male(s)/female (2005 est.).

Religions: Church of Tuvalu (Congregationalist) 97%, Seventh-Day Adventist 1.4%, Baha'i 1%, others 0.6%.

Languages: Tuvaluan, English, Samoan, Kiribati (on the island of Nui).

Infant mortality rate: 20.03 deaths/ 1,000 live births (2005 est.)

Life expectancy: Total 68.01 years, Male 65.79 years, Female 70.33 years (2005 est.).

Government

Capital: Funafuti.

Government type: Constitutional monarchy with a parliamentary democracy.

Independence: 1 October 1978 (from UK).

Executive branch:
Chief of state: Queen Elizabeth II (since 6 February 1952), represented by Governor General Filoimea Telito (since 15 April 2005).

Head of government: Prime Minister Maatia Toafa (since 11 October 2004).

Economy

Currency: Australian dollar; there is also a Tuvaluan dollar.

GDP: Purchasing power parity—$12.2 million (2000 est.).

GDP—real growth rate: 3% (2000 est.).

GDP—per capita: Purchasing power parity—$1,100 (2000 est.).

Inflation rate: 5% (2000 est.).

Exports: $1 million f.o.b. (2002)— copra, fish.

Imports: $79 million c.i.f. (2002)— food, animals, mineral fuels, machinery, manufactured goods.

Transport and Communications

Railways: None.

Roads: 8 km.

Telephones: 700 (2002).

Internet users: 1,300 (2002).

Internet country code: .tv

Uganda

History

By the 1800s, the Buganda kingdom gained control of a vast stretch of territory bordering Lake Victoria. Arab traders reached the area in the 1840s and European explorers arrived soon afterwards. In 1894, Uganda became a British protectorate. In 1921, Uganda gained its own legislative council and in 1958, it was given internal self-government. In 1962, Uganda became independent with Milton Obote as prime minister. In 1963, Uganda became a republic with Sir Edward Mutesa, the King of Buganda, as the first President. In 1966, Milton Obote seized control of the government from President Mutesa.

In 1971, General Idi Amin seized power from President Milton Obote. Amin ruled directly with hardly any delegation of power. His expulsion of all Asians from Uganda in 1972 led to a breakdown of Uganda's economy. A Muslim himself, Amin reversed Uganda's friendly relations with Israel and built up new links with Libya and the Palestinians.

Some 100,000 to 300,000 Ugandans were allegedly tortured or murdered during Amin's presidency. Amin's downfall came about when, in 1978, he invaded Tanzania to annex its Kagera region. Tanzania responded in 1979 by invading Uganda. This had the effect of unifying the various anti-Amin forces under the Uganda National Liberation Front. Amin fled the country, first to Libya and finally to Saudi Arabia, where he passed away in August 2003.

Geography

Location: Eastern Africa, west of Kenya.

Area: 236,040 sq. km.

Terrain: Plateau with a rim of mountains.

Natural resources: Copper, cobalt, hydropower, limestone, salt, arable land.

Climate: Generally rainy tropical climate with two dry seasons from December to February and June to August.

People

Population: 27,269,482 (July 2005 est.).

Population growth rate: 3.31% (2005 est.).

Sex ratio: 1 male(s)/female (2005 est.).

Religions: Roman Catholic 33%, Protestant 33%, Muslim 16%, indigenous beliefs 18%.

Languages: English (official national language), Ganda or Luganda (most widely used of the Niger–Congo languages), other Niger–Congo languages, Nilo-Saharan languages, Swahili, Arabic.

Literacy rate: Total 69.9%, Male 79.5%, Female 60.4% (2003 est.).

Infant mortality rate: 67.83 deaths/1,000 live births (2005 est.).

Life expectancy: Total 51.59 years, Male 50.74 years, Female 52.46 years (2005 est.).

Government

Capital: Kampala.

Government type: Republic.

Independence: 9 October 1962 (from UK).

Legal system: In 1995, the government restored the legal system to one based on English common law and customary law.

Executive branch:
Chief of state: President Lt Gen. Yoweri Kaguta Museveni (since he seized power on 26 January 1986). The president is both chief of state and head of government.

Economy

Currency: Ugandan shilling.

GDP: Purchasing power parity—$39.39 billion (2004 est.).

GDP—real growth rate: 5% (2004 est.).

GDP—per capita: Purchasing power parity—$1,500 (2004 est.).

Inflation rate: 3.5% (2004 est.).

Population below poverty line: 35% (2001 est.).

Exports: $621.7 million f.o.b. (2004 est.)—coffee, fish and fish products, tea, gold, cotton, flowers, horticultural products.

Imports: $1.306 billion f.o.b. (2004 est.)—capital equipment, vehicles, petroleum, medical supplies, cereals.

External debt: $3.865 billion (2004 est.).

Transport and Communications

Railways: 1,241 km.

Roads: 27,000 km.

Telephones: 61,000 (2003).

Mobile cellular: 776,200 (2003).

Internet users: 125,000 (2003).

Internet country code: .ug

Ukraine

History

A major state emerged in the area from the ninth century onwards. This is referred to as the Kievan Rus. Kiev became a major political and cultural centre in the 10th century. A Mongol invasion that culminated with the sack of Kiev in 1240 ended the glory days.

In the 15th century, a new martial society called the Cossacks emerged in the southern steppe frontier region of Ukraine. Although the Polish government availed of their services as an effective fighting force, the Cossacks eventually rose in revolt. The Polish authorities subdued them, but only after much difficulty.

In 1645, Ukraine requested protection against the Polish from Moscow. The treaty they signed recognized the suzerainty of Moscow and led to the annexation of Kiev. The state of Ukraine was subsequently absorbed into the Russian Empire.

Ukraine took advantage of the confusion resulting from the Russian Revolution and in January 1918, it declared independence from the Empire. In 1920, the Soviets gained control of Ukraine once again. The 1930s saw large-scale death and deportations, as the Stalinist regime implemented its policies of collectivization and purges. More suffering was to follow when Nazi Germany occupied the country during World War II while Stalin deported some 200,000 Crimean Tatars to Siberia and Central Asia following accusations of collaboration with Nazi Germany.

The worst nuclear accident in history took place on the morning of 26 April 1986 at the Chernobyl nuclear power station in Ukraine. It was later estimated that five million people were exposed to radiation in Ukraine, Belarus and Russia.

In 1991, Ukraine declared its independence following an attempted coup in Moscow.

Geography

Location: Eastern Europe, bordering the Black Sea, between Poland, Romania, and Moldova in the west and Russia in the east.

Area: 603,700 sq. km.

Terrain: Mostly fertile plains (steppes) and plateaus. Carpathian Mountains in the west, and the Crimean Peninsula in the south.

Natural resources: Iron ore, coal, manganese, natural gas, oil, salt, sulphur, graphite, titanium, magnesium, kaolin, nickel, mercury, timber, arable land.

Climate: Temperate continental climate.

People

Population: 47,425,336 (July 2005 est.).

Population growth rate: −0.63% (2005 est.).

Sex ratio: 0.86 male(s)/female (2005 est.).

Religions: Ukrainian Orthodox, Moscow Patriarchate, Kiev Patriarchate, Ukrainian Autocephalous Orthodox, Ukrainian Catholic (Uniate), Protestant, Jewish.

Languages: Ukrainian, Russian, Romanian, Polish, Hungarian.

Literacy rate: 99.7% (2003 est.).

Infant mortality rate: 20.34 deaths/1,000 live births (2005 est.).

Life expectancy: Total 66.85 years, Male 61.6 years, Female 72.38 years (2004 est.).

Government

Capital: Kiev (Kyyiv).

Government type: Republic.

Independence: 24 August 1991 (from the Soviet Union).

Legal system: Based on civil law system; judicial review of legislative acts.

Executive branch:
Chief of state: President Viktor A. Yushchenko (since 23 January 2005).

Head of government: Prime Minister Yuliya Tymoshenko (since 4 February 2005).

Economy

Currency: Hryvnia.

GDP: Purchasing power parity—$299.1 billion (2004 est.).

GDP—real growth rate: 12% (2004 est.).

GDP—per capita: Purchasing power parity—$6,300 (2004 est.).

Inflation rate: 12% (2004 est.).

Population below poverty line: 29% (2003 est.).

Unemployment rate: 3.5% (2004 est.).

Exports: $32.91 billion (2004 est.)—ferrous and nonferrous metals, fuel and petroleum products, chemicals, machinery and transport equipment, food products.

Imports: $31.45 billion (2004 est.)—energy, machinery and equipment, chemicals.

External debt: $16.37 billion (2004 est.).

Transport and Communications

Railways: 22,473 km.

Roads: 169,679 km.

Ports and harbours: Berdyans'k,

Telephones: 10,833,300 (2002).

Mobile cellular: 4,200,000 (2002).

Internet users: 3.8 million (2003).

Internet country code: .ua

United Arab Emirates

History

Initially, seafaring people inhabited the area that is today United Arab Emirates. Later, a sect called the Carmathians formed a powerful sheikhdom in the area. Following the disintegration of this sheikhdom, the people resorted to piracy. When they provoked Muscat and Oman, the British intervened and enforced peace. This area along the coast of the Eastern Arabian Peninsula came to be known as the Trucial Coast.

Although the British came to administer the region from 1853, each of the constituent states had full internal control. In 1960, the states formed the Trucial States Council. This was followed by the formation of the six-member federation. Bahrain and Oman opted out while Ra's-al-Khaymah joined in 1972.

Geography

Location: Middle East, bordering the Gulf of Oman and the Persian Gulf, between Oman and Saudi Arabia.

Area: 82,880 sq. km.

Terrain: Flat, barren coastal plain that merges into the sand dunes of a desert wasteland. Mountains lie in the east.

Natural resources: Petroleum, natural gas.

Climate: Desert climate but the eastern mountains are cooler.

People

Population: 2,563,212 including an estimated 1,606,079 non-nationals (July 2005 est.).

Population growth rate: 1.54% (2005 est.).

Sex ratio: 1.44 male(s)/female (2005 est.).

Religions: Muslim 96% (Shi'a 16%), Christian, Hindu, and others 4%.

Languages: Arabic (official), Persian, English, Hindi, Urdu.

Literacy rate: Total 77.9%, Male 76.1%, Female 81.7% (2003 est.).

Infant mortality rate: 14.51 deaths/1,000 live births (2005 est.).

Life expectancy: Total 75.24 years, Male 72.73 years, Female 77.87 years (2005 est.).

Government

Capital: Abu Dhabi.

Government type: Federation.

Independence: 2 December 1971 (from UK).

Legal system: A federal court system.

Executive branch:

Chief of state: President Sheikh Khalifa bin Zayed al-Nahyan (since November 2004).

Head of government: Prime Minister Maktum bin Rashid al-Maktum (since 8

October 1990), ruler of Dubayy (Dubai).

Economy

Currency: Dirham.

Economy—overview:
The country has an open economy. The country boasts of a high per capita income and substantial annual trade surplus. The country's prosperity is based on oil and gas output that accounts for about 33% of GDP. At the present levels of production, the country's oil and gas reserves should last for more than 100 years.

GDP: Purchasing power parity—$63.67 billion (2004 est.).

GDP—real growth rate: 5.7% (2004 est.).

GDP—per capita: Purchasing power parity—$25,200 (2004 est.).

Inflation rate: 3.2% (2004 est.).

Unemployment rate: 2.4% (2001).

Exports: $69.48 billion f.o.b. (2004 est.)—crude oil, natural gas, re-exports, dried fish, dates.

Imports: $45.66 billion f.o.b. (2004 est.)—machinery and transport equipment, food, chemicals.

External debt: $5.9 billion (2004 est.).

Transport and Communications

Railways: None.

Roads: 1,088 km.

Telephones: 1,135,800 (2003).

Mobile cellular: 2,972,300 (2003).

Internet users: 1,110,200 (2003).

Internet country code: .ae

United Kingdom

History

Romans invaded UK in the first century BC. The Roman withdrawal in the fifth century AD led to a series of invasions by Scandinavians and people from the Low Countries. Several large Anglo-Saxon kingdoms were established all over the country. In 1066, a succession dispute led to the Norman Conquest when William of Normandy (William the Conqueror) invaded the country and defeated the Saxon king, Harold II at the Battle of Hastings. This led to the establishment of French law and traditions in the country.

The rule of the Plantagenets saw an increasing degree of centralization of powers in the crown and the removal of much of the powers of the nobles. However, in 1215, King John was forced to sign the Magna Carta that awarded civil rights to the common people.

In 1284, England and Wales joined together in a union. This was formalized in 1536 through an Act of Union.

Edward III's claim to the French throne led to the Hundred Years War between 1338 and 1453 and the subsequent loss of most large British territories in France. In the 14th century, the Black Death plague epidemic swept UK, along with other parts of Europe. This reduced the British population by almost one-third.

The War of the Roses took place between 1455 and 1485. It arose from the struggle for the throne between the House of York and the House of Lancaster and ended in victory for Henry Tudor (later Henry VII). The reign of Henry VIII saw the breaking away of the Church of England from the Roman Catholic Church.

The reign of Elizabeth I between 1558 and 1603 is referred to as the Elizabethan Age, and saw the emergence of England as a major European power in politics, trade and commerce, and the arts. This period also saw the development of a more moderate Church of England. In 1588, the Spanish sent a huge fleet, the Spanish Armada to invade England. But the invasion failed and resulted in the rise of UK as a maritime power.

In 1642, a civil war erupted between Charles I and the Parliament. It resulted in the defeat and execution of Charles I in 1649. Between 1649 and 1653, a Council of States led the country. Oliver Cromwell, who led the parliamentarians in the civil war, ruled the country as 'lord protector' of England, Scotland, and Ireland from 1653 to 1658. Oliver Cromwell's death was followed by the restoration of the monarchy. Charles II became the new Stuart king in 1660. His brother, James I succeeded him but was ousted in the Revolution of 1688. During the reign of Queen Anne, England fought in the War of Spanish Succession.

In 1707, England and Scotland was joined together in an Act of the Union. The 16th and 17th centuries also saw the emergence of the British Empire all over the world. The Empire continued to grow thorough the 18th and 19th centuries.

The country fought with France in the Napoleonic Wars of the 18th century. It ended with French defeat at the Battle of Waterloo in 1815.

Queen Victoria ruled as the queen of the United Kingdom of Great Britain and Ireland from 1837 to 1901 and as the Empress of India from 1876–1901. The Victorian Era saw the emergence of a strong democratic system of government and the gradual transformation of the British monarchy to a largely ceremonial function.

In 1920, the British Parliament passed the Government of Ireland Act that established one Parliament for the six counties of Northern Ireland and another for the rest of Ireland. In 1921, the Anglo-Irish Treaty established the Irish Free State as an independent dominion of the British Crown with full internal self-government. However, the Free State was separated from Northern Ireland that remains part of the United Kingdom even today.

The United Kingdom emerged victorious in both World War I and World War II. Coalition governments were formed for much of the two World Wars. The resignation of Prime Minister Neville Chamberlain in 1950 led to the formation of a coalition government headed by Sir Winston Churchill. He served as the prime minister from 1940–5 and again from 1951–5. He is widely regarded as UK's greatest prime minister.

Edward VIII succeeded to the throne in January 1936. However, he abdicated the throne in December 1936, in order to marry a divorcee, Wallis Simpson. The throne passed on to his brother who became George VI. On 6 February 1952, King George VI's daughter, Elizabeth Alexandra Mary was coronated as Queen Elizabeth II.

In 1973, UK joined the European Economic Community. In 1979, Margaret Thatcher became the country's first woman prime minister. In 1981, she began a programme of privatization of state-run industries.

In 1982, the UK fought Argentina in the Falklands War. It ended in British victory and the surrender of Argentine forces on the Falklands Islands.

In 1992, the separation between Princess Diana and Prince Charles, heir to the British throne, was announced. In May 1997, the Labour Party won a landslide election victory under its new leader, Tony Blair.

In 2003–4, the Blair government was hit by the controversy over the Iraq invasion. The prime minister was accused of misleading the country by exaggerating the threat that Iraq really posed and its arsenal of weapons of mass destruction. It later emerged that the dossier that the prime minister's office compiled to convince the Parliament was based on inaccurate intelligence. The prime minister, the defence secretary and other government officials and aides, senior BBC officials and journalists had to testify at an inquiry into the death of Dr David Kelly, a government scientist who had first revealed to the press that the government had probably exaggerated claims regarding Iraqi weapons.

Geography

Location: Group of islands in Western Europe, including the northern one-sixth of the island of Ireland, between the North Atlantic Ocean and the North Sea, north-west of France.

Area: 244,820 sq. km.

Terrain: Consists largely of rugged hills and low mountains. There are plains in the east and the south-east.

Natural resources: Coal, petroleum, natural gas, iron ore, lead, zinc, gold, tin, limestone, salt, clay, chalk, gypsum, potash, silica sand, slate, arable land.

Climate: Temperate climate moderated by prevailing south-west winds over the North Atlantic Current.

People

Population: 60,441,457 (July 2005 est.).

Population growth rate: 0.28% (2005 est.).

Sex ratio: 0.98 male(s)/female (2005 est.).

Religions: Anglican and Roman Catholic (around 40 million), Muslim (around 1.5 million), Presbyterian (around 800,000), Methodist 760,000, Sikh (around 500,000), Hindu (around 500,000), Jew (around 350,000).

Languages: English, Welsh, Scottish form of Gaelic.

Literacy rate: 99% (2000 est.).

Infant mortality rate: 5.16 deaths/1,000 live births (2005 est.).

Life expectancy: Total 78.38 years, Male 75.94 years, Female 80.96 years (2005 est.).

Government

Capital: London.

Government type: Constitutional monarchy.

Independence: 1284 (date of union between England and Wales, formalized in 1536 through an Act of Union); 1707 (date of joining together of England and Scotland as Great Britain through an Act of Union); 1801 (date of legislative union of Great Britain and Ireland implemented with the adoption of the name The United Kingdom of Great Britain and Ireland).

Constitution: UK has no written constitution. Instead, there are statutes and common law and practice.

Legal system: Common law tradition with early Roman and modern continental influences.

Executive branch:
Chief of state: Queen Elizabeth II (since 6 February 1952). Heir Apparent Prince Charles (son of the queen; born 14 November 1948).

Head of government: Prime Minister Anthony (Tony) Blair (since 2 May 1997).

Legislative branch:
UK has a bicameral parliament. The parliament has two chambers. The House of Commons has 646 members, elected for a five year term in single-

seat constituencies. The House of Lords has 675 members, 557 life peers and 118 hereditary members (June 2001).

Elections and election results: In the House of Lords, elections are held only when vacancies in the hereditary peerage arise. The last such election was held in 1999 to determine the 92 hereditary peers. Elections to the House of Commons were last held on 5 May 2005.

Economy

Currency: British pound.

Economy—overview:
The British economy is among the largest in Europe. UK and its capital city of London is one of the most important trading and financial centres of the world. The country boasts of an efficient and highly mechanized agricultural sector, substantial mineral resources, and a well-developed services sector. It has one of the strongest economies in the world with low inflation, interest rates, and unemployment. However, the British population remains opposed to joining the European Economic and Monetary Union (EMU) and the euro common currency.

GDP: Purchasing power parity—$1.782 trillion (2004 est.).

GDP—real growth rate: 3.2% (2004 est.).

GDP—per capita: Purchasing power parity—$29,600 (2004 est.).

Inflation rate: 1.4% (2004 est.).

Population below poverty line: 17% (2002 est.).

Unemployment rate: 4.8% (2004 est.).

Exports: $347.2 billion f.o.b. (2004 est.)—manufactured goods, fuels, chemicals, food, beverages, tobacco.

Imports: $439.4 billion f.o.b. (2004 est.)—manufactured goods, machinery, fuels, foodstuff.

External debt: $4.71 billion (2003).

Transport and Communications

Railways: 17,186 km.

Roads: 392,931 km.

Telephones: 34,898,000 (2002).

Mobile cellular: 49,677,000 (2002).

Internet users: 25,000,000 (2002).

Internet country code: .uk

United States of America

History

Christopher Columbus never set foot on the mainland United States. However, the first European explorations of the continental United States were staged from the Spanish bases that Columbus had helped establish in the region.

In 1585, Walter Raleigh established the first British colony in North America. The settlement was later abandoned. It was finally in 1607 that English settlers succeeded when they set up Jamestown in present-day Virginia. In 1620, the Pilgrim Fathers, a group of European settlers, set up Plymouth Colony, near present-day Cape Cod.

In 1609, the Dutch East India Company hired Henry Hudson to explore the area around what is today New York City and Hudson River. In 1624, the Dutch purchased the island of Manhattan from local Indians for the reported price of $24. They renamed it New Amsterdam. The new diseases the Europeans brought with them and their desire for land posed a serious challenge to the native population. The initial cordial relations soon gave way to conflict, war and, almost always, further loss of land.

Meanwhile, in the 17th and 18th centuries, Europeans imported hundreds of thousands of Africans and sold them into slavery to work on cotton and tobacco plantations. British imperialist designs on the New World received a boost in 1763 when it gained control of territory up to the Mississippi river, following victory over France in the Seven Years War. Thereafter, the British government decided to raise the costs of administering and protecting its North American colonies from the colony itself. It therefore set out to impose new taxes. This led to widespread opposition and hatred for British rule. Dissent soon gave way to fighting between the British and Americans in 1775. The following year, the 13 North American colonies declared their independence from Britain. The document that announced this separation is the famous Declaration of Independence. In 1789, George Washington, who had served as the commander in chief of the American forces during the War of Independence, was elected the first President of USA.

In 1860, the anti-slavery Republican Party candidate Abraham Lincoln was elected President. The 11 pro-slavery southern states reacted by breaking away from the Union and forming the Confederate States of America under the leadership of Jefferson Davis. This was the flash point for the US Civil War. The Confederate forces surrendered in April 1965. Within a week, Abraham Lincoln was assassinated.

In 1898, USA gained territory when it received Puerto Rico, Guam, the Philippines and Cuba following the Spanish–American war. The same year, it annexed Hawaii. In 1920, the US government banned the manufacture and sale of alcoholic liquors. This was the Prohibition Era and it lasted till 1933.

In 1929, USA, along with the rest of North America, Europe and other industrialized economies plunged into the Great Depression. It was triggered by the Wall Street stock market crash of 1929 and resulted in the unemployment of 13 million people.

In 1932, Franklin D. Roosevelt was elected as the new US President. He launched the 'New Deal' recovery programme that aimed to restore the economy. He also lifted the ban on sale of alcohol.

In 1941, Japanese warplanes attacked a US military base at Pearl Harbour in Hawaii. This led the US to declare war on Japan. Soon thereafter, Germany declared war on US. USA's entry into World War II on a massive scale eventually led to the defeat of the Axis powers led by Germany, Japan and Italy. In 1945, USA became the first, and so far only country, to use nuclear weapons in war when it dropped two atomic bombs on the Japanese cities of Hiroshima and Nagasaki. It caused horrendous casualties and led to the surrender of Japan.

The post-World War II years saw the polarization of the world into a pro-USA block and a pro-Soviet Union block. This marked the start of the Cold War, that only ended with the collapse of the Soviet Union in the 1990s. In 1950–3, USA played a leading role in the Korean War.

The 1950s were marked by the campaign of civil disobedience to secure civil rights for Americans of African descent. In 1960, Democratic Party candidate John F. Kennedy was elected US President. The following year, USA organized and sponsored the unsuccessful Bay of Pigs invasion of Cuba by Cuban exiles. In 1962, USA and USSR came to the brink of nuclear war following the Cuban missile crisis.

In 1963, President John F. Kennedy was assassinated. Between 1955 and

1975, USA fought the prolonged and unsuccessful Vietnam War along with South Vietnam to prevent the communists of North Vietnam from uniting South Vietnam with North Vietnam.

On 11 September 2001, four US passenger aircraft were hijacked and crashed into the World Trade Center in New York, the US Defence Department headquarters and the Pentagon, in Washington DC. More than 3000 people were estimated killed. This led USA to declare its 'War on Terror'. In October 2001, USA lead a military campaign in Afghanistan to defeat the Taliban regime and find Osama bin Laden, who was suspected of masterminding the 9/11 attacks.

Geography

Location: North America, bordering both the North Atlantic Ocean and the North Pacific Ocean, between Canada and Mexico.

Area: 9,629,091 sq. km.

Terrain: Mountains in the west, hills and low mountains in the east, a vast central plain, mountains and broad river valleys in Alaska. Hawaii has a rugged, volcanic topography.

Natural resources: Coal, copper, lead, molybdenum, phosphates, uranium, bauxite, gold, iron, mercury, nickel, potash, silver, tungsten, zinc, petroleum, natural gas, timber.

Climate: Mostly temperate, tropical in Hawaii and Florida, arctic in Alaska, semi-arid in the Great Plains west of the Mississippi River and arid in the Great Basin of the south-west.

People

Population: 295,734,134 (July 2005 est.).

Population growth rate: 0.92% (2005 est.).

Sex ratio: 0.97 male(s)/female (2005 est.).

Religions: Protestant 56%, Roman Catholic 28%, Jewish 2%, others 4%, none 10%.

Languages: English, Spanish (spoken by a sizable minority).

Literacy rate: 97% (1979 est.).

Infant mortality rate: 6.5 deaths/1,000 live births (2005 est.).

Life expectancy: Total 77.71 years, Male 74.89 years, Female 80.67 years (2005 est.).

Government

Capital: Washington DC.

Government type: Constitution-based federal republic.

Independence: 4 July 1776 (from Great Britain).

Legal system: Based on English common law; judicial review of legislative acts.

Executive branch:
Chief of state: President George W. Bush (since 20 January 2001) and Vice-President Richard B. Cheney (since 20 January 2001). Both re-elected in November 2004. The President is both the chief of state and head of government.

Elections and election results: President and vice-president are elected on the same ticket by a college of representatives who are elected directly from each state. President and vice-president serve four-year terms. Last elections were held on 2 November 2004.

Legislative branch:
USA has a bicameral Congress. It consists of the Senate that has 100 seats, one-third of which are renewed every two years. Two members are elected from each state by popular vote to serve six-year terms. The other chamber is the House of Representatives that has 435 seats. Members are di-

rectly elected by popular vote to serve two-year terms.

Elections and Election Results: Elections to the Senate were last held in November 2004. Elections to the House of Representatives were last held in November 2004.

Economy

Currency: US Dollar.

Economy—overview:
The US has the largest and the most technologically powerful economy in the world, with a per capita GDP of over $40,000.

GDP: Purchasing power parity—$11.75 trillion (2004 est.).

GDP—real growth rate: 4.4% (2004 est.).

GDP—per capita: Purchasing power parity—$40,100 (2004 est.).

Inflation rate: 2.5% (2004).

Population below poverty line: 12% (2004 est.).

Unemployment rate: 5.5% (2004 est.).

Exports: $795 billion f.o.b. (2004 est.)—capital goods, automobiles, industrial supplies and raw materials, consumer goods, agricultural products.

Imports: $1.476 trillion f.o.b. (2004 est.)—crude oil and refined petroleum products, machinery, automobiles, consumer goods, industrial raw materials, food and beverages.

External debt: 1.4 trillion (2001 est.).

Transport and Communications

Railways: 228,464 km.

Roads: 6,393,603 km.

Telephones: 181,599,900 (2003).

Mobile cellular: 158,722,000 (2003).

Internet users: 16,575,000 (2002).

Internet country code: .us

Uruguay

History

European explorers arrived in the area in the 16th century. These included Ferdinand Magellan who came in 1520 and Sebastian Cabot who came in 1526. In 1726, the Spanish founded the city of Montevideo and took control of Uruguay from the Portuguese. In 1776, Uruguay became a part of the viceroyalty of La Plata, with its capital at Buenos Aires, Argentina. In 1808, Uruguay rebelled against the viceroyalty of La Plata after Napoleon Bonaparte overthrew the Spanish monarchy in Europe.

The early part of the 19th century saw a struggle between Argentina and

Brazil to control Banda Oriental, as Uruguay was then known. Uruguay became independent in 1825 with Argentine assistance and in 1828 it became a republic. During 1838–65, the country was hit by a civil war between the 'Whites' and 'Colorados' or 'Reds'. During 1865–70, Uruguay joined Argentina and Brazil in the War of the Triple Alliance, also called the Paraguayan War. It ended with the decimation of Paraguay. In 1903, Uruguay set up a welfare state under the leadership of Jose Batlley Ordonez who served as the country's President between 1903–7 and 1911–15.

A Marxist urban guerrilla movement called the Tupamaros began in the early

1960s and lasted till 1975. In 1973, the armed forces overthrew the civilian government. This initiated a period of brutal repression during which Uruguay came to be known as 'the torture chamber of Latin America' and was believed to have the largest number of political prisoners per capita in the world. A civilian government returned in 1985 with Julio Maria Sanguinetti as the President.

Geography

Location: South America, bordering the South Atlantic Ocean, between Argentina and Brazil.

Area: 176,220 sq. km.

Terrain: Rolling plains and low hills, and a fertile coastal lowland.

Natural resources: Arable land, hydropower, minor minerals, fisheries.

Climate: Warm temperate climate.

People

Population: 3,415,920 (July 2005 est.).

Population growth rate: 0.47% (2005 est.).

Sex ratio: 0.95 male(s)/female (2005 est.).

Religions: Roman Catholic 66%, Protestant 2%, Jewish 1%, non-professing or others 31%.

Languages: Spanish, Portunol or Brazilero.

Literacy rate: Total 98%, Male 97.6%, Female 98.4% (2003 est.).

Infant mortality rate: 11.95 deaths/1,000 live births (2005 est.).

Life expectancy: Total 76.13 years, Male 72.92 years, Female 79.45 years (2005 est.).

Government

Capital: Montevideo.

Government type: Constitutional republic.

Independence: 25 August 1825 (from Brazil).

Legal system: Based on Spanish civil law system.

Executive branch:
Chief of state: President Tabare Vazquez (since 1 March 2005) and Vice-President Rodoifo Nin Noua (since 1 March 2005). The president is both the chief of state and head of government.

Economy

Currency: Uruguayan peso.

GDP: Purchasing power parity—$49.27 billion (2004 est.).

GDP—real growth rate: -10.2% (2004 est.).

GDP—per capita: Purchasing power parity—$14,500 (2004 est.).

Inflation rate: 7.6% (2004 est.).

Population below poverty line: 21% (2003).

Unemployment rate: 13% (2004 est.).

Exports: $2.2 billion f.o.b. (2003 est.)—meat, rice, leather products, wool, vehicles, dairy products.

Imports: $2.071 billion f.o.b. (2003 est.)—machinery, chemicals, road vehicles, crude petroleum.

External debt: $12.8 billion (2004 est.).

Transport and Communications

Railways: 2,073 km.

Roads: 8,983 km.

Telephones: 946,500 (2002).

Mobile cellular: 652,000 (2002).

Internet users: 400,000 (2002).

Internet country code: .uy

Uzbekistan

History

The land that is today Uzbekistan formed parts of the Persian Empire and Tamerlane's empire. The area remained under the control of the successors of Tamerlane till the Uzbeks invaded it in the 16th century and merged it with neighbouring areas. However, upon their downfall, the territory fragmented into smaller units. In the 19th century, the Russians invaded the region.

In 1924, the area was formed into the Uzbek Republic and in 1925 the Uzbekistan Soviet Socialist Republic was formed. In June 1990, Uzbekistan issued its own laws and in December 1991, it declared its independence.

Geography

Location: Central Asia, north of Afghanistan.

Area: 447,400 sq. km.

Terrain: Mostly flat or rolling sandy desert with sand dunes. There are also broad, flat irrigated river valleys.

Natural resources: Natural gas, petroleum, coal, gold, uranium, silver, copper, lead and zinc, tungsten, molybdenum.

Climate: Mostly of the mid-latitude desert type with long and hot summers and mild winters.

People

Population: 26,851,195 (July 2005 est.).

Population growth rate: 1.67% (2005 est.).

Sex ratio: 0.98 male(s)/female (2003 est.).

Religions: Muslim 88% (mostly Sunnis), Eastern Orthodox 9%, others 3%.

Languages: Uzbek 74.3%, Russian 14.2%, Tajik 4.4%, others 7.1%.

Literacy rate: 99.3% (2003 est.).

Infant mortality rate: 71.1 deaths/ 1,000 live births (2005 est.).

Life expectancy: Total 64.19 years, Male 60.82 years, Female 67.73 years (2005 est.).

Government

Capital: Tashkent (Toshkent).

Government type: Republic with an authoritarian presidential rule. There is very little power outside the executive branch.

Independence: 1 September 1991 (from Soviet Union).

Legal system: An evolution of Soviet civil law.

Executive branch:
Chief of state: President Islom Karimov (since 24 March 1990).

Head of government: Prime Minister Shavkat Mirziyayev (since 11 December 2003).

Economy

Currency: Uzbekistani sum.

Economy—overview:
Uzbekistan is one of the world's largest cotton exporters and also a significant producer of gold and oil. Besides, it is

a key producer of chemicals and machinery in the region. After independence, the government attempted to retain its Soviet-type economy with subsidies and strict controls on production and prices. The adverse conditions generated by the Asian and Russian financial crises by promoting import substitute industrialization and by monitoring and tightening export and currency controls.

GDP: Purchasing power parity—$47.59 billion (2004 est.).

GDP—real growth rate: 4.4% (2004 est.).

GDP—per capita: Purchasing power parity—$1,800 (2004 est.).

Inflation rate: 36% (2004 est.).

Population below poverty line: 28% (2004 est.).

Unemployment rate: 0.6% officially, blows 20% underemployment (2004 est.).

Exports: $3.7 billion f.o.b. (2004 est.)—cotton 41.5%, gold 9.6%, energy products 9.6%, mineral fertilizers, ferrous metals, textiles, food products, automobiles (1998 est.).

Imports: $2.5 billion f.o.b. (2002 est.)—machinery and equipment 49.8%, foodstuff 16.4%, chemicals, metals (1998 est.).

External debt: $4.6 billion (2002 est.).

Transport and Communications

Railways: 3,950 km.

Roads: 81,600 km.

Telephones: 1,717,100 (2003).

Mobile cellular: 320,800 (2003).

Internet users: 492,000 (2003).

Internet country code: .uz

Vanuatu

History

In 1606, the Portuguese Pedro Fernandes de Queiros sighted the islands while in 1774, the British explorer James Cook charted them. It was Cook who named the archipelago New Hebrides. A joint Anglo-French government ruled the islands from 1906. During World War II, the islands served as a major base for the Allied forces. In 1980, the islands were granted independence as Vanuatu.

Geography

Location: Oceania, group of islands in the South Pacific Ocean, north-east of Queensland, Australia.

Area: 12,200 sq. km.

Terrain: Mountainous islands of volcanic origins.

Natural resources: Manganese, hardwood forests, fish.

Climate: Tropical climate moderated by south-east trade winds.

People

Population: 205,754 (July 2005 est.).

Population growth rate: 1.52% (2005 est.).

Sex ratio: 1.05 male(s)/female (2005 est.).

Religions: Presbyterian 36.7%, Anglican 15%, Roman Catholic 15%, indigenous beliefs 7.6%, Seventh-Day Adventist 6.2%, Church of Christ 3.8%, others 15.7%.

Languages: English, French, pidgin (known as Bislama or Bichelama).

Literacy rate: Total 53%, Male 57%, Female 48% (1979 est.).

Infant mortality rate: 55.16 deaths/1,000 live births (2005 est.).

Life expectancy: Total 62.49 years, Male 61 years, Female 64.05 years (2005 est.).

Government

Capital: Port-Vila.

Government type: Parliamentary republic.

Independence: 30 July 1980 (from France and UK).

Legal system: Unified system created from former dual French and British systems.

Executive branch:
Chief of state: President Kalkot Matas Kelekele (since 16 August 2004).

Head of government: Prime Minister Ham Lini (since 11 December 2004).

Economy

Currency: Vatu.

GDP: Purchasing power parity—$580 million (2003 est.).

GDP—real growth rate: −1.1% (2003 est.).

GDP—per capita: Purchasing power parity—$2,900 (2003 est.).

Inflation rate: 3.1% (2003 est.).

Exports: $26.6 million f.o.b. (2003)—copra, beef, cocoa, timber, kava, coffee.

Imports: $138 million c.i.f. (2003).

External debt: $83.7 million (2002 est.).

Transport and Communications

Railways: None.

Roads: 1,070 km.

Telephones: 6,500 (2003).

Mobile cellular: 7,800 (2003).

Internet users: 7,500 (2003).

Internet country code: .vu

Vatican City

History

The Vatican City state is the sole surviving remnant of the Papal States that, at one point of time, occupied thousands of square kilometres in Italy. During the Risorgimento (the 19th century movement for Italian unification), most of the area of the Papal States were absorbed into Italy. The Lateran Treaty of 1929 set up an independent state of Vatican City.

Geography

Location: Southern Europe, an enclave of Rome (Italy).

Area: 0.44 sq. km.

Natural resources: None.

Climate: Temperate climate.

People

Population: 921 (July 2005 est.).

Population growth rate: 0.01% (2005 est.).

Religions: Roman Catholic.

Languages: Italian, Latin, French, various other languages.

Literacy rate: 100%.

Government

Capital: Vatican City.

Government type: Ecclesiastical.

Independence: 11 February 1929.

Legal system: Based on Code of Canon Law and its revised forms.

Executive branch:
Chief of state: Pope Benedick XVI (since 19 April 2005).

Head of government: Secretary of State Cardinal Angelo Sodano (since 2 December 1990).

Economy

Currency: Euro.

Economy—overview:
The Vatican City has a unique, non-commercial economy that is supported financially by an annual contribution from Roman Catholic dioceses all over the world, by special collections (known as Peter's Pence), museum admission fees, sale of postage stamps, medals, coins, and tourist mementos, sale of publications, investments and real estate income also account for a sizable portion of revenue.

Transport and Communications

Railways: 0.86 km.

Roads: City streets.

Internet country code: .va

Venezuela

History

Spanish colonization of the area began in the 1520s. Napoleon's invasion of Spain encouraged Venezuelans to declare their independence in 1810.

Venezuela was part of the Republic of Gran Colombia that was proclaimed on 17 December 1819, with Simon Bolivar as President. However, Venezuela seceded from Gran Colombia in 1829 and became an independent republic with its capital at Caracas.

For almost a century between 1830 and 1935, a series of warlord-like leaders, locally referred to as caudillos, ruled over Venezuela. This period, marked by repeated internal strife, ended with the death of dictator Juan Vicente Gomez in 1935.

Meanwhile, towards 1928, Venezuela emerged as the world's second largest producer of petroleum and the leading petroleum exporter. The Venezuelan economy experienced a boom in the 1970s due to high global oil prices.

Geography

Location: Northern South America, bordering the Caribbean Sea and the North Atlantic Ocean, between Colombia and Guyana.

Area: 912,050 sq. km.

Terrain: The Andes Mountains and Maracaibo Lowlands in the north-west, a central plain (llanos) and the Guiana Highlands in the south-east.

Natural resources: Petroleum, natural gas, iron ore, gold, bauxite, other minerals, hydropower, diamonds.

Climate: Hot and humid tropical that is more moderate in the highlands.

People

Population: 25,375,281 (July 2005 est.).

Population growth rate: 1.4% (2005 est.).

Sex ratio: 1.02 male(s)/female (2005 est.).

Religions: Nominally Roman Catholic 96%, Protestant 2%, others 2%.

Languages: Spanish (official), numerous indigenous dialects.

Literacy rate: Total 93.4%, Male 93.8%, Female 93.1% (2003 est.).

Infant mortality rate: 22.2 deaths/1,000 live births (2005 est.).

Life expectancy: Total 74.31 years, Male 71.27 years, Female 77.58 years (2005 est.).

Government

Capital: Caracas.

Government type: Federal republic.

Independence: 5 July 1811 (from Spain).

Legal system: Based on organic laws.

Executive branch:
Chief of state: President Hugo Chavez Frias (since 3 February 1999). Vice-President Jose Vicente Rangel (since 28 April 2002). The president is both the chief of state and head of government.

Economy

Currency: Bolivar.

Economy—overview:
Venezuela's petroleum sector accounts for around one-third of the country's GDP, over half of the government's operating revenues and around 80% of export earnings. However, internal instability, followed by a two-month national oil strike between December 2002 and February 2003 seriously damaged the Venezuelan economy.

GDP: Purchasing power parity—$145.2 billion (2004 est.).

GDP—real growth rate: −16.8% (2004 est.).

GDP—per capita: Purchasing power parity—$5,800 (2004 est.).

Inflation rate: 22.4% (2004 est.).

Population below poverty line: 47% (1998 est.).

Unemployment rate: 17.1% (2004 est.).

Exports: $35.84 billion f.o.b. (2004 est.)—petroleum, bauxite and aluminum, steel, chemicals, agricultural products, basic manufactures.

Imports: $14.98 billion f.o.b. (2004 est.)—raw materials, machinery and equipment, transport equipment, construction materials.

External debt: $33.29 billion (2004 est.).

Transport and Communications

Railways: 682 km.

Roads: 96,155 km.

Telephones: 2,841,800 (2002).

Mobile cellular: 6,463,600 (2002).

Internet users: 1,274,400 (2002).

Internet country code: .ve

Vietnam

History

In the early 17th century, the area that is today Vietnam was divided into two parts. While the northern part was called Tonkin, the southern part was called Cochin China. In 1802, the two parts were unified under a single dynasty.

The French gained control of Saigon (now Ho Chi Minh City) in 1859. Soon after, they came to control much of the remaining area of the country and ruled it till World War II. During 1940–5, the Japanese controlled Vietnam and declared the country independent. The French opposed this and this led to the first Indochina War. The French evacuated Vietnam after defeat at Dien Bien Phu in 1954.

The defeat of the French led to the division of the nation into North Vietnam (Democratic Republic of Vietnam, under Ho Chi Minh) and South Vietnam (Republic of Vietnam, under emperor Bao Dai). In 1955, Bao Dai's premier Ngo Dinh Diem deposed him and established a strong authoritarian rule with US backing.

Ngo Dinh Diem refused to hold a combined north–south election in 1956. His decision met with US approval. Consequently, North Vietnam decided to use military force as the means of unification of the South with the North. This led to the Vietnam War that raged on till 1975.

On 30 April 1975, the remains of the South Vietnamese government surrendered unconditionally to North Vietnamese forces that promptly occupied Saigon. On 2 July 1976, the country was officially united as the Socialist Republic of Vietnam with Hanoi as its capital.

Geography

Location: Vietnam lies in South-eastern Asia, bordering the Gulf of Thailand, Gulf of Tonkin and South China Sea, alongside China, Laos and Cambodia.

Area: 329,560 sq. km.

Terrain: Low and flat delta in the south and north of the country. There are highlands in the central part while the hilly mountainous region lies in the north and north-west.

Natural resources: Phosphates, coal, manganese, bauxite, chromate, offshore oil and gas deposits, forests, hydropower.

Climate: Tropical in the south, monsoon type in the north.

People

Population: 83,535,576 (July 2005 est.).

Population growth rate: 1.04% (2005 est.).

Sex ratio: 0.98 male(s)/female (2005 est.).

Religions: Buddhist, Hoa Hao, Cao Dai, Christian (predominantly Roman Catholic, some Protestant), indigenous beliefs, Muslim.

Languages: Vietnamese (official), English, French, Chinese, and Khmer; mountain area languages (Mon-Khmer and Malayo-Polynesian).

Literacy rate: Total 94%, Male 95.8%, Female 92.3% (2003 est.).

Infant mortality rate: 25.95 deaths/ 1,000 live births (2005 est.).

Life expectancy: Total 70.61 years, Male 67.82 years, Female 73.6 years (2005 est.).

Government

Capital: Hanoi.

Government type: Communist state.

Independence: 2 September 1945 (from France).

Legal system: Based on communist legal theory and French civil law system.

Executive branch:
Chief of state: President Tran Duc Luong (since 24 September 1997).

Head of government: Prime Minister Phan Van Khai (since 25 September 1997).

Economy

Currency: Dong.

Economy—overview:
Vietnam has a centrally planned economy that was dealt a blow by the collapse of the Soviet Union as it used to provide substantial assistance to it. During 1993–7, growth averaged around 9% per year. The 1997 Asian financial crisis revealed the flaws in the Vietnamese economy. GDP growth of 8.5% in 1997 shrank to 6% in 1998 and 5% in 1999 but then rose to 6%–7% during 2000–2. Many of Vietnam's domestic industries such as coal, cement, steel, and paper are reported to suffer from large stockpiles of inventory.

GDP: Purchasing power parity—$227.2 billion (2004 est.).

GDP—real growth rate: 7.7% (2004 est.).

GDP—per capita: Purchasing power parity—$2,700 (2004 est.).

Inflation rate: 9.5% (2004 est.).

Population below poverty line: 28.9% (2002 est.).

Unemployment rate: 1.9% (2004 est.).

Exports: $23.72 billion f.o.b. (2004 est.)—crude oil, marine products, rice, coffee, rubber, tea, garments, shoes.

Imports: $26.31 billion f.o.b. (2004 est.)—machinery and equipment, petroleum products, fertilizer, steel products, raw cotton, grain, cement, motorcycles.

External debt: $16.55 billion (2004 est.).

Transport and Communications

Railways: 2,600 km.

Roads: 93,300 km.

Telephones: 4,402,000 (2003).

Mobile cellular: 2,742,000 (2003).

Internet users: 3.5 million (2003).

Internet country code: .vn

Yemen

History

Ancient Yemen was centred on the port of Aden and was an important centre of trade in myrrh and frankincense. Romans invaded Yemen in the first century AD and so did the Persians and Ethiopians in the sixth century. In 628, the people of the area converted to Islam and in the 10th century, it came under the control of the Rassite dynasty of the Zaidi sect. The Ottoman Turks ruled over the area from 1538 until their decline in 1918.

Imams ruled the northern part of Yemen till a pro-Egyptian coup took place in 1962. A Yemen Arab Republic was declared. Meanwhile, in the south, the strategically located port of Aden came under the control of the British. By 1937, it came to be called Aden Protectorate. The Nationalist's Liberation Front fought against the British and this led to the formation of the People's Republic of Southern Yemen in 1967. In 1979, it became the only Marxist state of the Arab world. On 22 March 1990, the two countries, pro-West Yemen and Marxist Yemen Arab Republic, united after 300 years of separation.

Geography

Location: Middle East, bordering the Arabian Sea, Gulf of Aden, and Red Sea, between Oman and Saudi Arabia.

Area: 527,970 sq. km.

Terrain: Narrow coastal plain with flat-topped hills and rugged mountains. There are also dissected upland desert plains.

Natural resources: Petroleum, fish, rock salt, marble, small deposits of coal, gold, lead, nickel, copper, and fertile soil.

Climate: Mostly desert type of climate.

People

Population: 20,727,063 (July 2005 est.).

Population growth rate: 3.45% (2005 est.).

Sex ratio: 1.04 male(s)/female (2005 est.).

Religions: Muslim including Shaf'i (Sunni) and Zaiydi (Shi'a), small numbers of Jew, Christian, and Hindu.

Literacy rate: Total 50.2%, Male 70.5%, Female 30% (2003 est.).

Infant mortality rate: 61.5 deaths/ 1,000 live births (2005 est.).

Life expectancy: Total 61.75 years, Male 59.89 years, Female 63.71 years (2005 est.).

Government

Capital: Sana'a.

Government type: Republic.

Independence: 22 May 1990. The merger of the Yemen Arab Republic and the Marxist-dominated People's Democratic Republic of Yemen created the Republic of Yemen.

Legal system: Based on Islamic law, Turkish law, English common law, and local tribal customary law.

Executive branch:

Chief of state: President Field Marshall Ali Abdallah Salih (since 22 May 1990, the former President of North Yemen. He assumed office following the merger of North and South Yemen). Vice-President Maj. Gen. Abd al-Rab Mansur al-Hadi (since 3 October 1994).

Head of government: Prime Minister Abd al-Qadir Ba Jamal (since 4 April 2001).

Economy

Currency: Yemeni rial.

Economy—overview:
Yemen reported strong growth in the mid-1990s largely due to oil production, but periodic fluctuations in oil prices have harmed the economy. Yemen has started out on an IMF-supported structural adjustment programme meant to modernize and streamline the economy. This has led to significant foreign debt relief and restructuring.

GDP: Purchasing power parity—$16.25 billion (2004 est.).

GDP—real growth rate: 1.9% (2004 est.).

GDP—per capita: Purchasing power parity—$800 (2004 est.).

Inflation rate: 12.2% (2004 est.).

Unemployment rate: 35% (2003 est.).

Exports: $4.468 billion f.o.b. (2004 est.)—crude oil, coffee, dried and salted fish.

Imports: $3.734 billion f.o.b. (2004 est.)—food and live animals, machinery and equipment, chemicals.

External debt: $5.4 billion (2004 est.).

Transport and Communications

Railways: None.

Roads: 67,000 km.

Telephones: 542,200 (2002).

Mobile cellular: 411,100 (2002).

Internet users: 100,000 (2003).

Internet country code: .ye

Zambia

History

In the 12th century, Shona people arrived in the area and established the empire of the Mwene Mutapa. In the 16th century, people from the Luba and Lunda empires of present day Democratic Republic of Congo arrived to set up small kingdoms. Portuguese explorers arrived in the late 18th century. British missionary David Livingstone came in 1851. In 1889, UK established control over the area (as Northern Rhodesia). It administered the area through a system of indirect rule that left power in the hands of local rulers. The Federation of Rhodesia and Nyasaland was created in 1953. It consisted of Northern Rhodesia, Southern Rhodesia (now Zimbabwe) and Nyasaland (now Malawi). The Federation was dissolved in 1963. Zambia gained independence in 1964 with Kenneth Kaunda as President. In the 1970s, Zambian support for the independence struggle in Rhodesia proved to be crucial to the creation of an independent Zimbabwe.

Geography

Location: Southern Africa, east of Angola.

Area: 752,614 sq. km.

Terrain: High plateau with some hills and mountains.

Natural resources: Copper, cobalt, zinc, lead, coal, emerald, gold, silver, uranium, hydropower.

Climate: Tropical climate with a rainy season from October to April.

People

Population: 11,261,795 (July 2005 est.).

Population growth rate: 2.12% (2005 est.).

Sex ratio: 0.99 male(s)/female (2005 est.).

Religions: Christian 50%–75%, Muslim and Hindu 24%–49%, indigenous beliefs 1%.

Languages: English (official), Bemba, Kaonda, Lozi, Lunda, Luvale, Nyanja, Tonga, about 70 other indigenous languages.

Literacy rate: Total 80.6%, Male 86.8%, Female 74.8% (2003 est.).

Infant mortality rate: 88.29 deaths/1,000 live births (2005 est.).

Life expectancy: Total 39.7 years, Male 39.43 years, Female 39.98 years (2005 est.).

Government

Capital: Lusaka.

Government type: Republic.

Independence: 24 October 1964 (from UK).

Legal system: Based on English common law and customary law.

Executive branch:
Chief of state: President Levy Mwanawasa (since 2 January 2002); Vice-President Nevers Mumba (since May 2003). The president is both the chief of state and head of government.

Economy

Currency: Zambian kwacha.

GDP: Purchasing power parity—$9.409 billion (2004 est.).

GDP—real growth rate: 4.6% (2004 est.).

GDP—per capita: Purchasing power parity—$900 (2004 est.).

Inflation rate: 18.3% (2004 est.).

Population below poverty line: 86% (1993).

Unemployment rate: 50% (2000 est.).

Exports: $1.548 billion f.o.b. (2004 est.)—copper, cobalt, electricity, tobacco, flowers, cotton.

Imports: $1.519 billion f.o.b. (2004 est.)—machinery, transportation equipment, petroleum products, electricity, fertilizer, foodstuff, clothing.

External debt: $5.353 billion (2004 est.).

Transport and Communications

Railways: 2,173 km.

Roads: 91,440 km.

Telephones: 88,400 (2003).

Mobile cellular: 241,000 (2003).

Internet users: 68,200 (2003).

Internet country code: .zm

Zimbabwe

History

Europeans arrived in the region in the 19th century. In 1889, Cecil Rhodes's British South Africa Company obtained a British mandate to colonize part of the region that subsequently became Southern Rhodesia. In 1922, British South Africa Company administration came to an end and the white minority opted for self-government. Meanwhile, black opposition to colonial rule grew and led to the emergence of two nationalist groups in the 1960s. These were the Zimbabwe African People's Union (ZAPU) and the Zimbabwe African National Union (ZANU).

In 1953, UK established the Central African Federation, consisting of Southern Rhodesia (Zimbabwe), Northern Rhodesia (Zambia) and Nyasaland (Malawi). However, the Federation disintegrated in 1963 when Zambia and Malawi became independent.

In 1964, Ian Smith of the Rhodesian Front (RF) became the prime minister. The following year, Smith unilaterally declared independence under white minority rule. This caused widespread international outrage and led to the imposition of economic sanctions. It also triggered guerrilla warfare against white rule that intensified in 1972 as the rival ZANU and ZAPU forces launched operations out of Zambia and Mozambique.

In 1979, British-brokered all-party talks in London led to a peace agreement and a new Constitution that guaranteed minority rights. In 1980, pro-independence leader Robert Mugabe and his ZANU party won British-supervised independence elections. Mugabe became prime minister. Zimbabwe finally gained independence on 18 April 1980.

Geography

Location: Southern Africa, between South Africa and Zambia.

Area: 390,580 sq. km.

Terrain: High plateau, with mountains in the east.

Natural resources: Coal, chromium ore, asbestos, gold, nickel, copper, iron ore, vanadium, lithium, tin, platinum group metals.

Climate: Tropical climate.

People

Population: 12,746,990 (July 2005 est.).

Population growth rate: 0.51% (2005 est.).

Sex ratio: 1.02 male(s)/female (2005 est.).

Religions: Syncretic (partly Christian, partly indigenous beliefs) 50%, Christian 25%, indigenous beliefs 24%, Muslim and others 1%.

Languages: English (official), Shona, Sindebele (the language of the Ndebele, sometimes called Ndebele), and many tribal dialects.

Literacy rate: Total 90.7%, Male 94.2%, Female 87.2% (2003 est.).

Infant mortality rate: 67.69 deaths/ 1,000 live births (2005 est.).

Life expectancy: Total 36.67 years, Male 37.21 years, Female 36.11 years (2005 est.).

Government

Capital: Harare.

Government type: Parliamentary democracy.

Independence: 18 April 1980 (from UK).

Legal system: Mixture of Roman–Dutch and English common law.

Executive branch:

Chief of state: Executive President Robert Gabriel Mugabe (since 31 December 1987). The president is both the chief of state and head of government.

Economy

Currency: Zimbabwean dollar.

GDP: Purchasing power parity—$24.37 billion (2004 est.).

GDP—real growth rate: −8.2% (2004 est.).

GDP—per capita: Purchasing power parity—$1,900 (2004 est.).

Inflation rate: 133% (2004 est.).

Population below poverty line: 70% (2002 est.).

Unemployment rate: 70% (2002 est.).

Exports: $1.409 billion f.o.b. (2004 est.)—tobacco, gold, ferro alloys, textiles/clothing.

Imports: $1.599 billion f.o.b. (2004 est.)—machinery and transport equipment, other manufactures, chemicals, fuels.

External debt: $4.086 billion (2004 est.).

Transport and Communications

Railways: 3,077 km.

Roads: 18,338 km.

Telephones: 300,900 (2003).

Mobile cellular: 379,100 (2003).

Internet users: 500,000 (2002).

Internet country code: .zw

Countries at a Glance

Country	Location	Capital	Currency
Afghanistan	Asia	Kabul	Afghani
Albania	Europe	Tirana	Lek
Algeria	Africa	Algiers	Algerian Dinar
Andorra	Europe	Andorra la Vella	Euro
Angola	Africa	Luanda	Kwanza
Antigua and Barbuda	Central America	Saint John's	East Caribbean Dollar
Argentina	South America	Buenos Aires	Argentine Peso
Armenia	Asia	Yerevan	Dram
Australia	Australia	Canberra	Australian Dollar
Austria	Europe	Vienna	Euro
Azerbaijan	Asia	Baku	Azerbaijani Manat
The Bahamas	Central America	Nassau	Bahamian Dollar
Bahrain	Asia	Manama	Bahraini Dinar
Bangladesh	Asia	Dhaka	Taka
Barbados	Central America	Bridgetown	Barbadian Dollar
Belarus	Europe	Minsk	Belarusian Ruble
Belgium	Europe	Brussels	Euro
Belize	Central America	Belmopan	Belizean Dollar
Benin	Africa	Porto Novo	CFA Franc
Bhutan	Asia	Thimphu	Ngultrum
Bolivia	South America	La Paz	Boliviano
Bosnia and Herzegovina	Europe	Sarajevo	Marka
Botswana	Africa	Gaborone	Pula
Brazil	South America	Brasilia	Real
Brunei	Asia	Bandar Seri Begawan	Bruneian Dollar
Bulgaria	Europe	Sofia	Lev
Burkina Faso	Africa	Ouagadougou	CFA Franc
Burundi	Africa	Bujumbura	Burundi Franc
Cambodia	Asia	Phnom Penh	Riel
Cameroon	Africa	Yaounde	CFA Franc
Canada	North America	Ottawa	Canadian Dollar
Cape Verde	Africa	Praia	Cape Verdean Escudo
Central African Republic	Africa	Bangui	CFA Franc
Chad	Africa	N'Djamena	CFA Franc
Chile	South America	Santiago	Chilean Peso
China	Asia	Beijing	Yuan
Colombia	South America	Bogota	Colombian Peso
Comoros	Africa	Moroni	Comoran Franc
Democratic Republic of the Congo	Africa	Kinshasa	Congolese Franc

Country	Location	Capital	Currency
Republic of the Congo	Africa	Brazzaville	CFA Franc
Costa Rica	Central America	San Jose	Costa Rican Colon
Cote d'Ivoire	Africa	Yamoussoukro	CFA Franc
Croatia	Europe	Zagreb	Kuna
Cuba	Central America	Havana	Cuban Peso
Cyprus	Europe	Nicosia	Cypriot Pound
Czech Republic	Europe	Prague	Czech Koruna
Denmark	Europe	Copenhagen	Danish Krone
Djibouti	Africa	Djibouti	Djiboutian Franc
Dominica	Central America	Roseau	East Caribbean Dollar
Dominican Republic	Central America	Santo Domingo	Dominican Peso
East Timor	Asia	Dili	US Dollar
Ecuador	South America	Quito	US Dollar
Egypt	Africa	Cairo	Egyptian Pound
El Salvador	South America	San Salvador	US Dollar
Equatorial Guinea	Africa	Malabo	CFA Franc
Eritrea	Africa	Asmara	Nakfa
Estonia	Europe	Tallinn	Estonian Kroon
Ethiopia	Africa	Addis Ababa	Birr
Fiji	Oceania	Suva	Fijian Dollar
Finland	Europe	Helsinki	Euro
France	Europe	Paris	Euro
Gabon	Africa	Libreville	CFA Franc
The Gambia	Africa	Banjul	Dalasi
Georgia	Asia	T'bilisi	Lari
Germany	Europe	Berlin	Euro
Ghana	Africa	Accra	Cedi
Greece	Europe	Athens	Euro
Grenada	Central America	Saint George's	East Caribbean Dollar
Guatemala	Central America	Guatemala City	Quetzal
Guinea	Africa	Conakry	Guinean Franc
Guinea-Bissau	Africa	Bissau	CFA Franc
Guyana	South America	Georgetown	Guyanese Dollar
Haiti	Central America	Port-au-Prince	Gourde
Honduras	Central America	Tegucigalpa	Lempira
Hungary	Europe	Budapest	Forint
Iceland	Europe	Reykjavik	Icelandic Krona
India	Asia	New Delhi	Rupee
Indonesia	Asia	Jakarta	Indonesian Rupiah
Iran	Asia	Tehran	Iranian Rial
Iraq	Asia	Baghdad	New Iraqi Dinar
Ireland	Europe	Dublin	Euro
Israel	Asia	Jerusalem	New Israeli Shekel
Italy	Europe	Rome	Euro
Jamaica	Central America	Kingston	Jamaican Dollar
Japan	Asia	Tokyo	Yen

Country	Location	Capital	Currency
Jordan	Asia	Amman	Jordanian Dinar
Kazakhstan	Asia	Astana	Tenge
Kenya	Africa	Nairobi	Kenyan Shilling
Kiribati	Oceania	Tarawa	Australian Dollar
Kuwait	Asia	Kuwait City	Kuwaiti Dinar
Kyrgyzstan	Asia	Bishkek	Kyrgyzstani Som
Laos	Asia	Vientiane	Kip
Latvia	Europe	Riga	Latvian Lat
Lebanon	Asia	Beirut	Lebanese Pound
Lesotho	Africa	Maseru	Loti
Liberia	Africa	Monrovia	Liberian Dollar
Libya	Africa	Tripoli	Libyan Dinar
Liechtenstein	Europe	Vaduz	Swiss Franc
Lithuania	Europe	Vilnius	Litas
Luxembourg	Europe	Luxembourg	Euro
Macedonia	Europe	Skopje	Macedonian Denar
Madagascar	Africa	Antananarivo	Malagasy Franc
Malawi	Africa	Lilongwe	Malawian Kwacha
Malaysia	Asia	Kuala Lumpur	Ringgit
Maldives	Asia	Male	Rufiyaa
Mali	Africa	Bamako	CFA Franc
Malta	Europe	Valletta	Maltese Lira
Marshall Islands	Oceania	Majuro	US Dollar
Mauritania	Africa	Nouakchott	Ouguiya
Mauritius	Africa	Port Louis	Mauritian Rupee
Mexico	North America	Mexico City	Mexican Peso
Federated States of Micronesia	Oceania	Palikir	US Dollar
Moldova	Europe	Chisinau	Moldovan Leu
Monaco	Europe	Monaco	Euro
Mongolia	Asia	Ulaanbaatar	Togrog
Morocco	Africa	Rabat	Moroccan Dirham
Mozambique	Africa	Maputo	Metical
Myanmar	Asia	Yangon	Kyat
Namibia	Africa	Windhoek	Namibian Dollar
Nauru	Oceania		Australian Dollar
Nepal	Asia	Kathmandu	Nepalese Rupee
The Netherlands	Europe	Amsterdam	Euro
New Zealand	Oceania	Wellington	New Zealand Dollar
Nicaragua	Central America	Managua	Gold Cordoba
Niger	Africa	Niamey	CFA Franc
Nigeria	Africa	Abuja	Naira
North Korea	Asia	Pyongyang	Won
Norway	Europe	Oslo	Norwegian Krone
Oman	Asia	Muscat	Omani Rial
Pakistan	Asia	Islamabad	Pakistani Rupee

Country	Location	Capital	Currency
Palau	Oceania	Koror	US Dollar
Panama	Central America	Panama City	Balboa
Papua New Guinea	Oceania	Port Moresby	Kina
Paraguay	South America	Asuncion	Guarani
Peru	South America	Lima	Nuevo Sol
The Philippines	Asia	Manila	Philippine Peso
Poland	Europe	Warsaw	Zloty
Portugal	Europe	Lisbon	Euro
Qatar	Asia	Doha	Qatari Rial
Romania	Europe	Bucharest	Leu
Russia	Europe/Asia	Moscow	Rouble
Rwanda	Africa	Kigali	Rwandan Franc
Saint Kitts and Nevis	Central America	Basseterre	East Caribbean Dollar
Saint Lucia	Central America	Castries	East Caribbean Dollar
Saint Vincent and the Grenadines	Central America	Kingstown	East Caribbean Dollar
Samoa	Oceania	Apia	Tala
San Marino	Europe	San Marino	Euro
Sao Tome and Principe	Africa	Sao Tome	Dobra
Saudi Arabia	Asia	Riyadh	Saudi Riyal
Senegal	Africa	Dakar	CFA Franc
Serbia and Montenegro	Europe	Belgrade	New Yugoslav Dinar
Seychelles	Africa	Victoria	Seychelles Rupee
Sierra Leone	Africa	Freetown	Leone
Singapore	Asia	Singapore	Singapore Dollar
Slovakia	Europe	Bratislava	Slovak Koruna
Slovenia	Europe	Ljubljana	Tolar
Solomon Islands	Oceania	Honiara	Solomon Islands Dollar
Somalia	Africa	Mogadishu	Somali Shilling
South Africa	Africa	Pretoria	Rand
South Korea	Asia	Seoul	Won
Spain	Europe	Madrid	Euro
Sri Lanka	Asia	Colombo	Sri Lankan Rupee
Sudan	Africa	Khartoum	Sudanese Dinar
Suriname	South America	Paramaribo	Surinamese Guilder
Swaziland	Africa	Mbabane	Lilangeni
Sweden	Europe	Stockholm	Swedish Krona
Switzerland	Europe	Berne	Swiss Franc
Syria	Asia	Damascus	Syrian Pound
Tajikistan	Asia	Dushanbe	Somoni
Tanzania	Africa	Dar es Salaam	Tanzanian Shilling
Thailand	Asia	Bangkok	Baht
Togo	Africa	Lome	CFA Franc
Tonga	Oceania	Nuku'alofa	Pa'anga

Country	Location	Capital	Currency
Trinidad and Tobago	Central America	Port of Spain	Trinidad and Tobago Dollar
Tunisia	Africa	Tunis	Tunisian Dinar
Turkey	Asia/Europe	Ankara	Turkish Lira
Turkmenistan	Asia	Ashgabat	Turkmen Manat
Tuvalu	Oceania	Funafuti	Australian Dollar
Uganda	Africa	Kampala	Ugandan Shilling
Ukraine	Europe	Kiev	Hryvnia
United Arab Emirates	Asia	Abu Dhabi	Dirham
United Kingdom	Europe	London	British Pound
United States of America	North America	Washington DC	US Dollar
Uruguay	South America	Montevideo	Uruguayan Peso
Uzbekistan	Asia	Tashkent	Uzbekistani Sum
Vanuatu	Oceania	Port Vila	Vatu
Vatican City	Europe	Vatican City	Euro
Venezuela	South America	Caracas	Bolivar
Vietnam	Asia	Hanoi	Dong
Yemen	Asia	Sana'a	Yemeni Rial
Zambia	Africa	Lusaka	Zambian Kwacha
Zimbabwe	Africa	Harare	Zimbabwean Dollar

India

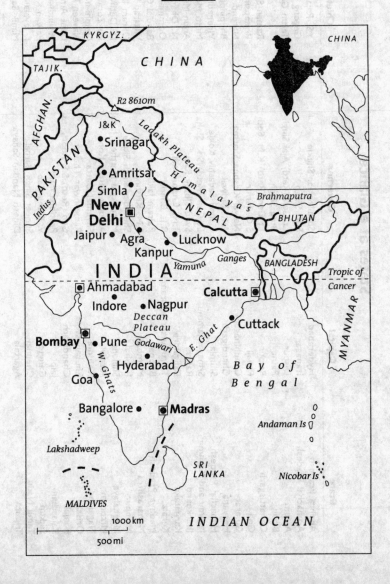

States at a Glance

State	Capital	Governor	Chief Minister
Andhra Pradesh	Hyderabad	Sushilkumar Shinde	Y.S. Rajasekhar Reddy
Arunachal Pradesh	Itanagar	S.K. Singh	Gegong Apang
Assam	Dispur	Lt Gen (Retd) Ajai Singh	Tarun Gogoi
Bihar	Patna	Buta Singh	
Chhattisgarh	Raipur	Lt Gen (Retd) K.M. Seth	Raman Singh
Goa	Panaji	S.C. Jamir	Pratapsingh Rane
Gujarat	Gandhinagar	Nawal Krishna Sharma	Narendra Modi
Haryana	Chandigarh	A.R. Kidwai	Bhupinder Singh Hooda
Himachal Pradesh	Shimla	Vishnu Sadashiv Kokje	Virbhadra Singh
Jammu and Kashmir	Srinagar/Jammu	Lt Gen (Retd) S.K. Sinha	Mufti Mohammed Sayeed
Jharkhand	Ranchi	Syed Sibtey Razi	Arjun Munda
Karnataka	Bangalore	T.N. Chaturvedi	N. Dharam Singh
Kerala	Thiruvananthapuram	R.L. Bhatia	Oommen Chandy
Madhya Pradesh	Bhopal	Balram Jakhar	Babulal Gour
Maharashtra	Mumbai	S.M. Krishna	Vilasrao Deshmukh
Manipur	Imphal	Shivinder Singh Sidhu	Okram Ibobi Singh
Meghalaya	Shillong	Mundakkal Matthew Jacob	D. Dethwelson Lapang
Mizoram	Aizawl	Amolak Rattan Kohli	Pu Zoramthanga
Nagaland	Kohima	Shyamal Datta	Neiphi-u Rio
Orissa	Bhubaneswar	Rameshwar Thakur	Naveen Patnaik
Punjab	Chandigarh	Gen (Retd) S.F. Rodrigues	Capt Amarinder Singh
Rajasthan	Jaipur	Pratibha Patil	Vasundhara Raje Scindia
Sikkim	Gangtok	V. Rama Rao	Pawan Kumar Chamling
Tamil Nadu	Chennai	Surjeet Singh Barnala	J. Jayalalithaa
Tripura	Agartala	Dinesh Nandan Sahaya	Manik Sarkar

State	Capital	Governor	Chief Minister
Uttaranchal	Dehradun	Sudarshan Agarwal	N.D. Tiwari
Uttar Pradesh	Lucknow	T.V. Rajeswar	Mulayam Singh Yadav
West Bengal	Kolkata	Gopalkrishna Gandhi	Buddhadeb Bhattacharya

National Capital Territory

		Lt Governor	**Chief Minister**
Delhi	Delhi	Banwari Lal Joshi	Sheila Dikshit

Union Territory

		Lt Governor/Administrator	
Andaman and Nicobar	Port Blair	Ramchandra Ganesh Kapse	
Chandigarh	Chandigarh	Gen (Retd) S.F. Rodrigues	
Dadra and Nagar Haveli	Silvassa	Arun Mathur	
Daman and Diu	Daman	Arun Mathur	
Lakshadweep	Kavaratti	Parimal Rai	
Pondicherry	Pondicherry	Lt Gen (Retd) M.M. Lakhera	Thiru N. Rangasamy

States

Between 26 January 1950 and 1 November 1956 there were four types of divisions in India: states (governor as head), states (under a rajpramukh), states (under a chief commissioner), and one territory; from 1956 there were only states and union territories. Currently, there are 28 states with Rajasthan being the largest and Goa the smallest in area.

Andhra Pradesh

Key Statistics

Capital: Hyderabad.
Area: 276,754 sq. km.
Population: Total: 76,210,007, Male: 38,527,413, Female: 37,682,594.
Population density: 275 per sq. km.
Sex ratio: 978 females per 1000 males.
Principal languages: Telugu, Urdu, Hindi.
Literacy rates: Total: 60.5%, Male: 70.3%, Female: 50.4%.

Government

Governor: Sushilkumar Shinde. He assumed office on 1 November 2004.

Chief Minister: Y.S. Rajasekhar Reddy (INC). He was sworn in on 14 May 2004.

Geography

Physical characteristics: Andhra Pradesh has three main physiographic regions: a coastal plain lying in the eastern part of the state, the Eastern Ghats, which form the western flank of the coastal plain, and a plateau west of the Eastern Ghats. The coastal plain extends from the Bay of Bengal to the mountain ranges and runs nearly the entire length of Andhra Pradesh. A number of rivers flow across the coastal plain, through the hills into the bay, from west to east. The Krishna and the Godavari Deltas form the central part of the plains. The Eastern Ghats are broken up by the numerous river valleys and do not form a continuous range in Andhra Pradesh. They are a part of the larger mountain system that extends from central India to the south, lying parallel to the east coast. The plateau region to the west of the ranges has an average elevation of 500 metres above sea level.

Neighbouring States and Union territories:
States: Chhattisgarh, Karnataka, Maharashtra, Orissa, Tamil Nadu.

Union territories: Pondicherry.

Major rivers: The most important rivers of the state include Krishna, Godavari, Musi, Penneru and Tungabhadra.

Climate: In Andhra Pradesh, the summer is from March to June, the rainy season from July to September and the winter from October to February. Maximum and minimum temperatures in most parts of the state range from 23°C to 28°C and from 10°C to 12°C respectively. The coastal plain region experiences very warm summers with temperatures rising to 42°C in some places. Summers are cooler and winters colder still in the plateau region. Rainfall is largely due to the south-west monsoon winds and some places receive a maximum of 1,400mm of rain while other parts get less than half of that. Rainfall is heavier in the coastal areas but scanty in the northern and western parts of the plateau.

Flora and Fauna:

Flora: Forests occupy nearly 63,000 sq. km. in the state. Mangrove swamps and palm trees are found in the coastal plain. Cultivation of food crops, fruits, and tobacco are carried out in the deltas. Thorny vegetation is found on the hills of the plateau region. The forests in the state consist of both moist deciduous and dry savanna vegetation. Plants like teak, bamboo, rosewood, and those bearing wild fruits are found. Cashew is grown in the coastal districts. Common trees found in the state include the banyan, mango, neem and pipal and flowering plants like rose and jasmine.

Fauna: Tigers, leopards, bears and deer are found in the hills and forest areas of the state.

History

Although references to people called 'Andhras', who lived south of the central Indian mountain ranges, can be found in Sanskrit writings dating back to about 1000 BC, the earliest definitive historical evidence of the Andhras dates only from the times of the Mauryan dynasty, around the third century BC. Emperor Asoka had sent Buddhist missions to the Andhras. Around the first century AD, the Satakarnis (or the Satavahanas) came to power. They were one of the most well known Andhra dynasties and ruled over almost the entire Deccan Plateau. They even established trade relations with Rome. In the eleventh century, large expanses of Andhra were united under the reign of the eastern Chalukyas. The Kakatiya dynasty of Warangal spread Andhra power in the twelfth and thirteenth centuries. Their regime witnessed the rise of the Andhras as a commercial power to parts of South-East Asia. Muslim invasion of south India led to the downfall of Warangal in 1323. However, the rise of the kingdom of Vijayanagar to the south-west of Warangal prevented Muslim domination to some extent. The Vijayanagar kingdom is often regarded as the greatest kingdom in Andhra history. Its greatest ruler was Krishna Deva Raya who reigned from 1509 to 1529. However, the glory of the Vijayanagar kingdom came to an end when it succumbed to an alliance of the neighbouring Muslim states in 1565.

In 1687, the Mughal emperor Aurangzeb invaded Golconda and annexed it to the Mughal Empire. The Mughals appointed 'Nazims' as agents of the Mughal emperor. For about thirty-five years the Nazims ruled the area. Then came the Asaf Jahi Nizams.

When the Europeans arrived in India and gained power, the Nizams of Hyderabad sought their help against their rivals. In this process, they acquired French and later British support. In exchange, the British acquired vast stretches of land from the Nizams. Over a period of time the British gained control over most parts of Andhra territory and only parts of the Telugu-speaking areas, the Telangana region, remained with the Nizams. Even the French acquired a few towns.

At the time of Independence in 1947, the Nizams held sway over Hyderabad and desired to gain independence. Hyderabad was then one of the most prosperous of the princely states and had substantial armed forces. For this purpose, Nizam Osman Ali enlisted the help of Kasim Razvi of the Ittehadul Muslimeen and its private army, the Razakars. Even as the Hindus of the state campaigned to join India, the Nizam banned the Congress party in the state. As 15 August 1947 approached, negotiations between India and the Nizam reached a stalemate as Osman Ali refused to join India. Meanwhile, the Nizam's police, the Razakars and the supporters of the Nizam perpetrated a reign of terror in the state. On 29 November 1947, Hyderabad signed a Stand Still Agreement with India. It established a period of status quo. Hyderabad was allowed to maintain the status that existed between the British and the Nizam before 15 August 1947. The Nizam sent representations to other nations to seek their support and even approached the United Nations Security Council.

The Indian armed forces launched Operation Polo on 13 September 1948. It ended just over 100 hours later, when the Nizam asked his forces to cease fire, allowed Union troops into the Hyderabad territories and banned the Razakars. On 18 September, the Hyderabad Army surrendered and Major General J.N. Chaudhuri of the Indian Amy was appointed Military Governor of the state. The merger of Hyderabad state with the Indian Dominion followed. In January 1950, M.K. Vellodi, a Senior Civil Servant, was appointed the Chief Minister of the State. The first General Elections were held in 1952 and B. Rama Krishna Rao became the first popularly elected Chief Minister.

Meanwhile, the demand for a separate Andhra state gained momentum. To complicate matters, a local Gandhian leader, Potti Sreeramulu, fasted to death in 1953. On 1 October 1953, the Andhra state, which included the Telugu-speaking districts of the former Madras state, was formed with its capital at Kurnool. Andhra Pradesh was formed on 1 November 1956 when the erstwhile state of Hyderabad was split up and its Telugu-speaking districts were joined to the Andhra state. Neelam Sanjiva Reddy was the first Chief Minister of Andhra Pradesh.

In 1960, 221.4 square miles in the Chingleput and Salem districts of Madras state were transferred to Andhra Pradesh in exchange for 410 square miles from Chittoor district.

Politics

The Andhras had long cherished a demand for the formation of Visalandhra, which would incorporate the outlying Telugu-speaking areas of Orissa, Madhya Pradesh, Mysore and Madras into a greater Andhra state. However, the States Reorganisation Committee, set up by the Government of India in 1953, favoured the formation of a separate state for Telangana. The Congress High Command favoured Visalandhra and prevailed upon the Andhra and Telangana lobbies to sort out their differences. The two parties entered into a 'Gentlemen's Agreement', one of the provisions of which was the creation of a Regional Council for the all-round development of Telangana. Consequent to this, the enlarged state of Andhra Pradesh was formed in 1956, merging nine Telugu-speaking districts with eleven districts of the Andhra state.

During the years 1969 and 1972, Andhra Pradesh was rocked by two political agitations popularly known as the Telangana movement and the Jai Andhra movement. The Telangana agitation was started by the people of the region when they felt that the Andhra leaders had flouted the Gentlemen's Agreement which facilitated the formation of Andhra Pradesh. The agitation took a new turn when Congress legislators from Telangana supported the movement. Dr Channa Reddy formed the Telangana Praja Samity to lead the movement. But the movement petered out after it became clear that Prime Minister Indira Gandhi was not in favour of a separate Telangana state. In September 1971, Brahmanand Reddy, the then chief minister, resigned to make room for a leader from Telangana to become chief minister. P.V. Narasimha Rao became the new chief minister.

The Jai Andhra movement was a sequel to the Telangana agitation, and demanded that only 'Mulkis' should be appointed to posts in Telangana including Hyderabad city.

'Mulki' was defined as one who was born in the State of Hyderabad or resided there continuously for fifteen years and had given an affidavit that he abandoned the idea of returning to his native place. Even after the formation of Andhra Pradesh, the Mulki rules continued to be in force in the Telangana region. As these rules stood in the way of the people of the Andhra region to compete for the posts, their validity was challenged in the High Court. A full bench of the High Court by a four-one majority held that the Mulki rules were not valid and operative after the formation of Andhra Pradesh. But on an appeal by the state government, the Supreme Court declared on 3 October 1972 that the Mulki rules were valid and were in force. The judgment created a great political crisis in the state. The people of the Andhra region felt that they were reduced to the status of second class citizens in their own state capital. They felt that the only way to uphold their dignity was by severing their connection with Telangana and started a movement for the separation of the Andhra region from Andhra Pradesh. As the agitation continued, President's Rule was imposed in the state on 10 January 1973. Finally, a political settlement was arrived at under the aegis of the Central government. On 10 December 1973, President's Rule in the state was revoked and a popular ministry with Jalagam Vengala Rao as the chief minister was inducted.

N.T.Rama Rao, a leading figure of the film world, formed a regional party called 'Telugu Desam' in January 1983 and contested the elections to the Andhra Pradesh Legislative Assembly held in 1983. His party became victorious and Rama Rao was sworn in as the tenth chief minister of the state. But on 16 August 1984, Nadendla Bhaskara Rao, a cabinet colleague of Rama Rao, succeeded in becoming the chief minister by engineering the dismissal of Rama Rao by the Governor. However, Rama Rao was reinstated on 16 September 1984 consequent on the severe criticism on the action of Governor. In the elections of March 1985, Rama Rao proved that he continued to enjoy the confidence of the people by winning an absolute majority in the House.

The Congress returned to power in 1989 with a good majority. During the following five years, three chief ministers, Dr M.Channa Reddy, N.Janardhana Reddy and K.Vijaya Bhaskara Reddy held the reins of power. The discontentment of the Telugu public was reflected in pushing the Congress out and handing over the power again to the Telugu Desam Party in 1994. In 1995 N.T.Rama Rao was succeeded by N.Chandrababu Naidu of the same party. In May 2004 the Congress won the Assembly elections and Y.S. Rajashekhara Reddy was sworn in as the chief minister.

Culture

One of the six classical dance forms of India, Kuchipudi, is indigenous to Andhra Pradesh. The state is also well known for its banjara embroidery, bidri metalwork, Budithi metalwork and Dokra metal craft. Nirmal in Adilabad district is famous for its Nakash craftsmen, who specialize in painting scenes from the *Mahabharata* and the *Ramayana*. The state is also known for its Ikat textiles. Besides these, Andhra Pradesh is also reputed for its wood and stone carvings, kalamkari fabrics, puppets, toys, dolls and filigree work.

Fairs and festivals: Hindu festivals such as Dasara, Deepavali, Sri Ramanavami, Krishna Janmastami, Vinayaka Chavithi (Ganesh Chaturthi) and Maha Sivarathri are celebrated in the state. But the celebrations of Ugadi

(Telugu New Year's day), Sankranti, Dasara and Vinayaka Chavithi in the state are unique.

Economy, Industry and Agriculture

Economy: The net state domestic product at current prices for 2002–03 (provisional) was Rs 143,975 crores. The per capita net state domestic product at current prices for 2002–03 (provisional) was Rs 18,661.

Minerals and industry: The significant industries of the state include IT industry, auto-component manufacturing, chemical synthesis and process engineering, and horticulture. Smaller industries that have developed in the state from locally available agricultural raw materials include rice flour, rice-bran oil, soaps and detergents, cardboard and other packaging materials, paints and varnishes, and cattle feed.

Minerals found in the state include oil and natural gas, coal, limestone, iron ore, manganese, gold, diamonds, asbestos, ball clay, fire clay, graphite, dolomite, quartz, tungsten, feldspar and silica sand. Much of the state's mineral resources remain unexploited.

Agriculture: Production of food grains dominates agriculture in Andhra Pradesh and forms the mainstay of the state's economy. The state is one of the leading producers of rice and tobacco in the country. Sugarcane is also produced in the state. Other agricultural commodities now grown in different parts of Andhra Pradesh include pulses (peas, beans and lentils), chili peppers, castor beans, sorghum, groundnut and cotton, as well as fruits like mangoes, grapes, bananas and oranges.

Power: Andhra Pradesh has one of the highest installed power capacities in the country.

Education

Prominent educational institutions of Andhra Pradesh include the Andhra University (Vishakhapatnam), Central Institute of English and Foreign Languages (Hyderabad), Dr B.R. Ambedkar Open University (Hyderabad), Dravidian University (Chitoor), University of Hyderabad (Hyderabad) , Jawaharlal Nehru Technological University (Hyderabad), Kakatiya University (Warangal), Maulana Azad National Urdu University (Hyderabad), Nagarjuna University (Guntur), Nizam's Institute of Medical Sciences (Hyderabad), N.T.R. University of Health Sciences (Vijayawada), Osmania University (Hyderabad), Potti Sreeramulu Telugu University (Hyderabad), Rashtriya Sanskrit Vidyapeetha (Tirupati), Sri Krishnadevaraya University (Anantapur), Sri Sathya Sai Institute of Higher Learning (Prasanthinilayam), Sri Padmavati Mahila Visvavidyalayam (Tirupati) and Sri Vinkateswara Institute of Medical Sciences (Tirupati).

Tourism

Major tourist attractions:

1. Hyderabad: Charminar, Salarjung Museum, Hussein Sagar Lake, Durgam Ceruvu (Secret Lake), Shamirpet Lake, Qutb Shahi Tombs, Statue of Lord Buddha in Hussein Sagar Lake, Golconda Fort.

2. Tirupati: Lord Venkateswara Temple, Sri Agastheswara Swamy Temple, Govindarajaswami Temple, Goddess Alamelumanga Temple, Kodandarama Swamy Temple.

3. Vishakhapatnam: Simhachalam Temple, Rishikonda Beach, Dolphin's Nose.

4. Chittor: Horsley Hills, Chandragiri Fort, Lord Venkateswara Temple, Sri Venkateswara Sanctuary, Govindarajaswami Temple.

5. Cuddapah: Bhagavan Mahavir Government Museum, Chand Phira Gumbadh, Gandikota Fort.

6. Vijayawada: Prakasam Barrage, Kanakadurga Temple, St. Mary's Church, Moghalrajapuram caves, Hazrat Bal Mosque, Kondapalli Fort, Victoria Jubilee Museum.

Airports:

International: Hyderabad.

Domestic: Rajahmundry, Tirupati, Vijaywada, Vishakhapatnam, Warangal, Cuddapah, Donakonda and Nadrigul.

National Parks: Kasu Brahma Reddy National Park in Hyderabad district (1.42 sq. kms), Mahavir Harina Vanasthal National Park in Rangareddi district (14.59 sq. kms), Mrugavani National Park in Rangareddi district (3.6 sq. kms), Sri Venkateshwara National Park in Chittoor and Cuddapah districts (353.62 sq. kms).

Administration

Legislature: Andhra Pradesh has a unicameral legislature with only the legislative assembly. The assembly has 295 seats including 39 seats reserved for SCs, 15 seats reserved for STs and one member who is nominated from the Anglo-Indian community.

The current party position is as follows:

Name of Party	Seats
Indian National Congress	185
Telugu Desam Party	47
Telangana Rashtra Samithi	26
Communist Party of India (Marxist)	9
Communist Party of India	6
All India Majlis-E-Ittehadul Muslimeen	4
Bharatiya Janata Party	2
Janata Party	2
Bahujan Samaj Party	1
Samajwadi Party	1
Independent	11
Nominated	1
Total	**295**

Judiciary: The seat of the Andhra Pradesh High Court is in Hyderabad. The present acting Chief Justice is Bilal Nazki.

Districts:

District	Area (sq. km)	Population	Headquarters	Urban Agglomerations
Adilabad	16128	2,479,347	Adilabad	Adilabad
Anantapur	19130	3,639,304	Anantapur	Anantapur
Chittoor	15151	3,735,202	Chittoor	Madanapalle, Tirupati
Cuddapah	15359	2,573,481	Cuddapah	Cuddapah
East Godavari	10807	4,872,622	Kakinada	Kakinada, Rajahmundry
Guntur	11391	4,405,521	Guntur	Narasaraopet
Hyderabad	217	3,686,460	Hyderabad	Hyderabad
Karimnagar	11823	3,477,079	Karimnagar	Ramagundam, Karimnagar
Khammam	16029	2,565,412	Khammam	Kothagudem, Khammam
Krishna	8727	4,218,416	Machilipatnam	Vijayawada
Kurnool	17658	3,512,266	Kurnool	Adoni, Kurnool, Nandyal
Mahbubnagar	18432	3,506,876	Mahbubnagar	Mahbubnagar, Gadwal
Medak	9700	2,662,296	Sangareddy	
Nalgonda	14240	3,238,449	Nalgonda	Miryalguda, Nalgonda, Suryapet
Nellore	13076	2,659,661	Nellore	Guduru, Kavali, Nellore
Nizamabad	7956	2,342,803	Nizamabad	

Prakasam	17626	3,054,941	Ongole	Chirala, Ongole
Rangareddi	7493	3,506,670	Hyderabad	Hyderabad
Srikakulam	5837	2,528,491	Srikakulam	Srikakulam
Visakhapatnam	11161	3,789,823	Visakhapatnam	Bheemunipatnam, Visakhapatnam
Vizianagaram	6539	2,245,103	Vizianagaram	Vizianagaram
Warangal	12847	3,231,174	Warangal	Warangal
West Godavari	7742	3,796,144	Eluru	Palacole, Tanuku, Eluru, Bheemavaram

Arunachal Pradesh

Key Statistics

Capital: Itanagar.

Area: 83,743 sq. km.

Population: Total: 1,097,968, Male: 579,941, Female: 518,027.

Population density: 13 per sq. km.

Sex ratio: 893 females per 1000 males.

Principal languages: Nissi/Daffla, Nepali, Bengali.

Literacy rates: Total: 54.3%, Male: 63.8%, Female: 43.5%.

Government

Governor: S.K. Singh. He was sworn in on 16 December 2004.

Chief Minister: Gegong Apang (INC). He was sworn in on 16 October 2004.

Geography

Physical characteristics: Arunachal Pradesh is a land of lush green forests, deep river valleys and plateaus. The land is mostly mountainous with the Himalayan ranges lying along the northern borders criss-crossed with north-south running ranges. These divide the state into five river valleys: the Kameng, the Subansiri, the Siang, the Lohit and the Tirap. A series of foothills lie in the southernmost part of the state, rising from the Assam plains to touch altitudes of 300 to 1000 metres. These hills rise northward to the Lesser Himalayas to reach heights of more than 3000 metres. The main ranges of the Great Himalayas lie further north along the Chinese border.

Neighbouring States and Union territories:

International borders: Bhutan, China, Myanmar.

States: Assam, Nagaland.

Major rivers: The Brahmaputra, known as the Siang in Arunchal Pradesh, and its tributaries which include the Lohit, Subansiri, Dibang, Kameng, Tirap, Kamla, Siyum, Noa-Dihing and Kamlang.

Climate: The climate of Arunachal Pradesh varies from subtropical in the south to alpine in the north. Arunachal Pradesh receives heavy rainfall varying from 1000mm in the higher altitudes to 5750mm in the foothills. Average rainfall is more than 3500mm. It is spread over eight to nine months with the exception of a dry period in winter. The average temperature ranges from 15 to 21°C during winter and 22 to 30°C during monsoon. Between June and August the temperature sometimes rises to 40–42°C (in some regions).

Flora and Fauna:

Flora: Almost 60 per cent of the state is covered with evergreen forests. Arunachal Pradesh has seven types of forests. These are: tropical, subtropical, pine, temperate, alpine, bamboo and degraded forests. Besides these forests, there are grasslands in the riverine plains and higher altitudes.

The state is home to a variety of timber species, orchids, oaks, rhododendrons, medicinal plants, ferns, bamboos and canes.

Fauna: Arunachal Pradesh has a rich wildlife population. It is home to the mithun, elephant, tiger, leopard, snow leopard, clouded leopard, white browed gibbon, red panthers, musk deer, gaur and wild buffalo. The species of primates found in the state include slow loris, hoolock gibbon, rhesus macaque, pigtailed macaque, Assamese macaque, stump-tailed macaque, and capped langur. Three species of goat-antelopes, serow, goral and takin, are found in the state. Significant species of birds found in the state are hornbill, Sclater's monal, white winged duck, Bengal florican, Temminck's tragopan and green pigeon.

History

The history of Arunachal Pradesh is rich in myths and traditions. The recorded history of this state is available only from the sixteenth century onwards. It was at this point of time that the Ahom kings began to rule Assam. The modern history of the state begins with the imposition of British rule in Assam following the Treaty of Yandaboo (1826). Between 1947 and 1962, it was a part of the North East Frontier Agency that was constitutionally a part of Assam. Because of its strategic importance, the ministry of external affairs administered Arunachal Pradesh till 1965, with the governor of Assam acting as an agent to the President of India. The administrative head was the advisor to the governor. Later, in August 1965, the ministry of home affairs gained administrative control. In 1972, it became a Union territory under the name of Arunachal Pradesh. In 1975, it got its own legislature. Arunachal Pradesh attained full-fledged statehood on 20 February 1987. At that time, Gegong Apang was its Chief Minister.

Politics

Though the history of the political process in Arunachal Pradesh dates back to 1875 when the British-India government started to define the administrative jurisdiction by drawing an Inner Line in relation to the frontier tribes inhabiting the North Frontier Tract, the area was kept outside the purview of regular laws of the country. Thereafter, the British followed the policy of gradual penetration to bring more areas under normal administration. By the year 1946, the North East Frontier Tracts were reorganized into four Frontier Tracts namely Sadiya, Lakhimpur, Tirap and Sela Sub Agency and Subansiri, and administrated by the Governor of Assam in his discretion. The government of Assam administered the North East Frontier Tracts during the period 15 August 1947 to 26 January 1950. In 1950, Frontier Tract, Tirap Frontier Tract, Abor Hill District and Mishimi Hills Districts were transferred to the government of Assam. In 1951, the units of the tracts were reconstituted again and Tuensang Frontier Division was created, which later merged with Nagaland. The remaining portion of the Tracts after the introduction of the North East Frontier (Administration) Regulation 1954 was designated as the North East Frontier Agency, the NEFA. Thereafter, the administration was brought under the Ministry of External Affairs and in August 1965, it was brought under the supervision and control of the Ministry of Home Affairs. It remained so till the attainment of union territory status by Arunachal Pradesh in 1972. It was only in 1975 that by virtue of the enactment of 37th Constitutional Amendment Act that the Pradesh Council was constituted as a separate Legislative Assembly. In November 1979, the Assembly was dissolved and President's Rule was imposed which continued till January 1980. On 18 January 1980 Gegong Apang became the chief minister. He was the chief minister for a record nineteen years. The union territory of Arunachal Pradesh became a full-fledged state with effect from 20 February 1987.

Culture

The various tribes of Arunachal Pradesh have their own dance forms. Some of the more popular folk dances include Roppi (Nishing Tribe), Aji Lamu (Monpa), Hiirii Khaniing (Apatani), Chalo (Nocte), Lion and Peacock dance (Monpa), Ponung (Adi), Popir (Adi), Pasi Kongki (Adi) and Rekham Pada (Nishing). Most of the dance forms of the state are group dances performed by both men and women. However there are some dance forms, such as the war dances of the Adis, Noctes and Wanchos, Igu dance of the Mishmi priests and ritualistic dance of the Buddhist tribes, that are exclusive male dances. The state has a notable tradition of bamboo and cane handicrafts, as well as pottery, carpet weaving and woodcarving. Handloom is a significant aspect of the state's culture and tradition.

Fairs and festivals: Important festivals of the state include Lossar, Si-Donyi, Mopin, Solung, Nyokum, Dree, Sipong Yong, Reh, Boori-boot, Kshyatsowai, Tamladu, Sarok, Chalo-loku, Nichido, Sangken, Mopin and Oriah. Parashuram Kund Mela (Parashuram Kund) and Malinithan Mela (Likabali) are two notable fairs of the state.

Economy, Industry and Agriculture

Economy: The net state domestic product at current prices for 2002–03 (provisional) was Rs 1747 crores. The per capita net state domestic product at current prices for 2002–03 (provisional) was Rs 15,616.

Minerals and industry: Notable among the industries of the state are timber-based industries, tourism, tea-based industries, coal mines and fruit processing plants.

Coal reserves at the Namchik-Namphuk coalfield are estimated at 90 million tonnes. Petroleum crude reserves are estimated at 1.5 million tonnes. Besides these, there are reported deposits of iron, copper, limestone, graphite, dolomite, quartzite, kyanite and mica.

Agriculture: The major crops grown in the state are rice, maize, millet, wheat, pulses and sugarcane. There are rubber, coffee and tea plantations. The state also grows banana, ginger, chillies, turmeric, pineapple, plum, orange, apple, walnut, guava, grapes and potato.

Power: Most of the state's power requirements are met by hydroelectric power plants. As a matter of fact, the hydel power potential of Arunachal Pradesh is estimated at 30,000 MW. There are a large number of mini and micro hydel power plants in the state. A certain amount of the state's power needs are met by diesel power plants.

Education

Educational institutes: Arunachal University (Itanagar), North Eastern Regional Institute of Science and Technology (Itanagar).

Tourism

Major tourist attractions: Tawang Monastery, Bhismaknagar, Malinithan, Parashuram Kund, Tipi Orchid Research Centre, Akashiganga, Gekar Sinyi (Ganaga lake), Talley Valley, Dr D. Ering Wildlife Sanctuary, Bomdila.

Airports: Along, Daporijo, Pasighat, Teju, Ziro.

National Parks: Mouling National Park in Upper Siang district (483 sq. km) and Namdapha National Park in Changlang district (1985.23 sq. km).

Administration

Legislature: The state has a 60-seat legislative assembly, out of which 59 are reserved for STs. Elections were held in October 2004. The current party position is:

Name of Party	Seats
Indian National Congress	34
Bharatiya Janata Party	9
Nationalist Congress Party	2
Arunanchal Congress	2
Independent	13
Total	**60**

Judiciary: Arunachal Pradesh is under the jurisdiction of the Itanagar Bench of the Gauhati High Court at Guwahati, Assam. Binod Kumar Roy is the current chief justice.

Districts:

District	Area (sq. km)	Population	Headquarters	Urban Agglomerations
Changlang	4,662	124,994	Changlang	–
Dibang Valley	1,302	57,543	Anini	–
East Kameng	4,134	57,065	Seppa	–
East Siang	3,895	87,430	Pasighat	–
Kurung Kumey	NA	NA	Laying-Yangte	–
Lohit	11,402	143,478	Teju	–
Lower Subansiri	9,548	97,614	Ziro	–
Papum Pare	3,462	121,750	Yupia	–
Tawang	2,172	34,705	Tawang	–
Tirap	2,362	100,227	Khonsa	–
Upper Siang	6,590	33,146	Yingkiong	–
Upper Subansiri	7,032	54,995	Daporijo	–
West Kameng	7,422	74,595	Bomdila	–
West Siang	8,033	103,575	Along	–

Assam

Key Statistics

Capital: Dispur.
Area: 78,438 sq. km.
Population: Total: 26,655,528, Male 13,777,037, Female: 12,878,491.
Population density: 340 per sq. km.
Sex ratio: 935 females per 1000 males.
Principal languages: Assamese, Bengali, Bodo/Boro.
Literacy rates: Total: 63.3%, Male: 71.3%, Female: 54.6%.

Government

Governor: Lt Gen. (Retd) Ajai Singh. He was sworn in on 5 June 2003.

Chief Minister: Tarun Gogoi. He was sworn in on 18 May 2001.

Geography

Physical characteristics: Assam can be broadly divided into three geographical units: the alluvial Brahmaputra Valley covering large parts of the state in the north, the Barak Valley in the southern part of the state, and the hilly region that separates the two valleys.

Neighbouring States and Union territories:
International borders: Bangladesh, Bhutan.

States: Arunachal Pradesh, Nagaland, Manipur, West Bengal, Meghalaya, Mizoram, Tripura.

Major rivers: Brahmaputra, Barak, Sonai, Dhaleswari, Kapili, Jamuna and Dhansiri.

Climate: While the hilly regions have a pleasant subalpine climate, the plains experience tropical climatic conditions making them uncomfortably humid. Maximum temperatures in summers are 35 to 38°C. Minimum temperatures in winters drop to 6°C. The normal annual rainfall is 2850mm.

Flora and Fauna:

Flora: Assamese flora includes bamboo, lac and valuable timber trees like sal and teak. The state's forests have about 74 species of trees, of which two-thirds are commercially exploited.

Fauna: Wildlife found in Assam includes one-horned rhinoceros, elephant, wild buffalo, wild boar, swamp deer, sambar, hog deer, sloth bear, tiger, leopard, leopard cat, jungle cat, hog badger, capped langur, hispid hare, pigmy hog and golden langur, hoolock gibbon, jackal, goose, hornbill, ibis, pelican, duck, cormorants, egret, river chats (white capped redstars), forktail, heron, fishing eagle, etc.

History

In ancient times, Assam was a part of the kingdom of Kamarupa that had its capital at Pragjyotishpura. Chinese traveller Hiuen-Tsang's account of AD 640 describes a powerful Kamarupa under King Bhaskaravarman. From the seventh to thirteenth century, the region was ruled by different dynasties—the Palas, Koches, Kacharis, and the Chutiyas—who constantly raged wars among themselves till the coming of the Ahoms in the thirteenth century who then became the dominant power. The power and prosperity of the Ahoms reached a zenith during the rule of King Rudra Singh in the late seventeenth century. It then went into a decline due to internal uprisings and invasions from Myanmar. The British drove out the Myanmar invaders and restored order. After the Treaty of Yandabo in 1826, Assam became a part of British India.

In 1874, a separate chief commissioner's province of Assam was created with its capital at Shillong. Assam was amalgamated with eastern Bengal at the time of Bengal's partition in 1905, but was again made a separate province in 1912.

Assam became a constituent state of the Indian Union after Independence and has had many states carved out of it since: Nagaland in 1963, Meghalaya and Mizoram in 1971, and Arunachal Pradesh in 1972. Assam's first Chief Minister was Gopinath Bardoloi.

Politics

The legislature of Assam remained bicameral from 1937 to 1946. Under the India (Provincial Legislatures) Order 1947, the Legislative Council was abolished on 14 August 1947. The Assam legislature has been unicameral since then. In the years that followed, Assam was truncated to create several smaller states. Gopinath Bardoloi from the Congress party was the first chief minister of Assam who remained in office from 15 August 1947 to 6 August 1950. The Congress has ruled the state for the longest period since 1952. It lost to the Asom Gana Parishad in the 1985 Assembly elections held immediately after the Assam Accord was signed in the wake of a violent anti-foreigner agitation, which lasted from 1979 to 1985. However, the Congress returned to power in 1991 and ruled the state until 1996.

Following Indian independence in 1947, the Assamese won control of their state assembly and launched a campaign to reassert the preeminence of Assamese culture in the region and improve employment opportunities for native Assamese. This led to the alienation of some tribal districts. In addition, many in the tribal districts were demanding independence from India. Thinking it would satisfy the tribals, the Indian government parititioned former Assamese territories into the tribal states of Nagaland, Mizoram, Meghalaya, Manipur and Arunachal Pradesh over the next twenty years. This was seen by Assamese leaders as a deliberate division of their constituency. Following the Pakistan war in 1971, nearly two million Bengali Muslim refugees migrated to Assam. Their illegal settlement and then their electoral support for Indira Gandhi's Congress government further aggravated Assamese fears of Bengali cultural domination and central government's ambitions to undermine Assamese regional autonomy. In the late 1970s and early 1980s, there were persistent disputes between the government and Assamese students and some Assamese political factions over the rights of illegal immigrants to citizenship and suffrage. The state government and the Government of India responded by the use of force to suppress the movement. Many demonstrators were killed. This led to some of India's worst communal violence since Partition towards the end of the movement. The central government's effort to hold a constitutionally mandated election to the state assembly in 1983 led to its near total boycott, a complete breakdown of order, and the worst killings since 1947. The election proved to be a complete failure with less than 2 per cent of the voters casting their votes in the constituencies with Assamese majority. The Congress party formed the government and on 27 February 1983 Hiteshwar Saikia became the chief minister of the state.

In 1985, a treaty was signed between the Assamese and the Government of India. According to it all those foreigners who had entered Assam between 1951 and 1961 were to be given full citizenship, including the right to vote; those who had done so after 1971 were to be deported; the entrants between 1961 and 1971 were to be denied voting rights for ten years but would enjoy all other rights of citizenship. This was followed by an election. A new party, Asom Gana Parishad, formed by the leaders of anti-foreigners movement, was elected to power, winning 64 of the 126 assembly seats. Prafulla Mahanta became at the age of thirty-two the youngest chief minister of independent India. There was a lot of expectation among the people. But the victory of the AGP did not end the controversy over Assamese nationalism. The AGP was unable to implement the accord's provisions for disenfranchising and expelling illegal aliens, in part because Parliament passed legislation making it more difficult to prove illegal alien status. The AGP's failure to implement the accord along with the general ineffectiveness with which it operated the state government undercut its popular support, and in November 1990 was dismissed and President's Rule declared.

As the AGP floundered, other nationalist groups of agitators flourished. The United Liberation Front of Assam (ULFA) became the primary torchbearer of militant Assamese nationalism while the All Bodo Students' Union (ABSU) and Bodo People's Action Committee (BPAC) led an agitation for a separate homeland for the central plain tribal people of Assam (often called Bodos). By 1990 ULFA militants ran virtually a parallel government in the state, extorting huge sums from businesses in Assam, especially the Assamese tea industry. The ULFA was ultimately subdued through a combination of military action and generous terms of surrender for many of its leaders. The Government of India has classified it a terrorist organization and had banned it under the Unlawful Activities (Prevention) Act in 1990. On the other hand the ABSU/BPAC-led mass agitation lasted from March 1987 until February 1993 when the ABSU signed an accord with the state government that had been under Congress (I) control since 1991. The accord provided for the creation of a Bodoland Autonomous Council with jurisdiction over an area of 5,186 square kilometers and 2.1 million people within Assam. Nevertheless, the Bodo agitation continued in the mid-1990s as a result of the demands of many Bodo leaders, who insisted that more territory be included under the Bodoland Autonomous Council.

On 30 Jun 1991 Hiteshwar Saikia of the Congress party returned to power, becoming the chief minister for the second time and remained in power till 22 April 1996. Prafulla Kumar Mahanta regained the chief ministership in May 1996. He remained in power till 18 May 2001. In the 2001 elections the Congress(I) came back to power in Assam. It defeated the four-party alliance led by Asom Gana Parishad (AGP), winning 71 of the 125 seats. The alliance, which included the AGP, the BJP, the All Bodo Students Union (ABSU) and the Autonomous State Demand Committee (United) secured 39 seats. Tarun Gogoi was sworn in as the 15th chief minister of Assam. Despite large-scale violence by ULFA and the National Democratic Front of Bodoland (NDFB), more than 70 per cent of the electorate exercised its franchise in largely peaceful polling.

Culture

Assam has a large number of tribal groups who exhibit great cultural variety. Among them are the Boro-Kacharis, Deoris, Misings, Dimassas, Karbis, Lalungs and Rabhas. The three Bihus or agricultural festivals—Rongali Bihu, Bhogali Bihu and Kongali Bihu—are an important aspect of Assamese culture. Apart from Bihu, popular dance forms include Ojapali, Satriya, Ghosa Dhemali, Ras Nritya and Bagrumba.

Handloom weaving of fine silk and cotton cloths is a popular activity. Other ethnic products include cane and bamboo articles, brass and bell metal products, pottery, woodcraft, masks, jewellery and terracotta articles.

Fairs and festivals: Important festivals and fairs are the three Bihus, Durga Puja, Bathow Puja, Kherai Puja, Ali-ai-ligang, Po-rag, Baishagu, Bohaggiyo Bishu, Jonbeel Mela and Ambubasi Mela.

Economy, Industry and Agriculture

Economy: Net state domestic product at current prices for for 2002–03 (provisional) was Rs 31,721 crores. The per capita net state domestic product at current prices for 2002–03 (provisional) was Rs 11.755.

Minerals and industry: Industrial scenario in Assam is dominated by two major industries: tea and oil and natural gas. Other industries include jute, silk, fertilizers, petrochemicals, paper, matchsticks, cement, iron pipes, asbestos sheets and pipes, pan masala, cosmetics, plastics processing and moulded articles, polyester yarn, acrylic yarn, sugar, plywood, handloom and handicrafts.

The mineral wealth of Assam includes coal, petroleum, limestone, granite, sillimanite, iron ore, quartzite, feldspar and clay.

Agriculture: Rice, maize, wheat, jute, cotton, sugar cane and pulses are the major crops. Important plantation crops are tea, rubber and coffee. Major horticultural crops are banana, pineapple, orange, potato, sweet potato, papaya, cabbage, onion, tapioca, arecanut, coconut, ginger, jackfruit, guava and mango.

Power: Assam has great potential for development of power sector based on hydel, oil, natural gas and coal resources. At present the Assam State Electricity Board has a total installed capacity of 574 MW.

Education

Prominent educational institutions are Gauhati University, Guwahati; Dibrugarh University, Diburgarh; Tezpur University, Tezpur; Assam University, Silchar; Assam Agriculture University, Jorhat; Indian Institute of Technology, Guwahati and National Institute of Technology, Silchar.

Tourism

Major tourist attractions:

1. Kamrup: Guwahati (Kamakhya and Bhubaneswari Temples, Basishthashram, Navagraha Temple, Gandhimandap); Hajo (Hayagriva-Madhab Temple, Poa Macca); Chandubi; Sualkuchi; Madan Kamdev.

2. Darrang: Bhairabkunda.

3. Morigaon: Pobitora Wildlife Sanctuary.

4. Nagaon: Nagaon; Batadrawa; Laokhowa Wildlife Sanctuary.

5. North Lakhimpur: Pobha Wildlife Sanctuary; Garampani.

6. Golaghat: Kaziranga National Park.

7. Tinsukia: Dibru Saikhowa National Park; Digboi (National Oil Park, War Cemetery).

8. Sonitpur: Orang Wildlife Sanctuary; Nameri National Park; Bhalukpun; Tezpur (Bamuni Hill, Hazara Tank, Chitralekha Udyan, Cole Park, Agnigarh, Da-Parbatiya, Maha Bhairav Temple).

9. Barpeta: Barpeta Satra and Kirtan Ghar; Manas National Park.

10. Sibsagar: Sibsagar (Shivadol, Vishnudol and Devidol Temples, Kareng Ghar and Talatal Ghar, Gorgaon Palace, Rang Ghar, Joysagar Tank and Temples, Charaideo).

11. NC Hills: Haflong; Jatinga; Maibong; Umrangshu.

12. Jorhat: Majuli, the world's largest riverine island.

Airports: Guwahati, Tezpur, Jorhat, Dibrugarh, Silchar, North Lakhimpur.

National Parks: Kaziranga National Park in Golaghat, Nagaon districts (471.71 sq. km); Manas National Park in Barpeta, Bongaigaon districts (500 sq. km); Nameri National Park in Sonitpur District (200 sq. km); Dibru Saikhowa Naional Park in Tinsukia, Dibrugarh districts (340 sq. km); Orang National Park in Darrang and Sonitpur districts (78.808 sq. km).

Administration

Legislature: The Assam state legislative assembly has 126 members elected from as many constituencies. Of the 126 seats, eight are reserved for scheduled castes and 16 for scheduled tribes. The term of the current assembly ends on 29 May 2006. The present party position is as follows:

Name of Party	Seats
Indian National Congress	71
Asom Gana Parishad	20
Bharatiya Janata Party	8
Nationalist Congress Party	3
Autonomous State Demand Committee (United)	2
All India Trinamool Congress	1
Samata Party	1
Samajwadi Party	1
Independents	19
Total	**126**

Judiciary: The Gauhati High Court, Guwahati, is the high court of Assam, Nagaland, Meghalaya, Manipur, Tripura, Mizoram, and Arunachal Pradesh. The present chief justice is Binod Kumar Roy.

Districts:

District	Area (sq. km)	Population	Headquarters	Urban Agglomerations
Barpeta	3245	1,642,420	Barpeta	
Bongaigaon	2510	906,315	Bongaigaon	Bongaigaon
Cachar	3786	1,442,141	Silchar	Silchar
Darrang	3481	1,503,943	Mangaldoi	
Dhemaji	3237	569,468	Dhemaji	
Dhubri	2798	1,634,589	Dhubri	
Dibrugarh	3381	1,172,056	Dibrugarh	Dibrugarh
Goalpara	1824	822,306	Goalpara	
Golaghat	3502	945,781	Golaghat	
Hailakandi	1327	542,978	Hailakandi	
Jorhat	2851	1,009,197	Jorhat	Jorhat
Kamrup	4345	2,515,030	Guwahati	Guwahati
Karbi Anglong	10434	812,320	Diphu	
Karimganj	1809	1,003,678	Karimganj	
Kokrajhar	3169	930,404	Kokrajhar	
Lakhimpur	2277	889,325	North Lakhimpur	
Marigaon	1704	775,874	Marigaon	
Nagaon	3831	2,315,387	Nagaon	Lumding, Nagaon
Nalbari	2257	1,138,184	Nalbari	
North Cachar Hills	4888	186,189	Haflong	
Sibsagar	2668	1,052,802	Sibsagar	
Sonitpur	5324	1,677,874	Tezpur	Tezpur
Tinsukia	3790	1,150,146	Tinsukia	Digboi, Tinsukia

Bihar

Key Statistics

Capital: Patna.

Area: 94,163 sq. km.

Population: Total: 82,998,509, Male: 43,243,795, Female: 39,754,714.

Population density: 880 per sq. km.

Sex ratio: 919 females per 1000 males.

Principal languages: Hindi, Urdu, Santhali.

Literacy rates: Total: 47%, Male: 59.7%, Female: 33.1%.

Government

Governor: Buta Singh. He was sworn in on 3 November 2004.

Chief Minister: None. The state is under President's Rule.

Geography

Physical characteristics: Located in the eastern part of the country, Bihar is a landlocked state. The outlet to the sea is through the port of Kolkata. The river Ganga flows through the middle of the Bihar plain from west to east and divides it into two halves.

Bihar lies midway between the humid West Bengal in the east and the sub-humid Uttar Pradesh in the west, which gives it a transitional position in terms of climate.

The north Gangetic Plain consist of a flat alluvial region, and are prone to floods. The Kosi river, due to its tendency to cause dangerous floods, was previously referred to as the 'Sorrow of Bihar', before the construction of artificial embankments.

The soil in the Bihar plain is composed mainly of new alluvium, which is mostly non-chalky and heavy-textured (clay and clay loam) towards the east, and chalky and light-textured (mostly sandy loam) towards the west of the Old Burhi Gandak river.

Apart from floods, another hazard is that this region lies in the Himalayan earthquake zone. The earthquakes of 1934 and 1988 caused widespread damage here.

In the south, the Gangetic Plain is more diversified than in the north. Many hills rise from the level alluvium that constitutes the Gangetic Plain. Except for Son, all the rivers are small, and their water is diverted into irrigation channels. The soil of the land is usually made up of older alluvium.

The Kaimur Plateau lies in the extreme northwest. It consists of nearly horizontal sandstone strata that are underlain by limestone. The soil of the plateau is typically red, and is sandy in the Damodar valley.

Neighbouring States and Union territories:
International border: Nepal.

States: West Bengal, Uttar Pradesh, Jharkhand.

Major rivers: Ganga, Kamla-Balan, Mahananda, Saryu (Ghaghra), Gandak, Budhi Gandak and Bagmati.

Climate: Bihar's climate is in keeping with the Indian subcontinent's climatic pattern. Due to its great distance from the sea, Bihar enjoys a continental monsoon type of climate.

There are many factors that affect its climate. For one, the Himalayan mountains in the north affect the distribution of monsoon rainfall in Bihar. It records an average annual rainfall of about 1200mm.

Also, Bihar extends from 22° to 27°N latitude, i.e. in the tropical to subtropical region.

The cold weather season in Bihar lasts from December to February. Summer lasts from March to May. The southwest monsoon lasts from June to September, and the retreating southwest monsoon from October to November.

Flora and Fauna:
Flora: Deciduous forests in the state can be found in the sub-Himalayan foothills of Someshwar and the Dun ranges in Champaran. These forests are also largely made of grass, reeds and scrub. Other important trees include Semal, Khair, shisham, *Cedrela Toona*, and *Shorea robusta* (sal). These places register a rainfall of above 1600 mm, which is responsible for the presence of sal forests in certain areas.

Fauna: Many wildlife sanctuaries and reserves can be found in Bihar. Sambar, gaur, nilgai, munjtac, elephants, tigers and the Indian wolf are some of the animals that can be seen in the sanctuaries. The birds, fish and reptiles consist of species common throughout peninsular India.

History

The history of Bihar dates back to the dawn of human civilization. The earliest myths and legends of Hinduism are associated with Bihar, including the Sanatana (eternal) Dharma. Sita, the consort of Lord Rama, is believed to have been a princess from Bihar.

In the 3rd century BC, the state was part of Ashoka's kingdom.

During the British rule in India, Bihar was a part of the Bengal Presidency and governed from Calcutta, and was separated from it in 1912. Together with Orissa, Bihar formed a single province, until the Government of India Act of 1935, which made Orissa into a separate province, and led to the formation of the province of Bihar as an individual administrative unit of British India.

At the time of independence in 1947, Bihar was constituted with the same geographic boundary into the Republic of India. In 1956, during the linguistic reorganization of Indian states, the south-east area of Bihar known as Purulia was separated from the state, and was added to the territory of West Bengal. Sri Krishna Sinha became the first Chief Minister of Bihar.

In the year 2000, Bihar was bifurcated and the state of Jharkhand was carved out.

Politics

The Bihar Legislative Assembly came into existence in 1937. Bihar had a Congress government from 1937. After Independence, Srikrishna Sinha was the chief minister from 15 August 1947 to 31 January 1961. Unexpectedly, the Congress party could not win a majority of seats in 1967 elections. A coalition government came to power under the leadership of Mahamaya Prasad Sinha of the Bharatiya Kranti Dal. President's Rule was imposed for the first time in the State on 29 June 1968 when Bhola Paswan Shastri, succumbing to pulls and pressures from various constituents of his Sanyukta Vidhayak Dal (SVD), resigned. Bihar was brought under Central rule for the fourth time on 30 April 1977 when Jagannath Mishra's Congress government was dismissed after Morarji Desai became prime minister. With the failure of the Janata experiment and the return of Indira Gandhi, President's Rule was imposed for the fifth time on 17 February 1980, after which Jagannath Mishra became the chief minister for the second time and remained in the position till 14 August 1983. Laloo Prasad Yadav became the chief minister for the first time in 1990 and remained in power till the 1995 elections. Shortly after winning the 1995 election, Laloo Prasad Yadav came under pressure from senior leaders in the Janata Dal and its alliance partners to resign as chief minister following his alleged involvement in the fodder scam. He was charge-sheeted by the Central Bureau of Investigation (CBI), but remained in power until July 1997 when he floated the Rastriya Janata Dal, resigned as chief minister and appointed his wife Rabri Devi his successor. Rabri Devi had three tenures as chief minister. In between her second and third tenures Nitish Kumar was the chief minister for seven days in March 2000. After the 2005 election which resulted in a hung Assembly it was for the eighth time that Bihar was brought under President's Rule on 8 March 2005. Elections have been scheduled in Bihar for October-November 2005.

A students' agitation which began in Bihar in 1974 is popularly known as the Jayaprakash Narayan or JP movement. Today's Bihar is dominated by leaders who were once the chief actors in the JP movement - Lalu Prasad Yadav of the Rashtriya Janata Dal (RJD), Sushil Modi of the Bharatiya Janata Party (BJP), Ram Jatan Sinha of the Congress, and Nitish Kumar of the Janata Dal (United). The JP movement's ideological thrust was to fashion a new Bihar, free from corruption and casteism. The movement catalysed some revolutionary social changes, such as inter-caste marriages and the breaking of the sacred thread worn by upper-caste Hindus. Jayaprakash Narayan wanted a 'total revolution', not political change alone but also transformations in the social and cultural attitudes of the people. But even today the caste factor is the most potent social and political force in the state. Bihar has never been free of caste in politics. Even during the freedom movement, Bhumihars dominated politics; there were intense rivalries in Congress politics between Bhumihars and Rajputs, on the one hand, and Brahmins on the other. Even the state's greatest politicians couldn't rid themselves of narrow casteism. Veteran Congress leader Srikrishna Sinha, the first chief minister of Bihar, credited with the abolition of the zamindari system, was accused by Jayaprakash Narayan of promoting people from the Bhumihar caste and, thus, creating bottlenecks in the progressive evolution of politics and society. Even today, elections in Bihar are contested with formulations of caste-based alliances.

Culture

Writers from Bihar like Shiva Pujan Sahay, Ram Briksha Benipuri, Raja Radhika Raman Singh, Ramdhari Singh Dinakar, and Divakar Prasad Vidyarthy contributed greatly to Hindi literature and culture, which flourished around the mid-19th century, with Bhartendu Babu Harischandra's drama 'Harischandra'. 'Indumati' by Pundit Kishorilal Goswami was published in 1900, and is considered to be one of the very first short stories in Hindi.

Bihar also has a variety of dance forms including religious dances and the dances of the tribals and the famous Chhau dance. Karma, Jatra and Paika dances are some other important dances.

Fairs and festivals: Bihar has a long tradition of festivals. The most popular festival 'Chatt Puja', is a unique form of worship of the 'sun god'. The people of Bihar have immense faith in this festival, which is celebrated twice a year, once in 'Chaitra' (according to the Hindu Calendar, in March) and in 'Kartik' (November).

The other popular festivals include Sama-Chakeva festival, Ramnavami and the Makar Sankranti, also known as the Tila Sankranti, to mark the beginning of summer.

Economy, Industry and Agriculture

Economy: The net state domestic product at current prices in 2002–03 (advance estimate) is Rs 51,345 crores, whereas the per capita net state domestic product at current prices in 2000–03 (advance estimate) is Rs 6015.

Minerals and industry: Some of the major industries in Bihar are agro-based industries, oil refineries, textiles, engineering, and oil mills.

Industries that are dependent on agriculture are the edible oil mills located at Araria, rice mills located in Buxar Karbisganch in Purnia district, spice industires, sugar mills located at Banmankhi in Purnia district, jute mills and other agro-based industries.

One of the biggest oil refineries in the country is situated at Barauni in Bihar. It is managed and controlled by the Indian Oil Corporation Ltd, and was built in collaboration with the erstwhile Soviet Union at a cost of Rs 49.40 crores, and went into operation in 1964.

After West Bengal, Bihar is the largest producer of jute and jute textiles. This is largely due to the availability of sufficient power, raw jute, water, transportation, and cheap labour. Jute mills are located in Katihar and Muktapur in Samastipur district, and at Karsbisganj in Purnia district.

Engineering industries are located at Madora in the district of Saran, Muktapur in Samastipur district, Dumaro in Bhojpur district, and Fatuha in Patna district. Railway carriages and goods factories are located in Rohtas district at Dehri-on-Son.

Due to the availability of kendu leaves and cheap labour, biri manufacturing industries are located at Bihar Sarif in Nalanda district. Bihar is also the sixth largest producer of tobacco in the country.

The important minerals found in Bihar are limestone, pyrites, quartzite and steatite.

Agriculture: Bihar has plenty of farmlands and orchards. The important crops include paddy, sugarcane, wheat and lentils. Jute or hemp, a source of tough fibres used for 'gunny bags', are also grown. Some of the important fruits grown in the state are banana, jackfruit, mangoes, and litchis.

Paddy is the important crop in all the regions. Supplementary crops include oilseeds, pulses (legumes), barley, gram, wheat and corn (maize). Sugarcane is grown in a well-defined belt in the north-west.

Vegetables include potatoes grown near Bihar Sharif, in Patna district, which produces the best variety of seed potato in India. Other important cash crops include tobacco and chillies that are grown on the banks of the Ganga.

Power: Thermal power is the main source of electricity in the state. Hydroelectric power ranks a distant second.

Education

Prominent institutes of higher education include B.N. Mandal University (Madhepura), Babasaheb Bhimrao Ambedkar Bihar University (Muzaffarpur), Jai Prakash Vishwavidyalaya (Chapra), Kameshwar Singh Darbhanga Sanskrit University (Darbhanga), Lalit Narayan Mithila University (Darbhanga), Magadh University (Bodh Gaya), Nalanda Open University (Patna), Patna University, Rajendra Agricultural University (Samastipur), Tilka Manjhi Bhagalpur University (Bhagalpur) and Veer Kunwar Singh University (Arrah).

Tourism

Major tourist attractions: Bodh Gaya, Rajgir, Nalanda, Vaishali, Pawapuri, Lauria Nandangarh, Vikramshila.

Airports: Patna, Gaya.

National Parks: Valmiki National Park in Pashchim Champaran district (335.65 sq. km).

Administration

Legislature: Bihar has a bicameral legislature consisting of the Vidhan Parishad and the Vidhan Sabha. The governor is appointed by the President of India and acts as the head of the state. The Chief Minister heads the council of ministers. There are 243 seats in the Vidhan Sabha, of which 39 seats are reserved for SC candidates. No seats are reserved for ST candidates.

The current party position is as follows:

Name of Party	Seats
Bharatiya Janata Party	37
Indian National Congress	10
Nationalist Congress Party	3
Communist Party of India	3
Bahujan Samaj Party	2
Communist Party of India (Marxist)	1
Rashtriya Janata Dal	75
Janata Dal (United)	55
Communist Party of India (Marxist-Leninist) (Liberation)	7
Samajwadi Party	4
Lok Jan Shakti Party	29
Independent	17
Total	**243**

Judiciary: The main seat for the judiciary is the high court of judicature at Patna. The chief justice is Ravi S. Dhawan.

Districts:

District	Area (sq. km)	Population	Headquarters	Urban Agglomerations
Araria	2,830	2,124,831	Araria	
Aurangabad	3,305	2,004,960	Aurangabad	
Banka	3,020	1,608,778	Banka	
Begusarai	1,918	2,342,989	Begusarai	Begusarai
Bhagalpur	2,569	2,430,331	Bhagalpur	Bhagalpur
Bhojpur	2,474	2,233,415	Arrah	
Buxar	1,624	1,403,462	Buxar	
Darbhanga	2,279	3,285,473	Darbhanga	
Gaya	4,976	3,464,983	Gaya	Gaya
Gopalganj	2,033	2,149,343	Gopalganj	
Jamui	3,098	1,397,474	Jamui	
Jehanabad	1,569	1,511,406	Jehanabad	
Kaimur (Bhabua)	3,362	1,284,575	Bhabua	
Katihar	3,057	2,389,533	Katihar	Katihar
Khagaria	1,486	1,276,677	Khagaria	
Kishanganj	1,884	1,294,063	Kishanganj	
Lakhisarai	1,228	801,173	Lakhisarai	
Madhepura	1,788	1,524,596	Madhepura	
Madhubani	3,501	3,570,651	Madhubani	
Munger	1,419	1,135,499	Munger	
Muzaffarpur	3,172	3,743,836	Muzaffarpur	
Nalanda	2,355	2,368,327	Biharsharif	
Nawada	2,494	1,809,425	Nawada	
Pashchim Champaran	5,228	3,043,044	Bettiah	
Patna	3,202	4,709,851	Patna	Patna
Purba Champaran	3,968	3,933,636	Motihari	Motihari
Purnia	3,229	2,540,788	Purnia	Purnia
Rohtas	3,851	2,448,762	Sasaram	
Saharsa	1,702	1,506,418	Saharsa	
Samastipur	2,904	3,413,413	Samastipur	Samastipur
Saran	2,641	3,251,474	Chapra	
Sheikhpura	689	525,137	Sheikhpura	
Sheohar	443	514,288	Sheohar	
Sitamarhi	2,200	2,669,887	Sitamarhi	Sitamarhi
Siwan	2,219	2,708.840	Siwan	
Supaul	2,410	1,745,069	Supaul	
Vaishali	2,036	2,712,389	Hazipur	

Chhattisgarh

Key Statistics

Capital: Raipur.
Area: 135,191 sq. km.
Population: Total: 20,833,803, Male: 10,474,218, Female: 10,359,585.
Population density: 154 per sq. km.
Sex ratio: 989 females per 1000 males.
Principal language: Hindi.
Literacy rates: Total: 64.7%, Male: 77.4%, Female: 51.9%.

Government

Governor: Lt Gen. K.M. Seth, (Retd). He was sworn in on 2 June 2003.

Chief Minister: Dr Raman Singh (BJP). He was sworn in on 8 December 2003.

Geography

Physical characteristics: The state can be divided into three agro-climatic zones. These are the Chhattisgarh plains, the northern hills of Chhattisgarh and the Bastar plateau.

The Satpura mountain range lies in the northern part of the state; the plains of river Mahanadi and its tributaries lie in the central part of the state, while in the south lies the plateau of Bastar. Uttar Pradesh borders the state towards the north; Jharkhand in the north-east; Orissa in the east; Andhra Pradesh in the south and south-east; Maharashtra in the south-west and Madhya Pradesh in the west.

Neighbouring States and Union territories:
States: Madhya Pradesh, Jharkhand, Orissa, Uttar Pradesh, Andhra Pradesh, Maharashtra.

Major rivers: The Mahanadi and the Indravati are the two most important rivers of the state. The Narmada, the Son, the Hasdeo, the Sabari, the Sheonath, the Ib and the Arpa also provide water to the state.

Climate: Chhattisgarh has a generally sub-humid climate. It has hot, dry summers and cold winters. Annual rainfall ranges from 1200 to 1500mm.

Flora and Fauna:
Flora: Chhattisgarh has deciduous forests of two types: tropical moist deciduous forests and tropical dry deciduous forests. The state has about 22 forest subtypes. The two major tree species in the state are sal and teak. The other notable species are saja, dhawra, mahua, bija, tendu, amla, karra and bamboo.

Fauna: The notable species of animals found in Chhattisgarh are tiger, gaur, sambar, wild buffalo, hill myna, chital, nilgai, wild boar and leopard.

History

In ancient times, the region that is today Chhattisgarh was called Dakshin Kosala. Its history can be traced back to the *Ramayana* and the *Mahabharata*. It was called Ratanpur during the reign of the Mughals.

In the 10th century AD, a powerful Rajput family ruled at Tripuri, near Jabalpur. A member of the Kalchuri dynasty, Kalingraja, settled at Tuman around AD 1000. His grandson Ratanraja founded Ratanpur, which became the capital of a large part of the area now known as Chhattisgarh. This Rajput family called itself the Haihaya dynasty and it continued to rule Chhattisgarh for six centuries until about the 14th century, when it disintegrated.

In the middle ages, the Chalukya dynasty established its rule in Bastar. The Chalukya ruler Annmdev established his dynasty in Bastar in 1320.

One branch of the dynasty continued

at Ratanpur, while the other settled in Raipur. At the end of the 16th century the latter branch acknowledged the domination of the Mughals.

In 1741, the Marathas attacked Chhattisgarh and destroyed the Haihaya power. In 1745, they conquered the region and deposed Raghunathsinghji, the last survivor of the Ratanpur house. In 1758, the Marathas ultimately annexed Chhattisgarh and it came directly under Maratha rule. The Maratha rule was a period of chaos and misrule, marked by widespread loot and plunder by the Maratha army. The Gonds resisted the Marathas, leading to conflicts and hostility between them. In the early 19th century, the Pindaris from Gwalior attacked and plundered the region.

In 1818, Chhattisgarh came under British control for the first time. When the province of Nagpur lapsed to the British government in 1854, Chhattisgarh was put under a deputy commissioner and Raipur made the headquarters. The tribals of Bastar resisted British overlordship and this resulted in the Halba Rebellion, which lasted nearly five years (1774–79).

A demand for a separate Chhattisgarh state was first raised in 1924 by the Raipur Congress unit. It was later raised at the Tripuri session of the Indian National Congress. In 1955, a demand for a separate state was made in the Nagpur assembly of the then state of Madhya Bharat.

On 18 March 1994, a resolution for a separate Chhattisgarh was tabled in the Madhya Pradesh Vidhan Sabha. Both the INC and the BJP supported the resolution and it was unanimously approved.

In 1998, the Union government drafted a bill for the creation of a separate state of Chhattisgarh carved out from 16 districts of Madhya Pradesh. The Madhya Pradesh assembly unanimously approved the draft bill in 1998, with some modifications.

Chhattisgarh became a separate state on 1 November 2000. Ajit Jogi was the first Chief Minister of Chhattisgarh.

Politics

The Congress government of Madhya Pradesh took the first institutional and legislative initiative for the creation of Chhattisgarh. On 18 March 1994, a resolution demanding a separate Chhattisgarh was tabled and unanimously approved by the Madhya Pradesh Vidhan Sabha. Both the Congress and the Bhartiya Janta Party supported the resolution. The election manifestos of the Congress and the BJP for both the 1998 and the 1999 parliamentary elections as well as the Madhya Pradesh assembly election of 1998 included the demand for the creation of a separate Chhattisgarh. The state of Chhattisgarh came into existence on 1 November 2000, with the enactment of the Madhya Pradesh (Reorganisation) Act, 2000, by the Parliament. The State fulfils the long-cherished demand of the tribal people. This is the twenty-sixth state of India. Ajit Jogi of the Congress was sworn in the first chief minister of the state. In the 2003 Assembly elections the BJP won 50 seats in the 90-member Chhattisgarh state assembly, while the ruling Congress party had to content itself with a mere 37 seats. Raman Singh, president of the BJP in Chhattisgarh, was sworn in as the chief minister on 7 December 2003.

Culture

The state is well known for its tribal art forms, dance forms and handicrafts. These include handicrafts made out of wood, bamboo, terracotta, bell metal items, wrought iron items and cotton fabrics. The state is also renowned for its Kosa silk fabric. Local dance forms include the Suga dance, Saila, Ravat Nacha and Karma.

Fairs and festivals: Besides Diwali, Dussehra and Holi, various districts have their own distinct festivals. These include Charta, Navakhana, Surhul, Mati Puja, Goncha, Madai Hareli, Pola, Cherchera, Dev Uthni, Gouri-gour and Surti Teeja.

Economy, Industry and Agriculture

Economy: The net state domestic product at current prices for 2002–03 (provisional) was Rs 25,094 crores. The per capita net state domestic product at current prices for 2002–03 (provisional) was Rs 11,893.

Minerals and industry: The famous Bhilai Steel Plant is located in this state. Apart from this, there are cement plants, food-processing plants, engineering works, chemical plants, plastics units, and fabrication units.

The minerals mined in the state include iron ore, coal, corundum, bauxite, diamond, gold, dolomite, limestone, tin and granite.

Agriculture: The most important crops are paddy, maize, pulses like tur and kulthi, kodo-kutki, small millets, oilseeds like sunflower, groundnut, soyabean and niger. The state also produces jowar, gram, urad, moong and moth in the rabi season.

Power: Most of the state's power comes from thermal power plants, while hydroelectric plants generate the rest.

Education

Educational institutes: The most well known among the institutes of higher education in the state are Pandit Ravishankar Shukla University (Raipur), Guru Ghasidas University (Bilaspur), Indira Gandhi Agriculture University (Raipur), Indira Kala Sangeet University (Khairagarh), Jawaharlal Nehru Krishi Vishwavidyalaya (Jabalpur) and Rani Durgavati Vishwavidyalaya (Jabalpur).

Tourism

Major tourist attractions: Chitrakot Waterfalls, Bastar dist.; Tirathgarh Falls, Bastar dist.; Kutumsar Caves and Kailash Gufa, Bastar dist.; Danteshwari Temple, Bastar dist.; Ratanpur, Bilaspur dist.; Mallhar, Bilaspur dist.; Deorani-Jethani Temple, Talagram, Bilaspur dist.; Maitry Bagh, Durg dist.; Amrit Dhara Waterfalls, Koriya dist.; Ramdaha Waterfalls, Koriya dist.; Gavar Ghat Waterfalls, Koriya dist.; Akuri Nala, Koriya dist.; Radha Krishna Temple, Raipur dist.; Chandi Temple, Raipur dist.; Swastik Vihar Monastery, Raipur dist.; Anand Premkuti Vihar Monastery, Raipur dist.; Maa Bambleshwari Temple, Dongargarh, Rajnandgaon dist.; Thinthini Patthar, Surguja dist.

Airports: Raipur, Bilaspur.

National Parks: Indravati National Park in Dantewada dist. (1,258.37 sq. km), Sanjay National Park in Surguja and Koriya dists (1,471.13 sq. km) and Kangerghati National Park in Kanker dist. (200 sq. km).

Administration

Legislature: Chhattisgarh has a unicameral legislature. There are 90 seats in the Legislative Assembly, of which 10 are reserved for SCs and 34 for STs. The tenure of the present House ends on 21 December 2008. The current party position is:

Name of Party	Seats
Bharatiya Janata Party	50
Indian National Congress	37
Bahujan Samaj Party	2
Nationalist Congress Party	1
Total	**90**

Judiciary: Chhattisgarh High Court is at Bilaspur. Ananga Kumar Patnaik is the chief justice.

Districts:

District	Area (sq. km)	Population	Headquarters	Urban Agglomerations
Bastar	14,974	13,02,253	Jagdalpur	Jagdalpur
Bilaspur	8,270	19,93,042	Bilaspur	Bilaspur, Mungeli
Dantewada	17,634	7,19,065	Dantewada	
Dhamtari	3,385	7,03,569	Dhamtari	
Durg	8,549	28,01,757	Durg	Dalli-Rajhara, Durg, Bhilainagar
Janjgir-Champa	3,852	13,16,140	Janjgir	
Jashpur	5,838	7,39,780	Jashpur	
Kanker	6,506	6,51,333	Kanker	Kanker
Kawardha	4,223	5,84,667	Kawardha	Kawardha
Korba	6,599	10,12,121	Korba	
Koriya	6,604	5,85,455	Baikunthpur	Chirmiri
Mahasamund	4,789	30,09,042	Mahasamund	
Raigarh	7,086	12,65,084	Raigarh	Raigarh
Raipur	13,083	30,09,042	Raipur	Raipur, Tilda Newra
Rajnandgaon	8,068	12,81,811	Rajnandgaon	
Surguja	15,731	19,70,661	Ambikapur	Ambikapur

Goa

Key Statistics

Capital: Panaji.

Area: 3,702 sq. km.

Population: Total: 1,347,668, Male: 687,248, Female: 660,420.

Population density: 363 per sq. km.

Sex ratio: 961 females per 1000 males.

Principal languages: Konkani, Marathi, Kannada.

Literacy rates: Total: 82.32%, Male: 88.88%, Female: 75.51%.

Government

Governor: S.C. Jamir. He became the governor on 2 July 2004.

Chief Minister: Pratapsingh R. Rane (INC) was sworn in on 2 February 2005. On 4 March 2005 the assembly was dissolved and President's Rule was declared. Pratapsingh Rane was reinstated on 7 June.

Geography

Physical characteristics: Goa, situated on the Konkan coast of India, has a coastline of 131 km. It has a partly hilly terrain, with the Western Ghats rising to nearly 1200 metres in some parts of the state. In the north, the Terekhol river separates Goa and Maharashtra. Karnataka lies to the south, with the Arabian Sea to the west and the Western Ghats to the east. The island of Goa lies between the mouths of the Mandovi and Zuari rivers, which are connected on the landward side by a creek. The island is triangular in shape, with a cape in the form of a rocky headland that divides the harbour of Goa into two parts—Aguada at the mouth of the Mandovi, on the north, and Mormugao or Marmagao at the mouth of the Zuari, on the south.

Neighbouring States and Union territories:

States: Maharashtra, Karnataka.

Major rivers: Mandovi and Zuari.

Climate: Summer temperatures vary from 24°C to 32.7°C. Winter temperatures vary from 21.3°C to 32.2°C. Rainfall 3200mm (June–September).

History

Goa first appears in the Puranas as 'Gove', 'Govapuri', and 'Gomant'. The medieval Arab geographers called it 'Sindabur'. The Portuguese called it 'Velha Goa'. From the 2nd century AD to 1312, it was ruled by the Kadamba dynasty. The Muslim invaders of the Deccan held sway between 1312 and 1367, after which it was annexed by the Hindu kingdom of Vijayanagar. Later, it was conquered by the Bahmani dynasty, which founded Old Goa in 1440. After 1482, Goa passed into the hands of Yusuf Adil Khan, the king of Bijapur. It was during his reign that the Portuguese first reached India. In March 1510 the city surrendered to the Portuguese under Afonso de Albuquerque. A violent struggle between the Portuguese and Yusuf Adil Khan ensued, but the Portuguese had the last laugh. Goa was the first territorial possession of the Portuguese in Asia. It later became the capital of the entire Portuguese empire in the East.

In 1603 and 1639 the Dutch Navy blockaded the city, but never managed to capture it. In 1683 a Mughal army saved it from capture by the Maratha. The latter attacked the area again in 1739 but it was saved once again.

In 1809, the British temporarily occupied the city, as a result of Napoleon's invasion of Portugal.

At the time of independence in 1947, Goa was still a Portuguese colony. On 18 December 1961, Indian military forces invaded and occupied Goa, Daman, and Diu. They were incorporated into the Indian Union in 1962. On 30 May 1987, Goa was granted statehood, Daman and Diu remaining as a separate Union territory. Goa's first Chief Minister was Pratapsingh Rane.

Politics

Portuguese rule was so oppressive and exploitative that during 450 years of Portuguese rule, there were forty armed revolts in Goa. Although these revolts were put down with a heavy hand, the urge for freedom could not be suppressed forever. A movement for the liberation of Goa gained momentum in the 1900s. The main leaders of the movement were Tristao Bragansa Cunha, Purushottam Kakodkar, Laxmi Kant Bhembre, Divakar Kakodkar and Dayanand Bandodkar. The liberation movement became stronger after Indian independence in 1947.

India's new government claimed Goa in 1948. In 1955, nonviolent protesters attempted a peaceful annexation. The resulting casualties led to a breakdown of relations between India and Portugal. Indian troops invaded Goa in December 1961. Within three days Goa was integrated into India in a near bloodless operation—'Operation Vijay' on 19 December 1961. The other Portuguese territories of Daman and Diu were also taken over at around the same time and thus was formed the 'Union territory of Goa, Daman and Diu' which became a part of the Indian Union. Initially the liberated territory was under the army administration of Lt. Gen. Candeth, the Military Governor who was assisted by the Chief Civil Administrator. On 8 June 1962, the military government gave place to civil rule. The Lt. Governor formed an informal

Consultative Council consisting of 29 nominated members to assist him in the administration of the territory. Goa attained full statehood on 30 May1987 when Daman and Diu retained separate identity as a Union Territory.

In 1963 the Maharashtrawadi Gomantak Party, which had won the first Assembly elections, was led by Dayanand Bandodkar. On 20 December 1963 the first Chief Minister of Goa, Daman and Diu (Union Territory), Dayanand Bandodkar was sworn in. He had three tenures as the Chief Minister of Goa, Daman and Diu. Bhausaheb Bandodkar was the Chief Minister from 20 December 1963 to 2 December 1966. His second tenure was from 5 April 1967 to 23 March 1972. His third tenure was from 23 March 1972 till his death on 12 August 1973. The Maharashtrabadi Gomantak Party believed in the merger of Goa with neighbouring Maharashtra as they believed in the similarities of culture but at the same time underscored Konkani as being an under-developed dialect of Marathi. The United Goans party had the exact opposite view; they believed in retaining and preserving Goa's unique identity. They were led by Dr Jack Sequeira. They firmly believed that Konkani was an independent language and not a dialect of Marathi. The party insisted on maintaining its unique historical identity of its own with statehood as its long term goal, without being a part of neighbouring Maharashtra. On 16 January 1967 an opinion poll was held and the unanimous opinion of the people was to retain Goa's unique identity and not to merge with Maharashtra. The United Goans party won the elections by 34,021 votes.

After the death of Dayanand Banodkar his daughter, Shashikala Kakodkar was subsequently voted into power and she became the Chief Minister (India's first woman to do so). She was in power until April 1979. After a brief eight months of President's Rule, elections were held in January 1980. For the first time, the MG party was voted out of power and the mainstream Congress party came to power with the election of Pratapsingh Rane of the Congress party as Chief Minister. This was the first time the Congress party had made an entry into Goa's political scene. A scion of the Rane family of Sattari, Pratapsingh Rane remained in power, winning the election again in 1985 and 1990. Goa attained another political milestone by becoming a state on 30 May 1987. Daman and Diu remained as a separate Union territory. Pratapsingh Rane was sworn in as the first Chief Minister of the new Goa state. In 1992 Konkoni was declared as the official language of the state of Goa.

On 27 March 1990 Churchill Alemao of United Goans Democratic Party took over as the Chief Minister of Goa. His rule lasted for 18 and a half days till 14 April 1990. From 14 April 1990 to 14 December 1990, Dr Luis Proto Barbosa was the Chief Minister of Goa, followed by President's Rule. On 25 January 1991 Ravi Naik took over as the Chief Minister and was the CM till 18 May 1993. Ravi Naik was followed by Dr Wilfred or Willy D'Souza from 18 May 1993 to 2 April 1994. Shri Ravi Naik came back as the CM from 2 April 1994, to 8 April 1994. Ravi Naik's second tenure as the CM lasted for six and a half days. Once again Dr Wilfred D'Souza was the CM from 8 April 1994 to 16 December 1994. Pratapsingh Rane's fifth tenure as the Chief Minister of Goa came on 16 December 1994 and lasted till 29 July 1998. Dr Wilfred D'Souza came for the third time as the Chief Minister from 29 July 1998 to 23 November 1998. On 26 November 1998 Luizinho Faleiro took over as the Chief Minister and ruled till 8 February 1999 followed by President's Rule. On 9 June 1999 once again Luizinho Faleiro took over as the CM till 24 November 1999. From 24 November 1999 to 24 October 2000 Francisco Sardinha was the Chief Minister. From 24 October 2000 to 3 June 2002 Manohar Parrikar of the Bharatiya Janata Party was the Chief Minister. Parrikar's second tenure as the CM was from 3 June 2002 till 2 February 2005. Again Pratapsingh Rane was sworn in as Chief Minister on 2 February 2005. President's Rule was proclaimed on 4 March, but Pratapsingh Rane returned as Chief Minister on 7 June 2005.

Culture

Goa is well known for its folk dances like Dhalo, Fugdi, Mando, Corridinho and performing folk arts like Khell-Tiatro and Jagar-perani. It is also well known for rosewood and teak furniture, terracotta figurines, brass items and jewellery designs. Folk paintings of Goa mostly depict scenes from the *Mahabharata*, the *Ramayana* and the Puranas and also scenes from the New Testament. Goa is also an important centre for Konkani literature.

Fairs and festivals: The Goan Hindu community celebrates Ganesh Chathurti, Krishna Janmashtami, Rakshabandhan, Gudi Padwa, Diwali, Dussehra, Holi, and Ramnavmi.

In Goa, the most widely celebrated festival is Ganesh Chaturthi, or Chovoth. In the month of Phalgun, Goa celebrates Holi, or Shigmoutsav. In the month of Shravan, the town of Vasco celebrates Vasco Saptah. The Lairai Jatra takes place in early May. The Goa Carnival is usually celebrated in the month of February or March.

Economy, Industry and Agriculture

Economy: The net state domestic product at current prices (new series) in 2001–02 (quick estimate) was Rs 6,736 crores. The per capita net state domestic product at current prices (new series) in 2001–02 (quick estimate) was Rs 49,673. At Rs 45,000, Goa has the highest per capita income in India.

Minerals and industry: There are over 5000 small-scale industrial units in the state. Mineral resources of the state include bauxite, iron ore and ferro-manganese.

Agriculture: Rice, millets and pulses are the most widely grown food grains. Coconuts, cashew nuts and oilseeds are also grown.

Education

Educational institutes: Prominent institutes of higher education include Goa University, National Institute of Oceanography, National Institute of Water Sports, Goa Institute of Management and the Indian Council of Agricultural Research.

Tourism

Major tourist attractions: Calangute Beach, Colva Beach, Dona Paula Beach, Miramar Beach, Anjuna Beach, Palolem Beach, Vagator Beach, Arambol Beach, Agonda Beach, Basillica of Bom Jesus, Se Cathedral, Church of St Francis of Assisi, Dudhsagar Waterfalls, Aguada Fort.

Airports: Goa, Mormugao.

National Parks: Bhagwan Mahavir (107 sq. km).

Administration

Legislature: Goa has a unicameral legislature, with a legislative assembly. There are 40 seats in the assembly, including one seat reserved for SCs. The term of the current assembly expires on 11 June 2007. The present party position in the assembly is as follows:

Name of Party	Seats
Bharatiya Janata Party	17
Indian National Congress	16
United Gomantwadi Democratic Party	3
Maharashtrabadi Gomantak Party	2
Nationalist Congress Party	1
Independent	1
Total	**40**

Judiciary: Goa falls under the jurisdiction of the Goa bench of the Mumbai High Court. The chief justice is Dalveer C. Bhandari. There is one district court and other subordinate courts.

Districts:

District	Area (sq. km)	Population	Headquarters	Urban Agglomerations
North Goa	1,736	757,407	Panaji	Panaji
South Goa	1,966	586,591	Margao	Margao, Mormugao

Gujarat

Key Statistics

Capital: Gandhinagar.
Area: 196,024 sq. km.
Population: Total: 50,671,017, Male: 26,385,577, Female: 24,285,440.
Population density: 258 per sq. km.
Sex ratio: 920 females per 1000 males.
Principal languages: Gujarati, Hindi, Sindhi.
Literacy rates: Total: 69.1%, Male: 79.7%, Female: 57.8%.

Government

Governor: Nawal Krishna Sharma. He was sworn in on 24 July 2004.

Chief Minister: Narendra Damodardas Modi. He was sworn in on 22 December 2002.

Geography

Physical characteristics: One of the most striking geographical features of the state is the Rann of Kutch, a vast salt marsh that stretches for about 18,000 sq km. In the dry season, it is a sandy salt plain prone to dust storms, but during the rainy season even light rainfall floods the Rann and the region becomes an island.

The expansive Kathiawar Peninsula lies to the south of Kutch, between the Gulf of Kutch and the Gulf of Khambhat. This is another arid region and the coastal region gives way to a low area of wooded hilly region in the central part. The rivers of the state are mostly seasonal streams. The northeastern part of the state is primarily a region of plains and low hills. The highest point in the state is in the Girnar Hills (1,117 metres).

Neighbouring States and Union territories:
International border: Pakistan.

States: Rajasthan, Maharashtra, Madhya Pradesh.

Union territories: Daman and Diu, Dadra and Nagar Haveli.

Major rivers: Narmada, Tapti, Mahi, Sabarmati, Banas and Bhadar are the most important rivers. Other rivers include Heran, Orsang, Karad, Saidak, Mohar and Vatrak.

Climate: The climate in Gujarat varies

from humid in the coastal areas, to very hot in areas like Kutch. It can get extremely hot in the summers and extremely cold in the winters.

The climate of Gujarat is moist in the southern districts and dry in the northern region. The state's climate can be divided into a winter season from November to February, a summer season from March to May and a south-west monsoon season from June to September.

Flora and Fauna:

Flora: Roughly 10 per cent of the area of Gujarat is under forest cover. The state's flora includes dry deciduous forests, moist deciduous forests, grasslands, wetlands and marine ecosystems.

Fauna: Gujarat is home to some rare species. The Asiatic lion is found only in the Gir Forest, while the wild ass is found in the Rann of Kutch. Besides these, the great Indian bustard, the world's only four-horned antelope, the black buck, the dugong and the boralia are all found in different habitats across the state.

History

The settlements of Lothal, Rangpur, Amri, Lakhabaval and Rozdi in Gujarat have been linked with the Indus Valley Civilization.

Asokan rock edicts of around 250 BC show that in ancient times, the region that is today Gujarat came under the rule of the Mauryan dynasty. After the fall of the Mauryan empire, Gujarat came under the rule of the Sakas between AD 130–390. At its height, the Sakas held sway over what is today Malwa, Saurashtra, Kutch and Rajasthan.

In the 4th and 5th centuries, Gujarat constituted a part of the Gupta empire. The Guptas were succeeded by the Maitraka dynasty of the kingdom of Valabhi. The Maitrakas ruled over Gujarat and Malwa for three centuries.

The Maitraka dynasty was succeeded by the Gurjara-Pratiharas of Kannauj, who ruled during the 8th and 9th centuries. Following the Gurjara-Pratiharas came the Solanki dynasty, which was followed by the Vaghela dynasty. In about 1297, Ala-ud-Din Khalji, the sultan of Delhi, defeated Karnadeva Vaghela and the area came under Muslim influence. In 1401, Zafar Khan, whom the Tughluqs had appointed governor of the province, declared independence. His grandson Ahmad Shah, founded Ahmedabad in 1411. From the end of the 16th century to the mid-18th century, Gujarat was under Mughal rule. Then came the Marathas, who overran the region in the mid-18th century.

In 1818, Gujarat came under the administration of the British East India Company. After the Revolt of 1857, the area became a province of the British crown and was divided into Gujarat province and numerous smaller states.

When India became independent, all of Gujarat except for the states of Kutch and Saurashtra was included in Bombay state. In 1956, the provinces of Kutch and Saurashtra were also included.

On 1 May 1960, Bombay state was bifurcated into present-day Gujarat and Maharashtra. Jivraj Mehta was the state's first Chief Minister.

Politics

After Independence, the British-ruled Gujarat and several princely states were clubbed together to form the state of Bombay. The States Reorganisation Act was passed by parliament in November 1956. Bombay state was enlarged by merging the states of Kutch and Saurashtra and the Maratha-speaking areas of Hyderabad with it. The strongest reaction against the States Reorganisation Act came from Maharashtra where widespread rioting broke out; eighty people were killed in Bombay city in police firings in January 1956. Under pressure, the government decided in June 1956 to divide Bombay state into two linguistic states of Maharashtra and Gujarat with Bombay city forming a separate, centrally administered state. This move too was, however, opposed by the people of both Maharashtra and Gujarat. The government finally agreed in May 1960 to bifurcate the state of Bombay into Maharashtra and Gujarat, with Bombay city being included in Maharashtra, and Ahmedabad being made the capital of Gujarat.

On bifurcation of the Greater Bombay state on 1 May 1960, under the Bombay Reorganization Act, 1960, the new state of Gujarat came into existence.

The Congress dominated Gujarat's corridors of power for most of the time from 1960 to 1995. Chimanbhai Patel and Chhabildas Mehta were the last Congress chief ministers of the state. Keshubhai Patel of the BJP became chief minister after elections in 1995. Narendra Damodardas Modi took over as the fourteenth chief minister of Gujarat on 7 October 2001 after Keshubhai Patel stepped down on the directive of BJP high command. He is the current chief minister. The imposition of President's Rule on five occasions so far and frequent outbreaks of communal violence has played a vital role in shaping the state's politics over the years. On 27 February 2002, a sleeper coach in the Sabarmati Express, coming from Faizabad and proceeding towards Ahmedabad, caught fire a few minutes after it left the Godhra railway station. The coach that was ravaged in the fire was occupied predominantly by members and sympathizers of the Sangh Parivar called kar sevaks who were returning after a pilgrimage to Ayodhya. This incident was a precursor to a spate of widepsread riots in the state, which lasted nearly three months.

Culture

Gujarat is famous for its 'Garba' dance form, which is performed on Navratri. The state is also famous for its 'bandhni' tie-and-dye technique, Patola saris, toys of Idar, perfumes of Palanpur, the handloom products of Konodar and woodwork from Ahmedabad and Surat.

Fairs and festivals: The festivals of the state include the International Kite Festival of Ahmedabad, Somnath Festival, Navratri, Tarnetra Festival and Janmastami.

Economy, Industry and Agriculture

Economy: The net state domestic product at current prices for 2002–03 (provisional) was Rs 114,405 crores. The per capita net state domestic product at current prices for 2002–03 (provisional) was Rs 22,047.

Minerals and industry: The important minerals found in the state are bauxite, manganese, limestone, lignite, bentonite, dolomite, crude oil, granite, silica, china clay and fireclay.

The major industries in the state are petrochemicals, engineering, electronics, chemicals and fertilizers. Surat is an important centre for the diamond trade while Anand is home to Amul, the milk giant.

Agriculture: Major food crops in the state are rice, wheat, jowar, bajra, maize, tur, gram and groundnut. The most important non-food crops are cotton and tobacco.

Power: Gujarat gets its power mainly from thermal power plants, as well as partially from nuclear and hydroelectric power plants.

Education

Educational institutes: Notable institutes for higher education in the state include the Indian Institute of Management (Ahmedabad), Gujarat University (Ahmedabad), Gujarat Agricultural University (Sardar Krushinagar), Maharaja Sayaji Rao University (Vadodara), North Gujarat University (Patan), Saurashtra University (Rajkot), Indian Institute of Rural Management (Anand), Mudra Institute of Communications (Ahmedabad).

Tourism

Major tourist attractions: Mandvi Beach, Palitana Temple, Hatheesing Temple, Akshardham Temple, Somnath Temple, Sasan Gir, Modhera Sun Temple, Lothal, Bala Sinor, Saputara Hill Station.

Airports:
International: Ahmedabad.

Domestic:: Bhuj, Kandla, Jamnagar, Keshoo, Bhavnagar, Rajkot , Vadodara, Palanpur, Porbandar.

National Parks: Marine National Park and Sanctuary in Jamnagar dist. (162.89 sq. km and 295.03 sq. km respectively); Gir National Park and Sanctuary in Junagadh dist. (258.71 sq. km and

1153.42 sq. km respectively); Velavadhar National Park in Bhavnagar dist. (34.08 sq. km) and Vansda National Park in Valsad dist. (23.99 sq. km).

Administration

Legislature: Gujarat has a unicameral legislature. There are 182 seats of which 13 are reserved for SCs and 26 for STs. The tenure of the present house ends on 26 December 2007.

The party position in the current Vidhan Sabha is as follows:

Name of Party	Seats
Bharatiya Janata Party	128
Indian National Congress	49
Janata Dal	2
Independents	2
Vacant	1
Total	**182**

Judiciary: The High Court of Gujarat is at Ahmedabad. The chief justice is Bhawani Singh, sworn in on 25 August 2003.

Districts:

District	Area (sq. km)	Population	Headquarters	Urban Agglomerations
Ahmedabad	8,086	5,808,378	Ahmedabad	Ahmedabad, Dholka
Amreli	7,397	1,393,295	Amreli	Amreli
Anand	2,940	1,856,712	Anand	Anand, Khambhat
Banas Kantha	10,757	2,502,843	Palanpur	Palanpur
Bharuch	6,527	1,370,104	Bharuch	Anklesvar, Bharuch
Bhavnagar	9,980.9	2,469,264	Bhavnagar	Bhavnagar, Mahuva
Dohad	3,646.1	1,635,374	Dohad	Dohad
Gandhinagar	2,163.4	1,334,731	Gandhinagar	Ahmadabad, Kalol
Jamnagar	14,125	1,913,685	Jamnagar	Jamnagar
Junagadh	8,846	2,448,427	Junagadh	Junagadh, Mangrol, Veraval
Kutch	45,652	1,526,321	Bhuj	Bhuj
Kheda	4,218.8	2,023,354	Nadiad	Dakor, Nadiad
Mahesana	4,382.8	1,837,696	Mahesana	Kadi, Mahesana, Vijapur, Visnagar
Narmada	2,755.5	514,083	Rajpipla	
Navsari	2,209.2	1,229,250	Navsari	Bilimora, Navsari
Panch Mahals	5,219.9	2,024,883	Godhra	Godhra, Halol, Kalol
Patan	5,730.4	1,181,941	Patan	Patan, Sidhpur

Porbandar	2,297.8	536,854	Porbandar		Porbandar, Ranavav
Rajkot	11,203	3,157,676	Rajkot		Gondal, Morvi,
Rajkot Sabar Kantha		7,390	2,083,416		Himatnagarldar
Surat	7,657	4,996,391	Surat		Surat
Surendranagar	10,489	1,515,147	Surendranagar		Wadhwan
The Dangs	1,764	186,712	Ahwa		
Vadodara	7,549.5	3,639,775	Vadodara		Padra, Vadodara
Valsad	3,034.8	1,410,680	Valsad		Valsad

Haryana

Key Statistics

Capital: Chandigarh.

Area: 44,212 sq. km.

Population: Total: 21,144,564, Male: 11,369,953, Female: 9,780,611.

Population density: 477 per sq. km.

Sex ratio: 861 females per 1000 males.

Principal languages: Hindi, Punjabi, Urdu.

Literacy rates: Total: 67.9%, Male: 78.5%, Female: 55.67%.

Government

Governor: A.R. Kidwai. He became governor on 5 July 2004.

Chief Minister: Bhupinder Singh Hooda (INC). He was sworn in on 5 March 2005.

Geography

Physical characteristics: Haryana is surrounded by Himachal Pradesh in the north, Punjab in the west, Uttar Pradesh in the east and Delhi and Rajasthan in the south. The state has four main geographical features: (i) The Shivalik hills in the north, source of main seasonal rivers; (ii) The Ghaggar–Yamuna plain, which is divided into two parts—the higher one called 'Bangar' and the lower one 'Khadar'; (iii) A semi-desert plain, bordering the state of Rajasthan and (iv) The Aravalli Hills in the south, a dry area with uneven landscape.

Neighbouring States and Union territories:

States: Rajasthan, Punjab, Uttar Pradesh, Uttaranchal, Himachal Pradesh.

Union territories: Chandigarh, Delhi.

Major rivers: The Yamuna, Haryana's only perennial river, flows along the eastern boundary of the state. Ghaggar, the main seasonal river, flows along the northern boundary. Some other important seasonal rivers are Markanda, Tangri and Sahibi.

Climate: Haryana has very hot summers with maximum temperatures going up to 50°C in May and June in some areas. December and January are the coldest, minimum temperatures dropping as low as 1°C in parts of the state.

Rainfall is varied with the Shivalik region receiving the most rain and the Aravalli region being the driest. Nearly 80 per cent of the total rainfall occurs in the monsoon season, from July to September. The tributaries of the Yamuna and Ghaggar cause occasional floods.

Flora and Fauna:

Flora: Forests, mostly thorny dry deciduous forest, cover about 3.5 per cent of the total area. Common trees are babul, neem, shisham, pipal and banyan.

Fauna: Animals and birds found in the state include: leopard, jackal, the Indian fox, barking deer, sambar, chital, black buck, wild boar, seh or Indian porcupine, blue jay, northern green barbet, coppersmith, rose-ringed parakeet, kingfisher, Indian krait and Russell's viper.

History

The word 'Hariana' occurs in a Sanskrit inscription dated AD 1328. The region now known as Haryana was the scene of many important battles in Indian history. These include the three battles of Panipat: the first in 1526, when Babur defeated Ibrahim Lodi to establish Mughal rule in India; the second in 1556, when Emperor Akbar's army defeated the Afghans; and the third in 1761, when Ahmad Shah Abdali defeated the Marathas.

In 1803, the area included in the present state was ceded to the British East India Company and was subsequently transferred to the North-Western Provinces in 1832. Haryana became a part of Punjab in 1858, and remained so well after independence. Demands for states on a linguistic basis started to gain momentum in the early 1960s. On 1 November 1966, with the passage of the Punjab Reorganization Act, Haryana became the 17th state of India. Bhagwat Dayal Sharma was the first Chief Minister of the state.

Politics

In 1956, the states of PEPSU had been merged with Punjab, which remained a trilingual state having three language speakers—Punjabi, Hindi and Pahari—within its borders. In the Punjabi-speaking part of the state, there was a strong demand for carving out a separate Punjabi Suba (Punjabi-speaking state). The State Reorganisation Commission had refused to accept the demand for a separate Punjabi-speaking state on the ground that this would

not solve the language problem of Punjab. Finally, in 1966, Indira Gandhi agreed to the division of Punjab into two Punjabi- and Hindi-speaking states of Punjab and Haryana, with the Pahari-speaking district of Kangra and a part of Hoshiarpur district being merged with Himachal Pradesh. Thus Haryana was created on 1 November 1966, when PEPSU was split between a Hindu majority state and a Sikh majority state. The mostly Hindu and Hindi-speaking eastern portion of Punjab became Haryana, while the mostly Sikh and Punjabi-speaking western portion remained as Punjab. Today, Haryana has the vast majority of the ethnic Hindu population. Chandigarh, on the linguistic border, was made a union territory that serves as capital of both these states.

Five chief ministers in the state have had more than two tenures though most of them did not last the complete tenure of five years. Jat strongman Devi Lal was chief minister twice. Congress Leader Bansi Lal assumed charge for the first time in 1968 and remained chief minister till 1975. He was again Chief Minister between 1987 and 1989. His last tenure was from 1996-99. Banarsi Dass Gupta who succeeded Bansi Lal in 1975 also was chief minister twice. Devi Lal succeeded him on 21 May 1977. Devi Lal had played an active and decisive role in the formation of Haryana as a separate state. In 1971 he left the Congress after being in it for thirty-nine years. In 1977 he was elected on a Janata Party ticket and became the chief minister of Haryana. He formed the Lok Dal and started the programme Nyaya Yudh under the Haryana Sangharsh Samiti which became hugely popular among the masses. In the 1987 state elections, the alliance led by Devi Lal won a record victory winning 85 seats in the 90-member house. Bhajan Lal first became chief minister in 1979; he continued till 1985. He was again chief minister from 1991 to 1996. Om Prakash Chautala served the state four times as chief minister. He was elected unanimously as the president of the Haryana unit of the Indian National Lok Dal in 1999. Chautala's Indian National Lok Dal was routed in the 2005 Assembly polls. Bhupinder Singh Hooda of the Congress took oath on 5 March 2005 as the nineteenth chief minister of Haryana.

Culture

Haryana has a tradition of folklore expressed through mimes, dramas, ballads and songs such as Phag dance, Loor, Saang, Chupaiya and so on.

Fairs and festivals: Prominent festivals of Haryana are Holi, Diwali, Teej, Gugga Pir and Sanjhi. Popular fairs include Gopal-Mochan fair, Masani fair and Surajkund crafts fair. The Mango Festival and the Kurukshetra Festival are other popular annual events.

Economy, Industry and Agriculture

Economy: The net state domestic product at current prices for 2002–03 (provisional) was Rs 57,937 crores. The per capita net state domestic product at current prices for 2002–03 (provisional) was Rs 26,632.

Minerals and industry: The manufacturing sector's contribution to the state economy was 21.3 per cent during 1998–99. Major industries include passenger cars, motorcycles, tractors, sanitary ware, GI pipes, scientific instruments and gas stoves. In thirty years, the number of large and medium units has gone up from 162 to 1023, while the number of small-scale units increased from 4500 to 80,000. In recent years, many multinational companies have set up Business Process Outsourcing (BPO) operations in Gurgaon. Major minerals of the state are limestone, dolomite, china clay and marble.

Agriculture: Apart from meeting its own requirements, Haryana contributes about 45 lakh tonnes of food grain (mostly wheat and paddy) to the Central pool each year. Other important crops are sugarcane, cotton and maize.

Animal husbandry is a significant component of agriculture in the state. Apart from the 'Murrah' breed of buffaloes, the state regularly supplies eggs, layer-chicks and broilers to other Indian states.

Power: Most of Haryana's power is generated by thermal power plants. The rest comes from hydroelectric plants.

Education

Educational institutes: Notable institutions include the Maharshi Dayanand University (Rohtak), Kurukshetra University (Kurukshetra), Guru Jambheshwar University (Hissar), Chaudhary Charan Singh Agriculture University (Hissar) and National Dairy Research Institute (NDRI) (Karnal).

Tourism

Major tourist attractions: Surajkund, Kurukshetra, Panipat.

Airports: Chandigarh.

National Parks: Sultanpur National Park in Gurgaon dist. (1.43 sq. km).

Administration

Legislature: The state has a unicameral legislature with 90 members. Out of this 17 seats are reserved for SCs. The tenure of the current house ends on 8 March 2005. The current party position is as follows:

Name of Party	Seats
Indian National Congress	67
Indian National Lok Dal	9
Bharatiya Janata Party	2
Bahujan Samaj Party	1
Nationalist Congress Party	1
Independents	10
Total	**90**

Judiciary: The seat of the Punjab and Haryana High Court is at Chandigarh. The current chief justice is D.K. Jain.

Districts:

District	Area (sq. km)	Population	Headquarters	Urban Agglomerations
Ambala	1,574	1,013,660	Ambala	Ambala
Bhiwani	4,778	1,424,554	Bhiwani	
Faridabad	2,151	2,193,276	Faridabad	
Fatehabad	2,538	806,158	Fatehabad	
Gurgaon	2,766	1,657,669	Gurgaon	Gurgaon
Hisar	3,983	1,536,417	Hisar	Hisar
Jhajjar	1,834	887,392	Jhajjar	Bahadurgarh
Jind	2,702	1,189,725	Jind	
Kaithal	2,317	945,631	Kaithal	
Karnal	2,520	1,274,843	Karnal	Karnal
Kurukshetra	1,530	828,120	Kurukshetra	Thanesar
Mahendragarh	1,859	812,022	Narnaul	
Panchkula	898	469,210	Panchkula	Pinjore
Panipat	1,268	967,338	Panipat	Panipat
Rewari	1,582	764,727	Rewari	
Rohtak	1,745	940,036	Rohtak	Rohtak
Sirsa	4,277	1,111,012	Sirsa	
Sonipat	2,122	1,278,830	Sonipat	Sonipat
Yamunanagar	1,768	982,369	Yamunanagar	Yamunanagar

Himachal Pradesh

Key Statistics

Capital: Shimla.

Area: 55,673 sq. km.

Population: Total: 6,077,900, Male: 3,087,940, Female: 2,989,960.

Population density: 109 per sq. km.

Sex ratio: 968 females per 1000 males.

Principal languages: Hindi, Punjabi, Kinnauri.

Literacy rates: Total: 76.5%, Male: 85.3%, Female: 67.4%.

Government

Governor: Vishnu Sadashiv Kokje. He assumed the office of the governor on 8 May 2003.

Chief Minister: Virbhadra Singh (INC). He was sworn in on 6 March 2003.

Geography

Physical characteristics: Almost completely mountainous, with altitudes varying from 350 m to 6,975 m above sea level, Himachal Pradesh can be divided into five zones: (i) Wet sub-temperate zone (parts of Kangra, Mandi and Chamba districts); (ii) Humid sub-temperate zone (Kullu and Shimla districts; parts of Mandi, Solan, Chamba, Kangra and Sirmaur districts); (iii) Dry temperate alpine highlands (parts of Lahaul and Spiti district); (iv) Humid subtropical zone (Sirmaur district; parts of Chamba, Solan and Kangra districts); and (v) Sub-humid subtropical zone (parts of Kangra district).

Neighbouring States and Union territories:

International border: China.

States: Jammu and Kashmir, Uttaranchal, Punjab, Haryana, Uttar Pradesh.

Major rivers: Sutlej, Beas, Ravi, Chenab and Yamuna.

Climate: The climate varies from hot and humid in the valley areas to freezing cold in the alpine zone, which remains under snow for five to six months a year. Temperatures range from 40°C in plains during summer to −20°C in the alpine zone during winters. The average annual rainfall is about 1600mm.

Flora and Fauna:

Flora: Vegetation varies from dry scrub forests at lower altitudes to alpine pastures at higher altitudes. Between these two extremes, there are zones of mixed deciduous forests with deodar, chil, oak, bamboo, kail, spruce and fir.

Fauna: Wildlife found in Himachal Pradesh includes musk deer (the state animal), himalayan tahr, brown bear, snow leopard, ibex, western tragopan, sambhar, barking deer, wild boar, ghoral, leopard, monal (the state bird), cheer, snow cock and white crested kaleej.

History

The earliest known inhabitants of this mountainous region were a tribe called Dasas and later, Aryans. Successive Indian empires such as the Mauryans, the Kushans, the Guptas and the Mughals exercised varying degrees of control over the area. British domination of the region followed the Anglo-Sikh wars of the 1840s and continued for the next 100 years. After independence, 30 princely states were united to form the chief commissioner's province of Himachal Pradesh, which went on to become a Union territory in 1956.

With the reorganization of Punjab in 1966, Kangra and some other hill areas of Punjab were included in Himachal Pradesh, though its status remained that of a Union territory. Himachal Pradesh became the eighteenth state of the Indian Union on 25 January 1971. Yashwant Singh Parmar was the first Chief Minister.

Politics

Himachal Pradesh was formed as a union territory in 1948 by the merger of thirty former Punjabi princely states. In 1951, it became a part 'C' state. In 1956, despite majority recommendation of the States Reorganisation Commission for its merger with Punjab, Himachal Pradesh retained its separate identity, thanks to the famous dissenting note of the Chairman of the Commission, Justice Sh. Fazal Ali. But a great price had to be paid as Himachal was made a union territory sans a Legislative Assembly and was placed under an Administrator designated as Lt. Governor. Thereafter, the people and the political leadership of the state had to literally move heaven and earth for the restoration of a democratic edifice. Their efforts finally bore fruit in 1963, when a bill was passed by the Union parliament for providing Legislative Assemblies and Councils of Ministers to certain union territories including Himachal Pradesh. Himachal Pradesh attained statehood in the year 1971, emerging as the eighteenth state of the

Indian Union. Virbhadra Singh of the Congress party, the current chief minister, has had three tenures as chief minister of Himachal Pradesh.

Culture

Dances of Himachal include the Rakshasa (demon) dance, Kayang, Jataru Kayang, Chohara, Shand, Shabu, Lang-dar-ma, Jhanjhar and Rasa. These are accompanied by instruments like the Ranasingha, Karna, Turhi, Kindari, Jhanjh and Ghariyal. Popular weaving and handicrafts traditions include the Kullu and Kinnauri shawls, tweeds and blankets, carpets, traditional dresses, metal craft and pottery. Himachal is also famous for the Kangra Valley School of Painting.

Fairs and festivals: Prominent fairs and festivals of the state include Kullu Dussehra, Shimla's Summer Festival, Lohri or Maghi, Basant Panchami, Mandi Shivratri, Holi, Nalwari fair, Baisakhi, Phulech (Festival of Flowers), Minjar fair and Lahaul Festival.

Economy, Industry and Agriculture

Economy: The net state domestic product at current prices in 2002–03 (advance estimate) was Rs 14,202 crores. The per capita net state domestic product at current prices in 2002–03 (advance estimate) was Rs 22,576.

Minerals and industry: Major industries of Himachal Pradesh are chemicals and chemical products, textile, electronics, steel and steel products, paper and paper products, cement, beverages and plastic products. Minerals found in the state include limestone (light grade), quartzite, gold, pyrites, copper, rock salt, natural oil, gas, mica, barytes and gypsum.

Agriculture: Himachal Pradesh is predominantly an agricultural state with nearly 70% of the total population getting direct employment from agriculture. Important crops include maize, paddy, wheat, barley, vegetables, ginger and potato. Main fruits under cultivation are apple, pear, apricot, plum, peach, mango, litchi, guava and strawberry.

Power: Himachal has a huge identified hydroelectric potential in its five river basins. All of the state's power comes from hydroelectric plants.

Education

Educational institutes: Prominent educational institutions include Himachal Pradesh University, Shimla; Dr Y.S. Parmar University of Horticulture and Forestry, Solan; C.S.K. H.P. Krishi Vishva Vidyalaya, Palampur; Jaypee University of Information Technology (JUIT), Solan; Indian Institute of Advanced Studies, Shimla; National Institute of Technology, Hamirpur and Indira Gandhi Medical College, Shimla.

Tourism

Major tourist attractions:

1. Shimla: The Ridge, The Mall, Kali Bari Temple, State Museum, Chadwick Falls, Mashobra, Naldehra.
2. Chamba: Dalhousie, Laxmi Narayan Temple, Champavati Temple, Akhand Chandi Palace, Panchpula, Kalatop, Khajiar, Banikhet.
3. Kangra: Dharamshala, Kangra Fort, Palampur.
4. Solan: Kasauli, Chail.
5. Sirmaur: Nahan, Suketi Fossil Park, Paonta Sahib, Renuka.
6. Kullu: Manali, Bijli Mahadev Shrine, Raghunathji Temple, Camping Sight Raison, Hadimba Temple, Tibetan Monasteries, Rohtang Pass.
7. Kinnaur: Sangla Valley, Chitkul, Recong Peo, Rakchham.
8. Lahaul and Spiti: Gondla, Tandi, Shashur Monastery, Kardang Monastery, Thang. Yug Gompa.

Airports: Shimla, Kullu, Kangra (Gaggal).

National Parks: Great Himalayan National Park, Kullu (754 sq. km) and Pin Valley National Park, Lahaul-Spiti (675 sq. km).

Administration

Legislature: The Himachal Pradesh Legislative Assembly has 68 seats, of which 16 are reserved for SCs and 3 for STs. The term of the current house expires on 9 March 2008. The current party position is as follows:

Name of Party	Seats
Indian National Congress	43
Bharatiya Janata Party	16
Himachal Vikas Congress	1
Lok Jan Shakti Party	1
Loktantrik Morcha Himachal Pradesh	1
Independents	6
Total	**68**

Judiciary: The seat of the Himachal Pradesh High Court is in Shimla. The current chief justice is Justice V.K. Gupta.

Districts:

District	Area (sq. km)	Population	Headquarters	Urban Agglomerations
Bilaspur	1,167	340,735	Bilaspur	
Chamba	6,528	460,499	Chamba	
Hamirpur	1,118	412,009	Hamirpur	
Kangra	5,739	1,338,536	Dharamshala	
Kinnaur	6,401	83,950	Recong Peo	
Kullu	5,503	379,865	Kullu	
Lahaul and Spiti	13,835	33,224	Keylong	
Mandi	3,950	900,987	Mandi	
Shimla	5,131	721,745	Shimla	Shimla
Sirmaur	2,825	458,351	Nahan	
Solan	1,936	499,380	Solan	
Una	1,540	447,967	Una	

Jammu and Kashmir

Key Statistics

Capital: Summer (May–October)—Srinagar; Winter (November–April)—Jammu.

Area: 222,236 sq. km.

Population: Total: 10,069,917, Male: 5,300,574, Female: 4,769,343.

Population density: 99 per sq. km.

Sex ratio: 900 females per 1000 males.

Principal languages: Urdu, Kashmiri, Dogri.

Literacy rates: Total: 54.46%, Male: 65.75%, Female: 41.82%.

Government

Governor: Lt Gen. (Retd) Sriniwas Kumar Sinha. He took over as governor on 4 June 2003.

Chief Minister: Mufti Mohammed Sayeed (PDP). He was sworn in on 2 November 2002.

Geography

Physical characteristics: The northern extremity of India, Jammu and

Kashmir is bounded by Pakistan, Afghanistan and China from west to east. Himachal Pradesh and Punjab are on its south. The state has four geographical zones: (i) The submountainous and semi-mountainous plain known as Kandi; (ii) The Shivalik ranges; (iii) The high mountain zone constituting the Kashmir valley, the Pir Panjal range and its offshoots; (iv) The middle run of the Indus river comprising Leh and Kargil.

Neighbouring States and Union territories:
International border: Pakistan, Afghanistan, China.

States: Himachal Pradesh, Punjab.

Major rivers: Indus, Chenab, Jhelum and Ravi.

Climate: The climate varies from tropical in the plains of Jammu to semi-arctic cold in Ladakh. The mountainous tracts in Kashmir and Jammu have temperate climatic conditions. Annual rainfall varies from 92.6mm in Leh to 650.5mm in Srinagar and 1115.9mm in Jammu.

Flora and Fauna:
Flora: Flora in Jammu and Kashmir ranges from the thorn bush type in arid plains to the temperate and alpine flora in higher altitudes. Maple, horse chestnuts and silver fir are the common broad-leaf trees. Birch, rhododendron, berbers and a large number of herbs are found on higher altitudes. The state is also famous for its Chinar tree that is found all over the valley. Other trees found in the state include almond, walnut, willow and cedar. The mountain ranges have deodar, pine and fir.

Fauna: Wildlife in the state include leopard, hangul or Kashmir stag, wild sheep, bear, brown musk shrew, musk rat, varieties of snakes, chakor, snow partridge, pheasants and peacock. The fauna in Ladakh includes yak, Himalayan ibex, Tibetan antelope, snow leopard, wild ass, red bear and gazelle. Besides these, the state is known for its trout population.

History

Legend has it that Kashyapa Rishi reclaimed the land that now comprises Kashmir from a vast lake. It came to be known as Kashyapamar and, later, Kashmir. Emperor Asoka introduced Buddhism to the region in 3 BC. Subsequently, the valley became parts of the empires of Kanishka and Mihiragula. Around 7th century AD, a local dynasty, the Karkotas, believed to have been founded by Durlabhavardhana, came to power in the region. According to Kalhana, the famous historian of Kashmir, this dynasty spread its power under the reign of Lalitaditya. He is believed to have defeated Kanauj, the Tibetans and even the Turks in the Indus area. His grandson, Jayapada Vinyaditya, achieved victories over Gauda and Kanauj. This dynasty came to an end around 855. The house of Utpalas followed. Its founder was Avantivarman. His son, Sankaravarmana expanded the state's territorial limits and is believed to have even annexed a part of Punjab from the Gurjaras. A period of turmoil followed his death during which the widowed queen, Sugandha, attempted to rule. She faced fierce opposition from the Tantrins, a powerful military faction. They emerged as the virtual military dictators of the territory. But ultimately a group of Brahmanas elevated Yasaskara, a member of their order, to the throne of Kashmir. The lien started by Yasaskara was succeeded by the dynasty started by Parva Gupta.

The Hindu rule over Kashmir came to an end in the 14th century. In around 1339 or 1346, a Muslim adventurer named Shah Mirza seized power and assumed the title of Shams-ud-din Shah. The Sultanate of Kashmir thus established ruled till about 1540 when a relative of Humayun, Mirza Haidar, annexed Kashmir. He ruled Kashmir virtually as a sovereign although in theory he ruled on behalf of Humayun. In

1551, the local nobles ousted Mirza Haidar. In around 1555, the Chakks seized the throne. Kashmir ultimately became a part of the Mughal Empire in Akbar's reign.

In 1819, Kashmir was annexed to the Sikh kingdom of Punjab and later on to the Dogra kingdom of Jammu in 1846. In 1846, the treaties of Lahore and Amritsar that were signed at the conclusion of the First Sikh War made Raja Gulab Singh, the Dogra ruler of Jammu, the ruler of an extensive Himalayan kingdom. The state was under Dogra rule till 1947, when Maharaja Hari Singh signed the Instrument of Accession in favour of the Indian union.

Much drama surrounds Jammu and Kashmir's accession to the Indian Union. Jammu and Kashmir was one of the princely states of India on which British paramountcy lapsed at midnight on 15 August 1947. When power was transferred to the people in British India, the rulers of the princely states were given an option to join either India or Pakistan. The ruler of Jammu and Kashmir, Maharaja Hari Singh, did not exercise the option immediately. Instead, he offered a 'Standstill Agreement' to both India and Pakistan, pending a final decision. On 12 August 1947 the Prime Minister of Jammu and Kashmir sent identical communications to the governments of India and Pakistan, offering to enter into Standstill Agreements with both the countries. While Pakistan entered into a Standstill Agreement, India declined and instead asked the state to send its emissary for talks. Meanwhile, a 'Quit Kashmir' movement was active under the leadership of Sheikh Mohammad Abdullah. Sheikh Abdullah was against the Kashmir ruler's autocratic rule as well as an accession to Pakistan and enjoyed public support.

When Pakistani designs on acquiring the state failed, they sent in thousands of tribals along with regular Pakistani troops who entered the state on 22 October 1947. This finally caused the Maharaja to sign the Instrument of Accession in favour of India on 26 October 1947, agreeing to the prescribed terms and conditions. On 30 October 1947, an Emergency Government was formed in the state with Sheikh Mohammad Abdullah as its head. The Indian Army was sent in and it successfully flushed out the invaders. On 1 January 1948, India took up the issue of Pakistani aggression in Jammu and Kashmir at the United Nations. Consequently, a ceasefire came into operation on the midnight of 1 January 1949. At the time of ceasefire, Pakistan was in illegal possession of 78,114 sq. km. It remains in possession of this territory even today.

On 5 March 1948, the Maharaja announced the formation of an interim popular government with Sheikh Mohammad Abdullah as the Prime Minister. The Maharaja then signed a proclamation making Yuvraj Karan Singh the Regent. Pakistan waged two more wars, in 1965 and 1971, with the intention of annexing all of Jammu and Kashmir, but was beaten back.

In 1959, Chinese troops occupied the Aksai Chin part of Ladakh. In 1963, a Sino-Pakistani agreement defined the Chinese border with Pakistani Kashmir and ceded Indian-claimed territory to China.

Politics

Jammu and Kashmir was one of about 565 princely states of India on which the British paramountcy lapsed at the stroke of midnight on 15 August 1947. While the power was transferred to the people in British India, the rulers of the princely states were given an option to join either of the two Dominions – India or Pakistan. Moreover, in the Indian Independence Act, 1947, there was no provision for any conditional accession. The ruler of Jammu and Kashmir, Maharaja Hari Singh, did not exercise the option immediately and instead offered a proposal of Standstill Agreement to both the Dominions, pending a final decision on the state's accession. India did not agree to the offer and advised the Maharaja to send his authorized representative to Delhi for discussions on the offer. The Maharaja was already facing a formidable challenge from the people who had launched the Quit Kashmir movement under the leadership of Sher-i-Kashmir Sheikh Mohammad Abdullah against the Maharaja's rule. The Quit Kashmir movement ran parallel to the national movement with Sheikh Mohammad Abdullah having close associations with the leaders of the national movement against British rule. National leaders like Mahatma Gandhi and Pandit Nehru too espoused the cause of the people of Kashmir seeking political freedom from autocratic rule. To deal with the people's upsurge, the Maharaja had even detained Sheikh Abdullah on 20 May 1946. Faced with the new alarming situation arising out of repeated violations of the Standstill Agreement by Pakistan and blocking of the Pindi-Srinagar road, the Maharaja set him free on 29 September 1947. Mohammad Abdullah deputed his close aide Kh.G.M. Sadiq to Pakistan to tell Pak leaders about the sentiments of the people who could not be taken for granted and coerced to join them. This plain speaking did not deter Pakistan from pursuing its designs. At last, bowing before the wishes of the people as reflected by the Muslim dominated National Conference, and to resist the invaders, the Maharaja signed the Instrument of Accession in favour of India on 26 October 1947. This was accepted by the Governor General of India, Lord Mountbatten, the next day. With J&K becoming a legal and constitutional part of the Union of India, Indian troops were rushed to the state to push back the invaders and vacate aggressors from the territory of the state. On 30 October 1947 an emergency government was formed in the state with Sheikh Mohammad Abdullah as its head. The Army fought a sustained battle with the intruders and after several sacrifices pushed them out of the Valley and other areas in the Jammu region. On 1 January 1948 India took up the issue of Pak aggression in Jammu and Kashmir in the UNO under Article 35 of its charter. The Government of India requested the Security Council to call upon Pakistan to put an end immediately to the giving of such assistance, which was an act of aggression against India. If Pakistan did not do so, the Government of India said it may be compelled, in self defence, to enter Pakistani territory to take military action against the invaders. After long debates, a cease-fire came into operation on the midnight of 1 January 1949. At the time of the cease-fire, Pakistan was holding 78,114 sq. km of Kashmir territory illegally and this illegal possession of that territory (Pakistan Occupied Kashmir) continues even today. So far India and Pakistan have been to war three times in Kashmir (1947-1948, 1965, 1971) and clashed there again during the Kargil conflict of 1999.

On 5 March 1948, the Maharaja announced the formation of an interim popular government with Sheikh Mohammad Abdullah as the prime minister. Subsequently, the Maharaja signed a proclamation making Yuvraj Karan Singh the Regent. After attaining political freedom, Jammu and Kashmir marched ahead to strengthen the democratic structure. In 1951, the State Constituent Assembly was elected by the people. Close on the heels of this, the Delhi Agreement was signed between the two prime ministers of India and Jammu and Kashmir giving special position to the state under the Indian Constitutional framework. The Constituent Assembly elected the Yuvraj as the Sadar-I-Riyasat on 15

November 1952, thus bringing to end the 106-year old hereditary rule in Jammu and Kashmir. The State Constituent Assembly ratified the accession of the state to the Union of India on 6 February 1954 and the President of India subsequently issued the Constitution (Application to J&K) Order under Article 370 of the Indian Constitution extending the Union Constitution to the state with some exceptions and modifications. The state's own Constitution came into force on 26 January 1957 under which the elections to the state Legislative Assembly were held for the first time on the basis of adult franchise the same year. Since then eight assembly elections have been held in the state besides Lok Sabha elections where the people exercised their franchise freely.

Bakshi Ghulam Mohammad held the reins of government in the wake of Sheikh Abdullah's deposition in 1953. Bakshi had to face unprecedented challenges from the forces of disintegration and secessionism, which got a new lease of life after Sheikh Abdullah stepped down from office. He remained in power till 12 October 1963. The state's Constitution was amended on 30 March 1965 to rename the Sadr-e-Riyasat (president) as governor and the prime minister as the chief minister. Ghulam Mohammad Sadiq was the last prime minister and became the first chief minister of the state on 10 April 1965. Syed Mir Qasim held the post between December 1971 and February 1975. The founder president of National Conference Shiekh Mohammad Abdullah held the post twice from 1975 to 1982. He was succeeded by Farroq Abdullah who held the post thrice heading a National Conference government from 1982-84, 1987-90 and 1996-2002. In between, Abdullah's brother-in-law Ghulam Mohammad Shah held the top office in 1984-86. A nine-member ministry headed by People's Democratic Party president Mufti Mohammad Sayeed was sworn-in as chief minister in Jammu and Kashmir on 2 November 2002. Mufti Mohammad, who heads the PDP-Congress coalition government, is the sixth chief minister of the state. His government has the outside support of the Peoples' Democratic Front comprising independents and CPI(M) legislators.

Culture

Popular performing traditions of the Jammu region include Kud, a ritual dance performed in honour of local deities and the traditional theatre form Heren. Folk traditions in the Kashmir region include the theatre-style Bhand Pather and the Chakri form of music. There is also a rich tradition in Sufiana music. Jabro and Alley Yate are popular dance forms in the Ladakh region.

Fairs and festivals: Principal festivals of the state include Lohri, Baisakhi and Bahu Mela in the Jammu region; Id-ul-Fitr, Id-ul-Zuha and Miraj Alam in the Kashmir region; and Mela Losar and Hemis festival in the Ladakh region.

Economy, Industry and Agriculture

Economy: The net state domestic product at current prices for 2001–02 was Rs 13,697crore. The per capita net state domestic product at current prices for 2001–02 was Rs 13,320.

Minerals and industry: Handicrafts production and export, mainly papier mache, wood carving, carpets, shawls, copper and silverware have been the traditional industry of the state. Other important industries include plastic products, cricket bats and other sports items, chemicals and basic drugs, electronics and precision engineering. The state has small mineral and fossil fuel resources largely concentrated in the Jammu region. There are bauxite and gypsum deposits in Udhampur district. Other minerals include limestone, coal, zinc, and copper.

Agriculture: Nearly 80 per cent of the state's population depends on agriculture. Major crops include paddy, wheat, maize, pulses, cotton and barley. Horticulture is also widespread. Large orchards in the Kashmir valley produce apples, pears, peaches, walnuts, almonds, cherries, apricots, strawberries and saffron.

Power: Nearly all of Jammu and Kashmir's power comes from hydroelectric plants.

Education

Educational institutes: Notable educational institutes include University of Jammu, Jammu, University of Kashmir, Srinagar and Sher-e-Kashmir University of Agricultural Sciences and Technology, Srinagar.

Tourism

Major tourist attractions:

1. Jammu: Bahu Fort, Mubarak Mandi Complex, Ziarat Baba Buddan Shah, Raghunath Temple, Vaishno Devi Shrine, Mansar Lake, Patnitop.

2. Kashmir: Dal Lake, Hazratbal Shrine, Shankarcharya Temple, Gulmarg, Pahalgam, Sonamarg, Charar-i-Sharief, Amarnath.

3. Ladakh: Buddhist Gompas or monasteries at Hemis, Alchi, Thikse, and Spituk; Shey Palace, Jama Masjid, Leh Palace.

Airports: Srinagar, Jammu, Leh.

National Parks: Dachigam in Srinagar (141 sq. km); Hemis Leh (4100 sq. km) and Kishtwar Doda (310 sq. km).

Administration

Legislature: Jammu and Kashmir has a special status within the Union government: the state has its own Constitution (adopted in 1956) that affirms its integrity within the Republic of India.

The state assembly has a total of 87 seats, with seven seats reserved for scheduled castes. As per Article 52 of the Constitution of J&K, the term of the state assembly is for six years. The term of the current house expires on 20 November 2008. The current party position is as follows:

Name of Party	Seats
Jammu and Kashmir National Conference	28
Indian National Congress	20
Peoples Democratic Party	16
J and K National Panthers Party	4
Communist Party of India (Marxist)	2
Jammu and Kashmir Awami League	1
Democratic Movement	1
Bahujan Samaj Party	1
Bharatiya Janata Party	1
Independent	13
Total	**87**

Judiciary: The headquarters of the Jammu and Kashmir High Court is at Srinagar from May to October, and at Jammu from November to April. However, court sections of both Jammu and Srinagar wings of the High Court function throughout the year. The current chief justice is Sachchidanand Jha.

Districts:

District	Area (sq. km)	Population	Headquarters	Urban Agglomerations
Anantanag	3,984	1,170,013	Anantanag	Anantnag
Badgam	1,371	593,768	Badgam	
Baramula	4,588	1,166,722	Baramula	Baramula, Sopore
Doda	11,691	690,474	Doda	
Jammu	3,097	1,571,911	Jammu	Jammu

Kargil	14,036	115,227	Kargil	
Kathua	2,651	544,206	Kathua	Kathua
Kupwara	2,379	640,013	Kupwara	
Leh	45,110	117,637	Leh	
Pulwama	1,398	632,295	Pulwama	
Punch	1,674	371,561	Punch	
Rajauri	2,630	478,595	Rajauri	
Srinagar	2,228	1,238,530	Srinagar	Srinagar
Udhampur	4,550	738,965	Udhampur	Udhampur

Jharkhand

Key Statistics

Capital: Ranchi.

Area: 79,714 sq. km.

Population: Total: 26,945,829, Male: 13,885,037, Female: 13,060,792.

Population density: 338 per sq. km.

Sex ratio: 941 females per 1000 males.

Principal languages: Local languages like Santhali, Hindi, Urdu.

Literacy rates: Total: 53.6%, Male: 67.3%, Female: 38.9%.

Government

Governor: Syed Sibte Razi. He was sworn in on 10 June 2004.

Chief Minister: Arjun Munda (BJP). He was sworn in on 18 March 2003.

Geography

Physical characteristics: The Jharkhand region lies to the south of Bihar and encompasses Santhal Parganas and Chota Nagpur. It is a plateau region about 1000 metres above sea level, which features densely forested hill ranges. The highest part of the plateau is Netarhat (1100 metres). The Parasnath Hill is the highest point in the state (1500 metres). Bihar lies to the north, Chhattisgarh and Uttar Pradesh to the west, Orissa to the south and West Bengal to the east of the state.

Neighbouring States and Union territories:

States: Bihar, West Bengal, Orissa, Chhattisgarh, Uttar Pradesh.

Major rivers: Damodar and Subarnarekha.

Climate: The state's climate is of the hot tropical type, with hot summers and cold winters. Most of the rainfall takes place in the period between July and September. Maximum temperatures range from 30°C to 44°C in summer; winter temperatures range from 1°C to 28°C.

Flora and Fauna:

Flora: Forests extend over 23,605 sq. km, which is 29.61 per cent of the state's total geographical area. Of this, 82 per cent is categorized as 'Protected Forest' and 17.5 per cent as 'Reserve Forest'. A small portion (33.49 sq. km) is not categorized.

The state's forests consist largely of the tropical moist deciduous type. The state is home to a large number of threatened orchids. Sal and bamboo are the two key constituents of the state's forests.

Fauna: Important members of the state's animal population include gaur, chital, tiger, panther, wild boar, sambar, sloth bear, nilgai and deer.

History

In 1929 the Simon Commission was presented with a memorandum that demanded the formation of a separate Jharkhand state. In December 1947, the All India Jharkhand Party was formed and in 1951, it was elected to the Vidhan Sabha as the main opposition party. In 1971, A.K. Roy set up the MCC to demand a separate Jharkhand state. In 1973, N.E. Horo named his party the Jharkhand Party and presented the then prime minister with a memorandum for a separate Jharkhand state. The year 1980 saw the establishment of the Jharkhand Kranti Dal. In 1987, the home minister of India directed the Bihar government to prepare a detailed report on the profile of all districts of Chota Nagpur and Santhal Parganas. In January 1994, Laloo Prasad Yadav declared that the Jharkhand Development Autnomous Council Bill would be passed in the budget session of the legislature. In 1995, the Jharkhand Area Autonomous Council was formed, comprising as 18 districts of Santhal Parganas and Chota Nagpur, with Shibu Soren nominated as the chairman.

In July 1997, Shibu Soren offered his party's support to the minority government of Laloo Prasad Yadav, on the condition of a separate Jharkhand Bill in the assembly. In August 2000, the bill to create a separate state of Jharkhand out of the state of Bihar was passed in the Lok Sabha by a voice vote. Later that month, the Rajya Sabha cleared the formation of Jharkhand as well. On 25 August, the then President, K.R. Narayanan, approved the Bihar Reorganization Bill, 2000. The state of Jharkhand came into existence on 15 November 2000. The state's first Chief Minister was Babulal Marandi.

Politics

The Jharkhand movement started with the organizational activities of the Chhotanagpur Unnati Samaj (CUS), founded in 1921, and subsequently of the Adivasi Mahasabha, founded in 1939. Among those who spearheaded the Jharkhand movement was Jaipal Singh, an Oxford-returned tribal Christian who helped the regional aspiration gain national recognition. On 28 December 1947 the All India Jharkhand Party came into being under the leadership of Jaipal Singh. It was with the emergence of this party that the Jharkhand movement became purely political. In 1951, the Jharkhand party became the largest opposition party in the Bihar Assembly winning all the 32 seats from south Bihar and giving a fresh impetus to the demand for a separate Jharkhand state. The movement's original demand was for the formation of a separate state with 16 districts of south Bihar's Chhotanagpur and Santhal Pargana regions. The Jharkhand Party also wanted three contiguous, tribal-dominated districts of adjoining West Bengal, four districts of Orissa and two districts of Madhya Pradesh to be included in the proposed state. West Bengal, Orissa and Madhya Pradesh, however, refused to part with any territory. In 1955, the Jharkhand Party submitted a memorandum to the States Reorganisation Commission, reiterating the statehood demand. But it was turned down by the Commission. Subsequently the Jharkhand Party suffered a series of splits. In 1970, Sibu Soren of Santhal Pargana quit the party to form the Jharkhand Mukti Morcha, with Benode Behari Mahato as its chairman. In 1971 A.K.Roy founded the Marxist M.C.C. to demand a separate Jharkhand state. In 1973 N.E.Horo named his party the Jharkhand Party and presented the prime minister a memorandum for a separate Jharkhand state. The year

1980 saw the establishment of the Jharkhand Kranti Dal. On 25 September 1986 the All Jharkhand Students Union gave its first call for a Jharkhand bandh, which was a huge success. In 1987 the home minister of India directed the Bihar government to prepare a detailed profile of all districts of Chhotnagpur and Santhal Pargana. In 1995 the Jharkhand Area Autonomous Council was formed comprising 18 districts of Santhal Pargana and Chhotnagpur and Shibu Soren was nominated as the Chairman. In July 1997, Shibu Soren offered support to the minority government of Laloo Prasad Yadav with a condition of a separate Jharkhand bill in the assembly. In the year 2000 the bill to create a separate state of Jharkhand to be carved out of Bihar was passed in the Lok Sabha. The long cherished demand of people of the region was fulfilled and the new state Jharkhand was formed on 15 November 2000. Jharkhand is the twenty-eighth state of the Indian Union. Babulal Marandi of the Bharatiya Janata Party was sworn in as the first chief minister of Jharkhand. On 18 March 2003 Arjun Munda was sworn in as the chief minister. Sibu Soren replaced him after the assembly elections in 2005 but failed to prove his majority in the assembly and resigned. On 12 March 2005 Arjun Munda was again sworn in as the chief minister of the state.

Culture

Folk music forms of Jharkhand include Akhariya Domkach, Dohari Domkach, Janani Jhumar, Mardana Jhumar and Faguwa. Folk dance forms include Paika, Chhau, Jadur and Karma. Santhali Bhittichitra, Oraon Bhittichitra, Jado Patiya are some local forms of painting.

Fairs and festivals: Sarhul, Karma, Sohrai, Badna and Tusu (or Makar) are notable among the local festivals.

Economy, Industry and Agriculture

Economy: The net state domestic product at current prices (new series) in 2002–03 (advance estimate) was Rs 27,358 crores. The per capita net state domestic product at current prices (new series) in 2002–03 (advance estimate) was Rs 9955.

Minerals and industry: Jharkhand has some of the richest deposits of minerals in the country. The steel plants at Bokaro and Jamshedpur are also in this state. Minerals mined in the state include iron ore, coal, copper ore, mica, bauxite as well as fireclay, graphite, kyanite, sillimanite, limestone and uranium.

Agriculture: The main crops grown in the state are paddy, wheat, pulses and maize.

Power: The state gets its power from both thermal and hydroelectric sources.

Education

Educational institutes: Prominent institutes in the state include Ranchi University, Siddhu Kanhu University (Dumka), Vinoba Bhave University (Hazaribagh), Birsa Agricultural University (Ranchi), Birla Institute of Technology and Science (Ranchi), Xavier Labour Relations Institute (Jamshedpur), National Metallurgical Laboratory (Jamshedpur), Central Mining Research Institute (Dhanbad) and Research and Development Centre for Iron and Steel (Ranchi).

Tourism

Major tourist attractions: Dassam Falls, Netarhat, Hazaribagh National Park, Baidyanath Temple, Deoghar, Basakinath Temple, Deoghar, Topchanchi Lake, Dhanbad.

Airports: Ranchi.

National Parks: Palamau National Park (Betla) in Palamau dist. (226.32 sq. km) and Hazaribagh National Park in Hazaribagh dist. (183.89 sq. km).

Administration

Legislature: Jharkhand has a unicameral legislature consisting of 81 seats, out of which 9 are reserved for SCs and 28 for STs. However, the tenure of the existing members of Legislative Council (MLCs) was carried over from Bihar at the time of the formation of the state, and were maintained.

The party position in the state assembly is as follows:

Name of Party	Seats
Bharatiya Janata Party	30
Indian National Congress	9
Nationalist Congress Party	1
Jharkhand Mukti Morcha	17
Rashtriya Janata Dal	7
Janata Dal (United)	6
United Goans Democratic Party	2
All India Forward Bloc	2
Communist Party of India (Marxist-Leninist) (Liberation)	1
All Jharkhand Students Union	2
Jharkhand Party	1
Independent	3
Total	**81**

Judiciary: The Jharkhand High Court is located at Ranchi. The chief justice is Altamas Kabir.

Districts:

District	Area (sq. km)	Population	Headquarters	Urban Agglomerations
Bokaro	2,861	1,775,961	Bokaro Steel City	Bokaro Steel City, Phusro
Chatra	3,706	790,680	Chatra	
Deoghar	2,479	1,161,370	Deoghar	Deoghar
Dhanbad	2,052	2,394,434	Dhanbad	Chirkunda, Dhanbad
Dumka	6,212	1,754,571	Dumka	
Garhwa	4,044	1,034,151	Garhwa	
Giridih	4,975	1,901,564	Giridih	Giridih
Godda	2,110	1,047,264	Godda	
Gumla	9,077	1,345,520	Gumla	
Hazaribagh	6,147	2,277,108	Hazaribagh	Hazaribag, Ramgarh
Kodarma	1,312	498,683	Kodarma	
Lohardaga	1,491	364,405	Lohardaga	
Pakur	1,806	701,616	Pakur	
Palamau	8,705	2,092,004	Daltonganj	
Pashchimi Singhbhum	9,907	2,080,265	Chaibasa	Chakradharpur, Jamshedpur
Purbi Singhbhum	3,533	1,978,671	Jamshedpur	Jamshedpur
Ranchi	7,698	2,783,577	Ranchi	Ranchi
Sahibganj	1,599	927,584	Sahibganj	

Karnataka

Key Statistics

Capital: Bangalore.
Area: 191,791 sq. km.
Population: Total: 52,850,562, Male: 26,898,918, Female: 25,951,644.
Population density: 275 per sq. km.
Sex ratio: 965 females per 1000 males.
Principal languages: Kannada, Urdu, Telugu.
Literacy rates: Total: 66.6%, Male: 76.1%, Female: 56.9%.

Government

Governor: T.N. Chaturvedi. He assumed office of the governor on 21 August 2002.

Chief Minister: N. Dharam Singh (INC), sworn in on 28 May 2004.

Geography

Physical characteristics: About 750 km from north to south and 400 km from east to west, Karnataka can be divided in four physiographic regions: (i) The Northern Plateau, with a general elevation of 300 to 600 metres from the mean sea level; (ii) The Central Plateau, with a general elevation of 450 to 700 metres; (iii) The Southern Plateau, with a general elevation of 600 to 900 metres; and (iv) The Coastal Region, comprising the plains and the Western Ghats.

Among the tallest peaks of the state are Mullayyana Giri, Bababudangiri and Kudremukh.

Neighbouring States and Union territories:
States: Goa, Maharashtra, Andhra Pradesh, Tamil Nadu, Kerala.

Major rivers: Krishna, Cauvery, North Pennar, South Pennar, Palar, Hemavati, Kalinadi, Gagavali and Tungabhadra.

Climate: The climate varies from hot with excessive rainfall in the coastal belt and adjoining areas to hot and seasonally dry tropical climate in the southern half, and to hot and semi-arid in the northern half. April and May are the hottest months with maximum temperatures going above 40°C. The period from October to March is generally pleasant over the entire state. The average annual rainfall for the state is 1390mm, with Bijapur, Raichur and Bellary receiving the minimum rainfall and Shimoga and Kodagu receiving the maximum.

Flora and Fauna:
Flora: Around 20 per cent of the state area is under forests, with teak, rosewood, honne, mathi, bamboo and sandal trees in abundance.

Fauna: Wildlife found in Karnataka include gaur, sambar, barking deer, elephant, tiger, leopard, wild dog, sloth bear, black buck, open-bill stork, white ibis, egret, heron, partridge, peafowl, quail and hornbill.

History

Around the mid-3rd century BC, the Mauryas ruled over major parts of present-day Karnataka. After the Mauryas up until the 11 century AD, the principal dynasties in the region were the Kadambas, the Gangas and the Pallavas. They were followed by the Chalukyas, the Hoysalas and the Rashtrakutas. After the 13th century, Mysore gradually came under the influence of the Vijayanagar empire.

Towards the end of the 16th century, the Vijayanagar empire declined, resulting in Mughal domination of the territory lying north of the Tungabhadra and the rajas of Mysore controlling the south. Hyder Ali rose to power in 1761 and his invasions extended

Mysore's dominion. After his son Tipu Sultan was killed in 1799, the area came under British control which continued until independence.

After independence, Mysore state went through two territorial reorganizations: in 1953 and in 1956. The state was renamed Karnataka on 1 November 1973. Arcot Ramaswami Mudaliar was the first Chief Minister of Karnataka.

Politics

After Indian independence, the Wodeyar Maharaja of Mysore acceded to India. In 1950, Mysore became an Indian state, and the former Maharaja became its Rajpramukh or governor. After accession to India, the Woyedar family was given a pension by the Indian government until 1975, and members of the family still reside in part of their ancestral palace in Mysore. On 1 November 1956, Mysore state was enlarged to its present boundaries, incorporating the state of Coorg and the Kannada-speaking portions of neighboring Madras, Hyderabad, and Bombay states. On 1 November 1973 the name of the state was changed to Karnataka.

Karnataka's first Assembly started functioning from 18 June 1952 and lasted till 31 March 1957. During this period Karnataka had the highest dignitaries as its chief minister, including K.H. Hanumanthaiah, Kadidal Manjappa and S. Nijalingappa. Ramakrishna Hegde started his first term as chief minister from 1983. H.D. Deve Gowda was chief minister from 1994 to 1996, and subsequently became prime minister of India. J.H. Patel succeeded him as chief minister. S.M. Krishna became chief minister in 1999. After the 2004 Assembly elections, Dharam Singh came to power as chief minister.

Culture

Karnataka boasts a fascinating variety of folk theatre, called Bayalata.

Dasarata, Sannata, Doddata, Parijata and Yakshagana are the most popular forms of Bayalata.

Fairs and festivals: Prominent festivals of the state include Ugadi, Dussehra, Kar Hunnive, Nagapanchami, Navaratri or Nadahabb, Yellu Amavasya, Ramzan and Deepavali. Major fairs are Sri Vithappa fair, Sri Shidlingappa's fair, the Godachi fair and Banashankari Devi fair.

Economy, Industry and Agriculture

Economy: The net state domestic product at current prices for 2002–03 (provisional) was Rs 100,406crores. The per capita net state domestic product at current prices for 2002–03 (provisional) was Rs 18,521.

Minerals and industry: Prominent industries in Karnataka are aeronautics, automobiles, biotechnology, electronics, textiles, sugar, iron and steel, information technology, pharmaceuticals, leather, cement and processed foods. Minerals found in the state include gold, silver, iron ore, manganese, chromite, limestone, bauxite, copper and china clay.

Agriculture: Important crops include paddy, jowar, bajra, ragi, maize, pulses, groundnut, sunflower, soyabean, cotton, sugarcane and tobacco. Principal plantation crops are coffee, cashew, coconut, arecanut and cardamom.

Power: With an installed capacity of 3066 MW, a large part of Karnataka's power comes from hydroelectric plants. The rest comes from thermal and nuclear power plants.

Education

Educational institutes: Prominent educational institutions of Karnataka include the Indian Institute of Management, Bangalore; Indian Institute of Science, Bangalore; National Law

School of India University, Bangalore; National Institute of Mental Health and Neuro Sciences, Bangalore; University of Agricultural Sciences, Bangalore; Bangalore University, Bangalore; National Institute of Technology, Surathkal; Indian Statistical Institute, Bangalore; Central Institute of Indian Languages, Mysore; Gulbarga University, Gulbarga; Mangalore University, Mangalore; Manipal Academy of Higher Education, Manipal and University of Mysore, Mysore.

Tourism

Major tourist attractions:

1. Bangalore: Vidhana Soudha, Cubbon Park, Palace of Tipu Sultan, Ulsoor Lake.
2. Mysore: Mysore Palace, Srirangapatna, Gumbaz, St Philomena's Church, Brindavan Gardens.
3. Badami: The cave temples.
4. Aihole and Pattadakal.
5. Madikeri: Tipu's Fort, Omkareshwara Temple, Abbey Falls.
6. Hampi: Virupaksha Temple, Vittala Temple.
7. Belur and Halebid: Chennakeshava Temple, Shiva Temple.
8. Beaches: Karwar, Marwanthe, Malpe.
9. Jog falls.
10. Bijapur.
11. Sravanabelagola.
12. Sringeri.
13. Nandi Hills.

Airports:
International: Bangalore

Domestic:: Belgaum, Hubli, Mangalore.

National Parks: Anshi (Uttarakanada) —250 sq. km.; Bandipur Tiger Reserve (Mysore)—874.20 sq. km.; Bannerghatta (Bangalore)—104.27 sq. km.; Kudremukh (South Kanada and Chikmagalur)—600.32 sq. km.; Nagarhole (Mysore Kodagu)—643.39 sq. km.

Administration

Legislature: The Karnataka legislature comprises two houses: the 75 member legislative council and the 225 member legislative assembly. Of the 225 assembly seats, 224 are for elected members (33 reserved for SCs, 2 for STs) and 1 for a nominated member. The current party position is:

Name of Party	Seats
Bharatiya Janata Party	79
Indian National Congress	65
Janata Dal (S)	58
Janata Dal (U)	5
Communist Party of India (Marxist)	1
Republican Party of India	1
Kannada Nadu Paksha	1
Kannada Chalarali Vatal Paksha	1
Independent	13
Nominated	1
Total	**225**

Judiciary: The seat of the Karnataka High Court is in Bangalore. The present chief justice is Nauvdip Kumar Sodhi.

Districts:

District	Area (sq. km)	Population	Headquarters	Urban Agglomerations
Bagalkot	6,575	1,652,232	Bagalkot	
Bangalore	2,190	6,523,110	Bangalore	Bangalore
Bangalore Rural	5,815	1,877,416	Bangalore	
Belgaum	13,415	4,207,264	Belgaum	Athni, Belgaum, Ramdurg
Bellary	8,450	2,025,242	Bellary	
Bidar	5,448	1,501,374	Bidar	Bidar
Bijapur	10,494	1,808,863	Bijapur	Bijapur
Chamarajanagar	5,101	964,275	Chamarajanagar	

Chikmagalur	7,201	1,139,104	Chikmagalur	
Chitradurga	8,440	1,510,227	Chitradurga	Chitradurga
Dakshina Kannada	4,560	1,896,403	Mangalore	Mangalore
Davanagere	5,924	1,789,693	Davanagere	Harihar
Dharwad	4,260	1,603,794	Dharwad	
Gadag	4,656	971,955	Gadag	
Gulbarga	16,224	3,124,858	Gulbarga	Gulbarga, Shahabad, Wadi
Hassan	6,814	1,721,319	Hassan	Arsikere, Channarayapattana, Hassan
Haveri	4,823	1,437,860	Haveri	
Kodagu	4,102	545,322	Madikere	
Kolar	8,223	2,523,406	Kolar	Robertson Pet
Koppal	7,189	1,193,496	Koppal	Gangawati
Mandya	4,961	1,761,718	Mandya	
Mysore	6,854	2,624,911	Mysore	Mysore
Raichur	6,827	1,648,212	Raichur	
Shimoga	8,477	1,639,595	Shimoga	
Tumkur	10,597	2,579,516	Tumkur	
Udupi	3,880	1,109,494	Udupi	Udupi
Uttara Kannada	10,291	1,353,299	Karwar	Ankola, Bhatkal, Karwar, Kumta, Sirsi

Kerala

Key Statistics

Capital: Thiruvananthapuram.
Area: 38,863 sq. km.
Population: Total: 31,841,374, Male: 15,468,614, Female: 16,372,760.
Population density: 819 per sq. km.
Sex ratio: 1058 females per 1000 males.
Principal languages: Malayalam, Tamil, Kannada.
Literacy rates: Total: 90.9%, Male: 94.2%, Female: 87.7%.

Government

Governor: R.L. Bhatia. He was sworn on 23 June 2004.

Chief Minister: Oommen Chandy (INC). He was sworn in on 31 August 2004.

Geography

Physical characteristics: Kerala is a narrow strip of land on the south-west coast of India. The Lakshadweep Sea lies on the west, while the Western Ghats lie on the east. Karnataka is towards the north and northeast of the state while Tamil Nadu is to the east and the south. The Western Ghats are densely forested and have extensive ridges and ravines.

Anai Peak (2695 metres) is the highest peak of peninsular India. An interconnected chain of lagoons and backwaters is a feature of the coastline of Kerala.

Neighbouring states and Union territories:
States: Karnataka, Tamil Nadu.

Union territories: Pondicherry.

Major rivers: Periyar, Bharatapuzha, Chalakudi and Pamba.

Climate: Kerala has a tropical climate. The summer season is from February to May (24°C to 33°C). The monsoon season is from June to September (22°C to 28°C). The winter lasts between October and January (22°C to 32°C).

Kerala lies directly in the path of the south-west monsoon, but also receives rain from the north-east monsoon. Rainfall averages about 3000 mm annually, although some parts receive much more.

Flora and Fauna:

Flora: The state has 1,081,509 hectares of forest area. These are mostly rain forest, tropical deciduous forest and upland temperate grassland.

Fauna: The animal population of the state includes sambar, gaur, Nilgiri tahr, elephant, leopard, tiger, hanuman, Nilgiri langur, spectacled and king cobras, peafowl, bonnet monkey, lion-tailed macaque and hornbill.

History

Kerala has been mentioned in a rock inscription, dating back to the third century BC, of the Mauryan Emperor Asoka as 'Keralaputra'. Jewish immigrants arrived in the area in the first century AD, while Syrian Orthodox Christians believe that St Thomas the Apostle visited Kerala at around the same time. In the first five centuries AD, the region that is today Kerala was a part of Tamilakam and was at different times controlled by the eastern Pandya, Chola and the Chera dynasties.

Arab traders introduced Islam to the region in the latter part of the period between the sixth to eighth centuries AD. It was under the Kulasekhara dynasty that reigned between the years 800 and 1102 that Malayalam emerged as a distinct language.

In the early 14th century, Ravi Varma Kulasekhara of Venad established a short-lived domination over southern India. His death ushered in an era of confusion characterized by chieftains who constantly fought each other.

In 1498, the Portuguese explorer Vasco da Gama landed near Calicut (now Kozhikode). In the 16th century the Portuguese dominated trade and commerce in the Malabar region, successfully overtaking the Arab traders. Their attempts to establish political rule, however, were foiled by the hereditary rulers of Calicut, called 'zamorins'.

In the 17th century, the Dutch ousted the Portuguese. But even their ambition of imposing Dutch supremacy in the region was foiled by Marthanda Varma in 1741, in the Battle of Kolachel. Marthanda Varma adopted a system of martial discipline and expanded the new state of Travancore.

However, by 1806, Cochin, Travancore and Malabar had all become subject states under the British Madras Presidency. At the time of independence in 1947, the region that is today Kerala consisted of three separate territories: Cochin, Travancore and Malabar. On 1 July 1949, Cochin and Travancore were merged to form the Travancore–Cochin state. The present state of Kerala was formed on a linguistic basis, when Malabar along with the Kasargod taluka was added to the Cochin-Travancore state.

The new state was inaugurated on 1 November 1956. When Kerala was formed, the state was under President's rule. Elections were held for the first time in 1957 and E.M.S. Namboodiripad became the first Chief Minister.

Politics

The move towards democracy and social change started in Kerala towards the end of the nineteenth century. By the early twentieth century, leaders like E.M. Sankaran Namboodiripad, A.K. Gopalan and T.M. Varghese used Communist ideologies to organize political mass movements both against British rule and the Travancore state. In 1949, the two separate states of Tranancore and Cochin were united. On 1 November 1956 the boundaries of the newly-united states were revised to include neighbouring Malayalam-speaking areas, and the whole territory was officially named Kerala. In the first elections that followed the Communists gained a majority and the first Kerala ministry was sworn in under the leadership of E.M. Sankaran Namboodiripad (known as EMS), head of the Communist Party of India-Marxist. On 16 March 1957 for the first time in the history of the world, the Communists had come to power through democratic means. The ministry, however, lasted only until July 1959. The ministry was dismissed because the opposition parties launched an agitation called 'Vimochana Samaram' (Liberation Struggle) which led to clashes between the police and mass protesters. The state came under Presidential Rule. In February 1960 the second Assembly was formed with the coalition of the Congress Party and the Praja Socialist Party, with Pattom Thanu Pillai as chief minister. In 1967 E. M. S. Namboodiripad became the chief minister again with the Indian Communist Party (Marxist) getting an absolute majority in the assembly elections. In October 1969 EMS resigned and C. Achutha Menon became the chief minister. K. Karunakaran of the Congress became the chief minister in March 1977. In January 1980 seven political parties formed a coalition, the Left Democratic Front (LDF) under the leadership of the Communist Party of India-Marxist and won the election. E.K. Nayanar became the chief minister. In May 1982, an election was held

and a political coalition, the United Democratic Front (UDF), under the leadership of the Congress, got the majority. K. Karunakaran became the chief minister again. Power exchanged hands between the LDF and UDF subsequently. In 2004, Oommen Chandy was sworn in as the 19th chief minister of Kerala.

Culture

The dance form of Kathakali, which is one of the six classical dance forms of India, is indigenous to the state of Kerala, as in Mohiniattam. There are also more than 50 well-known folk dances in Kerala. The most popular among these are the Kaliyattom, Kolam Thullal, Kolkli, Mudiettu. Poorakkali, Velakali, Kamapadavukali, Kanniyarkali, Parichmuttukali, Thappukali, Kuravarkali and Thiruvathirakali. Other folk dance forms include Arjuna Nritham, Thullal and Theyyam.

The state is also the birthplace of the Kalaripayuttu martial art form.

Aranmula is famous for its metal mirrors. The state is also famous for its brass lamps and Kathakali masks.

Fairs and festivals: Important festivals of the state are Onam, Vishu, Thiruvathira, Navarathri, Sivarathri, Oachira, Kettukazcha, Vallom Kali, Christmas, Easter, Bakrid, Idul Fitr, Miladi Sharif and Muharram.

Economy, Industry and Agriculture

Economy: The net state domestic product at current prices for 2002–03 (provisional) was Rs 71,064 crores. The per capita net state domestic product at current prices for 2002–03 (provisional) was Rs 21,853.

Minerals and industry: The state's industries are mostly based on its natural resources. It is noted for handloom, cashewnut processing, food processing, coir and handicrafts. Tourism is also a major industry. Other industries of the state include rubber, tea, ceramics, electronics, electronic appliances, engineering, bricks and tiles, tobacco products, precision engineering products, petroleum-based industries, drugs and chemicals, plywood and soaps and oils. The state's mineral resources include zircon, monazite, ilmenite, rutile, sillimanite, clay and quartz sand.

Agriculture: The agricultural pattern of Kerala is unique for the predominance of cash crops. The state is a major producer of coconut (the most important cash crop of the state), rubber, pepper, coffee, cardamom, ginger, cocoa, cashew, arecanut, nutmeg, cinnamon, cloves and tea. The state is also noted for the production of fruits like banana, plantain, mango, jackfruit and pineapple.

Power: Most of the state's power comes from hydroelectric sources, while the rest comes from thermal power plants.

Education

Educational institutes: The major institutes for higher education in the state include the Indian Institute of Management (Kozhikode), Kerala Institute of Tourism and Travel Studies (Thiruvananthapuram), Cochin University of Science and Technology (Kochi), Central Institute of Fisheries, Nautical and Engineering Training (Kochi), Central Marine Fisheries Research Institute (Kochi), Kerala Agricultural University (Trichur), University of Kerala (Thiruvananthapuram), University of Calicut (Kozhikode), Mahatma Gandhi University (Kottayam), Sree Chitra Tirunal Institute of Medical Sciences and Technology (Thiruvananthapuram), Sree Sankaracharya University of Sanskrit (Sree Sankarapuram), Kannur University

(Kannur) and Central Plantation Crops and Research Institute (Kudlu, near Kasargod).

Tourism

Major tourist attractions: Vembanad Lake; Kappad Beach, Kozhikode; Kottayam; Kovalam Beach, Trivandrum; Munnar; Ponmudi; Cheeyappara and Valara waterfalls; Thattekkad Bird Sanctuary, Idukki; Thekkady; Kasaragod; Periyar; Silent Valley.

Airports:
International: Thiruvananthapuram, Nedumbassery (Kochi).

Domestic:: Kozhikode.

National Parks: Periyar National Park (part of the Tiger Reserve) in Idukki dist. (Tiger Reserve Area—777 sq. km, National Park—350 sq. km); Eravikulam National Park in Idukki dist. (97 sq. km); Silent Valley National Park in Palakkad dist. (89.52 sq. km).

Administration

Legislature: Kerala has a unicameral legislature. There are 140 seats in the Kerala Legislative Assembly. This includes 13 seats reserved for SCs and one seat reserved for STs, and one member nominated by the Governor from the Anglo-Indian community. The term of the current assembly expires on 4 June 2006.

The current party position is as follows:

Name of Party	Seats
Indian National Congress	62
Communist Party of India (Marxist)	23
Muslim League Kerala State Committee	16
Kerala Congress (M)	9
Communist Party of India	7
Janadhipathiya Samrekshna Samiti	4
Janata Dal (Secular)	3

Kerala Congress	2
Revolutionary Socialist Party	2
Nationalist Congress Party	2
Kerala Congress (B)	2
Kerala Congress (J)	2
Revolutionary Socialist Party of Kerala (Bolshevik)	2
Communist Marxist Party Kerala	

State Committee	1
Independent	3
Total	**140**

Judiciary: The High Court of Kerala has its seat at Ernakulam. Its jurisdiction also includes the Union territory of Lakshadweep. The acting chief justice is K.S. Radhakrishnan.

Districts:

District	Area (sq. km)	Population	Headquarters	Urban Agglomerations
Alappuzha	1,414	2,105,349	Alappuzha	Alappuzha, Cherthala
Ernakulam	2,950	3,098,378	Ernakulam	Kochi
Idukki	4,476	1,128,605	Kuyilimala	
Kannur	2,966	2,412,365	Kannur	Kannur
Kasargod	1,992	1,203,342	Kasargod	Kanhangad, Kasargod
Kollam	2,491	2,584,118	Kollam	Kollam
Kottayam	2,208	19,52,901	Kottayam	Kottayam
Kozhikode	2,344	28,78,498	Kozhikode	Kozhikode, Vadakara
Malappuram	3,550	36,29,640	Malappuram	Malappuram
Palakkad	4,480	26,17,072	Palakkad	Chittur-Thathamangalam, Palakkad
Pathanamthitta	2,637	12,31,577	Pathanamthitta	
Thiruvananthapuram	2,192	32,34,707	Thiruvananthapuram	Thiruvananthapuram
Thrissur	3,032	29,75,440	Thrissur	Guruvayoor, Kodungallur, Thrissur
Wayanad	2,131	7,86,627	Kalpetta	

Madhya Pradesh

Key Statistics

Capital: Bhopal.

Area: 308,000 sq. km.

Population: Total: 60,348,023, Male: 31,443,652, Female: 28,904,371.

Population density: 196 per sq. km.

Sex ratio: 919 females per 1000 males.

Principal languages: Hindi, Bhili/Bhilodi, Gondi.

Literacy rates: Total: 63.7%, Male: 76.1%, Female: 50.3%.

Government

Governor: Balram Jakhar. He was sworn in as the governor of Madhya Pradesh on 30 June 2004.

Chief Minister: Babulal Gour (BJP). He was sworn in on 23 August 2004.

Geography

Physical characteristics: Madhya Pradesh is the second largest Indian state covering 9.5 per cent of the country's area. It lies between the Indo-Gangetic Plain in the north and the Deccan Plateau in the south. Its landscape, which is largely made up of wide-ranging plateaus, low hills and river valleys, ranges from 100 to 1200 metres.

The land rises from south to north in the northern part of the state. In the southern part, its elevation increases towards the west. The Kaimur Hills and the Vindhya Range are situated in the north and the west respectively. To the northwest side of the Vindhya Range is the Malwa Plateau, which rises up to 100 metres. The Bundelkhand Plateau lies to the north of the Vindhya Range. There is also the Baghelkhand Plateau in the northeast, and Madhya Bharat Plateau in the extreme northeast. Various rivers originate from the state and flow into the adjoining states.

Neighbouring States and Union territories:

States: Gujarat, Maharashtra, Chhattisgarh, Rajasthan, Uttar Pradesh.

Major rivers: Narmada, Chambal, Betwa, Tapti and Wainganga are some of the major rivers.

Climate: The climate of Madhya Pradesh is mostly tropical, and largely governed by the monsoon. From March to May it experiences a hot, dry and windy summer, when the temperature can reach a maximum of about 48°C in some parts of the state. From June to September comes the southwest monsoon, when the rainfall fluctuates from region to region. The state has been divided into five crop zones and seven agro-climatic zones due to this reason. The total annual rainfall varies from 600mm (in the extreme northwestern areas) to about 1200mm (southern areas). Winters (between October and February) are usually pleasant.

Flora and Fauna:

Flora: Madhya Pradesh is rich in forest resources. There are four important types of forest, namely the tropical dry forest, the tropical moist forest, the subtropical broadleaved hill forest, and the tropical thorn forest. Based on the composition of the forest and the terrain of the region, it is possible to classify forests into three types: teak forests, sal forests and miscellaneous forests. Bamboo, small timber, fodder and fuelwood also grow in many areas.

Fauna: Madhya Pradesh is famous for its tiger population and is known as the 'Tiger State'. It has 19 per cent of the tiger population in India, and 17 per cent of the tiger population in the world. Satpura, Bandhavgarh, Pench, Panna, and Kanha are the five Project Tiger areas in the state. Apart from these projects, there is the Ghatigaon Sanctuary, which is set up for the conservation of the great Indian bustard, also known as the Son Chiriya. The Ken-gharial and Son-gharial sanctuaries are home to the mugger and gharial, while the Sardarpur Sanctuary houses the kharmor or lesser florican. Other creatures found in the state include the bison, panthers, chital (spotted deer), wild buffalo, sambar, black buck, bears and many species of birds.

History

Madhya Pradesh was founded on 1 November 1956, and forty-four years later, on 1 November 2000, the new state of Chhattisgarh was carved out of it. Madhya Pradesh occupies some of the oldest inhabited parts of India. At Bhimbhetka, close to Bhopal, some fascinating paintings are preserved in pre-historic caves dating back to the Paleolithic times.

The whole state came under the territory of the Guptas during the ascendancy of the Gupta dynasty. It also constituted part of Harshavardhan's empire. During the decline of the imperial power, small principalities created out of the province began fighting each other to establish their superiority. The Chandel dynasty emerged out of this, and later constructed the great temples of Khajuraho, creating a prosperous kingdom after the fall of the imperial power.

The Pratihara and Gaharwar Rajput dynasties followed the Chandels, but lost out to the expanding Muslim power. Emperor Akbar finally subdued all the other contenders in the region, and with Aurangzeb, Mughal rule was established in the region.

With the decline of the Mughals the Marathas reigned supreme, but they were finally replaced by the British who entered into treaty relationships with the rulers of the princely states in the area and went on to gain power over them.

After independence, many such princely states were merged into the Union. With the reorganization of states, the boundaries were rationalized and the state of Madhya Pradesh came into existence. Pandit Ravishankar Shukla was the first Chief Minister of the state.

Politics

Madhya Pradesh was created in 1950 from the former British Central Provinces and Berar and the princely states of Makrai and Chhattisgarh, with Nagpur as the capital of the state. The state of Madhya Pradesh was formed on 1 November 1956, on the basis of the Report of the States Reorganisation Commission by merging the territories of the states of Madhya Bharat, a union of princely states in the Malwa plateau region; Vindhya Pradesh, a union of states in the Vindhya region; Bhopal, a centrally administered princely state; the Hindi-speaking areas popularly known as Mahakoshal; and the Chhattisgarh region of the state of Central Provinces and Berar. Bhopal became the new capital. The state was bifurcated into two states, Madhya Pradesh and Chhattisgarh, on 1 November 2000.

Sunderlal Patwa of the Bharatiya Janata Party had two tenures as chief minister, in 1980 and from 1990 to 1992. From 1980 to 1985 Arjun Singh of the Congress party was the chief minister. He served as chief minister of the state again from 1988 to 1989. Motilal Vora of the Congress party became the chief minister twice, in 1985 and 1989. In 1993, Digvijay Singh of the Congress became chief minister. He was the longest serving chief minister in the history of Madhya Pradesh after winning the people's mandate for the second consecutive term in the year 1998. The victory of the ruling Congress party in the election in Madhya Pradesh was more significant because the political parties in power were losing elections in state after state in India in that year in the face of an anti-incumbency wave. Uma Bharti of the Bharatiya Janata Party was sworn-in on 8 December 2003 as the first woman chief minister of Madhya Pradesh. Babulal Gaur of the Bharatiya Janata Party was sworn in as the chief minister on 23 August 2004.

Culture

In Madhya Pradesh, the Gwalior *gharana* is one of the most important propagators of style in Indian music. Madhya Pradesh is famous for the rivalry of Tansen and Baiju Bawra, and is also well known for the patronage of the Dhrupad singers by Raja Mansingh.

Other great musicians from Madhya Pradesh include the legendary Ustad Alauddin Khan, the guru of the famous sitarist Pandit Ravi Shankar; the sarod players Ali Akbar Khan and Ustad Hafiz Khan; and the *beenkar* Ustad Hussu Khan.

Madhya Pradesh is also famous for its craftsmen, including the sari weavers from Chanderi town, who are also regarded as true artists. Their silk and cotton saris, delicately woven with silver and gold threads, are extremely popular. Maheshwar in Madhya

Pradesh is popular for sari making, while Bhopal is renowned for the bead work and embroidery, and Ujjain for its *chippa* work (block printing by hand). Other popular forms of craft include woodwork, terracotta display and metalware in the tribal areas of Bastar.

In the year 1980, the state government constituted a separate department for culture in Madhya Pradesh.

Fairs and festivals: Shivratri in Khajuraho, Ujjain, Pachmarhi and Bhojpur, the annual festival of dances at Khajuraho, Bhagoriya in Jhabua, Dussehra in Bastar, the Malwa Festival in Mandu, Ujjain and Indore, Ramnavami in Orchha and Chitrakoot, and the Pachmarhi Festival are some of the important cultural events in Madhya Pradesh. Some of the important cultural festivals held in the state include the All India Kalidasa Festival, Alauddin Khan Samaroh (Maihar), Tansen Sam-aroh (Gwalior), Lokranjan (Khajuraho), Miwar Utsav (Maheshwar), Khajuraho Dance Festival, Kumar Gandharva Samaroh (Dewas) and Shankara Samaroh.

Economy, Industry and Agriculture

Economy: The net state domestic product at current prices in 2002–03 (advance estimate) was Rs 71,387 crores. The per capita net state domestic product at current prices in 2002–09 (advance estimate) was Rs 11,438.

Minerals and industry: Madhya Pradesh is one of the largest producers of forest products, agricultural products, and minerals. Its important industries also include its modern biotech industries, horticulture, agro-industries, and its eco-tourist and tourist industry, which are especially aided by the presence of world heritage sites like Khajuraho and Sanchi, and various tiger reserves in the state.

The state consists of 19 Industrial Growth Centres, and its infrastructure is an advantage, in terms of its railways and roads connecting all the important cities. The strongest optical fibre backbone is present in every district in Madhya Pradesh. Important minerals of Madhya Pradesh include limestone, bauxite, coal, manganese ore, diamond, base metals, dolomite, rock phosphate and granite.

Agriculture: In Madhya Pradesh, 49.5 per cent of its population depend on agriculture. The state produces about 2.19 million tonnes of sugar cane, 2.38 million tonnes of cotton, 3.969 million tonnes of oil seed, and nine million tonnes of food grain. Food grain production in Madhya Pradesh is about 260 kg per person, compared to the all-India production figure of about 200 kg per person per year. On the other hand, food grain yield in Madhya Pradesh, when compared to the all-India figure of 1.70 tonne per hectare (ha), is quite low at 1.14 tonnes per ha. Wheat, rice, a few varieties of coarse millets, and jowar (sorghum) are the main food crops in the state. Soyabean is produced on a large scale throughout the state.

Power: Thermal power is the main source of energy in the state. The rest of the energy is provided by hydroelectric sources.

Education

Educational institutes: Some of the important institutions of higher education are Awadhesh Pratap Singh University (Rewa), Barkatullah Vishwavidyalaya (Bhopal), Devi Ahilya Vishwavidyalaya (Indore), Dr Harisingh Gour Vishwa-vidyalaya (Sagar), Jawaharlal Nehru Krishi Vishwavidyalaya (Jabalpur), Jiwaji University (Gwalior), Lakshmibai National Institute of Physical Education (Gwalior), Madhya Pradesh Bhoj Open University

(Bhopal), Maharishi Mahesh Yogi Vedic University (Jabalpur), Mahatma Gandhi Gramoday Vishwavidyalaya (Chitrakoot), Makhanlal Chaturvedi National University of Journalism (Bhopal), Rani Durgavati Vishwa-vidyalaya (Jabalpur) and Vikram University (Ujjain).

Tourism

Major tourist attractions: Khajuraho; Amarkantak; The marble rocks at Bhedaghat, near Jabalpur; Bhimbhetka; Bhojpur; Chanderi; Chitrakoot; Mandu; Omkareshwar; Sanchi; Pachmarhi.

Airports: Gwalior, Indore, Jabalpur, Bhopal, Khajuraho.

National Parks: Bandhavgarh National Park in Umaria and Jabalpur districts (448.85 sq. km) • Fossil National Park in Mandla district (0.27 sq. km), Kanha National Park in Mandla and Balaghat districts (940 sq. km), Madhav National Park in Shivpuri district (375.22 sq. km), Panna National Park in Panna and Chhatarpur districts (542.67 sq. km), Pench (Priyadarshini) National Park in Seoni and Chhindwara districts (292.85 sq. km), Sanjay National Park in Sidhi district (466.88 sq. km), Satpura National Park in Hoshangabad district (585.17 sq. km) and Van Vihar National Park in Bhopal district (4.45 sq. km).

Administration

Legislature: Madhya Pradesh has a unicameral legislature. There are 230 seats in the Madhya Pradesh assembly, of which 33 are reserved for SCs and 41 for STs.

The current party position is as follows:

Name of Party	Seats
Bharatiya Janata Party	173
Indian National Congress	38
Samajwadi Party	7
Gondvana Gantantra Party	3
Bahujan Samaj Party	2
Rashtriya Samanta Dal	2
Communist Party of India (Marxist)	1
Nationalist Congress Party	1
Janata Dal—United	1
Independent	2
Total	**230**

Judiciary: The High Court of Madhya Pradesh has its seat at Jabalpur. Justice Rajiv Gupta is the acting chief justice of the Madhya Pradesh High Court.

Districts:

District	Area (sq. km)	Population	Headquarters	Urban Agglomerations
Balaghat	9,229	1,445,760	Balaghat	Balaghat, Wara Seoni
Barwani	5,422	1,081,039	Barwani	
Betul	10,043	1,394,421	Betul	Betul
Bhind	4,459	1,426,951	Bhind	
Bhopal	2,772	1,836,784	Bhopal	Bhopal
Chhatarpur	8,687	1,474,633	Chhatarpur	Chhatarpur
Chhindwara	11,815	1,848,882	Chhindwara	Chhindwara, Chiklikalan Parasia Damoh 7,306
1,081,909	Damoh	Damoh		
Datia	2,691	627,818	Datia	
Dewas	7,020	1,306,617	Dewas	
Dhar	8,153	1,740,577	Dhar	
Dindori	7,470	579,312	Dindori	
East Nimar (Khandwa)	10,776	1,708,170	Khandwa	
Guna	11,064	1,665,503	Guna	

Gwalior	4,560	1,629,881	Gwalior	Gwalior
Harda	3,330	474,174	Harda	Harda
Hoshangabad	6,707	1,085,011	Hoshangabad	Itarsi, Pipariya
Indore	3,898	2,585,321	Indore	Indore, Mhow Cantt
Jabalpur	5,211	2,167,469	Jabalpur	Jabalpur
Jhabua	6,778	1,396,677	Jhabua	
Katni	4,950	1,063,689	Katni	
Mandla	5,800	893,908	Mandla	Mandla
Mandsaur	5,535	1,183,369	Mandsaur	Mandsaur
Morena	4,989	1,587,264	Morena	Joura, Sabalgarh
Narsimhapur	5,133	957,399	Narsimhapur	Gadarwara, Narsimhapur Neemuch
4,256	725,457	Neemuch	Neemuch	
Panna	7,135	854,235	Panna	Panna
Raisen	8,466	1,120,159	Raisen	Baraily
Rajgarh	6,153	1,253,246	Rajgarh	
Ratlam	4,861	1,214,536	Ratlam	Jaora, Ratlam Rewa
6,314	1,972,333	Rewa		
Sagar	10,252	2,021,783	Sagar	Bina-Etawa, Garhakota, Khurai, Sagar
Satna	7,502	1,868,648	Satna	Satna
Sehore	6,578	1,078,769	Sehore	Ashta, Sehore
Seoni	8,758	1,165,893	Seoni	
Shahdol	9,952	1,572,748	Shahdol	Burhar-Dhanpuri,
Shajapur	6,195	1,290,230	Shajapur	Shajapur
Sheopur	6,606	559,715	Sheopur	Sheopur
Shivpuri	10,277	1,440,666	Shivpuri	
Sidhi	10,526	1,830,553	Sidhi	
Tikamgarh	5,048	1,203,160	Tikamgarh	
Ujjain	6,091	1,709,885	Ujjain	Badnagar, Mahidpur, Ujjain
Umaria	4,076	515,851	Umaria	
Vidisha	7,371	1,214,759	Vidisha	Basoda
West Nimar (Khargone)	8,030	1,529,954	Khargone	Barwaha, Khargone

Maharashtra

Key Statistics

Capital: Mumbai.

Area: 307,713 sq. km.

Population: Total: 96,878,627, Male: 50,400,596, Female: 46,478,031.

Population density: 314 per sq. km.

Sex ratio: 922 females per 1000 males.

Principal languages: Marathi, Hindi, Urdu.

Literacy rates: Total: 76.9%, Male: 86.0%, Female: 67.0%.

Government

Governor: S.M. Krishna. He was sworn in on 6 December 2004.

Chief Minister: Vilasrao Deshmukh (INC). He became the Chief Minister on 1 November 2004.

Geography

Physical characteristics: The dominant physical feature of the state is its plateau. The western upturned edges of this plateau rise to form the Sahyadri Range. The major rivers and their main tributaries have eroded the plateau into alternating river valleys and intervening higher-level interfluves, such as the Ahmadnagar, Buldana and Yavatmal plateaus.

The Sahyadri Range, with an average elevation of 1000m, forms the topographical backbone of Maharashtra. Its steep cliffs descend to the Konkan coast in the west, while on the east it descends in steps through a transitional area called Mawal till it reaches the plateau level.

The Konkan area is a narrow coastal lowland that is hardly 50 km wide and 200m high. It lies between the Arabian Sea and the Sahyadri Range.

The Satpuras that lie along the northern border and the Bhamragad-Chiroli-Gaikhuri Range that lies along the eastern border serve as the natural limits of Maharashtra.

The flat topography of the state is a result of the outpouring of lava through fissures in the ground around 60 to 90 million years ago. This formed horizontal layers of basalt over extensive areas.

Neighbouring States and Union territories:

States: Gujarat, Madhya Pradesh, Karnataka, Andhra Pradesh, Goa, Chhattisgarh.

Union territories: Dadra, Nagar Haveli.

Major rivers: Godavari, Tapi, Wainganga, Penganga, Ulhas, Wardha and Bhima.

Climate: Maharashtra has a tropical monsoon climate. The summers are hot and commence from March onwards and continue till June, when the monsoon season arrives. This lasts till October when the transition to winter takes place. Seasonal rains from sea clouds are intensive and rainfall exceeds 4000mm in the Sahyadri region.

The Konkan region also gets heavy rainfall, but the intensity follows a decreasing trend northwards. Rainfall is low east of the Sahyadris, around 700mm in the western plateau areas. The Solapur–Ahmadnagar region forms the heart of the dry zone. The rains increase marginally later in the season, mainly eastwards in the Marathwada and Vidarbha regions.

Flora and Fauna:

Flora: The forest cover of Maharashtra is 47,482 sq. km. It is interesting that the forest cover in the state has been showing increasing trends. Teak trees are found to occur over an area of approximately 10,180 sq. km, while bamboo plants cover an area of in excess of 10,100 sq. km.

The forests of the state are of the following types: (i) southern tropical semi-evergreen forests, (ii)) southern tropical moist deciduous forests, (iii) southern tropical dry deciduous forests, (iv) southern tropical thorn forests, and (v) littoral and swamp forests.

Fauna: Animals found in the state include tigers, bison, panthers, deer, antelopes, wild boar, blue bull, great Indian bustard, sloth bear, wild dog, jackal, hyena, chausingha, sambar, gaur, barking deer, ratel, pangolin, cheetal, mouse deer, flying squirrel and civet cat. Reptiles found in the state include monitor lizard, python, cobra, Russell's viper and pit viper.

A large variety of birds are found in the Sanjay Gandhi National Park. These include Tickell's flower pecker, sunbird, white-bellied sea eagle, paradise flycatcher, trogon, various species of kingfisher, woodpeckers, and drongos. Besides these, the green barbet, the parakeet, the Malabar whistling thrush and spotted babbler are also found.

History

The name Maharashtra appeared in a seventh-century inscription and in the account of the Chinese traveller, Hiuen-Tsang.

During the early period, the territory that forms the modern state of Maharashtra was ruled over by several Hindu kingdoms. The Satavahanas, the Rashtrakutas, the Yadavas, the Vakatakas, the Kalachuris and the Chalukyas. After 1307 came the Muslim dynasties.

By the middle of the 16th century, Maharashtra was broken up into several smaller states and ruled by several independent, warring Muslim rulers. Shivaji was born in 1627. He set up a large Maratha empire that rivalled the Mughals in might and power. During the 18th century, almost the entire region of western and central India, as well as large parts of north and even eastern India were brought under Maratha control. Ultimately, even the mighty Marathas had to give way to the British in the 19th century.

At the time of independence in 1947, Bombay Presidency became the state of Bombay with B.G. Kher as its first Chief Minister. On 1 May 1960, the state was divided into two parts creating Gujarat in the north and Maharashtra in the south, with Y.B. Chavan as its Chief Minister.

Politics

During British rule, portions of the western coast of India under direct British rule were part of the Bombay Presidency. In 1937, the Bombay Presidency became a province of British India. After Indian independence in 1947, many former princely states, including the Gujarat states and the Deccan states, were merged with the former Bombay province. Bombay state was significantly enlarged on 1 November 1956, expanding eastward to incorporate the Marathi-speaking Marathwada region of Hyderabad state, the Marathi-speaking Vidarbha region of southern Madhya Pradesh, and Gujarati-speaking Saurashtra and Kutch. The southernmost, Kannada-speaking portion of Bombay state became part of the new linguistic state of Karnataka. Yashwantrao Chavan and later Morarji Desai were its only two chief ministers. Bombay state was partitioned into Gujarat and Maharashtra states on 1 May 1960, after an agitation for a separate Marathi state turned violent.

Yashwantrao Balwantrao Chavan of the Congress Party became the Bombay's chief minister (1956) and was the first chief minister of the new state of Maharashtra (1960-62). Shankarrao Bhaurao Chavan served two times as chief minister, from 1975 to 1977, and from 1986 to 1988. In 1978, Sharad Pawar toppled the Congress government in Maharashtra led by Vasantdada Patil and formed a government in coalition with the Janata Party under the banner of the Progressive Democratic Front. He was also chief minister from 1988 to 1991 and from 1993 to 1994. Sharad Pawar is the president of the Nationalist Congress Party, which he formed in 1999. Shiv Sena, a Hindu nationalist party strongly associated with Maratha identity, was founded in 1966 by Bal Thackeray who is the president of the party. The party came to power in 1995 in alliance with the BJP and Manohar Joshi was the chief minister till 1999. Vilasrao Deshmukh of the Congress became chief minister in 1999. He had to step down in January 2003 and make way for Sushilkumar Shinde, a prominent Dalit face of Congress, following factionalism in the state unit of the party. Vilasrao Deshmukh again came back to the office of chief minister on 1 November 2004.

Culture

The tamasha form of folk drama is indigenous to this state. Marathi literature is also well known. Mumbai is also the most important centre of the Indian film industry.

Fairs and festivals: Ganesh Chaturthi is one of the most important festivals of the state. Modern festivals of the state include Pune Festival, Banganga Festival, Elephanta Festival, Ellora Festival (near Aurangabad), Kalidas Festival (Nagpur).

Economy, Industry and Agriculture

Economy: The net state domestic product at current prices for 2002–03 (provisional) was Rs 263,225 crores. The per capita net state domestic product at current prices for 2002–03 (provisional) was Rs 26,386.

Minerals and industry: Mumbai is regarded as the financial capital of India. The state is home to a wide range of manufacturing industries such as chemicals, textiles, automobiles, food products, machinery, electrical products, printing and publishing, paper and paper products, tobacco and related products. The film and tourism industries have an important place in the economic and social life of Maharashtra.

The districts of Chandrapur, Gadchiroli, Bhandara and Nagpur as constitute the main mineral-bearing areas of Maharashtra. Coal and manganese are the major minerals mined in the state. There are deposits of iron ore and limestone as well. Substantial deposits of ilmenite are found in the coastal area of Ratnagiri.

Agriculture: Major crops grown in the state are rice, jowar, bajra, wheat, pulses, oilseeds, cotton, sugar cane and turmeric. The main fruit crops are oranges, grapes, mangoes and bananas.

Power: The state gets most of its power from thermal power plants. Hydroelectric power plants are the second most important source while nuclear power plants are the third.

Education

Educational institutes: Prominent institutes of higher education in the state include the University of Mumbai, University of Pune, Nagpur University, Indian Institute of Technology (Powai), Jamnalal Bajaj Institute of Management Studies (Mumbai), Narsee Monjee Institute of Management Studies (Mumbai), SNDT Women's University (Mumbai), Amravati University (Amravati), Bharati Vidyapeeth (Pune), Central Institute of Fisheries Education (Mumbai), Deccan College Post Graduate and Research Institute (Pune), Dr Babasaheb Ambedkar Marathwada University (Aurangabad), Dr Babasaheb Ambedkar Technological University (Raigad), Dr Panjabrao Deshmukh Krishi Vidyapeeth (Akola), Gokhale Institute of Politics and Economics (Pune), Indira Gandhi Institute of Development Research (Mumbai), International Institute for Population Sciences (Mumbai), Kavikulguru Kalidas Sanskrit Vishwavidyalaya (Ramtek), Konkan Krishi Vidyapeeth (Ratnagiri) • Maharashtra University of Medical Sciences (Nashik), Mahatma Gandhi Antarrashtriya Hindi Vishwavidyalaya (Wardha), Mahatma Phule Krishi Vidyapeeth (Ahmadnagar), Marathwada Krishi Vidyapeeth (Parbhani), North Maharashtra University (Jalgaon), Shivaji University (Kolhapur), Swami Ramanand Teerth Marathwada University (Nanded), Tata Institute of Social Sciences (Mumbai), Tilak Maharshtra Vidyapeeth (Pune), Yahswantrao Chavan Maharasthra Open Univeristy (Nashik).

Tourism

Major tourist attractions: Mahabaleshwar, Lonavla, Elephanta Caves,

Gateway of India, Ganapatiphule, Alibag, Raigad Fort, Sinhadurg Fort, Panchgani, Ajanta and Ellora.

Airports:
International: Mumbai.
Domestic: Pune, Nagpur, Akola, Sholapur, Kolhapur, Aurangabad.

National Parks: Sanjay Gandhi National Park in Thane dist. (86.96 sq. km). Gugamal National Park in Amaravati district. It is a part of Melghat Tiger Reserve. The Tiger Reserve covers an area of 1676.93 sq. km while the National Park has an area of 361.28 sq. km. Pench National Park in Nagpur dist. (257.26 sq. km). Navegaon National Park in Bhandara dist. (133.88 sq. km). Tadoba National Park in Chandrapur dist. (116.55 sq. km). The Andhari Wildlife Sanctuary (508.85 sq. km). Tadoba National Park together form the Tadoba-Andhari Tiger Reserve.

Administration

Legislature: Maharashtra has a bicameral legislature, which means that there is a legislative assembly as well as a legislative council. There are 288 seats in the assembly, of which 18 are reserved for SCs and 22 for STs. Elections were held in October 2004.

The current party position is as follows:

Name of Party	Seats
Nationalist Congress Party	71
Indian National Congress	69
Shiv Sena	62
Bharatiya Janata Party	54
Jan Surajya Sharti	4
Communist Party of India (Marxist)	3
Peasants and Workers Party of India	2
Akhil Bharatiya Sena	1
Bharipa Bahujan Mahasangha	1
Republican Party of India (A)	1
Swatantra Bharat Paksha	1
Independent	19
Total	**288**

Judiciary: The Bombay High Court has jurisdiction over Maharashtra, Goa, and Daman and Diu. Besides Mumbai, it has benches at Aurangabad, Nagpur and Panaji (Goa). Dalveer Bhandari is the chief justice.

Districts:

District	Area (sq. km)	Population	Headquarters	Urban Agglomerations
Ahmadnagar	17,048	4,088,077	Ahmadnagar	Ahmadnagar, Shrirampur
Akola	5,429	1,629,305	Akola	
Amravati	12,210	2,606,063	Amravati	
Aurangabad	10,107	2,920,548	Aurangabad	Aurangabad
Bhandara	3,895	1,135,835	Bhandara	
Beed	10,693	2,159,841	Beed	
Buldana	9,661	2,226,328	Buldana	
Chandrapur	11,443	2,077,909	Chandrapur	
Dhule	8,063	1,708,993	Dhule	
Gadchiroli	14,412	969,960	Gadchiroli	
Gondiya	5,425	1,200,151	Gondiya	
Hingoli	4,524	986,717	Hingoli	
Jalgaon	11,765	3,679,936	Jalgaon	Bhusawal
Jalna	7,718	1,612,357	Jalna	
Kolhapur	7,685	3,515,413	Kolhapur	Ichalkaranji, Kolhapur

Latur	7,157	2,078,237	Latur	
Mumbai	157	3,326,837	Mumbai	Greater Mumbai
Mumbai (Suburban)	446	8,587,561	Mumbai	Greater Mumbai
Nagpur	9,802	4,051,444	Nagpur	Kamptee, Nagpur
Nanded	10,528	2,868,158	Nanded	
Nandurbar	5,034	1,309,135	Nandurbar	
Nashik	15,530	4,987,923	Nashik	Nashik
Osmanabad	7,569	1,472,256	Osmanabad	
Parbhani	6,517	1,491,109	Parbhani	
Pune	15,643	7,224,224	Pune	Pune
Raigarh	7,152	2,205,972	Alibag	
Ratnagiri	8,208	1,696,482	Ratnagiri	
Sangli	8,572	2,581,835	Sangli	Sangli
Satara	10,480	2,796,906	Satara	
Sindhudurg	5,207	861,672	Oras	
Solapur	14,895	3,855,383	Solapur	
Thane	9,558	8,128,833	Thane	Bhiwandi, Greater Mumbai, Vasai
Wardha	6,309	1,230,640	Wardha	
Washim	5,153	1,019,725	Washim	
Yavatmal	13,582	2,460,482	Yavatmal	Yavatmal

Manipur

Key Statistics

Capital: Imphal.
Area: 22,327 sq. km.
Population: Total: 2,166,788, Male: 1,095,634, Female: 1,071,154.
Population density: 107 per sq. km.
Sex ratio: 978 females per 1000 males.
Principal languages: Manipuri, Thado, Tangkhul.
Literacy rates: Total: 70.5%, Male: 80.3%, Female: 60.5%.

Government

Governor: Shivender Singh Sidhu. He was sworn in on 6 August 2004.

Chief Minister: Okram Ibobi Singh (INC). He was sworn in on 7 March 2002.

Geography

Physical characteristics: Manipur can be divided into two distinct physical regions—the outlying area of rugged hills and narrow valleys, and the inner area of flat plains. The Loktak Lake is an important geographic feature of the central plain area. The total area occupied by all the lakes is about 600 sq. km. The highest point of the state is the Iso Peak near Mao (2,994m).

Neighbouring States and Union territories:
International border: Myanmar.

States: Assam, Mizoram, Nagaland.

Major rivers: Manipur (also called Imphal) and Barak.

Climate: The average annual rainfall varies from 933mm at Imphal to 2593mm at Tamenglong. The temperature ranges from sub-zero to 36°C. Depending on the altitude, the climatic conditions vary from tropical to subalpine.

Flora and Fauna:

Flora: About 67 per cent of the geographical area of Manipur is hilly and covered with forests. The wet forests and the pine forests occur between 900–2700m above mean sea level. Manipur is home to 500 varieties of orchids. 'Siroi Lily', which is the only terrestrial lily in India, grows on the hilltops of the Siroi Hill.

Fauna: The rich fauna of Manipur includes the sangai (or dancing deer), slow loris, hornbill, hoolock gibbon, the clouded leopard, Mrs Hume's barbacked pheasant, spotted linshang, blyths tragopan, Burmese peafowl and salamander.

History

In 1762 the ruler of Manipur, Raja Jai Singh, made a treaty with the British to thwart a Myanmarese invasion. Again in 1824, the services of the British were sought to expel invaders from Myanmar. Political turmoil continued for some time until 1891, when Chura Chand, a five-year-old member of the ruling family, was nominated as the raja. The administration was henceforth conducted under British supervision for the next few years.

In 1907, the raja and the durbar regained control of the government. It is noteworthy that the vice-president of the durbar was a member of the Indian Civil Service. The administration was eventually transferred to the raja and the vice-president of the durbar became its president.

An uprising of the Kuki hill tribes in 1917 resulted in the adoption of a new system of government. The region was divided into three subdivisions. Each of these subdivisions was put under an officer from the government of the neighbouring state of Assam.

In 1947 Manipur joined the Indian Union and the political agency of Assam was abolished. In 1949 Manipur became a Union territory administered by a chief commissioner and an elected territorial council. In 1969, the office of the chief commissioner was replaced by a lieutenant governor. This in turn was converted to a governorship when Manipur became full-fledged state of the Indian Union on 21 January 1972. M. Koireng Singh as the first Chief Minister of Manipur.

Politics

The year 1934 marked a turning point in the political history of Manipur when a political organization called the Nikhil Manipuri Mahasabha under the Presidentship of Maharaja Churchand Singh came into existence. The Mahasabha was initially a social organization, but in 1938 it became the first political party of Manipur, thus becoming a harbinger of regional parties in Manipur. At the time of Independence, the king of Manipur was one of the few rulers who refused to sign the merger agreement but was later reportedly coaxed and compelled to sign on 21 September 1949, and subsequently endorsed the formal merger of Manipur with the dominion of India on 15 October 1949. The Manipur People's Party (MPP), the state's most important regional party, was composed of the defectors of the Indian National Congress (INC) and was formed in 1968. Emphasizing its regional character, the MPP claimed that it alone could bring prosperity to the people of Manipur. The MPP entered the arena of electoral tug-of-war for the first time in 1972. There was a tremendous excitement in the contest since it was also the first election after the conferment of statehood to Manipur. In the 60-member Assembly, the MPP won 15 out of the 42 seats it contested. The MPP utilized the fractured verdict and thus formed a coalition government with the help of Socialist Party, Congress (O), and Independents. A ministry headed by Md Alimuddin under the name of United Legislature Party (ULP) was installed on 20 March 1972. However, dissensions soon cropped up in the government. As a result some members of the ULP ministry defected to the Opposition. Later on, the Opposition moved a non-confidence motion against the government. Subsequently, the Assembly was dissolved and President's Rule was imposed. In the next elections, no party was able to secure an absolute majority in the house and political instability continued to plague Manipur as before. On 29 June 1977 a new Janata ministry under Yangmaso Shaiza was installed. All the members of the Congress party and the MPP joined the Janata Legislature Party and the Janata Party's strength was raised to 55 in the House. Again, after the 1990 Assembly election, a new ministry was sworn in under the leadership of MPP stalwart R.K. Ranbir Singh making an event in the political history of Manipur of being the first non-Congress government in more than a decade. A Congress ministry came to power under Okram Ibobi Singh after the 2002 elections.

Culture

The Manipuri dance form is indigenous to the state. For example, the Anal community have the Kamdom and the Ludem dance forms, while the Chote community has the Hucham Pulak. Different communities and tribes have varied art forms, folk dances, folk songs and folklore of their own.

Fairs and festivals: Important festivals of the state include Ningol Chakouba, Yaoshang (the most important festivals of Hindus of the state), Ramzan Id, Kut (a festival of Kuki-Chin-Mizo), Gang-Ngai (a festival of Kabui Nagas), Chumpha (festival of Tangkhul Nagas), Christmas, Cheiraoba (the Manipuri New Year), Kang (the Rathayatra of Manipur) and Heikru Hitongba.

Economy, Industry and Agriculture

Economy: The net state domestic product at current prices in 2002–03 (advance estimate) was Rs 3047 crores. The per capita net state domestic product at current prices (new series) in 2002–03 (advance estimate) was Rs 12,230.

Minerals and industry: Occurrences of asbestos, copper ore, coal, bog iron, lignite, chromite, limestone, nickel ore and petroleum are reported from the state. Iron and steel products, consumer products and cement are also produced in the state.

Agriculture: About 80 per cent of the state's population depends on agriculture for their livelihood. Rice and maize are the most important food crops. Besides this, the state is well known for its fruit production—orange, pineapple, jackfruit, peach, plum, pears and banana. Potato, turmeric, ginger, black pepper, tapioca, cotton, oilseeds, jute and mesta, cashew nut, tea, mushrooms, orchids and arecanut are also grown.

Power: The state mainly utilizes hydroelectric power, but thermal power is also used.

Education

Educational institutes: Prominent institutes of higher education are the Manipur University and the Central Agricultural University, both located at Imphal.

Tourism

Major tourist attractions: Ima Market, Imphal; Khomghampat Orchidarium, Imphal; Manipur Zoological Gardens, Imphal; Bishnupur; Moirang; Loktak Lake and Sendra Island; Waithou Lake; Kangchup; Ukhrul; Tamenglong.

Airport: Imphal.

National Parks: Keibul Lamjao National Park in Bishnupur district (40 sq. km). It is the world's only floating national park and Shiroi Hill National Park in Ukhrul district (41 sq. km).

Administration

Legislature: Manipur has a unicameral legislature. There are 60 seats of which 1 is reserved for SCs and 19 are reserved for STs. The tenure of the present house ends on 11 March 2007. The current party position is as follows:

Name of Party	Seats
Indian National Congress	20
Federal Party of Manipur	13
Manipur State Congress Party	7
Communist Party of India	5
Bharatiya Janata Party	4
Nationalist Congress Party	3
Samata Party	3
Manipur Peoples Party	2
Democratic Revolutionary Peoples Party	2
Manipur National Conference	1
Total	**60**

Judiciary: The state comes under the Mizoram bench of the Guwahati High Court. Binod Kumar Roy is the chief justice.

Districts:

District	Area (sq. km)	Population	Headquarters	Urban Agglomerations
Bishnupur	496	205,907	Bishnupur	
Chandel	3,313	122,714	Chandel	
Churachandpur	4,570	228,707	Churachandpur	
Imphal East	709	393,780	Porompat	Imphal
Imphal West	519	439,532	Lamphel	Imphal
Senapati	3,271	379,214	Senapati	
Tamenglong	4,391	111,493	Tamenglong	
Thoubal	514	366,341	Thoubal	
Ukhrul	4,544	140,946	Ukhrul	

Meghalaya

Key Statistics

Capital: Shillong.

Area: 22,429 sq. km.

Population: Total: 2,318,822, Male: 1,176,087, Female: 1,142,735.

Population density: 103 per sq. km.

Sex ratio: 972 females per 1000 males.

Principal languages: Khasi, Garo, Bengali, Assamese.

Literacy rates: Total: 62.6%, Male: 65.4%, Female: 59.6%.

Government

Governor: Mundakkal Matthew Jacob. He has been the governor of Meghalaya since 19 June 1995.

Chief Minister: D. Dethwelson Lapang (INC). He was sworn in on 4 March 2003.

Geography

Physical characteristics: The state of Meghalaya is a region of uplands that has been formed by a detached part of the Deccan Plateau. In the western part of Meghalaya, the Garo Hills rise abruptly from the Brahmaputra valley to about 300 metres. They merge with the Khasi Hills and Jaintia Hills. These adjacent highlands together form a single tableland region that is separated by a series of eastward-running ridges. The steep southern face of the plateau overlooks the lowlands of Bangladesh. A number of rivers and streams flow out of the plateau, to create deep, narrow valleys with steep sides. These include the Umiam–Barapani, a major source of hydroelectric power for Assam and Meghalaya.

Neighbouring States and Union territories:
International border: Bangladesh.

States: Assam

Major rivers: Although there are a number of rivers in Meghalaya, none of them are fit for navigation. In the Garo Hills, the Manda, the Janjiram and the Damring flow towards the north while the Ringge and the Ganol flow westwards. The south flowing rivers are the Simsang, the biggest river in Garo Hills, and the Bhogai.

Significant north-flowing rivers in the Khasi and Jaintia hills are the Khri, the Umkhem, the Umtrew and the Umiam. The Kulpi lies on the border between Jainita Hills and North Cachar Hills. The Kynshi, the Umiam Mawphlang and the Umngot flow south into Bangladesh.

Climate: This region experiences tropical monsoonal climate, that varies from the western to the eastern parts of the plateau. The Garo Hills district has a tropical climate characterized by high rainfall and humidity. Summers are generally warm while winters are moderately cold. The Khasi and Jaintia Hills have high rainfall, moderately warm summers and severely cold winters when temperature sometimes dips to below freezing point in the higher altitudes. The mean summer temperature in Meghalaya is 26°C and the mean winter temperature is 9°C.

A maximum rainfall of 12,000mm has been recorded on the southern slope of Khasi Hills along the Cherrapunjee–Mawsynram belt. The average annual rainfall is about 2600mm in western Meghalaya, between 2500 and 3000mm in northern Meghalaya and about 4000mm in south-eastern Meghalaya. There is substantial variation of rainfall in the central and southern parts of the state.

Flora and Fauna:
Flora: Meghalaya has a widely varied and unique flora. The vegetation of Meghalaya ranges from tropical and subtropical to temperate or near temperate. This is largely due to the diverse topography, abundant rainfall and climatic and soil conditions of the state.

The forest types found in the state are: (i) Tropical forests: tropical evergreen forests, tropical semi-evergreen forests, tropical moist and dry deciduous forests, and grasslands and savannas; and (ii) Temperate forests.

The different types of plants found in the state are: parasites and epiphytes, succulent plants, and trees and shrubs.

Meghalaya also produces timber, fuelwood, resin, fibre, latex, tannin, fodder, gums, shellac, essential oils, fats, edible fruits, honey and a large number of medicinal plants. Some of the important tree species that yield timber are Khasi pine, teak, sal, and bamboos. Meghalaya is also well known for a large variety of flowers, bay leaves, orchids and cinnamon.

Fauna: Meghalaya is home to a wide variety of animals. These include the elephant, serow, sambar, hoolock, leopard, golden cat, barking deer, pangolin, jungle cat, large Indian civet, binturong or bear cat and Himalayan black bear. Notable among the reptile population found in the state are Indian cobra, king cobra, coral snake, viper, green tree racer, red-necked kulback, copperhead, blind snake and python.

Some of the significant species of birds found in the state are hoopoe, black-breasted Kalij pheasant, jungle mynas, hill mynas, long-tailed broadbill, red jungle fowl, spotted forktail, Himalayan whistling thrush, Burmese roller, blue-throated barbet, and Himalayan black bulbul. Besides these, the great Indian hornbill, florican and black drongo are also found in the state. Meghalaya is also famous for its large butterfly population.

History

When the British came to Sylhet (now in Bangladesh) in 1765, the Khasis used to go to Pandua on the border of Sylhet to trade in various commodities in exchange for rice, salt and dried fish. At that time, limestone from the Khasi Hills was taken to Bengal. The British officials of the East India Company came in contact with the Khasis when they began trading in Khasi Hill limestone.

In 1824, the Burmese invaded Cachar and reached the border of the Jaintia Hills. The British sent a force to reinforce the Jaintia ruler's troops. This paved the way for a friendship treaty to be signed on 10 March 1824, whereby the Jaintia ruler accepted British protection. This led to other Khasi chiefs to allow the passage of the British troops through their territories. After the end of the Burmese invasion, the Khasi chiefs agreed to a British demand for a route through the Khasi and Jaintia Hills that would connect Assam Valley with Surma Valley. The road was completed in March 1929, but only after suppressing an uprising led by U Tirot Sing. This led to the signing of several treaties with different Khasi chiefs. These treaties let the British slowly take control of the mineral deposits and at the same time subjugate the chiefs and also gain control of the judiciary. In 1862 the Jaintias rose in revolt under U Kiang Nongbah.

Shillong, the present-day capital of Meghalaya was made the capital of Assam in 1874. It remained so till January 1972, when Meghalaya was created. At the time of independence in 1947, the rulers of the region acceded to India. The region was given special protection in the Indian constitution. It was included within the state of Assam but was granted a substantial amount of autonomy. On 2 April 1970, Meghalaya became an autonomous state within Assam and attained full statehood on 21 January 1972. Captain Williamson A. Sangma was the state's first Chief Minister.

Politics

With the partition of Bengal in 1905, Meghalaya became a part of the new province of Assam and Eastern Bengal. In 1912, when the partition of Bengal was reversed, Meghalaya became a part of the revived province of Assam. In 1921, following the Montagu-Chelmsford Report of 1917 and the Government of India Act of 1919 the Governor-General-in-Council declared the areas now in Meghalaya, excluding the Khasi states, as backward tracts. On 2 April 1970 an autonomous state of Meghalaya was created within the state of Assam by the Assam Reorganisation (Meghalaya) Act, 1969. Williamson A. Sangma, the first chief minister of Meghalaya, had three tenures as chief minister, from 1970 to 1978, from 1981 to 1983 and from 1988 to 1990. In 1979, B.B. Lyngdoh split the All-Party Hill Leaders' Conference (APHLC) to form a coalition government with the Congress. Lyngdoh and Sangma agreed to share the chief minister's post for two years each. D.D. Lapang, the current chief minister, came to power in 2003.

Culture

A common and unique cultural tradition of all the tribes of Meghalaya is the matriarchal law of inheritance, whereby custody of property and succession of family position runs through the female line. It passes from the mother to the youngest daughter. The traditional costume of the state is the 'Jainsem' and the 'Dhara', although Western clothes are gaining popularity amongst the younger generation.

The different tribes have their own set of traditions and art forms. Phawar is one of the basic forms of Khasi music. It is more of a 'chant' than a song and is often composed on the spot to suit the occasion. Other forms of songs include the exploits of legendary heroes, ballads and verses based on historical events and laments for martyrs. Khasi musical instruments include the tangmuri, shaw shaw, nakra, ksing padiah, besli, sharati, shyngwiang and duitara.

Fairs and festivals: The different Khasi festivals are Ka Shad Suk Mynsiem, Ka Pom-Blang Nongkrem, Ka-Shad Shyngwiang-Thangiap, Ka-Shad-Kynjoh Khaskain, Ka Bam Khana Shnong, Umsan Nongkharai and Shad Beh Sier. The key Jaintia festivals include Behdienkhlam, Laho Dance and the sowing ritual ceremony. Other festivals commemorated by the Jaintias include the Tiger Festival, Bam Phalar/Bam Doh, Rong Belyngkan, Durga Puja, Seng Kut Snem and Christmas. The main festivals of the Garos are Wangala, Den Bilsia, Rongchu gala, Mangona, Grengdik BaA, Mi Amua, Jamang Sia, Ja Megapa, Sa Sat Ra Chaka, Ajeaor Ahaoea, Chambil Mesara, Dore Rata Dance, Saram Cha'A, Do'KruSua and A Se Mania.

Economy, Industry and Agriculture

Economy: The net state domestic product at current prices (new series) in 2002–03 (advance estimate) was Rs 3842 crores. The per capita net state domestic product at current prices (new series) in 2002–03 (advance estimate) was Rs 15,983.

Minerals and industry: The main industries of the state are tourism, iron and steel, consumer products, cement, handloom, silk production, lime and granite cutting and polishing. Small scale industries in the state include wooden furniture making, cane and bamboo works, tailoring, flour and rice mills, weaving and bakeries. There are six industrial estates, one designated industrial area and one export promotion industrial park in Meghalaya.

The significant mineral resources that are currently being exploited in the state are coal, limestone, clay and sillimanite. Other mineral resources found to occur in the state include phosphorite, glass sand, granite, quartz, feldspar, gypsum, gold, iron ore, uranium, base metal and gypsum.

Agriculture: Agriculture is the main occupation of the people of Meghalaya. Over 80 per cent of the total population is dependent on agriculture for their livelihood. Rice and maize are the major food crops. Millets and pulses are also grown, but in lesser quantities. Potato is a major cash crop of Meghalaya. Oilseeds such as rapeseed, mustard, soyabean and sesame are also grown. Important fruits grown here are orange, pineapple, lemon, guava, litchi, plum, peach, pear, jackfruit and bananas. Jute, mesta and cotton are the main fibre crops grown in the state. Areca nut and betelvine are also grown. The most prominent spices of the state are ginger, chillies, turmeric, black pepper and bay leaf. Jhum or 'shifting system' of cultivation is now being replaced with scientific methods, thereby bringing more land under permanent cultivation.

Power: Hydroelectric power plants meet all of Meghalaya's power requirements. However, the state has a high thermal power generation potential.

Education

Educational institutes: North Eastern Hill University, Shillong; Sacred Heart Theological College, Hawlai; Jowai Polytechnic School and North Eastern Indira Gandhi Regional Institute of Health and Medical Sciences.

Tourism

Major tourist attractions:

1. Khasi Hills: Cherrapunjee (Sohra), Shillong Peak, Mawsynram, Ward's Lake, Sohpetbneng Peak, Botanical Garden, Lady Hydari Park, Umiam Water Sports Complex, Shillong Cathedral, Dwarksuid, Bishop and Beadon Falls, Elephant Falls, Sweet Falls, Nongkhnum Island, Crinoline Falls, Diengiei Peak, Spread Eagle Falls, Kyllang Rock, Noh Kalikai Falls, Ranikor.

2. Jaintia Hills: Megalithic Remnants at Nartiang, Syndai, Syntu Ksiar, Jowai, Thadlaskein Lake.

3. Garo Hills: Nokrek Peak, Imilchang Dare Waterfalls, Tura Peak, Naphak Lake.

Airport: Umroi.

National Parks: Balphakram National Park in South Garo Hills district (220 sq. km) and Nokrek National Park in East, West and South Garo Hills districts (47.48 sq. km).

Administration

Legislature: Meghalaya has a 60-seat unicameral legislature of which 55 are reserved for STs. The term of the current house expires on 10 March 2008. The present party position is as under:

Name of Party	Seats
Indian National Congress	22
Nationalist Congress Party	14
United Democratic Party	9
Meghalaya Democratic Party	4
Bharatiya Janata Party	2
Hill State People's Democratic Party	2
Khun Hynnieutrip National Awakening Movement	2
Independent	5
Total	**60**

Judiciary: Meghalaya is under the jurisdiction of the Gauhati High Court at Guwahati, Assam. The principal seat of the High Court is at Guwahati and there is a circuit bench at Shillong. Binod Kumar Roy is the chief justice.

Districts:

District	Area (sq. km)	Population	Headquarters	Urban Agglomerations
East Garo Hills	260	247,555	Williamnagar	
East Khasi Hills	2,748	660,994	Shillong	Shillong
Jaintia Hills	3,819	295,692	Jowai	
Ri Bhoi	2,448	192,795	Nongpoh	
South Garo Hills	1,887	99,105	Baghmara	
West Garo Hills	3,677	515,813	Tura	
West Khasi Hills	5,247	294,115	Nongstoin	

Mizoram

Key Statistics

Capital: Aizawl.

Area: 21,087 sq. km.

Population: Total: 888,573, Male: 459,109, Female: 429,464.

Population density: 42 per sq. km.

Sex ratio: 935 females per 1000 males.

Principal languages: Lushai/Mizo, Bengali, Lakher.

Literacy rates: Total: 88.49% (second highest in the country), Male: 90.69%, Female: 86.13%.

Government

Governor: Amolak Rattan Kohli. He took over as governor on 18 May 2001.

Chief Minister: Pu Zoramthanga (MNF). He was sworn in on 4 December 2003.

Geography

Physical characteristics: Mizoram is bounded by Myanmar on the east and south and Bangladesh on the west. It is a mountainous region with steep hills separated by rivers that create deep gorges between them. Phawngpui or the Blue Mountain is the highest peak (2210m). The Tropic of Cancer runs through the state.

Neighbouring States and Union territories:

International borders: Myanmar, Bangladesh.

States: Assam, Tripura, Manipur.

Major rivers: Tlawng is the longest river of the state. Tlau, Chhimtuipui, Tuichang and Tuirial are other important rivers.

Climate: The hilly areas are cooler during summer, while the lower reaches are relatively warm and humid. The average maximum temperature in summer is 30°C. The average minimum temperature during winter is around 11°C. The months of May to September see heavy rains, with an average annual rainfall of 2500mm.

Flora and Fauna:

Flora: Three-fourths of the state's area is under forest cover. Prominent trees include the Himalayan maple, champak, ironwood, bamboo and gurjun. The region also abounds in various species of shrubs. About 150 species of orchids have also been identified.

Fauna: Wildlife found in the state include tiger, leopard, elephant, Malayan sun bear, Himalayan black bear, serow, wild boar, slow loris, Assamese macaque, capped langur, owl, pheasant, partridge, hawk, eagle, egret and heron.

History

Like many other northeast Indian tribes, the origin of the Mizos is shrouded in mystery. They are generally accepted as part of a great Mongoloid wave of migration from China. These include the Kuki, New Kuki and Lushai tribes. In 1895, the Mizo Hills were formally declared as a part of British India and subsequently marked as Lushai Hills district, with Aizawl as the headquarters.

At the time of India's independence, a subcommittee was formed under the chairmanship of Gopinath Bordoloi to advise the Constituent Assembly on the tribal affairs in the north-east. The region became a district of Assam.

In 1959, a great famine, known in Mizo history as the 'Mautam Famine', struck the Mizo Hills. The cause of the famine was the flowering of bamboos and the consequent manifold increase in the rat population which infested the villages and destroyed crops.

Movements for sovereignty for the region gained momentum in 1961, with the birth of the Mizo National Front (MNF). After a decade of insurgency, the region was declared a Union territory in 1972. Insurgency continued for another 14 years, and ended with MNF leader Laldenga signing an accord with the Union government. Mizoram became India's 23rd state on 20 February 1987. Laldenga was the state's first Chief Minister.

Politics

It was during the British regime that a political awakening among the Mizos in Lushai Hills started taking shape. The first political party, the Mizo Common People's Union, was formed on 9 April 1946. At the time of Independence a sub-committee under the chairmanship of Gopinath Bordoloi was formed to advise the Constituent Assembly on the tribal affairs in the North-East. The Mizo Union submitted a resolution to this sub-committee demanding inclusion of all Mizo inhabited areas adjacent to Lushai Hills. However, a new party called the United Mizo Freedom (UMFO) came up to demand that Lushai Hills join Burma after Independence. After independence of India, Mizoram continued to be part of Assam. The Lushai Hills Autonomous District Council came into being in 1952. Representatives of the District Council and the Mizo Union pleaded with the States Reorganisation Commission (SRC) in 1954 for integrating the Mizo-dominated areas of Tripura and Manipur with their District Council in Assam. The tribal leaders in the North East were unhappy with the SRC's recommendations. They met in Aizawl in 1955 and formed a new political party, Eastern India Union (EITU) and raised the demand for a separate state comprising of all the hill districts of Assam. The Mizo Union split and the breakaway faction joined the EITU. By this time, the UMFO also joined the EITU; the demand for a separate Hill state by EITU was kept in abeyance.

A new political organization, the Mizo National Front (MNF) was born on 22 October 1961 under the leadership of Laldenga with the specified goal of achieving sovereign independence of Greater Mizoram. While the MNF took to violence to secure its goal of establishing a sovereign land, other political forces in the hills of Assam were striving for a separate state. The search for a political solution to the problems facing the hill regions in Assam continued. In 1966 the Mizos resorted to the use of armed struggle to put forth their demands to set up a homeland. The Mizo National Front was outlawed in 1967. A Mizo District Council delegation, which met Prime Minister Indira Gandhi in May 1971 demanded a full-fledged state for the Mizos. The Union government on its own offered to turn Mizo Hills into a union territory in July 1971. The union territory of Mizoram came into being on 21 January 1972. On 3 May 1972 L. Chal Chhunga was sworn in as the first chief minister of Mizoram. In 1986 a peace agreement was signed between the Government of India and the MNF. Mizoram was created as a separate state within India, and Pu Laldenga became chief minister. The formalization of Mizoram state took place on 20 February 1987. However, in 1989, the MNF lost the first elections following the peace agreement. In 1998 and 2003 the MNF won the state assembly elections, and Pu Zoramthanga is currently the chief minister.

Culture

Popular dance forms of Mizoram are Khuallam, Cheraw or bamboo dance, Chailam and Tlanglam. These are accompanied by instruments like the gong and drum. Traditional crafts include exquisite cane and bamboo work and handloom weaving.

Fairs and festivals: Most Mizo festivals are connected with harvest or other agricultural operations. These include Mim Kut, Pawl Kut and Chapchar Kut.

Economy, Industry and Agriculture

Economy: The net state domestic product at current prices in 2001–02 was Rs 1777 crores. The per capita net state domestic product at current prices in 2001–02 was Rs 19,696.

Minerals and industry: Mizoram has no major industry. The small-scale sector comprises handloom, handicrafts, rice, oil and flour milling, mechanized bamboo workshops and sericulture. Major minerals include coal, limestone and natural gas.

Agriculture: Nearly 60 per cent of the population is engaged in agriculture. Shifting cultivation, or jhum, is the usual practice. Important crops include paddy, maize, soyabean, mustard, pulses, sugarcane, chilli, ginger, tobacco, turmeric, potato, banana and pineapple.

Power: The two main sources of power in the state are hydroelectric plants and diesel power plants.

Education

Educational institutes: The North Eastern Hill University, which is headquartered at Shillong, has a campus at Aizawl.

Tourism

Major tourist attractions: The Blue Mountain (Phawngpui); The famous caves: Pukzing Cave, Milu Puk, Lamsial Puk, and Kungawrhi Puk; Sibuta Lung; Thangliana Lung; Suangpuilawn Inscriptions; Mangkhai Lung; Buddha's Image near Mualcheng village.

Airport: Aizawl.

National Parks: Murlen (200 sq. km) and Phawngpui (50 sq. km).

Administration

Legislature: The Mizoram Legislative Assembly comprises 40 seats, of which 39 are reserved for STs. The term of the current assembly expires on 14 November 2008. Party position of the current house is as follows:

Name of Party	Seats
Mizo National Front	21
Indian National Congress	12
Mizoram People's Conference	3
Zoram Nationalist Party	2
Hmar Peoples Convention	1
Maraland Democratic Front	1
Total	**40**

Judiciary: Mizoram falls under the jurisdiction of the Gauhati High Court. There is a permanent bench located at Aizawl. Binod Kumar Roy is the chief justice.

Districts:

District	Area (sq. km)	Population	Headquarters	Urban Agglomerations
Aizawl	3,576.3	339,812	Aizawl	–
Champhai	3,185.8	101,389	Champhai	–
Kolasib	1,382.5	60,977	Kolasib	–
Lawngtlai	2,557.1	73,050	Lawngtlai	–
Lunglei	4,538.0	137,155	Lunglei	–
Mamit	3,025.8	62,313	Mamit	–
Chhimtuipui	1,399.9	60,823	Saiha	–
Serchhip	1,421.6	55,539	Serchhip	–

Nagaland

Key Statistics

Capital: Kohima.

Area: 16,579 sq. km.

Population: Total: 1,990,036, Male: 1,047,141, Female: 942,895.

Population density: 120 per sq. km.

Sex ratio: 900 females per 1000 males.

Principal languages: Ao, Sema, Konyak.

Literacy rates: Total: 66.6%, Male: 71.2%, Female: 61.5%.

Government

Governor: Shyamal Datta. He assumed the office of the governor of Nagaland on 28 January 2002.

Chief Minister: Neiphi-u Rio (NPF). He became Chief Minister on 6 March 2003.

Geography

Physical characteristics: Nagaland has state boundaries with Assam, Arunachal Pradesh and Manipur. On the east, it has an international boundary with Myanmar. The Naga Hills run through this state. Saramati (3840m) is the highest peak.

Neighbouring States and Union territories:
International border: Myanmar.

States: Arunachal Pradesh, Assam, Manipur.

Major rivers: Dhansiri, Doyang, Dikhu, Barak and tributaries of the Chindwin of Myanmar. Others include Milak, Zungki and Tizu.

Climate: Temperature varies between 16°C and 31°C in summer and between 4°C and 24°C in winter. Average rainfall is 2000mm to 2500mm. It rains heavily from May to August, as well as occasionally in September and October. November to April is the dry season.

Flora and Fauna:

Flora: Evergreen and coniferous forests, medicinal plants, bamboo, cane and orchids make up the state's flora.

Fauna: Animals like Asian elephant, clouded leopard, binturong, musk deer, macaque, common langur, gaur (Indian bison), tiger, sambar, barking deer, hoolock, serow, sloth bear and wild boar can be found in the state. Reptiles include the monitor lizard, tortoise, reticulated python, king cobra, common krait, banded krait, viper and common cobra.

The greyheaded fishing eagle, crested serpent eagle, forest eagle owl, tragopan and hornbill are notable among the birds found in Nagaland. Amongst the animals, the Asian elephant, spotted linsang, tiger civet, sloth bear, tiger and the tailed pig are endangered species. The gaur or Indian bison is also facing extinction in Nagaland. The diverse hornbills and tortoise are also endangered.

History

Medieval chronicles of the Ahom kingdom of Assam talk of the Naga tribes. The Myanmar invasion of Assam in 1816 was followed by the establishment of British rule in 1826. By 1892, British administration covered the entire Naga territory, with the exception of the Tuensang area.

After independence in 1947, Naga territory initially remained a part of Assam, after which there was a strong nationalist pressure for the political union of the Naga tribes. In 1957, an agreement was signed between the Naga leaders and the Indian government, following which the Naga Hill districts of Assam and the Tuensang division to the north-east were brought together under a single unit, directly administered by the Indian government. However, unrest continued and another accord was reached at the Naga People's Convention meeting of July 1960. According to this accord, it was decided that Nagaland should become a constituent state of the Indian Union. Nagaland became a state on 1 December 1963 and a democratically elected government took office in 1964. Shilu Ao was the first Chief Minister.

Politics

The Naga territory remained split between Assam and the North East Frontier Agency after Indian independence in 1947, despite a vocal movement advocating the political union of all the Naga tribes. The government of the newly independent India refused to accept such a demand, and some Nagas took to armed rebellion in an effort to gain independence. The area remained in a rebellious political condition for much of the 1950s. A voluntary plebiscite was held in 1951 to determine whether the Nagas would join the Indian Union, or remain by themselves. The result was 99.9 in favour of independence. In persuance of their declared national decision, the Naga people launched a civil disobedience movement and successfully boycotted the general elections of free India. Nagaland was just a district in the state of Assam until 1957, known to others as 'The Naga Hills'. Not satisfied with such an obscure status, the leaders of various Naga tribes, in August 1957, formed the Naga People's Convention (NPC). In its first session held at Kohima on 21 August 1957, under the presidentship of Imkongliba Ao, the NPC proposed the formation of a separate administrative unit by merging the Tuensang division of NEFA with Naga Hills district. The Government of India agreed to the proposal. In July 1960, a delegation of the NPC met Jawaharlal Nehru and discussed the formation of a separate state for the Nagas within the Indian Union to be known as Nagaland. On 18 February 1961 an interim body of 42 members was constituted to function as the de-facto legislature. On 1 December 1963, President S. Radhakrishnan inaugurated the state of Nagaland. The first Assembly election in Nagaland was held in 1964 and the Naga National Organization (NNO) came to power. Following a grave political crisis in the state, President's Rule was imposed in Nagaland on 22 March 1975; Nagaland was under President's Rule for 32 months, so far the longest in the country. The state has come under President's Rule several more times. Neiphi-u Rio, leader of the Democratic Alliance of Nagaland (DAN), was sworn in as the present chief minister on 6 March 2003.

Culture

Each of the several tribes and communities of Nagaland has its own unique folk dances, folk songs and folklore. They are skilful craftsmen specializing in woodcarving, weaving, spinning, metalwork and stonework. Pottery is considered a taboo among certain sections of the Ao community.

Fairs and festivals: The major festivals of the state are Sekrenyi of the Angamis, Moatsu of the Aos, Phom-Monyu of the Phom tribe and the Hornbill festival of Nagaland.

Economy, Industry and Agriculture

Economy: The net state domestic product at current prices in 2001–02 was Rs 3864 crores. The per capita net state domestic product at current prices in 2001–02 was Rs 18,911.

Minerals and industry: The process of industrialization of the state is in its infancy. There is a need for more industries in the state. There are several plans in the pipeline to increase industrial investment and activity in the state. Coal, limestone, petroleum and marble are the main minerals found in the state.

Agriculture: Agriculture is the most important occupation of the people. Rice, wheat, maize and pulses are the chief agricultural products of the state. Fruits like banana, orange, passion fruit, pears, plum and jackfruit are grown. Vegetables like ginger, cabbage, chilli, tomato, potato and garlic are also grown.

Power: The main sources of power in the state are diesel power plants and hydroelectric plants.

Education

Educational institutes: Nagaland University is at Kohima.

Tourism

Major tourist attractions: Shangnyu village; Longwa village; Veda peak; Naginimora; Dzukou Valley; Kohima village; War Cemetry, Kohima; Dzulekie; Ruins of medieval Kachari kingdom, Dimapur; Chumukedima.

Airport: Dimapur.

National Parks: Intanki National Park in Kohima district (202.02 sq. km).

Administration

Legislature: Nagaland has a unicameral legislature. The Nagaland Legislative Assembly has 60 seats out of which 59 are reserved for STs. The term of the present house runs out on 13 March 2008. The current party position is:

Name of Party	Seats
Indian National Congress	21
Nagaland Peoples Front	19
Bharatiya Janata Party	7
Nationalist Democratic Movement	5
Janata Dal (United)	3
Samata Party	1
Independent	4
Total	**60**

Judiciary: Nagaland falls under the jurisdiction of the Gauhati High Court with a bench at Kohima. Binod Kumar Roy is the chief justice.

Districts:

District	Area (sq. km)	Population	Headquarters	Urban Agglomerations
Dimapur	927	308,382	Dimapur	–
Kohima	3,114	314,366	Kohima	–
Mokokchung	1,615	227,230	Mokokchung	–
Mon	1,786	259,604	Mon	–
Phek	2,026	148,246	Phek	–
Tuensang	4,228	414,801	Tuensang	–
Wokha	1,628	161,098	Wokha	–
Zunheboto	1,255	154,909	Zunheboto	–

Orissa

Key Statistics

Capital: Bhubaneswar.
Area: 155,707 sq. km.
Population: Total: 36,804,660, Male: 18,660,570, Female: 18,144,090.
Population density: 236 per sq. km.
Sex ratio: 972 females per 1000 males.
Principal languages: Oriya, Hindi, Telugu.
Literacy rates: Total: 63.1%, Male: 75.3%, Female: 50.5%.

Government

Governor: Rameshwar Thakur. He was sworn in on 16 November 2004.

Chief Minister: Naveen Patnaik (BJD). He was sworn in on 16 May 2004.

Geography

Physical characteristics: The state is surrounded by the Bay of Bengal on the east, Chhattisgarh in the west, Jharkhand and West Bengal in the north and Andhra Pradesh in the south. It has a coastline of about 450 km. Orissa is divided into five major physiographic regions: the central plateaus, the coastal plain in the east, the western rolling uplands, the middle mountainous and highland regions, and the flood plains. The middle mountainous and highland region covers about three-fourths of the entire state and is a part of the Eastern Ghats.

Neighbouring States and Union territories:
States: West Bengal, Chhattisgarh, Jharkhand, Andhra Pradesh.

Major rivers: Subarnarekha, Mahanadi, Baitarani, Burabalang, Brahmani, Rushikulya and Vamsadhara.

Climate: The coastal lowland receives substantial rainfall every year because it comes directly under the influence of tropical depressions originating in the Bay of Bengal in the monsoon season. This is a distinctive climatic feature of this region. The state is sometimes hit by tropical cyclones which cause a lot of damage to property and human life. Summers are extremely hot, with temperatures rising up to 45°C; winters are temperate.

Flora and Fauna:
Flora: The state has tropical semi-evergreen, tropical moist deciduous, tropical dry deciduous, littoral and swamp forests.

Fauna: Wildlife found in the state includes tiger, elephant, gaur, chital, leopard, mouse deer, flying squirrel, mugger, salt water crocodile, monitor lizards, snakes, fishing cat, hyena, wild pig, water birds and Ridley sea turtle.

History

At various points in ancient and medieval times, the land corresponding roughly with modern Orissa was known as Utkala, Kalinga, and Odra Desa. These names were initially associated with peoples. The Okkala or Utkala, the Kalinga, and the Odra or Oddaka were mentioned in literature as tribes. Later on these names became identified with territories. For many centuries preceding and following the birth of Christ, Kalinga was a very strong political power. Its territories extended from the Ganga to the Godavari. At some point of time between the 11th and the 16th centuries, the name fell into disuse. In its place came the name Odra Desa, which was gradually transformed into

Uddisa, Udisa, or Odisa and ultimately, Orissa.

In 260 BC, Asoka fought the famed Kalinga War and this is now considered the turning point in Asoka's own life. The bloodshed and loss of life in this war led him to renounce warfare and violence. It was after this that he took up Buddhism and preached the gospel of peace and harmony.

In the 1st century BC, the Kalinga emperor Kharavela achieved great power by conquering vast tracts of land and setting up a Kalinga empire. In the eighth, ninth and 10th centuries AD, the area was ruled by the Bhuma-Kara dynasty and in the 10th and 11th centuries by the Soma dynasty.

Between 1028 and 1434–35, Kalinga was ruled by the Ganga dynasty followed by the Surya dynasty. After the fall of the Surya kings, Orissa passed into the hands of the Afghan rulers of Bengal.

In the 1590s, the Mughal emperor Akbar conquered Orissa from the Afghans. With the decline and fall of the Mughal empire in the 1760s, a part of Orissa remained under the Bengal nawabs and the rest went to the Marathas. The Bengal region passed into British rule in 1757, after the Battle of Plassey. The British conquered the Maratha areas in 1803. After 1803, the British controlled the entire Oriya-speaking area and it was administered as two separate units, the Northern Division and the Southern Division. It was only in April 1936 that the British constituted Orissa as a separate province on a linguistic basis, with the exception of 26 princely states that stayed outside provincial administration. After independence in 1947, all these princely states (except Saraikela and Kharsawan that merged with Bihar) became parts of Orissa. The first Chief Minister of Orissa was Harekrushna Mahatab.

Politics

Orissa became a separate province on 1 April 1936 by the Government of India (Constitution of Orissa) Order 1936. It comprised certain portions of the Bihar and Orissa Province, Madras Presidency and the Central Provinces. On 1 January 1948, 24 princely states merged with the province of Orissa. Harekrushna Mahtab became the first chief minister of Orissa in 1947 and was chief minister two more times. Biju Patnaik of the Congress first became chief minister in 1961. In 1967 a new party called Jana Congress was formed under the leadership of Harekrushna Mahtab and came to power. Utkal Congress was formed in 1969 when Biju Patnaik left the Indian National Congress. After the 1971 Orissa elections Utkal Congress took part in the Biswanath Das ministry in the state. In 1977 Utkal Congress merged into Janata Party. The Jana Congress too merged into Janata Party. In a mid-term poll, the Janata Party led by Biju Patnaik secured 110 seats out of 147. Nilamani Routray was made the chief minister. In 1981 the Congress party won a resounding victory and Janaki Ballav Patnaik became the chief minister. Under the leadership of Biju Patnaik, the Janata Dal won an astounding victory in the elections held in 1990. J.B. Patnaik was the chief minister again from 1995 to 1999. On 5 March 2000 Naveen Patnaik of the Biju Janata Dal was elected the chief minister.

Culture

The state is home to the Odissi and Chhau dance forms as well as the Patachitra art form. It is the home of renowned weaves of saris like Sambalpuri, Katki, Behrampuri, Bomkai and Baragaht.

Fairs and festivals: The major festivals of the state include Dola Purnima

(Holi), Ratha Yatra, Chandan Yatra, Snana Yatra, Konark Dance Festival, Puri Beach Festival, Bali Yatra and Dhanu Yatra.

Economy, Industry and Agriculture

Economy: The net state domestic product at current prices for 2002–03 (provisional) was Rs 38,737 crores. The per capita net state domestic product at current prices for 2002–03 (provisional) was Rs 10,340.

Minerals and industry: Orissa has substantial mineral resources such as dolomite, chromite, limestone, high quality iron ore, coal and manganese. The state is home to steel mills, non-ferrous smelting, paper mills, fertilizer industries, cement plants, foundries and glass works. The famous steel plant at Rourkela is in Orissa.

Agriculture: About 80 per cent of the area sown is under rice cultivation. Other important crops are oilseeds, pulses, jute, sugar cane, and coconut. Adverse crop-growing conditions such as poor soil quality and low availability of sunlight combine to hamper agriculture in the state.

Power: Most of Orissa's power is generated by hydroelectric plants. The rest comes from thermal power plants.

Education

Educational institutes: Notable educational institutes in the state include Utkal University, Bhubaneswar; Fakir Mohan University, Balasore; Orissa University of Agriculture and Technology, Bhubaneswar; Regional Engineering College (National Institute of Technology), Rourkela and Xavier Institute of Management, Bhubaneswar.

Tourism

Major tourist attractions: Bhitarkanika National Park; Simlipal National Park; Lingaraj Temple, Bhubaneswar; Mukteswar Temple, Bhubaneswar; Rajarani Temple, Bhubaneswar; Shanti Stupa, Bhubaneswar; Jagannath Temple, Puri; Sun Temple, Konark; Barabati Fort, Cuttack; Chilka Lake; Puri beach.

Airports: Bhubaneswar, Jharsuguda.

National Parks: Simlipal (Mayurbhanj) —845.7 sq. km, Bhitarkanika (Cuttack) —367 sq. km.

Administration

Legislature: The state has a unicameral legislature of 147 members. Out of this, 22 seats are reserved for SCs and 34 for STs. The tenure of the current house ends on 29 June 2009. The current party position is:

Name of Party	Seats
Biju Janata Dal	61
Indian National Congress	38
Bharatiya Janata Party	32
Jharkhand Mukti Morcha	4
Orissa Gana Parishad	2
Communist Party of India	1
Communist Party of India (Marxist)	1
Independent	8
Total	**147**

Judiciary: The Orissa High Court is situated at Cuttack. The chief justice is Sujit Burman Ray.

Districts:

District	Area (sq. km)	Population	Headquarters	Urban Agglomerations
Anugul	6,375	1,139,341	Anugul	
Balangir	6,575	1,335,760	Balangir	Titlagarh
Baleshwar	3,806	2,023,056	Baleshwar	Baleshwar

Bargarh	5,837	1,345,601	Bargarh	
Baudh	3,098	373,038	Baudh	
Bhadrak	2,505	1,332,249	Bhadrak	
Cuttack	3,932	2,340,686	Cuttack	Cuttack
Debagarh	2,940	274,095	Debagarh	
Dhenkanal	4,452	1,065,983	Dhenkanal	
Gajapati	4,325	518,448	Parlakhemundi	
Ganjam	8,206	3,136,937	Chatrapur	
Jagatsinghapur	1,668	1,056,556	Jagatsinghapur	
Jajapur	2,899	1,622,868	Panikoili	Byasanagar
Jharsuguda	2,081	509,056	Jharsuguda	
Kalahandi	7,920	1,334,372	Bhawanipatna	
Kandhamal	8,021	647,912	Phulbani	
Kendrapara	2,644	1,301,856	Kendrapara	
Kendujhar	8,303	1,561,521	Kendujhar	
Khordha	2,813	1,874,405	Khordha	Bhubaneswar, Jatani
Koraput	8,807	1,177,954	Koraput	
Malkangiri	5,791	480,232	Malkangiri	
Mayurbhanj	10,418	2,221,782	Baripada	Baripada
Nabarangapur	5,291	1,018,171	Nabarangapur	
Nayagarh	3,890	863,934	Nayagarh	
Nuapada	3,852	530,524	Nuapada	
Puri	3,479	1,498,604	Puri	
Rayagada	7,073	823,019	Rayagada	Gunupur
Sambalpur	6,657	928,889	Sambalpur	Sambalpur
Sonapur	2,337	540,659	Sonapur	
Sundargarh	9,712	1,829,412	Sundargarh	Raurkela

Punjab

Key Statistics

Capital: Chandigarh.

Area: 50,362 sq. km.

Population: Total: 24,358,999, Male: 12,985,045, Female: 11,373,954.

Population density: 482 per sq. km.

Sex ratio: 876 females per 1000 males.

Principal languages: Punjabi, Hindi, Urdu.

Literacy rates: Total: 69.7%, Male: 75.2%, Female: 63.4%.

Government

Governor: Gen. S.F. Rodrigues. He was sworn in on 16 November 2004.

Chief Minister: Captain Amarinder Singh. He was sworn in on 27 February 2002.

Geography

Physical characteristics: Punjab is largely a flat plain that rises gently from about 150 metres in the southwest to about 300 metres in the northeast. Physiographically, it can be divided into three parts: (i) The Shiwalik Hills in the northeast rising from about 300 to 900 metres; (ii) The zone of narrow, undulating foothills dissected by seasonal rivers terminating in the plains and not flowing into bigger waterbodies and (iii) The flat tract with fertile alluvial soils. The low-lying floodplains lie along the rivers while the slightly elevated flat uplands lie between them. Sand dunes are found in the southwest and west of the Sutlej.

Neighbouring States and Union territories:
International border: Pakistan.

States: Haryana, Himachal Pradesh, Jammu and Kashmir, Rajasthan.

Union territories: Chandigarh.

Major rivers: Ravi, Beas, Sutlej and Ghaggar with their numerous small and seasonal tributaries.

Climate: Punjab has three major seasons. These are: (i) The hot weather from April to June with temperatures rising as high as 45°C; (ii) The rainy season from July to September with average annual rainfall in the state ranging between 960mm in the submontane region to 580mm in the plains and (iii) The cold weather from October to March with temperatures going down to 4°C.

Flora and Fauna:
Flora: The rapid growth of human settlement resulted in the clearing out of most of the forest cover of the state. Consequently, trees have been replaced by bush vegetation in the Shiwalik Hills. Attempts at aforestation have been made on the hills while eucalyptus trees have been planted along major roads.

Fauna: Wildlife faces intense competition from agriculture for its natural habitat. Many species of birds, some monkeys, rodents, and snakes have adapted to the farmland environment.

History

Punjab was the site of the Indus Valley Civilization. Archaeological excavations all over the state have revealed evidences of the cities belonging to the civilization that also included Harappa and Mohenjodaro, which are now in Pakistan. The *Mahabharata* contains rich descriptions of the land and people of Punjab. It is also believed that parts of the *Ramayana* were written around the Shri Ram Tirath Ashram near Amritsar and that it was in the forests of what is today Punjab that Lav and Kush, the sons of Rama, grew up.

Other important historical centres are at Ropar, Kiratpur, Dholbaha, Rohira and Ghuram. Sanghol, in Fatehgarh Sahib district near Ludhiana, is home to sites associated with Mauryan Dynasty. Relics found here record the presence of Buddhism in the region.

The Vedic and the later epic periods of the Punjab are of great significance. The Rig Veda was composed here. Numerous cultural and educational centres were established in the region during the period.

A few years before the birth of Buddha (556 BC), the armies of Darius I, King of Persia, had arrived in Punjab and made the area a protectorate of the Persian empire. The Buddhists referred to Punjab as 'Uttar Path' or the way to the north, namely the valleys of Afghanistan, Central Asia and China. In 327 BC Alexander invaded Punjab, defeating Raja Paurava. In subsequent centuries, there were more invasions from the north. This happened during the rules of the Mauryas, the Sungas, the Guptas and the Pushpabhuti.

Modern-day Punjab owes its origin to Banda Singh Bahadur who led a group of Sikhs to free parts of the region from Mughal rule in 1709–10. In 1716, however, the Mughals defeated and killed Banda Singh. This sparked off a prolonged struggle between the Sikhs and the Mughals and Afghans.

By 1764–65, the Sikhs established their dominance in the region. Ranjit Singh led Punjab into a powerful kingdom and also added the provinces of Multan, Kashmir, and Peshawar. In 1849, Punjab had passed into the hands of the British East India Company. It later became a province of the British empire in India.

Many Punjabis played significant roles during India's freedom struggle. These included Baba Ram Singh (of the Kuka or Namdhari movement fame), Lala Lajpat Rai, Madan Lal Dhingra, Bhagat Singh and Bhai Parmanand. The nationalist fervour was kept alive by several movements, such as the Singh Sabha, Arya Samaj and the Akali movements and by organizations like Bharat Mata Society, Naujawan Bharat Sabha and Kirti Kisan Sabha.

It was in Punjab that the infamous Jallianwala Bagh massacre took place at Amritsar on 13 April 1919. Hundreds of peaceful demonstrators were killed and over a thousand were injured when General Reginald Dwyer ordered his troops to open fire on civilians who had gathered in a peaceful protest meeting. This incident proved to be a turning point in the history of India.

At the time of independence in 1947, the province was divided between India and Pakistan. The smaller eastern portion was allocated to India. Gopichand Bhargava was the first Chief Minister of the state. In November 1956 the Indian state of Punjab was enlarged by the addition of the Patiala and East Punjab States Union (PEPSU). Pepsu was a collection of the erstwhile princely states of Faridkot, Jind, Kalsia, Kapurthala, Malerkotla, Nabha, Nalagarh and Patiala.

The present-day state of Punjab came into existence on 1 November 1966 when Punjab was divided on a linguistic basis. The Hindi-speaking parts were formed into a new state, Haryana. The northernmost districts were transferred to Himachal Pradesh.

Politics

With the partition of India in 1947, the East Punjab Legislative Assembly came into existence. On 15 July 1948 eight princely states of East Punjab grouped together to form a single state called PEPSU (Patiala and the East Punjab States Union) which merged with Punjab on the Reorganisation of States on 1 November 1956. Later, the state of Punjab was reorganized on 1 November 1966 when Haryana was carved out of it and some of its areas were transferred to Himachal Pradesh.

Following the partition of India in 1947, the Sikhs were concentrated in India in east Punjab. Sikh leaders demanded a Punjabi language majority state, which would have included most Sikhs. Fearing that a Punjabi state might lead to a separatist Sikh movement, the government opposed the demand. In 1966 a compromise was reached, when two new states of Punjab and Haryana were created. Punjabi became the official language of Punjab, and Chandigarh became the shared capital of the two states. However the agreement did not resolve the Sikh question.

The Congress ruled the state for the first two decades. From the late 1960s the Akali Dal won power in the state. Prakash Singh Badal formed an Akali government in Punjab in 1970. From 1972 to 1977 Zail Singh of the Congress arty served as the chief minister; he later became the President of India. Prakash Singh Badal became the chief minister for the second time in 1977 and remained in the post till 1980.

From the early 1980s to the early part of the 1990s the state was ravaged by Khalistani terrorism. In 1977, Sant Jarnail Singh Bhindranwale, an obscure but charismatic religious leader, made his appearance. He preached strict fundamentalism and armed struggle for national liberation. His speeches inflamed both young students and small farmers dissatisfied with their economic lot. Tensions between Sikhs and New Delhi heightened during the early 1980s. Over the years that followed, Punjab was faced with escalating confrontations and increased terrorist incidents. The Akali Dal only achieved limited concessions from the government and Sikh separatists prepared for battle. In the Golden Temple enclosure 10,000 Sikhs took an oath to lay down their lives if necessary in the struggle. Renewed confrontations in October 1983 resulted in Punjab being placed under central government authority. The violence continued and hundreds of Sikhs were detained in the first part of 1984. Followers of Jarnail Singh Bhindranwale established a terrorist stronghold inside the Golden Temple. The prime minister Indira Gandhi then initiated Operation Blue Star, which took place on 5-6 June 1984. The Golden Temple was shelled and besieged by the army to dislodge the terrorists. The fighting continued for five days. Bhindranwale was killed and there was serious damage to sacred buildings. The intervention had disastrous consequences for the Sikh community and the whole country. Sikh-Hindu communalism was aggravated, Sikh extremism was reinforced, and political assassinations increased. On 31 October 1984 Indira Gandhi was assassinated in New Delhi by two Sikh bodyguards. A peace agreement was concluded between the Indian government and moderate Akali Dal Sikhs led by Harchand Singh Longowal in July 1985, which granted many of the Sikh community's longstanding demands. However the extremists regarded Longowal as a traitor to the Sikh cause and he was assassinated in August 1985. In 1987 the state government was dismissed and Punjab was placed under President's Rule. Extremists spread terror throughout Punjab and the Indian government mounted a campaign of anti-terrorist measures designed to restore the situation in Punjab to normal. In May 1988 the Punjab police and Indian paramilitary forces launched Operation Black Thunder against armed extremists who had again created a fortified stronghold within the Golden Temple. At least 40 extremists and several police officers were killed during the battle. President's Rule was finally brought to an end following elections in February 1992, which were won by the Congress (I). However the elections were boycotted by the leading factions of Akali Dal and attracted an extremely low turnout. Beant Singh of the Congress (I) was sworn in as chief minister. On 31 August 1995 Beant Singh was killed by a car bomb in Chandigarh.

Rajinder Kaur Bhattal who became chief minister on 21 November 1996 was the first woman chief minister of Punjab. After the February 1997 state election, Prakash Singh Badal became chief minister a third time, being chosen by the Akali Dal party. He remained in power till 27 February 2002. In state elections in Punjab in 2002, the Congress Party won 64 out of 117 seats. Amarinder Singh was sworn in as chief minister.

Culture

Patiala and Muktsar are famous for *juttis*, the traditional shoes worn by Punjabis. Punjab's most famous example of handicraft, phulkari, is a shawl that is completely covered in silk embroidery, with folk motifs in jewel tones on an ochre background.

Punjabi ornaments include the sagi, which is a central head stud. There are many varieties of sagi. These include the sagi uchhi, sagi motianwali, sagi phul, sagi chandiari, sagi meenawali. The state is famous for its gold and silver ornaments and objects made out of these metals.

Punjab is also noted for its weaving of durries which are cotton bedspreads or floor spreads in a variety of motifs and designs. The state's needlework is also unique. These include baghs, phulkaris, handkerchiefs and scarfs. In Punjab, needlework is done on a wide variety of objects. Punjabi hand fans are also well known. Punjab is famous for its woodwork. These include elaborate decorated beds called pawas, low seats called peeras. Besides furniture, the state's woodwork is also noted for boxes, toys and decorative pieces.

The state's many dance forms include Bhangra, Gidda, Jhumar, Luddi, Julli, Dankara, Dhamal, Sammi, Jaago, Kikli and Gatka.

In the 18th and 19th centuries a new school of classical music grew up around Patiala. This is known today as the Patiala Gharana. The founders of this gharana were Ustaad Ali Bux and Ustaad Fateh Ali, singers at the Patiala Darbar. Notable amongst their disciples were Ustaad Bade Ghulam Ali and his brother Barkat Ali. The gharana of tabla playing which is known as the Punjab style also developed in the state. Ustaad Alla Rakha was its best-known exponent.

Various songs are associated with Punjabi weddings. These include suhag, sehra, ghodi, sithaniya and patal kaavya, The instruments used in Punjabi folk art forms include the toombi, algoza, chheka, chimta, kaanto, daphali, dhad and manjira.

Fairs and festivals: Lohri, Baisakhi and Maaghi Da Mela are the most significant among the Punjabi festivals.

Economy, Industry and Agriculture

Economy: The net state domestic product at current prices for 2002–03 (provisional) was Rs 64,621 crores. The per capita net state domestic product at current prices for 2002–03 (provisional) was Rs 25,855.

Minerals and industry: The main industrial products of the state include engineering goods, pharmaceuticals, leather goods, food products, textiles, electronic goods, sugar, machine tools, hand tools, agricultural implements, sports goods, paper and paper packaging.

Agriculture: Agriculture is the most important component of Punjab's economy. As much as 97 per cent of the total cultivable area is under the plough. The main crops grown in the state are wheat, rice and cotton. Sugar cane and oilseeds are also grown. In recent times, impetus is being given to horticulture and forestry. The state has recorded highest yield per hectare of wheat, rice, cotton and bajra. It also has the highest per capita milk and egg production in the country.

Power: Punjab gets its power requirements both from thermal and from hydroelectric sources.

Education

Educational institutes: Well-known institutions of higher education in Punjab include Baba Farid University of Health Sciences (Faridkot), Guru Nanak Dev University (Amritsar), Punjab Agricultural University (Ludhiana), Punjab Technical University (Jalandhar), Punjabi University (Patiala) and Thapar Institute of Engineering and Technology (Patiala).

Tourism

Major tourist attractions:
Religious centres: Golden Temple, Amritsar; Ram Tirth, Amritsar; Durgiana Mandir, Amritsar; Bhagwathi Mandir, Maisar Khanna, Bathinda City; Shiv Mandhir, Gur-mandi, Jalandhar; Sodal Mandir, Jalandhar City; Panch Mandir, Kapurthala Town; Kali Devi Temple, Patiala; Mazaar, Pir Baba Haji Rattan, Bathinda City; Rauza Sharif, Sirhind; Qadian; The Moorish Mosque, Kapurthala City; Imam Nasir Mausoleum and Jamma Masjid, Jalandhar City; Chilla Baba Seikh Farid, Faridkot City;

Gurudwaras at Kiratpur Sahib; Gurudwaras at Anandpur Sahib; Bhaini Sahib; Radha Soami Dera Baba Jaimal Singh; Swetamber Jain Temple, Zira, Ferozpur District; Budhist Caves, Doong, Gurdaspur; Catholic Cathedral, Jalandhar Cantt.

Archaeological centres: Ghuram, Patiala Dist.; Sanghol, Fatehgarh Sahib Dist.; Ropar; Dholbaha.

Forts: Govindgarh Fort, Amritsar; Bathinda Fort; Faridkot Fort; Qila Mubark, Patiala; Bhadurgarh Fort; Anandpur Sahib Fort, Ropar; Phillaur Fort, Ludhiana; Shahpur Kandi Fort, near Pathankot.

Palaces: Summer Palace of Maharaja Ranjit Singh, Amritsar; Sheesh Mahal, Patiala.

Museums: Maharaja Ranjit Singh Museum, Amritsar; Sanghol Museum; Angol Sikh War Memorial, Ferozeshah; Government Museum, Hoshiarpur; Rural Museum, Punjab Agricultural University, Ludhiana; Qila Mubarak Patiala, Museum of Armoury and Chandeliers; Art Gallery at Sheesh Mahal, Patiala; Sports Museum, National Institute of Sports, Patiala; Guru Teg Bahadur Museum, Anandpur Sahib, Ropar.

Others: Jallianwala Bagh Martyr's Memorial, Amritsar; Bhagat Singh, Sukhdev and Rajguru Memorial, Ferozepur; The Sargarhi Memorial at Ferozepur; Desh Bhagat Hall, Jalandhar.

Airports:
International: Amritsar.
Domestic: Chandigarh, Ludhiana.

National Parks: None.

Administration

Legislature: The state has a 117-seat legislative assembly of which 29 are reserved for SCs. The term of the current house expires on 20 March 2007. The party position is as under:

Name of Party	Seats
Indian National Congress	62
Shiromani Akali Dal (Badal)	41
Bharatiya Janata Party	3
Communist Party of India	2
Independent	9
Total	**117**

Judiciary: The High Court of Punjab and Haryana is at Chandigarh. The chief justice is D.K. Jain.

Districts:

District	Area (sq. km)	Population	Headquarters	Urban Agglomerations
Amritsar	5,094	3,074,207	Amritsar	Amritsar
Bhatinda	3,382	1,181,236	Bhatinda	Rampur Phul
Faridkot	1,469	552,466	Faridkot	Faridkot, Jaitu
Fatehgarh Sahib	1,180	539,751	Fatehgarh Sahib	Gobindgarh
Firozpur	5,300	1,744,753	Firozpur	Jalalabad, Zira
Gurdaspur	3,569	2,096,889	Gurdaspur	Batala, Gurdaspur, Pathankot, Qadian
Hoshiarpur	3,364	1,478,045	Hoshiarpur	
Jalandhar	2,634	1,953,508	Jalandhar	Jalandhar
Kapurthala	1,633	752,287	Kapurthala	Phagwara
Ludhiana	3,767	3,030,352	Ludhiana	
Mansa	2,169	688,630	Mansa	
Moga	2,216	886,313	Moga	Moga

Muktsar	2,615	776,702	Muktsar		
Nawanshahr	1,266	586,637	Nawanshahr		Nawanshahr
Patiala	3,627	1,839,056	Patiala		Patiala
Rupnagar	2,056	1,110,000	Rupnagar		Kharar, Nangal
Sangrur	5,021	1,998,464	Sangrur		Sunam

Rajasthan

Key Statistics

Capital: Jaipur.

Area: 342,239 sq. km.

Population: Total: 56,507,188, Male: 29,420,011, Female: 27,087,177.

Population density: 165 per sq. km.

Sex ratio: 921 females per 1000 males.

Principal languages: Hindi, Bhili/Bhilodi, Urdu.

Literacy rates: Total: 60.4%, Male: 75.7%, Female: 43.9%.

Government

Governor: Pratibha Patil. She was sworn in on 8 November 2004.

Chief Minister: Vasundhara Raje Scindia (BJP). She is the first woman Chief Minister of the state, and was sworn in on 8 December 2003.

Geography

Physical characteristics: Rajasthan shares an international boundary with Pakistan in the west. On the Indian side there is a border with Punjab and Haryana in the north, Uttar Pradesh and Madhya Pradesh in the east and Gujarat in the south. The southern part of the state is about 225km from the Gulf of Kutch and about 400km from the Arabian Sea. The Aravalli mountain range divides the state into two regions. The north-west region mostly consists of a series of sand dunes and covers two-thirds of the state, while the eastern region has large fertile areas. The state includes The Great Indian (Thar) Desert.

Neighbouring States and Union territories:

International border: Pakistan.

States: Punjab, Haryana, Uttar Pradesh, Madhya Pradesh, Gujarat.

Major rivers: Chambal is the only river that flows throughout the year. Banas, the only river that has its entire course in Rajasthan, is one of its main tributaries. Other important rivers of the state are Banganga, Gambhiri, Luni, Mahi, Sabarmati and Ghaghar.

Climate: The climate of Rajasthan is warm and dry, with peak summer temperatures in the west reaching 49°C. In June, the arid zone of the west and the semi-arid zone of the mid-west have an average maximum temperature of 45°C. January is the coldest month of the year, with minimum temperatures as low as minus 2°C.

The annual rainfall west of the Aravallis ranges from less than 100mm in the Jaisalmer region to more than 400mm in Sikar, Jhunjhunu and Pali regions. On the eastern side, rainfall ranges from 550mm in Ajmer to 1020mm in Jhalawar. Mount Abu in the southwest usually receives the highest rainfall. Notably, Rajasthan's climate and parched landscape are undergoing significant changes because of developmental efforts like the Indira Gandhi Nahar. As a result, Rajasthan is today a major producer of a number of agricultural crops.

Flora and Fauna:

Flora: The flora of Rajasthan includes the semi-green forests of Mount Abu, dry grasslands of the desert, the dry deciduous thorn forest of the Aravallis and the wetlands of Bharatpur. 16,367 sq. km of area is under forest cover.

Fauna: Notable among the fauna of Rajasthan are black buck, chinkara, tigers, the rare desert fox, the endangered caracal, gharial, monitor lizard, wild boars, porcupine and the great Indian bustard.

In the winter months, migratory birds like the common crane, coots, pelicans, ducks, the rare Siberian cranes, imperial sand grouse, falcons and buzzards flock to this state.

History

Before AD 700, the region corresponding with present-day Rajasthan was a part of several republics including the Mauryan empire, the Malavas, Kushans, Saka satraps, Guptas and Huns. The Rajput clans, primarily the Pratihars, Chalukyas, Parmars and Chauhans, rose to ascendancy from the eighth to the 12th century AD.

A part of the region came under Muslim rule around AD 1200, Nagaur and Ajmer being the centres of power. Mughal dominance reached its peak at the time of Emperor Akbar, who created a unified province comprising different princely states. The decline of Mughal power after 1707 was followed by political disintegration and invasions by the Marathas and Pindaris.

From 1817–18, almost all the princely states of Rajputana, as the state was then called, entered treaties of alliance with the British, who controlled their affairs till the time of independence. The erstwhile Rajputana, comprising 19 princely states and the British administered territory of Ajmer–Merwara, became the state of Rajasthan after a long process of integration that began on 17 March 1948 and ended on 1 November 1956. Rajasthan's first Chief Minister was Gokul Lal Asawa.

Politics

After independence Sardar Vallabhbhai Patel, deputy prime minister, persuaded the ruling princes of the Indian states to merge their principalities into the Indian Union. The merger of the states was considered a major triumph towards the establishment of a democratic nation. Though the twenty-two princely states of Rajputana region were declared to have been annexed to the Union of India on 15 August 1947, the process of merger and their unification became complete only in April 1949, in five phases. The Union of Rajasthan was inaugurated by Jawaharlal Nehru on 18 April 1948. The Maharana of Udaipur was appointed as Rajpramukh and the Kota Naresh was appointed as Up-Rajpramukh of this Union. The formation of the Union of Rajasthan paved the way for the merger of big states like Bikaner, Jaisalmer, Jaipur and Jodhpur with the Union and the formation of Greater Rajasthan. It was formally inaugurated on 30 March 1949 by Sardar Vallabhbhai Patel. Rajasthan attained its current dimensions in November 1956. The princes of the former kingdoms were constitutionally granted handsome remuneration in the form of privy purses to assist them in the discharge of their financial obligations. In 1970, Indira Gandhi, who had come to power in 1966, commenced under-takings to discontinue the privy purses, which were abolished in 1971.

Mohanlal Sukhadia of the Congress held the post of chief minister for the longest duration, from 1954 to 1971. Bhairon Singh Shekhawat, the present Vice President of India, became the state's first non-Congress chief minister in 1977, and remained in office till 1980, when he was dismissed after the change of government at the Centre. He became chief minister again in 1990, only to be dismissed again on 15

December 1992, in the aftermath of the demolition of the Babri Masjid at Ayodhya. In 1998 the Congress (I) Legislature Party elected state party president Ashok Gehlot to be the chief minister. Gehlot, at 47, was the youngest chief minister Rajasthan has had. BJP leader Vasundhara Raje came to power as the first woman chief minister of Rajasthan in 2003.

Culture

Communities of musicians like the Mirasis, Manganiyars and Langas have preserved the rich traditions that exist in folk music and dance, like the Maand style of singing. The state is also home to different schools of painting like the Mewar school, the Bundi–Kota *kalam*, and the Jaipur school. The Kishengarh school is best known for its Bani Thani paintings.

Fairs and festivals: The major festivals of the state include Holi, Diwali, the Desert Festival (Jaisalmer), Gangaur and Teej (Jaipur), Urs Ajmer Sharif (Ajmer) and the Pushkar Fair.

Economy, Industry and Agriculture

Economy: The net state domestic product at current prices for 2002–03 (provisional) was Rs 75,048 crores. The per capita net state domestic product at current prices for 2002–03 (provisional) was Rs 12,753.

Minerals and industry: Textiles are the major industry in the large and medium category of industries, followed by agro-food and allied products, as well as cement. Other important industries are chemical gases, lubricants and plastics, heavy machinery and metal and allied products. Tourism is also a major industry. More than half the heritage hotels in India are located in Rajasthan.

Major minerals include zinc, gypsum, silver ore, asbestos, mica, rock phosphate, limestone and marble. Recently, oil reserves have been discovered around Barmer. Rajasthan holds a share of about 24 per cent in the total national production of non-metallic minerals.

Agriculture: Rajasthan produces a wide variety of cereals, oilseeds, pulses, cash crop like cotton, vegetables and fruits. The state accounts for a large proportion of the seed spices grown in the country, mainly coriander, cumin, fennel, chillies and garlic. The state produces jowar, maize, wheat, rice and millet and it is amongst the largest producers of bajra in the country.

Power: The majority of the state's power requirements are met by thermal power plants. Besides these, nuclear and hydroelectric power plants also contribute to the state's power needs.

Education

Educational institutes: Notable educational institutes include Rajasthan University (Jaipur), Jai Narayan Vyas University (Jodhpur), Birla Institute of Technology and Science (Pilani), Vanasthali Vidyapeeth (Tonk), Kota Open University, Maharshi Dayanand Saraswati University (Ajmer), Mohanlal Sukhadia University (Udaipur), Rajasthan Agricultural University (Bikaner) and Rajasthan Vidyapeeth (Udaipur).

Tourism

Major tourist attractions:

1. Ajmer: The Dargah of Khawaja Moinuddin Chisti, Adhai-din-ka-jhonpra, Taragarh Fort, Pushkar.

2. Alwar: City Palace, Government Museum, Vijai Mandir Palace, Sariska Wildlife Reserve, Ranthambore National Park, Keoladeo Ghana National Park.

3. Bharatpur: Lohagarh Fort, Deeg Palace, Jawahar Burj and Fateh Burj.

4. Chittorgarh: Vijay Stambh, Rana Khumbha's Palace, Saas–Bahu Temple, Meerabai Temple.

5. Jaipur: The City Palace, Jantar Mantar, Hawa Mahal, Amer Palace, Jaigarh and Nahargarh.

6. Jaisalmer: The Fort, Manak Chowk and Havelis, Sam Sand Dunes.

7. Jodhpur: Mehrangarh Fort, Umaid Bhawan Palace, Mandore.

8. Kota: Chambal Garden, Maharao Madho Singh Museum, Jag Mandir.

9. Mount Abu: Gaumukh Temple, Delwara Jain Temple, Guru Shikhar.

10. Udaipur: City Palace, Haldighati, Eklingji, Nathdwara, Kumbhalgarh Fort, Ranakpur Jain Temples.

Airports: Jaipur, Udaipur, Jodhpur, Jaisalmer.

National Parks: Keoladeo Ghana National Park in Bharatpur dist. (29 sq. km), Ranthambhor National Park in Sawai Madhopur dist. (392 sq. km), Sariska Tiger Reserve in Alwar dist. (866 sq. km), Desert National Park in Jaisalmer dist. (3162 sq. km).

Administration

Legislature: The state has a unicameral legislature. The legislative assembly consists of 200 members, of which 57 seats are reserved for SCs (33) and STs (24).

The party position of the current assembly is as follows:

Name of Party	Seats
Bharatiya Janata Party	120
Indian National Congress	56
Indian National Lok Dal	4
Bahujan Samaj Party	2
Janata Dal (United)	2
Communist Party of India (Marxist)	1
Lok Jan Shakti Party	1
Rajasthan Samajik Nyaya Manch	1
Independent	13
Total	**200**

Judiciary: The seat of the Rajasthan High Court is at Jodhpur, with a bench at Jaipur. The acting chief justice is Y.R. Meena.

Districts:

District	Area (sq. km)	Population	Headquarters	Urban Agglomerations
Ajmer	8,481.0	2,180,526	Ajmer	Ajmer, Beawar
Alwar	8,380.0	2,990,862	Alwar	Alwar
Banswara	5,037.0	1,500,420	Banswara	Banswara
Baran	6,992.0	1,022,568	Baran	
Barmer	28,387.0	1,963,758	Barmer	
Bharatpur	5,066.0	2,098,323	Bharatpur	Bharatpur
Bhilwara	10,455.0	2,009,516	Bhilwara	
Bikaner	27,284.0	1,673,562	Bikaner	
Bundi	5,550.0	961,269	Bundi	Lakheri
Chittaurgarh	10,856.0	1,802,656	Chittaurgarh	
Churu	16,830.0	1,922,908	Churu	Churu, Rajgarh
Dausa	3,432.0	1,316,790	Dausa	
Dhaulpur	3,033.0	982,815	Dhaulpur	Dhaulpur
Dungarpur	3,770.0	1,107,037	Dungarpur	
Ganganagar	7,984.0	1,788,487	Ganganagar	Ganganagar
Hanumangarh	12,650.0	1,517,390	Hanumangarh	
Jaipur	11,143.0	5,252,388	Jaipur	
Jaisalmer	38,428.0	507,999	Jaisalmer	
Jalor	10,640.0	1,448,486	Jalor	
Jhalawar	6,219.0	1,180,342	Jhalawar	

Jhunjhunu	5,928.0	1,913,099	Jhunjhunu	Khetri, Pilani
Jodhpur	22,783.0	2,880,777	Jodhpur	Jodhpur, Phalodi
Karauli	5,524.0	1,205,631	Karauli	
Kota	5,443.0	1,568,580	Kota	Kota
Nagaur	17,718.0	2,773,894	Nagaur	Nagaur, Makrana
Pali	12,387.0	1,819,201	Pali	
Rajsamand	3,860.0	986,269	Rajsamand	
Sawai Madhopur	4,498.0	1,116,031	Sawai Madhopur	Sawai Madhopur, Gangapur City
Sikar	7,732.0	2,287,229	Sikar	Sikar, Khandela
Sirohi	5,136.0	850,756	Sirohi	Abu Road
Tonk	7,194.0	1,211,343	Tonk	Malpura
Udaipur	13,419.0	2,632,210	Udaipur	

Sikkim

Key Statistics

Capital: Gangtok.

Area: 7096 sq. km.

Population: Total: 540,851, Male: 288,484, Female: 252,367.

Population density: 76 per sq. km.

Sex ratio: 875 females per 1000 males.

Principal languages: Nepali, Bhutia, Lepcha.

Literacy rates: Total: 68.8%, Male: 76.0%, Female: 60.4%.

Government

Governor: V. Rama Rao. He was appointed on 23 September 2002.

Chief Minister: Pawan Kumar Chamling (SDF). He was sworn in on 21 May 2004.

Geography

Physical characteristics: Sikkim is a small hilly state situated in the Eastern Himalayas. It is a basin surrounded on three sides by steep mountain walls. It extends for approximately 114km from north to south and 64km from east to west. The state is surrounded by the Tibetan Plateau towards the north, the Chumbi Valley of China and Bhutan towards the east, Darjeeling district of West Bengal in the south and Nepal towards the west. The state is a part of the inner ranges of the Himalayas and as such it has no open valley or plains. Within a distance of 80 km, the elevation rises from 200 metres in the Teesta river valley to 8598 metres at Kanchenjunga, India's highest peak and the world's third highest. The 31-km long Zemu glacier lies on the western side of the peak.

Besides the Kanchenjunga, other major peaks in the state include Jongsang (7459m), Tent Peak (7365m), Pauhunri (7125m), Sinioulchu (6887m), Pandim (6691m), Rathong (6679m), Talung (6147m) and Koktang (6147m). The Singalila range forms the barrier between Sikkim and Nepal in the west, while the Dongkya range is at the border with China on the east. There are many passes across this range that allow access to the Chumbi Valley.

Neighbouring States and Union territories:
International borders: China, Nepal, Bhutan.

States: West Bengal.

Major rivers: The Teesta and Rangit are the two most important rivers of the state. Other significant rivers include Rongni Chu, Talung and Lachung. Sikkim is also home to many hot water springs like Ralang Sachu, Phur-Cha, Yumthang and Momay.

Climate: The climate of Sikkim can be divided into tropical, temperate and alpine zones. For most of the year, the climate is cold and humid as rainfall occurs in each month.

In Sikkim, temperatures tend to vary with altitude and slope. The maximum temperature is usually recorded in July and August, while the minimum is usually registered during December and January. Fog is a common feature, mainly between May and September. Intense cold is experienced at high altitudes in the winter months and snowfall is also not uncommon during this period.

The state gets well-distributed heavy rainfall between May and early October. The wettest month is usually July in most parts of the state. Mean annual rainfall varies between a minimum of 82mm at Thangu and a maximum of 3494mm at Gangtok. The intensity of rainfall during the southwest monsoon decreases from south to north. The distribution of winter rainfall is in the reverse pattern.

Flora and Fauna:

Flora: Forests cover 36 per cent of the land. The plants vary with altitude. The flora at altitudes between 1500 m and 4000 m is largely temperate forest of oak, birch, alder, chestnut, magnolia maple, and silver fir. The alpine zone lies above 4000 m with plants like juniper, cypress and rhododendron. The perpetual snowline lies at 5000 m. More than 4000 species of plants have been recorded in Sikkim. Sikkim is also home to over 600 species of orchids.

Fauna: Notable among the animals found in Sikkim are the snow leopard, the red panda, the musk deer, the Himalayan black bear, the tahr, the yak, the wild ass and the blue sheep. The state is also home to many species of birds like vulture, eagle, whistling thrush, giant lammergeier, minivets, bulbuls and pheasants.

History

In pre-historic times, land that is today Sikkim was inhabited by three tribes—the Naongs, the Changs and the Mons. The Lepchas who entered Sikkim later absorbed them completely. The Lepchas were organized into a society by a person named Tur Ve Pa No who was eventually elected the leader or the king 'Punu', in 1400. After his death in battle three kings succeeded him—Tur Song Pa No, Tur Aeng Pa No and Tur Alu Pa No. After the death of Tur Alu Pa No, the monarchy came to an end. From then on, the Lepchas resorted to an elected leader. The area witnessed a major migration from Tibet later on.

In 1642, a young man named Phuntsok was crowned the king. He was named Namgyal and also endowed with the title of Chogyal or religious king. The Namgyal dynasty ruled over Sikkim as hereditary rulers for about 332 years. Phuntsok Namgyal ruled over a vast territory, much larger than present-day Sikkim. In his times, the kingdom extended till Thang La in Tibet in the north, Tagong La near Paro in Bhutan in the east, Titalia on the West Bengal–Bihar border in the south and Timar Chorten on the Timar river in Nepal in the west. Even the Dalai Lama recognized Phuntsok Namgyal as the ruler of the southern slopes of the Himalayas and sent ceremonial gifts to him. At the time the capital city was at Yoksom.

In 1670, Phuntsok Namgyal's son, Tensung Namgyal, succeeded his father. He moved the capital to Rabdentse.

Chador Namgyal, a minor son from Tensung's second of three wives, succeeded to the throne upon the death of his father. This led to much conflict as Pedi, the daughter from the first wife, challenged the succession and secretly invited Bhutan, her mother's homeland, to intervene. A loyal minister named Yungthing Yeshe ferreted away the minor king to Lhasa. In Tibet, Chador Namgyal made his mark as a scholar of Buddhist learning and Tibetan literature. He even became a state astrologer to the sixth Dalai Lama. When Bhutanese forces imprisoned Yugthing Yeshe's son, Tibet intervened and forced Bhutan to withdraw.

Chador Namgyal evicted the rest of the invading Bhutanese forces on his return. Although the Bhutanese made a second attempt to capture Sikkim territory, Chador Namgyal put up a worthy resistance but certain areas were lost forever. However, the old family feud returned to cost Chador Namgyal his life. He was killed in 1716 as a result of a conspiracy hatched by Pedi.

The next few years saw rebellions, internal conflicts and border disputes. Gurkhas encroached into Sikkimese territory under the leadership of Raja Prithvi Narayan Shah of Nepal. They also incited the rebellious factions within Sikkim. But they were repelled 17 times. In 1775, a peace treaty was signed, whereby Gurkhas promised to refrain from attacks and also stay away from collaborating with the Bhutanese. Nevertheless, they violated the treaty when they took land in western Sikkim. The period also saw a Bhutanese invasion. They captured all areas east of the Teesta river, but later retreated following negotiations.

In the 19th century, the British struck up a friendship with Sikkim. This was largely due to the fact that they had a common enemy—the Gorkhas. The British defeated Nepalese forces in the Anglo-Nepalese War (1814–16). In 1817, British India signed the Treaty of

Titalia with Sikkim. Consequently, territories that the Nepalis had taken away were restored to Sikkim. By the treaty, British India gained a position of great power and influence in the state and Sikkim almost became a British protectorate.

Sikkim even gifted Darjeeling to British India in return for an annual payment and Chogyal Tsudphud Namgyal signed the gift deed in 1835. The British however, did not pay the compensation. This led to a deterioration in relations between the two countries. There were also differences between the British government and Sikkim over the status of the people of Sikkim. The relations deteriorated to the extent that in 1849, when the Superintendent of Darjeeling visited Sikkim along with a scientist on a research trip, they were taken prisoner. They were later freed after the British issued an ultimatum. In 1850, British India stopped the annual grant of Rs 6000 to the Maharaja of Sikkim and also annexed part of Darjeeling and a large portion of Sikkim.

When India became independent, the then Chogyal, Tashi Namgyal, obtained the status of a protectorate for Sikkim. However, local parties like the Sikkim State Congress wanted a democratic set-up and the accession of Sikkim to the Union of India. After Tashi Namgyal died in 1963, demands for the removal of the monarchy and the establishment of a democratic set-up intensified. By 1973, the agitation against the Sikkim Durbar had taken a serious turn and resulted in a collapse of the administration. This led the Indian government to intervene, and Sikkim was transformed from a protectorate to an associate state.

In 1975, a referendum was held. More than 97 per cent of the electorate voted for the merger of Sikkim with India. Sikkim became the 22nd state of the Indian Union on 15 May

1975. Kazi Lhendup Dorji was the first Chief Minister.

Politics

In 1947, after the British withdrew from India Tashi Namgyal of the Chogyal dynasty was successful in getting a special status of protectorate for Sikkim. On 4 September 1947, the leader of Sikkim Congress, Kazi Lendup Dorji, was elected the chief minister of the state. The Chogyal however still remained as the constitutional figurehead monarch in the new setup. Troubles arose in 1973, when the Sikkim National Congress demanded fresh elections and establishment of a democratic set-up. The Kazi was elected by the council of ministers, which was unanimous in its opposition to the retention of the monarchy. After a period of unrest in 1972-73, matters came to a head in 1975, when Kazi appealed to the Indian parliament for representation and change of status to statehood. A referendum was held in which 97.5% of the people voted to join the Indian Union. Sikkim became a full-fledged state of the Indian Union on 16 May 1975; it was India's twenty-second state. Kazi was elected chief minister.A popular ministry headed by Nar Bahadur Bhandari, leader of the Sikkim Parishad Party, came into power in 1979. Bhandari held on to power in the 1984 and 1989 elections. After the 1994 elections Pawan Kumar Chamling from the Sikkim Democratic Front became the chief minister of the state. The party has since held on to power by winning the 1999 and 2004 elections. In 2003, China officially recognized Indian sovereignty over Sikkim as the two nations moved toward resolving their border disputes. Sikkim no longer figures as an 'independent nation' in the world map and index of the annual yearbook published by the Chinese Foreign Ministry.

Culture

Sikkim is famous for its mask dance that is performed by lamas in gompas. The state is also known for its handicrafts and handloom objects. The Kagyat dance is performed every 28th and 29th day of the Tibetan calendar. The dance is one of solemnity interspersed with comic relief provided by jesters.

Fairs and festivals: Different communities in the state have different festivals. Saga Dawa is an auspicious day for the Mahayana Buddhists and they go to monasteries to offer butter lamps and worship. Monks take out a procession that goes around Gangtok with holy scriptures.

Phang Lhabsol is a unique festival that is celebrated to offer thanks to Mount Kanchenjunga. The biggest and most important festival of the Hindu–Nepali population is Dasain. It is celebrated in September/October and symbolizes the victory of good over evil. Tyohar or Dipavali is the festival of lights and is celebrated 10 days after Dasain. Other festivals include Drupka Tseshi that is celebrated around August. Losoong is the Sikkimese New Year which is celebrated in the last week of December, while Losar is the Tibetan New Year and is celebrated around February.

Economy, Industry and Agriculture

Economy: The net state domestic product at current prices for 2002–03 (provisional) was Rs 1139 crores. The per capita net state domestic product at current prices for 2002–03 (provisional) was Rs 20,456.

Minerals and industry: Sikkim is an industrially underdeveloped state. There are public–sector undertakings for the manufacture of precision instruments and watches. Besides these, there are handicrafts, handlooms, liquor, and pisciculture ventures in the state.

Agriculture: Maize, rice, wheat, barley, pulses, potato and cardamom are the most important crops grown in the state. The economy is based largely on agriculture and animal husbandry.

Power: The state mainly utilizes hydroelectric power.

Education

Educational institutions: The Sikkim Manipal University of Health, Medical and Technology Sciences is at Gangtok. Other institutes of learning in the state include the Directorate of Handicraft and Handloom and the Sikkim Research Institute of Tibetology (SRIT).

Tourism

Major tourist attractions:

1. North Sikkim: Singba Rhododendron Sanctuary, Yumthang, Chungthang, Singiek, Kabi Lungtsok.

2. South Sikkim: Namtse, Varsey Rhododendron Sanctuary, Borong Tsa-Chu hot spring, Maenam Hill, Ravangla.

3. East Sikkim: White Hall, Ridge Garden, Do-Drul Chorten, Rumtek Dharma Chakra Centre, Kyongnosla Alpine Sanctuary, Fambong La Wildlife Sanctuary.

4. West Sikkim: Pelling, Ruins of Rabdentse, Yuksom.

Airports: None.

National Parks: Kanchenjunga National Park in North Sikkim dist. (850 sq. km).

Administration

Legislature: There are 32 seats in the legislative assembly, out of which two are reserved for SCs and 12 for STs (for the Bhutia and Lepcha community). One general seat is reserved for the Sangha community. The term of the current house expires on 14 October 2004. The current party position is:

Name of Party	Seats
Sikkim Democratic Front	31
Indian National Congress	1
Total	**32**

Judiciary: The High Court of Sikkim is at Gangtok. N. Surjawani Singh is the acting chief justice.

Districts:

District	Area (sq. km)	Population	Headquarters	Urban Agglomerations
East	954.0	244,790	Gangtok	–
North	4,226.0	41,023	Mangan	–
South	750.0	131,506	Namchi	–
West	1,166.0	123,174	Gyalshing	–

Tamil Nadu

Key Statistics

Capital: Chennai.
Area: 1,30,058 sq. km.
Population: Total: 62,405,679, Male: 31,400,909, Female: 31,004,770.

Population density: 478 per sq. km.
Sex ratio: 987 females per 1000 males.
Principal languages: Tamil, Telugu, Kannada.

Literacy rates: Total: 73.5%, Male: 82.4%, Female: 64.4%.

Government

Governor: Surjeet Singh Barnala. He assumed the office on 1 November 2004.

Chief Minister: J. Jayalalithaa (AIADMK). She was sworn in on 2 March 2002.

Geography

Physical characteristics: Tamil Nadu is divided between the flat areas along the eastern coast and the hilly regions in the north and west. The Kavery delta is the broadest part of the eastern plains, with the arid plains of Ramanathapuram and Madurai towards the south. The Western Ghats run along the state's western border, while the lower hills of the Eastern Ghats run through the centre.

Neighbouring States and Union territories:

States: Andhra Pradesh, Karnataka, Kerala..

Union territories: Pondicherry.

Major rivers: Kavery, Palar, Ponnaiyar, Pennar, Vaigai and Tamiraparani.

Climate: Excepting the hills, Tamil Nadu's climate can be classified as semi-arid tropic monsoonal. Maximum temperatures in the plains go up to 45°C in summer, with minimum temperatures in the winter hovering around 10°C. The average annual rainfall ranges between 650mm and 1900mm. The hill areas have maximum temperatures around 30°C in the summer and minimum temperatures as low as 3°C in the winter and also receive substantially higher rainfall.

Flora and Fauna:

Flora: Nearly 18 per cent of the area of Tamil Nadu is under forests. Dry deciduous forests, thorn forests, scrub, mangroves and wetlands cover most of the plains and lower hills. Moist deciduous and wet evergreen forests as also shoal and grassland occupy most of the hills in the moister parts, particularly in the Western Ghats. Sandalwood, pulpwood, rubber and bamboo are important forest products.

Fauna: Wildlife found in the state includes elephant, tiger, leopard, striped hyena, jackals, Indian pangolin, slender loris, lion-tailed macaque, sloth bear, bison or gaur, black buck, Nilgiris tatur, grizzled giant squirrel, dugong and mouse deer.

History

The early history of the region can be traced to a trinity of powers: the Cheras, the Cholas and the Pandyas. From the sixth to the ninth centuries, the Chalukyas and the Pallavas also established their dominance with a series of wars in the region. From the midninth century, Chola rulers dominated the region, the most prominent among them being Rajendra I. Around the 12th century, Muslim rulers also strengthened their position, leading to the establishment of the Bahamani sultanate. The Vijayanagar kingdom came into prominence in the mid-14 century and ruled for nearly 300 years. The British control over the region began from the mid-17th century and continued until independence.

After independence, the areas of present-day Tamil Nadu, Andhra Pradesh and some territorial areas of Kerala came under the governance of Madras state. In 1953, the Telugu-speaking areas of Madras state were carved out into the state of Andhra Pradesh. In 1956, the Madras state was further divided into the states of Kerala, Mysore and Madras. In August 1968, Madras state was renamed Tamil Nadu. O.P. Ramaswamy Reddyar was the first Chief Minister.

Politics

Modern Tamil Nadu has emerged from Madras Presidency of the British administration. At the time of Indian independence, Madras state comprised of Tamil Nadu, Andhra Pradesh and some territorial areas of present Kerala. In 1953, however, the Madras state bifurcated into two states, Andhra state, comprising of Telugu speaking areas and Madras state, comprising of Tamil speaking areas. The old capital city of Madras was retained in the Madras state. Under the States Reorganisation Act, 1956, Madras state was further divided into the states of Kerala, Mysore and Madras. Later, on 1 April 1960, territories comprising of Chittoor district in Andhra Pradesh was transferred to Madras state in exchange of territories from the Chingleput and Salem district. In 1968, Madras state was renamed Tamil Nadu.

Regional political parties have been strongest in Tamil Nadu, where they have dominated state politics since 1967. Regional parties in the state trace their roots to the establishment of the Justice Party by non-Brahman social elites in 1916 and the development of the non-Brahman Self-Respect Movement, founded in 1925 by E.V. Ramaswamy Naicker. As leader of the Justice Party, in 1944 Ramaswamy renamed the party the Dravida Khazagam (Dravidian Federation) and demanded the establishment of an independent state called Dravidasthan. In 1949, charismatic film script writer C.N. Annadurai, who was chafing under Ramaswamy's authoritarian leadership, split from the DK to found the DMK (Dravida Munnetra Khazagam) in an attempt to achieve the goals of Tamil nationalism through the electoral process. During the fifties and sixties, however, there were several developments which gradually led to a change in the basic political thrust of DMK.

Naicker gave up his opposition to Congress when in 1954, K. Kamraj, a non-Brahmin, displaced C. Rajagopalachari, the dominant leader of the Congress party in Tamil Nadu and became the chief minister. He remained in power till 2 October 1963. DMK participated in the 1957 and 1962 elections. That a change was coming became visible when, in the 1962 elections, it entered into an alliance with Swatantra Party and CPI and did not make a separate Dravidasthan a campaign issue. Although the DMK dropped its demand for Dravidasthan in 1963, it played a prominent role in the agitations that successfully defeated attempts to impose the northern Indian language of Hindi as the official national language in the mid-1960s. With each election the DMK kept expanding its social base and increasing its electoral strength. With the deterioration of Annadurai's health, M. Karunanidhi became chief minister in 1969. Karunanidhi's control over the party was soon challenged by M.G. Ramachandran (best known by his initials, MGR), one of South India's most popular film stars. In the 1971 elections to the Lok Sabha and the state assembly, DMK teamed up with the Indira Gandhi-led Congress (R), which surrendered all claims to assembly seats in return for DMK's support to it in 9 parliamentary seats, which it won. In 1972 MGR split from the DMK to form the All-India Anna Dravida Munnetra Kazhagam (AIADMK). Under his leadership, the AIADMK dominated Tamil politics at the state level from 1977 through 1989. The importance of personal charisma in Tamil politics was dramatized by the struggle for control over the AIADMK after MGR's death in 1988. MGR's wife Janaki Ramachandran, herself a film star, succeeded MGR and vied for control with Jayalalitha, an actress who had played MGR's leading lady in several films. The rivalry allowed the DMK to gain control over the state government in

1989. The AIADMK, under the leadership of Jayalalitha, recaptured the state government in 1991. From 1996 to 2001 Karunanidhi returned to power. Jayalalitha came back to power in 2001 and, on being jailed on charges of corruption, appointed O. Paneerselvam as the chief minister for a year. Since 2002 Jayalalitha has been the chief minister of Tamil Nadu again.

Culture

Tamil Nadu has more than 30,000 temples, for which reason the state is sometimes called 'A Land of Temples'. The festivals held in many of them attract large congregations of devotees throughout the year.

The Bharatnatyam form of classical dancing has its origin in the temples of Tamil Nadu and continues to be followed with a lot of fervour. Another reputed art form that has flourished over the ages is Carnatic music.

Fairs and festivals: Prominent festivals and fairs include Pongal, Chithirai Festival, Navarathri, Saral Vizha, Kanthuri Festival, Mahamagam Festival, Thyagaraja Festival and Mamallapuram Dance Festival.

Economy, Industry and Agriculture

Economy: The net state domestic product at current prices for 2002–03 (provisional) was Rs 135,252 crores. The per capita net state domestic product at current prices for 2002–03 (provisional) was Rs 21,433.

Minerals and industry: Important industries of Tamil Nadu include cement, automobiles and auto components, railway coaches, leather, cotton textiles, sugar, software, biotechnology, agrobased industries and paper. Major minerals found in the state include garnet, lignite, magnesite, monazite, quartz/silica sand, gypsum, ilmenite, rutile, vermiculite, zircon, graphite.

Agriculture: Paddy, millets and other cereals, pulses, sugar cane, groundnut, gingelly, tea, rubber, cashew and cotton are the principal crops of the state.

Power: A large part of Tamil Nadu's power comes from thermal power plants and hydroelectric plants.

Education

Educational institutes: Prominent educational institutions of the state include Alagappa University, Karaikudi; Annamalai University, Annamalainagar; Bharathiar University, Coimbatore; Bharthidasan University, Tiruchirapalli; Chennai Medical College and Research Institute, Chennai; Indian Institute of Technology Madras, Chennai; University of Madras, Chennai; Madurai Kamraj University, Madurai; Periyar University, Salem; Sri Ramachandra Medical College and Research Institute, Chennai; Tamil Nadu Dr Ambedkar Law University, Chennai and Tamil Nadu Dr MGR Medical University, Chennai.

Tourism

Major tourist attractions:

1. Chennai: Planetorium, Vandalur zoo, Art gallery, Snake park, Marina beach.

2. Chidambaram: Poompuhar, Tarangambadi, The Church of Zion, Masilamaninathar Temple.

3. Coimbatore: Indira Gandhi National Park, Maruthamalai Temple.

4. Kancheepuram: Tiruttani, Vellore, Vedanthangal, Elagiri Hills.

5. Kanniyakumari: Suchindram, Nager- coil, Pechipara Dam, Padmanabhapuram, Valluvar Statue, Udayagiri Fort, Vivekananda Rock.

6. Kodaikkanal: Palani, Hill range.

7. Madurai: Alagarkoil, Pazhamudircholai, Thiruparankunram, Thiruvadavur, Tiruvedagam.

8. Mamallapuram: Tirukkalukunram, Crocodile bank.

9. Pondicherry: Auroville, Cuddalore, Tiruvannamalai, Sathanur, Gingee Fort.

10. Rameswaram: Kurusadai islands.

11. Thanjavur: Thiruvaiyaru, Swamimalai, Tirubuvanam, Kumbakonam, Kodikkarai.

12. Tiruchirappally: Srirangam, Thiruvanaikkaval, Gangaikondancholapuram.

13. Udagamandalam (Ooty): Mudumalai, Coonoor.

Airports:
International: Chennai.

Domestic: Tiruchirappally, Madurai, Coimbatore, Tuticorin.

National Parks: Guindy (Chennai)— 2.82 sq. km, Indira Gandhi National Park (Coimbatore)—117.10 sq. km, Gulf of Mannar Biosphere Reserve and National Park—6.23 sq. km, Mudumalai (Nilgiris)—103.23 sq. km and Mukurthi (Nilgiris)—78.46 sq. km.

Administration

Legislature: The unicameral Tamil Nadu state assembly comprises 234 elected members and one nominated member (Anglo-Indian). Of the 234 seats 42 are reserved for SCs and three for STs. The term of the current house expires on 21 May 2006.

The current party position is as follows:

Name of Party	Seats
All India Anna Dravida Munnetra Kazhagam	132
Dravida Munnetra Kazhagam	31
Tamil Maanila Congress (Moopanar)	23
Pattali Makkal Katchi	20
Indian National Congress	7
Communist Party of India (Marxist)	6
Communist Party of India	5
Bharatiya Janata Party	4
M.G.R. Anna D.M. Kazhagam	2
All India Forward Bloc	1
Independent	3
Total	**234**

Judiciary: Madras High Court, with its seat in Chennai, has jurisdiction over Tamil Nadu and Pondicherry. The present chief justice is Markandey Katju.

Districts:

District	Area (sq. km)	Population	Headquarters	Urban Agglomerations
Chennai	178.2	4,216,268	Chennai	Chennai
Coimbatore	7,470.8	4,224,107	Coimbatore	Coimbatore, Pollachi, Tiruppur
Cuddalore	3,645.0	2,280,530	Cuddalore	Chidambaram, Neyveli
Dharmapuri	4,497.8	1,286,552	Dharmapuri	
Dindigul	6,058.0	1,918,960	Dindigul	
Erode	8,209.0	2,574,067	Erode	Erode, Bhavani
Kancheepuram	4,433.0	2,869,920	Kancheepuram	Kancheepuram
Kanniyakumari	1,684.0	1,669,763	Nagercoil	
Krishnagiri	5,143.0	1,546,700	Krishnagiri	
Karur	3,003.5	933,791	Karur	Karur
Madurai	3,497.8	2,562,279	Madurai	Madurai
Nagapattinam	2,715.8	1,487,055	Nagapattinam	
Namakkal	3,363	1,495,661	Namakkal	Erode, Bhavani, Mallasamudram
Perambalur	3,690	1,181,029	Perambalur	
Pudukkottai	4,651.0	1,452,269	Pudukkottai	
Ramanathapuram	4,129.0	1,183,321	Ramanathapuram	

Salem	5,219.6	2,992,754	Salem	Mallasamudram, Salem
Sivaganga	4,189.0	1,150,753	Sivaganga	Karaikkudi
Thanjavur	3,396.6	2,205,375	Thanjavur	Kumbakonam
The Nilgiris	2,549.0	764,826	Udhagamandalam	Coonoor, Devarshola
Theni	3,243.6	1,094,724	Theni	
Thiruvallur	3,424.0	2,738,866	Thiruvallur	Thiruvallur
Thiruvarur	2,167.6	1,165,213	Thiruvarur	
Tiruchirappalli	4,403.8	2,388,831	Tiruchirappalli	Tiruchirappalli
Tirunelveli	6,810.0	2,801,194	Tirunelveli	Ambasamudram, Tirunelveli
Tiruvanamalai	6,191.0	21,81,853	Tiruvanamalai	
Toothukudi	4,621.0	1,565,743	Toothukudi	Toothukudi, Tiruchendur
Vellore	6,077.0	3,482,970	Vellore	Arcot, Gudiyatham, Vaniyambadi, Vellore
Viluppuram	7,250.0	2,943,917	Viluppuram	
Virudhunagar	4,283.0	1,751,548	Virudhunagar	Sivakasi

Tripura

Key Statistics

Capital: Agartala.
Area: 10,491.69 sq. km.
Population: Total: 3,199,203, Male: 1,642,225, Female: 1,556,978.
Population density: 304 per sq. km.
Sex ratio: 948 females per 1000 males.
Principal languages: Bengali, Tripuri, Hindi.
Literacy rates: Total: 73.2%, Male: 81.0%, Female: 64.9%.

Government

Governor: Dinesh Nandan Sahaya. He assumed office on 2 June 2003.

Chief Minister: Manik Sarkar (CPIM). He was sworn in on 7 March 2003.

Geography

Physical characteristics: Tripura is a land of hills, plains and valleys. The central and northern part of the state is a hilly region that is intersected by four major valleys. These are the Dharma-nagar, Kailashahar, Kamalpur and Khowai valleys. These valleys are formations resulting from northward-flowing rivers. The valleys in the western and southern part of the state are marshy. The terrain is densely forested and highly dissected in southern Tripura. Ranges running north–south cross the valleys. These hills are a series of parallel north–south ranges that decrease in elevation southwards and finally merge into the eastern plains. These are the Deotamura range, followed by the Atharamura, Langtarai, and Sakhan Tlang ranges. Of these peaks, Deotamura is the lowest and the height of each successive range increases eastwards. The 74-km-long Jamrai Tlang mountains have the highest peak, Betalongchhip (1097m).

The Tripura plains are also called the Agartala plains. The plains lie in the south-western part of the state and extend over approximately 4,150 sq. km. The Tripura plains are situated on a part of the bigger Ganga–Brahmaputra lowlands to the west of the Tripura Hills. The plains have extensive forest cover and have numerous lakes and marshes.

Neighbouring States and Union territories:
International border: Bangladesh.

States: Assam, Mizoram.

Major rivers: Gomti, Muhuri, Howrah, Juri, Manu, Deo, Dhalai, Khowai, Feni and Longai.

Climate: Summer temperatures range between 20°C and 36°C. In winter, the range is between 7°C and 27°C. Average annual rainfall in 2000 was 2500mm.

Flora and Fauna:
Flora: In 2000–01, Tripura had a forest area of 6,292.68 sq. km or around 60 per cent of the total land area. Sal is found extensively in the state. There are rubber, tea and coffee plantations as well.

Fauna: Tiger, elephant, jackal, leopard, wild dog, boar, wild buffalo and gaur are the most notable members of the state's animal population.

History

The early history of Tripura is described in the *Rajamala*, an account of people who are supposed to be the early rulers of Tripura. The *Rajamala*, written in Bengali verse, was compiled by the courtiers of Dharma Manikya, one of the greatest rulers of Tripura.

During the reign of Dharma Manikya and his successor, Dhanya Manikya, in the 15th and 16th centuries, rule of Tripura was extended over large portions of Bengal, Assam, and what is today Myanmar as a consequence of a string of military conquests.

It was only in the 17th century that the Mughal empire extended its rule over Tripura. The British East India Company gained control of parts of Tripura when it obtained the diwani of Bengal in 1765. But this was limited to the parts that were under Mughal control. From 1808 onwards, the rulers of Tripura had to be approved by the British government. In 1905, Tripura was attached to the new province of Eastern Bengal and Assam. It came to be known as Hill Tippera.

After independence, the Regent Maharani signed an agreement of merger with the Indian Union on 9 September 1947. Consequently, the administration of the state was taken over by the Government of India on 15 October 1949. On 1 November 1956, Tripura became a Union territory without legislature. A popular ministry took power on 1 July 1963. Tripura attained statehood on 21 January 1972. Sachindra Lal Singh was the first Chief Minister.

Politics

The princely state of Tripura was ruled by Maharajas of Manikya dynasty. It was an independent administrative unit under the Maharaja even during the British rule in India though this independence was qualified, being subject to the recognition of the British of each successive ruler. After India's independence, an agreement of merger of Tripura with the Indian Union was signed by the Regent Maharani on 9 September 1947. Tripura was merged with the Indian Union as a part 'C' state. Tripura became a union territory with effect from 1 November 1956. On 21 January 1972, Tripura became a full-fledged state. After annexation by India the Tripuri people became microscopic minority in the state because of the huge Hindu Bengali influx from the then East Pakistan (present Bangladesh). Therefore the Tripura Peoples Democratic Front (TPDF) and National Liberation Front of Tripura (NLFT) started an armed national liberation struggle against Indian colonialism. Until 1977 the state was governed by Indian National Congress. The Left Front governed from 1978 to 1988 and then returned to power in 1993. Comrade Nripen Chakraborty became the chief minister of the state's first Left Front government in 1978 and also of the second one in 1983. From 1988 to 1993 the state was governed by a coalition of Indian National Congress and Tripura Upajati Juba Samiti. A Left Front ministry was sworn-in on 7 March 2003 headed by Manik Sarkar, who assumed the office of chief minister for the second consecutive term.

Culture

Tripura has a rich heritage of folk dances of the different communities of the state. The main folk dances of Tripura are Garia, Maimita, Masak Sumani, Jhum and Lebang Boomani dances of the Tripuri community, Hozagiri dance of the Reang community, Cheraw and Welcome dances of the Lusai community, Bizu dance of the Chakma community, Sangraiaka, Chimithang, Padisha and Abhangma dances of the Mog community, Hai-Hak dance of the Malsum community, Wangala dance of the Garo community, Basanta Rash and Pung Chalam dances of Manipuri community, Garia dances of Kalai and Jamatia communities, Gajan, Sari, Dhamail, and Rabindra dances of the Bengali community. The state is also well known for its cane and bamboo handicrafts and household items such as furniture, baskets and ornaments.

Fairs and festivals: In Tripura, Garia and Gajan festivals, Manasa Mangal, Durga Puja, Rabindra Jayanti and Nazrul Jayanti are celebrated all over the state. Events of specific places include Ashokastami Festival of Unakoti, Kharchi Festival of Old Agartala, Dewali Festival of Mata Tripureswari Temple in Udaipur, Rasha Festival of Kamalpur, Kailashahar, Khowai and Agartala, Orange and Tourism Festival of Jampui Hill range and the Pous Sankranti Mela of Tirthamukh.

Economy, Industry and Agriculture

Economy: The net state domestic product at current prices (new series) in 2001–02 (quick estimates) was Rs 5660 crores. The per capita net state domestic product at current prices (new series) in 2001–02 (quick estimates) was Rs 17,459.

Minerals and industry: Jute, tourism, handicrafts, handloom and food products are the most notable among the existing industrial ventures of the state. There are five industrial estates and two industrial growth centres in Tripura. Both the state and the Central governments offer various incentives for the setting up of new industrial ventures in Tripura. It is also being promoted as the international gateway to the north-east region of India, given its proximity to Bangladesh, mainly the latter's port at Chittagong.

The two most important mineral resources of Tripura are oil and natural gas. Other significant minerals are glass sand, shale, plastic clay and sand.

Agriculture: The main crops grown in the state are rice, sugar cane, cotton, jute and mesta. Key plantation crops are tea, rubber and coffee. Besides these, banana, pineapple, cashew nuts, orange, mango, guava, litchi, potato, papaya and tomato are also grown.

Power: Thermal power plants contribute the biggest share of the energy produced in the state. Hydroelectric power plants are the second most important source.

Education

Educational institutions: Tripura University is at Agartala.

Tourism

Major tourist attractions: Sephahijala Wildlife Sanctuary, Trishna Wildlife Sanctuary, Gumti Wildlife Sanctuary, Roa Wildlife Sanctuary, Rudra Sagar (Neer Mahal), Kamala Sagar, Brahmakund, Udaipur, Deotamura, Dumbur, Pilak, Jampui Hills, Unakoti, Tripura Sundari Temple, Ujjayanta Palace.

Airports: Agartala, Kailashahar, Khowai, Kamalpur.

National Parks: None.

Administration

Legislature: The legislative assembly of Tripura has 60 seats, out of which 20 seats are reserved for STs and seven reserved for SCs. The term of the current house expires on 19 March 2008.

The current party position is as follows:

Name of Party	Seats
Communist Party of India (Marxist)	38
Indian National Congress	13
Indigenous Nationalist Party of Tripura	6
Revolutionary Socialist Party	2
Communist Party of India	1
Total	**60**

Judiciary: The jurisdiction is of the Agartala Bench of the Gauhati High Court. Binod Kumar Roy is the chief justice.

Districts:

District	Area (sq. km)	Population	Headquarters	Urban Agglomerations
Dhalai	2,212.3	307,417	Ambassa	–
North Tripura	2,100.7	590,655	Kailashahar	–
South Tripura	3,140.0	762,565	Udaipur	–
West Tripura	3,033.0	1,530,531	Agartala	–

Uttaranchal

Key Statistics

Capital: Dehradun (provisional).
Area: 53,483 sq. km.
Population: Total: 8,489,349, Male: 4,325,924, Female: 4,163,425.
Population density: 159 per sq. km.
Sex ratio: 962 females per 1000 males.
Principal languages: Hindi, Garhwali, Kumaoni.
Literacy rates: Total: 71.6%, Male: 83.3%, Female: 59.6%.

Government

Governor: Sudarshan Agarwal. He was appointed on 8 January 2003.

Chief Minister: N.D. Tiwari. He was sworn in on 2 March 2002.

Geography

Physical characteristics: Uttaranchal is located in the foothills of the Himalayas. The state has international boundaries with China in the north and Nepal in the east. On its north-west lies Himachal Pradesh while Uttar Pradesh lies to the south. The region is mostly mountainous with a major portion covered with forests. Based on topographic characteristics, specific availability of land resources for urban development and economic mobility, the 13 districts in Uttaranchal can be segregated into three broad categories. These are:

1. The high mountain region (these would include significant port-ions of Uttarkashi, Champawat, Pithoragarh, Chamoli and Rudra-prayag districts).
2. The mid-mountain region (major parts of Pauri Garhwal, Tehri, Almora, Bageshwar districts).
3. The Doon, Terai region and Hardwar (lower foothills and plains of Dehradun, Nainital, Udhamsingh Nagar and Hardwar districts).

The significant peaks of the Great Himalayan range in the state are Nanda Devi, Panchachuli, Kedarnath, Chaukhamba, Badrinath, Trishul, Bandarpunch and Kamet. Pindari, Gangotri, Milam and Khatling are the important glaciers.

Neighbouring States and Union territories:

International borders: China, Nepal.

States: Himachal Pradesh, Uttar Pradesh.

Major rivers: Ganga, Yamuna, Ramganga and Kali (Sharda).

Climate: The climate of the state is generally temperate but varies greatly from tropical to severe cold, depending upon altitude. Different parts of the state experience temperature variations due to difference in elevation. Summers are pleasant in the hilly regions but in the Doon area, it can get very hot. It can get even hotter in the plains of the state. Temperature drops to below freezing point not only at high altitudes but also at places like Dehradun in the winters. Average rainfall experienced in the state is around 1079mm. Average temperature ranges between a minimum of 1.9°C and a maximum of 40.5°C.

Flora and Fauna:

Flora: Different types of forests found in the state are: deodar forests, blue pine forests, chir forests, teak forests, bamboo forests, oak forests, fir and spruce forests, and sal forests.

The region is also rich in medicinal plants. These can be classified on the basis of the altitude at which they can be found growing.

1. Medicinal plants growing upto 1000m: bel, chitrak, kachnar, pipali, babul, ashok, amaltas, sarpagandha, bhringraj, harar, behera, malu, siris, amla and mossli.
2. Medicinal plants growing from 1000m to 3000m: banspa, sugandhabala, tejpat, dalchini, jhoola, kuth, timru and painya.
3. Medicinal plants growing above 3000m: atis, mitha, gugal, jamboo, mamira, gandrayan, bajradanti and salammishri.

Fauna: The animal population of Uttaranchal includes tiger, leopard, other members of the cat family, Indian elephant, dhole (wild dog), antelopes like nilgai and ghoral, Himalayan tahr, deer like hog deer, sambar, chital or spotted deer and barking deer and primates like rhesus monkey and langur. Other animals found in the state include jackals, foxes, civets, wild boar, sloth bear and black bear. Reptiles like the cobra and python are found in the state. Ramganga river is home to two species of crocodile, namely gharial and mugger, as well as fishes like the famous mahaseer and the malee.

Uttaranchal is also home to hundreds of species of birds including water fowl, many types of woodpecker and predatory birds like the Pallas's fishing eagle, harriers and kites. Peafowl, kalij pheasant, chir pheasant, red jungle fowl, minivets, shrikes, cuckoos, drongos and barbets are also found in the state. Corbett National Park is home to various species of birds like brown fish owl, Himalayan kingfisher, brown dipper and plumbeous/white-capped redstarts. The bird population of the National Park also includes the little/staty backed forktails and mountain/rufous-bellied hawk-eagles, blue whistling thrush and red jungle fowl, oriental white-eye, jungle owlet, Alexandrine parakeet, Himalayan swiftlet, lesser fish-eagle and great thick-knee, stork-billed kingfisher.

History

Uttaranchal has been mentioned in ancient texts as Kedarkhand and Kurmanchal. The region's history is older than that of the *Ramayana* and the *Mahabharata*. It is also a site of popular myths, like that of Lord Shiva appearing as Kirat, of Urvashi, Shakuntala as well as the Kauravas and Pandavas. In those days, the area that is today Garhwal was known as Kedarkhand, or the region of Kedarnath. On the other hand, Kumaon was Kurmanchal, the land of the Kurmavatar—Lord Vishnu in his incarnation as tortoise.

Rock paintings, rock shelters, palaeoliths and megaliths bear evidence of human habitation in this region from the prehistoric period. Various texts also mention a number of tribes that inhabited the region. These include the Sakas, Kol-Munds, the Nagas, Khasas, Hunas, Kirats, Gujars and Aryans. After the era of the Kols and the Kirats, the Khasas attained a position of dominance in the Garhwal and Kumaon Himalayas, till the arrival of the Rajputs and Brahmins from the plains.

With the arrival of the Aryans came the establishment of later Vedic culture and most of these people got absorbed into the caste system. The sages living in the region made it an important point of origin of Indo-Aryan culture.

What is Uttaranchal today was earlier a part of the United Provinces of Agra and Awadh. This province came into existence in 1902 and in 1935, it was renamed United Provinces. In 1950, it was renamed once again, this time as Uttar Pradesh. The socio-economic disparities of this region led to a demand for a separate state for many years. The students' protest at Pauri in August 1994 against 27 per cent OBC reservation in education subsequently led to widespread agitations. Later on, it turned into a full-fledged mass movement for a separate state.

Uttaranchal came into existence on 9 November 2000 as the 27th state of the Indian Union. Nityanand Swami was the first Chief Minister of the state.

Politics

The first demand for a separate Uttarakhand state was voiced by P.C. Joshi, a member of the Communist Party of India (CPI), in 1952. However, a movement did not develop in earnest until 1979 when the Uttarakhand Kranti Dal (Uttarakhand Revolutionary Front) was formed to fight for separation. In 1991 the Uttar Pradesh legislative assembly passed a resolution supporting the idea, but nothing came of it. In 1994 student agitation against the state's implementation of the Mandal Commission report increasing the number of reserved government positions and university places for lower caste people (the largest caste of Kumaon and Garhwal is the high-ranking Rajput Kshatriya group) expanded into a struggle for statehood. Violence spread on both sides, with attacks on the police, police firing on demonstrators, and rapes of female Uttarakhand activists. In 1995 the agitation was renewed, mostly peacefully, under the leadership of the Uttarakhand Samyukta Sangharsh Samiti (Uttarakhand United Struggle Association), a coalition headed by the Uttarakhand Kranti Dal. The Bharatiya Janata Party (BJP), seeing the appeal of statehood to its high-caste constituencies, also supported the movement, but wanted to act on its own. To distinguish its activities, the BJP wanted the new state to be called Uttaranchal, essentially a synonym for Uttarakhand. In 1995 various marches and demonstrations of the Uttarakhand movement were tense with the possibility of conflict not just with the authorities, but also between the two main political groups. Actual violence, however, was rare. Uttaranchal became the twenty-seventh state of the Republic of India on 9 November 2000. The BJP came to power under the leadership of Nityanand Swamy. Narain Dutt Tiwari was sworn in as the chief minister on 2 March 2002.

Culture

The arts, crafts, dance forms and music of Uttaranchal revolve around gods and goddesses and seasonal cycles. In recent times, however, historical events of the freedom struggle and national life have come to be based as the topic for art forms.

Fairs and festivals:

1. Almora: Shrawan Mela (Jageshwar), Doonagiri Mela (Ranikhet), Gananath Mela, Dwarhat Mela, Kasar Devi Mela, Somnath Fair.

2. Bageshwar: Uttarayani Mela, Shivratri Fair, Kartik Purnima, Dussehra Fair.

3. Champawat: Purnagiri Fair, Devidhura Fair, Mata Murti Ka Mela.

4. Dehradun: Jhanda Fair, Tapakeshwar Fair, Lakshman Siddha Fair, Bissu Fair, Mahasu Devta's Fair, Shadheed Veer Kesari Chand's Fair, Lakhawar Fair, Hanol Mela, Neelkanth Mahadev Mela.

5. Hardwar: Ardh Kumbh and Kumbh Mela, Kavand Mela.

6. Nainital: Vasantotsav, Nandadevi Fair, Hariyali Devi Fair, Ranibagh Fair, Chhota Kailash Fair, Garjiadevi Fair, Sharadotsav, Holi Mahotsav.

7. Pithoragarh: Jauljibi and Thal Fairs, Punyagiri Mela, Hatkalika Fair.

8. Tehri Garhwal: Chandrabadni Fair, Surkhanda Devi Fair, Kunjapuri Fair.

9. Udham Singh Nagar: Tharuwat Buxad Mahotsav, Ataria Fair, Chaiti Fair, Terai Utsav.

10. Uttarkashi: Magh Mela.

Economy, Industry and Agriculture

Economy: The net state domestic product at current prices in 2001–02 was Rs 11,361 crores. The per capita net state domestic product at current prices in 2001–02 was Rs 13,260.

Minerals and industry: Sheep development, weaving and fruit processing are the predominant industries of this industrially backward state. Most of the industrial enterprises of the state belong to the small-scale and household sector like khadi and handicrafts.

According to estimates, there are deposits of limestone, dolomite, magnesite, rock phosphate, gypsum and soapstone in different areas of the state.

Agriculture: Agriculture is the main source of livelihood of the rural population. The state grows foodgrains (like rice, wheat, barley, jowar, bajra, maize, manduwa, sanwan and kodo). The state also grows pulses (like urad, moong-moth, masoor, gram, mattar, arhar), oilseeds (like rape, mustard, sesame, groundnut, sunflower and soyabean). Besides these, sugar cane, potato, tobacco and cotton are also grown.

Power: The state's power requirements are mainly met by hydroelectric power plants. The state is home to the Tehri Dam Project.

Education

Educational institutions: Hemwati Nandan Bahuguna Garhwal University, Srinagar; G.B. Pant Kumaon University, Nainital; Gurukul Kangri University, Hardwar; G.B. Pant University of Agriculture and Technology, Pantnagar; Roorkee Engineering University, Roorkee; Forest Research Institute, Dehradun; Indian Institute of Petroleum, Dehradun; Keshav Dev Malviya Institute of Petroleum Exploration, Dehradun; Oil and Natural Gas Corporation Ltd., Dehradun; Wadia Institute of Himalayan Geology, Dehradun; Wildlife Institute of India, Dehradun; Indira Gandhi National Forest Academy, Dehradun; Survey of India, Dehradun; Indian Institute of Remote Sensing, Dehradun; Instrument Research and Development Establishment, Dehradun; L.B.S. National Academy of Administration, Mussoorie; Defence Electronics Applications Laboratory, Dehradun; Indian Military Academy, Dehradun; Central Soil and Water Conservation Research and Training Institute, Dehradun; National Institute of Visually Handicapped, Dehradun; Rashtriya Indian Military College, Dehradun; Nehru Institute of Mountaineering, Uttarkashi, Central Building Research Institute, Roorkee.

Tourism

Major tourist attractions:

I. Nature tourism:

a. Wildlife: Askot Sanctuary, Corbett National Park, Govind Wildlife Sanctury, Nanda Devi National Park, Rajaji National Park, Valley of Flowers, Assan Barrage.

b. Glaciers: Bandarpunch Glacier, Chorbari Bamak Glacier, Dokriani Glacier, Doonagiri Glacier, Gangotri Glacier, Pindari Glacier, Maiktoli Glacier, Sunderdhunga Glacier, Milam Glacier, Ralam Glacier, Namik Glaciers, Khatling Glaciers, Nandadevi Glacier, Satopnath, Bhagirathi-Khark Glacier, Tiprabamak Glacier.

II. Pilgrimage tourism:

a. Yatras: Char Dham Yatra, Nanda Devi Yatra, Kailash Mansarovar Yatra.

b. Pilgrimage centres

i. Almora: Doonagiri Temple, Jageshwar Temple, Chitai Temple, Hairakhan.

ii. Bageshwar: Bagnath Temple, Chandika Temple, Shri Haru Temple, Gauri Udiyar.

iii. Chamoli: Badrinath, Hemkund Saheb, Gopeshwar, Prayags.

iv. Champawat: Baleshwar Temple, Gwal Devta, Devidhura, Kranteshwar Mahadev, Meetha Reetha Saheb, Purnagiri.

v. Dehradun: Bhadraj Temple, Surkhanda Devi, Jwalaji Temple, Nag Devta Temple, Parkasheshwar Temple, Bharat Mandir, Kailash Niketan Mandir, Satya Narayan Temple, Shatrughan Temple, Neelkanth Mahadev.

vi. Haridwar: Har ki Pauri, Sapt Rishi Ashram and Sapt Sarovar, Mansa Devi Temple, Chandi Devi Temple, Maya Devi Temple, Daksha Mahadev Temple.

vii. Nainital: Garjiya Devi Temple, Naina Devi Temple, Seeta Bani Temple.

viii. Pauri: Siddhibali Temple, Durga Devi Temple, Medanpuri Devi Temple, Shri Koteshwar Mahadev, Tarkeshwar Mahadev, Keshorai Math, Kamleshwar Temple, Shankar Math, Devalgarh, Dhar Devi.

ix. Pithoragarh: Dhwaj Temple, Narayan Ashram, Patal Bhaubaneshwar, Thal Kedar, Kapileshwar Mahadev.

x. Rudraprayag: Kedarnath Temple, Shankaracharya Samadhi, Gaurikund, Son Prayag, Panch Kedar, Madmaheshwar, Tungnath, Koteshwar, Guptkashi.

xi. Tehri Garhwal: Surkhanda Devi Temple.

xii. Udham Singh Nagar: Atariya Temple, Nanak Matta, Purnagiri, Chaiti.

xiii. Uttarkashi: Gangotri, Yamunotri.

III. Adventure tourism:

a. Skiing: Auli, Mundali, Dayara Bagyal, Munsya.

b. Water sports:

i. Still water sports: Asan Barrage Water Sports Resort, Nainital Lake Paradise, Nanaksagar Matta.

ii. Rafting:

a. Garhwal: River Yamuna: Barkot to Bernigad, Damta to Yamuna Bridge, Mori to Tuni (Khoonigad). River Alaknanda: Kaliasaur to Srinagar, Srinagar to Bagwan, Kaliasaur to Rishikesh. River Bhagirathi: Matli to Dunda, Harsil to Uttarkashi, Dharasu to Chham, Jangla to Jhala, Bhaldyana to Tehri. River Bhilangana: Ghansali to Gadolia. River Mandakini: Chandrapuri to Rudraprayag.

b. Kumaon: River Maha Kali, Kaudiyala Rafters Camp.

Airports: Dehradun, Pant Nagar.

National Parks: Corbett National Park in Nainital and Garhwal districts (520.82 sq. km), Gangotri National Park in Uttarkashi district (1,552 sq. km), Govind National Park in Uttarkashi district (472.08 sq. km), Nanda Devi National Park in Chamoli district (630.00 sq. km), Rajaji National Park in Dehradun Garhwal and Haridwar districts (820.00 sq. km), Valley of Flowers National Park in Chamoli district (87.50 sq. km).

Administration

Legislature: Uttaranchal has a unicameral legislature of 70 seats of which 12 are reserved for SCs and 3 for STs. The term of the current house ends on 17 March 2007. The present party position is as under:

Name of Party	Seats
Indian National Congress	36
Bharatiya Janata Party	19
Bahujan Samaj Party	7
Uttarakhand Kranti Dal	4
Nationalist Congress Party	1
Independent	3
Total	**70**

Judiciary: The High Court of Uttaranchal is at Nainital. The chief justice is Cyriac Joseph.

Districts:

District	Area (sq. km)	Population	Headquarters	Urban Agglomerations
Almora	3,082.8	630,446	Almora	Almora
Bageshwar	2,302.5	249,453	Bageshwar	
Chamoli	7,613.8	369,198	Gopeshwar	
Champawat	1,781.0	224,461	Champawat	
Dehradun	3,088.0	1,279,083	Dehradun	Dehradun, Mussouri, Rishikesh
Garhwal	5,399.6	696,851	Pauri	
Hardwar	2,360.0	1,444,213	Hardwar	Hardwar, Roorkee
Nainital	3,860.4	762,912	Nainital	Nainital, Haldwani-cum-Kathgodam
Pithoragarh	7,100.0	462,149	Pithoragarh	
Rudraprayag	1,890.6	227,461	Rudraprayag	
Tehri Garhwal	4,080.0	604,608	New Tehri	
Udhamsingh Nagar (Rudrapur)	2,908.4	1,234,548	Udhamsingh Nagar	
Uttarkashi	8,016.0	294,179	Uttarkashi	

Uttar Pradesh

Key Statistics

Capital: Lucknow.

Area: 2,36,286 sq. km.

Population: Total: 166,197,921, Male: 87,565,369, Female: 78,632,552.

Population density: 689 per sq. km.

Sex ratio: 898 females per 1000 males.

Principal languages: Hindi, Urdu, Punjabi.

Literacy rates: Total: 56.3%, Male: 68.8%, Female: 42.2%.

Government

Governor: T.V. Rajeshwar. He was sworn in on 8 July 2004.

Chief Minister: Mulayam Singh Yadav (SP). He was sworn in on 29 August 2003.

Geography

Physical characteristics: On the basis of its physiography, the main regions of Uttar Pradesh are the central plains of the Ganga and its tributaries, the southern uplands, the Himalayan region, and the submontane region between the Himalayas and the plains.

The Gangetic Plain occupies about three-fourths of the total area of Uttar Pradesh. It largely consists of a fertile plain which is featureless, and varies in elevation, rising up to 300 metres in the northwest, and 60 metres in the extreme east. It is composed of alluvial deposits which are brought down by the Ganga and its tributaries from the Himalayas.

The southern uplands constitute a part of the Vindhya Range, which is rugged, largely dissected, and rises towards the south-east. The elevation in this region reaches up to 300 metres. The submontane region consists of the Bhabar, a narrow bed of alluvium and gravel, which along its southern fringes joins into the Terai area. The Terai area, which previously consisted of tall grass and thick forests, is a marshy and damp tract. A definite portion of the Terai region has been subject to deforestation.

The topography of the Himalayan region is vastly varied. There are deep canyons, turbulent streams, large lakes and snow-capped peaks.

Neighbouring States and Union territories:
International border: Nepal.

States: Uttaranchal, Madhya Pradesh, Haryana, Rajasthan, Himachal Pradesh, Bihar.

National Capital Territory: Delhi.

Major rivers: Ganga, Yamuna, Gomti, Ramganga, Ghaghara, Chambal, Betwa, Ken and Son.

Climate: Uttar Pradesh has a varying climate. The Himalayan region experiences a moderately temperate climate, while the southern uplands and the central plains experience tropical monsoon. The highest temperature recorded in the state was 49.9°C at Gonda in 1958. The average temperatures in the plains vary from 12.5°C to 17.5°C in January to 27.5°C to 32.5°C in May and June.

Uttar Pradesh registers a rainfall between 1000–2000mm in the east and 600–1000mm in the west. Around 90 per cent of the rainfall occurs between June and September, during the time of the southwest monsoon. Floods are a recurring problem due to the concentrated rainfall during these four months, and cause heavy destruction to life, property and crops, especially in the eastern part of Uttar Pradesh. On the other hand, the periodic failure of monsoons leads to droughts and failure of crops.

Flora and Fauna:

Flora: The plains of Uttar Pradesh are rich in mineral vegetation, which is diminishing due to the various requirements of the people. While natural forests can be found in the mountainous regions of Uttaranchal on a very large scale, Uttar Pradesh has very few patches of natural forest that lie scattered in the plains.

Tropical moist deciduous forests grow in regions that register 1000 to 1500 mm of annual rainfall and an average temperature between 26°–27°C. In Uttar Pradesh, these forests can be found in Terai. Deciduous trees of uneven sizes grow in regions of higher altitude. This is a special feature of these forests.

In the lower regions, there are climbers, bamboo, evergreen shrubs and cand. The important trees that grow here are dhak, gular, jamun, jhingal, sal, palas, amla, and mahua semal. In all parts of the plains, especially in the central, eastern and western regions, tropical dry deciduous forests can be found, and they consist of trees that are mostly deciduous. Important trees include amaltas, anjeer, palas, bel, and sal. In other moist regions, and especially along river banks, sheesham, jamun, babool, imli (tamarind), peepal, mango, and neem can be found.

In the southwestern parts of the state can be found tropical thorny forests, which are confined to areas that experience low humidity (below 47 per cent), low annual rainfall (between 500–700mm), and a mean annual temperature between 25° to 27°C. Euphorbias, thorny legumes, babool, and especially thorny trees can be found extensively in these areas. Short grasses grow during rains. In these regions, the trees are normally small, and form open dry forests. Some of the trees that can be found in this region are kokke, khair, dhaman, neem, phulai, and danjha. These trees also produce various types of gum and resin.

Fauna: Uttar Pradesh has a variety of fauna. Important species of fish include rohu, einghi, trout, cuchia, labi, parthan, mirror carp, kata, eel, hilsa, magur, mirgal, mahaser, vittal and tengan. Birds include pigeon, vulture, owl, nightingale, sparrow, parrot, nilkanth, cheel and peacock. Other common species found in the state are black deer, nilgai, kastura, sambar, chinkara, snow leopard, hill dog, elephant, mountain goat, cheetal, hyena, tiger, and black-brown bear.

The submontane region of the state is rich in animal life. Animals like wild boars, crocodiles, sloth bears, partridges, wild ducks, quails, peafowls, woodpeckers doves, pigeons, blue jays, leopards and tigers can be found in these regions.

History

During the British rule in India, there were certain pockets in Uttar Pradesh that were governed by the English equity and common law. In 1773, the Mughal Emperor transferred the districts of Banaras and Ghazipur to the East India Company.

The East India Company acquired the area of modern-day Uttar Pradesh over a period of time. The territories occupied from the nawabs, the Scindias of Gwalior and the Gurkhas were initially placed within the Bengal Presidency. In 1833, they were separated and the North-Western Provinces, originally called Agra Presidency, were created. In 1877, the kingdom of Awadh was united with the North-Western Provinces and the province was renamed North-Western Provinces of Agra and Oudh. In 1902, the province was renamed yet again, when it became 'United Provinces of Agra and

Oudh'. In 1937, the name was shortened to 'United Provinces'.

In 1947, the United Provinces became an administrative unit of Independent India. In 1949, the autonomous states of Rampur and Tehri-Garhwal were incorporated into the United Provinces. When the new Constitution was adopted in 1950, United Provinces got its present name, Uttar Pradesh. Gobind Ballabh Pant was the first Chief Minister of Uttar Pradesh

In 2000, the state of Uttaranchal was carved out from Uttar Pradesh.

Politics

The state was made a Governor's province in 1921 and after some time its capital was shifted to Lucknow. Its name was changed to United Provinces in 1937. It got its present name of Uttar Pradesh in 1950. Uttar Pradesh has held the centre-stage in the country's politics mainly because it provides the biggest chunk of 85 MPs in the 545-member Indian parliament. Its 425-member state assembly holds a perpetual live-wire political situation. Heavyweight chief ministers like Sampurnanand, C.B. Gupta, Sucheta Kriplani, Charan Tribhuvan Narain Singh, Kamlapati Tripathi, H.N. Bahuguna and N.D. Tiwari kept the Congress flag flying high in Uttar Pradesh for nearly thirty years. The state had by 1977 produced all the three prime ministers of the country. But by mid-March 1977, the political setting of Uttar Pradesh saw the Congress as a humiliated party. The Janata Party made a clean sweep of the 85 Lok Sabha seats, with 68 per cent of the voters backing it. Subsequent Assembly elections proved no different for the Congress. The Janata Party won 352 seats of the 425 seats in the assembly. But soon infighting and bickering crippled the Janata Party. The going proved tough for the first backward chief minister Ram Naresh Yadav. Already bogged down with the Shia-Sunni riots of October 1977, Yadav seemed completely at a loss with the outbreak of communal violence in Varanasi on the Dussehra day. Banarsi Das was the chief minister from 1979 to 1980. This was a period of political instability. At this time Sanjay Gandhi capitalized on the Janata Party's failures and helped his mother Indira Gandhi to take over the reins of the country for the second time in January 1980. The Congress won 51 of the 85 UP Lok Sabha seats in 1980. Vishwanath Pratap Singh set his foot in big time politics when he became the chief minister on 9 June 1980. Sanjay Gandhi himself handpicked his huge 61-member ministry. The air crash on 23 June abruptly ended Sanjay Gandhi's soaring rise. This presented Singh with unexpected challenges from within the Congress in the state. Many severe tests were waiting. The violent Moradabad riots, which started on 13 August 1980, proved the worst ever. The riots continued for more than 45 days and necessitated intermittent curfew situations in and around the district. A visibly upset V.P. Singh tendered his resignation but it was not accepted. 1981 was even worse for V.P. Singh. Sripati Misra was chosen as Singh's alternative in 1982. A virtual revolt by Congress MLAs sealed Misra's fate. The Congress chose its old hand N.D. Tiwari, a union minister, to replace Misra in August 1984.

The Vishwa Hindu Parishad had launched Ek-atmata Yatras in late 1983. These yatras criss-crossed Uttar Pradesh to receive an overwhelming response. There were repeated religious build ups in Ayodhya. The Vishwa Hindu Parishad's major onslaught was unveiled with the announcement of a Ram Janm Bhumi Mukti (freeing of the temple) agitation on 7 October 1984. A huge crowd of kar sevaks (RSS volunteers) collected at the banks of the Sarayu River in Ayodhya and vowed to sacrifice their lives for the cause. A truck carrying idols of Ram and Sita, called the Ram Rath yatra, started from Ayodhya to Lucknow the next day on its way to Delhi. The yatra had to be abandoned in Ghaziabad, on the Delhi borders, as Indira Gandhi was assassinated, riddled with bullets by her own bodyguards.

Rajiv Gandhi's entry worked as a soothing balm for hurt sentiments. The Congress won a whopping 415 of the total 542 Lok Sabha seats; the biggest ever haul by a single party. Uttar Pradesh responded in Rajiv's favour almost unilaterally. The party lost just 3 of the 85 Lok Sabha seats in the state with an incredible 50.71% votes. The BJP, in turn, stood nowhere with merely 6.37% votes. The Dalit Mazdoor Kisan Party (DMKP), formed by dissolving Lok Dal, was the only party which survived the hurricane with only 3 seats but a more respectable vote percentage of 24.47%. But the Congress could not fair well in the Vidhan Sabha elections in 1985. One reason for the Congress's dip in performance compared to the 1980 elections could have been Rajiv's determination of lending a clean image to the party. Nearly half the 306 MLAs of 1980 were denied tickets and they worked against the party's interest in most cases during the campaign. The Congress won 268 seats. It was time for Narayan Datt Tiwari to move out. He made way for Bir Bahadur Singh as chief minister.

In 1989, the National Front comprising seven parties, on an electoral understanding with the BJP, came to power. The Congress's downfall in UP had begun. And so had the era of political instability in Uttar Pradesh. Mulayam Singh Yadav of the Samajvadi Party became the chief minister and remained in the post till 1991. His government fell when the government at the Centre changed. Mulayam Singh Yadav was succeeded by Kalyan Singh on 24 June 1991. The Kalyan Singh government was dismissed on 6 December 1992

after the demolition of the Babri Masjid at Ayodhya, and a Governor's rule was imposed. Two governors—Satyanarain Reddy and Motilal Vora—ruled the state over the next nine months. On 5 December 1993 Mulayam Singh Yadav was back on the seat of chief minister. Mayawati of the Bahujan Samaj Party became the chief minister in 1995, but President's Rule was soon imposed in the state.

The 1997 Assembly elections produced a hung assembly. The BJP and the BSP carved out a peculiar unheard-of arrangement: the chief minister's position was to be shared by the two parties in rotation in the block period of six months each. The BSP was to get the CM's position first. Mayawati took over as chief minister once again on 20 March 1997. Kalyan Singh took over on 21 September 1997 and reversed some of the decisions made by the Mayawati government. Mayawati withdrew support from the Kalyan Singh government on 19 October. On 21 February 1998, twelve members of the rebel Congress group Loktantrik Congress Party (LCP), which was supporting the BJP government, called on the governor along with some other rebel MLAs of other splinter groups along with Mayawati and Congress Legislature Party leader Pramod Tewari. Representatives of the Samajvadi Party were also in the delegation. Congress MLAs submitted a memorandum claiming that the LCP had withdrawn support from the BJP. The governor of UP Romesh Bhandari immediately invited Jagdambika Pal to form the government. On 22 February the court reinstated the Kalyan Singh government by setting the governor's order null and void. The Vidhan Sabha met on 26 February as both the chief ministers occupied the podium along with the Speaker. Kalyan Singh proved his strength in the House and emerged the winner. Mayawati came to power for the third time on 3 May 2002. She was succeeded by Mulayam Singh Yadav on 29 August 2003.

Culture

Apart from possessing a variety of geographical regions and cultures, Uttar Pradesh is also one of the most ancient centres of Indian culture. The antiquities discovered at Mirzapur, Meerut and Banda or Bundelkhand connect its history to the early stone age and the Harappan culture. In the Vindhyan Range, chalk drawings or dark red drawings by primitive men can be found.

The state also features popular holy shrines and pilgrim centres, and also plays an important role in education, culture, politics, tourism, industry, and agriculture. It is also well known for the contribution of its people to the national freedom movement.

Fairs and festivals: There are about 2250 fairs that are held every year in Uttar Pradesh. Mathura has the largest number of fairs (86). Other major venues of fairs are Kanpur, Hamirpur, Jhansi, Agra and Fatehpur.

The Kumbh Mela at Prayag (Allahabad) attracts pilgrims and tourists from around the world. At Prayag, the Kumbh fair is held once in twelve years, and the Ardh Kumbh is held every six years.

Festivals of other religions are also celebrated in Uttar Pradesh, and it is renowned for its composite culture. As many as 40 festivals are celebrated by various communities. Hindu festivals include Shivaratri, Makar Sankranti, Krishna Janmashtami, Karthik Purnima, Vijaya Dashmi, Holi, Deepawali, Ganesha Chaturthi, Ganga Dashahara, Ram Navami, Vaishakhi Purnima, Raksha Bandhan, Sheetla Ashtami, Naag Panchami, and Vasant Panchami. Major Muslim festivals celebrated in the state are Shab-e-Barat, Barawafat, Bakr-Id, Id and Muharram. Christian festivals include Christmas, Good Friday, Easter and New Year's Day.

Some of the important fairs and festivals held in Uttar Pradesh include the Bateshwar Fair, festivals organised by the UP Tourism Department, the Ganga Mahotsava at Varanasi, the Buddha Mahotsava at Sarnath and Kushinagar, and the Water Sports Festival at Allahabad.

Economy, Industry and Agriculture

Economy: The net state domestic product at current prices for 2002–03 (provisional) was Rs 176,076 crores. The per capita net state domestic product at current prices for 2002–03 (provisional) was Rs 10,289.

Minerals and industry: Textiles and sugar refining, both long-standing industries in Uttar Pradesh, employ nearly one-third of the state's total factory labour. Most of the mills, however, are old and inefficient. Other resource-based industries in Uttar Pradesh include vegetable oil, jute and cement.

A number of large factories manufacturing heavy equipment, machinery, steel, aircraft, telephone and electronics equipment, and fertilizers have been set up in the state. An oil refinery at Mathura and the development of coalfields in the southeastern district of Mirzapur are also major Union government projects.

The state government has promoted medium and small scale industries. Industries that contribute most to the state's exports include handicrafts, carpets, brassware, footwear, and leather and sporting goods. Carpets from Bhadohi and Mirzapur are prized worldwide. Silks and brocades of Varanasi, ornamental brassware from Moradabad, chikan (a type of embroidery) work from Lucknow, ebony work from Nagina, glassware from Firozabad, and carved woodwork from

Saharanpur are also important.

Tourism in the state has great potential, but much of it is untapped.

The minerals found in Uttar Pradesh include limestone, dolomite, glass-sand, marble, bauxite and uranium

Agriculture: The economy of Uttar Pradesh is largely dependent on agriculture. The main crops are rice, sugar cane, millet, wheat and barley. High-yielding varieties of seed for rice and wheat were introduced in the 1960s, along with a greater availability of fertilizers, and an increased use of irrigation in the state.

Two chief problems still affect the farmers, namely small, non-economic landholdings and lack of resources needed to invest in the state's technology, in order to increase production. The yield of milk is low, but livestock and dairy still manage to provide a supplementary means of income. Most of the agricultural landholdings are insufficient for the subsistence of the farmers in the state.

Forests in the state yield timber, which is used in construction, and also as firewood and raw materials for producing a number of industrial products like paper, matches and plywood. The government's reforestation programmes in Uttar Pradesh have contributed to some increase in the forest area, and the subsequent availability of forest products useful for industries.

Power: Uttar Pradesh is mainly dependent on thermal power, which provides bulk of the energy to the state. However, hydroelectric and nuclear power (from the Narora Atomic Power Station) also contribute to the total power scenario.

Education

Educational institutes: Aligarh Muslim University (Aligarh), University of Allahabad, Babasaheb Bhimrao Ambedkar University (Lucknow), Banaras Hindu University (Varanasi) , Bundelkhand University (Jhansi), Central Institute of Higher Tibetan Studies (Varanasi), Ch. Charan Singh University (Meerut), Chandra Shekhar Azad University of Agriculture and Technology (Kanpur), Chhatrapati Sahu Ji Maharaj Kanpur University (Kanpur), Dayalbagh Educational Institute (Agra), Deendayal Upadhyaya Gorakhpur University (Gorakhpur), Dr Bhim Rao Ambedkar University (Agra), Dr Ram Manohar Lohia Avadh University (Faizabad), Indian Institute of Technology (Kanpur), Indian Veterinary Research Institute (Izatnagar), University of Lucknow, Mahatma Gandhi Kashi Vidyapeeth (Varanasi), M.J.P. Rohilkhand University (Bareilly), Narendra Deva University of Agriculture and Technology (Faizabad), Purvanchal University (Jaunpur), University of Roorkee, Sampurnanand Sanskrit Vishwavidyalaya (Varanasi) and the Sanjay Gandhi Postgraduate Institute of Medical Sciences (Lucknow).

Tourism

Major tourist attractions: Chitrakoot, Ayodhya, Jhansi, Kushinagar, Kapilavastu, Varanasi, Sarnath, Fathepur Sikri, Braj-Bhoomi, Vrindavan, Agra.

Airports: Lucknow, Kanpur, Varanasi, Agra.

National Parks: Dudhwa National Park in Lakhimpur Kheri district (490.00 sq. km).

Administration

Legislature: Uttar Pradesh has a bicameral legislature. The Lower House is called Vidhan Sabha and the Upper House Vidhan Parishad. The state legislative assembly has 403 seats, of which 89 are reserved for the SCs. No seats are reserved for STs. The present party positions are:

Name of Party	Seats
Samajwadi Party	143
Bahujan Samaj Party	98
Bharatiya Janata Party	88
Indian National Congress	25
Rashtriya Lok Dal	14
Rashtriya Kranti Party	4
Apna Dal	3
Communist Party of India (Marxist)	2
Akhil Bhartiya Lok Tantrik Congress	2
Janata Dal (United)	2
Akhil Bharat Hindu Mahasabha	1
Janata Party	1
Lok Jan Shakti Party	1
National Loktantrik Party	1
Rashtriya Parivartan Dal	1
Samajwadi Janata Party (Rashtriya)	1
Independent	16
Total	**403**

Judiciary: The Allahabad High Court is the seat of judiciary. A.N. Roy is the chief justice.

Districts:

District	Area (sq. km)	Population	Headquarters	Urban Agglomerations
Agra	4,027.0	3,611,301	Agra	Agra
Aligarh	3,747.0	2,990,388	Aligarh	
Allahabad	5,425.1	4,941,510	Allahabad	Allahabad
Ambedkar Nagar	2,372.0	2,025,373	Akbarpur	
Auraiya	2,051.9	1,179,496	Auraiya	
Azamgarh	4,210.0	3,950,808	Azamgarh	Mubarakpur
Baghpat	1,389.4	1,164,388	Baghpat	
Bahraich	5,751.0	2,384,239	Bahraich	
Ballia	2,981.0	2,752,412	Ballia	
Balrampur	2,927.0	1,684,567	Balrampur	
Banda	4,418.1	1,500,253	Banda	Banda
Barabanki	3,825.0	2,673,394	Barabanki	Barabanki
Bareilly	4,120.0	3,598,701	Bareilly	Bareilly
Basti	3,033.8	2,068,922	Basti	
Bijnor	4,561.0	3,130,586	Bijnor	Bijnor, Kiratpur, Seohara
Budaun	5,168.0	3,069,245	Budaun	
Bulandshahar	3,717.7	2,923,290	Bulandshahar	
Chandauli	2,554.1	1,639,777	Chandauli	Mughalsarai
Chattrapati Shahuji Maharaj Nagar			Gauriganj	
Chitrakoot	3,205.9	800,592	Chitrakoot	
Deoria	2,535.0	2,730,376	Deoria	
Etah	4,446.0	2,788,270	Etah	
Etawah	2,288.2	1,340,031	Etawah	
Faizabad	2,764.0	2,087,914	Faizabad	Faizabad
Farrukhabad	2,279.5	1,577,237	Fatehgarh	Farrukhabad-cum-Fatehgarh
Fatehpur	4,152.0	2,305,847	Fatehpur	
Firozabad	2,361.0	2,045,737	Firozabad	Firozabad, Sirsaganj, Tundla

Gautam Buddha Nagar	1,268.6	1,191,263	Noida
Ghaziabad	1,955.8	3,289,540	Ghaziabad	Modinagar
Ghazipur	3,377.0	3,049,337	Ghazipur	Ghazipur
Gonda	4,425.0	2,765,754	Gonda
Gorakhpur	3,321.0	3,784,720	Gorakhpur
Hamirpur	4,316.5	1,042,374	Hamirpur
Hardoi	5,986.0	3,397,414	Hardoi
Hathras	1,751.0	1,333,372	Hathras	Hathras, Sasni
Jalaun	4,565.0	1,455,859	Orai
Jaunpur	4,038.0	3,911,305	Jaunpur
Jhansi	5,024.0	1,746,715	Jhansi	Jhansi
Jyotiba Phule Nagar	2,320.5	1,499,193	Amroha
Kannauj	1,994.5	1,385,227	Kannauj
Kanpur Dehat	3,146.0	1,584,037	Akbarpur
Kanpur Nagar	3,030.0	4,137,489	Kanpur	Kanpur
Kaushambi	1,835.9	1,294,937	Kaushambi
Kheri	7,680.0	3,200,137	Kheri
Kushinagar	2,910.0	2,891,933	Padarauna
Lalitpur	5,039.0	977,447	Lalitpur
Lucknow	2,528.0	3,681,416	Lucknow	Lucknow
Maharajganj	2,951.0	2,167,041	Maharajganj
Mahoba	2,849.6	708,831	Mahoba
Mainpuri	2,746.0	1,592,875	Mainpuri	Mainpuri
Mathura	3,332.0	2,069,578	Mathura	Mathura
Mau	1,713.0	1,849,294	Mau	Muhammadabad Gohna
Meerut	2,521.6	3,001,636	Meerut	Meerut
Mirzapur	4,522.0	2,114,852	Mirzapur
Moradabad	3,646.5	3,749,630	Moradabad	Bilari
Muzaffarnagar	4,008.0	3,541,952	Muzaffarnagar	Muzaffarnagar, Purquazi
Pilibhit	3,499.0	1,643,788	Pilibhit
Pratapgarh	3,717.0	2,727,156	Pratapgarh
Rae Bareli	4,586.0	2,872,204	Rae Bareli
Rampur	2,367.0	1,922,450	Rampur
Saharanpur	3,689.0	2,848,152	Saharanpur
Sant Kabir Nagar	1,442.3	1,424,500	Khalilabad
Sant Ravidas Nagar	959.8	1,352,056	Bhadohi
Shahjahanpur	4,575.0	2,549,458	Shahjahanpur	Shahjahanpur
Shravasti	1,126.0	1,175,428	Shravasti
Siddharth Nagar	2,752.0	2,038,598	Navgarh
Sitapur	5,743.0	3,616,510	Sitapur
Sonbhadra	6,788.0	1,463,468	Robertsganj	Renukoot
Sultanpur	4,436.0	3,190,926	Sultanpur
Unnao	4,558.0	2,700,426	Unnao
Varanasi	1,578.0	3,147,927	Varanasi	Varanasi

West Bengal

Key Statistics

Capital: Kolkata.
Area: 88,752 sq. km.
Population: Total: 80,176,197, Male: 41,465,985, Female: 38,710,212.
Population density: 904 per sq. km.
Sex ratio: 934 females per 1000 males.
Principal languages: Bengali, Hindi, Urdu.
Literacy rates: Total: 68.6%, Male: 77.0%, Female: 59.6%.

Government

Governor: Gopalkrishna Gandhi. He was sworn in on 14 December 2004.

Chief Minister: Buddhadeb Bhattacharya (CPIM). He was sworn in on 18 May 2001.

Geography

Physical characteristics: Stretching from the Himalayas in the north to the Bay of Bengal in the south, West Bengal is primarily composed of plain land, except the north where the southern flank of the Himalayas extends into the state. Part of the Ganga–Brahmaputra delta constitutes the eastern part of West Bengal. From the northern highlands to the tropical forests of Sunderbans, variations in altitude result in great variety in nature and climate.

Neighbouring States and Union territories:
International borders: Bangladesh, Nepal, Bhutan.

States: Sikkim, Assam, Bihar, Jharkhand, Orissa

Major rivers: Hooghly and its tributaries (Mayurakshi, Damodar, Kangsabati and Rupnarayan) and Teesta, Torsa, Subarnarekha, Joldhara and Ranjit.

Climate: Climate in the state varies from the relatively cooler northern part to the warm region in the south. Maximum and minimum temperatures vary between 30°C–44°C and 4°C–12°C respectively. Annual rainfall is about 4000–5000mm in the northern districts and about 1100–1600mm in the western districts. The average annual rainfall is 1750mm.

Flora and Fauna:
Flora: The forests of West Bengal could be classified under seven categories: tropical semi-evergreen, tropical moist deciduous, tropical dry deciduous, littoral and swampy, subtropical hill forest, eastern Himalayan wet temperate, and alpine.

The Sunderbans, which derives its name from sundari trees, have large numbers of genwa, dhundal, passur, garjan and kankra trees.

Fauna: Wildlife found in the state include Royal Bengal Tiger, elephant, one-horned rhino, sambar, barking deer, spotted deer, hog deer, wild boar, rhesus monkey, mongoose, crocodile, bison, Olive Ridley sea turtle, python, salvator lizard, chequered killback, heron, egret, cormorant, fishing eagle, white-bellied sea eagle, seagull, tern, kingfisher, Eastern knot, curlew, sandpiper, golden plover, pintail, white-eyed pochard and whistling teal.

History

The state gets its name from the ancient kingdom of Vanga, or Banga. Around 3 BC, it formed part of the extensive Mauryan empire. The region was then taken over into the Gupta empire and later came under the rule of the Pala dynasty. From the 13th to the 18th centuries Bengal was under Muslim rule, and came under British control following Robert Clive's conquest over the region in 1757.

In 1773, Warren Hastings, the governor of Bengal, became the first Governor General of Bengal with powers over the Madras and Bombay Presidencies as well. In 1905, Bengal was partitioned into two provinces in spite of violent protests. Continued opposition to the partition led to the reunification of the state in 1911.

At the time of independence, the eastern part of Bengal became East Pakistan (later Bangladesh) and the western part became the Indian state of West Bengal. The princely state of Cooch Behar was integrated with West Bengal in 1950. The state also gained some territory from Bihar after the reorganization of Indian states in 1956.

Politics

After India's independence partition led to two nations, India and Pakistan with two halves—East Pakistan and West Pakistan. Bengal was partitioned and the western half became the state of West Bengal in the Indian Union. The eastern half of Bengal became East Pakistan and in 1971, became an independent nation—Bangladesh. The first chief minister of the Indian state of West Bengal, Dr Prafulla Chandra Ghosh, was sworn in as the chief minister on 15 August 1947. Dr Bidhan Chandra Roy became the new chief minister on 14 January 1948. Dr B.C. Roy is credited with the planning and implementation of many of West Bengal's major projects. In 1962, with the death of Dr B.C. Roy, Prafulla Chandra Sen, the food minister, became the chief minister and his government lasted till 1967. During the late sixties and early seventies widespread poverty and dissatisfaction led to a major political turbulence in the state. The breakdown of infrastructure and resentment against the

Delhi-based Congress government led to the strengthening of the Left parties in West Bengal. The Communist Party of India (CPI), formed in 1920, split in 1964 and the Communist Party of India (Marxist) (CPIM) was formed. The United Front, a combination of Left and other parties came to power in West Bengal in 1967. Ajoy Mukherjee of the Bangla Congress became the new chief minister in the UF government. The government was short lived and Dr Prafulla Chandra Ghosh (the first chief minister and the food minister in Ajoy Mukherjee's cabinet) formed the Progressive Democratic Front and became the new chief minister. In 1969 the United Front returned to power with Ajoy Mukherjee as the chief minister for a second time. The second UF government survived till 1971, followed by a Congress coalition with Ajoy Mukherjee remaining the chief minister. The Congress Party returned to power in 1972 under the leadership of Siddhartha Shankar Ray. A leftist movement called the Naxalite movement (named after its birthplace Naxalbari) gathered huge support amongst the frustrated urban youth. The leader of this movement was Charu Chandra Majumder. The uprising was clamped down with a heavy hand leading to widespread middle class resentment. The period of uncertainty, instability and lawlessness led to an economic decline as major companies and business houses shifted their investments and offices from Calcutta to other states.

In 1977 the state elections were won by the Left Front, a coalition of ten parties. The CPI(M) led by Jyoti Basu was the dominant party in the coalition. Jyoti Basu was elected chief minister and remained in that position till 2000. The turbulent situation of the seventies slowly improved and from the late eighties the political situation in the state has stabilized. Today West Bengal is one of the few remaining strongholds of the Left parties of India. Buddhadeb

Bhattacharya succeeded Jyoti Basu as the chief minister of West Bengal in 2000. The main opposition in the state –the Indian National Congress (INC)– suffered a setback when a former Congress party member and popular leader Mamata Banerjee founded her own Trinamool (grassroots) Congress (TMC) Party in 1997. In the 1998 and the 1999 national elections she allied with the Bharatiya Janata Party. It is interesting to note that the BJP (founded in 1980) has its origins in the Bharatiya Jana Sangha which was founded by prominent Bengali leader Dr Shymaprasad Mukherjee (1901-1953). The 1999 national elections saw the Left maintaining its comfortable lead from the state, followed by the TMC, the INC and the BJP. The TMC won all the three seats from Calcutta. In 1999 Calcutta's name was changed to Kolkata by the state legislature. Just before the 2001 state assembly elections there was a realignment of political parties with the TMC dumping the BJP and joining hands with the INC. The Kolkata media had predicted a tough fight by the TMC-INC alliance and a possibility of the government changing hands. However the Left Front won 199 of the 294 seats and was voted back to power for a record sixth time.

Culture

The rich traditions in art and culture in West Bengal are reflected in numerous ways in theatre, folk music, literature, films and paintings. The state has seen many great writers and artists, including the Nobel prize-winning poet Rabindranath Tagore.

Jatra, the hugely popular theatre form, has a range of themes: from mythological to historical to contemporary. Rabindrasangeet, consisting of songs written and composed by Tagore, has a strong influence on Bengali culture. Bengali filmmakers— most notably Satyajit Ray, Tapan Sinha and Mrinal Sen—have also earned worldwide acclaim.

Popular handicrafts include leather craft, brass and bell metal, articles from bamboo and cane, clay dolls, jute products and silver filigree. Handloom saris, notably the Baluchari and Dhakai, are well known.

Fairs and festivals: Important festivals of West Bengal include Durga Puja, Id, Diwali, Rasajatra, Navanna, Christmas, Saraswati Puja, Vasanta Utsav, Holi and Charak. Important fairs include Gangasagar Mela, Kenduli Mela, Jalpesh Mela, Rash Mela and Poush Mela.

Economy, Industry and Agriculture

Economy: The net state domestic product at current prices for 2002–03 (provisional) was Rs 153,781 crores. The per capita net state domestic product at current prices for 2002–03 (provisional) was Rs 18,756.

Minerals and industry: Major industries in the state include chemicals, cotton textiles, coal, iron and steel products, heavy and light Engineering products, leather and footwear, papers, tea, jute products, breweries, drugs and pharmaceuticals, electrical and electronics, plastics, software and infotech, locomotives, vegetable oils, gems and jewellery, poultry products and frozen marine products.

The state is rich in coal deposits located in the districts of Bardhaman and Birbhum. Other mineral deposits include iron ore, manganese, silica, limestone, China clay and dolomite.

Agriculture: Principal crops include rice, food grains, oilseeds, jute, potato, tea, mango, pineapple, banana, papaya, orange, guava and litchi. With an annual production of 58,000 tonnes, floriculture is another important activity.

Power: With an installed capacity of 6877 MW, West Bengal is a power surplus state. It supplies power to its neighbouring states. Most of the state's power comes from thermal power plants, and a small amount from hydroelectric plants.

Education

Educational institutes: University of Calcutta, Kolkata; Jadavpur University, Kolkata; Visva Bharati, Santiniketan; Rabindra Bharati University, Kolkata; Indian Institute of Technology, Kharagpur; Indian Institute of Management, Kolkata; Indian Statistical Institute, Kolkata; Bengal Engineering College, Howrah; University of Burdwan, Burdwan; Netaji Subhash Open University, Kolkata; University of North Bengal, Darjeeling • Vidyasagar University, Medinipur; Marine Engineering and Research Institute, Kolkata; West Bengal University of Animal and Fisheries Sciences, Kolkata.

Tourism

Major tourist attractions:

1. Kolkata and Howrah: Victoria Memorial, Indian Museum, Kalighat Temple, Dakshineswar Kali Temple, Belur Math, Ramakrishna Mission Institute of Culture, St. John's Church, Birla Planetarium, Shahid Minar, Howrah Bridge (Rabindra Setu), Vidyasagar Setu, Science City, Botanical Gardens.

2. Santiniketan.

3. Darjeeling: Tiger Hill, Batasia Loop, Lloyds Botanical Garden.

4. Murshidabad: Nimak Haram Deohri, Khusbagh, Hazarduari, Plassey.

5. Dooars Valley: Jaldapara, Buxa Tiger Project, Gorumara and Chapramari Wildlife Sanctuaries.

6. Kalimpong: Dr Graham's Homes, Durpin Dara, Kalibari, Thongsha Gumpha, Tharpa Choling Monastery.

7. Vishnupur: Rasmancha, Pancha Ratna Temple, Jorebangla Temple.

8. Siliguri.

9. Beaches: Digha, Shankarpur, Junput, Bakkhali, Sagardwip.

Airports:
International: Kolkata.

Domestic: Bagdogra.

National Parks: Neora Valley National Park (Darjeeling)—88.00 sq. km, Singalila National Park (Darjeeling)—78.60 sq. km, Sunderbans Tiger Reserve (South 24 Paraganas)—1330.10 sq. km, Buxa Tiger Reserve (Jalpaiguri)—117.10 sq. km, Gorumara National Park (Jalpaiguri)—79.45 sq. km.

Administration

Legislature: The unicameral West Bengal legislature comprises 294 elected seats, of which 59 are reserved for SCs and 17 for STs. One member can be nominated by the governor to represent the Anglo-Indian community. The term of the current house expires on 13 June 2006. The present party-wise break-up is as follows:

Name of Party	Seats
Communist Party of India (Marxist)	143
All India Trinamool Congress	60
Indian National Congress	26
All India Forward Bloc	25
Revolutionary Socialist Party	17
Communist Party of India	7
West Bengal Socialist Party	4
Gorakha National Liberation Front	3
Independent	9
Total	**294**

Judiciary: The Calcutta High Court is the seat of judiciary. The present chief justice is V.S. Sirpurkar.

Districts:

District	Area (sq. km)	Population	Headquarters	Urban Agglomerations
Bankura	6,882.0	3,191,822	Bankura	
Bardhaman	7,024.0	6,919,698	Bardhaman	Asansol, Kalna, Katwa
Birbhum	4,545.0	3,012,546	Suri	
Cooch Behar	3,387.0	2,478,280	Cooch Behar	Dinhata, Cooch Behar
Darjeeling	3,149.0	1,605,900	Darjeeling	Darjeeling
East Midnapore	NA	NA	NA	NA
Hooghly	3,149.0	5,040,047	Chinsurah	Kolkata
Howrah	1,467.0	4,274,010	Howrah	Kolkata
Jalpaiguri	6,227.0	3,403,204	Jalpaiguri	Alipurduar
Kolkata	185.0	4,580,544	Kolkata	Kolkata
Maldah	3,733.0	3,290,160	English Bazar	English Bazar
Murshidabad	5,324.0	5,863,717	Behrampore	Behrampore
Nadia	3,927.0	4,603,756	Krishnanagar	Birnagar, Chakdaha, Kolkata, Krishnanagar, Nabadwip, Ranaghat
North Twenty Four Parganas	4,094.0	8,930,295	Barasat	Gobardanga, Habra, Kolkata
North Dinajpur	3,140.0	2,478,280	Raiganj	Raiganj
Puruliya	6,259.0	2,535,233	Puruliya	
South Twenty Four Parganas	9,960.0	6,909,015	Alipur	Kolkata
South Dinajpur	2,219.0	1,502,647	Balurghat	Balurghat, Jaynagar-Mazilpur
West Midnapore	NA	NA	NA	NA

National Capital Territory

The approval of the Union Cabinet to grant statehood to Delhi has sparked off a fresh debate in the political circles. Here are some essential facts about the National Capital Territory.

Delhi

Key Statistics

Capital: Delhi.
Area: 1483 sq. km.
Population: Total: 13,850,507, Male: 7,607,234, Female: 6,243,273.
Population density: 9294 per sq. km.
Sex ratio: 821 females per 1000 males
Principal languages: Hindi, Punjabi, Urdu.

Literacy rates: Total: 81.7%, Male: 87.3%, Female: 74.7%.

Government

Lt Governor: Banwari Lal Joshi. He was sworn in as Lt Governor on 9 June 2004.

Chief Minister: Sheila Dikshit (INC). She was sworn in on 15 December 2003.

Geography

Physical characteristics: Delhi, the National Capital Territory of India, is divided into two zones: the extension of the Aravali Hills and the plains. Altitudes vary between 200 to 300 metres.

Neighbouring States and Union territories:

States: Haryana, Uttar Pradesh

Major rivers: Yamuna.

Climate: Delhi witnesses hot summers characterized by extreme dryness, with maximum temperatures going up to 46°C. Cold waves from the north make winters in Delhi very chilly, with minimum temperatures of around 4°C. Winters also witness thick fog on some mornings. Rainfall varies between 400–600mm.

Flora and Fauna:

Flora: Forest and tree cover constitutes about 151 sq. km of the area. The Ridge, with trees like dhak and amaltas, is classified as a tropical thorn forest. Delhi is also known for numerous flowering plants, mainly chrysanthemums, verbenas, violas, and phlox.

Fauna: The Indira Priyadarshini Wildlife Sanctuary at Asola is the main habitat for most animal species. These include nilgai, common mongoose, small Indian civet, porcupine, rufus tailed hare and monitor lizards. There's also a variety of birds including cormorants, egrets, grebes, falcons, partridges, quail, peafowl, waterhens, lapwings, sandpipers, woodpeckers, doves, parakeets, cuckoos, owls, nightjars, barbets, swallows, shrikes, orioles, drongos, mynahs, flycatchers, warblers, babblers, wagtails, pipits and buntings.

History

The earliest historical reference to Delhi date back to the first century BC, when Raja Dhilu built a city near the site of present-day Qutab Minar and named it after himself. Around AD 12, the city became the capital of Prithviraj Chauhan and passed into Muslim rule by the end of that century. It became the capital of Qutab-ud-din Aibak. The city was then ruled by the Khaljis followed by the Tughluqs. Babur established Mughal rule in India in 1526 with Delhi as the seat of his empire.

Mughal emperors Akbar and Jahangir moved their headquarters to Fatehpur Sikri and Agra respectively, but the city was restored to its former glory in 1638, when Shah Jahan laid the foundations of Shahjahanabad, which is now known as Old Delhi.

After the fail of the Mughal Empire during the mid-18th century, Delhi faced many raids by the Marathas and an invasion by Nadir Shah before the British rise to prominence in 1803. In 1912 the British moved the capital of British India from Calcutta to Delhi.

After independence, Delhi remained a chief commissioner's province till 1956, when it was converted into a Union territory. The chief commissioner was replaced by a Lt Governor.

In 1991, the National Capital Territory Act was passed by the Parliament and the elected government was given wider powers.

Delhi was divided into nine revenue districts in 1997.

Politics

After Independence, Delhi was given the status of a part-C state. In pursuance of the recommendations of the State Reorganisation Commission (1955), Delhi ceased to be a part-C state with effect from 1 November 1956. Delhi became a union territory under the direct administration of the President. In December 1987, the Government of India appointed the Sarkaria Committee (later on called Balakrishan Committee) to go into the various issues connected with the administration of the union territory of Delhi and to recommend measures for streamlining the administrative set-up. The committee submitted its report on 14 December 1989. After detailed enquiries and examinations, it recommended that Delhi should continue to be a union territory but should be provided with a Legislative Assembly and a Council of Ministers. The committee also recommended that with a view to ensuring stability and permanence, the arrangements should be incorporated in the Constitution to give the national capital a special status among the union territories. Delhi was granted a special statehood and an elected Legislative Assembly in 1991 under the 69th Constitutional amendment. Delhi is headed by a Lieutenant Governor nominated by the President of India and is administered by a chief minister appointed from the elected party.

In 1993, the BJP wrested the state from the Congress in a big way securing 49 of the 70 seats while Congress got just 14. The veteran BJP leader Madanlal Khurana became the chief minister. Sahib Singh Verma replaced him after a few years following intense infighting. Finally, just months before the 1998 polls, the high profile union minister Sushma Swaraj was brought in as the chief minister. The ruling BJP led by Sushma Swaraj was routed in the polls bagging just 15 seats while the Congress walked away with 52 seats. The credit for the Congress victory went to its Delhi chief Sheila Dikshit, who became the chief minister. In the Assembly elections held in 2003 the Congress emerged victorious again and Sheila Dikshit remained chief minister of the National Capital Territory of Delhi.

Culture

Migrations from various parts of India has led to pockets of diverse culture coming together in Delhi. Many of the country's prominent cultural institutions are located in Delhi. Popular handicrafts include zari zardozi, stone carving, paper craft and papier mache, and metal engraving.

Fairs and festivals: Major festivals and fairs include Holi, Dussehra, Lohri, Deepawali, Qutub festival, Phoolwalon Ki Sair, Roshnara and Shalimar Bagh festivals, and Mango festival.

Economy, Industry and Agriculture

Economy: The net state domestic product at current prices in 2002–03 (provisional) was Rs 68,747 crores. The per capita state domestic product at current prices in 2002–03 (provisional) was Rs 47,477.

Minerals and industry: Delhi is the largest centre of small industries in India. These manufacture a wide variety of goods like plastic and PVC goods, sports goods, radio and TV parts, razor blades, textiles, chemicals, fertilizers, soft drinks, and hand and machine tools. The new industrial policy focuses on areas like electronics, telecommunications, software and IT-enabled services.

Agriculture: The main crops are wheat, jawar, bajra and paddy. Vegetable cultivation, floriculture and mushroom cultivation are also important activities. The main livestock products are milk, eggs and meat.

Power: Delhi's own resources amount to an installed capacity of about 1000 MW, all of which come from thermal power plants. The balance of the power demand, which exceeds 3000 MW, is met by purchases from NTPC and other sources.

Education

Educational institutes: All India Institute of Medical Sciences, University of Delhi, Indian Agricultural Research Institute, Indian Institute of Technology, Delhi, Indira Gandhi National Open University, Jamia Millia Islamia, Jawaharlal Nehru University, School of Planning and Architecture, Shri Lal Bahadur Shastri Rashtriya Sanskrit Vidyapeetha, TERI School of Advanced Study and Indian Institute of Foreign Trade.

Tourism

Major tourist attractions: Red Fort, Puarana Qila, Qutab Minar (World Heritage Site), India Gate, Bahai's House Of Worship, Rashtrapati Bhavan, Rajghat, Humayun's Tomb (World Heritage Site), Parliament House, Jama Masjid, Jantar Mantar, Firoz Shah Kotla, Safdurjung's Tomb, Dilli Haat, Mughal Gardens, Lodi Gardens, National Museum.

Airports:
International: Indira Gandhi International Airport.
Domestic: Palam Airport, Safdarjung Airport.

National Parks: None.

Administration

Legislature: Two acts passed by the Parliament have been instrumental in providing for a legislative assembly for Delhi and supplementing the provisions relating to it: the Constitution (69th Amendment) Act, 1991; and the Government of National Capital Territory of Delhi Act, 1991.

The Delhi Legislative Assembly has 70 members, all chosen by direct election from as many constituencies, of which 13 are reserved for SCs. The term of the present house ends on 17 December 2008. Party position in the present assembly is as follows:

Name of Party	Seats
Indian National Congress	47
Bharatiya Janata Party	20
Nationalist Congress Party	1
Janata Dal (Secular)	1
Independent	1
Total	**70**

Judiciary: The Delhi High Court was established in 1966. The present chief justice is B.C. Patel.

Districts:

District	Area (sq. km)	Population
Central	25	644,005
East	64	1,448,770
New Delhi	35	171,806
North	60	779,788
North East	60	1,763,712
North West	440	2,847,395
South	250	2,258,367
South West	420	1,749,492
West	129	2,119,641

Union Territories

There are six Union Territories in India and only one—Pondicherry—has an assembly.

Andaman and Nicobar Islands

Key Statistics

Capital: Port Blair.
Area: 8,249 sq. km.

Population: Total: 356,152, Male: 192,972, Female: 163,180.
Population density: 43 per sq. km.
Sex ratio: 846 females per 1000 males.

Principal languages: Bengali, Tamil, Hindi.

Literacy rates: Total: 81.3%, Male: 86.3%, Female: 75.2%.

Government

Lieutenant Governor: Prof. Ramchandra Ganesh Kapse. He was sworn in on 5 January 2004.

Geography

Physical characteristics: The Andaman and Nicobar Islands lie along an arc in a long broken chain, approximately north–south over a distance of about 800km.

The Andamans are a group of more than 300 islands and islets, of which only 26 are inhabited. The three main islands, namely North, Middle and South Andaman, are collectively known as Great Andaman, since they are closely positioned. The Andaman Islands have a rough landscape, with hills enclosing its longitudinal, narrow valleys. The islands are covered by dense tropical forests. The deeply indented coral-fringed coasts form tidal creeks and harbours, which are surrounded by mangrove swamps. Saddle Peak (737m) is the highest in the Andaman Islands. About 135 km from Port Blair is Barran Island, India's only active volcano.

The Nicobar Islands consist of a group of islands, of which 12 are inhabited and seven are uninhabited. The uninhabited islands in the central and southern group are Battimaly, Tileangchong and Merore, Trak, Treis, Menchal and Kabna respectively. Inhabited islands include Kamorta and Nancowry, which form the central group; Car Nicobar, which belongs to the northern group; and Great Nicobar, the largest and the southernmost of all. Undulating landscapes and intervening valleys characterize the physiography of these islands. However,

Car Nicobar and Trinket are flat islands.

The Great Nicobar is hilly, and contains many fast-flowing streams. A few of the other islands have flat surfaces covered with coral. Great Nicobar rises to a height of 642m. It is isolated from the Nicobars and the Nancowries group by the Sombero channel.

The Ten Degree Channel (145 km wide) separates the Andamans from the Nicobars. The principal harbours in Andaman and Nicobar are Port Blair, Neil, Diglipur, Mayabandar and Rangat in the Andamans and Car Nicobar and Kamorta in the Nicobars. The Union Territory has a total of 572 islands and islets. To the extreme south of the Nicobars is Indira Point, the southernmost point of India.

Neighbouring States and Union territories: The Andaman and Nicobar Islands have no neighbouring states or union territories. They lie on the southeastern margins of the Bay of Bengal. Port Blair is connected to Kolkata and Chennai by air as well as by sea routes.

Major rivers: Alexendra, Dagmar and Galathea rivers (Great Nicobar) and Kalpong (North Andaman) are the perennial freshwater rivers in these islands.

Climate: The Andaman and Nicobar Islands enjoy warm, moist and tropical climate. The abundant rainfall and the presence of the sea prevent the islands from experiencing extremes of heat, though the amount of rainfall may vary from island to island. Humidity is high, and varies from 66 per cent to 85 per cent. The temperature ranges from 18°C to 34°C. The islands receive an average annual rainfall of about 3000mm from southwest and northeast monsoons, extending over a period of about eight months.

A reporting station was set up at Port Blair in 1868, in order to provide accurate meteorological data for shipping in the Bay of Bengal.

Flora and Fauna:

Flora: The Andaman and Nicobar Isalnds are covered with evergreen tropical rainforests containing some 2200 varieties of plants. Out of these, 200 are endemic and 1300 cannot be found in mainland India. North Andamans have wet evergreen forests that contain plenty of woody climbers. South Andaman forests have a luxuriant growth of orchids, ferns and other epiphytic vegetation, while the Middle Andamans mostly contain deciduous forests.

Evergreen forests are absent in north Nicobar, including Battimaly and Car Nicobar, but form the dominant vegetation in central and southern Nicobar. Grasslands, not found in the Andamans, are present in the Nicobar group, whereas deciduous forests common in Andamans, can hardly be found in the Nicobars.

This uncharacteristic forest coverage consists of different types, including the giant evergreen forest, the southern hilltop tropical evergreen forest, the wet bamboo brakes, the Andaman tropical evergreen forest, the Andaman semi-evergreen forests and the cane brakes.

Andaman forest is abundant in timber of more than 200 species. Of these, 30 varieties are considered to be commercial. Major commercial varieties are padauk (*Pterocarpus dalbergioides*), and gurjan. There are a few kinds of ornamental wood noted for their pronounced grain formation. These include silver grey, kokko, padauk, chooi and marble wood.

Fauna: The Andaman and Nicobar Islands have a rich variety of animal species. These include about 50 varieties of forest mammals, most of which have been brought in from outside. Rats constitute the largest group of animals (26 species), followed by 14 species of bat. The larger mammals include two endemic varieties of wild pig, the spotted deer, sambar, barking deer and elephants.

Other than mammals, there are more than 225 species of moths and butterflies in the Andaman and Nicobar islands. Shells, corals and fishes are also found in abundance.

History

The Andaman and Nicobar islands have been the home of aboriginals since prehistoric times. According to a British Survey conducted here in 1777, Negritos and Mongoloids occupied the Islands for many centuries, till people from outside arrived.

The history of these islands can be divided into four broad periods: British intrusion and settlement, the Japanese regime, and the post-independence period. In 1788, the Governor General of India, Lord Cornwallis, according to the recommendation of two of his navy officers, founded the British settlement in 1789 on Chatham Island near Port Cornwallis (which is now Port Blair, named after Lt. Reginald Blair who conducted a survey of the area in 1789).

After the Revolt of 1857, the British government wanted to establish a penal settlement here, which they did in 1858. Two hundred prisoners, mostly rebels from the Indian Army, were kept in a jail at Viper island, which had a jail, gallows, and areas for residence. This jail was later abandoned in favour of the Cellular Jail built at Port Blair in 1906.

During the Second World War, the Japanese occupied Andamans on 21 March 1942 and kept the region under their control till 1945. Many innocent people were killed by the Japanese, including the massacre at Humfreygunj. The Japanese occupation however made the Andamans self-sufficient, in terms of food production. On 30 December 1943, Subhash Chandra Bose hoisted the National Flag at Port Blair, making it the first instance during British rule in India. The Japanese finally surrendered to the South East Asia Command at Port Blair on 8 October 1945.

The Andaman and Nicobar Islands together with the rest of India became independent on 15 August 1947.

Culture

Two distinct native cultures dominate the Andaman and Nicobar Islands. One is that of the Negrito population, and the other is of the Mongoloid Nicobarese and Shompen. Both before and after independence, these cultures retained their separate identities.

The Onges of Negrito origin form the main aboriginal group in the Andamans. Their main occupations include honey collecting, fishing and food gathering and hunting. They are the only tribe who accept contact with people from outside the islands. Till 1998, the Jarwas remained hostile but now they voluntarily seek medical assistance.

In the Nicobars, the Shompens are the only aboriginals. They are averse to contact with people from outside the island. The largest group, the Nicobarese are probably a mixture of Malay, Mon, Shan and Burmese origins. They still engage in the barter system.

Fairs and Festivals: The noteworthy fairs and festivals in these islands include the Island Tourism Festival, Subhash Mela (organized to commemorate the birth anniversary of Subhash Chandra Bose) and Vivekananda Mela. Festivals like Panguni Uthiram and Pongal for the Tamils, Durga Puja for the Bengalis, and Onam for the Malayalis are also celebrated.

Economy, Agriculture and Industry

Economy: The net state domestic product at current prices for 2000–01 (new series) was Rs 872 crores (provisional). The per capita net state domestic product at current prices for 2000–01 (new series) was Rs 24,560 (provisional).

Minerals and industry: The main industry is fisheries which, the Union territory occupying a coastline of 1912 km, has potential for further development. More than 1100 species of fish are identified in these islands of which about 30 species are commercially exploited at present. The estimated annual exploited stock is around 1.6 lakh tonnes, while the level of exploitation is only 26,000 tonnes. Fish culture, fish processing and other industries like fish meal, fish pickling, and fish oil are encouraged.

Another important industry is tourism, with the islands coming up as major tourist attractions. This also generates large employment. The other industries include production of cane, bamboo, coir, coconut and rubber. Industries like boat building, automobile body building, electronics and packaging are also coming up. The mineral wealth is negligible.

Agriculture: Paddy is the main food crop of the Andaman Islands. About 50,000 hectares of land is cultivated. Areca nut and coconut are the main cash crops of the Nicobar group of islands. Fruits such as sapota, pineapple, mango, papaya, orange and root crops are also grown in these islands. Coffee, rubber and tapioca are also important. About 7,171 sq. km of the total area is under forest cover.

Power: Presently, diesel power generation meets the requirements of commercial and household establishments in the territory.

Education

Educational institutes: The Andaman and Nicobar Islands has a few colleges affiliated to the Pondicherry University, and two polytechnics—the Dr B.R. Ambedkar Government Polytechnic at Port Blair, and the Second Government Polytechnic at Port Blair.

Tourism

Major tourist attractions:

1. Andaman: Long Island, Neil Island, Mayabander, Rangat, Diglipur, Little Andaman Island, Cellular Jail, Sippighat Farm, National Memorial Museum, Ross Island, Andaman Water Sports Complex.

2. Nicobar: Car Nicobar, Katchal, Great Nicobar. Scuba-diving and snorkelling are added attractions here.

Airports: Port Blair, Car Nicobar.

National Parks:

Andaman district: Mahatma Gandhi Marine National Park (281.50 sq. km), Rani Jhansi Marine National Park (256.14 sq. km), Middle Button Island National Park (0.64 sq. km), Mount Harriet National Park (0.46 sq. km), North Button Island National Park (0.44 sq. km), Saddle Peak National Park (32.54 sq. km), South Button Island National Park (0.03 sq. km).

Nicobar district: Campbell Bay National Park (426.23 sq. km), Galathea National Park (110.00 sq. km).

Administration

Legislature: The territory is administered by a lieutenant governor, appointed by the President of India.

Judiciary: The Union territory of Andaman and Nicobar Islands is under the jurisdiction of the Calcutta High Court. The chief justice of the Calcutta High Court is V.S. Sirpurkar.

Districts:

District	Area (sq. km)	Population	Headquarters	Urban Agglomerations
Andaman	6,408	314,239	Port Blair	–
Nicobar	1,841	42,026	Car Nicobar	–

Chandigarh

Key Statistics

Capital: Chandigarh.
Area: 114 sq. km.
Population: Total: 900,635, Male: 506,938, Female: 393,697.
Population density: 7,902 per sq. km.
Sex ratio: 777 females per 1000 males.
Principal languages: Hindi, Punjabi, Tamil.
Literacy rates: Total: 81.9%, Male: 86.1%, Female: 76.5%.

Government

Administrator: Gen. (Retd) S.F. Rodrigues. He was sworn in on 16 November 2004.

Geography

Physical characteristics: Situated at the foot of the Shivalik Range, Chandigarh lies on the Indo-Gangetic plain. The Union territory is positioned between two seasonal hill torrents: the Patiali Rao and the Sukhna Choe.

The city of Chandigarh (area 56 sq. km) covers about half of the land area of the territory. It has the distinction of being the first planned city of independent India. The city, built in 47 rectangular sectors, has a modern infrastructure. No sector was given the unlucky number '13'. Every sector consists of shopping centres and marketplaces, and the sectors are interconnected by buses and auto- rickshaws. Most of the important government buildings are in Sector 1, in the northern part of the city, whereas the industrial areas are mainly located in the south-east.

Neighbouring States and Union territories:

States: Haryana, Punjab.

Major rivers: There are no major rivers.

Climate: Chandigarh has hot summers and cold winters. During summer, the maximum temperature goes up to 44°C, the temperature range being 37°C–44°C. In winter, the temperature is generally within 4°C–14°C. Chandigarh sees monsoon from July to September, with an average annual rainfall of 1110mm.

Flora and Fauna: The Union territory of Chandigarh has 3,245 hectares under forest area. These forest areas are mostly situated around Patiala ki Rao, Sukhna Choe and Sukhna Lake. On the outskirts of Chandigarh towards the hills, next to the village of Kansal, is a reserve forest. Another reserve forest, known as Nepli, is located at a short distance from Kansal forest, and has a variety of wild life including hyena, antelopes, jackals, nilgais, and hares.

History

After India attained independence in 1947, the province of Punjab was divided and its capital Lahore fell within the Pakistani borders. As a result, the Indian state of Punjab was left without a capital and the need to construct a new capital city was felt. In March 1948, a 114.59 sq. km tract of land at the foot of the Shivalik Hills was approved for the purpose. The chosen site was a tract of agricultural land marking the sites of 24 villages—one of which was called 'Chandigarh' since it had a temple dedicated to the goddess Chandi. The chosen site got its name from that village.

American town planner Albert Mayer was initially approached by the Government of Punjab to create the new capital. Though he showed a lot of initial interest and also conceived a master plan for the city, he could not continue with the project due to the death of Matthew Nowicki, an architect who was involved with Mayer in the execution of the plan. In 1950, renowned French architect Le Corbusier was selected to replace Mayer, which he successfully did, giving India its first 'planned' city. Other than Corbusier, the work was carried out by three other foreign architects—Maxwell Fry, his wife Jane Drew and Corbusier's cousin Pierre Jeanneret.

On 21 September 1953, the capital of Punjab was officially shifted to Chandigarh from Shimla, and President Dr Rajendra Prasad inaugurated the city on 7 October 1953. When Punjab was again divided in 1966, leading to the creation of Haryana, Chandigarh became the capital of both Punjab and Haryana. However, the city became a Union territory, administered by the Government of India, and Mani Majra town and some villages of Kharar tehsil of Ambala district were added to the city.

Culture

The city of Chandigarh has a cosmopolitan character. It is home to many painters and writers, and houses frequently held exhibitions and performances by musicians, dancers, singers and actors. The city also has many associations and halls devoted to the culture of other states. Numerous institutions in the city offer instruction in classical, folk and instrumental music. Chandigarh also has several noted potters, sculptors, photographers and graphic designers. Street theatre is quite popular in Chandigarh, and there are many active groups in the realm of theatre.

Fairs and festivals: Other than the traditional religious festivals, Chandigarh celebrates several unique festivals. The Festival of Gardens (initially called the Rose Festival) is one of the main cultural events in Chandigarh and attracts thousands of visitors. On April Fools' Day, poets from all over the country gather to take part in the 'Maha Moorkh Sammelan'. The other popular festivals are Baisakhi, the Mango Festival, Indo-Pak Mushaira, Teej, the Plaza Carnival, the Chrysanthemum Show and the Chandigarh Carnival.

Economy, Industry and Agriculture

Economy: The net state domestic product at current prices for 2001–02 was Rs 935 crores. The per capita net state domestic product at current prices for 2002–03 was Rs 52,795.

Minerals and industry: Chandigarh has about 15 medium and large-scale industrial units. These units mainly manufacture steel and wooden furniture, antibiotics, electric meters, electronic components and equipment, machine tools, soaps and detergents, biomedical equipment, tractor parts, cement pipes and tiles, washing machines, sports goods, plastic goods etc. These units employ close to 30,000 people. There are also about 20 major exporting units. The mineral wealth is negligible.

Agriculture: The agricultural produce in Chandigarh includes crops like wheat, maize and rice. Fruits like lemon, litchi, mango, orange, guava, pear, plum, grape and peach are also cultivated.

Power: In order to meet its power requirement, Chandigarh gets power from Central generation projects and neighbouring states.

Education

Educational institutes: Punjab University, Post Graduate Institute of Medical Education and Research, The Government Medical College , Punjab Engineering College, Chandigarh College of Architecture, The Government College of Art, Chandigarh College of Engineering and Polytechnic (The Central Polytechnic College), The Government Polytechnic for Women, Industrial Training Institute, The Government Central Crafts Institute for Women and the Food Craft Institute.

Tourism

Major tourist attractions: Government Museum and Art Gallery, Museum of the Evolution of Life, International Dolls Museum, Punjab Kala Kendra, The Rock Garden, Sukhna Lake, Zakir Rose Garden, Leisure Valley.

Airports: Chandigarh.

National Parks: There are no national parks. The Sukhna Lake Wildlife Sanctuary was established in 1986 and has an area of 25.42 sq. km.

Administration

Legislature: Chandigarh has no legislature; instead, it is administered by an administrator appointed by the President of India (under the provisions of Article 239 of the Constitution). The Parliament is directly responsible for legislating for Chandigarh, and administrative control of the Union territory rests with the Union ministry of home affairs.

Regarding policy matters concerning Chandigarh, the ministry receives advice from a committee constituted by the Union home minister.

Judiciary: The High Court of Punjab and Haryana is at Chandigarh. The chief justice is D.K. Jain.

Districts:

District	Area (sq. km)	Population	Headquarters	Urban Agglomerations
Chandigarh	114	900,635	Chandigarh	Chandigarh

Dadra and Nagar Haveli

Key Statistics

Capital: Silvassa.
Area: 491 sq. km.
Population: Total: 220,490, Male: 121,666, Female: 98,824.
Population density: 449 per sq. km.
Sex ratio: 812 females per 1000 males.
Principal languages: Gujarati, Hindi, Konkani.
Literacy rates: Total: 57.6%, Male: 71.2%, Female: 40.2%.

Government

Administrator: Arun Mathur.

Geography

Physical characteristics: Reaching elevations of about 305m in the northeast and east near the Western Ghats, the territory of Dadra and Nagar Haveli is hilly and undulating. The lowland areas are generally restricted to the central plains.

Neighbouring States and Union territories:
States: Maharashtra, Gujarat.

Union territories: Daman and Diu.

Major rivers: The Damanganga is the only navigable river in Dadra and Nagar Haveli. It flows through the territory towards Daman in the north-west.

Climate: From November to March, the climate is very pleasant in Dadra and Nagar Haveli. The region otherwise experiences hot summers with the average maximum temperature in May approaching 34°C. Most of the rainfall takes place between June and September, averaging about 3000mm annually.

Flora and Fauna:
Flora: Around 40 per cent of the total geographical area spread over 58 villages is covered with forests. Teak, khair, sisam, sadra and mahara constitute the main vegetation of the territory, of which teak and khair are the most predominant. Teak is the main source of timber, whereas a forest-based industry producing 'Katha' from khair wood helps the local economy.

History

The recorded history of Dadra and Nagar Haveli starts from the medieval period. A Rajput invader became the ruler of a small state called Ramnagar (which included Nagar Haveli in its territory) in AD 1262, by defeating the Koli chieftains of the area. The region continued to remain under Rajput rule till the mid-18th century, when it was conquered by the Marathas. In 1783, Nagar Haveli was ceded to the Portuguese, as compensation for a Portuguese vessel that the Maratha navy had destroyed. In 1785, Dadra was also acquired by the Portuguese. After the independence of India, Goan nationalists tried to break away from Portuguese control, and their first success was the possession of Dadra on 21 July 1954. Two weeks later, they also captured Nagar Haveli, and a pro-Indian administration was formed in Dadra and Nagar Haveli. On 1 June 1961, the administration requested accession to the Indian Union, and the government of India that had already acknowledged their induction to the union from the day of liberation, made it official on 11 August 1961.

Culture

The Dhol dance (incorporating aerobatics and rhythm), the Gheria dance of the Dubla tribe, the Mask dance or Bhavada, the Bohada mask dance performed by the Koknas and the human pyramid formations by the Tur dancers are some of the prominent dance forms.

Fairs and festivals: The Union territory of Dadra and Nagar Haveli normally celebrates all festivals of Hindus, Muslims and Christians, while the tribal communities celebrate their own festivals. The Dhodia and Varli tribes celebrate Diwaso, while the Dhodia tribe also celebrates Raksha Bandhan. The 'Gram Devi' and 'Khali Puja' are celebrated by all tribes before and after harvest respectively.

Economy, Industry and Agriculture

Economy: The net state domestic product at current prices is not available.

Minerals and industry: There was no industry in Dadra and Nagar Haveli before 1965–66, except for a few traditional craftsmen who made pots, leather items and some other items made of bamboo. It was only between 1967–68 that industrial development started on a low-key basis. An industrial estate was established under the cooperative sector by Dan Udyog Sahakari Sangh Ltd, after which three Government Industrial Estates were developed at Masat, Silvassa and Khadoli. As on March 2003, there were 1617 industries in the region including cottage, village and small scale industries, and 406 medium scale industries in engineering, textiles, electronics, pharmaceuticals and plastics.

Agriculture: Dadra and Nagar Haveli is mainly rural, with 79 per cent of its population consisting of tribals. There are about 22,850 hectares of area under cultivation. Paddy, small millets, pulses and ragi are the main crops, and the agricultural production is mainly dependent on rain, and mostly on a single crop system. Other than the main crops, additional crops like wheat, jowar, tuvr, sugar cane and oilseeds are also cultivated. Among vegetables, cauliflower, brinjal, tomato, and cabbage are grown. The tribals have been given exclusive rights for collection of minor forest produce for free, since they depend mainly on forests.

Power: The Central sector power generating stations located in the western region handle the power requirement of the territory.

Education

Educational institutes: Lions English School, Prabhat Scholar's Academy.

Tourism

Major tourist attractions: Khanvel; The Tribal Cultural Museum, Silvassa; Vanganga Lake.

Airports: None.

National Parks: There are no National Parks in Dadra and Nagar Haveli, and there is only one wildlife sanctuary—the Dadra and Nagar Haveli

Wildlife Sanctuary. It has an area of 92.16 sq. km and is located in the Dadra and Nagar Haveli district.

Administration

Legislature: An administrator, appointed by the Government of India, heads the Union territory.

Judiciary: Dadra and Nagar Haveli comes under the jurisdiction of the Bombay High Court. The chief justice of the Bombay High Court is Dalveer Bhandari.

Districts: There is only one district, which is Dadra and Nagar Haveli.

District	Area (sq. km)	Population	Headquarters	Urban Agglomerations
Dadra and Nagar Haveli	491	220,490	Silvassa	–

Daman and Diu

Key Statistics

Capital: Daman.

Area: 112 sq. km.

Population: Total: 158,204, Male: 92,512, Female: 65,692.

Population density: 1411 per sq. km.

Sex ratio: 710 females per 1000 males.

Principal languages: Gujarati, Hindi, Marathi.

Literacy rates: Total: 78.2%, Male: 86.8%, Female: 65.6%.

Government

Administrator: Arun Mathur.

Geography

Physical characteristics: Daman is situated on an alluvial coastal plain, even though headlands and low plateaus are created in the area due to outcrops of basalt. The area surrounding the town of Daman is traversed by River Damanganga which flows through the territory. A marshy creek separates the island of Diu from the Kathiawar Peninsula in Gujarat, though the territory of Diu also encompasses a small part of the mainland. The island is about 11 km long and 2 km wide.

Neighbouring States and Union territories:

States: Gujarat, Maharashtra.

Union territories: Dadra and Nagar Haveli.

Major rivers: Damanganga, Kalai and Kolak.

Climate: In Daman, the average daily maximum temperatures range from 29°C in January to 34°C in May, which is quite similar to that of Diu. However, Daman receives more rainfall than Diu; it averages 2000mm annually in Daman whereas Diu has an annual rainfall of about 585mm. The rainfall is mainly received between the months of June and September.

Flora and Fauna:

Flora: The flora of the island mainly consists of vegetation ranging from fuliflora, tortolis, acasias, palm trees (locally referred to as hokka), casuarina, equistifolia, procofis, and several groves of coconut palms.

Fauna: The island has different varieties of birds, including koels, doves, blue rock pigeons, parrots, crows and sparrows, making it a bird watchers' delight. A large number of migratory birds fly into the island from August and stay on until February, which constitutes a major attraction. The inland and the coastal waters are rich in fishes, especially hilsa, Bombay duck, shark, dara, prawns, and the popular pomfret.

History

The town of Daman possibly gets its name from the Damanganga River, whereas 'Diu' is derived from the Sanskrit word 'dvipa', which means 'island'. Daman, in the 13th century, formed part of the state of Ramnagar, which then became a tributary of the sultans of Gujarat. Diu was taken over by the sultan of Gujarat in the 15th century, which then had been ruled over by many dynasties of Kathiawar (Saurashtra). Both Daman and Diu were acquired by the Portuguese in order to control the trade of the Indian Ocean. The Portuguese in 1535 signed a treaty with Bahadur Shah of Gujarat in order to build a fort at Diu. Towards the middle of the 1550s, all Gujarati ships entering and leaving the Gulf of Khambhat (Cambay) ports were required to pay Portuguese duties at Diu. Daman was renowned for its shipbuilding yards and docks, and was conquered by the Portuguese in 1559. Daman and Diu were subject to the Governor General of Goa as part of the Portuguese province Estado da India (State of India). The Portugese ruled them for more than four centuries, and they remained as outposts of Portuguese overseas territory until December 1961, when 'Operation Vijay' was launched by India restoring Daman and Diu to India to make them an integral part of the country. It initially became part of the erstwhile Union territory of Goa, Daman and Diu, but became a separate Union territory once statehood was given to Goa on 30 May 1987.

Culture

Dance and music are a part of the daily life of the people of Daman. Different Portuguese dances are still widely prevalent and performed, and they reflect the distinct fusion of tribal, urban, European and Indian cultures.

Fairs and festivals: Some of the important festivals in Daman and Diu are Holi, Diwali, Bhai Duj, Raksha Bandhan, Id-ul-Fitr, Navratri, Moharram, Id-ul-Zuha, Carnival, Feast of St Francis Xavier, Good Friday and Easter.

Economy, Industry and Agriculture

Economy: The net state domestic product at current prices is not available.

Minerals and industry: Daman and Diu has 2707 small and medium-scale industries. Omnibus Industrial Development Corporation at Daman has developed two industrial areas. The other industrial areas are Kadaiya, Bhimpore, Kanchigam and Dabhel.

Agriculture: The important crops of Daman include rice, ragi (finger millet), beans and pulses (legumes); however, Diu only has 20 per cent of cultivated land area, and crops such as wheat and bajra (pearl millet) are more suited to the dry climate.

Power: The Central sector power stations in the western region have granted power allocation to the Union territory of Daman and Diu, with which all villages have been electrified.

Education

Educational institute: Daman Government Arts College.

Tourism

Major tourist attractions: Fort of Moti Daman, Jampore Beach, Kadaiya Lake Garden.

Airports: Daman, Diu.

National Parks: Though there are no National Parks here, it has a wildlife sanctuary—Fudam Wildlife Sanctuary (area 2.18 sq. km in Diu).

Administration

Legislature: Daman and Diu does not have a legislative assembly. They are each organized as administrative districts and the Government of India appoints an administrator to govern these districts.

Judiciary: The Union Territory of Daman and Diu is under the jurisdiction of the Bombay High Court. The chief justice is Dalveer Bhandari.

Districts:

District	Area (sq. km)	Population	Headquarters	Urban Agglomerations
Daman	72	113,949	Daman	–
Diu	40	44,110	Diu	–

Lakshadweep

Key Statistics

Capital: Kavaratti.

Area: 32 sq. km.

Population: Total: 60,650, Male: 31,131, Female: 29,519.

Population density: 1,894 per sq. km.

Sex ratio: 948 females per 1000 males.

Principal languages: Malayalam, Tamil, Hindi.

Literacy rates: Total: 86.7%, Male: 92.5%, Female: 80.5%.

Government

Administrator: Parimal Rai. He assumed charge on 22 November 2004.

Geography

Physical characteristics: Lakshadweep is an archipelago of 12 atolls, three reefs and five submerged banks. It lies scattered over 45,000 sq. km of the Indian Ocean. There are 27 coral islands—India's only coral islands. In all, there are 10 inhabited islands, 17 uninhabited islands with attached islets, four newly formed islets and five submerged reefs. The easternmost island lies about 300 km off the western coast of Kerala. Lakshadweep has a lagoon area of about 4,200 sq. km and territorial waters of 20,000 sq. km. Only 10 of the islands are inhabited. The 10 inhabited islands are Andrott, Amini, Agatti, Bitra, Chetlat, Kadmath, Kalpeni, Kavaratti, Kiltan and Minicoy. Bitra is the smallest of all, with a nominal population. The main islands are Kavaratti, Minicoy and Amini.

The Amindivis are the northernmost islands of the group and Minicoy Island the southernmost. The eastern sides of the islands are higher and hence more suitable for human habitation. The low-lying lagoons on the western sides protect the islanders from the south-west monsoon. None of the islands exceed 1.5 km in width. They have sandy soils, derived from corals.

Neighbouring States and Union territories: None. The Union Territory lies in the Indian Ocean with no land borders. However, Kerala is the closest state. Kochi in Kerala is the usual point of origin for scheduled ships and aircraft travelling to the state.

Major rivers: There are no major rivers.

Climate: Lakshadweep has a tropical climate. Summer temperatures range between 22°C and 35°C while winter temperature varies between 20°C and 32°C. The monsoon season is between October and November. Normal rainfall is around 1600mm in the Minicoy group of islands and 1500mm in the Amindivi group of islands.

Flora and Fauna:

Flora: Coconut is the only crop of economic importance in the Union territory. Different varieties of coconut found in Lakshadweep include Laccadive micro, Laccadive ordinary and green dwarf. Banana, vazha, breadfruit, chakka, colocassia, chambu, drumstick moringakkai and wild almond grow extensively in Lakshadweep. It is also home to shrub jungle plants like kanni, chavok, punna and cheerani. Two different varieties of sea grass are seen adjacent to the beaches. These prevent sea erosion and movement of the beach sediments.

Fauna: The seas around Lakshadweep are rich in marine life. Sharks, tuna, flying fish, devil ray, bonito, octopus, sail fish, turtles, sea cucumber and snapper are found here. Colourful coral fish such as butterfly fish, parrotfish and surgeonfish are also found in plenty. Oceanic birds are also found in Lakshadweep. These include tharathasi and karifetu. Other species of birds found in Lakshadweep include seagull, tern, teal, heron and water heron. Money cowry is widely found in the shallow lagoons and reefs. The hermit crab is commonly found.

History

It is commonly believed that Cheraman Perumal, the last king of Kerala, set up the first settlement on what is today Lakshadweep, after he was shipwrecked. However, there are historical records to show that a Muslim saint named Ubaidullah was shipwrecked around the 7th century and it was he who converted the inhabitants to Islam.

Control over the islands remained with the Hindu ruler of Chirakkal for some years, after which it passed on to the Muslim rulers of Arakkal, in Cannanore, around the middle of the 16th century. The oppressive nature of the Arakkal rule resulted in the islanders seeking refuge with

in 1783. Tipu Sultan was on friendly terms with the Beebi of Arakkal and the Amini islands passed into his control. After Tipu Sultan's defeat at the battle of Seringapattam in 1799, the British East India Company annexed the islands and administered them from Mangalore.

In 1847, a severe cyclone hit the island of Andrott. When the Raja of Chirakkal found it difficult to pay for the damages, the East India Company granted a loan. The Raja was however unable to repay the loan or the mounting interest and in 1854 all the remaining islands were handed over to the British, who administered the islands till India became independent in 1947. Till 1956, the islands were a part of the erstwhile Madras state. On 1 November 1956, the islands became a Union territory of the Indian Union. The headquarters of the administration was shifted from Kozhikode/Calicut in Kerala to Kavaratti Island in March 1964. Between 1956 and 1973, the territory was called Laccadive, Minicoy, and Amindivi Islands. In 1973, it was renamed Lakshadweep.

Culture

Most of the people on Lakshadweep are Muslims with a small number of Hindus. The commonly spoken languages include Mahl, similar to old Sinhalese. The Hindu society is characterized by the matrilineal system of kinship and a rigid caste system. The folklore and customs are largely derived from the sea. Kiltan Island has a rich tradition of folk dances, namely kolkali and parichakali. Other dance forms of the Union territory include Lava dance, Ulakamut, Bhandiya, Kottuvili, Oppana, Duff and Attam. Opana is a well-known form of music performed at marriages. The Union territory is noted for carpentry and woodcarving. A variety of handicrafts are also made out of material like tortoise-shell, coconut shell, coconut fibre and corals. However, picking of corals from their natural habitat is a punishable offence.

Fairs and festivals: Id-ul-Fitr, Bakrid, Muharram, Id-e-Milad-un-Nabi and Dussehra are important festivals of Lakshadweep.

Economy, Industry and Agriculture

Economy: Figures not available.

Minerals and industry: The two most important industries of the state revolve around the coconut plant and fishes. Extraction of coconut fibre and its conversion into fibre products is a main industry of Lakshadweep. There are many fibre factories, coir production-cum-demonstration centres and fibre curling units in different islands. Fishing is the other important industrial activity. The huge potential that Lakshadweep possesses in fishing has resulted in the setting up of boat-building yards, fish-processing factories and the adoption of mechanized fishing boats. Tourism is also a major industry.

Two handicraft training centres were established at Kavaratti and Kalpeni in 1973 and 1979 respectively. A hosiery factory was established in 1967 at Kalpeni.

Agriculture: Agriculture is the most important component of the economy of Lakshadweep. The key products are coconut and coir. Coconut is the Union territory's only major crop.

Power: Lakshadweep gets most of its power supply from diesel generating sets. There are a few solar power plants while wind power plants are also planned for the Union territory.

Education

There are no universities or major institute of higher education in the Union territory.

Tourism

Major tourist attractions: Lighthouse, Minicoy; Ujra Mosque, Kavaratti; Hazrat Ubaidullah, Andrott; Buddhist archaeological remains, Andrott; Water Sport Institute, Kadmat.

Airports: Agatti.

National Parks: None.

Administration

Legislature: The President of India appoints an administrator to govern the territory.

Judiciary: Lakshadweep is under the jurisdiction of the High Court of Kerala. The acting chief justice is K.S. Radhakrishnan.

Districts:

District	Area (sq. km)	Population	Headquarters	Urban Agglomerations
Lakshadweep	32	60,650	Kavaratti	–

Pondicherry

Key Statistics

Capital: Pondicherry.

Area: 492 sq. km.

Population: Total: 974,345, Male: 486,961, Female: 487,384.

Population density: 2029 per sq. km.

Sex ratio: 1001 females per 1000 males.

Principal languages: Tamil, Malayalam, Telugu.

Literacy rates: Total: 81.2%, Male: 88.6%, Female: 73.9%.

Government

Lieutenant Governor: Lt. Gen. (Retd.) M.M. Lakhera was sworn in on 3 June 2004.

Chief Minister: Thiru N. Rangasamy. He was sworn in on 27 October 2001.

Geography

Physical characteristics: The Union territory of Pondicherry has four constituent parts: Pondicherry, Karaikal, Mahe and Yanam. Podichery and Karaikal are bordering Tamil Nadu, Mahe is situated on the Malabar Coast surrounded by the state of Kerala and Yanam is surrounded by the East Godavari district of Andhra Pradesh.

A canal divides the town of Pondicherry into two parts. The main streets run parallel to one another. The port of Pondicherry does not have a harbour and ships are anchored at some distance offshore. The Pondicherry area has about 300 villages.

Karaikal lies on Coromandel Coast, about 300km south of Chennai, at a distance of about 135km from Pondicherry town. It is located near the mouth of River Arasalar, in the Kaveri delta. The Nagappattinam and Thiruvarur districts of Tamil Nadu surround Karaikal.

Mahe consists of two parts. The town of Mahe lies on the left bank of River Mahe near its mouth while the area called Naluthrara is on the right bank and consists of the villages of Chambara, Chalakara, Palour, and Pandaquel. Mahe town is situated 647km away from Pondicherry town, between Badagara and Thalassery.

The town of Yanam lies at the spot where River Koringa (Atreya) branches off from Gauthami into two parts, about 870km from Pondicherry town.

Neighbouring States and Union territories:
1. Karaikal
   States: Tamil Nadu.
2. Mahe
   States: Kerala.
3. Pondicherry
   States: Tamil Nadu.
4. Yanam
   States: Andhra Pradesh.

Major rivers: Arasalar (Karaikal), Mahe (Mahe), Koringa and Gauthami (Yanam).

Climate: Pondicherry has a hot and humid climate for most of the year. Temperature varies between 26°C and 38°C. It is mostly dry. The short monsoon season is between July and September. The months of May and June can be very humid. The summer is between March and July, when temperatures can touch 40°C and higher, mainly in May and June. On the west coast (Mahe), the monsoon season lasts between July and October. The winter usually starts in November, but sometime in mid-October, which is also when the north-east monsoon brings some rainfall. Temperatures remain in the region of 30°C.

Flora and Fauna:
Flora: The flora of Pondicherry can be listed under seven categories. These

are: hydrophytes (aquatic plants), halophytes (plants that grow in salty soil), plants on sand dunes, plants on sandstones, avenue trees, hedge plants and ornamental plants.

Hydrophytes or aquatic plants found in Pondicherry include the lotus, akasathamarai and vettiver. Halophytes found in the Union territory include muttaikkorai, sattaranai, thakkali, thumbai, kanavalai, mayil kondai pul, karisalankanni, tutti and gilugilupai. Plants on sand dunes occurring in Pondicherry include woody plants like casuarina and eucalyptus. They grow along the sea coast. This category of plants also includes some herbs. The vegetative landscape of Pondicherry comprises mostly tall palms.

The Union territory also possesses a limited variety of mangrove species, mainly in the estuaries and the riverine sides of Ariyankuppam river and Malattar. A mangrove patch is also present in Thengaithittu and Murthikuppam.

Another striking feature of the flora of Pondicherry is the sacred groves. Pondicherry does not have natural forest cover. However, there are patches of sacred groves. These may be termed as natural islands of vegetation that are maintained and preserved for centuries for a religious purpose. Such groves are usually looked after by the local communities. The distribution of species varies from grove to grove. Pondicherry is also home to some tropical dry evergreen species and some medicinal plants.

Fauna: The marine biodiversity of the Union territory include mackerel, shrimps, sardines, perches, ribbonfish and flying fish.

History

Remains of an ancient port town have been excavated at Arikamedu, 6 km from Pondicherry town. There are evidences here to suggest that it had trade connections with Rome and Greece around the period between 100 BC and AD 100. Pondicherry flourished during the Chola period, as indicated by the discovery of the Chola coins from the 11th and 12th centuries. Karaikal was also a part of the Chola empire but was successively occupied by the Vijayanagar, Marathas, Muslims and finally the French.

The history of modern Pondicherry starts with the arrival of the French in 1673, who ruled for most of the next 281 years. In 1674, the French East India Company established a settlement at Pondicherry. Mahe was founded in 1725, Yanam in 1731, and Karaikal in 1739.

Mahe was the site of prolonged conflict between the British and French troops in the 18th and 19th centuries. In 1726, the French captured the town. Later however, it was added several times to the British Madras Presidency. It was finally restored to the French in 1817.

Yanam was also a part of the Chola empire but came under Muslim occupation in the 16th century. In the 17th and 18th centuries it was the scene of conflict between Muslim, British, and French troops. When much of the coastal plain region that includes Yanam was incorporated into the Madras Presidency in 1765, Yanam remained a French enclave.

At the time of independence in 1947, the French restored Pondicherry, Mahe, Karaikal and Yanam to the Union of India. De facto transfer of these four French possessions to the Union of India took place on 1 November 1954 while de jure transfer took place on 28 May 1956. The instruments of ratification were signed on 16 August 1962.

Politics

With India becoming independent in August 1947, the citizens of French India hoisted the Indian national flag all over the French settlements. The Jaipur session of the Indian National Congress passed a resolution for the peaceful merger of Pondicherry with India. The Indo-French agreement of June 1948 was signed and the French gave freedom to the French Indian population to choose their political status by a referendum. While Chandannagar (another French colony) merged with India on the basis of referendum, Pondicherry could not enjoy that facility because of a different system and practice of elections. As per the understanding reached between the Government of India and France, the question of the merger of Pondicherry with the Indian Union was referred to the elected representatives of the people for decision in a secret ballot on 18 October 1954. 170 out of 178 elected representatives favoured the merger. This was the de facto transfer of power, which took place on 1 November 1954, while the de jure transfer took place on 16 August 1962. As the people aspired for a popular government, the parliament enacted the Government of Union Territories Act, 1963 which came into force on 1 July 1963, and the pattern of government prevailing in the rest of the country was introduced in Pondicherry, subject to certain limitations. The Congress has consistently won the elections in Pondicherry ever since the former French enclave became a part of the Indian Union. In the twelve elections held between 1962 and 1999, the Congress won nine times, the All India Anna Dravida Munnetra Kazhagam (AIADMK) twice and the DMK once.

Culture

There is a strong French influence in Pondicherry even today. Pondicherry was home to the famous poets, Subramania Bharathi and Bharathidasan. Pondicherry is also fa-

mous for the Aurobindo Ashram and Auroville. Pondicherry is well known for its handmade paper, the use of dried flowers on stationery items, aromatic candles and candles with pressed-in dried flowers. Incense sticks made at the Ashram and in Auroville are also famous.

Fairs and festivals: Festivals of Pondicherry are unique in the sense that the French influence still remains in its festivals and celebrations. The mask festival, Masquerade, is held in March–April. During this festival, the inhabitants wear costumes and masks and dance down the streets to accompanying music. On the eve of Bastille Day (14 July), retired soldiers parade in the streets singing the French and Indian national anthems. The Maasi Magam Festival is celebrated during the full moon period around mid-March. In Yanam, Vishnu Festival is celebrated in March. In March–April (first week after Easter), the Villianur Lourdes Festival is held. The Chitrai Kalai Vizha summer festival is held in April. The Villianur Temple Car Festival is usually celebrated around the middle of May but its exact date depends on the appearance of the full moon. During the Mangani Festival Karaikal experiences a month-long period of festivity that accompanies a feast dedicated to Karaikal Ammaiyar. The Virampattinam Car Festival takes place in August while the Fete de Pondicherry coincides with the Indian Independence Day. Other festivals celebrated in the Union territory are St Theresa Festival in Mahe and Isai Vizha, both celebrated in October.

Economy, Industry and Agriculture

Economy: The net state domestic product at current prices (new series) in 2002–03 (advance estimates) was Rs 3828 crores. The per capita state domestic product at current prices (new series) in 2002–03 (advance estimates) was Rs 38,162.

Minerals and industry: The significant industrial products of the Union territory include food products, cotton products, wood products, paper products, leather, rubber, plastic products, chemical and chemical products, non-metallic mineral products, metal products and machinery products. There are seven industrial estates in Pondicherry.

Agriculture: Around 35 per cent of the population is dependent on agriculture. Paddy is the most important crop in the territory, followed by pulses. Coconut, spices, condiments and areca nut are grown in Mahe while Yanam grows spices, chilli, pulses and groundnut.

Power: Pondicherry draws its power requirements from the southern grid. A gas-based power plant is being established at Karaikal.

Education

Educational institutes: Pondicherry University is at Pondicherry, Ecole Français d' Extrème Orient Institute for Indology, French Institute, Jawaharlal Institute of Post-graduate Medical Education and Research (JIPMER), Pondicherry Institute of Linguistics and Culture, Vinayaka Mission Medical College (Karaikal).

Tourism

Major tourist attractions:

1. Pondicherry: Auroville and Shri Aurobindo Ashram, Pondicherry Museum, Botanical Garden, Sri Gokilambal Thirukameswarar Temple, Mansion of Ananda Rangapillai, Eglise De Sacre Coeur De Jesus.

2. Karaikal: Lord Darbaraneswara Temple, Karaikal Ammaiyar Temple, Jadaayupureeswar Temple, Dargah of Mastan Syed Dawood, Our Lady Angel's Church.

3. Mahe: Tagore Park, St Theresa's Church, Puthalam, Othenan's Fort, St George Fort, Sree Krishna Temple, Choodikotta.

4. Yanam: Annavaram, Draksharamam, Padagaya Temple.

Airports: None.

National Parks: None.

Administration

Legislature: Pondicherry has a 30-seat legislative assembly of which five seats are reserved for SCs. The tenure of the current house expires on 8 June 2006. The present party position is as under:

Name of Party	Seats
Indian National Congress	11
Dravida Munnetra Khazagam	7
Pudhucherry Makkal Congress	4
All India Anna Dravida Munnetra Khazagam	3
Tamil Maanila Congress (Moopanar)	2
Bharatiya Janata Party	1
Independent	2
Total	**30**

Judiciary: Pondicherry falls under the jurisdiction of the Madras High Court. The chief justice is Thiru Markandey Katju.

Districts:

District	Area (sq. km)	Population	Headquarters	Urban Agglomerations
Karaikal	161.0	31,362	Karaikal	–
Mahe	9.0	36,823	Mahe	–
Pondicherry	290.0	735,004	Pondicherry	Pondicherry
Yanam	20.0	170,640	Yanam	–

Governors and Chief Ministers since Independence

Andhra Pradesh

1 Oct 1953	Andhra Part A State created from part of Madras
1 Nov 1956	Andhra Pradesh

Governors

1 Oct 1953–1 Aug 1957	Sir Chandulal Madhavlal Trivedi
1 Aug 1957–8 Sep 1962	Bhim Sen Sachar
8 Sep 1962–4 May 1964	Satyavant Mallannah Srinagesh
4 May 1964–11 Apr 1968	Pattom Thanu Pillai
11 Apr 1968–25 Jan 1975	Khandubhai Kasanji Desai
26 Jan 1975–10 Jan 1976	S. Obul Reddy
10 Jan 1976–16 Jun 1976	Mohan Lal Sukhadia
16 Jun 1976–17 Feb 1977	R.D. Bhandare
17 Feb 1977–5 May 1977	B.J. Diwan
5 May 1977–15 Aug 1978	Sharada Mukherjee
15 Aug 1978–15 Aug 1983	Kochakkan Chacko Abraham
15 Aug 1983–29 Aug 1984	Thakur Ram Lal
29 Aug 1984–26 Nov 1985	Shankar Dayal Sharma
26 Nov 1985–7 Feb 1990	Kumudben Joshi
7 Feb 1990–22 Aug 1997	Krishan Kant
22 Aug 1997–24 Nov 1997	Gopala Ramanujam
24 Nov 1997–3 Jan 2003	Chakravarti Rangarajan
3 Jan 2003–4 Nov 2004	Surjit Singh Barnala
4 Nov 2004–	Sushil Kumar Shinde

Chief Ministers

1 Oct 1953–15 Nov 1954	Tanguturi Prakasam
28 Mar 1955–1 Nov 1956	Bezawada Gopala Reddy
1 Nov 1956–11 Jan 1960	N. Sanjiva Reddy
11 Jan 1960–12 Mar 1962	Damodaram Sanjivayya
12 Mar 1962–29 Feb 1964	N. Sanjiva Reddy
29 Feb 1964–30 Sep 1971	Kasu Brahmananda Reddy
30 Sep 1971–10 Jan 1973	P.V. Narasimha Rao
10 Dec 1973–6 Mar 1978	Jalagam Vengala Rao
6 Mar 1978–11 Oct 1980	Marri Channa Reddy
11 Oct 1980–24 Feb 1982	Tanguturi Anjaiah
24 Feb 1982–20 Sep 1982	Bhavanam Venkatram
20 Sep 1982–9 Jan 1983	Kotla Vijaya Bhaskara Reddy
9 Jan 1983–16 Aug 1984	N.T. Rama Rao
16 Aug 1984–16 Sep 1984	N. Bhaskara Rao
16 Sep 1984–3 Dec 1989	N.T. Rama Rao
3 Dec 1989–17 Dec 1990	Marri Channa Reddy

17 Dec 1990–9 Oct 1992	N. Janardhan Reddy
9 Oct 1992–12 Dec 1994	Kotla Vijaya Bhaskara Reddy
12 Dec 1994–1 Sep 1995	N.T. Rama Rao
1 Sep 1995–14 May 2004	Nara Chandrababu Naidu
14 May 2004–	Y.S. Rajasekhara Reddy

Hyderabad

Chief Ministers

26 Jan 1950–6 Mar 1952	M.K. Vellodi
6 Mar 1952–31 Oct 1956	Burgula Ramakrishna Rao

Arunachal Pradesh

21 Jun 1972	Union territory created from part of Assam
20 Feb 1987	State

Lieutenant Governors

15 Aug 1975–18 Jan 1979	K.A.A. Raja
18 Jan 1979–23 Jul 1981	R.N. Haldipur
23 Jul 1981–10 Aug 1983	H.S. Dubey
10 Aug 1983–21 Nov 1985	Thanjavelu Rajeshwar
21 Nov 1985–20 Feb 1987	Shiva Swaroop

Governors

20 Feb 1987–19 Mar 1987	Bhishma Narain Singh (acting)
19 Mar 1987–17 Mar 1990	R.D. Pradhan
17 Mar 1990–9 May 1990	Gopal Singh (acting)
9 May 1990–17 Mar 1991	D.D. Thakur (acting)
17 Mar 1991–26 Mar 1991	Loknath Mishra (acting)
26 Mar 1991–5 Jul 1993	Surendra Nath Dwivedi
5 Jul 1993–21 Oct 1993	Madhukar Dighe (acting)
21 Oct 1993–17 May 1999	Mata Prasad
17 May 1999–2 Aug 1999	S.K. Sinha
2 Aug 1999–13 Jun 2003	Arvind Dave
13 Jun 2003–16 Dec 2004	Vinod Chandra Pande
16 Dec 2004–	S.K. Singh

Chief Ministers

13 Aug 1975–18 Sep 1979	Prem Khandu Thungon
18 Sep 1979–3 Nov 1979	Tomo Riba
18 Jan 1980–19 Jan 1999	Gegong Apang
19 Jan 1999–3 Aug 2003	Mukut Mithi
3 Aug 2003–	Gegong Apang

Assam

15 Aug 1947	Province
26 Jan 1950	State (until 1956: Part A)

Governors

15 Aug 1947–28 Dec 1948	Sir Akbar Hydari

30 Dec 1948–16 Feb 1949	Sir Ronald Francis Lodge (acting)
16 Feb 1949–27 May 1950	Sri Prakasa
27 May 1950–15 May 1956	Jairamdas Daulatram
15 May 1956–22 Aug 1959	Sir Saiyid Fazl Ali
23 Aug 1959–14 Oct 1959	Chandreswar Prasad
14 Oct 1959–12 Nov 1960	Satyavant Mallannah Srinagesh
12 Nov 1960–13 Jan 1961	Vishnu Sahay
13 Jan 1961–7 Sep 1962	Satyavant Mallannah Srinagesh
7 Sep 1962–17 Apr 1968	Vishnu Sahay
17 Apr 1968–19 Sep 1973	Braj Kumar Nehru
19 Sep 1973–10 Aug 1981	Lallan Prasad Singh
10 Aug 1981–28 Mar 1984	Prakash Chandra Mehrotra
28 Mar 1984–15 Apr 1984	T.S. Mishra
15 Apr 1985–10 May 1989	Bhishma Narain Singh
10 May 1989–21 Jul 1989	Harideo Joshi
21 Jul 1989–2 May 1990	Anisetti Roghuvir
2 May 1990–17 Mar 1991	D.D. Thakur
17 Mar 1991–1 Sep 1997	Loknath Mishra
1 Sep 1997–21 Apr 2003	S.K. Sinha
21 Apr 2003–5 Jun 2003	Arvind Dave
5 Jun 2003–	Ajai Singh

Chief Ministers

15 Aug 1947–6 Aug 1950	Gopinath Bardoloi
9 Aug 1950–28 Dec 1957	Bishnuram Medhi
28 Dec 1957–6 Nov 1970	Bimali Prasad Chaliha
11 Nov 1970–31 Jan 1972	Mahendra Mohan Choudhury
31 Jan 1972–12 Mar 1978	Sarat Chandra Sinha
12 Mar 1978–4 Sep 1979	Golap Borbora
9 Sep 1979–11 Dec 1979	Jogendra Nath Hazarika
12 Dec 1980–29 Jun 1981	Anwara Taimur
13 Jan 1982–19 Mar 1982	Keshav Chandra Gogoi
27 Feb 1983–24 Dec 1985	Hiteshwar Saikia
24 Dec 1985–27 Nov 1990	Prafulla Kumar Mahanta
30 Jun 1991–22 Apr 1996	Hiteshwar Saikia
22 Apr 1996–15 May 1996	Bhumidhar Barman
15 May 1996–18 May 2001	Prafulla Kumar Mahanta
18 May 2001–	Tarun Gogoi

Bihar

15 Aug 1947	Province
26 Jan 1950	State (until 1956: Part A)

Governors

1947	Jairamdas Daulatram
12 Jan 1948–16 Jun 1952	Madhavrao Srihari Aney
16 Jun 1952–1957	Ranganath Ramachandra Diwakar
1957–12 May 1962	Zakir Husain
12 May 1962–Dec 1967	M. Ananthasayanam Ayyangar
Dec 1967–1 Feb 1971	Nityanand Kanungo

1 Feb 1971–Feb 1973	Dev Kanta Borooah
1974–Jun 1976	R.D. Bhandare
Jun 1976–11 Sep 1979	Jagannath Kaushal
11 Sep 1979–1985	A.R. Kidwai
1985–Feb 1988	Pendekanti Venkatasubbaiah
Feb 1988–1989	Govind Narayan Singh
1989–Feb 1990	Jagannath Pahadia
Feb 1990–Feb 1991	Mohammad Yunus Saleem
Feb 1991–1991	B. Satyanarayan Reddy
1991–Aug 1993	Mohammed Shafi Qureshi
Aug 1993–Apr 1998	A.R. Kidwai
27 Apr 1998–15 Mar 1999	Sunder Singh Bhandari
15 Mar 1999–6 Oct 1999	Brij Mohan Lal (acting)
6 Oct 1999–23 Nov 1999	Suraj Bhan
23 Nov 1999–12 Jun 2003	Vinod Chandra Pande
12 Jun 2003–1 Nov 2004	M. Rama Jois
1 Nov 2004–5 Nov 2004	Ved Marwah
5 Nov 2004–	Buta Singh

Chief Ministers

15 Aug 1947–31 Jan 1961	Srikrishna Sinha
1 Feb 1961–18 Feb 1961	Deep Narayan Singh
18 Feb 1961–1 Oct 1963	Binodanand Jha
1 Oct 1963–5 Mar 1967	Krishna Ballabh Sahay
5 Mar 1967–28 Jan 1968	Mahamaya Prasad Sinha
28 Jan 1968–1 Feb 1968	Satish Prasad Sinha
1 Feb 1968–23 Feb 1968	Bindeyyeshwari Prasad Mandal
23 Feb 1968–29 Jun 1968	Bhola Paswan Shastri
29 Feb 1969–22 Jun 1969	Harihar Prasad Singh
22 Jun 1969–4 Jul 1969	Bhola Paswan Shastri
17 Feb 1970–22 Dec 1970	Daroga Prasad Rai
22 Dec 1970–2 Jun 1971	Karpoori Thakur
2 Jun 1971– 9 Jan 1972	Bhola Paswan Shastri
19 Mar 1972–2 Jul 1973	Kedar Pandey
2 Jul 1973–11 Apr 1975	Abdul Ghafoor
11 Apr 1975–30 Apr 1977	Jagannath Mishra
24 Jun 1977–21 Apr 1979	Karpoori Thakur
21 Apr 1979–17 Feb 1980	Ram Sundar Das
8 Jun 1980–14 Aug 1983	Jagannath Mishra
14 Aug 1983–25 Mar 1985	Chandra Shekhar Singh
25 Mar 1985–14 Feb 1988	Bindeshwari Dubey
14 Feb 1988–11 Mar 1989	Bhagwat Jha Azad
11 Mar 1989–6 Dec 1989	Satyendra Narain Sinha
6 Dec 1989–10 Mar 1990	Jagannath Mishra
10 Mar 1990–28 Mar 1995	Laloo Prasad Yadav
4 Apr 1995–25 Jul 1997	Laloo Prasad Yadav
25 Jul 1997–12 Feb 1999	Rabri Devi
9 Mar 1999–3 Mar 2000	Rabri Devi
3 Mar 2000–10 Mar 2000	Nitish Kumar
10 Mar 2000–7 Mar 2005	Rabri Devi

Chhattisgarh

15 Aug 1947	Province
1 Jan 1948	Part of Central Provinces and Berar (later Madhya Pradesh)
1 Nov 2000	State

Chief Commissioner

1947–1 Jan 1948	S.N. Mehta

Governors

1 Nov 2000–2 Jun 2003	Dinesh Nandan Sahay
2 Jun 2003–	Krishna Mohan Seth

Chief Ministers

1 Nov 2000–7 Dec 2003	Ajit Jogi
7 Dec 2003–	Raman Singh

Goa

16 Mar 1962	Goa, Daman and Diu union territory (formerly Portuguese India)
30 May 1987	Split into Goa state and Daman and Diu Union territory

Lieutenant Governors

7 Jun 1962–2 Sep 1963	Tumkur Sivasankar
2 Sep 1963–8 Dec 1964	M.R. Sachdev
12 Dec 1964–24 Feb 1965	Hari Sharma
24 Feb 1965–18 Apr 1967	Kashinath Raghunath Damle
18 Apr 1967–16 Nov 1972	Nakul Sen
16 Nov 1972–16 Nov 1977	S.K. Banerjee
16 Nov 1977–31 Mar 1981	Pratap Singh Gill
31 Mar 1981–30 Aug 1982	Jagmohan
30 Aug 1982–24 Feb 1983	Idris Hasan Latif
24 Feb 1983–4 Jul 1984	Kershasp Tehmurasp Satarawala
4 Jul 1984–24 Sep 1984	Idris Hasan Latif (acting)
24 Sep 1984–29 May 1987	Gopal Singh

Governors

30 May 1987–18 Jul 1989	Gopal Singh
18 Jul 1989–18 Mar 1991	Khurshed Alam Khan
18 Mar 1991–4 Apr 1994	Bhanu Prakash Singh
4 Apr 1994–4 Aug 1994	B. Rachaiah
4 Aug 1994–16 Jun 1995	Gopala Ramanujam
16 Jun 1995–19 Jul 1996	Romesh Bhandari
19 Jul 1996–16 Jan 1998	P.C. Alexander
16 Jan 1998–19 Apr 1998	Tumkur Ramaiya Satish Chandran
19 Apr 1998–26 Nov 1999	J.F.R. Jacob
26 Nov 1999–26 Oct 2002	Mohammed Fazal
26 Oct 2002–2 Jul 2004	Kidar Nath Sahani

2 Jul 2004–17 Jul 2004	Mohammed Fazal
17 Jul 2004–	S.C. Jamir

Chief Ministers

8 Jun 1962–2 Dec 1966	Dayanand B. Bandodkar
5 Apr 1967–12 Aug 1973	Dayanand B. Bandodkar
12 Aug 1973–27 Apr 1979	Shashikala G. Kakodkar
16 Jan 1980–27 Mar 1990	Pratapsing Rane
27 Mar 1990–14 Apr 1990	Churchill Braz Alemao
14 Apr 1990–14 Dec 1990	Luis Proto Barbosa
25 Jan 1991–18 May 1993	Ravi Naik
18 May 1993–2 Apr 1994	Wilfred D'Souza
2 Apr 1994–8 Apr 1994	Ravi Naik
8 Apr 1994–16 Dec 1994	Wilfred D'Souza
16 Dec 1994–30 Jul 1998	Pratapsing Rane
30 Jul 1998–26 Nov 1998	Wilfred D'Souza
26 Nov 1998–9 Feb 1999	Luizinho Faleiro
9 Jun 1999–24 Nov 1999	Luizinho Faleiro
24 Nov 1999–24 Oct 2000	Francisco Sardinha
24 Oct 2000–2 Feb 2005	Manohar Parrikar
2 Feb 2005–4 Mar 2005	Pratapsing Rane
7 Jun 2005–	Pratapsing Rane

Gujarat

1 May 1960	State crated from part of Bombay (see Maharashtra)

Governors

1 May 1960–1 Aug 1965	Mehdi Nawaz Jung
1 Aug 1965–7 Dec 1967	Nityanand Kanungo
7 Dec 1967–26 Dec 1967	P.N. Bhagwati (acting)
26 Dec 1967–17 Mar 1973	Shriman Narayan
17 Mar 1973–4 Apr 1973	P.N. Bhagwati (acting)
4 Apr 1973–14 Aug 1978	Kambanthodath Kunhan Vishwanatham
14 Aug 1978–6 Aug 1983	Sharada Mukherjee
6 Aug 1983–26 Apr 1984	Kizhekethil Mathew Chandy
26 Apr 1984–26 Feb 1986	Braj Kumar Nehru
26 Feb 1986–2 May 1990	Ram Krishna Trivedi
2 May 1990–21 Dec 1990	Mahipal Shastri
21 Dec 1990–1 Jul 1995	Sarup Singh
1 Jul 1995–1 Mar 1996	Naresh Chandra
1 Mar 1996–25 Apr 1998	Krishna Pal Singh
25 Apr 1998–16 Jan 1999	Anshuman Singh
16 Jan 1999–18 Mar 1999	K.G. Balakrishnan (acting)
18 Mar 1999–7 May 2003	Sunder Singh Bhandari
7 May 2003–2 Jul 2004	Kailashpati Mishra
2 Jul 2004–24 Jul 2004	Balram Jakhar
24 Jul 2004–	Nawal Kishore Sharma

Chief Ministers

1 May 1960–18 Sep 1963	Jivraj Mehta
18 Sep 1963–19 Sep 1965	Balwantrai Mehta

1 Oct 1965–13 May 1971	Hitendra Kanaiyalal Desai
17 Mar 1972–20 Jul 1973	Ghanshyam Oza
20 Jul 1973–9 Feb 1974	Chimanbhai Patel
18 Jun 1975–12 Mar 1976	Babubhai Jashbhai Patel
24 Dec 1976–11 Apr 1977	Madhavsinh Solanki
11 Apr 1977–17 Feb 1980	Babubhai Jashbhai Patel
7 Jun 1980–6 Aug 1985	Madhavsinh Solanki
6 Aug 1985–10 Dec 1989	Amarsinh Chaudhary
10 Dec 1989–4 Mar 1990	Madhavsinh Solanki
4 Mar 1990–17 Feb 1994	Chimanbhai Patel
17 Feb 1994–14 Mar 1995	Chhabildas Mehta
14 Mar 1995–21 Oct 1995	Keshubhai Patel
21 Oct 1995–19 Sep 1996	Suresh Chandra Mehta
23 Oct 1996–28 Oct 1997	Shankersinh Vaghela
28 Oct 1997–4 Mar 1998	Dilip Parikh
4 Mar 1998–7 Oct 2001	Keshubhai Patel
7 Oct 2001–	Narendra Modi

Saurashtra

Chief Ministers

1948–1954	Uchharangray Navalshankar Dhebar
19 Dec 1954–1956	Rasiklal Umedchand Parikh

Haryana

1 Nov 1966	State created from part of Punjab

Governors

1 Nov 1966–15 Sep 1967	Dharma Vira
15 Sep 1967–27 Mar 1976	Birendra Narayan Chhakravarti
27 Mar 1976–14 Aug 1976	Ranjit Singh Narula
14 Aug 1976–24 Sep 1977	Jaisukh Lal Hathi
24 Sep 1977–10 Dec 1979	Harcharan Singh Brar
10 Dec 1979–28 Feb 1980	S.S. Sandhawalia
28 Feb 1980–14 Jun 1984	Ganpatrao Devji Tapase
14 Jun 1984–22 Feb 1988	S.M.H. Burney
22 Feb 1988–7 Feb 1990	Hara Anand Barari
7 Feb 1990–14 Jun 1995	Dhanik Lal Mandal
14 Jun 1995–19 Jun 2000	Mahabir Prasad
19 Jun 2000–2 Jul 2004	Babu Parmanand
2 Jul 2004–7 Jul 2004	Om Prakash Verma
7 Jul 2004–	A.R. Kidwai

Chief Ministers

1 Nov 1966–24 Mar 1967	Bhagwat Dayal Sharma
24 Mar 1967–21 Nov 1967	Rao Birendra Singh
21 May 1968–7 Dec 1975	Bansi Lal
7 Dec 1975–21 May 1977	Banarsi Das Gupta
21 May 1977–28 Jun 1979	Devi Lal
28 Jun 1979–5 Jul 1985	Bhajan Lal
5 Jul 1985–19 Jun 1987	Bansi Lal

17 Jul 1987–2 Dec 1989	Devi Lal
2 Dec 1989–22 May 1990	Om Prakash Chautala
22 May 1990–12 Jul 1990	Banarsi Das Gupta
12 Jul 1990–17 Jul 1990	Om Prakash Chautala
17 Jul 1990–22 Mar 1991	Hukam Singh
22 Mar 1991–6 Apr 1991	Om Prakash Chautala
23 Jul 1991–11 May 1996	Bhajan Lal
11 May 1996–24 Jul 1999	Bansi Lal
24 Jul 1999–5 Mar 2005	Om Prakash Chautala
5 Mar 2005–	Bhupinder Singh Hooda

Himachal Pradesh

15 Apr 1948	Province
26 Jan 1950	Part C state
1 Nov 1956	Union territory
25 Jan 1971	State

Chief Commissioners

Apr 1948–1951	E.P. Menon
1951–1952	Bhagwan Sahay

Lieutenant Governors

1 Mar 1952–1 Jan 1955	M.S. Himmatsinhji
1 Jan 1955–14 Aug 1963	Bajrang Bahadur Singh Bhadri
14 Aug 1963–26 Feb 1966	Bhagwan Sahay
26 Feb 1966–7 May 1967	Venkata Vishwanathan
7 May 1967–16 May 1967	Om Prakash
16 May 1967–25 Jan 1971	Kanwar Bahadur Singh

Governors

25 Jan 1971–17 Feb 1977	Subramaniam Chhakravarti
17 Feb 1977–26 Aug 1981	Aminuddin Ahmad Khan
26 Aug 1981–16 Apr 1983	Asoka Nath Banerji
16 Apr 1983–8 Mar 1986	Hokishe Sema
8 Mar 1986–17 Apr 1986	Prabodh Dinkarrao Desai (acting)
17 Apr 1986–16 Feb 1990	Rustom Khusro Shampoorjee Gandhi
16 Feb 1990–20 Dec 1990	B. Rachaiah
20 Dec 1990–30 Jan 1993	Virendra Verma
30 Jan 1993–11 Feb 1993	Surendra Nath
11 Feb 1993–30 Jun 1993	Bali Ram Bhagat
30 Jun 1993–27 Nov 1993	Gulsher Ahmed
27 Nov 1993–10 Jul 1994	Surendra Nath
10 Jul 1994–30 Jul 1994	Viswanathan Ratnam
30 Jul 1994–18 Sep 1995	Sudhakarrao Naik
18 Sep 1995–17 Nov 1995	Mahabir Prasad
17 Nov 1995–23 Apr 1996	Sheila Kaul
23 Apr 1996–26 Jul 1997	Mahabir Prasad
26 Jul 1997–2 Dec 1999	V.S. Rama Devi
2 Dec 1999–24 Nov 2000	Vishnu Kant Shastri
24 Nov 2000–8 May 2003	Suraj Bhan
8 May 2003–	Vishnu Sadashiv Kokje

Chief Ministers

8 Mar 1952–1956	Yashwant Singh Parmar
1 Jul 1963–28 Jan 1977	Yashwant Singh Parmar
28 Jan 1977–22 Jun 1977	Ram Lal Chauhan
22 Jun 1977–14 Feb 1980	Shanta Kumar
14 Feb 1980–8 Apr 1983	Thakur Ram Lal
8 Apr 1983–5 Mar 1990	Virbhadra Singh
5 Mar 1990–3 Dec 1993	Shanta Kumar
3 Dec 1993–24 Mar 1998	Virbhadra Singh
24 Mar 1998–6 Mar 2003	Prem Kumar Dhumal
6 Mar 2003– Virbhadra Singh	

Jammu & Kashmir

Governors

30 Mar 1965–15 May 1967	Karan Singh
15 May 1967–3 Jul 1973	Bhagwan Sahay
3 Jul 1973–22 Feb 1981	Lakshmi Kant Jha
22 Feb 1981–26 Apr 1984	Braj Kumar Nehru
26 Apr 1984–Jul 1989	Jagmohan
Jul 1989–19 Jan 1990	K.V. Krishna Rao
19 Jan 1990–26 May 1990	Jagmohan
26 May 1990–12 Mar 1993	Girish Chandra Saxena
12 Mar 1993–2 May 1998	K.V. Krishna Rao
2 May 1998–4 Jun 2003	Girish Chandra Saxena
4 Jun 2003–	S.K. Sinha

Prime Ministers

11 Aug 1947–15 Oct 1947	Janak Singh (acting)
15 Oct 1947–5 Mar 1948	Meher Chand Mahajan
5 Mar 1948–9 Aug 1953	Sheikh Mohammad Abdullah
9 Aug 1953–12 Oct 1963	Bakshi Ghulam Mohammad
12 Oct 1963–29 Feb 1964	Khwaja Shams-ud-Din
29 Feb 1964–30 Mar 1965	Ghulam Mohammad Sadiq

Chief Ministers

30 Mar 1965–12 Dec 1971	Ghulam Mohammad Sadiq
12 Dec 1971–25 Feb 1975	Syed Mir Qasim
25 Feb 1975–26 Mar 1977	Sheikh Mohammad Abdullah
9 Jul 1977–8 Sep 1982	Sheikh Mohammad Abdullah
8 Sep 1982–2 Jul 1984	Farooq Abdullah
2 Jul 1984–6 Mar 1986	Ghulam Mohammad Shah
7 Nov 1986–19 Jan 1990	Farooq Abdullah
9 Oct 1996–18 Oct 2002	Farooq Abdullah
2 Nov 2002–	Mufti Mohammad Sayeed

Jharkhand

15 Nov 2000	State created from part of Bihar

Governors

15 Nov 2000–1 Feb 2002	Prabhat Kumar
1 Feb 2002–15 Jul 2002	Vinod Chandra Pande
15 Jul 2002–12 Jun 2003	M. Rama Jois
12 Jun 2003–10 Dec 2004	Ved Marwah
10 Dec 2004–	Syed Sibtey Razi

Chief Ministers

15 Nov 2000–18 Mar 2003	Babulal Marandi
18 Mar 2003–2 Mar 2005	Arjun Munda
2 Mar 2005–12 Mar 2005	Shibu Soren
12 Mar 2005–	Arjun Munda

Karnataka

15 Aug 1947	Mysore state (1950–56: part B)
1 Nov 1973	Renamed Karnataka

Rajpramukh

1947–1 Nov 1956	Jayachamarajendra Wodeyar

Governors

1 Nov 1956–4 May 1964	Jayachamarajendra Wodeyar
4 May 1964–2 Apr 1965	Satyavant Mallannah Srinagesh
2 Apr 1965–13 May 1967	Varahagiri Venkata Giri
13 May 1967–30 Aug 1969	Gopal Swarup Pathak
23 Oct 1969–1 Feb 1972	Dharma Vira
1 Feb 1972–10 Jan 1976	Mohan Lal Sukhadia
10 Jan 1976–2 Aug 1977	Uma Shankar Dikshit
2 Aug 1977–15 Apr 1983	Govind Narain Singh
16 Apr 1983–25 Feb 1988	Asoka Nath Banerji
26 Feb 1988–5 Feb 1990	Pendekanti Venkatasubbaiah
8 May 1990–6 Jan 1991	Bhanu Pratap Singh
6 Jan 1991–2 Dec 1999	Khurshed Alam Khan
2 Dec 1999–21 Aug 2002	V.S. Rama Devi
21 Aug 2002–	T.N. Chaturvedi

Chief Ministers

1946–25 Oct 1947	Arcot Ramaswami Mudaliar
25 Oct 1947–30 Mar 1952	Kysasambally Chengalaraya Reddy
30 Mar 1952–19 Aug 1956	Kengal Hanumanthaiah
19 Aug 1956– 1 Nov 1956	Kadidal Manjappa
1 Nov 1956–16 May 1958	Siddhavvanahalli Nijalingappa
16 May 1958– 9 Mar 1962	Basappa Danappa Jatti
14 Mar 1962–21 Jun 1962	Shivalingappa Rudrappa Kanthi
21 Jun 1962–3 Mar 1967	Siddhavvanahalli Nijalingappa
29 May 1968–27 Mar 1971	Veerendra Patil
20 Mar 1972–31 Dec 1977	Devaraj Urs
28 Feb 1978–12 Jan 1980	Devaraj Urs
12 Jan 1980–10 Jan 1983	R. Gundu Rao
10 Jan 1983–13 Aug 1988	Ramakrishna Hegde
13 Aug 1988–21 Apr 1989	Somappa R. Bommai

30 Nov 1989–10 Oct 1990	Veerendra Patil
17 Oct 1990–20 Nov 1992	S. Bangarappa
20 Nov 1992–11 Dec 1994	M. Veerappa Moily
11 Dec 1994–31 May 1996	H.D. Deve Gowda
31 May 1996–11 Oct 1999	Jayadevappa Halappa Patel
11 Oct 1999–28 May 2004	S.M. Krishna
28 May 2004–	Dharam Singh

Coorg

Chief Minister

17 Mar 1952–1956	Cheppudira Muthana Poonacha

Kerala

1 Jul 1949	Travancore-Cochin state formed (from 1950: Part B)
1 Nov 1956	Kerala state

Rajpramukh

1 Jul 1949–31 Oct 1956	Sir Bala Rama Varma II

Governors

22 Nov 1956–1 Jul 1960	Burgula Ramakrishna Rao
1 Jul 1960–2 Apr 1965	Varahagiri Venkata Giri
2 Apr 1965–6 Feb 1966	Ajit Prasad Jain
6 Feb 1966–15 May 1967	Bhagwan Sahay
15 May 1967–1 Apr 1973	Venkata Vishwanathan
1 Apr 1973–14 Oct 1977	Niranja Nath Wanchoo
14 Oct 1977–27 Oct 1982	Jyoti Venkatachalam
27 Oct 1982–23 Feb 1988	Parthasarathy Ramachandran
23 Feb 1988–12 Feb 1990	Ram Dulari Sinha
12 Feb 1990–20 Dec 1990	Sarup Singh
20 Dec 1990–12 Nov 1995	B. Rachaiah
12 Nov 1995–4 May 1996	P. Shiv Shanker
4 May 1996–25 Jan 1997	Khurshed Alam Khan
25 Jan 1997–18 Apr 2002	Sukhdev Singh Kang
18 Apr 2002–23 Feb 2004	Sikander Bakht
25 Feb 2004–23 Jun 2004	T.N. Chaturvedi
23 Jun 2004–	Raghunandan Lal Bhatia

Chief Ministers (of Travancore to 1 Jul 1949)

24 Mar 1948–20 Oct 1948	Pattom Thanu Pillai
20 Oct 1948– Jan 1951	T.K. Narayan Pillai
Jan 1951–12 Mar 1952	C. Kesavan
12 Mar 1952–16 Mar 1954	Anapparambul Joseph John
16 Mar 1954–10 Feb 1955	Pattom Thanu Pillai
10 Feb 1955–23 Mar 1956	Panampilly Govinda Menon
5 Apr 1957–31 Jul 1959	E.M. Sankaran Namboodiripad
22 Feb 1960–25 Sep 1962	Pattom Thanu Pillai
25 Sep 1962– 9 Sep 1964	R. Sankar
5 Mar 1967– 1 Nov 1969	E.M. Sankaran Namboodiripad
1 Nov 1969– 4 Aug 1970	C. Achutha Menon

4 Oct 1970–11 Apr 1977	C. Achutha Menon
11 Apr 1977–25 Apr 1977	K. Karunakaran
25 Apr 1977–29 Oct 1978	A.K. Antony
29 Oct 1978–12 Oct 1979	P.K. Vasudevan Nair
12 Oct 1979– 5 Dec 1979	C.H. Mohammed Koya
25 Jan 1980–20 Oct 1981	E.K. Nayanar
28 Dec 1981–17 Mar 1982	K. Karunakaran
24 May 1982–25 Mar 1987	K. Karunakaran
25 Mar 1987–24 Jun 1991	E.K. Nayanar
24 Jun 1991–22 Mar 1995	K. Karunakaran
22 Mar 1995–20 May 1996	A.K. Antony
20 May 1996–18 May 2001	E.K. Nayanar
18 May 2001–31 Aug 2004	A.K. Antony
31 Aug 2004–	Oommen Chandy

Madhya Pradesh

15 Aug 1947	Central Province and Berar
26 Jan 1950	Madhya Pradesh state (until 1956: Part A)

Governors

1947–1952	Mangaldas Mancharam Pakvasa
1952–14 Jun 1957	B. Pattabhi Sitaramayya
14 Jun 1957–11 Feb 1965	Hari Vinayaha Pataskar
11 Feb 1965–8 Mar 1971	Kysasambally Chengalaraya Reddy
8 Mar 1971–14 Oct 1977	Satya Narayan Sinha
14 Oct 1977–17 Aug 1978	Niranja Nath Wanchoo
17 Aug 1978–30 Apr 1980	Cheppudira Muthana Poonacha
30 Apr 1980–15 May 1984	Bhagwat Dayal Sharma
15 May 1984–31 Mar 1989	Kizhekethil Mathew Chandy
31 Mar 1989–6 Feb 1990	Serla Grewal
6 Feb 1990–24 Jun 1993	Kunwar Mahmood Ali Khan
24 Jun 1993–22 Apr 1998	Mohammed Shafi Qureshi
22 Apr 1998–7 May 2003	Bhai Mahavir
7 May 2003–1 May 2004	Ram Prakash Gupta
2 May 2004–30 Jun 2004	Krishna Mohan Seth
30 Jun 2004–	Balram Jakhar

Chief Ministers

15 Aug 1947–31 Dec 1956	Ravi Shankar Shukla
1 Jan 1957–31 Jan 1957	Bhagwantrao Mandloi
31 Jan 1957–11 Mar 1962	Kailash Nathi Katju
11 Mar 1962–30 Sep 1963	Bhagwantrao Mandloi
30 Sep 1963–30 Jul 1967	Dwarka Prasad Mishra
30 Jul 1967–13 Mar 1969	Govind Narayan Singh
13 Mar 1969–26 Mar 1969	Raja Naresh Chandra Singh
26 Mar 1969–29 Jan 1972	Shyama Charan Shukla
29 Jan 1972–23 Dec 1975	Prakash Chandra Sethi
23 Dec 1975–29 Apr 1977	Shyama Charan Shukla
26 Jun 1977–18 Jan 1978	Kailash Chandra Joshi
18 Jan 1978–20 Jan 1980	Virendra Kumar Saklecha
20 Jan 1980–17 Feb 1980	Sunderlal Patwa

9 Jun 1980–14 Mar 1985	Arjun Singh
14 Mar 1985–14 Feb 1988	Motilal Vora
14 Feb 1988–25 Jan 1989	Arjun Singh
25 Jan 1989– 9 Dec 1989	Motilal Vora
9 Dec 1989– 5 Mar 1990	Shyama Charan Shukla
5 Mar 1990–15 Dec 1992	Sunderlal Patwa
7 Dec 1993–8 Dec 2003	Digvijay Singh
8 Dec 2003–23 Aug 2004	Uma Bharti
23 Aug 2004–	Babulal Gaur

Madhya Bharat

Chief Ministers

Jan 1948– May 1949	Lilasthar Joshi
May 1949–18 Oct 1950	Gopikrishnan Vijayavargiya
18 Oct 1950–3 Mar 1952	Takhatmal Jain
3 Mar 1952–16 Apr 1955	Mishrilal Gangwal
16 Apr 1955–31 Oct 1956	Takhatmal Jain

Bhopal

Chief Ministers

Apr 1948–Jan 1949	Oudhnarain Bisatya
Jan 1949–1952	Pandit Chatur Narain Malviya
1952–1956	Shankar Dayal Sharma

Vindhya Pradesh

Chief Ministers

1948–1949	Awadesh Pratap Singh
13 Mar 1952–31 Oct 1956	Shambhunath Shukla

Maharashtra

15 Aug 1947	Bombay province
26 Jan 1950	State (unitl 1956: Part A)
1 May 1960	Divided into Maharashtra and Gujarat

Governors

15 Aug 1947–6 Jan 1948	David John Colville, Baron Clydesmuir
Jan 1948–30 May 1952	Raja Maharaj Singh
30 May 1952–5 Dec 1954	Sir Girja Shankar Bajpai
5 Dec 1954–1 Mar 1955	Mangaldas Mancharam Pakvasa
1 Mar 1955–14 Oct 1956	Harekrushna Mahatab
14 Oct 1956–10 Dec 1956	Mohomedali Currim Chagla
10 Dec 1956–16 Apr 1962	Sri Prakasa
16 Apr 1962–6 Oct 1962	P. Subbarayan
6 Oct 1962–5 Dec 1962	H.K. Chainani
5 Dec 1962–5 Sep 1963	Vijaya Lakshmi Pandit
5 Sep 1963–18 Dec 1963	H.K. Chainani
18 Dec 1963–8 Oct 1964	Vijaya Lakshmi Pandit
8 Oct 1964–14 Nov 1964	Mangaldas Mancharam Pakvasa

14 Nov 1964–9 Nov 1969	P.V. Cherian
9 Nov 1969–26 Feb 1970	S.P. Kotval
26 Feb 1970–11 Dec 1976	Ali Yavar Jung Bahadur
12 Dec 1976–30 Apr 1977	R.M. Kantawala
30 Apr 1977–3 Nov 1980	Sadiq Ali
3 Nov 1980–5 Feb 1982	Om Prakash Mehra
6 Mar 1982–18 Apr 1985	Idris Hasan Latif
18 Apr 1985–30 May 1985	K. Madhava Reddy
30 May 1985–3 Apr 1986	Kona Prabhakara Rao
3 Apr 1986–3 Sep 1987	Shankar Dayal Sharma
3 Sep 1987–6 Nov 1987	S.K. Desai
6 Nov 1987–20 Feb 1988	Chittatosh Mookerjee
20 Feb 1988–15 Feb 1989	Kasu Brahmananda Reddy
15 Feb 1989–12 Jan 1993	Chidambaram Subramaniam
12 Jan 1993–13 Jul 2002	P.C. Alexander
13 Jul 2002–10 Oct 2002	C.K. Thakkar (acting)
10 Oct 2002–6 Dec 2004	Mohammed Fazal
6 Dec 2004–	S.M. Krishna

Chief Ministers

15 Aug 1947–21 Apr 1952	Bal Gangadhar Kher
21 Apr 1952–1 Nov 1956	Morarji Desai
1 Nov 1956–19 Nov 1962	Yashwantrao Balwantrao Chavan
19 Nov 1962–25 Nov 1963	Marotrao Sambashio Kannamwar
5 Dec 1963–20 Feb 1975	Vasantrao Phulsing Naik
20 Feb 1975–1 Apr 1977	Shankarrao Chavan
1 Apr 1977–18 Jul 1978	Vasantrao Patil
18 Jul 1978–9 Jun 1980	Sharad Pawar
9 Jun 1980–20 Jan 1982	Abdul Rahman Antulay
20 Jan 1982–2 Feb 1983	Babasaheb Bhosale
2 Feb 1983–2 Jun 1985	Vasantrao Patil
2 Jun 1985–13 Mar 1986	Shivajirao Patil Nilangekar
13 Mar 1986–24 Jun 1988	Shankarrao Chavan
25 Jun 1988–25 Jun 1991	Sharad Pawar
25 Jun 1991–3 Mar 1993	Sudhakarrao Naik
3 Mar 1993–14 Mar 1995	Sharad Pawar
14 Mar 1995–1 Feb 1999	Manohar Joshi
1 Feb 1999–18 Oct 1999	Narayan Rane
18 Oct 1999–18 Jan 2003	Vilasrao Deshmukh
18 Jan 2003–1 Nov 2004	Sushil Kumar Shinde
1 Nov 2004–	Vilasrao Deshmukh

Manipur

15 Oct 1949	State (from 1950: Part C)
1 Nov 1956	Union territory
21 Jan 1972	State

Chief Commissioners (from 19 Dec 1969, lieutenant governors)

15 Oct 1949–18 Oct 1949	Rawal Amar Singh
18 Oct 1949–Dec 1950	Himmat Singh K. Maheswari
Jan 1951–22 Sep 1952	E.P. Moon Jan

22 Sep 1952–3 Jan 1955	Rameshwar Prasad Bharagava
3 Jan 1955–25 Apr 1958	P.C. Mathew
26 Apr 1958–23 Nov 1963	Jagat Mohan Raina
23 Nov 1963–Jan 1970	Baleshwar Prasad
Jan 1970–21 Jan 1972	Dalip Rai Kohli

Governors

21 Jan 1972–21 Sep 1973	Braj Kumar Nehru
21 Sep 1973–12 Aug 1981	Lallan Prasad Singh
12 Aug 1981–12 Jun 1984	S.M.H. Burney
12 Jun 1984–10 Jul 1989	K.V. Krishna Rao
10 Jul 1989–20 Mar 1993	Chintamani Panigrahi
20 Mar 1993–31 Aug 1993	K.V. Raghunatha Reddy
31 Aug 1993–23 Dec 1994	V.K. Nayar
23 Dec 1994–2 Dec 1999	Oudh Narain Shrivastava
2 Dec 1999–12 Jun 2003	Ved Marwah
12 Jun 2003–6 Aug 2004	Arvind Dave
6 Aug 2004–	Shivinder Singh Sidhu

Chief Ministers

1 Jul 1963–12 Jan 1967	M. Koireng Singh
20 Mar 1967–4 Oct 1967	M. Koireng Singh
13 Oct 1967–25 Oct 1967	Longjam Thambou Singh
19 Feb 1968–17 Oct 1969	M. Koireng Singh
23 Mar 1972–28 Mar 1973	Mohammed Alimuddin
4 Mar 1974–10 Jul 1974	Mohammed Alimuddin
10 Jul 1974–6 Dec 1974	Yangmasho Shaiza
6 Dec 1974–16 May 1977	R.K. Dorendra Singh
29 Jun 1977–14 Nov 1979	Yangmasho Shaiza
14 Jan 1980–27 Nov 1980	R.K. Dorendra Singh
27 Nov 1980–28 Feb 1981	Rishang Keishing
19 Jun 1981–4 Mar 1988	Rishang Keishing
4 Mar 1988–23 Feb 1990	R.K. Jaichandra Singh
23 Feb 1990–7 Jan 1992	Raj Kumar Ranbir Singh
8 Apr 1992–11 Apr 1993	R.K. Dorendra Singh
11 Apr 1993–31 Dec 1993	Dasarath Deb
14 Dec 1994–16 Dec 1997	Rishang Keishing
16 Dec 1997–15 Feb 2001	W. Nipamacha Singh
15 Feb 2001–2 Jun 2001	Radhabinod Koijam
7 Mar 2002–	Okram Ibobi Singh

Meghalaya

2 Apr 1970	State within Assam
21 Jan 1972	Separate state

Governors

1970–Sep 1973	Braj Kumar Nehru
Sep 1973–10 Aug 1980	Lallan Prasad Singh
10 Aug 1980–1984	Prakash Chandra Mehotra
1984	Triveni Sahai Misra
1984–1989	Bhishma Narain Singh

1989	Harideo Joshi
1 Jul 1989–1990	Abubakar Abdul Rahim
1990–1995	Madhukar Dighe
19 Jun 1995–	M.M. Jacob

Chief Ministers

2 Apr 1970–10 Mar 1978	Williamson A. Sangma
10 Mar 1978–7 May 1979	Darwin Diengdoh Pugh
7 May 1979–7 May 1981	Brington Buhai Lyngdoh
7 May 1981–2 Mar 1983	Williamson A. Sangma
2 Mar 1983–2 Apr 1983	Brington Buhai Lyngdoh
2 Apr 1983–6 Feb 1988	Williamson A. Sangma
6 Feb 1988–26 Mar 1990	Purno Agitok Sangma
26 Mar 1990–11 Oct 1991	Brington Buhai Lyngdoh
5 Feb 1992–19 Feb 1993	D.D. Lapang
19 Feb 1993–10 Mar 1998	Salseng C. Marak
10 Mar 1998–8 Mar 2000	Brington Buhai Lyngdoh
8 Mar 2000–8 Dec 2001	E.K. Mawlong
8 Dec 2001–4 Mar 2003	Flinder Anderson Khonglam
4 Mar 2003–	D.D. Lapang

Mizoram

21 Jan 1972	Union territory created from part of Assam
20 Feb 1987	State

Chief Commissioner

21 Jan 1972–24 Apr 1972	S.J. Das

Lieutenant Governors

24 Apr 1972–13 Jun 1974	Shanti Priya Mukherjee
13 Jun 1974–27 Sep 1977	S.K. Chhibbar
27 Sep 1977–1980	Mohan Prakash Mathur
1980–16 Apr 1981	K.A.A. Raja
16 Apr 1981–10 Aug 1983	S.N. Kohli
10 Aug 1983–11 Dec 1986	Mari Shankar Dhube
11 Dec 1986–20 Feb 1987	Hiteshwar Saikia

Governors

20 Feb 1987–30 Apr 1989	Hiteshwar Saikia
1 Jul 1989–8 Feb 1990	Williamson A. Sangma
8 Feb 1990–10 Feb 1993	Swaraj Kaushal
10 Feb 1993–29 Jan 1998	Paty Ripple Kyndiah
29 Jan 1998–2 May 1998	Arun Prasad Mukherjee
2 May 1998–22 Nov 2000	Anandam Padmanabhan
22 Nov 2000–18 May 2001	Ved Marwah
18 May 2001–	Amolak Rattan Kohli

Chief Ministers

3 May 1972–10 May 1977	L. Chal Chhunga
2 Jun 1978–10 Nov 1978	Thenphunga Sailo
8 May 1979–4 May 1984	Thenphunga Sailo

5 May 1984–20 Aug 1986	Lal Thhanhawla
21 Aug 1986–7 Sep 1988	Laldenga
24 Jan 1989–3 Dec 1998	Lal Thhanhawla
3 Dec 1998–	Zoramthanga

Nagaland

1 Dec 1963	State created from part of Assam

Governors

1 Dec 1963–17 Apr 1968	Vishnu Sahay
17 Apr 1968–19 Sep 1973	Braj Kumar Nehru
19 Sep 1973–10 Aug 1981	Lallan Prasad Singh
10 Aug 1981–13 Jun 1984	S.M.H. Burney
13 Jun 1984–20 Jul 1989	K.V. Krishna Rao
20 Jul 1989–4 May 1990	Gopal Singh
4 May 1990–9 May 1990	Chintamani Panigrahi
9 May 1990–13 Apr 1992	M.M. Thomas
13 Apr 1992–2 Oct 1993	Loknath Mishra
2 Oct 1993–5 Aug 1994	V.K. Nayar
5 Aug 1994–12 Nov 1996	Oudh Narain Shrivastava
12 Nov 1996–28 Jan 2002	Om Prakash Sharma
28 Jan 2002–	Shyamal Datta

Chief Ministers

1 Dec 1963–14 Aug 1966	Shilu Ao
14 Aug 1966–22 Feb 1969	T.N. Angami
22 Feb 1969–26 Feb 1974	Hokishe Sema
26 Feb 1974–10 Mar 1975	Vizol
10 Mar 1975–22 Mar 1975	John Bosco Jasokie
25 Nov 1977–18 Jan 1980	Vizol
18 Jan 1980–18 Apr 1980	George A. Pang
18 Apr 1980–5 Jun 1980	S.C. Jamir
5 Jun 1980–18 Nov 1982	John Bosco Jasokie
18 Nov 1982–29 Oct 1986	S.C. Jamir
29 Oct 1986–7 Aug 1988	Hokishe Sema
25 Jan 1989–15 May 1990	S.C. Jamir
15 May 1990–19 Jun 1990	K.L. Chishi
19 Jun 1990–2 Apr 1992	Vamuzo Phesao
22 Feb 1993–6 Mar 2003	S.C. Jamir
6 Mar 2003–	Neiphiu Rio

Orissa

15 Aug 1947	Province
26 Jan 1950	State (unitl 1956: Part A)

Governors

15 Aug 1947–20 Jun 1948	Kailash Nathi Katju
21 Jun 1948–6 Jun 1952	Janab M. Asaf Ali
7 Jun 1952–9 Feb 1954	Sir Saiyid Fazl Ali

10 Feb 1954–11 Sep 1956	Poosapati S. Kumaraswamy Raja
12 Sep 1956–31 Jul 1957	Bhim Sen Sachar
31 Jul 1957–15 Sep 1962	Yeshwant Narayan Sukthankar
16 Sep 1962–30 Jan 1968	Ajudhia Nath Khosla
31 Jan 1968–20 Sep 1971	Shaukatullah Shah Ansari
20 Sep 1971–30 Jun 1972	Sardar Jogendra Singh
1 Jul 1972–8 Nov 1972	Gatikrisina Misra (acting)
8 Nov 1972–20 Aug 1974	Basappa Danappa Jatti
21 Aug 1974–25 Oct 1974	Gatikrisina Misra (acting)
25 Oct 1974–17 Apr 1976	Akbar Ali Khan
17 Apr 1976–7 Feb 1977	Shiva Narayin Sankar (acting)
7 Feb 1977–22 Sep 1977	Harcharan Singh Brar
23 Sep 1977–30 Apr 1980	Bhagwat Dayal Sharma
30 Apr 1980–17 Aug 1983	Cheppudira Muthana Poonacha
17 Aug 1983–20 Nov 1988	Bishambhar Nath Pande
20 Nov 1988–6 Feb 1990	Nurul Hasan
7 Feb 1990–1 Feb 1993	Yagya Dutt Sharma
1 Feb 1993–31 May 1993	Nurul Hasan
1 Jun 1993–17 Jun 1995	B. Satyanarayan Reddy
18 Jun 1995–27 Apr 1998	Gopala Ramanujam
27 Apr 1998–14 Nov 1999	Chakravarti Rangarajan
15 Nov 1999–17 Nov 2004	M.M. Rajendran
17 Nov 2004–	Rameshwar Thakur

Chief Ministers

15 Aug 1947–12 May 1950	Harekrushna Mahatab
12 May 1950–15 Oct 1956	Nabakrushna Choudhury
15 Oct 1956–25 Feb 1961	Harekrushna Mahatab
28 Jun 1961–2 Oct 1963	Bijayananda Patnaik
2 Oct 1963–21 Feb 1965	Biren Mitra
21 Feb 1965–8 Mar 1967	Sadasiva Tripathy
8 Mar 1967–11 Jan 1971	Rajendra Narayana Singh Deo
3 Apr 1971–14 Jun 1972	Biswanath Das
14 Jun 1972–3 Mar 1973	Nandini Satpathy
6 Mar 1974–16 Dec 1976	Nandini Satpathy
29 Dec 1976–25 Jun 1977	Binayak Acharya
25 Jun 1977–17 Feb 1980	Nilamani Routray
9 Jun 1980–7 Dec 1989	Janaki Ballabh Patnaik
7 Dec 1989–5 Mar 1990	Hemananda Biswal
5 Mar 1990–15 Mar 1995	Bijayananda Patnaik
15 Mar 1995–15 Feb 1999	Janaki Ballabh Patnaik
15 Feb 1999–6 Dec 1999	Giridhar Gomango
6 Dec 1999–5 Mar 2000	Hemananda Biswal
5 Mar 2000–	Naveen Patnaik

Punjab

15 Aug 1947	Province
26 Jan 1950	State (until 1956: part A)

Governors

15 Aug 1947–11 Mar 1953	Sir Chandulal Madhavlal Trivedi

11 Mar 1953–15 Sep 1958	C.P.N. Singh
15 Sep 1958–1 Oct 1962	Narhar Vishnu Gadgil
1 Oct 1962–4 May 1964	Pattom Thanu Pillai
4 May 1964–1 Sep 1965	Hafiz Muhammad Ibrahim
1 Sep 1965–26 Jun 1966	Sardar Ujjal Singh
27 Jun 1966–1 Jun 1967	Dharma Vira
1 Jun 1967–16 Oct 1967	Mehar Singh
16 Oct 1967–21 May 1973	Dadasaheb Chintanani Pavate
21 May 1973–1 Sep 1977	Mahendra Mohan Choudhury
1 Sep 1977–24 Sep 1977	Ranjit Singh Narula
24 Sep 1977–26 Aug 1981	Jaisukh Lal Hathi
26 Aug 1981–21 Apr 1982	Aminuddin Ahmad Khan
21 Apr 1982–7 Feb 1983	Marri Channa Reddy
7 Feb 1983–21 Feb 1983	S.S. Sandhawalia
21 Feb 1983–10 Oct 1983	Anant Prasad Sharma
10 Oct 1983–3 Jul 1984	Bhairab Dutt Pande
3 Jul 1984–14 Mar 1985	Kershasp Tehmurasp Satarawala
14 Mar 1985–14 Nov 1985	Arjun Singh
14 Nov 1985–26 Nov 1985	Hokishe Sema
26 Nov 1985–2 Apr 1986	Shankar Dayal Sharma
2 Apr 1986–8 Dec 1989	Siddharta Shankar Ray
8 Dec 1989–14 Jun 1990	Nirmal Mukarji
14 Jun 1990–18 Dec 1990	Virendra Verma
18 Dec 1990–7 Aug 1991	Om Prakash Malhotra
7 Aug 1991–9 Jul 1994	Surendra Nath
10 Jul 1994–18 Sep 1994	Sudhakar Panditrao Kurdukar
18 Sep 1994–27 Nov 1999	B.K.N. Chhibber
27 Nov 1999–8 May 2003	J.F.R. Jacob
8 May 2003–3 Nov 2004	Om Prakash Verma
3 Nov 2004–16 Nov 2004	A.R. Kidwai
16 Nov 2004–	S.F. Rodrigues

Chief Ministers

15 Aug 1947–13 Apr 1949	Gopichand Bhargava
13 Apr 1949–18 Oct 1949	Bhim Sen Sachar
18 Oct 1949–20 Jun 1951	Gopichand Bhargava
17 Apr 1952–23 Jan 1956	Bhim Sen Sachar
23 Jan 1956–21 Jun 1964	Sardar Pratap Singh Kairon
21 Jun 1964–6 Jul 1964	Gopichand Bhargava
6 Jul 1964–5 Jul 1966	Ram Kishan
1 Nov 1966–8 Mar 1967	Gurumukh Singh Musafir
8 Mar 1967–25 Nov 1967	Sardar Gurnam Singh
25 Nov 1967–23 Aug 1968	Sardar Lachhman Singh Gill
17 Feb 1969–27 Mar 1970	Sardar Gurnam Singh
27 Mar 1970–14 Jun 1971	Prakash Singh Badal
17 Mar 1972–30 Apr 1977	Zail Singh
20 Jun 1977–17 Feb 1980	Prakash Singh Badal
6 Jun 1980–6 Oct 1983	Darbara Singh
29 Sep 1985–11 May 1987	Surjit Singh Barnala
25 Feb 1992–31 Aug 1995	Beant Singh
31 Aug 1995–21 Nov 1996	Harcharan Singh Brar
21 Nov 1996–12 Feb 1997	Rajinder Kaur Bhattal

12 Feb 1997–27 Feb 2002	Prakash Singh Badal
27 Feb 2002–	Amarinder Singh

Patiala and East Punjab States Union

Chief Ministers

22 Apr 1952–5 Mar 1953	Sardar Gian Singh Rarewala
8 Mar 1954–7 Jan 1955	Sardar Raghbir Singh
12 Jan 1955–31 Oct 1956	Brish Bhan

Rajasthan

25 Mar 1948	Rajasthan Union
18 Apr 1948	United states of Rajasthan
30 Apr 1949	United states of Greater Rajasthan (from 1950: Part B)
1 Nov 1956	Rajasthan

Rajpramukhs

25 Mar 1948–18 Apr 1948	Bhim Singh II
18 Apr 1948–4 Jul 1955	Sir Bhopal Singh
(from 1 Apr 1949, maharajpramukh)	

Governors

1 Nov 1956–16 Apr 1962	Gurumukh Nihal Singh
16 Apr 1962–16 Apr 1967	Sampurnanand
16 Apr 1967–1 Jul 1972	Sardar Hukam Singh
1 Jul 1972–15 Feb 1977	Sardar Jogendra Singh
15 Feb 1977–11 May 1977	Vedpal Tyagi (acting)
17 May 1977–8 Aug 1981	Raghukul Tilak
8 Aug 1981–6 Mar 1982	K.D. Sharma (acting)
6 Mar 1982–4 Jan 1985	Om Prakash Mehra
20 Nov 1985–15 Oct 1987	Vasantrao Patil
20 Feb 1988–3 Feb 1990	Sukhdev Prasad
3 Feb 1990–14 Feb 1990	Milap Chand Jain (acting)
14 Feb 1990–26 Aug 1991	Debi Prasad Chattopadhyaya
26 Aug 1991–5 Feb 1992	Swarup Singh (acting)
5 Feb 1992–31 May 1993	Marri Channa Reddy
31 May 1993–30 Jun 1993	Dhanik Lal Mandal (acting)
30 Jun 1993–1 May 1998	Bali Ram Bhagat
1 May 1998–24 May 1998	Darbara Singh
25 May 1998–16 Jan 1999	Navrang Lal Tibrewal (acting)
16 Jan 1999–14 May 2003	Anshuman Singh
14 May 2003–22 Sep 2003	Nirmal Chandra Jain
22 Sep 2003–14 Jan 2004	Kailashpati Mishra
14 Jan 2004–1 Nov 2004	Madan Lal Khurana
1 Nov 2004–8 Nov 2004	Thanjavelu Rajeshwar
8 Nov 2004–	Pratibha Patil

Chief Ministers

25 Mar 1948–18 Apr 1948	Gokul Lal Asawa
18 Apr 1948–7 Apr 1949	Manikya Lal Verma
7 Apr 1949–6 Jan 1951	Hiralal Shastri

6 Jan 1951–26 Apr 1951	Cadambi Seshachar Venkatachari (acting)
26 Apr 1951–3 Mar 1952	Jai Narayan Vyas
3 Mar 1952–1 Nov 1952	Tikaram Palliwal
1 Nov 1952–13 Nov 1954	Jai Narayan Vyas
13 Nov 1954–13 Mar 1967	Mohan Lal Sukhadia
26 Apr 1967–9 Jul 1971	Mohan Lal Sukhadia
9 Jul 1971–11 Oct 1973	Barkatullah Khan
23 Oct 1973–22 Jun 1977	Harideo Joshi
22 Jun 1977–16 Feb 1980	Bhairon Singh Shekhawat
6 Jun 1980–14 Jul 1981	Jagannath Pahadia
14 Jul 1981–23 Feb 1985	Shiv Charan Mathur
23 Feb 1985–10 Mar 1985	Heera Lal Devpura
10 Mar 1985–20 Jan 1988	Harideo Joshi
20 Jan 1988–4 Dec 1989	Shiv Charan Mathur
4 Dec 1989–4 Mar 1990	Harideo Joshi
4 Mar 1990–15 Dec 1992	Bhairon Singh Shekhawat
4 Dec 1993–1 Dec 1998	Bhairon Singh Shekhawat
1 Dec 1998–8 Dec 2003	Ashok Gehlot
8 Dec 2003–	Vasundhara Raje

Matsya

Matsya Union formed by merger of former princely states of Alwar, Bharatpur, Dholpur, and Karauli

Chief Minister

18 Mar 1948–15 May 1949	Shobha Ram

Ajmer

Chief Minister

24 Mar 1952–1956	Hari Bhau Upadhyay

Sikkim

16 May 1975	State

Governors

16 May 1975–10 Jan 1981	Bipen Bihari Lal
10 Jan 1981–16 Jun 1984	Homi J.H. Taleyarkhan
16 Jun 1984–31 May 1985	Kona Prabhakara Rao
31 May 1985–21 Nov 1985	Bhishma Narain Singh
21 Nov 1985–2 Mar 1989	Thanjavelu Rajeshwar
2 Mar 1989–8 Feb 1990	S.K. Bhatnagar
8 Feb 1990–21 Sep 1994	R.H. Tahiliani
21 Sep 1994–12 Nov 1995	P. Shiv Shanker
12 Nov 1995–10 Mar 1996	K.V. Raghunatha Reddy
10 Mar 1996–18 May 2001	Chaudhury Randhir Singh
18 May 2001–25 Oct 2002	Kidar Nath Sahani
25 Oct 2002–	V. Rama Rao

Chief Ministers

16 May 1975–18 Aug 1979	Kazi Lhendup Dorji

18 Oct 1979–11 May 1984	Nar Bahadur Bhandari
11 May 1984–25 May 1984	B.B. Gurung
8 Mar 1985–18 May 1994	Nar Bahadur Bhandari
18 May 1994–12 Dec 1994	Sanchaman Limboo
12 Dec 1994–	Pawan Chamling

Tamil Nadu

15 Aug 1947	Madras province
26 Jan 1950	State (until 1956: Part A)
14 Jan 1969	Renamed Tamil Nadu

Governors

15 Aug 1947–7 Sep 1948	Sir Archibald Edward Nye
7 Sep 1948–12 Mar 1952	Sir Krishnakumarsinhji Bhavsinhji
12 Mar 1952–10 Dec 1956	Sri Prakasa
10 Dec 1956–30 Sep 1957	Anapparambul Joseph John
24 Jan 1958–4 May 1964	Bishnuram Medhi
4 May 1964–26 Jun 1966	Jayachamarajendra Wodeyar
26 Jun 1966–27 May 1971	Sardar Ujjal Singh
27 May 1971–16 Jun 1976	Kodardas Kalidas Shah
16 Jun 1976–8 Apr 1977	Mohan Lal Sukhadia
8 Apr 1977–27 Apr 1977	C.P.N. Singh (acting)
27 Apr 1977–4 Nov 1980	Prabhudas Balubhai Patwari
4 Nov 1980–3 Sep 1982	Sadiq Ali
3 Sep 1982–17 Feb 1988	Sundar Lal Khurana
17 Feb 1988–24 May 1990	P.C. Alexander
24 May 1990–15 Feb 1991	Surjit Singh Barnala
15 Feb 1991–31 May 1993	Bhishma Narain Singh
31 May 1993–2 Dec 1996	Marri Channa Reddy
2 Dec 1996–25 Jan 1997	Krishan Kant
25 Jan 1997–3 Jul 2001	Fathima Beevi
3 Jul 2001–18 Jan 2002	Chakravarti Rangarajan
18 Jan 2002–3 Nov 2004	P.S. Ramamohan Rao
3 Nov 2004–	Surjit Singh Barnala

Chief Ministers

15 Aug 1947–6 Apr 1949	Amandur Ramaswami Reddiar
6 Apr 1949–10 Apr 1952	Poosapati S. Kumaraswamy Raja
10 Apr 1952–13 Apr 1954	Chakravarti Rajagopalachari
13 Apr 1954–2 Oct 1963	Kumaraswami Kamaraj
2 Oct 1963–4 Mar 1967	M. Bhaktavatsalam
4 Mar 1967–3 Feb 1969	C.N. Annadurai
10 Feb 1969–31 Jan 1976	Kalaignar Muthuvel Karunanidhi
30 Jun 1977–17 Feb 1980	Marudur Gopala Ramachandran
9 Jun 1980–24 Dec 1987	Marudur Gopala Ramachandran
7 Jan 1988–30 Jan 1988	Janaki Ramachandran
27 Jan 1989–30 Jan 1991	Kalaignar Muthuvel Karunanidhi
24 Jun 1991–13 May 1996	Jayaram Jayalalitha
13 May 1996–14 May 2001	Kalaignar Muthuvel Karunanidhi
14 May 2001–21 Sep 2001	Jayaram Jayalalitha
21 Sep 2001–2 Mar 2002	O. Paneerselvam
2 Mar 2002–	Jayaram Jayalalitha

Tripura

15 Oct 1949	Province
26 Jan 1950	Part C state
1 Nov 1956	Union territory
21 Jan 1972	State

Chief Commissioners

15 Oct 1949–1951	R.K. Ray
1951–1955	Venkatasubrami Nanjappa
1955–1956	H.L. Atal
1956–1958	Kalka Prasad Bhargawa
1958–1962	N.M. Patnaik
15 Nov 1962–17 Jan 1967	Shanti Priya Mukherjee
17 Jan 1967–5 Nov 1967	U.N. Sharma
5 Nov 1967–31 Jan 1970	D.K. Bhattacharya
31 Jan 1970–8 Aug 1971	Anthony Lancelot Dias
8 Aug 1971–21 Jan 1972	Baleshwar Prasad

Governors

21 Jan 1972–22 Sep 1973	Braj Kumar Nehru
22 Sep 1973–10 Aug 1980	Lallan Prasad Singh
10 Aug 1980–14 Aug 1981	Prakash Chandra Mehotra
14 Aug 1981–14 Jun 1984	S.M.H. Burney
14 Jun 1984–12 Jul 1989	K.V. Krishna Rao
12 Jul 1989–12 Feb 1990	Sultan Singh
12 Feb 1990–15 Aug 1993	K.V. Raghunatha Reddy
15 Aug 1993–16 Jun 1995	Romesh Bhandari
16 Jun 1995–23 Jun 2000	Siddheswar Prasad
23 Jun 2000–2 Jun 2003	Krishna Mohan Seth
2 Jun 2003–	Dinesh Nandan Sahay

Chief Ministers

1 Jul 1963–1 Nov 1971	Sachindra Lal Singh
20 Mar 1972–1 Apr 1977	Sukhamoy Sen Gupta
1 Apr 1977–26 Jul 1977	Prafullah Kuma Das
26 Jul 1977– 5 Nov 1977	Radhika Ranjan Gupta
5 Jan 1978–5 Feb 1988	Nripen Chakraborty
5 Feb 1988–19 Feb 1992	Sudhir Ranjan Majumdar
19 Feb 1992–11 Mar 1993	Samir Ranjan Barman
10 Apr 1993–11 Mar 1998	Dasarath Deb
11 Mar 1998–	Manik Sarkar

Uttar Pradesh

15 Aug 1947	United province
26 Jan 1950	Uttar Pradesh state (until 1956: Part A)

Governors

15 Aug 1947–2 Mar 1949	Sarojini Naidu

3 Mar 1949–2 May 1949	Bidhubhusan Malik (acting)
2 May 1949–2 Jun 1952	Sir Hormasji Peroshaw Mody
2 Jun 1952–10 Jun 1957	Kanaiyalal Maneklal Munshi
10 Jun 1957–1 Jul 1960	Varahagiri Venkata Giri
1 Jul 1960–16 Apr 1962	Burgula Ramakrishna Rao
16 Apr 1962–1 May 1967	Biswanath Das
1 May 1967–1 Jul 1972	Bezawada Gopala Reddy
1 Jul 1972–14 Nov 1972	Shashi Kanta Verma (acting)
14 Nov 1972–25 Oct 1974	Akbar Ali Khan
25 Oct 1974–2 Oct 1977	Marri Channa Reddy
2 Oct 1977–28 Feb 1980	Ganpatrao Devji Tapase
28 Feb 1980–31 Mar 1985	C.P.N. Singh
31 Mar 1985–12 Feb 1990	Mohammed Usman Arif
12 Feb 1990–27 May 1993	B. Satyanarayan Reddy
27 May 1993–3 May 1996	Motilal Vora
3 May 1996–19 Sep 1996	Mohammed Shafi Qureshi
19 Sep 1996–17 Mar 1998	Romesh Bhandari
17 Mar 1998–20 Apr 1998	Mohammed Shafi Qureshi
20 Apr 1998–24 Nov 2000	Suraj Bhan
24 Nov 2000–2 Jul 2004	Vishnu Kant Shastri
2 Jul 2004–8 Jul 2004	Sudarshan Agarwal
8 Jul 2004–	Thanjavelu Rajeshwar

Chief Ministers

15 Aug 1947–28 Dec 1954	Govind Ballabh Pant
28 Dec 1954–7 Dec 1960	Sampurnanand
7 Dec 1960–2 Oct 1963	Chandra Bhanu Gupta
2 Oct 1963–14 Mar 1967	Sucheta Kriplani
14 Mar 1967–3 Apr 1967	Chandra Bhanu Gupta
3 Apr 1967–17 Feb 1968	Charan Singh
26 Feb 1969–18 Feb 1970	Chandra Bhanu Gupta
18 Feb 1970–2 Oct 1970	Charan Singh
18 Oct 1970–4 Apr 1971	Tribhuvan Narain Singh
4 Apr 1971–12 Jun 1973	Kamlapati Tripathi
8 Nov 1973–30 Nov 1975	Hemwati Nandan Bahuguna
21 Jan 1976–30 Apr 1977	Narain Dutt Tiwari
23 Jun 1977–28 Feb 1979	Ram Naresh Yadav
28 Feb 1979–17 Feb 1980	Banarsi Das
9 Jun 1980–19 Jul 1982	Vishwanath Pratap Singh
19 Jul 1982–3 Aug 1984	Sripati Mishra
3 Aug 1984–24 Sep 1985	Narain Dutt Tiwari
24 Sep 1985–25 Jun 1988	Bir Bahadur Singh
25 Jun 1988–5 Dec 1989	Narain Dutt Tiwari
5 Dec 1989–24 Jun 1991	Mulayam Singh Yadav
24 Jun 1991–6 Dec 1992	Kalyan Singh
5 Dec 1993–3 Jun 1995	Mulayam Singh Yadav
3 Jun 1995–18 Oct 1995	Mayawati
21 Mar 1997–21 Sep 1997	Mayawati
21 Sep 1997–21 Feb 1998	Kalyan Singh
21 Feb 1998–23 Feb 1998	Jagadambika Pal
23 Feb 1998–12 Nov 1999	Kalyan Singh
12 Nov 1999–28 Oct 2000	Ram Prakash Gupta

28 Oct 2000–8 Mar 2002	Rajnath Singh
3 May 2002–29 Aug 2003	Mayawati
29 Aug 2003–	Mulayam Singh Yadav

Uttaranchal

9 Nov 2000	State created from part of Uttar Pradesh

Governors

9 Nov 2000–8 Jan 2003	Surjit Singh Barnala
8 Jan 2003–	Sudarshan Agarwal

Chief Ministers

9 Nov 2000–30 Oct 2001	Nityanand Swamy
30 Oct 2001–2 Mar 2002	Bhagat Singh Koshiyari
2 Mar 2002–	Narain Dutt Tiwari

West Bengal

15 Aug 1947	Province
26 Jan 1950	State (until 1956: Part A)

Governors

15 Aug 1947–21 Jun 1948	Chakravarti Rajagopalachari
21 Jun 1948–1 Nov 1951	Kailash Nathi Katju
1 Nov 1951–8 Aug 1956	Harendra Coomar Mookerjee
8 Aug 1956–3 Nov 1956	Phani Bhusan Chakraborty
3 Nov 1956–1 Jun 1967	Padmaja Naidu
1 Jun 1967–1 Apr 1969	Dharma Vira
1 Apr 1969–19 Sep 1969	Deep Narayan Sinha
19 Sep 1969–21 Aug 1971	Shanti Swaroop Dhavan
21 Aug 1971–6 Nov 1977	Anthony Lancelot Dias
6 Nov 1977–12 Sep 1981	Tribhuvana Narayana Singh
12 Sep 1981–10 Oct 1983	Bhairab Dutt Pande
10 Oct 1983–16 Aug 1984	Anant Prasad Sharma
16 Aug 1984–1 Oct 1984	Satish Chandra
1 Oct 1984–12 Aug 1986	Uma Shankar Dikshit
12 Aug 1986–20 Mar 1989	Nurul Hasan
20 Mar 1989–7 Feb 1990	Thanjavelu Rajeshwar
7 Feb 1990–12 Jul 1993	Nurul Hasan
13 Jul 1993–14 Aug 1993	B. Satyanarayan Reddy
14 Aug 1993–27 Apr 1998	K.V. Raghunatha Reddy
27 Apr 1998–18 May 1999	A.R. Kidwai
18 May 1999–4 Dec 1999	Shyamal Kumar Sen
4 Dec 1999–14 Dec 2004	Viren J. Shah
14 Dec 2004–	Gopalkrishna Gandhi

Chief Ministers

15 Aug 1947–14 Jan 1948	Prafulla Ghosh
14 Jan 1948– 1 Jul 1962	Bidhan Chandra Roy
8 Jul 1962–15 Mar 1967	Prafulla Sen
15 Mar 1967–2 Nov 1967	Ajoy Kumar Mukherjee

2 Nov 1967–20 Feb 1968	Prafulla Ghosh
25 Feb 1969–19 Mar 1970	Ajoy Kumar Mukherjee
2 Apr 1971–28 Jun 1971	Prafulla Ghosh
19 Mar 1972–21 Jun 1977	Siddharta Shankar Ray
21 Jun 1977–6 Nov 2000	Jyoti Basu
6 Nov 2000–	Buddhadev Bhattacharya

Delhi

15 Aug 1947	Province
26 Jan 1950	Part C state
1 Nov 1956	Union territory
1 Feb 1992	National Capital Territory of Delhi

Lieutenant Governors

1 Nov 1966–1970	Adity Nath Jha
1970–1971	M.C. Pimputkar
1971–1974	Baleshwar Prasad
1974–1978	Krishan Chand
1978–1979	Dalip Rai Kohli
Feb 1980–1981	Jagmohan
1981–Sep 1982	Sundar Lal Khurana
Sep 1982–Mar 1984	Jagmohan
Mar 1984–Nov 1984	P.G. Gavai
Nov 1984–Nov 1985	Mohan M.K. Wali
Nov 1985–Aug 1988	Harkishan Lal Kapoor
Aug 1988–Dec 1989	Romesh Bhandari
Dec 1989–Dec 1990	Arjun Singh
Dec 1990–1992	Markandey Singh
4 May 1992–4 Jan 1997	Prasannabhai Karunashankar Dave
4 Jan 1997–20 Apr 1998	Tejendra Khanna
20 Apr 1998–9 Jun 2004	Vijai Kapoor
9 Jun 2004–	B.L. Joshi

Chief Ministers

17 Mar 1952–12 Feb 1955	Chaudhary Brahm Prakash
12 Feb 1955–Nov 1956	G.N. Singh
1993–26 Feb 1996	Madan Lal Khurana
26 Feb 1996–12 Oct 1998	Sahib Singh Verma
12 Oct 1998–3 Dec 1998	Sushma Swaraj
3 Dec 1998–	Sheila Dikshit

Andaman and Nicobar Islands

15 Aug 1947	Province
26 Jan 1950	Part D territory
1 Nov 1956	Union Territory

Lieutenant Governors

12 Nov 1982–3 Dec 1985	Manohar L. Kampani
4 Dec 1985–Dec 1989	Tirath Singh Oberoi

Dec 1989–24 Feb 1990	Romesh Bhandari
25 Feb 1990–Dec 1990	Ranjit Singh Dayal
Dec 1990–18 Mar 1993	Surjit Singh Barnala
19 Mar 1993–18 Mar 1996	Vakkom Purushothaman
19 Mar 1996–25 May 2001	Ishwari Prasad Gupta
26 May 2001–4 Jan 2004	Nagendra Nath Jha
5 Jan 2004–	Ram Kapse

Chandigarh

1 Nov 1996	Union territory created from part of Punjab

Chief Commissioners

1 Nov 1966–31 Oct 1968	M.S. Randhava
31 Oct 1968–8 Apr 1969	Damodar Dass
8 Apr 1969–1 Sep 1972	B.P. Bagchi
1 Sep 1972–Dec 1975	Mohan Prakash Mathur
Dec 1975–15 Jun 1976	G.P. Gupta
15 Jun 1976–Jun 1978	T.N. Chaturvedi
Jun 1978–19 Jul 1980	J.C. Agrawal
19 Jul 1980–8 Mar 1982	B.S. Sarao
8 Mar 1982–2 Jun 1984	Krishna Banerji
2 Jun 1984–2 Aug 1984	The Governor of Punjab (administrator)
2 Aug 1984–30 May 1985	Krishna Banerji
30 May 1985–	The Governor of Punjab (administrators)

Dadra and Nagar Haveli

2 Aug 1954	End of Portuguese rule
11 Aug 1961	Union territory

Administrators

1962–2 Sep 1963	Tumkur Sivasankar
2 Sep 1963–8 Dec 1964	M.R. Sachdev
12 Dec 1964–24 Feb 1965	Hari Sharma
24 Feb 1965–18 Apr 1967	Kashinath Raghunath Damle
18 Apr 1967–16 Nov 1972	Nakul Sen
16 Nov 1972–16 Nov 1977	S.K. Banerjee
16 Nov 1977–31 Mar 1981	Pratap Singh Gill
31 Mar 1981–30 Aug 1982	Jagmohan
30 Aug 1982–24 Feb 1983	Idris Hasan Latif (acting)
24 Feb 1983–4 Jul 1984	Kershasp Tehmurasp Satarawala
4 Jul 1984–24 Sep 1984	Idris Hasan Latif (acting)
24 Sep 1984–18 Jul 1989	Gopal Singh
18 Jul 1989–25 Mar 1991	Khurshed Alam Khan
25 Mar 1991–16 Mar 1992	Bhanu Prakash Singh
16 Mar 1992–28 Mar 1994	K.S. Baidwan
28 Mar 1994–15 Jul 1995	Ramesh Chandra
15 Jul 1995–26 Jun 1998	S.P. Aggarwal
26 Jun 1998–23 Feb 1999	Ramesh Negi (acting)
23 Feb 1999–23 Apr 1999	Sanat Kaul
23 Apr 1999–19 Jul 1999	Ramesh Negi (acting)

19 Jul 1999–   O.P. Kelkar

Daman and Diu

6 May 1962	Part of Goa, Daman, and Diu Union territory (see Goa)
30 May 1987	Separate Union territory

Administrators

30 May 1987–	The Administrators of Dadra and Nagar Haveli

Lakshadweep

1 Nov 1956	Laccadive, Minicoy, and Amindivi Islands Union territory (separated from Madras [see Tamil Nadu])
1 Nov 1973	Renamed Lakshadweep

Administrators

1 Nov 1956–7 Nov 1956	U.R. Panicker
8 Nov 1956–21 Sep 1958	S. Moni
22 Sep 1958–5 Dec 1961	C.K. Balakrishna Nair
6 Dec 1961–8 Apr 1965	M. Ramunny
9 Apr 1965–31 Oct 1969	C.H. Nayar
1 Nov 1969–30 Apr 1973	K.D. Menon
22 May 1973–21 Jun 1975	W. Shaiza
22 Jun 1975–14 Feb 1977	M.C. Verma
21 Feb 1977–30 Jul 1978	S.D. Lakhar
31 Jul 1978–15 Jun 1981	P.M. Nair
15 Jun 1981–21 Jul 1982	Pradip Mehra
21 Jul 1982–9 Jul 1985	Omesh Saigal
9 Jul 1985–8 Sep 1987	J. Sagar
8 Sep 1987–31 Jan 1990	Wajahat Habibullah
1 Feb 1990–1 May 1990	Pradip Singh
2 May 1990–3 May 1992	S.P. Aggarwal
4 May 1992–9 Sep 1994	Satish Chandra
9 Sep 1994–14 Jun 1996	G.S. Chima
1 Aug 1996–1 Jun 1999	Rajeev Talwar
1 Jun 1999–20 Aug 1999	R.K. Verma
21 Aug 1999–30 Apr 2001	Chaman Lal
30 Apr 2001–19 Jun 2001	R.K. Verma
19 Jun 2001–	K.S. Mehra

Pondicherry

1 Nov 1954	French India becomes de facto part of India
16 Aug 1962	De jure transfer to India
2 Jan 1963	Pondicherry Union territory

High Commissioners

1 Nov 1954–1957	Kewal Singh

1957–1958	M.K. Kripalani
1958–1958*	L.R.S. Singh
1960	A.S. Bam
1961–1961*	Sarat Kumar Dutta

Lieutenant Governors

14 Oct 1963–14 Oct 1968	S.L. Sailam
14 Oct 1968–8 Nov 1972	Basappa Danappa Jatti
8 Nov 1972–30 Aug 1976	Cheddy Lal
30 Aug 1976–1 Nov 1980	Bidesh T. Kulkarni
1 Nov 1980–16 Apr 1981	Ram Kishore Vyas
16 Apr 1981–27 Jul 1981	Sadiq Ali
27 Jul 1981–15 May 1982	R.N. Haldipur
15 May 1982–5 Aug 1983	Kizhekethil Mathew Chandy
19 Aug 1983–18 Jun 1984	Kona Prabhakara Rao
18 Jun 1984–1 Oct 1984	Sundar Lal Khurana
1 Oct 1984–22 Jun 1988	Thiru Tribhuvan Prasad Tewary
22 Jun 1988–19 Feb 1990	Ranjit Singh Dayal
19 Feb 1990–19 Dec 1990	Chandrawati
19 Dec 1990–6 Feb 1993	Swarup Singh
6 Feb 1993–31 May 1993	Bhishma Narain Singh
31 May 1993–2 May 1995	Marri Channa Reddy
2 May 1995–23 Apr 1998	Rajendra Kumari Bajpai
23 Apr 1998–31 Jul 2002	Rajani Rai
31 Jul 2002–27 Oct 2003	K.R. Malkani
31 Oct 2003–5 Jan 2004	P.S. Ramamohan Rao (administrator)
5 Jan 2004–7 Jul 2004	Nagendra Nath Jha
7 Jul 2004–	M.M. Lakhera

Chief Ministers

1 Jul 1963–11 Sep 1964	Edouard Goubert
11 Sep 1964–9 Apr 1967	V. Venkatasubha Reddiar
9 Apr 1967–6 Mar 1968	M.O. Hasan Farook Maricar
6 Mar 1968–18 Sep 1968	V. Venkatasubha Reddiar
17 Mar 1969–3 Jan 1974	M.O. Hasan Farook Maricar
6 Mar 1974–28 Mar 1974	Subramanyan Ramaswamy
2 Jul 1977–12 Nov 1978	Subramanyan Ramaswamy
16 Jan 1980–24 Jun 1983	D. Ramachandran
16 Mar 1985–19 Jan 1989	M.O. Hasan Farook Maricar
5 Mar 1990–12 Jan 1991	D. Ramachandran
4 Jul 1991–14 May 1996	V. Vaithilingam
26 May 1996–18 Mar 2000	R.V. Janakiraman
22 Mar 2000–27 Oct 2001	P. Shanmugam
27 Oct 2001–	N. Rangaswamy

POLITICAL INDIA

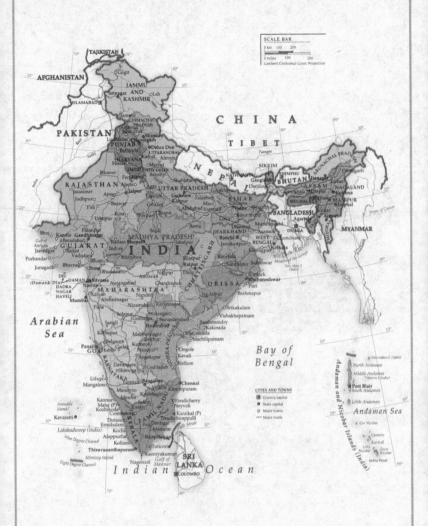

The following pertains to all maps showing the external boundaries and coastlines of India:

PHYSICAL INDIA

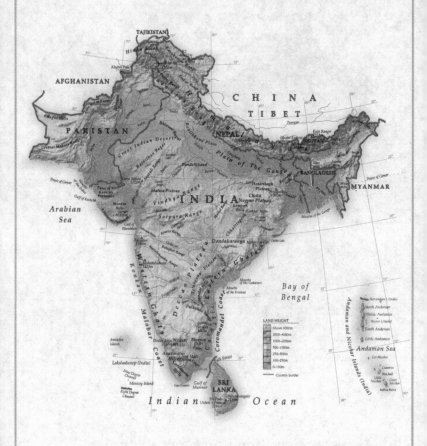

LAND HEIGHT

- Above 4000m
- 2000-4000m
- 1000-2000m
- 500-1000m
- 250-500m
- 100-250m
- 0-100m
- Country border

SCALE BAR

0 km 100 200

0 miles 100 200

Lambert Conformal Conic Projection

Education loans for a better tomorrow.

- 1% interest rebate for girl students ■ Loans upto Rs. 15 lakhs
- No processing & documentation fees ■ Simple interest during moratorium period.

बैंक ऑफ़ बड़ौदा
Bank of Baroda
India's International Bank

www.bankofbaroda.com

In a very real sense, **people who have read good literature** **have lived more** than people who cannot or will not read.

— S. I. Hayakawa

much more than a

books | music | gifts | cha bar | gallery | internet

Kolkata: 17 Park Street, Kolkata 700016 Phone 033 22297662 Mumbai: 3 Dinsha Vachha Road, Churchgate, Mumbai 400020 Phone 022 56364477 Bangalore: The Leela Galleria, 23 Airport Road, Bangalore 560008 Phone 080 51155222 New Delhi: Statesman House, 148 Barakhamba Road, New Delhi 110001 Phone 011 23766080 Goa: 'Panverica' House No 156, Opp. St Anthony's Chapel, Calangute, Bardez, Goa 40351€
Visit us at: www.oxfordbookstore.com

NORTHERN INDIA
Delhi, Uttar Pradesh, Uttaranchal

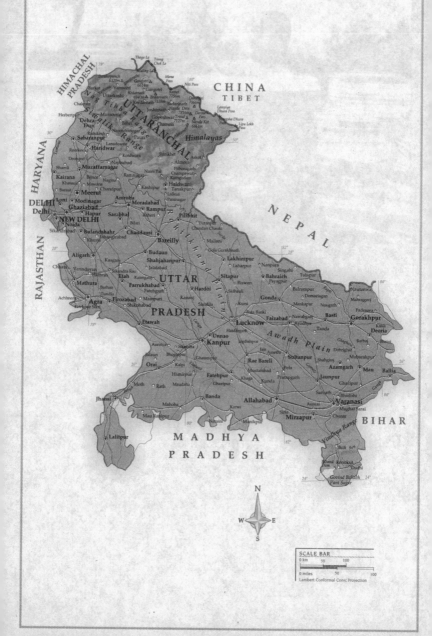

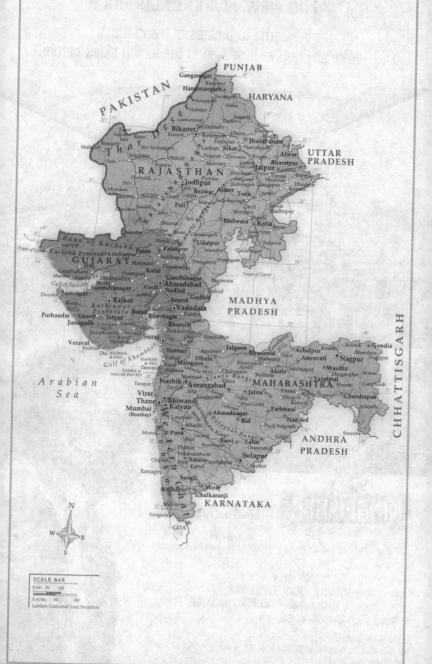

WESTERN INDIA
DADRA & NAGAR HAVELI, DAMAN & DIU, GUJARAT, MAHARASHTRA, RAJASTHAN

PUNJAB

PAKISTAN

HARYANA

UTTAR PRADESH

RAJASTHAN

Ganganagar
Hanumangarh
Karanpur
Suratgarh
Anupgarh
Nohar
Lunkaransar
Raghach
Dudhwa
Sardarshahr
Chirawa
Bilani
Kolayat
Churu
Ratangarh
Fatehpur
Jhunjhunun
Nawalgarh
Ladnun
Sikar
Kot Putli
Alwar
Nagaur
Didwana
Makrana
Kishangarh
Sambhar
Salt Lake
Jaipur
Bharatpur
Dhaulpur
Kuchaman
Phalodi
Jaisalmer
Shri Mohangarh
Jodhpur
Beawar
Ajmer
Tonk
Dausa
Hindaun
Gangapur
Karauli
Pokaran
Phalsund
Shiv
Balotra
Pali
Marwar Jodh Raisingh
Devli
Shahpura
Bundi
Kota
Sawai Madhopur
Bhilwara
Baran
Munabao
Barmer
Jalor
Bhinmal
Bali
Chittaurgarh
Rana Pratap Sagar
Jhalawar
Chohtan
Sanchar
Gundri
Sirohi
Udaipur
Salumbar
Dungarpur
Pratapgarh
Gandhi Sagar
Banswara

THAR DESERT
Thar Desert
Aravalli Range
Luni

GUJARAT

Rann of Kachchh
Kachchh Peninsula
Gulf of Kachchh
Palanpur
Sidhpur
Himatnagar
Mahesana
Kalol
Gandhinagar
Dungarpur
Tropic of Cancer
Gandhidham
Mandvi
Kandla
Morbi
Viramgam
Kheda
Ahmadabad
Nadiad
Anand
Godhra
Dabhoi
Dahod
Dwarka
Jamnagar
Rajkot
Botad
Bhavnagar
Vadodara
Porbandar
Junagadh
Jetpur
Amreli
Talaja
Bharuch
Ankleshwar
Veraval
Kodinar
Diu
Surat
Nandurbar

MADHYA PRADESH

Barda Hills
Kathiawar Peninsula
Girnar Hills
Saurashtra Range

Gulf of Khambhat

Arabian Sea

DADRA & NAGAR HAVELI
DAMAN & DIU
Daman
Silvassa
Tarapur
Valsad
Bardi
Navsari
Virar
Thane
Mumbai (Bombay)
Kalyan
Bhiwandi
Nashik
Deolali
Igatpuri
Pune
Lonavale
Khadki
Phaltan
Bhor
Mahabaleshwar
Satara
Karad
Chiplun
Ratnagiri
Sangli
Miraj
Kolhapur
Ichalkaranji
Malvan
Vengurla
Murud

Amalner
Dhule
Malegaon
Manmad
Chalisgaon
Jalgaon
Bhusawal
Maikagon
Khamgaon
Buldana
Ajanta
Akola
Aurangabad
Jalna
Sillod
Sangamner
Ahmadnagar
Bid
Parli Vaijnath
Latur
Osmanabad
Barsi
Solapur
Akalkot
Pandharpur
Kurduvadi
Daund

MAHARASHTRA

Satmala Hills
Ajanta Range
Godavari
Balaghat Range
Bhima

ANDHRA PRADESH

Achalpur
Amravati
Murtazapur
Wardha
Yavatmal
Warora
Hinganghat
Pusad
Hingoli
Kinwat
Nanded
Parbhani
Udgir
Umri
Sironcha

Kamthi
Nagpur
Bhandara
Dugdpur
Warsa
Gondia
Ramtek
Gadchiroli
Chandrapur
Allapalli

CHHATTISGARH

KARNATAKA

GOA

SCALE BAR
0 km 50 100
0 miles 50 100
Lambert Conformal Conic Projection

N
W E
S

KNOWLEDGE ALONE
HAS THE ABILITY
TO SHELTER THE MIND .

Pure Oxygen

THE BOOK STORE

2nd Flr, Citi Center, S. V. Road, Goregaon (W), Mumbai-62. Tel - 022 28768585/8989.

Shortly Opening Second Store at Juhu, Mumbai.

www.granth.com

ON LINE BUYING SIMPLIFIED.

Free Home Delivery within BMC limits.

CENTRAL INDIA
Madhya Pradesh, Chhattisgarh

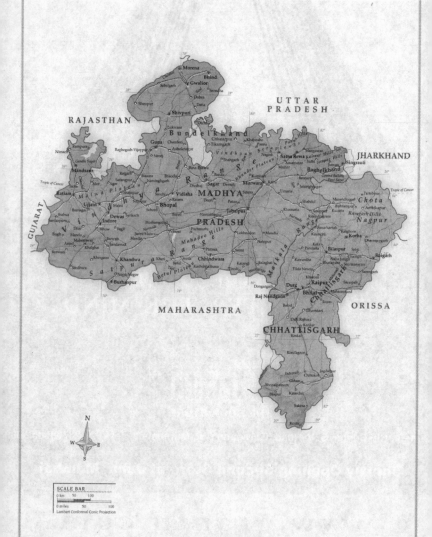

SCALE BAR
0 km   50   100
0 miles   50   100
Lambert Conformal Conic Projection

EASTERN INDIA

Bihar, Jharkhand, Orissa, Sikkim, West Bengal

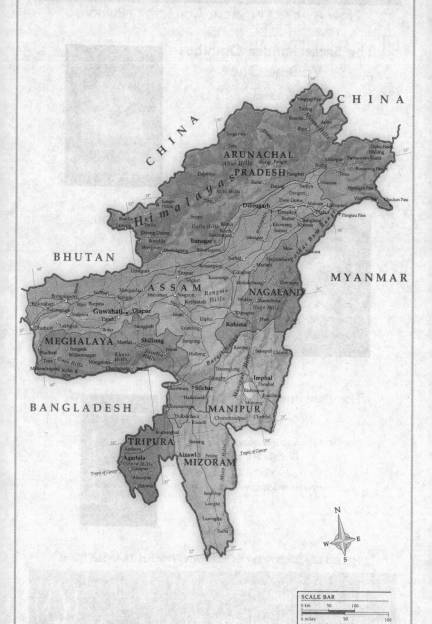

SOUTHERN INDIA

ANDHRA PRADESH, GOA, KARNATAKA, KERALA, PONDICHERRY, TAMIL NADU

SCALE BAR
0 km   50   100
0 miles   50   100
Lambert Conformal Conic Projection

Cover Story: Building Confidence

Becoming Independent

A.P.J. Abdul Kalam

This year India celebrates fifty-eight years of independence. I met 137 freedom fighters from 27 States and Union Territories on 9 August 2005 at Rashtrapati Bhavan. I saw their enthusiasm even at their ripe age, to bring back the nationalism as a living movement. Today our country is free, because the freedom fighters gave their best to the nation in their prime of youth. Honouring the freedom fighters is honouring the independent nation and its spirit of nationalism. We must thank them with respect and make their lives happy.

Nature's fury and its management

While we are celebrating the 58th anniversary of our hard earned political independence, we have to remember the sufferings of our people affected by the recent rain and flood in Maharashtra, Gujarat, Madhya Pradesh, Himachal Pradesh, Karnataka and Orissa. The city of Mumbai and other areas in Maharashtra bore the brunt of nature's fury. The people of these areas are meeting the challenge with courage and fortitude. The Prime Minister had visited some of the affected areas. I spoke to the Chief Minister of Maharashtra while he was visiting various places affected by the floods and I also shared my concern with other Chief Ministers. Maharashtra needs help at this critical juncture to mitigate the sufferings arising out of loss of life and properties inflicted by the fury of rain and flood. All the States need to express their solidarity with the people of Maharashtra in their time of distress and suffering, and collectively help in removing the pain of the people. Mumbai needs an urgent reconstruction to face unexpected heavy rain, as it happened this year.

Rainfall and floods

Rainfall and floods are annual features in many parts of the country. Instead of thinking on interlinking of rivers only at times of flood and drought, it is time that we implement this programme with a great sense of urgency. We need to make an effort to overcome various hurdles in our way to the implementation of this major project. I feel that it has the promise of freeing the country from the endless cycle of floods and droughts. Also, as a measure for preventing flooding of the streets in the cities due to heavy sustained downpour, I would suggest the Ministry of Urban Development at the Centre and the State governments to mount a programme to rebuild and modernize the infrastructure and storm-water drainage systems including construction of underground water silos to store the excess water. This water can be treated, processed and used at the time of shortage as practiced in many other countries. Fortunately India has adequate technology and expertise in making underground tunnels for a metro rail system. This technology can be used for constructing underground water storage systems.

Earthquake forecasting

Another natural phenomenon that affects and causes damages of high magnitude without pre-warning in many parts of our country is the earthquake. To prevent heavy damage to the people and property, we need to accelerate research for forecasting earthquakes. Research work on earthquake forecasting is being done in many countries. We in India should have an integrated research team consisting of experts drawn from academia, meteorology and Space Departments for creating earthquake forecast modelling using pre-earthquake and post-earthquake data collected from various earthquake occurrences in our country. This can be validated periodically with the proven forecasting data available from other countries.

Earth Systems Science

Many of the countries in the world have experienced successive calamities driven by nature. Till recently, researchers the world over had been pursuing research in unconnected ways, in Climate, Earthquake Forecasting, Ocean Sciences and Earth Sciences, without realizing the latent but tight coupling between these areas. This new realization has prompted many countries to pursue the interdisciplinary area of research which is now known as Earth Systems Science. It is in fact fast emerging as an area of convergence between Earth, Climate, Ocean, Environment, Instrumentation and Computer Sciences. I strongly suggest that India should mount a programme in this emerging area of Earth Systems Science. This will call for a dedicated, cohesive and seamless integration between researchers in multiple areas and in multiple organizations. Further, Earth Systems Science doesn't obey political or geographical borders. It is truly a science and its intensive results would make our planet safe and prosperous.

Unlike research in strategic areas, wherein the nations have to maintain superiority over other nations, Earth Systems Science is the ultimate realization of the human kind to collaborate since no nation is safe if its neighbours are not. Nature's fury knows no borders.

Energy independence

This year, on Republic Day, I discussed the potential for employment generation in eight areas. I am happy that a number of actions are evolving in this regard. Today I would like to discuss with all of you another important area that is 'Energy Security', a transition to total 'Energy Independence'. Energy is the lifeline of modern societies. But today, India has 17 per cent of the world's population, and just 0.8 per cent of the world's known oil and natural gas resources. We might expand the use of our coal reserves for some time and that too at a cost and with environmental challenges. The climate of the globe as a whole is changing. Our water resources are also diminishing at a faster rate. As it is said, energy and water demand will soon surely be a defining characteristic of our people's lives in the twenty-first century.

Energy Security rests on two principles. The first, to use the least amount of energy to provide services and cut down energy losses. The second, to secure access to all sources of energy including coal, oil and gas supplies worldwide, till the end of the fossil fuel era which is fast approaching. Simultaneously we should access technologies to provide a diverse supply of reliable, affordable and environmentally sustainable energy.

As you all know, our annual requirement of oil is 114 million tonnes. A significant part of this is consumed in the transportation sector. We produce only about 25 per cent of our total requirement. The presently known resources and future exploration of oil and gas may give mixed results. The import cost today of oil and natural gas is over Rs 120,000 crore. Oil and gas prices are escalating; the barrel cost of oil has doubled within a year. This situation has to be combated.

Energy security, which means ensuring that our country can supply the lifeline of energy to all its citizens, at affordable costs at all times, is thus a very important and significant need and is an essential step forward. But it must be considered as a transition strategy, to enable us to achieve our real goal, that is energy independence or an economy which will function well with total freedom from oil, gas or coal imports. Is it possible?

Energy independence has to be our nation's first and highest priority. We must be determined to achieve this within the next twenty-five years i.e by the year 2030. This one major, twenty-five-year national mission must be formulated, funds guaranteed, and the leadership entrusted without delay as public-private partnerships to our younger generation, now in their thirties, as their lifetime mission in a renewed drive for nation-building.

Energy consumption pattern in India

We have to critically look at the need for energy independence in different ways in its two major sectors: electric power generation and transportation. At present, we have an installed capacity of about 121,000 MW of electricity, which is 3 per cent of the world capacity. We also depend on oil to the extent of 114 million tonnes every year, 75 per cent of which is imported, and used almost entirely in the transportation sector. Forecasts of our energy requirements by 2030, when our population may touch 1.4 billion, indicate that the demand from the power sector will increase from the existing 120,000 MW to about 400,000 MW. This assumes an energy growth rate of 5 per cent per annum.

Electric power generation in India now accesses four basic energy sources: fossil fuels such as oil, natural gas and coal; hydroelectricity; nuclear power; and renewable energy sources such as bio-fuels, solar, biomass, wind and ocean.

Fortunately for us, 89 per cent of the energy used for power generation today is indigeneous, sourced from coal (56 per cent), hydroelectricity (25 per cent), nuclear power (3 per cent) and renewable (5 per cent). The solar energy segment contributes just 0.2 per cent of our energy production.

Thus it would be seen that only 11 per cent of electric power generation is dependent on oil and natural gas which is mostly imported at enormous cost. Only 1 per cent of oil (about 2-3 million tonnes of oil) is being used every year for producing electricity. However, power generation to the extent of 10 per cent is dependent on high cost gas supplies. We are making efforts to access natural gas from other countries.

Even though India has abundant quantities of coal, it is constrained to regional locations, high ash content, affecting the thermal efficiency of our power plants, and also there are environmental concerns. Thus, a movement towards energy independence would demand accelerated work in operationalizing the production of energy from the coal sector through an integrated gasification and combined cycle route. In 2030, the total energy requirement would be 400,000 MW. At that time, the power generated from coal-based power plants would increase from the existing 67,000 MW to 200,000 MW. This would demand a significant build-up of thermal power stations and large scale expansion of coal fields.

Changing structure of energy sources

The strategic goals for energy independence by 2030 would thus call for a shift in the structure of energy sources. Firstly, fossil fuel imports need to be minimized and secure access has to be ensured. Maximum hydro and nuclear power potential should be tapped. The most significant aspect, however, would be that the power generated through renewable energy technologies may target 20 to 25 per cent against the present 5 per cent. It would be evident that for true energy independence, a major shift in the structure of energy sources from fossil to renewable energy sources is mandated.

Solar farms

Solar energy in particular requires unique, massive applications in the agricultural sector, where farmers need electricity exclusively in the daytime. This could be the primary demand driver for solar energy. Our farmers' demand for electric power today is significantly high to make solar energy economical on a large scale.

Shortages of water, both for drinking and farming operations, can be met by large scale seawater desalination and pumping inland using solar energy, supplemented by bio-fuels wherever necessary.

The current high capital costs of solar power stations can be reduced by grid-locked 100 MW sized Very Large Scale Solar Photovoltaic (VLSPV) or Solar Thermal Power Stations. In the very near future, breakthroughs in nanotechnologies promise significant increase in solar cell efficiencies from the current 15 per cent values to over 50 per cent levels. These would in turn reduce the cost of solar energy production. Our science laboratories should mount a R&D programme for developing high efficiency CNT based Photo Voltaic Cells.

We thus need to embark on a major national programme in solar energy systems and technologies, for both large, centralized applications as well as small, decentralized requirements concurrently, for applications in both rural and urban areas.

Nuclear energy

Nuclear power generation has been given a thrust by the use of uranium based fuel. However there would be a requirement for a tenfold increase in nuclear power generation even to attain a reasonable degree of energy self-sufficiency for our country. Therefore it is essential to pursue the development of nuclear power using Thorium, reserves of which are higher in the country. Technology development has to be accelerated for Thorium based reactors since the raw material for Thorium is abundantly available in our country. Also, Nuclear Fusion research needs to be progressed with international cooperation to keep that option for meeting the large power requirement, at a time when fossil fuels get depleted.

Power through municipal waste

In the power generation sector of the energy economy, we need to fully use the technologies now available for generating power from municipal waste. Today, two plants are operational in India, each plant generating 6.5 MW of electric power. Studies indicate that as much as 5800 MW of power can be generated by setting up 900 electric power plants spread over different parts of the country which can be fuelled by municipal waste. The electric power generation and the creation of a clean environment are the twin advantages.

Power system loss reduction

Apart from generating power and running power stations efficiently without interruption, it is equally essential to transmit and distribute the power with minimum loss. The loss of power in transmission and distribution in our country is currently in the region of 30-40 per cent for a variety of reasons. Of about one thousand billion units of electrical energy produced annually, only 600 billion units reach the consumer. This is the result of transmission loss and unaccounted loss. We need to take urgent action to bring down this loss to 15 per cent from 30-40 per cent by close monitoring of the losses, improving efficiency, and increasing the power factor through modern technology. By this one action alone we will be able to avoid the need for additional investment of around Rs 70,000 crores for establishing additional generating capacity.

Transportation sector

The transportation sector is the fastest growing energy consumer. It now consumes nearly 112 million tonnes of oil annually, and is critically important to our nation's economy and security. The complete substitution of oil imports for the transportation sector is the biggest and toughest challenge for India.

Use of biofuels

We have nearly 60 million hectares of wasteland, of which 30 million hectares are available for energy plantations like Jatropha. Once grown, the crop has a life of fifty years. Each acre will produce about 2 tonnes of bio-diesel at about Rs 20 per litre. Bio-diesel is carbon neutral and many valuable by-products flow from this agro-industry. Intensive research is needed to burn bio-fuel in internal combustion engines with high efficiency, and this needs to be an urgent R&D programme. India has the potential to produce nearly 60 million tones of bio-fuel annually, thus making a significant and important contribution to the goal of energy independence. Indian Railways has already taken a significant step of running two passenger locomotives (Thanjavur to Nagore section) and six trains of diesel multiple units (Tiruchirapalli to Lalgudi, Dindigul and Karur sections) with a 5 per cent blend of bio-fuel sourced from its in-house esterification plants. In addition, they have planted 75 lakh Jatropha saplings in Railway land which is expected to give yields from the current year onwards. This is a pioneering example for many other organizations to follow. Similarly many states in our country have energy plantations. What is needed is a full economic chain from farming, harvesting, extraction to esterification, blending and marketing. Apart from employment generation, bio-fuel has a significant potential to lead our country towards energy independence.

The other critical options are development of electric vehicles; hydrogen based vehicles; electrification of Railways and urban mass transportation.

Conclusion

By 2020 the nation should achieve comprehensive energy security through enhancement of our oil and gas exploration and production worldwide. By the year 2030, India should achieve energy independence through solar power and other forms of renewable energy; maximize the utilization of hydro and nuclear power and enhance the bio-fuel production through large scale energy plantations like Jatropha.

We need to evolve a comprehensive renewable energy policy for energy independence within a year. This should address all issues relating to generation of energy through wind, solar, geothermal, bio-mass and ocean. The nation should also work towards establishment of thorium based reactors. Research and technology development of thorium based reactors is one of the immediate requirements for realizing self-reliance in nuclear power generation and long term energy security for the nation.

We should operationalize a 500 MW capacity power plant using integrated gasification and combined cycle route within the next three years from the existing pilot plant stage.

Bio-fuel research should be extended in collaboration with R&D laboratories, academic institutions and the automobile industry to make it a full fledged fuel for the fleet running in the country in a time bound manner. This should lead to a mission mode integrated programme encompassing various ministries and industries. Also there is a need to formulate a comprehensive bio-fuel policy from research and development to production and marketing.

Energy security leading to energy independence is certainly possible and is within the capability of the nation. India has the knowledge and natural resources; what we need are planned integrated missions to achieve the target in a time bound manner. Let us all work for self-sufficient environment-friendly energy independence for the nation.

Adapted from the text of the president's address to the nation on the eve of Independence Day, 2005. Copyright © A.P.J. Abdul Kalam 2005. Used with permission.

Building the Nation

Manmohan Singh

Next year, we will commence the celebrations of the 150th anniversary of the First Battle of Independence. Through the celebrations, we will have a chance to once again remember the glorious freedom fighters of that great battle who had laid the foundations for our independence.

In 1857, Bahadurshah Zafar had declared the Battle for Independence from the historic Red Fort. The battle cry of Rani of Jhansi

Lakshmi Bai, Peshwa Nana Saheb, Tantia Tope and Begum Hazrat Mahal of Lucknow was 'Delhi Chalo'. This cry was renewed with vigour and force by Netaji Subhash Chandra Bose and in 1947 this ambition was fulfilled.

Today, we have the opportunity of remembering their sacrifices. We can also learn from their enthusiasm and self-confidence, a number of traits which will be useful in facing today's challenges as well.

Mahatma Gandhi had also dreamt of the same independence when he launched the Dandi March seventy-five years ago. Through that struggle, he shook the foundations of the greatest and most powerful empire the world had ever seen.

Today, we need to once again remember the sacrifice and commitment of the Father of the Nation and also his dreams for an independent nation. We also need to reflect on how far we have been successful in fulfilling his dreams.

What was the dream Gandhiji had of an independent India? He had said, 'I will work for an India where the poorest of the poor feel that this country and this nation belongs to them and that they have a major role in its construction. An India where there is no higher class or lower class among all people. An India where all communities live in friendship and harmony. An India where women have the same rights as men.'

He had also said: 'The Swaraj I dream of is a Swaraj of poor people. I have not the slightest hesitation in saying that Swaraj cannot be complete till the poorest have a guarantee of being provided with the basic necessities of life.'

Have we come anywhere near this dream? In the last one year, our attempt has been to build the India of Gandhiji's dream. The goal of our government's National Common Minimum Programme is also the same.

In order to fulfil our promises, we have taken many important steps and have taken major decisions which will contribute to our nation's progress. While taking these decisions, the focus of our thoughts and attention has always been the aam aadmi. The effort of our government has been that while we continue to make rapid economic progress, the benefits of this progress and growth must reach all sections of society in a fair manner.

Our vision is not just of economic growth, but also of a growth which would improve the life of the aam aadmi.

Our country is witnessing unprecedented economic growth at this point in time. Last year, our economic growth rate was 7 per cent and it is likely to be similar this year as well. Our country has never witnessed such consistently high growth rates in the past. I am confident that if we maintain this momentum of growth for the next 5-10 years, then it would be possible for us to eradicate poverty, ignorance, hunger and disease from our country. This is not a dream but something that is possible in our times.

It is not only us but the entire world, which is viewing India as an emerging power of these times. The whole world is eagerly watching the manner in which India is making rapid economic progress. And this economic growth is happening within the framework of a liberal democracy.

Our country is a multi-cultural, multi-religious, multi-lingual and multi-ethnic nation. Nowhere in the world do we have an example of a country of a 100 crore people seeking their economic and social destiny within the framework of a democracy.

It is because of this that the entire world's attention is riveted on us. It is the result of our combined hard work that India today has made its mark on the world stage and we feel proud of our standing in the comity of nations.

It is my belief that India's future is extremely bright and that this future is indeed possible. In order to achieve this, we need to focus on achieving rapid economic growth and on ensuring social justice.

It is only by walking on these two legs will we be able to ensure that the benefits of growth reach all sections of society.

Last year, while addressing the nation on Independence Day, I had mentioned that our growth is critically dependent on seven sectors which I called the 'Saat Sutras'. These seven sectors are agriculture, irrigation, education, health, employment, urban renewal and infrastructure.

Today, we can review the progress made in these 7sevenareas. Our maximum emphasis has been on agriculture. Farmers are the backbone of our country and of our economy. It is the result of their tireless efforts that we do not have any shortage of foodgrains in our country.

The entire country is grateful to them for this.

We must admit that the economic growth we have been referring to earlier has not yet fully reached every individual in our society. This is particularly true in our rural areas. The growth in agriculture has not been at the required pace.

Even today, over 60 per cent of our population is dependent on agriculture and every farmer has a right to be a participant in our economic growth processes.

Hence, we have talked about giving a 'new deal' to our farmers. We have taken a number of steps to alleviate the problems of our farmers, such as improving and enhancing the flow of agricultural credit, increasing investment opportunities and storage facilities, launching a National Horticulture Mission to increase the output and trade in fruits and vegetables, and promoting research and training in agriculture.

It is our goal that by 2007, there should be a Krishi Vigyan Kendra in every district. Through this, the benefits of advanced research and training will reach all our rural bretheren. Large parts of our country are still dependent on rainfall and we will focus on removing the problems of farmers in dry land areas.

We are considering setting up a National Rainfed Area Authority for this purpose. It is our hope that in the coming years, agricultural growth becomes rapid and we have a new green revolution. We are fully committed to achieving this.

It is not possible for our rural areas to develop in the absence of basic infrastructural facilities. In order to improve basic infrastructure in rural areas, we have conceived an ambitious programme called 'Bharat Nirman'.

In Bharat Nirman, I crore hectares of unirrigated land will be irrigated. All villages whose population is 1000 or more, and 500 or more in hilly areas, will be connected with roads. Two and a half crore houses will be given electricity connections, and through this, the entire country will be electrified. Over 60 lakh houses will be built in villages.

The remaining 74,000 habitations which do not have access to safe drinking water will be provided these facilities. Each and every village will have at least one telephone connection. I am confident that Bharat Nirman will ensure the rapid economic development of our rural areas.

In all our economic programmes, our policy has been to ensure the participation of the common man, particularly of those in rural areas. They should feel that all programmes belong to them.

We have believed that the proper institutional mechanism to ensure their participation is the panchayat system. Shri Rajiv Gandhi had dreamt of Panchayati Raj many years ago.

Today, zila, tehsil and village panchayats have a major responsibility to discharge. Our Constitution has placed the responsibility on panchayats, not only of ensuring economic development but also delivering social justice.

Bharat Nirman provides a unique opportunity to our panchayats to shoulder this immense responsibility by effectively implementing this programme. I am confident that panchayats will ensure Bharat Nirman becomes a milestone in our development process.

We are giving importance not only to our rural areas but also to the economic conditions in our urban areas. Today, a third of our population lives in urban areas and keeping in mind the speed at which urbanization is taking place, the day is not far off when over 50 per cent of India's population will be residing in urban areas.

The foundations of our culture and society were laid thousands of years ago in the cities on the banks of Indus River. We taught the world the basic concepts of urban planning. However, today our cities are often unable to meet the basic needs of their residents on many counts. We will be investing in urban areas and for this, a National Urban Renewal Mission has been launched.

We have a large proportion of young people in our population. We will need to invest in their education and health so that their future prospects are bright. By doing so, our population will become our biggest asset.

It is necessary for every section of society to be literate and educated so that they can take advantage of our growth processes. By strengthening Sarva Shiksha Abhiyan, we are trying to ensure universalization of primary education.

We are giving special emphasis to the education of the girl child. We need to make education joyful, interesting and meaningful so that children develop a desire to go to school.

We need to pay particular attention to the education of first generation learners. We are resolute in our commitment to see that no child is deprived of the benefit of primary education. It is our hope that in the near future, women are as literate as men. In order to achieve these goals, resources shall not be a constraint. We are committed to providing education to disabled children as well.

Along with primary education, we also need to pay attention to higher education. If India is seen around the world as a rising knowledge power, it is because of our universities and research institutions. If we want to maintain our rapid economic growth, we need to improve the quality of these institutions and also create many more such institutions.

Let us resolve to achieve excellence in academic work in the 150th anniversary year of the Universities of Kolkata, Mumbai and Chennai.

However educated an individual may be, it is necessary for the person to be healthy in order to lead a happy life. Through the National Rural Health Mission, we will provide the best primary health care facilities in each and every village. We are confident that by providing excellent primary health care, we will be able to improve the health of young mothers and children which will then lead to a consequent reduction in our population growth rate.

In the last fifty years, we have been able to control and eliminate many diseases which have been a scourge in our country. Leprosy has been eliminated in twenty-five states. Polio and tuberculosis are also being gradually brought under control.

AIDS is now becoming a major national problem and we need to tackle this on a war-footing. We need to have a mass movement to ensure that this disease is rapidly checked and its growth arrested. We will also ensure that medicines are available to common people at reasonable prices.

As I had mentioned earlier, the true test of development is the number of people who have secured employment and the number of families who have prospered as a result. As long as there is widespread unemployment in the country, we cannot claim that we are truly independent. It is with this goal in mind that Indira Gandhi had given the nation the goal of 'Garibi Hatao'.

Today, if we need to remove poverty, we need to create employment: 'Rozgar Badhao'. In order to ensure that a minimum level of employment is available to everyone in rural areas, it is necessary to have an employment guarantee.

The National Rural Employment Guarantee Bill has been prepared with this goal in mind. We hope that this act will bring about a revolutionary change in the lives of people in rural India. We are also revamping the Khadi and Village Industries Commission so that more employment is generated through small and village industries.

In order to ensure that our economic growth does not slow down, it is necessary to have a strong infrastructure. Economic growth is intrinsically linked to the availability of infrastructure. Railways, roads and electricity are important elements of infrastructure. In order to improve our railways, a rail modernization programme has been prepared so that our railways become one of the best in the world. A dedicated freight corridor is being developed between Delhi-Kolkata and Delhi-Mumbai by investing over Rs 25,000 crore rupees.

The development of our national highways is progressing at a rapid pace. We have begun work on an additional 30,000 km of highways and we will soon be six-laning the Golden Quadrilateral. There has been tremendous progress in civil aviation. World class airports are being constructed in many cities. Ports are being modernized and many new ports are under construction.

Shortage of electricity is still a major inconvenience. Electricity is an essential ingredient of economic development. We need to ensure that electricity generation grows rapidly and that power shortages are eliminated. We need far greater investment in this sector. I have often said that, excepting for the poorest sections of society, giving electricity free of cost to other sections will worsen the financial condition of our electric utilities.

We need to get used to paying a reasonable price for electricity just as we do for petroleum products. Through this, we can ensure supply of electricity in the right quantity, at the right time and of right quality.

In my visit to the United States, we have managed to reduce some of the constraints which have been hampering the growth of our nuclear energy programme and in the next ten years, in addition to the 1,50,000 MW of capacity being added in the thermal and hydro sectors, another 40,000 MW could be generated through nuclear energy.

While rapid economic growth is one facet of our vision for the nation, social justice and equitable development is the other facet. Last year, our greatest contribution to the nation has been to bring it back on the path of rapid economic growth.

There is a ray of hope in the lives of all weaker sections of society. There is an atmosphere of calm, peace and communal harmony all around the country. We believe that this is an important achievement.

In our country, scheduled castes, scheduled tribes, backward classes and women suffer from many disabilities. Many of them have been discriminated against for centuries. It is essential that they are made stakeholders and participants in our development processes. We are committed to paying attention to their education, health and basic necessities.

We have taken some steps to improve their economic and social status. A bill has been introduced in Parliament on reservation in government employment. It will be our effort now to increase the opportunities for employment and equal opportunities in employment outside government.

Our Adivasi brothers have been cultivating land near forests for many generations. However, they do not have any rights on this land owing to which they live in constant fear of eviction. Their rights were snatched away from them 150 years ago during British rule. In order to correct this, we are bringing a legislation which will benefit scheduled tribes living in forests while at the same time ensuring conservation of our natural heritage.

Our Constitution provides for equality of all religions. All religions are safe and secure within our Republic. It is essential that minorities should have every opportunity of carrying on their daily activities with a feeling of security and happiness. This is also our goal. Hence we have repealed POTA, the Prevention of Terrorism Act.

As a result, many sections of society are able to breathe easy.

We have commissioned a report on the social economic status of minorities. This is being done for the first time and will be the basis for all our policy interventions for improving their status. We will also revive and revamp the 15 Point Programme for Minorities. The New 15 Point Programme will have definite goals which are to be achieved in a specific time frame.

We are going to start a special development programme which will focus on the skill enhancement of artisans and weavers, many of whom are minorities. This will help improve their incomes.

Industrial growth is the result of the sweat and toil of our working classes. This year, our industrial growth in May has exceeded 10 per cent. I would like to congratulate all our workers for this magnificent result. The government will pay specific attention towards addressing the problems of workers, particularly those in the unorganized sector.

It is our hope that we will be able to provide a social security net for them so that they do not feel insecure in times of distress. However, I would like to emphasize that workers too have a responsibility. Wherever they may be working, in factories or in firms, they should work in cooperation with the management so that profitability of enterprises increases and they also benefit from this.

Women are the backbone not only of our homes but also of our nation. We need to strengthen their hands and empower them fully. We have brought legislation to prevent domestic violence against women and to secure their property rights. We will also ensure reservation for women in Parliament and Legislative Assemblies.

In order to provide an opportunity for our youth and sportspersons to demonstrate their skills, we will make all possible efforts to ensure that India once again hosts the Asian Games in Delhi, the first time since 1982.

In this new phase of development, we are acutely aware that all regions of the country should develop at the same pace. It is unacceptable for us to see any region of the country left behind other regions in this quest for development. In every scheme of the government, we will be making all efforts to ensure that backward regions are adequately taken care of. This has been ensured in the Food for Work Programme and the National Rural Health Mission.

We will also focus on the development of our border areas. We will ensure that these regions are provided basic infrastructure such as roads, electricity and telephone connectivity in the next 3-4 years.

Our rivers are the lifelines of the country. They are the foundations of our ancient civilization. Today the demand for water is growing all around. In the twenty-first century, water will be the most precious commodity and its shortage will be felt all around. We need to launch a national movement to prevent the wastage of water and for its efficient use. This is an absolute necessity. It is also necessary that all states of our country work together in a spirit of give and take and a spirit of mutual understanding to sort out all contentious issues amicably so that everyone is benefited.

We also need to pay special attention to our environment. We need to start a national campaign for cleanliness so that our cities, towns, villages, roads, streets and homes are neat and clean. Gandhiji used to emphasize this aspect in his ashram as well. We need to stop the pollution of our rivers and atmosphere. We need to protect our forests and natural heritage. We must remember that we are only the custodians of our environment and it is our responsibility to preserve and pass it on to our future generations.

In the recent past, natural calamities have affected many parts of our country with disastrous effects on people and property. A tsunami in December, snowfall in January and floods in July.

A lot of people have lost their precious lives in these calamities. The entire nation's sympathies are with the bereaved families. I am confident that we will face the problems of floods in a united manner, just as we faced the devastation caused by the tsunami.

I would like to assure that we will provide whatever assistance is required to ensure that Mumbai, Maharashtra, Gujarat and Karnataka are restored to normalcy. In order to effectively tackle such natural calamities, we have constituted a National Disaster Management Authority. Through this, and by using the latest technologies, we hope to face future calamities in a much better manner.

In the country, we still have regions such as Jammu & Kashmir and the North-East where complete peace and tranquillity does not exist. The people in these regions are the victims of violence and terrorism.

Wherever conditions deteriorate we take the assistance of our armed forces.

As a result of our policy in Jammu & Kashmir, the state is once again on the path of peace and progress. It is our humanitarian obligation that we assist the state in all possible ways so that the people there can live in peace and harmony. Terrorists have never been the friends of the people of Kashmir. As long as they continue their terrorist attacks, our armed forces will be alert and give them a fitting response.

In this conflict, common citizens may also be affected at times. I have said before and I am repeating once again, that there is no issue that cannot be resolved through a process of discussion and dialogue. Our doors are always open and will continue to be open for anyone interested in dialogue. I invite everyone to join us to discuss the problems of the state of Jammu & Kashmir so that its people can lead a life of peace and dignity.

But if violence continues, then our response too will be hard. I am aware that the Government of Pakistan has put some checks on the activities of terrorists from its soil. However, it is not possible to achieve success through half-hearted efforts. It is necessary that the entire infrastructure of terrorism is totally dismantled.

In the context of terrorism and extremism, development and security have an intrinsic relationship. We have managed to face extremism successfully through a democratic process. However, it is imperative that a democratic government should be able to differentiate between the genuine problems of people and the designs of terrorists.

Today, there are a number of challenges in our security environment such as terrorism, communal violence, atrocities on women and exploitation of dalits and adivasis. Our security forces have been facing the daunting task of controlling extremist violence admirably. Extremism is a challenge which requires a united response from all of us. However, it is also necessary to look at a political resolution of this problem.

Often extremism has its roots in backwardness and lack of economic development. It is not easy to handle the problem of extremism in isolation. However, by addressing it in all its dimensions—social, political, economic and security-related—in an integrated manner, I am confident that we will be successful in checking it.

India has always been a country which loves peace. Its destiny is intrinsically linked to those of its neighbours. Our goal has always been the prosperity and happiness of our citizens. Hence, we have always sought the friendship of our neighbours, although at times, this has not been fully successful.

There seems to be some success in our search for peace and harmony now. Many problems of South Asia are similar, of which poverty and illiteracy are the most widespread. It is possible for us to eliminate these in the region by working together.

The composite dialogue process with Pakistan is continuing. As a result, we have been able to reopen the Srinagar-Muzaffarabad highway which was a long pending demand of the people and restarted the bus service on this route, a step which has been widely welcomed. Talks are going on to open similar links from points in other states.

Discussions are also going on a gas pipeline from Iran to India via Pakistan. Once this is completed, we will be able to address a major constraint affecting our economy.

It is our sincere hope that we work with all our neighbours in South Asia to effectively address the challenges of poverty, unemployment and disease. If India and Pakistan are able to work together, than we will have many opportunities for making our countries prosperous. I am confident that we will be able to fulfil this vision.

Our largest neighbour is China with whom we have a centuries old relationship, a relationship from which both of us have learnt a lot and imbibed a lot. We are today willing and ready to deepen our trade and cultural relations with China for the benefit of the two nations. The agreement arrived at between our two countries in April has paved the way for a closer relationship.

My visit to the United States has been a major step in promoting friendship with that country. By deepening our economic and technological relations, we will be accelerating our own growth. Simultaneously, our two democracies can work together to strengthen democracy in the world.

We also wish to deepen our relations with the countries to the east. The recently concluded trade agreement with Singapore is a major step in improving our economic engagement with the region. We will be entering into many more such agreements in future.

I would like to emphasize that the contribution of Indians and persons of Indian origin settled abroad in ensuing that our efforts are successful is enormous. They have not only travelled to far off lands to achieve their dreams of prosperity for themselves and their children, but have also played a stellar role in changing the world's perception of India.

The world today sees India as a major knowledge power whose people are skilled, competent, hard working and peace loving. Even within our own country, our scientists, doctors, engineers and scholars have contributed substantially in the achievements of our nation. We are proud of all of them.

The biggest challenge in running a government is to ensure that development programmes are implemented in an effective manner. We will ensure that our outlays of expenditure are visible to citizens as outcomes of progress. The central government, state governments and panchayats have to work together so that the expectations of people are fulfilled. If we have to achieve results, there is a need to change the manner in which governments function.

There is no space in our government or in our society for corruption and arbitrary action. We are not prepared to tolerate this at any cost. Government servants must work with a sense of public service and they should be held accountable to the people. Governments will have to be made more transparent and accountable. The recently passed Right to Information Act is a landmark step in this direction.

India is on the road to progress. The whole world is watching us with expectation. It is possible for us to eradicate poverty, ignorance and disease within our lifetime. This has been made possible by the advances in science and technology.

There comes a time in the history of a nation when it can be said that the time has come to make history. We are today at the threshold of such an era. The world wants us to do well and take our rightful place on the world stage. There are no external constraints on our development. If there are any hurdles, they are internal.

We must seize this moment and grab this opportunity. We need to have the resolve to make our country prosperous. We must have the self-confidence to realize that we are second to none, that Indians are as good as the best.

Our political system and leadership must show sagacity, wisdom and foresight so that we are able to make the best of this moment and make India a truly great nation.

Let us come together, as one nation, strengthened by our plurality, to work shoulder to shoulder and build a new India. An India where there are no barriers between the government and the people. An India where each and every Indian can stand proudly and proclaim that he is an Indian. Let us work together to build such a nation.

Adapted from the text of the prime minister's address to the nation on Independence Day, 2005. Copyright © Manmohan Singh 2005. Used with permission.

The Way to Economic Development

Amartya Sen

There is indeed much about the process of economic growth and development that India can learn from the experience of China. Making good use of global trade opportunities is among the lessons that China offers to India, and the lessons here can be critically important for India's economic progress. A similar message had already emerged from the economic success of other east Asian economies, including South Korea, but given China's size and the intensity of its pre-existing poverty, China's experiences are particularly relevant for India's economic policy-making. The general lesson that good use can be made of global opportunities of trade and commerce to enhance domestic income and to reduce poverty has emerged very clearly from the success of economies in East and South-East Asia – led now by China.

It is, however, important to avoid the much-aired simplification that argues that all India needs to do to achieve fast economic growth and speedy reduction of poverty is greater reliance on the global market and on international trade. This reflects, in fact, a serious misreading of the variety of factors that have contributed to the kind of economic success achieved in China, South Korea, Thailand and other countries in East and South-East Asia. These countries did emphasize international trade and made fine use of the global market mechanism. But they also made it possible to have broad-based public participation in economic expansion, through such policies as extensive schooling and high literacy, good health care, widespread land reforms, and some considerable fostering of gender equity (not least through female education and employment).

This is not to doubt that India can achieve reasonably high growth rates of aggregate GNP even with the rather limited social opportunities that exist in India. For one thing, it can continue to do extremely well in industries that make excellent use of India's accomplishments in higher education and technical training. New centres of technical excellence, like Bangalore and Hyderabad, can prosper and flourish, and India can even accelerate its progress along the lines that it has already established well. This will be a substantial achievement of considerable economic importance.

Yet even a hundred Bangalores and Hyderabads will not, on their own, solve India's tenacious poverty and deep-seated inequality. The very poor in India get a small – and basically indirect – share of the cake that information technology and related developments generate.

The removal of poverty, particularly of extreme poverty, calls for more participatory growth on a wide basis, which is not easy to achieve across the barriers of illiteracy, ill health, uncompleted land reforms and other sources of severe societal inequality. The process of economic advance cannot be divorced from the cultivation and enhancement of social opportunities over a broad front.

The products that China exports to the outside world include a great many that are made by not particularly highly skilled labour, but schooled and literate labour nevertheless. Their production generates much employment, with a great deal of income going to poorer sections of the community. Utilization of the world market for such exports requires production according to specification, quality control and an informed consciousness of the economic tasks involved. Good school education is central for these tasks. Similarly, good health is extremely important if productive effort and economic schedules are not to be affected by illnesses and intermittent absence.

Basic education, good health and other human attainments are not only directly valuable as constituent elements of human capabilities and quality of life (these are the direct pay-offs of schooling, health care and other social arrangements), but these capabilities can also help in generating economic success of a more standard kind, which in turn can contribute to enhancing the quality of human life even more. If there is something that India can learn from China's post-reform experience in the 1980s onwards about making skilful use of global markets, there is also much that India can assimilate from China's pre-reform experience in rapidly expanding the delivery of basic education and elementary health care.

The Economic Role of the State

Bimal Jalan

The main political problem in the making of economic policy in India is not the weakness of its political institutions or its form of government, but the wrong assumptions about the real political interests at the ground level. For as long as four decades of central planning after independence, the primary assumption of planners, economists and development advisers was that of a welfare-maximizing State, strenuously seeking to reconcile differences among the competing demands by various groups, and selflessly promoting the greatest good of the greatest number. Based on this assumption, it was assumed that the greater the intervention of the State (and its agent, the government of the day) in the economy, the greater would be the benefit to the people. Thus, it was assumed that if the government-owned banks allocated credit, prescribed the pattern of output by giving out industrial licences and determined the pattern of consumption, the scarce economic resources of the country could be used to produce goods and services at affordable prices for the common man.

Similarly, it was assumed that if the means of production were owned by the State and were under the control of its political leaders, the entire value added in production would flow to the people. Savings and investment would also be maximized, leading to the emergence of a virtuous circle of a large public sector, leading to higher public investment, which in turn would lead to higher growth with redistributive Justice. The political motivations in the use of resources were, however, vastly different, inward-looking, narrow and self-centred. Instead of a virtuous circle, the expansion of economic power by self-centred agencies of the State, over time, trapped India in a vicious circle of low growth, higher poverty and periodic economic crises.

A priority for the future is to further reduce the political role of the government in the economy. The process of reform, initiated in the early 1980s and accelerated haltingly since then, needs to be firmly pursued. The political role of the government, in so far as the economy is concerned, should be to ensure a stable and competitive environment with a strong external sector and a transparent domestic financial system. Since the balance of payments position, unlike in the past, is now strong with low external debt, India must also adopt an aggressive 'open economy' policy with as low a level of protection as most competitive economies in the world. Open competition is the most effective deterrent to the emergence of monopolistic practices and monopoly rents. A reduction in the political role of the government and its ministers also implies a reduction in the ownership of commercial enterprises. The high-sounding term 'public sector' is really a misnomer in this connection.

The public sector does not really work for the public at large. The value added by the enterprises has been low, and instead of adding to public savings, they are now a major drain on the fiscal resources available to the government.

At the same time, the political role of the government in ensuring the availability of public goods (such as roads or water) and essential services (such as health and education) must expand substantially. A reduction in the role of the government in managing commercial enterprises and an expansion of its role in the supply of public services are two sides of the same coin. A reduction in public sector deficit and elimination of ministerial access to commercial activities will facilitate larger fiscal expenditure on public services and promote stronger ministerial responsibility for the implementation of anti-poverty and people-oriented programmes.

A related political imperative is the need for a joint agreement between leaders of major political parties and the trade unions of government employees to improve the services of the State to its people. Such an agreement to improve service to the people should be possible through a democratic process. Unfortunately, this has not been attempted and trade unions continue to press for more benefits for those who are already employed without a corresponding improvement in their duties to the public. Some public-spirited heads of municipal- and state-level government departments have made attempts to meet some of the most basic requirements of the people (such as birth certificates or the renewal of trade licences) without delay or corruption. However, even these efforts have not yielded results because of the non-cooperation of government employees. A recent example is the failure of the so-called Citizen Service Bureaus set up by the Municipal Corporation of Delhi (MCD). According to an investigative report, this is what some citizens had to say about the service being provided by the bureaus: 'I want my daughter's birth certificate, but every time I come, the officials ask me to get some new papers ... corruption cannot be checked even in a computerized office. I am being asked to pay extra money to get the work done faster ... The Bureaus were supposed to cut red tape, but more than a year later, they are anything but [*sic*] convenience.' There cannot be a more severe indictment of the insensitivity of government organizations and their employees to the requirements of citizens. A political campaign, with the support of civil society organizations, is now necessary to make the unions and government leaders more responsive to the needs of their voters and to make public servants more accountable.

There is also a case for reducing the number of ministries and ministers in the governments. In 2004, some state governments had nearly a hundred ministers, and the central government has sixty-six (the number would have been considerably larger if some of the parties that are supporting the present government from outside were also inside). Naturally, the larger the number of ministries and ministers, the greater the scope for interference, conflicts and duplication. A legislative amendment to restrict the size of ministries to 15 per cent of the members of the legislatures is welcome. But even this percentage is too high. However, since this amendment has been adopted only recently, with considerable opposition from some states, it is unlikely that the number of ministries and ministers can be reduced further any time soon. An alternative approach may be to keep the numbers of ministries as they are, but redefine their functions and responsibility.

A worthwhile principle to follow in streamlining the working of ministries may be to abolish all commercial and regulatory functions which are handled by other autonomous bodies (such as the Reserve Bank, the Securities and Exchange Board, the Telecom Commission, Electricity Commissions, the Public Sector Enterprises Board, and so on). In their place, ministries should assume the responsibility for monitoring the progress of programme implementation in physical quantitative terms in areas that are of interest to the public and where there is a need for the government to assume greater responsibility.

The 'rule-making' powers of the government under the Acts of Parliament, and the complexity of various legislative provisions and rules notified by the government also require a review. Many of the Acts, including Acts for the regulation of financial or economic contracts and the development of capital markets, are more than a hundred years old. These laws are anachronistic and out of line with the current realities of global trade, commerce and industry. What has made the situation worse is a plethora of rules notified by the government over several decades, many of which are not even accessible (but nevertheless remain in force). Cleaning up the legislative mess, abolishing outdated laws and simplifying the notified rules, particularly in the economic and financial areas, are essential. For this purpose, it may be desirable to set up a separate Standing Committee of Parliament, with sufficient powers and legal support, to complete this task within one year.

Over time, the 'rule-making' powers of the government, without any effective parliamentary oversight, have grown immensely. The main legislative sections of an Act may be precisely defined or formulated to indicate the purpose and coverage of various provisions. However, it has become the general practice to add an explanatory section or an omnibus clause which gives powers to the government to notify various rules to give effect to legislative provisions. These rule-making powers are very wide. The legislation often prescribes that the government has the power to prescribe rules 'notwithstanding any other provisions of the Act or any other laws in force'. These omnibus powers provide sufficient scope for the arbitrary exercise of powers (or vendettas against political opponents and particular classes of persons, including taxpayers). In some states, as political rivalries among parties have intensified, these rule-making powers have been used to defeat the original purpose of the Act itself.

An example of the misuse of a central legislation at the state level is the 'Prevention of Terrorism Act 2002', or POTA (which the new government has rightly withdrawn). The relevant sections of the Act (Chapter II, Sections 3[I][a] and 3[I][b]) were careful to define a terrorist act precisely by identifying the means by which such an act could be perpetrated (that is, by using bombs, dynamite and other explosive substances). At the same time, an explanatory provision to these sections had the effect of conferring unlimited discretionary powers on the government to regard almost any action by a citizen as a terrorist activity. Thus, anyone who was believed to 'advocate, abet, or advise' or did any act 'preparatory' to a terrorist act could also be apprehended as a conspirator and sent to prison! Any citizen, however innocent, could thus be brought under the purview of such an omnibus provision if the government wished to do so. And this is precisely how the POTA provisions were used in some states by governments in power to harass political opponents. It must now be made mandatory for all legislative provisions to be precisely defined. The rule-making powers of the government under the various Acts should be abolished. There is no reason why all essential and relevant rules cannot be included in the legislation itself. If further amendments in the rules are necessary, these can also be brought before Parliament for adoption.

Building Confidence

Derek O'Brien

Many years ago, on a cold and smoggy winter's morning in Calcutta I remember driving down to my school with my parents in the red family Standard Herald. The reason I remember this morning more than most other winter mornings was because of what was to happen next. It was promotion day; time for me to climb the stairs from Class 8 to Class 9. Or so I thought. My Dad, Mum and I reached the entrance to the hallowed staff room and I quickly found out all was not right. The wiry Class 8 teacher who we had fondly nicknamed 'Lal Murgi' (a take off on his name Redden, i.e. red hen!) was all set to gleefully deliver the bad news: your son is not being promoted to Class 9. He is quite useless in science and maths; in fact he is quite useless, period.

Words enough to shatter the confidence of any thirteen-year old.

The thirteen-year-old soon turned eighteen. It was time to seek admission to one of Calcutta's premier colleges, an extension of the same school that was my alma mater. One quick look at the final list of students selected to join this elite Jesuit institution gave me the bad news: my name was missing. The distinguished priest who headed the department and was in charge of admissions did not rustle his cassock when he delivered the blow: you are just not good enough to join the college.

Words enough to shatter the confidence of any eighteen-year old.

What is confidence? Although my favourite dictionary may define it as 'a positive feeling arising from an appreciation of one's own abilities', you will agree, there cannot be one single definition to describe this state of mind. Confidence means different things to different people.

What does confidence mean to Sania Mirza? This pop star cum tennis icon has been flashing forehands and smoothening serves on tennis courts when most other girls her age are cramming for exams or burning the dance floor. There is a story doing the rounds, that when her parents first took her to a coach, she was dismissed as 'too young to even hold a racquet properly'. However, one look at her swing and the coaches swiftly rectified their double fault. They realized that there was something special in that pint-sized package. Before her seventh birthday, Sania was already playing in local tournaments. At age thirteen, she got her first sponsor. The other milestones too are worth recording.

2001: Sania started playing in professional tournaments in India.

2003: She won the Wimbledon junior doubles title, with Russian Alisa Kleybanova as her partner.

2004: she became the first Indian woman to win a WTA Tour event (a doubles title). A star was born.

2005: she then becomes the first Indian woman to reach the third round at a Grand Slam—the 2005 Australian Open.

There was more to follow. More records to tumble. More confidence to build upon. The Hyderabad heart-throb became the first Indian woman to win a Tour singles title, when she defeated the number 9 seed Alyona Bondarenko of Ukraine in a three setter in the final of the Hyderabad Open. Months later in Dubai she wrapped up a sizzling year by stunning reigning US Open champion and number 4 seed Svetlana Kuznetsova at the Dubai Open. Here was Miss Confidence now in the stratosphere of the Top 35 players in the world.

Rather than give you theories and cold definitions of that magical ten-letter word called confidence, allow me to walk you through the career of another iconic Indian, Shah Rukh Khan.

This Delhi-born actor first appeared on the public radar with his performances in the television programmes, *Fauji* and *Circus*. SRK then made the switch to the big screen with *Deewana*, *Raju Ban Gaya Gentleman* and *Maya Memsaab*. Then came the dual superhits: *Darr* and *Baazigar*. It was not about macho looks or typical Bollywood pancake that took Khan to dizzying heights. It was what critics called the X-factor. They could not define it, but the man had 'something that worked, something that connected'. Soon more hits followed: *Dilwale Dulhania Le Jayenge* (1995), *Pardes* (1997), *Dil To Pagal Hai* (1997), *Dil Se..* (1998), *Kuch Kuch Hota Hai* (2000), *Kabhi Khushi Kabhie Gham...* (2001), *Devdas* (2002), *Kal Ho Naa Ho* (2003), *Veer-Zaara* (2004).

So what does confidence mean to the man Amitabh Bachchan calls the Badshah of Bollywood? What does confidence mean to the man who, by his own admission, only has a few standard facial expressions to offer? I don't have a ready answer. And neither does, probably, Mr Khan. Let's make a feeble attempt though at finding an answer.

Maybe it is the sheer versatility of the man and his confidence to handle a wide range of characters that have provided the cutting edge. From a star-crossed lover to a scheming, murderous anti-hero; from a legendary king to a NASA scientist – it has been an unreal journey for this student of St Columbas School, Delhi. Here is someone who inspires the confidence of the world's largest film industry because they know that the shortest cut to box office success is to have those three magical letters on Friday first day first show: SRK.

Sania and tennis. Shah Rukh and tinsel town. Now, cricket. Who is my favourite Indian icon? Without a doubt, Irfan Pathan. May I ask you that question again? What does confidence mean to this twenty-year old from Baroda? Maybe you will find the answer in two photographs of this handsome man. One, taken when he wrecked Bangladesh in the Asian Under-19s (remember?—a nine-wicket haul including a hat-trick) and another picture taken in October 2005 at the launch of a television brand in Mumbai. Two very different Irfans, one Arjunesque mission. The small-town boy from Baroda was now a brand ambassador, complete with fizzy hair and screeching female fans. Irfan had walked (correction, run) the plank of confidence.

Pathan's was a confidence not gained from personality development classes or makeover clinics. His confidence was built on *champion performances*. Consider this. Irfan made his Test debut against Australia at Adelaide in December 2003, only after playing a handful of matches at the domestic first class level.

Performance equal confidence. Seven five-wicket hauls (Tests plus ODIs, till October 2005) and two 10-wicket hauls (Tests plus ODIs, till October 2005) means that he is now regarded as a certainty for selection to the national squad. Welcome to the confidence club, Irfan Pathan. It's not about which school you went to or which car your father drives, it, perhaps, is about knowing and believing *I can*.

We could address the confidence question to the much-loved A.P.J. Abdul Kalam. Or, to another youth icon Narain Karthikeyan. Or, to your elder brother who is your hero. Or, to my father, my hero. They would all give us different answers. No right answers, no wrong answers, but points of view that help us understand and inspire us to be more confident.

This writer (and there is no false modesty here) is hardly qualified to provide you the interpretations of confidence our youth icons have. At best, on a personal level, a first step towards gaining confidence is to experience failure. How you react to failure; how you emerge stronger from it is the cornerstone of confidence. It is this paradox which makes the development of confidence such a challenging process.

I am quite sure, if you ask any hero or heroine (and I don't mean only the Shah Rukh Khans and Sania Mirzas), or someone in your family you look up to, they will tell you that they have experienced failure in some form or the other. Confidence lies in the positives you take out of this failure.

Let me leave you with one last thought. Can anyone be one hundred percent confident? Here's a classic cricketing story which provides the answer.

In his last international innings, Sir Donald Bradman needed four runs to be able to retire with a batting average of 100. He was dismissed for a duck by spin bowler Eric Hollies. So, Bradman's batting average from 52 Tests was 99.94.

He still remains the cricketing world's greatest legend ever. As he would have been with that 'perfect' average of 100.

Copyright © Derek O'Brien 2005.

Politics

Government

India has a parliamentary form of government with its foundations in the principle of universal adult franchise. The sovereignty of the country rests with the people of India and the executive authority is responsible to the elected representatives of the people in the Parliament for all its decisions and actions. The Parliament of India has two houses: the Rajya Sabha, or the Council of States and the Lok Sabha, the House of the People.

The Rajya Sabha consists of not more than 250 members, of whom the President of India nominates 12 and the rest are elected. It is not subject to dissolution and one-third of its members retire at the end of every second year. The elections to Rajya Sabha are indirect, with the members of the Legislative Assembly of each state electing its members in accordance with the system of proportional representation by means of a single transferable vote. The Vice-President of India presides over the Rajya Sabha.

The Lok Sabha consists of 545 members. Of these, 530 are directly elected from the 28 states and 13 from the six Union territories and the National Capital territory of Delhi. Two members are nominated by the President to represent the Anglo-Indian community. Unless dissolved sooner, the term of the House is five years from the date appointed for its first meeting. The Lok Sabha elects its own presiding officer, the Speaker.

The President of India is the Head of State and the Commander-in-Chief of the Armed Forces. He is elected by an electoral college comprising both Rajya Sabha and Lok Sabha members, as well as the legislatures of the constituent states. The President holds office for five years and can be re-elected. The members of both houses of Parliament jointly elect the Vice-President.

The President does not normally exercise any constitutional powers on his own initiative. These are exercised by the Council of Ministers, headed by the Prime Minister, which is responsible to the popularly elected Parliament. The President appoints the person enjoying majority support in the Lok Sabha as the Prime Minister. The former then appoints other ministers on the advice of the Prime Minister. The cabinet appointed by the President can remain in office only as long as it enjoys majority support in the Parliament.

The judiciary: The judiciary is independent of the executive. It is viewed as the guardian and interpreter of the Constitution. The Supreme Court is the highest judicial tribunal positioned at the top of a single unified system for the whole country. Each state has its own High Court. A uniform code of civil and criminal laws applies to the whole country.

The states: The states have their own legislative assemblies and in some cases, a second legislative council. All members of the legislative assemblies are elected on the principle of universal adult franchise. The Governor, appointed by the President, is the head of the state. All 28 states, the Union territory of Pondicherry and NCT of Delhi have state assemblies with a cabinet headed by the Chief Minister responsible to the elected state legislature.

Presidents of India

Name	Tenure
Dr Rajendra Prasad (1884–1963)	26 January 1950–13 May 1962
Dr Sarvepalli Radhakrishnan (1888–1975)	13 May 1962–13 May 1967
Dr Zakir Husain (1897–1969)	13 May 1967–3 May 1969
Varahagiri Venkatagiri (1884–1980)	3 May 1969–20 July 1969 (Acting)
Justice Mohammad Hidayatullah (1905–1992)	20 July 1969–24 August 1969 (Acting)
Varahagiri Venkatagiri (1884–1980)	24 August 1969–24 August 1974
Fakhruddin Ali Ahmed (1905–1977)	24 August 1974–11 February 1977
B.D. Jatti (1913–2002)	11 February 1977–25 July 1977 (Acting)
Neelam Sanjiva Reddy (1913–1996)	25 July 1977–25 July 1982
Giani Zail Singh (1916–1994)	25 July 1982–25 July 1987
R. Venkataraman (b 1910)	25 July 1987–25 July 1992
Dr Shanker Dayal Sharma (1918–1999)	25 July 1992–25 July 1997
K.R. Narayanan (b 1920)	25 July 1997–25 July 2002
Dr A.P.J. Abdul Kalam (b 1931)	25 July 2002–till date

Vice-Presidents of India

Name	Tenure
Dr Sarvepalli Radhakrishnan (1888–1975)	1952–1962
Dr Zakir Husain (1897–1969)	1962–1967
Varahagiri Venkatagiri (1884–1980)	1967–1969
Gopal Swarup Pathak (1896–1982)	1969–1974
B.D. Jatti (1913–2002)	1974–1979
Justice Mohammad Hidayatullah (1905–1992)	1979–1984
R. Venkataraman (b 1910)	1984–1987
Dr Shanker Dayal Sharma (1918–1999)	1987–1992
K.R. Narayanan (b 1920)	1992–1997
Krishan Kant (1927–2002)	1997–2002
Bhairon Singh Shekhawat (b 1923)	2002–till date

Prime Ministers of India

Name	Tenure
Jawaharlal Nehru (1889–1964)	15 August 1947–27 May 1964
Gulzari Lal Nanda (1898–1997)	27 May 1964–9 June 1964 (Acting)
Lal Bahadur Shastri (1904–1966)	9 June 1964–11 January 1966
Gulzari Lal Nanda (1898–1997)	11 January 1966–24 January 1966 (Acting)
Indira Gandhi (1917–1984)	24 January1966–24 March 1977

Morarji Desai (1896–1995)	24 March 1977–28 July 1979
Charan Singh (1902–1987)	28 July 1979–14 January 1980
Indira Gandhi (1917–1984)	14 January 1980–31 October 1984
Rajiv Gandhi (1944–1991)	31 October 1984–1 December 1989
Vishwanath Pratap Singh (b 1931)	2 December 1989–10 November 1990
Chandra Shekhar (b 1927)	10 November 1990–21 June 1991
P.V. Narasimha Rao (b 1921)	21 June 1991–16 May 1996
Atal Bihari Vajpayee (b 1926)	16 May 1996–1 June 1996
H.D. Deve Gowda (b 1933)	1 June 1996–21 April 1997
I.K. Gujral (b 1933)	21 April 1998–18 March 1998
Atal Bihari Vajpayee (b 1926)	19 March 1998–22 May 2004
Manmohan Singh(b 1932)	22 May 2004–till date

Chief Justices of India

Name	Tenure
Harilal J. Kania	26 January 1950–6 November 1951
M. Patanjali Sastri	7 November 1951–3 January 1954
Mehar Chand Mahajan	4 January 1954–22 December 1954
B.K. Mukherjea	23 December 1954–31 January 1956
S.R. Das	1 February 1956–30 September 1959
Bhuvaneshwar Prasad Sinha	1 October 1959–31 January 1964
P.B. Gajendragadkar	1 February 1964–15 March 1966
A.K. Sarkar	16 March 1966–29 June 1966
K. Subba Rao	30 June 1966–11 April 1967
K.N. Wanchoo	12 April 1967–24 February 1968
M. Hidayatullah	25 February 1968–16 December 1970
J.C. Shah	17 December 1970–21 January 1971
S.M. Sikri	22 January 1971–25 April 1973
A.N. Ray	26 April 1973–27 January 1977
M.H. Beg	28 January 1977–21 February 1978
Y.V. Chandrachud	22 February 1978–11 July 1985
Prafullachandra Natvarlal Bhagwati	12 July 1985–20 December 1986
R.S. Pathak	21 December 1986–18 June 1989
E.S. Venkataramiah	19 June 1989–17 December 1989
S. Mukharjee	18 December 1989–25 September 1990
Ranganath Mishra	26 September 1990–24 November 1991
K.N. Singh	25 November 1991–12 December 1991
M.H. Kania	13 December 1991–17 November 1992
L.M. Sharma	18 November 1992–11 February 1993
M.N. Venkatachaliah	12 February 1993–24 October 1994
A.M. Ahmadi	25 October 1994–24 March 1997
J.S. Verma	25 March 1997–17 January 1998
M.M. Punchhi	18 January 1998–9 October 1998
A.S. Anand	10 October 1998–till date
S.P. Bharucha	1 November 2001–5 May 2002
B.N. Kirpal	6 May 2002–7 November 2002
G.B. Pattanaiak	8 November 2002–18 December 2002
V.N. Khare	19 December 2002–2 May 2004
S. Rajendra Babu	2 May 2004–1 June 2004
Ramesh Chandra Lahoti	1 June 2004–till date

The Constitution of India

Introduction

The Constitution of India is one of the world's lengthiest written constitutions with 395 articles and 12 schedules. It was passed on 26 November 1949 by the Constituent Assembly and became fully applicable from 26 January 1950.

The Constitution of India draws from Western legal traditions in the way that it outlines the principles of liberal democracy. It provides for a bicameral parliament (a lower house and an upper house) along the lines of the British parliamentary pattern. It contains the Fundamental Rights, similar to the Bill of Rights contained in the United States Constitution. It also provides for a Supreme Court, as in the US Constitution.

India has a federal system, in which the residual powers of legislation are vested in the central government. This is similar to the Canadian set-up. The Constitution also contains detailed lists (the state list, the union list and the concurrent list), dividing powers between the central and state governments, similar to Australia. It contains a set of Directive Principles of State Policy. This is similar to the Irish Constitution.

The Constitution has the provision for the addition of Schedules by means of amendments. At present, the Constitution has 12 schedules. The assent of at least two-thirds of the Lok Sabha and the Rajya Sabha is needed to review the Constitution.

The Indian Constitution has been frequently amended. The first amendment was passed after only a year of the adoption of the Constitution, and it came into force on 18 June 1951. The most recent amendment, the Ninety-second Amendment, came into force on 1 July 2004. Most parts of the Constitution can be amended after a quorum of more than half of the members of each house in the Parliament passes an amendment with a two-thirds majority vote. However, articles relating to the distribution of legislative authority between the central and state governments must also be approved by 50 per cent of the state legislatures.

Preamble

WE, THE PEOPLE OF INDIA, having solemnly resolved to constitute India into a SOVEREIGN, SOCIALIST, SECULAR, DEMOCRATIC, REPUBLIC and to secure to all its citizens:

JUSTICE, social, economic and political;

LIBERTY of thought, expression, belief, faith and worship;

EQUALITY of status and of opportunity; and to promote among them all

FRATERNITY assuring the dignity of the individual and the unity and integrity of the nation;

IN OUR CONSTITUENT ASSEMBLY this twenty-sixth day of November 1949, do HEREBY ADOPT, ENACT AND GIVE TO OURSELVES THIS CONSTITUTION.

Schedules

FIRST SCHEDULE
    I. The States.
    II. The Union Territories.

SECOND SCHEDULE
    Part A
Provisions as to the President and the Governors of States.
    Part B
    (Repealed)
    Part C
Provisions as to the Speaker and the Deputy Speaker of the House of the People and the Chairman and the Deputy Chairman of the Council of States and the Speaker and the Deputy Speaker of the Legislative Assembly and the Chairman and the Deputy Chairman of the Legislative Council of a State.
    Part D
Provisions as to the Judges of the Supreme Court and of the High Courts.
    Part E
Provisions as to the Comptroller and Auditor-General of India.

Parts of the Constitution

THIRD SCHEDULE
Forms of Oaths or Affirmations.

FOURTH SCHEDULE
Allocation of Seats in the Council of States.

FIFTH SCHEDULE
Provision as to the Administration and Control of Scheduled Areas and Scheduled Tribes.
Part A
General.
Part B
Administration and Control of Scheduled Areas and Scheduled Tribes.
Part C
Scheduled Areas.
Part D
Amendment of the Schedule.

SIXTH SCHEDULE
Provisions as to the Administration of Tribal Areas in the States of Assam, Meghalaya, Tripura and Mizoram.

SEVENTH SCHEDULE
List I: Union List.
List II: State List.
List III: Concurrent List.

EIGHTH SCHEDULE
Languages.

NINTH SCHEDULE
Validation of certain Acts and Regulations.

TENTH SCHEDULE
Provisions as to disqualification on ground of defection.

ELEVENTH SCHEDULE
Powers, authority and responsibilities of Panchayats.

TWELFTH SCHEDULE
Powers, authority and responsibilities of Municipalities, etc.

Appendix

APPENDIX I
The Constitution (Application to Jammu and Kashmir) Order, 1954.

APPENDIX II
Re-statement with, reference to the present text of the Constitution, of the exceptions and modifications subject to which the Constitution applies to the State of Jammu and Kashmir.

APPENDIX III
Extracts from the Constitution (Forty-fourth Amendment) Act, 1978.

Speakers of the Lok Sabha

The Indian Parliament had its first communist Speaker in Somnath Chatterjee in 2004. The office of the Speaker occupies a pivotal position in India's parliamentary democracy. In the Warrant of Precedence the Speaker comes after only the President, the Vice-President and the Prime Minister. Through the guidelines laid down by the Constitution, the Rules of Procedure and Conduct of Business in Lok Sabha and through established practices and conventions, adequate powers are vested in the office of the Speaker to enable him to ensure the smooth conduct of parliamentary proceedings and protect the independence and impartiality of the office. One of the first acts of a newly constituted House is to elect the Speaker. Usually, a member belonging to the ruling party is elected the Speaker. It has been the practice through the years that the ruling party nominates its candidate after informal consultations with the leaders of other opposition parties and groups in the Lok Sabha. This convention ensures that once elected, the Speaker enjoys the respect of all sections of the House. The Constitution of India provides that the Speaker's salary and allowances are to be charged to the Consolidated Fund of India. The Speaker holds office from the date of his election until immediately before the first meeting of the Lok Sabha after the dissolution of the one to which he was elected. He is eligible for re-election. The Speaker does not vacate his office on the dissolution of the Lok Sabha, unless he ceases to be a member of the House.

However, the Speaker may, at any time, resign from office by writing under his hand to the Deputy Speaker. The Speaker can be removed from office only on a resolution of the House passed by a majority of all members of the House.

List of Speakers

G.V. Mavalankar
   (15.5.1952–27.2.1956)
M.A. Ayyangar
   (08.3.1956–10.5.1957) (11.5.1957–16.4.1962)
Sardar Hukam Singh
   (17.4.1962–16.3.1967)
N. Sanjiva Reddy
   (17.3.1967–19.7.1969)

(26.03.1977–13.7.1977)
G.S. Dhillon
   (8.8.1969–17.3.1971) (22.3.1971–1.12.1975)
Bali Ram Bhagat
   (15.1.1976–25.3.1977)
K.S. Hegde (21.7.1977–21.1.1980)
Bal Ram Jakhar
   (22.1.1980–15.1.1985) (16.1.1985–18.12.1989)
Rabi Ray
   (19.12.1989–09.7.1991)
Shivraj V. Patil
   (10.7.1991–22.5.1996)
P.A. Sangma
   (25.3.1996–23.3.1998)
G.M.C. Balyogi
   (24.3.1998–19.10.1999)
   (22.10.1999–3 3.2002 died in office)
Manohar Joshi
   (10.5.2002–2.6.2004)
Somnath Chatterjee
   (4.6.2004–till date)

List of Council of Ministers (as on 10.8.2005)

Cabinet Ministers

1. Dr. Manmohan Singh	Prime Minister and also in-charge of the Ministries/Departments not specifically allocated to the charge of any Minister viz.:
	(i) Ministry of Personnel, Public Grievances & Pensions
	(ii) Ministry of Planning
	(iii) Department of Atomic Energy
	(iv) Department of Space
	(v) Ministry of Coal
	(vi) Ministry of Youth Affairs and Sports
	(vii) Ministry of Overseas Indian Affairs
2. Pranab Mukherjee	Minister of Defence
3. Arjun Singh	Minister of Human Resource Development
4. Sharad Pawar	Minister of Agriculture and Minister of Consumer Affairs, Food & Public Distribution
5. Lalu Prasad Yadav	Minister of Railways
6. Shivraj V. Patil	Minister of Home Affairs
7. Ram Vilas Paswan	Minister of Chemicals & Fertilizers and Minister of Steel
8. Ghulam Nabi Azad	Minister of Parliamentary Affairs and Minister of Urban Development

9.	S. Jaipal Reddy	Minister of Information & Broadcasting and Minister of Culture
10.	Sis Ram Ola	Minister of Mines
11.	P. Chidambaram	Minister of Finance
12.	Mahavir Prasad	Minister of Small Scale Industries and Minister of Agro & Rural Industries
13.	P.R. Kyndiah	Minister of Tribal Affairs and Minister of Development of North Eastern Region
14.	T.R. Baalu	Minister of Shipping,Road Transport & Highways
15.	Shankersinh Vaghela	Minister of Textiles
16.	K. Natwar Singh	Minister of External Affairs
17.	Kamal Nath	Minister of Commerce & Industry
18.	H.R. Bhardwaj	Minister of Law & Justice
19.	P.M. Sayeed	Minister of Power
20.	Raghuvansh Prasad Singh	Minister of Rural Development
21.	Priyaranjan Dasmunsi	Minister of Water Resources
22.	Mani Shankar Aiyar	Minister of Petroleum & Natural Gas and Minister of Panchayati Raj
23.	Meira Kumar	Minister of Social Justice & Empowerment
24.	K. Chandra Sekhar Rao	Minister of Labour & Employment
25.	A. Raja	Minister of Environment & Forests
26.	Dayanidhi Maran	Minister of Communications & Information Technology
27.	Dr. Anbumani Ramdoss	Minister of Health & Family Welfare

Ministers of State (Independent Charge)

1.	Santosh Mohan Dev	Minister of State (Independent Charge) of the Ministry of Heavy Industries & Public Enterprises
2.	Oscar Fernandes	Minister of State (Independent Charge) of the Ministry of Statistics & Programme Implementation
3.	Renuka Chowdhury	Minister of State (Independent Charge) of the Ministry of Tourism
4.	Subodh Kant Sahay	Minister of State (Independent Charge) of the Ministry of Food Processing Industries
5.	Kapil Sibal	Minister of State (Independent Charge) of the Ministry of Science & Technology and Minister of State (Independent Charge) of the Department of Ocean Development
6.	Vilas Muttemwar	Minister of State (Independent Charge) of the Ministry of Non-Conventional Energy Sources
7.	Kumari Selja	Minister of State (Independent Charge) of the Ministry of Urban Employment & Poverty Alleviation
8.	Praful Patel	Minister of State (Independent Charge) of the Ministry of Civil Aviation

9. Prem Chand Gupta — Minister of State (Independent Charge) of the Ministry of Company Affairs

Ministers of State

1. E. Ahammed — Minister of State in the Ministry of External Affairs

2. Suresh Pachouri — Minister of State in the Ministry of Personnel, Public Grievances & Pensions and Minister of State in the Ministry of Parliamentary Affairs

3. B.K. Handique — Minister of State in the Ministry of Defence and Minister of State in the Ministry of Parliamentary Affairs

4. Panabaka Lakshmi — Minister of State in the Ministry of Health & Family Welfare

5. Dr. Dasari Narayan Rao — Minister of State in the Ministry of Coal and Minister of State in the Ministry of Mines

6. Dr. Shakeel Ahmad — Minister of State in the Ministry of Communications & Information Technology

7. Rao Inderjit Singh — Minister of State in the Ministry of External Affairs

8. Naranbhai Rathwa — Minister of State in the Ministry of Railways

9. K.H. Muniappa — Minister of State in the Ministry of Shipping, Road Transport & Highways

10. M.V. Rajasekharan — Minister of State in the Ministry of Planning

11. Kantilal Bhuria — Minister of State in the Ministry of Agriculture and Minister of State in the Ministry of Consumer Affairs, Food & Public Distribution

12. Manikrao Gavit — Minister of State in the Ministry of Home Affairs

13. Shriprakash Jaiswal — Minister of State in the Ministry of Home Affairs

14. Prithviraj Chavan — Minister of State in the Prime Minister's Office

15. Taslimuddin — Minister of State in the Ministry of Agriculture and Minister of State in the Ministry of Consumer Affairs, Food & Public Distribution

16. Suryakanta Patil — Minister of State in the Ministry of Rural Development and Minister of State in the Ministry of Parliamentary Affairs

17. Md. Ali Ashraf Fatmi — Minister of State in the Ministry of Human Resource Development

18. A. Narendra — Minister of State in the Ministry of Rural Development

19. R. Velu — Minister of State in the Ministry of Railways

20.	S.S. Palanimanickam	Minister of State in the Ministry of Finance
21.	S. Regupathy	Minister of State in the Ministry of Home Affairs
22.	K. Venkatapathy	Minister of State in the Ministry of Law & Justice
23.	Subbulakshmi Jagadeesan	Minister of State in the Ministry of Social Justice & Empowerment
24.	E.V.K.S. Elangovan	Minister of State in the Ministry of Commerce & Industry
25.	Kanti Singh	Minister of State in the Ministry of Human Resource Development
26.	Namo Narain Meena	Minister of State in the Ministry of Environment & Forests
27.	Jay Prakash Narayan Yadav	inister of State in the Ministry of Water Resources
28.	Dr. Akhilesh Prasad Singh	Minister of State in the Ministry of Agriculture and Minister of State in the Ministry of Consumer Affairs, Food & Public Distribution

Ministry of Home Affairs

The Ministry of Home Affairs discharges certain vitally important responsibilities that are becoming increasingly onerous and complex.

Article 355 of the Constitution of India requires the Union Government to protect every State against external aggression and internal disturbance. The Union Government is also required to ensure that the government of every State is carried on in accordance with the provisions of the Constitution. It is in pursuance of these obligations that the Ministry of Home Affairs provides financial support, manpower guidance and expertise to the State Governments for maintenance of security, peace and harmony without affecting the constitutional rights of the States and its citizens. Under the Government of India (Allocation of Business) Rules, 1961, the Ministry of Home Affairs has the following constituent Departments:-

(a) Department of Internal Security
(b) Department of States
(c) Department of Official Language
(d) Department of Home
(e) Department of Jammu & Kashmir Affairs
(f) Department of Border Management

Ministers for Home Affairs

Tenure	Name
15–26 December 1950	Jawaharlal Nehru
26 December 1950–5 November 1951	Chakravarti Rajagopalachari
5 November 1951–9 January 1955	Kailash Nath Katju
10 January 1955–7 March 1961	Govind Ballabh Pant
1 September 1963–9 November 1966	Gulzari Lal Nanda
10–13 November 1966	Indira Gandhi
14 November 1966–26 June 1970	Yeshwantrao Balwantrao Chavan
27 June 1970–4 February 1973	Indira Gandhi.

5 February 1973–10 October 1974	Uma Shankar Dikshit
10 October 1974–24 March 1977	Reddy Kasu Brahamananda
1 July 1978–23 January 1979	Morarji Ranchhodji Desai
24 January–28 July 1979	H.M. Patel
22 June–2 September 1982	Ramasamy Venkataraman
2 September 1982–19 July 1984	Prakash Chand Sethi
19 July–31 December 1984	Pamulaparti Venkata Narasimha Rao
31 December 1984–13 March 1986	Shakarrao Bhaorao Chavan
14 March–12 May 1986	Pamulaparti Venkata Narasimha Rao
12 May–22 October 1986	Ghulam Nabi Azad
22 October1986–2 December 1989	Buta Singh
21 June 1991–16 May 1996	Shankarrao Bhaorao Chavan
16 May–1 June 1996	Murli Manohar Joshi
1–29 June 1996	H.D. Deve Gowda
28 June 1996–19 March 1998	Indrajit Gupta
20 March 1998–6 February 2004	L.K. Advani
24 May 2004–till date	Shivraj Patil

Ministry of Finance

The Ministry of Finance is responsible for administration of finances of the Government. It is headed by the Finance Minister (appointed by the Prime Minister of India). The Ministry comprises four departments

1. Economic Affairs
2. Expenditure
3. Revenue
4. Company Affairs

The Finance Minister presents annual Financial Statement or Budget. R.K. Shanmukham Chetty presented the first Budget of independent India on 26 November 1947.

List of Finance Ministers

1. R.K. Shanmukham Chetty 1947–49
2. John Mathai 1949–51
3. C.D. Deshmukh 1951–57
4. T.T. Krishnamachari 1957–58
5. Jawaharlal Nehru 1958–59
6. Morarji Desai 1959–64
7. T.T. Krishnamachari 1964–66
8. Sachindra Chowdhury 1966–67
9. Morarji Desai 1967–70
10. Indira Gandhi 1970–71
11. Y.B. Chavan 1971–75
12. C. Subramaniam 1975–77
13. H.M. Patel 1977–78
14. Charan Singh 1979–80
15. R. Venkataraman 1980–82
16. Pranab Mukherjee 1982–85
17. V.P. Singh 1985–87
18. N.D. Tiwari 1988–89
19. S.B. Chavan 1989–90
20. Madhu Dandavate 1990–91
21. Yashwant Sinha (Vote on Account) 1991–92
22. Manmohan Singh 1991–96
23. P. Chidambaram 1996–98
24. Yashwant Sinha 1998–2002
25. Jaswant Singh 2002–04
26. P. Chidambaram 2004–till date

Ministry of External Affairs

The Ministry of External Affairs is concerned with foreign affairs and is responsible for some aspects of foreign policy making, actual implementation of policy and daily conduct of international relations. The ministry's duties include providing information and analyses to the prime minister and minister of external affairs, recommending specific measures, planning policy for the future, and maintaining communications with foreign missions in New Delhi. The ministry is headed by the minister of external affairs, who holds cabinet rank. The Ministry of External Affairs is mainly housed in South Block.

Ministers for External Affairs

Tenure	Name
15 August 1947–27 May 1964	Jawaharlal Nehru
27 May–9 June 1964	Gulzari Lal Nanda
18 July 1964–14 November 1966	Sardar Swaran Singh
14 November 1966–5 September 1967	Mahomedali Currin Chagla
6 September 1967–13 February 1969	Indira Gandhi
14 February 1969–27 June 1970	Dinesh Singh
27 June 1970–10 October 1974	Swaran Singh
10 October 1974–24 March 1977	Yeshwantrao Balwantrao Chavan
26 March 1977–28 July 1979	Atal Behari Vajpayee
14 January 1980–19 July 1984	Pamulaparti Venkata Narasimha Rao
31 October 1984–24 September 1985	Rajiv Gandhi
25 September 1985–12 May 1986	Bhagat Bali Ram
12 May–22 October 1986	P. Shiv Shankar
22 October 1986–25 July 1987	Narayan Datt Tiwari
25 July 1987–25 June 1988	Rajiv Gandhi
25 June 1988–2 December 1989	Pamulaparti Venkata Narasimha Rao
5 December 1989–10 November 1990	Inder Kumar Gujral
21 November 1990–20 February 1991	Vidya Charan Shukla
21 June 1991–31 March 1992	Madhavsinh Solanki
31 March 1992–18 January 1993	Pamulaparti Venkata Narasimha Rao
18 January 1993–10 February 1995	Dinesh Singh
10 February 1995–16 May 1996	Pranab Kumar Mukherjee
21 May–1 June 1996	Sikander Bakht
1 June 1996–21 April 1997	Inder Kumar Gujral
19 March–5 December 1998	Atal Behari Vajpayee
5 December 1998–23 June 2002	Jaswant Singh
1 July 2002–22 May 2004	Yashwant Sinha
23 May 2004–till date	Natwar Singh

Table Of Precedence

1. President
2. Vice-President
3. Prime Minister
4. Governors of States (within their respective States)
5. Former Presidents
5A. Deputy Prime Minister
6. Chief Justice of India
   Speaker of Lok Sabha
7. Cabinet Ministers of the Union.
   Chief Ministers of States (within their respective States)
   Deputy Chairman, Planning Commission

Former Prime Ministers
Leaders of Opposition in Rajya Sabha and Lok Sabha

7A. Holders of Bharat Ratna decoration

8. Ambassadors Extraordinary and Plenipotentiary and High Commissioners of Commonwealth countries accredited to India
Chief Ministers of States (outside their respective States)
Governors of States (outside their respective States)

9. Judges of Supreme Court

9A. Chief Election Commissioner
Comptroller & Auditor General of India

10. Deputy Chairman, Rajya Sabha
Deputy Chief Ministers of States
Deputy Speaker, Lok Sabha
Members of the Planning Commission
Ministers of State of the Union +{and any other Minister in the Ministry of Defence for defence matters}.

11. Attorney General of India.
Cabinet Secretary.
Lieutenant Governors(within their respective Union Territories.

12. Chiefs of Staff holding the rank of full General or equivalent rank.

13. Envoys Extraordinary and Ministers Plenipotentiary accredited to India.

14. Chairmen and Speakers of State Legislatures within their respective States.
Chief Justices of High Courts within their respective jurisdictions.

15. Cabinet Ministers in States within their respective States.
Chief Ministers of Union Territories and Chief Executive Councilor, Delhi, within their respective Union Territories.
Deputy Ministers of the Union.

16. Officiating Chiefs of Staff holding the rank of Lieutenant General or equivalent rank.

17. Chairman, Central Administrative Tribunal.
Chairman, Minorities Commission.
Chairman, Scheduled Castes and Scheduled Tribes Commission.
Chairman, Union Public Service Commission.
Chief Justices of High Courts outside their respective jurisdictions.
Puisne Judges of High Courts within their respective jurisdictions.

18. Cabinet Ministers in States outside their respective States.
Chairmen and Speakers of State Legislatures outside their respective States.
Chairman, Monopolies and Restrictive Trade Practices Commission.
Deputy Chairman and Deputy Speakers of State Legislatures within their respective States.
Legislatures within their respective States.
Ministers of State in States within their respective States.
Ministers of Union Territories and Executive Councilors, Delhi, within their respective Union Territories.
Speakers of Legislative Assemblies in Union Territories and Chairman of Delhi Metropolitan Council within their respective Union Territories.

19. Chief Commissioners of Union Territories not having Councils of Ministers, within their respective Union Territories.
Deputy Ministers in States within their respective States.
Deputy Speakers of Legislative Assemblies in Union Territories and Deputy Chairman of metropolitan Council Delhi, within their respective Union Territories.

20. Deputy Chairmen and Deputy Speakers of State Legislatures, outside their respective states.

Ministers of State in States outside their respective States.

Puisne Judges of High Courts outside their respective jurisdictions.

21. Members of Parliament.

22. Deputy Ministers in State outside their respective States.

23. Army Commanders/ Vice-Chief of the Army Staff or equivalent in other services

Chief Secretaries to State Governments within their respective States.

Commissioner for Linguistic Minorities.

Commissioner for Scheduled Castes and Scheduled Tribes.

Members, Minorities Commission.

Members, Scheduled Castes and Scheduled Tribes Commission.

Officers of the rank of full General or equivalent rank.

Secretaries to the Government of India (including officers holding this office ex-officio).

Secretary, Minorities Commission.

Secretary, Scheduled Castes and Scheduled Tribes Commission.

Secretary to the President.

Secretary to the Prime Minister.

Secretary, Rajya Sabha/Lok Sabha

Solicitor General.

Vice-Chairman, Central Administrative Tribunal.

24. Officers of the rank of Lieutenant General or equivalent rank.

25. Additional Secretaries to the Government of India.

Additional Solicitor General.

Advocate Generals of States.

Chairman, Tariff Commission.

Charge d' Affairs and Acting High Commissioners a pied and ad interim.

Chief Ministers of Union Territories and Chief Executive Councillor, Delhi, outside their respective Union Territories.

Chief Secretaries of State Governments outside their respective States.

Deputy Comptroller and Auditor General.

Deputy Speakers of Legislative Assemblies in Union Territories and Deputy Chairman, Delhi Metropolitan Council, outside their respective Union Territories.

Director, Central Bureau of Investigation.

Director General, Border Security Force.

Director General, Central Reserve Police.

Director, Intelligence Bureau.

Lieutenant Governor outside their respective Union Territories.

Members, Central Administrative Tribunal.

Members, Monopolies and Restrictive Trade Practices Commission.

Members, Union Public Service Commission.

Ministers of Union Territories and Executive Councillors, Delhi, outside their respective Union Territories.

Principal Staff Officers of the Armed Forces of the rank of major General or equivalent rank.

Speakers of Legislative Assemblies in Union Territories and Chairman of Delhi, Metropolitan Council, outside their respective Union Territories.

26. Joint Secretaries to the Government of India and officers of equivalent rank.

Officers of the rank of Major-General or equivalent rank.

Party Position in the Fourteenth Lok Sabha Elected in 2004

(Party position at the time of dissolution of Thirteenth Lok Sabha in brackets)

Congress and its allies	Total 218
Indian National Congress (INC)	145 (114)
Rashtriya Janata Dal (RJD)	21 (7)

Dravida Munnetra Kazhagam
(AIADMK)   16 (12)
Nationalist Congress Party
(NCP)   9 (8)
Pattali Makkal Katchi (PMK)   6 (5)
Jharkhand Mukti Morcha (JMM)   5
Telengana Rashtra Samity (TRS)   5
Lok Jan Sakthi Party (LJNSP)   4
Marumalarchi Dravida Munnetra
Kazhagam (MDMK)   4 (4)
Muslim League (MUL)   1 (2)
People's Democratic Party (PDP)   1 (2)
Republican Party of India-A
(RPIA)   1 (1)

National Democratic Alliance

	Total 187
Bharatiya Janata Party (BJP)	138 (182)
Shiv Sena (SHS)	12 (15)
Biju Janata Dal (BJD)	11 (10)
Janata Dal-United (JDU)	8 (21)
Shiromani Akali Dal (SAD)	8 (2)
Telugu Desam Party (TDP)	5 (29)
All India Trinamool Congress (AITC)	2 (8)
Indian Federal Democratic Party (IFDP)	1
Mizo National Front (MNF)	1
Nagaland People's Front (NPF)	1

Left parties and allies

	Total 60
Communist Party of India-Marxist (CPM)	43 (33)
Communist Party of India (CPI)	10 (4)
Revolutionary Socialist Party (RSP)	3 (3)
All India Forward Block (FBL)	3 (2)
Kerala Congress-Joseph (KEC)	1 (1)

Others

	Total 74
Samajvadi Party (SP)	36 (26)
Bahujan Samaj Party (BSP)	19 (14)
Janata Dal-Secular (JDS)	3 (1)
Rashtriya Lok Dal (RLD)	3 (2)
Asom Gana Parishad (AGP)	2
Jammu and Kashmir National Conference (JKN)	2 (4)
Sikkim Democratic Front (SDF)	1 (1)
Bharatiya Navshakti party (BNP)	1

All India Majilis-E-Ittehadul
Muslimeen (AIMIM)   1 (1)
Samajvadi Janata Party (Rashtriya) 1 (1)
National Loktantrik Party (NLP)   1
Independents   4 (6)

National Parties in India

According to the Election Commission, a political party will be treated as a recognized political party in a state, if and only if either the party fulfils the conditions specified in Clause (A) or the condition specified in Clause (B).

(A) A political party will be considered a state party if it ...

• has been engaged in political activity for a continuous period of five years; and

• has, at the last general election in that State to the House of the People, or, as the case may be, to the Legislative Assembly of the State, returned either

o at least one member to the House of the People for every 25 members of that House or any fraction of that number from that State, or

o at least one member to the Legislative Assembly of that State for every 30 members of that Assembly or any fraction of that number

(B) The total number of valid votes polled by all the contesting candidates set up by such party at the last general election in the State to the House of the People, or, to the Legislative Assembly of the State, as the case may be, is not less than six per cent of the total number of valid votes polled by all the contesting candidates at such general election in the State.

A political party is treated as a 'National Party' throughout the whole of India if it is a recognized political party in four or more States, but only as long as the political party continues to fulfill the conditions for recognition in four or more States on the results of any subsequent general election thereafter, either to the House of the People or to the Legislative Assembly of any State.

National Parties

	Name	Symbol
1.	Bharatiya Janata Party	Lotus
2.	Bahujan Samaj Party	Elephant
3.	Communist Party of India	Ears of Corn & Sickle
4.	Communist Party of India (Marxist)	Hammer Sickle & Star
5.	Indian National Congress	Hand
6.	Nationalist Congress Party	Clock

CPI(M) General Secretaries

Prakash Karat is the new General Secretary of the Communist Party of India (Marxist). The CPI(M) was formed at the Seventh Congress of the Communist Party of India held in Calcutta from 31 October to 7 November 1964. The party has emerged as the main Leftist party in the country. The membership of the Party, which was 118,683 at the time of its formation, has grown to 814,408 (2002). The 18th party congress of CPI(M), held in Delhi 6-11 April 2005 elected a Central Committee with 85 members. The Central Committee later elected a 17-member Politburo.

CPI(M) General Secretaries:

Puchalapalli Sundarayya	1964–1976
E.M.S. Namboodiripad	1977–1992
Harkishan Singh Surjeet	1992–2005
Prakash Karat	2005–till date

Assembly Elections 2004

Arunachal Pradesh: Gegong Apang was sworn in as the chief minister of Arunachal Pradesh on 16 October 2004. Apang's name was proposed by Pradesh Congress Committee president Mukut Mithi. The Congress retained power in the state winning 34 seats in the 60-member assembly elections for which elections were held on 7 October. The Bharatiya Janata Party secured nine seats while Independent candidates won in 13 seats.

Maharashtra: Vilasrao Deshmukh was sworn-in as the new chief minister of Maharashtra on 1 November 2004, as the state's 23rd chief minister, while the state Nationalist Congress Party legislature unit leader R.R. Patil was sworn-in as the new deputy chief minister. The oath-taking ceremony was held 15 days after assembly election results were announced on 16 October. The Congress-NCP led alliance won 141 seats in the 288-member assembly. The alliance submitted a list of 165 legislators to the governor while staking claim to form the government.

Assembly Elections 2005

Haryana: Bhupinder Singh Hooda was sworn in as the 19th chief minister of Haryana on 5 March 2005.Haryana Governor A.R. Kidwai administered the oath of office and secrecy to the 57-year-old Hooda at the Raj Bhavan in Chandigarh. The Congress party took 67 seats in the 90-member assembly of Haryana, while the Indian National Lok Dal (INLD) got nine. This enabled the Congress to return to power in the state for the first time in nine years.

Bihar: Elections to the Bihar Assembly were held in three phases in February 2005. The Rashtriya Janata Dal (RJD) contested 170 seats and won 75, while the Bhartiya Janata Party (BJP)-Janata Dal United (JD-U) combine won 92 seats. The hung assembly that this election produced was dissolved on 23 May. The Election Commission announced a four-phase re-election starting 18 October.

Jharkhand: Jharkhand's first ever assembly elections resulted in a hung parliament. The NDA won 36 seats (only five short of the majority mark) while the JMM-Congress combine won 26 seats. Both of these were pre-poll combinations. The RJD had no pre-poll tie-up with either the Congress or the JMM and finished with seven seats. The Forward Bloc won two while the CPI(ML) and the NCP had one each.

Jharkhand Mukti Morcha chief Shibu Soren presented the governor with a list of 42 members of Legislative Assembly, compared to the 41 of the NDA, and was invited by the governor Syed Sibtey Razi to form the government. The governor asked Soren to prove his majority on the floor of the 81-member assembly by 21 March 2005. On 11 March 2005, Shibu Soren resigned after he failed to obtain a vote of confidence in the assembly, as directed by the Supreme Court. The governor then sent an invitation to Bharatiya Janata Party's Arjun Munda to form the government. Arjun Munda was appointed the fourth chief minister of Jharkhand on 12 March 2005.

Chief Election Commissioners Of India

Name	Tenure
Sukumar Sen	21 March 1950–19 December 1958
K.V.K. Sundaram	20 December 1958–30 September 1967
S.P. Sen Verma	1 October 1967–30 September 1972
Dr Nagendra Singh	1 October 1972–6 February 1973
T. Swaminathan	7 February 1973–17 June 1977
S.L. Shakdhar	18 June 1977–17 June 1982
R.K. Trivedi	18 June 1982–31 December 1985
R.V.S. Peri Sastri	1 January 1986–25 November 1990
Smt V.S. Rama Devi	15 November 1990–12 December 1990
T.N. Seshan	12 December 1990–11 December 1996
M.S. Gill	12 December 1996–13 June 2001
J.M. Lyngdoh	13 June 2001–7 February 2004
T.S. Krishnamurthy	8 February 2004–15 May 2005
B.B. Tandon	6 May 2005–till date

Number of Assembly Seats in States and UTs

Name	Number of Seats
State	
Andhra Pradesh	295
Arunachal Pradesh	60
Assam	126
Bihar	243
Chhattisgarh	90
Goa	40
Gujarat	182

Haryana	90
Himachal Pradesh	68
Jammu and Kashmir	87
Jharkhand	81
Karnataka	225
Kerala	140
Madhya Pradesh	230
Maharashtra	288
Manipur	60
Meghalaya	60
Mizoram	40
Nagaland	60
Orissa	147
Punjab	117
Rajasthan	200
Sikkim	32
Tamil Nadu	234
Tripura	60
Uttaranchal	70
Uttar Pradesh	403
West Bengal	294

National Capital Territory

Delhi	70

Union Territory

Andaman and Nicobar	
Chandigarh	
Dadra and Nagar Haveli	
Daman and Diu	
Lakshadweep	
Pondicherry	30

Number of Lok Sabha Seats in States and UTs

Name	Number of Seats
State	
Andhra Pradesh	42
Arunachal Pradesh	2
Assam	14
Bihar	40
Chhattisgarh	11
Goa	2
Gujarat	26
Haryana	9
Himachal Pradesh	4
Jammu and Kashmir	6
Jharkhand	14
Karnataka	28
Kerala	19

Madhya Pradesh	29
Maharashtra	47
Manipur	2
Meghalaya	2
Mizoram	1
Nagaland	1
Orissa	21
Punjab	13
Rajasthan	25
Sikkim	1
Tamil Nadu	39
Tripura	2
Uttar Pradesh	80
Uttranchal	5
West Bengal	42

National Capital Territory

Delhi	7

Union Territories

Andaman and Nicobar	1
Chandigarh	1
Dadra and Nagar Haveli	1
Daman and Diu	1
Lakshadweep	1
Pondicherry	1

Others

Nominated Members	2
Total	**542**

Number of Rajya Sabha Seats in States and UTs

Name	Number of Seats
State	
Andhra Pradesh	18
Arunachal Pradesh	1
Assam	7
Bihar	16
Chhattisgarh	5
Goa	1
Gujarat	11
Haryana	5
Himachal Pradesh	3
Jammu and Kashmir	4
Jharkhand	6
Karnataka	12
Kerala	9
Madhya Pradesh	11

Maharashtra	19
Manipur	1
Meghalaya	1
Mizoram	1
Nagaland	1
Orissa	10
Punjab	7
Rajasthan	10
Sikkim	1
Tamil Nadu	18
Tripura	1
Uttaranchal	3
Uttar Pradesh	31
West Bengal	16

National Capital Territory

Delhi	3

Union Territories

Pondicherry	1

Others

Nominated members	12
Total	**245**

The Armed Forces

Army

The Indian Army has about one million personnel and 34 divisions. In 2002, the Indian Army was estimated to have about 980,000 active troops, along with an Army Reserve consisting of 300,000 first line troops (those within five years of full time service) and another 500,000 second line troops (subject to recall to service until 50 years of age). The Territorial Army has about 40,000 first line troops and 160,000 second line troops. The army is headquartered in New Delhi and is under the direction of the chief of the army staff, who is always a full general.

The Army consists of a number of arms and services like Armoured Corps, Regiment of Artillery, Corps of Engineers, Corps of Signals, and Mechanized Infantry, among many others. It also has its own Military Nursing Service, Army Medical Corps, and Army Dental Corps. The Army also has its own Recruiting Organization, Record Offices, Depots, Boys Establishments and Selection Centres and training institutions. These units are organized in twelve corps-level formations.

As of early 2002 the Indian Army was estimated to have between 3,300 and 4,900 tanks. Some estimates put the number of tanks in storage at 1,500. Such high figures of vehicles in storage make it difficult to estimate India's armored vehicle inventory. The Indian Army operates indigenously manufactured Vijayanta tanks as well as T-55, T-72, T-72M1 and PT-76 tanks. The army plans to phase out the Vijayanta and T-55 tanks by 2010 and replace them with upgraded T-72M1s and T-90 tanks. The new Russian T-90 tanks (re-christened Bhishma) are being inducted into the army. The army has also ordered 124 models of the indigenously developed Arjun main battle tank. The army possesses sizable artillery forces, with estimates placing the army's towed artillery capabilities at over 4,000 pieces. The army also has self-propelled artillery and field guns, howitzers, multi-barrel rocket launchers like the indigenous Pinaka and surface-to-air missiles.

Navy

The Indian Navy is one of the largest navies in the world. It is a three-dimensional force equipped with sophisticated missile-capable warships, aircraft carriers, advanced submarines and aircraft. A large number of the warships are of indigenous design and have been constructed in Indian shipyards. The navy also possesses modern dockyard facilities with state-of-the-art technology. At present, the Navy has two major Naval bases at Mumbai and Visakhapatnam. The naval headquarters is in New Delhi and is under the command of the chief of naval staff who is a full admiral.

In 1994, the total strength of the navy was estimated to be 54,000, including 5,000 naval aviation personnel and 1,000 marines. The navy currently operates one aircraft carrier (INS Viraat), over 40 surface combatants, and more than a dozen submarines. However, the navy faces the challenges of an aging fleet and a slow rate of replacement of ships and aircraft.

India also has a coast guard set-up that is organized along the lines of the US Coast Guard. Besides the aircraft carrier, the navy also has cruisers, destroyers, frigates, minesweepers, survey ships, store carriers, tankers, and submarines. It also has shore establishments like training institutions, dockyard, storage deposits and other technical and administrative establishments. The navy also has a separate Aviation Wing consisting of Naval Air Stations and a Fleet Requirement Unit. The Indian Navy is under the command of the Chief of Naval Staff (CNS), located in New Delhi. It consists of two fleets, each commanded by a Rear Admiral. The Eastern Fleet is primarily based in Visakhapatnam on the Bay of Bengal. The Western Fleet is primarily based in Mumbai on the Arabian Sea.

In addition to the principal naval commands, there are three large sub-commands under the direct charge of flag officers. These are:

1. Naval Aviation and Goa Area (in Goa)
2. Submarines (in Visakhapatnam), and
3. 'Fortress' in the Andaman and Nicobar Islands (Port Blair).

The navy has recently made a number of significant acquisitions. These include the Russian aircraft carrier Admiral Gorshkov (along with MiG-29K fighter jets that will operate out of the ship). The vessel is currently undergoing retrofitting in Russia and is expected to be ready by 2008–9. It has been reported that India has entered into an agreement with Russia for the lease-purchase of Russian Akula-class nuclear-powered submarines (SSNs). The first submarine would reportedly be delivered by 2005. However, both Indian and Russian authorities have refused to comment on these reports. Other recent significant acquisitions include the Talwar-class frigate, INS *Tabar* and the stealth frigate INS *Satpura*. Construction projects that are either underway or planned include the indigenous aircraft carrier, the 'Air Defence Ship', French Scorpene submarines and more stealth frigates.

Air Force

The Indian Air Force is one of the world's largest air forces with over 600 combat aircraft and more than 500 transports and helicopters. In 1994, it was estimated to have 110,000 personnel. The air force is headquartered in New Delhi and is headed by the chief of air staff, an air chief marshal.

The air force operates a wide variety of aircraft, support equipment, weapon systems, communication and detection systems. The aircraft in the air force inventory include air superiority fighters like the MiG-29 and MiG-23 aircraft, multi-role combat aircraft like the Sukhoi SU-30 and Mirage 2000 aircraft, tactical strike fighter aircraft like MiG-27, strategic reconnaissance aircraft like MiG-25, multirole fighter and ground attack aircraft like MiG-21, and deep penetration strike aircraft like Jaguar. It also uses older generation aircraft like Hunter and Canberra (tactical bomber and interdictor) but in ancillary roles. The transport fleet of the air force consists of aircraft like Ilyushin IL-76, Antonov AN-32 and AVRO and Dornier 228 aircraft. The air force also has Boeing 737 aircraft that are used for VIP transport. The helicopter fleet consists of Cheetah and Chetak helicopters, Mi-17 and Mi-26 helicopters as well as attack helicopters like Mi-25 and Mi-35. Newly inducted aircraft include IL-78 mid-air refueling tanker aircraft and the indigenous Dhruv Advanced Light Helicopter. India also intends to acquire more Mirage 2000-5 aircraft. The indigenous Light Combat Aircraft is undergoing development. India has also entered into a deal with UK for 66 Hawk Advanced Jet Trainer aircraft and for the Israeli Phalcon AWACS system.

Terrorist Incidents in the Recent Past

5 July 2005

Five terrorists attack the disputed Ram Janmabhoomi in Ayodhya with explosives. All five are shot down in a gunfight with the security forces guarding the area. One civilian dies in the bomb blast triggered by the terrorists to breach the cordon wall.

15 August 2004

17 persons, including 16 school children, are killed as suspected ULFA activists detonate explosives at the venue of Independence Day celebrations in Dhemaji town in Assam.

23 May 2004

Twenty-nine Border Security Force personnel and their family members die when their bus hits an improvised explosive device on Jammu-Srinagar highway; Hizbul Mujahideen claims responsibility.

25 August 2003

At least 48 people are killed and 150 injured in two blasts in south Mumbai—one near the Gateway of India and the other at Zaveri Bazaar.

21 July 2003

At least six devotees, including a child are killed, while 48 others suffer injuries in powerful twin explosions set off at Banganga, on way to Vaishno Devi shrine in Jammu.

24 September 2002

Two heavily armed men enter the Akshardham temple complex in Gujarat and kill 29 visitors.

22 January 2002

Heavily armed men riding a motorcycle attack the United States Information Centre in Kolkata, killing four security personnel and injuring 17 others.

13 December 2001

Terrorist attack on Indian Parliament.

2 October 2001

A massive explosion near the main entrance of the Jammu and Kashmir state assembly leaves at least 29 persons dead and 40 injured.

2 December 2000

Suspected militants storm New Delhi's high-security Red Fort. Three die in the attack.

24 December 1999

Indian Airlines flight IC-814 flying out of Kathmandu, carrying 178 passengers, is hijacked and taken to Kandahar in Afghanistan.

Opinions

The demolition of the Babri Masjid at Ayodhya in 1992 remains one of the key events in the social and political history of India in the recent past. P.V. Narasimha Rao was prime minister of India when kar sevaks attacked and demolished the mosque, leading to widespread communal riots. Here for the first time he reveals his insights into the events of 6 December 1992.

The issue of human rights is linked inextricably to acts of vandalism and terrorism, which threaten the lives and possessions of citizens which the nation-state and courts of law are dutybound to protect. Vinay Lal's perceptive article analyses the implications of such protection in detail.

What Happened in Ayodhya on 6 December 1992

P.V. Narasimha Rao

On the morning of 6 December 1992 the situation at Ayodhya was reportedly peaceful. The *Kar sevaks* were engaged in washing and chiselling the platform and reciting of mantras by sadhus/saints was going on. Later, when Shri L.K. Advani was addressing a gathering of about 45,000 *Kar sevaks* at Ram Katha Kunj, a section of the crowd reportedly rushed towards the disputed structure through the wall near the Lakshman Temple after breaking through the cordon of RSS volunteers. The police were unable or did not make the effort to control the crowd. A mob of about 5,000 were able to overwhelm the security arrangements and occupied the structure. According to subsequent information, the crowd had caused some damage to the structure and such activities were continuing, the police having been withdrawn from the spot. The communication systems in Ayodhya were at that time out of operation and the entire logistic infrastructure for the *Kar sevaks* had become non-functional.

On the morning of 6 December 1992 itself, the Director General of ITBP who was heading the Para-military Forces at Ayodhya had been instructed by the Union Home Secretary to be in readiness and also make available forces if requested by the State Government promptly. It was reported that the State Government asked for 3 battalions of the Para-military Forces in the afternoon which was made available, but when this force was proceeding towards Ayodhya from Faizabad, it was sent back by the Magistrate on duty stating that his orders were not to use force under any circumstances and it was not possible to move in without using force. The exact timing of this incident is given below:-

2-20 p.m. DG, ITDP informed MHA that 3 battalions, which had moved from DRC, had met resistance and obstruction. En route there were a lot of road blocks and people stopped vehicles. The convoy reached with great difficulty at Saket Degree College where the force was again stopped and the road was blocked. Minor pelting of stones also took place. The magistrate asked them in writing to return. DG, ITDP further informed that the 3 battalions had returned accordingly. The Commissioner had been contacted who informed that CM, UP had ordered that there would be no firing under any circumstances.

2-25 p.m. HS spoke to DGP, UP informing him of the sending back of the force by the local administration and requested for necessary instructions to use necessary force. DGP, UP informed that CM's instructions were that firing should not be resorted to but other kinds of force could be used. HS asked DGP, UP that the State Government should issue necessary instructions immediately. DGP promised to attend to this matter immediately.

2-30 p.m. HS spoke to Chief Secretary, UP and requested him also similarly. Evidently, nothing happened thereafter from the State Government.

According to latest reports, the State Government had requested for 15 companies of Para-military Forces and the same was made available to them. The Union Home Secretary and DGP of UP had brought to their notice that the Central Para-military Forces were unable to move to Ayodhya because of the above-mentioned stand of the local administration. As stated above there was no action on this and thereafter, the crowds carried out the demolition of the structure without let or hindrance.

As already stated, the Central force was all ready to move from Faizabad since the morning of 6 December, but in spite of repeated requests from the commander of the force as well as from the Union Home Secretary in Delhi, a Magistrate, as required by law, to accompany the force in its effort to reach the disputed structure (a distance of about 8 kilometres) with a view to protecting it, was neither refused, nor actually made available by the State Government. After the storming of the structure by the crowd had actually commenced and there was no trace of the State Police on the spot and the crowd had been left in full run of the place—then only, a Magistrate at last reached Faizabad—at 1-15 p.m. to be exact. The force started at once towards the Babri structure, but on the plea of crowd resistance the Magistrate gave them *written* orders to return to Faizabad.

It will thus be seen that on 6 December, until the very last moments the Central Government kept pressurizing the UP State authorities to make use of the Central force available with them to save the Babri structure. Even at the very last moment when the force had actually moved halfway towards the structure, at 2-20 p.m., by which time the demolition was going on, but could have been stopped even then, the deliberate act of the Magistrate in not allowing the Central force to proceed further and thus officially aborting the very last possibly successful attempt to save the structure, became transparently visible, and will always be cited as a wanton and mala fide step to stop the saving of the structure.

Until late in the evening of 6 December, the Supreme Court was reviewing the happenings at Ayodhya. When the final news of the demolition reached the Court, they expressed their extreme annoyance and distress at the unfortunate turn of events. The State Government all those days had deliberately misled the Supreme Court and when the ultimate vandalism took place, the Court called the Senior Counsel of the State Government and called for an explanation. To this, the Counsel replied, 'I was misled by the party and my head hangs in shame.'

In this context the Supreme Court held that 'the demolition of Babri Masjid in brazen defiance of the order of this Court is indeed a challenge to the majesty of law and the Constitution. This act of defiance is indeed a defiance of the Constitution and also the powers of the constitutional authorities of the Centre and the State. The demolition is an unprecedented attack on the secular foundation of democracy, the authority and dignity of this Court. The Court thus stands betrayed as never before.' The Court went on to hold that, 'having regard to the developments in this case which, prima facie, indicate that in spite of repeated undertakings made to the Court by no less an authority than a constitutional Government of a State and its officers, have committed or permitted to be committed acts of a very serious magnitude that it is necessary to issue suo motu notice calling upon Shri Kalyan Singh, the then Chief Minister of the State of Uttar Pradesh and its officers who had filed affidavits in this Court or otherwise said to be associated with the events, to show cause why proceedings for contempt of Court should not be initiated against them.'

Further, going into the contempt aspect in detail, the Supreme Court held that 'we find that the undertaking given by Shri Kalyan Singh was both in his personal capacity and on behalf of his Government. There has been a flagrant breach of that undertaking. There has been willful disobedience of the order.'

While concluding the verdict, the Hon'ble Supreme Court held, 'It is unhappy that a leader of a political party and their Chief Minister has to be convicted of the offence of contempt of Court, but it has to be done to uphold the majesty of law, so we convict him of the offence of the contempt of Court. Since the contempt raises larger issue, which is the foundation of the secular foundation of our nation, we sentence him to a token imprisonment of one day. We also sentence him to pay a fine of Rs 2000.'

From the above chronology of events and explanations given, it should be clear that there was no lapse whatever on the part of the Central Government and that if the State Government had at least made use of the Central force in time and meaningfully, the Babri structure could certainly have been saved on 6 December 1992. The UP Government and the BJP, the party of the State government, would have to be held completely responsible for this wanton vandalism perpetrated on the secular credentials of the nation on that unfortunate day.

Human Rights
Vinay Lal

The notion of human rights is deeply embedded in modern legal and political thought and could well be considered one of the most significant achievements of contemporary civilization. Certain classes of people in all societies have from the beginning of time been endowed with 'rights' which others could not claim. Diplomatic emissaries, for instance, were conferred with 'rights' that even an alien state could not abrogate, and elites arrogated to themselves certain rights and privileges. *The Declaration of the Rights of Man and Citizen* (1789), Thomas Paine's *Rights of Man* (1791) and the 'Bill of Rights' attached to the US Constitution are conventionally seen as having extended rights to a much broader class of people, and the post-Second-World-War Universal Declaration of Human Rights is described as the rightful culmination of these democratic propensities. Some 'rights' were such which the citizen could claim against the state, others placed restraints on the state's agenda to produce conformity and contain dissent.

In this liberal vision of human rights, what is uniquely modern is that never before have Individual rights been so squarely placed under the protection of the law. Moreover, it is only in recent times that the 'International community' seems prepared to enforce sanctions against a state for alleged violations of such rights. With the demise of communism, the principal foes of human rights appeared to have been crushed, and the very notion of 'human rights' seemed sovereign. Should we then unreservedly endorse the culture of 'human rights', as it has developed in the liberal-democratic framework of the modern West, as a signifier of the 'end of history' and the emergence of what V.S. Naipaul called 'our universal civilization' ? Or, rather than acquiescing in the suggestion that the notion of human rights is the most promising avenue to a new era in human relations, is there warrant for considering the discourse of human rights as the most evolved form of Western imperialism? Is it the latest masquerade of the West, particularly the United States, the torch-bearer since the end of the Second World War of 'Western' values, which appears to the rest of the world as the epitome of civilization and as the only legitimate arbiter of human values?

The 'individual' and the 'rule of law' are the two central notions from which the modern discourse of human rights is derived. Since at least the Renaissance it has been a staple of Western thought that while the West recognizes the individual as the true unit of being and the organic building block of society, non-Western cultures have been built around collectivities, conceived as religious, linguistic, ethnic, tribal or racial groups. 'Whatever may be the political atom in India,' we find unabashedly stated in the 27 February 1909 issue of the *Economist*, 'it is certainly not the individual of Western democratic theory, but the community of some sort.' In the West the individual stands in singular and splendid isolation, the promise of the inherent perfectibility of man; in the non-West, the individual is nothing, always a part of a collectivity in relation to which his or her existence is defined, never an entity unto himself or herself. Where the 'individual' does not exist, one cannot speak of his or her rights; and where there are no rights, it is perfectly absurd to speak of their denial or abrogation.

Regarding the Western view, moreover, if the atomistic conception of the 'individual' is a prerequisite for a concern with human rights, so too is the 'rule of law' under which alone such rights can be respected. In a society which lives by the 'rule of law', such laws as the government might formulate are done so in accordance with certain normative criteria—for example, they shall be nondiscriminatory, blind to considerations of race, gender, class, linguistic competence and so on. These laws are then made public, so that no person might plead ignorance of the law; and the judicial process under which the person charged for the infringement of such laws is tried must hold out the promise of being fair and equitable. As in the case of the 'individual', the 'rule of law' is held to be a uniquely Western contribution to civilization, on the twofold assumption that democracy is an idea and institution of purely Western origins, and that, contrariwise, the only form of government known to non-Western societies was absolutism. In conditions of 'Oriental despotism', the only law was the law of the despot, and the life and limb of each of his subjects was hostage to the tyranny of his pleasures and whims. In the despotic state, there was perhaps only one 'individual', the absolute ruler; under him were the masses, particles of dust on the distant horizon. What rights were there to speak of then?

Having suggested how the notions of the 'individual' and the 'rule of law' came to intersect in the formulation of the discourse of human rights, we can proceed to unravel some of the more disturbing and insidious aspects of this discourse. Where once the language of liberation was religion, today the language of emancipation is law. Indeed, the very notion of 'human rights', as it is commonly understood in the international forum today, is legalistic. Customs and traditional usages have in most 'Third World' countries functioned for centuries in place of 'law'. Even without the 'rule of law' in a formalistic sense, there were conventions and traditions which bound one person to respect the rights of another. However, this is not something that proponents of the 'rule of law', convinced of the uniqueness of the West, are generally prepared to concede. By what right, with what authority, and with what consequences, do certain states brand other states as 'outlaw' or 'rogue' states, living outside the pale of the 'rule of law', allegedly oblivious to the rights of their subjects, and therefore subject to sanctions from the 'international community' ?

There is, as has been argued, one 'rule of law' for the powerful, and an altogether different one for those states and non-state actors that do not speak the 'rational', 'diplomatic' and 'sane' language that the West has decreed as the universal form of linguistic exchange. It is not only the case that when Americans retaliate against their foes, they are engaged in 'Just war' or purely 'defensive' measures in the interest of national security, but that when Libyans or Iraqis do so, they are transformed into 'terrorists' or ruthless and self-aggrandizing despots in the pursuit of international dominance. The problem is more acute: who is to police the police? Or, in the more complex variant of that query, how do certain particularisms acquire the legitimacy of universalisms, and why is it that Western universalisms have monopolized our notion of universalisms? In an astounding judgment rendered in the early 1990s, which was barely noticed in the American press, the United States Supreme Court upheld the constitutionality of a decision of a circuit court in Texas which allowed American law enforcement officers to kidnap nationals of a foreign state for alleged offences under American law, and bring them to the United States for trial. Such a decision arbitrarily proclaims the global jurisdiction of American law. Some centuries ago, such occurrences on the high seas were referred to as piracy.

There are still more significant problems with the legalistic conception of a world order where 'human rights' will be safeguarded. The present conception of 'human rights' largely rests on a distinction between state and civil society, a distinction here fraught with hazardous consequences. The rights which are claimed are rights held against the state or, to put it another way, with the blessing of the state: the right to freedom of speech and expression, the right to gather in public, the right to express one's grievances within the limits of the constitution, and so forth. The state becomes the guarantor of these rights, when in fact it is everywhere the state which is the most flagrant violator of human rights. Not only does the discourse of 'human rights' privilege the state, but the very conception of 'rights' must of necessity remain circumscribed. The right to a fair hearing upon arrest, or to take part in the government of one's country, is acknowledged as an unqualified political and civil right. However, the right to housing, food, clean air, an ecologically sound environment, free primary and secondary education, public transportation, a high standard of health, the preservation of one's ethnic identity and culture, and security in the event of unemployment or impairment due to disease and old age is not accorded parity. Such an ecumenical conception of human rights is admitted to by no state, and is infrequently encountered in the vast literature. Nor is it amiss to suggest that the 'individual' rather than the 'human person' predominates in human rights precisely because the individual is an abstraction, while the person is present in every gesture, action, word, relationship and transaction.

Certainly there are organizations, such as the Minority Rights Group (London), Cultural Survival (Boston) and Doctors without Borders, among others, which have adopted a broader conception of 'human rights' and whose discourse is as concerned with the numerous rights of 'collectivities', whether conceived in terms of race, gender, class, ethnic or linguistic background, as it is with the rights of 'individuals'. But this is not the discourse of 'human rights' in the main, and it is emphatically not the discourse of Western powers, which have seldom adhered to the standards that they expect others to abide by, and would use even food and medicine, as the long-lasting embargo against Iraq so vividly demonstrates, to retain their political and cultural hegemony even as they continue to deploy the rhetoric of 'human rights'. Never mind that state formation in the West was forged over the last few centuries by brutally coercive techniques—colonialism, genocide, eugenics, the machinery of 'law and order'—to create homogeneous groups. One could point randomly to the complete elimination of the Tasmanian Aboriginals, the extermination of many Native American tribes, the Highland Clearances in Scotland, even the very (seemingly 'natural') processes by which a largely Breton-speaking France became, in less than a hundred years, French-speaking. The West homogenized itself before it colonized various others; it is now homogenizing these others. Thus the Western discourse of human rights is entirely abstracted from the language of duty, with which the notion of rights is inextricably linked, partly because the West absolved itself of its duties to those whom it colonized.

We should be emphatically clear that what are called the 'Third World' countries should not be allowed the luxury, the right if you will, of pointing to the excesses of state formation in the West to argue (in a parody of the ludicrous evolutionary model where the non-Western world is destined to become progressively free and democratic) that they too must ruthlessly forge ahead with 'development' and 'progress' before their subjects can be allowed 'human rights'. One has, in some respects, heard too much of 'Asian values'; the idea of 'human rights' is noble and its denial an effrontery to humankind. Yet our fascination with this idea must not deflect us from the recognition that 'human rights' is the Maxim gun of the twenty-first century. Perhaps, before 'human rights' is flaunted by the United States as what most of the rest of the world must learn to respect, the movement for 'human rights' should first come home to roost. As Noam Chomsky (1991) has written, people in the Third World 'have never understood the deep totalitarian strain in Western culture, nor have they ever understood the savagery and cynicism of Western culture'. The further rejoinder to these critiques cannot lie in the recourse taken by some to endow their pets with rights while humans are shunned as incurables. Human rights will only flourish when there is a plurality of knowledges and each is furnished with its ecological niche—when, that is, different cultures put forth their own universalisms, and thereby set their own terms for a fruitful engagement with Western human rights discourse.

Economy

Indian Economy

The Indian economy is currently one of the fastest growing economies in the world and encompasses an agriculture sector that sustains much of the rural population, a modern and varied industrial sector and a sizable service sector. Since the initiation of economic reforms and the subsequent liberalization in 1991, the economy has been growing at an average annual rate of around 6 per cent, as compared to 5.4 per cent in the 1980s and 3.5 per cent prior to that. This in turn has led to a sizable growth in GDP and a reduction in poverty. According to Planning Commission estimates, the percentage of India's population living below the poverty line has declined substantially from 51.3 per cent in 1977–78 to 26.1 per cent in 1999–2000. However, there are wide rural-urban and state-wise disparities in poverty reduction. There is a lot of work to be done, mainly in the rural areas, home to the biggest portion of India's population (and consequently, the vote bank) and some of the worst living conditions and incidences of poverty in the country. It is perhaps with a view to this that the new UPA government has announce a wide variety of plans and schemes to improve the conditions in rural India. The country also needs large doses of infrastructure additions—roads and highways, power plants and distribution networks, airports and ports, if it is to sustain rapid growth and attract sizable Foreign Direct Investments.

India's GDP grew 8.1 per cent in the first quarter of FY 2005–06. This is substantially higher, compared to the 7 per cent rise seen in the previous quarter. The key driver of this high growth rate was an 11.3 per cent rise in manufacturing.

The Union Budget 2005–06

Presented by P. Chidambaram, Minister of Finance, on 28 February 2005.

Key Features of Budget 2005–06

Poverty and Unemployment

- The funds allocated for the National Food for Work programme has been increased from Rs 4,020 crore in 2004–05 to Rs 11,000 crore in 2005–06 and the programme will be converted into the **National Rural Employment Guarantee Scheme**.
- The **National Rural Health Mission** will be launched in the next fiscal and will include components like training of health volunteers, supplying more medicines and augmenting the primary and community health centre system. Work will also start on six new AIIMS-like institutions next year.
- The coverage of the **Antyodaya Anna Yojana** will be increased to cover 2.5 crore families.
- The **ICDS** scheme will be expanded through the creation of 1,88,168 additional *anganwadi* centers while the supplementary

nutrition norms will be doubled. The Centre will share one-half of the States' costs.

- The allocation for the **Mid-day Meal Scheme** *will* increase from Rs 1,675 crore in BE 2004–05 to Rs 3,010 crore in 2005–06.
- A non-lapsable fund called 'Prarambhik Shiksha Kosh' will be created for funding the **Sarva Shiksha Abhiyan** and allocation will increase to Rs 7,156 crore in 2005–06.
- **Drinking Water and Sanitation:** All drinking water schemes will be brought under the aegis of Rajiv Gandhi National Drinking Water Mission and stress will be laid on providing drinking water facilities in those rural habitations which have not been covered yet. Another priority area will be tackling water quality in about 2.16 lakh habitations. The 'Total Sanitation Campaign' will be extended to all districts.
- **Scheduled Castes and Scheduled Tribes:** The scholarship scheme programme will be widened so that any student securing admission in one of the shortlisted institutes of excellence will be awarded a larger scholarship for tuition fees, living expenses, books and a computer. The Rajiv Gandhi National Fellowship to be introduced for SC and ST students for pursuing M.Phil and Ph.D courses in selected universities.
- **Women and Children:** Departments will be required to present gender budgets and make make benefit-incidence analyses.
- **Minorities:** The equity support for the National Minorities Development and Finance Corporation will be raised. A certain percentage of new schools under the *Sarva Shiksha Abhiyan* and the *Kasturba Balika Vidyalaya Scheme*

and new *anganwadi* centres will be set up in districts, blocks or villages with a sizable minority population. Assistance will be provided for appointing Urdu language teachers in primary and upper-primary schools. Schemes for pre-examination coaching will include reputed private coaching institutes.

- A **Backward Regions Grant Fund** will be established with an allocation of Rs 5,000 crore in 2005–06, followed by an equal sum of money allocated every subsequent year, for the following four years.
- **Bihar:** The transition arrangements under the *Rashtriya Sam Vikas Yojana* (RSVY) will continue until 2006–07. The Backward Regions Grant Fund will grant Rs 7,975 crore for the period 2005–10.
- **Jammu & Kashmir:** A special plan assistance will be provided under a Reconstruction Plan, in addition to the usual State Plan. The Baglihar project will be provided with adequate funds and the Udhampur — Baramulla rail line will be implemented as a 'project of national importance'.
- **North Eastern Region:** The Kumarghat—Agartala and Lumding—Silchar—Jiribam—Imphal projects will be supported with additional funds, outside the railway budget. The region will also be provided with a special package for highway development amounting to Rs 450 crore.
- Rs 8000 crore will be provided for the **Rural Infrastructure Development Fund** in 2005–06.

Bharat Nirman
Goals:

1. To bring an additional one crore hectares under assured irrigation
2. To connect all villages that have a population of 1000 (or 500 in hilly/tribal areas) with a road

3. To construct 60 lakh more houses for the poor
4. To provide drinking water to the remaining 74,000 habitations that are not already uncovered
5. To provide electricity to the remaining 1,25,000 villages and offer electricity connection to 2.3 crore households
6. To provide telephone connectivity to the remaining 66,822 villages.

Investment

- Equity support of Rs 14,040 crore and loans of Rs 3,554 crore will be provided to Central Public Sector Enterprises, including Railways, in 2005–06.

Agriculture

- A **Roadmap for Agricultural Diversification** will be prepared. It will focus on fruits, flowers, vegetables, dairy, poultry, fisheries, pulses and oilseeds.
- Rs 630 crore will be allocated to the National Horticulture Mission in 2005–06 for the purposes of research, production, post-harvest management, processing and marketing.
- **Agricultural Marketing Infrastructure:** The Budget proposed a new scheme for Development/ Strengthening of Agricultural Marketing Infrastructure. It also proposed that grading and standardization be introduced to attract large investments from the private and cooperative sectors for setting up agricultural markets, marketing infrastructure and support services. These will be implemented through NABARD and NCDC, in those States which amend their APMC Acts.
- **Water Resources, Flood Management and Erosion Control:** A National Project for the repair, renovation and restoration of wa-

ter bodies to be launched in March 2005. The pilot project will cover nearly 700 water bodies in 16 districts across 9 States. 20,000 hectares of additional land will come under irrigation. Rs 180 crore will be provided in 2005–06 for flood management and erosion control in the Ganga basin and in the Brahmaputra and Barak valleys. Rs 52 crore will be provided for the Farakka Barrage Project. The outlay for AIBP will increase to Rs 4,800 crore in 2005–06.

- **Micro Irrigation:** The coverage will increase to 3 million hectares in the Tenth Plan and to 14 million hectares in the Eleventh Plan.
- **Rural Credit and Indebtedness:** RBI will look into the issue of allowing banks to adopt the agency model by using the infrastructure of civil society organizations, rural kiosks and village knowledge centres to provide credit support. Rs 108,500 crore will be disbursed as agricultural credit in the current year. Public sector banks to increase the number of borrowers by an additional 50 lakh.
- **Farm Insurance:** The National Agricultural Insurance Scheme will continue for *kharif* and *rabi* 2005–06.
- **Micro Finance:** The target for credit-linking will be increased from 2 lakh Self Help Groups (SHGs) to 2.5 lakh SHGs. Micro Finance Development Fund will be renamed as the 'Micro Finance Development and Equity Fund' with an increased outlay of Rs 200 crore. RBI will facilitate qualified NGOs to use the External Commercial Borrowing (ECB) window.
- **Micro Insurance:** NGOs, SHGs, cooperatives and MFIs will be invited to become micro insurance

agents.

- **A Knowledge Centre in Every Village:** The Government will particpate in Mission 2007—a national initiative launched to set up a Knowledge Centre in every village by 2007. Rs 100 crore to be provided out of the RIDF.
- **Agricultural Research:** Rs 50 crore will be provided for the National Fund for Strategic Agricultural Research.

Manufacturing

- A 'Manufacturing Competitiveness Programme' will be launched to help small and medium enterprises. The National Manufacturing Competitiveness Council will evolve the model in consultation with the industry.
- **Textiles:** Rs 435 crore will be allocated for the Technology Upgradation Fund. A 10 per cent capital subsidy scheme will be introduced for the textile processing sector. A 'cluster development' approach will be adopted for the production and marketing of handloom products. 20 clusters to be taken up in the first phase at a cost of Rs 40 crore. The life insurance scheme for handloom weavers will be widened to to cover 20 lakh weavers in two years at a cost of Rs 30 crore per year. The coverage of the health insurance package for weavers will be increased to 2 lakh weavers at a recurring cost of Rs 30 crore per year.
- **Sugar industry:** NABARD, in consultation with State Governments, RBI, banks and financial institutions will work out a scheme for providing a financial package with a moratorium for two years, on both principal and interest, and a schedule of payment with regard to the commercial viability of each unit. An interest rate of 2 percentage points below the bank rate will be applicable to outstanding loans as on 21 October 2004. Indian Banks' Association (IBA) and NABARD will work out a scheme under which factories may renegotiate their past high interest loans.
- **Pharmaceuticals and Biotechnology:** Funds allocated to research and development fund will be increased in phases. A stable policy environment and incentives wil be provided to help the two industries become world leaders.
- **Small and Medium enterprises:** 108 items will be identified for dereservation. A provision for 'Promotion of SSI Schemes' will be enhanced to Rs 173 crore in 2005–06. Units in knowledge-based industries like IT, pharma and biotech will be provided equity support through the SME Growth Fund.
- **Skills Training:** 100 ITIs will be identified for upgradation. Of these, 67 ITIs in 15 States/Union Territories linked with industry will be upgraded at a cost of Rs 1.6 crore each. A Skills Development Initiative will be introduced as Public-Private Partnership.
- **Foreign Trade:** Target of US$ 150 billion for exports by the year 2008–09 has been fixed to double India's share in world exports to 1.5 per cent.

Infrastructure

- **Telecommunications:** A provision of Rs 1,200 crore will be made for Universal Service Obligation Fund in 2005–06. 1,687 subdivisions will get support for rural household telephones. BSNL will provide public telephones in the next three years to the remaining 66,822 revenue villages.
- **National Highway Development Project:** NHDP III will be

launched in 2005–06 to target selected high density highways not forming part of the Golden Quadrilateral or the North-South and East-West corridors; Rs 1,400 crore provided in 2005–06 to four-lane 4000 kms.

- **Rural Electrification:** This will cover 1.25 lakh villages in five years with a focus on deficient States. A rural electricity distribution backbone will be created. A 33/11 KV substation will be set up in each block and at least one distribution transformer in each village. Rs 1,100 crore will be provided in 2005–06 for this purpose.

- **Indira Awas Yojana:** The allocation will be increased to Rs 2,750 crore in 2005–06. About 15 lakh houses will be constructed in the next year.

- **Special Purpose Vehicle:** A financial Special Purpose Vehicle (SPV) will be established to finance infrastructure projects that are financially viable. The SPV will lend funds, mainly long term debt, directly to eligible, appraised projects to supplement other loans. The limit for 2005–06 will be fixed at Rs 10,000 crore.

- **Provision of Urban Amenities in Rural Areas (PURA) clusters:** The National Commission on Enterprises in the Unorganized/Informal Sector has proposed pilot projects for 'growth poles' applying the PURA principles. The creation of a few growth poles, as pilot projects will be started in 2005–06.

- **National Urban Renewal Mission:** This will cover the seven mega cities, with a population of over a million and some other towns. Rs 5,500 crore will be provided in 2005–06, including a grant of Rs 1,650 crore.

Financial Sector

Banking

- The Banking Regulation Act, 1949 will be amended to remove the lower and upper limits to statutory liquidity ratio (SLR) and provide flexibility to RBI to prescribe prudential norms, to allow banking companies to issue preference shares, to introduce provisions to enable the consolidated supervision of banks and their subsidiaries by RBI. The Reserve Bank of India Act, 1934, will be amended to remove the limits of the cash reserve ratio (CRR) to facilitate more flexible conduct of monetary policy, to enable RBI to lend or borrow securities by way of repo, reverse repo or other methods.

Capital Market

- FIIs will be allowed to submit appropriate collateral (cash or otherwise) as prescribed by SEBI, when trading in derivatives on the domestic market.

- The Definition of 'securities' under the Securities Contracts (Regulation) Act, 1956 will be amended to provide a legal framework for trading of securitized debt including mortgage backed debt.

- A high level Expert Committee on corporate bonds and securitization will be appointed to look into the legal, regulatory, tax and market design issues in the development of the corporate bond market.

- A one-time exemption from stamp duty on the notional transfer of assets will be granted to the three stock exchanges that are not yet corporatized.

- A high powered Expert Committee will be appointed in consultation with RBI, with the goal of turning Mumbai into a regional financial centre.

- SEBI to be asked to permit mutual funds to introduce Gold Exchange Traded Funds (GETFs) with gold as the underlying asset, in order to enable any household to buy and sell gold in units for a minimum amount of Rs 100.

Other Proposals

- **Higher Education:** Indian Institute of Science (IISc), Bangalore will be upgraded to a world class university with an additional grant of Rs 100 crore.
- **VAT:** All States have agreed to introduce the value added tax (VAT) with effect from 1 April 2005. The Central Government will compensate the States any revenue loss, according to an agreed formula.
- **Twelfth Finance Commission:** Packages covering higher devolution of taxes, debt relief and grants will be made.
- **Defence Expenditure:** The defence expenses allocation will be raised to Rs 83,000 crore in 2005–06. This will include Rs 34,375 crore for capital expenditure.

Fiscal Consolidation

- A mechanism will be instituted to measure the development results of all major programmes. Schemes will not to be allowed to continue from one Plan period to the next without an independent, in-depth evaluation.
- The Ministry of Agriculture will make procurement of food grains more cost effective through decentralized procurement, mainly in the non-traditional States, without harming the present MSP-based procurement.
- A Working Group will be set up by the Department of Fertilizers

to examine issues for implementing the next stage of the New Pricing Scheme for fertilizers starting from 1 April 2006.

Indirect Taxes

Customs

- The customs duty structure will be brought closer to that of East Asian neighbours and the peak rate for non-agricultural products will be reduced from 20 per cent to 15 per cent.
- Customs duties on selected capital goods and their parts will be reduced to below 15 per cent, to 10 per cent in some cases and to 5 per cent in some others.
- The duty on textile machinery and refrigerated vans will be reduced from 20 per cent to 10 per cent.
- Duties on seven specified machinery used in leather and footwear industry will be reduced from 20 per cent to 5 per cent. The duty on ethyl vinyl acetate (EVA) will be reduced from 20 per cent to 10 per cent.
- The duty on nine specified machinery used in pharma and biotech sectors will be reduced to 5 per cent.
- Duties on specified parts of battery-operated road vehicles and for printing presses will be reduced from 20 per cent to 10 per cent.
- Duties on primary and secondary metals will be reduced from 15 per cent to 10 per cent and industrial raw materials like catalysts, refractory raw materials, basic plastic materials, molasses and industrial ethyl alcohol will be liable to a customs duty rate of 10 per cent. The duty on lead will be reduced to 5 per cent.
- The duty on coking coal with high ash content will be reduced to 5 per cent.

- The duty on polyester and nylon chips, textile fibres, yarns and intermediates, fabrics, and garments will be reduced from 20 per cent to 15 per cent.
- Duty to be removed on specified capital goods and all inputs required for the manufacture of Information Technology Agreement (ITA) bound items.
- A CVD of 4 per cent will be levied on the imports of ITA bound items and their inputs that attract nil duty; credit for the CVD to be available against payment of excise duty; IT software will be exempt from the proposed CVD.
- The duty on atmospheric drinking water generators will be reduced from 20 per cent to 5 per cent.

Excise

- The duty on polyester filament yarn, tyres and air conditioners will be reduced to 16 per cent.
- Independent texturizers will be given the option to avail the exemption route or pay 8 per cent excise duty with CENVAT credit.
- Duty of 2 per cent will be applicable on branded jewellery. Duty on mosaic tiles will be levied at 8 per cent. Road tractors for semi trailers of engine capacity exceeding 1800 cc will attract 16 per cent duty. Agricultural tractors will continue to be exempt.
- The surcharge of Re1 per kg on tea and duty of Re1 per kg on refined edible oils and Rs 1.25 per kg on vanaspati will be abolished.
- The ceiling for SSI exemption based on turnover will be raised from Rs 3 crore per year to Rs 4 crore per year. SSI units will be either fully exempt on the first clearance of Rs 1 crore or attract normal duty on the first clearance of Rs 1 crore with CENVAT credit.
- Duty on iron and steel will be reduced to 16 per cent.

- Duty on molasses will be increased from Rs 500 per MT to Rs 1000 per MT. Duty on cement clinkers will be increased from Rs 250 per MT to Rs 350 per MT as an anti-avoidance measure.
- The cess on petrol and diesel will be increased by 50 paise per litre.
- The specific rate on cigarettes will be raised by about 10 per cent and a surcharge of 10 per cent will be imposed on ad valorem duties on other tobacco products including gutka, chewing tobacco, snuff and pan masala; biris not to be subject to this levy.

Taxes on petroleum products

- The customs duty on crude petroleum will be reduced from 10 per cent to 5 per cent.
- There will be no customs duty and excise duty on LPG for domestic consumption and on subsidized kerosene.
- The customs duty on other petroleum products, including motor spirit (MS) and diesel (HSD) will be reduced from 20 or 15 per cent to 10 per cent. Excise duty on petrol and diesel will be fixed as a combination of ad valorem and specific duties.

Service Tax

- Service providers with gross turnover under Rs 4 lakh per year will be exempt.
- Some additional services to be covered.

Direct Taxes

The new tax brackets and the new rates are:

Up to Rs 1 lakh	Nil
Rs 1 lakh to Rs 1.5 lakh	10 per cent
Rs 1.5 lakh to Rs 2.5 lakh	20 per cent
Above Rs 2.5 lakh	30 per cent

- The surcharge of 10 per cent will now apply to a level of Rs 10 lakh taxable income.

- The exemption level for women will be Rs 1.25 lakh. The exemption level for senior citizens will be Rs 1.5 lakh.
- Every tax payer to be allowed a consolidated limit of Rs 1 lakh for savings which will be deducted from the income before tax is calculated. All prevailing sectoral caps will be removed. Rebate under Section 88 will be eliminated and Section 80L will be brought in line with the new regime.
- The exemption from tax on interest earned on accounts maintained by Non Resident Indians will continue.
- A 'Fringe Benefits Tax' will be introduced, at 30 per cent on an appropriately defined base It will be applicable to benefits that are usually enjoyed collectively by employees and which cannot be attributed to individual employees. Such benefits will be taxed in the hands of the employer. However, transport services for workers and staff and canteen services in office or factory will remain outside the scope of this tax net.
- The corporate income tax rate for domestic companies will be 30 per cent plus a surcharge of 10 percent. The rate of depreciation will be 15 per cent for general machinery and plant, but the initial depreciation rate will be increased to 20 per cent. The requirement of 10 per cent increase in installed capacity for availing of the benefit of initial depreciation will be removed.
- The withholding tax on technical services will be reduced from 20 per cent to 10 per cent.
- Credit to be allowed for the Minimum Alternate Tax (MAT) paid under Section 115 JB of the Income Tax Act.
- The Terminal date on exemptions given for specific purposes, will be extended from 31 March 2005 to 31 March 2007 in the following cases:
  - Weighted deduction of 150 per cent of expenditure on in-house research and development facilities of companies engaged in the business of biotechnology, telecommunication, electronics, pharmaceuticals, chemicals or any other notified product.
  - In the case of deduction of profits of new industrial undertakings in Jammu & Kashmir.
  - 100 per cent deduction of profits will be allowed to companies carrying on scientific research and development and approved by the Department of Scientific and Industrial Research.
- Tax exemption on agreements to acquire aircraft or aircraft engines on lease will be extended up to 30 September 2005.
- There will be a Nominal increase in the rates of STT for all categories of transactions.
- Income Tax Act to be amended to provide that trading in derivatives in specified stock exchanges will not be treated as 'speculative transactions' for the purposes of the Income Tax Act.
- Mobile telephone will be removed from the one-in-six criteria for filing income tax returns and replaced with payment for electricity of more than Rs 50,000 per year.
- Two anti tax-evasion measures to be introduced. Firstly, a 0.1 per cent tax will be levied on withdrawal of cash on a single day of over Rs 10,000 or more from banks. Secondly, banks will be required to report all deposits which are exempt from TDS on interest.

- Large taxpayer units (LTUs) will be established in major cities. Help Centres for small taxpayers to be setup in cooperation with industry associations, professional bodies and NGOs.

Railway Budget 2005–06

Presented by Laloo Prasad Yadav, Minister of Railways, on 26 February 2005.

Review of Performance in 2004–05

- 7.67 per cent growth in loading in the first nine months. The revised target for freight loading will be raised from 580 mt to 600 mt. The target for freight earnings will be increased from Rs 28,745 cr to Rs 30,450 cr.
- The target of 396 billion tkm for Tenth Plan end year will be surpassed in 2004–05 itself.
- Growth in originating passenger traffic was around 6 per cent, compared to budget target of 3 per cent.
- There has been a growth of 8.3 per cent in total earnings in the period ending December 2004, as compared to 4.1 per cent growth in the previous financial year. The total earnings in the Revised Estimates are fixed at Rs 46,635 cr (Rs 1,838 cr higher than Budget Estimates.)
- Ordinary Working Expenses will increase by Rs 400 cr, mainly due to increase in fuel prices.
- Operating Ratio will improve to 91.2 per cent, compared to the budgeted target of 92.6 per cent.
- Fund balances expected to close with a healthy figure of Rs 6,963 cr.

Freight Business Initiatives

- Wagon turn round will be brought down to 5 days in the near future, compared to 6 days in the current year.

- Preferential traffic schedule for supply of wagons will be rationalized and simplified.
- Electrification of diesel sidings will be located on electrified sections at Railways' cost where justified by traffic.
- Engine-on-Load Scheme will be further liberalized and made attractive. The scheme will be extended to selected goods sheds and for customers not having their own private sidings.
- The Terminal Incentive Scheme including cash incentives, aimed at reduction of detention at terminals, will be formulated in consultation with industry.
- Facilities at freight train examination centres will be upgraded for qualitative improvement in examination and for providing longer intervals between successive examinations.
- Rules relating to demurrage/wharfage and loading/unloading time will be rationalized.
- Incentives will be provided to customers adopting mechanized loading and round the clock working.
- Electronic Payment Gateway facility will be implemented for BTPS. It will be extended to major customers.

Public-Private Partnership

- Freight customers will be encouraged to develop their private sidings through cost sharing.
- Scheme for development of Integrated Warehouse Complexes to provide single window service will be provided to customers
- Organizations other than CONCOR will be considered for running container trains.
- Introduction of double stack container trains on one of the identified routes connecting North India with Gujarat Ports is being considered.

- Rail Land Development Authority (RLDA) will develop surplus Railway land.
- RailTel will exploit its upgraded OFC network to increase its revenue earning capability by providing various broadband services.

Parcel Business Initiatives

- Additional parcel space will be leased in certain nominated trains.
- Vacant compartment of guard in front of SLR coach will be given on lease.
- Short term lease and lower lease price are being considered for trains with poor SLR utilization.

Passenger Business–Initiatives and Amenities

- A countrywide extension of universal enquiry number (139) at local call rates will be made.
- A system to book tickets through landline phones will be started. Internet booking timings will now be from 4 a.m. to 11.30 p.m. without a break.
- Reservation status will be made available in advance. The display of vacant berth position, renewal of season tickets on Internet will be provided for Mumbai suburban passengers.
- PRS facility will be extended further. 45 of the remaining district headquarters will be covered in 2005–06. The balance will be covered in the following year.
- UTS will be expanded by over 300 locations.

IT Steps oriented towards MIS

- MIS through data warehouse will be developed from UTS, PRS and FOIS, Implementation of Control charting system on 15 divisions, unified computerized crew management system to be developed.
- COIS timetable module under development will be web-enabled.

- Computerization of Railway Claims Tribunals, Goods Refund Offices for online registration and quick settlement of claims will be implemented. Claims management system will be web-enabled.

Integrated Railway Modernization Plan (IRMP)

A Five year Integrated Railway Modernization Plan costing Rs 24,000 cr has been formulated. It aims at running of 150 kmph passenger trains and 100 kmph freight trains on the golden quadrilateral and its diagonals. It also plans to introduce higher axle load trains, double stack containers, light weight corrosion resistant aluminium wagons, modernization of track, bridge, signaling and telecommunication, etc.

Accounting Initiatives

An Accounting Reforms process has been initiated. The modification in the accounting system will be carried out so that the true nature of lease transaction and their contribution to railway revenues will be reflected.

A rationalization of the capital structure of Indian Railways will be carried out. A chair for studies in Railway finance at one of the IIMs will be established. Actuarial assessment of pension liability has been proposed.

- Transparency in purchase and sale.
- New vendors will be developed.

Safety

- Medical relief trains and trains carrying equipment for restoration will be upgraded to run at 100 kmph.
- State of the art modern track recording car for better monitoring and maintenance of track will be deployed.
- The first ACD worked section on Indian Railways designed to prevent collisions likely to be ready in Northeast Frontier Railway by March 2005.

Security

The recruitment drive for filling up vacancies in RPF and modernization programme of RPF is in full swing for improving security to passengers and their belongings.

Concessions

- Full concession in second class will be extended to unemployed youth appearing for interviews of state government jobs.
- 50 per cent concession in second class will be allowed to farmers and milk producers for travel to national level institutes for training/learning better agricultural practices/dairy farming.
- 75 per cent concession in second class will be allowed to rural school students in government schools, once in a year, for study tour.
- 75 per cent concession in second class will be allowed to girls from rural areas studying in government schools for attending national level entrance examination for professional courses.
- Transportation of relief material will be allowed on priority basis and free of cost in notified cases, free second class transportation to stranded persons for their evacuation.
- 50 per cent concession in the normal tariff rates will be allowed for carrying dead bodies of patients who die while undergoing treatment in major government hospitals.

Recruitment

Recruitment for Group D posts will be done by field units instead of RRBs.

Reservation

- Appropriate representation of Scheduled Tribes and Other Backward Castes in Railway Services will be ensured.
- 25 per cent reservation in licences of small catering units at 'A', 'B' and 'C' category stations and 49.5 per cent reservation at other categories of stations for under privileged categories.
- 25 per cent reservation to under privileged categories in new bookstall policy.

Staff welfare

A Corporate Welfare Programme is being formulated. This will include a 10 year plan for improvement of staff quarters.

Upgradation of health units/ hospitals

- A provision for sale of dairy products under Catering policy will be made.
- 'Clean Train Station System' will be implemented on at least one station of each zonal railway in 2005–06. Stainless steel EMU coaches will be introduced for Mumbai Suburban area.
- Composite Sleepers will be developed from waste material.

Passenger Services

New Service in 2005–06

- 54 pairs of new train services will be introduced.
- 28 pairs of trains will be extended.
- The frequency of 10 pairs of trains will be increased.
- 30 trains will be speeded up.
- Trains with low usage will be reviewed.
- About 400 additional coaches will be deployed in well-patronized trains.

Surveys

In addition to 72 surveys announced in the last Budget, 20 more surveys will be sanctioned this year.

New Plants

- A wheel manufacturing plant will be set up at Chapra.
- 12 new concrete sleeper plants are being planned contemplated. Five of these will be set up at Dauram Madhepura, Chak Sikander, Sitamarhi, Palghat and Harihar, on an immediate basis.

Annual Plan 2005–06

- Plan outlay: Rs 15,349 cr, consisting of:
  - Rs 7230.81 cr from General Exchequer (including Rs 2699 cr from SRSF and Rs 710.81 cr from Central Road Fund),
  - Rs 4718.19 cr from internal resources,
  - Rs 3400 cr through market borrowings.
- Besides this, the Railways will be allowed access to extra budgetary resources of Rs 3000 cr for financially viable schemes.
- Additional funds of Rs 1365 cr for national projects in Jammu & Kashmir/North-east Region and Rs 358 cr for RVNL works will be released during the course of the year.
- Appropriation to Development Fund will be raised significantly for making available adequate funds for throughput enhancement works including traffic facility works.

Projects

Achievements of current year and targets for next year as below:

Kumarghat-Agartala and Jiribam-Imphal Road (Tupul) new lines and Lumding-Silchar-Jiribam gauge conversion will be declared as national projects.

Budget Estimates 2005–06

- Freight loading target 635 mt, originating passenger traffic will increase by 4 per cent.
- Gross Traffic Receipts are estimated at Rs 50,968 cr, Rs 4,183 cr higher than RE 2004–05.
- Ordinary Working Expenses are estimated at Rs 35,600 cr. Appropriation to DRF kept at Rs 3,604 cr., 60 per cent more than BE of 2004–05.
- Net Revenue is estimated to be Rs 5,914 cr.
- Operating Ratio will improve to 90.8 per cent.

Freight Services

- There will be no increase in freight rates across the board.
- Goods tariff will be simplified, rationalised and made transparent. Goods tariff to contain only 80 group of commodities instead of over 4000 commodities at present.
- Freight will be charged now based upon the carrying capacity of wagons, for all commodities.
- Introduction of three new classes viz. 90-W1, 90-W2 and 90-W3 will be made to avoid appreciable increase in freight for lighter commodities.

	Likely in 2004–05	Target for 2005
Total BG lines to be added	1400 kms	1692 kms
New Lines	205 kms	219 kms
Gauge Conversion	885 kms	935 kms
Doubling	307 kms	538 kms
Electrification	375 kms	350 kms

- The total number of classes will be reduced from 27 to 19 with uniform interval between successive classes. The highest class will be reduced from Class-250 to Class-240. Freight for kerosene and LPG will be reduced.
- A single uniform Class-100 will be made for the entire group of Chemical Manures.
- Classification for foodgrains and pulses will be revised to Class-120. However, foodgrains for Public Distribution System and Poverty Alleviation Programmes and for other relief works will be charged at Class-100 to avoid increase in their freight rates. They will be charged at Class-90 if carried in open wagons.
- Iron ore will be charged at Class-160 instead of Class-140. However, transportation of programmed Iron-ore, with private sidings will continue to be charged at Class-140.
- New Premium Registration Scheme will be drawn up. Those willing to pay freight at two classes higher than the prescribed class will be given higher preference in allotment of rakes within the same class of priority.
- Two days in a week will be reserved for allotment of rakes strictly as per the date of registration.
- 'Wagon Investment Scheme' will be introduced. This will assure guaranteed supply of wagons to customers investing in railway wagons. The scheme also aims to set certain freight rebates and higher priority for such customers.

Passenger Services

There will be no increase in passenger fares.

The Five Year Plans

The Plans at a Glance

Item	VIII Plan (1992–97) Targets	VII Plan (1985–90) Estimates	VI Plan (1980–85)
	Rs Crores		
Overall outlay	871100	389584	185177
Public outlay	434100	221436*	110467*
Private investment	437000	168148#	74710#
Total investment	798000	322366#	158710#
Public sector	361000	154218#	84000#
Private sector	437000	168148#	74710#
Break-up of public outlay:			
Center	247865	127520*	57825*
States and Union Territories	186235	93916*	52642*
Financing of public outlay:			
Internal resources	405400	205930	102292
External resources	28700	20708	8529

Item	V Plan (1974–79)	IV Plan (1969–74)	III Plan (1961–66)	II Plan (1956–61)
	Estimates		Actuals	
	Rs Crores			
Overall outlay	66474	24882	12677	7742
Public outlay	39303*	15902*	8577	4672
Private investment	27171#	8980#	4100#	3100
Total investment	63751#	22635#	11280	6831
Public sector	36703#	13655#	7180	3731
Private sector	27408#	8980#	4100#	3100
Break-up of public outlay:				
Center	19954	7826*	4212	2534
States and Union Territories	19349	7952*	4365	2138
Financing of public outlay:				
Internal resources	32115	12438	6154	3623
External resources	5834	2614	2423	1049

*Resource gap was bridged by deficit finance
Original targets

Macro Parameters for the 10th Plan

Item	IX Plan (1997–02)	X Plan (2002–07)	Post Plan
	%		
GDP (Growth rate per annum)	5.4	7.9	9.4
Investment rate	24.2	28.4	36.1
Domestic savings rate	23.3	26.8	33.0
International capital output ratio	4.5	3.6	3.8
Current account deficit	0.9	1.6	3.1
Export (Growth rate per annum)	6.9	12.4	–
Import (Growth rate per annum)	9.8	17.1	–

Note: Savings, investment and current account deficit are % of GDP at market price.

Central Government Receipts (Major Components)

(Rs Million)

Year	2001–02	2002–03	2003–04	2004–05 (RE)	2005–06 (BE)
Tax revenue	133532	158544	186982	225804	273466
Direct Tax	48421	61592	76572	97344	129779
Personal income tax	22588	27759	30739	36514	47687
Corporation tax	25355	33893	45706	60609	81873
Indirect tax	85112	96952	110410	128460	143687
Excise duties	53849	62388	70245	78836	94320
Customs duty	28243	31898	34586	40450	37961
Non-tax revenue	67774	72290	76896	75100	77734

Interest receipts	35538	37622	38517	31538	25500
Revenue receipts	201306	230834	263878	300904	351200
Capital receipts	162500	180531	207490	204887	163144
Total receipts	363806	411365	471368	505791	514344

(RE) = Revised estimates
(BE) = Budget estimates
*Net of states' share

Major Heads of Expenditure of the Central Government

(Rs Million)

Year	2001–02	2002–03	2003–04	2004–05 (RE)	2005–06 (BE)
Revenue expenditure	301468	338713	362140	386069	446512
Defence expenditure	38059	40709	43203	43517	48625
Interest payments	107460	117804	124088	125905	133945
Subsidies	31210	43533	44256	46514	47432
Capital expenditure	60842	74535 *	109228 *	119722 *	67832
Loans and advances	34284	31668	28768	30442	5652
Capital outlay	26558	29101	34249	56615	62180
Defence expenditure	16207	14953	16863	33483	34375
Total expenditure	362310	413248	471368	505791	514344

(RE) = Revised estimates
(BE) = Budget estimates

Market Exchange Rate of Indian Rupee
(Average of Buying and Selling Rates)

Month-end	US$	Pound Sterling	Euro	Japanese Yen
		Rupees Per Unit of Foreign Currency		
March, 1998	39.50	65.62	–	0.3070
December, 1998	42.55	70.92	–	0.3643
March, 1999	42.44	68.85	46.07	0.3529
December, 1999	43.51	70.28	43.84	0.4248
March, 2000	43.61	69.51	41.80	0.4148
December, 2000	46.74	69.75	43.42	0.4073
March, 2001	46.64	66.58	41.02	0.3593
December, 2001	48.18	69.89	42.65	0.3669
March, 2002	48.80	69.59	42.64	0.3681
December, 2002	48.04	77.09	50.36	0.4053
March, 2003	47.51	74.92	51.50	0.3990
December, 2003	45.62	78.59	55.17	0.4210

(*Source*: Statistical Outline of India, 2004–05, Tata Services Limited)

India's Exports and Imports

A Secretary heads the Department of Commerce in the Ministry of Commerce and Industry, Government of India. The Department is responsible for the country's external trade and all matters connected with it, such as commercial relations with other countries, state trading, export promotional measures and the development and regulation of certain export oriented industries and commodities. It formulates policies in the sphere of foreign trade, in particular, the import and export policy of the country. Foreign trade has played a crucial role in India's economic growth. India's total external trade in the year 1950–51 stood at Rs 1,214 crores. It reached Rs 537,433 crores during 2002–03. Despite the appreciation of the Rupee, the exports in 2003–04 increased by 17.3 per cent reaching $61.8 billion. Imports for the same period increased by 25 per cent to $75.2 billion. The Government of India operates FOCUS-LAC (Latin America Caribbean), FOCUS-Africa and Focus-CIS Programmes to promote trade with the emerging markets of these three regions.

Export of Principal Commodities: April–March, 2003–04

(Rs crores)

Commodities	April–March 2002–03	April–March 2003–04	Percentage Growth	Weight
I. Plantations	2646.04	2676.78	1.16	0.92
1. Tea	1652.07	1594.56	−3.48	0.55
2. Coffee	993.98	1082.22	8.88	0.37
II. Agri and allied prdts	22848.97	24474.22	7.11	8.39
1. Cereal	7682.17	6858.36	−10.72	2.35
a) Rice	5831.24	4133.08	−29.12	1.42
b) Wheat	1759.87	2349.37	33.5	0.81
c) Others	91.06	375.91	312.82	0.13
2. Pulses	345.02	322.57	−6.51	0.11
3. Tobacco	1022.89	1090.82	6.64	0.37
a) Unmanufactured	733.52	801.5	9.27	0.27
b) Manufactured	289.37	289.31	−0.02	0.1
4. Spices	1655.49	1525.6	−7.85	0.52
5. Nuts and seeds	2690.68	2987.49	11.03	1.02
a) Cashew incl. CNSL	2061.5	1700.18	−17.53	0.58
b) Sesame and niger seed	450.88	743.22	64.84	0.25
c) Groundnut	178.3	544.09	205.16	0.19
6. Oil Meals	1487.35	3271.63	119.96	1.12
7. Guergum Meal	486.64	503.72	3.51	0.17
8. Castor Oil	609.81	635.56	4.22	0.22
9. Shellac	89.85	163.12	81.55	0.06
10. Sugar and mollasses	1814.54	1220.55	−32.74	0.42
11. Processed foods	2929	3543.58	20.98	1.22
a) Fresh fruits and vegetables	1090.11	1700.35	55.98	0.58
b) Fruits/vegetable seeds	97.96	52.3	−46.61	0.02
c) Processed and misc.				

Processed items	1740.93	1790.93	2.87	0.61
12. Meat and preparations	1377.19	1602.44	16.36	0.55
13. Poultry and dairy product	358.52	407.38	13.63	0.14
14. Floriculture products	180.77	220.8	22.14	0.08
15. Spirit and beverages	119.06	120.63	1.32	0.04
III. Marine products	6928.05	6067.84	−12.42	2.08
IV. Ores and minerals	9659.92	10755.74	11.34	3.69
1. Iron ore	4200.44	5133.63	22.22	1.76
2. Mica	40.85	76.67	87.69	0.03
3. Processed minerals	2662.87	2827.77	6.19	0.97
4. Other ores and minerals	2497.47	2451.39	−1.85	0.84
5. Coal	258.29	266.29	3.1	0.09
V. Leather and mfrs.	8945.02	9306.66	4.04	3.19
1. Footwear	3107.08	3407.08	9.66	1.17
2. Leather and mfrs.	5837.94	5899.58	1.06	2.02
VI. Gems and jewellery	43700.65	48293.86	10.51	16.56
VII. Sports goods	351.38	429	22.09	0.15
VIII. Chemicals and related products	38030.65	44993.05	18.31	15.43
1. Basic chemls.,Pharma & cosmetics	22544.58	25791.9	14.4	8.85
2. Plastics and linoleum	5912.31	7991.57	35.17	2.74
3. Rubber, glass & other products	7749.4	9404.58	21.36	3.23
4. Residual chemls. & allied products	1824.36	1805	−1.06	0.62
IX. Engineering goods	37211.02	47853.28	28.6	16.41
A. Machinery	16759.94	22063.18	31.64	7.57
1. Machine tools	584.6	631.36	8	0.22
2. Machinery and instruments	9719.91	12735.61	31.03	4.37
3. Transport equipments	6455.44	8696.21	34.71	2.98
B. Iron and steel	8982.32	11322.1	26.05	3.88
4. Iron and steel bar rod etc	1135.13	1486.39	30.94	0.51
5. Primary and semi-fnshd iron and steel	7847.19	9835.7	25.34	3.37
C. Other engineering items	11468.75	14468	26.15	4.96
6. Ferro Alloys	250.8	391.55	56.12	0.13
7. Aluminium other than prods.	740.26	709.6	−4.14	0.24
8. Non-ferrous metals	1394.09	2097.28	50.44	0.72
9. Manufacture of metals	8941.63	11065.05	23.75	3.79
10. Residual Engineering Items	141.96	204.52	44.07	0.07
X. Electronic goods	6265.07	7992.39	27.57	2.74
1. Electronics	6062.64	7749.29	27.82	2.66
2. Computer software in physical form	202.43	243.1	20.09	0.08
XI. Project goods	239.32	275.06	14.93	0.09
XII. Textiles	53627.52	55003.7	2.57	18.86
1. Readymade garments	27536.5	27977.07	1.6	9.59
2. Cotton,yarn,fabrics,				

made-ups, etc.	16217.49	15275.87	−5.81	5.24
3. Manmade textiles made-ups, etc.	6859.97	8351.96	21.75	2.86
4. Natural silk textiles	1504.35	1698.66	12.92	0.58
5. Wool & woollen mfrs.	246.43	271.67	10.24	0.09
6. Coir & coir mfrs.	355	360.44	1.53	0.12
7. Jute mfrs.	907.77	1068.03	17.65	0.37
XIII. Handicrafts	3800.64	2032.46	−46.52	0.7
XIV. Carpets	2577.5	2616.93	1.53	0.9
1. Hand-made excl. silk	1940.76	2495.3	28.57	0.86
2. Mill-made excl. silk	540.61	0	−100	0
3. Silk carpets	96.13	121.63	26.53	0.04
XV. Cotton raw incl. waste	50.28	811.47	1513.9	0.28
XVI. Petroleum products	12469.22	16168.04	29.66	5.54
XVII. Unclassified exports	5784.73	11831.13	104.52	4.06
Grand Total	**255137.3**	**291581.9**	**14.28**	**100**

Import of Principal Commodities: April–March, 2003–04

(Rs crores)

Commodities	April–March 2002–03	April–March 2003–04	Percentage Growth	Weight
I. Bulk imports	115864.8	134067.4	15.71	37.87
1. Cereals and preparations	118.55	88.11	−25.68	0.02
a) Rice	1.09	0.17	−84.73	0
b) Wheat	0	0.24		0
c) Other cereals	0.67	1.94	190.37	0
d) Preparations	116.79	85.76	−26.57	0.02
2. Fertilizers	3028.49	3303.37	9.08	0.93
a) Crude	894.42	614.99	−31.24	0.17
b) Sulphur and un-roasted pyrites	403.35	396.25	−1.76	0.11
c) Manufactured	1730.72	2292.12	32.44	0.65
3. Edible Oil	8779.64	11674.41	32.97	3.3
4. Sugar	32.83	42.83	30.46	0.01
5. Pulp and waste paper	1661.76	1876.54	12.93	0.53
6. Paper board and mfrs.	2043.92	2769.18	35.48	0.78
7. Newsprint	1134.66	1535.9	35.36	0.43
8. Crude rubber	882.98	1286.6	45.71	0.36
9. Non-ferrous Metals	3225.63	4330.94	34.27	1.22
10. Metalliferrous ores & metal scrap	5022.38	5746.43	14.42	1.62
11. Iron and steel	4566.92	6893.12	50.94	1.95
12. Petroleum crude and products	85367	94520	10.72	26.7
II. Pearls, precious and semi-precious stones	29340.9	32755.51	11.64	9.25
III. Machinery	30847.4	37627.31	21.98	10.63
1 Machine tools	1195.07	2111.51	76.69	0.6
2 Machinery other than electrical	17255.9	21701.17	25.76	6.13

3 Electrical machinery	3213.92	3969.51	23.51	1.12
4 Transport equipment	9182.51	9845.13	7.22	2.78
IV. Project goods	2626.34	1744.88	−33.56	0.49
V. Others	118526.5	147780.5	24.68	41.75
1. Cashew nuts	1236.24	1371.8	10.96	0.39
2. Fruits and nuts	641.76	815.51	27.07	0.23
3. Wool raw	801.83	870.61	8.58	0.25
4. Silk raw	647.15	626.29	−3.22	0.18
5. Synth. and reg. fibres	364.15	268.51	−26.26	0.08
6. Pulses	2737.09	2251.15	−17.75	0.64
7. Raw hides and skins	269.64	228.75	−15.17	0.06
8. Leather	688.01	786.39	14.3	0.22
9. Coal, coke and briquettes	5999.27	6478.77	7.99	1.83
10. Non-metallic mnl. mfrs.	1135.71	1500.12	32.09	0.42
11. Other crude minerals	499.21	589.43	18.07	0.17
12. Organic and inorganic chmls.	14640.36	18482.97	26.25	5.22
13. Dyeing, tanning matrl.	1339.65	1600.53	19.47	0.45
14. Medicinal and pharma prds.	2865.2	2955.63	3.16	0.83
15. Artf. resins, etc.	3783.71	4962.81	31.16	1.4
16. Chemical products	2187.38	2898.67	32.52	0.82
17. Other textile yarn, fabrics, etc	1647.54	1949.38	18.32	0.55
18. Manufactures of metals	2363.1	3157.93	33.64	0.89
19. Profl. instruments, etc.	5484.09	5635.56	2.76	1.59
20. Electronic goods	27098.53	34442.91	27.1	9.73
21. Wood and wood products	1945.99	3268.45	67.96	0.92
22. Gold and silver	20753.13	31326.69	50.95	8.85
23. Tea	125.3	64.52	−48.5	0.02
24. Wollen yarn and fabrics	100.96	167.93	66.33	0.05
25. Cotton yarn and fabrics	424.9	652.01	53.45	0.18
26. Man made f'mnt spun yarn	1922.42	1905.14	−0.9	0.54
27. Made up textile articles	191.26	373.22	95.13	0.11
28. Ready made garments (wov.)	115.93	172.65	48.92	0.05
29. Silk yarn and fabrics	293.04	521.11	77.83	0.15
30. Milk and cream	9.547	89.47	837.11	0.03
31. Spices	586.44	581.92	−0.77	0.16
32. Oil seeds	11.49	13.89	0	0
33. Jute raw	134.77	49.62	−63.18	0.01
34. Woollen and cotton rags	83.9	134.29	60.06	0.04
35. Veg. and animal fats	11.61	12.68	9.17	0
36. Cottow raw and waste	1237.61	1570.01	26.86	0.44
37. Essential oils & cos. prep	486.44	418.13	−14.04	0.12
38. Cement	4.18	9.28	122.21	0
39. Computer soft. physical form	2389.74	1749.2	−26.8	0.49
40. Other commodities	11268.21	12826.56	13.83	3.62
Total Imports	**297205.9**	**353975.6**	**19.1**	**100**

Agriculture

The Indian agriculture sector has achieved significant progress since independence in terms of crop yields, growth in output, and area under different crops. According to the Department of Agriculture and Co-operation, Ministry of Agriculture, Government of India, India is presently the world's largest producer of tea, milk, fruits, coconuts, and cashewnuts, the second largest producer of wheat, sugar, vegetables, and fish and the third largest producer of rice and tobacco. The per capita availability of foodgrains in the country has grown from 350 gms. in 1951 to about 500 gms. per day. In the case of milk, it has grown from less than 125 gms. to 210 gms. per day while the availability of eggs has jumped from 5 to 30 per annum. All this growth has taken place even though the population itself has leaped to over 100 crores. However, Indian agriculture still has a long way to go. The sector suffers from numerous problems. These drawbacks relate to the size of landholdings which make it difficult to introduce automation and achieve efficient yields, difficulty in obtaining agricultural credit from banks, scarcity of seeds, the evils of poor handling, inadequate storage facilities and spillage, and natural calamities like floods, droughts, pests, and crop diseases. The system is not yet free of exploitative factors like moneylenders and trading cartels. The Common Minimum Programme (CMP) of the UPA government that came to power in 2004 stated the government's intentions of ensuring substantial and rapid public investment in agricultural research and the development of rural infrastructure. The CMP also states that steps will be taken to revive the rural cooperative credit system to achieve a doubling of the flow of rural credit over a timeframe of the next three years. The government will also address the issues of the easing of the burden of debt on farmers and increasing the efficiency of crop and livestock insurance schemes. The Government also announced its intention to ensure sufficient protection to farmers from imports, mainly in the scenario of sharp dips in international prices. The CMP also pledged the fast clearing of dues to all farmers including sugarcane farmers.

Targets and Achievements of Production of Major Crops During 2002-03 and 2003-04

(Million Tonnes)

Crop	2002-03		2003-04	
	Targets	Achievements	Targets	Achievements*
Rice	93.00	72.66	93.00	87.00
Wheat	78.00	65.10	78.00	72.06
Coarse Ceareals	33.00	25.29	34.00	37.76
Pulses	16.00	11.14	15.00	15.23
Foodgrains	220.00	174.19	220.00	212.05
Oilseeds	27.00	15.06	24.70	25.14
Sugarcane	320.00	281.58	320.00	236.18
Cotton #	15.00	8.72	15.00	13.79
Jute & Mesta@	12.00	11.38	12.00	11.20

Million Bales of 170 kg. each.
@ Million Bales of 180 kg. each.
* Advance Estimates as on 05.08.2004 2002-03 2003-04

Production of Major Livestock Products and Fish

Year	Milk (Million Tonnes)	Eggs (Million Tonnes)	Fish (Thousand Nos.)
2000–01	80.8	36600	5656
2001–02	84.8	39100	5956
2002–03*	87.3	40300	6200
2003–04(A)	91.1	43100	–

* Provisional

Foodgrains Production

(Million tonnes)

Crop/Year	1999–2000	2000–01	2001–02	2002–03	2003–04*	2004–05*
Rice	89.7	85.0	93.3	72.7	87.0	87.8
Wheat	76.4	69.7	72.8	65.1	72.1	73
Coarse Cereals	30.3	31.1	33.4	25.3	37.8	31.9
Pulses	13.4	11.1	13.4	11.1	15.2	13.7
Food grains						
Kharif	105.5	102.1	112.1	87.8	112.0	102.9
Rabi	104.3	94.7	100.8	86.4	100.0	103.5
Total	209.8	196.8	212.9	174.2	212.0	206.4

Irrigation

In India, irrigation has played an important role in the development of agriculture and of various states. The full irrigation potential of the country has been estimated at 139.5 million hectares (mha). This consists of 58.5 mha from major and medium schemes, 15 mha from minor irrigation schemes and 66 mha from ground water exploitation. India's irrigation potential has increased from 22.6 mha in 1951 to about 90 mha at the end of 1995-96. The utilization of irrigation potential at the end of 1995 was 78.5 mha. Most irrigation projects are operating at an efficiency level of 30-40 per cent. It is estimated that even after achieving the full irrigation potential, nearly 50 per cent of the total cultivated area will remain rain fed. Of the net canal irrigated area of 17 mha, 3.4 mha are estimated to be under varying degrees of waterlogging and soil salinity.

Statewise Ultimate Irrigation Potential from Major, Medium and Minor Irrigation

(in Thousand Hectares)

State Name	Ultimate Irrigation Potential (UIP)				
	Major and MediumIrri.	Minor Irrigation			Total (UIP)
		Surface Water	Ground Water	Total (M.I)	
Andhra Pradesh	5000	2300	3960	6260	11260
Arunachal Pradesh	0	150	18	168	168
Assam	970	1000	900	1900	2870

Bihar	6500	1900	4947	6847	13347
Goa	62	25	29	54	116
Gujarat	3000	347	2756	3103	6103
Haryana	3000	50	4462	1512	4512
Himachal Pradesh	50	235	68	303	353
Jammu & Kashmir	250	400	708	1108	1358
Karnataka	2500	900	2574	3474	5974
Kerala	1000	800	879	1679	2679
Madhya Pradesh	6000	2200	9732	11932	17932
Maharashtra	4100	1200	3652	4852	8952
Manipur	135	100	369	469	604
Meghalaya	20	85	63	148	168
Mizoram	0	70	-	70	70
Nagaland	10	75	-	75	85
Orissa	3600	1000	4203	5203	8803
Punjab	3000	50	2917	2967	5967
Rajasthan	2750	600	1778	2378	5128
Sikkim	20	50	-	50	70
Tamil Nadu	1500	1200	2832	4032	5532
Tripura	100	100	81	181	281
Uttar Pradesh	12500	1200	16799	17999	30499
West Bengal	2300	1300	3318	4618	6918
Total States	58367	17337	64045	81382	139749
Total Uts	98	41	5	46	144
Grand Total	58465	17378	64050	81428	139893

Coal Reserves in India

The Ministry of Coal is responsible for determining policies and strategies related to exploration and development of coal and lignite reserves, sanctioning important projects of high value and for deciding all related issues. India has a long history of commercial coal mining covering nearly 220 years starting from 1774 by M/s Sumner and Heatly of East India Company in the Raniganj Coalfield along the Western bank of Damodar River. However, for about a century the growth of Indian coal mining remained slow for lack of demand. The introduction of steam locomotives in 1853 put it on the rise. Within a short span, production rose to an annual average of 1 million tonnes (mt) and India could produce 6.12 mts. per year by 1900 and 18 mts. per year by 1920. The production got a sudden boost from the First World War but went through a slump in the early thirties. It again reached a level of 29 mts. by 1942 and 30 mts. by 1946. Unscientific mining practices adopted by some of the mine owners and poor working conditions for labourers in some of the private coalmines became matters of concern for the Government. Due to these reasons, the Central Government took a decision to nationalize private coalmines. The nationalization was done in two phases, the first with the coking coalmines in 1971–72 and then with the non-coking coalmines in 1973. 55 per cent of the country's energy consumption is met by coal. The country's industrial heritage was built upon indigenous coal. Commercial primary energy consumption in India has grown by about 700 per cent in the last four decades. The current per capita commercial primary energy consumption in India is about 350 kgoe/year (kilogram of oil equivalent per year) that is well below that of developed countries. Driven by the rising population, expanding economy and a quest for improved quality of life, energy usage in India is expected to rise to around 450 kgoe/year in 2010. Considering the limited reserve potentiality of petroleum and natural gas, eco-conservation restriction on hydel project and geo-political perception of nuclear power, coal will continue to occupy centre-stage in India's energy scenario.

Inventory of Coal Reserves of India

As a result of exploration carried out down to a depth of 1200m by the GSI and other agencies, a cumulative total of 245.69 billion tonnes of coal resources have been estimated in the country as on 1 January 2004.

The state-wise distribution of coal resources and its categorization are as follows:

Statewise Resources of Indian Coal

State	Coal Resources in Million Tonnes			
	Proved	Indicated	Inferred	Total
Andhra Pradesh	8263	6079	2584	16926
Arunachal Pradesh	31	40	19	90
Assam	279	27	34	340
Bihar	0	0	160	160
Chhattisgarh	9373	26191	4411	39975
Jharkhand	35417	30439	6348	72204
Madhya Pradesh	7513	8815	2904	19232
Maharashtra	4653	2309	1620	8582
Meghalaya	117	41	301	459
Nagaland	4	1	15	20
Orissa	15161	30976	14847	60984
Uttar Pradesh	766	296	0	1062
West Bengal	11383	11876	4554	27813
Total	92960	117090	37797	247847

Indian Power Sector

The Indian power sector was one of the first sectors in which private participation was allowed in the early 1990s. At first, the focus was on private sector investments in power generation projects but the government later allowed private organizations to invest in distribution and transmission projects as well. As on March 2002, India has around 104,000 MW of installed power generating capacity. As much as 80 per cent of this installed capacity comes from thermal power plants while hydroelectric plants account for about 16 per cent. Nuclear plants account for the remaining installed capacity. Non-conventional energy sources contribute only a relatively small percentage. There are a large number of private power projects either at the planning stages or under construction. The Central Electricity Authority (CEA) has granted techno-economic clearances (TECs) to over 50 private power projects that account for a total of around 30,000 MW. India needs substantial addition of power generation capacities, given its economic growth targets. According to Planning Commission estimates, India needs to add around 47,000 MW of power generation facilities in the near future, requiring an investment of around US$ 73 billion.

Energy and Power Supply Scenario in India

	2002–03*	2003–04	2004–05 (up to January)
Energy (MU)			
Requirement	545983	559264	491348
Availability	497890	519398	456009
Shortage (%)	8.8	7.1	7.2
Power (MW)			
Peak demand	81492	84574	87906
Peak demand Met	71547	75066	77281
Shortage (%)	12.2	11.2	12.1

(*Source*: Statistical Outline of India, 2003–04, Tata Services Limited)

Petroleum Industry in India

The Ministry of Petroleum & Natural Gas is involved in exploration & production of oil & natural gas (including import of Liquefied Natural Gas), refining, distribution & marketing, import, export and conservation of petroleum products. Crude oil production in the country in 2003–04 was 33.37 million metric tonnes (MMT) and gas production was 31.96 billion cubic metres (BCM) as against a production of 33.04 MMT of crude oil and 31.39 BCM of natural gas in 2002-03. Crude oil production and natural gas production targets for 2004-05 are 33.64 MMT and

31.07 BCM respectively. Availability of oil is vital to national security. Oil security is very important for a country like India that has a high oil import dependency (at present over 70 per cent). The gap between domestic crude availability and demand for crude indicates the vulnerability of the Indian economy to oil imports. At present, about 67 per cent of India's crude oil imports come from the Middle East region. The general political instability in this region is another cause of worry from the oil supply security perspective. The Government has decided to set up a 5 million metric tonne (MMT) strategic crude oil storage facilities at various locations in the country.

Production of Crude Oil and Natural Gas

	2002–03	2003–04	2004–05* (Apr.–Dec.)
I. Crude Oil Production ++ ('000' Tonnes)			
(a) Onshore:			
Gujarat	6043	6131	4655
Assam/Nagaland	4660	4592	3526
Arunachal Pradesh	74	77	63
Tamil Nadu	395	375	286
Andhra Pradesh	300	281	170
Total	11472	11456	8700
(b) Offshore:			
ONGC	17559	17677	13678

JVC/Private	4013	4240	3178
Total	21572	21917	16856

2. **Natural Gas Production** (Million Cubic Metres)

(a) Onshore:			
Gujarat	3531	3517	2652
Assam/Nagaland	2047	2247	1680
Arunachal Pradesh	36	–	29
Tripura	446	508	362
Tamil Nadu	466	605	489
Andhra Pradesh	2038	1927	1283
Rajasthan	162	168	149
Total	8726	8972	6644
(b) Offshore:			
ONGC	18373	17806	13351
JVC/Private	4290	5184	3864
Total	22663	22990	17215

* Provisional

Stock Exchanges of India

The Indian Securities Market originated in 1875, when 22 brokers established the Bombay Stock Exchange (BSE) under a banyan tree. Presently, there are two national level exchanges in India— the Bombay Stock Exchange (BSE) and National Stock Exchange (NSE), along with 21 regional exchanges. There are around 9400 broking outfits, with about 9600 companies listed on the exchanges. The market capitalization is close to US$ 125.5 billion.

The Securities and Exchange Board of India (SEBI) is the statutory body, operating within the legal framework of Securities and Exchange Board of India Act, 1992. It exercises its powers under the Securities and Exchange Board of India Act, 1992; the Securities Contract (Regulation) Act, 1956; the Depositories Act, 1996; and also the delegated powers under the Companies Act, 1956.

The headquarters of SEBI are located in Mumbai. It has three regional offices at Chennai, New Delhi and Kolkata. Its board is its main decision-making body, headed by the Chairman and comprising five other members.

List of Stock Exchanges in India

North Zone

Uttar Pradesh Stock Exchange Assoc. Ltd., Kanpur
Ludhiana Stock Exchange Assoc. Ltd.
Delhi Stock Exchange Assoc. Ltd.
Jaipur Stock Exchange Ltd.

East Zone

Bhubaneswar Stock Exchange Assoc Ltd.
Calcutta Stock Exchange Assoc Ltd.
Gauhati Stock Exchange Ltd.
Magadh Stock Exchange Association, Patna

West Zone

The Stock Exchange, Ahmedabad
Vadodara Stock Exchange Ltd.
Madhya Pradesh Stock Exchange Ltd., Indore
The Stock Exchange, Mumbai
OTC Exchange of India, Mumbai
National Stock Exchange of India Ltd., Mumbai
Pune Stock Exchange Ltd.
Saurashtra Kutch Stock Exchange Ltd., Rajkot
Inter-connected Stock Exchange of India, Mumbai

South Zone

Bangalore Stock Exchange Ltd.
Madras Stock Exchange Ltd.
Cochin Stock Exchange Ltd.
Coimbatore Stock Exchange
Hyderabad Stock Exchange Ltd.
Mangalore Stock Exchange Ltd.

Insurance Industry in India

In India, the insurance business is divided into four categories. These are:

1. Life Insurance
2. Fire Insurance
3. Marine Insurance
4. Miscellaneous Insurance

While life insurers transact life insurance business, general insurers transact the business regarding the other forms of insurance. Insurance is a federal subject in India. The business of life insurance in India in its present form began in 1818 with the setting up of the Oriental Life Insurance Company in Calcutta. The first general insurance company set up in India was the Triton Insurance Company Ltd. in 1850 in Calcutta. The primary legislations dealing with insurance business in India are the Insurance Act, 1938, and the Insurance Regulatory and Development Authority Act, 1999.

State Insurers

Life insurer

1. Life Insurance Corporation of India (LIC)

General insurers

2. General Insurance Corporation of India (GIC)

GIC had four subsidiary companies. These were:

1. The Oriental Insurance Company Limited
2. The New India Assurance Company Limited
3. National Insurance Company Limited
4. United India Insurance Company Limited

However, with the General Insurance Business (Nationalization) Amendment Act 2002 (40 of 2002) coming into force from 21 March 2002, GIC ceased to be a holding company of its subsidiaries and Government of India became the owner of these four organizations.

Private insurers

Life insurers (in the sequence of date of registration)

1. HDFC Standard Life Insurance Company Ltd.
2. Max New York Life Insurance Co. Ltd.
3. ICICI Prudential Life Insurance Company Ltd.
4. OM Kotak Mahindra Life Insurance Co. Ltd.
5. Birla Sun Life Insurance Company Ltd.
6. Tata AIG Life Insurance Company Ltd.
7. SBI Life Insurance Company Ltd.
8. ING Vysya Life Insurance Company Private Ltd.
9. Allianz Bajaj Life Insurance Company Ltd.
10. Metlife India Insurance Company Pvt. Ltd.
11. AMP SANMAR Assurance Company Ltd.
12. Aviva Life Insurance Co. India Pvt. Ltd.
13. Sahara India Insurance Company Ltd.

Private general insurers (in the sequence of date of registration)

1. Royal Sundaram Alliance Insurance Company Limited
2. Reliance General Insurance Company Limited.
3. IFFCO Tokio General Insurance Co. Ltd.

4. TATA AIG General Insurance Company Ltd.
5. Bajaj Allianz General Insurance Company Limited
6. ICICI Lombard General Insurance Company Limited.
7. Cholamandalam General Insurance Company Ltd.
8. Export Credit Guarantee Corporation Ltd.
9. HDFC-Chubb General Insurance Co. Ltd.

Banking System

Although different forms of banking, mainly in the form of money lending, existed in India since ancient times, banking in the form that we know today only began around 100 years back. The earliest such institutions under the British regime were agency houses that carried on banking business besides their trading activities. However, most of these agency houses were closed down between 1929–32. In 1919, the three presidency banks (Bank of Bengal, Bank of Bombay, and Bank of Madras) were amalgamated into the Imperial Bank of India. Later on, in 1955, the Imperial Bank of India became the State Bank of India. Oudh Commercial Bank, founded in 1881, was the first bank of limited liability to be managed by Indians. The Swadeshi movement that began in 1906 inspired the formation of a number of commercial banks. The Banking Companies (Inspection Ordinance) and the Banking Companies (Restriction of Branches) Act were passed in January and February 1946 respectively. The Banking Companies Act was passed in February 1949. It was later renamed the Banking Regulation Act. On 19 July 1969, the Government issued an ordinance, acquiring the ownership and control of 14 major banks in the country, with deposits above Rs 50 crore each. The aim was to bring commercial banks into the mainstream of economic development with definite social obligations and objectives. On 15 April 1980, six more commercial banks were nationalized. The government laid down the objectives of public sector banking system on 21 July 1969. A high-level committee was set up on 14 August 1991 to examine all aspects relating to the structure, organization, functions and procedures of the financial system, in view of the changing economic scenario of the country. Based on the recommendations of this committee, headed by Chairman M. Narasimham, a comprehensive reform of the banking system was introduced in 1992–93. The objective of this reform programme was to ensure that the balance sheets of banks reflected their real financial health. Another important measure of the reforms process was the introduction of capital adequacy norms in line with international standards. The setting up of new private sector banks was not allowed in the post-nationalization era. However, this was allowed in 1993. The aim was to introduce greater competition that in turn would lead to higher productivity and efficiency. In December 1997, the Government of India set up a high-level committee under the chairmanship of Shri M. Narasimham to review the implementation of financial system reforms as initiated in the post-liberalization era and to plan the reforms necessary in the future. The committee submitted its report to the Government in April 1998.

The Reserve Bank of India (RBI) was established under the Reserve Bank of India Act, 1934 on 1 April 1935 and nationalized on 1 January 1949. The RBI is the sole authority for issue of currency in India other than one rupee coins and subsidiary coins and notes. As the agent of the Central government, the Reserve Bank also undertakes the distribution of one-rupee notes and coins and small coins that the Government issues. The Reserve Bank also performs a variety of developmental and promotional functions and also handles the borrowing programme of the Government of India.

Nationalized Banks in India

1. Allahabad Bank
2. Andhra Bank
3. Bank of Baroda
4. Bank of India
5. Canara Bank
6. Central Bank of India
7. Corporation Bank
8. Dena Bank
9. Indian Bank
10. Indian Overseas Bank
11. Punjab and Sind Bank
12. Syndicate Bank
13. UCO Bank
14. Union Bank of India
15. United Bank of India

State Bank of India and its Associate Banks

1. State Bank of India
2. State Bank of Bikaner and Jaipur
3. State Bank of Hyderabad
4. State Bank of Mysore
5. State Bank of Travancore
6. State Bank of Patiala

Private Indian Banks

1. Bank of Rajasthan
2. Bharat Overseas Bank Ltd.
3. Catholic Syrian Bank Ltd.
4. Federal Bank Ltd
5. Karnataka Bank Ltd.
6. Development Credit Bank Ltd.
7. Global Trust Bank Ltd.
8. HDFC Bank Ltd.
9. ICICI Banking Corporation Ltd.
10. IDBI Bank Ltd.
11. IndusInd Bank Ltd.
12. Jammu and Kashmir Bank
13. Ratnakar Bank Ltd.
14. Sangli Bank Ltd.
15. SBI Commercial and International Bank Ltd.
16. South Indian Bank Ltd.
17. United Western Bank
18. UTI Bank Ltd.
19. Vysya Bank Ltd.

Important foreign banks operating in India

1. ABN AMRO Bank N.V
2. American Express Bank Ltd.
3. Arab Bangladesh Bank Ltd.
4. Bank of Bahrain and Kuwait BSC
5. Bank of Tokyo—Mitsubishi Ltd.
6. Bank of Muscat
7. Banque Nationale de Paris
8. Barclays Bank plc
9. Cho Hung Bank
10. Citibank NA
11. Commerz Bank
12. Credit Lyonnais Bank
13. Deutsche Bank
14. Development Bank of Singapore
15. Fuji Bank Ltd.
16. Hongkong and Shanghai Banking Corporation Ltd.
17. ING Bank N.V
18. KBC Bank N.V
19. Krung Thai Bank plc
20. Mashreq Bank PSC
21. Oman International Bank SAOG
22. Overseas-Chinese Banking Corporation Ltd.
23. Sakura Bank
24. Sanwa Bank Ltd.
25. Societe Generale
26. Standard Chartered Bank
27. Standard Chartered Grindlays Bank Ltd.
28. Sumitomo Bank
29. The Chase Manhattan Bank N.V
30. The Toronto Dominion Bank

Value Added Tax

Value Added Tax (VAT) is a sales tax levied on the sale of goods and services. VAT was invented by Maurice Lauré, joint director of the French tax authority in the 1950s. A common VAT system is compulsory for member states of the European Union. The EU VAT system is imposed by a series of European Union directives.

List of countries that have introduced VAT.

1. Albania
2. Algeria
3. Bangladesh
4. Barbados
5. Belarus
6. Belgium
7. Benin
8. Bolivia
9. Botswana
10. Brazil
11. Bulgaria
12. Burkina Faso
13. Cambodia
14. Cameroon
15. Chad
16. Chile
17. China
18. Colombia
19. Congo
20. Costa Rica
21. Croatia
22. Cyprus
23. Czech Republic
24. Dominican Republic
25. Denmark
26. Ecuador
27. El Salvador
28. Estonia
29. Ethiopia
30. Finland
31. France
32. Gabon
33. Georgia
34. Germany
35. Ghana
36. Greece
37. Guatemala
38. Hungary
39. Iceland
40. India
41. Indonesia
42. Ireland
43. Israel
44. Italy
45. Kazakhstan
46. Kenya
47. Peoples Republic of South Korea
48. Kyrgyzstan
49. Latvia
50. Lebanon
51. Lesotho
52. Liechtenstein
53. Lithuania
54. Luxembourg
55. Macedonia
56. Madagascar
57. Mali
58. Malta
59. Mauritania
60. Mauritius
61. Mexico
62. Moldova
63. Monaco
64. Mongolia
65. Morocco
66. Mozambique
67. Namibia
68. Nepal
69. Netherlands
70. Nicaragua
71. Nigeria
72. Norway
73. Paraguay
74. Peru
75. Philippines
76. Poland
77. Romania
78. Russia
79. Senegal
80. Serbia & Montenegro
81. Slovakia
82. Slovenia
83. South Africa
84. Spain
85. Sri Lanka
86. Suriname
87. Sweden
88. Switzerland
89. Tajikistan
90. Tanzania
91. Thailand
92. Togo
93. Trinidad & Tobago
94. Tunisia
95. Turkey
96. Turkmenistan
97. Uganda
98. Ukraine
99. United Kingdom
100. Uruguay

101. Uzbekistan
102. Vanuatu
103. Venezuela
104. Vietnam
105. Zambia
106. Zimbabwe

Opinions

Globalization of world economies, accompanied by aggressive consumerism, characterize market trends in the world today. Here are two analyses of this phenomenon by two world-renowned scholars.

The World is Flat
Thomas L. Friedman

No one ever gave me directions like this on a golf course before: 'Aim at either Microsoft or IBM.' I was standing on the first tee at the KGA Golf Club in downtown Bangalore, in southern India, when my playing partner pointed at two shiny glass-and-steel buildings off in the distance, just behind the first green. The Goldman Sachs building wasn't done yet; otherwise he could have pointed that out as well and made it a threesome. HP and Texas Instruments had their offices on the back nine, along the tenth hole. That wasn't all. The tee markers were from Epson, the printer company, and one of our caddies was wearing a hat from 3M. Outside, some of the traffic signs were also sponsored by Texas Instruments, and the Pizza Hut billboard on the way over showed a steaming pizza, under the headline 'Gigabites of Taste!'

No, this definitely wasn't Kansas. It didn't even seem like India. Was this the New World, the Old World, or the Next World?

I had come to Bangalore, India's Silicon Valley, on my own Columbus-like journey of exploration. Columbus sailed with the *Niña*, the *Pinta*, and the *Santa María* in an effort to discover a shorter, more direct route to India by heading west, across the Atlantic, on what he presumed to be an open sea route to the East Indies—rather than going south and east around Africa, as Portuguese explorers of his day were trying to do. India and the magical Spice Islands of the East were famed at the time for their gold, pearls, gems, and silk—a source of untold riches. Finding this shortcut by sea to India, at a time when the Muslim powers of the day had blocked the overland routes from Europe, was a way for both Columbus and the Spanish monarchy to become wealthy and powerful. When Columbus set sail, he apparently assumed the Earth was round, which was why he was convinced that he could get to India by going west. He miscalculated the distance, though. He thought the Earth was a smaller sphere than it is. He also did not anticipate running into a landmass before he reached the East Indies. Nevertheless, he called the aboriginal peoples he encountered in the new world 'Indians'. Returning home, though, Columbus was able to tell his patrons, King Ferdinand and Queen Isabella, that although he never did find India, he could confirm that the world was indeed round.

I set out for India by going due east, via Frankfurt. I had Lufthansa business class. I knew exactly which direction I was going thanks to the GPS map displayed on the screen that popped out of the armrest of my airline seat. I landed safely and on schedule. I too encountered people called Indians. I too was searching for the source of India's riches. Columbus was searching for hardware—precious metals, silk, and spices—the source of wealth in his day. I was searching for software, brainpower, complex algorithms, knowledge workers, call centres, transmission protocols, breakthroughs in optical engineering—the sources of wealth in our day. Columbus was happy to make the Indians he met his slaves, a pool of free manual labor. I just wanted to understand why the Indians I met were taking our work, why they had become such an important pool for the outsourcing of service and information technology work from America and other industrialized countries. Columbus had more than one hundred men on his three ships; I had a small crew from the Discovery Times channel that fit comfortably into two banged-up vans, with Indian drivers who drove barefoot. When I set sail, so to speak, I too assumed that the world was round, but what I encountered in the real India profoundly shook my faith in that notion. Columbus accidentally ran into America but thought he had discovered part of India. I actually found India and thought many of the people I met there were Americans. Some had actually taken American names, and others were doing great imitations of American accents at call centres and American business techniques at software labs.

Columbus reported to his king and queen that the world was round, and he went down in history as the man who first made this discovery. I returned home and shared my discovery only with my wife, and only in a whisper.

'Honey,' I confided, 'I think the world is flat.'

How did I come to this conclusion? I guess you could say it all started in Nandan Nilekani's conference room at Infosys Technologies Limited. Infosys is one of the jewels of the Indian information technology world, and Nilekani, the company's CEO, is one of the most thoughtful and respected captains of Indian industry. I drove with the Discovery Times crew out to the Infosys campus, about forty minutes from the heart of Bangalore, to tour the facility and interview Nilekani. The Infosys campus is reached by a pockmarked road, with sacred cows, horse-drawn carts, and motorized rickshaws all jostling alongside our vans. Once you enter the gates of Infosys, though, you are in a different world. A massive resort-size swimming pool nestles amid boulders and manicured lawns, adjacent to a huge putting green. There are multiple restaurants and a fabulous health club. Glass-and-steel buildings seem to sprout up like weeds each week. In some of those buildings, Infosys employees are writing specific software programs for American or European companies; in others, they are running the back rooms of major American- and European-based multinationals—everything from computer maintenance to specific research projects to answering customer calls routed there from all over the world. Security is tight, cameras monitor the doors, and if you are working for American Express, you cannot get into the building that is managing services and research for General Electric. Young Indian engineers, men and women, walk briskly from building to building, dangling ID badges. One looked like he could do my taxes. Another looked like she could take my computer apart. And a third looked like she designed it!

After sitting for an interview, Nilekani gave our TV crew a tour of Infosys's global conferencing centre—ground zero of the Indian outsourcing industry. It was a cavernous wood-paneled room that looked like a tiered classroom from an Ivy League law school. On one end was a massive wall-size screen and overhead there were cameras in the ceiling for teleconferencing. 'So this is our conference room, probably the largest screen in Asia—this is forty digital screens [put together],' Nilekani explained proudly, pointing to the biggest flat-screen TV I had ever seen. Infosys, he said, can hold a virtual meeting of the key players from its entire global supply chain for any project at any time on that supersize screen. So their American designers could be on the screen speaking with their Indian software writers and their Asian manufacturers all at once. 'We could be sitting here, with somebody from New York, London, Boston, San Francisco, all live. And maybe the implementation is in Singapore, so the Singapore person could also be live here ... That's globalization,' said Nilekani. Above the screen there were eight clocks that pretty well summed up the Infosys workday: 24/7/365. The clocks were labeled US West, US East, GMT, India, Singapore, Hong Kong, Japan, Australia.

'Outsourcing is just one dimension of a much more fundamental thing happening today in the world,' Nilekani explained. 'What happened over the last [few] years is that there was a massive investment in technology, especially in the bubble era, when hundreds of millions of dollars were invested in putting broadband connectivity around the world, undersea cables, all those things.' At the same time, he added, computers became cheaper and dispersed all over the world, and there was an explosion of software—e-mail, search engines like Google, and proprietary software that can chop up any piece of work and send one part to Boston, one part to Bangalore, and one part to Beijing, making it easy for anyone to do remote development. When all of these things suddenly came together around 2000, added Nilekani, they 'created a platform where intellectual work, intellectual capital, could be delivered from anywhere. It could be disaggregated, delivered, distributed, produced, and put back together again—and this gave a whole new degree of freedom to the way we do work, especially work of an intellectual nature ... And what you are seeing in Bangalore today is really the culmination of all these things coming together.'

We were sitting on the couch outside of Nilekani's office, waiting for the TV crew to set up its cameras. At one point, summing up the implications of all this, Nilekani uttered a phrase that rang in my ear. He said to me, 'Tom, the playing field is being leveled.' He meant that countries like India are now able to compete for global knowledge work as never before—and that America had better get ready for this. America was going to be challenged, but, he insisted, the challenge would be good for America because we are always at our best when we are being challenged. As I left the Infosys campus that evening and bounced along the road back to Bangalore, I kept chewing on that phrase: 'The playing field is being leveled.'

What Nandan is saying, I thought, is that the playing field is being flattened ... Flattened? Flattened? My God, he's telling me the world is flat!

Here I was in Bangalore—more than five hundred years after Columbus sailed over the horizon, using the rudimentary navigational technologies of his day, and returned safely to prove definitively that the world was round—and one of India's smartest engineers, trained at his country's top technical institute and backed by the most modern technologies of his day, was essentially telling me that the world was *flat*—as flat as that screen on which he can host a meeting of his whole global supply chain. Even more interesting, he was citing this development as a good thing, as a new milestone in human progress and a great opportunity for India and the world—the fact that we had made our world flat!

In the back of that van, I scribbled down four words in my notebook: 'The world is flat.' As soon as I wrote them, I realized that this was the underlying message of everything that I had seen and heard in Bangalore in two weeks of filming. The global competitive playing field was being leveled. The world was being flattened.

As I came to this realization, I was filled with both excitement and dread. The journalist in me was excited at having found a framework to better understand the morning headlines and to explain what was happening in the world today. Clearly, it is now possible for more people than ever to collaborate and compete in real time with more people on more different kinds of work from more different corners of the planet and on a more equal footing than at any previous time in the history of the world—using computers, e-mail, networks, teleconferencing, and dynamic new software. That is what Nandan was telling me. That was what I discovered on my journey to India and beyond.

When you start to think of the world as flat, a lot of things make sense in ways they did not before. But I was also excited personally, because what the flattening of the world means is that we are now connecting all the knowledge centres on the planet together into a single global network, which—if politics and terrorism do not get in the way—could usher in an amazing era of prosperity and innovation.

Copyright © Thomas L. Friedman 2005. Excerpted with permission from *The World is Flat: A Brief History of the Globalized World in the 21st Century*, Allen Lane 2005.

Consumerism
Ashis Nandy

Consumerism is not the first choice of human beings. Nor is it a basic need. There is not an iota of evidence in contemporary psychology, anthropology or ethnology to confirm that consumerism is a part of human nature, that we cannot survive without unending consumption. Not even the great champions of free market have dared to claim that human happiness is inescapably hitched to the kind of consumption that the prosperous are encouraged to practice in the name of development today. Even much of the West, identified the world over with infinite consumption, had no genuine tradition of

heavy consumption before the beginning of this century, probably not till the 1940s.

Consumption was discovered as a value and a lifestyle only about five decades ago. Previously, it had been a character trait of profligate rulers and the spoilt children of a few super-rich; now it was made a marker of social achievement and, thus, a part of everyday life. People now consumed stories of super-consumption through newspapers, journals and television—the way they earlier read of, fantasized about and vicariously entered the harems of Oriental potentates. Earlier, the aristocracy, when it consumed mindlessly, did not dare to advertise the fact, for it was incongruent with class status. Only the newly rich were expected to flaunt their wealth. High consumption now became a marker of social status and success and a patented remedy for feelings of social inadequacy and personal inferiority.

Perhaps no other country has become so deeply identified with consumption in our times as the United States, though some of the most powerful critiques of consumption, too, have come from that country. The reason for both these facts may be that in no other country has consumption been so systematically institutionalized as a need in itself. A few city states like Hong Kong and Singapore, and a few small kingdoms acting as city states, such as Dubai, have also jumped on the bandwagon of 'consuming societies'. These are societies where not only is consumption an end in itself but the entire country often looks to a casual observer like a huge supermarket, and the country's political economy, if not life itself, is organized around consumption. However, the global cultural impact of such city states is not a fraction of that of the United States.

In America the successful institutionalization of consumption might have come about perhaps because it is mainly a society of immigrants that has tried to build a public culture hitched to the psychological and social needs of the exiled and decultured. The institutionalization of consumption is an incidental byproduct of this larger cultural process that has been going on for the last 200 years thanks to the changing colour of industrial capitalism, erosion of communities and the emergence of 'lonely crowds' in the large parts of the world. As I have already said, consumption has anxiety-binding properties, particularly in the lives of the uprooted, the lonely and the massified.

This culture of exile also provides a clue to the unique status that the United States has began to enjoy as everyone's second country. In pre-war Europe Paris claimed the status, I am told, of being every European's second city. For many subjects of British and French colonies as well, London and Paris had a similar status. Today, it seems that only the United States can claim this prerogative. The size of the American market (including the market for conformity and deviance and for new faiths, ideologies and creeds) has a role to play in this. The United States is the consumer's paradise. Even dissent has a better market there than elsewhere; it is consumed more avidly and widely there than almost anywhere else. This critique of consumption can also be consumed.

In the 1940s, the psychoanalyst Erich Fromm coined the term 'marketing orientation' to describe a personality type that included people who sold their selves, rather than things in the modern marketplace. He did not foresee that one day we shall have another personality type that would consider it 'normal' to consume for the sake of consuming. The consuming orientation is now a hallmark of style and high fashion; there are persons and groups in the world famous only for their flamboyant consumption. These hyperconsumers would have put to shame the greediest rich before the Second World War.

Usually when justifying consumption, the marketeers claim that it will lead to greater consumption of the physical essentials of life by the poor. Alternatively, they extol the technological growth or economic modernization that follows a consumption explosion, allegedly serving as an engine of development. It has, however, already become obvious that the kind of consumption they have in mind—or are comfortable with—has nothing to do with any such grand social vision. For, once built, a culture of consumption becomes a self-perpetuating affair. As has been the case with the super-consuming rich, it becomes an end in itself. This is not unknown to the development experts; they expect consumption to lead to a consumption-oriented development and technology. I am not saying that their economic logic is faulty. I am arguing that their justifications of consumption only capture a small part of the phenomenon and spirit of consumption.

To understand that spirit, one must first face the fact that to make consumption a value, human beings have to be re-engineered. The first step in this process is to isolate or uproot a person from his or her community, traditions and family. In their place, he or she has to be given a large, anonymous quasi-community called the nation, a more manageable set of cultural artefacts called traditions (artefacts that can be consumed in a theatre, gallery, classroom or a tourist resort) and a nuclearized unit called family where the elderly and the underaged both become either intrusions or liabilities that have to be sometimes borne but never treated on the same footing as the conjugal pair, bonded together by a commodified concept of sex.

Simultaneously, an ideological basis has to be laid for consumption. The possessive individual who, according to many European scholars, provides the very basis of modern liberal capitalism, has to be redefined as the consuming individual. Simultaneously, the right to property has to be redefined as the right to consumption. The sovereignty of this consuming individual has to be declared so that the apparent sacredness that attaches to the individual in many theories of the state, freedom and rights begins to attach to the act of and the right to consumption. Some social and political activists claim that standardized production systems are now producing standardized consumption patterns, for only such patterns now make economic sense. Many popular ideas of democracy in the global mass culture seem, on closer scrutiny, to be an attempt to protect this pattern and the particular form of individualism that goes with it. Speaking of the Kyoto protocol on world environment, which the United States refused to sign, President George Bush, Sr, once said, 'Gentlemen, the American way of life is not negotiable.' As some others put it, 'dollarized poverty' is now matched by dollarized wealth and dollarized individuals.

To such an individual—lonely, narcissistic and decoupled from community ties—consumption becomes the ultimate value, a guarantor of social belonging and status. He or she compensates for an empty social life by consuming. One is, because one consumes.

This lonely individual is the basic constituent of all projects of global marketing. Marketing is all about creating needs. Basic needs do not have to be advertised; people automatically try to meet them and are willing to work or pay for them. Advertisements become necessary to create artificial needs. Marketing is the art and science of creating such needs by linking them to basic human needs. This linkage is often not noticed. Many talk of consumerism as a form of a conspiracy to cheat the ordinary innocent citizen with the help of smart, high-pitched advertisements. Ordinary citizens are not that easily cheated. They are influenced by advertisements, but first a void has to be created in their lives so that the seductive properties of advertisement can work on them.

It is crucial to create this void. Only when his or her life is emptied of a deep sense of belonging to a community, family or tradition does the atomized individual begin to seek meaning in various pseudo-solidarities. One of the most important of these today is the solidarity of the consumers. Presidents and prime ministers in the First World are now made or unmade on the basis of the threat they pose to—or the promises they offer of—mega consumption. Consumption, or the hope of it, now gives meaning to the lives of many, however odd that may sound to a large proportion of the world. This has even produced a new internationalism which, paradoxically, relieves one from any responsibility to learn about other countries or communities. You do not have to, for others also consume, and therefore they are. They also can be known through their consumption patterns.

Yet, consumerism is not anti-cultural. Being a world view, it has a place for culture. The place is not for culture as we have known it—vibrant, unmanageable, fuzzy and often subversive of the projects called modernity and development—but for a consumable culture. Once such a culture becomes triumphant, many known entities in our world acquire new meanings. For instance, I notice remarkable and rapid changes taking place in ancient civilizations such as China and India. There are already signs that, under a consumerist dispensation, the Indianness of India may become a liability and yet, at the same time, a capital. Much effort, we may presume, will be made in the coming years to encash that Indianness as a form of commodified classicism or ethnic chic, 'viewable' on the weekends and saleable in the tourist market.

Do cultures resist consumerism? I do not really know. But I like to believe that they can hit back when threatened with extinction, whether the threat is real or imaginary. Human biology can be even more aggressively resistant. A large majority of the fatal diseases in the First World have to do with over-consumption. Worse is the fate of those ethnic groups in the First World which have not developed any scepticism towards consumption. The incidence of cardiac diseases among expatriate South Asians in some of the Western societies today is three times that among the native whites. This is probably the way nature and culture seek to restore balance and ensure their survival.

Copyright © Ashis Nandy 2005. Excerpted with permission from *The Future of Knowledge and Culture: A Dictionary for the 21st Century*, edited by Vinay Lal and Ashis Nandy, Viking 2005.

Some Famous Business Personalities

Bezos, Jeff; (1964–); US; founder of Amazon.com.

Gates III (Bill), William H; (1955–); US; co-founder and current Chairman and Chief Software Architect of Microsoft Corporation.

Ellison (Larry), Lawrence J; (1944–); US; founder and CEO of the major database software firm Oracle Corporation.

Jobs, Steven (Steve) P; (1955–); US; co-founder and CEO of Apple Computer and Pixar Animation Studios.

Buffett, Warren E; (1930–);US; investor and amassed a substantial fortune from astute investments through his company Berkshire Hathaway, of which he holds 38%.

Disney, Walter (Walt) E; (1901–1966); US; animated film producer, cartoon artist, and the creator of an American-based theme park called Disneyland.

Tata, Ratan N.; (1937–); India; executive chairman of the Tata group (1991-2002), now non-executive chairman of the Tata Group.

Narayana Murthy, N.R.; (1946–); India; chairman of the Board and Chief Mentor of Infosys Technologies Ltd.

Premji, Azim H.; (1945–); India; chairman, Wipro Technologies.

Murdoch, Rupert K.; (1931–); Australia; media mogul, major shareholder and managing director of the News Corporation.

Branson, Richard; (1950–); UK; founder and Chairman of Virgin Group.

Hirachand, Walchand; (1882–1953); India; industrialist who established a number of industries.

Birla, Ghanshyam D; (1894–1983); Indian; industrialist who established a number of industries.

Godrej, Pirojsha; (1882–1972); India; co-founder of Godrej Group of companies.

Trump, Donald J; (1946–); US; real estate magnet.

Drucker, Peter F; (1909–); Austrian; living in USA, famous management theorist.

Welch Jr. (Jack), John F; (1935–); US; CEO of General Electric between 1981 and 2001.

Morita, Akio; (1921–1999); Japanese; co-founder of Sony Corporation.

Carnegie, Andrew; (1835–1919); US; born in UK, businessman and philanthropist.

Lalbhai, Kasturbhai; (1894–1980); Indian; industrialist who established a number of industries.

Ford, Henry; (1863–1947); US; founder of the Ford Motor Company and one of the first to apply assembly line manufacturing to the mass.

Morgan, John P; (1837–1913); US; investment banker, art collector, and philanthropist.

Getty, Jean P; (1892–1976); US; industrialist and founder of the Getty Oil Company.

Ferrari, Enzo A; (1898–1988); Italian; founder of Ferrari car-manufacturing company.

Agnelli, Giovanni; (1866–1945); Italian; founder of Fiat.

Tata, Jehangir R.D.; (1904–1993); Indian; chairman of Tata Sons, Indian civil aviation pioneer.

Mittal, Lakshmi N.; (1950–); Indian living in UK; founder, Chairman of the Board of Directors and Chief Executive Officer of LNM Group.

Roy, Subroto; Indian; Managing Worker and Chairman, Sahara India Pariwar.

Ambani, Dhirajlal (Dhirubhai) H.; (1932–2002); Indian; founder and Chairman, Reliance Group.

Rockefeller, John D.; (1839–1937); US; industrialist and philanthropist, founder of the Standard Oil Company.

Rothschild, Mayer A.; (1744–1812); German; founder of the Rothschild family banking empire.

Some Famous Economists

Bhagwati, Jagdish; (1934–); Indian; famous works include A Stream of Windows: Unsettling Reflections on Trade, Immigration, and Democracy (1998) and India in Transition: Freeing the Economy (1993).

Black, Fischer; (1938–1995); American; famous for Black-Scholes equation.

Böhm-Bawerk, Eugen von; (1851–1914); Austrian; made important contributions to the development of Austrian School; famous for Capital and Interest.

De Soto, Hernando; (1941–); Peruvian; famous for The Other Path (1986) and The Mystery of Capital (2000).

Dupuit, Jules; (1804–1866); French; self-taught economist who introduced 'diminishing marginal utility' curve.

Engels, Friedrich; (1820–1895); German; published The Communist Manifesto together with Karl Marx.

Fisher, Irving; (1867–1947); American; proposed the Phillips curve, the indifference curve, and the Fisher separation theorem.

George, Henry; (1839–1897); American political economist, famous for proposing the 'single tax' on land.

Galbraith, John Kenneth; (1908–); American; famous for American Capital-ism: The concept of countervailing power, The Affluent Society. He was U.S. ambassador to India from 1961 to 1963.

Greenspan, Alan; (1926–); American; Chairman of the Federal Reserve; On 18 May 2004, he was nominated by US President George W. Bush to serve for an unprecedented fifth term.

Hayek, Friedrich August von; (1899–1992); Austrian; famous for his defence of free-market capitalism; noted for The Road to Serfdom.

Jevons, William Stanley; (1835–1882), English; famous for The Theory of Political Economy (1871) and utility theory of value.

Keynes, John Maynard; (1883–1946); English; famous for The General Theory of Employment, Interest and Money (1936), often viewed as the foundation of modern macroeconomics. He argued in favour of a central bank for the world and a common unit of currency, the 'Bancor'.

Knight, Frank Hyneman; (1885–1972); American; a founder of the Chicago school; author of Risk Uncertainty and Profit.

Krugman, Paul; (1953–); American; famous for zero interest rate policy.

Malthus, Thomas Robert; (1766–1834); English demographer and economist; famous for Essay on Population (1798) and his hypothesis—unchecked population growth always exceeds the growth of means of subsistence.

Marshall, Alfred; (1842–1924); English; famous for *Principles of Political Economy* (1890).

Marx, Karl Heinrich; (1818–1883); German political philosopher and social theorist; wrote the multi-volume *Das Kapital (Capital: A Critique of Political Economy)*.

Menger, Carl; (1840–1921); Austrian; founder of the Austrian School; noted work *Principles of Economics (Grundsaetze der Volkswirtschaftslehre)*.

Mill, John Stuart; (1806–1873); English philosopher and economist; advocate of utilitarianism; famous for *On Liberty* and *System of Logic*.

Molinari, Gustave de; (1819–1912); Belgian-born associated with the 'économistes'; noted works *The Production of Security*, and *Les Soirées de la Rue Saint-Lazare*.

Neumann, John von Neumann; (1903–1957); Hungarian-American mathematician; father of game theory and published the classic book *Theory of Games and Economic Behavior* with Oskar Morgenstern.

Pareto, Vilfredo; (1848–1923); Italian; introduced Pareto efficiency and indifference curves; well known for the 'Pareto principle'—20% of the population owned 80% of the property in Italy.

Pigou, Arthur Cecil; (1877–1959); British; noted for his studies in welfare economics; significant work *The Economics of Welfare* (1920).

Ricardo, David; (1772–1823); British; systemized economics, famous for *Principles of Political Economy and Taxation* (1817).

Say, Jean-Baptiste; (1767–1832); French; famous for Say's Law—'Supply creates its own demand'.

Schumacher, Ernst Friedrich; (1911–1977); German-born British founder of Intermediate Technology Development Group; best known for the collection of essays entitled *Small is Beautiful*.

Schumpeter, Joseph A.; (1883–1950); Austrian capital theorist; most popular work in English is probably *Capitalism, Socialism, and Democracy*.

Smith, Adam; (1723–1790); Scottish; famous for *The Wealth of Nations* and is generally thought of as the 'father of modern economics'.

Walras, Marie-Esprit-Léon; (1834–1910); French mathematical economist from the Lausanne school; famous for the general equilibrium theory and *Elements of Pure Economics* (1874).

Science

The Nine Members of the Solar System

Mercury

Criteria	Value
Mass (10^{24}kg)	0.33
Diameter (km)	4879
Density (kg/m^3)	5427
Gravity (m/s^2)	3.7
Rotation Period (hours)	1407.6
Length of Day (hours)	4222.6
Distance from Sun (10^6 km)	57.9
Orbital Period (days)	88
Number of Moons	0
Ring System	No

Venus

Criteria	Value
Mass (10^{24}kg)	4.87
Diameter (km)	12,104
Density (kg/m^3)	5243
Gravity (m/s^2)	8.9
Rotation Period (hours)	−5832.5
Length of Day (hours)	2802
Distance from Sun (10^6 km)	108.2
Orbital Period (days)	224.7
Number of Moons	0
Ring System	No

Earth

Criteria	Value
Mass (10^{24}kg)	5.97
Diameter (km)	12,756
Density (kg/m^3)	5515
Gravity (m/s^2)	9.8
Rotation Period (hours)	23.9
Length of Day (hours)	24
Distance from Sun (10^6 km)	149.6
Orbital Period (days)	365.2

Number of Moons	1
Ring System	No

Mars

Criteria	Value
Mass (10^{24}kg)	0.642
Diameter (km)	6794
Density (kg/m^3)	3933
Gravity (m/s^2)	3.7
Rotation Period (hours)	24.6
Length of Day (hours)	24.7
Distance from Sun (10^6 km)	227.9
Orbital Period (days)	687
Number of Moons	2
Ring System	No

Jupiter

Criteria	Value
Mass (10^{24}kg)	1899
Diameter (km)	142,984
Density (kg/m^3)	1326
Gravity (m/s^2)	23.1
Rotation Period (hours)	9.9
Length of Day (hours)	9.9
Distance from Sun (10^6 km)	778.6
Orbital Period (days)	4331
Number of Moons	61
Ring System	Yes

Saturn

Criteria	Value
Mass (10^{24}kg)	568
Diameter (km)	120,536
Density (kg/in^3)	687
Gravity (m/s^2)	9
Rotation Period (hours)	10.7
Length of Day (hours)	10.7
Distance from Sun (10^6 km)	1433.5
Orbital Period (days)	10,747

Number of Moons	31
Ring System	Yes

Uranus

Criteria	Value
Mass (10^{24}kg)	86.8
Diameter (km)	51,118
Density (kg/m³)	1270
Gravity (m/s²)	8.7
Rotation Period (hours)	−17.2
Length of Day (hours)	17.2
Distance from Sun (10^6 km)	2872.5
Orbital Period (days)	30,589
Number of Moons	26
Ring System	Yes

Neptune

Criteria	Value
Mass (10^{24}kg)	102
Diameter (km)	49,528
Density (kg/m³)	1638
Gravity (m/s²)	11
Rotation Period (hours)	16.1
Length of Day (hours)	16.1
Distance from Sun (10^6 km)	4495.1
Orbital Period (days)	59,800
Number of Moons	13
Ring System	Yes

Pluto

Criteria	Value
Mass (10^{24}kg)	0.0125
Diameter (km)	2390
Density (kg/m³)	1750
Gravity (m/s²)	0.6
Rotation Period (hours)	−153.3
Length of Day (hours)	153.3
Distance from Sun (10^6 km)	5870
Orbital Period (days)	90,588
Number of Moons	1
Ring System	No

Glossary

Mass (10^{24}kg): This is the mass of the planet in septillion—1 followed by 24 zeros—kilogrammes.

Diameter (km): The distance through the center of the planet from one point on the equator to the opposite side, in kilometres.

Density (kg/m³): The average density—mass divided by volume—of the whole planet, not including the atmosphere for the terrestrial planets in kilogrammes per cubic metre.

Gravity (m/s²): The gravitational acceleration on the surface at the equator in meters per second squared or feet per second squared, including the effects of rotation. For the gas giant planets such as Jupiter the gravity is given at the 1 bar pressure level in the atmosphere.

Rotation Period (hours): Time it takes for the planet to complete one rotation relative to the fixed background stars, not relative to the Sun, in hours. Negative numbers indicate retrograde (backwards relative to the Earth) rotation.

Length of Day (hours): The average time in hours for the Sun to move from the noon position in the sky at a point on the equator back to the same position.

Distance from Sun (10^6 km): This is the average distance from the planet to the Sun in millions of kilometres. All planets have orbits which are egg-shaped or elliptical so there is a point in the orbit at which the planet is closest to the Sun and a point furthest from the Sun. The average distance from the Sun is midway between these two values.

Orbital Period (days): This is the time in Earth days for a planet to orbit the Sun from one vernal equinox to the next. Also known as the tropical orbit period, this is equal to a year on Earth.

Number of Moons: This gives the number of International Astronomical Union officially confirmed natural satellites orbiting the planet.

Ring System: This tells whether a planet has a set of rings around it.

Note: *All data and information courtesy NASA*

A Tenth Member of Our Solar System?

Nearly 75 years after Clyde Tombaugh's discovery of Pluto in 1930, an astronomer at the California Institute of Technology in Pasadena, working at Palomar Observatory, Pasadena on 14 November 2003 discovered a mysterious planet-like body orbiting our Sun. The object was also detected on sky photographs taken in 2001 and 2002. It is much bigger than an average asteroid and smaller than a planet. The object, unofficially named 'Sedna', is 13 billion kilometres (8 billion miles) away from Earth. Sedna is of reddish colour; it is the second reddest object in the solar system, after Mars. According to International Astronomical Union's press note: 'Orbit computations show that the object's distance from the Sun varies between 11.4 and 15 billion km. Its current distance is 13 billion km, about twice Pluto's distance. A very uncertain diameter of around 1800 km has been estimated from the brightness of the object. Since the object appears to be somewhat smaller than Pluto and has an extremely elongated orbit with a period of around 10,000 years, compared to 248 years for Pluto, it seems appropriate to designate the object as an asteroid and not as the 10th planet. The name Sedna has been proposed after an Inuit ocean goddess, but the name has not yet been endorsed by the IAU and needs to be reviewed first by the IAU Committee on Small Bodies Nomenclature.'

More on the Solar System

The Moon is the Earth's sole natural satellite. It takes 1.3 seconds for the moon's light to reach us. The moon, however, has no light of its own, but merely reflects the rays of the sun. It takes exactly 27 days, 7 hours and 43 minutes to complete one lunar revolution of the Earth. Neil Armstrong and Edwin Aldrin were the first two men to set foot on the moon on 21 July 1969, having reached there in the spacecraft *Apollo XI*.

Other significant features of the solar system are **Asteroids**, which are thought to be debris from the formation of the inner planets. There is a large 'asteroid belt' that lies between Mars and Jupiter. When asteroids enter the atmosphere of the Earth, they burn up due to friction and are known as meteors or meteorites.

Comets are occasional visitors to the solar system. They are relatively small extraterrestrial bodies consisting of a frozen mass that travels around the sun in a highly elliptical orbit. Some important comets include Hailey's Comet, named after its discoverer Edmund Hailey. It is believed to orbit the sun every 76 years. Comet Smith-Tuttle has been in the news as it is thought to be headed straight for Earth, with an impact date set at 17 August 2116. In case of impact, the comet would have the destructive power of a 20 million megaton bomb, or 1.6 million Hiroshima bombs. Comet Shoemaker-Levy 9 broke up into 21 fragments before hitting Jupiter in 1994, a rare celestial event that was widely observed by astronomers worldwide.

Space Explorations

Humans have been looking up to the sky much before the recorded history. However, since the middle of 20th century exploring the skies have taken off. Initially, it was a race to reach the moon between the US and the former USSR. Now, words such as Black Hole and time warps have become a part of the common man's lexicon. Here is a brief overview of what the humans have been doing in the past five decades.

4 October 1957: The Soviet Union launches *Sputnik* I, becoming the first nation to successfully launch an artificial satellite.

31 January 1958: The United States launches its first artificial satellite, *Explorer I*.

3 November 1957: Laika, the first animal sent to space, travels into orbit on board *Sputnik II*.

1 October 1958: National Aeronautics and Space Administration (NASA) is christened as the successor to the National Advisory Committee for Aeronautics. The latter was responsible for researching the growing aeronautical industry since 1915. NASA was given the task of overseeing the civilian space program in USA.

2 January 1959: USSR launches *Luna I*, which was meant to reach the Moon. Although *Luna I* failed to reach the Moon, it became the first artificial object to escape Earth orbit.

14 September 1959: Soviet *Luna 2* becomes the first artificial object to reach the Moon.

12 April 1961: Soviet cosmonaut Yuri Gagarin becomes the first man in space. This began the era of manned space flights.

5 May 1961: Alan Shepard becomes the first American in space when he completes a 15-minute sub-orbital flight. Nine months later, John Glenn becomes the first American man to orbit the Earth. USA's first manned flight programme Project Mercury was launched with Shepard and Glen.

25 May 1961: US President John F. Kennedy commits the US to landing an astronaut on the moon before the end of the decade. The Apollo Programme was announced.

16 June 1963: Valentina Tereshkova, the first woman to travel in space, was launched into space on board *Vostok 6*.

18 March 1965: *Voskhod 2* cosmonaut Aleksey Leonov executes the first 'space walk'.

March 1966: Soviet *Venera 3* crashlands on the Martian surface becoming the first spacecraft to strike another planet.

27 January 1967: Project Apollo suffers a setback when a fire in the *Apollo* command module kills three astronauts, holding up manned flights for nearly two years.

24 December 1968: *Apollo 8* circles the moon on Christmas Eve.

20 July 1969: Neil Armstrong and Edwin 'Buzz' Aldrin of the *Apollo 11* mission become the first humans to walk on the moon.

14 April 1970: The *Apollo 13* spacecraft loses its main power supply after an on board explosion on its way to the moon. However, the spacecraft and its astronauts are safely brought back to Earth.

19 April 1971: USSR launches the world's first space station, *Salyut 1*. However, it could not stay in space because of its low orbit. It was followed by *Salyut 2* (that disintegrated soon after launch). *Salyut 3* and *Salyut 5* were military space stations, while *Salyut 4* and *Salyut 6* were meant for civilian purposes.

14 May 1973: US launches its first space station, *Skylab*.

12 April 1981: The first space shuttle, *Columbia*, is launched from Kennedy Space Center with astronauts John Young and Robert Crippen at the helm. The space shuttle is a winged, re-usable manned spacecraft meant for scientific missions and for carrying payloads in its cargo bay.

28 January 1986: The space shuttle *Challenger* explodes within seconds of lift-off, killing all seven aboard. The dead included teacher Christa McAuliffe, the first private citizen chosen for space flight. This accident grounded the shuttle programme for many years.

20 February 1986: Russia launches the first part of the space station *Mir*.

15 November 1988: The first and only orbital launch of the Soviet space shuttle *Buran* takes place. It was an unmanned. The Soviet space shuttle

programme was sanctioned in 1976 in response to the US shuttle programme. No further flights were carried out after the funding was cut following the collapse of the Soviet Union. Although construction of two more orbiters were started, the remained unfinished and were ultimately dismantled.

24 April 1990: NASA launches the Hubble Space Telescope.

21 August 1993: The first US mission to Mars since 1975, Mars Observer, disappears three days before its scheduled entry into orbit around Mars.

7 November 1996: USA launches Mars Global Surveyor that enters Martian orbit in 1998 and started mapping the planet.

4 July 1997: The US Pathfinder spacecraft lands on Mars. Its miniature rover vehicle named Sojourner explores the surface of the planet. The Pathfinder transmits back a huge amount of new data about Mars that includes colour images of the surface of the planet.

29 May 1999: The Discovery becomes the first shuttle to dock with the International Space Station (ISS).

23 July 1999: The space shuttle Columbia deploys the Chandra X-Ray Observatory. Air Force Colonel Eileen Collins becomes the first woman to command a shuttle mission.

August 1999: Mir is abandoned after its 27th expedition due to a lack of government funding.

14 February 2000: A probe named Near Earth Asteroid Rendezvous (NEAR) Shoemaker conducts the first long-term, close-up study of an asteroid, Eros.

23 March 2001: The abandoned Russian space station, Mir, re-enters the Earth's atmosphere and falls into the South Pacific Ocean. It had remained in orbit for over 14 years. The aging Mir was abandoned in 1999 due to a lack of funding from the Russian government.

27 April 2001: Dennis Tito, the first space tourist, blasted off on his trip to the International Space Station.

1 February 2003: The Columbia space shuttle explodes over Texas minutes before its scheduled landing in Florida. The seven-person crew that includes Kalpana Chawla and the first Israeli to go into space, are killed.

15 October 2003: China sends its first manned spacecraft into orbit, making it the third country to send a human into space. Yang Liwei, a 38-year-old army lieutenant travels into space on board a spacecraft named Shenzhou V.

2 March 2004: Europe's Rosetta cometary probe is successfully launched into orbit around the Sun. Rosetta is the first probe ever designed to enter orbit around a comet's nucleus and release a landing craft onto its surface. It is scheduled to reach the comet 67P/Churyumov-Gerasimenko in 2014 after three flybys of the Earth and one of Mars.

1 April 2004: NASA's Mars Exploration Rover Spirit finds hints of past water on Mars.

5 August 2004: The US Cassini spacecraft makes new discoveries around Saturn including a new radiation belt.

Space Shuttle

The US space shuttle is officially referred to as the 'Space Transportation System' (STS). At present, the Shuttle is the United States government's only manned launch vehicle currently in service. The Space Shuttle consists of three main components: the reusable Orbiter, an expendable external fuel tank and a pair of reusable solid-fuel booster rockets. The fuel tank and booster rockets are jettisoned during launch and only the Orbiter goes into orbit. The North American Rockwell company (now part of the Boeing Company) built the Space Shuttle orbiter. The Martin Marietta (now part of Lockheed Martin) company designed the external fuel tank and Morton Thiokol (now the Thiokol corporation) designed the solid rocket boosters. The

Shuttle is the first orbital spacecraft designed for partial reusability. Its main functions are carriage of large payloads to various orbits, crew rotation for the International Space Station (ISS), and performance of servicing missions. The Shuttle has also been designed to recover satellites and other payloads from orbit and return them to Earth. Each Shuttle was designed for a projected lifespan of 100 launches or 10-years operational life. The Shuttle programme was launched on 5 January 1972, with an announcement from then US President Richard M. Nixon. The first orbiter to be built was named *Enterprise* and was rolled out on 17 September 1976. It later conducted a series of successful tests. However, the *Enterprise* never made a space flight. The first fully functional Shuttle Orbiter was the *Columbia*, which was delivered to Kennedy Space Center in March 1979. It was first launched on 12 April 1981—the 20th anniversary of Yuri Gagarin's space flight. *Challenger* was delivered in July 1982, *Discovery* was delivered in November 1983, and *Atlantis* was delivered in April 1985. Two Shuttles have been lost till date. *Challenger* was destroyed in an explosion during launch on 28 January 1986. *Columbia* was destroyed during reentry on 1 February 2003. All on board, including Kalpana Chawla perished in the accident.

Indian Space Research Centres

The Government of India set up its Space Commission and Department of Space (DOS) in June 1972. The Indian Space Research Organisation (ISRO) under DOS carries out India's space programme through its establishments located in different places in India. The primary objectives of the Indian space programme include development of satellites, launch vehicles, sounding rockets and related ground systems. Since its inception, the space programme has passed many milestones. ISRO enjoys co-operative arrangements with several countries and space agencies. ISRO also provides training to personnel from other countries while its hardware and services are commercially available through Antrix Corporation Ltd., which is the commercial arm of Department of Space (DOS). It was incorporated in September 1992 for the promotion and commercial exploration of products and services from the Indian Space Programme.

The various space centres of Department of Space are as follows:

Name	Place
Vikram Sarabhai Space Centre	Thiruvananthapuram
ISRO Satellite Centre	Bangalore
Satish Dhawan Space Centre	Hassan
Liquid Propulsion Systems Centre	Mahendragiri and Thiruvananthapuram
Space Applications Centre	Ahmedabad
Development and Educational Communication Unit	Ahmedabad
ISRO Telemetry, Tracking and Command Network	Bangalore and Lucknow
INSAT Master Control Facility	Hassan
ISRO Inertial Systems Unit	Thiruvananthapuram
National Remote Sensing Agency	Hyderabad
Regional Remote Sensing Service Centres	Bangalore, Kharagpur, Nagpur, Jodhpur and Dehradun
Physical Research Laboratory	Ahmedabad
National Mesosphere/ Stratosphere Troposphere Radar Facility	Tirupati

Indian Eyes in Space

Name	Date	Achievements
Aryabhata	19.04.1975	First Indian satellite. Launched by Russian launch vehicle Intercosmos from USSR.
Bhaskara-I	07.06.1979	First experimental remote sensing satellite. Carried TV and Microwave cameras. Launched by Russian launch vehicle Intercosmos from USSR.
Bhaskara-II	20.11.1981	Second experimental remote sensing satellite similar to Bhaskara-1. Launched by Russian launch vehicle Intercosmos from USSR.
Ariane Passenger Payload Experiment (APPLE)	19.06.1981	First experimental communication satellite. Launched by the European Ariane from French Guiana.
Rohini (RS-1)	18.07.1980	Used for measuring in-flight performance of second experimental launch of SLV-3 from India.
Rohini (RS-D1)	31.05.1981	Used for conducting some remote sensing technology studies. Launched by the first developmental launch of SLV-3 from India.
Rohini (RS-D2)	17.04.1983	Identical to RS-D1. Launched by the second developmental launch of SLV-3 from India.
Stretched Rohini Satellite Series (SROSS-C)	20.05.1992	Launched by third developmental flight of ASLV from India. Carried Gamma Ray astronomy and aeronomy payload.
Stretched Rohini Satellite Series (SROSS-C2)	04.05.1994	Launched by fourth developmental flight of ASLV from India. Identical to SROSS-C. Still in service.
Indian National Satellite (INSAT-1A)	10.04.1982	First operational multi-purpose communication and meteorology satellite procured from USA. Was operational for six months. Launched from USA
Indian National Satellite (INSAT-1B)	30.08.1983	Identical to INSAT-1A. Served for more than its design life of seven years. Launched from USA.
Indian National Satellite (INSAT-1C)	21.07.1988	Same as INSAT-1A. Served for one and a half years. Launched by European Ariane launch vehicle from French Guiana.
Indian National Satellite (INSAT-1D)	12.06.1990	Identical to INSAT-1A. Launched from USA. Still in service.
Indian National Satellite (INSAT-2A)	10.07.1992	First satellite in the second-generation Indian-built INSAT-2 series. Has enhanced capability than INSAT-1 series. Launched by European Ariane launch vehicle from French Guiana. Still in service.

Indian National Satellite (INSAT-2B)	23.07.1993	Second satellite in INSAT-2 series. Identical to INSAT-2A. Launched by European Ariane launch vehicle from French Guiana. Still in service.
Indian National Satellite (INSAT-2C)	07.12.1995	Has additional capabilities such as mobile satellite service, business communication and television outreach beyond Indian boundaries. Launched by European launch vehicle from French Guiana. Still in service.
INSAT-2E	03.04.1999	Multipurpose communication and meteorological satellite launched by Ariane from French Guiana.
Indian Remote Sensing Satellite (IRS-1A)	17.03.1988	First operational remote sensing satellite. Launched from USSR.
Indian Remote Sensing Satellite (IRS-1B)	29.08.1991	Same as IRS-1A. Launched from USSR Still in service.
Indian Remote Sensing Satellite (IRS-P2)	15.10.1994	Carried remote sensing payload. Launched by second developmental flight of PSLV from India.
Indian Remote Sensing Satellite (IRS-1C)	28.12.1995	Carries advanced remote sensing cameras. Launched from former USSR. Still in service.
Indian Remote Sensing Satellite (IRS-P3)	21.03.1996	Carries remote sensing payload and an X-ray astronomy payload. Launched by third developmental flight of PSLV from India. Still in service.
Indian Remote Sensing Satellite (IRS-1D)	29.09.1997	Same as IRS-1C. Launched from India. Still in service.

(Source: ISRO)

Physics

100 Years of the Special Theory of Relativity

Many consider the year 1905 as Albert Einstein's *annus mirabilis* or miracle year. In that year the Swiss patent clerk published in a German physics monthly four papers that changed how physicists looked at time and space. These papers were *Annalen der Physik*: -*Über einen die Erzeugung und Verwandlung des Lichtes betreffenden heuristishen Gesichtspunkt*, on the quantum of light and the photo-electric effect; *Die von der molekularkinetischen Theorie der Wärme geforderte Bewegung von in ruhenden Flüssigkeiten suspendierten Teilchen*, on Brownian motion of particles and atomic theory; *Elektrodynamic bewegter Körper*, the special theory of relativity; *Ist die Trägheit eines Körpers von seinem Energieeinhalt abhängig?* on equivalence of mass and energy that included the famous equation $e = mc^2$. Since this publication theoretical physics has progressed at the speed of light. There have been controversies and bitter debates. Here are some significant advances both before and after Albert Einstein that tries to put this *tour de force* publication in perspective.

Before Einstein

1589: Galileo Galilei studies the motion of objects and begins a book *De Motu* (On Motion) which he never finishes.

1609: Johannes Kepler claims in the journal *Astronomia Nova* that the orbit of Mars is an ellipse with the Sun at one focus, and sweeps out equal areas in equal time.

1640: Ismael Bullialdus suggests an inverse-square gravitational force law.

1665: Isaac Newton introduces an inverse-square universal law of gravitation.

1684: Newton proves that planets moving under an inverse-square force law will obey Kepler's laws.

1798: Henry Cavendish measures the gravitational constant.

1855: Urbain Le Verrier explains an unusual characteristic of the motion of Mercury.

1876: William Clifford suggests that the motion of matter may be due to changes in the geometry of space.

1887: Albert Michelson-Edward Morley experiment fails to detect any ether drift.

1889: FitzGerald suggests what is now called the FitzGerald-Lorentz contraction to explain the 'Michelson-Morley experiment'.

1893: Ernst Mach states Mach's principle; attacks Newton's view of absolute space.

1905: French mathematician Henri Poincaré shows that Lorentz transformations in space and time plus rotations in space form a group.

1905: On 5 June Poincaré theorizes that there seems to be a general law of nature, that it is impossible to demonstrate absolute motion.

Einstein and After

1905: On 30 June Einstein postulates special relativity. In September, Einstein publishes the short article 'Does the Inertia of a Body Depend upon Its Energy-Content?' in which he derives the formula $e=mc^2$.

1907: Minkowski publishes *Raum und Zeit* (Space and Time), and establishes the idea of a space-time continuum.

1915: Albert Einstein completes his theory of general relativity; the theory explains Mercury's strange motions observed by Le Verrier.

1916: German Karl Schwarzschild mails Einstein his paper on the Schwarzschild metric.

1919: Arthur Eddington leads a solar eclipse expedition that claims to detect gravitational deflection of light by the Sun. Relativity receives its observational backing.

1921: Theodor Kaluza demonstrates that a five-dimensional version of Einstein's equations unifies gravitation and electromagnetism.

1927: Belgian priest Georges Lemaître proposes that the universe began with the explosion of a primeval atom.

1929: Edwin Hubble observes the redshift of distant galaxies and concludes that the universe is expanding.

1931: Einstein stops using the cosmological constant to keep the universe from expanding.

1935: Subrahmanyan Chandrasekhar is attacked by Eddington for his report that there is a mass limit for a star beyond which it collapses to a black hole.

1937: Fritz Zwicky states that galaxies could act as gravitational lenses.

1948: Hermann Bondi, Thomas Gold, and Sir Fred Hoyle propose the steady-state theory.

1955: Einstein dies at Princeton.

1960: Robert Pound and Glen Rebka test the gravitational redshift.

1962: Robert Dicke, Peter Roll, and R. Krotkov use a torsion fiber balance to test the weak equivalence principle to 2 parts in 100 billion.

1964: Irwin Shapiro predicts a gravitational time delay of radiation travel as a test of general relativity.

1964: Roger Penrose proves that a black hole space-time must contain a singularity where space-time physics ceases to make good sense.

1965: Joseph Weber puts the first Weber bar gravitational wave detector into operation.

1971: Soviet physicists Yuri Gol'fand and E. Likhtman extend the Poincaré algebra into a superalgebra and discover supersymmetry in four space-time dimensions.

1974: Stephen Hawking combines quantum field theory with classical general relativity and predicts that black holes radiate through particle emission and decay with a finite lifetime.

1974: Joel Scherk and John Schwarz propose string theory as a theory of quantum gravity.

1976: Robert Vessot and Martin Levine use a hydrogen maser clock on a Scout D rocket to test the gravitational redshift.

1980: Alan Guth puts forward the idea of an inflationary phase of the early universe, before the Big Bang.

1981: Michael Green and John Schwarz develop superstring theory.

1982: Joseph Taylor and Joel Weisberg show that the rate of energy loss from the binary pulsar PSR1913+16 agrees with that predicted by the general relativistic quadrupole formula to within 5 per cent.

2003: Experiment by a scientific collaboration between NASA and the Italian Space Agency using data from NASA's *Cassini* spacecraft confirms Einstein's theory of general relativity with a precision that is 50 times greater than previous measurements.

2004: Gravity Probe B (GP-B) launched by NASA to measure two parts of Einstein's general theory of relativity by assessing how the presence of Earth warps space and time, and how Earth's rotation drags space and time.

Note: There are several areas of theoretical physics that have been left out. Most notable among them are efforts to find a 'final theory' that will answer all the questions of the universe. Einstein spent 30 years of his life looking for such a theory that can 'only' happen through a successful marriage between gravitational physics and quantum theory. Currently there are two theoretical frameworks that experts feel can effect the marriage— Superstrings and/or Quantum Gravity.

Science News

The Tenth Planet has a Moon A satellite has been found around the newly discovered possible tenth planet. The object was discovered on 10 September 2005 with an adaptive optics system on the Keck II telescope. However, 2003 UB_{313} is yet to be recognized as a planet. By convention, the International Astronomical Union designated its 'moon' as S/2005 (2003 UB313) 1. But Mike Brown, the Caltech astronomer who revealed 2003 UB_{313} in July 2005 and nicknamed it Xena after the television warrior princess, is calling the moon Gabrielle, after the princess's companion. With the discovery of the satellite, vital information about 2003 UB_{313} can possibly now be obtained.

Red Blood Cells are the First Living Cells to be Fitted with an Artificial Tail Red blood cells have become the first living cells to be fitted with an artificial tail. The cell moves tail-first at 6 micrometres per second. This is about 10 times slower than a sperm cell. The tail consists of a filament of tiny magnetic beads held rigidly together by strands of DNA. When an oscillating magnetic field is applied to the cells, they move through the fluid as their tails bend to align themselves with the constantly reversing direction of the magnetic field. According to Remi Dreyfus, who created the device with colleagues at France's Ecole Supérieure of industrial physics and chemistry in Paris, this innovation may one day help to direct medicines through the bloodstream to specific spots.

Nobel for Ulcer Discovery Two Australians named Barry Marshall and Robin Warren have won the 2005 Nobel Prize in Physiology or Medicine for establishing that bacteria cause stomach ulcers. They showed that ulcers could be completely cured by killing the bacteria with antibiotics. By revealing a simple cure, this discovery can spell the end for the huge and lucrative global markets for existing anti-ulcer drugs, which merely ease the symptoms, but do not eliminate the problem. Marshall and Warren established that the organism was almost always present in patients with gastric inflammation, duodenal ulcers or gastric ulcers. The pair then proved that patients could be cured, but only by eradicating the bacteria with antibiotics. Since their discovery, it has been accepted beyond all dispute that H. pylori causes more than 90 per cent of duodenal ulcers and 80 per cent of gastric ulcers. Half of all humans carry the bugs in their stomachs for life, but on average only 10 to 15 per cent of those infected develop gastric inflammation or ulcers. In some individuals, infections can even lead to stomach cancer.

Chimpanzee Genome Sequenced The Chimpanzee Sequencing and Analysis Consortium, a body of 67 scientists from Germany, the United States, Israel, Italy, and Spain has released a draft version of its report on the chimpanzee genome in the September 2005 edition of the scientific journal *Nature*. The researchers have mapped 94 per cent of the genome. The report centres on comparisons between chimpanzee and human DNA. The fresh decoding of the chimpanzee's DNA allows an unprecedented 'gene-to-gene' comparison with the human genome, which was mapped in 2001. It also elucidates the evolutionary processes through which chimpanzees and humans arose from a common ancestor about 6 million years ago. By placing the two codes alongside each other, scientists were able to identify all 40 million molecular changes that separate the two species today and also pinpointed the 250,000 changes that seem most responsible for the differences between chimpanzee and humans.

Physics Nobel Prize Awarded for Insights into Light Research on the quantum nature of light and harnessing lasers to measure the physical world with greater accuracy has been honoured with the 2005 Nobel Prize in Physics. Roy Glauber at Harvard University in the USA receives half of the •1.1 million award for his work marrying quantum physics with traditional optics. John Hall at the University of Colorado, USA, and Theodor Hänsch at the Max Planck Institute in Garching, Germany, share the other half of the prize for advancing laser spectroscopy, which can be used to measure physical phenomena very precisely.

Admixture Mapping Pinpoints the Likely Location of Genes for Diseases A technique called admixture mapping uses the genomes of people of mixed ethnic ancestry to pinpoint the likely location of genes for diseases such as multiple sclerosis. It is giving geneticists a powerful tool for understanding the genetic basis of diseases such as multiple sclerosis, schizophrenia, diabetes and prostate cancer. These and other diseases are caused by multiple genetic and environmental causes. This makes the links between gene and disease hard to detect, virtually impossible. But now, David Reich, a geneticist at Harvard Medical School, and his colleagues have found a better way to search for genes that increase the risk of multiple sclerosis (MS), using the technique of admixture mapping.

Electronic Nose Sniffs out Infections
An electronic nose has been developed to help 'sniff' out infections. It could potentially help hospitals tackle outbreaks of the antibiotic-resistant superbug, MRSA. Culture tests routinely used to identify MRSA (Methicillin-Resistant Staphylococcus Aureus) take two or three days to complete. This hampers attempts to manage outbreaks as infected patients remain untreated and pose a risk infection to others. UK-based researchers have come up with a test using an electronic 'sniffer' that could cut the time required to detect MRSA to just 15 minutes. University of Warwick and doctors at the Heart of England Hospital, Birmingham, say the electronic nose can recognise the unique cocktail of volatile organic compounds that S. aureus strains excrete. 'E-noses' analyse gas samples by passing the gas over an array of electrodes coated with different conducting polymers. Each electrode reacts to specific substances by changing its electrical resistance in a characteristic way. Combining the signals from all the electrodes gives a 'smell-print' of the chemicals in the mixture that neural network software built into the 'e-nose' can learn to recognize. Each 'e-nose' is about the size of a pair of desktop PCs and costs about £60,000.

Human Genes Implanted in Mice
Scientists have successfully transplanted human chromosomes into mice for the first time. The mice were genetically engineered to carry a genetic anomaly that causes Down's syndrome. Genetic studies of the mice will help scientists identify the genes that give rise to medical conditions prevalent among people with Down's syndrome. They include impaired brain development,

behavioural abnormalities, heart defects, Alzheimer's disease and leukaemia. Elizabeth Fisher of the Institute of Neurology and Victor Tybulewicz at the National Institute for Medical Research in London spent 13 years perfecting the technique.

Key Computer Breakthrough Russian scientists have invented a computer keyboard where each key has its own tiny video screen. This would enable the symbols on the keys to be changed to show different languages or symbols. Every single key of the Moscow-based Art.Lebedev Studio's all-purpose Optimus keyboard is a 32x32 pixel OLED (Organic Light Emitting Diode) display. According to the company's director Artemy Lebedev, the Optimus keyboard will enable the users to switch from the Arabic, Cyrillic or Latin alphabet or HTML code in a matter of seconds. It could also be programmed for the use of any given software, games or music composition programmes. The keyboard will have an aluminium case and polycarbonate keys. It is due to be released in the market in 2006 with an estimated price of about £200.

Atom-swapping Reaction Wins Chemistry Nobel Yves Chauvin at the French Petroleum Institute in Rueil-Malmaison, France, Robert H. Grubbs at the California Institute of Technology, California, USA, and Richard R. Schrock at the Massachusetts Institute of Technology in Massachusetts, USA, will share the •1.1 million Chemistry Nobel prize for 2005. They won the prize for their contributions towards understanding and harnessing an important type of organic reaction called 'metathesis', meaning 'to change places'. In these reactions double bonds between carbon atoms – the basis of all life on Earth – are broken and formed in such a way that atom groups can be made to change places. This molecular partner swapping occurs with the help of special catalysts. These catalysts are molecules which speed a reaction without being altered themselves.

Heart-imaging Revolution The Hospital of the University of Pennsylvania (HUP) is now utilizing a new high-tech tool to quickly and efficiently screen for coronary disease when patients complaining of chest pain come into the emergency room. It's a move that could save lots of time and money, reducing unnecessary testing and hospital stays. The 64-slice CT scanner at HUP is now being used by the emergency department (ED) and could prove to be an effective tool in giving quick results to physicians—so they can identify the 15 per cent of patients whose chest pain is being caused by heart disease (and, conversely, weed out the other 85 per cent of presenting patients who visit hospital emergency rooms each year complaining of chest pains and are eventually found not to have heart and coronary diseases). The new multi-slice CT scan supplies experts with an exquisitely detailed 3-D image of the heart by utilizing unparalleled resolution and speed. Multi-slice CT is a new application of computed tomography technology, which can look at the coronary arteries as well as actual heart function, helping doctors to identify problems without invasive diagnostic procedures. The 64-slice CT scanner at HUP is the fastest available in the world at this point.

Novel Mechanism for DNA Replication Discovered Since the discovery of the structure of DNA by James Watson and Francis Crick in 1953, the paradigm for DNA replication has stated that the DNA codes itself for the appropriate pairings for replication. In a study published in *Science*, researchers from Mount Sinai School of Medicine report on the first instance in which a protein, rather than the DNA, provides the coding information. The study offers a specific mechanism by which cells cope with some of the most destructive carcinogens in the environment, including those in cigarette smoke. Many of these carcinogens preferentially damage DNA guanine—one of the four bases in DNA—blocking, in some cases, the ability of the guanine to partner with cytosine, which can lead to mistakes during replication. Aneel Aggarwal, PhD, and Deepak Nair, PhD, of the Department of Physiology and Biophysics at Mount Sinai School of Medicine and their colleagues at University of Texas Medical Branch, Galveston discovered that a protein called Rev1 DNA polymerase itself codes for a cytosine to be placed on the replicating strand. The cytosine is inserted based upon the coding information in Rev1 regardless of whether a guanine or another base is present on the DNA.

First Partial Pancreas Transplant A 56-year-old Japanese woman has donated half of her pancreas to treat her daughter's diabetes. It is the first time a living donor has donated part of this organ. After removing the pancreatic tissue at Kyoto University Hospital in Japan on 19 January, James Shapiro of the University of Alberta in Canada and his colleagues extracted the islet cells and transplanted them into the woman's 27-year-old daughter. The islet cells began producing insulin minutes after the transplant, says James Shapiro, who in 2000 developed the so-called 'Edmonton protocol'. This is a procedure for isolating and transplanting islet cells taken from cadavers or people pronounced brain dead, and a cocktail of drugs to prevent rejection. It appears to cure diabetes—although patients have to take the anti-rejection drugs for life—but so far only 500 people have been treated worldwide because of a severe shortage of islet cells from the usual sources.

Earth's Inner Core is Solid, Not Liquid This long-standing presumption has finally been confirmed by studying seismic waves travelling through the core. Previously, seismologists had inferred that the inner core was solid by looking at how the Earth resonates after a major earthquake. But the proof scientists were looking for to confirm their suspicions has come from the detection of seismic shear waves in the core. Pressure waves such as sound waves can pass through both solids and liquids, but shear waves, which are side-to-side oscillations like those generated by wiggling one end of a rope, can only exist in solids. Shear waves move more slowly than pressure waves. Aimin Cao of the University of California, Berkeley, and colleagues analysed nearly 20 years of data from the extremely sensitive Gräfenberg Seismic Array in Germany. They calculated the speed at which seismic waves generated by large earthquakes in the south Pacific Ocean travelled through the Earth and found it agreed with theoretical predictions that assume a solid inner core.

Interactions of Quantum Clouds Measured for First Time For the first time, physicists have measured interactions between two exotic clouds of atoms known as Bose-Einstein condensates (BECs) without completely destroying the clouds. BECs form when a gas is chilled to a few billionths of a degree above absolute zero. The atoms in the gas settle into a single quantum state and behave as one quantum mechanical wave. Each such wave has a phase and if two of these waves interact, their phase difference should produce an interference pattern. But previous attempts to produce this pattern have ruined the clouds. Now Michele Saba's team at the Massachusetts Institute of Technology in Cambridge has measured the difference in phase of two BECs without destroying them. They used yellow laser light to nudge out a stream of atoms from each cloud and make them interfere. This allowed them to measure the phase difference between the two clouds and follow its evolution over time. The clouds would eventually run out of atoms.

New Lifespan Extension Genes Found Researchers from UC Davis and Harvard Medical School in USA have identified new genes tied to lifespan extension in yeast. They drastically reduce calorie intake, or caloric restriction, and is known to extend the lifespan of species including yeast, worms and rodents. Previous research linked a gene called Sir2 with lifespan extension due to caloric restriction. However, worms and yeast that lack Sir2 also live longer when put on a tough diet, showing that some other genes must be at work. Researchers led by David Sinclair at Harvard Medical School and Su-Ju Lin at UC Davis' Center for Genetics and Development and Section of Microbiology screened for other life-extending genes in yeast. They found a gene called Hst2 that accounts for most of the difference. Eliminating Hst2 and Sir2 blocked most of the beneficial effect of caloric restriction. When Hst2 was over expressed, so that the gene was more active than normal, the yeast lived longer than normal. A third gene, Hst1, appears to act when both Sir2 and Hst2 are missing. Sir2 and the newly identified Hst genes account for all of the life-prolonging effects of caloric restriction in yeast.

Inventions and Inventors

Invention	Year	Inventor	Note
Aeroplane	1903	Orville and Wilbur Wright (the Wright brothers)	A Brazillian named Alberto Santos-Dumont was the first person to achieve the first officially observed powered flight in Europe (1906). At that point of time, most of continental Europe was unaware of the 1903 feat of the Wright brothers and Santos-Dumont was widely credited as the inventor of the airplane. In 1991, a Brazilian government decree declared him the 'Father of Aviation'.
Aerosol can	1926	Erik Rotheim	The concept of an aerosol originated in the 1790s with the introduction of pressurized carbonated beverages in France. In 1837, a man named Perpigna invented a soda siphon incorporating a valve.
Air conditioning	1911	Willis Carrier	Willis H. Carrier is regarded as the father of air conditioning. However, a textile engineer named Stuart H. Cramer of Charlotte North Carolina used the term 'air conditioning' in a patent claim filed for a device that added water vapour to air in textile plants to 'condition' the yarn and used the term in a convention of cotton manufacturers in May 1906.
Antibiotics	1928	Alexander Fleming	Louis Pasteur and Jules-Francois Joubert made the first demonstration of antibiotic effect in1887.
Antiseptic medicine	1865	Joseph Lister	Ignaz Philipp Semmelweis made the first introduction of antisepsis into medical practice in 1847. Joseph Lister first successfully used this new method in August 1865.
Aqualung	1943	Jacques-Yves Cousteau and Émile Gagnan	
Aspirin	1899	Felix Hoffmann	Hippocrates, the 'father of medicine', made the first use of salicyn, an active component of

			Aspirin. In 1853, French chemist Charles Frederic Gerhardt was the first to synthesize the drug. Hoffmann rediscovered Gerhardt's formula.
Atomic theory	1808	John Dalton	Aristotle and Theophrastus credited Leucippus with having originated the theory of atomism.
Atomic structure	1911	Ernest Rutherford	The Rutherford atomic model has been alternatively called the nuclear atom, or the planetary model of the atom. Neils Bohr's atomic model, the Bohr atomic model, was created in 1913 and was the first that incorporated quantum theory.
Automobile	1769	Nicolas-Joseph Cugnot	In 1769 and 1770, Cugnot made two huge steam-powered tricycles that are today recognized as the first true auto-mobiles. These were tractors intended for hauling artillery. Karl Benz ran his first three-wheeled car with an internal combustion engine in in 1885. He built his first four-wheeled car in 1890. Gottlieb Daimler and Wilhelm Maybach launched their first car also in 1885.
Bicycle	1818	Karl de Drais de Sauerbrun	
Bifocal lens	1760	Benjamin Franklin	
Bridges	1800	James Finley (Suspension, Iron chains)	Marc Séguin originated the wire-cable suspension bridge in 1825. Ithiel Town invented the lattice truss bridge in 1820.
Calculating machine (Analytical Engine)	1835	Charles Babbage	
Calculating machine (Digital calculator)	1642	Blaise Pascal	
Camera	1814	Joseph Nicéphore Niépce	
Camera (Polaroid)	1947	Edwin Herbert Land	
Chewing gum	1848	John Curtis	The ancient Mayans chewed chicle the sap of the sapodilla tree. Thomas Adams invented a chicle based chewing gum in 1871.

Integrated circuit	1959	Jack Kilby and Robert Noyce	In the same year, 1959 Jack Kilby received a US patent for miniaturized electronic circuits and Robert Noyce received US patent #2,981,877 for a silicon based integrated circuit. However, these were for two different types of integrated circuits.
Digital compact Disc (CD)	1965	James Russell	
Electric motor	1822	Michael Faraday	
Electromagnet	1823	William Sturgeon	
Frozen foods	1824	Clarence Birdseye	
Heart (artificial)	1957	Willem Kolff	
Helicopter	1939	Igor Sikorsky	Paul Cornu originated the first piloted helicopter in 1907. However, this design was not successful.
Hot-air balloon	1783	Joseph and Étienne Montgolfier	In 1709, a Brazillian named Padre Bartolomeu Lourenço de Gusmão presented a miniature balloon made of glued paper sections to King João V of Portugal and his court and ambassadors of other countries. However, inspite of experimental success, he could not attain much success with his aeronautical studies.
Laser	1960	Theodore Maiman	In 1958, Charles Townes and Arthur Schawlow theorized a visible laser, an invention that would use infrared and/or visible spectrum light.
Liquid crystal Displays (LCDs)	1970	James Fergason	
Lightning rod	1752	Benjamin Franklin	
Locomotive	1804	Richard Trevithick (Steam powered)	George Stephenson invented the first practical locomotive with a multiple-fire-tube boiler in 1829.
Lock (cylinder)	1861	Linus Yale	
Loom (Jacquard loom)	1804	Joseph-Marie Jacquard	
Machine gun	1884	Hiram Maxim (first satisfactory fully automatic machine gun)	Richard Gatling invented the multi-barrel machine gun in 1862.
Optical Telescope	1608	Hans Lippershey	In 1609, Galileo Galilei built his first refracting telescope using a glass lens. He was also the first to

			use the telescope for astronomical purposes. In 1668, Sir Isaac Newton built a new type of telescope, the reflecting telescope, using mirrors. However, the first description of a practical reflecting telescope was made in 1663 by James Gregory.
Pen	1884	L.E. Waterman	Ball-point pens were invented by Lazlo Biro in 1944.
Plastics	1862	Alexander Parkes	In 1870, John W. Hyatt made the first plastic made of nitrocellulose, celluloid.
Polio vaccine	1914	Jonas Edward Salk	
Pressure cooker	1679	Denis Papin	
Radar	1904	Christian Hulsmeyer	British physicist Robert Watson-Watt made the first practical radar system in 1935.
Radio	1895	Guglielmo Marconi	Nikola Tesla had demonstrated a workable model of radio in 1893. In 1943, the US patent office granted him the patent for radio overturning Marconi's claim.
Refrigerator	1748	William Cullen	American inventor Oliver Evans designed the first refrigeration machine in 1805. Jacob Perkins built a practical refrigerating machine in 1834.
Revolver	1835	Samuel Colt	
Rocket (liquid-fueled)	1926	Robert Goddard	
Safety pin	1849	Walter Hunt	
Sewing Machine	1790	Thomas Saint	The first American patent was issued to Elias Howe in 1846.
Star catalogue	1572	Tycho Brahe	First modern star catalogue.
Steam engine	1639	Thomas Savery	James Watt made his double-acting engine in 1782.
Steamship	1783	Marquis Claude de Jouffroy d'Abbans	
Stethoscope	1819	R.T.H. Laënnec	
Tape recorder	1898	Valdemar Poulsen	
Television	1884	Paul G. Nipkow	In 1925, Charles Jenkins and John L. Baird, both demonstrated the mechanical transmission of images over wire circuits.
Teflon	1938	Roy J. Plunkett	
Telegraph	1837	Samuel Morse	
Telephone	1876	Alexander Graham Bell	

Thermometer	1593	Galileo Galilei	Daniel Gabriel Fahrenheit produced mercury thermometers in 1714. The first centigrade scale is attributed to Anders Celsius, who developed it in 1742.
Tyre (pneumatic)	1888	John Dunlop	
Transistor	1947	John Bardeen, Walter H. Brattain, and William B. Shockley	
Typewriter	1867	Christopher Latham Sholes	
Vacuum cleaner	1869	Ives McGaffey	Hubert Cecil Booth received a British patent for a vacuum cleaner in 1901.
World Wide Web	1989	Tim Berners-Lee	
Xerography	1938	Chester Carlson	
Zero	5th–6th century	Indian mathematicians	Indian mathematicians of the 5th and 6th centuries are credited with the origin of the base-10 number system complete with a symbol and a position for zero. However, the concept of zero appeared earlier, in the Mayan and Babylonian number systems. But these were faulty. In the Mayan case, their inconsistency in base notation made it virtually useless for computations. The Babylonians used it only between two numbers to indicate an empty position and never at the end of a number.
Zipper	1891	W.L. Judson	

Some Famous Scientists

d'Alembert, Jean Le Rond; 1717–1783; French mathematician and physicist; a method for the wave equation is named after him.

Ali, Dr Salim; 1896–1987; Indian ornithologist; famous works *The Book of Indian Birds* and *Handbook of the Birds of India and Pakistan*.

Ampère, André-Marie; 1775–1836; French physicist; generally credited as one of the discoverers of electromagnetism; unit of measurement of electric current is named after him.

Ångström, Anders J.; 1814–1874; Swedish physicist; one of the founders of the science of spectroscopy.

Archimedes of Syracuse; c. 287–212 BC; Greek mathematician, astronomer, philosopher, physicist and engineer; famous for principles of density and buoyancy.

Aristarchus; lived in 4th or 3rd century BC; Greek astronomer and mathematician; first recorded person to propose a heliocentric model of the solar system.

Avogadro, Amedeo; 1776–1856; Italian scientist; stated the hypothesis of what we now call Avogadro's law: equal volumes of gases, at the same temperature and pressure, contain the same number of molecules.

Bernoulli, Daniel; 1700–1782; was a Dutch-born Swiss mathematician; famous for Bernoulli's principle in aerodynamics.

Berzelius, Jöns Jacob; 1779–1848; Swedish chemist; invented modern chemical notation.

Bhabha, Homi J.; 1906–1966; Indian physicist; proposed the cascade theory which explains why electrons are found in cosmic rays at sea level; architect of India's atomic energy program.

Bhatnagar, Shanti S.; 1894–1958; Indian chemist; contributions range from his theories on emulsions and colloids, research on industrial chemistry and magneto-chemistry.

Black, Joseph; 1728–1799; Scottish physicist and chemist; discovered carbon dioxide.

Boltzmann, Ludwig; 1844–1906; Austrian physicist; famous for the invention of statistical mechanics.

Bose, Satyendranath; 1894–1974; Indian scientist; noted for Bose-Einstein statistics and a new state of matter known as Bose-Einstein condensate. The particle 'boson' is named after him.

Bose, Sir Jagadish C.; 1858–1937; Indian experimental scientist and inventor; produced a compact apparatus for generating electromagnetic waves of wavelengths 25 to 5 mm; researched on response to external stimuli in living and non-living organisms.

Boyle, Robert; 1627–1691; Irish natural philosopher; noted for his work in physics and chemistry, especially Boyle law for gases.

Brahe, Tycho; 1546–1601; Danish nobleman, astrologer, astronomer, and alchemist; in November, 1572, Tycho had observed a supernova Cassiopeia; helped Kepler with his observation.

Brahmachari, Sir Upendranath; 1873–1941; Indian; Chemist and Physician; discovered Urea Stibamine as a drug against Kala-azar.

Braun, Wernher von; 1912– 1977; German; leading figures in the development of rocket technology.

Buffon; 1707–1788; French naturalist, mathematician, biologist and cosmologist; best remembered for his *Histoire naturelle, générale et particulière.*

Cavendish, Henry; 1731–1810; British scientist; generally credited with having discovered hydrogen; calculated G, Newton's gravitational constant.

Copernicus, Nicolaus; 1473–1543; Polish; astronomer and mathematician; developed the heliocentric theory of the solar system.

Coulomb, Charles A.; 1736–1806; French physicist; Noted for Coulomb's inverse-square laws of electrical and magnetic force.

Dalton, John; 1766–1844; British chemist and physicist; noted for Atomic Theory.

Darwin, Charles R.; 1809–1882; English naturalist; laid the foundation for both the modern theory of evolution; famous work *The Origin of Species.*

Davy, Sir Humphry; 1778–1829; English chemist; separated elemental potassium, sodium, calcium, strontium, barium, and magnesium; also designed Davy's safety lamp for miners.

Doppler, Christian A.; 1803–1853; Austrian mathematician, most famous for the discovery of the Doppler effect.

Faraday, Michael; 1791–1867; British scientist; contributed to the fields of electromagnetism and electrochemistry.

Fahrenheit, Daniel Gabriel; 1686–1736; English physicist and an engineer; the Fahrenheit scale of temperature is named after him.

Fraunhofer, Joseph von; 1787–1826; German physicist; invented the spectroscope in 1814 and was the first to investigate the absorption lines in the solar spectrum.

Galilei, Galileo; 1564–1642; Italian astronomer, philosopher, and physicist; closely associated with the Scientific Revolution; his achievements include perfecting the telescope, the first law of motion; confirming the heliocentric model.

Goddard, Robert Hutchins; 1882–1945; American; modern rocketry pioneer; launched the first liquid-fuelled rocket.

Halley, Edmond; 1656–1742; English astronomer and mathematician; Halley's comet is named after him; contributed to the development of actuary science.

Herschel, Sir William; 1738–1822; English; an astronomer and composer; discovered the planet Uranus.

Hertz, Heinrich R.; 1857–1894; German physicist; first to demonstrate the existence of electromagnetic radiation; the SI unit of frequency is named after him.

Hipparchus; lived around 2nd century BC; Greek astronomer, astrologer and mathematician; first Greek to develop quantitative and accurate models for the motion of the Sun and Moon.

Hippocrates of Cos; c. 460–377 BC; Ancient Greek physician.

Hooke, Robert; 1635–1703; English; discovered Hooke's law of elasticity.

Hubble, Edwin Powell; 1889–1953; American astronomer, generally credited for discovering and proving redshift and that universe is expanding.

Huygens, Christiaan; 1629–1695; Dutch mathematician and physicist; notable for his arguments that light consisted of waves.

Jansky, Karl G.; 1905–1950; American physicist and radio engineer; discovered that the Milky Way galaxy emanates radio waves.

Johanson, Donald C.; 1943–; American, paeleoanthropologist; discoverer of Lucy the skeleton of a 3.18 million year old female hominid in the Afar Triangle of Ethiopia.

Joule, James Prescott; 1818–1889; English physicist, studied the nature of heat, and discovered its relationship to mechanical work that led to the theory of conservation of energy.

Kepler, Johannes; 1571–1630; German astronomer, mathematician and astrologer; best known for his three laws of planetary motion.

Lemaître, Georges-Henri; 1894–1966; Belgian Roman Catholic priest and astronomer; credited with proposing the Big Bang theory of the origin of the universe.

Lamarck, Jean-Baptiste; 1744–1829; French naturalist, first to use the term biology in its modern sense also proposed a now discredited theory of heredity, the 'inheritance of acquired traits'.

Lavoisier, Antoine-Laurent de; 1743–1794; French; stated the first version of the Law of Conservation of Matter, recognized and named oxygen.

Leeuwenhoek, Anton van; 1632 – 1723; Dutch businessman and scientist; best known for his contribution to improvement of the microscope and was observe and describe muscles fibres, bacteria and spermatozoa.

Linnaeus, Carolus; 1707–1778; Swedish scientist; laid the foundations for the modern scheme of taxonomy.

Mahalanobis, Prasanta C.; 1893–1972; Indian scientist and applied statistician; best known for his Mahalanobis distance, a statistical measure; founded the Indian Statistical Institute and actively involved in Five-year Plans.

Maxwell, James Clerk; 1831–1879; Scottish physicist; developed a set of equations expressing the basic laws of electricity and magnetism and Maxwell distribution in the kinetic theory of gases.

Mendeleev, Dmitri Ivanovich; 1834–1907; Russian chemist; one of two scientists who created the first version of the Periodic Table of Elements.

Messier, Charles; 1730–1817; French astronomer; created the catalogue of 110 deep sky objects.

Narlikar, Jayant V.; 1938–; Indian astrophysicist; noted for 'conformal theory of gravity'; with Fred Hoyle and Geoffrey Burbidge, he proposed, the 'Quasi-Steady State Cosmology'.

Newton, Sir Isaac; 1643–1727; English physicist, mathematician, astronomer, philosopher, and alchemist; published the *Philosophiae Naturalis Principia Mathematica* where he described universal gravitation and, via his laws of motion, laid the groundwork for classical mechanics. He also shares credit with Gottfried Wilhelm Leibniz for the development of differential calculus.

Ørsted, Hans C.; 1777–1851; Danish physicist and chemist; discovered the relationship between electricity and magnetism.

Pasteur, Louis; 1822–1895; French microbiologist and chemist; advocated the germ theory of disease and developed techniques of inoculation.

Ptolemy; AD c. 85–165; Greek geographer, astronomer and astrologer; best known for the astronomical treatise *Almagest.*

Ramanujan, Srinivasa Iyengar; 1887–1920; Indian mathematician; noted for researches in analytical theory of numbers, elliptic functions, continued fractions, infinite series and hypergeometric functions. He also gave his name to two constants, the Landau-Ramanujan constant and the Nielsen-Ramanujan constant.

Ray, Prafulla Chandra; 1861–1944; Indian scientist and educationist; succeeded in isolating mercurous nitrite; set up 'The bengal Chemicals And Pharmaciutical Works Ltd; also noted for *History of Hindu Chemistry.*

Richter, Charles Francis; 1900–1985; American seismologist, famous as the creator of the Richter Magnitude Scale, which quantifies the size of earthquakes.

Sagan, Carl E.; 1934–1996; American astronomer and science popularizer; pioneered exobiology and promoted the Search for Extraterrestrial Intelligence (SETI).

Saha, Meghnad; 1893–1956; Indian physicist; noted for an instrument to measure the weight and pressure of solar rays and Saha's 'thermo-ionization equation'.

Sarabhai, Vikram A.; 1919–1971; Indian physicist and administrator; noted for research on cosmic rays; founded the Physical Research Laboratory (PRL); drew up plans to set up the Satellite Instructional Television Experiment (SITE).

Scheele, Karl W.; 1742–1786; Swedish chemist, discoverer of many chemical substances, most notably oxygen before Joseph Priestley.

Sushruta; lived around 7 century BC; Ancient Indian surgeon; noted for *Sushruta Samhita*; credited with performing cosmetic surgery and especially with using forehead skin to reconstruct noses.

Tombaugh, Clyde W.; 1906–1997; American astronomer; discovered the planet Pluto in 1930.

Torricelli, Evangelista; 1608–1647; Italian physicist and mathematician; discovered the principle of the barometer.

Tsiolkovsky, Konstantin E.; 1857–1935; Russian; rocket scientist and pioneer of cosmonautics.

Volta, Alessandro G.A.A.; 1745–1827; Italian physicist; known for the development of the voltaic cell.

Swaminathan, Monkombu S.; 1925–; Indian geneticist, civil servant and international administrator; regarded as the father of the Green Revolution in India.

Career

Major Examinations

A. All India Entrance Examination for BE/B.Tech courses

Some of the notable institutions that offer four-year B.Tech courses to students after 10+2 with Physics, Chemistry, and Mathematics on the basis of the All India Entrance Examination for BE/B.Tech courses:

1. Indian Institutes of Technology
2. Banaras Hindu University
3. School of Mines, Dhanbad
4. Birla Institute of Technology, Ranchi
5. Birla Institute of Technology and Science, Pilani
6. University of Roorkee
7. Manipal Institute of Technology
8. Annamallai University, Faculty of Engineering and Technology.
9. Naval College of Engineering
10. National Dairy Institute, Karnal
11. Aligarh Muslim University

B. All India Pre-Medical/Pre-Dental Entrance Examination

Some of the notable institutions that give admission on the basis of the All India Pre-Medical/Pre-Dental Entrance Examination:

1. The Central Board of Secondary Education, New Delhi
2. All India Institute of Medical Sciences, New Delhi
3. The Armed Forces Medical College, Pune
4. Christian Medical College, Vellore
5. The Mahatma Gandhi Institute of Medical Science, Sevagram
6. Jawaharlal Nehru Medical College, Aligarh
7. Jawaharlal Institute of Post Graduation Medical Education and Research, Pondicherry
8. Banaras Hindu University
9. Kasturba Medical College, Mangalore
10. Medical College and Dental College, Pune

C. Joint Entrance Examination, the admission test conducted by Indian Institutes of Technology

List of the Indian Institutes of Technology that give admission on the basis of the Joint Entrance Examination:

1. Indian Institute of Technology, Powai, Mumbai
2. Indian Institute of Technology, Hauzkhas, New Delhi
3. Indian Institute of Technology, Guwahati, Assam
4. Indian Institute of Technology, Kanpur
5. Indian Institute of Technology, Kharagpur
6. Indian Institute of Technology, Chennai
7. Indian Institute of Technology, Roorkee

D. Some examinations conducted by Staff Selection Commission (SSC)

1. Combined Matric level Examination for recruitment to the posts of:

   a. Lower Division Clerks in Ministries/Departments, Attached and Subordinate offices of the

Govt. of India

b. Stenographer Grade 'D' in Ministries/Departments, Attached and Subordinate offices of the Govt. of India, and

c. Stenographer Grade 'C ' in Ministries/Departments, Attached and Subordinate offices of the Govt. of India

2. Combined Graduate level Examination for recruitment to the posts of:

   a. Assistants in Ministries/Departments, Attached and Subordinate office of the Govt. of India

   b. Inspectors of Central Excise and Customs

   c. Inspectors of Income Tax

   d. Preventive Officers in Customs

   e. Examiner in Customs

   f. Sub-Inspectors in Delhi Police and CBI

   g. Sub-Inspectors in BSF, CRPF, ITBP and CISF

   h. Divisional Accountant, Jr. Accountant, Auditor and UDCs in various offices of Govt. of India

3. Section Officer (Audit) in various offices under Comptroller and Auditor General of India

4. Section Officer (Commercial) in the offices under Comptroller and Auditor General of India

5. Investigator in National Sample Survey Organization, M/o Planning

6. Junior Hindi Translators

E. Some examinations conducted by Union Public Service Commission (UPSC)

1. Civil Services (Preliminary) Examination

2. Civil Services (Main) Examination

3. Indian Forest Service Examination

4. Engineering Services Examination

5. Geologist Examination

6. Special Class Railway Apprentices Examination

7. National Defence Academy and Naval Academy Examination

8. Combined Defence Services Examination

9. Combined Medical Services Examination

10. Indian Economic Service/Indian Statistical Service Examination

11. Section Officers/Stenographers (Grade-B/Grade-I) Limited Departmental Competitive Examination

12. Central Police Forces (Assistant Commandants) Examination

F. Defence Competitive Exams

1. Combined Defence Services Exam

2. National Defence Academy Exam

3. I.A.F. Airman (Technical Trades) Exam

4. I.A.F. Airman (Non-Technical Trades) Exam

5. I.A.F. Airman (Educational Instructors Trade) Exam

6. Indian Navy Sailors Matric Entry Recruitment Exam

7. Indian Navy Artificer Apprentices Exam

8. Indian Navy Dockyard Apprentices Exam

9. Indian Army Soldiers (Technical) Exam

10. Indian Army Soldiers Nursing Assistant's Exam

11. Indian Army Soldiers General Duty Exam

12. Indian Army Soldiers Clerks Exam

G. Insurance Competitive Exams

1. L.I.C/G.I.C Competitive Exams

2. L.I.C Officers' Exam

3. G.I.C Officers' Exam

4. L.I.C Development Officers' Exam

5. G.I.C Assistants Exam

H. SLET and NET

State Eligibility Test for Lectureship Eligibility (SLET)

States conducting SLET:

1. Maharashtra

2. Goa

3. Tamil Nadu (under consideration as on 14-07-2005)
4. Madhya Pradesh
5. Andhra Pradesh
6. Himachal Pradesh
7. Jammu & Kashmir
8. Rajasthan
9. West Bengal
10. NE-SLET (Which includes all North Eastern states and Sikkim)
11. Karnataka (Under consideration as on 14-07-2005)

It was resolved in the UGC's Commission Meeting that commencing from the SLET examinations scheduled in or after June 2002, SLET-qualified candidates will be eligible for appointment to the post of lecturer only in the universities/colleges belonging to the state from where they have passed the SLET examination. The status of SLET shall remain unchanged for SLET examinations conducted prior to 1 June 2002. In other words, candidates clearing SLET before June 2002 were eligible for appointment to the post of lecturer anywhere in India.

National Eligibility Test (NET)

The University Grants Commission (UGC) conducts the National Eligibility Test (NET) to determine eligibility for lectureship and to endow Junior Research Fellowships (JRF) for Indian nationals, with the object of ensuring minimum standards for entrants in the teaching profession and research field. The examination is conducted in Humanities (including languages), Social Sciences, Forensic Science, Environmental Sciences, Computer Science and Applications and Electronic Science. The Council of Scientific and Industrial Research (CSIR) conducts the UGC-CSIR NET for other Science subjects. These include Life Sciences, Physical Sciences, Chemical Sciences, Mathematical Sciences and Earth Atmospheric Ocean & Planetary Sciences and are held jointly with the UGC. The tests are conducted twice a year, usually in the months of June and December. For research candidates, the Junior Research Fellowship (JRF) is available for five years, subject to fulfilment of certain conditions. UGC has allocated a number of fellowships to universities for candidates who qualify the test for JRF. JRFs are awarded to meritorious candidates from among those who qualify in NET, provided they have opted for it at the time of application. The JRF test has been conducted since 1984. The Government of India, through a notification dated 22 July 1988, has entrusted the task of conducting the eligibility test for lectureship to UGC. Consequently, UGC conducted the first National Eligibility Test, common to both eligibility for Lectureship and Junior Research Fellowship in two parts, in December 1989 and in March 1990.

I. Admission Tests for Management Programmes

1. Common Admission Test (CAT)

List of institutions accepting CAT scores for admission:

1. IIM, Ahmedabad
2. IIM, Bangalore
3. IIM, Kolkata
4. IIM, Lucknow
5. IIM, Kozhikode
6. IIM, Indore
7. Management Development Institute, Gurgaon
8. National Institute of Industrial Engineering, Mumbai
9. S.P. Jain Institute of Management and Research, Mumbai
10. Mudra Institute of Communication, Ahmedabad
11. Institute of Management Technology, Ghaziabad
12. T.A. Pai Management Institute, Manipal
13. Indian Institute of Forest Management, Bhopal
14. Indian Institute of Social Welfare and Business Management, Kolkata

15. International Management Institute, New Delhi
16. K.J. Somaiya Institute of Management Studies and Research, Mumbai
17. Institute of Management Development and Research, Pune
18. Nirma Institute of Management, Ahmedabad
19. Principal L.N. Welingkar Institute of Management Development and Research, Mumbai
20. Institute for Financial Management and Research, Chennai
21. Fore School of Management, New Delhi
22. Indian Institute of Tourism and Travel Management, Gwalior
23. New Delhi Institute of Management, New Delhi
24. Institute for Integrated Learning in Management, New Delhi
25. National Institute of Management, Kolkata
26. Institute of Engineering and Management, Kolkata
27. Motilal Nehru National Institute of Technology, Allahabad
28. Globsyn Business School, Kolkata
29. International School of Business, Burhanpur
30. EMPI Business School, New Delhi
31. International Institute for Special Education, Lucknow
32. Alliance Business Academy, Bangalore
33. Kirloskar Institute of Advanced Management Studies, Devangere
34. Institute of Management Studies, Dehradun
35. Birla Institute of Technology, Ranchi
36. Institute of Management Studies, Ghaziabad
37. SDM Institute for Management Development, Mysore
38. Institute of Public Enterprise, Hyderabad
39. N.L. Dalmia Institute of Management Studies and Research, Mumbai
40. Ishan Institute of Management and Technology, New Delhi
41. Indian Institute of e-Business Management, Pune
42. Institute of Marketing and Management, New Delhi
43. NIILM Centre for Management Studies, New Delhi
44. Institute of Business Administration and Training, Bhubaneswar
45. DC School of Management and Technology, Idukki
46. National Insurance Academy, Pune
47. National Institute of Bank Management, Pune
48. Indian School of Mines, Dhanbad
49. Lal Bahadur Shastri Institute of Management, New Delhi
50. Indian Institute of Management Training, Pune
51. EMPI Institute of Advertising, Communication and Management, New Delhi
52. Aravali Institute of Management, Jodhpur
53. Amrita Institute of Management, Coimbatore
54. United Institute of Management, Allahabad,
55. College of Agri Business Management, Pantnagar
56. Hindustan Inst of Management and Computer, Agra
57. Department of Business Administration, Lucknow
58. Institute of Finance and International Management Bangalore, Karnataka
59. Thakur Institute of Management Studies and Research, Mumbai
60. Pailan College of Management and Technology, Kolkata
61. School of Management Sciences, Varanasi
62. Jaipuria Institute of Management, Lucknow
63. Management Education Centre, Kolkata

2. XLRI Aptitude Test (XAT)

List of institutions accepting XAT scores for admission:

1. Xavier Labour Relations Institute (XLRI), Jamshedpur
2. Xavier Institute of Management (XIM), Bhubaneswar
3. Bharathidasan Institute of Management, Trichy
4. Goa Institute of Management, Panjim
5. Principal L.N. Welingkar Institute of Management Development and Research, Mumbai
6. Institute of Technology and Management, Chennai
7. Loyola Institute of Business Administration, Chennai
8. International School of Business and Media, Pune
9. Akson Institute of Management Studies, Bangalore
10. Asia-Pacific Institute of Management, New Delhi
11. Institute for Technology and Management, Mumbai
12. Institute of Management and Information Science, Bhubaneswar
13. Xavier Institute of Social Service (XISS), Ranchi
14. Indira Group of Institutes, Pune
15. AICAR Business School, Mumbai

3. Institute of Rural Management, Anand (IRMA)

List of institutions accepting IRMA scores for admission:

1. Institute of Rural Management, Anand
2. Xavier Institute of Management (XIM), Bhubaneswar

4. Joint Management Entrance Test (JMET)

List of institutions accepting JMET scores for admission:

1. Shailesh Mehta School of Management, IIT Powai, Mumbai
2. Department of Management Studies, IIT Delhi
3. Vinod Gupta School of Management (IIT Kharagpur)
4. Department of Humanities and Social Sciences, IIT Madras
5. Department of Management Studies, IISc Bangalore
6. Department of Industrial and Management Engineering, IIT Kanpur
7. Department of Management Studies, IIT Roorkee

5. Indian Institute of Foreign Trade (IIFT)

List of institutions accepting IIFT test scores for admission:

1. Indian Institute of Foreign Trade, New Delhi
2. K.J. Somaiya Institute of Management Studies and Research, Mumbai
3. Geetam Institute of Foreign Studies, Visakhapatnam
4. Gandhi Institute of Technology and Management, Delhi

6. AIMS (Association of Indian Management Schools) Test for Management Admissions (ATMA)

Institutes accepting ATMA scores for admission:

1. Alliance Business Academy, Bangalore
2. Indian Business Academy, Bangalore
3. Institute of Business Management and Technology, Bangalore
4. MATS School of Business and MATS School of Information Technology, Bangalore
5. Bhubaneswar Institute of Management and Information Technology (BIMIT), Bhubaneswar
6. M.O.P Vaishnav College for Women (Madras University MBA), Chennai
7. SSN School of Management and Computer Applications, (SSN College of Engineering) (Anna University MBA), Chennai
8. Institute of Technology and Science, Ghaziabad
9. Integrated Academy of Management and Technology (INMANTEC), Ghaziabad
10. Jagan Institute of Management Studies, New Delhi

11. Shiva Institute of Management Studies, Ghaziabad
12. Institute of Marketing and Management Marketing, New Delhi
13. Education and Research Institute, New Delhi
14. Govindram Seksaria Institute of Management and Research, Indore
15. Prestige Institute of Management, Gwalior
16. Prestige Institute of Management and Research, Indore
17. Khandesh College Education Society's Institute of Management and Research, Jalgaon
18. B.P.H.E. Society's Institute of Management Studies, Career Development and Research, Ahmednagar
19. N.L. Dalmia Institute of Management Studies and Research, Mumbai
20. S.I.E.S College of Management Studies, Mumbai
21. Amrutvahini Institute of Management and Business Administration, Pune
22. Audyogik Shikshan Mandal's Institute of Business Management and Research, Pune
23. Apex Institute of Management, Pune
24. Indian Institute of Cost and Management Studies and Research, Pune
25. Indian Institute of Management Training (IIMT), Pune
26. Institute of International Business and Research, Pune
27. Indian Institute of Science and Management, Ranchi
28. Vasantraodada Patil Institute of Management Studies and Research, Sangli
29. Maharshi Karve Stree Shikshan Samstha's Smt. Hiraben Nanavati Insitute of Management and Research, Pune
30. Suryadatta Group of Institutes, Pune (Pune University)
31. Shri Shivaji Maratha Society's Institute of Management and Research, Pune (Pune University)
32. Bharati Vidyapeeth's Institute of Management and Rural Development Administration, Sangli
33. Bharati Vidyapeeth's Abhijit Kadam Institute of Management and Social Sciences, Solapur
34. Bharati Vidyapeeth's Institute of Management, Kolhapur
35. Bharati Vidyapeeth's Yashwantrao Mohite Institute of Management, Karad
36. Indo-American School of Business, Visakhapatnam
37. Indian Institute of Tourism and Travel Management, Gwalior
38. Institute of Business Management, Bangalore
39. Prestige Institute of Management, Dewas (Vikram University, Ujjain MBA)
40. SCMS—School of Technology and Management (Mahatma Gandhi University MBA)
41. SCMS—School of Communication and Management Studies, Management House, Cochin
42. Shikshana Prasaraka Mandali's Prin. N.G. Naralkar Institute of Career Development and Research, Pune
43. Dr. Vikhe Patil Foundation's Centre for Management Research and Development, Pune
44. Rajiv Gandhi Vocational Education Training College, Gwalior
45. Department of Business Administration, Awadesh Pratap Singh University, Rewa (Awadhesh Pratap Singh University MBA)
46. Institute of Business Management and Research, Bangalore
47. Institute of Business Management Research, Hubli
48. Sinhgad Institute of Management, Pune
49. Teerthanker Mahaveer Institute of Management and Technology,

Moradabad (U.P Technical University MBA)

50. University Institute of Management, Rani Durga University, Jabalpur
51. Bansilal Ramnath Agarwal Charitable Trust's Vishwakarma Institute of Management, Pune
52. NIILM University, New Delhi
53. Vidyasagar Institute of Management, Bhopal
54. Ambedkar Institute of Management Studies, Visakhapatnam
55. EMPI Business School, Chattarpur
56. Data Systems Research Foundation, Pune
57. Deen Dayal Upadhyaya Institute of Management and Higher Studies, Kanpur
58. Indian Institute of Tourism and Travel Management, Gwalior (MP Bhoj Open University, Bhopal MBA)
59. Technocrats Institute of Technology, Bhopal (Barkatullah University MBA)
60. Pioneer Institute of Professional Studies, Indore (Devi Ahilya Vishwavidyalaya MBA)
61. BVM College of Management Education, Gwalior (Jiwaji University MBA)
62. Medi-Caps Institute of Technology and Management, Indore (Devi Ahilya Vishwavidyalaya MBA)
63. Lakshmi Narain College of Technology, Bhopal
64. Pandit Jawaharlal Nehru Institute of Business Management, Vikram University, Ujjain (Vikram University MBA)
65. VNS Institute of Management, Bhopal (Barkatullah University MBA)
66. Samrat Ashok Technological Institute, Vidisha (Barkatullah University MBA)
67. Maharishi Centre Educational Excellence, Bhopal (Barkatullah University MBA)

68. Institute of Professional Education and Research (IPER), Bhopal (Barkatullah University MBA)
69. Bansal MBA College, Bhopal (Barkatullah University MBA)
70. Institute of Management Studies (IMS), Indore (Devi Ahilya Vishwavidyalaya MBA)
71. Anna University, Chennai
72. Department of Management Studies, Adhiyamaan College of Engineering, Hosur (Anna University MBA)
73. MEPCO Schlenk Engineering College, Dist. Virudhunagar (Anna University MBA)
74. Akson Academie, Bangalore (Bangalore University MBA)
75. Institute for Development and Research in Banking Technology (IDRBT), Hyderabad
76. M.O.P Vaishnav College for Women, Chennai (University of Madras MBA)
77. National Institute of Technology (Formerly Regional Engineering College), Tiruchirapalli
78. Symbiosis Institute of Business Management, Pune
79. L.N. Welingkar Institute of Management Development and Research, Mumbai
80. Bansilal Ramnath Agarwal Charitable Trust's Vishwakarma Institute of Management, Pune
81. Symbiosis Institute of Computer Studies and Research, Pune
82. Shri Shivaji Maratha Society's Institute of Management and Research, Pune (University of Pune MBA)
83. Department of Management Sciences, University of Pune, Pune (University of Pune MBA)
84. Thakur Institute of Management Studies and Research, Mumbai
85. Faculty of Management, International University for Human Transformation, Raipur
86. University Institute of Management, Rani Durgavati Vishwavidyalaya, Jabalpur

87. Mahatma Gandhichitrakoot Gramoday Vishwavidyalaya, Satna
88. Institute of Management, Jiwaji University, Gwalior
89. Faculty of Management Studies, Dr. Hari Singh Gour University, Sagar
90. Institute of Professional Studies, Indore
91. Department of Business Administration, Awadhesh Pratap Singh University, Rewa
92. Hindu Institute of Management, Sonepat (M.D. University, Rohtak MBA)
93. Crescent Institute of Management, Bhopal (Barkatullah University MBA)
94. IILM Institute for Higher Education, Gurgaon
95. IILM Institute for Higher Education, Lucknow
96. IILM Academy of Higher Learning, Greater Noida
97. Prestige Institute of Management, Gwalior (Jiwaji University MBA)
98. Prestige Institute of Management, Dewas (Vikram University, Ujjain MBA)
99. C.R. Institute of Management (C.R.I.M), University Teaching Department, Barkatullah University, Bhopal
100. Govindram Seksaria Institute of Management and Research, Indore (Devi Ahilya Vishwavidyalaya MBA)
101. Shri Vaishnav Institute of Management, Indore (Devi Ahilya Vishwavidyalaya MBA)
102. Mahakal Institute of Management, Ujjain (Vikram University MBA)
103. Institute of Business Management and Research, Indore (Devi Ahilya Vishwavidyalaya MBA)
104. Xavier Institute of Development Action and Studies (XIDAS), Jabalpur (Rani Durgavati Vishwavidyalaya MBA)
105. RKDF Institute of Management, Bhopal (Barkatullah University MBA)
106. Sri Satya Sai Institute of Management, Bhopal (Barkatullah University MBA)
107. Bhabha Management Research Institute, Bhopal (Barkatullah University MBA)

7. Under Graduate Aptitude Test (UGAT)

Institutes accepting UGAT score for admission to Bachelor Programmes:

1. University of Petroleum and Energy Studies, Dehradun/New Delhi
1. Amity Business School, Noida
2. Jagannath International Management School, New Delhi
4. International Management Centre, New Delhi
4. EMPI Business School, New Delhi
5. NIILM Centre for Management Studies, New Delhi
6. R.K. College of Systems and Management, New Delhi
7. Institute of Marketing and Management, New Delhi
8. AIM University, New Delhi
9. Apeejay Institute of Management and Information Technology, New Delhi
10. New Delhi Institute of Management, New Delhi
11. Delhi School of e-Learning, New Delhi
12. Jagan Institute of Management Studies, New Delhi
13. The Delhi School of Communication, New Delhi
14. S.G.S.S.—IIT New Delhi
15. Institute of Management Studies Noida
16. Army Institute of Management and Technology, Greater Noida
17. Ansal Institute of Technology, Gurgaon
18. Unique Institute of Management and Technology, Ghaziabad
19. Shiva Institute of Management Studies and Technology, Ghaziabad
20. NIMT Institute of Management and Technology, Ghaziabad

21. Mewar University, Ghaziabad
22. Integrated Academy of Management and Technology, Ghaziabad
23. BLS Institute of Education Ghaziabad
24. Jaipuria Institute of Management Ghaziabad
25. Institute of Environment and Management, Lucknow
26. Sherwood College of Management, Lucknow
27. Graduate School of Business and Administration, Greater Noida
28. Invertis Institute of Management Studies, Bareilly
29. Institute of Media, Management and Technology, Dehradun
30. Ram Institute of Hotel Management and Catering Technology, Dehradun
31. Institute of Technology and Management, Dehradun
32. Beehive College of Advance Studies, Dehradun
33. SD College of Management Studies, Muzzaffar Nagar
34. Amrapali Institute of Management and Computer Applications, Haldwani
35. NIMT Institute of Management and Technology, Jaipur
36. MES College of Arts and Commerce, Goa
37. Rosary College of Commerce and Arts, Goa
38. SVS College of Commerce and Management Studies, Goa
39. Suryadatta College of Management, Information Research and Technology Pune
40. IPS Academy, Indore
41. Christian Eminent Academy of Management, Professional Education and Research, Indore
42. International Institute of Foreign Trade and Research, Indore
43. MATS University, Raipur
44. IIAS International University, Bhilai
45. University of Technology and Science, Raipur
46. International University for Human Transformation, Raipur
47. Alliance Business Academy, Bangalore
48. Dayananda Sagar College of Management and Information Technology, Bangalore
49. T John College, Bangalore
50. Acharya Institute of Management and Sciences, Bangalore
51. Sri Bhagwan Mahaveer Jain College Bangalore
52. KLE Society, Belgaum
53. Rajarajan Academy of Higher Learning Ltd., Chennai
54. Annex College of Management Studies, Kolkata
55. International School of Business, Kolkata
56. Indian Institute of Hotel Management and Catering Bhubaneswar
57. Rourkela Institute of Management Studies, Rourkela
58. RJ School of Management Studies, Balasore
59. Durgapur Society of Management Science, Durgapur
60. RAI University

8. Management Aptitude Test

The Government of India has approved MAT as a National Entrance Test for admission to MBA and equivalent programmes. MAT is necessary for admission into the Post Graduate Diploma in Management (PGDM), Post Graduate Diploma in Information Technology & Management (PGDITM) and equivalent programmes offered by the All India Management Association (AIMA-CME) or other Management Institutes.

Participating Management Institutes / Universities (MAT of 4 December 2005).

Northern Region

1. Academy of Management Studies, Dehradun
2. AIMA-Centre for Management Education (PGDM), New Delhi

3. AIMA-Centre for Management Education (PGDITM), New Delhi
4. Amity Business School, Noida
5. Amrapali Institute of Management & Computer Applications, Haldwani
6. Apeejay Institute of Management & Information Technology, New Delhi
7. Apeejay School of Management, New Delhi
8. Asia Pacific Institute of Management, New Delhi
9. Asian School of Media Studies, Noida
10. Bhai Gurdas Institute of Management & Technolgy, Sangrur
11. Birla Institute of Management Technology, Greater Noida
12. BLS Institute of Education, Ghaziabad
13. BLS Institute of Management, Ghaziabad
14. Centre for Management Development, Modinagar
15. Centre for Management Technology, Greater Noida
16. Cosmic Business School, New Delhi
17. CT Institute of Management & IT, Jalandhar
18. DPC Institute of Management, New Delhi
19. Dr Gaur Hari Singhania Institute of Management & Research, Kanpur
20. EMPI Institutions, New Delhi
21. Fortune Institute of International Business, New Delhi
22. Global Institute of Management Technology, New Delhi
23. Graduate School of Business & Administration, Greater Noida
24. Guru Nanak Institute of Management, New Delhi
25. Gurukul Kangri Vishwavidyalaya, Haridwar
26. IBAT School of Management, Greater Noida
27. IILM Institute for Higher Education, Gurgaon
28. IIMR Pharma Business School, Delhi
29. IIMT Management College, Meerut
30. Indian Institute of Finance, New Delhi
31. Institute for Integrated Learning in Mgmt, New Delhi
32. Institute of Business Administration & Management, New Delhi
33. Institute of Environment & Management, Lucknow
34. Institute of Informatics & Management Sciences, Meerut
35. Institute of Management & Development, New Delhi
36. Institute of Management Education, Ghaziabad
37. Institute of Management Studies, Ghaziabad
38. Institute of Management Studies, Dehradun
39. Institute of Marketing & Mgmt, New Delhi
40. Institute of Productivity & Management, Meerut
41. Institute of Productivity & Management, Ghaziabad
42. Institute of Productivity & Management, Lucknow
43. Institute of Productivity & Management, Kanpur
44. Institute of Professional Excellence & Management, Ghaziabad
45. Institute of Technology & Science, Ghaziabad
46. Integrated Academy of Management & Technology, Ghaziabad
47. International Institute for Special Education, Lucknow
48. International Management Centre, New Delhi
49. Ishan Institute of Management & Technology, New Delhi
50. Jagan Instt of Management Studies, Delhi
51. Jagannath Institute of Management Sciences, New Delhi
52. Jaipuria Institute of Management, Ghaziabad

53. Jamia Hamdard, New Delhi
54. Landmark Foundation, Dehradun
55. Maharishi Institute of Management, Noida
56. Management Education & Research Institute, New Delhi
57. Master School of Management, Meerut
58. Motilal Rastogi School of Management, Lucknow
59. Netaji Subhash Institute of Management Sciences, New Delhi
60. New Delhi Institute of Management, New Delhi
61. NICE Management College, Meerut
62. NIILM School of Business, New Delhi
63. Nimbus Academy of Management, Dehradun
64. NIMT, Ghaziabad
65. NIMT, Greater Noida
66. Rai Business School, New Delhi
67. RIMT-Institute of Management & Computer Technology, Mandigobindgarh
68. Shiva Institute of Management Studies, Ghaziabad
69. Shri Guru Ram Rai Institute of Technology & Science, Dehradun
70. Skyline Business School, New Delhi
71. Sri Sringeri Sharda Institute of Management, New Delhi
72. SRM Institute of Management & Technology, Modinagar
73. Teerthankar Mahaveer Institute of Management & Technology, Moradabad
74. The Delhi School of Communication, New Delhi
75. Unique Institute of Management & Technology, Modinagar
76. University of Petroleum & Energy Studies, New Delhi

Western Region

1. AIMA-Centre for Management Education (PGDM), New Delhi
2. AIMA-Centre for Management Education (PGDITM), New Delhi
3. Asia Pacific Institute of Management, Jaipur
4. College of Commerce, Science & Information Technology, Pune
5. IBAT School of Management, Pune
6. Indian Institute of Education & Business Management, Chandigarh
7. Indian Institute of Management Training, Pune
8. Indian Institute of Rural Management, Jaipur
9. Institute of Business Management & Research, Pune
10. Institute of Health Management Research, Jaipur
11. Institute of Management & Computer Studies, Mumbai
12. Institute of Rural Management, Jodhpur
13. International Institute of Foreign Trade & Research, Indore
14. International School of Business Management, Jaipur
15. JK Institute of Technology & Management, Navi Mumbai
16. Maharishi Arvind Institute of Science & Management, Jaipur
17. MKM Indian Institute of Management, Jaipur
18. Mody Institute of Technology, Laxmangarh
19. NIMT, Kotputli
20. Rai Business School, Mumbai
21. Rai Business School, Pune
22. School of International Business & Management, Jaipur
23. Som-Lalit Institute of Management Studies, Ahmedabad
24. Suryadatta Group of Institutions, Pune

Eastern Region

1. Academy for Professional Excellence, Kolkata
2. Annex College of Management Studies, Kolkata
3. Arya School of Management & Information Technology, Bhubaneswar

4. Bengal College of Engineering & Technology, Durgapur
5. Bharatiya Vidya Bhavan, Kolkata
6. BRM Institute of Management & Information Technology, Bhubaneswar
7. CMCE College, Bokaro
8. Eastern Institute for Integrated Learning in Management, Kolkata
9. Eastern Institute of Management, Kolkata
10. Future Institute of Engineering & Management, Kolkata
11. Global Institute of Management, Bhubaneswar
12. Heritage Institute of Technology, Kolkata
13. IBAT School of Management, Bhubaneswar
14. Indian Institute of Business Management, Patna
15. Institute of Business Management, Kolkata
16. Institute of Management & Information Sciences, Bhubaneswar
17. Institute of Management Bhubaneswar, Bhubaneswar
18. Institute of Professional Studies & Research, Cuttack
19. Institute of Science & Management, Ranchi
20. International Institute of Management Sciences, Kolkata
21. Lalit Narayan Mishra College of Business Management, Muzaffarpur
22. North Eastern Regional Institute of Management, Guwahati
23. Rajdhani College of Engineering & Management, Bhubaneswar
24. Regional College of Management, Bhubaneswar
25. Rourkela Institute of Management Studies, Rourkela
26. Sairam College, Bhubaneswar
27. Sikkim Manipal Institute of Technology, Rangpo
28. Tezpur University, Tezpur
29. The University of Burdwan, Burdwan
30. Vaishali Institute of Business & Rural Management, Muzaffarpur
31. Xavier Institute of Social Service, Ranchi

Southern Region

1. Academy for Management Studies, Tirupati
2. Acharya Institute of Management & Sciences, Bangalore
3. Acharya Institute of Technology, Bangalore
4. Alliance Business Academy, Bangalore
5. Alliance International College, Coimbatore
6. Ambedkar Institute of Management Studies, Visakhapatnam
7. Asan Memorial Institute of Management, Chennai
8. Asia Pacific Institute of Management, Hyderabad
9. Balla Institute of Technology & Management, Visakhapatnam
10. Bangalore Institute of Management Studies, Bangalore
11. Bharatiya Vidya Bhavan, Bangalore
12. Bhavan-SIET Institute of Management, Bangalore
13. CBM College, Coimbatore
14. Christ College, Bangalore
15. CMR Group of Institutions, Bangalore
16. Coimbatore Institute of Management & Technology, Coimbatore
17. Dayananda Sagar Business School, Bangalore
18. DC School of Management & Technology, Kottayam
19. Farook Institute of Management Studies, Calicut
20. Fatima College, Madurai
21. Guru Nanak Institute of Management, Chennai
22. Guruvayurappan Institute of Management, Coimbatore
23. IBAT School of Management, Bangalore
24. Indian Institute of Plantation Management, Bangalore
25. Institute of Business Management & Research, Bangalore

26. Institute of Business Management & Technology, Bangalore
27. Institute of Finance & International Management, Bangalore
28. INTECH Institute of Business Management, Bangalore
29. Mar Athanasios College for Advanced Studies, Tiruvalla
30. MATS School of Business & IT, Bangalore
31. MES College of Engineering, Malappuram (Dist)
32. MP Birla Institute of Management, Bangalore
33. MS Ramaiah Institute of Management, Bangalore
34. NIILM Business School, Bangalore
35. Park's College, Coimbatore
36. PES Institute of Technolgy, Bangalore
37. R L Institute of Management Studies, Madurai
38. Rai Business School, Bangalore
39. Rai Business School, Chennai
40. Rajagiri School of Management, Kochi
41. Rajalakshmi Engineering College, Chennai
42. RJS Institute of Management Studies, Bangalore
43. SCMS School of Communication & Management Studies, Cochin
44. SCMS School of Technology & Management, Cochin
45. Sidvin School of Business Institute of Technology, Bangalore
46. Sir M Visvesvaraya Institute of Technology, Bangalore
47. Siva Sivani Institute of Management, Secunderabad
48. Sona School of Management, Salem
49. Sree Narayana Guru Institute of Science & Technology, North Paravur
50. Sree Narayana Gurukulam College of Engineering, Ernakulam
51. T John College, Bangalore
52. TKM Institute of Management, Kollam
53. Vael's Institute of Business Administration, Chennai

Exams for Education Abroad

Most institutes of higher education abroad assess the performance of students through certain tests before admitting her/his application for consideration. Different institutions have different requirements. These tests are prepared by professional testing organizations, like the US Educational Testing Service (ETS), that administers a wide array of tests including SAT, GRE, TOEFL and TSE. These tests are valid for admission to universities in USA, Canada, UK, and Australia, among others.

Notable exams for the purpose of gaining admission in educational institutes abroad:

1. Graduate Record Examinations (GRE)
2. Graduate Management Admission Test (GMAT)
3. The International English Language Testing System (IELTS)
4. Test of English as a Foreign Language (TOEFL)
5. Scholastic Aptitude Test (SAT)
6. Michigan English Language Assessment Battery (MELAB)
7. American College Testing Programme (ACT)

Indian Institutes of Management

After 1947, India focused on the development of science and technology education within the country. It soon became apparent that the country needed to train personnel to help grow and manage the talent pool of technologists and scientists. This led to the creation of the Indian Institutes of Management in the country. The Indian Institute of Management Calcutta was set up in 1961. It launched a two-year full time post graduate programme. The first batch of stu-

List of IIMs

	Name	Established in
1.	Indian Institute of Management Ahmedabad	1961
2.	Indian Institute of Management Calcutta	1961
3.	Indian Institute of Management Bangalore	1973
4.	Indian Institute of Management Lucknow	1984
5.	Indian Institute of Management Kozhikode	1996
6.	Indian Institute of Management Indore	1997

dents graduated in 1966. The institute was established in collaboration with Alfred P Sloan School of Management, Ford Foundation, the Government of India and the Government of West Bengal. The Indian businesses also played a major role in the setting up of IIM Calcutta.

Indian Institutes of Technology (IIT)

In 1946 a committee was set up by Jogendra Singh, member, Viceroy's Executive Council, Department of Education, Health and Agriculture to consider the setting up of Higher Technical Institutions for post World War II industrial development in India. The 22-member committee, headed by N.R. Sarkar, in its report recom-mended the establishment of four higher technical institutions in the Eastern, Western, Northern and Southern regions, on the lines of the Massachusetts Institute of Technology, USA, with a number of secondary institutions affiliated to it. The committee also suggested that the institutes would not only produce undergraduates but they should be engaged in research, producing research workers and technical teachers. They felt that the proportion of undergraduates and postgraduate students should be 2:1. With the recommendations of the Sarkar Committee in view, the first Indian Institute of Technology was set up in May 1950 at Kharagpur, in West Bengal. Since then six other institutes have come up in the country.

List of IITs

	Name	Established in
1.	Indian Institute of Technology Kharagpur	1950
2.	Indian Institute of Technology Bombay	1958
3.	Indian Institute of Technology Madras	1959
4.	Indian Institute of Technology Kanpur	1960
5.	Indian Institute of Technology Delhi	1961
6.	Indian Institute of Technology Guwahati	1994
7.	Indian Institute of Technology Roorkee	2001

UPSC – Programme of Examinations to be Held in 2006

S. No	Name of Examination	Date of Notification/ Last date for receipt of applications	Date of Commencement and its duration	Minimum academic qualifications prescribed	Age Limits	Remarks
1.	Combined Medical Services Exam, 2006	—	— 1 Day	MBBS Degree	Below 32 years as on 1.1.2006	Candidates appearing at the final MBBS Examination also eligible to compete subject to certain conditions. Selected candidates will be appointed only after they have completed compulsory rotating internship.
2.	CDS Exam (I), 2006	17 Sept 2005 17 Oct 2005	19 Feb 2006 1 Day	i) For IMA & OTA :- Degree of a recognized university or equivalent ii) For Naval Academy :- B.Sc. (with Physics & Mathematics) or Bachelor of Engineering iii) For Air Force Academy :- Degree of a recognized University (with Physics and Mathematics at 10+2 level) or Bachelor of Engineering	19-24 years as on 1.1.2007 for IMA; 19-22 years as on 1.1.2007 for Naval Academy; 19-23 years as on 1.1.2007 for Air Force Academy; and 19-25 years as on 1.1.2007 for OTA	Candidates appearing at the degree or equivalent examination also eligible to compete subject to certain conditions.

No.	Examination	Dates	Exam Date / Duration	Educational Qualification	Age	Remarks
3.	NDA & NA Exam (I), 2006	15 Oct 2005 14 Nov 2005	16 Apr 2006 1 Day	i) For Army Wing of NDA :- 12th Class pass of the 10+2 pattern of School Education or equivalent examination conducted by a State Education Board or a University ii) For Air Force and Naval Wings of NDA and for 10+2 (Executive Branch) Course at Naval Academy : 12th Class pass of the 10+2 pattern of School Education or equivalent with Physics and Mathematics conducted by a State Education Board or a University	16-1/2 to 19 years as on 1.1.2007	Candidates appearing at the 12th Class under the 10+2 pattern of School Education or equivalent examination also eligible to compete subject to certain conditions.
4.	Civil Services (Prel) Exam, 2006	19 Nov 2005 19 Dec 2005	14 May 2006 1 Day	A degree from a recognized university or equivalent	21-30 years as on 1.8.2006	Candidates appearing at the degree examination also eligible to compete subject to certain conditions.
5.	Engineering Services Exam 2006	07 Jan 2006 06 Feb 2006	10 Jun 2006 3 Days	A degree in Engineering from a recognized university or equivalent. M.Sc. Degree or its equivalent with Wireless Communications, Electronics, Radio Physics or Radio Engineering as special subject acceptable for certain Services/ posts only.	21-30 years as on 1.8.2006	Candidates appearing at Engineering Degree or equivalent also eligible to compete subject to certain conditions.

No.	Exam	Dates	Exam Date / Duration	Qualification	Age Limit	Remarks
6.	IFS Exam, 2006	04 Feb 2006 06 Mar 2006	08 July 2006 10 Days	A Bachelor's degree with atleast one of the subjects namely Animal Husbandry & Veterinary Science, Botany, Chemistry, Geology, Mathematics, Physics, Statistics and Zoology or a degree in Agriculture or Forestry or Engineering of a recognized University or equivalent.	21-30 years as on 1.7.2006	Candidates appearing at degree examination (with prescribed subject) also eligible to compete subject to certain conditions.
7.	SCRA Exam, 2006	18 Feb 2006 20 Mar 2006	23 July 2006 1 Day	Intermediate or Senior Secondary (12 years) Examination under 10+2 pattern of School Education or equivalent with Mathematics and at least one of the subjects Physics and Chemistry as subjects of the Examination in Ist or IInd Division.	17-21 years as on 1.8.2006	Candidates appearing at the Intermediate/Senior Secondary (12 years) examination under 10+2 pattern of School Education/Ist year of the 3 years degree course or equivalent examination with the prescribed subjects also eligible subject to certain conditions.
8.	NDA & NA Exam (II), 2006	18 Mar 2006 17 Apr 2006	20 Aug 2006 1 Day	i) For Army Wing of NDA :- 12th Class pass of the 10+2 pattern of School Education or equivalent examination conducted by a State Education Board or a University ii) For Air Force and Naval Wings of NDA and for 10+2	16-1/2 to 19 years as on 1.7.2007	Candidates appearing at the 12th Class under the 10+2 pattern of School Education or equivalent examination also eligible to compete subject to certain conditions.

No.	Exam	Dates	Exam Date	Educational Qualification	Age	Remarks
9.	CDS Exam (II), 2006	22 Apr 2006, 22 May 2006	17 Sep 2006, 1 Day	(Executive Branch) Course at Naval Academy : 12th Class pass of the 10+2 pattern of School Education or equivalent with Physics and Mathematics conducted by a State Education Board or a University i) For IMA & OTA :- Degree of a recognized university or equivalent ii) For Naval Academy :- B.Sc. (with Physics & Mathematics) or Bachelor of Engineering iii) For Air Force Academy :- Degree of a recognized University (with Physics and Mathematics at 10+2 level) or Bachelor of Engineering	19-24 years as on 1.7.2007 for IMA; 19-22years as on 1.7.2007 for Naval Academy; 19-23 years as on 1.7.2007 for Air Force Academy; and 19-25 years as on 1.7.2007 for OTA	Candidates appearing at the degree or equivalent examination also eligible to compete subject to certain conditions.
10.	Central Police Forces (AC) Exam 2006	06 May 2006, 05 June 2006	08 Oct 2006, 1 Day	A degree from recognized University or equivalent	20-25 years as on 1.8.2006	Candidates appearing at the Degree or equivalent examination also eligible to compete subject to certain conditions.
11.	Civil Services (Main) Exam, 2006	—	13 Oct 2006, 21 Days	A degree from recognized University or equivalent	21-30 years as on 1.8.2006	Only such of the candidates as are declared qualified on the results of Preliminary Examination are eligible to take the Main Examination.

	Examination	Dates	Qualification	Age	Conditions
12.	IES/ISS Exam, 2006	10 Jun 2006 10 July 2006	A post-graduate degree in Economics/Applied Economics/ Business Economics/ Econometrics for the IES and a Post-graduate degree in Statistics/ Mathematical Statistics/Applied Statistics for the ISS, from a recognized University or equivalent.	21-30 years as on 1.1.2006	Candidates appearing at the Post-graduate degree or equivalent examination in the relevant disciplines also eligible to compete subject to certain conditions.
13.	Geologists' Exam, 2006	17 Jun 2006 17 July 2006	Master's Degree in Geology or Applied Geology or Marine Geology from a recognized University or equivalent	21-32 years as on 1.1.2006	Candidates appearing at their Master's Degree or equivalent examination (with prescribed subjects) also eligible to compete subject to certain conditions.
14.	SO/Steno (Gd B/ Gd-I) Ltd Deptt Competitive Exam, 2006	24 Jun 2006 21 Aug 2006			Departmental Examination open to only certain categories of Government Servants.

Sports

World Cup Football

On 21 May 1904, the Fédération Internationale de Football Association (FIFA) was founded in Paris by representatives of seven countries—Belgium, Denmark, France, Netherlands, Spain, Sweden and Switzerland. On 28 May 1928, the FIFA Congress in Amsterdam decided to stage a world championship of football and Uruguay was finally chosen as the host country in 1929. The original world cup trophy bore Frenchman Jules Rimet's name since he proposed the tournament. In 1970, the trophy was awarded to Brazil permanently when it became the first country to win the world cup thrice and a new trophy called the 'FIFA World Cup' was put up for competition. The tournament was not held for twelve years during the Second World War. Though the tournament was held alternately in Europe and the Americas since 1958, it broke new ground when it was held in Japan and Korea in 2002. Since 1930, only seven teams have been able to win the trophy. Germany will host the 2006 edition of the FIFA World Cup.

List of World Cup Winners

Year	Host	Winner	Runner-up
1930	Uruguay	Uruguay	Argentina
1934	Italy	Italy	Czechoslovakia
1938	France	Italy	Hungary
1950	Brazil	Uruguay	Brazil
1954	Switzerland	West Germany	Hungary
1958	Sweden	Brazil	Sweden
1962	Chile	Brazil	Czechoslovakia
1966	England	England	West Germany
1970	Mexico	Brazil	Italy
1974	West Germany	West Germany	Netherlands
1978	Argentina	Argentina	Netherlands
1982	Spain	Italy	West Germany
1986	Mexico	Argentina	West Germany
1990	Italy	West Germany	Argentina
1994	United States	Brazil	Italy
1998	France	France	Brazil
2002	South Korea and Japan	Brazil	Germany

UEFA European Championship

In 1956, the groundwork for an international competition among European teams began, and two years later the initial matches of the first European Nations' Cup (now known as the UEFA European Championship) got under way. The trophy is named after Frenchman Henri Delaunay who served as UEFA's first general secretary.

Greece were the surprise winners of the 2004 Euro Cup.

List of Winners

Year	Winner	Runner-up
1960	USSR	Yugoslavia
1964	Spain	USSR
1968	Italy	Yugoslavia
1972	West Germany	USSR
1976	Czechoslovakia	West Germany
1980	West Germany	Belgium
1984	France	Spain
1988	Netherlands	USSR
1992	Denmark	Germany
1996	Germany	Czech Republic
2000	France	Italy
2004	Greece	Portugal

India's Notable Achievements in Football

At the London Olympics in 1948, India made its Olympic debut in football. This is a list of notable performances by the Indian football team till today.

Tournament	Year	Venue	Position
Asian Games	1951	Delhi	Gold
Olympic Games	1956	Melbourne	4th
Merdeka Cup	1959	Kuala Lumpur	2nd
Asian Games	1962	Jakarta	Gold
Asia Cup	1964	Tel Aviv	2nd
Merdeka Cup	1964	Kuala Lumpur	2nd
Merdeka Cup	1965	Kuala Lumpur	3rd
Merdeka Cup	1966	Kuala Lumpur	3rd
Merdeka Cup	1970	Kuala Lumpur	3rd
Asian Games	1970	Bangkok	Bronze
L.G. Cup	2002	Ho Chi Minh City	Winner

Federation Cup

In 1977, the Federation Cup was inaugurated in India. It continues to be one of the most eagerly watched tournaments in India.

List of Federation Cup Winners

Year	Venue	Winners	Runners-up
1977	Ernakulam	ITI (Bangalore)	Mohun Bagan
1978	Coimbatore	East Bengal/Mohun Bagan joint winners	
1979	Guwahati	BSF	Mafatlal
1980	Calcutta	East Bengal/Mohun Bagan joint winners	
1981	Madras	Mohun Bagan	Md Sporting
1982	Calicut	Mohun Bagan	Mafatlal
1983	Cannanore	Md Sporting	Mohun Bagan
1984	Tiruchi	Md Sporting	East Bengal
1985	Bangalore	East Bengal	Mohun Bagan
1986	Srinagar	Mohun Bagan	East Bengal
1987	Cuttack	Mohun Bagan	Salgaocar
1988	Delhi	Salgaocar	BSF
1989	Coimbatore	Salgaocar	Md Sporting

1990	Trichur	Kerala Police	Salgaocar
1991	Cannanore	Salgaocar	Mahindras
1992	Calcutta	Mohun Bagan	East Bengal
1993	Calicut	Mohun Bagan	Mahindras
1994	Goa	Mohun Bagan	Salgaocar
1995	Calcutta	JCT	East Bengal
1996	Kannur	JCT	East Bengal
1997 (Jan)	Calcutta	East Bengal	Dempo
1997 (July-Aug)	Calcutta	Salgaocar	East Bengal
1998	Calcutta	Mohun Bagan	East Bengal
1999	Tournament not held		
2000	Tournament not held		
2001	Chennai	Mohun Bagan	Dempo
2002/03	Calcutta	Mahindra United	Mohammedan Sporting
2004/05	Bangalore	Dempo Sports Club	Mohun Bagan

National Football League

In 1996, the National Football League was started in India by the All India Football Federation to encourage the development of the sport in the country. The tournament features the top football clubs of the country. In 1997–98, relegation was introduced on the basis of performance. Presently, the league has twelve teams of which the last two are relegated annually.

List of National Football League Winners

Year	Winners	Runner-up
1996–97	JCT Mills	Churchill Brothers
1997–98	Mohun Bagan	East Bengal
1998–99	Salgaocar	East Bengal
1999–2000	Mohun Bagan	Churchill Brothers
2000–01	East Bengal	Mohun Bagan
2001–02	Mohun Bagan	Churchill Brothers
2002–03	East Bengal	Salgaocar
2003–04	East Bengal	Dempo
2004–05	East Bengal	Sporting Club de Goa

Indian Cricket

Here are the statistics tracking India's performances in both versions of the game (updated till 1 October 2005).

Tests—Highest Innings Totals by India

Home

Score	Opponent	Venue	Year
676-7	Sri Lanka	Kanpur	1986/87
657-7d	Australia	Kolkata	2000/01
644-7d	West Indies	Kanpur	1978/79
633-5d	Australia	Kolkata	1997/98
609-6d	Zimbabwe	Nagpur	2000/01

Away

705-7d	Australia	Sydney	2003/04
675-5d	Pakistan	Multan	2003/04
628-8d	England	Leeds	2002
606-9d	England	The Oval	1990
600-4d	Australia	.Sydney	1985/86
600	Pakistan	Rawalpindi	2003/04

Tests—Lowest Innings Totals by India

Home

Score	Opponent	Venue	Year
75	West Indies	Delhi	1987/88
83	England	Chennai	1976/77
83	New Zealand	Chandigarh	1999/00
88	New Zealand	Mumbai	1964/65
89	New Zealand	Hyderabad	1969/70

Away

42	England	Lord's	1974
58	Australia	Brisbane	1947/48
58	England	Manchester	1952
66	South Africa	Durban	1996/97
67	Australia	Melbourne	1947/48

India—First Test Wins Against Each Opponent

Opponent	Date	Venue	Test	Margin
England	10th Feb 1952	Madras	15th	Inns and 8 runs
Pakistan	18th Oct 1952	Delhi	1st	Inns and 70 runs
New Zealand	7th Dec 1955	Mumbai	2nd	Inns and 27 runs
Australia	24th Dec 1959	Kanpur	10th	119 runs
West Indies	10th Mar 1971	Trinidad	25th	7 wickets
Sri Lanka	31st Dec 1986	Nagpur	6th	Inns and 106 runs
Zimbabwe	17th Mar 1993	Delhi	2nd	Inns and 13 runs
South Africa	20th Nov 1996	Ahmedabad	5th	64 runs
Bangladesh	10th Nov 2000	Dhaka	1st	9 wickets

India—First Tests Against Each Opponent

Opponent	Date	Venue	Result
England	27th June 1932	Lord's	Lost
Australia	28th Nov 1947	Brisbane	Lost
West Indies	10th Nov 1948	Delhi	Draw
Pakistan	16th Oct 1952	Delhi	Won
New Zealand	19th Nov 1955	Hyderabad	Draw
Sri Lanka	17th Sep 1982	Madras	Draw
Zimbabwe	18th Oct 1992	Harare	Draw
South Africa	13th Nov 1992	Durban	Draw
Bangladesh	10th Nov 2000	Dhaka	Won

India's Overall Performance in Tests

	Played	Won	Lost	Tied	Draw
Overall	387	84	127	1	175
Home	201	59	46	1	95
Away	182	21	81	0	80
1930s	7	0	5	0	2
1940s	13	0	6	0	7
1950s	44	6	17	0	21
1960s	52	9	21	0	22
1970s	64	17	19	0	28
1980s	81	11	21	1	48
1990s	69	18	20	0	31
2000s	57	23	18	0	16

India's Series Wins in India

Pakistan in India, 1952/53

Played	Won	Lost	Draw
5	2	1	2

New Zealand in India, 1955/56

Played	Won	Lost	Draw
5	2	0	3

England in India, 1961/62

Played	Won	Lost	Draw
5	2	0	3

New Zealand in India, 1964/65

Played	Won	Lost	Draw
4	1	0	3

England in India, 1972/73

Played	Won	Lost	Draw
5	2	1	2

New Zealand in India, 1976/77

Played	Won	Lost	Draw
3	2	0	1

West Indies in India, 1978/79

Played	Won	Lost	Draw
6	1	0	5

Australia in India, 1979/80

Played	Won	Lost	Draw
6	2	0	4

Pakistan in India, 1979/80

Played	Won	Lost	Draw
6	2	0	4

England in India, 1981/82

Played	Won	Lost	Draw
6	1	0	5

Sri Lanka in India, 1986/87

Played	Won	Lost	Draw
3	2	0	1

New Zealand in India, 1988/89

Played	Won	Lost	Draw
3	2	1	0

Sri Lanka in India, 1990/91

Played	Won	Lost	Draw
1	1	0	0

England in India, 1992/93

Played	Won	Lost	Draw
3	3	0	0

Zimbabwe in India, 1992/93

Played	Won	Lost	Draw
1	1	0	0

Sri Lanka in India, 1993/94

Played	Won	Lost	Draw
3	3	0	0

New Zealand in India, 1995/96

Played	Won	Lost	Draw
3	1	0	2

Border-Gavaskar Trophy (Aus/Ind) in India, 1996/97

Played	Won	Lost	Draw
1	1	0	0

South Africa in India, 1996/97

Played	Won	Lost	Draw
3	2	1	0

Border-Gavaskar Trophy (Aus/Ind) in India, 1997/98

Played	Won	Lost	Draw
3	2	1	0

New Zealand in India, 1999/2000

Played	Won	Lost	Draw
3	1	0	2

Zimbabwe in India, 2000/01

Played	Won	Lost	Draw
2	1	0	1

Border-Gavaskar Trophy (Aus/Ind) in India, 2000/01

Played	Won	Lost	Draw
3	2	1	0

England in India, 2001/02

Played	Won	Lost	Draw
3	1	0	2

Zimbabwe in India, 2001/02

Played	Won	Lost	Draw
2	2	0	0

West Indies in India, 2002/03

Played	Won	Lost	Draw
3	2	0	1

South Africa in India, 2004/05

Played	Won	Lost	Draw
2	1	0	1

India's Series Wins Abroad

India in New Zealand, 1967/68

Played	Won	Lost	Draw
4	3	1	0

India in West Indies, 1970/71

Played	Won	Lost	Draw
5	1	0	4

India in England, 1971

Played	Won	Lost	Draw
3	1	0	2

India in England, 1986

Played	Won	Lost	Draw
3	2	0	1

India in Sri Lanka, 1993

Played	Won	Lost	Draw
3	1	0	2

India in Bangladesh, 2000/01

Played	Won	Lost	Draw
1	1	0	0

India in Pakistan, 2003/04

Played	Won	Lost	Draw
3	2	1	0

India in Bangladesh, 2004/05

Played	Won	Lost	Draw
2	2	0	0

India in Zimbabwe, 2005/06

Played	Won	Lost	Draw
2	2	0	0

Indian Captains and Results

	Tenure	Tests	Won	Lost	Drawn	Tied
C.K. Nayudu	1932–34	4	0	3	1	0
Vijaya Anand (Maharajah of Vizianagram)	1936	3	0	2	1	0
I.A.K. Pataudi	1946	3	0	1	2	0
L. Amarnath	1947–53	15	2	6	7	0
V.S. Hazare	1951–53	14	1	5	8	0
M.H. Mankad	1953–59	6	0	1	5	0
Ghulam Ahmad	1955–59	3	0	2	1	0
P.R. Umrigar	1955–59	8	2	2	4	0
H.R. Adhikari	1958–59	1	0	0	1	0
D.K. Gaekwad	1959	4	0	4	0	0
Pankaj Roy	1959	1	0	1	0	0
G.S. Ramchand	1959–60	5	1	2	2	0
N.J. Contractor	1960–62	12	2	2	8	0
M.A.K. Pataudi	1961–75	40	9	19	12	0
C.G. Borde	1967–68	1	0	1	0	0
A.L. Wadekar	1970–74	16	4	4	8	0
S. Venkataraghavan	1975–79	5	0	2	3	0
S.M. Gavaskar	1975–85	47	9	8	30	0
B.S. Bedi	1975–78	22	6	11	5	0
G.R. Viswanath	1979–80	2	0	1	1	0
Kapil Dev	1982–87	34	4	7	22	1

D.B. Vengsarkar	1987–89	10	2	5	3	0
R.J. Shastri	1987–88	1	1	0	0	0
K. Srikkanth	1989–90	4	0	0	4	0
M. Azharuddin	1989–99	47	14	14	19	0
S.R. Tendulkar	1996–2000	25	4	9	12	0
S.C. Ganguly	2000–till date	49	21	13	15	0
R.S. Dravid	2003–04	5	2	2	1	0

Indian Wisden Cricketers of the Year

1897	K.S. Ranjitsinhji
1930	K.S. Duleepsinhji
1932	Nawab of Pataudi (Sr)
1933	C.K. Nayudu
1937	Vijay Merchant
1947	Vinoo Mankad
1968	Nawab of Pataudi (Jr)
1972	B.S. Chandrasekhar
1980	Sunil Gavaskar
1983	Kapil Dev
1984	Mohinder Amarnath
1987	Dilip Vengsarkar
1991	Mohd. Azharuddin
1996	Anil Kumble
1997	Sachin Tendulkar
2000	Rahul Dravid
2002	V.V.S. Laxman

India's Overall Performance in ODIs

	Played	Won	Lost	Tied	No Result	Victory %
Total	594	277	290	3	24	49%
Home	194	103	85	1	5	55%
Away	180	61	108	0	11	36%
Neutral	220	113	97	2	8	54%
1970s	13	2	11	0	0	15%
1980s	155	69	80	0	6	46%
1990s	257	122	120	3	12	50%
2000s	169	84	79	0	6	52%

Top Ten Batsmen in Tests (Runs Scored)

	M	I	Runs	HS	Ave	100s
A.R. Border	156	265	11174	205	50.56	27
S.R. Waugh	168	260	10927	200	51.06	32
B.C. Lara	117	206	10818	400*	54.09	30
S.R. Tendulkar	123	198	10134	248*	57.25	34
S.M. Gavaskar	125	214	10122	236*	51.12	34
G.A. Gooch	118	215	8900	333	42.58	20
Javed Miandad	124	189	8832	280*	52.57	23
I.V.A. Richards	121	182	8540	291	50.23	24
A.J. Stewart	133	235	8463	190	39.54	15
D.I. Gower	117	204	8231	215	44.25	18

Five Highest Individual Scores in Tests

400*	B.C. Lara	West Indies v England at St John's, 4th Test, 2003/04
380	M.L. Hayden	Australia v Zimbabwe at Perth, 1st Test, 2003/04
375	B.C. Lara	West Indies v England at St John's, 5th Test, 1993/94
365*	G.S. Sobers	West Indies v Pakistan at Kingston, 3rd Test, 1957/58
364	L. Hutton	England v Australia at The Oval, 5th Test, 1938

Five Highest Individual Scores by Indians in Tests

309	V. Sehwag Pakistan at Multan, 1st Test, 2003/04
281	V.V.S. Laxman v Australia at Calcutta, 2nd Test, 2000/01
270	R. Dravid v Pakistan at Rawalpindi, 3rd Test, 2003/04
248*	S.R. Tendulkar v Bangladesh at Dhaka, 1st Test, 2004/05
241*	S.R. Tendulkar v Australia at Sydney, 4th Test, 2003/04

Top Ten Batsmen in ODIs (Runs Scored)

	M	I	Runs	HS	Ave	SR	100s	50s
S.R. Tendulkar	348	339	13642	186*	44.43	86.15	38	69
Inzamam-ul-Haq	347	322	10971	137*	39.89	74.28	10	81
S.C. Ganguly	279	270	10123	183	40.65	73.79	22	60
S.T. Jayasuriya	339	330	10122	189	32.13	88.55	18	58
M. Azharuddin	334	308	9378	153*	36.92	73.99	7	58
B.C. Lara	258	251	9359	169	41.59	79.46	19	57
P.A. de Silva	308	296	9284	145	34.90	81.13	11	64
Saeed Anwar	247	244	8823	194	39.21	80.66	20	43
D.L. Haynes	238	237	8648	152*	41.37	63.09	17	57
M.E. Waugh	244	236	8500	173	39.35	76.83	18	50

Five Highest Individual Scores in ODIs

194	Saeed Anwar Pakistan v India at Chennai, Independence Cup, 1996/97
189*	I.V.A. Richards West Indies v England at Manchester, Texaco Trophy, 1984
189	S.T. Jayasuriya Sri Lanka v India at Sharjah, Champions Trophy, 2000/01
188*	G. Kirsten South Africa v United Arab Emirates at Rawalpindi, World Cup, 1995/96
186*	S.R. Tendulkar India v New Zealand at Hyderabad, 2nd ODI, 1999/00

Top Ten Bowlers in Tests (Wickets Taken)

	M	W	Ave	Best	5w
S.K. Warne	128	623	25.16	8-71	32
M. Muralitharan	95	563	22.15	9-51	47
C.A. Walsh	132	519	24.44	7-37	22
G.D. McGrath	112	518	21.29	8-24	28
A. Kumble	97	465	28.38	10-74	29
N. Kapil Dev	131	434	29.64	9-83	23
R.J. Hadlee	86	431	22.29	9-52	36
Wasim Akram	104	414	23.62	7-119	25
C.E.L. Ambrose	98	405	20.99	8-45	22
I.T. Botham	102	383	28.40	8-34	27

Top Five Bowlers in ODIs (Wickets Taken)

	M	W	Ave	Best
Wasim Akram	356	502	23.52	5-15
Waqar Younis	262	416	23.84	7-36
M. Muralitharan	249	384	22.23	7-30
A. Kumble	264	329	30.76	6-12
G.D. McGrath	215	326	22.20	7-15

Hockey World Cup

The concept for an international hockey competition at the world level originated in a joint proposal made by India and Pakistan at an FIH (International Hockey Federation) Council meeting on 30 March 1969. The proposal called for a tournament in between the Olympic years. Pakistan was chosen to host the inaugural World Cup in October 1971. However India and Pakistan were locked in a tense standoff over the situation in East Pakistan. The prevailing political situation resulted in the shifting of the site to the Spanish city of Barcelona. From 1978 onwards, the tournament has been held once in four years. The eleventh Hockey World Cup will be held in Germany in 2006. India has won the tournament only once, in 1975.

	Year	Host	Winner	Runner-up
1.	1971	Spain	Pakistan	Spain
2.	1973	The Netherlands	The Netherlands	India
3.	1975	Malaysia	India	Pakistan
4.	1978	Argentina	Pakistan	The Netherlands
5.	1982	India	Pakistan	West Germany
6.	1986	England	Australia	England
7.	1990	Pakistan	The Netherlands	Pakistan
8.	1994	Australia	Pakistan	The Netherlands
9.	1998	The Netherlands	The Netherlands	Spain
10.	2002	Malaysia	Germany	Australia

Commonwealth Games

The Commonwealth Games were initially known as the British Empire Games (from 1930–1950). From 1954, their name was modified to 'British Empire and Commonwealth Games', the name being retained till 1962. From 1966 to 1974, they took on the title 'British Commonwealth Games' and from 1978 onwards they was finally renamed the 'Commonwealth Games'. In 1930, the first Commonwealth Games were held in Hamilton, Canada where 400 athletes from 11 countries took part. Since 1930, the Games have been conducted at four-year intervals excepting 1942 and 1946, because of World War II. The 2006 Commonwealth Game will be held in Melbourne, Australia. Delhi will host the 2010 Commonwealth Games.

India's Performance at the Commonwealth Games

Year	Medals Won			
	Gold	Silver	Bronze	Total
1934	0	0	1	1
1938	0	0	0	0
1954	0	0	0	0
1958	2	1	0	3
1966	3	4	3	10
1970	5	3	4	12
1974	4	8	3	15
1978	5	4	6	15
1982	5	8	3	16
1990	13	8	11	32
1994	6	11	7	24
1998	7	10	8	25
2002	30	22	17	69
Total Medals	**80**	**79**	**63**	**222**

Tennis

2005 Grand Slam Winners

Tournament	Men's Singles	Women's Singles
Australian Open	Marat Safin	Serena Williams
French Open	Rafael Nadal	Justine Henin-Hardene
Wimbledon	Roger Federer	Venus Williams
U.S. Open	Roger Federer	Kim Clijsters

Indian Grand Slam Winners

Over the years, Indians have come up with some commendable performances in the Grand Slam tournaments—Australian Open, French Open, Wimbledon and the US Open. Here is a list of some notable performances by some Indian tennis players.

Australian Open

Championship Category	Name	Year
Mixed Doubles (Sr.)	Leander Paes (IND) and Martina Navratilova (USA)	2003

French Open

Championship Category	Name	Year
Boy's Singles	Ramesh Krishnan	1979

Championship Category	Name	Year
Mixed Doubles (Sr.)	Mahesh Bhupathi and Rika Hiraki	1997
Men's Doubles (Sr.)	Mahesh Bhupathi and Leander Paes	1999
Men's Doubles (Sr.)	Mahesh Bhupathi and Leander Paes	2001

Wimbledon

Championship Category	Name	Year
Boy's Singles (Jr.)	Ramanathan Krishnan	1954
Boy's Singles (Jr.)	Ramesh Krishnan	1979
Boy's Singles (Jr.)	Leander Paes	1990
Girls Doubles (Jr.)	Sania Mirza (IND) and A Kleybanova (RUS)	2003

Championship Category	Name	Year
Mixed Doubles (Sr.)	M.S. Bhupathi (IND) and Mary Pierce (FRA)	1999
Men's Doubles (Sr.)	M.S. Bhupathi and L.A. Paes (IND)	1999
Mixed Doubles (Sr.)	L.A. Paes (IND) and L.M. Raymond (USA)	1999
Mixed Doubles (Sr.)	M. Bhupathi (IND) and E Likhovteva (RUS)	2002
Mixed Doubles (Sr.)	L. Paes (IND) and M. Navratilova (USA)	2003

US Open

Championship Category	Name	Year
Boy's Singles (Jr.)	Leander Paes	1991

Championship Category	Name	Year
Mixed Doubles (Sr.)	Ai Sugiyama and Mahesh Bhupathi	1999
Men's Doubles (Sr.)	Mahesh Bhupathi and Max Mirnyi	2002

Indian International Grandmasters in Chess

FIDE, the world chess body, awards the title 'International Grandmaster'. It is a lifetime title.

List of Indian International Grandmasters

Name	Year
1. Viswanathan Anand	1987
2. Dibyendu Barua	1991
3. Praveen M. Thipsay	1997
4. Krishnan Sasikiran	2000
5. Abhijit Kunte	2000
6. P. Harikrishna	2001
7. R.B. Ramesh	2001
8. Koneru, Humpy	2002
9. Surya Shekhar Ganguly	2002
10. Sandipan, Chanda	2003
11. Tejas Bakre	2004
12. Magesh Chandran	2005

Billiards

IBSF World Champions in Billiards (The Indian winners and runner-up)

(Point Format)

Year	Winner	Runner-Up
2005	Pankaj Advani	Geet Sethi
2002	-	Geet Sethi
2001	Geet Sethi	Ashok Shandilya
1997	-	Ashok Shandilya
1990	Manoj Kothari	Ashok Shandilya
1987	Geet Sethi	-
1985	Geet Sethi	-
1983	Michael Ferreira	Subhash Agrawal

1981	Michael Ferreira	-
1975	-	Michael Ferreira
1973	-	Satish Mohan
1969	-	Michael Ferreira
1964	Wilson Jones	-
1962	-	Wilson Jones
1958	Wilson Jones	-

(Frame Format)

Year	Winner	Runner-Up
2005	Pankaj Advani	Devendra Joshi
2003	-	Geet Sethi
2002	Ashok Shandilya	-

IBSF World Champions in Snooker (The Indian winners and runner-up)

Year	Winner	Runner-Up
2003	Pankaj Advani	-
1984	O.B. Agrawal	-

Arjuna Awards

Instituted in 1961, the Arjuna Awards are given in honour of outstanding performances in sports and games. The Government has recently revised the scheme for the Arjuna Awards. According to revised guidelines, a sportsperson, in order to be eligible for this award, should not only perform consistently for the previous three years at the international level while excelling for the year in which the award is given, but also exhibit qualities of sportsmanship, leadership and discipline. The award consists of a statuette, a cash award of Rs 3 lakhs, a scroll of honour and a ceremonial dress.

From 2001, the award is only given in disciplines that fall under the following categories:

1. Olympic Games/Asian Games/Commonwealth Games/World Cup/World Championship Disciplines and Cricket
2. Indigenous games
3. Sports for the physically challenged

Award List from 2003 to 2005

Discipline	Year	Awardees
Athletics	2003–04	Soma Biswas
Athletics	2003–04	Madhuri Saxena
Billiards and Snooker	2003–04	Pankaj Advani
Boxing	2003–04	M.C. Mary Kom
Chess	2003–04	Koneru Humpy
Equestrian	2003–04	Rajesh Pattu
Hockey	2003–04	Devesh Chauhan
Hockey	2003–04	Suraj Lata Devi
Judo	2003–04	Akram Shah
Kabaddi	2003–04	Sanjeev Kumar

Shooting	2003–04	Rajyavardhan Singh Rathore
Cricket	2003–04	Harbhajan Singh
Cricket	2003–04	Mithali Raj
Wrestling	2003–04	Shokinder Tomar
Paralympic games	2003–04	Madasu Srinivas Rao
Athletics	2004–05	Ms. J.J. Shobha
Athletics	2004–05	Anil Kumar
Badminton	2004–05	Abhinn S. Gupta
Golf	2004–05	Jyoti Randhawa
Equestrian	2004–05	Deep Ahlawat
Hockey	2004–05	Deepak Thakur
Hockey	2004–05	Innocent Helen Mary
Judo	2004–05	Angom Anita Chanu
Kabaddi	2004–05	Sundar Singh
Rowing	2004–05	J. Krishnan
Shooting	2004–05	Deepali Deshpande
Table Tennis	2004–05	Achanta S. Kamal
Tennis	2004–05	Sania Mirza
Wrestling	2004–05	Anuj Kumar
Athletics-Paralympics	2004–05	Devendra

Dronacharya Awards

Instituted in 1985, the Dronacharya Award honours reputed coaches who have successfully coached sportspersons and teams helping them accomplish outstanding results in international competitions. The recipient of this award is given a statuette of Guru Dronacharya, a cash prize of Rs 3 lakhs, a ceremonial dress, and a scroll of honour.

List of Awardees 2003–05

Sports	Year	Winner
Athletics	2003–04	Robert Bobby George
Boxing	2003–04	Anoop Kumar
Hockey	2003–04	Rajinder Singh
Wrestling	2003–04	Sukhchain Singh Cheema
Billiards	2004–05	Arvind Savur
Cricket	2004–05	Sunita Sharma
Squash	2004–05	Cyrus Poncha

Rajiv Gandhi Khel Ratna Awards

In 1991–92, the Rajiv Gandhi Khel Ratna Award was instituted by the Indian Government. The award is given for the most outstanding and spectacular performance by a sportsperson or a team in a year. The award comprises a medal, a cash prize of 5 lakhs and a scroll of honour.

List of Awardees

Year	Sports	Winner
2004–05	Shooting	Rajyavardhan Singh Rathore
2003–04	Athlete	Anju Bobby George
2002–03	Athletics	K.M. Beenamol
2002–03	Shooting	Anjali R. Bhagwat
2001–02	Shooting.	Abhinav Bindra
2000–01	Badminton	Pullela Gopi Chand
1999–2000	Hockey	Dhanraj Pillay
1998–99	Athlete	Jyotirmoyee Sikdar
1997–98	Cricket	Sachin Tendulkar
1996–97	Tennis	Leander Peas
1996–97	Weight Lifting	Kunjurani Devi
1995–96	Weight lifting	Karnam Malleshwari
1994–95	Yachting (Team Events)	Cdr. Homi D. Motiwala and Lt. Cdr. P.K. Garg
1992 –93	Billiards	Geet Sethi
1991–92	Chess	Vishwanathan Anand

Dhyan Chand Award for Lifetime Achievement in Sports and Games

From 2002, a new Dhyan Chand Award for Lifetime Achievement in Sports and Games has been instituted, in order to honour sportsmen who, by their performances have contributed and continue to contribute to sports in India, even after retirement. The award consists of a cash prize of Rs 1.50 lakhs, a scroll of honour and a plaque. The awardees are:

Sport	Year	Winners
Athletics	2003–04	Labh Singh
Hockey	2003–04	Hardayal Singh
Hockey	2003–04	Mehendale Digambor Parasuram (physically handicapped)
Wrestling	2004–05	Maruti Dnyanu Mane Patil
Hockey	2004–05	Rajinder Singh (Jr.)
Billiards & Snooker	2004–05	Manoj Kumar Kothari

Some Famous Sportspersons

Schumacher, Michael; (1969–); Germany; he is the only driver to win seven championships in Formula One history and his records include most career wins, most podium finishes, most fastest laps and most wins in a season.

Nascimento (Pele), Edson A do; (1940–); Brazil; scorer of 1,283 first-class goals—12 of them in World Cup final tournaments; a member of Brazilian squads that won World Cup in 1958, 1962 and 1970.

Maradona, Diego A; (1960–); Argentina; winner of 1986 Golden Ball for Player of the FIFA World Cup.

Cruyff, Johannes H; (1947–); The Netherlands; he was Player of the Tournament in the 1974 FIFA World Cup.

Yashin, Lev; (1929–); USSR; he was the European Footballer of the Year 1963.

Puskas, Ferenc; (1927–); Hungary; scored 83 goals in 84 internationals and first player to have scored four goals in a European Cup final.

Moore, Bobby; (1941–1993); UK; played for England 108 times, captained them in a record 90 matches.

Woods (Tiger), Eldrick; (1975–); US; greatest golfers of all time and has won 53 tournaments, 40 of those on the PGA Tour.

Di Stefano, Alfred; (1926–); Argentina; was the European Footballer of the Year 1957, 1959.

Bradman, Donald G; (1908–2001); Australia; universally regarded as the greatest cricket player of all time, retired with a Test cricket average of 99.94.

Richards, Isaac VA; (1952); Antigua; he has received an honorary knighthood for his services to cricket, and was named in *Wisden* 2000 as one of the five Cricketers of the Century.

Sobers, Garfield; (1936–); Barbados; an all-rounder, set a Test cricket record by scoring 365 runs in a single innings and in 1975 was awarded a knighthood for his services to the sport.

Hutton, Leonard; (1916–1990); UK; in 79 Test matches he scored 6,971 runs with an average of 56.67, hitting nineteen hundreds and twice carrying his bat.

Hobbs, John B; (1882–1963); UK; one of the most prolific batsman and was selected as one of five *Wisden* Cricketers of the Century, 2000.

Grace, William G; (1848–1915); UK; scored more than 54,000 first-class runs spreading across 44 seasons.

Ranjitsinhji, Kumar; (1872–1933); India; played for England and was *Wisden* Cricketer of the Year 1897.

Hadlee, Richard J; (1951–); New Zealand; he was the first bowler to take 400 Test wickets.

Walsh, Courtney A; (1962–); Jamaica; he was the first bowler to take 500 Test wickets.

Niazi, Imran Khan; (1952–); Pakistan; famous all-rounder and was *Wisden* Cricketer of the Year 1983.

Mohammad, Hanif; (1934–); India; famous Pakistan cricketer, played the longest innings in Test history—in 970-minutes he scored 337 against West Indies in Bridgetown in 1957–58.

Tendulkar, Sachin R; (1973–);India; one of the all-time great cricketers, he is India's second highest run-getter in Tests and has scored the most centuries in ODIs.

Gavaskar, Sunil M; (1949–); India; one of the greatest opening batsmen of all time, and still holds the record for the highest number of Test hundreds.

Ganguly, Sourav C; (1972–); India; till date India's most successful Test captain.

Lenglen, Suzanne; (1899–1938); France; famous tennis player and winner of six Wimbledon and six French Open title.

Budge (Donald), John D; (1915–2000); US; a champion tennis player who became famous as the first man to win in a single year the four tournaments that comprise the Grand Slam of tennis.

McEnroe, John; (1959–); US; No. 1 player in the world 4 times and 4-time US Open champion and 3-time Wimbledon champion.

King, Billie J; (1943–); US; tennis player who has a record 20 Wimbledon titles.

Navratilova, Martina, (1956–); Czechoslovakia; American tennis player who won 18 Grand Slam singles titles and 37 Grand Slam doubles titles.

Sampras, Pete; (1971–); US; tennis star and winner of 14 grand slam singles titles for his career, more than any other male player.

Amritraj, Vijay; (1953–); India; tennis star who played at Wimbledon and made it to the quarterfinals in 1973 and 1981.

Lendl, Ivan; (1960–); Czechoslovakia; tennis player who won both French and US Opens 3 times and Australian Open twice.

Senna, Ayrton; (1960–1994); Brazil; racing driver who won the Formula 1 world championship title three times.

Fangio, Juan M; (1911–1995); Argentina; racing car driver and winner of the Formula One championship five times, including four in a row from 1954 to 1957.

Nicklaus, Jack W; (1940–); US; a major force in professional golf and was the first person in the history of the PGA to win the same Senior Tour (now the Champions Tour) event four times.

Palmer, Arnold D; (1929–); US; a golfer who has won numerous events on both the PGA TOUR and Champions Tour, dating back to 1955.

Berra (Yogi), Lawrence P; (1925–); US; famous baseball player and is generally considered to be one of the five best catchers in history.

DiMaggio, Joe; (1914–1999); US; an American baseball star and first baseball pro athlete to sign for $100,000.

Ruth (Babe), George H; (1895–1948); US; baseball player who was the first player to hit over 50 home runs in one season.

Jordan, Michael J; (1963–); US; a former National Basketball Association player and was Most Valuable Player five times.

Johnson (Magic), Earvin; (1959–); US; an American professional basketball star and is the first NBA rookie to win the NBA Finals Most Valuable Player Award.

Abdul-Jabbar, Kareem; (1947–); US; a professional basketball player and winner of NBA Most Valuable Player Award 6 times.

Bird, Larry J; (1956–); US; a former NBA basketball player who was a three-time league Most Valuable Player.

Owens (Jesse), James Cleveland; (1913–1980); US; an athlete most famous for wining four gold medals in the 1936 Summer Olympics.

Erving, Julius; (1950–); US; basketball great who scored over 30,000 points in his professional career.

Zátopek, Emil; (1922–2000); Czechoslovakia; athlete, was the first to break the 29-minute barrier in the 10,000 meter run in 1954.

Rudolph, Wilma G; (1940–94); US; track and field athlete who won three gold medals at the 1960 Olympics in the 100-metre and 200-metre races and the 4×100 metre relay.

Beamon (Bob), Robert; (1946); US; track and field athlete, best known for his world record for the long jump at the 1968 Summer Olympics in Mexico City with a jump of 8.90 metre. His world record stood for 23 years.

Bubka, Sergei; (1964–); Ukraine; pole-vaulter, who broke the world record in pole-vaulting more than 30 times.

Thompson (Daley), Francis M; (1958–); UK; a former British decathlete who won consecutive gold medals at the 1980 and 1984 Olympic Games, and broke the world record for the event four times.

Johnson, Michael D; (1967–); US; a former athlete who holds world records for the 200m, 400m and 4×400 relay.

Moses, Edwin C; (1955–); US; a track and field athlete who won gold medals in the 400-metre hurdles at the 1976 and 1984 Summer Olympics and won 107 consecutive finals.

Lewis (Carl), Frederick C; (1961–); US; won 10 Olympic medals, of which 9 are gold, from 1984 to 1996.

Otto, Kristin; (1966–); Germany; an Olympic medal-winning swimmer who became the first woman to win six gold medals at one Olympic Games.

Ender, Kornelia; (1958–); Germany; first woman to win 4 gold medals at one Olympics (1976), all in world-record time.

Fraser, Dawn; (1937–); Australia; famous swimmer who won eight Olympic and eight Commonwealth Games medals.

Spitz, Mark A; (1950–); US; famous swimmer who won most gold medals in a single Olympics (seven).

Comaneci, Nadia E; (1961–); Romania; noted gymnast, a winner of five Olympic medals and the first to be awarded a perfect score of 10 in an Olympic gymnastic event.

Sherbo, Vitali; (1972–); Belaruss; famous gymnast who became the first gymnast to win six gold medals in one Olympics.

Bikila, Abebe; (1932–); Ethiopia; first to win consecutive Olympic marathons (1960, 1964).

Bannister, Roger G; (1929–); UK; famous athlete best known as the first man to run the mile in less than four minutes.

Coe, Sebastian N; (1956–); UK; won four Olympic medals and set eight world records in middle distance track events.

Virén, Lasse; (1949–); Finland; was the winner of four gold medals at the 1972 Summer Olympics and 1976 Summer Olympics.

Usha, P T; (1964–); India; first Indian woman (and the fifth Indian) to reach the final of an Olympic event.

Singh, Milkha; (1935–); India; famous athlete who won a gold medal in the Asian Games.

Suleymanoglu, Naim; (1967–); Bulgaria; competing at the 1992 Olympic Games in Barcelona, Spain, he won three gold medals for Turkey.

Kurniawan (Hartono), Rudy H; (1949–); Indonesia; famous badminton player who won the world championship in 1980, and the All-England Champions trophy 8 times in the 1960s and 1970s.

Susanti, Susi; (1971–); Indonesia; famous badminton player who was a Olympic Gold medallist and World Champion.

Joyner-Kersee, Jackie; (1962–); US; generally considered the best all-around female athlete in the world and winner of three gold, one silver and one bronze Olympic medals.

Padukone, Prakash; (1955–); India; noted Badminton player; in 1980, he won the All England Badminton Championship.

Kasparov, Garry K; (1963–); Azerbaijan; chess legend who became the world chess champion in 1985.

Karpov, Anatoly E; (1951–); Russia; famous chess player who won (1975) the world championship by default when Bobby Fischer, the titleholder, refused to agree to terms for a match.

Fischer, Robert J; (1943–); US; broke the Soviet domination of the World Championship when he became the first American chess player to win the title by defeating Boris Spassky of the USSR.

Botvinnik, Mikhail M; (1911–1995); Russia; was the first Russian to hold the World Championship title after he won the 1948 tournament following the death of Alexander Alekhine.

Chand, Dhyan; (1905–1979); India; field hockey player who was considered to be one of the greatest players of all time and is most remembered for his three Olympic gold medals (1928, 1932, and 1936).

Charlesworth, Richard; (1952–); Australia; represented Australia in four Olympic hockey teams and received the Order of Australia in 1987.

Anand, Viswanathan; (1969–); India; the first Asian to win the World Chess Champion, ending many years of Soviet domination.

Louis, Joe; (1914–1981); US; held the world's heavyweight boxing title from 22 June 1937 until 25 June 1948 and made a division-record 25 successful title defences.

Ali, Muhammad; (1942–); US; became the first man to win the heavyweight boxing title three times.

Marciano, Rocky; (1923–1969); US; the only world champion boxer to complete his career undefeated (49-0).

Armstrong, Lance; (1971–); US; won the Tour de France a record six consecutive times from 1999 to 2004.

Surtees, John; (1934–); UK; racing driver and winner of seven world titles in motorcycle racing.

Gretzky, Wayne D; (1961–); Canada; a professional ice hockey player who holds 61 NHL records: 40 regular season, 15 playoff, and 6 All-Star.

Tomba, Alberto; (1966–); Italy; Alpine skier, winner of three gold medals at the Olympic Games.

Louganis, Greg; (1960–); US; a diver who won platform and springboard gold medals at both 1984 and 1988 Olympics.

Sethi, Geet; (1961–); India; famous billiards player who won the World Professional Billiards Championship.

Davis, Steve; (1957–); UK; a professional snooker player who won the Embassy World Snooker Championship 6 times during the 1980s.

Khan, Jansher; (1969–); Pakistan; dominated the sport of squash and won six successive British Open.

Khan, Jahangir; (1963–); Pakistan; a squash player who won the world open championship a record six times.

Piggott, Lester; (1935–); UK; he was one of the world's leading jockeys in thoroughbred flat racing and was the British riding champion 11 times.

Taro, Akebono; (1969–); US; a Sumo wrestler who became the first non-Japanese wrestler ever to reach yokozuna, the highest rank in Sumo.

Fifty Years of *Pather Panchali*

2005 marks the fiftieth anniversary of the theatrical release of *Pather Panchali*, Satyajit Ray's masterpiece which is a landmark in Indian cinema. Here are selections from a previously unpublished article by the great film-maker on his art, from his new book *Speaking of Films*.

Breaking Barriers in Cinema
Satyajit Ray

On the strength of my first film and the wide success it won, I have heard it said that I was a born film-maker. And, yet, I had no thoughts, and no ambitions, of ever becoming one even as late as three or four years before I actually took the plunge. I loved going to the cinema ever since I can remember, but I must have shared this love with millions of others, or there wouldn't be such a flourishing film business in India for such a long time.

I was born in the heyday of silent cinema. Chaplin, Keaton and Harold Lloyd were producing what *then* were uproarious comedies, and are *now* seen as timeless masterpieces. Living in North Calcutta then, and most of the cinemas showing foreign films being around Chowringhee, going to the 'Bioscope' was a rare event. So I never had a surfeit of films. Every visit was a very special occasion, and every film was followed by weeks of musing on its wonders.

When the talkies came, I was just old enough to realize that a revolution had taken place. There were two kinds of talkies to start with: Partial Talkies, which had bursts of dialogue, followed by long stretches of silence; and One Hundred Per Cent Talkies. Newspapers in those days carried large pictorial ads of the foreign films. One look at them and a glance at the headlines were enough to tell the elders whether or not the films were likely to tarnish innocent minds. Those were the days of the flamboyant Hollywood stars, and what they were good at was not considered particularly suitable for a boy barely in his teens. So 'sizzling romance' was out, and so was 'tempestuous, hot-blooded passion'. I saw jungle stories, slapstick comedies, and swashbuckling adventures. But occasionally there were chance visits to supposedly adult movies. Ernst Lubitsch was a great name in cinema those days. As an Austrian who had settled in Hollywood, he had a highly sophisticated approach to romantic comedy. I saw three of his films, around the age of ten: *Love Parade*, *The Smiling Lieutenant* and *One Hour With You*—a forbidden world, only half understood, but observed with a tingling curiosity.

Films remained a great attraction right through college. But by then I had discovered something which was to grow into an obsession. This was western classical music. I had grown up in an atmosphere of Bengali songs, mainly Rabindrasangeet and Brahmo Samaj hymns. Even as a child, the ones that I liked most had a western tinge to them. A Vedic hymn like

Sangachhadhwam, or the song by Rabindranath with a rather similar tune, *Anandalokay mangalalokay*; or the stately chorus, *Padoprantay rakho shebokey*, which came as a wonderful relief after three exhausting hours of sermon on Maghotsab day. My response to western classical music was immediate and decisive. As a small boy, I had read about Beethoven in the *Book of Knowledge*, and developed an admiration for him which amounted to hero-worship. Now I was listening enraptured to his sonatas and symphonies. If films were fun and thrills and escape, the pursuit of music was something undertaken with deadly seriousness. It was a great voyage of discovery, and it transported me to a world of ineffable delight. Films were at the most a once-a-week affair, while music, played on the hand-cranked gramophone, took up all my spare time at home. At an age when the Bengali youth almost inevitably writes poetry, I was listening to European classical music. My reading was then confined to light English fiction. I hardly read any Bengali those days; not even the classics.

When I finally decided to become a film-maker, I was well aware that I would be up against a relatively backward audience. And yet I had set my mind on breaking all manner of conventions.

I had discussed the project with a number of professionals, and, to a man, they had discouraged me by saying that it couldn't be done the way we wanted to do it. 'You can't shoot entirely on location,' they had said. 'You need the controlled conditions of a studio.' 'You can't shoot in cloudy weather; you can't shoot in the rain; you can't shoot with amateur actors,' and so on and so forth.

So one of the first things we did was to borrow a 16mm camera and go to a village and take test shots. Subrata, who was to be my cameraman, and I went to Bibhuti Bhushan's village Gopalnagar, the Nishchindipur of *Pather Panchali*. It was in the middle of the rainy season, and we had to squelch through knee-deep mud to reach our destination. But once we got there, we lost no time. We took shots in the dim light of a mango grove, we shot in pouring rain, and we shot in the failing light of dusk. Everything came out.

I shall not go into the various ordeals we had to face in the two-and-a-half years it took to make *Pather Panchali*. The story has been told often enough. But what I have probably not mentioned elsewhere is that it was in a way a blessing that the film took so long to make. We learnt film-making as we went along, and since we went on for so long, it gave us that much more time to learn.

With all my knowledge of Western cinema, the first thing I realized was that none of the films I had ever seen was remotely like the story I was about to film. *Pather Panchali* had its roots deep in the soil of Bengal. The life it described had its own pace and its own rhythm, which in turn had to mould the pace and the rhythm of the film. The inspiration had to come from the book, and from the real surroundings in which we had decided to place the story.

If the books on film-making helped, it was only in a general sort of way. For instance, none of them tells you how to handle an actor who has never faced a camera before. You had to devise your own method. You had to find out yourself how to catch the hushed stillness of dusk in a Bengali village, when the wind drops and turns the ponds into sheets of glass, dappled by the leaves of shaluk and shapla, and the smoke from ovens settles in wispy trails over the landscape, and the plaintive blows on conch shells from homes far and near are joined by the chorus of crickets, which rises as the light falls, until all one sees are the stars in the sky, and the stars that blink and swirl in the thickets.

We wanted to show fireflies in *Aparajito*. The books didn't tell us that the light they gave off was too weak to be photographed. Our own tests with the camera proved that. So we had to invent a way of showing them. What we did was photograph a group of bare-bodied assistants in black loin cloths, who hopped about in total darkness, holding in their hands tiny electric bulbs which flashed on and off in a simulation of the dance of the fireflies.

If film books didn't help much, I was helped enormously by Bibhuti Bhushan. He is one writer whose stories are a gold mine of cinematic observation, and it is fortunate that I developed a taste for him right at the start of my career. Another quality which Bibhuti Bhushan had was a wonderful ear for lifelike speech. A vital and unending pursuit for a film-maker is the study of speech patterns: speech as a reflection of class, and speech as revealing states of mind. The best film dialogue is where one doesn't feel the presence of the writer at all. I am talking here of the kind of film that tries to capture the feel of reality. There are also films which attempt a larger-than-life style, or an oblique, fractured or expressionist style: I myself wrote dialogue with end rhymes in *Hirok Rajar Deshe*, which was a fantasy. But the overwhelming majority of narrative films belong in the tradition of realism, where the dialogue sustains the feeling of lifelikeness that is conveyed through the camera.

This realism in films is not the naturalism of the painter who sets up his easel before his subject and proceeds to record faithfully what he sees. For a film-maker, there is no readymade reality which he can straightaway capture on film. What surrounds him is only raw material. He must at all times use this material selectively. Objects, locales, people, speech, viewpoints—everything must be carefully chosen, to serve the ends of his story. In other words, creating reality is part of the creative process, where the imagination is aided by the eye and the ear.

A film, on the other hand, presents information in lumps, as it were. At any given moment, the image on the screen may be filled with a plethora of details, each carrying information. In other words, the language here is far more diffused than the language of words, and it is the film-maker's job to direct the attention of the audience to the dominant idea contained in the image.

If the idea is conveyed through dialogue, there is usually no ambiguity. But when it is conveyed in non-verbal terms—through gestures, objects, pure sounds, and so on—precise communication becomes difficult. When a writer is at a loss for words, he can turn to his thesaurus; but there is no thesaurus for the film-maker. He can of course fall back on clichés—goodness knows how many films have used the snuffed-out candle to suggest death—but the really effective language is both fresh and vivid at the same time, and the search for it is an inexhaustible one.

Translated from the Bengali by Gopa Majumdar. Copyright © The Estate of Satyajit Ray 2005. This translation copyright © Penguin Books India 2005. Excerpted with permission from *Speaking of Films*, Penguin India 2005.

Indian Cinema

In July 1896, the Lumiere Brothers screened a number of films using their new invention, the first commercially viable cinema projector, at Watson's Hotel in Mumbai. This is regarded as the first screening of motion pictures in India. India's first indigenous feature film was Dadasaheb Phalke's *Raja Harishchandra*, released in 1913. Over the years, a number of awards have been instituted to give due recognition to achievements in the world of films and filmmaking. The Filmfare Awards is one of India's oldest national level film awards.

National Film Awards

The National Film Awards was started on the recommendation of the Film Enquiry Committee as an annual event in 1954. Initially, only three awards were instituted—the President's Gold Medal for the best feature film and the best documentary and the Prime Minister's Silver Medal for the best children's film. The medallions were later changed to Swarna Kamal (Golden Lotus) and Rajat Kamal (Silver Lotus). Cash prizes were later added. Separate awards for artists and film technicians were introduced in 1968.

Best Feature Films

Year	Film
2004	Page 3
2003	Shwaas
2002	Mondo Meyer Upakhyan
2001	Dweepa
2000	Shantam
1999	Vaanaprastham
1998	Samar
1997	Thai Saheba
1996	Lal Darja
1995	Kathapurushan
1994	Unishe April
1993	Charachar
1992	Bhagwat Geeta
1991	Agantuk
1990	Marupakkam
1989	Bagh Bahadur
1988	Piravi
1987	Halodhia Choraye Baodhan Khai
1986	Tabarana Kathe
1985	Chidambaram
1984	Damul
1983	Adi Shankaracharya
1982	Chokh
1981	Dakhal
1980	Akaler Sandhane
1979	Ekdin Pratidin
1978	Ganadevata
1977	Ghattashraddha
1976	Mrigayaa
1975	Chomana Dudi
1974	Chorus
1973	Nirmalayam
1972	Swayamvaram
1971	Simabaddha
1970	Samskskara
1969	Bhuvan Shome
1968	Goopy Gyne Bagha Byne
1967	Hatey Bazarey
1966	Teesri Kasam
1965	Chemmen
1964	Charulata
1963	Shehar Aur Sapna
1962	Dada Thakur
1961	Bhagini Nivedita
1960	Anuradha
1959	Apur Sansar
1958	Sagar Sangame
1957	Do Ankhen Barah Haath
1956	Kabuliwala
1955	Pather Panchali
1954	Mirza Ghalib
1953	Shyamchi Aai

Dada Saheb Phalke Award

The Dada Saheb Phalke Award was instituted in 1969, in honour of the late Shri Dada Saheb Phalke, in order to commemorate his contribution to the Indian film industry. The award is given to recognize an individual's lifetime contribution to Indian films. The award is decided by the Government of India and presented at the National Awards ceremony every year. The Dada Saheb Phalke Award consists of a cash prize of Rs 2 lakhs, a Swarna Kamal and a shawl.

Recipients of the Dada Saheb Phalke Award

Year	Recipient
1969	Devika Rani Roerich
1970	B.N. Sircar
1971	Prithviraj Kapoor
1972	Pankaj Mullick
1973	Sulochana (Ruby Myers)
1974	B.N. Reddi
1975	Dhiren Ganguly
1976	Kanan Devi
1977	Nitin Bose
1978	R.C. Boral
1979	Sohrab Modi
1980	P. Jairaj
1981	Naushad Ali

1982	L.V. Prasad
1983	Durga Khote
1984	Satyajit Ray
1985	V. Shantaram
1986	B. Nagi Reddy
1987	Raj Kapoor
1988	Ashok Kumar
1989	Lata Mangeshkar
1990	Akkineni Nageshwara Rao
1991	Balachandra Govind Pendharakar
1992	Dr. Bhupen Hazarika
1993	Majrooh Sultanpuri
1994	Dilip Kumar
1995	Dr. Rajkumar
1996	Shivaji Ganesan
1997	Kavi Pradeep
1998	B.R. Chopra
1999	Hrishikesh Mukherjee
2000	Asha Bhosle
2001	Yash Chopra
2002	Dev Anand
2003	Mrinal Sen
2004	Adoor Gopalkrishnan

Filmfare Awards

The Filmfare Awards were established to honour the best talents of the Hindi film industry and provide them with substantial encouragement. The winners of the awards are decided by the readers of the film magazine by polling their opinions.

The Metro Theatre in Mumbai hosted the first Filmfare Awards on 21 March 1954 with Hollywood actor Gregory Peck being the guest of honour. Only five awards were presented at the first ceremony—Best Film, Best Director, Best Male Performance, Best Female Performance and Best Music Director. Every award winner receives a trophy.

List of Filmfare Winners

Best Director (Popular Choice)

Year	Film	Director
1953	Do Bigha Zamin	Bimal Roy
1954	Parineeta	Bimal Roy
1955	Biraj Bahu	Bimal Roy
1956	Jhanak Jhanak Payal Baaje	V. Shantaram
1957	Mother India	Mehboob Khan
1958	Madhumati	Bimal Roy
1959	Sujata	Bimal Roy
1960	Parakh	Bimal Roy
1961	Kanoon	B.R. Chopra
1962	Sahib Bibi Aur Ghulam	Abrar Alvi
1963	Bandini	Bimal Roy
1964	Sangam	Raj Kapoor
1965	Waqt	Yash Chopra
1966	Guide	Vijay Anand
1967	Upkar	Manoj Kumar
1968	Ankhen	Ramanand Sagar
1969	Ittefaq	Yash Chopra
1970	Safar	Asit Sen
1971	Mera Naam Joker	Raj Kapoor
1972	Be-Imaan	Sohanlal Kanwar
1973	Daag	Yash Chopra
1974	Roti Kapada Aur Makaan	Manoj Kumar
1975	Deewaar	Yash Chopra
1976	Mausam	Gulzar
1977	Swami	Basu Chatterji

1978	Shatranj Ke Khilari	Satyajit Ray
1979	Junoon	Shyam Benegal
1980	Aakrosh	Govind Nihalani
1981	Umrao Jaan	Muzaffar Ali
1982	Prem Rog	Raj Kapoor
1983	Ardh Satya	Govind Nihalani
1984	Sparsh	Sai Paranjpye
1985	Ram Teri Ganga Maili	Raj Kapoor
1988	Qayamat Se Qayamat Tak	Mansoor Khan
1989	Parinda	Vidhu Vinod Chopra
1990	Ghayal	Rajkumar Santoshi
1991	Saudagar	Subhash Ghai
1992	Khuda Gawah	Mukul Anand
1993	Damini	Rajkumar Santoshi
1994	Hum Aapke Hain Koun..!	Sooraj Barjatya
1995	Dilwale Dulhania Le Jayenge	Aditya Chopra
1996	Bandit Queen	Shekhar Kapoor
1997	Border	J.P. Dutta
1998	Kuch Kuch Hota Hai	Karan Johar
1999	Hum Dil De Chuke Sanam	Sanjay Leela Bansali
2000	Kaho Naa Pyaar Hai	Rakesh Roshan
2001	Lagaan	Ashutosh Gowarikar
2002	Devdas	Sanjay Leela Bhansali
2003	Koi Mil Gaya	Rakesh Roshan
2004	Hum Tum	Kunal Kohli

Best Film (Popular Choice)

Year	Film
1953	Do Bigha Zamin
1954	Boot Polish
1955	Jagriti
1956	Jhanak Jhanak Payal Baaje
1957	Mother India
1958	Madhumati
1959	Sujata
1960	Mughal-E-Azam
1961	Jis Desh Men Ganga Behti Hai
1962	Sahib Bibi Aur Ghulam
1963	Bandini
1964	Dosti
1965	Himalay Ki God Mein
1966	Guide
1967	Upkar
1968	Brahmachari
1969	Aradhana
1970	Khilona
1971	Anand
1972	Be-Imaan
1973	Anuraag
1974	Rajnigandha
1975	Deewaar
1976	Mausam
1977	Bhumika
1978	Main Tulsi Tere Aangan Ki
1979	Junoon
1980	Khubsoorat
1981	Kalyug
1982	Shakti
1983	Ardh Satya
1984	Sparsh
1985	Ram Teri Ganga Maili
1988	Qayamat Se Qayamat Tak
1989	Maine Pyar Kiya
1990	Ghayal
1991	Lamhe
1992	Jo Jeeta Wohi Sikandar
1993	Hum Hain Rahi Pyar Ke
1994	Hum Appke Hain Koun..!
1995	Dilwale Dulhania Le Jayenge
1996	Raja Hindustani
1997	Dil To Pagal Hai
1998	Kuch Kuch Hota Hai
1999	Hum Dil De Chuke Sanam

2000	Kaho Naa Pyaar Hai	2003	Koi Mil Gaya
2001	Lagaan	2004	Veer-Zaara
2002	Devdas		

Best Actor (Popular Choice)

Year	Film	Actor
1953	Daag	Dilip Kumar
1954	Shri Chaitanya Mahaprabhu	Bharat Bhooshan
1955	Azaad	Dilip Kumar
1956	Devdas	Dilip Kumar
1957	Naya Daur	Dilip Kumar
1958	Kala Pani	Dev Anand
1959	Anari	Raj Kapoor
1960	Kohinoor	Dilip Kumar
1961	Jis Desh Men Ganga Behti Hai	Raj Kapoor
1962	Rakhi	Ashok Kumar
1963	Mujhe Jeene Do	Sunil Dutt
1964	Leader	Dilip Kumar
1965	Khandaan	Sunil Dutt
1966	Guide	Dev Anand
1967	Ram Aur Shyam	Dilip Kumar
1968	Brahmachari	Shammi Kapoor
1969	Ashirwad	Ashok Kumar
1970	Sacha Jhutha	Rajesh Khanna
1971	Anand	Rajesh Khanna
1972	Be-Imaan	Manoj Kumar
1973	Bobby	Rishi Kapoor
1974	Aavishkar	Rajesh Khanna
1975	Aandhi	Sanjeev Kumar
1976	Arjun Pandit	Sanjeev Kumar
1977	Amar Akbar Anthony	Amitabh Bachchan
1978	Don	Amitabh Bachchan
1979	Gol Maal	Amol Palekar
1980	Aakrosh	Naseeruddin Shah
1981	Chakra	Naseeruddin Shah
1982	Shakti	Dilip Kumar
1983	Masoom	Naseeruddin Shah
1984	Saaransh	Anupam Kher
1985	Saagar	Kamal Haasan
1988	Tezaab	Anil Kapoor
1989	Parinda	Jackie Shroff
1990	Ghayal	Sunny Deol
1991	Hum	Amitabh Bachchan
1992	Beta	Anil Kapoor
1993	Baazigar	Shah Rukh Khan
1994	Krantiveer	Nana Patekar
1995	Dilwale Dulhania Le Jayenge	Shah Rukh Khan
1996	Raja Hindustani	Aamir Khan
1997	Dil To Pagal Hai	Shah Rukh Khan

1998	Kuch Kuch Hota Hai	Shah Rukh Khan
1999	Vaastav	Sunjay Dutt
2000	Kaho Naa Pyar Hai	Hrithik Roshan
2001	Lagaan	Aamir Khan
2002	Devdas	Shah Rukh Khan
2003	Koi Mil Gaya	Hrithik Roshan
2004	Swades	Shah Rukh Khan

Best Actress (Popular Choice)

Year	Film	Actress
1953	Baiju Bawra	Meena Kumari
1954	Parineeta	Meena Kumari
1955	Biraj Bahu	Kamini Kaushal
1956	Seema	Nutan
1957	Mother India	Nargis
1958	Sadhna	Vyjayanthimala
1959	Sujata	Nutan
1960	Ghunghat	Bina Rai
1961	Gunga-Jumna	Vyjayanthimala
1962	Sahib Bibi Aur Ghulam	Meena Kumari
1963	Bandini	Nutan
1964	Sangam	Vyjayanthimala
1965	Kaajal	Meena Kumari
1966	Guide	Waheeda Rehman
1967	Milan	Nutan
1968	Neel Kamal	Waheeda Rehman
1969	Aradhana	Sharmila Tagore
1970	Khilona	Mumtaz
1971	Kati Patang	Asha Parekh
1972	Seeta Aur Geeta	Hema Malini
1973	Bobby	Dimple Kapadia
	Abhimaan	Jaya Bhaduri
1974	Kora Kaagaz	Jaya Bhaduri
1975	Julie	Lakshmi
1976	Tapasya	Raakhee
1977	Swami	Shabana Azmi
1978	Main Tulsi Tere Aangan Ki	Nutan
1979	Nauker	Jaya Bhaduri
1980	Khubsoorat	Rekha
1981	Chakra	Smita Patil
1982	Prem Rog	Padmini Kolhapure
1983	Arth	Shabana Azmi
1984	Bhavna	Shabana Azmi
1985	Saagar	Dimple Kapadia
1988	Khoon Bhari Maang	Rekha
1989	Chaalbaaz	Sridevi
1990	Dil	Madhuri Dixit
1991	Lamhe	Sridevi
1992	Beta	Madhuri Dixit
1993	Hum Hain Rahi Pyar Ke	Juhi Chawla

1994	Hum Aapke Hain Koun..!	Madhuri Dixit
1995	Dilwale Dulhania Le Jayenge	Kajol
1996	Raja Hindustani	Karisma Kapoor
1997	Dil To Pagal Hai	Madhuri Dixit
1998	Kuch Kuch Hota Hai	Kajol
1999	Hum Dil De Chuke Sanam	Aishwarya Rai
2000	Fiza	Karisma Kapoor
2001	Kabhie Khushi Kabhie Gham	Kajol
2002	Devdas	Aishwarya Rai
2003	Kal Ho Na Ho	Preity Zinta
2004	Hum Tum	Rani Mukherji

International Cinema

Today the Academy Awards, better known as the Oscars, are the most well known film industry awards in the world and is often considered to be the pinnacle of achievement in the world of films. However, the road to many an Oscar has started with a screening at one of the famous film festivals of the world, such as the festivals held at Cannes, Berlin, Karlovy Vary or Venice. While these festivals enjoy the position of eminence in the pantheon of international film festivals, other well known film festivals are held at London, Chicago and New York.

Oscars

The Academy of Motion Pictures Arts and Sciences gives the Academy Awards. The first awards were handed out on 16 May 1929 at a ceremony during a banquet held in the Blossom Room of the Hollywood Roosevelt Hotel. The awardees were given what is officially named the Academy Award of Merit, the statuette is better known by a nickname, Oscar. The first Oscar went to Emil Jannings, who was named best actor for his roles in *The Last Command* and *The Way of All Flesh*. In 1929, 15 Oscars were awarded. All voting for the Academy Awards is conducted by secret ballot and tabulated by the international auditing firm of PricewaterhouseCoopers.

Oscar Winners

Best Actor

Year	Actor	Film
1927/28	Emil Jannings	The Last Command, The Way of All Flesh
1927/28	Charles Chaplin	The Circus (Special Award)
1928/29	Warner Baxter	In Old Arizona
1929/30	George Arliss	Disraeli
1930/31	Lionel Barrymore	A Free Soul
1931/32	Wallace Beery	The Champ
	Fredric March	Dr. Jekyll and Mr. Hyde
1932/33	Charles Laughton	The Private Life of Henry VIII
1934	Clark Gable	It Happened One Night
1935	Victor McLaglen	The Informer
1936	Paul Muni	The Story of Louis Pasteur
1937	Spencer Tracy	Captains Courageous

1938	Spencer Tracy	Boys Town
1939	Robert Donat	Goodbye, Mr. Chips
1940	James Stewart	The Philadelphia Story
1941	Gary Cooper	Sergeant York
1942	James Cagney	Yankee Doodle Dandy
1943	Paul Lukas	Watch on the Rhine
1944	Bing Crosby	Going My Way
1945	Ray Milland	The Lost Weekend
1946	Fredric March	The Best Years of Our Lives
1947	Ronald Colman	A Double Life
1948	Laurence Olivier	Hamlet
1949	Broderick Crawford	All the King's Men
1950	José Ferrer	Cyrano de Bergerac
1951	Humphrey Bogart	The African Queen
1952	Gary Cooper	High Noon
1953	William Holden	Stalag 17
1954	Marlon Brando	On the Waterfront
1955	Ernest Borgnine	Marty
1956	Yul Brynner	The King and I
1957	Alec Guinness	The Bridge on the River Kwai
1958	David Niven	Separate Tables
1959	Charlton Heston	Ben-Hur
1960	Burt Lancaster	Elmer Gantry
1961	Maximilian Schell	Judgment at Nuremberg
1962	Gregory Peck	To Kill a Mockingbird
1963	Sidney Poitier	Lilies of the Field
1964	Rex Harrison	My Fair Lady
1965	Lee Marvin	Cat Ballou
1966	Paul Scofield	A Man for All Seasons
1967	Rod Steiger	In the Heat of the Night
1968	Cliff Robertson	Charly
1969	John Wayne	True Grit
1970	George C. Scott	Patton
1971	Gene Hackman	The French Connection
1972	Marlon Brando	The Godfather
1973	Jack Lemmon	Save the Tiger
1974	Art Carney	Harry and Tonto
1975	Jack Nicholson	One Flew over the Cuckoo's Nest
1976	Peter Finch	Network
1977	Richard Dreyfuss	The Goodbye Girl
1978	Jon Voight	Coming Home
1979	Dustin Hoffman	Kramer vs. Kramer
1980	Robert De Niro	Raging Bull
1981	Henry Fonda	On Golden Pond
1982	Ben Kingsley	Gandhi
1983	Robert Duvall	Tender Mercies
1984	F. Murray Abraham	Amadeus
1985	William Hurt	Kiss of the Spider Woman
1986	Paul Newman	The Color of Money
1987	Michael Douglas	Wall Street
1988	Dustin Hoffman	Rain Man

1989	Daniel Day-Lewis	My Left Foot
1990	Jeremy Irons	Reversal of Fortune
1991	Anthony Hopkins	The Silence of the Lambs
1992	Al Pacino	Scent of a Woman
1993	Tom Hanks	Philadelphia
1994	Tom Hanks	Forrest Gump
1995	Nicolas Cage	Leaving Las Vegas
1996	Geoffrey Rush	Shine
1997	Jack Nicholson	As Good As It Gets
1998	Roberto Benigni	Life Is Beautiful
1999	Kevin Spacey	American Beauty
2000	Russell Crowe	Gladiator
2001	Denzel Washington	Training Day
2002	Adrien Brody	The Pianist
2003	Sean Penn	Mystic River
2004	Jamie Foxx	Ray

Best Actress

Year	Actor	Film
1927/28	Janet Gaynor	Sunrise, 7th Heaven, Street Angel
1928/29	Mary Pickford	Coquette
1929/30	Norma Shearer	The Divorcee
1930/31	Marie Dressler	Min and Bill
1931/32	Helen Hayes	The Sin of Madelon Claudet
1932/33	Katharine Hepburn	Morning Glory
1934	Claudette Colbert	It Happened One Night
1935	Bette Davis	Dangerous
1936	Luise Rainer	The Great Ziegfeld
1937	Luise Rainer	The Good Earth
1938	Bette Davis	Jezebel
1939	Vivien Leigh	Gone with the Wind
1940	Ginger Rogers	Kitty Foyle
1941	Joan Fontaine	Suspicion
1942	Greer Garson	Mrs. Miniver
1943	Jennifer Jones	The Song of Bernadette
1944	Ingrid Bergman	Gaslight
1945	Joan Crawford	Mildred Pierce
1946	Olivia de Havilland	To Each His Own
1947	Loretta Young	The Farmer's Daughter
1948	Jane Wyman	Johnny Belinda
1949	Olivia de Havilland	The Heiress
1950	Judy Holliday	Born Yesterday
1951	Vivien Leigh	A Streetcar Named Desire
1952	Shirley Booth	Come Back, Little Sheba
1953	Audrey Hepburn	Roman Holiday
1954	Grace Kelly	The Country Girl
1955	Anna Magnani	The Rose Tattoo
1956	Ingrid Bergman	Anastasia
1957	Joanne Woodward	The Three Faces of Eve
1958	Susan Hayward	I Want To Live!

1959	Simone Signoret	Room at the Top
1960	Elizabeth Taylor	Butterfield 8
1961	Sophia Loren	Two Women
1962	Anne Bancroft	The Miracle Worker
1963	Patricia Neal	Hud
1964	Julie Andrews	Mary Poppins
1965	Julie Christie	Darling
1966	Elizabeth Taylor	Who's Afraid of Virginia Woolf?
1967	Katharine Hepburn	Guess Who's Coming to Dinner
1968	Katharine Hepburn	The Lion in Winter
	Barbra Streisand	Funny Girl
1969	Maggie Smith	The Prime of Miss Jean Brodie
1970	Glenda Jackson	Women in Love
1971	Jane Fonda	Klute
1972	Liza Minnelli	Cabaret
1973	Glenda Jackson	A Touch of Class
1974	Ellen Burstyn	Alice Doesn't Live Here Anymore
1975	Louise Fletcher	One Flew over the Cuckoo's Nest
1976	Faye Dunaway	Network
1977	Diane Keaton	Annie Hall
1978	Jane Fonda	Coming Home
1979	Sally Field	Norma Rae
1980	Sissy Spacek	Coal Miner's Daughter
1981	Katharine Hepburn	On Golden Pond
1982	Meryl Streep	Sophie's Choice
1983	Shirley MacLaine	Terms of Endearment
1984	Sally Field	Places in the Heart
1985	Geraldine Page	The Trip to Bountiful
1986	Marlee Matlin	Children of a Lesser God
1987	Cher	Moonstruck
1988	Jodie Foster	The Accused
1989	Jessica Tandy	Driving Miss Daisy
1990	Kathy Bates	Misery
1991	Jodie Foster	The Silence of the Lambs
1992	Emma Thompson	Howards End
1993	Holly Hunter	The Piano
1994	Jessica Lange	Blue Sky
1995	Susan Sarandon	Dead Man Walking
1996	Frances McDormand	Fargo
1997	Helen Hunt	As Good As It Gets
1998	Gwyneth Paltrow	Shakespeare in Love
1999	Hilary Swank	Boys Don't Cry
2000	Julia Roberts	Erin Brockovich
2001	Halle Berry	Monster's Ball
2002	Nicole Kidman	The Hours
2003	Charlize Theron	Monster
2004	Hilary Swank	Million Dollar Baby

Best Direction

Year	Director	Film
1927/28	Lewis Milestone	Two Arabian Knights (Comedy-Picture category)
1927/28	Frank Borzage	7th Heaven (Dramatic-Picture category)
1927/28	Charles Chaplin	The Circus (Honorary award)
1928/29	Frank Lloyd	The Divine Lady
1929/30	Lewis Milestone	All Quiet on the Western Front
1930/31	Norman Taurog	Skippy
1931/32	Frank Borzage	Bad Girl
1932/33	Frank Lloyd	Cavalcade
1934	Frank Capra	It Happened One Night
1935	John Ford	The Informer
1936	Frank Capra	Mr. Deeds Goes to Town
1937	Leo McCarey	The Awful Truth
1938	Frank Capra	You Can't Take It with You
1939	Victor Fleming	Gone with the Wind
1940	John Ford	The Grapes of Wrath
1941	John Ford	How Green Was My Valley
1942	William Wyler	Mrs. Miniver
1943	Michael Curtiz	Casablanca
1944	Leo McCarey	Going My Way
1945	Billy Wilder	The Lost Weekend
1946	William Wyler	The Best Years of Our Lives
1947	Elia Kazan	Gentleman's Agreement
1948	John Huston	The Treasure of the Sierra Madre
1949	Joseph L. Mankiewicz	A Letter to Three Wives
1950	Joseph L. Mankiewicz	All about Eve
1951	George Stevens	A Place in the Sun
1952	John Ford	The Quiet Man
1953	Fred Zinnemann	From Here to Eternity
1954	Elia Kazan	On the Waterfront
1955	Delbert Mann	Marty
1956	George Stevens	Giant
1957	David Lean	The Bridge on the River Kwai
1958	Vincente Minnelli	Gigi
1959	William Wyler	Ben-Hur
1960	Billy Wilder	The Apartment
1961	Robert Wise and Jerome Robbins	West Side Story
1962	David Lean	Lawrence of Arabia
1963	Tony Richardson	Tom Jones
1964	George Cukor	My Fair Lady
1965	Robert Wise	The Sound of Music
1966	Fred Zinnemann	A Man for All Seasons
1967	Mike Nichols	The Graduate
1968	Carol Reed	Oliver!
1969	John Schlesinger	Midnight Cowboy
1970	Franklin J. Schaffner	Patton
1971	William Friedkin	The French Connection

1972	Bob Fosse	Cabaret
1973	George Roy Hill	The Sting
1974	Francis Ford Coppola	The Godfather Part II
1975	Milos Forman	One Flew over the Cuckoo's Nest
1976	John G. Avildsen	Rocky
1977	Woody Allen	Annie Hall
1978	Michael Cimino	The Deer Hunter
1979	Robert Benton	Kramer vs. Kramer
1980	Robert Redford	Ordinary People
1981	Warren Beatty	Reds
1982	Richard Attenborough	Gandhi
1983	James L. Brooks	Terms of Endearment
1984	Milos Forman	Amadeus
1985	Sydney Pollack	Out of Africa
1986	Oliver Stone	Platoon
1987	Bernardo Bertolucci	The Last Emperor
1988	Barry Levinson	Rain Man
1989	Oliver Stone	Born on the Fourth of July
1990	Kevin Costner	Dances With Wolves
1991	Jonathan Demme	The Silence of the Lambs
1992	Clint Eastwood	Unforgiven
1993	Steven Spielberg	Schindler's List
1994	Robert Zemeckis	Forrest Gump
1995	Mel Gibson	Braveheart
1996	Anthony Minghella	The English Patient
1997	James Cameron	Titanic
1998	Steven Spielberg	Saving Private Ryan
1999	Sam Mendes	American Beauty
2000	Steven Soderbergh	Traffic
2001	Ron Howard	A Beautiful Mind
2002	Roman Polanski	The Pianist
2003	Peter Jackson	The Lord of the Rings: The Return of the King
2004	Clint Eastwood	Million Dollar Baby

Best Picture

Year	Film	Producer
1927/28	Wings	Paramount Famous Lasky
1928/29	The Broadway Melody	Metro-Goldwyn-Mayer
1929/30	All Quiet on the Western Front	Universal
1930/31	Cimarron	RKO Radio
1931/32	Grand Hotel	Metro-Goldwyn-Mayer
1932/33	Cavalcade	Fox
1934	It Happened One Night	Columbia
1935	Mutiny on the Bounty	Metro-Goldwyn-Mayer
1936	The Great Ziegfeld	Metro-Goldwyn-Mayer
1937	The Life of Emile Zola	Warner Bros.
1938	You Can't Take It with You	Columbia
1939	Gone with the Wind	Selznick International Pictures
1940	Rebecca	Selznick International Pictures

1941	How Green Was My Valley	20th Century-Fox
1942	Mrs. Miniver	Metro-Goldwyn-Mayer
1943	Casablanca	Warner Bros.
1944	Going My Way	Paramount
1945	The Lost Weekend	Paramount
1946	The Best Years of Our Lives	Samuel Goldwyn Productions
1947	Gentleman's Agreement	20th Century-Fox
1948	Hamlet	J. Arthur Rank-Two Cities Films
1949	All the King's Men	Robert Rossen Productions
1950	All about Eve	20th Century-Fox
1951	An American in Paris	Arthur Freed
1952	The Greatest Show on Earth	Cecil B. DeMille
1953	From Here to Eternity	Buddy Adler
1954	On the Waterfront	Sam Spiegel
1955	Marty	Harold Hecht
1956	Around the World in 80 Days	Michael Todd
1957	The Bridge on the River Kwai	Sam Spiegel
1958	Gigi	Arthur Freed
1959	Ben-Hur	Sam Zimbalist
1960	The Apartment	Billy Wilder
1961	West Side Story	Robert Wise
1962	Lawrence of Arabia	Sam Spiegel
1963	Tom Jones	Tony Richardson
1964	My Fair Lady	Jack L. Warner
1965	The Sound of Music	Robert Wise
1966	A Man for All Seasons	Fred Zinnemann
1967	In the Heat of the Night	Walter Mirisch
1968	Oliver!	John Woolf
1969	Midnight Cowboy	Jerome Hellman
1970	Patton	Frank McCarthy
1971	The French Connection	Philip D'Antoni
1972	The Godfather	Albert S. Ruddy
1973	The Sting	Tony Bill, Michael Phillips and Julia Phillips
1974	The Godfather Part II	Francis Ford Coppola
1975	One Flew over the Cuckoo's Nest	Saul Zaentz and Michael Douglas
1976	Rocky	Irwin Winkler and Robert Chartoff
1977	Annie Hall	Charles H. Joffe
1978	The Deer Hunter	Barry Spikings, Michael Deeley, Michael Cimino and John Peverall
1979	Kramer vs. Kramer	Stanley R. Jaffe
1980	Ordinary People	Ronald L. Schwary
1981	Chariots of Fire	David Puttnam
1982	Gandhi	Richard Attenborough
1983	Terms of Endearment	James L. Brooks
1984	Amadeus	Saul Zaentz
1985	Out of Africa	Sydney Pollack
1986	Platoon	Arnold Kopelson
1987	The Last Emperor	Jeremy Thomas
1988	Rain Man	Mark Johnson

1989	Driving Miss Daisy	Richard D. Zanuck and Lili Fini Zanuck
1990	Dances With Wolves	Jim Wilson and Kevin Costner
1991	The Silence of the Lambs	Edward Saxon, Kenneth Utt and Ron Bozman
1992	Unforgiven	Clint Eastwood
1993	Schindler's List	Steven Spielberg, Gerald R. Molen and Branko Lustig
1994	Forrest Gump	Wendy Finerman, Steve Tisch and Steve Starkey
1995	Braveheart	Mel Gibson, Alan Ladd, Jr. and Bruce Davey
1996	The English Patient	Saul Zaentz
1997	Titanic	James Cameron and Jon Landau
1998	Shakespeare in Love	David Parfitt, Donna Gigliotti, Harvey Weinstein, Edward Zwick and Marc Norman
1999	American Beauty	Bruce Cohen and Dan Jinks
2000	Gladiator	Douglas Wick, David Franzoni and Branko Lustig
2001	A Beautiful Mind	Brian Grazer and Ron Howard
2002	Chicago	Martin Richards
2003	The Lord of the Rings: The Return of the King	Barrie M. Osborne, Peter Jackson and Fran Walsh
2004	Million Dollar Baby	Clint Eastwood, Albert S. Ruddy and Tom Rosenberg

Berlin International Film Festival

The first Berlin International Film Festival opened on 6 June 1951. The Berlin Festival appointed an international jury for the first time in 1956 that awarded the 'Golden Bear' and the 'Silver Bear' awards.

Notable Indian Winners

Year	Category	Film	Director
1957	Silver Bear for background music (The music director was Ravi Shankar)	Kabuliwala	Tapan Sinha
1958	Silver Bear (Special Prize)	Do Ankhen Barah Haath	V. Shantaram
1964	Silver Bear Best Director	Mahanagar	Satyajit Ray
1965	Silver Bear Best Director	Charulata	Satyajit Ray
1967	Golden Bear Short Film	Through the Eyes of a Painter	M.F. Husain
1973	Golden Bear	Ashani Sanket	Satyajit Ray
1981	Silver Bear Special Jury	Akaler Sandhane	Mrinal Sen

Karlovy Vary International Film Festival

The Karlovy Vary International Film Festival is one of the oldest film festivals of all times (the first festival was held in 1946).

Notable Indian Winners

1957: Grand Prix–Crystal Globe—*Jagte Raho*—Directed by Sombhu Mitra
1958: Best Actress Award—Nargis (*Mother India*)
1972: Best Actor Award—Ranjit Mullick (*Interview*)
1978: Special Jury Prize—*Oka Oori Katha*—Directed by Mrinal Sen
1984: Best Actor Award—Om Puri (*Ardh Satya*)

Venice Film Festival

The Venice Film Festival is the oldest international film festival—it was organized for the first time in 1932.

Indian Winners

Lifetime Achievement Award: Satyajit Ray (1982).
Golden Lion: *Aparajito* by Satyajit Ray (1957); *Monsoon Wedding* by Mira Nair (2001).
Special Director's Award: Buddhadeb Dasgupta (*Uttara*, 2000).

Cannes Film Festival

The Cannes Film Festival started on 20 September 1946. It quickly became a major meeting point for buyers and sellers from all over the world.

Notable Indian Winners

Year	Category	Film	Director
1946	Grand Prix du Festival International du Film	Neecha Nagar	Chetan Anand
1954	Prix International	Do Bigha Zamin	Bimal Roy
1955	Mention	Boot Polish	Prakash Arora
1956	Prix du document humain	Pather Panchali	Satyajit Ray
1957	Mention exceptionnelle	Gotoma the Buddha	Rajbans Khanna
1983	Prix du Jury	Kharij	Mrinal Sen
1988	Prix de la Caméra d'Or	Salaam Bombay!	Mira Nair
1989	Mention d'honneur-Caméra d'Or	Piravi	Shaji N. Karun
1999	Prix de la Caméra d'Or	Marana Simhasanam	Murli Nair
2002	Prix du Jury-court métrage (Ex-aequo)	A Very Very Silent Film	Manish Jha (Short Film)

Bollywood: Top Grossing Films of All Time

1950s

Rank	Film Name	Inflation Adjusted All India Net
1.	Mother India	Rs 1,08,75,95,050
2.	Naya Daur	Rs 64,08,16,340
3.	Awaara	Rs 63,64,86,434
4.	Do Bigha Zameen	Rs 57,84,21,039
5.	Pyaasa	Rs 57,67,34,709

1960s

Rank	Film Name	Inflation Adjusted All India Net
1.	Mughal E Azam	Rs 89,33,06,421
2.	Aradhana	Rs 86,72,38,106

3.	Sangam	Rs 75,48,07,653
4.	Ganga Jamuna	Rs 68,26,08,642
5.	Do Raaste	Rs 67,28,57,146

1970s

Rank	Film Name	Inflation Adjusted All India Net
1.	Sholay	Rs 1,96,35,00,000
2.	Muqaddar Ka Sikandar	Rs 87,22,22,239
3.	Bobby	Rs 77,94,32,590
4.	Amar Akbar Anthony	Rs 77,27,97,929
5.	Dharam Veer	Rs 69,14,50,780

1980s

Rank	Film Name	Inflation Adjusted All India Net
1.	Coolie	Rs 63,18,88,533
2.	Naseeb	Rs 58,80,14,974
3.	Qurbani	Rs 53,22,03,366
4.	Shaan	Rs 51,88,98,279
5.	Laawaris	Rs 49,98,12,735

1990s

Rank	Film Name	Inflation Adjusted All India Net
1.	Hum Aapke Hai Kaun	Rs 1,13,22,11,563
2.	Dilwale Dulhaniya Le Jayenge	Rs 85,51,19,824
3.	Raja Hindustani	Rs 70,65,00,020
4.	Kuch Kuch Hota Hai	Rs 55,00,82,443
5.	Karan Arjun	Rs 54,72,76,680

2004

Rank	Film Name	Inflation Adjusted All India Net
1.	Veer Zaara	Rs 39,70,48,552
2.	Main Hoon Na	Rs 34,46,84,692
3.	Dhoom	Rs 30,43,94,900
4.	Lakshya	Rs 28,75,52,997
5.	Mujhse Shaadi Karogi	Rs. 28,10,78,368

Note: All figures are subject to change with time.

Hollywood: All Time Top Grossing Films

Rank	Title	Worldwide Box Office
1.	Titanic (1997)	$1,835,300,000
2.	The Lord of the Rings: The Return of the King (2003)	$1,129,219,252
3.	Harry Potter and the Sorcerer's Stone (2001)	$968,600,000
4.	Star Wars: Episode I—The Phantom Menace (1999)	$922,379,000
5.	The Lord of the Rings: The Two Towers (2002)	$921,600,000
6.	Jurassic Park (1993)	$919,700,000
7.	Shrek 2 (2004)	$880,871,036

8.	Harry Potter and the Chamber of Secrets (2002)	$866,300,000
9.	Finding Nemo (2003)	$865,000,000
10.	The Lord of the Rings: The Fellowship of the Ring (2001)	$860,700,000

2004

Rank	Title	Total Gross
1.	The Lord of the Rings: The Return of the King	$741,452,679
2.	Harry Potter and the Azkaban	$540,263,485
3.	Shrek 2	$479,439,411
4.	Spider-Man 2	$410,180,516
5.	The Incredibles	$370,027,373
6.	Troy	$364,031,596

Note: All figures are approximate and subject to change with time.

On Printing and Books

The invention of printing is recognized as one of the most important technical advances in history. A German crafts-man named Johann Gutenberg is widely credited with this feat when he origi-nated a method of printing from mov-able type in the 1450s. The first book that he printed is now called the Gutenberg Bible, or the Forty-two-line Bible, or the Mazarin Bible. However, it was William Caxton who published the first book in English, *The Recuyell of the Historyes of Troye* in 1474-75. In spite of the arrival of new, more high-tech means, printing remains the most widely used medium for the storage and distribution of information.

Jnanpith Award

The Jnanpith Award is regarded as the highest literary award in India. It is awarded for the best creative literary writing by an Indian, in one of the lan-guages included in the eighth schedule of the Indian Constitution. The award carries a bronze replica of Vagdevi, a citation and a cash prize of Rs 5 lakh. The Award was the brainchild of Rama Jain, and was instituted on 22 May 1961, though the first award was given in 1965. The award is given by an or-ganization called 'Bharatiya Jnanpith', of which Rama Jain was the first presi-dent.

Jnanpith Laureates	Year
G. Shankara Kurup for his poems *Odakkuzhal* in Malayalam	1965
Tarashankar Bandopadhyaya for the novel *Ganadevta* in Bengali	1966
Dr K.V. Puttappa for *Sri Ramayana Darshanam* in Kannada	1967
Uma Shankar Joshi for *Nishitha* in Gujarati	1967
Sumitra Nandan Pant for *Chidambara* in Hindi	1968
Firaq Gorakpuri for *Gul-e-Naghma* in Urdu	1969
Vishwanath Satyanarayan for *Ramayana Kalpavrikshamu* in Telugu	1970
Bishnu Dey for *Smriti Satta Bhavishyat* in Bengali	1971
Ramdhari Singh Dinkar for *Urvashi* in Hindi	1972
Dattatreya Ramachandran Bendre for *Nakutanti* in Kannada	1973
Gopinath Mohanty for *Mattimatal* in Oriya	1973
Vishnu Sakaram Khandekar for *Yayati* in Marathi	1974

P.V. Akilandam for his novel *Chittirappavai* in Tamil	1975
Asha Purna Devi for *Pratham Pratisruti*, in Bengali	1976
K. Shivaram Karanth for *Mukajjiya Kanasugalu* in Kannada	1977
S.H.V. Ajneya for his novel *Kitni Navon men Kitni Bar* in Hindi	1978
Birendra Kumar Bhattacharya for his novel *Mrityunjay* in Assamese	1979
S.K. Pottekkatt for his novel *Oru Desattinte Katha* in Malayalam	1980
Amrita Pritam for her literary collection *Kagaz te Canvas* in Punjabi	1981
Mahadevi Varma (Hindi)	1982
Masti Venkatesh Ayengar (Kannada)	1983
Takazhi Sivashankar Pillai (Malayalam)	1984
Pannalal Patel (Gujarati)	1985
Sachidanand Rout Roy (Oriya)	1986
Vishnu Vaman Shirwadkar Kusumagraj (Marathi)	1987
Dr C. Narayanan Reddy (Telugu)	1988
Qurratulain Hyder (Urdu)	1989
V.K. Gokak (Kannada)	1990
Subhash Mukhopadhyay (Bengali)	1991
Naresh Mehta (Hindi)	1992
Sitakant Mahapatra (Oriya)	1993
UR Anantha Murthy (Kannada)	1994
M.T. Vasudevan Nair (Malayalam)	1995
Mahesweta Devi (Bengali)	1996
Ali Sardar Jafri (Urdu)	1997
Girish Karnad (Kannada)	1998
Nirmal Verma (Hindi)	1999
Gurdial Singh (Punjabi)	1999
Dr Indira Goswami (Assamese)	2000
Rajendra Keshavlal Shah (Gujarati)	2001
D. Jayakanthan (Tamil)	2002

Note: From 1982, the award was given for overall contribution to literature.
[The award for 2002 was awarded in 2005; in 2006 the winner for 2003 would be announced]

The Sahitya Akademi Award

The Sahitya Akademi was formally launched by the Government of India on 12 March 1954 and later registered as a society on 7 January 1956. It was instituted in order to coordinate and encourage literary activities in all Indian languages, thereby contributing to the cultural unity of the country. According to the Government of India Resolution, the Akademi is a national organization set up in order to work for the development of Indian letters, thereby setting high literary standards. Since 1954, the Sahitya Akademi awards are given to books of outstanding literary merit published in any of the major Indian languages, as recognized by the Akademi. The award comprises a monetary component of Rs 40,000 along with a plaque. The Akademi gives 22 awards to literary works in the languages recognized by it. It also gives an equal number of awards to literary translations from and into the languages of India. All these awards are given after a year-long process of discussion, scrutiny and selection. The Akademi intends to awards literary works that are a reflection of current tastes, and also contribute to the establishment of a distinct Indian sensibility.

The languages that the Akademi recognizes are: Assamese, Bengali, Dogri, English, Gujarati, Hindi, Kannada, Kashmiri, Konkani, Maithili, Malayalam, Manipuri, Marathi, Nepali, Oriya, Punjabi, Rajasthani, Sanskrit, Sindhi, Tamil, Telugu and Urdu.

The Sahitya Akademi awards for 2004 are as follows:

Language	Book	Author
Assamese	Manuh Anukule (Poetry)	Hirendra Nath Dutta
Bengali	Baul Fakir Katha (Essay)	Sudhir Chakraborty
Dogri	Cheten Di Chitkabri (Essays)	Shiv Nath
English	The Mammaries of the Welfare State (Novel)	Upamanyu Chatterjee
Gujarati	Saundaryani Nadi Narmada (Travelogue)	Amritlal Vegad
Hindi	Dushchakra Mein Srista (Poetry)	Viren Dangwal
Kannada	Baduku (Novel)	Geetha Nagabhushana
Kashmiri	Sada Te Samandar (Poetry)	Gh. Nabi Firaq
Konkani	Athang (Short Stories)	Jayanti Naik
Maithili	Shakuntala (Epic)	Niraja Renu (Khamakhya Devi)
Malayalam	Zachariyayute Kathakal (Short Stories)	Paul Zachariah
Manipuri	Lanthengnariba Lanmee (Poetry)	Birendrajit Naorem
Nepali	Shanti Shandeha (Poetry)	Jos Yonjan 'Pyasi'
Oriya	Bharatiya Sanskruti O Bhagwadgita (Essays)	Prafulla Kumar Mohanty
Punjabi	Kavita Di Bhumika (Criticism)	Sutinder Singh Noor
Rajasthani	Samhi Khulto Marag (Novel)	Nand Bhardwaj
Sanskrit	Âkhyanavallari (Fiction)	Kala Nath Shastri
Sindhi	Kavita Khan Kavita Tain (Criticism)	Satish Rohra
Tamil	Vanakkam Valluva (Poetry)	Tamilanban
Telugu	Kalarekhalu (Novel)	Naveen
Urdu	Shikasta Buton Ke Darmiyan (Short Stories)	Salam Bin Razzak

The Booker Prize

The Booker Prize is one of the most prestigious awards in the world of literature. The award was set up in 1968 when publisher Tom Maschler, inspired by the French literary award Prix Goncourt, approached the Booker Brothers (who had a highly successful 'Authors' Division' publishing a lot of celebrated writers) and persuaded them to establish a literary prize. This resulted in the establishment of the Booker Prize.

The Booker Prize is awarded to the best full-length novel of the year, decided by a panel of judges. Only a novel written by a citizen of the Commonwealth or the Republic of Ireland is eligible for the award. The book must be a unified and substantial piece of work; neither a novella nor a book of short stories is eligible. Further, an English translation of a book written originally in another language is not eligible; neither is a self-published book. A book submitted on behalf of an author who was deceased at the date of publication is also not considered for selection. The award is sponsored by Man Group plc; hence it is called 'Man Booker Prize for Fiction'. The winner of the Booker Prize receives £ 50,000.

List of Winners

Year	Author	Country	Book
1969	P.H. Newby	United Kingdom	Something to Answer For
1970	Bernice Rubens	United Kingdom	The Elected Member 1971
	V.S. Naipaul	United Kingdom	In a Free State
1972	John Berger	United Kingdom	G
1973	J.G. Farrell	United Kingdom	The Siege of Krishnapur
1974	Stanley Middleton	United Kingdom	Holiday
	Nadine Gordimer	South Africa	The Conservationist
1975	Ruth Prawer Jhabvala	United Kingdom	Heat and Dust
1976	David Storey	United Kingdom	Saville Saville
1977	Paul Scott	United Kingdom	Staying On
1978	Iris Murdoch	United Kingdom	The Sea, The Sea
1979	Penelope Fitzgerald	United Kingdom	Offshore
1980	William Golding	United Kingdom	Rites of Passage
1981	Salman Rushdie	United Kingdom	Midnight's Children
1982	Thomas Keneally	Australia	Schindler's Ark
1983	J.M. Coetzee	South Africa	Life and Times of Michael K
1984	Anita Brookner	United Kingdom	Hotel du Lac
1985	Keri Hulme	New Zealand	The Bone People
1986	Kingsley Amis	United Kingdom	The Old Devils
1987	Penelope Lively	United Kingdom	Moon Tiger
1988	Peter Carey	Australia	Oscar and Lucinda
1989	Kazuo Ishiguro	United Kingdom	The Remains of the Day
1990	A.S. Byatt	United Kingdom	Possession
1991	Ben Okri	United Kingdom	The Famished Road
1992	Michael Ondaatje	Canada	The English Patient
	Barry Unsworth	United Kingdom	Sacred Hunger
1993	Roddy Doyle	Ireland	Paddy Clarke Ha Ha Ha
1994	James Kelman	United Kingdom	How Late It Was, How Late
1995	Pat Barker	United Kingdom	The Ghost Road
1996	Graham Swift	United Kingdom	Last Orders
1997	Arundhati Roy	India	The God of Small Things
1998	Ian McEwan	United Kingdom	Amsterdam
1999	J.M. Coetzee	South Africa	Disgrace
2000	Margaret Atwood	Canada	The Blind Assassin
2001	Peter Carey	Australia	True History of the Kelly Gang
2002	Yann Martel	Canada	Life of Pi
2003	DBC Pierre	Australia	Vernon God Little
2004	Alan Holinghurst	United Kingdom	The Line of Beauty
2005	John Banville	Ireland	The Sea

Man Booker International Prize

Albanian novelist Ismail Kadaré became the first ever winner of the Man Booker International Prize on 2 June 2005. The Man Booker International Prize is unique in the world of literature in that it can be won by an author of any nationality, provided that his or her work is available in the English language. It will be awarded every second year.

Commonwealth Writers Prize

In 1987 the Commonwealth Writers Prize was established by the Commonwealth Foundation to encourage and reward the rise of new Commonwealth fiction. The prize is administered by Cumberland Lodge (at the invitation of the Commonwealth Foundation) in association with Booktrust. The Commonwealth Writers Prize amounts to £10,000, and is financed by the Commonwealth Foundation, an inter-governmental organization funded by the governments of the Commonwealth.

In order to be eligible, the author must be a citizen of one of the member countries of the Commonwealth. Any work of fiction written in prose (i.e. a short story collection or a novel) is eligible for the award, but drama and poetry are not. The work must be in English. Further, the author must be alive on the closing date for entries. The award ceremony is held in a different Commonwealth country every year.

Winners in the Best Book Category

Year	Author	Country	Book
1987	Olive Senior	Canada	Summer Lightning
1988	Festus Iyayi	Nigeria	Heroes
1989	Janet Frame	New Zealand	The Carpathians
1990	Mordechai Richler	Canada	Solomon Gursky Was Here
1991	David Malouf	Australia	The Great World
1992	Rohinton Mistry	Canada	Such a Long Journey
1993	Alex Miller	Australia	The Ancestor Game
1994	Vikram Seth	India	A Suitable Boy
1995	Louis de Bernieres	United Kingdom	Captain Corelli's Mandolin
1996	Rohinton Mistry	Canada	A Fine Balance
1997	Earl Lovelace	Trinidad and Tobago	Salt
1998	Peter Carey	Australia	Jack Maggs
1999	Murray Bail	Australia	Eucalyptus
2000	J.M. Coetzee	South Africa	Disgrace
2001	Peter Carey	Australia	True History of the Kelly Gang
2002	Richard Flanagan	Australia	Gould's Book of Fish
2003	Austin Clarke	Canada	The Polished Hoe
2004	Caryl Phillips	United Kingdom	A Distant Shore
2005	Andrea Levy	United Kingdom	Small Island

Bestsellers of 2005

This is a representative list of the significant bestselling books of 2005. Please note that this is an alphabetical list and not a ranking.

Fiction

Name	Author
1. The Da Vinci Code	Dan Brown
2. Eldest: Inheritance, Book II	Christopher Paolini
3. Harry Potter and the Half-Blood Prince	J.K. Rowling
4. The Historian	Elizabeth Kostova
5. Lipstick Jungle	Candace Bushnell
6. Point Blank	Catherine Coulter
7. Polar Shift	Clive Cussler and Paul Kemprecos

8. Straken	Terry Brooks
9. Thud!	Terry Pratchett
10. Widow of the South	Robert Hicks

Non-Fiction

Name	Author
1. Big Russ and Me	Tim Russert
2. Blink: The Power of Thinking Without Thinking	Malcolm Gladwell
3. Freakonomics	Steven D. Levitt, Stephen J. Dubner
4. Natural Cures They Don't Want You to Know About	Kevin Trudeau
5. The Purpose-Driven Life	Rick Warren
6. 1776	David McCullough
7. Where God Was Born	Bruce Feiler
8. The World Is Flat: A Brief History of the Twenty-first Century	Thomas L. Friedman
9. You: The Owner's Manual	Michael Roizen and Mehmet Oz
10. Your Best Life Now	Joel Osteen

Some Famous Film Personalities

Antonioni, Michelangelo; (1912–); Italian; famous film director; his best known works include *Le amiche*, *L'avventura*, *L'eclisse*, and *Blow-up*.

Ashok Kumar (real name Kumudlal K. Ganguly); (1911–2001); Indian; predominantly Hindi film actor; best known films include *Jeevan Naiya*, *Achhut Kanya*, *Kismet*, *Mahal*, *Chalti Ka Naam Gaadi*; helped set up Filmistan studio.

Benegal, Shyam; (1934–); Indian; director; famous films include *Ankur*, *Charandas Chor* and *Manthan*.

Bergman, Ingmar (full name Ernst Ingmar Bergman); (1918–); Swedish; director and writer; best known works include *Det sjunde inseglet* (*The Seventh Seal*), *Smultronstället* (*Wild Strawberries*), the *Såsom i en spegel* trilogy (*Through a Glass Darkly*), *Nattsvardsgästerna* (*The Communicants*, or *Winter Light*), *Tystnaden* (*The Silence*) and *Viskingar och rop* (*Cries and Whispers*).

Chaplin, Charles 'Charlie' S.; (1889–1977), British-born US actor; one of the most famous actors and directors in early Hollywood cinema; famous films include *The Tramp*, *The Kid*, *The Gold Rush*, *City Lights*, *Modern Times*, and *The Great Dictator*.

Connery, Sean (full name Thomas Sean Connery); (1930–); British-born actor; achieved fame by playing the role of James Bond (in *Dr. No*, *From Russia With Love*, *Goldfinger*, *Thunderball*, *You Only Live Twice*, *Diamonds Are Forever*, *Never Say Never Again*); notable among the other films are *Another Time Another Place*, *The Untouchables*, *The Man Who Would Be King*, *Murder on the Orient Express*, *A Bridge Too Far*, *The Great Train Robbery*, *Indiana Jones and the Last Crusade*, *The Hunt for Red October*, *Rising Sun*, *The Rock* and *The Avengers*.

Davis, Bette (real name Ruth Elizabeth Davis); (1908–1989); US; actor; her films include *Of Human Bondage*, *Dangerous*, *Jezebel* and *All About Eve*.

Dutt, Nargis (real name Fatima A. Rashid); (1929–1981); Indian; Hindi film actor; best known films include *Mother India*, *Barsaat*, *Awara*, and *Shri 420*.

Eisenstein, Sergei M.; (1898–1948); Latvian-born Russian director; famous works include *Bronenosets Potyomkin(Battleship Potemkin)*.

Fellini, Federico; (1920–1993), Italy, famous director who helped launch the Neorealist movement; best known works include *La dolce vita (The Sweet Life)*, *Otto e mezzo (8 1/2)*, *La Strada (The Road)*, and *Le notti di Cabiria (The Nights of Cabiria)*.

Ganesan, Villupuram C. 'Sivaji'; (1928–2001); Indian; predominantly Tamil film actor and politician; most well known films include *Parasakthi*, *Veerapandiya Kattaboman*, and *Rangoon Radha*.

Godard, Jean-Luc; (1930–); French; one of the most influential members of the New Wave cinema in France; works include *Le Petit Soldat (The Little Soldier)*, *Vivre sa vie (My Life to Live)* and *Le Mépris (Contempt)*.

Griffith, David L.W.; (1875–1948); US; producer and director; famous films include *The Birth of a Nation*, and *Intolerance*.

Hepburn, Katharine H.; (1907–2003); US; actor; notable films include *Morning Glory*, *The Philadelphia Story*, *The African Queen*, *Guess Who's Coming to Dinner*, *The Lion in Winter*, and *On Golden Pond*.

Hitchcock, Alfred J.; (1899–1980); British-born director who made a number of successful films in suspense thriller genre; best known works include *The Man Who Knew Too Much*, *The Thirty-nine Steps*, *Rebecca*, *Spellbound*, *Dial M for Murder*, *Rear Window*, *Psycho*, and *The Birds*.

Kapoor, Raj (full name Ranbir Raj Kapoor); (1924–1988); Indian; actor, producer, director; famous films include *Awara*, *Shri 420*, *Boot Polish*, *Sangam* and *Mera Naam Joker*.

Kishore Kumar (real name Abhas K. Ganguly); (1929–1987); Indian; playback singer, music composer, actor, producer, and director; best known films include *Chalti Ka Naam Gaadi*, *Padosan*, *Jhumroo* and *Half Ticket*.

Kubrick, Stanley; (1928–1999); US; director and writer; best known works include *Spartacus*, *Dr. Strangelove*, *2001: A Space Odyssey*, *A Clockwork Orange*, and *Full Metal Jacket*.

Kurosawa, Akira; (1910–1998), Japanese; prominent director, producer, and screenwriter; best known works include *Rashomon*, *Seven Samurai*, *Kagemusha*, and *Ran*.

Leigh, Vivien (real name Vivian Mary Hartley); (1913–1967), Indian-born British actor; played the role of Scarlett O'Hara in *Gone with the Wind*.

Loren, Sophia (real name Sofia Villani Scicolone); (1934–); Italian; actor; best known films are *Ieri, oggi, domani (Yesterday, Today and Tomorrow)*, and *Matrimonio all'italiana (Marriage, Italian Style)*.

Lucas Jr., George W.; (1944–); US; director, producer, and screenwriter; famous for his epic *Star Wars* and *Indiana Jones* trilogies; other notable works include *American Graffiti*.

Madhubala (real name Begum Mumtaz Jehan Dehlavi); (1933–1969); Indian; Hindi film actor; most notable films include *Mughal-E-Azam*, *Howrah Bridge*, *Chalti Ka Naam Gaadi*, *Mahal*, and *Half Ticket*.

Mammootty (Mohammed Kutty); (1953–); Indian; predominantly Malayalam film actor; well known films include *Lekhayude Maranam Oru Flashback*, *Anantaram*, *Akkare*, and *America America*.

Mangeshkar, Lata; (1929–); Indian; playback singer; since her first recording in the 1940s, she has recorded thousands of songs in a range of Indian languages; also acted in a number of films in the 1940s.

Olivier, Laurence K.; (1907–1989); British; actor and director; notable films include *Wuthering Heights*, *Hamlet*, *Richard III*, and *The Prince and the Showgirl*.

Peck, Gregory (full name Eldred Gregory Peck); (1916–2003); US; actor; best known films include *Spellbound, The Snows of Kilimanjaro, To Kill a Mockingbird,* and *MacArthur.*

Phalke, Dhundiraj Govind 'Dadasaheb'; (1870–1944); Indian; pioneering director; his 1913 film *Raja Harishchandra* is considered to be the first feature length Indian film.

Rafi, Mohammed; (1924–1980); Indian; playback singer; famous films featuring his songs include *Shahjehan, Baiju Bawra, Mughal-E-Azam, Pyaasa, Kaagaz Ke Phool, Junglee,* and *Kashmir Ki Kali.*

Rama Rao, Nandamuri T.; (1923–1996); Indian; predominantly Telugu film actor, director, producer; later became a politician; founded the Telugu Desam Party and served as Chief Minister of Andhra Pradesh; best known films include *Shri Venkateswara Mahatyam, Patala Bhairavi,* and *Daana Veera Shura Karna.*

Ray, Satyajit; (1921–1992); Indian; director, writer, and illustrator; famous for *Pather Panchali, Aparajito, Apur Sansar, Charulata* and *Ghare Baire.*

Sinatra, Francis A.'Frank'; (1915–1998); US; singer and actor; famous films include *Anchors Aweigh, From Here to Eternity,* and *The Man with the Golden Arm.*

Spielberg, Steven A; (1946–); US; director and producer; best known works include *Jaws, Close Encounters of the Third Kind, Raiders of the Lost Ark, E.T.—the Extraterrestrial, Jurassic Park, Schindler's List* and *The Color Purple.*

Taylor, Elizabeth R.; (1932–); British; actor; famous films include *National Velvet, Cat on a Hot Tin Roof, Cleopatra,* and *Who's Afraid of Virginia Woolf?*

Truffaut, François; (1932–1984); French; film critic and producer; considered to be one of the founders of the French New Wave movement in filmmaking; best known works include *Les Quatre Cents Coups* (*The 400 Blows*), *Tirez sur le pianiste* (*Shoot the Piano Player*), *Baisers volés* (*Stolen Kisses*), *L'Enfant sauvage* (*The Wild Child*), and *Le Dernier Métro* (*The Last Metro*).

Uttam Kumar (real name Arun K. Chatterjee); (1926–1980); Indian; predominantly Bengali film actor and National Award (Best Actor) winner; best known among his Bengali films are *Sharey Chuattar, Saptapadi, Nayak,* and *Chidiyakhana;* Hindi films include *Amanush.*

Wilder, Billy (real name Samuel Wilder); (1906–2002); Polish-born US screenwriter, film director and producer; famous works include *Double Indemnity, Stalag 17, Irma La Douce, Sunset Boulevard, The Seven Year Itch,* and *Some Like It Hot.*

Some Famous Dancers

Arundale, Rukmini Devi; (1904–1986); Indian bharatanatayam dancer; popularized dance dramas; started Kalakshetra dance academy.

Baryshnikov, Mikhail N.; (1948–); Russian dancer and actor born in Riga now in Latvia.

Birju Maharaj; (1937–); Indian Kathak dancer and singer.

Diaghilev, Sergei P.; (1872–1929); often referred to as Serge; Russian ballet manager and organizer; founder of the Ballets Russes ballet company which introduced, among others, Vaslav Nijinsky and Anna Pavlova.

Fonteyn, Margot (born Margaret Hookham); (1919–1991); British ballet dancer; associated with Rudolf Nureyev; they appeared together in a film version of *Swan Lake;* she served as the chancellor of the University of Durham in UK from 1981 to 1990.

Krishnamurthy, Yamini P.T.; (1940–); Indian bharatanatayam dancer; studied at Kalakshetra dance academy.

Nijinsky, Vaslav F.; (1890–1950); Ukrainian ballet dancer and choreographer, born in Kiev, Ukraine. Associated with Sergei Diaghilev and Anna Pavlova; suffered from mental illness in the last years of his life.

Nureyev, Rudolf K.; (1938–1993); Russian-born dancer; widely regarded as the greatest male dancer of the 20th century; defected to the West in June 1961 and appeared in a number of films. He was appointed director of the Paris Ballet Opera in 1983. Closely associated with Margot Fonteyn.

Pavlova, Anna; (born Anna Matveyevna); (1881–1931); Russian ballet dancer of the early 20th century; worked briefly for Serge Diaghilev before starting her own company and performing throughout the world.

Some Famous Painters

Bosch, Hieronymus; (also spelled as Jheronimus Bos, real name Jerome Van Aeken); (c. 1450–1516); Dutch painter; said to have been an inspiration to the surrealism movement in the 20th century; famous works include *The Garden of Earthly Delights*, *The Seven Deadly Sins*, *The Crowning with Thorns*, *St. John the Evangelist in Patmos* and *St. Jerome in Prayer*.

Bose, Nandalal; (1882–1966); Indian painter; famous works include the *Haripura Posters*.

Cézanne, Paul; (1839–1906); French painter; his most famous works include *Rideau, Cruchon et Compotier*, *The Sea at L'Estaque*, and *The House of the Suicide*.

Da Vinci, Leonardo; (1452–1519); Italian; Renaissance architect, inventor, engineer, sculptor and painter, well known for his masterly paintings, such as *The Last Supper* and *Mona Lisa*.

Dalí, Salvador FJD (full name Salvador Felipe Jacinto Dalí Y Domenech); (1904–1989); Spanish, Surrealist artist; most famous works include *The Persistence of Memory*; also made two Surrealistic films—*Un Chien andalou (An Andalusian Dog)* and *L'Âge d'or (The Golden Age)*.

Dürer, Albrecht; (1471–1528); German; painter, wood carver and engraver; best known for his woodcuts in series; famous works include *Apocalypse*, two series on the crucifixion of Christ, and the *Four Apostles*.

El Greco ('the Greek') (real name Domenikos Theotocopoulos); (1541–1614); Greek-born painter, architect and sculptor who settled in Spain; best known works include *Burial of the Conde de Orgaz*.

Gauguin, Paul (full name Eugène-Henri-Paul Gauguin); (1848–1903); French; famous works include *Vision After the Sermon* and *Where Do We Come From? What Are We? Where Are We Going?*

Goya, Francisco (in full Francisco José de Goya y Lucientes); (1746–1828); Spanish; painter and engraver; famous works include *The Clothed Maja* and *The Naked Maja*.

Husain, Maqbool F.; (1915–); Indian painter and filmmaker; best known works include the *Sufi* paintings, *Sunhera Sansaar*, the *Sansad* portfolio, the *Gaja Gamini* series; his films include *Through the Eyes of a Painter*, *Gaja Gamini* and *Meenaxi: Tale of Three Cities*.

Manet, Édouard; (1832–1883); French; most famous works include *Le déjeuner sur l'herbe*, *Olympia* and *A Bar at the Folies-Bergère*.

Michelangelo (in full Michelangelo di Lodovico Buonarroti Simoni); (1475–1564); Italian; Renaissance painter, sculptor, and architect, famous for creating the fresco ceiling of the Sistine Chapel and sculptures which includes the *Pieta* and *David*.

Monet, Oscar-Claude; (1840–1926); French painter, key leader of the Impressionist movement; famous for *Impression, soleil levant* and the water-lily series.

Picasso, Pablo; (in full Pablo Ruiz y Picasso); (1881–1973); Spanish; founder, along with Georges Braque, of Cubism; one of his most famous works is his depiction of the German bombing of Guernica, Spain.

Pollock, Jackson (full name Paul Jackson Pollock); (1912–1956); US painter; key exponent of the abstract expressionism movement; famous works include *The Moon-Woman Cuts the Circle;* nicknamed 'Jack the Dripper' because of his painting style.

Raphael (Italian full name Raffaello Sanzio); (1483–1520); Italian; painter and architect of the Florentine school, best known for his Madonnas and Holy families and for his large frescoes in the Vatican Palace.

Rembrandt (full name Rembrandt Harmenszoon van Rijn); (1606–1669); Dutch; painter, draftsman and etcher; considered as one of the all time greats; most famous works include *The Militia Company of Captain Frans Banning Cocq* (also known as the *Night Watch*).

Renoir, Pierre-Auguste; (1841–1919); French impressionist painter; most famous work is *Le Bal au Moulin de la Galette.*

Roy, Jamini; (1887–1972); Indian painter; best known works include *Mother Helping the Child to Cross the Pool, Ploughman, At Sunset Prayer.*

Sher-Gil, Amrita; (1913–1941); Hungarian-born Indian painter; famous works include the *Bramhacharis, South Indian Villagers Going to Market,* and *Three Sisters.*

Tagore, Abanindranath; (1871–1951); Indian painter; well known works include *Nirbasita Yaksa, Bharatmata* and *Shahjahaner Mrtyu.*

Turner, Joseph M.W.; (1775–1851); British; landscape artist; famous works include *The Fighting Temeraire Tugged to Her Last Berth to Be Broken up, Dort, or Dortrecht: The Dort Packet Boat from Rotterdam Becalmed* and *Snow Storm: Hannibal and His Army Crossing the Alps.*

Warhol, Andy (real name Andrew Warhola); (1928–1987); US artist and filmmaker; credited with launching the Pop art movement of the 1960s; his painting include commercial objects like Campbell soup cans and Coca-Cola bottles, silkscreen prints of celebrities like Marilyn Monroe (including the famous *Turquoise Marilyn*), Chinese leader Mao Tse-Tung and Elvis Presley.

Whistler, James A.M.; (1834–1903); US; painter and etcher; best known for a portrait of his mother, titled *Arrangement in Gray and Black, No. 1,* usually referred to as *Whistler's Mother.*

Some Famous Authors

Munshi Premchand (born as Dhanpat Rai Srivastava); (1880–1936); Indian poet, novelist and writer of short stories in Hindi and Urdu; notable works include *Prema, Sevasadan, Nirmala, Gaban,* and *Godaan.*

Menon, Vallathol Narayana; (1878–1958); Indian; famous works include *Bandhanasthanaya Aniruthan, Sishyanum Makanum, Magdalanamariam;* shorter lyrics are contained in the early volumes of *Sahityamanjari.*

Seth, Vikram; (1952–); Indian; novelist and poet; best known works are *The Golden Gate* (written in verse but as a long sonnet sequence), *A Suitable Boy* and *An Equal Music.*

Tendulkar, Vijay; (1928–); Indian; author of many full-length plays and one-act plays; famous works are *Shantata! Court Chalu Ahe, Sakharam Binder, Kamala,* and *Ghashiram Kotwal;* also wrote original scripts and dialogue for numerous Hindi films in the 1970s and 1980s including *Nishant, Manthan, Akrosh, Ardha-satya.*

Wells, Herbert G.; (1866–1946); English; novelist, journalist, sociologist, and historian; famous for his science fiction works; most famous works are *The Time Machine*, *The Invisible Man*, and *The War Of The Worlds*.

Vatsyayana; Indian; best known for the text of *Kama Sutra*.

Hugo, Victor; (1802–1885); French; author; famous works are *Les Misérables* and *The Hunchback of Notre Dame*.

Verne, Jules; (1828–1905); French; one of the earliest science fiction authors; best known works are *From the Earth to the Moon*, *A Journey to the Center of the Earth*, *Around the World in Eighty Days* and *20,000 Leagues Under the Seas*.

Maugham, William Somerset; (1874–1965); British; novelist, playwright, short-story writer; famous works are *Of Human Bondage*, *The Razor's Edge*, *The Lotus Eater and The Summing Up*, and *The Moon and Sixpence*.

Huxley, Aldous L.; (1894–1963); British; author and poet; famous works include *Point Counter Point*, *Brave New World*, and *Eyeless in Gaza*.

Zola, Émile; (1840–1902); French; novelist; famous works include *Les Rougon-Macquart*, the collective title given to a twenty-novel cycle, tracing the activities of the various members of an extended family during the French Second Empire.

Pushkin, Aleksandr S.; (1799–1837); Russian; author; most famous works are *The Captive of the Caucasus* and *The Fountain of Bakhchisaray*.

Alexandre Dumas; (born Dumas Davy de la Pailleterie); (1802–1870); French; novelist, best known works are *The Three Musketeers*, *The Count of Monte Cristo* and *The Man in the Iron Mask*.

Narayan, Rasipuram K; (1906–2001); Indian; famous author, best known for *Swami and Friends* and *Malgudi Days*.

Genet, Jean; (1910–1986); French novelist, playwright, and poet, notable for *Our Lady of the Flowers*.

Arouet, François-Marie; (1694–1778); French; better known by the pen-name Voltaire, his two important works are *Lettres philosophiques sur les Anglais* and *Temple du gout* appeared.

Proust, Marcel; (1871–1922); French; novelist, essayist and critic, best known as the author of *In Search of Lost Time*.

Turgenev, Ivan S.; (1818–1883); Russian; poet, and writer, most famous for his novel *Fathers and Sons*.

Rousseau, Jean-Jacques; (1712–1778); Swiss-French; philosopher, writer, political theorist, notable for *The Social Contract*.

Rimbaud, Arthur; (1854–1891); French; *Une Saison en Enfer* is one of his major works.

Baudelaire, Charles-Pierre; (1821–1867); French; his famous work is *Les fleurs du mal* and *Les paradis artificiels*.

Andersen, Hans Christian; (1805–1875); Danish; famous for his fairy tales like *The Ugly Duckling*, *The Little Mermaid* and *Thumbelina*.

Austen, Jane; (1775–1817); British; novelist, noted for her novels *Sense and Sensibility*, *Pride and Prejudice* and *Mansfield Park*.

Balzac, Honoré de; (1799–1850); French; famous author; noted for *La peau de chagrin* and *Cousine Bette*.

Chaucer, Geoffrey; (c. 1343–1400); British; author, philosopher, diplomat, and poet, best remembered as the author of *The Canterbury Tales*.

Brontë, Emily; (1818–1848); British; noted for the literary classic *Wuthering Heights*.

Camus, Albert; (1913–1960); French, author and philosopher; best remembered as the author of *The*

Stranger and The Myth of Sisyphus and *The Fall.*

Cervantes, Miguel de; (1547–1616); Spanish; best known for his novel *Don Quixote de la Mancha.*

Dickens, Charles; (1812–1870); British; author, best known for his work named *Great Expectations, David Copperfield, Oliver Twist, A Tale of Two Cities* and *Great Expectations.*

Alighieri, Dante; (1265–1321); Italian; famous poet whose greatest work is *The Divine Comedy.*

Dostoevsky, Fyodor; (1821–1881); Russian, best remembered as the author of *Crime and Punishment* and *The Brothers Karamazov*

Eliot, George; (1819–1880); British; his most famous work is *Middlemarch* and *The Mill on the Floss.*

Goethe, Johann W.; (1749–1832); German; writer, humanist, and philosopher; author of *Faust* and *Theory of Colors.*

Hemingway, Ernest M; (1899–1961); US; best remembered as the author of *The Sun Also Rises* and *A Farewell To Arms.*

Joyce, James A.A.; (1882–1941); Irish; he is best known for his short story collection *Dubliners* and for his novels *A Portrait of the Artist as a Young Man, Ulysses* and *Finnegans Wake.*

Kafka, Franz; (1883–1924); Czech-born German author; his most famous works include the short stories *The Metamorphosis, A Hunger Artist,* and novels *The Trial* and *The Castle.*

Kalidas; Indian; considered one of India's greatest Sanskrit poets and dramatists; famous plays attributed to him are *Malavikaagnimitra, Vikramorvashiiyaand* and *Abhigyaanashaakuntalam.*

Lawrence, David H.; (1885–1930); British; his best known works are *Lady Chatterley's Lover* and *Women In Love.*

Melville, Herman; (1819–1891), US; he is best known for his masterpiece *Moby-Dick.*

Nabokov, Vladimir; (1899–1977), Russian; *Lolita* and *Pale Fire* are his best known works.

Poe, Edgar A.; (1809–1849); US; poet, novelist and short story writer; famous for *The Murders in the Rue Morgue.*

Rabelais, François; (c. 1493–1553); French; he is best known for his masterpiece *Gargantua and Pantagruel.*

Shakespeare, William; (1564–1616); British; considered as one of the greatest writers of the English language, his famous works include *Macbeth, Hamlet, Tempest, Romeo and Juliet,* and *Merchant of Venice.*

Swift, Jonathan; (1667–1745); Irish; most famous for his work *Gulliver's Travels.*

Tolstoy, Leo N.; (1828–1910); Russian; author, reformer and moral thinker, notable for his work *War and Peace* and *Anna Karenina.*

Chekhov, Anton; (1860–1904); Russian; playwright, famous works include *Uncle Vanya, The Cherry Orchard, The Island: A Journey to Sakhalin.*

Clemens, Samuel L; (1835–1910); US; better known by his pen name Mark Twain; most famous works are *The Adventures of Tom Sawyer* and *The Adventures of Huckleberry Finn.*

Valmiki; Indian; the author of *Ramayana* written in Sanskrit.

Woolf, Virginia; (1882–1941); British; her best-known works are *A Room of One's Own* and *Three Guineas.*

Adams, Douglas, N.; (1952–2001) ; British; most famous work is *The Hitchhiker's Guide to the Galaxy.*

Aesop, or Æsop; (c. 620–560 BC); Greek; famous for *Aesop's Fables.*

Alcott, Louisa, M.; (1832–1888); US; most famous work is *Little Women.*

Amis, Kingsley; (1922–1995); British; famous works include *Lucky Jim.*

Aristophanes; (c. 446–385 BC); Greek; famous works include *The Birds.*

Asimov, Isaac; (c. 1920–1992); Russian-born American science fiction writer; most famous works are *Foundation, Foundation and Empire*, and *Second Foundation* (the Foundation Trilogy).

Barrie, James, M.; (1860–1937); British; creator of *Peter Pan*.

Wodehouse, Pelham G.; (1881–1975); British; comic novelist best known for the Jeeves and Wooster and Blandings Castle novels and short stories.

Doyle, Arthur Conan; (1859–1930); British; most famous for his Sherlock Holmes detective stories.

Christie, Agatha M.C.; (1890–1976); British; crime fiction writer most famous or her stories about the detectives Hercule Poirot and Miss Marple.

Jerome, Jerome K.; (1859–1927); British; best known for *Three Men in a Boat*.

Shelley, Percy B.; (1792–1822); British; Romantic poet, most famous for poems such as *Ozymandias, Ode to the West Wind, To a Skylark*, and *The Masque of Anarchy*.

Keats, John; (1795–1821); British; Romantic poet, famous works are *Ode to Psyche, Ode on a Grecian Urn* and *Ode to a Nightingale*.

Wordsworth, William; (1770–1850); UK, Romantic poet; famous works include *Lyrical Ballads* (with Samuel Coleridge) and *The Prelude*.

Byron, George G.; (1788–1824); British; popularly known as Lord Byron, his best-known works are *Childe Harold's Pilgrimage* and *Don Juan*.

Tennyson, Alfred; (1809–1892); British; poet, most famous for his work *The Charge of the Light Brigade* and *The Lady of Shalott*.

Scott, Walter; (1771–1832); British; historical novelist most notable for his works *Rob Roy, Ivanhoe* and *Waverly*.

Frost, Robert L.; (1874–1963); US; poet, famous for *Stopping by Woods on a Snowy Evening, Mending Wall* and *Birches*.

Cummings, Edward E.; (1894–1962); US; famous for *The Enormous Room* and for *Tulips and Chimneys*.

Munro, Hector H., (Saki); (1870–1916); the short story such as *The Open Window*.

Khayyám, Omar; (1048–1131); Iranian; best known for the *The Rubáiyát of Omar Khayyám*.

Ghalib, Mirza A.K.; (1797–1869); Indian; *Urdu-i-Hindi* and *Urdu-i-Muallah* are his two famous books of collection of letters.

Chatterjee, Sarat C.; (1876–1938); Indian; author is best known for the *Srikanta* works, *Charitrahin, Biraj Bau, Palli Samaj*, and *Devdas*.

Chatterjee, Bankim C.; (1838–94); Indian; his famous work include *Anandamath, Rajmohan's Wife, Durgeshnandini* and *Kapalkundala*.

The Grimm Brothers, Jacob L.C., (1785–1863), **Wilhelm C.**, (1786–1859); German; They are well known for publishing collections of German fairy tales.

Rushdie, Salman; (1947–); Indian-born author; most famous works are *Midnight's Children, Haroun and the Sea of Stories, The Moor's Last Sigh* and *The Ground Beneath Her Feet*.

Naipaul, Vidiadhar S.; (1932–); Trinidadian writer of Indian descent; famous works include *The Mystic Masseur, A House for Mr. Biswas, In a Free State*, and *A Bend in the River*.

Roy, Arundhati; (1961–); Indian; author of *The God of Small Things*.

Eliot, Thomas S.; (1888–1965); American-English; poet, playwright, literary critic, and editor; leader of the modernist movement in poetry; most famous works are *The Waste Land* and *The Four Quartets*.

Coleridge, Samuel T.; English poet, philosopher and critic; wrote *Lyrical Ballads* with William Wordsworth.

Plath, Sylvia; (1932–1963); American poet and novelist; best known works include *The Bell Jar*, *Johnny Panic and the Bible of Dreams*, *The Colossus* and *Ariel*.

Beckett, Samuel B.; (1906–1989); Irish-born author, critic, and playwright who wrote both in English and French; best known for *Waiting for Godot*.

Yeats, William B.; (1865–1939); Irish poet, dramatist, and author; his most important collections of poetry include *The Green Helmet* and *Responsibilities*.

Kamban; (9th century); Indian; Tamil poet; author of *Ramavataram*, commonly known as *Kambaramayanam*.

General Knowledge

Nobel Prize

The Nobel Prize is the first international award given annually since 1901 for achievements in physics, chemistry, medicine, literature and peace. The prize consists of a medal, a personal diploma, and a prize amount. In 1968, the Sveriges Riksbank (Bank of Sweden) instituted the Prize in Economic Sciences in memory of Alfred Nobel, founder of the Nobel Prize. The festival day of the Nobel Foundation is on the 10th of December, the death anniversary of the testator.

Winners of the Nobel Prize:

Economics

Year	Name	Country
2005	Robert J. Aumann	Israel/United States of America
	Thomas C. Schelling	United States of America
2004	Finn E. Kydland	United States of America
	Edward C. Prescot	United States of America
2003	Robert F. Engle	United States of America
	Clive W.J. Granger	United Kingdom
2002	Daniel Kahneman	United States of America
	Vernon L. Smith	United States of America
2001	George A. Akerlof	United States of America
	A. Michael Spence	United States of America
	Joseph E. Stiglitz	United States of America
2000	James J. Heckman	United States of America
	Daniel L. McFadden	United States of America
1999	Robert A. Mundell	Canada
1998	Amartya Sen	India
1997	Robert C. Merton	United States of America
	Myron S. Scholes	United States of America
1996	James A. Mirrlees	United Kingdom
	William Vickrey	United States of America
1995	Robert E. Lucas Jr.	United States of America
1994	John C. Harsanyi	United States of America
	John F. Nash Jr.	United States of America
	Reinhard Selten	Germany
1993	Robert W. Fogel	United States of America
	Douglass C. North	United States of America
1992	Gary S. Becker	United States of America
1991	Ronald H. Coase	United States of America
1990	Harry M. Markowitz	United States of America
	Merton H. Miller	United States of America

	William F. Sharpe	United States of America
1989	Trygve Haavelmo	Norway
1988	Maurice Allais	France
1987	Robert M. Solow	United States of America
1986	James M. Buchanan Jr.	United States of America
1985	Franco Modigliani	United States of America
1984	Richard Stone	United Kingdom
1983	Gerard Debreu	United States of America
1982	George J. Stigler	United States of America
1981	James Tobin	United States of America
1980	Lawrence R. Klein	United States of America
1979	Theodore W. Schultz	United States of America
	Sir Arthur Lewis	United Kingdom
1978	Herbert A. Simon	United States of America
1977	Bertil Ohlin	Sweden
	James E. Meade	United Kingdom
1976	Milton Friedman	United States of America
1975	Leonid Vitaliyevich Kantorovich	Union of Soviet Socialist Republics
	Tjalling C. Koopmans	United States of America
1974	Gunnar Myrdal	Sweden
	Friedrich August von Hayek	United Kingdom
1973	Wassily Leontief	United States of America
1972	John R. Hicks	United Kingdom
	Kenneth J. Arrow	United States of America
1971	Simon Kuznets	United States of America
1970	Paul A. Samuelson	United States of America
1969	Ragnar Frisch	Norway
	Jan Tinbergen	The Netherlands

Medicine

Year	Name	Country
2005	Barry J. Marshall	Australia
	J. Robin Warren	Australia
2004	Richard Axel	United States of America
	Linda B. Buck	United States of America
2003	Paul C. Lauterbur	United States of America
	Sir Peter Mansfield	United Kingdom
2002	Sydney Brenner	United Kingdom
	H. Robert Horvitz	United States of America
	John E. Sulston	United Kingdom,
2001	Leland H. Hartwell	United States of America
	Tim Hunt	United Kingdom
	Sir Paul Nurse	United Kingdom
2000	Arvid Carlsson	Sweden
	Paul Greengard	United States of America
	Eric R. Kandel	United States of America
1999	Günter Blobel	United States of America
1998	Robert F. Furchgott	United States of America
	Louis J. Ignarro	United States of America
	Ferid Murad	United States of America

1997	Stanley B. Prusiner	United States of America
1996	Peter C. Doherty	Australia
	Rolf M. Zinkernagel	Switzerland
1995	Edward B. Lewis	United States of America
	Christiane Nüsslein-Volhard	Germany
	Eric F. Wieschaus	United States of America
1994	Alfred G. Gilman	United States of America
	Martin Rodbell	United States of America
1993	Richard J. Roberts	United Kingdom
	Phillip A. Sharp	United States of America
1992	Edmond H. Fischer	United States of America
	Edwin G. Krebs	United States of America
1991	Erwin Neher	Germany
	Bert Sakmann	Germany
1990	Joseph E. Murray	United States of America
	E. Donnall Thomas	United States of America
1989	J. Michael Bishop	United States of America
	Harold E. Varmus	United States of America
1988	Sir James W. Black	United Kingdom
	Gertrude B. Elion	United States of America
	George H. Hitchings	United States of America
1987	Susumu Tonegawa	Japan
1986	Stanley Cohen	United States of America
	Rita Levi-Montalcini	Italy
1985	Michael S. Brown	United States of America
	Joseph L. Goldstein	United States of America
1984	Niels K. Jerne	Denmark
	Georges J.F. Köhler	Germany
	César Milstein	Argentina
1983	Barbara McClintock	United States of America
1982	Sune K. Bergström	Sweden
	Bengt I. Samuelsson	Sweden
	John R. Vane	United Kingdom
1981	Roger W. Sperry	United States of America
	David H. Hubel	United States of America
	Torsten N. Wiesel	Sweden
1980	Baruj Benacerraf	United States of America
	Jean Dausset	France
	George D. Snell	United States of America
1979	Allan M. Cormack	United States of America
	Godfrey N. Hounsfield	United Kingdom
1978	Werner Arber	Switzerland
	Daniel Nathans	United States of America
	Hamilton O. Smith	United States of America
1977	Roger Guillemin	United States of America
	Andrew V. Schally	United States of America
	Rosalyn Yalow	United States of America
1976	Baruch S. Blumberg	United States of America
	D. Carleton Gajdusek	United States of America
1975	David Baltimore	United States of America
	Renato Dulbecco	United States of America

	Howard M. Temin	United States of America
1974	Albert Claude	United States of America
	Christian de Duve	Belgium
	George E. Palade	United States of America
1973	Karl von Frisch	Austria
	Konrad Lorenz	Austria
	Nikolaas Tinbergen	United Kingdom
1972	Gerald M. Edelman	United States of America
	Rodney R. Porter	United kingdom
1971	Earl W. Sutherland, Jr.	United States of America
1970	Sir Bernard Katz	United Kingdom
	Ulf von Euler	Sweden
	Julius Axelrod	United States of America
1969	Max Delbrück	United States of America
	Alfred D. Hershey	United States of America
	Salvador E. Luria	United States of America
1968	Robert W. Holley	United States of America
	H. Gobind Khorana	United States of America
	Marshall W. Nirenberg	United States of America
1967	Ragnar Granit	Sweden
	Haldan K. Hartline	United States of America
	George Wald	United States of America
1966	Peyton Rous	United States of America
	Charles B. Huggins	United States of America
1965	François Jacob	France
	André Lwoff	France
	Jacques Monod	France
1964	Konrad Bloch	United States of America
	Feodor Lynen	Germany
1963	Sir John Eccles	Australia
	Alan L. Hodgkin	United Kingdom
	Andrew F. Huxley	United Kingdom
1962	Francis Crick	United Kingdom
	James Watson	United States of America
	Maurice Wilkins	United kingdom
1961	Georg von Békésy	United States of America
1960	Sir Frank Macfarlane Burnet	Australia
	Peter Medawar	United Kingdom
1959	Severo Ochoa	United States of America
	Arthur Kornberg	United States of America
1958	George Beadle	United States of America
	Edward Tatum	United States of America
	Joshua Lederberg	United States of America
1957	Daniel Bovet	Italy
1956	André F. Cournand	United States of America
	Werner Forssmann	Germany
	Dickinson W. Richards	United States of America
1955	Hugo Theorell	Sweden
1954	John F. Enders	United States of America
	Thomas H. Weller	United States of America
	Frederick C. Robbins	United States of America

Year	Name	Country
1953	Hans Krebs	United Kingdom
	Fritz Lipmann	United States of America
1952	Selman A. Waksman	United States of America
1951	Max Theiler	South Africa
1950	Edward C. Kendall	United Staes of America
	Tadeus Reichstein	Switzerland
	Philip S. Hench	United Staes of America
1949	Walter Hess	Switzerland
	Egas Moniz	Portugal
1948	Paul Müller	Switzerland
1947	Carl Cori	United States of America
	Gerty Cori	United States of America
	Bernardo Houssay	Argentina
1946	Hermann J. Muller	United States of America
1945	Sir Alexander Fleming	United Kingdom
	Ernst B. Chain	United Kingdom
	Sir Howard Florey	Australia
1944	Joseph Erlanger	United States of America
	Herbert S. Gasser	United States of America
1943	Henrik Dam	Denmark
	Edward A. Doisy	United States of America
1942	The prize money was 1/3 allocated to the Main Fund and 2/3 to the Special Fund of this prize section	
1941	The prize money was 1/3 allocated to the Main Fund and 2/3 to the Special Fund of this prize section	
1940	The prize money was 1/3 allocated to the Main Fund and 2/3 to the Special Fund of this prize section	
1939	Gerhard Domagk	Germany
1938	Corneille Heymans	Belgium
1937	Albert Szent-Györgyi	Hungary
1936	Sir Henry Dale	United Kingdom
	Otto Loewi	Germany
1935	Hans Spemann	Germany
1934	George H. Whipple	United States of America
	George R. Minot	United States of America
	William P. Murphy	United States of America
1933	Thomas H. Morgan	United States of America
1932	Sir Charles Sherrington	United Kingdom
	Edgar Adrian	United Kingdom
1931	Otto Warburg	Germany
1930	Karl Landsteiner	United States of America
1929	Christiaan Eijkman	The Netherlands
	Sir Frederick Hopkins	United kingdom
1928	Charles Nicolle	France
1927	Julius Wagner-Jauregg	Austria
1926	Johannes Fibiger	Denmark
1925	The prize money was allocated to the Special Fund of this prize section	
1924	Willem Einthoven	The Netherlands
1923	Frederick G. Banting	Canada
	John Macleod	United Kingdom

1922	Archibald V. Hill	United Kingdom
	Otto Meyerhof	Germany
1921	The prize money was allocated to the Special Fund of this prize section	
1920	August Krogh	Denmark
1919	Jules Bordet	Belgium
1918	The prize money was allocated to the Special Fund of this prize section	
1917	The prize money was allocated to the Special Fund of this prize section	
1916	The prize money was allocated to the Special Fund of this prize section	
1915	The prize money was allocated to the Special Fund of this prize section	
1914	Robert Bárány	Austria
1913	Charles Richet	France
1912	Alexis Carrel	France
1911	Allvar Gullstrand	Sweden
1910	Albrecht Kossel	Germany
1909	Theodor Kocher	Switzerland
1908	Ilya Mechnikov	Russia
	Paul Ehrlich	Germany
1907	Alphonse Laveran	France
1906	Camillo Golgi	Italy
	Santiago Ramón y Cajal	Spain
1905	Robert Koch	Germany
1904	Ivan Pavlov	Russia
1903	Niels Ryberg Finsen	Denmark
1902	Ronald Ross	United Kingdom
1901	Emil von Behring	Germany

Peace

Year	Name	Country
2005	International Atomic Energy Agency	Austria
	Mohamed El Baradei	Egypt
2004	Wangari Muta Maathai	Kenya
2003	Shirin Ebadi	Iran
2002	Jimmy Carter	United States of America
2001	United Nations	United States of America
	Kofi Annan	Ghana
2000	Kim Dae-jung	South Korea
1999	Médecins Sans Frontières	Belgium
1998	John Hume	United Kingdom
	David Trimble	United Kingdom
1997	International Campaign to Ban Landmines	United States of America
	Jody Williams	United States of America
1996	Carlos Filipe Ximenes Belo	East Timor
	José Ramos-Horta	East Timor
1995	Joseph Rotblat	United Kingdom

	Pugwash Conferences on Science and World Affairs	Canada
1994	Yasser Arafat	Palestine
	Shimon Peres	Israel
	Yitzhak Rabin	Israel
1993	Nelson Mandela	South Africa
	F.W. de Klerk	South Africa
1992	Rigoberta Menchú Tum	Guatemala
1991	Aung San Suu Kyi	Myanmar
1990	Mikhail Gorbachev	Union of Soviet Socialist Republics
1989	The 14th Dalai Lama	China (Tibet)
1988	United Nations Peacekeeping Forces	United States of America
1987	Oscar Arias Sánchez	Costa Rica
1986	Elie Wiesel	United States of America
1985	International Physicians for the Prevention of Nuclear War	United States of America
1984	Desmond Tutu	South Africa
1983	Lech Walesa	Poland
1982	Alva Myrdal	Sweden
	Alfonso García Robles	Mexico
1981	Office of the United Nations High Commissioner for Refugees	Switzerland
1980	Adolfo Pérez Esquivel	Argentina
1979	Mother Teresa	India
1978	Anwar al-Sadat	Egypt
	Menachem Begin	Israel
1977	Amnesty International	United Kingdom
1976	Betty Williams	Northern Ireland
	Mairead Corrigan	Northern Ireland
1975	Andrei Sakharov	Union of Soviet Socialist Republics
1974	Seán MacBride	Ireland
	Eisaku Sato	Japan
1973	Henry Kissinger	United States of America
	Le Duc Tho	North Vietnam
1972	The prize money for 1972 was allocated to the Main Fund	
1971	Willy Brandt	Germany
1970	Norman Borlaug	United States of America
1969	International Labour Organization	United Kingdom
1968	René Cassin	France
1967	The prize money was with 1/3 allocated to the Main Fund and with 2/3 to the Special Fund of this prize section	
1966	The prize money was allocated to the Special Fund of this prize section	
1965	United Nations Children's Fund	United States of America
1964	Martin Luther King	United States of America
1963	International Committee of the Red Cross	Switzerland
	League of Red Cross Societies	Switzerland
1962	Linus Pauling	United States of America

1961	Dag Hammarskjöld	Sweden
1960	Albert Lutuli	South Africa
1959	Philip Noel-Baker	United kingdom
1958	Georges Pire	Belgium
1957	Lester Bowles Pearson	Canada
1956	The prize money was 1/3 allocated to the Main Fund and 2/3 to the Special Fund of this prize section	
1955	The prize money was allocated to the Special Fund of this prize section	
1954	Office of the United Nations High Commissioner for Refugees	Switzerland
1953	George C. Marshall	United States of America
1952	Albert Schweitzer	France
1951	Léon Jouhaux	France
1950	Ralph Bunche	United States of America
1949	Lord Boyd Orr	United Kingdom
1948	The prize money was 1/3 allocated to the Main Fund and 2/3 to the Special Fund of this prize section	
1947	Friends Service Council	United Kingdom
	American Friends Service Committee	United States of America
1946	Emily Greene Balch	United States of America
	John R. Mott	United States of America
1945	Cordell Hull	United States of America
1944	International Committee of the Red Cross	Switzerland
1943	The prize money was 1/3 allocated to the Main Fund and 2/3 to the Special Fund of this prize section	
1942	The prize money was 1/3 allocated to the Main Fund and 2/3 to the Special Fund of this prize section	
1941	The prize money was 1/3 allocated to the Main Fund and 2/3 to the Special Fund of this prize section	
1940	The prize money was 1/3 allocated to the Main Fund and 2/3 to the Special Fund of this prize section	
1939	The prize money was 1/3 allocated to the Main Fund and 2/3 to the Special Fund of this prize section	
1938	Nansen International Office for Refugees	Switzerland
1937	Robert Cecil	United Kingdom
1936	Carlos Saavedra Lamas	Argentina
1935	Carl von Ossietzky	Germany
1934	Arthur Henderson	United Kingdom
1933	Sir Norman Angell	United Kingdom
1932	The prize money was allocated to the Special Fund of this prize section	
1931	Jane Addams	United States of America
	Nicholas Murray Butler	United States of America
1930	Nathan Söderblom	Sweden
1929	Frank B. Kellogg	United States of America
1928	The prize money was allocated to the Special Fund of this prize section	

1927	Ferdinand Buisson	France
	Ludwig Quidde	Germany
1926	Aristide Briand	France
	Gustav Stresemann	Germany
1925	Sir Austen Chamberlain	United Kingdom
	Charles G. Dawes	United States of America
1924	The prize money was allocated to the Special Fund of this prize section	
1923	The prize money was allocated to the Special Fund of this prize section	
1922	Fridtjof Nansen	Norway
1921	Hjalmar Branting	Sweden
	Christian Lange	Norway
1920	Léon Bourgeois	France
1919	Woodrow Wilson	United States of America
1918	The prize money was allocated to the Special Fund of this prize section	
1917	International Committee of the Red Cross	Switzerland
1916	The prize money was allocated to the Special Fund of this prize section	
1915	The prize money was allocated to the Special Fund of this prize section	
1914	The prize money was allocated to the Special Fund of this prize section	
1913	Henri La Fontaine	Belgium
1912	Elihu Root	United States of America
1911	Tobias Asser	Netherlands
	Alfred Fried	Austria
1910	Permanent International Peace Bureau	Switzerland
1909	Auguste Beernaert	Belgium
	Paul Henri d'Estournelles de Constant	France
1908	Klas Pontus Arnoldson	Sweden
	Fredrik Bajer	Denmark
1907	Ernesto Teodoro Moneta	Italy
	Louis Renault	France
1906	Theodore Roosevelt	United States of America
1905	Bertha von Suttner	Austria
1904	Institute of International Law	Belgium
1903	Randal Cremer	United Kingdom
1902	Élie Ducommun	Switzerland
	Albert Gobat	Switzerland
1901	Henri Dunant	Switzerland
	Frédéric Passy	France

Chemistry

Year	Name	Country
2005	Yves Chauvin	France
	Robert H. Grubbs	United States of America
	Richard R. Schrock	United States of America
2004	Aaron Ciechanover	Israel
	Avram Hershko	Israel
	Irwin Rose	United States of America
2003	Peter Agre	United States of America
	Roderick MacKinnon	United States of America
2002	John B. Fenn	United States of America
	Koichi Tanaka	Japan
	Kurt Wüthrich	Switzerland
2001	William S. Knowles	United States of America
	Ryoji Noyori	Japan
	K. Barry Sharpless	United States of America
2000	Alan Heeger	United States of America
	Alan G. MacDiarmid	United States of America
	Hideki Shirakawa	Japan
1999	Ahmed Zewail	Egypt
1998	Walter Kohn	United States of America
	John Pople	United Kingdom
1997	Paul D. Boyer	United States of America
	John E. Walker	United Kingdom
	Jens C. Skou	Denmark
1996	Robert F. Curl Jr.	United States of America
	Sir Harold Kroto	United Kingdom
	Richard E. Smalley	United States of America
1995	Paul J. Crutzen	The Netherlands
	Mario J. Molina	United States of America
	F. Sherwood Rowland	United States of America
1994	George A. Olah	United States of America
1993	Kary B. Mullis	United States of America
	Michael Smith	Canada
1992	Rudolph A. Marcus	United States of America
1991	Richard R. Ernst	Switzerland
1990	Elias James Corey	United States of America
1989	Sidney Altman	United States of America
	Thomas R. Cech	United States of America
1988	Johann Deisenhofer	West Germany
	Robert Huber	West Germany
	Hartmut Michel	West Germany
1987	Donald J. Cram	United States of America
	Jean-Marie Lehn	France
	Charles J. Pedersen	United States of America
1986	Dudley R. Herschbach	United States of America
	Yuan T. Lee	United States of America
	John C. Polanyi	Canada
1985	Herbert A. Hauptman	United States of America
	Jerome Karle	United States of America

1984	Bruce Merrifield	United States of America
1983	Henry Taube	United States of America
1982	Aaron Klug	United Kingdom
1981	Kenichi Fukui	Japan
	Roald Hoffmann	United Stats of America
1980	Paul Berg	United States of America
	Walter Gilbert	United States of America
	Frederick Sanger	United Kingdom
1979	Herbert C. Brown	United States of America
	Georg Wittig	West Germany
1978	Peter Mitchell	United Kingdom
1977	Ilya Prigogine	Belgium
1976	William Lipscomb	United States of America
1975	John Cornforth	United Kingdom
	Vladimir Prelog	Switzerland
1974	Paul J. Flory	United States of America
1973	Ernst Otto Fischer	Germany
	Geoffrey Wilkinson	United Kingdom
1972	Christian Anfinsen,	United States of America
	Stanford Moore	United States of America
	William H. Stein	United States of America
1971	Gerhard Herzberg	Canada
1970	Luis Leloir	Argentina
1969	Derek Barton	United Kingdom
	Odd Hassel	Norway
1968	Lars Onsager	United States of America
1967	Manfred Eigen	Germany
	Ronald G.W. Norrish	United Kingdom
	George Porter	United Kingdom
1966	Robert S. Mulliken	United States of America
1965	Robert B. Woodward	United States of America
1964	Dorothy Crowfoot Hodgkin	United Kingdom
1963	Karl Ziegler	Germany
	Giulio Natta	Italy
1962	Max F. Perutz	United Kingdom
	John C. Kendrew	United Kingdom
1961	Melvin Calvin	United States of America
1960	Willard F. Libby	United States of America
1959	Jaroslav Heyrovsky	Czechoslovakia
1958	Frederick Sanger	United Kingdom
1957	Lord Todd	United Kingdom
1956	Sir Cyril Hinshelwood	United Kingdom
	Nikolay Semenov	Union of Soviet Socialist Republics
1955	Vincent du Vigneaud	United States of America
1954	Linus Pauling	United States of America
1953	Hermann Staudinger	Germany
1952	Archer J.P. Martin	United Kingdom
	Richard L.M. Synge	United Kingdom
1951	Edwin M. McMillan	United States of America
	Glenn T. Seaborg	United States of America

1950	Otto Diels, Kurt Alder	Germany
1949	William F. Giauque	United States of America
1948	Arne Tiselius	Sweden
1947	Sir Robert Robinson	United Kingdom
1946	James B. Sumner	United States of America
	John H. Northrop	United States of America
	Wendell M. Stanley	United States of America
1945	Artturi Virtanen	Finland
1944	Otto Hahn	Germany
1943	George de Hevesy	Hungary
1942	The prize money was 1/3 allocated to the Main Fund and 2/3 to the Special Fund of this prize section	
1941	The prize money was 1/3 allocated to the Main Fund and 2/3 to the Special Fund of this prize section	
1940	The prize money was 1/3 allocated to the Main Fund and 2/3 to the Special Fund of this prize section	
1939	Adolf Butenandt	Switzerland
	Leopold Ruzicka	Germany
1938	Richard Kuhn	Germany
1937	Norman Haworth	United Kingdom
	Paul Karrer	Switzerland
1936	Peter Debye	The Netherlands
1935	Frédéric Joliot	France
	Irène Joliot-Curie	France
1934	Harold C. Urey	United States of America
1933	The prize money was 1/3 allocated to the Main Fund and 2/3 to the Special Fund of this prize section	
1932	Irving Langmuir	United States of America
1931	Carl Bosch	Germany
	Friedrich Bergius	Germany
1930	Hans Fischer	Germany
1929	Arthur Harden	United Kingdom
	Hans von Euler-Chelpin	Sweden
1928	Adolf Windaus	Germany
1927	Heinrich Wieland	Germany
1926	The Svedberg	Sweden
1925	Richard Zsigmondy	Austria
1924	The prize money was allocated to the Special Fund of this prize section	
1923	Fritz Pregl	Austria
1922	Francis W. Aston	United Kingdom
1921	Frederick Soddy	United Kingdom
1920	Walther Nernst	Germany
1919	The prize money was allocated to the Special Fund of this prize section	
1918	Fritz Haber	Germany
1917	The prize money was allocated to the Special Fund of this prize section	
1916	The prize money was allocated to the Special Fund of this prize section	
1915	Richard Willstätter	Germany

1914	Theodore W. Richards	United States of America
1913	Alfred Werner	Switzerland
1912	Victor Grignard	France
	Paul Sabatier	France
1911	Marie Curie	France
1910	Otto Wallach	Germany
1909	Wilhelm Ostwald	Germany
1908	Ernest Rutherford	United Kingdom
1907	Eduard Buchner	Germany
1906	Henri Moissan	France
1905	Adolf von Baeyer	Germany
1904	Sir William Ramsay	United Kingdom
1903	Svante Arrhenius	Sweden
1902	Emil Fischer	Germany
1901	Jacobus H. van 't Hoff	The Netherlands

Physics

Year	Name	Country
2005	Roy J. Glauber	United States of America
	John L. Hall	United States of America
	Theodor W. Hänsch	Germany
2004	David J. Gross	United States of America
	H. David Politzer	United States of America
	Frank Wilczek	United States of America
2003	Alexei A. Abrikosov	Russia
	Vitaly L. Ginzburg	Russia
	Anthony J. Leggett	United Kingdom
2002	Raymond Davis Jr.	United States of America
	Masatoshi Koshiba	Japan
	Riccardo Giacconi	United States of America
2001	Eric A. Cornell	United States of America
	Wolfgang Ketterle	Germany
	Carl E. Wieman	United States of America
2000	Zhores I. Alferov	Russia
	Herbert Kroemer	Germany
	Jack S. Kilby	United States of America
1999	Gerardus 't Hooft	The Netherlands
	Martinus J.G. Veltman	The Netherlands
1998	Robert B. Laughlin	United States of America
	Horst L. Störmer	Germany
	Daniel C. Tsui	United States of America
1997	Steven Chu	United States of America
	Claude Cohen-Tannoudji	France
	William D. Phillips	United States of America
1996	David M. Lee	United States of America
	Douglas D. Osheroff	United States of America
	Robert C. Richardson	United States of America
1995	Martin L. Perl	United States of America
	Frederick Reines	United States of America
1994	Bertram N. Brockhouse	Canada
	Clifford G. Shull	United States of America

1993	Russell A. Hulse	United States of America
	Joseph H. Taylor Jr.	United States of America
1992	Georges Charpak	France
1991	Pierre-Gilles de Gennes	France
1990	Jerome I. Friedman	United States of America
	Henry W. Kendall	United States of America
	Richard E. Taylor	Canada
1989	Norman F. Ramsey	United States of America
	Hans G. Dehmelt	United States of America
	Wolfgang Paul	Germany
1988	Leon M. Lederman	United States of America
	Melvin Schwartz	United States of America
	Jack Steinberger	United States of America
1987	J. Georg Bednorz	West Germany
	K. Alex Müller	Switzerland
1986	Ernst Ruska	West Germany
	Gerd Binnig	West Germany
	Heinrich Rohrer	Switzerland
1985	Klaus von Klitzing	West Germany
1984	Carlo Rubbia	Italy
	Simon van der Meer	The Netherlands
1983	Subramanyan Chandrasekhar	United States of America
	William A. Fowler	United States of America
1982	Kenneth G. Wilson	United States of America
1981	Nicolaas Bloembergen	United States of America
	Arthur L. Schawlow	United States of America
	Kai M. Siegbahn	Sweden
1980	James Cronin	United States of America
	Val Fitch	United States of America
1979	Sheldon Glashow	United States of America
	Abdus Salam	Pakistan
	Steven Weinberg	United States of America
1978	Pyotr Kapitsa	Union of Soviet Socialist Republics
	Arno Penzias	United States of America
	Robert Woodrow Wilson	United States of America
1977	Philip W. Anderson	United States of America
	Sir Nevill F. Mott	United kingdom
	John H. van Vleck	United States of America
1976	Burton Richter	United States of America
	Samuel C.C. Ting	United States of America
1975	Aage N. Bohr	Denmark
	Ben R. Mottelson	Denmark
	James Rainwater	United States of America
1974	Martin Ryle	United Kingdom
	Antony Hewish	United Kingdom
1973	Leo Esaki	Japan
	Ivar Giaever	United States of America
	Brian D. Josephson	United Kingdom
1972	John Bardeen	United States of America
	Leon N. Cooper	United States of America

	Robert Schrieffer	United States of America
1971	Dennis Gabor	United Kingdom
1970	Hannes Alfvén	Sweden
	Louis Néel	France
1969	Murray Gell-Mann	United States of America
1968	Luis Alvarez	United States of America
1967	Hans Bethe	United States of America
1966	Alfred Kastler	France
1965	Sin-Itiro Tomonaga	Japan
	Julian Schwinger	United Stats of America
	Richard P. Feynman	United States of America
1964	Charles H. Townes	United States of America
	Nicolay G. Basov	Union of Soviet Socialist Republics
	Aleksandr M. Prokhorov	Union of Soviet Socialist Republics
1963	Eugene Wigner	United States of America
	Maria Goeppert-Mayer	United States of America
	J. Hans D. Jensen	Germany
1962	Lev Landau	Union of Soviet Socialist Republics
1961	Robert Hofstadter	United States of America
	Rudolf Mössbauer	Germany
1960	Donald A. Glaser	United States of America
1959	Emilio Segrè	United States of America
	Owen Chamberlain	United States of America
1958	Pavel A. Cherenkov	Union of Soviet Socialist Republics
	Il´ja M. Frank	Union of Soviet Socialist Republics
	Igor Y. Tamm	Union of Soviet Socialist Republics
1957	Chen Ning Yang	China
	Tsung-Dao Lee	China
1956	William B. Shockley	United States of America
	John Bardeen	United States of America
	Walter H. Brattain	United States of America
1955	Willis E. Lamb	United States of America
	Polykarp Kusch	United States of America
1954	Max Born	United Kingdom
	Walther Bothe	Germany
1953	Frits Zernike	The Netherlands
1952	Felix Bloch	United States of America
	E.M. Purcell	United States of America
1951	John Cockcroft	United Kingdom
	Ernest T.S. Walton	Ireland
1950	Cecil Powell	United Kingdom
1949	Hideki Yukawa	Japan
1948	Patrick M.S. Blackett	United Kingdom
1947	Edward V. Appleton	United Kingdom
1946	Percy W. Bridgman	United States of America
1945	Wolfgang Pauli	Austria
1944	Isidor Isaac Rabi	United States of America
1943	Otto Stern	United States of America
1942	The prize money was 1/3 allocated to the Main Fund and 2/3 to the Special Fund of this prize section	

1941	The prize money was 1/3 allocated to the Main Fund and 2/3 to the Special Fund of this prize section	
1940	The prize money was 1/3 allocated to the Main Fund and 2/3 to the Special Fund of this prize section	
1939	Ernest Lawrence	United states of America
1938	Enrico Fermi	Italy
1937	Clinton Davisson	United States of America
	George Paget Thomson	United kingdom
1936	Victor F. Hess	Austria
	Carl D. Anderson	United States of America
1935	James Chadwick	United Kingdom
1934	The prize money was 1/3 allocated to the Main Fund and 2/3 to the Special Fund of this prize section	
1933	Erwin Schrödinger	Austria
	Paul A.M. Dirac	United Kingdom
1932	Werner Heisenberg	Germany
1931	The prize money was allocated to the Special Fund of this prize section	
1930	Chandrasekhara Venkata Raman	India
1929	Louis de Broglie	France
1928	Owen Willans Richardson	United Kingdom
1927	Arthur H. Compton	United States of America
	C.T.R. Wilson	United Kingdom
1926	Jean Baptiste Perrin	France
1925	James Franck	Germany
	Gustav Hertz	Germany
1924	Manne Siegbahn	Sweden
1923	Robert A. Millikan	United States of America
1922	Niels Bohr	Denmark
1921	Albert Einstein	Switzerland
1920	Charles Edouard Guillaume	Switzerland
1919	Johannes Stark	Germany
1918	Max Planck	Germany
1917	Charles Glover Barkla	United Kingdom
1916	The prize money was allocated to the Special Fund of this prize section	
1915	William Bragg	United Kingdom
	Lawrence Bragg	United Kingdom
1914	Max von Laue	Germany
1913	Heike Kamerlingh Onnes	The Netherlands
1912	Gustaf Dalén	Sweden
1911	Wilhelm Wien	Germany
1910	Johannes Diderik van der Waals	The Netherlands
1909	Guglielmo Marconi	Italy
	Ferdinand Braun	Germany
1908	Gabriel Lippmann	France
1907	Albert A. Michelson	United States of America
1906	J.J. Thomson	United Kingdom
1905	Philipp Lenard	Germany
1904	Lord Rayleigh	United Kingdom

1903	Henri Becquerel	France
	Pierre Curie	France
	Marie Curie	France
1902	Hendrik A. Lorentz	The Netherlands
	Pieter Zeeman	The Netherlands
1901	Wilhelm Conrad Röntgen	Germany

Literature

Year	Name	Country
2005	Harold Pinter	United Kingdom
2004	Elfriede Jelinek	Austria
2003	J.M. Coetzee	South Africa
2002	Imre Kertesz	Hungary
2001	V.S. Naipaul	United Kingdom
2000	Gao Xingjian	France
1999	Günter Grass	Germany
1998	Jose Saramago	Portugal
1997	Dario Fo	Italy
1996	Wislawa Szymborska	Poland
1995	Seamus Heaney	Ireland
1994	Kenzaburo Oe	Japan
1993	Toni Morrison	United States of America
1992	Derek Walcott	St. Lucia (In the Caribbean)
1991	Nadine Gordimer	South Africa
1990	Octavio Paz	Mexico
1989	Camilo Jose Cela	Spain
1988	Naguib Mahfouz	Egypt
1987	Joseph Brodsky	United States of America
1986	Wole Soyinka	Nigeria
1985	Claude Simon	France
1984	Jaroslav Seifert	Czechoslovakia
1983	William Golding	United Kingdom
1982	Gabriel Garcia Marquez	Colombia
1981	Elias Canetti	Bulgaria
1980	Czeslaw Milosz	United States of America
1979	Odysseus Elytis	Greece
1978	Isaac Bashevis Singer	United States of America
1977	Vicente Aleixandre	Spain
1976	Saul Bellow	United States of America
1975	Eugenio Montale	Italy
1974	Eyvind Johnson	Sweden
	Harry Martinson	Sweden
1973	Patrick White	Australia
1972	Heinrich Boll	Germany
1971	Pablo Neruda	Chile
1970	Alexander Solzhenitsyn	Union of Soviet Socialist Republic
1969	Samuel Beckett	Ireland
1968	Yasunari Kawabata	Japan
1967	Miguel Angel Asturias	Guatemala
1966	Samuel Agnon	Israel

	Nelly Sachs	Sweden
1965	Michail Sholokhov	Union of Soviet Socialist Republic
1964	Jean-Paul Sartre (declined)	France
1963	Giorgos Seferis	Greece
1962	John Steinbeck	United States of America
1961	Ivo Andric	Yugoslavia
1960	Saint-John Perse	France
1959	Salvatore Quasimodo	Italy
1958	Boris Pasternak (declined)	Union of Soviet Socialist Republic
1957	Albert Camus	France
1956	Juan Ramon Jimenez	Spain
1955	Halldor Laxness	Iceland
1954	Ernest Hemingway	United States of America
1953	Winston Churchill	United Kingdom
1952	François Mauriac	France
1951	Par Lagerkvist	Sweden
1950	Bertrand Russell	United Kingdom
1949	William Faulkner	United States of America
1948	T.S. Eliot	United Kingdom
1947	Andre Gide	France
1946	Hermann Hesse	Switzerland
1945	Gabriela Mistral	Chile
1944	Johannes V. Jensen	Denmark
1943	No award	
1942	No award	
1941	No award	
1940	No award	
1939	Frans Eemil Sillanpaa	Finland
1938	Pearl Buck	United States of America
1937	Roger Martin du Gard	France
1936	Eugene O'Neill	United States of America
1935	No award	
1934	Luigi Pirandello	Italy
1933	Ivan Bunin	Union of Soviet Socialist Republic
1932	John Galsworthy	United Kingdom
1931	Erik Axel Karlfeldt	Sweden
1930	Sinclair Lewis	United States of America
1929	Thomas Mann	Germany
1928	Sigrid Undset	Norway
1927	Henri Bergson	France
1926	Grazia Deledda	Italy
1925	George Bernard Shaw	Ireland
1924	Wladyslaw Reymont	Poland
1923	William Butler Yeats	Ireland
1922	Jacinto Benavente	Spain
1921	Anatole France	France
1920	Knut Hamsun	Norway
1919	Carl Spitteler	Switzerland
1918	No award	
1917	Karl Gjellerup	Demmark

	Henrik Pontoppidan	Denmark
1916	Verner von Heidenstam	Sweden
1915	Romain Rolland	France
1914	No award	
1913	Rabindranath Tagore	India
1912	Gerhart Hauptmann	Germany
1911	Maurice Maeterlinck	Belgium
1910	Paul Heyse	Germany
1909	Selma Lagerlof	Sweden
1908	Rudolf Eucken	Germany
1907	Rudyard Kipling	United Kingdom
1906	Giosue Carducci	Italy
1905	Henryk Sienkiewicz	Poland
1904	Frederic Mistral	France
	Jose Echegaray	Spain
1903	Bjørnstjerne Bjørnson	Norway
1902	Theodor Mommsen	Germany
1901	Sully Prudhomme	France

Padma Awardees 2005

Padma Vibhushan (9)

1. Dr Bal Krishan Goyal
2. Dr Bhai Mohan Singh
3. Jyotindra Nath Dixit (posthumous)
4. Dr Karan Singh
5. Marthanda Varma Sankaran Valiathan
6. Milon Kumar Benerji
7. Mohan Dharia
8. Pandit Ram Narayan
9. Rasipuram Krishnaswami Laxman

Padma Bhushan (30)

1. A. Ramachandran
2. Dr Andre Beteille
3. Dr Anil Kohli
4. Azim Premji
5. Balraj Puri
6. Dr Brijmohan Lall Munjal
7. Chandi Prasad Bhatt
8. G.V. Ramakrishna
9. Girish Chandra Saxena
10. Dr Hari Mohan
11. Irfan Habib
12. K. Srinath Reddy
13. Kiran Majumdar Shaw
14. M.T. Vasudevan Nair
15. Mrinal Miri
16. Dr Mrinal Datta Chaudhuri
17. Dr Narasimhiah Seshagiri
18. Probodh Chandra Dey alias Manna Dey
19. Qurratulain Hyder
20. Romila Thapar
21. S.R. Sankaran
22. Dr Sardar Anjum
23. Syed Mir Qasim (posthumous)
24. T.R. Satish Chandran
25. Dr Tarlochan Singh Kler
26. Valangiman Subramanian Ramamurthy
27. Varaprasad K. Reddy
28. William Mark Tully
29. Yash Chopra
30. Dr Yusuf Khwaja Hamied

Padma Shri (57)

1. Amin Kamil
2. Amiya Kumar Bagchi
3. Anil Kumble
4. Banwarilal Chouksey
5. Bhagavatula Dattaguru
6. Bilat Paswan Vihangam
7. Chaturbhuj Meher
8. Dr Cyrus Soli Poonawalla
9. Darchhawna
10. Dr Dipankar Banerjee
11. Dr G. Bakthavathsalam
12. Gadul Singh Lama

13. Ustad Ghulam Sadiq Khan
14. Gladys Staines
15. Gurbachan Singh Randhawa
16. Hema Bharali
17. Indira Jaisingh
18. Dr J.M. Hans
19. Dr Jagtar Singh Grewal
20. K.C. Reddy
21. Kanaksen Deka
22. Kavita Krishnamurti Subramaniam
23. Guru Kedarnath Sahu
24. Komala Varadan
25. Krishnan Nair Santhakumari Chitra
26. Kumkum Mohanty
27. Kunnakudi R. Vaidyanathan
28. Kunnakudi R. Vaidyanathan
29. Rev (Dr) Lalsawma
30. Dr Lavu Narendranath
31. Madhu Sudan Kanungo
32. Mahadevappa Madappa
33. Mammen Mathew
34. Manas Chaudhuri
35. Manuel Santana alias M. Boyer Aguior
36. Mehrunnisa Parvez
37. Muzaffar Ali
38. Nana Chudasama
39. Dr P.N. Vasudeva Kurup
40. Pullela Gopichand
41. Puna Ram Nishad
42. Puran Chand Wadali
43. Rachel Thomas
44. Rajyavardhan Singh Rathore
45. Swami Ram Swaroop Sharma
46. Shah Rukh Khan
47. Shameem Dev Azad
48. Dr Shantaram Balwant Mujumdar
49. Shobhana Bhartia
50. Sougaijam Thanil Singh
51. Srikumar Banerjee
52. Sunita Narain
53. Sushil Sahai
54. Theilin Phanbuh
55. Vasudevan Gnana Gandhi
56. Veer Singh Mehta
57. Yumlembam Gambhini Devi

Bharat Ratna

The Bharat Ratna is India's highest civilian honour. It is generally conferred on 23 January each year for rendering outstanding services to the world community. The award was instituted by the President of India on 2 January 1954. The Bharat Ratna medallion is made of bronze and shaped like a pipal leaf. The ribbon is white in colour. The replica of the sun with radiating rays can be seen on the obverse of the medallion with the words 'Bharat Ratna' inscribed beneath it. Our National Emblem (the lion capital of Sarnath) is embossed on the reverse with the motto 'Satyameva Jayate' (Only truth shall prevail). The award can also be granted posthumously. The awards are produced at the Kolkata Mint.

Bharat Ratna Recipients

Person	Year
Dr Sarvepali Radhakrishnan (1888–1975)	1954
Chakravarti Rajagopalachari (1878–1972)	1954
Dr Chandrasekhar Venkat Raman (1888–1970)	1954
Dr Bhagwan Das (1869–1958)	1955
Dr Mokshagundam Visvesvaraya (1861–1962)	1955
Jawaharlal Nehru (1889–1964)	1955
Govind Ballabh Pant (1887–1961)	1957
Dr Dhondo Keshave Karve (1858–1962)	1958
Dr Bidhan Chandra Roy (1882–1962)	1961
Purushottam Das Tandon (1882–1962)	1961
Dr Rajendra Prasad (1884–1963)	1962
Dr Zakir Husain (1897–1969)	1963
Dr Pandurang Vaman Kane (1880–1972)	1963

Lal Bahadur Shastri (Posthumous) (1904–1966)	1966
Indira Gandhi (1917–1984)	1971
Varahagiri Venkatagiri (1894–1980)	1975
Kumaraswami Kamraj (Posthumous) (1903–1975)	1976
Mary Taresa Bojaxhiu (Mother Teresa) (1910–1997)	1980
Acharya Vinobha Bhave (Posthumous) (1895–1982)	1983
Khan Abdul Ghaffar Khan (1890–1988)	1987
Marudu Gopalan Ramachandran (Posthumous) (1917–1987)	1988
Dr Bhim Rao Ramji Ambedkar (Posthumous) (1891–1956)	1990
Dr Nelson Rolihlahla Mandela (b 1918)	1990
Rajiv Gandhi (Posthumous) (1944–1991)	1991
Sardar Vallabhbhai Patel (Posthumous) (1875–1950)	1991
Morarji Ranchhodji Desai (1896–1995)	1991
Maulana Abul Kala Azad (1888–1958)	1992
Jehangir Ratanji Dadabhai Tata (1904–1993)	1992
Satyajit Ray (1922–1992)	1992
A.P.J. Abdul Kalam (b 1931)	1997
Gulzarilal Nanda (1898–1998)	1997
Aruna Asaf Ali (Posthumous) (1909–1996)	1997
MS Subbulakshmi (b 1916)	1998
C Subramaniam (1910–2000)	1998
Jayaprakash Narayan (Posthumous) (1902–1979)	1999
Ravi Shankar (b 1920)	1999
Amartya Sen (b 1933)	1999
Gopinath Bordoloi (Posthumous) (1927–1950)	1999
Lata Mangeshkar (b 1929)	2001
Bismillah Khan (b 1916)	2001

Note: From 2002–05, no one has been conferred the Bharat Ratna

Param Vir Chakra

Param Vir Chakra is India's highest gallantry award. It is awarded for the highest degree of valour in presence of the enemy. Officers and other enlisted personnel of all the military branches of India are eligible for this award. The award was established on January 26, 1950, by the President of India, with effect from August 15, 1947. The Param Vir Chakra medal was designed by Savitri Khanolankar, whose son-in-law Major Somnath Sharma, coincidentally became the first recipient of the award. The medal symbolizes Rishi Dadhichi who donated his thigh bones to make Indra's weapon 'Vajra'. It has a radius of 1-3/8 inch and is made of bronze. The words 'Param Vir Chakra' are written on it in English and Hindi. A purple color ribbon of 32 mm length holds the medal. The award is India's post-independence equivalent of the Victoria Cross.

Param Vir Chakra Recipients

1. Major Somnath Sharma, Kumaon Regiment, November 1947 (Kashmir Operations 1947–48) (given posthumously)

2. Lance Naik Karham Singh M.M., I Sikh Regiment, October, 1948 (Kashmir Operations 1947–48)

3. Second Lt Rama Raghobe Rane, Corps of Engineers, April, 1948, Naushera (Kashmir Operations 1947–48)

4. Naik Jadu Nath Singh, I Rajput Regiment, February 1948, posthumous (Kashmir Operations 1947–48)

5. Company Havildar Major Piru Singh, 6 Rajputana Rifles, July, 1948,

posthumous (Kashmir Operations 1947–48)

6. Captain Gurbachan Singh Salaria, 3/I Gurkha Rifles, December, 1961, posthumous (Congo)

7. Major Dhan Singh Thapa, 1/8 Gurkha Rifles, October, 1962 (Ladakh)

8. Subedar Joginder Singh, I Sikh Regiment, October, 1962, posthumous (Northeast Frontier Agency)

9. Major Shaitan Singh, Kumaon Regiment, November, 1962, posthumous (Ladakh)

10. Company Havildar Major Abdul Hamid, 4 Grenadiers, September, 1965, posthumous (Operation against Pakistan)

11. Lieutenant-Colonel Ardeshir Burzorji Tarapore, 17 Poona Horse, September, 1965, posthumous (Operation against Pakistan)

12. Lance Naik Albert Ekka, 14 Guards, December, 1971, posthumous (Indo-Pakistan conflict)

13. Flying Officer Nirmal Jit Singh Sekhon, Indian Air Force, December, 1971, posthumous (Indo-Pakistan conflict)

14. Lieutenant Arun Khetarpal, 17 Poona Horse, December, 1971, posthumous (Indo-Pakistan conflict)

15. Major Hoshiar Singh, Grenadiers, December, 1971 (Indo-Pakistan conflict)

16. Naib Subedar Bana Singh, 8 Jammu and Kashmir Light Infantry, June, 1987 (Operations in Siachen Glacier)

17. Major Ramaswamy Parmeshwaran, 8 Mahar Regiment, November, 1987, posthumous (IPKF Operations in Sri Lanka)

18. Captain Vikram Batra, 13 Jammu and Kashmir Rifles, July, 1999, posthumous (Operation Vijay in Kargil)

19. Lt Manoj Kumar Pandey, 1/11 Gorkha Rifles, July, 1999, posthumous (Operation Vijay in Kargil)

20. Grenadier Yogendra Singh Yadav, 18 Grenadiers, July, 1999 (Operation Vijay in Kargil)

21. Rifleman Sanjay Kumar, 13 Jammu and Kashmir Rifles, July, 1999 (Operation Vijay in Kargil)

Ramon Magsaysay Award

Conceived by John D. Rockefeller III, in April 1957 the trustees of the Rockefeller Brothers Fund based in New York City established the Ramon Magsaysay Award to commemorate president of Philippines Ramon Magsaysay and to perpetuate his example of integrity in government and pragmatic idealism within a democratic society. The award is given to any person living in Asia without regard to race, gender, or religion. However, heads of state and heads of government (and their spouses) are not eligible during their terms of office. Each September, the Foundation solicits award nominations. Awards themselves are determined following evaluation by the Foundation's president and board of trustees. Presentation ceremonies are held in Manila on 31 August. The annual award is given in six categories:

1. Government Service; 2. Public Service; 3. Community Leadership; 4. Journalism, Literature, And Creative Communication Arts; 5. Peace and International Understanding; and 6. Emergent Leadership

Over the years many Indians have featured on list of awardees for their distinguished services. They are:

Government Service

Name	Year
1. C.D. Deshmukh	1959
2. Kiran Peshawaria Bedi	1994
3. Tirunellai N. Seshan	1996
4. James Michael Lyngdoh	2003

Public Service

Name	Year
1. Jayaprakash Narayan	1965
2. M.S. Subbulakshmi	1974
3. Manibhai B. Desai	1982
4. Murlidhar Devidas Amte	1985
5. Lakshmi Chand Jain	1989
6. Banoo Jehangir Coyaji	1993
7. Mahesh Chander Mehta	1997

Community Leadership

Name	Year
1. Vinoba Bhave	1958
2. Dara N. Khurody	1963
3. Verghese Kurien	1963
4. Tribhuvandas K. Patel	1963
5. K. Chattopadhyay	1966
6. M.S. Swaminathan	1971
7. Ela Ramesh Bhatt	1977
8. Mabelle Rajanikant Arole	1979
9. Rajanikant S. Arole	1979
10. Pramod Karan Sethi	1981
11. Chandi Prasad Bhatt	1982
12. Pandurang S. Athavale	1996
13. Aruna Roy	2000
14. Rajendra Singh	2001
15. Shantha Sinha	2003

Journalism, Literature, and Creative Communication Arts

Name	Year
1. Amitabha Chowdhury	1961
2. Satyajit Ray	1967
3. B. George Verghese	1975
4. Sombhu Mitra	1976
5. Gour Kishore Ghosh	1981
6. Arun Shourie	1982
7. Rasipuram K. Laxman	1984
8. K.V. Subbanna	1991
9. Ravi Shankar	1992
10. Mahasweta Devi	1999

Peace and International Understanding

Name	Year
1. Mother Teresa	1962
2. Jockin Arputham	2000
3. Laxminarayan Ramdas	2004

Emergent Leadership

Name	Year
1. Sandeep Pandey	2002

International Gandhi Peace Prize

In 1995, on the occasion of the 125th birth anniversary of Mahatma Gandhi, Government of India established the International Gandhi Peace Prize. The annual award, given to individuals and institutions for their contributions towards social, economic and political transformation through non-violence and other Gandhian methods, carries a cash prize of Rs 1 crore, convertible in any currency in the world, a plaque and a citation. The award is open to any person regardless of nationality, race, creed or sex. Only achievements within 10 years immediately preceding the nomination are considered for the award. The jury for the award consists of the Prime Minister of India, the Leader of the Opposition in the Lok Sabha, Chief Justice of India and two other eminent persons.

The past recipients of the Award are:

Name	Year
1. Dr Julius K. Nyerere	1995
2. Dr A.T. Ariyaratne	1996
3. Dr Gerhard Fischer	1997
4. Ramakrishna Mission	1998
5. Shri Murlidhar Devidas Amte	1999
6. Dr Nelson Mandela and Grameen Bank, Bangladesh	2000
7. John Hume	2001
8. Bhartiya Vidya Bhawan	2002
9. Vaclav Havel	2003
10. Ellen Moxley and Helen Steven	2004

British Prime Ministers

Prime Minister	Period
1. Sir Robert Walpole	1721–1742
2. Spencer Compton	1742–1743
3. Henry Pelham	1743–1754
4. Thomas Pelham-Holles	1754–1756

5.	William Cavendish	1756–1757
6.	Thomas Pelham-Holles	1757–1762
7.	John Stuart	1762–1763
8.	George Grenville	1763–1765
9.	Charles Watson-Wentworth	1765–1766
10.	William Pitt	1766–1768
11.	Augustus Henry Fitzroy	1768–1770
12.	Frederick North	1770–1782
13.	Charles Watson-Wentworth	1782–1782
14.	William Petty	1782–1783
15.	William Henry Cavendish-Bentinck	1783–1783
16.	William Pitt The Younger	1783–1801
17.	Henry Addington	1801–1804
18.	William Pitt the Younger	1804–1806
19.	William Wyndham Grenville	1806–1807
20.	William Henry Cavendish-Bentinck	1807–1809
21.	Spencer Perceval	1809–1812
22.	Robert Banks Jenkinson	1812–1827
23.	George Canning	1827–1827
24.	Frederick John Robinson	1827–1828
25.	Arthur Wellesley	1828–1830
26.	Charles Grey	1830–1834
27.	William Lamb	1834–1834
28.	Arthur Wellesley	1834–1834
29.	Sir Robert Peel	1834–1835
30.	William Lamb	1835–1841
31.	Sir Robert Peel	1841–1846
32.	Lord John Russell	1846–1852
33.	Edward Geoffrey Smith Stanley	1852–1852
34.	George Hamilton Gordon	1852–1855
35.	Henry John Temple	1855–1858
36.	Edward Geoffrey Smith Stanley	1858–1859
37.	Henry John Temple	1859–1865
38.	John Russell	1865–1866
39.	Edward Geoffrey Smith Stanley	1866–1868
40.	Benjamin Disraeli	1868–1868
41.	William Ewart Gladstone	1868–1874
42.	Benjamin Disraeli	1874–1880
43.	William Ewart Gladstone	1880–1885
44.	Robert Arthur Talbot Gascoyne-Cecil	1885–1886
45.	William Ewart Gladstone	1886–1886
46.	Robert Arthur Talbot Gascoyne-Cecil	1886–1892
47.	William Ewart Gladstone	1892–1894
48.	Archibald Philip Primrose	1894–1895
49.	Robert Arthur Talbot Gascoyne-Cecil	1895–1902
50.	Arthur Balfour	1902–1905
51.	Sir Henry Campbell-Bannerman	1905–1908
52.	Herbert Henry Asquith	1908–1915
53.	Herbert Henry Asquith	1915–1916
54.	David Lloyd George	1916–1922
55.	Andrew Bonar Law	1922–1923

56.	Stanley Baldwin	1923–1924
57.	Ramsay MacDonald	1924–1924
58.	Stanley Baldwin	1924–1929
59.	Ramsay MacDonald	1929–1931
60.	Ramsay MacDonald	1931–1935
61.	Stanley Baldwin	1935–1937
62.	Neville Chamberlain	1937–1940
63.	Winston Churchill	1940–1945
64.	Clement Atlee	1945–1951
65.	Sir Winston Churchill	1951–1955
66.	Sir Anthony Eden	1955–1957
67.	Harold Macmillan	1957–1963
68.	Sir Alec Douglas-Home	1963–1964
69.	Harold Wilson	1964–1970
70.	Edward Heath	1970–1974
71.	Harold Wilson	1974–1976
72.	James Callaghan	1976–1979
73.	Margaret Thatcher	1979–1990
74.	John Major	1990–1997
75.	Tony Blair	1997–present

Presidents of the United States of America

Chronological List of Presidents

1. George Washington (1789–97)
2. John Adams (1797–1801)
3. Thomas Jefferson (1801–09)
4. James Madison (1809–17)
5. James Monroe (1817–25)
6. John Adams (1825–29)
7. Andrew Jackson (1829–37)
8. Martin Van Buren (1837–41)
9. William Henry Harrison (1841)
10. John Tyler (1841–45)
11. James Polk (1845–49)
12. Zachary Taylor (1849–50)
13. Millard Fillmore (1850–53)
14. Franklin Pierce (1853–57)
15. James Buchanan (1857–61)
16. Abraham Lincoln (1861–65)
17. Andrew Johnson (1865–69)
18. Ulysses S. Grant (1869–77)
19. Rutherford B. Hayes (1877–81)
20. James Garfield (1881)
21. Chester Arthur (1881–85)
22. Grover Cleveland (1885–89)
23. Benjamin Harrison (1889–93)
24. Grover Cleveland (1893–97)
25. William McKinley (1897–1901)
26. Theodore Roosevelt (1901–09)
27. William H. Taft (1909–13)
28. Woodrow Wilson (1913–21)
29. Warren Harding (1921–23)
30. Calvin Coolidge (1923–29)
31. Herbert Hoover (1929–33)
32. Franklin D. Roosevelt (1933–45)
33. Harry Truman (1945–53)
34. Dwight Eisenhower (1953–61)
35. John F. Kennedy (1961–63)
36. Lyndon Johnson (1963–69)
37. Richard Nixon (1969–74)
38. Gerald Ford (1974–77)
39. Jimmy Carter (1977–81)
40. Ronald Reagan (1981–89)
41. George H.W. Bush (1989–93)
42. William J. Clinton (1993–2001)
43. George W. Bush (2001–present)

Non-Aligned Movement (NAM)

The Non-Aligned Movement traces its origins in 1955 when heads of states of 29 African and Asian countries met at Bandung, Indonesia to discuss common concerns, including colonialism and western influence. In 1961, the criteria for NAM membership were set up which stated that the member countries of NAM could not be involved in defence pacts or alliances with the major world powers. This was done to distance NAM from the Soviet and Western power blocks and prevent its members from becoming pawns in the Cold War.

Member States of NAM

1. Afghanistan, 2. Algeria, 3. Angola, 4. Bahamas, 5. Bahrain, 6. Bangladesh, 7. Barbados, 8. Belarus, 9. Belize, 10. Benin, 11. Bhutan, 12. Bolivia, 13. Botswana, 14. Brunei, 15. Burkina Faso, 16. Burundi, 17. Cambodia, 18. Cameroon, 19. Cape Verde, 20. Central African Republic, 21. Chad, 22. Chile, 23. Colombia, 24. Comoros, 25. Congo, 26. Cote d'Ivoire, 27. Cuba, 28. Cyprus, 29. Democratic People's Rep of Korea (North Korea), 30. Democratic Republic of the Congo, 31. Dominican Republic, 32. Djibouti, 33. Ecuador, 34. Egypt, 35. Equatorial Guinea, 36. Eritrea, 37. Ethiopia, 38. Gabon, 39. Gambia, 40. Ghana, 41. Grenada, 42. Guatemala, 43. Guinea, 44. Guinea-Bissau, 45. Guyana, 46. Honduras, 47. India, 48. Indonesia, 49. Iran, 50. Iraq, 51. Jamaica, 52. Jordan, 53. Kenya, 54. Kuwait, 55. Laos, 56. Lebanon, 57. Lesotho, 58. Liberia, 59. Libya, 60. Madagascar, 61. Malawi, 62. Malaysia, 63. Maldives, 64. Mali, 65. Malta, 66. Mauritania, 67. Mauritius, 68. Mongolia, 69. Morocco, 70. Mozambique, 71. Myanmar, 72. Namibia, 73. Nepal, 74. Nicaragua, 75. Niger, 76. Nigeria, 77. Oman, 78. Pakistan, 79. Palestine, 80. Panama, 81. Papua New Guinea, 82. Peru, 83. Philippines, 84. Qatar, 85. Rwanda, 86. Saint Lucia, 87. Saint Vincent and the Grenadines, 88. Sao Tome and Principe, 89. Saudi Arabia, 90. Senegal, 91. Seychelles, 92. Sierra Leone, 93. Singapore, 94. Somalia, 95. South Africa, 96. Sri Lanka, 97. Sudan, 98. Suriname, 99. Swaziland, 100. Syria, 101. Thailand, 102. Timor Leste (East Timor), 103. Togo, 104. Trinidad and Tobago, 105. Tunisia, 106. Turkmenistan, 107. Uganda, 108. United Arab Emirates, 109. Tanzania, 110. Uzbekistan, 111. Vanuatu, 112. Venezuela, 113. Vietnam, 114. Yemen, 115. Zambia, 116. Zimbabwe,

List of NAM Summits

First Conference—Belgrade, September 1–6, 1961

Second Conference—Cairo, October 5–10, 1964

Third Conference—Lusaka, September 8–10, 1970

Fourth Conference—Algiers, September 5–9, 1973

Fifth Conference—Colombo, August 16–19, 1976

Sixth Conference—Havana, September 3–9, 1979

Seventh Conference—New Delhi, March 7–12, 1983

Eighth Conference—Harare, September 1–6, 1986

Ninth Conference—Belgrade, September 4-7, 1989

Tenth Conference—Jakarta, September 1–7, 1992

Eleventh Conference—Cartagena de Indias, October 18–20, 1995

Twelfth Conference—Durban, September 2–3, 1998

Thirteenth Conference—Kuala Lumpur, February 20–25, 2003

Commonwealth of Independent States

The agreement of the establishment of the Commonwealth of Independent States (CIS) was signed in Viskuli, Belarus by the leaders of Belarus, Russia and Ukraine on December 8, 1991. The charter of the CIS was adopted on January 22, 1993 by the Council of Heads of States. The Charter stipulates the principles and goals of the Commonwealth and rights and the obligations of the countries that established it. According to the charter, the Commonwealth was formed on the basis of sovereign equality of all the member states that were independent and equal subjects of international law. The Commonwealth serves further development and strengthening of relations of friendship, inter-ethnic accord, neighbourhood, trust and mutual understanding and cooperation between the states.

Members

1. Azerbaijan, 2. Armenia, 3. Belarus, 4. Georgia, 5. Kazakhstan, 6. Kyrgyzstan, 7. Moldova, 8. Russia, 9. Tajikistan, 10. Turkmenistan, 11. Uzbekistan, 12. Ukraine.

North Atlantic Treaty Organization (NATO)

NATO or the North Atlantic Treaty Organization is an alliance committed to fulfilling the initiatives and goals of the North Atlantic Treaty signed on April 4, 1949. It consists of 26 member countries from Europe and North America.

The fundamental role of NATO is to protect the security and freedom of its member countries by military and political means. It also plays an important role in peacekeeping and crisis management.

Member Countries of NATO

1. Belgium, 2. Bulgaria, 3. Canada, 4. Czech Rep, 5. Denmark, 6. Estonia, 7. France, 8. Germany, 9. Greece, 10. Hungary, 11. Iceland, 12. Italy, 13. Latvia, 14. Lithuania, 15. Luxembourg, 16. Netherlands, 17. Norway, 18. Poland, 19. Portugal, 20. Romania, 21. Slovakia, 22. Slovenia, 23. Spain, 24. Turkey, 25. United Kingdom, 26. United States.

Association of Southeast Asian Nations (ASEAN)

On August 8, 1967, ASEAN or The Association of Southeast Asian Nations was established in Bangkok by five countries—Philippines, Thailand, Malay-

sia, Singapore, and Indonesia. Later, five other countries joined the organization—Brunei (on 8 January 1984), Vietnam (on 28 July 1995), Laos and Myanmar (both on 23 July 1997), and Cambodia (on 30 April 1999).

Member Countries

1. Brunei, 2. Cambodia, 3. Indonesia, 4. Laos, 5. Malaysia, 6. Myanmar, 7. Philippines, 8. Singapore, 9. Thailand, 10. Vietnam.

European Union

List of Member Countries

1. Austria, 2. Belgium, 3. Cyprus, 4. Czech Republic, 5. Denmark, 6. Estonia, 7. Germany, 8. Greece, 9. Finland, 10. France, 11. Hungary, 12. Ireland, 13. Italy, 14. Latvia, 15. Lithuania, 16. Luxembourg, 17. Malta, 18. Poland, 19. Portugal, 20. Slovakia, 21. Slovenia, 22. Spain, 23. Sweden, 24. The Netherlands, 25. United Kingdom.

The applicant countries: 1. Bulgaria, 2. Romania, 3. Turkey.

Arab League

Member States

1. Jordan, 2. United Arab Emirates, 3. Bahrain, 4. Tunisia, 5. Algeria, 6. Djibouti, 7. Saudi Arabia, 8. The Sudan, 9. Syria, 10. Somalia, 11. Iraq, 12. Oman, 13. Palestine, 14. Qatar, 15. Comoros, 16. Kuwait, 17. Lebanon, 18. Libya, 19. Egypt, 20. Morocco, 21. Mauritania, 22. Yemen.

Organization of the Islamic Conference

Member Countries of the Organization of the Islamic Conference and their year of Joining

1. Afghanistan (1969), 2. Albania (1992), 3. Algeria (1969), 4. Azerbaijan (1992), 5. Bahrain (1972), 6. Bangladesh (1974), 7. Benin (1983), 8. Brunei (1984), 9. Burkina Faso (1974),

10. Cameroon (1974), 11. Chad (1969), 12. Comoros (1976), 13. Cote d'Ivoire (2001), 14. Djibouti (1978), 15. Egypt (1969), 16. Gabon (1974), 17. The Gambia (1974), 18. Guinea (1969), 19. Guinea-Bissau (1974), 20. Guyana (1998), 21. Indonesia (1969), 22. Iran (1969), 23. Iraq (1975), 24. Jordan (1969), 25. Kazakhstan (1995), 26. Kuwait (1969), 27. Kyrgyzstan (1992), 28. Lebanon (1969), 29. Libya (1969), 30. Malaysia (1969), 31. Maldives (1976), 32. Mali (1969), 33. Mauritania (1969), 34. Morocco (1969), 35. Mozambique (1994), 36. Niger (1969), 37. Nigeria (1986), 38. Oman (1972), 39. Pakistan (1969), 40. Palestine (1969), 41. Qatar (1972), 42. Saudi Arabia (1969), 43. Senegal (1969), 44. Sierra Leone (1972), 45. Somalia (1969), 46. The Sudan (1969), 47. Suriname (1996), 48. Syria (1972), 49. Tajikistan (1992), 50. Togo (1997), 51. Tunisia (1969), 52. Turkey (1969), 53. Turkmenistan (1992), 54. Uganda (1974), 55. United Arab Emirates (1972), 56. Uzbekistan (1996), 57. Yemen (1969).

G8

Member Nations of G8

1. Canada, 2. France, 3. Germany, 4. Italy, 5. Japan, 6. Russia, 7. United Kingdom, 8. United States of America.

Secretary General of the UN

The activities of the United Nations are coordinated and administered by the Secretariat, which is headed by the UN Secretary-General. On the recommendation of the Security Council, the General Assembly appoints the Secretary-General, whose selection can be vetoed by any of the five permanent members in the Security Council.

The Secretary-General and his staff carry out functions entrusted by the General Assembly, Security Council, the Trusteeship Council and the Economic and Social Council. He is the chief administrative officer at all the meetings of these organs, and submits an annual report to the General Assembly on the work of the UN. The Secretary-General may also bring to the notice of the Security Council any issue that he considers to be a threat to international peace and security.

The Secretary-General is the most authoritative and visible figure of the UN in international affairs. He is regarded as the chief spokesman for the UN, and his headquarters are located at the UN building in New York City.

List of Secretaries-General of the United Nations

1. Trygve Lie (Norway) (1946–1952), 2. Dag Hammarskjöld (Sweden) (1953–1961), 3. U Thant (Myanmar) (1961–1971), 4. Kurt Waldheim (Austria) (1972–1981), 5. Javier de Perez de Cuellar (Peru) (1982–1991), 6. Boutros Boutros-Ghali (Egypt) (1992–1996), 7. Kofi Annan (Ghana) (1997–present).

Geography

Height of Some Important Indian Mountain Peaks

S.No.	Peak Height	From Sea Level in Metres
1.	K2	8,611 in Pak-occupied territory
2.	Kanchenjunga	8,598
3.	Nanga Parbat	8,126
4.	Gasher Brum	8,068 in Pak-occupied territory
5.	Broad Peak	8,047 in Pak-occupied territory
6.	Disteghil Sar	7,885 in Pak-occupied territory

7.	Masher Brum East	7,821
8.	Nanda Devi	7,817
9.	Masher Brum West	7,806 in Pak-occupied territory
10.	Rakaposhi	7,788 in Pak-occupied territory
11.	Kamet	7,756
12.	Saser Kangri	7,672
13.	Skyang Kangri	7,544 in Pak-occupied territory
14.	Sia Kangri	7,422 in Pak-occupied territory
15.	Chaukhamba (Badrinath)	7,138
16.	Trisul West	7,138
17.	Nunkun	7,135
18.	Pauhunri	7,128
19.	Kangto	7,090
20.	Dunagiri	7,066

Ten Largest Islands of the World (Excluding Continents)

Name	Size	Location
1.	Greenland	822,700 sq miles	North Atlantic Ocean
2.	New Guinea	309,000 sq miles	Papua New Guinea-Indonesia
3.	Borneo	283,400 sq miles	Indonesia-Malaysia-Brunei
4.	Madagascar	226,658 sq miles	Indian Ocean
5.	Baffin Island	195,928 sq miles	Northwest Territories, Canada
6.	Sumatra	167,600 sq miles	Indonesia
7.	Honshu	87,805 sq miles	Japan
8.	Victoria Island	83,897 sq miles	Northwest Territories, Canada
9.	Great Britain	83,698 sq miles	United Kingdom
10.	Ellesmere Island	75,767 sq miles	Northwest Territories, Canada

Longest Rivers of the World

Name	Outflow	Length in Kilometres
1.	Nile	Mediterranean Sea	6,650
2.	Amazon-Ucayali-Apurimac	South Atlantic Ocean	6,400
3.	Yangtze	East China Sea	6,300
4.	Mississippi-Missouri- Red Rock	Gulf of Mexico	5,971
5.	Yenisey-Baikal-Selenga	Kara Sea	5,540
6.	Huang Ho	Gulf of Chihli	5,464
7.	Ob-Irtysh	Gulf of Ob	5,410
8.	Parana	Río de la Plata	4,880
9.	Congo South	Atlantic Ocean	4,700
10.	Amur-Argun	Sea of Okhotsk	4,444

Largest Lakes by Area

Lake	Country	Area (Sq. km)
1.	Caspian Sea	Azerbaijan, Iran, Kazakhstan, Russian Federation, Turkmenistan	436,000
2.	Superior	Canada, United States of America	82,100
3.	Victoria	Kenya, Tanzania, Uganda	68,870
4.	Huron	Canada, United States of America	59,600

5.	Michigan	United States of America	57,800
6.	Tanganyika	Burundi, Congo (Democratic Republic), Tanzania, Zambia	32,600
7.	Baikal	Russian Federation	31,500
8.	Great Bear Lake	Canada	31,000
9.	Malawi	Malawi, Mozambique, Tanzania	29,500
10.	Great Slave	Canada	27,000
11.	Erie	Canada, United States of America	25,700
12.	Winnipeg	Canada	24,500
13.	Ontario	Canada, United States of America	18,960
14.	Balkhash	Kazakhstan	17,580
15.	Aral Sea	Kazakhstan, Uzbekistan	17,158
16.	Ladoga	Russian Federation	16,400
17.	Maracaibo	Venezuela	13,010
18.	Tonle Sap	Cambodia	13,000
19.	Agassiz	Canada, United States of America	11,911
20.	Patos	Brazil	10,140

Some Famous Volcanoes of the World

Name	Location	Elevation (ft.)
Guallatiri	Chile	19,876
Cotopaxi	Ecuador	19,347
Kilimanjaro	Tanzania	19,340
El Misti	Peru	19,101
Citlaltépetl	Mexico	18,406
Popocatépetl	Mexico	17,930
Klyuchevskaya	Russia	15,584
Mauna Kea	Hawaii	13,796
Mauna Loa	Hawaii	13,678
Fuji	Japan	12,388
Etna	Italy	10,902
St. Helens	United States of America	8,360
Vesuvius	Italy	4,198
Stromboli	Italy	3,038

Ten Largest Countries

Country	Area (sq. km)
Russia	17075200
Canada	9984670
China	9629021
USA	9596960
Brazil	8511965
Australia	7686850
India	**3300000**
Argentina	2766890
Kazakhstan	2717300
Sudan	2505810

Ten Most Populous Countries

Country	Population
China	1306313812
India	**1028610328**
USA	295734134
Indonesia	241973879
Brazil	186112794
Pakistan	162419946
Russia	144319628
Bangladesh	143420309
Japan	128771988
Nigeria	127417244
Mexico	106202903

Countries with Highest GDPs (Purchasing Power Parity)

Country	GDP (Purchasing Power Parity in $ billion)
USA	11750
China	7262
Japan	3745
India	**3022**
Germany	2362
France	1782
UK	1737
Italy	1609
Brazil	1492
Russia	1408

Countries with Highest Per Capita GDPs

Country	GDP (Purchasing Power Parity in $)
Luxembourg	58900
Norway	40100
USA	40000
Switzerland	33800
Denmark	32200
Ireland	31900
Iceland	31900
Austria	31500
Canada	31300
Netherlands	30700
India	**2900**

[2005 estimates]

Dams in India

Some major projects constructed in India during pre-independence period:

Projects	Year
1. Tajewala Barrage	1873
2. Grand Anicut	1889
3. Bhandardara Dam	1926
4. Mettur Dam	1934

Some large projects constructed after independence:

Projects	Year
1. Hirakud	1957
2. Tungabhadra	1958
3. Matatila	1958
4. Kota Barrage	1960
5. Gandhi Sagar	1960
6. Bhakra	1963
7. Jawahar Sagar	1973
8. Nagarjuna Sagar	1974
9. Farakka Barrage	1974
10. Paithan	1976
11. Dehar Power House	1977
12. Ghataprabha	1979
13. Mahi Bajaj Sagar	1985
14. Salal Projects	1987
15. Chamera	1994

Tallest Buildings of the World

Building	City	Height	Floors	Year
1. Taipei 101	Taipei	509 m	101	2004
2. Petronas Tower 1	Kuala Lumpur	452 m	88	1998
3. Petronas Tower 2	Kuala Lumpur	452 m	88	1998
4. Sears Tower	Chicago	442 m	108	1974
5. Jin Mao Tower	Shanghai	421 m	88	1998
6. Two International Finance Center	Hong Kong	415 m	88	2003
7. CITIC Plaza	Guangzhou	391 m	80	1997
8. Shun Hing Square	Shenzhen	384 m	69	1996
9. Empire State Building	New York City	381 m	102	1931
10. Central Plaza	Hong Kong	374 m	78	1992

Major Indian Ports

Along India's 5,560-km coastline there are 12 major ports and 184 minor/intermediate ports. The ports at Kolkata, Mumbai, Chennai and Mormugao are more than 100 years old, while the Kochi and Visakhapatnam ports are over 60 years old. The ports at Kandla, New Mangalore, Tuticorin, Paradip and Haldia were developed after Independence and the Jawaharlal Nehru Port Trust at Mumbai was commissioned in 1989. Major ports handle about 75 per cent of the country's port traffic.

The major ports are: Kolkata/Haldia, Mumbai, Jawaharlal Nehru Port Trust (JNPT) at Nahava Sheva in Mumbai, Chennai, Kochi, Vishakhapatnam, Kandla, Mormugao, Paradip, New Mangalore, Tuticorin, Ennore Port.

Indian Railways

The first railway train in India ran between Bombay (now Mumbai) and Thane on April 16, 1853, carrying 400 people in 14 carriages. Presently, India has the largest railway system in Asia and the second largest in the world under a single management. It is also the fourth largest on the basis of route kilometrage. In India, 13,000 trains run every day on 63,000 route kilometres of track. 1.3 crore passengers travel daily and about 14 lakh metric tonnes of goods are transported all over the country.

Indian Railways is now organized into sixteen zones and Metro Railway, Kolkata. They are all coordinated and managed by the Railway Board, the apex body. The Railway Board is also known as the Ministry of Railways.

There are more than 7000 stations in India. With regard to the number of passenger coaches, India ranks first in the world. It ranks second in terms of employees, and third in terms of freight wagons, number of passengers carried and the number of locomotives. Indian Railways is a multi-gauge, multi-traction system.

Some Facts on Indian Railways

Track Kilometres

Broad Gauge (1676 mm): 86,526
Metre Gauge (1000 mm): 18,529
Narrow Gauge (762/610 mm): 3651
Total: 108,706

Route	Kilometres
Electrified	16,001
Total	63,028

Indian Railways have:

1. Locomotives: 7566
2. Coaching vehicles: 37,840
3. Freight wagons: 222,147
4. Stations: 6853
5. Good sheds: 2300
6. Repair shops: 700
7. Workforce: 1.54 million

Indian Railway's Zones and Their Divisions with Heaquarters

S.No.	Name of the Zone	Headquarter	Divisions
1.	Central Railway	Mumbai	Bhusawal, Nagpur, Mumbai (CST)*, Solapur*, Pune ^
2.	Eastern Railway	Kolkata	Malda, Howarh, Sealdah, Asansol
3.	Northern Railway	New Delhi	Ambala, Ferozpur, Lucknow, Moradabad, Delhi
4.	North Eastern Railway	Gorakhpur	Lucknow, Varanasi, Izatnagar*
5.	Northeast Frontier Railway	Guwahati	Katihar, Lumding, Tinsukhia, Alipurduar*, Rangiya ^
6.	Southern Railway	Chennai	Chennai, Madurai, Palghat, Trichy, Trivandrum
7.	South Central Railway	Secunderabad	Secunderabad*, Hyderabad*, Guntakal*, Vijaywada*, Guntur ^, Nanded ^
8.	South Eastern Railway	Kolkata	Kharagpur, Chakradharpur*, Adra*, Ranchi ^
9.	Western Railway	Mumbai	Bhavnagar, Mumbai Central, Ratlam*, Rajkot*, Vadodara*, Ahemdabad ^
10.	East Central Railway	Hajipur**	Danapur, Dhanbad, Sonepur, Mughalsarai, Samastipur
11.	East Coast Railway	Bhubaneswar ^	Khurda Road, Waltair, Sambalpur
12.	North Central Railway	Allahabad ^	Allahabad*, Jhansi*, Agra ^
13.	North Western Railway	Jaipur**	Bikaner*, Jodhpur, Jaipur*, Ajmer*
14.	South East Central Railway	Bilaspur ^	Nagpur, Bilaspur*, Raipur ^

15.	South Western Railway	Hubli ^	Bangalore, Mysore, Hubli*
16.	West Central Railway	Jabalpur ^	Jabalpur, Bhopal, Kota*

* : Reorganized Divisions w.e.f 1.4.2003
** : New Zones operationalized on 1.10.2002
^ : New Zones/Divisions operationalized on 1.4.2003

Major Railway Disasters in India

Indian Railways extends for 63,140 route kms, comprising broad gauge (45,099 kms), meter gauge (14,776 kms) and narrow gauge (3,265 kms). It has a fleet strength of nearly 2,17,000 wagons (units), 40,000 coaches and 7,750 locomotives. The system runs 14,444 trains daily, of which about 8,702 are passenger trains. The network carries more than a million tonne of freight traffic and about 14 million passengers, connecting over 6,800 stations. One of the major problems affecting the Railways is the high accident rate. The major forms of mishaps are rake accidents (including derailment and collisions) and incidents of running over of pedestrians. According to the Indian Railways, 'human error' is the cause of 83 per cent of the train accidents in India. The Railways claims that the number of accidents has declined in absolute and relative terms to 0.55 per million train kilometres. The number of consequential train accidents per million train kilometres has also come down to 0.39. The Special Railway Safety Fund (SRSF) of Rs. 17,000 crore was created with effect from 1.10.2001 to eliminate arrears in renewal of overage assets including track, bridges, rolling stock & signaling equipment, as well as safety enhancement works, over a six-year period. The Railways has started the work of rehabilitation and strengthening of old bridges on a priority basis. Around 2700 bridges will be rehabilitated or rebuilt through the Special Railway Safety Fund. It is planned to convert over 1280 unmanned level crossings into manned crossings, over a period of time.

Number of Train Accidents

Year	Accidents
2000–01	473
2001–02	414
2002-03	351
2003-04	325

Major Accidents

Date	Casualty	Comments
6 June 1981	800 dead, over 100 injured	Cyclone blows a train off its tracks and into a river in Bihar
8 July 1987	53 dead	Dakshin Express derails near Macherial in Andhra Pradesh
8 July 1988	107 dead	Island Express plunges into Ashtamudi Lake in Kerala
18 April 1988	75 dead	Karnataka Express derails near Lalitpur in Uttar Pradesh
1 November 1988	48 dead	Udyan Abha Toofan Express derails at Sakaldiha in Bihar
31 October 1991	30 dead	Karnataka Express derails near Makaligurga in Karnataka
21 September 1993	71 dead	Kota-Bina passenger train collides with a goods train near Chhabra in Rajasthan

14 May 1995	52 dead	Madras-Kanyakumari Express collides with a goods train near Salem in Tamil Nadu
20 August 1995	400 dead	Puroshottam Express collides with Kalindi Express near Firozabad railway station in Uttar Pradesh
18 April 1996	60 dead	Gorakhpur-Gonda passenger train collides with a stationary goods train near Gorakhpur in Uttar Pradesh
14 May 1996	35 dead	Bus carrying the victims collides with a Ernakulam-Kayamkulam train at an unmanned level-crossing near Alappuzha in Kerala
14 September 1997	81 dead	Five bogies of Ahmedabad-Howrah express falls into a river in Bilaspur district of Madhya Pradesh
3 August 1999	285 dead	Brahmaputra Mail collides with a stationary Awadh-Assam Express at Gaisal in West Bengal.
22 June 2001	52 dead	Three coaches of Mangalore-Madras Mail tumbled into the Kadalundi river, near Kozhikode in Kerala
9 September 2002	100 dead, 150 hurt	A bogie of Howrah-Delhi Rajdhani Express falls into the Dhave river in Bihar's Aurangabad district
5 January 2002	21 dead, 41 hurt	Secunderabad-Manmad Express hits a stationary goods train at Ghatnandur station in Maharashtra
15 May 2003	38 dead, 13 hurt	Three coaches of Amritsar-bound Frontier Mail catches fire
22 June 2003	53 dead, 25 hurt	First major accident on Konkan Railway; three coaches and engine of the Karwar-Mumbai Central Holiday Special train derails in Sindhudurg district in Maharashtra
14 December 2004	At least 34 dead, around 50 hurt	Head-on collision between Jammu Tawi Ahmedabad Express and Jalandhar-Pathankot Diesel Multiple Unit passenger train in Hoshiarpur district of Punjab
3 October 2005	16 dead, 60 seriously hurt	Bundelkhand Express derails and hits a railway signal cabin in Datia district, Madhya Pradesh

Road Network in India

With a total length of approximately 3.3 million kilometres, India has the second largest road network in the world. Roads have played a vital role in transportation and also enhancing trade. The government has taken initiatives to improve and strengthen the network of National Highways, State Highways and roads in major districts and rural areas. In terms of private sector participation in road projects, the government has received an encouraging response from private investors, both foreign and domestic.

Indian Road Network	Length (in km)
National Highways	58,112*
State Highways	137,119
Major District Roads	470,000
Village and Other Roads	2,650,000
Total Length	3,315,231

*National Highways are less than 2% of network but carry 40% of total traffic

State-wise Distribution of National Highways

Name of the State/ Union Territory	Length (kms)
Andhra Pradesh	4,002
Arunachal Pradesh	392
Assam	2,836
Bihar	3,301
Chandigarh	24
Chhatisgarh	1,810
Delhi	72
Goa	269
Gujarat	2,461
Haryana	1,361
Himachal Pradesh	1,188
Jammu & Kashmir	823
Jharkhand	1,614
Karnataka	3,570
Kerala	1,440
Madhya Pradesh	4,664
Maharashtra	3,626
Manipur	954
Meghalaya	717
Mizoram	927
Nagaland	369
Orissa	3,301
Pondicherry	53
Punjab	1,553
Rajasthan	4,597
Sikkim	62
Tamil Nadu	3,758
Tripura	400
Uttar Pradesh	4,941
Uttaranchal	1,076
West Bengal	1,951
Total	**58,112**

Airlines operating in India

Air traffic in India is growing at a rate of over 20 per cent a year. A key factor behind this growth is the rise of new 'low-cost' airlines. In the last half of 2005, private and public sector airlines from India have placed orders constituting a growth of more than a 170 per cent from a present fleet strength of 158 aircraft. Foreign equity up to 49 per cent and NRI investment of up to 100 per cent is now allowed in domestic airlines, without the requirement of any government approval. At present, India has a low base of 18 million passengers. However, there exists huge growth potential. Tourist arrivals in India are expected to grow exponentially, mainly due to the open sky policy between India and the SAARC countries and the increase in bilateral entitlements with European countries and USA. According to the Directorate-General of Civil Aviation statistics (DGCA), the total size of the domestic market was 18 million in 2003. The scheduled domestic airlines in India carried 42,590 passengers a day in 2003-04, which was 11 per cent more than the previous year's figure of 38,222 per day. The average load factor, an indicator of passenger demand and efficiency of the airlines' sales and marketing efforts, was 58 per cent, a small improvement over the previous year's average of 56 per cent. As per DGCA statistics, domestic airlines were able to record revenue per kilometre (RPKM) higher than costs, for the first time in 2003-04, with a positive operating margin of 3 per cent, compared to a negative margin of 3 per cent in previous years.

List of Scheduled Indian Domestic/ International Airlines:

1. Air-India
2. Air Deccan
3. Air Sahara
4. Indian Airlines
5. Jet Airways
6. Kingfisher Airlines
7. SpiceJet Airlines

Subscriber Trunk Dialing Services

The Subscriber Trunk Dialing (STD) service started in India in 1960. It is presently available in more than 19,500 stations across the country, in all the district headquarters and in more than 97 per cent of the sub-divisional headquarters. In 1976, the International Subscriber Dialing Services or ISD was started between Mumbai and London, and is now available throughout India to almost every other country in the world.

List of Some STD Codes Across India

STD Codes for Andaman and Nicobar Islands

Place	Code
Andaman Island	3192
Nicobar Island	3193

STD Codes for Andhra Pradesh

Place	Code
Hyderabad	40
Vishakhapatnam	891

STD Codes for Arunachal Pradesh

Place	Code
Itanagar	360

STD Codes for Assam

Place	Code
Dispur	360
Digboi	3751
Guwahati	361

STD Codes for Bihar

Place	Code
Patna	612

STD Codes for Chandigarh

Place	Code
Chandigarh	172

STD Codes for Chhattisgarh

Place	Code
Raipur	771

STD Code for Dadra and Nagar Haveli

Place	Code
Dadra And Nagar Haveli	260

STD Code for Daman and Diu

Place	Code
Daman and Diu	260

STD Code for Delhi

Place	Code
Delhi	11

STD Codes for Goa

Place	Code
Panaji	832

STD Codes for Gujarat

Place	Code
Ahmedabad	79
Gandhinagar	2712
Surat	261
Vadodara	265

STD Codes for Haryana

Place	Code
Ambala	171

STD Codes for Himachal Pradesh

Place	Code
Shimla	177

STD Codes for Jammu and Kashmir

Place	Code
Jammu	191
Kargil	1985
Srinagar	194

STD Codes for Jharkhand

Place	Code
Jamshedpur	657
Ranchi	651

STD Codes for Karnataka

Place	Code
Bangalore	80
Mangalore	824

STD Codes for Kerala

Place	Code
Kottayam	481
Thiruvananthapuram	471

STD Code for Lakshadweep

Place	Code
Lakshadweep	486

STD Codes for Madhya Pradesh

Place	Code
Bhopal	755
Gwalior	751
Indore	731

STD Codes for Maharashtra

Place	Code
Mumbai	22
Pune	20

STD Codes for Manipur

Place	Code
Imphal	385

STD Codes for Meghalaya

Place	Code
Cherrapunji	3637
Shillong	364

STD Codes for Mizoram

Place	Code
Aizawl	389

STD Codes for Nagaland

Place	Code
Dimapur	3862
Kohima	370

STD Codes for Orissa

Place	Code
Cuttack	671
Puri	6752
Bhubaneshwar	674

STD Codes for Pondicherry

Place	Code
Pondicherry	413

STD Codes for Punjab

Place	Code
Amritsar	183
Ludhiana	161
Jalandhar	181

STD Codes for Rajasthan

Place	Code
Bhilwara	1482
Jaipur	141

STD Codes for Sikkim

Place	Code
Gangtok	3592

STD Codes for Tamil Nadu

Place	Code
Chennai	44
Coimbatore	422
Ootacamund	423

STD Codes for Tripura

Place	Code
Agartala	381

STD Codes for Uttar Pradesh

Place	Code
Agra	562
Allahabad	532
Kanpur	512
Lucknow	522

STD Codes for Uttaranchal

Place	Code
Dehradun	135
Nainital	5942

STD Codes for West Bengal

Place	Code
Asansol	341
Burdwan	342
Calcutta	33

PIN Codes

The Postal Index Number Code system was introduced in India by the Postal Department on 15 August 1972. Under the scheme, every post office (head or sub) that delivered mails was allotted an individual six-digit Postal Index Number (PIN) Code number. PIN Code digits from left to right progressively pinpoint and locate the geographical position of the Post Office and have a definite role.

I) The first digit represents a zone in the country.

II) The second a sub zone and the manner of routing mails.

III) The first three digits taken together indicate a Sorting District.

IV) The last three digits pinpoint post office of delivery within District.

Branch Post Offices do not have separate PIN Codes that of Sub Post Offices cover branch post offices under it.

The first digit of PIN indicates as below:

First Digit	Region	States Covered
1	Northern	Delhi, Haryana, Punjab, Himachal Pradesh, Jammu and Kashmir
2	Northern	Uttar Pradesh and Uttaranchal
3	Western	Rajasthan, Gujarat, Daman and Diu, and Dadra and Nagar Haveli
4	Western	Chattisgarh, Maharastra and Madhya Pradesh
5	Southern	Andhra Pradesh and Karnataka
6	Southern	Kerala, Tamil Nadu, Laccadive, Minicoy and Amindive Islands and Pondicherry
7	Eastern	Orissa, West Bengal, Assam, Arunachal Pradesh, Mizoram, Manipur, Meghalaya, Nagaland, Tripura, Sikkim, Andaman and Nicobar Islands
8	Eastern	Bihar and Jharkand

The first 2 digits of PIN indicates as below:

First 2 Digits of PIN	Circle
11	Delhi
12 and 13	Haryana
14 to 16	Punjab
17	Himachal Pradesh
18 to 19	Jammu and Kashmir
20 to 28	Uttar Pradesh
30 to 34	Rjasthan
36 to 39	Gujarat
40 to 44	Maharastra
45 to 49	Madhya Pradesh
50 to 53	Andhra Pradesh
56 to 59	Karnataka
60 to 64	Tamil Nadu
67 to 69	Kerala
70 to 74	West Bengal
75 to 77	Orissa
78	Assam
79	North Eastern
80 to 85	Bihar

Weights and Measures

The name International System of Units (SI) was adopted at the 11th General Conference on Weights and Measures. Following an international inquiry by the Bureau of Weights and Measures, which began in 1948, the 10th General Conference on Weights and Measures (1954) approved the introduction of the 'ampere', the 'kelvin' and the 'candela' as base units for electric current, thermodynamic temperature and luminous intensity respectively. At the 14th General Conference on Weights and Measures in 1971 the current version of the SI was completed by adding 'mole' as base unit for amount of substance, bringing the total number of base units to seven.

Quantity	Unit	Symbol	Definition
Length	Meter	m	The metre is the length of the path traveled by light in vacuum during a time interval of 1/299,792,458 of a second

Mass	Kilogram	kg	The kilogram is the unit of mass; it is equal to the mass of the international prototype of the kilogram
Time	Second	s	The second is the duration of 9,192,631,770 periods of the radiation corresponding to the transition between the two hyperfine levels of the ground state of the caesium 133 atom
Electric Current	Ampere	A	The ampere is that constant current which, if maintained in two straight parallel conductors of infinite length, of negligible circular cross-section, and placed 1 m apart in vacuum, would produce between these conductors a force equal to 2×10^{-7} newton per metre of length
Thermodynamic temperature	Kelvin	K	The kelvin, unit of thermodynamic temperature, is the fraction 1/273.16 of the thermodynamic temperature of the triple point of water
Amount of substance	Mole	mol	The mole is the amount of substance of a system which contains as many elementary entities as there are atoms in 0.012 kilogram of carbon 12
Luminous intensity	Candela	cd	The candela is the luminous intensity, in a given direction, of a source that emits monochromatic radiation of frequency 540×10^{12} hertz and that has a radiant intensity in that direction of 1/683 watt per steradian

Derived units

Derived units are units that may be expressed in terms of base units by means of the mathematical symbols of multiplication and division. Certain derived units have been given special names and symbols, and these special names and symbols may themselves be used in combination with those for base and other derived units to express the units of other quantities.

SI Derived Units Expressed in Terms of Base Units

Derived quantity	SI derived unit	
	Name	Symbol
Area	square metre	m^2
Volume	cubic metre	m^3
Speed, Velocity	metre per second	m/s
Acceleration	metre per second squared	m/s^2
Wavenumber	reciprocal metre	m^{-1}
Density, Mass density	kilogram per cubic metre	kg/m^3
Specific volume	cubic metre per kilogram	m^3/kg
Current density	ampere per square metre	A/m^2
Magnetic field strength	ampere per metre	A/m
Concentration (of amount of substance)	mole per cubic metre	mol/m^3
Luminance	candela per square metre	cd/m^2
Refractive index	(the number) one	$1^{(a)}$

SI Derived Units with Special Names and Symbols

Derived quantity	SI derived unit			
	Name	Symbol	Expressed in terms of other SI units	Expressed in terms of SI base units
Plane angle	radian[a]	rad	-	$m \cdot m^{-1} = 1^{(b)}$
Solid angle	steradian[a]	$sr^{(c)}$	-	$m^2 \cdot m^{-2} = 1^{(b)}$
Frequency	hertz	Hz	-	s^{-1}
Force	newton	N	-	$m \cdot kg \cdot s^{-2}$
Pressure, Stress	pascal	Pa	N/m^2	$m^{-1} \cdot kg \cdot s^{-2}$
Energy, Work, Quantity of heat	joule	J	$N \cdot m$	$m^2 \cdot kg \cdot s^{-2}$
Power, Radiant flux	watt	W	J/s	$m^2 \cdot kg \cdot s^{-3}$
Electric charge, Quantity of electricity	coulomb	C	-	$s \cdot A$
Electric potential difference, Electromotive force	volt	V	W/A	$m^2 \cdot kg \cdot s^{-3} \cdot A^{-1}$
Capacitance	farad	F	C/V	$m^{-2} \cdot kg^{-1} \cdot s^4 \cdot A^2$
Electric resistance	ohm	Ω	V/A	$m^2 \cdot kg \cdot s^{-3} \cdot A^{-2}$
Electric conductance	siemens	S	A/V	$m^{-2} \cdot kg^{-1} \cdot s^3 \cdot A^2$
Magnetic flux	weber	Wb	$V \cdot s$	$m^2 \cdot kg \cdot s^{-2} \cdot A^{-1}$
Magnetic flux density	tesla	T	Wb/m^2	$kg \cdot s^{-2} \cdot A^{-1}$
Inductance	henry	H	Wb/A	$m^2 \cdot kg \cdot s^{-2} \cdot A^{-2}$
Celsius temperature	degree Celsius[d]	°C	-	K
Luminous flux	lumen	lm	$cd \cdot sr^{(c)}$	$m^2 \cdot m^{-2} \cdot cd = cd$
Illuminance	lux	lx	lm/m^2	$m^2 \cdot m^{-4} \cdot cd = m^{-2} \cdot cd$
Activity (referred to a radionuclide)	becquerel	Bq	-	s^{-1}

Absorbed dose, specific energy (imparted), kerma	gray	Gy	J/kg	$m^2 \cdot s^{-2}$
Dose equivalent, ambient dose equivalent, directional dose equivalent, personal dose equivalent, organ equivalent dose	sievert	Sv	J/kg	$m^2 \cdot s^{-2}$
Catalytic activity	katal	kat	-	$s^{-1} \cdot mol$

(a) The radian and steradian may be used with advantage in expressions for derived units to distinguish between quantities of different nature but the same dimension.

(b) In practice, the symbols rad and sr are used where appropriate, but the derived unit "1" is generally omitted in combination with a numerical value.

(c) In photometry, the name steradian and the symbol sr are usually retained in expressions for units.

(d) This unit may be used in combination with SI prefixes, e.g. millidegree Celsius, m°C.

SI Derived Units Whose Names and Symbols Include SI Derived Units with Special Names and Symbols

Derived quantity	SI derived unit Name	Symbol	Expressed in terms of SI base units
Dynamic viscosity	pascal second	Pa · s	$m^{-1} \cdot kg \cdot s^{-1}$
Moment of force	newton metre	N · m	$m^2 \cdot kg \cdot s^{-2}$
Surface tension	newton per metre	N/m	$kg \cdot s^{-2}$
Angular velocity	radian per second	rad/s	$m \cdot m^{-1} \cdot s^{-1} = s^{-1}$
Angular acceleration	radian per second squared	rad/s²	$m \cdot m^{-1} \cdot s^{-2} = s^{-2}$
Heat flux density, Irradiance	watt per square metre	W/m²	$kg \cdot s^{-3}$
Heat capacity, Entropy	joule per kelvin	J/K	$m^2 \cdot kg \cdot s^{-2} \cdot K^{-1}$
Specific heat capacity, Specific entropy	joule per kilogram kelvin	J/(kg·K)	$m^2 \cdot s^{-2} \cdot K^{-1}$
Specific energy	joule per kilogram	J/kg	$m^2 \cdot s^{-2}$
Thermal conductivity	watt per metre kelvin	W/(m·K)	$m \cdot kg \cdot s^{-3} \cdot K^{-1}$
Energy density	joule per cubic metre	J/m³	$m^{-1} \cdot kg \cdot s^{-2}$
Electric field strength	volt per metre	V/m	$m \cdot kg \cdot s^{-3} \cdot A^{-1}$
Electric charge density	coulomb per cubic metre	C/m³	$m^{-3} \cdot s \cdot A$

Electric flux density	coulomb per square metre	C/m^2	$m^{-2} \cdot s \cdot A$
Permittivity	farad per metre	F/m	$m^{-3} \cdot kg^{-1} \cdot s^4 \cdot A^2$
Permeability	henry per metre	H/m	$m \cdot kg \cdot s^{-2} \cdot A^{-2}$
Molar energy	joule per mole	J/mol	$m^2 \cdot kg \cdot s^{-2} \cdot mol^{-1}$
Molar entropy, molar heat capacity	joule per mole kelvin	$J/(mol \cdot K)$	$m^2 \cdot kg \cdot s^{-2} \cdot K^{-1} \cdot mol^{-1}$
Exposure (x and y rays)	coulomb per kilogram	C/kg	$kg^{-1} \cdot s \cdot A$
Absorbed dose rate	gray per second	Gy/s	$m^2 \cdot s^{-3}$
Radiant intensity	watt per steradian	W/sr	$m^4 \cdot m^{-2} \cdot kg \cdot s^{-3} = m^2 \cdot kg \cdot s^{-3}$
Radiance	watt per square metre steradian	$W/(m^2 \cdot sr)$	$m^2 \cdot m^{-2} \cdot kg \cdot s^{-3} = kg \cdot s^{-3}$
Catalytic (activity) concentration	katal per cubic metre	kat/m^3	$m^{-3} \cdot s^{-1} \cdot mol$

General Knowledge Quiz

1. Whom did AIFF recently appoint as the coach of the Indian national team?

2. Who is the present President of Interpol?

3. In which Indian city was India's only WTA tournament, the Sunfeast Open, held?

4. Who recorded his seventh consecutive win at the 2005 Tour de France?

5. Who did Roger Federer defeat to lift the 2005 US Open men's singles title for a second consecutive time?

6. Which actress, director and actor was a member of the jury for international competition at Locarno 2005?

7. Who was awarded the Rajiv Gandhi Khel Ratna Award for the year 2004?

8. Which Indian film was shown on the opening day of the 2005 Locarno Film Festival?

9. Who was the only Indian to reach the final of an event in the 2005 World Athletics Championship?

10. Who won the awards for Best Actress and Best Actor at the 52nd National Film Awards?

11. Which film bagged the Best Film award at the 52nd National Film Awards?

12. Who won the 2005 edition of the ICC Trophy?

13. What is the name of the latest or sixth book in the Harry Potter series?

14. Which city will host the the 2012 Summer Olympics?

15. Where did the 2005 FIFA World Youth Championship take place?

16. Who was the men's singles champion at the 2005 Wimbledon tennis championship?

17. From which seat did Sunil Dutt serve five terms as Lok Sabha MP?

18. Who is the only Indian in the top 10 of 2005 Forbes list of world's richest people?

19. Who won the Best Actor and Best Actress awards at the 2005 Oscar Awards?

20. Which famous Englishman gave the most accepted theory about the formation of Lakshadweep?

21. Whom did Mahesh Bhupathi pair up with to lift the mixed doubles trophy at Wimbledon for the second time?

22. Till date, the American Red Cross launched the largest mobilization of resources for which single natural disaster?

23. The post office of which European country is to issue the world's first postage stamps with images sent in to it via camera phones using MMS?

24. What is the name of the nationwide campaign, launched by Ministry of Tourism, that aims at sensitizing key stakeholders towards tourists, through a process of training and orientation?

25. Till 31 July 2005, the maximum number of AIDS cases in India were reported from which state?

26. Which United Nations organization is celebrating its sixtieth anniversary in 2005?

27. Whose record did Fernando Alonso break to become Formula One's youngest World champion?

28. In which country capital did the SAF Games take place in 2004?

29. On the birth anniversary of which Indian sportsperson is 'National Sports Day' celebrated in India?

30. In 2004, which famous Indian monument completed 350 years of existence?

31. Which famous Indian building has four floors and 340 rooms with a floor area of 200,000 square feet and was built by using 700 million bricks and 3 million cubic feet of stone?

32. Who is the ex officio president of the Indian Parliamentary Group (IPG) and the chairman of the Conference of Presiding Officers of Legislative Bodies in India?

33. Which famous Indian drafted the first petition sent by the Indians to a South African legislature in 1894?

34. Whose birth anniversary is observed as the National Day of Patriotism in India every year?

35. Which continent has the most number of countries?

36. The name of which natural phenomenon comes from the Japanese language meaning 'harbour' and 'wave'?

37. Which country has got the largest number of permanent post offices in the world?

38. Who is the oldest pope since Clement XII (elected 1730)?

39. Which government fund was set up in the wake of the Chinese aggression in 1962?

40. Which is the last language to appear on the language panel of any bank note?

41. The Man of the Series of the Test series between which two teams receives the Compton-Miller Medal?

42. What is the internet country code for India?

43. Which is the oldest among the contemporary classical dance forms of India?

44. Which UNESCO World Heritage Site serves as the headquarters of the Central Railways in India?

45. Which lady formed the 'Vanar Sena', a children's brigade to help freedom fighters in the 1930s?

46. Which present North-Eastern state of India was known as Lushai Hills District before independence?

47. Which is the most extracted metal in the world?

48. What fraction of the Rajya Sabha retires every second year?

49. Which is the oldest locomotive in India still in operation?

50. The Legislative Assembly of which state has the highest number of seats?

51. Which famous dance form derived its name from an earthen lamp?

52. Which town was built by Akbar in honour of Shaikh Salim Chisti?

53. Which monument has pink honeycombed 953 sandstone windows known as 'jharokhas'?

54. Who served as the first Indian municipal commissioner of Ahmedabad from 1917 to 1924?

55. Which was the first affiliated specialized agency of the United Nations?

56. 'Abhanga' and 'Tribhanga' are postures of which dance form?

57. According to a survey of the British Council, which six letter word was nominated as the most beautiful word in the English language?

58. Which Nobel Laureate is the chief of the political party 'National League for Democracy' and has been under house arrest from 1989?

59. Which state of USA originally abstained from voting in favour of the Declaration of Independence on 2 July 1776?

60. In January 1776, who published a pamphlet titled 'Common Sense' in which the issue of American independence was made the main agenda?

61. If you want to visit the cities in the Golden Triangle, which city, apart from Delhi and Jaipur, would you visit?

62. According to NASA, who is the first fare-paying passenger to space who went aboard the STS-41D space craft on 30 August 1984?

63. What was the name of the space exploration facility of the former Soviet Union in which Yuri Gagarin acted as deputy training director during the mid-1960s?

64. Forces from which country forced hundreds of thousands of Armenians to flee their country during World War I?

65. The Potsdam Conference authorized the expulsion of 12 million people of which ethnic origin from different parts of Europe after World War II?

66. When is the UN World Refugee Day?

67. What is the total limit of questions admitted for a particular day in the Rajya Sabha?

68. How many members constitute the quorum of the Rajya Sabha?

69. What is the name of the tennis museum located beneath Court no. 3 at Roland Garros?

70. Which South American Nobel Prize winner in Literature translated Rabindranath Tagore's works into Spanish in 1924?

71. In which year did Rabindranath Tagore start a school in Shantiniketan with no more than 5 students?

72. In 1961, what replaced Oxygen as a standard of comparison for the atomic weight of each element?

73. In 1791, for supporting which political movement was Joseph Priestley ousted from the city of Birmingham?

74. In 2002, which well-known playwright wrote and directed the film called *Mango Souffle*?

75. On which specific day you might get to witness the 'muhurat' trading on Indian stock exchanges?

76. Who is the first woman to be among the BSE board of directors?

77. Of the seven countries that have nuclear capabilities, which two did not sign the Comprehensive Test Ban Treaty (CTBT) in 1996?

78. Which African country claims to have dismantled all its nuclear weapons?

79. Which country developed a missile warhead with nuclear capabilities named 'Red Snow'?

80. What is the name for the most important industrial region along the north Rhine- Westphalia state of western Germany?

81. The 1944 Anglo-Ethiopian Agreements ended the colonial rule of which country in Ethiopia?

82. This country gained independence in two parts; Tanganaika in 1961 and Zanzibar in 1963. In 1964, they merged together to form which new entity?

83. Before its independence in 1990, which country was known as 'South-West Africa'?

84. Which south-east Asian country celebrates its Independence Day on 31 August?

85. Which place in the Indian subcontinent once recorded a temperature of 52 degrees centigrade?

86. Which specific sensory organ in the 'Giant Squid' is the largest among all animals?

87. From which language did the word hurricane originate?

88. On the Beaufort Scale of wind speed, which number is assigned to hurricanes?

89. In which country is a national holiday celebrated on the third Monday of September called Respect for the Aged Day?

90. Which equinox occurs in September in the northern hemisphere?

91. Which was the third country to launch an artificial satellite in 1965 and named it 'Asterix'?

92. According to Hindu mythology, which day marks the triumph of Lord Rama over Ravana?

93. Hourly time signals from which observatory were first broadcast on 5 February 1924?

94. How many time zones are observed around the world?

95. The hospital St Mary of Bethlehem in London, an asylum for the insane, gave rise to which word in modern usage?

96. Which city has an underground railway system stretching 265 kilometres and 170 stations?

97. Geoffrey Dummer, a Rudder scientist from UK, was the first person to conceive and publish a paper on which aspect of modern computers?

98. In 1877, on what did Emil Berliner obtain a patent on in Paris?

99. In 1992, who won the inaugural Confederations Cup in football?

100. In Homer's epic *Odyssey*, what was the name of the dog who was the only one to recognize Odysseus after his return to Ithaca after 19 years?

101. Who is the only Pakistani scientist to win a physics Nobel?

102. Which discourse of the Buddha is believed to be the earliest printed image with an authenticated date?

103. Which film institute, directly financed by the Ministry of Information and Broadcasting, was established in Kolkata in 1995?

104. Which was the first organ to be transplanted successfully in humans?

105. In which state is the National Institute of Oceanography located?

106. In 1885, nine-year-old Joseph Meister received the first vaccination against which disease?

107. In 2000, the president of which Asian country was awarded the Nobel Prize for Peace?

108. On 10 October 2000, to which country did USA grant 'Permanent Normal Trade Relations' (PNTR)?

109. From which US city was the then US First Lady, Hillary Clinton, elected to the US Senate in November 2000?

110. Who is the first author to be included in the Forbes billionaire list?

111. With which dance form is Birju Maharaj associated?

112. Which was the last to be set up amongst all the IIMs (Indian Institutes of Management) in India?

113. According to Linus Pauling, high daily doses of which vitamin could ward off cancer?

114. Name the Australian athlete who lit the Olympic flame at the Opening Ceremony and also won the gold in the women's 400-metre dash event at the 2000 Olympic Games.

115. Who was the first Indian to win an Oscar?

116. The government of which state, other than Maharashtra, gives the Lata Mangeshkar Award?

117. Along with Rahul Dravid, which cricketer was awarded the Padma Shri in 2004?

118. Who was the first chief election commissioner of India?

119. In May 2000, which country marked the birth of its billionth citizen?

120. Who was crowned king of Nepal after the death of King Birendra?

121. In March 2000, which US President visited India?

122. Who was the first president of the BJP?

123. Which Indian state did a massive earthquake hit on Republic Day in 2001?

124. Which political party's symbol has remained the same through 14 general elections?

125. In December 2002, which Indian chief minister was acquitted of all corruption charges in the TANSI land deal case and the Pleasant Stay Hotel case?

126. What was the name of Saddam Hussein's political outfit?

127. In January 2000, Ricardo Lagos became the president of which South American country?

128. Which Indian politician founded the Telugu Desam Party?

129. In January 2000, which Asian country issued bans on posting and distribution of what it described as 'state secrets' on the Internet?

130. In January 2000, which Internet company agreed to buy media giant Time Warner for $ 165 billion?

131. In April 2002, which party won a landslide victory in the Tamil Nadu Assembly polls?

132. In January 2000, more than 130 countries established the first treaty regulating trade in which type of products?

133. To which party does US presidential candidate John Kerry belong?

134. In March 2000, who was formally elected the new president of Russia?

135. Who was the youngest person to become the chief minister of Assam?

136. In February 2000, in which European country did a nationalist leader named Jorg Haider attract controversy for praising Nazis?

137. In February 2000, the Kurdistan People's Party announced an end of their war on which West Asian country?

138. Which independent candidate has won the maximum number of terms to the Lok Sabha?

139. In February 2000, the British government suspended self-government in which region?

140. King Jigme Singye Wangchuck rules which Asian country?

141. In 2000, US General Wesley Clark served as the head of NATO troops maintaining order in which Yugoslav province?

142. Vice-President Bhairon Singh Shekhawat was the chief minister of which Indian state?

143. In December 2003, which former Indian prime minister was acquitted in the Lakhubhai Pathak case?

144. Where was the 2004 edition of the ICC Champions Trophy held?

145. In 2000, who succeeded Jyoti Basu as the chief minister of West Bengal?

146. In May 2002, who was re-elected the president of France?

147. Which Indian golfer was the first to qualify and play on the 2004 US PGA tour?

148. In February 2002, where was the Sabarmati Express train set on fire, sparking off widespread violence in Gujarat?

149. In December 2001, terrorists attacked which New Delhi landmark that led to a near-war situation between India and Pakistan?

150. In 2004, who became the youngest Test captain for Zimbabwe?

151. Who was the first author to submit a typewritten manuscript?

152. Against which team did Brian Lara score his 400 runs in a Test match?

153. Charles M. Schulz, who passed away in 2000, was the creator of which famous comic strip?

154. What is the name of the consortium of genetic researchers who mapped the first draft of the human genetic code in 2000?

155. Which theatre training institution was set up by the Sangeet Natak Akademi in 1959 in New Delhi?

156. In April 2002, in which state did the Left Front win is sixth successive term in the Assembly elections?

157. In March 2001, the remaining pieces of the Russian space station, Mir, splashed down into which ocean?

158. Which California millionaire became the world's first paying space tourist when the Russian space agency launched him aboard a rocket in April 2001?

159. From which state have the most Indian prime ministers come?

160. By what name is the Hindi author Sachchidananda Hirananda Vatsyayana better known?

161. Which Marathi playwright is well known for plays like *Sakharam Binder* and *Ghashiram Kotwal*?

162. Which noted Tamil poet died in 1921 after being hit by a temple elephant in Triplicane, Madras?

163. Which Persian-language poet is sometimes called the 'Parrot of India'?

164. Which country won the Euro 2004 Championship in Portugal?

165. In July 2000, which famous aircraft crashed for the first time since its launch?

166. Name the Russian submarine that sank in August 2000, killing 118.

167. In which country did the Summer Olympic Games take place in 2000?

168. In which country is the resort city of Cannes, where the Cannes Film Festival is held every year, located?

169. Which Yugoslav president was overthrown in an uprising in October 2000?

170. *My Son's Father* is the autobiography of which well-known Indian author?

171. Which US corporate giant lost an anti-trust suit in April 2000?

172. Which Indian musician developed a guitar with 19 strings and named it after himself?

173. In May 2000, Ken Livingstone became the first elected mayor of which European capital?

174. Which eminent film director has made the film *Netaji Subhash Chandra Bose: The Forgotten Hero*?

175. In June 2000, the merger of Phillip Morris and which other US food giant was announced?

176. Which author-cartoonist wrote *Khasakinte Ithihasam* (The Legends of Khasak)?

177. Who is the Nobel Prize-winning French author whose last incomplete novel was called *The First Man*?

178. In which dialect is the poet Maithili Sharan Gupt regarded a pioneer of verse?

179. In February 2000, which spacecraft became the first artificial satellite to circle an asteroid?

180. Who along with Podolsky and Rosen constructed a thought experiment to challenge the Copenhagen interpretation of quantum theory?

181. Name the longest running musical in New York's Broadway that shut in June 2000, after running for 18 years?

182. In March 2003, Horst Kohler became the new managing director of which international organization?

183. Where is the Indian Institute of Science located?

184. Where was India's first nuclear power station constructed?

185. Which is the first individual event in which an Indian won an Olympic medal?

186. *Madhushala* is a creation of which Indian poet?

187. What were the four subsidiaries of General Insurance Corporation?

188. In which Iraq jail did US private Lynndie England, currently under trial, take pictures of POWs in humiliating poses?

189. Who was the first Indian filmmaker to win a Golden Lion at the Venice Film Festival?

190. From which modern-day Indian state does the dance form Mohiniattam originate?

191. Which South African author has won two Booker prizes as well as the Nobel Prize?

192. Which Indian author's autobiography is titled *Rashidi Ticket*?

193. Which group was formed after independence in Bombay, by artists F.N. Souza, M. F. Husain, K. H. Ara, S. K. Bakre and H. A. Gade?

194. By what name is Haribhai Jariwala better known in the world of Hindi films?

195. Which Indian musician was awarded the Grammy Award for *Full Circle – Carnegie Hall 2000*, in the Best World Music Album category at the 2001 Grammy Awards?

196. By what name is Dhanpat Rai Shrivastava better known?

197. In which Indian state is folk music known as Baul mostly performed?

198. What was the name of the first National Academy of the Arts set up in India, which was inaugurated on 28 January 1953 in a special function held in Parliament House?

199. Which Indian director made the film *Bhuvan Shome* (1969), which started the new-wave cinema movement in India?

200. Which famous 18th century-born German composer became deaf in the latter part of his life?

201. Which film did Alfred Hitchcock make twice?

202. Which painter is famous for the Renaissance frescoes painted by him in the Sistine Chapel?

203. Which Indian musician is the son of Ustad Hafiz Ali Khan?

204. Which instrument was patented by Antoine-Joseph Sax in Paris in 1846?

205. Which Nobel Laureate introduced the Manipuri form of dance to the rest of India in the early 20th century?

206. Which Odissi dancer established a dance village called Nrityagram, 30 km north-west of Bangalore in the 1990s?

207. By what name is the 400-year-old ritualistic dance drama of Karnataka, of which the themes are based on Hindu epics, known?

208. What was the nationality of Vincent van Gogh?

209. Which term was coined in the 1970s by economist Dr Raj Krishna to describe the inability of the Indian economy to grow at more than a modest rate of 3 per cent per annum?

210. Which is the first communications school in India to offer post-graduate diploma courses focusing on communications, advertising, media and market research?

211. Which T.S. Eliot work ends with the words 'Shantih Shantih Shantih'?

212. Name the Assamese author who was awarded the 36th Bharatiya Jnanpith Award in 2002.

213. Which significant portfolio in the Central government was L.K. Advani holding when he was elevated to the post of the deputy prime minister in June 2002?

214. From where was India's first exclusive Meteorological Satellite (METSAT) successfully launched in Spetember 2002?

215. Which service would you have to join if you wanted to be the principal chief conservator of forests in a state?

216. 23 April is celebrated by UNESCO as 'World Book Day' each year to commemorate the death of three celebrated authors. Who are they?

217. National Sports Day is celebrated in India on the birth anniversary of which Indian sportsman?

218. In July 2004, which former Miss India committed suicide in Mumbai?

219. Till today, which is the only Indian city to have hosted the Asian Games?

220. Who appoints the comptroller and auditor general of India?

221. Who is the first IPS officer to head Mumbai's Crime Branch?

222. What are the two cities in Charles Dicken's *A Tale of Two Cities*?

223. Who was the first Indian to win the All-England Badminton Championships?

224. On which internationally famous institution are the IITs of India modelled?

225. Name the Indian Vice-President who passed away in July 2002.

226. Which famous French thinker and author declined the Nobel Prize in 1964?

227. In which city did India win the Hockey World Cup in 1975?

228. In December 2001, which US utility giant filed for bankruptcy protection?

229. To which business house does Spectramind, a leading outsourcing company belong?

230. Which Australian author has won the Booker Prize twice?

231. If the HIV virus affects humans, what animal does SIV affect?

232. In June 2001, whom did Pervez Musharraf replace as Pakistan's president?

233. Which economic doctrine that opposes unnecessary regulation or market influence by government means 'allow to do' in French?

234. Other than Life Insurance and General Insurance, which is the other insurance sector in India?

235. Which author of Indian origin won the Pulitzer Prize for her collection of short stories titled *The Interpreter of Maladies*?

236. Which German scientist formulated the 'uncertainty principle'?

237. Which club won the English Premier League title in the 2003-04 season?

238. Who was the first Indian woman to receive the Jnanpith Award?

239. In January 2002, which former Indian Air Force chief was made the first- ever Marshal of the Indian Air Force?

240. Which Northern Ireland leader and a key player in the peace settlement was presented the Gandhi Peace Prize in 2002?

241. Who was the famous coach of Indian 'golden girl' P.T. Usha?

242. Which famous Irish poet wrote the introduction to Rabindranath Tagore's *Gitanjali*?

243. Traditionally, who is the chairman of the Planning Commission of India?

244. In which Olympic Games did Milkha Singh break an Olympic record to achieve the 4th position in 400 metres?

245. Who captained India in the first two cricket World Cups?

246. Who is the author of 'An Inquiry into the nature and causes of the Wealth of Nations' (1776), the first comprehensive system of political economy?

247. Who was the first Indian to play in 100 Test matches?

248. In which novel by Bankim Chandra Chatterjee would you find the phrase 'Vande Mataram'?

249. Which company launched Yisou, or 'Number One Search', a search engine exclusively for Chinese users?

250. India's Second Five-Year plan was based on the four-sector model developed by which famous statistician?

251. Athletes of which country have won the 100 metres race at the Olympics the most number of times?

252. What is the name of the first private manned spacecraft to fly to the edge of space and back?

253. In which celebrated Indian novel would you come across a village named 'Ayemenem'?

254. In 2000, whom did Vishwanathan Anand beat to win the FIDE World Championships?

255. Which Indian has served the longest period as president of India?

256. Who was the first Indian cricketer to win the Arjuna Award?

257. Who is the youngest MP in the 14th Lok Sabha?

258. Where are the headquarters of the Asian Development Bank?

259. Who wrote the historical chronicle *Rajatarangini*?

260. *Razm Namah* was a translation of which Indian epic into Persian?

261. In which Indian city is the Postgraduate Institute of Medical Education and Research (PGIMER) located?

262. Which professor of the London School of Economics received the Pravasi Bharatiya Samman Award in 2004?

263. Who won the 2004 general election by a record margin of nearly 6,00,000 votes?

264. Chevening Scholarships enable students to study in which country?

265. Who composed Rag Mian-ki Todi and Rag Darbari Todi?

266. Which was the earliest authoritative text on public finance, administration and fiscal laws in India?

267. What is the full form of BPO?

268. In January 2001, the Government conferred the Bharat Ratna on Lata Mangeshkar and which other musician?

269. In February 2001, who assumed charge as India's first-ever woman Foreign Secretary?

270. What is the name of the national award for wildlife protection that the Union Environment and Forests Ministry set up in February 2001?

271. In 2004, which Indian astronaut was posthumously awarded NASA's Congressional Space Medal of Honor?

272. In October 2003, whom did Pope John Paul II beatify in Vatican City?

273. What was the name of the British-built space probe that was launched into the atmosphere around Mars in December 2003 by the Mars Express orbiter?

274. What is unique about the Jamnagar-Loni pipeline that Prime Minister Atal Bihari Vajpayee dedicated to the nation in May 2001?

275. In September 2002, terrorists attacked which famous temple belonging to the Swaminarayan sect in Gandhinagar?

276. In May 2001, where did the world's highest ground-based telescope start functioning?

277. Which unique feat did an US investment banker named Steve Fossett complete in July 2002?

278. Name the highway project that seeks to connect the four metros: Delhi, Mumbai, Chennai and Kolkata.

279. On 27 August 2003 which planet came closer to earth than at any time during the last 60,000 years?

280. In December 2003, which East Asian country confirmed an outbreak of bird flu after the virus was discovered at a farm 80km south of its capital city?

281. In May 2003, who became the first Indian actress to be on the jury of the Cannes International Film Festival?

282. On January 1, 2002, the currency Euro was launched affecting the lives of people in how many countries?

283. In October 2003, which Hollywood star was elected the governor of California?

284. In February 2002, which country in the Arabian Gulf was proclaimed a 'kingdom'?

285. In August 2002, which Indian state was declared the world's first 'baby-friendly' state?

286. In Jan 2003, who became the first woman and also the first Indian to be appointed as United Nations Civilian Police Adviser?

287. In February 2003, after whom did Prime Minister Atal Bihari Vajpayee christen Meteorological Satellite (METSAT)?

288. Who is the first cricketer to take 500 wickets in one-day internationals?

289. In which city was 'The International Criminal Court', the world's first permanent war crimes court, launched?

290. In which Indian state was the first confirmed case of SARS reported?

291. Name India's first indigenously built stealth frigate.

292. Who is the youngest driver to win a Formula One Grand Prix?

293. What is the name of India's indigenous Light Combat Aircraft (LCA) - the smallest, lightweight, single-seat, single-engine, fourth generation combat aircraft?

294. Who is the first woman to head a political party in Jammu and Kashmir?

295. Which was the first former Soviet republic to vote itself into the European Union, after a referendum in the capital?

296. Which club did David Beckham join after quitting Manchester United?

297. Name the main accused in the multi-crore fake stamp paper scam.

298. In 2002, whose record did Sachin Tendulkar break by completing 30 centuries?

299. In December 2002, what post did Ratan Tata still hold after he gave up his executive posts in the Tata empire after he turned 65?

300. Name the world's largest and most expensive passenger ship that completed its maiden transatlantic voyage and arrived at the Florida port in January 2004.

301. Which author, believed to have been in the court of Chandragupta Vikramaditya, wrote *Abhijnana Sakuntalam*?

302. From which state was Reliance Industries Limited managing director, Anil Ambani, elected to the Rajya Sabha?

303. J J School of Arts (Mumbai) has six degree courses. If four of them are in Painting, Sculpture,

Metal Work and Textile Design, what are the other two in?

304. Which Indian helped create the United Nations' Human Development Index?

305. Till date, which is India's single largest foreign direct investment?

306. To which party did Morarji Desai belong when he became the prime minister of India?

307. Name the village in Kerala which is India's first 100 per cent computer-literate village.

308. Who was the first prime minister of India never to have faced Parliament?

309. 'Yokakshemam Vahamyaham' or 'Your Welfare is our Responsibility' is the motto of which Indian organization?

310. Kemal Ataturk was the first president of which country?

311. In the 20th century, who was the longest serving British prime minister?

312. Which economist developed the theory of 'Comparative Advantage'?

313. In July 2004, Where did Indian Air Force fighter aircraft participate in an international exercise outside the Indian subcontinent for the first time?

314. In 1972, with which president of Pakistan did Indira Gandhi sign the Simla Agreement?

315. Name India's first stealth warship that was commissioned at St. Petersburg, Russia.

316. Who was the first governor-general of Pakistan?

317. Which former head of state spent many years as a prisoner at Robben Island?

318. In August 2003, the fossil remains of which creature was found at Rhioli village near the river Narmada?

319. Which Indian chief minister created the record of ruling his state for 24 continuous years?

320. Which Indian state has the most number of Lok Sabha seats?

321. Which type of computing devices are targets of a Trojan horse virus known as Backdoor.Bardor.A or WinCE.Bradona?

322. What is the name of the party formed by the breakaway Hurriyat group leader Syed Ali Geelani?

323. What is the name of the low-cost airline floated by Vijay Mallya's UB Group?

324. Who was the first deputy prime minister of India?

325. Which is the only socialist country in the West Indies?

326. Who was the first socialist to become the president of France?

327. In 1981, President Anwar Sadat was assassinated. Which country did he rule?

328. What is the election symbol of the Nationalist Congress Party?

329. When Atal Bihari Vajpayee first became prime minister, whom did he succeed in office?

330. How is Badruddin Jamaluddin Kazi, the comedian of yesteryears, better known?

331. Which Congress politician has been the chief minister of two Indian states?

332. Visitors from which neighbouring country caused a rise in alcohol tax collections in Estonia?

333. According to Swedish geographer Ulf Erlingsson, which is the most likely match for Atlantis as described by Plato?

334. In which African country did poachers burn down nearly one-third of its largest national park?

335. Who was the first Speaker of the Lok Sabha?

336. Which country built the world's deepest and most silent nuclear submarine nicknamed 'Losharik'?

337. In which SAARC country is the legislative house called 'Majlis'?

338. Name the daughter of Sheikh Mujibur Rahman who also became the prime minister of Bangladesh?

339. In September 2003, the UN lifted 11 year old sanctions against which country?

340. Which country is the largest importer of gold?

341. In 1993, where was the National Stock Exchange of India set up?

342. Which Indian state has seen 21 chief ministers in the first 50 years of Independence?

343. Which music personality recently changed her name to Esther?

344. What was set up in the Department of Industrial Development by the Government of India in 1970 on the basis of the recommendations of the Administrative Reforms Commission?

345. Which physician led the team that performed the first successful heart transplant surgery in India?

346. Ben Metcalfe passed away on 14 October 2003. He was the founder of which international organization?

347. Which scientist designed the crescograph to measure the response of plants to external stimuli?

348. Which infamous criminal was arrested from Royale Casino in Durbarmarg in Nepal in September 2003?

349. What is the Russian name of the aircraft carrier that the Indian Navy bought from Russia?

350. Which airship of yesteryears did the Greek government use for surveillance in the Athens Olympic?

351. Which is the only subatomic particle to be named after an Indian scientist?

352. Who was sworn in as Malaysia's fifth prime minister after Mahathir Mohamad stepped down?

353. Who was the first US president to make an official visit to India?

354. In which city did Air India's first-ever commercial flight to China arrive?

355. What was the name of the traveling robotic geologist from NASA that landed on the 'Red Planet' on 3 January 2004?

356. Who was the first non-European to win the Nobel Prize for Literature?

357. In 2000, which state became the 28th state of the Indian Union?

358. What is the observation in economics that 'bad money drives our good' popularly called?

359. Who was India's captain in its inaugural cricket Test against England in 1932?

360. Which is the only country in Europe to have a 'restorative justice scheme' for every prison and crime?

361. In which year did India qualify for the football World Cup, but couldn't take part finally because of monetary reasons?

362. Which is the first Indian private sector company to feature on Fortune magazine's Global 500 list?

363. Who is the first Indian woman to win a junior Grand Slam title?

364. When emergency was declared in India in 1975, who was the President of India?

365. What was the name of the mascot of the 1982 Asian Games held in New Delhi?

366. Who was the prime minister of India at the time of nationalization of banks in 1969?

367. What is a market dominated by a single buyer popularly called?

368. Which non-Test playing qualified for the semi-finals of the 2003 cricket World Cup?

369. For what purpose do you need to fill up the Form no. 49A of the Income Tax Department of India?

370. What is the index that is the sum of a country's inflation and unemployment rates called?

371. Who wrote an article on war finance titled 'How to pay for the War'?

372. What is the name of the coefficient that measures the inequality of income distribution within a country?

373. What was founded when Klaus Schwab, a professor of Business Administration, convened a conference of European business leaders in Davos in 1971?

374. Which organization is the world's largest external source of funding for education and HIV/AIDS programmes?

375. What is the upper age limit for obtaining an Inlaks Scholarship which enables students to study abroad?

376. In which city is the Indian Diamond Institute located?

377. What was established in 1875 as 'The Native Share and Stock Brokers Association'?

378. What was formed to administer American and Canadian aid under the Marshall Plan for the reconstruction of Europe after the Second World War?

379. In 1999, which act for the insurance industry did the Indian Parliament pass on the recommendation of the Malhotra Committee?

380. What is the minimum height required to be an airhostess for Air India?

381. In 1993, which organization was formed in India to act as a capital market regulator?

382. Which street in the southern section of the borough of Manhattan, in New York City, is named for an earthen wall built by Dutch settlers in 1653 to repel an expected English invasion?

383. Who was the first Indian to describe the technique of rhinoplasty (reconstruction of the nose)?

384. After which Indian mathematician was the first Indian satellite named?

385. What is the name of India's first moon mission?

386. What is an economic good for which demand increases as its price rises popularly called?

387. In 1926, the Hilton Young Commission recommended the establishment of which bank?

388. Which stock exchange has a trading floor called the 'Garage'?

389. Who is the first person of Indian origin to be chosen by the International Monetary Fund as its chief economist?

390. In 1995, which currency was chosen as a new currency at the European Council in Madrid?

391. The book *The Double Helix*, written by James Watson, deals with which famous molecule?

392. The C60 allotrope of carbon is named after which American architect?

393. Which organization conducted the first economic census covering non-agricultural establishments in 1977?

394. In 1997, a team led by which embryologist created history by cloning the first adult mammal?

395. In simple terms, what can be defined as the absence of tariffs and import quotas on goods?

396. Which famous theory is built on the Irving Fisher equation $MV = PT$?

397. In which sport did Geet Sethi and Michael Ferreira win several world titles?

398. In 1977, who defeated Indira Gandhi in a Lok Sabha election?

399. Which British explorer became the first person to trek solo and unsupported to the North Pole?

400. What is the Amrita Devi Bishnoi National Award conferred for?

401. Which Bombay-born writer became the first English author to win the Nobel Prize in 1907?

402. In January 2004, in which city was the 12th SAARC Summit held?

403. What is the minimum age limit for those who wish to join the IAS?

404. In January 2004, which former Australian Test cricketer died after being attacked outside a hotel by a hotel security guard?

405. Which is the first and only academic institution in India to run a one-year diploma course in the Art of Private Investigation?

406. In December 2003, near which town was Saddam Hussein captured?

407. On 15 August 1993, of which profession in India did Hrishikesh Kannan become the first member?

408. In December 2003, who was sworn in as the first woman chief minister of Rajasthan?

409. Which Institute was established by the Reserve Bank of India in 1954 in a conscious effort towards systematic training of bank personnel?

410. In 2002, who succeeded N. R. Narayana Murthy as the CEO of Infosys Technologies?

411. Who was the first person of Indian origin to win the Booker Prize?

412. Which noted French sculptor is the creator of 'Le Penseur' (The Thinker) and 'Le Baiser' (The Kiss)?

413. On 1 February 2003, which space shuttle disaster ended the life of astronaut Kalpana Chawla?

414. Who became the first recipient of the Dadasaheb Phalke Award in 1970?

415. Which Indian state is renowned for the Madhubani style of painting?

416. On 1 January 2002, the largest Indian district was bifurcated to facilitate smooth administration. Name the district.

417. According to R.K. Narayan's Malgudi stories, which river flows by the fictional town of Malgudi?

418. Which is the only non-Commonwealth country whose authors are eligible for the Booker Prize?

419. If you want to take the CFA programme, you need to be a graduate in one of two subjects. If one is Economics, which is the other one?

420. Glove, rod, string-rod and shadow are different forms of which traditional art?

421. Which is the only team event in which India won consecutive gold medals at the Asian Games?

422. In which city was the first ever Afro-Asian Games held?

423. Which famous singer composed the theme song of the Athens Olympics?

424. Who was the first recipient of the Jnanpith Award?

425. Which was the first Hindi film to be entirely shot in Los Angeles?

426. For a sport to be included as an Olympic sport for men, it should be widely practised in at least how many countries?

427. What is the name of the web mail launched by Google?

428. What is the name of the supersonic cruise missile that India and Russia have jointly developed?

429. Who is the Russian owner of Chelsea Football Club of England?

430. In how many languages is the Sahitya Akademi Award presented?

431. Marc Ravalomanana was sworn in as the president of which African island nation in May 2002?

432. What is the name of India's indigenously built Advanced Light Helicopter (ALH)?

433. Before Sourav Ganguly, who was the last Indian cricket captain to lead an Indian side to Pakistan?

434. Which country has produced the most authors who have won the Nobel Prize for Literature?

435. In March 2002, which country became the first to legalize euthanasia or mercy killing for terminally ill persons wishing to die?

436. Who is the author of *Ignited Minds*?

437. *Meri Ekyavan Kavitayen* is a collection of poems by which famous personality?

438. Who quit as the defence minister in the wake of the tehelka.com scandal of 2001?

439. Which 11th century Persian scholar and scientist wrote a book on India named *Ta'rikh al-Hind*?

440. What are up, down, charm, strange, bottom and top?

441. Who was the chairman of the Atomic Energy Commission when the first nuclear test at Pokhran took place in 1974?

442. In 1969, which lunar module landed on the surface of the moon?

443. In which Indian city was the first official case of AIDS reported in the country?

444. Which is the most used product that we get from orchids?

445. Which Indian scientist successfully explained the duality problem in string theory?

446. Which commonplace sporting activity did the Central Government ban in February 2001?

447. The work on which technological innovation was started by Tim Berners-Lee and his colleagues at CERN in Geneva?

448. Who is Chairman of the General Council of NLSIU (National Law School of India University), Bangalore?

449. Which institute was established in 1926 by the Government of India to train mining engineers and geologists?

450. In February 2001, where was India's first corporatized port opened?

451. What is the full form of WiFi?

452. In which state is BITS (Birla Institute of Technology and Science), Pilani located?

453. Which two countries hosted the FIFA World Cup 2002?

454. On 2 November 2001, which activity did the Supreme Court of India ban from public places all over India, with immediate effect?

455. Indian Institute of Mass Communication (IIMC), New Delhi offers postgraduate diploma courses in journalism in three languages. If English and Hindi are two of them, which is the third?

456. In November 2001, who did the CBI arrest along with two of his brothers for alleged misappropriation of 27 lakh shares of 90 blue chip companies?

457. Which Indian metro was officially renamed on 1 January 2001?

458. In which Indian institute can you get an 'Executive Masters in International Business'?

459. Of which US university is the Kellog School of Management a part?

460. In which British university would the Rhodes scholarship enable you to study?

461. The Institute of Chartered Accountants of India (ICAI) has its headquarters in New Delhi as well as five Regional Offices. If four of them are located in Mumbai, Chennai, Kolkata and New Delhi, where is the fifth located?

462. How many times can you take the civil services examination?

463. If you get selected for the Combined Defence Sevices (CDS), you

can obtain direct entry to any of four training academies. If two of them are the Indian Military Academy (IMA), Dehradun (for permanent Commission in the Indian Army) and Officers Training Academy (OTA), Chennai (for short-service Commission in the Indian Army), what are the other two?

464. Where is the National Defence Academy located?

465. Three ISIs are located in India. If two of them are in Delhi and Kolkata, where is the third one?

466. To become a college lecturer in India, which exam conducted by the University Grants Commission (UGC) would you have to pass?

467. What was the name of the US reporter who was abducted and later killed while investigating a lead in Pakistan in January 2002?

468. What is the entry level rank for a fresh Marine Engineer (ME) in the Merchant Navy?

469. What is the full form of WAP?

470. Which European ruler marked her Golden Jubilee year on the throne on 6 February 2002?

471. What are the four sections in a TOEFL Test?

472. In March 2002, in which country did US troops launch a mission named Operation Anaconda?

473. In March 2001, which Indian musician received the Order of British Empire(OBE) for his contribution to music?

474. If you were taking the Scholastic Aptitude Test (SAT), which country would you be applying to study in?

475. In March 2002, who was re-elected the President of Zimbabwe?

476. The Indira Gandhi National Open University has 48 regional centers, of which 22 are IGNOU Regional Centres; 8 are IGNOU North-East Regional Centres; 5 are Army Command Centres; 8 are IAF Command Centres and 4 are Navy Command Centres. For which Indian paramilitary force does it have a centre?

477. What is the full form of SARS, that affected more than 8000 people between November 2002 and July 2003?

478. Which famous Indian wrote the novella *Burial at Sea*?

479. Which is the oldest school in the Jawaharlal Nehru University, which was established in 1955?

480. Where is the Lal Bahadur Shastri National Academy of Administration, India's premier research and training institute on administration and public policy, located?

481. Which famous Bengali novelist wrote the novel *Devdas*?

482. At what designation does a Foreign Service Officer begins his career abroad?

483. Who is the first Indian golfer to win a place on the US PGA tour?

484. Which was the first state in India to have a democratically elected communist government?

485. Which Bombay-born musician became the chief music adviser to the Israel Philharmonic Orchestra in 1968?

486. Which Indian institute was set up on the basis of a report (The India Report) by Charles and Ray Eames?

487. Who is the first woman to become the prime minister of a modern Muslim nation?

488. What is the popular folk theatre of Maharashtra called?

489. In which sport did Dingko Singh of Manipur win a gold medal for India at the 1998 Bangkok Asiad after a 16-year drought?

490. Which speaker of the Lok Sabha later became the president of India?

491. Which Indian composed the music for Andrew Llyod Webber's musical production *Bombay*

Dreams (2002)?

492. Who is the first Indian spinner to take 300 wickets in Test cricket?

493. In 2002, which Lok Sabha Speaker died after his private helicopter crashed while trying to make an emergency landing at Kovvadalanka village in Kolluru area of Krishna district, in Andhra Pradesh?

494. Who is the first Indian to become the president of the International Cricket Council?

495. On 19 October 2002, which cellular service did Prime Minister Atal Bihari Vajpayee launch in Lucknow?

496. Name the country's first agricultural job portal, launched in New Delhi.

497. In 2003, which Indian shooter shared the Rajiv Gandhi Khel Ratna Award with athlete K.M. Beenamol?

498. Who is the famous Indian writer whose first book was titled *Mappings*?

499. What word describing the Hindi film industry was included in the Oxford English Dictionary in 2004?

500. In the presidential polls, who did A.P.J. Abdul Kalam defeat to become the president of India?

Answers

1. Syed Nayeemuddin
2. Jackie Selebi
3. Kolkata
4. Lance Armstrong
5. Andre Agassi
6. Aparna Sen
7. Rajyavardhan Singh Rathore
8. *The Rising - Ballad of Mangal Pandey*
9. Anju Bobby George (women's long jump)
10. Saif Ali Khan (for *Hum Tum*) and Tara (for Kannada film, *Haseena*)
11. *Page 3*
12. Scotland
13. *Harry Potter and the Half-Blood Prince*
14. London
15. The Netherlands
16. Roger Federer
17. Mumbai North-West
18. Lakshmi Mittal
19. Jamie Foxx (*Ray*) and Hilary Swank (*Million Dollar Baby*)
20. The most accepted theory is given by the English evolutionist Sir Charles Darwin. He concluded in 1842 that the subsidence of a volcanic island resulted in the formation of a fringing reef and the

continual subsidence allowed this to grow upwards

21. Mary Pierce
22. Hurricane Katrina
23. Switzerland
24. Atithi Devo Bhavah
25. Tamil Nadu. The number is 52,036 as reported to NACO
26. UNESCO
27. Emerson Fittipaldi
28. Islamabad
29. Dhyan Chand
30. Taj Mahal
31. Rashtrapati Bhavan
32. The Speaker of the Lok Sabha
33. Mahatma Gandhi
34. Netaji Subhash Chandra Bose, on 23 January
35. Africa is home to 53 independent countries, representing more than 25 per cent of the countries of the world
36. Tsunami
37. India. The number is 155,618
38. His Holiness Pope Benedict XVI (Joseph Alois Ratzinger), the current pope
39. National Defence Fund
40. Urdu
41. England and Australia (the Ashes series)
42. .in

43. Bharatanatyam
44. Chhatrapati Shivaji Terminus (formerly Victoria Terminus) in Mumbai
45. Indira Gandhi
46. Mizoram
47. Iron
48. One third
49. Fairy Queen; it goes from Delhi to Alwar in Rajasthan and back. It was built in 1855
50. Andhra Pradesh
51. Garba; from 'garabi', a decorated pot containing offerings
52. Fatehpur Sikri
53. Hawa Mahal in Jaipur
54. Sardar Vallabhbhai Patel
55. ILO
56. Odissi
57. Mother
58. Aung San Suu Kyi
59. New York
60. Thomas Paine
61. Agra
62. Charlie Walker
63. Star City
64. Turkey
65. German
66. 20 June
67. 175
68. 25 (One-tenth of the total number of members)
69. Tenniseum
70. Pablo Neruda
71. 1901
72. Carbon 12
73. French revolution
74. Mahesh Dattani
75. Diwali
76. Dina Mehta
77. India and Pakistan
78. South Africa
79. United Kingdom
80. Ruhr region
81. Italy
82. Tanzania
83. Namibia
84. Malaysia
85. Sibbi in Pakistan's Baluchistan province
86. Eyes
87. Spanish
88. 12
89. Japan
90. Autumnal equinox
91. France
92. Dussehra
93. Royal Greenwich Observatory
94. 24
95. Bedlam
96. Moscow
97. Integrated Circuits (Chips)
98. Telephone Exchange
99. Argentina
100. Argus
101. Dr Abdus Salam
102. A scroll of the Diamond Sutra printed by Wang Cheih in AD 868
103. Satyajit Ray Film and Television Institute
104. The kidney
105. Goa. The institute was founded on 1 January 1966, and is the largest formal oceanography laboratory in the Indian Ocean Region. It has three regional centres—Mumbai, Kochi, Vishakapatnam. It is located in Dona Paula, 7 km from Panjim
106. Rabies
107. South Korea; Kim Dae Jung was awarded the Nobel for his work for promoting democracy in South Korea and East Asia and for his peace initiatives with North Korea
108. China
109. New York City
110. The author of the Harry Potter series, J.K. Rowling
111. Kathak
112. IIM Indore, which was established in 1997. The other IIMs are located in Kolkata, Ahmedabad, Bangalore, Lucknow and Kozhikode
113. Vitamin C
114. Cathy Freeman
115. Costume designer Bhanu Athaiya. She shared an Oscar for *Gandhi* (1982) with John Mollo.

116. Madhya Pradesh
117. Sourav Ganguly
118. Sukumar Sen
119. India; the child, Astha Arora, was born to a Delhi couple
120. King Gyanendra
121. Bill Clinton; President Clinton's visit to India was the fourth by a US President. Earlier visits were by Presidents Dwight Eisenhower in 1959, Richard Nixon in 1969 and Jimmy Carter in 1978
122. Atal Bihari Vajpayee
123. Gujarat; the epicenter lay 20 kms northeast of Bhuj. It measured 6.9 on the Richter Scale
124. Communist Party of India (CPI)
125. Jayalalithaa
126. Ba'th Party
127. Chile; he was the first Socialist to hold the office in 27 years
128. N.T. Rama Rao
129. China
130. America Online (AOL); it was at that time the biggest merger in history
131. AIADMK
132. Genetically modified products
133. Democratic Party
134. Vladimir Putin; he was earlier designated acting-president by his predecessor, Boris Yetlsin, who had been the president of Russia since the fall of Communism
135. Prafulla Kumar Mahanta
136. Austria; he later had to resign as the head of the Freedom Party under international pressure
137. Turkey; they announced plans of self-rule without recourse to violence
138. Dr Karni Singh
139. Northern Ireland; this was announced after the Irish Republican Army (IRA) missed a disarmament deadline
140. Bhutan
141. Kosovo
142. Rajasthan
143. P.V. Narasimha Rao

144. England
145. Buddhadev Bhattacharya
146. Jacques Chirac
147. Arjun Atwal
148. Godhra
149. The Parliament building; several security personnel were killed in the incident which ended with the death of five gunmen. The situation led to the massing of troops on the Indo-Pak border
150. Tetenda Taibu
151. Mark Twain; it was the manuscript of *The Adventures of Tom Sawyer*
152. England
153. Peanuts
154. Human Genome Project (HGP)
155. The National School of Drama
156. West Bengal
157. Pacific Ocean; the name Mir means 'peace' or 'world'. Mir's core module was launched on 20 February 1986. It supported human habitation from March 1986 to June 2000.It was designed to have a life of five years
158. Dennis Tito; he was launched on board a Russian Soyuz rocket from the Baikonur cosmodrome in Kazakhstan on a mission to the International Space Station. He was accompanied by two Russian cosmonauts and was reported to have paid $20m for the trip
159. Uttar Pradesh
160. Agyeya. He won the Jnanpith Award for the Hindi novel *Kitni Navon Mein Kitni Bar* in 1978
161. Vijay Tendulkar
162. Subramania Bharati
163. Amir Khusrau
164. Greece
165. The Concorde; it was the only supersonic aircraft that was on regular scheduled service. This was the first crash of a Concorde since its commercial launch in 1976. All on board the aircraft died along with four on the

ground when the aircraft crashed soon after take off from Paris

166. Kursk; the nuclear-powered submarine sank to the bottom of the Barents Sea

167. Australia; in the city of Sydney

168. France

169. Slobodan Milosevic

170. Dom Moraes

171. Microsoft; the ruling said that it had shown anti-competitive behaviour and threatened to break up the giant organization

172. Pandit Vishwa Mohan Bhatt

173. London

174. Shyam Benegal

175. Nabisco

176. O.V. Vijayan

177. Albert Camus. He received the Nobel Prize for literature in 1957

178. Khari Boli

179. Near-Earth Asteroid Rendezvous (NEAR); it went into orbit around an asteroid named Eros

180. Albert Einstein; it is known as the famous EPR paradox

181. Andrew Lloyd Webber's *Cats*

182. International Monetary Fund (IMF)

183. Bangalore

184. Tarapur (in Maharashtra)

185. Wrestling (K.D. Jadhav won a bronze at the Helsinki Olympics in 1952)

186. Harivansh Rai Bachchan. It was published in 1935

187. National Insurance, New India Assurance, Oriental Insurance, United India Insurance

188. Abu Ghraib jail

189. Satyajit Ray, for his film *Aparajito* (1957)

190. Kerala

191. J.M. Coetzee. He won the Booker in 1983 (for *Life & Times of Michael K*) and then again in 1999 (for *Disgrace*); and was awarded the Nobel Prize in 2003

192. Amrita Pritam. It was published in 1976

193. Progressive Artists Group

194. Sanjeev Kumar

195. Pandit Ravi Shankar

196. Munshi Premchand

197. West Bengal

198. Sangeet Natak Akademi. It is India's national academy for music, dance and drama

199. Mrinal Sen

200. Ludwig Van Beethoven

201. *The Man Who Knew Too Much*. He originally made it in 1934 and then made it again in 1955

202. Michelangelo

203. Sarod maestro Ustad Amjad Ali Khan

204. The saxophone

205. Rabindranath Tagore

206. Protima Gauri Bedi

207. Yakshagana

208. Dutch

209. Hindu Rate of Growth

210. MICA, Ahmedabad. MICA stands for Mudra Institute of Communications

211. *The Waste Land*. It was published in 1922

212. Indira Goswami

213. Home Ministry

214. Sriharikota Space Centre; this was the first time the Indian Space Research Organisation used the Polar Satellite Launch Vehicle (PSLV) to launch a meteorological satellite in the geo-synchronous transfer orbit

215. Indian Forest Service

216. William Shakespeare, Cervantes and Garcilaso de la Vega. It is believed that they all died on the same date in 1616

217. Dhyan Chand

218. Nafisa Joseph

219. New Delhi

220. President of India

221. Meera Borwankar

222. London and Paris

223. Prakash Padukone

224. Massachusetts Institute of Technology (MIT), USA

225. Krishan Kant

226. Jean-Paul Sartre. He declined the prize as he felt that such honours could interfere with a writer's responsibilities to his readers

227. Kuala Lumpur

228. Enron Corporation; the collapse was triggered when rivals Dynegy Inc pulled out of a proposed $9bn merger deal

229. Wipro. The chairman of Wipro Spectramind helped start the Indian call centre boom in the '90s when he came up with a business plan for American companies to direct their calls to India. Spectramind was founded by Raman Roy in March 2000

230. Peter Carey. He won it in 1988 for *Oscar and Lucinda*, and then again in 2001 for *True History of the Kelly Gang*

231. Apes and monkeys; SIV stands for Simian Immunodeficiency virus

232. Rafiq Tarar

233. Laissez-faire

234. Postal Life Insurance

235. Jhumpa Lahiri. She was awarded the 2000 Pulitzer Prize for fiction

236. Werner Heisenberg

237. Arsenal

238. Ashapurna Devi, for her Bengali novel *Pratham Pratisruti*

239. Arjan Singh; he was made the Marshal in recognition of his services towards the development of the Indian Air Force

240. John Hume

241. O.M. Nambiar

242. William Butler Yeats. *Gitanjali* was published in 1912

243. Prime Minister of India

244. 1960 Rome Olympics

245. S. Venkataraghavan

246. Adam Smith

247. Sunil Gavaskar

248. *Ananda Math*. It was published in 1882

249. Yahoo

250. Prasanta Chandra Mahalanobis

251. USA

252. SpaceShipOne

253. *The God of Small Things* by Arundhati Roy

254. Alexei Shirov

255. Dr Rajendra Prasad

256. Salim Durrani

257. Sachin Pilot from Dausa, Rajasthan

258. Manila, Philippines

259. Kalhana. It was written in 1148 in Sanskrit verse

260. *Mahabharata*. It was translated during the reign of Akbar

261. Chandigarh

262. Lord Meghnad Desai

263. Anil Basu of CPI (M) from Arambagh, West Bengal

264. United Kingdom. These scholarships are funded by the Foreign and Commonwealth Offices and administered by the British Council

265. Tansen

266. Kautilya's *Arthasastra*

267. Business Process Outsourcing

268. Shehnai maestro, Ustad Bismillah Khan

269. Chokila Iyer of Sikkim

270. Amrita Devi Wildlife Protection Award

271. Kalpana Chawla

272. Mother Teresa; after her beatification, she is known as 'Blessed Mother Teresa'

273. Beagle 2; it was built by British scientists. The probe failed to respond or transmit data after it was released from Mars Express

274. It is the world's longest LPG pipeline

275. The Akshardham temple; 29 persons died in the raid

276. The Indian Astronomical Observatory at Hanle in Ladakh

277. The first solo round the world balloon flight

278. Golden Quadrilateral

279. Mars

280. South Korea; the virus was discovered 80 km south of Seoul.

Since then, more than 20 lakh chickens and ducks have been culled in order to erase the disease

281. Aishwarya Rai

282. Twelve. The twelve countries are – Belgium, Germany, Greece, Spain, France, Ireland, Italy, Luxembourg, The Netherlands, Austria, Portugal and Finland

283. Arnold Schwarzenegger; he ran as a Republican and beat the Democratic incumbent Gray Davis

284. Bahrain; it dropped the word 'emirate' from its name in favour of the word 'kingdom'

285. Kerala; it implies that more than 80 per cent of the maternity hospitals in the state 'protect, promote and support breastfeeding', and discourage using of baby foods

286. Kiran Bedi

287. Kalpana Chawla; it was named Kalpana-1 and dedicated to the nation

288. Wasim Akram

289. The Hague, the Netherlands

290. Goa

291. Shivalik; it was launched in Mumbai

292. Fernando Alonso; he won the Hungary Grand Prix at Budapest at the age of 22 years

293. Tejas

294. Mehbooba Mufti; she took over as president of the People's Democratic Party

295. Lithuania; the referendum was held in the capital Vilnius

296. Real Madrid

297. Abdul Karim Telgi

298. Don Bradman's. Bradman scored 29 centuries. Sachin scored his 30th century in the third Test match against England at Headingley, Leeds

299. Non-executive Chairman

300. Queen Mary 2

301. Kalidasa

302. Uttar Pradesh; he is an Independent

303. Interior Decoration and Ceramics

304. Nobel Prize-winning economist Amartya Sen

305. Dabhol Power Corporation

306. Janata Party

307. Chamravattom

308. Charan Singh

309. Life Insurance Corporation of India

310. Turkey

311. Margaret Thatcher

312. David Ricardo

313. Alaska, USA; the exercise was named 'Cooperative Cope Thunder-04-01'

314. Zulfikar Ali Bhutto

315. INS Talwar

316. Mohammed Ali Jinnah

317. Nelson Mandela

318. Dinosaur; it was named 'Rajasaurus Narmadensis', meaning 'princely reptile from the Narmada'

319. Jyoti Basu

320. Uttar Pradesh

321. Personal Digital Assistants or PDAs

322. Tehreek-e-Hurriyat Jammu and Kashmir

323. Kingfisher

324. Sardar Vallabhbhai Patel

325. Cuba

326. Francois Mitterrand

327. Egypt

328. A clock

329. P.V. Narasimha Rao

330. Johnny Walker; he passed away in 2003 in his Mumbai residence, after a prolonged illness

331. N.D. Tiwari

332. Finland

333. Ireland

334. Rwanda

335. G.V. Mavalankar

336. Russia

337. Maldives

338. Sheikh Hasina

339. Libya

340. India
341. Mumbai
342. Bihar
343. Madonna
344. The Bureau of Industrial Costs and Prices (BICP)
345. Dr K.M. Cherian
346. Greenpeace International
347. Sir Jagdish Chandra Bose
348. Charles Shobhraj
349. Admiral Gorshkov
350. A 200-foot zeppelin
351. Boson; named after S.N. Bose
352. Abdullah Ahmad Badawi
353. Dwight Eisenhower (in 1959)
354. Shanghai
355. Mars Exploration Rover Spirit
356. Rabindranath Tagore
357. Jharkhand
358. 'Gresham's law'
359. C.K. Nayudu
360. Belgium
361. 1950
362. Reliance Industries Limited
363. Sania Mirza
364. Dr Fakhruddin Ali Ahmed
365. Appu, a baby elephant
366. Indira Gandhi
367. Monopsony
368. Kenya
369. It has been prescribed for making an application for allotment of the Permanent Accounting Number or PAN
370. Misery Index
371. John Maynard Keynes
372. Gini Coefficient
373. The World Economic Forum
374. World Bank
375. 30 years
376. Surat, the centre of the Indian diamond-cutting industry
377. Bombay Stock Exchange
378. Organisation for European Economic Co-operation (OPEC)
379. Insurance Regulatory Development Act (IRDA)
380. 157.5 cms (5 feet 2 inches). There can be a relaxation of height requirement up to 2.54 cms (1") for Gorkhas, Garwalis and those hailing from Northeast states and hilly areas
381. The Securities & Exchange Board of India (SEBI)
382. Wall Street
383. Sushruta
384. Aryabhata
385. Chandrayan-1
386. Giffen goods, named after Robert Giffen
387. Reserve Bank of India
388. NYSE or New York Stock Exchange
389. Raghuram G. Rajan
390. Euro
391. The DNA molecule
392. R. Buckminister Fuller
393. Central Statistical Organisation (CSO)
394. Dr Ian Wilmut
395. Free Trade
396. Quantity Theory of Money
397. Billiards
398. Raj Narain
399. Pen Hadow
400. For wildlife conservation; it was conferred posthumously on Ganga Ram Bishnoi of Chirai village in Jodhpur
401. Rudyard Kipling
402. Islamabad
403. 21 years
404. David Hookes
405. Indore Christian College
406. Tikrit, his hometown; he was captured about nine miles from Tikrit
407. Radio jockey
408. Vasundhara Raje
409. Bankers Training College in Mumbai
410. Nandan Nilekani
411. V. S Naipaul
412. Auguste Rodin
413. The Columbia disaster
414. Devika Rani
415. Bihar
416. Midnapore in West Bengal; it was bifurcated into Midnapore East and Midnapore West

417. Sarayu
418. Ireland
419. Statistics
420. Puppetry
421. Kabaddi
422. Hyderabad
423. George Michael
424. G. Shankara Kurup, for his poem Odakkuzhal in Malayalam in 1965
425. *Kaante* (2002)
426. Seventy-five
427. G-mail
428. BrahMos; the name BrahMos comes from the names of the two rivers, the Brahmaputra and the Moskva
429. Roman Abramovich
430. Twenty-two; the languages are – Assamese, Bengali, Dogri, English, Gujarati, Hindi, Kannada, Kashmiri, Konkani, Maithili, Malayalam, Manipuri, Marathi, Nepali, Oriya, Punjabi, Rajasthani, Sanskrit, Sindhi, Tamil, Telugu and Urdu
431. Madagascar
432. Dhruv
433. Krishnamachari Srikkanth
434. France. French authors have won 13 Nobel Prizes for Literature
435. The Netherlands
436. President A.P.J. Abdul Kalam
437. Atal Bihari Vajpayee
438. George Fernandes
439. Al-Barauni
440. Names of quarks
441. Dr H.N. Sethna
442. Eagle
443. Chennai (in 1986)
444. Vanilla
445. Dr Ashoke Sen
446. Whipping of horses in a horse race
447. The World Wide Web
448. The Chairman of the Bar Council of India
449. Indian School of Mines, Dhanbad
450. Ennore, near Chennai
451. Wireless Fidelity
452. Rajasthan
453. South Korea and Japan
454. Smoking
455. Oriya. IIMC Dhenkanal was set up in August 1993 as the first branch of IIMC New Delhi, and presently runs two regular PG diploma courses in English and Oriya journalism
456. Harshad Mehta
457. Calcutta was renamed Kolkata
458. Indian Institute of Foreign Trade, New Delhi
459. Northwestern University
460. Oxford University
461. Kanpur
462. Four
463. Naval Academy, Goa (for Commission in the General Services in the Indian Navy) and Airforce Academy, Begumpet, Hyderabad (for Commission in the Indian Airforce)
464. Khadakvasla
465. Hyderabad
466. NET (National Eligibility Test)
467. Daniel Pearl; he was the South Asia bureau chief of the *Wall Street Journal*. He was investigating the alleged 'shoe bomber', Richard Reid
468. Fifth engineer or junior engineer
469. Wireless Application Protocol
470. Queen Elizabeth II; she became the Queen of England after the death of her father, King George VI in 1952
471. Listening, Structure, Reading and Writing
472. Afghanistan; the operation aimed to flush out remaining al-Qaeda and Taliban fighters in eastern Afghanistan
473. Pandit Ravi Shankar
474. USA
475. Robert Mugabe
476. Assam Rifles (The Assam Rifles Command Centre)
477. Severe Acute Respiratory Syndrome; SARS is a viral respiratory illness that first appeared in

Southern China in November 2002

478. Khushwant Singh. It was published in 2004
479. The School of International Studies
480. Mussoorie
481. Sarat Chandra Chatterjee
482. Third Secretary
483. Arjun Atwal
484. Kerala
485. Zubin Mehta
486. National Institute of Design, Ahmedabad
487. Benazir Bhutto of Pakistan
488. Tamasha
489. Boxing (in the bantamweight category)
490. Neelam Sanjiva Reddy
491. A. R. Rahman
492. Anil Kumble
493. G. M. C. Balayogi
494. Jagmohan Dalmiya
495. BSNL cellular service
496. agrijobsindia.com
497. Anil Bhagwat
498. Vikram Seth. *Mappings* was a book of poems published in 1980
499. Bollywood
500. Lakshmi Sahgal

Index

Essential Books on Contemporary Politics & Culture

American Power and the New Mandarins
by Noam Chomsky

Chomsky's first political book and widely considered to be among the most cogent and powerful statements against the American war in Vietnam.

Penguin India   ISBN 0143030183   Rs 375

For Reasons of State
by Noam Chomsky

Chomsky's second major collection of political writings.

Penguin India   ISBN 014303054X   Rs 395

Middle East Illusions: Peace, Security and Terror
by Noam Chomsky

This latest work includes chapters written by Chomsky just before the 2000 Intifada and up through October 2002.

Penguin India   ISBN 0143030019   Rs 295

On Language
by Noam Chomsky

Chomsky's classic works *Language and Responsibility* and *Responsibility on Language* in one volume.

Penguin India   ISBN 0143030000   Rs 325

Understanding Power
The Indispensable Chomsky
edited by John Schoeffel & Peter R. Mitchel

Characterized by Chomsky's accessible and informative style, this is the ideal book for those new to his work as well as for those who have been listening for years.

Penguin India   ISBN 0143029916   Rs 375

Penguin Books India
www.penguinbooksindia.com